Advertising

Principles & Practice

Tenth Edition

Global Edition

Advertising & IMC

Principles & Practice

Tenth Edition

Global Edition

Sandra Moriarty
University of Colorado

Nancy Mitchell
University of Nebraska-Lincoln

William Wells
University of Minnesota

Pearson

Original edition, entitled *Advertising & IMC: Principles and Practice*, 1st Edition, by Moriarty, Sandra; Mitchell, Nancy D; Wells, William D, published by Pearson Education, Limited. Copyright © 2014 by Pearson Education, Inc.

Indian edition

ISBN 978-93-325-7414-4

First Impression, 2016

This edition is manufactured in India and is authorized for sale only in India, Bangladesh, Bhutan, Pakistan, Nepal, Sri Lanka and the Maldives. Circulation of this edition outside of these territories is UNAUTHORIZED.

Published by Pearson India Education Services Pvt. Ltd, CIN: U72200TN2005PTC057128.
Formerly known as TutorVista Global Pvt. Ltd, licensees of Pearson Education in South Asia

Head Office: 7th Floor, Knowledge Boulevard, A-8(A) Sector-62, Noida (U.P) 201309, India
Registered Office:4th Floor, Software Block, Elnet Software City, TS -140, Block 2 & 9
Rajiv Gandhi Salai, Taramani, Chennai, Tamil Nadu 600113.

Fax: 080-30461003, Phone: 080-30461060
Website: www.pearson.co.in
Email: companysecetary.india@pearson.com

Printed in India by Saurabh Printers Pvt. Ltd.

The Tenth Edition is dedicated to all the students who have inspired us with their questions and ideas and all the colleagues who have challenged us with new thoughts and new findings. Most of all we dedicate this book to all our many contributors—the students, graduates, professors, and professionals who have contributed their thoughts, creative work, and professional experience to this edition.

Sandra Moriarty and Nancy Mitchell

Brief Contents

PART 1 Principle: Back to Basics

1 Advertising 34

2 Brand Communication 62

3 Brand Communication and Society 88

PART 2 Principle: Be True to Thy Brand—and Thy Consumer

4 How Brand Communication Works 120

5 Segmenting and Targeting the Audience 152

6 Strategic Research 180

7 Strategic Planning 206

PART 3 Practice: Developing Breakthrough Ideas in the Digital Age

8 The Creative Side 238

9 Promotional Writing 268

10 Visual Communication 300

PART 4 Principle: Media in a World of Change

11 Media Basics 334

12 Paid Media 362

13 Owned, Interactive, and Earned Media 398

14 Media Planning and Negotiation 432

PART 5 Principle: IMC and Total Communication

15 Public Relations 472

16 Direct Response 498

17 Promotions 530

18 The Principles and Practice of IMC 558

19 Evaluating IMC Effectiveness 588

Appendix 616

Glossary 621

Notes 639

Index 650

Contents

Preface 21

PART 1 Principle: Back to Basics

1. Advertising 34
   IT'S A WINNER: Old Spice: What It Takes to Be a Man 35

What Is Advertising? 36
What Are Advertising's Basic Functions? 37 | What Are the Key Components of Advertising? 38 | Common Types of Advertising 39 | Other Important Promotional Tools 39 | What Roles Does Advertising Perform? 40
A MATTER OF PRACTICE: The Greatest Commercial Ever Made 42

How Did Current Practices and Concepts Evolve? 43
Eras and Ages 43

The Advertising World 48
Who Are the Key Players? 48
A MATTER OF PRINCIPLE: *Mad Men*: The Inherent Drama of Advertising 49
THE INSIDE STORY: Freelancing: Two Sides of the Coin 52
Types of Agencies 52
How Are Agency Jobs Organized? 54
A DAY IN THE LIFE: The Day-to-Day Job in Content Management 55
How Are Agencies Paid? 56

How Is the Practice of Advertising Changing? 56
Consumer in Charge 57 | Blurring Lines and Converging Media 57 | Accountability and Effectiveness 57 | Integrated Marketing Communication 58 | Looking Ahead 58
IT'S A WRAP: Old Spice: The Smell of Success 59

Key Points Summary 59
Key Terms 60
Review Questions 60
Discussion Questions 61
Take-Home Projects 61
TRACE North America Case 61

2. Brand Communication 62
IT'S A WINNER: McDonald's Love Story 63
What Is Brand and Marketing Communication? 64
Brand Communication's Role in Marketing 65
Who Are the Key Players? 65 I What Are the Most Common Types of Markets? 66
A DAY IN THE LIFE: A View from the Marcom Front Line 67
How Does the Marketing Mix Send Messages? 68 I Added Value 70
What Is Integrated Marketing Communication? 71
What Is the Role of Communication in Branding? 72
THE INSIDE STORY: A Passion for the Business 73
How Does a Brand Acquire Meaning? 74 I How Does Brand Transformation Work? 75
A MATTER OF PRINCIPLE: It's Pure and It Floats 76
Brand Value and Brand Equity 79
A PRINCIPLED PRACTICE: PAUSE FOR THE CAUSE: *Boosting Brand Value with Cause Marketing* 79
Brand Communication in a Time of Change 81
Brand Relationships 82 I Accountability 82 I Global Marketing 82 I Word-of-Mouth Marketing 83 I Looking Ahead 84
IT'S A WRAP: Golden Arches, Golden Opportunity 84
Key Points Summary 85
Key Terms 85
Review Questions 86
Discussion Questions 86
Take-Home Projects 87
TRACE North America Case 87

3. Brand Communication and Society 88
IT'S A WINNER: To Tell the truth® 89
What Is the Social Impact of Brand Communication? 90
What Are the Key Debates about Impact on Society? 91 I What Are the Key Debates and Issues about Brand Communication Practices? 93
THE INSIDE STORY: Pepsi: Creating Culturally Relevant Programs 95
A PRINCIPLED PRACTICE: Tribute to Ivan L. Preston: 1931–2011 97
Communicators' Ethical Responsibilities 101
PRACTICAL TIPS: Brilliant or Offensive Advertising? 102
Personal and Professional Ethics 102
A MATTER OF PRACTICE: Advertising Gets No Respect! 103
Why and How Is Brand Communication Regulated? 105
Brand Communication's Legal Environment 105 I The Regulatory Environment 108 I The Impact of Regulation 109 I Media Review of Advertising 112 I Self-Regulation 112 I Looking Ahead 114
IT'S A WRAP: The truth® Wins Out in the End 114
Key Points Summary 115
Key Terms 115
Review Questions 116
Discussion Questions 116
Take-Home Projects 116

TRACE North America Case 117
Hands-On Case 117

PART 2 Principle: Be True to Thy Brand—and Thy Consumer

4. How Brand Communication Works 120
IT'S A WINNER: Anatomy of an Award-Winning Campaign for Chrysler 121
How Does Brand Communication Work? 122
The Mass Communication Foundation 123 | Adding Interaction to Brand Communication 124
THE INSIDE STORY: What Went Wrong at Office Depot? 126
Other Aspects of Communication 126 | What Are the Effects behind Effectiveness? 127
What Are the Facets of Impact? 129
The Perception Facet: See/Hear 130
A PRINCIPLED PRACTICE: Ice Cubes, Breasts, and Subliminal Ads 133
The Emotion or Affect Facet: Feel 134 | The Cognition Facet: Think/Understand 136
A MATTER OF PRINCIPLE: Thought vs. Feeling 138
The Association Facet: Connect 139 | The Persuasion Facet: Believe 141 | The Behavior Facet: Act/Do 143
A MATTER OF PRACTICE: May VW's Force Be with You 144
The Power of Brand Communication 146
Strong and Weak Effects 146 | Looking Ahead 148
IT'S A WRAP: Finding Chrysler's Heart and Soul 148
Key Points Summary 149
Key Terms 149
Review Questions 150
Discussion Questions 150
Take-Home Projects 151
TRACE North America Case 151

5. Segmenting and Targeting the Audience 152
IT'S A WINNER: Dove Audiences Redefine Beauty 153
Starting the Conversation 154
How Do Consumers Make Brand Decisions? 155 | Paths to a Brand Decision 155
What Influences Consumer Decisions? 156
Cultural Influences 156 |
A MATTER OF PRINCIPLE: "There Are No Ugly Women, Only Lazy Ones": Why Dove's Real Beauty Campaign Flopped in Taiwan 158
Social Influences 158
THE INSIDE STORY: Scotts Brand Comes Alive as Scott 159
Psychological Influences 160 | Influences on B2B Decision Making 162
How Do We Segment Markets and Target Audiences? 163
Segmentation Strategies 163 | Types of Segmentation 164 | Targeting the Best Audience 165
Profiling Markets and Target Audiences 166
Targeting and Profiling Using Demographics 166

A MATTER OF PRACTICE: Same-Sex Marriage: A Boon to the Economy? 168
Targeting and Profiling Using Psychographics 170 I Sociodemographic Segments 173 I Targeting and Profiling Using Behavioral Patterns 174 I Seeking Seekers 175 I Looking Ahead 177
IT'S A WRAP: The Beauty of a Campaign 177
Key Points Summary 177
Key Terms 178
Review Questions 178
Discussion Questions 179
Take-Home Projects 179
TRACE North America Case 179

6. Strategic Research 180
IT'S A WINNER: Domino's Cooks Up a Recipe for Success 181
How Do You Get Insights into Consumer Behavior? 182
What Are the Basic Types of Research? 183 I Basic Research Designs 185
A PRINCIPLED PRACTICE: Does Advertising Make Smoking Cool? 188
How Do We Use Research? 188
Market Information 189 I Consumer Insight 190 I Media Information 191 I Message Development and Diagnostics 192 I Evaluation 192
A MATTER OF PRINCIPLE: Finding Moments of Truth 193
What Are the Most Common Research Methods? 194
Ways of Contact: Quantitative Methods 194 I Ways of Contact: Qualitative Methods 195
A MATTER OF PRACTICE: Online Marketing Research 196
A DAY IN THE LIFE: A Stopwatch, Code Sheet, and Curiosity 199
How Do You Choose a Research Method? 201
Research Trends and Challenges 202
Sampling Challenges 202 I Global Issues 202 I IMC Research Challenges 203 I Looking Ahead 203
IT'S A WRAP: Domino's Gets Its Slice of the (Pizza) Pie 203
Key Points Summary 204
Key Terms 204
Review Questions 205
Discussion Questions 205
Take-Home Projects 205
TRACE North America Case 205

7. Strategic Planning 206
IT'S A WINNER: Re-telling a Tale 207
What Is Strategic Planning? 208
The Business Plan 209 I The Marketing Plan 211
A PRINCIPLED PRACTICE: "Just Give Me My One Vice" 212
A MATTER OF PRACTICE: "My SPAR": Letting Our Customers Lead 214
The Brand Communication/IMC Plan 215 I Plans for Marketing Communication Functions 216
Key Strategic Decisions 217
The Communication Objectives 217 I The Target Audience 218 I Brand Identity Strategy 218
THE INSIDE STORY: Mistake #1: Drinking and Driving Drunk 219
Brand Positioning Strategy 221

Consumer Insight and Account Planning 225
A MATTER OF PRINCIPLE: The 7-Up Uncola Story: A Classic in Repositioning 226
Account Planning 227 | The Consumer Insight Process 228 | The Creative Brief 230 | Looking Ahead 231
IT'S A WRAP: Re-telling a Tale 231
Key Points Summary 232
Key Terms 232
Review Questions 233
Discussion Questions 233
Take-Home Projects 233
TRACE North America Case 234
Hands-On Case 234

PART 3 Practice: Developing Breakthrough Ideas in the Digital Age

8. The Creative Side 238
IT'S A WINNER: A Tale of Brotherly Love and Sharp Thinking 239
Science and Art? 240
Who Are the Key Players? 242 | What Is the Role of Creativity? 242
A DAY IN THE LIFE: Tweets from the Front Line 243
The Creative Brief 243
Message Strategies 246
Which Strategic Approach to Use? 247
A MATTER OF PRINCIPLE: Six Message Strategies in Six Minutes 249
Strategic Formats 250 | Matching Messages to Objectives 253
Creative Thinking: So How Do You Do It? 256
Big Ideas 257
PRACTICAL TIPS: Checklist for Killer Ads 258
The ROI of Creativity 259 | The Creative Leap 260 | Dialing Up Your Creativity 260 | The Creative Process: How to Get an Idea 261 | Brainstorming 262
Managing Creative Strategies 263
Extension: An Idea with Legs 263 | Adaptation: Taking an Idea Global 263 | Evaluation: The Go/No-Go Decision 264 | Looking Ahead 265
IT'S A WRAP: Creating Ideas That Stick 265
Key Points Summary 265
Key Terms 266
Review Questions 266
Discussion Questions 267
Take-Home Projects 267
TRACE North America Case 267

9. Promotional Writing 268
IT'S A WINNER: Wildlife Blaze Trails for Frontier 269
The Writer's Role in Brand Communication 270
The Language of Brand Communication 270 | Writing Styles 273 | Strategy and Legal Imperatives 274

Types of Brand Communication Writing 274
The Ad Copywriter 275
PRACTICAL TIPS: So You Think You Want to Create a Funny Ad? 278
Public Relations Writing 279 I Direct-Response Writing 279

Writing for Various Media 279
Basics of Writing for Print Media 280
A MATTER OF PRINCIPLE: The Principle of Truth 285
Radio Messages and How to Write Them 287 I Television Messages and How to Write Them 289
A MATTER OF PRACTICE: How the Emotional Pivot Works in a Story 290
A DAY IN THE LIFE: A Copywriter's View of Television Production 293
The Internet and How to Write for It 294

Copywriting Challenges 295
Writing for a Global Brand 295 I Looking Ahead 296
IT'S A WRAP: And the Winner Is . . . Frontier 296

Key Points Summary 297
Key Terms 297
Review Questions 298
Discussion Questions 298
Take-Home Projects 298
TRACE North America Case 299

10. Visual Communication 300
IT'S A WINNER: A Strong Mint with a Curious Past Goes Digital 301

Why Is Visual Communication Important? 302
Visual Impact 302
A PRINCIPLED PRACTICE: An Imperative: Respect the Dignity of the Person 303
Brand Image and Position 305 I Visual Storytelling 306 I Emotion and Visual Persuasion 307
A MATTER OF PRINCIPLE: Save the Pandas! Save the Baby Seals! Save the Eagles! Save the Toads? 307

What Is Art Direction? 308
THE INSIDE STORY: Large or Small, Which Would You Choose? The Good, Bad and Ugly, Exposed 308
The Designer's Tool Kit 309 I Design Principles, Layout, and Styles 312
A MATTER OF PRACTICE: The Beautiful Messy 315
Composition 316 I Environmental Design 317

What Do You Need to Know about Production? 317
Print Media Requirements 317 I Print Art Reproduction 319 I Binding and Finishing 320 I 3D Printing 321

What Does an Art Director Need to Know about Video Production? 321
Filming and Editing 322 I The Process of Producing Videos 323 I The Television Production Process 324

Web Design Considerations 326
Action and Interaction 327 I Looking Ahead 327
IT'S A WRAP: Keeping the Altoids Brand in Mint Condition 328

Key Points Summary 328
Key Terms 329
Review Questions 329

Discussion Questions 330
Take-Home Projects 330
TRACE North America Case 331
Hands-On Case 331

PART 4 Principle: Media in a World of Change

11. Media Basics 334

IT'S A WINNER: Lottery of Life 335

What Do We Mean by Media? 336

A MATTER OF PRINCIPLE: The Engagement Strategy behind Sports Advertising 337

IMC and Media 338 | The Media Industry 338 | Media Types and Terms 339 | The Evolution of Media Forms and Functions 342 | Key Media Players 345

What Are the Fundamentals of Media Strategy? 346

The Media Plan 346 | Key Strategic Media Concepts 346

THE INSIDE STORY: "Warrior—A Three-Artist, One-Song Music Video for Converse" 348

The Basis for the Buy 349

Changing Patterns of Media Use 351

Consumer Use of Media 351

A MATTER OF PRACTICE: Connected Viewers + Multiscreen Marketers 352

Alternative Media Forms 353

A MATTER OF PRINCIPLE: Creative Use of Out-of-Home and Nontraditional Media 354

THE INSIDE STORY: The Animated Axe Effect in *City Hunters* 356

Looking Ahead 358

IT'S A WRAP: Lottery of Life 358

Key Points Summary 359
Key Terms 359
Review Questions 360
Discussion Questions 360
Take-Home Projects 360
TRACE North America Case 361

12. Paid Media 362

IT'S A WINNER: The Art of Laying an Egg and Making It Golden 363

Traditional Paid Media of Advertising 364

Published Print Media 364 | Published Media: Newspapers 365

THE INSIDE STORY: Tsunami Disaster: The Inherent Value of Newspapers and Their Ads 365

Published Media: Magazines 369 | Published Media: Directories 372

A MATTER OF PRINCIPLE: Directories: The Medium You Trust the Most 373

Broadcast Media: Radio 374 | Broadcast Media: Television 376

A MATTER OF PRACTICE: People Really Enjoy Their Large-Screen Televisions 377

Movie Advertising 382 | Video Game Advertising 383 | Place-Based Media 383

PRACTICAL TIPS: Outdoor: An Effective Brand Communication Mecium 386

Online Advertising 388
Cell Phone Advertising 389
THE INSIDE STORY: Indian Villagers Advertise on Mobile Phones 390
Website Advertising 390 | Search Advertising 392 | Online Advertising Sales 393 | Digital Issues for Traditional Media 394 | Looking Ahead 394
IT'S A WRAP: Aflac's Flap Ducks Disaster 395
Key Points Summary 395
Key Terms 396
Review Questions 397
Discussion Questions 397
Take-Home Projects 397
TRACE North America Case 397

13. Owned, Interactive, and Earned Media 398
IT'S A WINNER: Unleash Deadly 399
Beyond Paid Media 400
Owned Media: We Own It; We Control It 400
Corporate Presence Media 401 | Branded Media 402 | The Media of Retail 403
A MATTER OF PRINCIPLE: Using Chinese Folk Arts in Promotional Designs 404
The Owned Media of Public Relations and Promotions 405
Owned but Interactive: Let's Talk 407
Corporate Interactive Media 408 | Direct-Response Media 408 | Personal Contact Media 408 | Interactive Promotional Media 410
THE INSIDE STORY: Farmers Ending Hunger 411
Owned Digital Media 411
A MATTER OF PRACTICE: How Web Sites Build Brands (or Don't) 413
Mobile Marketing 416 | Our Mobile Future 416
A MATTER OF PRACTICE: Your Mobile Future 417
Earned Interactive Media: Let's Listen 418
Earned Publicity 418 | Word of Mouth 419 | Social Media Mentions 420 | The Media of Sharing 422 | Earned and Interactive Media Considerations 423
Multiplatform Brand Communication 424
Viral Marketing 425 | Social Media Marketing 426 | Integration of Platforms 426
A MATTER OF PRINCIPLE: Advertising at the Intersection of Digital and Physical Media 427
Looking Ahead 427
IT'S A WRAP: Unleash Deadly 428
Key Points Summary 428
Key Terms 429
Review Questions 430
Discussion Questions 430
Take-Home Projects 430
TRACE North America Case 431

14. Media Planning and Negotiation 432
IT'S A WINNER: A Hair-Raising Story about Men's Cancer 433
How Are Media Plans Created? 434
Media Engagement Research 435
Key Steps in Media Planning 440
Step 1: Target Audience 440
A DAY IN THE LIFE: What Do I *Do* as a Media Planner? 441

A MATTER OF PRACTICE: Toyota Taps the Do-It-Yourself Community 443
Step 2: Communication and Media Objectives 444
A MATTER OF PRACTICE: Horizontal and Vertical Reach 445
Step 3: Media Strategies 447 I Step 4: Media Metrics and Analytics 455
A MATTER OF PRACTICE: Integrating Advertising and Public Relations Media Planning 458

How Do Media Buying and Negotiation Work? 460
Media-Buying Basics 460
PRACTICAL TIPS: Interactive Media Buying 463
Multichannel Buying (and Selling) 463 I Global Media Buying 464

Media Planning and Buying Trends 465
Unbundled Media Planning and Buying 465 I Online Media Buying 465 I New Forms of Media Research 465 I Looking Ahead 466
IT'S A WRAP: Having a Ball and Saving Lives 466

Key Points Summary 467
Key Terms 467
Review Questions 468
Discussion Questions 468
Take-Home Projects 468
TRACE North America Case 468
Hands-On Case 469

PART 5 Principle: IMC and Total Communication

15. Public Relations 472

IT'S A WINNER: Häagen-Dazs Creates a Buzz about Bees 473

What Is Public Relations? 474
Public Opinion 475 I Reputation: Goodwill, Trust, and Integrity 475 I How Public Relations Contributes to Brand Perception 476
A MATTER OF PRACTICE: Content Management as a Career in Public Relations 477

Different Types of Public Relations Programs 477
Aspects of Public Relations That Focus on Relationships 478 I Aspects of Public Relations That Focus on Particular Functions 479

What Key Decisions Guide Public Relations Plans? 481
Research and SWOT Analysis 481 I Targeting 482 I Objectives and Strategies 482
A MATTER OF PRACTICE: Mudo City: A Successful Brand Expansion 483
The Big Idea 484

What Are Common Public Relations Tools? 484
Advertising 486
A PRINCIPLED PRACTICE: The Social Impact of Public Service Advertising 487
Publicity 489 I Publications 491 I Other Tools 491 I Online Communication 492
A MATTER OF PRACTICE: Engaging Word of Mouth through Online Influencers 493
Looking Ahead 494
IT'S A WRAP: Just Bee-Cause 495

Key Points Summary 495
Key Terms 496
Review Questions 496

Discussion Questions 497
Take-Home Projects 497
TRACE North America Case 497

16. Direct Response 498
IT'S A WINNER: The Gecko and His Pals Go Direct for Geico 499
What Is Direct-Response Brand Communication? 500
Who Are the Key Players? 502 | What Is Included in the DBC Process? 503
What Are the Primary Tools and Media of DBC? 506
Personal Sales 506 | Direct-Response Advertising Media 507 | Direct Mail 508
THE INSIDE STORY: Thinking outside the Mailbox 510
Catalogs 512 | Telemarketing 513 | The Internet and New Forms of Direct Response 514
Databases: The Foundation of DBC 517
Databases Drive a Circular Process 518 | Lists 519 | Data Mining 520 | Issue: Privacy 521
A PRINCIPLED PRACTICE: Privacy: Use but Don't Abuse Consumer Information 523
DBC Trends and Challenges 524
Integrated Direct Marketing 524 | Global Considerations in DBC 526 | Looking Ahead 526
IT'S A WRAP: The Gecko and Pals Deliver Direct Response 527
Key Points Summary 527
Key Terms 528
Review Questions 528
Discussion Questions 528
Take-Home Projects 529
TRACE North America Case 529

17. Promotions 530
IT'S A WINNER: The Power of Pink 531
Why Sales Promotion? 532
Why Is Sales Promotion Growing? 533 | Sales Promotion Planning 535 | Promotional Big Ideas 538
Consumer Promotions 538
Tools of Consumer Promotions 538 | How Are Consumer Promotions Used? 542
Trade Promotions 543
Types of Trade Promotion 544
THE INSIDE STORY: Explore. Discover. FEI and the World of Images 545
How Is Trade Promotion Used? 546
PRACTICAL TIPS: Planning Point-of-Purchase Promotions 547
Multiplatform Promotions 548
Sponsorships and Event Marketing 548 | Event Marketing 549
A MATTER OF PRACTICE: Active Engagement through Event Sponsorships 549
A MATTER OF PRINCIPLE: The Underdog Wins the Super Bowl Ad Championship 550
Loyalty Programs 552 | Partnership Programs 552

Sales Promotion and Integration 554
Looking Ahead 555
IT'S A WRAP: Positively Pink 555
Key Points Summary 555
Key Terms 556
Review Questions 556
Discussion Questions 557
Take-Home Projects 557
TRACE North America Case 557

18. The Principles and Practice of IMC 558
IT'S A WINNER: I'm Amazing 559
Key IMC Concepts 560
Stakeholders and Brand Relationships 560 | Total Communication 561
A MATTER OF PRINCIPLE: When Is Too Many Too Much? 561
Moving from Channels to Contact Points 562 | Message Synergy 562 | A Brand Is an Integrated Perception 563 | Unified Brand Vision 563 | Internal Integration 563 | Brand Integrity 564
IMC Campaign Planning 564
What Is a Campaign Plan? 565 | Situation Analysis 565
A MATTER OF PRACTICE: Doha: A New City 566
Campaign Strategy 567 | The IMC Mix 571 | Message Strategy 572
A MATTER OF PRACTICE: A Campaign with Legs (and Flippers) 572
IMC Media and Contact Points 573 | Management and Campaign Controls 576
THE INSIDE STORY: What in the World Is Marketing Portfolio Management? 577
International IMC Campaigns 578
Managing 360° Communication Programs 581
Cause and Mission Marketing 581 | Internal Integration 582
A MATTER OF PRINCIPLE: Who's the Integrator Here, Anyway? 583
Looking Ahead 584
IT'S A WRAP: I'm Amazing 585
Key Points Summary 585
Key Terms 586
Review Questions 586
Discussion Questions 587
Take-Home Projects 587
TRACE North America Case 587

19. Evaluating IMC Effectiveness 588
IT'S A WINNER: Gut-Checking Obesity 589
Brand Communication Impact: Did It Work? 590
First Things First: The Campaign Objectives 590
A MATTER OF PRACTICE: Can You Really Predict the Impact of Advertising on Sales? 591
The Campaign Purpose: Brand Building 592 | Why Evaluation Matters 593
A MATTER OF PRINCIPLE: Completing the Cycle 593
How Evaluation Fits into the Stages of Brand Communication Testing 594

Evaluating the IMC Message 594
Experts in Message Evaluation 596 I Message Evaluation Techniques 597

Evaluating the Performance of Various IMC Tools 599
Advertising 600 I Public Relations 601 I Consumer, Trade, and Point-of-Purchase Promotions 601
THE INSIDE STORY: The Best and Worst Website Designs 603

Evaluating the Performance of Media Vehicles 603
Media Optimization 604 I Evaluating Exposure 604 I Vehicle-by-Vehicle Evaluation 604

IMC Campaign Evaluation Challenges 606
Measuring ROI 606 I The Synergy Problem 606 I Digital Challenges 607
A PRINCIPLED PRACTICE: Can a Broken Guitar Really Hurt United? 608
International Challenges 609

Back to the Big Picture: Did the Campaign Work? 609
Connecting the Dots: Tying Measurement Back to Objectives 609 I Bringing It All Together 610
IT'S A WRAP: Results of Colorado's Gut Check 611

Key Points Summary 612
Key Terms 612
Review Questions 613
Discussion Questions 613
Take-Home Projects 613
TRACE North America Case 613
Hands-On Case 614

Appendix 616
Glossary 621
Endnotes 639
Index 650

About the Authors

Sandra Moriarty, Ph.D., ***Professor Emerita, University of Colorado at Boulder***

Sandra Moriarty is cofounder of the Integrated Marketing Communication graduate program at the University of Colorado. Now retired, she has also taught at Michigan State University, University of Kansas, and Kansas State University, where she earned her Ph.D. in education. She specialized in teaching the campaign course and courses on the creative side—both writing and design. She has worked in government public relations, owned an advertising and public relations agency, directed a university publications program, and edited a university alumni magazine. She has been a consultant on integrated marketing communication with agencies such as BBDO and Dentsu, the largest advertising agency in the world, and with their clients in the United States, Europe, and Asia. Professor Moriarty has published widely in scholarly journals on marketing communication and visual communication topics and has authored 12 books on advertising, integrated marketing communication, marketing, visual communication, and typography. A classic book on integrated marketing, *Driving Brand Value*, was written with coauthor Tom Duncan. Most recently she has authored the *Science and Art of Branding* with Giep Franzen, University of Amsterdam. International versions of her books include Spanish, Chinese, Taiwanese, Korean, Japanese, and an English-language version for India. She has spoken to groups and presented seminars in most European countries, as well as Mexico, Japan, Korea, India, New Zealand, and Turkey.

Nancy Mitchell, Ph.D., ***Professor, University of Nebraska-Lincoln***

Nancy Mitchell is professor of advertising in the College of Journalism and Mass Communications at the University of Nebraska-Lincoln, where she's taught since 1990. She served as chair of the advertising department for 11 years before heading the graduate program in her college. Prior to her tenure at the University of Nebraska, she taught at West Texas A&M University. She's taught a variety of courses, including advertising principles, design, copywriting, research and strategy, and campaigns and media ethics. She worked as an advertising professional for 15 years before entering academe. She gained experience as a copywriter, designer, editor, fund-raiser, and magazine editor in an array of businesses, including a large department store, a publishing company, an advertising agency, a newspaper, and a Public Broadcasting System affiliate. Her research focuses on creating effective advertising messages to underrepresented groups, ethical issues, and assessment of student learning. Nationally, she served as Advertising Division Head for the Association for Education in Journalism and Mass Communications. She serves on the editorial boards for *Journal of Advertising Education* and *Journalism and Mass Communication Educator*.

William Wells, Ph.D., ***Professor Emeritus, University of Minnesota, and former Executive Vice President, DDB, Chicago***

One of the industry's leading market and research authorities, Bill Wells is a retired Professor of Advertising at the University of Minnesota's School of Journalism and Mass Communication. Formerly Executive Vice President and Director of Marketing Services at DDB Needharn Chicago, he is the only representative of the advertising business elected to the Attitude Research Hall of Fame. He earned a Ph.D. from Stanford University and was formerly Professor of Psychology and Marketing at the University of Chicago. He joined Needham, Harper, Chicago as Director of Corporate Research. Author of the Needham Harper Lifestyle study as well as author of more than 60 books and articles, Dr. Wells also published Planning for ROI: Effective Advertising Strategy (Prentice Hall, 1989).

Preface

The Power of Liking

You know what—and who—you like. And your likes ripple through your friendship circles as you influence and are influenced by people you know and respect. That's what research in 2013 found about the practice of "liking" something on Facebook and other social media. A positive comment or action feeds on itself and sets off a cycle of friendly responses as it spins through a network of communication.

Why is that important to advertising and brand communication? It's because these "likes" may echo and amplify thoughts and feelings about brands and organizations as well as people and events.

Commercial communication has changed radically in the 21st century, moving from marketer-driven and product-focused brand messages to social media strategies that aim to inspire positive comments about brands and the organizations behind them. In this new world, the snowball effect of liking may spread the word about a brand faster and farther than traditional advertising—and with greater impact.

But liking is just the social face of emotion. On a deeper level, savvy marketers would like customers to fall in love with their brands.

That's the focus of a 2013 book called *Loveworks: How the World's Top Marketers Make Emotional Connections to Win in the Marketplace* by Brian Sheehan, one of this book's contributors. He's also a Syracuse University professor who spent 25 years working for Saatchi & Saatchi and its agencies in Japan, Australia, and Los Angeles. Based on a previous book called *Lovemarks* by Saatchi's CEO Kevin Roberts, Professor Sheehan's *Loveworks* uses case studies to prove that brands that engage consumer's deepest emotions are the ones that work—the brands that win in the marketplace.

For example, the idea that responses to communication are driven by emotion is demonstrated in the "Blood Relations" campaign by the Saatchi agency in Tel Aviv that showed Israelis and Palestinians giving blood together. The effort was sponsored by the Parents Circle Families Forum (both Israeli and Palestinian families whose relatives had been wounded or killed in the conflict) and the Peres Centre for Peace. The simplicity of the symbolism of "blood relations" and the imagery of blood donors sitting side by side was supported by the slogan "Could you hurt someone who has your blood running through their veins?" The "Blood Relations" videos led to an avalanche of coverage both in Israel and internationally on NBC, BBC, and Reuters, generating comments in blogs as well as other news publications and radio stations. The effort won the United Nations Gold Award and five Gold Lions at Cannes in 2012, but it also moved a few survivors and combatants to see each other in a more positive way.

That's why this textbook, *Advertising & IMC: Principles & Practice*, is dedicated not only to explaining advertising and other areas of brand communication—such as public relations, direct marketing, and sales promotion—but also to make you think about what works in commercial communication.

We'll look at the basic principles and best practices in an industry that is undergoing radical change—old media are shape-shifting, and new media are emerging and merging with old media. The practice of brand communication faces new and exciting challenges in an interactive age where consumers are more in charge—actively selecting and designing their own media worlds and engaging with their friends in new forms of social media.

This 10th edition reflects these changes as it challenges its readers to assume control not only of their media choices but also of their bigger role as consumers and creators of products, ideas, and media.

What's New in the 10th Edition

1. ***Liking, Loving, and Loyalty*** In recognition of the importance of brand liking, the 10th edition of *Advertising & IMC: Principles & Practice* focuses throughout on emotion-driven strategies that have relevance to consumers and that create feelings of liking for a brand or organization. It also focuses on brand relationship strategies that move consumers from targets to partners, moving away from one-way communication to interactive and experiential brand communication.
2. ***The New Media World*** The media world has changed so dramatically in the first decade of the 21st century that the old media categories we have used in the past, such as print or broadcast, are no longer valid. Media distinctions have blurred and expanded to include media other than advertising. Furthermore, consumers now exert more control over media selection as their role as consumers of media has expanded. This has driven the biggest change in the 10th edition, which is a total rewrite of the four chapters in Part 4.

   The media industry has a new concept that describes this broader and more interactive media world—POE, which stands for Paid, Owned, and Earned. With the guidance of the media experts on our Advisory Board, we have restructured the four media chapters in Part 4 around these concepts. We've also included Interactive as a defining media concept. In other words, we are now approaching media not in terms of the form (print or broadcast) but rather as functions—particularly how media function in consumers lives where they seek out entertainment, social connections, and information. This approach is discussed in Chapter 11 as part of the overview of the changes in the media marketplace. Here is how this totally rewritten presentation of the media world is presented in Chapters 12, 13, and 14:

   - ***Paid Media*** This category includes traditional advertising, which relies on the purchase of time and space from other media owners, as well as new media used to deliver advertising messages, such as cell phones, video games, and online ads. This is the focus of the new Chapter 12.
   - ***Owned Media*** The first part of Chapter 13 looks at media owned and controlled by the organization, such as corporate public relations materials, as well as media used in retail promotions and branded media, which are often used by consumers to engage in positive, entertaining experiences.
   - ***Interactive Owned Media*** Also in Chapter 13, we consider corporate interactive media (such as websites, Facebook, and Twitter pages), direct-response media, personal contact media and experiences (sales and customer service), and mobile marketing platforms. Although owned by the organization, consumers use them to gain information and participate in entertainment and social activities.
   - ***Earned Interactive Media*** The earned category has traditionally been the province of public relations, particularly through publicity and mentions in the news media. In addition, this discussion of earned media has been broadened in Chapter 13 to include word of mouth (such as referrals) and brand mentions in social media, such as Facebook and Twitter. The focus is on buzz—people talking about things that interest them, including brands.
   - ***Multiplatform Brand Communication Strategies*** Chapter 13 concludes with a discussion of new practices, such as mobile marketing, viral marketing, and social media marketing, that call for new approaches to platform integration as these new media forms overlap and, it is hoped, reinforce one another.
   - ***Media Planning and Negotiation*** Chapter 14 continues to provide a review of the media planning and buying functions; however, the buying operation is reframed to emphasize the important role of negotiation. In addition, this chapter is expanded to include the complexities of managing multimedia and multiplatform programs.

3. ***More In-Depth IMC Focus*** The title of this book was modified in the ninth edition to recognize the importance of integrated marketing communication (IMC) practices, many of which have been important in this book since its first edition. In the 10th edition, a number of other changes have been made to better align the content with an IMC philosophy:
   - ***More on Promotional Writing*** Chapter 9 was rewritten to include writing for all the areas of brand communication. So, instead of a focus on only advertising copywriting, writing for all areas of brand communication is discussed.
   - ***Broader Review of Media*** Similar to the advertising copywriting change in Chapter 9, media from all IMC disciplines and functions are discussed in the four media chapters in Part 4.
   - ***Principles of IMC*** A set of IMC principles was developed in the ninth edition. Instead of appearing throughout the book, as they did in ninth edition, in the 10th edition these principles have been grouped to form a more comprehensive presentation of the basic IMC concepts in Chapter 18. This is a wrap-up technique to pull the IMC discussion together into a more coherent conclusion about the essential IMC concepts and the principles on which they are based.
   - ***IMC Campaign Discussion as Summary*** Discussions about campaign planning were sprinkled through a number of chapters in the ninth edition. In the 10th edition, campaign planning is developed more comprehensively in Chapter 18 as a way to summarize the principles and practices discussed in the previous chapters.
   - ***IMC Management*** Chapter 18 concludes by making a distinction between the practice of IMC campaigns, which by their nature are more short term, and the management of IMC programs, which involves setting the direction and philosophy of an IMC operation for the long term.
4. ***New Evaluation Chapter (and Author)*** Chapter 19 introduces Regina Lewis, a member of the book's Advisory Board, as the author of the final chapter in the book, which wraps up the discussion of effectiveness and the evaluation of brand communication efforts. An expert in consumer insight, Professor Lewis has directed marketing communication research and evaluation programs for Dunkin' Brands and the Intercontinental Hotels Group. She uses her broad experience to shape our discussion of the critical area of evaluation and wrap up the discussion of effectiveness, which continues to be a central theme of *Advertising & IMC: Principles & Practice*.
5. ***New Examples of Award-Winning Brand Communication Campaigns*** Part of the added value of this textbook lies in the cohesive story that it tells about effective brand communication. This is particularly important as students face a radically changing and complex media environment. New and updated case studies open each chapter in the 10th edition to illustrate basic principles and best practices and show students how professionals design and execute effective strategies that work.
6. ***New Faces, New Cases, New Brands*** Throughout the book new stories have been added to update the discussions and illustrate the many changes in this new marketing communication environment.
   - In the 10th edition two new members of the Advisory Board have been involved not only with personal interviews and writing boxes, but also with critiquing and making suggestions about changing content and, in some cases, changing the organizational structure of the book.
   - We have seven new Ad Stars whose work and thoughts we feature, as well as eight new Pros and Profs who have written boxes about their research, professional work, and other projects.
   - All but two of the opening stories are new or have been completely rewritten. We also have five new part-ending cases.
   - We have a major new case adapted from the AAF National Student Advertising Competition in the Appendix with application and reflection questions at the end of every chapter.
   - With a total of 33 new or completely rewritten boxes, almost every chapter has new featured stories to support and further explain concepts in the text.
7. ***Contributions from Experts around the World*** Preparing students to become effective brand communicators requires a broad knowledge about many subjects in

a dramatically changing media environment. This edition expands the number of contributions from experts across the globe, exposing students to a vast array of contemporary thinking about current issues. These pieces are designed to pique readers' interest about exciting new possibilities related to brand communication and challenge students to think critically in their quest to apply enduring principles and develop effective practices.

The Central Themes

Although the introduction to this preface highlighted changes, the important thing in a textbook project of this size and scale is that there are central threads that weave key ideas across the chapters and throughout the book. So let's consider the foundation themes that make this book different from other introductory textbooks in advertising and marketing communication.

Brand Communication and IMC

This book started out many years ago as an introductory advertising textbook; however, it has always had an IMC slant with coverage of other marketing communication areas. Over the years, the scope of advertising has changed. Now we use the phrase *brand communication* (or *marketing communication*) because what used to be known as *advertising* has expanded beyond the familiar ads in print media and commercials on radio and television.

Electronic and social media have opened up new ways to communicate online with consumers about a brand. Alternative and nontraditional forms, such as *guerilla marketing*, which reaches people in surprising ways in unexpected places, have opened up new opportunities to engage people with brand messages through memorable experiences.

Creating buzz and dialogue have replaced the old practice of targeting messages at consumers. A new goal is to enlist word-of-mouth conversations to reinforce and extend the power of the more traditional marketing communication forms.

This wider view of *advertising* includes an array of communication tools used by a variety of organizations—nonprofit as well as for-profit—promoting consumer as well as business-to-business products and services. We mention public relations, direct marketing, and sales promotion, but those are just a few of the tools in the brand communication tool kit.

We will describe the use of these various forms of brand communication as IMC, which refers to the strategic use of multiple forms of communication to engage different types of consumers who have an interest in or a connection to a brand. The title of this book changed in the previous edition to recognize the importance of IMC in modern brand communication.

Effectiveness

During a Super Bowl some years ago, an ad for Anheuser-Busch called "Applause" showed people in an airport spontaneously applauding a group of American troops returning home. Even the audience watching from their living rooms were inclined to join in with applause as part of this graceful display of respect and appreciation. It was touching and memorable, and it might have nudged a few viewers to think well of Anheuser-Busch.

But was it an effective ad? What was it trying to accomplish? Did the viewers remember it as an Anheuser-Busch ad, and, if so, did it affect their opinions of that company and its brands?

What is effective? Is it marketing communication that gets talked about? Is it a message like the Anheuser-Busch commercial that touches your emotions and inspires you to applaud? What, exactly, does it mean to say that a brand message "works"?

Our answer is that brand communication is effective if it creates a desired response in the audience. A brand message *that works* is one that affects people; it gets results that can be measured.

Effective messages move people to like, love, laugh, dance, squirm in their seats, or even shed tears. But they can also cause you to stop and watch or even to stop and think. Commercial communication can't make you do something you don't want to do, but it can inspire you to read about a new product or remember a favorite brand when you're walking down the aisle in a supermarket.

This book uses the *Facets Model of Advertising Effects* to better explain brand communication strategies, consumer responses, and effectiveness. The facets model is like a diamond or a crystal whose surfaces represent the different types of responses generated by a brand message. This model and the ideas it represents are used throughout the book to help explain such things as how objectives are decided on, what strategies deliver what kind of effects, and how an advertisement and other forms of marketing communication are evaluated based on their objectives.

That's why this textbook is dedicated not only to explaining advertising and other areas of brand communication—such as public relations, direct marketing, and sales promotion—but also to make you think about what works in all commercial communication efforts.

The Facets Model of Effects

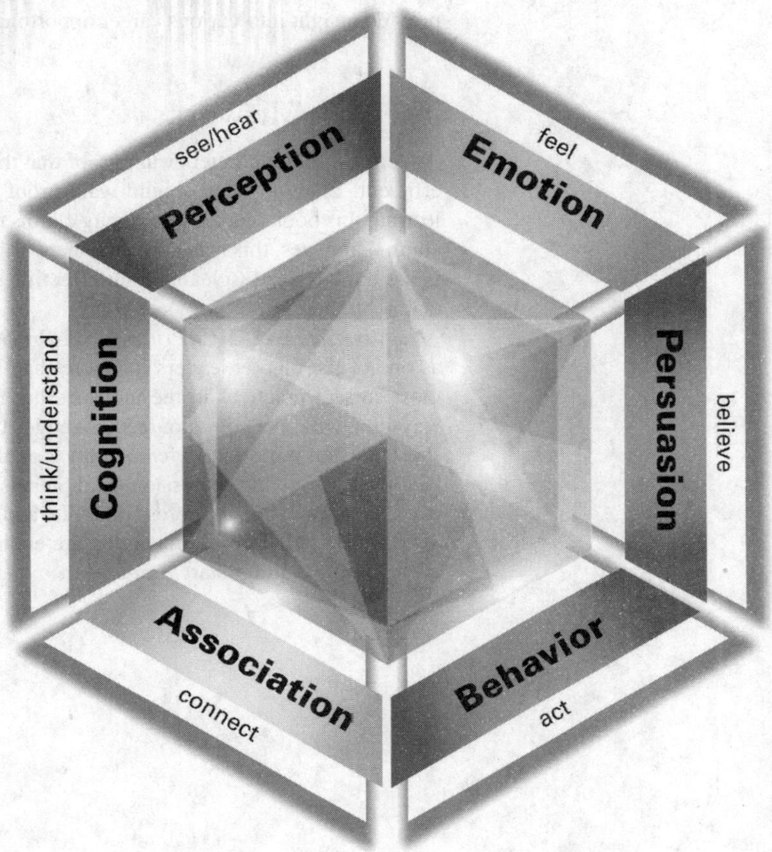

Enduring Principles and Best Practices

To help you better understand how effective communication is created, this textbook will highlight the principles and practices of the industry. Marketing communication messages are part inspiration and part hard work, but they are also a product of clear and logical thinking. In most cases, consumers have little idea what the objectives are because that information generally isn't made public—and you sometimes can't tell from the communication itself. But think about the "Applause" ad. From what we've told you, what do you think the ad's objectives are? To sell beer? To get viewers to run out and buy the brand? Actually, the ad seems to be a bit removed from a straight sales pitch.

An educated guess—and that's what you will be better able to make after reading this book—is that perhaps its objective is simply to make people feel good, to see the goodness in a simple patriotic gesture—and, ultimately, to associate that feeling of goodness and warmth with the brand. Does it work? How did you feel when you read over the description of the ad?

This book presents both principles and practices of effective brand communication. You will find principles in the margins of the text in every chapter. In addition, boxes and other features elaborate on both the principles and the practices related to the topic of each chapter.

In this 10th edition, we take you behind the scenes of many award-winning campaigns, such as the Aflac, Altoids, Geico, and McDonald's campaigns, to uncover the hard work and explain the objectives, the inspiration, and the creative ideas behind some great campaigns. You will see how the ideas come together; you will live through the decision making, and you will understand the risks the message creators faced.

We also have contributions from highly experienced professionals as well as our Ad Stars—graduates from advertising and marketing communication programs around the country who were nominated by their professors to be featured in this book. We showcase their work throughout the book. They also have written "Inside Stories" that explain strategies and what they have learned on the job as well as "A Day in the Life" features that provide insight into various career opportunities in marketing communication.

The Proof It Works

Advertisers and marketers want proof that their marketing communication is effective and efficient. Likewise, you should want proof about the value of your textbooks. You will learn in this book that all advertising claims need to be supported. That's why we make the claim—and, yes, this is an advertisement—that *Advertising & IMC: Principles & Practice* is the book to read to learn about effective brand communication. We are making a bold claim, but here is how we back it up.

Advertising & IMC: Principles & Practice is time-tested. That's why it has continued as one of the market leaders for more than 25 years. It continues to be in touch with the most current practices in the industry, but it also presents the fundamental principles in ways that will give you a competitive edge. That's why students keep this textbook on their shelves as an important reference book as they move through their major. One thing we hear from our young professional Ad Stars is that they continue to rely on this book as they make their transition to professional life, and you can find it on many of their office shelves as well. The principles in this book are enduring, and your understanding of the practices of the field can jump-start your career.

Contributors

Advisory Board VIPs

Shawn M. Couzens
Conceptual Engineer, AbbaSez, Yardley, Pennsylvania

Constance Cannon Frazier
Chief Operating Officer, AAF, Washington, D.C.

Larry Kelley
Partner, Media Director, and Chief Planning Officer, FKM, and Professor, University of Houston, Texas

Regina Lewis
Associate Professor, University of Alabama, and Contributing Author for Chapter 19

Ingvi Logason
Principal, H:N Marketing Communications, Reykjavik, Iceland

Harley Manning
Vice President of Research and Research Director, Forrester Research

Susan Mendelsohn
Ph.D., President, Susan Mendelsohn Consultants, Chicago, Illinois

David Rittenhouse
Worldwide Media Director, Ogilvy, New York

William H. Weintraub
Chief Marketing Officer (Retired), Coors Inc., Boulder, Colorado

Karl Weiss
President/CEO, Market Perceptions, Inc., Denver, Colorado

Robert Witeck
CEO, Witeck Communications, Washington, D.C.

Charles E. Young
Ph.D., Founder and CEO, Ameritest, Albuquerque, New Mexico

Contributors: Ad Stars

Masaru Ariga
Group Account Director, Dentsu Inc., Tokyo, Japan

Heather Beck
Photographer, Beck Impressions, Lewisburg, Tennessee

John Brewer
President and CEO, Billings Chamber of Commerce/CVB, Billings, Montana

Ed Chambliss
Vice President, Team Leader, The Phelps Group, Santa Monica, California

Diego Contreras
Art Director, Anomaly, New York

Jennifer L. Cunningham
Account Manager at Disney's Yellow Shoes Creative

Michael Dattolico
Owner, Musion Creative, LLC, Gainesville, Florida

Tammie DeGrasse-Cabrera
Management Supervisor, CP+B, Miami

Graham Douglas
Creative Director, Droga5, New York

Eric Foss
Director of Consulting Services, North America, Pcubed, Denver, Colorado

Amy Hume
Communications Consultant, University of Colorado–Denver

Mike Latshaw
President and Copywriter, Full Flannel Nudity, Pittsburgh, Pennsylvania

Melissa Lerner
Vice President, Director, Client Delivery and Data, Posterscope

Elisabeth Loeck
University of Nebraska–Lincoln

Lara Mann
Associate Creative Director, mcgarrybowen, Chicago

Mary Nichols
Founder and Chief Community Builder, Karmic Marketing, Portland, Oregon

Amy Niswonger
Design Instructor, School of Advertising Art, Dayton, Ohio; President, Ninth Cloud Creative & Little Frog Prints

Sonia Montes Scappaticci
Business Development Director, Branded Entertainment, Catmandu Entertainment, Detroit, Michigan

Karl Schroeder
Senior Writer, Coates Kokes, Portland, Oregon

Peter Stasiowski
Marketing and Communications Manager, Interprint, Inc., Pittsfield, Massachusetts

Kate Stein
University of Florida and Cornell Law School

Aaron Stern
Freelance Copywriter, New York, New York

Trent Walters
Brand Management Team Leader, The Richards Group, Dallas, Texas

Lisa Yansura
Marketing Coordinator, Gragg Advertising, Kansas City, MO

Wendy Zomnir
Creative Director and Founding Partner, Urban Decay, Costa Mesa, California

Contributors: Pros and Profs

Glenda Alvarado
Assistant Professor, Advertising and Public Relations, University of South Carolina

Nikki Arnell
Assistant Professor of Graphic Design, Arkansas State University

Bill Barre
Instructor, Central Michigan University

Ann Barry
Associate Professor, Boston College, Boston, Massachusetts

Fred Beard
Professor, Gaylord College of Journalism and Mass Communication, University of Oklahoma, Norman

Daryl Bennewith
Strategic Director, TBWA Group, Durban, South Africa

Edoardo Teodoro Brioschi
Professor and Chair of Economica and Techniques of Business Communication, Università Cattolica del Sacro Cuore, Milan, Italy

Sheri Broyles
Professor andInterim Chair, Department of Strategic Communications, Mayborn School of Journalism, University of North Texas, Denton

Clarke Caywood
Professor and Director, Graduate Program in Public Relations, Medill School of Journalism, Northwestern University, Evanston, Illinois

Jason Cormier
Cofounder and Managing Partner, Room214.com, Boulder, Colorado

Joel Davis
Professor, School of Journalism and Media Studies, San Diego State University

Bonnie Drewniany
Associate Professor, University of South Carolina, Columbia

Tom Duncan
IMC Founder and Director Emeritus, University of Colorado, and Daniels School of Business, University of Denver

Steve Edwards
Director and Professor, Termerlin Advertising Institute, Southern Methodist University, Dallas, Texas

Gary Ennis
Freelance Creative Director

Arlene Gerwin
Marketing Consultant and President, Bolder Insights, Boulder, Colorado

Thomas Groth
Professor, Department of Communication Arts, University of West Florida, Pensacola

Jean M. Grow
Associate Professor, Diederich College of Communication, Marquette University, Milwaukee, Wisconsin

Scott R. Hamula
Associate Professor and Program Director, Integrated Marketing Communications, Roy H. Park School of Communications, Ithaca College, Ithaca, New York

Michael Hanley
Associate Professor, Department of Journalism, Ball State University

Dean Krugman
Professor Emeritus, Department of Advertising and Public Relations, Grady College of Journalism and Mass Communication, University of Georgia, Athens

Hairong Li
Professor, Department of Advertising, Public Relations, and Retailing, Michigan State University, East Lansing

Qing Ma
Professor, Shejiang University City College, Hangzhou, China

Karen Mallia
Associate Professor, University of South Carolina, Columbia

James Maskulka
Associate Professor of Marketing, Lehigh University, Bethlehem, Pennsylvania

Michael McNiven
Managing Director and Portfolio Manager for Cumberland Advisors, Sarasota, Florida

George Milne
Professor, University of Massachusetts–Amherst

Keith Murray
Professor, College of Business, Bryant University, Smithfield, Rhode Island

Connie Pechmann
Professor, Paul Merage School of Business, University of California–Irvine

Jimmy Peltier
Professor, Marketing, University of Wisconsin–Whitewater

Joseph E. Phelps
Professor and Chair, Department of Advertising and Public Relations, University of Alabama, Tuscaloosa

James Pokrywczynski
Associate Professor, Strategic Communication, Diederich College of Communication, Marquette University

Jef I. Richards
Chair and Professor, Department of Advertising and Public Relations, Michigan State University

Herbert Rotfeld
Professor of Marketing, Auburn University, Alabama

Sheila Sasser
Professor of Advertising Creativity, IMC, and Marketing, College of Business, Eastern Michigan University, Ypsilanti

Brian Sheehan
Associate Professor, S. I. Newhouse School of Public Communications, Syracuse University, Syracuse, New York

Mark Stuhlfaut
Associate Professor, University of Kentucky

John Sweeney
Professor, Head of Advertising and Director of Sports Communication Program, University of North Carolina–Chapel Hill

Ronald E. Taylor
Professor, School of Advertising and Public Relations, University of Tennessee–Knoxville

Joe Tougas
Professor, Evergreen State College, Olympia, Washington

Wan-Hsiu Sunny Tsai
Assistant Professor, School of Communication, University of Miami, Florida

Bruce G. Vanden Bergh
Professor Emeritus, Department of Advertising and Public Relations, Michigan State University, East Lansing

Philip Willet
Assistant Professor, University of Oklahoma

Joyce M. Wolburg
Professor and Associate Dean, Diederich College of Communication, Marquette University, Milwaukee, Wisconsin

Acknowledgments

Thanks to Liz Williamson and Emily Zarybnisky for their invaluable editorial assistance and to Seonmin Bae for her help with research.

Pearson would like to thank and acknowledge the following people for their work on the Global Edition:

Contributors:

Rania Deeb, *Business Consultant, UAE*
Diane Sutherland, *Writer*
Jon Sutherland, *Writer*

Reviewers:

Kim Min-chung, *Hong Kong Polytechnic University*
Jayashree Sreenivasan, *Multimedia University*
Lilian Yap, *Wawasan Open University*

Advertising & IMC

Principles & Practice

Tenth Edition

Global Edition

PART

1 Principle: Back to Basics

This is one of the most exciting times to take an advertising course because of all the changes in the industry—new technology, new media, new types of consumers and media users, new ways of looking at brand communication, and new economic challenges. It's also a great time to be studying the basics of advertising and brand communication because this is the era of back to basics. Why do we say that?

Unchanging Truths in Times of Change

Bill Weintraub
is retired from Coors where he was chief marketing officer. Before that he spent 15 years managing a range of brands at Procter & Gamble, then he was chief marketing officer at Kellogg and Tropicana. He teaches about brands and brand communication at the University of Colorado and the Daniels School of Business at Denver University.

Rather than redefine the field to accommodate changing times, Bill Weintraub, one of this book's advisory board members and a marketing expert who led marketing teams at Procter & Gamble, Tropicana, Kellogg's, and Coors, insists that the basic truths in marketing communication are immutable.

He observes, "Whether the economy is strong or weak, the basic principles of strategy and persuasion remain in place. As economic conditions change, what might evolve is more or less strategic emphasis on 'price' vs. 'value added'—in product offering and formulation, promotion strategy, and advertising executions." He continues,

> I don't believe the underlying principles of marketing and communication should ever change. Regardless of the economy, new media, changes in culture, etc. I don't accept that these superficial changes in the marketing environment are relevant in terms of how intelligent business practices should be conducted.

The Basic Truth: Understand Your Brand

So what are the immutable principles that guide the practice of marketing communication? The most important is understanding your brand.

Advisory board member Regina Lewis, who has been in charge of consumer insights for InterContinental Hotel Group and Dunkin' Brands, says, "There is a very charged need for brand authenticity. With social media's power, brands are tasked with—among other things—achieving

CHAPTER 1 • Advertising
CHAPTER 2 • Brand Communication
CHAPTER 3 • Brand Communication and Society

perfect transparency." In other words, "There is an enhanced need for brand clarity—for brands to know exactly what they stand for and to communicate exactly what they stand for."

How is that brand strategy developed and delivered? Weintraub believes that "the essence of building a brand is a sound strategy that clearly differentiates a brand (in a positive way) to a specific group of consumers for whom the brand promise is relevant."

Lewis believes that the basics of successful branding lie with connecting with consumer values. Like, Weintraub, she sees that "uniquely positioning your brand (a strategy based on knowing how consumers think and feel about your brand versus competitive brands) is essential." But that's just the foundation of successful branding; the structure of a successful brand is built on effective communication. As Lewis explains, "Communicating about your brand in a way that is highly meaningful to consumers becomes even more important" in dynamic periods such as we see in this 21st century.

Dr. Regina Lewis has been vice president of Global Consumer Insights at InterContinental Hotels Group and vice president and director of the Consumer and Brand Insights Group at Dunkin' Brands, Inc. She is now an associate professor in the Department of Advertising and Public Relations at the University of Alabama.

The Enduring Principles

We agree with Weintraub and Lewis that branding, positioning, and communication are the foundations of brand success. We've elaborated on their thoughts to compile seven principles that we believe express marketing and marketing communication basics. These principles are central themes in this textbook:

1. ***Brand*** Build and maintain distinctive brands that your customers love.
2. ***Position*** Identify your competitive advantage in the minds of consumers.
3. ***Consumers*** Focus on consumers and match your brand's strengths to consumer needs and wants.
4. ***Message*** Identify your best prospects and engage them in a brand conversation
5. ***Media*** Know how to best reach and connect with your target audience.
6. ***Integrate*** Know how to connect the dots and make everything in the marketing communication toolkit work together.
7. ***Evaluate*** Track everything you do so you know what works.

As you will see throughout this book, effective advertising and marketing communication are founded on these basic, enduring principles. That doesn't mean that brand communication is unchanging. In fact, the practices are dynamic and continually adapting to changing marketplace conditions. But the basic principles are unchanging even in times of change. In the chapters that follow in Part 1, these principles and practices will be explained, as will the key concepts of advertising and brand communication.

CHAPTER

1 Advertising

Source: Ads reprinted courtesy of Wieden + Kennedy and the Procter & Gamble Co.

It's a Winner

Campaign	Company	Agency	Award
The Man Your Man Could Smell Like	*Old Spice/ Procter & Gamble*	*Wieden + Kennedy* **Contributing Agencies** *Paine PR, Landor*	*Grand Effie and Gold Effies in Beauty Products, Brand Experience, Media Innovation, Single Impact Engagement categories*

CHAPTER KEY POINTS

1. What is advertising, how has it evolved, and what does it do in modern times?
2. How have the key concepts of marketing communication developed over time?
3. How is the industry organized—key players, types of agencies, and jobs within agencies?
4. Why and how is the practice of advertising changing?

Old Spice: What It Takes to Be a Man

"The original. If your grandfather hadn't worn it, you wouldn't exist." This recent Old Spice slogan is part of an award-winning campaign that has become a cultural phenomenon. Old Spice advertising is a good starting point for this book because it lets us see advertising through a lens of change. What worked to convince your grandfather to use Old Spice probably wouldn't persuade guys to use it now.

This book explains and demonstrates principles and practices of effective advertising today. We are interested not only in ads that amuse us personally but also in ads that communicate effectively to achieve goals for the companies that sponsor them. Old Spice is a great example because it has demonstrated its effectiveness sufficiently to win the Grand Effie, the top prize in a competition that recognizes advertising and marketing communication that works.

As you read the book, you'll get a behind-the-scenes look at what makes advertising effective. You can see for yourself that a 1953 ad for Old Spice with the headline "Grand Shave? Looking Great!" and pictures of the shaving lotion bottle probably wouldn't cut it today to sell much shaving cream. Advertising has evolved to be much more complex than simply announcing that a brand of shaving cream is for sale, as the more recent "The Man Your Man Could Smell Like" campaign proves.

Procter & Gamble (P&G) and its agency Wieden + Kennedy faced a significant challenge to protect Old Spice's share in the male body wash segment and boost sales amid fierce competition, particularly from Dove Men+Care body wash, which was introduced during the 2010 Super Bowl.

To address this challenge, P&G took stock of the situation. Old Spice was perceived as a manly scent, not a feminine scent like other brands. P&G's research surprisingly revealed that women—not men—purchased 60 percent of men's body wash. The big idea driving the marketing communication: the campaign needed to spark conversations between men and women talking about a manly-scented body wash. If you want to "smell like a man," then the choice is obvious: Old Spice. Former NFL tight end Isaiah Mustafa (remember the bare-chested guy on the horse?) brought the message to life with his hilarious and over-the-top delivery about manhood.

Executing the idea in the digital age requires more than running an ad in a magazine or a commercial on television. P&G devised a strategy that involved using media in an innovative way, building buzz with social media and using YouTube, Facebook, Twitter, the Old Spice website, as well as television commercials to get people talking.

These commercials appeared on YouTube and Facebook a few days before—not during—the Super Bowl when airtime is superexpensive, and they ran in places where both sexes might be together and see them, such as during *Lost*, the Vancouver Winter Olympics, and *American Idol*.

Another component of this campaign was designed to generate buzz by letting the audience ask questions of "The Man Your Man Could Smell Like." Interactivity, getting people involved with a memorable message through a communication exchange, is a key to convincing the audience that Old Spice is cool.

Did it work? At the end of the chapter, the "It's a Wrap" section will report the results.

Sources: "The Man Your Man Could Smell Like," Effie Awards published case study, www.effie.org and www.oldspice.com; Bruce Watson, "Smells Like Viral Advertising: Old Spice through the Ages," July 16, 2010, www.dailyfinance.com; Brian Morrissey, "Old Spice's Agency Flexes Its Bulging Stats," August 4, 2010, www.adweek.com; "Online Video: Old Spice The Most Viral Brand of the Year—Again", December 28, 2011, www.adage.com.

In this chapter, we'll define advertising and its role in marketing and more generally in marketing communication. We'll also explain how advertising's basic concepts and practices evolved. Then we'll describe the agency world. We'll conclude by analyzing the changes facing the larger area of marketing communication.

What Is Advertising?

You've seen thousands, maybe millions, of commercial messages. Some of them are advertising, but others are different types of promotional messages, such as the design of a package or a sporting event sponsorship. But the heavyweight promotional tool in terms of dollars and impact is advertising, also the most visible of all the forms of marketing communication, and that's why we will start first with advertising.

So how would you define advertising? It may sound silly to ask such an obvious question. But where would you start if your instructor asked you for a definition?

At its most basic, the purpose of advertising has always been to sell a *product*, which can be *goods*, *services*, or *ideas*. Although there have been major changes in recent years, the basic premises of advertising remain unchanged even in the face of economic downturns and media convulsions. So how do we define it now, realizing that advertising is dynamic and that its forms are constantly changing to meet the demands of society and the marketplace? We can summarize a modern view of advertising with the following definition:

> **Advertising** is a paid form of persuasive communication that uses mass and interactive media to reach broad audiences in order to connect an identified sponsor with buyers (a target audience), provide information about products (goods, services, and ideas), and interpret the product features in terms of the customer's needs and wants.

This definition has a number of elements, and as we review them, we will also point out where the definition is changing because of new technology, media shifts, and cultural changes (see also the *American Marketing Association Dictionary* at www.marketingpower.com/_layouts/Dictionary.aspx).

Advertising is usually *paid* for by the advertiser (e.g., P&G) who has a product to *sell* (Old Spice), although some forms of advertising, such as public service announcements, use donated space and time. Not only is the message paid for, but the sponsor is identified. Advertising began as *one-way* communication—from an advertiser to a targeted audience. Digital, interactive media, however, have opened the door to interesting new forms of *two-way* and *multiple-way* brand-related communication, such as word-of-mouth conversations among friends or consumer-generated messages sent to a company.

Advertising generally reaches a *broad audience* of *potential customers*, either as a *mass audience* or in smaller *targeted* groups. However, *direct-response* advertising, particularly those practices that involve digital communication, has the ability to address individual members of the audience. So some advertising can deliver *one-to-one* communication but with a large group of people.

In traditional advertising, the message is conveyed through different kinds of *mass media*, which are largely *nonpersonal* messages. This nonpersonal characteristic, however, is changing with the introduction of more *interactive* types of media, as the Old Spice case demonstrates with its social media that created a great deal of buzz. Richard Edelman, chief executive officer (CEO) of the Edelman agency, emphasizes the emerging importance of *word of mouth*, which is personal communication through new media forms rather than what he describes as "scripted messages in a paid format."[1] In other words, the communication pattern is not just from a *business* to a *consumer*, which we sometimes describe in marketing shorthand as "B to C," but it can also be *business* to *consumer* to *consumer*, or "B to C to C," which recognizes the important role of personal communication—**word of mouth**—about a product or even an advertisement.

Most advertising has a defined strategy and seeks to *inform* consumers and/or make them *aware* of a brand, company, or organization. In many cases, it also tries to *persuade* or influence consumers to do something, such as buy a product or check out a brand's website. Persuasion may involve *emotional* messages as well as information. The Old Spice strategy was designed to recognize the negative messages associated with the brand's old image in order to turn the image around and make it cool for today's audience.

Keep in mind that, as we have said, a *product* can be a *good*, a *service*, or an *idea*. Some nonprofits, for example, use ads to "sell" memberships, inform about a cause and its need for donations and volunteers, or advocate on behalf of a position or point of view.

Advertising is not the only tool in a brand's promotional toolkit, although it may be the biggest. Advertising is a more than $500 billion industry worldwide and a $174 billion industry in the United States.[2] Advertising often is seen as the driving force in marketing communication because it commands the largest budget as well as the largest number of agencies and professionals.

What Are Advertising's Basic Functions?

To summarize the key parts of the definition and to better understand advertising's development as a commercial form of communication, it helps to see how advertising's definition has evolved over the years in terms of three critical functions.

- ***Identification*** *Advertising identifies a product and/or the store where it's sold.* In its earliest years, and this goes back as far as ancient times, advertising focused on identifying a product and where you could buy it. Some of the earliest ads were simply signs with the name or graphic image of the type of store—cobbler, grocer, or blacksmith.
- ***Information*** *Advertising provides information about a product.* Advances in printing technology at the beginning of the Renaissance spurred literacy and brought an explosion of printed materials in the form of posters, handbills, and newspapers. Literacy was no longer the badge of the elite, and it was possible to reach a general audience with more detailed information about products. The word **advertisement** first appeared around 1655, and by 1660 publishers were using the word as a heading in newspapers for commercial information. These messages announced land for sale, runaways (slaves and servants), transportation (ships arriving, stagecoach schedules), and goods for sale from local merchants. Because of the importance of commercial information, these ads were considered news and in many cases occupied more space in early newspapers than the news stories.
- ***Persuasion*** *Advertising may persuade people to buy things.* The Industrial Revolution accelerated social change as well as mass production. It brought the efficiency of machinery

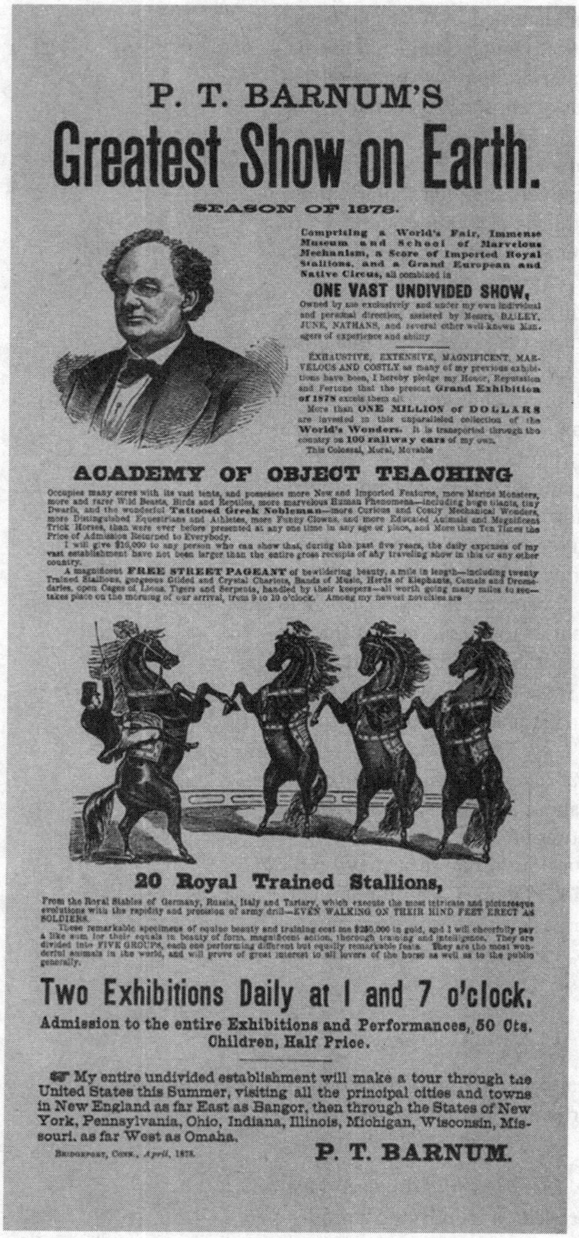

Source: Collection of the John and Mable Ringling Museum of Art Tibbals Collection.

CLASSIC

P. T. Barnum was a pioneer in advertising and promotion. His flamboyant circus posters were more than just hype. What are the other roles they performed?

Principle

Effectiveness means meeting the stated objectives, and that can be determined only if evaluation is built into the strategy.

not only to the production of goods but also to their distribution. Efficient production plus wider distribution meant manufacturers could offer more products than their local markets could consume. With the development of trains and national roads, manufacturers could move their products around the country. For widespread marketing of products, it became important to have a recognizable brand name, such as Ivory or, more recently, Old Spice. Also, large groups of people needed to know about these goods, so along with industrial mechanization and the opening of the frontier came even more use of new communication media, such as magazines, catalogs, and billboards that reached more people with more enticing forms of persuasion. P. T. Barnum and patent medicine makers were among the advertising pioneers who moved promotion from identification and information to a flamboyant version of persuasion called *hype*—graphics and language characterized by exaggeration, or hyperbole.

Over the years, these three functions—identification, information, and persuasion—have been the basic objectives of marketing communication and the focus of most advertising messages. Even though this first chapter focuses on advertising, note that many of the advertising basics, such as organization, compensation, and strategy, also apply to the other marketing communication functions.

What Are the Key Components of Advertising?

In this brief review of how advertising developed over some 300 years, a number of key concepts were introduced, all of which will be discussed in more detail in the chapters that follow. But let's summarize these concepts in terms of a simple set of key components that describe the practice of advertising: strategy, message, media, and evaluation (see Figure 1.1):

- ***Strategy*** The logic or **strategy** behind an advertisement or any type of marketing communication message is stated in measurable objectives that focus on areas such as sales, news, psychological appeals, emotion, branding, and brand reputation, as well as the position and differentiation of the product from the competition and segmenting and targeting the best prospects.
- ***Message*** The concept behind a message and how that message is expressed is based on research and consumer insights with an emphasis on creativity and artistry.
- ***Media*** Various media have been used by advertisers over the centuries including print (handbills, newspapers, and magazines), outdoor (signs and posters), broadcast (radio and television), and now digital media. Targeting ads to prospective buyers is done by matching their profiles to media audiences. Advertising agency compensation was originally based on the cost of buying time or space in the media.
- ***Evaluation*** Effectiveness means meeting the stated objectives, and in order to determine if that has happened, there must be evaluation methods planned into the strategy. Standards also are set by professional organizations and companies that rate the size and makeup of media audiences as well as advertising's social responsibility.

Common Types of Advertising

Advertising is not only a large industry but also a varied one. Different types of advertising have different roles. Considering all the different advertising situations, we can identify eight major types of advertising:

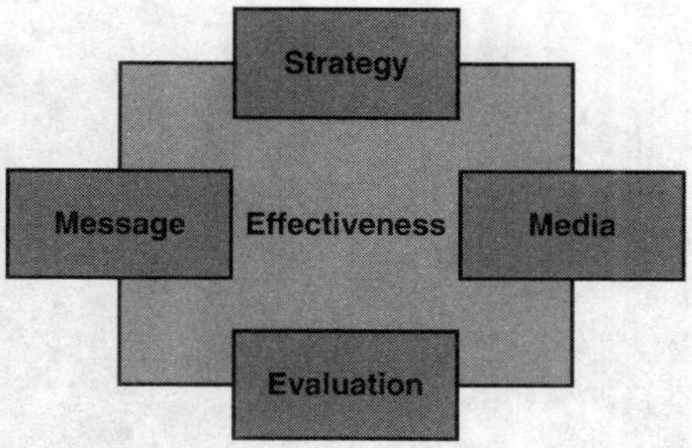

FIGURE 1.1
Four Components of Advertising

1. **Brand advertising**, the most visible type of advertising, is referred to as *national* or *consumer* advertising. Brand advertising, such as that for the Apple Macintosh in the classic "1984" commercial, focuses on the development of a long-term brand identity and image.
2. **Retail advertising** or **local advertising** focuses on retailers, distributors, or dealers who sell their merchandise in a certain geographical area; retail advertising has information about products that are available in local stores. The objectives focus on stimulating store traffic and creating a distinctive image for the retailer. Local advertising can refer to a retailer, such as T. J. Maxx; a service provider, such as KFC; or a manufacturer or distributor who offers products in a fairly restricted geographic area.
3. **Direct-response advertising** tries to stimulate an immediate response by the customer to the seller. It can use any advertising medium, particularly direct mail and the Internet. The consumer can respond by telephone, by mail, or over the Internet, and the product is delivered directly to the consumer by mail or some other carrier.
4. **Business-to-business (B2B) advertising**, also called *trade advertising,* is sent from one business to another. It includes messages directed at companies distributing products as well as industrial purchasers and professionals, such as lawyers and physicians. Advertisers place most business advertising in professional publications that reach these audiences.
5. **Institutional advertising**, also called **corporate advertising**, focuses on establishing a corporate identity or winning the public over to the organization's point of view. Tobacco companies, for example, run ads that focus on the positive things they are doing. The ads for a pharmaceutical company showcasing leukemia treatment also adopt that focus.
6. **Nonprofit advertising** is used by not-for-profit organizations, such as charities, foundations, associations, hospitals, orchestras, museums, and religious institutions, to reach customers (e.g., hospitals), members (the Sierra Club), and volunteers (Red Cross). It is also used to solicit donations and other forms of program participation. The "*truth*"® campaign for the American Legacy Foundation, which tries to reach teenagers with antismoking messages, is an example of nonprofit advertising.
7. **Public service advertising** provides messages on behalf of a good cause, such as stopping drunk driving (as in ads from Mothers Against Drunk Driving) or preventing child abuse. Also called **public service announcements**, advertising and public relations professionals usually create them **pro bono** (free of charge), and the media donate the space and time.
8. Specific advertising areas, such as health care, green marketing, agribusiness, and international, address specific situations or issues and have developed specialized advertising techniques and agencies. For example, some $262 million were spent for and against the health care reform legislation.[3]

Although these categories identify characteristics of various types of advertising, there are many commonalities. In practice, all types of advertising demand creative, original messages that are strategically sound and well executed, and all of them are delivered through some form of media. Furthermore, advertisements can be developed as single ads largely unrelated to other ads by the same advertiser, such as the "1984" ad for Apple, or as a **campaign**, a term that refers to a set of related ads that are variations on a theme. They are often used in different media at different times for different segments of the audience and to keep attracting the attention of the target audience over a period of time.

Principle
All types of advertising demand creative, original messages with a sound strategy delivered through some form of media.

Other Important Promotional Tools

As we said, advertising's original purpose was to sell something, but over the years, other promotional tools, with different sets of strengths, have developed to help meet that objective. For example, providing information, particularly about some new feature or a new product, is sometimes better handled through *publicity* or public relations. *Direct-response* advertising, such as catalogs and flyers sent to the home or office, can also provide more information in

Retail Retailers sometimes advertise nationally, but much of their advertising is targeted to a specific market, such as this direct-mail piece for T. J. Maxx.

Brand Advertising This ad promotes a brand, Crest Whitestrips, and provides information about the product as well as reasons to buy it.

more depth than traditional ads that are limited in space and time. *Specialties* that carry brand logos as reminders or incentives to buy are handled by *sales promotion* companies. Communication with employees and shareholders about brands and campaigns is usually handled by *public relations*.

In other words, a variety of promotional tools can be used to identify, inform, and persuade. Professionals see differences in all of these areas, but many people just see them all as *promotion* or lump them together and call them *advertising*. The proper name for this bundle of tools, however, is **marketing communication (marcom)**, an umbrella term that refers to the various types of promotional tools and communication efforts about a brand that appear in a variety of media. Although we are focusing on advertising in this chapter, the book will also introduce you to this expanded concept of marketing communication. Chapter 2 will provide more information about this wider world of brand communication.

What Roles Does Advertising Perform?

Advertising obviously plays a role in both communication and marketing, as we've been discussing. In addition to marketing communication, advertising also has a role in the functioning of the economy and society. Consider the launch of the Apple Macintosh in 1984, which was successful because of the impact of one advertisement, a television commercial generally considered to be the greatest ever made. As you read about this "1984" commercial in the "A Matter of Practice" feature, note how this commercial demonstrated all four roles—marketing, communication, social, and economic.

Marketing and Communication Roles In its marketing communication role, advertising provides information about a product. It can also transform a product into a distinctive brand by creating a **brand image** that goes beyond straightforward information about product features. The "1984" commercial demonstrated how a personality could be created for a computer

Photo: © 2004 The Pharmaceutical Research and Manufacturers of America (PhRMA). All rights reserved

Institutional This ad for a pharmaceutical trade association uses a heart-tugging visual and copy to show consumers the value of the organization's activities—producing drugs that help save lives.

Photo: Courtesy of Aflac Incorporated

Business-to-Business (B2B) Most people buy Aflac policies through payroll deduction at their workplace. Aflac used its memorable, quirky duck in B2B advertising to create a brand identity and help businesspeople understand how Aflac insurance can be part of an employee benefit package at no direct cost to the company.

(innovative), one that showcased it as a creative tool that breaks through the rigid systems of other computer brands. As advertising showcases brands, it also creates consumer demand (lines of customers the following day at stores where the Macintosh was sold) and makes statements that reflect social issues and trends (opening up the new category of personal computers for nonexperts). So, in addition to marketing and communication, advertising has economic and social roles.

Economic and Societal Roles Advertising flourishes in societies that enjoy economic abundance, in which supply exceeds demand. In these societies, advertising extends beyond a primarily informational role to create a demand for a particular brand. In the case of the Old Spice campaign, the decision was to invite people to ask questions in order to generate **buzz** as well as reinforce a high level of demand for the brand. Creating buzz—getting people to talk about the brand—has become an important goal of marketing communication in this era of social media.

Most economists presume that, because it reaches large groups of potential consumers, advertising brings cost efficiencies to marketing and, thus, lower prices to consumers. The more people know about a product, the higher the sales—and the higher the level of sales, the less expensive the product. Think about the high price of new products, such as a computer, HDTVs, and cell phones or other technologies. As demand grows, as well as competition, prices begin to drop. David Bell, retired CEO of the Interpublic Group, told a group of advertising educators in 2012 that "advertising is the motor of a successful economy. . . . But it isn't effective without trust . . . and ethics is critical to trust." In his view, the economic importance of advertising is a function of its social acceptance.[4] We'll talk about the critical role of ethics in Chapter 3 and trust in Chapter 4.

Principle
Advertising creates cost efficiencies by increasing demand among large groups of people resulting in higher levels of sales and, ultimately, lower prices.

Two contrasting points of view explain how advertising creates economic impact. In the first, the rational view, advertising is seen as a vehicle for helping consumers assess value through price cues and other information, such as quality, location, and reputation. Advocates of

A Matter of Practice

The Greatest Commercial Ever Made

The advertiser was Apple, the product was its new Macintosh, and the client—the person handling the advertising responsibility and making decisions—was Steve Jobs, Apple's CEO, who wanted a "thunderclap" ad. The agency was California-based Chiat/Day (now TBWA/Chiat/Day) with its legendary creative director Lee Clow (now global director for media arts at TBWA worldwide). The medium was the Super Bowl. The "supplier" was legendary British film director Ridley Scott of *Alien* and *Blade Runner* fame. The audience was the 96 million people watching Super Bowl XVIII that winter day in January 1984, and the target audience was all those in the audience who were trying to decide whether to buy a personal computer, a relatively new type of product for consumers.

It's a basic principle in advertising: The combination of the right product at the right time in the right place with all the right people involved can create something magical—in this case, Jobs's thunderclap. It also required a cast of 200 and a budget of $900,000 for production and $800,000 for the 60-second time slot. By any measure, it was a big effort.

The story line was a takeoff on George Orwell's science fiction novel about the sterile mind-controlled world of *1984*. An audience of mindless, gray-skinned drones (who were actually skinheads from the streets of London) watches a massive screen image of "Big Brother" spouting an ideological diatribe. Then an athletic young woman in bright red shorts runs in, chased by helmeted storm troopers, and throws a sledgehammer at the screen. The destruction of the image is followed by a burst of fresh air blowing over the open-mouthed drones as they "see the light." In the last shot, the announcer reads the only words in the commercial as they appear on screen:

> On January 24th, Apple Computer will introduce Macintosh. And you'll see why 1984 won't be like "1984."

Was it an easy idea to sell to the client?

First of all, some Apple executives who first saw the commercial were terrified that it wouldn't work because it didn't look like any commercial they had ever seen. After viewing it, several board members put their heads down in their hands. Another said, "Who would like to move on firing Chiat/Day immediately?" Legend has it that Apple's other founder, Steve Wozniak, took out his checkbook and told Jobs, "I'll pay for half if you pay for the other half." The decision to air the commercial finally came down to Jobs, whose confidence in the Chiat/Day creative team gave him the courage to run the ad. Recently, Clow and Steve Hayden, copywriter on "1984," said that Steve Jobs "put a stake in the ground," referring to how he wanted "technology in the hands of everybody."

Was it effective?

On January 24, long lines formed outside computer stores carrying the Macintosh, and the entire inventory sold out in one day. The initial sales goal of 50,000 units was easily surpassed by the 72,000 units sold in the first 100 days. More would have been sold if production had been able to keep up with demand.

The "1984" commercial is one of the most-talked-about and most-remembered commercials ever made. Every time someone draws up a list of best commercials, it sits at the top, and it continues to receive accolades more than two decades later.

Remember, the commercial ran only once—an expensive spot on the year's most-watched television program. The commercial turned the Super Bowl from just another football game into the advertising event of the year. What added to its impact was the hype before and after it ran. People knew about the spot because of press coverage prior to the game, and they were watching for it. Coverage after the game was as likely to talk about the "1984" spot as the football score. Advertising became news, and watching Super Bowl commercials became an event. That's why *Advertising Age* critic Bob Garfield calls it "the greatest TV commercial ever made."

Go to *YouTube.com* and search for 1984 Apple Hammer ad to view this award-winning commercial in its entirety as well as an interview with Ridley Scott about making this award-winning commercial.

Sources: "The Breakfast Meeting: What Olbermann Wrought, and Recalling Apple's '1984,'" *New York Times* Media Decoder, April 2, 2012, *http://mediadecoder.blogs.nytimes.com*; Kevin Maney, "Apple's '1984' Super Bowl Commercial Still Stands as Watershed Event," *USA Today*, January 28, 2004, 3B; Liane Hansen (host), "Steve Hayden Discusses a 1984 Apple Ad Which Aired during the Super Bowl," National Public Radio Weekend Edition, February 1, 2004; Bradley Johnson, "10 Years after '1984': The Commercial and the Product That Changed Advertising," *Advertising Age*, June 1994, 1, 12–14; Curt's Media, "The 1984 Apple Commercial: The Making of a Legend," *www.isd.net/cmcalone/cine/1984.html*.

this viewpoint see the role of advertising as a means to objectively provide price/value information, thereby creating more *rational economic decisions*. By focusing on images and emotional responses, the second approach appeals to consumers making a decision on *nonprice, emotional appeals*. This emotional view explains how images and psychological appeals influence consumer decisions. This type of advertising is believed to be so persuasive that it decreases the likelihood a consumer will switch to an alternative product, regardless of the price charged.

In addition to informing us about new and improved products, advertising also mirrors fashion and design trends and adds to our aesthetic sense. Advertising has an educational role in that it teaches about new products and their use. It may also expose social issues—some say the "1984" commercial symbolically proclaimed the value of computer literacy "for the rest of us," those who weren't slaves to the hard-to-operate PC systems of the time. It helps us shape an image of ourselves by setting up role models with which we can identify (a woman athlete liberating the gray masses), and it gives us a way to express ourselves in terms of our personalities (smash the screen image of Big Brother) and sense of style (red shorts—the only color in the drab environment) through the things we wear and use. It also presents images capturing the diversity of the world in which we live. These social roles have both negative and positive dimensions, which we will discuss in Chapter 3.

How Did Current Practices and Concepts Evolve?

As illustrated in the timeline in Figure 1.2, the advertising industry is dynamic and is affected by changes in technology, media, and the economic and social environment. But this history is far more than names and dates. The timeline reflects how the principles and practices of a multi-billion-dollar industry have evolved.[5]

Eras and Ages

The time line divides the evolution of advertising into five stages that reflect historical eras and the changes that led to different philosophies and styles of advertising. As you read through this, note how changing environments, in particular media advancements, have changed the way advertising functions. (For more historical information, check out the extensive time line at http://adage.com/century/timeline/index.html or http://library.duke.edu/digitalcollections/eaa. Another source for classic ads is www.vintageadbrowser.com.)

The Early Age of Print Industrialization and mechanized printing spurred literacy, which encouraged businesses to advertise beyond just their local place of business. Ads of the early years look like what we call **classified advertising** today. Their objective was to *identify products* and *deliver information* about them, including where they were being sold. The primary medium of this age was *print*, particularly newspapers, although handbills and posters were also important, as were hand-painted signs. The first newspaper ad appeared in 1704 for Long Island real estate, and Benjamin Franklin's *Pennsylvania Gazette* ran the first advertising section in 1729. The first *magazine* ads appeared in 1742 in Franklin's *General Magazine*.

The Early Age of Agencies The 19th century brought the beginning of what we now recognize as the advertising industry. Volney Palmer opened the *first ad agency* in 1848 in Philadelphia. The J. Walter Thompson agency formed in 1864, the oldest advertising agency still in existence. P. T. Barnum brought a Swedish singer to the United States and used a blitz of newspaper ads, handbills, and posters, one of the first *campaigns*. In 1868, the N. W. Ayer agency began the **commission system** for placing ads—advertising professionals initially were agents or brokers who bought space and time on behalf of the client for which they received a commission, a percentage of the media bill. The J. Walter Thompson agency invented *the* **account executive** position, a person who acts as a liaison between the client and the agency.

As advertisers and marketers became more concerned about creating ads that worked, professionalism in advertising began to take shape. Here, also, is when it became important to have a definition or a theory of advertising. In the 1880s, advertising was referred to by advertising

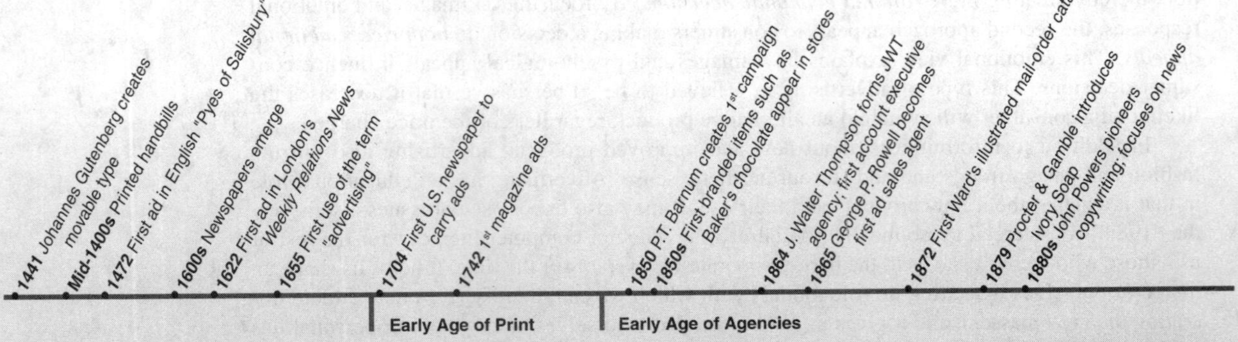

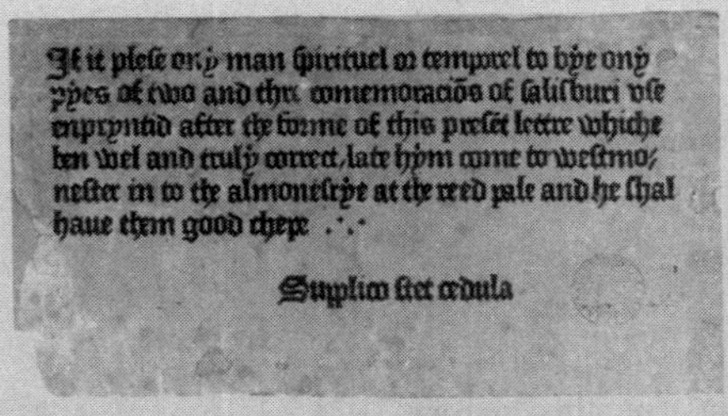

This early English ad, written by William Caxton in 1477, is an example of printed ads in the 15th century.

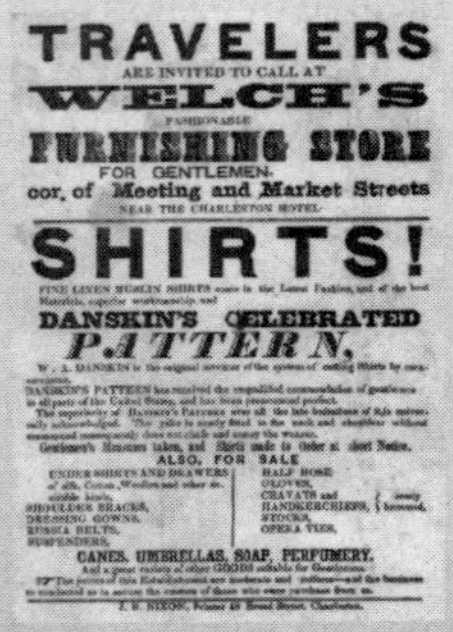

In this1869 ad, George P. Rowell's Ad-Wholesaling agency used testimonial from a satisfied customer to promote the agency.

FIGURE 1.2
Time Line
(Ads displayed by permission)

legend Albert Lasker as "*salesmanship in print* driven by a *reason why*." Those two phrases became the model for stating an ad *claim* and explaining the *support* behind it.

On the retail side, department store owner John Wanamaker hired John E. Powers in 1880 as the store's full-time **copywriter**, and Powers crafted an advertising strategy of "*ads as news*." The McCann agency, which began in 1902, also developed an agency philosophy stated as "*truth well told*" that emphasized the agency's role in crafting the ad message. *Printer's Ink*, the advertising industry's first trade publication, appeared in 1888. In the early 1900s, the J. Walter Thompson agency began publishing its "Blue Books," which explained how advertising works and compiled media data as an industry reference.

By the end of the 19th century, advertisers began to give their goods **brand names**, such as Baker's Chocolate and Ivory Soap. The purpose of advertising during this period was to create demand as well as a visual identity for these new brands. Inexpensive brand-name products, known as *packed goods*, began to fill the shelves of grocers and drug stores. The questionable ethics of hype and *puffery*, which is exaggerated promises, came to a head in 1892 when *Ladies Home Journal* banned patent medicine advertising. But another aspect of hype was the use of powerful graphics that dramatized the sales message.

In Europe, the visual quality of advertising improved dramatically as artists who were also *illustrators*, such as Toulouse-Lautrec, Aubrey Beardsley, and Alphonse Mucha, brought their craftsmanship to posters and print ads as well as magazine illustrations. Because of the artistry, this period is known as the *Golden Age*. The artist role moved beyond illustration to become the **art director** in 20th-century advertising.

The Scientific Era In the early 1900s, professionalism in advertising was reflected in the beginnings of a professional organization of large agencies, which was officially named the American Association of Advertising Agencies in 1917 (www.aaa.org). In addition to getting the industry organized, this period also brought a refining of professional practices. As 19th-century department store owner John Wanamaker commented, "Half the money I spend on advertising is wasted and the trouble is I don't know which half." That statement partly reflected a need to know more about how advertising works, but it also recognized the need to better target the message.

1888 George Eastman creates first Kodak camera.
1888 Printer's Ink founded
1890s Earnest Elmo Calkins and Ralph Holder develop image copy
1890s Lord & Thomas agency forms
1904–1940s Albert Lasker pioneers "reason-why" copy
1905 John E. Kennedy describes advertising as "Salesmanship in print"
1905–1930s Claude Hopkins develops scientific mail-order copy testing
1906 Pure Food and Drug Act
1908 Beginning of celebrity endorsements—Pepsi uses famed racecar driver Barney Oldfield
1912 "Truth in Advertising" movement
1914 FTC Act passed
1917 American Association of Advertising Agencies formed
1918 Stanley & Helen Resor develop account services, brand names, and status appeals
1923 Young & Rubicam agency formed

Scientific and Regulation Era

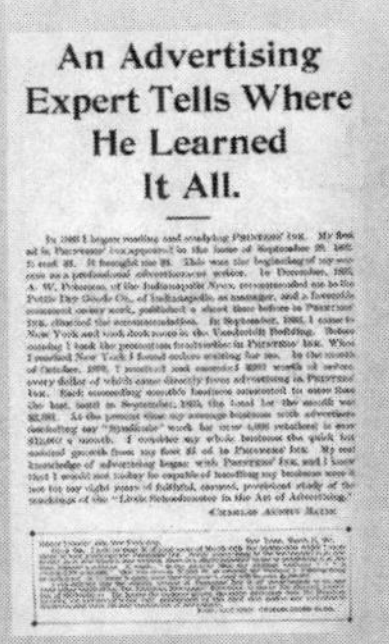
An Advertising Expert Tells Where He Learned It All.

After WW1, "I wanted to be happy" was the call of consumer, and jazz and dancing became popular, as this ad for Victor Talking Machine Co. illustrates.

In the early 20th century, modern professional advertising adopted scientific *research* techniques. Advertising experts believed they could improve advertising by blending science and art. Two leaders were Claude Hopkins and John Caples. At the height of Hopkins's career, he was Lord & Thomas's best-known copywriter. Highly analytical, he conducted *tests of his copy* to refine his advertising methods, an approach explained in his 1923 book *Scientific Advertising.* John Caples, vice president of Batten, Barton, Durstine and Osborn (BBDO), published *Tested Advertising Methods* in 1932. His theories about the *pulling power of headlines* also were based on extensive tests. Caples was known for changing the style of advertising writing, which had been wordy and full of exaggerations. During the 1930s and 1940s, Daniel Starch, A. C. Nielsen, and George Gallup founded research organizations that are still part of today's advertising industry.

During and after the Great Depression, Raymond Rubicam emerged as an advertising power and launched his own agency with John Orr Young, a Lord & Thomas copywriter, under the name of Young and Rubicam. Their work was known for intriguing headlines and fresh, original approaches to advertising ideas.

The idea that messages should be directed at particular groups of prospective buyers, a practice called **targeting**, evolved as media became more complex. Advertisers realized they could spend their budgets more efficiently by identifying those most likely to purchase a product as well as the best ways to reach them. The scientific era helped media better identify their audiences. In 1914, the Audit Bureau of Circulation, now known as Alliance for Audited Media, was formed to standardize the definition of paid circulation for magazines and newspapers. Media changes saw print being challenged by *radio advertising* in 1922. Radio surpassed print in ad revenue in 1938.

The world of advertising agencies and management of advertising developed rapidly in the years after World War II. The J. Walter Thompson agency, which still exists today, led the boom in advertising during this period. The agency's success was due largely to its *creative copy* and the *management* style of the husband-and-wife team of Stanley and Helen Resor. Stanley developed the concept of *account services* and expanded the account executive role into strategy development; Helen developed innovative copywriting techniques. The Resors also coined the brand-name concept as a strategy to associate a unique identity with a particular product as well as the concept of *status appeal* to persuade nonwealthy people to imitate the habits of rich people (www.jwt.com).

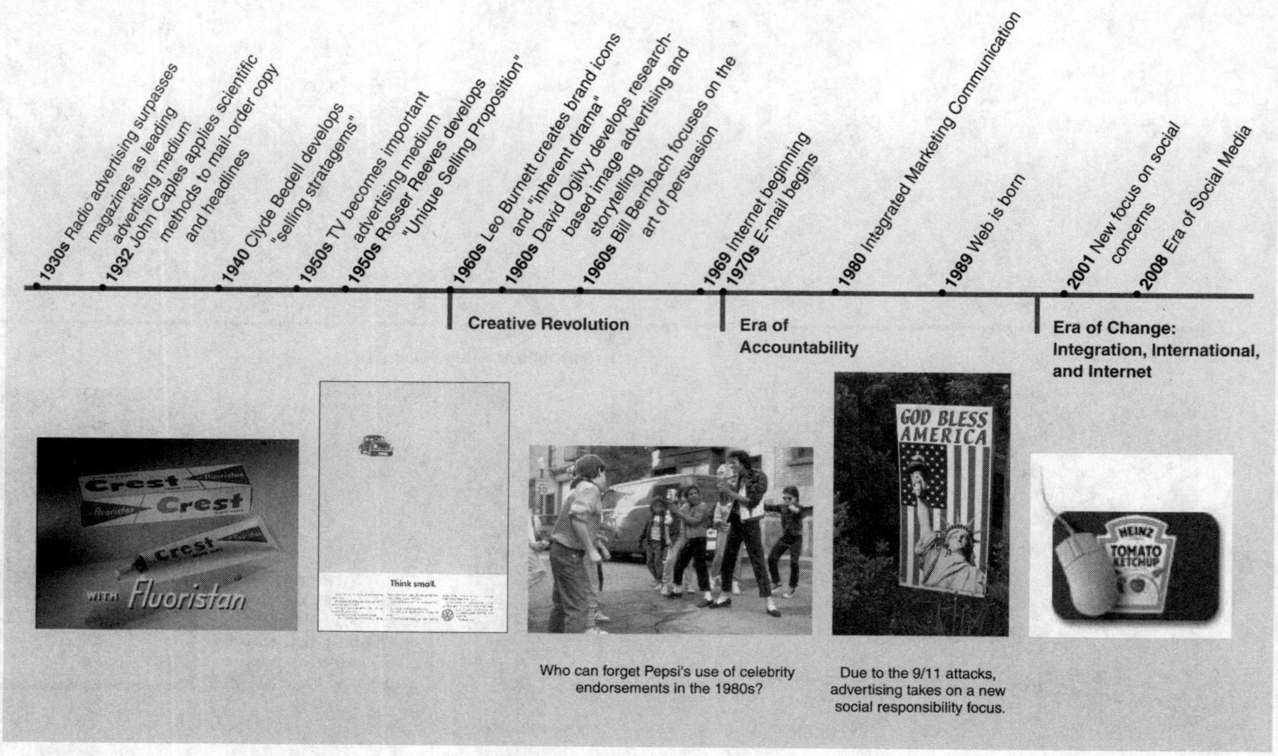

Who can forget Pepsi's use of celebrity endorsements in the 1980s?

Due to the 9/11 attacks, advertising takes on a new social responsibility focus.

FIGURE 1.2
(continued)

Television commercials came on the scene in the early 1950s and brought a huge new revenue stream to the advertising industry. In 1952, the Nielsen rating system for television advertising became the primary way to measure the reach of *television commercials*.

This period also saw marketing practices, such as **product differentiation** (identifying how a brand differs from its competition) and **market segmentation** (identifying groups of people who would likely buy the product) incorporated into advertising strategy. The idea of **positioning**, carving out a unique spot in people's minds for the brand relative to its competition, was developed by Al Ries and Jack Trout in 1969.

The Creative Era The creative power of agencies exploded in the 1960s and 1970s, a period marked by the resurgence of art, inspiration, and intuition. Largely in reaction to the emphasis on research and science, this revolution was inspired by three creative geniuses: Leo Burnett, David Ogilvy, and William Bernbach.

Leo Burnett was the leader of what came to be known as the *Chicago school of advertising*. He believed in finding the "*inherent drama*" in every product. He also believed in using *cultural archetypes* to create mythical characters who represented American values, such as the Jolly Green Giant, Tony the Tiger, the Pillsbury Doughboy, and his most famous campaign character, the Marlboro Man (www.leoburnett.com).

Ogilvy, founder of the Ogilvy & Mather agency, is in some ways a paradox because he married both the *image school* of Rubicam and the *claim school* of Lasker and Hopkins. He created enduring brands with *symbols*, such as the Hathaway Man and his mysterious eye patch for the Hathaway shirt maker, and handled such quality products as Rolls-Royce, Pepperidge Farm, and Guinness with product-specific and information-rich claims (www.ogilvy.com).

The Doyle, Dane, and Bernbach (DDB) agency opened in 1949. From the beginning, William Bernbach—with his acute sense of words, design, and creative concepts—was considered to be the most innovative advertising creative person of his time. His advertising touched people—and persuaded them—by focusing on *feelings and emotions*. He explained, "There are a lot of great technicians in advertising. However, they forget that advertising is persuasion, and persuasion is not a science, but an art. Advertising is the art of persuasion."[6] Bernbach is known for the understated Volkswagen campaign that ran at a time when car ads were full of glamour and bombast.

The campaign used headlines such as "Think Small" with accompanying picture of a small VW bug (www.ddb.com).

The Era of Accountability and Integration Starting in the 1970s, the industry-wide focus was on **effectiveness**. Clients wanted ads that produced sales, so the emphasis was on research, testing, and measurement. To be accountable, advertising and other marketing communication agencies recognized that their work had to prove its value. After the dot-com boom and economic downturn in the 1980s and 1990s, this emphasis on accountability became even more important, and advertisers demanded proof that their advertising was truly effective in accomplishing its *objectives* as stated in the strategy.

Social responsibility is another aspect of accountability. Although advertising regulation has been in place since the early 1900s with the passage of the Pure Food and Drug Act in 1906 and the creation of the Federal Trade Commission in 1914, it wasn't until 1971 that the National Advertising Review Board was created to monitor questions of *taste and socicl responsibility.* Charges of using sweatshops in low-wage countries and an apparent disregard for the environment concerned critics such as Naomi Klein, who wrote the best-selling book *No Logo*, and Marc Gobe, who wrote *Citizen Brands.* One powerful campaign that demonstrates social responsibility is the SORPA effort from Iceland.

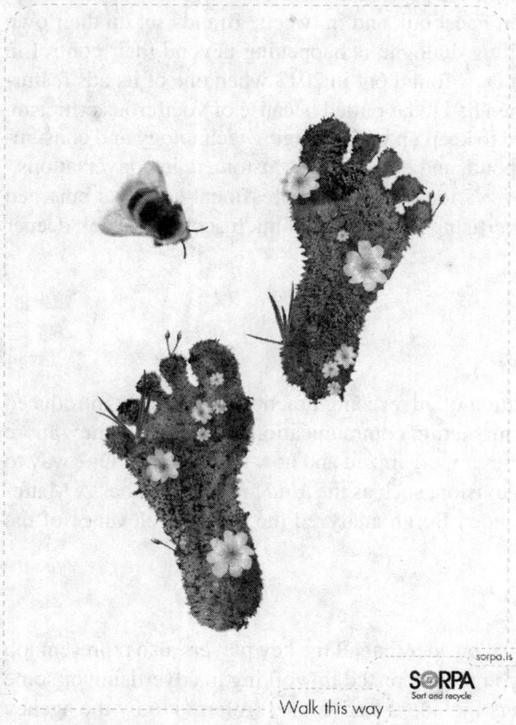

Photo: Courtesy of SORPA bs and Ingvi Logason. Used with permission

Photo: Courtesy of ngvi Logason

SHOWCASE

Contributed by Ingvi Logason, this work by his agency H:N Marketing Communication in Reykjavik, Iceland, for the local SORPA recycling center, urged people to participate in recycling. He explained, "From day one the marketing strategy, concept and platform has been very consistent—always positive, encouraging, and built around light colors. These two print ad examples were part of an overall image/reminder campaign that has the company aiming for even higher positive ratings, SORPA is now maintaining over a 90 percent positive rating."

A graduate of the University of West Florida, Ingvi Logason, who is a member of this book's Advisory Board, was nominated by Professor Tom Groth.

Ingvi Jökull Logason CEO and Strategy Director, H:N Marketing Communication, Reykjavík, Iceland

As the *digital era* brought nearly instantaneous means of communication, spreading *word of mouth* among a social network of consumers, companies became even more concerned about their practices and brand or corporate reputation. The recession that began in December 2007 and subsequent headlines about bad business practices, such as the Bernard Madoff "Ponzi" scheme and bank lending practices, made consumers even more concerned about *business ethics.*

We also characterize this as the era when integrated marketing communication became important. **Integrated marketing communication** (IMC) is another technique that managers began to adopt in the 1980s as a way to better coordinate their brand communication. Integration leading to consistency makes marketing communication more efficient and thus more financially accountable.

The Social Media Era Advertising and marketing communication practices have been turned upside down in the years since 2008. Digital and online communication became important in brand communication even earlier in the new century with most brands and companies setting up websites and experimenting with online advertising worldwide. But with the launch of Facebook, Twitter, YouTube, and other vehicles for sharing thoughts, photos, and even videos, the structure of consumer communication was radically altered.

No longer are brand messages dependent on planned and managed marketing communication programs with their targeted messages and one-way communication. In this new interactive world, consumers are generating brand messages and posting them to YouTube as well as sharing their thoughts and experiences with brands on Facebook and in tweets. Brands set up their own Facebook and Twitter accounts, but the exciting dialogue is happening beyond their control in person-to-person conversations, as Mountain Dew found out in 2013 when one of its ads featuring a battered woman and a lineup of black men had to be pulled because of vociferous criticism. Companies and organizations are hard pressed to keep up with changing technology and consumers as they search for new ways to listen, respond, and engage their customers in conversations.

This time line has briefly identified how various jobs and professional concepts emerged and changed over time. Let's now put the advertising world under a microscope and look deeper at the structure of the industry.

The Advertising World

In the discussion of definitions and the evolution of advertising practices, we briefly introduced agencies, but as a student of advertising and marketing communication, you need to know more about how the advertising industry and agencies are organized and how they operate. One way to get a peek at the field is through the lens of television, such as the *Mad Men* show. The "A Matter of Principle" feature explains how Bruce Vanden Bergh analyzed the cultural relevance of the popular award-winning drama *Mad Men.*

Who Are the Key Players?

As we discuss the organization of the industry, consider that all the key players also represent job opportunities you might want to consider if you are interested in working in advertising or some area of marketing communication. The players include the advertiser (referred to by the agency as the *client*) who sponsors the message, the agency, the media, and the *suppliers*, who provide expertise. The "A Matter of Practice" feature about "1984," the greatest television commercial ever made, introduced a number of these key players and illustrated how they all make different contributions to the final advertising.

The Organization Advertising begins with the organization behind the promotion message, or the **advertiser**. The company sponsors advertising and other promotional messages about its business. In the "1984" story, Apple Computer was the advertiser, and Steve Jobs, the company's CEO, made the final decision to run the then-controversial commercial. The advertiser is the number one key player. Management of the advertising function usually lies with the organization's marketing or advertising department.

In terms of the top advertisers in the United States, the list usually begins with P&G. The next leaders in 2012 who vary in importance from year to year are General Motors (moved up to second after its turnaround in 2010–2011), AT&T and Verizon, News Corp and Time Warner,

A Matter of Principle

Mad Men: The Inherent Drama of Advertising

Bruce Vanden Bergh, *Michigan State University*

Maybe we should be wondering why it took television so long to discover that a New York City advertising agency was a great place to set a dramatic series. We have had more than our share of emergency rooms, courtrooms, and crime scenes. Let's take a look at the dramatic elements of *Mad Men* and how naturally advertising serves its creator, Matthew Weiner.

A good drama requires action that is driven by the character and thought of the protagonists as they react to changes in their lives and the environment. *Mad Men* has these elements in spades. An advertising agency, by its very nature, is always a restless place as clients come and go, personnel switch agencies, and trends and fashions change in response to consumer wants and desires. Add to the mix the 1960s in New York City, and you have a backdrop of temptation and social change that provides much of the spectacle of the show. Advertising sits at this very precarious intersection of the forces of change.

A lot of our interest is in the spectacle of the 1960s that provides the setting for the show. The drinking, smoking, and carousing also add to the dramatic struggle between the good and bad choices the characters make. These vices look so bad from our current perspective that we ask if these things really did happen and if the show depicts what really happens in an agency. Yes and no, according to ad pros who worked during that era.

In a recent season, the principals of the New York City–based advertising agency started a new agency, Sterling Cooper Draper Pryce (SCDP). It was late 1963, President Kennedy had been assassinated, and change was in the air everywhere. In the next three years, a lot has happened in the personal lives of our friends at SCDP as well as in advertising and society as a whole. Part of our fascination with this series is that it permits us to view a slice of life as a cultural artifact. We can reflect on things from an historical perspective such as the recurring theme about the evolving role of women.

Matthew Weiner, the show's creator, said to the *New York Times* regarding the central theme of the show, "It's always been about change . . . and I'm starting to realize that that's all I am writing about."

Change is a fascinating, dramatic force that is at the heart of the advertising business. Some embrace it, some relish it, some tolerate it, and others resist it. This dynamic plays out in the personal and professional lives of the staff at SCDP while the world outside their corporate windows is changing in ways that, in hindsight, are clear to us but which they cannot predict.

Contemporary life in advertising, as in the series, is dynamic. Change is everywhere. That's part of the allure of the profession. Who will make the most of it? Where will it all go and end? That's what drives the action and our intrigue with *Mad Men* and advertising. Tune in.

Photo: Moviestore Collection/Alamy

Johnson & Johnson, and Pfizer. Other companies that periodically show up in the top 10 include General Electric, Ford, and L'Oreal. The top categories these companies represent include automotive, telecom, media, pharmaceuticals, and personal care and cosmetics. Other important categories are retail, financial services, food and candy, beverages, and restaurants.

Most advertisers have an executive or department that initiates the advertising effort by identifying a marketing problem advertising can solve. For example, Apple executives knew that the Macintosh easy-to-use computer platform needed to be explained and that information about the launch of the new computer would need to reach a large population of potential computer buyers. Advertising was essential to the success of this new product.

The marketing executive (with input from the corporate officers and others on the marketing team) also hires the advertising agency—for Old Spice this was Wieden + Kennedy—and other marketing communication agencies as needed. In professional jargon, the advertiser for Old Spice (P&G) becomes the agency's *client*. As the client, the advertiser is responsible for monitoring the work and paying the agency for its work on the account. That use of the word *account* is the reason agency people refer to the advertiser as *the account* and the agency person in charge of that advertiser's business as the *account manager*.

The marketing team, sometimes including the agency account people, makes the final decisions about strategy, including the target audience and the size of the advertising budget. The client team approves the advertising or marketing communication plan, which contains details outlining the message and media strategies. In Chapter 2, we'll explain more about how this marketing team functions.

Big companies may have hundreds of agencies working for them, although they normally have an **agency-of-record**, a lead agency that does most of their advertising business and may even manage or coordinate the work of other agencies.

The Agency The second player is the **advertising agency** (or other types of marketing communication agencies) that creates, produces, and distributes the messages. The working arrangement between advertiser and agency is known as the *agency–client partnership*. The "1984" story demonstrated how important it is to cultivate a strong sense of trust between the agency and its clients because the commercial involved risky ideas.

An advertiser uses an outside agency because it believes the agency will be more efficient in creating advertising messages than the advertiser would be on its own. Successful agencies such as Crispin Porter + Bogusky typically have strategic and creative expertise, media knowledge, workforce talent, and the ability to negotiate good deals for clients. The advertising professionals working for the agency are experts in their areas of specialization and passionate about their work.

Not all advertising professionals work in agencies. Large advertisers, either companies or organizations, manage the advertising process either by setting up an **advertising department** (sometimes called **marketing services**) that oversees the work of agencies or by setting up their own in-house agency, as Figure 1.3 illustrates. Tasks performed by the company's marketing services department include the following: set the budget and select the agencies; coordinate activities with vendors, such as media, production, and photography; make sure the work gets done as scheduled; and determine whether the work has achieved prescribed objectives.

The Media The third player in the advertising world is the media, the systems used to deliver messages and engage audiences. The emergence of mass media has been a central factor in the development of advertising because mass media offers a way to reach a widespread audience.

FIGURE 1.3
Two Advertising Organization Structures

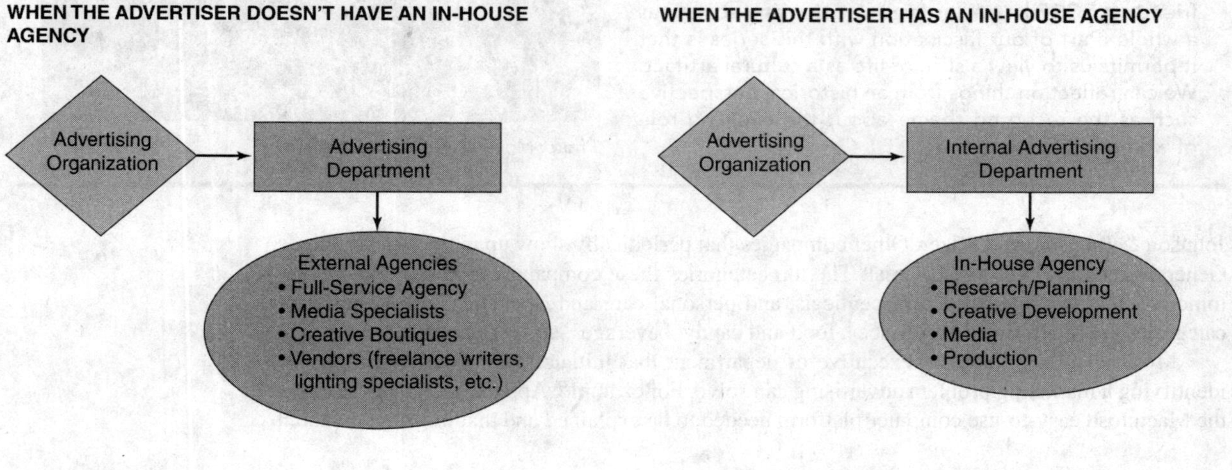

In traditional advertising, the term **media** refers to all of the channels of communication that carry the message from the advertiser to the audience and from consumers back to companies. We refer to these media as **channels** because they deliver messages, but they are also companies, such as your local newspaper or radio station.

Some of these media conglomerates are huge, such as Time Warner and Viacom. Time Warner, for example, is a $40 billion company with some 38,000 employees. It owns HBO, Time Inc., Turner Broadcasting, and Warner Brothers, among other media companies. You can learn more about this media conglomerate at www.timewarner.com. **Media vehicles** are the specific programs, such as *60 Minutes* or *The Simpsons*, or magazines, such as *The New Yorker*, *Advertising Age*, and *Woman's Day*.

Note that *media* is plural when it refers to various channels, but singular—*medium*—when it refers to only one form, such as newspapers.

Each medium (newspaper, radio or television station, billboard company, and so on) has a department that is responsible for selling ad space or time. These departments specialize in assisting advertisers in comparing the effectiveness of various media as they try to select the best mix of media to use. Many media organizations will assist advertisers in the design and production of advertisements. That's particularly true for local advertisers using local media, such as a retailer preparing an advertisement for the local newspaper.

The primary advantage of advertising's use of **mass media** is that the costs to buy time in broadcast media, space in print media, and time and space in digital media are spread over the tremendous number of people that these media reach. For example, $3 million may sound like a lot of money for one Super Bowl ad, but when you consider the advertisers are reaching more than 100 million people, the cost is not so extreme. One of the big advantages of mass-media advertising is that it can reach a lot of people with a single message in a very cost-efficient form.

Principle

Advertising is most cost efficient when it uses mass media to reach large numbers of prospective consumers.

Professional Suppliers and Consultants The fourth player in the world of advertising include artists, writers, photographers, directors, producers, printers, and self-employed freelancers and consultants. In the "1984" story, the movie director Ridley Scott was a supplier in that Chiat/Day contracted with him to produce the commercial.

This array of suppliers mirrors the variety of tasks required to put together an ad. Other examples include freelance copywriters (see "The Inside Story" by Aaron Stern) and graphic artists, songwriters, printers, market researchers, direct-mail production houses, telemarketers, and public relations consultants.

Why would the other advertising players hire an outside supplier? There are many reasons. The advertiser or the agency may not have expertise in a specialized area, their people may be overloaded with work, or they may want a fresh perspective. They also may not want to incur the overhead of full-time employees.

In the new world of digital media, another type of supplier has emerged and that is the consumer, people who supply what we call **user-generated content**. This is through YouTube contributions and contests sponsored by advertisers such as Doritos, which has sponsored a competition for the best commercial to be used on the Super Bowl.

Advertising relies on the expertise of many different people, such as television producers, graphic designers, photographers, printers, and musicians.

Photo sources (listed left to right): © Peter Atkins/Fotolia; JackF/Fotolia; ID1974/Fotolia; vukas/Fotolia

The Inside Story

Freelancing: Two Sides of the Coin

Aaron Stern, *Freelancer, New York City*

When I tell people I'm a freelance creative director, I usually get the same vaguely concerned look. In a time of economic uncertainty, many people assume that what I'm actually saying is, "I can't find a real job." But for the past five years, I've been consistently freelancing and turning down full time job offers along the way. Freelancing has some wonderful benefits. And it definitely has drawbacks.

One of the biggest benefits of being a freelancer is that, for the most part, I get to choose the projects I work on. If I get a call for a project that doesn't sound appealing to me, I can simply turn it down. If I was on staff, I probably wouldn't have that luxury.

Another nice aspect of freelance is that I have the opportunity to work with many different agencies on a variety of clients. In any given year, I may work at 10 agencies or more. It's a great way to learn about the range of approaches agencies use to tackle problems. In some cases, the best creative agencies aren't necessarily the best places to work. And sometimes I'm pleasantly surprised by agencies that are smaller and lesser known.

Freelancing also gives me a lot more flexibility with my time. I can take time off when I want to work on other projects. A lot of freelancers I know have personal projects in art, writing, or music that they are able to pursue more easily because freelance allows for that kind of flexibility.

As a rule of thumb, freelance pays better in the short term than staff jobs, which means that, say, in a month of freelance I'll make more than I would in a month of a salaried job. And if I work over a weekend, I get paid for that time.

Of course, there's always a flip side. Moving from agency to agency, project to project, means I constantly have to acclimate to a new environment. It's like starting a new job every time. I have to figure out how to navigate the politics, who to listen to, and what the new process is. Also, since the agency is paying me at an additional cost to them, I have to prove to them on a daily basis that I'm worth it.

Another drawback is that the projects usually given to freelancers aren't always the most exciting ones in the agency. Usually, those are given to the staff creatives. And freelancers are often brought in to help pitch new business, which can mean long hours and a lower chance of actually producing the work you do.

Finally, one of the hardest things for a freelancer to get used to is not knowing when the next job is going to come along. Even after five years, at the end of a project I still get a little nervous that I'll never work again. Fortunately, I've always proved myself wrong.

Freelancing isn't for everyone. Some people prefer the routine, teamwork, and security that come with a full-time job. And if you're just starting out in the business, it may make more sense to find a staff job that will give you the experience and portfolio you need to establish yourself. But I encourage you to try freelancing at some point in your career. After all, you can always go back to a "real" job.

Note: A graduate of the University of Colorado, Stern lives in New York as a freelance creative director. He was nominated by Professor Brett Robbs.

Types of Agencies

We are concerned primarily with advertising agencies in this chapter, but other areas, such as public relations, direct marketing, sales promotion, and the Internet, have agencies that provide specialized promotional help as well.

The A-List awards by *Advertising Age* recognize cutting-edge agencies that rank high in three areas. First, they are creative—*Ad Age* calls them "widely imaginative"—in developing brand strategies and executions. Second, they are fast growing and winners of some of the biggest new business pitches. Finally, they are recognized for their effectiveness. In other words, their work leads to measurable results. Note that the agencies in the following list represent big and small agencies as well as full-service and a variety of specialized agencies.

Advertising Age's A-List of Agencies[7]

1. ***McGarryBowen*** Identified as *Advertising Age*'s Agency of the Year in 2012, this agency has an enviable new-business record and a staggering 60 percent growth in revenue in 2011. Its clients describe it as a "jack-of-all-trades" in an era when clients want more integration and less specialization.

2. ***Droga5*** This five-year-old agency is sweeping award shows and signing up clients ranging from Amstel beer to Prudential with its avant-garde thinking.
3. ***BBDO*** In 2011, BBDO won every global pitch it participated in and about two-thirds of its U.S. pitches. Revenue was up 15 percent in the United States, while globally revenue increased 18 percent to an estimated $2.4 billion.
4. ***Razorfish*** A leading digital agency, its acquisition by the Publicis Group in 2009 has seen amazing successes.
5. ***72andSunny*** This agency's approach is far more democratic than that of most agencies. An understanding prevails in the agency that a great idea can come anywhere, not just the creative department.
6. ***Alma*** A knack for matching Hispanics' passion points with online efforts helped Alma's digital revenue soar 300 percent. Overall, revenue grew 10 percent with the agency bringing in 10 new accounts in 2011.
7. ***Grey*** A big, traditional agency that is part of the WPP group, Grey could have been mistaken for a typical insurance company, but the new president has created a new level of excitement that's changed the image and business success of Grey.
8. ***Edelman*** A giant public relations agency, Edelman's client retention is second to none, and its year-over-year growth and strong relationships make other agencies envious.
9. ***Huge*** This Brooklyn digital shop is growing into its name by creating products that connect marketers to consumers.
10. ***Arnold*** A pick for the Comeback Agency of the Year in 2010, Boston-based Arnold has grown even stronger boosted by marquee clients such as Volvo and Ocean Spray and a long list of new accounts including Dell and the Boston Bruins.

In addition to agencies that specialize in advertising and other areas of marketing communication, there are also consulting firms in marketing research and branding that offer specialized services to other agencies as well as advertisers. Since these various types of marketing communication areas are all part of an integrated marketing communication approach, we cover many of these functions in separate chapters later in the book.

Full-Service Agencies In advertising, a **full-service agency** includes the four major staff functions of account management, creative services, media planning, and account planning, which includes research. A full-service advertising agency also has its own finance and accounting department, a **traffic department** to handle internal tracking on completion of projects, a department for *broadcast* and *print production* (sometimes organized within the creative department), and a human resources department.

Let's take a minute to look inside one full-service agency, Crispin Porter + Bogusky (CP+B), which was named Agency of the Year by *Adweek* and *Advertising Age* as well as *Ad Age*'s sister publication *Creativity*. CP+B celebrates some $140 million in revenue and employs nearly 900 in its two offices in Miami and Boulder, Colorado. The agency is known for its edgy, pop-culture approach to strategy. You may remember Burger King's weird "king" character. That's the kind of provocative work that *Ad Age* calls "culturally primal."[8] It infiltrates the social scene and creates buzz. Although known for its creative work, CP+B also has an innovative product design think tank that has come up with such ideas as a public bike rental program, a portable pen version of WD-40, and Burger King's popular Burger Shots sliders.

In-House Agencies Like a regular advertising agency, an **in-house agency** produces ads and places them in the media, but the agency is a part of the advertiser's organization rather than an outside company. Companies that need closer control over their advertising have their own internal in-house agencies. An in-house agency performs most—and sometimes all—of the functions of an outside advertising agency and produce materials, such as point-of-sale displays, sales team literature, localized ads and promotions, and coupon books, that larger agencies have a hard time producing cost effectively. Retailers, for example, find that doing their own advertising and media placement provides cost savings as well as the ability to meet fast-breaking deadlines. Some fashion companies, such as Ralph Lauren, also create their own advertising in-house to maintain complete control over the brand image and the fashion statement it makes. Check out this in-house agency at http://about.ralphlauren.com/campaigns/default.asp.

Specialized Agencies Many agencies either specialize in certain functions (writing copy, producing art, or creating digital ads), audiences or markets (youth, minority groups, such as Asian, African American, or Hispanic), or industries (health care, computers, agriculture, or B2B communication). In addition, some agencies specialize in other marketing communication areas, such as branding, direct marketing, sales promotion, public relations, events and sports marketing, packaging, and point-of-sale promotions. Sometimes one-client agencies are created to handle the work of one large client. Let's take a look at two special types of agencies:

- **Creative boutiques** are agencies, usually small (two or three people to a dozen or more), that concentrate entirely on preparing the creative execution of the idea or the creative product. A creative boutique has one or more writers or artists on staff but generally no staff for media, research, or strategic planning. Typically, these agencies can prepare advertising to run in print and broadcast media as well as in out-of-home (such as outdoor and transit advertising), Internet, and alternative media. Creative boutiques usually serve companies directly but are sometimes retained by full-service agencies that are overloaded with work.
- **Media-buying services** specialize in the purchase of media for clients. They are in high demand for many reasons, but three reasons stand out. First, media have become more complex as the number of choices has grown—think of the proliferation of new cable channels, magazines, and radio stations. Second, the cost of maintaining a competent media department has escalated. Third, media-buying services often buy media at a low cost because they can group several clients' purchases together to get discounts from the media because of the volume of their media buys.

Agency Networks and Holding Companies Finally let's talk about **agency networks**, which are large conglomerations of agencies under a central ownership. Agency networks are all of the offices that operate under one agency name, such as DDB Worldwide (200 offices in 90 countries) or BBDO Worldwide (287 offices in 79 countries). You can read more about these agencies and their networks at www.ddb.com and www.bbdoworldwide.com.

Holding companies include one or more advertising agency network as well as other types of marketing communication agencies and marketing services consulting firms. The three largest after a merger in 2013 are WPP Group, Interpublic, and the newly combined Omnicom and Publicis—now known as Publicis Omnicom Group. WPP, for example, includes the J. Walter Thompson Group, Ogilvy & Mather Worldwide, Young & Rubicam, Grey Global Group, and Bates advertising networks as well as the Berlin Cameron creative agency; public relations agencies Hill and Knowlton, Ogilvy Public Relations, and Burson-Marsteller; direct-response company Wunderman; research firms Millward Brown and Research International; media firms Mindshare and Mediaedge:cia; and branding and corporate identity firms Landor and Lambie-Naim, to name a few. Most of those firms are also networks with multiple offices. For an inside look at a big holding company, check out WPP at www.wpp.com.

How Are Agency Jobs Organized?

In addition to the CEO, if the agency is large enough, it usually has one or more vice presidents as well as department heads for the different functional areas. We will concentrate on five of those areas: account management; account planning and research; creative development and production; media research, planning, and buying; and internal services.

Account Management The **account management** function (sometimes called **account services**) acts as a liaison between the client and the agency. The account team summarizes the client's communication needs and develops the basic "charge to the agency," which the account manager presents to the agency's creative team. Once the client and agency together establish the general guidelines for a campaign, the account management team supervises the day-to-day development of the strategy.

Account management in a major agency typically has three levels: the *management supervisor*, who provides leadership on strategic issues and looks for new business opportunities; the *account supervisor*, who is the key executive working on a client's business and the primary liaison between the client and the agency; and the *account executive* (as well as *assistant account executives*), who is responsible for day-to-day activities and operates like a project manager. A smaller agency will combine some of these levels.

At the CP+B agency, the account function is called *content management*. Similar to account management, this function is responsible for interpreting the client's marketing research and strategy for the rest of the agency. The "A Day in the Life" story by Tammie DeGrasse-Cabrera focuses on her work as a management supervisor in the content management system at CP+B.

Account Planning and Research Full-service agencies often have a separate department specifically devoted to planning and sometimes to research as well. Today the emphasis in agency research is on gaining insights into consumer thinking and behaviors in order to develop messages that focus on the consumer's perspective and relationship with the brand. The **account planning** group gathers all available intelligence on the market and consumers and acts as the voice of the consumer. Account planners are strategic specialists who prepare comprehensive information about consumers' wants, needs, and relationship to the client's brand and recommendations on how the advertising should work to satisfy those elements based on insights they derive from consumer research.

Creative Development and Production A creative group includes people who write (*copywriters*), people who design ideas for print ads or television commercials (*art directors*), and people who convert these ideas into television or radio commercials (*producers*). Shawn

A Day in the Life

The Day-to-Day Job in Content Management

Tammie DeGrasse-Cabrera, *Management Supervisor, CP+B, Miami*

"So what exactly do you do in advertising?" That is by far the most common question I am asked once someone finds out I'm in content management. "Do you create the ads?" "Do you choose the actors?" "Do you decide which magazines to run in?" To be honest, I don't think my own mother has it figured out yet.

I've since realized that the best way to define what we, as account people, do in advertising is to make it all happen. To use a simple analogy, an account person is like the supervisor in a car factory's assembly line. We don't physically connect part A to part B, but we do make sure every department fully understands what the car is supposed to look like, work with them on what drivers want and how it should run, and ensure it's built effectively and efficiently to make the sale.

I could break it down and give you an idea of my typical 9-to-5 day, but to be honest, in advertising and with today's technology, there's no such thing as a "typical" or "9 to 5."

We wear many hats in this job. I act like a train conductor, leading the team to keep all our projects moving forward, and at times as a translator, decoding consumers' responses on a new campaign idea to help solve for any issues and make the work even more powerful—always a problem solver, whether it's working with the clients on product innovations, offers, or promotions to help boost sales or with a producer and creative team on how to create the next best spot, app, event, or social media effort. This is a very creative and ever-evolving role that entails anything and everything to get the job done.

For those of you considering entering the advertising industry, deciding which area to concentrate in can be difficult. Each department—whether creative, technology, production, strategic planning, or media—is so equally interesting that anyone would have trouble figuring out what the best fit for him or her might be.

Since I possess leadership qualities, enjoy strategizing, and like to get my hands in just about everything, content management was the perfect fit for me. For others it may not be so easy, so I strongly suggest learning more about the specifics of every group. Keep in mind that there are pros and cons to each, and only you can decipher on which end of the factory assembly line you would be best to work.

That's all for now. Have to run and prep for our next television shoot. Best of luck to you all!

Note: Tammie DeGrasse-Cabrera was nominated by Professor Kartik Pashupti from the advertising program at Florida State University, where she graduated. Since then she has worked for McCann Erickson New York and is currently with CP+B.

Couzens, who is on the book's advisory board, prefers the title "conceptual engineer" for his work, which focuses on generating big ideas or concepts around which promotional campaigns may be built. Many agencies build a support group around a team of an art director and copywriter who work well together. In addition to these positions, the broadcast production department and art studio are two other areas where creative personnel can apply their skills.

Media Research, Planning, and Buying Agencies that don't rely on outside media specialists have a media department that recommends to the client the most efficient means of delivering the message to the target audience. That department has three functions: research, planning, and buying. Because the media world is so complex, it is not unusual for some individuals to become experts in certain markets or types of media.

Internal Operations The departments that serve the operations within the agency include the traffic department and print production as well as the more general financial services and human resources (personnel) departments. The traffic department is the lifeblood of the agency, and its personnel keep track of everything that happens.

How Are Agencies Paid?

Advertising agencies are a big business. P&G, for example, spends nearly $5 billion annually on global advertising. With that kind of money on the table, you can imagine that the agency-client relationship is under pressure from both sides. Agencies want to get more work and get paid more; clients want to cut costs and make their advertising as cost effective as possible.

Agencies derive their revenues and profits from four main sources: commissions, fees, retainers, and performance incentives. For years, a 15 percent *commission* on media billings was the traditional form of compensation. That's actually how agencies got started back in the 19th century. For those few accounts still using a commission approach, the rate is rarely 15 percent; it is more likely lower and subject to negotiation between agency and client.

Many advertisers now use a fee system either as the primary compensation tool or in combination with a commission system. The **fee system** is comparable to the system by which advertisers pay their lawyers and accountants. During the 1990s, it replaced commissions as the main compensation method.[9] The client and agency agree on an hourly fee or rate or may negotiate a charge for a specific project. Charges are also included for out-of-pocket expenses, travel, and other standard items.

An agency also may be put on a monthly or a yearly **retainer**. The amount billed per month is based on the projected amount of work and the hourly rate charged. This system is most commonly used by public relations agencies.

A more recent trend in agency compensation is for advertisers to pay agencies on the basis of their performance. One consultant recommends that this **performance incentive** approach be based on paying the agency either a percentage of the client's sales or a percentage of the client's marketing budget. Another approach is that agencies share in the profits of their client when they create a successful campaign, but that also means they have a greater financial risk in the relationship should the advertising not create the intended impact. Research in 2012 found an increase from 46 percent of U.S. marketers using the performance approach in 2010 to 49 percent in 2012.[10]

Another performance-related compensation innovation is **value billing**, which means that the agency is paid for its creative and strategic ideas rather than for executions and media placements. Sarah Armstrong, Coke's director of worldwide media and communication, urged the industry to shift to "value-based" forms of compensation that reward agencies based on effectiveness—whether they make the objectives they set for their advertising.[11]

How Is the Practice of Advertising Changing?

We would like to end this review of advertising basics by talking about the future of advertising. Because of the recent Great Recession, Mike Carlton, an industry commentator, says, "Clearly we are at a point in time when things will never be quite the same again for our industry." But there are still some exciting changes that open up opportunities for new professionals entering the field.

Consumer in Charge

As Jim Stengel, P&G's former global marketing officer, has said, "It's not just about doing great TV commercials: The days of pounding people with images, and shoving them down their eyeballs are over. The consumer is much more in control now."[12] This change, which was referred to earlier in our time line, is causing major shifts in the way the advertising business operates. We mentioned user-generated content, which illustrates how consumers are even taking charge of the ads they see.

For example, the East Coast grocery store Wegmans found itself the focus of a YouTube musical tribute, "Wegmans the Musical," written and produced by students at a high school in Northborough, Massachusetts, who were celebrating the opening of a new Wegmans store. You can see it at www.youtube.com.

That trend is occurring with the help of advertisers. It started in 2009 when CareerBuilder dismissed one of the most creative agencies—Portland-based Wieden + Kennedy, who had created five great Super Bowl ads for the job-posting website—and took its advertising in-house. The reason was that the company wanted ordinary consumers to create its commercials. That would not only bring publicity but also save bucks. CareerBuilder, through its in-house agency, still paid for production of the winning ad and bought the ad time. Not only did this move bring more opportunities for **consumer-generated advertising** (user-generated content), but the company estimated it saved around 15 to 20 percent of its annual marketing costs.[13]

Consumer involvement in advertising is a bigger issue than just ad agencies losing clients. In fact, consumers have been taking control of media and marketing for a number of years through Wikipedia, Twitter, and other newly democratized information sources. YouTube, MySpace, and Facebook have invited everyone into the ad distribution game.

Blurring Lines and Converging Media

One of the biggest changes impacting the advertising industry is the changing media environment. Television used to be the big gun, and it still eats up the biggest part of the budget, but the old networks (CBS, NBC, ABC, and FOX) are only half as important as they used to be as the number of cable channels has exploded.

The big bomb that has fragmented the media world is digital media, which appear in so many different forms that it's impossible to keep up with them. The newspaper industry has been particularly hurt as it has realized that much, if not most, of its content can be accessed more easily and quickly in a digital format. So are newspapers dead?

Traditional media are trying to adjust by transforming themselves into new digital formats as well. So what do you call online versions of newspapers and magazines? Are they still print when they appear on a screen? And new personal media—iPhones, iPods, iPads, BlackBerries, and Kindles—are real shape changers. They can be phones, music players, calendars, and sources of local and national information as well as cameras, video viewers, book readers, Web surfers, and video game players. Changes such as these need to be considered when putting together media plans, a challenge that will be discussed in Part 4.

Blurring also relates to marketing communication functions. In 2012, for example, a Washington public relations firm, APCO Worldwide, bought Strawberry Frog, a small boutique New York ad agency. The reason is because public relations firms are now being challenged to make more creative content for the clients in a variety of areas other than just public relations.[14] The line is even blurring between traditional marketing communication functions and tools.

Accountability and Effectiveness

Given the recent recession, you can guess that efficiency is an advantage in this new marketing communication world, which has been emphasizing accountability for a couple of decades. The other critical client concern is effectiveness, which is another way to look at accountability in marketing communication. A 2012 survey by the Association of National Advertisers found that 52 percent of marketers will challenge their agencies to cut costs and share more of the burden of cost efficiency.[15] We mentioned that CareerBuilder took its advertising in-house partly to save costs, which is critical in an economic downturn. Agencies that are creative in finding new ways to deliver cost efficiencies have a real advantage in their client dealings.

Along with the ongoing need for efficiencies, there's also a concern about effectiveness. The recent recession forced the advertising industry to become even more serious about creating advertising that delivers results and then proving the effectiveness of the advertising work once it's completed. Effectiveness is a theme that you will see discussed throughout this book. So what is effectiveness? Effective ads are ads that work. That is, they deliver the message the advertiser intended—as stated in its objectives—and consumers respond as the advertiser hoped they would. Ultimately, advertisers such as P&G want consumers to buy and keep buying their goods and services. To get to that point, ads must first effectively communicate a message that motivates consumers to respond.

Principle
Advertising is effective when it achieves its objectives and consumers respond as the advertiser hoped they would.

This chapter opened with the Old Spice campaign, and we'll discuss its effectiveness in the "It's a Wrap" chapter conclusion, but consider how we describe the impact of great advertising. The Nielsen media research company reported that sales of Old Spice products were up 107 percent in the month after the campaign began. Furthermore, the commercials not only were seen on television but also had more than 117 million upload views on YouTube.[16]

The Old Spice "Smell Like a Man" campaign also received a coveted Effie award. The Effie award, named for a shortened form of the word *effective*, is given by the New York Chapter of the American Marketing Association to advertising and other forms of marketing communication that have been proven to be not only creative but also, more importantly, effective. That means the campaigns were guided by measurable *objectives*, and evaluation after the campaign determined that the effort did, in fact, meet or exceed the objectives. (Check out the Effies at www.effie.org.) Other award shows that focus on effectiveness are the Advertising and Marketing Effectiveness awards by the New York Festivals company, Canada's Cassie Awards, and the London-based Institute of Practitioners awards. Check out these award programs at www.ameawards.com, www.cassies.ca, and www.ipa.co.uk, respectively.

Other award shows may focus on other aspects of advertising, such as creative ideas. For example, the Clios, which is a private award-show company; the One Show, which is sponsored by a New York–based advertising association; and the Cannes Lions Awards, an international competition from France. Awards are also given for media plans (*Adweek*'s Media Plan of the Year) and art direction (New York–based Art Directors Club award show). These awards can be found at www.clioawards.com, www.canneslions.com, www.adweek.com, and www.adcglobal.org/awards/annual, respectively. Other professional areas also have award shows that reward such things as clever promotional ideas. For example, the Reggies are given by the Promotion Marketing Association, and outstanding public relations efforts are recognized by the Public Relations Society of America's Silver Anvil Award.

Integrated Marketing Communication

We mentioned that effectiveness is a central theme for this book, but another concept that we will discuss throughout this book is *integration*. As we mentioned earlier in our time line, the search for effective communication has led many companies to focus on the consistency of their brand communication in order to more efficiently establish a coherent brand. As mentioned earlier, we call that practice *integrated marketing communication*—the primary tool of brand communication. To be effective, these brand messages need to complement one another and present the same basic brand strategy. This will be a main topic in Chapter 2.

Looking Ahead

The focus on effectiveness and results is the theme of this textbook, and throughout the book we will introduce you to practices that generate effectiveness. We'll end each chapter with the results of the campaign that introduced the chapter—in this case, the Grand Effie–winning "The Smell of Success " campaign for Old Spice.

This chapter has provided an introduction to many of the basic concepts of advertising. We'll continue that introduction of principles and practices in Chapter 2 later as we explain the bigger picture of advertising and its role in marketing communication and marketing. Essentially, these two first chapters introduce four major topics: advertising, marketing communication, integrated marketing communication, and brand communication.

It's a Wrap

Old Spice: The Smell of Success

At the beginning of this chapter, you read that P&G's Old Spice needed to fend off an attempt by Dove Men+Care to steal market share during its Super Bowl introduction.

Old Spice generated excitement with guys who were not current customers as well as the women who typically made most of the purchases of body wash by using research and generating an insight that drove the campaign: Old Spice needed to involve men and women in a conversation about what a guy should smell like. The tactic of using a hunk atop a horse captivated the audience (eye candy for the women and dry humor for the guys).

A far cry from what would have convinced your grandfather to buy Old Spice, this innovative interactive campaign effectively accomplished P&G's goals. Consider these stats:

- Old Spice won more than 75 percent of the online buzz during the first three months following the campaign's launch with half of the conversations generated by women.
- The YouTube videos received 10 million views from the launch in February to April.
- The "Response" (viral video megahit Q&A interactive sessions with "The Man Your Man Could Smell Like") garnered more than 40 million views on YouTube at the end of the first week following its introduction. Old Spice was twice named "most viral brand of the year" by *Advertising Age.*
- In one month, Twitter followers increased 2,700 percent, Facebook fans increased 60 percent (from 500,000 to 800,000), and Oldspice.com traffic increased 300 percent.

Becoming a cultural phenomenon, the campaign generated an incredible amount of free public relations. The six-month campaign resulted in 1.7 billion total impressions across traditional and online media outlets. Most importantly, sales soared. In five months, sales of its Red Zone body wash had more than doubled from the prior year.

In the chapters that follow, you will learn about the role of advertising as it relates to brands and other forms of marketing communication—and how brands like Old Spice make strategic choices to evolve their campaigns. You'll think about the role of advertising in society and learn what it takes to create campaigns such as this Grand Effie-winning effort.

Logo: Courtesy of the Procter & Gamble Co.

Key Points Summary

1. **What is advertising, how has it evolved, and what does it do in modern times?** The definition of advertising has evolved over time from identification to information and persuasion leading to selling. In modern times, advertising is persuasive communication that uses mass and interactive media to reach broad audiences in order to connect an identified sponsor with buyers and provide information about products. It performs communication, marketing, economic, and societal roles. Seven types of advertising define the industry: brand, retail or local, direct response, B2B, institutional, nonprofit, and public service.

2. **How have the key concepts and components of marketing communication developed over time?** A review of the evolution of advertising practice identifies the source of many of the key concepts currently used in advertising. These concepts can be grouped into the four key components of advertising: strategy (objectives, appeals, branding, positioning and differentiation, and segmenting and targeting), message (creative concept based on research and consumer insight, creativity, and artistry), media (the evolution of print, broadcast, outdoor, and digital as well as the practice of matching targets to media audiences and compensation based on the media buy), and evaluation (effectiveness in terms of meeting objectives,

testing, and standards). A time line from the earliest ages of print to the current era of social media illustrates how these components have developed and changed over time.

3. **How is the industry organized—key players, types of agencies, and jobs within agencies?** The key players begin with the advertiser, the organization, or the brand behind the advertising effort. Other players include the agency that prepares the advertising, the media that run it, and the professional suppliers and consultants who contribute expertise. The three types of agencies are full-service, in-house, and specialized agencies. There are also networks of agencies with many offices as well as holding companies that own many different kinds of agencies. Agency jobs are varied in expertise and provide a number of career opportunities for all kinds of skill sets: account management, planning and research, creative (writing, art direction, and production), and media (research, planning, and buying). Agencies are paid in different ways, including by commission based on a percent of media costs, with a fee system based on estimated project costs or hourly billing, or with a monthly retainer. Value billing is based on creative and strategic ideas rather than media costs.

4. **How is the practice of advertising changing?** A number of changes are creating new forms of advertising, such as the consumer-initiated ideas that have emerged with the new social media, blurring of lines between marcom areas and tools, media that are changing shape and merging with other media forms, new forms of client–agency relationships, and more accountable and effective marketing communication practices that emerged from the recession.

Key Terms

account executive, p. 43
account management, p. 54
account planning, p. 55
account services, p. 54
advertisement, p. 37
advertiser, p. 48
advertising, p. 36
advertising agency, p. 50
advertising department, p. 50
agency networks, p. 54
agency-of-record, p. 50
art director, p. 44
brand advertising, p. 39
brand image, p. 40
brand name, p. 44
business-to-business (B2B) advertising, p. 39
buzz, p. 41
campaign, p. 39
channels, p. 51
classified advertising, p. 43
commission system, p. 43
consumer-generated advertising, p. 57
copywriter, p. 44
corporate advertising, p. 39
creative boutique, p. 54
direct-response advertising, p. 39
fee system, p. 56
full-service agency, p. 53
holding companies, p. 54
in-house agency, p. 53
institutional advertising p. 39
integrated marketing communication, p. 48
local advertising, p. 39
marketing communication (marcom), p. 40
marketing services, p. 50
market segmentation, p. 46
mass media, p. 51
media, p. 51
media-buying services, p. 54
media vehicles, p. 51
nonprofit advertising, p. 39
performance incentive, p. 56
positioning, p. 46
pro bono, p. 39
product differentiation, p. 46
public service advertising, p. 39
public service announcements, p. 39
retail advertising, p. 39
retainer, p. 56
strategy, p. 38
targeting, p. 45
traffic department, p. 53
user-generated content, p. 51
value billing, p. 56
word of mouth, p. 37

Review Questions

✪ 1-4. Analyze the Old Spice campaign discussed in this chapter and compare it to key aspects of the modern definition of advertising.

1-5. What are the basic functions of advertising?

1-6. Explain the role of advertising in marketing communication.

1-7. Discuss the evolution of the concepts and practices in advertising.

1-8. What is the role of logic in advertising, and how is it related to the effectiveness of an ad?

1-9. Discuss the different agencies involved in advertising, and explain how the work involved varies among the agencies.

1-10. What challenges are affecting the current practice of advertising? Discuss why effectiveness is important to advertisers.

Discussion Questions

1-11. Many industry experts feel that Apple's "1984" commercial is the best television commercial ever made. Watch it online at www.youtube.com/watch?v=OYecfV3ubP8 and analyze how it works. How many of the basic advertising practices and concepts that we introduced in the historical time line in Figure 1.1 does it demonstrate? Why do you think the experts are so impressed with this ad?

1-12. In class, Mark tells the instructor that all this "history of advertising" stuff is irrelevant. The instructor asks the class to consider why it is important to understand the historical review of advertising definitions and practices. What would you say either in support of Mark's view or to change his mind?

Take-Home Projects

1-13. ***Portfolio Project:*** Leo Burnett, a giant of the advertising industry, always kept a file he called "Ads Worth Saving," ads that struck him as effective for some reason. This was his portfolio of ideas. He explained that he would go through that file, not looking for ideas to copy but because these great ads would trigger thoughts about how to solve some problem. So throughout this book, we will invite you to start your own portfolio. In some cases, the assignments will ask you to find good (or bad) work and explain why you evaluate them as you do. In other cases, we'll ask you to actually do something—write, design, or propose—or create something that you could take to an interview that demonstrates your understanding of the principles we talk about in this book.

A Facebook Profile: For this first assignment, choose one of the people from the historical discussions in this chapter, someone you believe influenced the development of modern marketing communication. Research this person on the Internet and build a personal profile including samples of work if you can find some. Present your report as if it were a Facebook page. Make sure your presentation explains why you believe this person was important.

1-14. ***Mini-Case Analysis:*** Every chapter in this textbook opens with an award-winning case. For this assignment, you will be asked to analyze why it was effective and, in many cases, come up with ideas for how that campaign could be extended to another year or another market.

Reread the Old Spice campaign that was introduced at the beginning of this chapter and wrapped up at the end of the chapter. Go online and see if you can find any other information about this campaign. What are the strong points of this campaign? Its weak points? Why has it won awards, and why was it deemed effective? If you were on the Old Spice team, would you recommend that this campaign be continued, or is it time to change it? In other words, what happens next? Is there a spin-off? Develop a one-page analysis and your proposal for the next year.

TRACE North America Case

A Multicultural Campaign

Read the TRACE case in the Appendix before coming to class.

1-15. In class, discuss the following:

a. In what ways does the TRACE case reflect the expanded definition of what advertising is?

b. How does the case illustrate the various roles that advertising campaigns can perform as well as the role of advertising in the broader area of marketing communication?

1-16. Write a one-page explanation of the campaign.

CHAPTER

2 Brand Communication

Photo: Courtesy of DDB and McDonald's

It's a Winner

Campaign	Company	Agency	Awards
I'm Lovin' It™	*McDonald's*	*DDB Chicago* **Contributing Agencies** *Tribal DDB and OMD*	*Gold Effie in Sustained Success category 2012, AdAge's Marketer of the Year 2004*

CHAPTER KEY POINTS

1. **What is the difference between marketing communication and brand communication?**
2. **How is the marketing mix related to marketing communication?**
3. **What is integrated marketing communication?**
4. **How does marketing communication contribute to the development of a brand?**
5. **What current trends affect marketing and brand communication?**

McDonald's Love Story

When you have 33,000 restaurants serving 68 million people in 119 countries every day and your name is McDonald's, you have to think big, not just Big Mac, when you want to communicate. What is it that you're selling? What do you stand for? Who are your customers?

You don't just sell burgers. You want to communicate with a wide spectrum of consumers from moms and their kids looking for nutritious Happy Meals to teens wanting a Big Mac and even old geezers who stop by for coffee. You want to let people know you want to give back to communities by supporting causes like Ronald McDonald House Charities. Most of all, as you state in your corporate mission statement, you are "committed to providing an exceptional customer experience—People, Products, Place, Price and Promotion."

In the olden days, marketers could control their message that told consumers what they wanted them to hear by placing advertising in media like newspapers and television. By 2003, you realized that McDonald's doesn't operate in that world any longer. Sales slumped, and analysts and popular media criticized the business.

McDonald's doesn't just sell Happy Meals to kids or Big Macs to teens. It expanded its menu with a host of new products, such as oatmeal, healthier Happy Meals, and McCafé Shamrock Shakes and Strawberry Lemonade. To further complicate things, it operates in a changing environment. Customers demand to know where their food is coming from and its nutritional value. Childhood obesity is a growing problem (fries, anyone?), and, oh, does McDonald's use "pink slime" in its burgers? What about sustainable supply chain practices and environmental responsibility?

McDonald's isn't one-dimensional, and a single, simple message won't communicate with all—or even most—of its vast audience. McDonald's wants to communicate broadly in a way that connects to everybody about things they care about. It is a multidimensional global corporation with a complex message situated in a digital age where communication can not only occur from the company to customer but also be exchanged between company and customer and, importantly in the digital age, between consumer and consumer.

To accomplish the overarching goal of reaching more consumers, McDonald's, under the direction of Larry Light, then executive vice president and global chief marketing officer, changed communication strategies from mass marketing a single message to multifaceted, multisegmented, many-sided marketing. In short, McDonald's needed to connect emotionally with its many audiences in different ways. What was needed was more than an ad campaign (series of related ads) about the products it sells; it needed to reflect the involvement with the McDonald's brand in its complexity from the customers' in-store experience to the quality of its products.

The answer was "I'm Lovin' It™," a worldwide brand campaign intended to link McDonald's with customers around the globe using a variety of relevant, culturally significant messages. The campaign kicked off in 2003 with five edgy commercials, some featuring vocals by Justin Timberlake, in 12 languages in more than 100 countries with a single brand message to customers. Since then, I'm Lovin' It has become a marketing classic as well as the company's most successful and longest-running campaign.

Light said, "It's much more than just a new tagline or commercials—it's a new way of thinking about and expressing our worldwide brand appeal to the consumer."

Using the over-(golden)-arching theme of "I'm Lovin' It™," McDonald's can help consumers feel/express the love for the brand in ways that are meaningful and interesting to them. As you read this chapter, you'll take a closer look at brands and how they are defined. You'll see how advertising relates to brand communication and read the latest thinking about what it takes to be an effective brand communicator.

See how successful this campaign has been for McDonald's and why it won a Gold Effie for Sustained Success by turning to the "It's a Wrap" feature at the end of this chapter.

Sources: "Rebuilding Icon: A Love Story," Effie Awards published case study (2012), www.effie.org; www.mcdonalds.com; McDonald's news release, "McDonald's Unveils "I'm Loving' It™" Worldwide Brand Campaign, September 2, 2003; McDonald's news release, "McDonald's Launches "I'm Lovin' It ™" Brand Campaign, September 29, 2003; "Is McDonald's Losing That Loving' Feeling?," adage.com, February 19, 2012; Emily Bryson York, "McDonald's Unveils 'I'm Lovin' It' 2.0," adage.com, April 22, 2010; "BrandZ™ Top 100 Most Valuable Global Brands," 2012, www.millwardbrown.com; Randall Ringer, "Who Is Jack Trout and What's He Done for Marketing Lately?," blog on http://narrativebranding.wordpress.com, May 18, 2011.

This chapter will give you a foundation for thinking about solving brand communication problems. The McDonald's story demonstrates how effective marketing communication can help accomplish marketing objectives. This chapter starts with an explanation of the basic principles of marketing communication and integrated marketing communication. We then explore the important concept of branding and why it is so heavily dependent on marketing communication.

What Is Brand and Marketing Communication?

We ended Chapter 1 by mentioning the trend toward integrated marketing communication (IMC). In order to understand that concept, we need to first explain what it is that gets integrated in an IMC program. What we call **marketing communication** (marcom for short) involves the use of a variety of tools and functions, such as advertising, public relations, sales promotion, direct response, events and sponsorships, point of sale, digital media, and the communication aspects of packaging, as well as personal sales and a number of new forms of online communication that have emerged recently. All of these are parts of a planned effort to deliver specific messages used strategically to promote a brand or organization. They deliver a complex system of brand messages we refer to as **brand communication**—all the various marketing communication messages and brand experiences that create and maintain a coherent brand.

For example, consider the Puma brand. The same creative spirit that drives Puma's cutting-edge product design also drives its marketing communication, which includes advertising—but also nontraditional ways to connect with customers, such as word of mouth, the Internet, and other marcom programs that promote the brand on the street and on the feet of its devotees. Retailers praise Puma for its eye-catching, in-store merchandising displays. Other clever ideas include promotions at sushi restaurants during the World Cup held in Japan and South Korea. Puma got a well-known sushi chef to create a special Puma sushi roll that was served in select Japanese restaurants in cities around the world. These restaurants also discretely announced the sponsorship through Puma-branded chopsticks, sake cups, and napkins. At the same time, Puma partnered with the U.K.-based Terence Conran design shop to sell an exclusive version of its World Cup soccer boot and held weekend sushi-making events at the Conran home furnishings store. In other words, Puma's brand communication extends well beyond advertising and traditional media, such as print advertising in newspapers and magazines, outdoor advertising, and television commercials.

The management challenge, then, is to manage all of the messages delivered by all the various types of marketing communication so they work together to present the brand in a coherent and consistent way.[1] In other words, advertising is only one element in a coordinated basket of messages.

Principle
The challenge is to manage all of the messages delivered by all aspects of marketing communication so that they work together to present the brand in a coherent and consistent way.

Brand Communication's Role in Marketing

Since marketing is a big topic and most advertising and marcom majors are expected to take an introductory course in marketing, we won't try to present Marketing 101 here in this chapter. Instead, we will review some of marketing's basic concepts and explain how they are important to understand how marketing communication works.

Marketing is designed to build brand and customer relationships that generate sales and profits or, in the case of nonprofits, memberships, volunteers, and donations. Traditionally, the goal of most marketing programs has been to sell products, defined as *goods*, *services*, or *ideas*. Marketing's sales goal is accomplished by responding to the marketplace matching a product's availability—and the company's production capabilities—to the consumer's need, desire, or demand for the product, as illustrated by the marketing program of Urban Decay, a line of cosmetics with a street-smart attitude that markets to fashionable young women. The *Wall Street Journal* says the cosmetics brand caught attention with its edgy packaging and product names, such as "Perversion" and "Stray Dog."[2]

Marketing accomplishes its goal by managing a set of operations and strategic decisions referred to as the **marketing mix** (or the **four Ps**). These include the design and performance of the *product*, its distribution (*place* available), its *pricing* strategies, and its *promotion*. We'll explain the communication dimensions of these four Ps in this chapter.

Marketing also focuses on managing customer relationships to benefit all of a brand's **stakeholders**—by stakeholders, we mean all the individuals and groups who have a stake in the success of the brand, including employees, investors, the community, business partners, and customers. As we'll explain later in the section on branding, positive stakeholder relationships create value for a brand.

Photo: Courtesy of Urban Decay

SHOWCASE

The Urban Decay line of cosmetics projects is designed to lead the market with edgy product designs and formulations that appeal to fashion-conscious young women. Its street-smart attitude is embodied in its packaging and product names.

A graduate of the University of North Texas, Wende Zomnir was nominated by Professor Sheri Broyles to be featured in this book.

Who Are the Key Players?

The marketing industry is a complex network of professionals, all of whom are involved in creating, producing, delivering, and selling something to customers. They are also involved in some way in delivering marketing communication messages. The four categories of key players include (1) marketers, (2) suppliers and vendors, (3) distributors and retailers, and (4) marketing partners, such as agencies. Consider also that these positions represent jobs, so you can use this information as a career guide should you be interested in working in marketing.

The **marketer**, also referred to from the agency's point of view as the *client*, is any company or organization behind the brand—that is, the organization, company, or manufacturer producing the product or service and offering it for sale. This is the same corporate source we referred to in Chapter 1 as "The Advertiser."

The materials and ingredients used in producing a product are obtained from other companies, referred to as *suppliers* or *vendors*. The phrase **supply chain** is used to refer to this complex network of suppliers who produce components and ingredients that are then sold to the manufacturer. The **distribution chain** or **channel of distribution** refers to the various companies involved in moving a product from its manufacturer to its buyers. Suppliers and distributors are also partners in the communication process, and their marketing communication often supports the brand. Marketing relationships also involve cooperative programs and alliances between two companies that work together as *marketing partners* to create products and promotions. For example, Leo Burnett created brand partnerships for Nintendo's Wii with 7-Eleven, Pringles, and Comedy Central.

What Are the Most Common Types of Markets?

The word **market** originally meant the place where the exchange between seller and buyer took place. Today, we speak of a market not only as a place (the New England market) but also as a particular type of buyer—for example, the youth market or the motorcycle market. The phrase **share of market** refers to the percentage of the total sales in a product category belonging to a particular brand.

As Figure 2.1 shows, the four main market types are (1) consumer, (2) business-to-business (industrial), (3) institutional, and (4) channel markets. We can further divide each of these markets by size or geography (local, regional, national, or international).

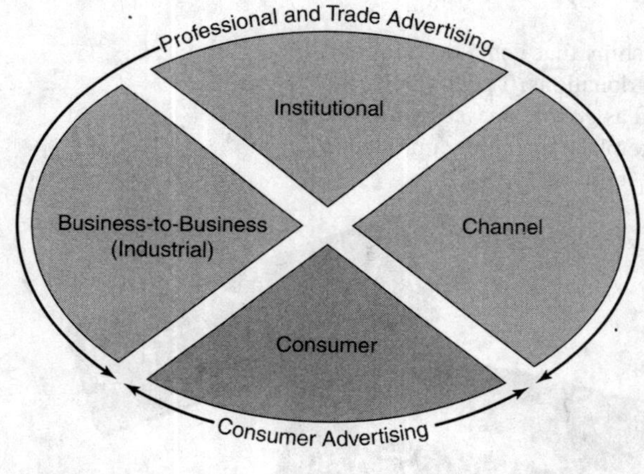

FIGURE 2.1
Four Types of Markets
The consumer market, which is the target of consumer advertising, is important but is only one of four types of markets. The other three are reached through professional and trade advertising.

- **Consumer markets** (business-to-consumer or B2C) refers to businesses selling to consumers who buy goods and services for personal or household use. As a student, you are considered a member of the consumer market for companies that sell jeans, athletic shoes, sweatshirts, pizza, music, textbooks, backpacks, computers, education, checking accounts, bicycles, and a multitude of other products that you buy at drugstores and grocery stores, which the marketing industry refers to as **package goods**. (In Europe, these are called **fast-moving consumer goods**.) Marcom programs vary with the product category—for example, advertising is addressed differently to buyers of cosmetics and buyers of dishwashers.
- **Business-to-business (B2B) markets** consist of companies that buy products or services to use in their own businesses or in making other products. General Electric, for example, buys computers to use in billing and inventory control, steel and wiring to use in the manufacture of its products, and cleaning supplies to use in maintaining its buildings. Advertising in this category tends to be heavy on factual content and information, but it can also be beautifully designed, as Peter Stasiowski's ads for Interprint demonstrate in the "A Day in the Life" story, which describes the job of a marketing and communication manager who works on the "client side." Stasiowski first started his career as an art director at Gargan Communications in Massachusetts before moving to the client side.
- **Institutional markets** include a wide variety of nonprofit organizations, such as hospitals, government agencies, and schools, that provide services for the benefit of society. Universities, for example, are in the market for furniture, cleaning supplies, computers, office supplies, groceries, audiovisual material, paper towels, and toilet paper, to name a few. Such ads are similar to B2B ads in that they are generally heavy on facts and light on emotional appeals.

- **Channel markets**, as discussed earlier, include members of the distribution chain, which is made up of businesses we call **resellers**, or intermediaries. **Channel marketing**, the process of targeting a specific campaign to members of the distribution channel, is more important now that manufacturers consider their distributors to be partners in their marketing programs. As giant retailers such as Walmart become more powerful, they can even dictate to manufacturers what products their customers want to buy and how much they are willing to pay for them.

Most marketing communication dollars are spent on consumer markets, although B2B advertising is becoming almost as important. Firms usually reach consumer markets through mass

A Day in the Life

A View from the Marcom Front Line

Peter Stasiowski, *Marketing and Communication Manager, Interprint, Inc.*

There's a big difference between working for an ad agency, where the focus is on promoting many clients, and becoming an individual company's lone marketing professional, where the focus is on promoting the company that signs your paycheck.

The most obvious changes, such as fine-tuning one marketing plan instead of juggling several, give way to more subtle and important differences. When I traded my agency title of art director and creative director for my current position as marketing and communications manager for an industrial printing company, I went from working with a group of people dedicated to practicing good marketing communications to working with a group dedicated to printing good decor paper for its customers in the laminate industry.

In my case, the opportunities to expand my marketing skills beyond commercial art into areas like copywriting and financial planning came with the responsibility to make good marketing decisions without the security of an ad agency's team behind me.

At its core, a day in my life as the marketing and communications manager for Interprint is spent communicating clear messages to the right markets as efficiently as possible. For example, to the broad laminate market, I write 90 percent of the articles for Interprint's promotional magazine about everything from our latest printing technologies to our environmental stewardship programs.

I'm also responsible for speaking with newspaper reporters, either to answer their questions or to promote a press release. Then there's coordinating the construction of trade show exhibits, planning press conferences, and, yes, designing print advertising. It's all meant to get the good word out to the right eyes and ears.

At the end of the day, my reward is knowing that as I dive deeper into the fabric of one company and learn what messages and media resonate with its customers, I gain both a broader skill set and the unfiltered feedback that ensures increasingly successful marketing efforts into the future. For more about Interprint, check out the company's fact sheet at http://usa.interprint.com/media.

Note: Peter Stasiowski is a graduate of the advertising program at the University of West Florida. He and his work were nominated by Professor Tom Groth to be featured in this book.

Photo: Courtesy of INTERPRINT, Inc.

Photo: Courtesy of INTERPRINT, Inc.

Principle

Every part of the marketing mix—not just marketing communication—sends a message.

media and other marketing communication tools. They typically reach the other three markets—industrial, institutional, and channel or reseller—through trade and professional advertising in specialized media, such as trade journals, professional magazines, and direct mail, but even more so through personal sales and trade shows and promotions.

What's important, however, is that marketing communication is used to reach customers in all four types of markets. The type of marketing communication and the way it is directed to the audience may differ, but strategic communication is essential to all four types of marketing.

The brand message coordination problem goes beyond all the varied marketing communication tools used in all these different markets because marketers have come to realize that other aspects of the marketing mix also send messages. So let's consider a basic concept of marketing: the marketing mix.

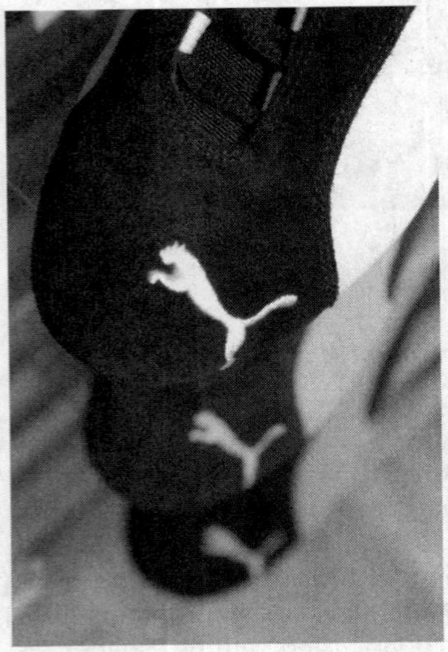

Photo: Christoph Papsch/Alamy

Founded in Germany in 1948, Puma was famous initially as a producer of innovative athletic-training shoes. A global brand that now includes fashion-statement apparel and accessories as well as footwear, it has left its paw prints in more than 80 countries. Go to www.puma.com to see Puma's newest designs. How important is design and performance to this manufacturer? Can you assess that and other marketing mix decisions from cues on this website?

How Does the Marketing Mix Send Messages?

As we mentioned in the chapter introduction, marketing managers construct the *marketing mix*, also called the four Ps, to accomplish marketing objectives. As shown in Figure 2.2, these marketing mix decisions are key elements of marketing strategy. (We'll talk more about strategy in Chapter 7.)

To a marketing manager, marketing communication is just one part of the marketing mix, but to a marcom manager all of these marketing mix elements also send messages that can sometimes contradict planned messages or even confuse consumers. The following sections explain these three other components of the marketing mix as providers of communication cues.

Product The focus of the four Ps is the product (goods, services, ideas). Design, performance, and quality are key elements of a product brand's success. When a product brand performs well, this sends a positive message that this brand is okay to repurchase. (And the opposite is also true—poor performance sends a negative message.) A positive brand experience also motivates the buyer to recommend the brand to others, extending the reach of the positive experience into personal communication, which we refer to as "word of mouth."

Some brands, such as Puma's products, are known for their design, which becomes a major **point of differentiation** from competitors. When this point of difference is of significant importance to customers, it also becomes a **competitive advantage**. Apple's personal digital products, such as the iPod, iPhone, and iPad, have built a fanatical following because of their innovativeness. The iPhone, for example, was characterized in the *Wall Street Journal* as "the defining consumer item of its age."[3]

A *product launch* for a new brand such as Apple's iPad depends on announcements in the media usually involving both publicity and advertising. The goals of the communication are to build awareness of the new brand and to explain how this new product works and how it differs from competitors. Performance is important for launching technical products, such as Nintendo's Wii, that are introduced to the market through ads that demonstrate how to use or play with this new technology.

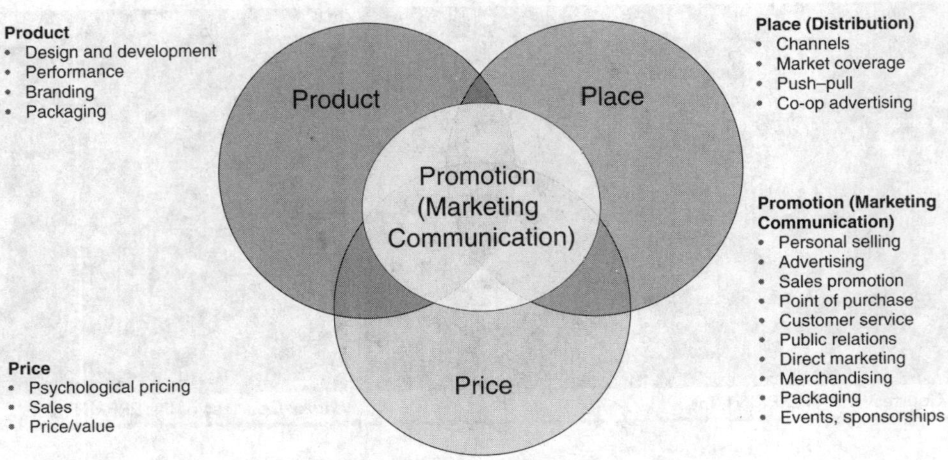

FIGURE 2.2

The Marketing Mix

The four marketing mix elements and their related tools and marketing communication techniques are basic components of marketing. Marketing communication is shown in the middle and overlapping because the other three Ps—product, place (distribution), and price—because all have communication effects.

Product performance—how it handles or is used—sends the loudest messages about a product or brand and determines whether the product is purchased again or whether the buyer recommends it to others. Computer buyers, for example, will assess performance by asking the following: Is it easy to use? Does it crash? How big is its memory? Quality is another product feature that is often linked to upscale brands, such as Mercedes and Rolex. The idea is that if the product is well engineered and its manufacturer maintains a high standard of quality, then the brand will last and perform at a high level.

Principle
Product performance sends the loudest message about a product or brand and determines whether it will be purchased again.

Related to product performance is product adaptions, particularly when innovation is driven by consumer needs. An example comes from Avon's bath oil, Skin So Soft, which has long been used as a bug repellent. Avon got the message and rolled out Skin So Soft Bug Guard.[4]

Pricing The price a seller sets for a product sends a "quality " or "status" message. The higher the price relative to the competition, the higher, supposedly, the quality or status will be. The price is based not only on the cost of making and marketing the product but also on the seller's expected margin of profit as well as the impact of the price on the brand image. Ultimately, the price of a product is based on what the market will bear, the competition, the economic well-being of the consumer, the relative value of the product, and the consumer's ability to gauge that value, which is referred to as the *price/value proposition*.

Principle
The treatment of the price in marketing communication cues a meaning that puts the price/value proposition in perspective.

Psychological pricing strategies use marketing communication to manipulate the customer's judgment of value. For example, ads showing *prestige pricing*—in which a high price is set to make the product seem worthy or valuable—may be illustrated by photographs of the "exceptional product" in luxury settings or by copy explaining the reasons for a high price. Consider a watch that costs $500—what does that price say? On one hand, it may say that it's a prestige or quality product; on the other hand, it might suggest that the watch is expensive, maybe too expensive. In fact, the meaning of the price is dependent on the context provided by the marketing communication, which puts the price in perspective.

With the exception of price information delivered at the point of sale, advertising is often the primary vehicle for telling the consumer about price, as the McDonald's sign demonstrates. The term **price copy**, which is the focus of much retail advertising, refers to advertising copy devoted primarily to this type of information. A number of other pricing strategies, however, can affect how the price is communicated or signaled in advertising. During the Great Recession, fast-food chains, as well as Walmart and, of course, discount and dollar stores, depended on a *value pricing* strategy using the $1 price to signal money-saving offers.[5] Some prices are relatively standard, such as those at movie theaters. In contrast, *promotional pricing* is used to communicate a dramatic or temporary price reduction through terms such as *sale*, *special*, and *today only*.

Photo: Jeff Greenberg/Alamy

This sign for McDonald's highlights its $1 items. The $1 menu has become a competitive battleground for the fast-food category.

Place (Distribution) Where or how a brand is made available also sends a message. The image of a watch, like Swatch, can be quite different if it's sold in Walmart as opposed to Nordstrom. The objective is to match the distribution to the product quality, brand personality, and price.

It does little good to offer a good or service that will meet customers' needs unless you have a mechanism for making the product available and handling the exchange of payment for the product. What marketers call **distribution** includes the channels used to make the product easily accessible to customers.

Puma, for example, is growing the market for its shoes and athletic apparel because of its unusual approach to distribution. Its channel marketing strategy delivers Puma products to exclusive and mass-market audiences, selling its edgy designs to trendy retailers and then placing its more mainstream products in mall stores. Foot Locker might sell the GV special, a style based on a retro Puma tennis shoe from its glory days 30 years ago; at the same time, an independent fashion store might carry a basketball shoe in fabrics like snakeskin or lizard. In recent years, Puma has expanded its distribution program to include its own stores, which greet customers with a unique shopping environment reflecting the personality of the Puma brand.

There are many routes to distribution and marketing managers consider a variety of channels when developing distribution strategies. A common distribution strategy involves the use of *intermediaries*, such as retailers. Some manufacturers, such as Apple, sell not only through other retailers but also in its very popular Apple stores. "Clicks or bricks" is a phrase used to describe whether a product is sold online (clicks) or in a traditional store (bricks). **Direct marketing** companies, such as Lands' End and Dell, distribute their products directly without the use of a reseller. The sale is totally dependent on the effectiveness of catalogs and direct-response advertising.

Another distribution-related strategy involves the distinction between push and pull strategies. A **push strategy** offers promotional incentives, such as discounts and money for advertising, to retailers. Distribution success depends on the ability of these intermediaries to market the product, which they often do with their own advertising. In contrast, a **pull strategy** directs marketing communication efforts at the consumer and attempts to pull the product through the channel by intensifying consumer demand. The decision to use a push or pull strategy determines, to some extent, the audience to be targeted and the nature of the demand to be addressed by the message.

Other Factors in the Mix The four Ps concept is useful in identifying the key marketing strategy decisions that support the promotion of a brand. But there are other areas that also are important in the brand's communication mix, such as personal sales and customer service.

Personal sales rely on face-to-face contact between the marketer and a prospective customer rather than contact through media. It's particularly important in B2B marketing and high-end retail. Self-service retailers (grocery stores, drugstores, and big-box stores like Costco) rely on customers to know what they want and where in the store to find it.

In contrast to most advertising, whose effects are often delayed, marketers use **personal selling** to create immediate sales to people who are shopping for a product. The different types of personal selling include sales calls at the place of business by a field representative (field sales), assistance at an outlet by a sales clerk (retail selling), and calls by a representative who goes to consumers' homes (door-to-door selling). Marketing communication works as a partner with sales programs to develop **leads**, the identification of potential customers, or **prospects. Lead generation** is a common objective for trade promotion and advertising. Personal sales are even more important in B2B marketing for reaching key decision makers within a company who can authorize a purchase.

Customer service refers to the help provided to a customer before, during, and after a purchase. It also refers to the company's willingness to provide such help. Most manufacturers have a customer service operation that provides follow-up services for many goods and also answers questions and deals with complaints about products. But it's more than just traditional face-to-face customer service. Many companies now provide more assistance to customers through online connections than face-to-face.

Photo: Image Courtesy of the National Library of Medicine

CLASSIC

Ads for Lydia Pinkham's Vegetable Compound appeared in newspapers in the 1870s with claims that the product "goes to the very root of all female complaints." How do products and advertising like this compare with modern-day pharmaceutical advertising?

Added Value

Information from the marketing mix and marketing communication can add value to a product both for consumers and for marketers. **Added value** refers to a strategy or activity that makes the product more useful or appealing to the consumer as well as distribution partners. The three Ps of product, price, and place add more tangible value. For example, the more convenient the product is to buy, the more valuable it is to the customer. Likewise, the lower the price, the more useful features a product has, or the higher its quality, the more a customer may value it.

Marketing communication adds psychological value by creating a brand that people remember, by delivering useful information, and by making a product appealing, as in the "Classic" ad for Lydia Pinkham's Vegetable Compound.

With no added value, why pay more for one brand over the competition? A motorcycle is a motorcycle, but a Harley-Davidson is a highly coveted bike because of the brand image created by its advertising. Advertising and other marketing communication not only showcase the product's inherent value but also may add value by making the product more desirable.

On the other hand, not all marketing mix decisions send positive messages and add value to products. In 2011, Netflix found to its horror that a clumsy plan designed to split the distribution of its streaming video service and DVD-via-mail services, as well as add a more expensive alternative system called Quickster, enraged its customers and drove its share price down.[6] Nothing in the proposal was seen as adding value for Netflix customers, who saw it, instead, as a way for Netflix to get more money for a more inconvenient form of the video service.

Let's now consider how this concept of the marketing mix relates to integrated marketing communication.

What Is Integrated Marketing Communication?

We mentioned earlier that advertising is only one type of marketing communication and that **integrated marketing communication** (IMC) is the practice of coordinating all brand communication messages as well as the messages from the marketing mix decisions. One of the important things IMC does is send a consistent message about the brand. IMC is like a musical score that helps all the various instruments play together. But before you decide what tune each individual instrument will play, you have to decide what the song is all about. In this book, we say the song is about the brand—its strategy and meaning. This concept will be developed in more detail in Chapter 18, where we explain the challenge of managing both IMC campaigns and programs.

Principle

IMC is like a musical score that helps the various instruments play together. The song is the meaning of the brand.

IMC is still evolving, and both professionals and professors are engaged in defining the field and explaining how it works. **Integration** means every message is focused and works together, as the ACW Ironworks campaign in the "Showcase" feature illustrates. This creates *synergy*, which is expressed in the common saying that "2 plus 2 equals 5." In other words, when the pieces are effectively coordinated, the whole has more impact than the sum of its parts. A simple example is McDonald's brand identity, where the "M" in the name is reflected in the shape of its iconic arches. A name, a logo, and a building design all work together to create the face of this familiar and highly successful brand.

The problem arises when the marcom tools are not aligned with other marketing mix communication messages that deliver brand communication. For example, how well does the activities of a function such as sales promotion reflect the brand image. Does it distract from the pricing strategy and the relationship of price to value? A high-priced status product, such as Lexus or Tiffany, can be undercut by poorly created sales promotions. Likewise, direct-response messages, whether by mail or online, can raise issues of privacy that can make a brand seem insensitive to its customers.

It might be helpful to consider how all of the communication we've been discussing fits together from a manager's viewpoint. Here's the scheme: advertising and other marcom areas comprise the tools of marketing communication in an IMC program. Those relationships are depicted in Figure 2.3. Note how we positioned marketing communication in the center of the four Ps. The point is that marketing communication is at the center of brand communication, and the effectiveness of the brand communication depends on how well all the pieces are integrated.

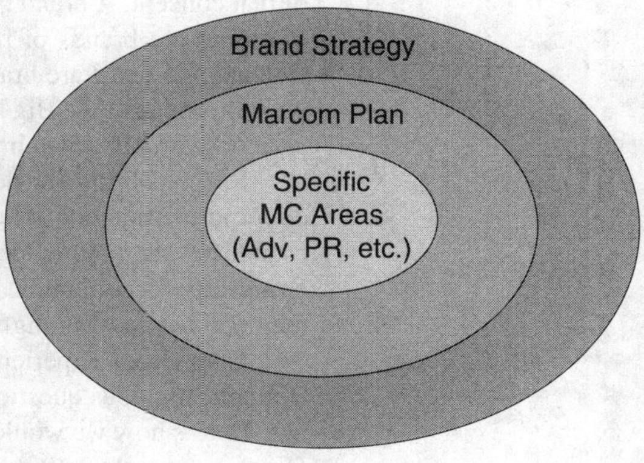

FIGURE 2.3

The Hierarchy of Brand Communication

Brand communication begins with a brand strategy that is outlined in a marketing plan. Then specific plans are developed for the relevant marcom areas that are needed to implement the marketing and brand strategy.

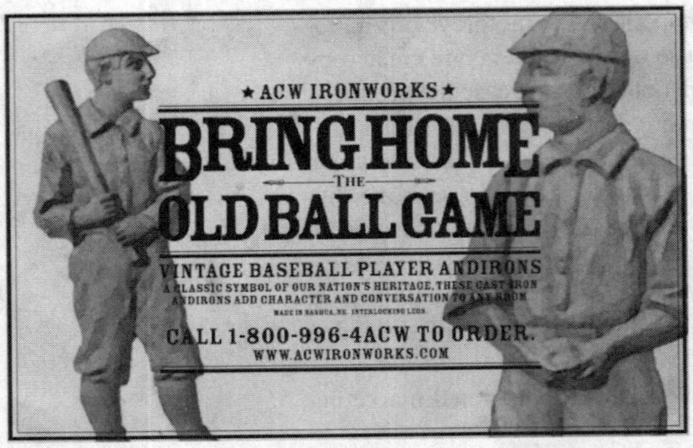

a.c.w. · ironworks ·

Photo: Courtesy of BU AdLab

SHOWCASE
This branding campaign by the AdLab student agency at Boston University for ACW Ironworks featured a logo design, a business card, and print advertising.

What Is the Role of Communication in Branding?

We've mentioned brands throughout this chapter, so let's take a minute to explain the importance of that concept. A brand is more than a product. Hamburgers are products—but the Big Mac and Whopper are brands of hamburgers. Toothpaste is a product (also the *product category*), but Colgate and Crest are brands of toothpaste. Branding applies to organizations (McDonald's) as well as products (the Big Mac) and to services—State Farm and the U.S. Postal Service—as well as goods. Brand is also important to nonprofits, such as United Way and Habitat for Humanity.

Responsibility for developing and maintaining a successful brand lies with the marketing or corporate function called **brand management**; however, effective marketing communication establishes the unique identity by which the brand engages the hearts and minds of consumers. **Branding** is a communication function that creates the intangible aspects of a brand that make it memorable and meaningful to a consumer.

Given your experience, how would you define a brand? You have pieces of a definition from our previous questions: past positive experience, familiarity, a promise, a position, an image. Here's how we would define a **brand**: *A perception, often imbued with emotion, that results from experiences with and information about a company or a line of products.* Other definitions point to a mixture of tangible and intangible attributes as well as the identity elements, such as the brand name and the trademark, that stand for the brand.

Said another way, a brand is something that lives in the heads and hearts of consumers and other stakeholders. Their heads hold brand information, and their hearts hold brand emotions and feelings (like or dislike, high or low status, sexy or boring, and so forth).

Think about these characteristics as you read "The Inside Story" feature about Urban Decay Cosmetics. For many brands, specifically smaller ones like Urban Decay, the communication

The Inside Story

A Passion for the Business

Wende Zomnir, *Creative Director and Founding Partner, Urban Decay Cosmetics*

Being the creative force behind a brand like Urban Decay makes me responsible for cranking out great ideas. And in the 13 years I've been doing this, I've figured out a few things about how to generate creative ideas with which people connect. It begins with a passion for the business. Here are my seven principles about how to run a business creatively:

1. *Feel a passion for your brand.* Everyone in product development, design, PR, merchandising, sales, and marketing at Urban Decay loves our makeup and deeply connects to our position as the counterculture icon in the realm of luxury makeup.
2. *Spot emerging trends.* Our best ideas don't start from analysts telling us what the trends are. My creative team and I talk about what kinds of colors, visual icons, textures, and patterns we are craving and start from there. Our job at Urban Decay is to lead graphically with our product design and formulation. Recently we launched a volumizing mascara called Big Fatty and played off the connotations in the name, infusing the formula with hemp oil and wrapping the mascara vial in an Age of Aquarius–inspired print. Shortly after the product's release, a supplier to the cosmetics industry came in to show us a version of our own mascara, giving us a presentation on the coming trends. It's annoying, but when this happens, we know we're doing our job.
3. *Cultivate your inner voice.* You also need to develop a gut instinct for what will work. I felt that skulls were going to be huge because everyone in the office was craving them on T-shirts, shoes, key rings, and so forth. We decided to put them on our seasonal holiday compacts in 2005. And the same season that Marc Jacobs launched them, so did we. We had distributors begging us to sell them a version without the skull, but we stood firm and wouldn't change it because we knew it was right. And you know what? The same distributors who balked placed the biggest reorders and complained that we couldn't stock them fast enough.
4. *Check your ego.* Listening to that inner voice *is* something you can cultivate, but you've got to check your ego at the door in order to do it. That can be hard because being a creative leader means you've probably generated a lot of great ideas that work. So, you've got confidence in your concepts and your ability to deliver, but you have to be able to admit others have great ideas, too.
5. *Cherry-pick the best ideas.* Gut instinct is important, *but*—and this is big—even more crucial is being able to listen to all the ideas and sort out the junk. After you sort through everything, then pick the very best concept, even if it's *not* your idea.
6. *Little ideas are important, too.* You've got to rally everyone behind your Big Idea, but realize that all those little ideas that prop up the big one are great, too. That's what makes so many of our products work in the marketplace: a big idea supported by little ideas—and the people who develop them.
7. *Be flexible.* My final important creative principle is flexibility. Knowing when to be flexible has resulted in some of the best work we've created here. While working on a body powder for summer that was to be impregnated with water for a cooling sensation on the skin, we ran into production problems. We wanted a powder, but I decided to add flavor instead. That edible body powder became a huge subbrand for us, spawning multiple flavors and generating huge amounts of press and revenue. The cooling powder would have been late, had quality control issues, and probably would have lasted a season.

Check out Urban Decay at *www.urbandecay.com*, *www.myspace.com/urbandecaycosmetics*, and *http://twitter.com/UrbanDecay411*.

Note: Wende Zomnir (aka Ms. Decay) graduated from the University of North Texas, where she was a student of Professor Sheri Broyles.

Photo: Courtesy of Urban Decay

The distinctive personality of Urban Decay Cosmetics is seen in its packaging as well as its products' names, such as the Ammo Group, and colors: "Smog," "Mildew," and "Oil Slick."

Photo: Ilan Ruben/Art Dept.

There are many different types of tennis shoes, and the advertising challenge is to create a distinctive brand image for the product. What do you think this ad says about the Keds brand?

decisions lie with the owner, founder, or partners in the business. Wende Zomnir is not only a founding partner of Urban Decay Cosmetics but also an advertising graduate and a marketing communication professional.

Branding also differentiates similar products from one another. Sometimes the difference between brands in the same product category lies in product features—the quality of the meat in the hamburger or the chemistry of the toothpaste—but often we choose one brand over another because of a difference in the brand impressions we carry. Companies make products but they sell brands. A brand differentiates a product from its competitors and makes a promise to its customers, as the Keds ad demonstrates.

In fact, all organizations with a name can be considered brands, and that includes organization brands, which are distinct from product brands. In particular, international branding expert Giep Franzen and his team of Dutch researchers found that "organizations should be aware that simply by existing and interacting with others, an organization is branding itself. So branding the organization is inevitable. It is going to happen whether the process is managed or not."[7] In other words, an organization cannot *not* communicate. Franzen identifies three components of brand perception for organizations:

- ***Organization Identity*** Identifiers, business category, physical identity, history, organization cultures, behaviors, ideology, performance, and reputation
- ***Consumer/Customer/Stakeholder Characteristics*** Sociodemographics, needs and goals, values, lifestyle situations, category experiences and attitudes, and brand relationships
- ***Brand Framework*** Brand signs, brand architecture (extensions), brand presence, brand experiences, brand meanings, brand essence, brand positioning, brand relationships, and market brand equity

Principle
An organization cannot *not* communicate. People create brand impressions whether or not the branding process is managed by the organization.

One thing that makes the practice of IMC different from traditional advertising is its focus on branding and the totality of brand communication. Duncan and Mulhern, the authors of a symposium report on IMC, explain that "IMC is, among other things, a process for doing advertising and promotion better and more effectively in the process of building brands."[8] Through IMC that considers all possible brand messages, marketing communication managers are able to ensure that the perception of their brand is clear and sharp rather than confused and mushy. How well the various messages delivered by marketing communication and the marketing mix are aligned determines the value and success of a brand. So let's consider next the communication foundation of branding.

How Does a Brand Acquire Meaning?

Principle
A brand is an integrated perception derived from personal experiences with and messages about the brand.

A brand is more than a name or logo; in fact, it is a perception—an identification that we assign to the products we know and use. In their book on the science and art of branding, Franzen and Moriarty explain that the meaning of a brand is "an integrated perception that is derived from experiences with and messages about the brand."[9] What do we mean by that?

Think about this: Why does one brand sell twice the number of products as another when there is no basic difference in product attributes or performance and both brands sell for the same price? The answer is, a difference in the brand meaning. Meaning-making cues and images are what marketing communication delivers to brands. This perception of the brand, this brand meaning, is the one thing a brand has that can't be copied. Competitors can make a similar product, but it's difficult for them to make the same brand because brand meaning is built on a collection of personal impressions.

A Brand Is a Perception A brand, then, is basically a perception loaded with emotions and feelings (intangible elements), not just a trademark or package design (tangible elements). Tangible features are things you can observe or touch, such as a product's design, ingredients, components, size, shape, and performance. Intangibles include the product's perceived value, its brand image, positive and negative impressions and feelings, and experiences customers have with the brand, product, or company, as the Wii ad illustrates. Intangibles, such as personal experiences, are just as important as the tangible features because they create the emotional bonds people have with their favorite brands.

Photo: Reuters Limited.

Brand perceptions are built on messages from marketing communication and the marketing mix but also from personal experiences and impressions. For the launch of the Wii video game, the marketing communicators felt it was important to demonstrate the experience of using the Wii.

But even intangibles can lend monetary value and legal protection to a brand's unique identity. All the impressions created by a brand's tangible and intangible features come together as a **brand concept**—the brand and what it stands for—that exists in people's hearts and minds. It results not only from experiences with the product but also from meanings acquired from marketing communication. Such impressions are particularly important in what we call **parity products**, such as soap, gasoline, and other products with few distinguishing features. For these products, feelings about the brand can become *the* critical point of difference.

The meaning of a brand, then, is an aggregation of everything a customer (or other stakeholder) sees, hears, reads, or experiences about an organization or a product brand. This meaning, however, cannot be totally controlled by management. A company can *own* a brand name and brand symbol and *influence* to some degree what people think about the brand, but it can't dictate brand impressions because they exist in people's minds and are derived, as we've said, from their personal experiences, as Mountain Dew found out in 2013 when one of its edgier ads brought charges of racism.

Branding Transforms Products A basic principle of branding is that brand communication transforms a product—goods as well as services—into something more meaningful than the product itself. A Whopper is something more than a hamburger. A brand adds personality and creates a brand identity that separates similar products and makes them unique. That simplifies shopping and adds value for the consumer. A Tiffany watch is more than a timepiece—it is also different from a Swatch even if both have the same basic components, and both are different from a generic Kmart watch with an unknown brand name. **Brand transformation** creates this difference by enriching the brand meaning. Brand meanings are more complex than impressions because of what they symbolize. The Tiffany brand symbolizes quality, sophistication, and luxury; a Swatch brand is fun and fashionable; and a generic watch from Walmart is inexpensive and utilitarian.

Principle
A brand transforms a product into something more meaningful than the product itself.

The development of the Ivory Soap brand by Procter & Gamble in 1879 represented a major advance in branding because of the way its makers built a meaningful brand concept to transform a parity product—soap—into a powerful brand—Ivory. Just as the Macintosh "1984" commercial mentioned in Chapter 1 represents one of the all-time great ads, Ivory represents one of the all-time great marketing and branding stories, which you can read about in the "A Matter of Principle" feature.

How Does Brand Transformation Work?

Although Franzen and his team of organizational branding researchers identified many elements in branding, for our discussion here we will consider only three key strategic decisions—identity, position and promise, and image and personality—that transform a product into a brand.

Brand Identity A critical function of branding is to create a separate **brand identity** for a product within a product category, and that assignment usually falls to designers and marketing communicators. Analyze the language you use in talking about your own things. Do you buy chips or Doritos? Do you drink a soft drink or a Pepsi? Do you wear tennis shoes or Nikes? If branding works, then you refer to a specific brand by name rather than a generic category when discussing a product. Brand identity cues are generally the brand name and the symbol used as a logo—think of the "swoosh" graphic that symbolizes Nike and the leaping cat for Puma.

Principle
If branding is successful, then you refer to a specific brand by name rather than its general category label.

The choice of a brand name for new products is tested for memorability and relevance. The idea is that the easier it is to recognize the identity cues, the easier it will be to create awareness

A Matter of Principle

It's Pure and It Floats

Soap is soap, right?

A basic principle of branding is that a brand takes on meaning when it makes a product distinctive within its product category. Procter & Gamble (P&G) accomplished that by creating identity elements for its soap brand Ivory before anyone had thought of making soap a distinctive product. The Ivory brand identity system also called attention to innovative features of the product. Here's the background story about how Ivory came to be one of the first and most successful brands of all time.

Before the Civil War, homemakers made their own soap from lye, fats (cooking grease), and fireplace ashes. It was a soft, jelly-like, yellowish soap that would clean things adequately, but if it fell to the bottom of a pail, it dissolved into mush. In Victorian times, the benchmark for quality soap was the highly expensive castile bar—a pure white soap imported from the Mediterranean and made from the finest olive oil.

William Procter and James Gamble, who were partners in a candle-making operation, discovered a formula that produced a uniform, predictable bar soap, which they provided in wooden boxes to both armies during the Civil War. This introduced the concept of mass production and opened up a huge market when the soldiers returned to their homes with a demand for the bars of soap. But back at home, the bars of soap were still yellow and sunk to the bottom.

Photo: Courtesy of Procter & Gamble Company.

of the brand. That also makes it easy to find and repurchase a brand, which is an important factor in customer repurchase decisions. Successful brand names have several characteristics:

- ***Distinctive*** A common name that is unrelated to a product category, such as Apple for a computer, ensures there will be no similar names creating confusion. It can also be provocative, as in the Virgin line.
- ***Association*** Subaru, for example, chose Outback as the name for its rugged SUV, hoping the name would evoke the adventure of the Australian wilderness.
- ***Benefit*** Some brand names relate to the brand promise, such as Slim-Fast for weight loss and Head & Shoulders for dandruff control shampoo.
- ***Heritage*** Some brand names reflect the maker, such as H&R Block, Kellogg's, and Dr. Scholl's. The idea is that there is credibility in a product when makers are proud to put their names on it, particularly in some international markets, such as Japan, where the company behind the brand is an important part of the brand image.
- ***Simplicity*** To make a brand name easier to recognize and remember, brand names are often short and easy to pronounce, such as Tide, Bic, and Nike. Because of the increase in multinational marketing, it is also important that names properly translate into other languages.

When Coke moved into the Chinese market in the late 1970s, it faced the immediate problem of translating its well-known brand name into Chinese. Of course, there are no equivalent Chinese words for *Coca* or *Cola*, and phonetic-based translations were meaningless. The ingenious solution was to use a group of four characters—可口可乐—the first half meaning "tasty" or "delicious" and the next two characters together meaning "really happy." Although it has come to stand as a generic phrase for cola, the name for Coke in Chinese is roughly "tasty happy" cola. So Coke owns the category. The effectiveness of the Chinese trademark has been an important factor in making Coca-Cola the leading soft drink in China.[10]

P&G hired a chemist to create a white-bar equivalent to the legendary castile bar. The chemist's work represented the first time scientific-based research and development was used to design a product. In 1878, P&G white soap was invented. It was a modest success until the company began getting requests for the "soap that floats." One legend is that a worker in 1879 accidentally left the soap-mixing machine operating during lunch, resulting in an unusually frothy mixture. Recent research, however, has found that James Gamble may have always intended for Ivory to float. Whether accident or intention, it led to one of the world's greatest statements of a product benefit: "It floats."

Photo: © 2007 Procter & Gamble Company. All rights reserved

Other decisions also helped make it a branding breakthrough. In 1879, one of the P&G family was in church listening to a scripture about ivory palaces and proposed that the white bar be renamed Ivory Soap. Now the great product had a great name as well as a great product benefit. Rather than asking for soap—soap was soap—and taking a bar from the barrel, customers could now ask for a specific product they liked by name.

But that wasn't the end of P&G's branding innovations. A grandson who was determined to match the quality of the legendary castile soap again turned to chemists and independent laboratories to determine the purity of both castile and Ivory. In 1882, the research found that the total impurities in Ivory added up to only 0.56 percent, which was actually lower than that of the castile bars. By turning that into a positive, Harley Procter wrote the legendary slogan that Ivory is "99 and 44/100 percent pure." Thus was born a pledge of quality that became one of the most famous brand slogans in marketing history.

To read more about the history of this famous brand, check out *www.ivory.com/purefun_history.htm.*

Sources: Charles Goodrum and Helen Dalrymple, *Advertising in America* (New York: Harry N. Abrams, 1990); Laurie Freeman, "The House That Ivory Built: 150 Years of Procter & Gamble," *Advertising Age*, August 20, 1987, 4–18, 164–220; "P&G History: History of Ivory," June 2004, *www.pg.com.*

Brand names are important, but recognition is often based on a distinctive graphic. In fact, the word *brand* comes from branding of cattle, a practice that used a distinctive design element to represent the name of the ranch to which the cattle belonged. A number of elements contribute to the visual identity—logos, trademarks, characters, and other visual cues, such as color and distinctive typefaces.

A **logo** is similar to a cattle brand in that it stands for the product's source. A **trademark** is a legal sign that indicates ownership. Originally these were simple symbols or initials that silversmiths etched into their products, the "mark of the trade." In modern times, trademarks may include logos, other graphic symbols, or even unusual renderings of the brand name, such as the distinctive Coca-Cola script. A trademark is registered with the government, and the company has exclusive use of its trademark as long as it is used consistently for that product alone.

Photo: Megapress/Alamy

Although the distinctive logo is known around the world, Coca-Cola's brand name needed to be represented in Chinese characters that had meaning for the Chinese market.

Problems can arise when a brand name dominates a product category, such as Kleenex and Xerox. In such situations, the brand name becomes a substitute label for the category label. Refrigerator, laundromat, zipper, and aspirin lost the legal right to their names when they became generic category names. Band-Aid and Q-tips, although legally registered as indicated by their use of the registration symbol (®), have also crept into common usage as generic names—"It's a band-aid for the budget"—so they, too, are in danger of having their brand names become generic category labels. That detracts from value of the brand both to the consumer who depends on the brand to identify a familiar product and to the organization behind

Photo: © 2013 Xerox Corporation. All rights reserved.

Xerox has a long-running campaign that seeks to protect its name as a brand. Ads such as this warn against using *Xerox* as a general term for a copy machine or as a verb for making a copy. The zipper is a reminder that the Zipper brand lost the rights to its name when the term became used as a category label.

the brand that has spent money and resources over many years to create a recognizable brand identity.

Brand Position and Promise Beyond the basic identification elements, another strategic decision in brand development involves deciding the correct **brand position**. We mentioned earlier that positioning is a way to identify the location a product or brand occupies in consumers' minds relative to its competitors—higher, lower, bigger, more expensive. Related to position is the **brand promise**. From a consumer viewpoint, the value of a brand lies in the promise it makes. Both "It floats" and "99 and 44/100 percent pure" are promises that identify key selling points for Ivory Soap. In other words, the brand through its communication sets expectations for what a customer believes will happen when the product is used. Because of past experience and advertising messages, you know what to expect—that's what a brand promise means.

Consistency is the backbone of a promise. The promise needs to be delivered not just by the advertising but at all points of contact with a brand. Furthermore, the brand has to deliver on the promise. Many weak brands suffer from overpromising. Using hype and exaggeration, they promise more than they can deliver, and consumers end up disappointed. If a cough drop promises relief from throat irritation, then it better deliver that relief. If it also promises good taste, then it better not disappoint with a bitter medicinal flavor. Successfully identifying and then delivering the promise are part of the platform for building a long-term brand relationship with customers.

Principle

Brand communication sets expectations for what will happen when the product is used through the virtual contract of a brand promise.

Brand Image and Personality Another aspect of brand meaning is brand image, which refers to something more complex than a brand impression. More specifically, a **brand image** is a mental picture or idea about a brand that contains associations—luxury, durable, cheap—as well as emotions. These associations and feelings result primarily from the content of advertising and other marketing communication. For example, what do you think of when you think of the Marines, Ben & Jerry's ice cream, the Chicago Cubs, or Celestial Seasonings teas?

A **brand personality** humanizes an organization or a brand. It symbolizes the personal qualities of people you know—bold, fun, exciting, studious, geeky, daring, boring, whatever. Probably the greatest brand personality ever created was for Harley-Davidson. How do you describe the Harley brand personality? Partly it's the people who you associate with the brand, people you may think of as black-leather, devil-may-care individuals who are a little on the outlaw side. It doesn't matter that in their real lives, Harley owners may be doctors, lawyers, or professors. When they put on that black jacket and climb on the bike, they are renegades of the road. The Harley brand personality reflects the people who ride it, and the people who ride it reflect—or adopt—the Harley brand personality.

Photo: Courtesy of Celestial Seasonings, Inc.

Celestial Seasonings® tea uses its distinctive packages to send messages to consumers about its brand image. In what way do packages like this reinforce the brand personality?

Each brand sends a different message because of the image or personality it projects through its marketing communication. If you give your mother a Tiffany watch, she knows you care and were willing to spend a lot of money to demonstrate your caring. If you give a friend a Swatch, you may be saying you think she's a *fashionista* and someone who likes to make a fashion statement. If you give your little brother a generic watch from Walmart, you might be saying that he needs a timepiece that works even though he may lose it or break it.

Brands speak to us through their images and personalities. A brand takes on a distinctive meaning as the branding elements—identity, position, promise, image, and personality—come together to create a coherent and unified perception.[11] The success of this brand effort is determined by the brand's *authenticity*—the genuineness and consistency of the brand's presentation and persona. It's particularly important with online communication and social media where brands need to use voices and ways of speaking that match perceiver personalities.[12] Can customers relate to this brand persona and create a positive, if not enduring, relationship with the brand? That's the basis for brand loyalty.

Brand Value and Brand Equity

Principle
Brands speak to us through their distinctive images and personalities.

For some products and categories, the brand identity is a huge factor in consumer decision making. Another type of added value, then, for a brand comes from associating the brand with a good cause, a practice called **cause marketing** as explained by Professor Scott Hamula. The primary goals, he says, are "to help communities and nonprofit organizations while generating goodwill, positive word of mouth, and the hope that people will look more favorably on these brands when making their next purchase decision." Customers feel good about themselves because they support a company or brand that is aligned with a good cause.

A spike in cause-related work is occurring as marketers increasingly strive for their brands to be "purpose driven" and demonstrate their commitment to social responsibility. The Cannes Lions International Festival of Creativity recognized the trend and honored many excellent cause-related campaigns with awards in 2013.

Hamula explains how cause marketing contributes to the value of a brand in the eyes of its customers in the "A Principled Practice" feature.

A PRINCIPLED PRACTICE

PAUSE FOR THE CAUSE: *Boosting Brand Value with Cause Marketing*

Scott Hamula, *Associate Professor, Roy H. Park School of Communications, Ithaca College*

Things are really tough out there for brands: lots of competition, savvier consumers, media messages that just don't break through the clutter like they used to, and occasional pieces of bad publicity. Today, though, some brands are turning to corporate social responsibility (CSR) not only because it is the right thing to do but also as a way for brands to more clearly differentiate themselves in this dynamic marketplace.

"Values-driven marketing is the next generation of business and an evolution of society," states Liz Brenna, founder of Socially Good Business. "Business practices that companies are implementing under the corporate responsibility or 'values-led business' umbrella are becoming more important to consumers, especially younger ones, and by adopting 'values-driven' strategies, like responsible sourcing initiatives and 'buy one, give one' (to an underserved population or charity), brands can connect with consumers' core values and create unparalleled brand loyalty."

An increasingly popular form of customer engagement is called cause-related marketing. From a local pizzeria donating money to pay for a neighborhood Little League team's baseball shirts to Ford Motor Company donating vehicles to an earthquake-ravaged disaster area in China, brands act as good corporate citizens.

This socially responsible promotional strategy occurs when a brand or company aligns itself with a nonprofit organization to generate both sales and charitable donations at the same time. Simply put, it's "buy my product, and I'll donate to your cause." This approach tends to make a lot of sense. Surveys continue to show that, given two very similar products, consumers are more likely to purchase the brand that is associated with a cause they care about.

American Express Company is often credited with starting cause-related marketing in the early 1980s when it pledged to donate 5 cents to the arts in San Francisco whenever a member used their American Express card to make a purchase and $2 for each new card member.

To launch and sustain a successful cause-related marketing program, a brand must first know what issues are important to its customers so as to align itself with a cause that's a good match. An example of this would be Yoplait yogurt's "Save Lids to Save Lives" campaign. Since this brand's primary target market is women, Yoplait linked itself with the Susan G. Komen Fight for the Cure organization, which is dedicated to fighting against breast cancer worldwide and is often recognized by its pink ribbon symbol. During Yoplait's annual drive, for every pink lid sent in, the brand donated 10 cents, up to $1.5 million. Some brands, like Pier 1 Imports, go as far as creating specific products for its annual partnership with Komen, including a candle whose design is remodeled every August, a pink jewelry box, and a pink shawl. For more information on these and other cause-related marketing programs, visit the Cause Marketing Forum at www.causemarketingforum.com.

What do you think? Is cause marketing limited to certain types of industries, or is this a strategy with more universal appeal for brands in a variety of categories?

Photo: Courtesy of Celestial Seasonings, Inc.

Celestial Seasonings ® tea supports the "Red Dress" campaign for women's heart health, which is part of the bigger American Heart Association's "Go Red for Women" campaign. The herbal tea company links its brand to the "Go Red" campaign using the symbol of the dress on its tea packages.

The added value that comes from brand communication and goodwill-building activities, such as cause marketing refers to the value of a brand to a consumer. But brands are also valued by the financial community. Google was the first $100 billion brand and has been in one of the top positions for years. Now there are many brands valued in the billions. The managing director of Landor, a branding firm, explains that brand value "is about how much would a consumer pay for a caramel-colored soda versus how much they would pay for a Coke."[13] Here is the 2012 BrandZ™ Top 20 list by Millward Brown, a brand consulting firm that calculates the value of global brands:[14]

Most Valuable Global Brands

1. Apple, $183 billion
2. IBM, $115 billion
3. Google, $107 billion
4. McDonald's, $95 billion
5. Microsoft, $76 billion
6. Coca-Cola, $74 billion
7. Marlboro, $73 billion
8. AT&T, $68 billion
9. Verizon, $49 billion
10. China Mobile, $47 billion
11. GE, $45 billion
12. Vodafone, $43 billion
13. IC Band of China, $41 billion
14. Wells Fargo, $39 billion
15. Visa, $38 billion
16. UPS, $37 billion
17. Walmart, $35 billion
18. Amazon.com, $34 billion
19. Facebook, $33 billion
20. Deutsche Telecom, $20 billion

Branding not only differentiates products but also increases their value. A brand and what it symbolizes can affect how much people are willing to pay for it—and that's true for computers as well as cars and cornflakes. Brand studies consistently find that in blind taste tests, people perceive the recognizable brand as tasting better than an unknown brand, even when the sample is identical. It's only a perception in their minds, not an actual taste. And when identical products carry different labels, people will pay more for the recognizable brand. Why do you suppose that's so?

Brand Value Branding not only differentiates products but also increases their value to consumers. The value of branding lies in the power of familiarity and trust to win and maintain consumer acceptance. If a well-known brand name has been tested over time, it's familiar and dependable, plus it carries the associations created through the marketing communication. All of these qualities add value to the brand and make it possible to give a familiar brand a premium price compared to unknown brands. The ACW Ironworks branding campaign is an example of how a brand identity is designed and conveyed through various types of marketing communication.

Brand value, in other words, comes in two forms—the value to a consumer and the value to the corporation. The first is a result of the experiences a customer has had with a brand; the second is a financial measure, which we call **brand equity**.

On the customer side, some brands have loyal users who purchase the brand repeatedly. Powerful brands are those that retain their customers who will repeatedly buy the product or service. **Brand relationship** programs that lead to *loyalty* are important brand strategies. **Brand loyalty** programs offer rewards for repeat business. The frequent-flyer and frequent-buy programs, for example, provide incentives to loyal customers.

Brands also have a financial value that can be plotted on corporate balance sheets. This brand equity is the intangible value of the brand based on the relationships with its stakeholders, as well as intellectual property, such as product formulations. These are intangible assets beyond the tangible ones of plants, equipment, and land. When a company is sold, a figure is calculated for the value of its brands—that's the intangible side of corporate valuation.

Another principle, then, is that *brand relationships drive brand value.* That's because brand relationships are built on a foundation of positive brand experiences and truthful brand communication. The part of brand equity that is based on relationships is also referred to as **goodwill.** It lies in the accumulation of positive brand relationships, which can be measured as a level of personal attachment to the brand that has revenue-producing potential.

Principle
Brand relationships drive brand value.

Leveraging Brand Equity People who manage brand marketing and communication, who we call **brand stewards**, will sometimes leverage brand equity through a **brand extension**, which is the use of an established brand name with a related line of products. In effect, they launch new products but use the established name because it is already recognized and respected. Because the brand is known, it carries with it associations and feelings as well as a certain level of trust. The disadvantage is that the extension may dilute the meaning of the brand or may even boomerang negatively. Usually the extension practice is used for related products, although Virgin, which started out as a brand name for an airline, has had some success adapting its brand name to various unrelated categories, including bottled beverages, mobile phone services, and music stores.

Another practice is **cobranding**, which is a strategy that uses two brand names owned by two separate companies to create a partnership offering. Cobranding is a common practice for credit cards, such as the Visa and United Airlines Mileage Plus card. The new brand name is Mileage Plus, but the card carries both the Visa and the United Airlines identity information. The idea is that the partnership provides customers with value from both brands.

A strong brand may be attractive to other business partners as well through a practice called **brand licensing**. In effect, a partner company rents the brand name and transfers some of its brand equity to another product. The most common example comes from sport teams whose names and logos are licensed to makers of all kinds of goods—shirts, caps, mugs, and other memorabilia. You may also be aware of the practice of brand licensing for your own school. Universities and colleges generate lots of money by licensing their names, logos, and mascots to apparel makers, among many others.

Logo: TP/Alamy

Intel Inside is an example of ingredient branding, in which a computer manufacturer advertises that it is using Intel chips as a testimony to the product's quality. On what brands have you seen this Intel Inside logo exhibited? Do you think ingredient branding like this works?

Another way to leverage a brand is through **ingredient branding**, which refers to the use of a brand name of a manufacturing component in another product's advertising and promotion. The most well-known example is the "Intel Inside" phrase and logo used by other computer makers to call attention to the quality of the chips it uses in manufacturing its products. Other examples of bragging about the quality of components are found in advertising for outdoor wear that announces the use of Gore-Tex, a lightweight, warm, water-resistant fabric, and in food advertising that promotes the use of NutraSweet or Hershey's chocolate. For ingredient branding to be successful, the ingredient must have a high level of awareness and be known as a premium product.

The point of this review of branding practices is that the way a product is made or how it performs its services is no longer the primary differentiating point. Marketing strategy isn't as much about promoting product features as it is about creating brand meanings. It isn't about gaining new customers but rather about building strong brand relationships. Ultimately, the stronger a brand is, the more value it has to all its stakeholders. Understanding how brands are built and managed requires an understanding of relationship-building communication, as the classic McGraw-Hill "client" ad in Chapter 1 illustrated. Most of the added value that comes from an effective brand strategy is driven by marketing communication. Since positive brand relationships generate profits and accumulate as brand equity, the success of branding depends on communication. In other words, advertising and other marketing communication tools are the drivers of strong brands and create marketing success stories.

Principle
Most of the added value that comes from an effective brand strategy is driven by marketing communication.

Brand Communication in a Time of Change

In Chapter 1, we concluded that advertising is a dynamic industry and subject to challenges and change. The same is true of marketing and all areas of marketing communication. The new digital technologies, as well as consumer-generated brand messages, and shared brand experiences through social media have opened up new worlds of communication possibilities. So let's consider ways in which the practice of marketing is changing, particularly in this new social media period.

Brand Relationships

We mentioned **relationship marketing** earlier, but let's come back to that topic because such programs are becoming much more important in marketing and because it has become clear that strong relationships are built on communication. Relationship-building communication programs are used to build strong relationships between loyal customers and the brands they purchase and repurchase. Brand relationship communication, therefore, aims to deliver reminders about familiar brands and build trust.

This kind of focus shifts the marketing strategy from focusing on one-time purchases to also include repeat purchases and the maintenance of long-term brand loyalty. In depends on the category, of course, but many areas, particularly in the services, have become much more concerned about strong relationships. You can see the results in the repeat business McDonald's enjoys from its fans who truly are "loving it."

Brand relationship programs can be directed to all the brand's critical stakeholders, such as employees, shareholders, distributors and suppliers, the community, and, of course, customers. This not only supports long-term brand growth but also contributes new voices to the marketing communication, as all stakeholders are communicators who send personal messages—either positive or negative—about a brand. Therefore, it is important to plan for multiaudience communication experiences and encourage fans of a brand to talk to their friends. In social media, this means using a network of fans to create a lot of "likes" for a brand.

Accountability

Similar to the concern for effectiveness in advertising, accountability is a hot issue in marketing. Marketing managers are being challenged by senior management to prove that their decisions lead to the most effective marketing strategies. Jim Stengel, retired global marketing officer for Proctor & Gamble and now a business professor at the University of California, Los Angeles, called attention to two major areas of concern—accountability and global marketing.[15] Accountability is what Stengel called for in his quest for better measurement.

Marketing managers are under pressure to deliver business results measured in terms of sales increases, the percentage share of the market the brand holds, and corporate **return on investment** (ROI). The calculation of ROI determines how much money the brand made compared to its expenses. In other words, what did the marketing program cost, and what did it deliver in sales?

Global Marketing

Marketers have moved into global markets, in some cases as a deliberate strategy and in other cases found themselves involved in global marketing because international competitors have moved into their own markets. General Mills survived the Great Recession by emphasizing its international markets and global brands as well as multicultural consumers in all the markets, including in the United States. Higher prices also pushed its profits higher.[16] As we mentioned in the beginning of this chapter, McDonald's is a strong global marketer with restaurants in 119 countries.

The growth in global marketing activities is increasing dramatically, so it's helpful to understand some of what makes global marketing different from national marketing. In most countries, markets are composed of local, regional, international, and global brands. A **local brand** is one marketed in a single country. A **regional brand** is one marketed throughout a region (e.g., North America, Europe, Asia). An **international brand** is available in a number of different countries in various parts of the world. A **global brand** is available virtually everywhere in the world, such as Coke.

International marketing and marketing communication are not the exclusive province of large companies. Bu Jin, a small, innovative company in Colorado, creates and markets martial arts products worldwide. With only eight full-time employees, its products serve a high-end international market. Most of Bu Jin's business is driven by its catalog and its website. (Check it out at www.bujindesign.com.) Service providers also market internationally. Airlines and transportation companies that serve foreign markets, such as United and UPS, are, in effect, exporting a service.

The choice of an agency or agencies for international marketing depends, in part, on whether the brand's messages are *standardized* across all markets or *localized* to accommodate cultural differences. If the company wants to take a highly standardized approach in international markets, it is likely to favor international agencies that can handle marketing communication for the product in both domestic and international markets. A localized effort, in contrast, favors

Photo: Redux Pictures

Photo: Getty Images, Inc - Liaison

Photo: Alamy Images

Here are a few brands that represent different types of geographical marketing strategies. Sainsbury's, an example of regional marketing, is the largest grocery retailer in the United Kingdom with stores in Great Britain, Wales, Scotland, and Northern Ireland. IKEA furniture stores are found in various countries, but the company keeps its base and image firmly anchored in Sweden and represents Scandinavian functional design and craftsmanship. Coca-Cola, of course, is one of the best-known brands in the world, and its logo is recognized everywhere.

use of local agencies for planning and implementation in all of the countries where the product is distributed.

Word-of-Mouth Marketing

A powerful new force in marketing communication, **word-of-mouth communication** has emerged because of its inherent persuasiveness—you tend to believe what you hear from a friend, family member, or other important person in your life. And comments from friend and family are more believable than most planned marketing communication messages, such as advertising, which is often seen by consumers as self-serving. A study of media use by the Business Information Group (BIG) that polled 15,000 consumers found the most influential form of media is word of mouth.[17] The goal is to get the right people talking about the brand and having them say things in support of the brand strategy.

Word-of-mouth communication is also called *buzz*, which, as we mentioned in Chapter 1, means people are talking about a brand. Buzz may be the most important factor in consumer decision making because the recommendations of others are so highly persuasive. Some marketing communication plans are specifically designed to generate excited talk about something new, particularly if the strategies can reach influential people whose opinions are valued by others. One idea is that buzz is best generated by disrupting common patterns of thinking, or schemas. In other words, we talk about things that surprise and don't fit into our standard mental models.[18]

Given the engaging work of its agency, Crispin Porter + Bogusky, Burger King is often lauded as the "king of buzz." Tia Lang, interactive director at Burger King, says, "Social media is very important in today's environment and we think generating buzz is a positive result in and of itself." She explained, "We have done some innovative campaigns that have helped lead to 20 consecutive quarters of positive sales."[19]

The power and reach of personal communication has been driven in the 21st century by the emergence of social media. So marketing messages—information as well as testimonials—are spread not only in face-to-face conversations but also online. And if the messages are quickly spread on the Internet through a wide network of contacts, then the phenomenon is referred to as **viral marketing**. Brands can instigate the viral process but can't control it.

Looking Ahead

Marketing communication is about more than just coordination. Effective brand communication not only determines the viability of a brand but also contributes to the integrity of a brand. Integration and integrity come from the same Latin root. Integrity means that the brand stands for something; it has a coherent presence; it has a brand reputation that honestly reflects the promise the brand concept signals to consumers. In this changing marketplace, how responsible the brand is seen to be in terms of its impact on society and the environment can be important to the brand's strategy. The idea of brand reputation and integrity leads to the discussion of ethics, social responsibility, and regulation, which are the topics we'll introduce in Chapter 3.

It's a Wrap

Golden Arches, Golden Opportunity

Ray Kroc had a vision for a system of McDonald's restaurants when he founded McDonald's Corporation in 1955, but he probably never dreamt of the impact the brand would have on so many people. The brand has evolved from "a restaurant that only served burgers, buns, fries, and beverages that tasted just the same in Alaska as they did in Alabama" to one with a much more extensive menu. The early model of the restaurant with the golden arches focused on grab-and-go menu items.

McDonald's realized it sells more than fast food; a positive customer experience is its goal. Now restaurants have been transformed to a decor that reflects a more contemporary look and feel with many of the restaurants featuring televisions and lounge areas to invite customers inside.

McDonald's has a good brand image. Millward Brown, a leading global research agency, ranked McDonald's as the fourth most valuable global brand for 2012, by far the highest-ranking fast-food company. It doesn't earn its brand reputation by being complacent. It has promoted itself with a dynamic, creative, and evolving narrative that involves customers, but it hasn't forgotten its core of who McDonald's is.

McDonald's Chief Marketing Officer Mary Dillon said, "We're making sure that we build both brand equity and drive sales with every piece of advertising . . . within a framework that gives us a consistent point of view about our brand."

Is the brand marketing approach working? McDonald's consistently ranks high on convenience and price in many studies. The challenge is to change the perception of people who aren't lovin' it in other areas, like healthfulness and quality. You can witness McDonald's ongoing efforts on its website with efforts to launch a campaign focused on growers and the quality of the food, healthier items on the menu, and even an effort to build trust with moms as quality correspondents.

The efforts are golden. Since the introduction of the "I'm Lovin' It" campaign, sales have soared. Global same-store sales rose 5.6 percent in 2011 over 2010, the eighth consecutive year of positive same-store sales. It's the 26th largest advertiser in the United States with a whopper (sorry, that's Burger King's word) of a budget of nearly $888 million.

Photo: Kevin Britland/Alamy

Key Points Summary

1. **What is brand communication, and how does it differ from marketing communication?** Marketing communication focuses on the use of a variety of functions, such as advertising, public relations, sales promotion, direct response, events, and sponsorships, among other promotional tools, as part of a planned effort to deliver strategic messages. Brand communication is a complex system of promotional messages that include all the marketing communication messages but also all the brand experiences that build and maintain a coherent brand presence.
2. **How is marketing defined, and what are marketing's key concepts that relate to marketing communication?** Marketing is the way a product is designed, branded, distributed, and promoted as well as a set of processes for creating customer relationships that benefit the organization and its stakeholders. Key concepts that affect the planning of marketing communication include the *marketing concept*, which refers to a focus on customers; the *exchange*, which refers to communication and interaction as well as money traded for goods or services; *competitive advantage*, which means that the product is differentiated and superior in some way to its competitors; and *added value*, which refers to the way that a product takes on features that are valued by consumers at each step of the marketing process.

   The *key players* are the marketer, the suppliers and vendors, the channels of distribution, and marketing partners, such as agencies. In addition to services marketing, the four *types of markets* are consumer, business-to-business, institutional, and channels. The *marketing process* leads to the development and execution of a marketing plan and the steps moved from research, including setting objectives, assessing consumer needs and wants, segmenting and targeting the market, differentiating and positioning the product, developing the marketing mix, and evaluating the effectiveness of the plan. The *marketing mix* includes the product, its pricing and distribution, and the marketing communication, all of which send messages. They also *add value*, which refers to the way that marketing mix decisions, such as the convenience of the distribution chain, make the product more valuable to consumers.
3. **What is integrated marketing communication (IMC), and what are its key concepts?** IMC can be described as total communication, which means that everything that sends a message is monitored for its impact on the brand image. Central to IMC is the practice of unifying all marketing communication messages and tools, as well as the marketing mix messages, to send a consistent brand message. Not only does this maximize consistency, but it also creates *synergy* such that a group of coordinated messages has more impact than marketing communications that are independent of each other. IMC recognizes a variety of *stakeholders* who contribute to the brand conversation as well as a multitude of *touch points* where messages are delivered, including marketing mix messages, as well as more formal planned marketing communication.
4. **How does IMC contribute to the development of a brand?** A brand is a perception created from information as well as experiences with the company and its line of products. It's intangible, but it generates value in the form of brand equity. A brand perception takes on meaning by *transforming* the product into something unique and distinctive and by making a *promise* that sets customers' expectations. The *branding process* includes establishing a brand *identity* through both name and symbols, defining the *brand image* and *personality*, value of the brand, called *brand equity*. Marketing communication is the primary driver of brand meanings and brand relationships.
5. **How is brand communication evolving during a time of change?** Accountability and global marketing are two key emergent themes. Tough economic times have led to increased calls for accountability. Investments in marketing communication must show that they are money well spent. This focus highlights the need for developing tools to measure the effectiveness of the investments. Growth in global marketing demonstrates a strategic opportunity to build business internationally. With this dramatic growth comes a need for marketing communicators to fully understand those audiences with whom they are trying to build relationships.

Key Terms

added value, p. 70
brand, p. 72
brand communication, p. 64
brand concept, p. 75
brand equity, p. 80
brand extension, p. 81
brand identity, p. 75
brand image, p. 78
brand licensing, p. 81
brand loyalty, p. 80
brand management, p. 72
brand personality, p. 78
brand position, p. 78
brand promise, p. 78
brand relationship, p. 80
brand steward, p. 81

brand transformation, p. 75
brand value, p. 80
branding, p. 72
business-to-business (B2B) markets, p. 66
cause marketing, p. 79
channel marketing, p. 67
channel markets, p. 67
channel of distribution, p. 66
cobranding, p. 81
competitive advantage, p. 68
consumer markets, p. 66
customer service, p. 70
direct marketing, p. 70
distribution, p. 79
distribution chain, p. 76
fast-moving consumer goods, p. 76
four Ps, p. 75
global brand, p. 82
goodwill, p. 81
ingredient branding, p. 81
institutional markets, p. 66
integrated marketing communication, p. 71
integration, p. 71
international brand, p. 82
lead generation, p. 70
leads, p. 70
local brand, p. 82
logo, p. 77
market, p. 66
marketer, p. 66
marketing, p. 65
marketing communication, p. 64
marketing mix, p. 65
package goods, p. 66
parity products, p. 75
personal sales, p. 70
personal selling, p. 70
point of differentiation, p. 68
price copy, p. 69
prospects, p. 70
psychological pricing, p. 69
pull strategy, p. 70
push strategy, p. 70
regional brand, p. 82
relationship marketing, p. 82
resellers, p. 67
return on investment, p. 82
share of market, p. 66
stakeholders, p. 65
supply chain, p. 66
trademark, p. 77
viral marketing, p. 84
word-of-mouth communication, p. 83

Review Questions

2-4. What is meant by branding, and why does it depend on marketing communication?

2-5. What is the definition of market, and what are the four main types of markets? Do marketing communication programs vary with each type of market?

2-6. Define brand transformation, and explain how it works.

2-7. Explain how marketing communication relates to the four key marketing concepts and to the marketing mix.

2-8. Define integrated marketing communication, and explain what integration contributes to brand communication.

✪ 2-9. Explain how brand meaning and brand value are created and how they relate to brand equity.

Discussion Questions

✪ 2-10. Apple is one of the most recognized brands in the world. How did the company achieve this distinction? What has the company done in its marketing mix in terms of product, price, distribution, and marketing communications that has created such tremendous brand equity and loyalty? How have advertising and other forms of marketing communication aided in building the brand?

2-11. Discuss the relation between marketing communication and pricing. Illustrate your discussion using an example.

2-12. List your favorite brands and, from that list, do the following analyses:

a. Think about the categories where it is important to you to buy your favorite brand. For which categories does the brand not make a difference? Why is that so?

b. In those categories where you have a favorite brand, what does that brand represent to you? Is it something that you've used and liked? Is it comfortable familiarity—you know it will be the same every time? Is it a promise—if you use this, something good will happen? Is it something you have always dreamed about owning? Why are you loyal to this brand?

Take-Home Projects

2-13. ***Portfolio Project:*** Look through the ads in this textbook or in other publications and find an example of an advertisement that you think adds value to a brand and another ad that you think does not effectively make the brand valuable to consumers. Compare the two and explain why you evaluated them as you did. Copy both ads and mount them and your analysis in your portfolio.

2-14. ***Mini-Case Analysis:*** In the "I'm Lovin' it" campaign, McDonald's needed a theme that was wide enough and broad enough to speak to all its various audiences both in the United States and around the world. This is a classic brand-building campaign. Go online and read what you can about the effectiveness of this effort. What are its strong points? Are there any points of criticism? Consider the components of a brand described in this chapter and analyze in communication team, do you think this campaign should be continued, or is it time to update or change the message? Develop a one-page proposal for next year, including your analysis that supports your ideas.

TRACE North America Case

Multicultural Millennials

Read the TRACE case in the Appendix before coming to class.

2-15. What aspects of the marketing mix are relevant to a campaign to Multicultural Millennials (ages 18–29)?

2-16. Why do you think TRACE would want a campaign directed to Multicultural Millennials?

2-17. Prepare a one-page statement explaining how the "Hard to Explain, Easy to Experience" campaign will actually help TRACE sales among Multicultural Millennials.

CHAPTER 3

Brand Communication and Society

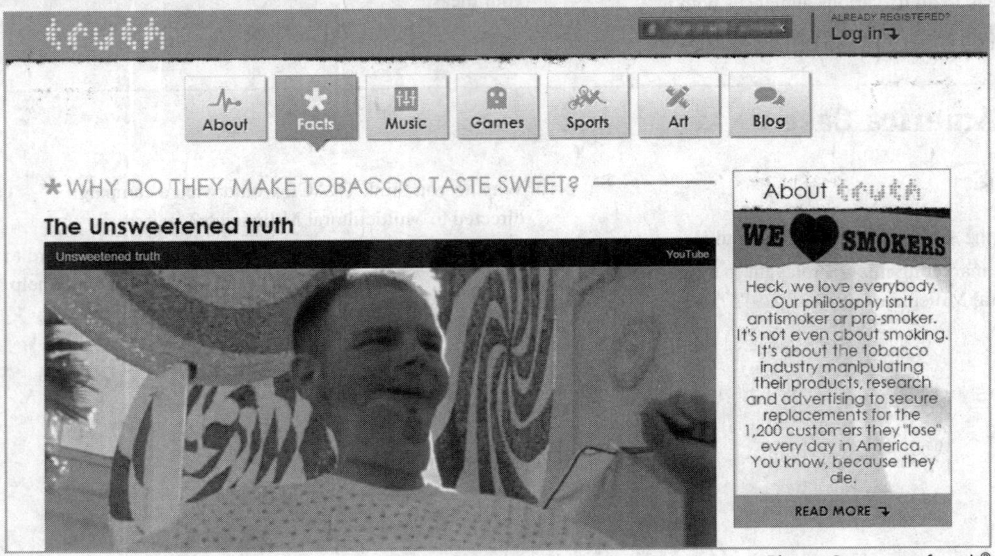

Photo: Courtesy of truth®

It's a Winner

Campaign	Company	Agency	Awards
Unsweetened truth®	The American Legacy Foundation	*Arnold Worldwide* **Contributing Agency** *PHD*	*5 Effies including the Grand Effie and more than 300 other awards*

CHAPTER KEY POINTS

1. What is the social impact of brand communication?
2. What ethical and social responsibilities do communicators bear?
3. Why and how is advertising regulated?

To Tell the truth®

Do you smoke? Do you have friends who smoke? Nearly 4 million teens in the United States smoke cigarettes. According to the Surgeon General and the Centers for Disease Control, every day more than 4,000 people ages 12 to 17 try a cigarette for the first time, and 90 percent of all smokers have their first cigarette before they turn 18.

As shocking as those numbers are, they used to be higher. According to the U.S. Department of Health and Human Services, the rate of past-month tobacco use among youths aged 12 to 17 dropped significantly from 15.2 percent in 2002 to 10.7 percent in 2010.

Even so, more than 400,000 Americans die annually from tobacco-related diseases, making smoking the leading cause of preventable death in the nation. In fact, the Federal Trade Commission (FTC) reported that tobacco kills more Americans each year than AIDS, alcohol, car accidents, murders, suicides, drugs, and fires combined. The alarming number of young smokers, coupled with the fact that so many people eventually die from tobacco-related illnesses, provides ample motivation to address the problem.

One of the most powerful campaigns of all time, the long-running, award-winning truth® project, has contributed to decreased teen smoking. The American Legacy Foundation, founded in 1999, aims to build a world where young people reject tobacco and anyone can quit. Its truth® campaign is a great example of using public communication as a social force to help change the world.

It has made a significant difference. After the first four years of the campaign, researchers documented that 450,000 fewer teens tried smoking. However, after a decade, new challenges emerged as states cut funding for tobacco prevention and cessation programs. Exacerbating the problem, big tobacco companies responded with new, innovative products, such as snus (Swedish snuff), flavored cigars, and little cigars to lure teens to try tobacco.

In a society where marketers spend billions trying to persuade teens to buy products, this campaign tries to get them not to buy something. Its goal is to empower teens to rebel against manipulation. The American Legacy Foundation teamed with the agency Arnold Worldwide to convince youth about the dangers of using the new tobacco products without preaching to them.

Agency researchers discovered that big tobacco was adding more than 45 flavors—like chocolate, strawberry, and cinnamon—to their products to sweeten the tobacco experience. Arnold used this insight to develop relevant ways to engage teens with American Legacy's brand and to expose big tobacco's newest tactic to hook customers by asking, "Why do they make tobacco taste sweet?"

The truth® campaign helps teen audiences learn the truth about the tactics of the tobacco industry and the truth about addiction, health effects, and social consequences of smoking. The message encourages teens to make informed choices about tobacco by giving them facts. Teens heard the "truth" at the cinema, on Web-exclusive "Day in the Life" videos, and social media sites Facebook, YouTube, MyYearbook, and MySpace. Teens were encouraged to interact with the message at www.thetruth.com. They could even access the videos and download ring tones via their cell phones.

The ads and commercials get right to the point, sometimes in stark ways. Viewers can see what happened to real people, such as a cast member who was diagnosed with mouth cancer at 17 as a result of having used the tobacco products.

The campaign has won more than 300 awards. We'll explain more about the impact of this campaign in the "It's a Wrap" section at the end of this chapter.

Sources: "Unsweetened truth," Effie Awards published case study, www.effie.org; "Preventing Tobacco Use among Youth and Young Adults: A Report of the Surgeon General," Centers for Disease Control and Prevention, 2012, www.surgeongeneral.gov/library/reports/preventing-youth-tobacco-use; "Results from the 2010 National Survey on Drug Use and Health: Summary of National Findings," www.samhsa.gov and www.thetruth.com; press releases available online at www.legacyforhealth.org.

With a huge potential to make a significant impact on society, brand communicators shoulder the responsibility for choosing what products and ideas they want to advertise, what messages they communicate, and how they want to communicate them. You'll explore the impact of brand communication on society in this chapter, reading about ongoing debates about the power of communication and looking at issues related to social and ethical responsibility. Finally, you will learn about some key legal and regulatory processes that ensure that harmful communication is minimized.

What Is the Social Impact of Brand Communication?

At its core, effective brand communication is about building brand integrity and a trustworthy reputation. Brands take on meaning when consumers see that all areas of marketing communication about the brand are consistent and authentic. Communicators want the recipients of their messages to feel positive about the brand but not at the expense of doing what is right both ethically and legally.

The truth® campaign is a good example of communicating authentically with its key audience. The campaign teaches us that messages do not necessarily need to be entertaining to be effective. It aims to reduce teen tobacco use, and truth® talks straightforwardly and believably to them to communicate the more sinister message underlying big tobacco companies—that they are literally candy-coating the effects of tobacco use. The message itself, in this case, has an important effect on society, specifically the health of teens.

Most of the time people use advertising for neutral or good purposes, meaning they value a brand's **social responsibility**. Examples of companies that aspire to be socially responsible with their brands are plentiful.[1] Premium ice cream maker Häagen-Dazs, a brand known for its all-natural ingredients, fittingly created a campaign to help find a solution to a mysterious disappearance of honeybees. (Read more about this in the opening case for Chapter 15.) General Electric's "ecomagination" campaign focuses on using renewable energy and reducing carbon emissions. Toms Shoes donates a pair of shoes to a child in need for every pair of its shoes that are sold.

These examples provide evidence that many brands strive to do good. Brand stewards work hard to protect the integrity of their brands and make sure the communication about the brand is consistent. One problem with brand consistency occurs when there are ethical questions about practices that undercut the brand.

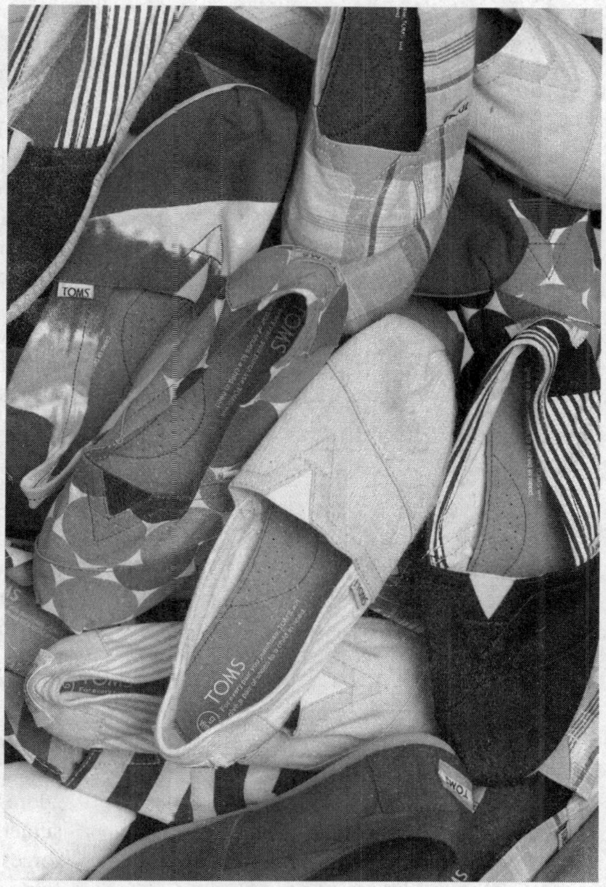

Photo: Adrian Lourie/Alamy

Toms was founded on the premise that everyday purchases could be a force for good around the world. What other examples of corporate social responsibility can you think of?

What Are the Key Debates about Impact on Society?

Marketing communication, particularly advertising, sometimes draws criticism for its social impact, so much of the discussion that follows is focused on advertising because it is highly visible. We review some of the debates related to advertising's role in society from the perspectives of advertising as an institution and as an applied practice. Our intention is to review the criticisms, but understand that we believe that advertising is a good force in society and in our economy even though it may sometimes be used in ways that generate concern.

To emphasize the importance of this topic, sprinkled throughout this book are "Principled Practice" boxes that discuss issues of social and ethical responsibility. The following are some of the key social responsibility issues that fuel debates.

Can Advertising Create Demand? Some critics charge that advertising causes **demand creation**, which results when an external message drives people to feel a need or want—sometimes unnecessarily. A 2009 Harris Poll indicated that two-thirds of Americans believed ad agencies were at least partially to blame for the recent economic crisis because they caused people to buy things they couldn't afford.[2] Others reject this notion. Does advertising create demand for products people don't need? Has advertising convinced you to buy products you don't need?

Let's start the discussion by considering deodorants. Did you know that no one used deodorants much before 1919? People didn't worry about having body odor. An ad for a new product, Odorono (great name, and it's still being used, by the way), targeted women because everyone assumed that men were supposed to emit bad odors and that women would be the more likely users of the product. The launch ad in *Ladies' Home Journal* so offended readers that about 200 people canceled their subscription. The ads were effective, however. Sales for the deodorant rose 112 percent.[3] Did advertising make women buy something they didn't even know they needed? Was that a bad thing?

If you think it doesn't happen today, think about Unilever's Axe product. Axe pioneered the new category of body spray for men in 2002. Did guys know before 2002 that they needed scented body spray? Is it a good thing that advertising entices people to buy products like deodorants and body sprays? Can such advertising improve consumers' lives?

Principle
If people do not want the products being marketed, they do not buy them.

Companies often conduct significant research to find out what consumers want before they launch new products. If people do not want the products being marketed, they do not buy them. Advertising may convince people to buy a product—even a bad one—once. If they try the product and don't like it, they won't buy it again. So, to some extent, advertising creates demand. At the same time, it is important to remember that audiences may refuse to purchase the product if they don't feel a need for it.

CLASSIC

A J. Walter Thompson ad for Odorono deodorant was so startling that readers bedded the Ladies' Home Journal to stop running the ad. It was considered disgusting then, but how do you see it now?

Does Advertising Mirror Social Values or Shape Them? Another important debate about advertising's role in society questions the limits of its influence. At what point does advertising cross the line between reflecting social values and creating them? Professionals believe they are reflecting the values of their society. Critics argue that advertising has repeatedly crossed this line, influencing vulnerable groups, such as children and young teenagers, too strongly.

A case in point: Do ultrathin models in advertising cause young women to have eating disorders, as some have claimed? While it is probable that the images women and girls see influence them in some ways, it's difficult to say that these images directly and solely cause the problem because many factors in a person's environment potentially influence eating choices. Some research, however, supports the view that advertising is partly to blame; advertising may contribute to the problem. What do you think?

Can advertising manipulate people's choices? Critics of advertising argue that advertising can create social trends and has the power to dictate how people think and act. They believe that even if an individual ad cannot control behavior, the cumulative effects of nonstop television, radio, print, Internet, and outdoor ads can be overwhelming. Others contend that effective brand communication spots trends and then develops messages that connect target audiences with the trends. In other words, if people are interested in achieving healthy lifestyles, you will see ads that use health appeals as an advertising strategy. In this way, advertising mirrors values rather than sets them. Do you agree with that argument?

This shape-versus-mirror debate is the most central issue we address in considering advertising's role in society. What drives consumers to behave or believe as they do? Is it advertising, or is it other forces? Why do women buy cosmetics, for example? Are they satisfying a deep cultural need for beauty, or were they manipulated by advertising to believe in the hope that cosmetics offer? Women can even purchase a product by the cosmetics company Philosophy called Hope in a Jar. Or have their families and friends socialized them to believe they look better with makeup than without? Advertising and society's values are interwoven, so the answer to the debate may simply be that advertising both mirrors and shapes values.

Does Advertising Cause People to Be Too Materialistic? The last 50 years are notable for the rise of a materialistic consumer culture in the Western world, and some argue that it is overly commercialized, too materialistic. Consider Nike's shoe the LeBron X, which costs more than $300. Do we need these shoes? Who will buy them? Did advertising create this culture, or does it simply reflect a natural striving for the good life?

Some argue that advertising heightens expectations and primes the audience to believe that the answer is always a product. If you have a headache, what do you do? You take a pill. The pill may actually make your headache vanish. What is left unsaid by an advertisement is that you might get rid of the headache just as easily by taking a nap, drinking less alcohol or more water, or taking a walk to relieve stress. Nobody pays for ads to tell you about free alternatives. Consumers, however, are not always passively doing what advertisers tell them. As we have said, they have the power to refuse to buy what is being sold if they think about it.

Should Some Audiences Be Protected from Advertising? Marketing to youth is one of the most controversial topics in the industry. One reason why advertising to children attracts so much attention is that children are seen as vulnerable. Children do not always know what is good for them and what is not. Concerned adults want to make sure that they protect impressionable minds from exploitative marketers. (A similar argument is made regarding older adults, who, some fear, are vulnerable to scams and other unscrupulous techniques.) They want to help children learn to make good choices. Do you think this is a valid argument? Are children highly impressed by advertising? How should marketing to vulnerable audiences be regulated? Who gets to decide what's good for these audiences?

A current issue that's being addressed relates to selling soft drinks, candy, and food with high fat and sugar content to children. Recognizing that obesity among youth is a major health problem, the Council of Better Business Bureaus launched the Children's Food and Beverage Advertising Initiative to help 10 major corporations set guidelines to cut down on junk-food advertising. The companies, which are responsible for producing almost two-thirds of the food and drink advertising for children under 12, include General Mills, McDonald's, Coca-Cola, PepsiCo, Hershey, and Kellogg. Marketing alcohol to black teens is another important issue because of the use of rappers like Ice-T to promote malt liquors and the dozens of pages of alcohol ads that appear in black youth–culture magazines such as *Vibe*. A Georgetown University study contends that the alcohol beverage industry is marketing far more heavily to African American young people than to others in that age-group.

You'll read more about the important issue of advertising to children in the regulation section of this chapter.

What Are the Key Debates and Issues about Brand Communication Practices?

Next we'll give you a checklist of issues that can have a negative impact on brands if the communication does not align with the brand image or respect the audience.

Does Brand Communication Fairly and Accurately Portray People? Stereotypes are a big issue, as are other problems, such as cultural relevance and honesty.

- ***Diversity and Stereotypes*** Athletic blacks, feeble seniors, sexy Italians, smart Asians. You're probably familiar with these and other examples of stereotypes. A **stereotype** is a representation of a cultural group that emphasizes a trait or group of traits that may or may not communicate an accurate representation of the group. Sometimes the stereotype is useful (athletes are fit) and aids communication by using easily understood symbolic meanings, but sometimes the stereotype relies on a characteristic that is negative or exaggerated and, in so doing, reduces the group to a caricature. Mountain Dew, for example, was charged with racial stereotyping in 2013 for an ad that showed a battered woman viewing suspects of black men in a police lineup. This is the problem with portraying older adults as all being absent-minded or feeble, for instance.

  Here's another example: Think about sports teams like the Washington Redskins, Kansas City Chiefs, or Cleveland Indians. Critics claim these sports images reduce Native Americans to a caricature and claim that racial and ethnic groups are stereotyped in their promotions. Do you believe these team names and logos represent negative stereotypes, and, if so, what should be done about them when millions of dollars have been invested in building these brands?

  The issue of stereotyping also raises the shape-versus-mirror question. For example, stereotyping women as sex objects is a practice that is deeply embedded in our culture. Using such strategies also makes advertising a participant in shaping and reinforcing that cultural value.

  Intentionally or not, communicators choose how they portray people in their ads. Even the absence of a particular group of people, such as seemingly invisible older adults, communicates a message. If they are not included, are they important?

  "The Inside Story" by Sonia Scappaticci offers a good example of Pepsi's efforts to create culturally relevant programs to reach its Hispanic market.
- ***Cultural Differences in Global Advertising*** In the global economy, advertisers seek worldwide audiences for their products. As they do so, advertisers sometimes make mistakes overlaying their worldview on that of another culture without thinking about the impact of the message.

  Concerns about the homogenization of cultural differences are expressed as **marketing imperialism** or **cultural imperialism**. These terms are used to describe what happens when Western culture is imposed on others, particularly Middle East, Asian, and African cultures. Some Asian and Middle Eastern countries are critical of what they see as America's materialism,

The blind are also color blind, Carson/Roberts, Inc., 1964.
Courtesy of AIGA Design Archives. designarchives.aiga.org.

CLASSIC

"Color Blind." This was an ad created by the Carson/Roberts agency in 1964 during debate over the Civil Rights Voting Guarantee Bill. It is included in the AIGA Design Archives. AIGA is the leading graphic design association.

disrespectful behavior toward elders, and appeals to sex. They worry that **international advertising** and media will encourage their young people to adopt these viewpoints.

Consider that respect for culture and local customs is so important that insensitivity to local customs can make an ad completely ineffective. Customs can be even stronger than laws. When advertising to children age 12 or older was approved in Germany, for example, local customs were so strong that companies risked customer revolt by advertising. In many countries, naming a competitor in comparative advertising is considered bad form.

- ***Sex Appeals and Body Image*** Advertising that portrays women (or men) as sex objects is considered demeaning and sexist, particularly if sex is not relevant to the product. Sometimes ads use sex appeals that are relevant, such as Victoria's Secret. The ethical question, then, is how sexy is too sexy? Transit authorities in two Canadian cities decided that Virgin Mobile's ads were too racy for the public and asked the company to pull risqué ads from bus shelters that showed embracing couples and invited viewers to "Hook up fearlessly."[4]

  Playing on consumers' insecurities about their appearance presents advertisers with a classic ethical dilemma because self-image advertising can be seen as contributing to self-improvement, but sometimes such advertising is questionable because it leads to dangerous practices. Some critics charge that women place their health at risk in order to cultivate an unrealistic or even unhealthy physical appearance. Supermodels don't always project healthy portrayals of women. Do you think advertising sends this message?

  The same problem of physical appearance exists for men, particularly young men, although the muscular ideal body may not lead to the same health-threatening reactions that young women face unless men resort to steroids to attain this image. The standard of attractiveness is a sociocultural phenomenon that both mirrors and shapes our ideals. Responsible advertisers, therefore, have begun using models of more normal size and weight as a way to reduce the pressure on young people. The "Dove Campaign for Real Beauty" that you'll read about in Chapter 5 defies the notion that women need to be thin to be beautiful.
- ***Poor Taste and Offensive Advertising*** Although certain ads might be in bad taste in any circumstance, viewer reactions are affected by such factors as sensitivity to the product category, timing (e.g., if the message is received in the middle of dinner), and other circumstances, such as whether the person is alone or with others when viewing the message. Some television ads, for example, might not bother adults watching alone but would make them uncomfortable if children were watching.

Also, some ads become offensive in the wrong context. Advertisers and media outlets must try to be sensitive to such objections. In 2009, outraged advertisers, including Applebee's, General Mills, and Kraft, pulled ads from Fox News Channel's *Glenn Beck* program after the host called President Obama a "racist" with a "deep-seated hatred for white people."

We all have our own ideas about what constitutes good taste. Unfortunately, these ideas vary so much that creating general guidelines for good taste in advertising is difficult. Different things offend different people at different times. In addition, taste changes over time. What was

The Inside Story

Pepsi: Creating Culturally Relevant Programs

Sonia Scappaticci, *Business Development Director for Branded Entertainment, Catmandu Entertainment*

Hispanics are the fastest-growing demographic segment of the U.S. population, according to the 2010 census, and so is their purchasing power. By 2050, estimates have Hispanics representing 24 percent of the U.S. population, making roughly one of every four Americans having Hispanic ethnicity. With the changing appearance of the U.S. population, marketers must be smarter about reaching this market and create culturally relevant programs.

Pepsi, historically one of the first brands to reach U.S. Hispanics, continued this tradition in 2012. This time, the goal was to encourage Hispanic communities across the country to incorporate spontaneity and fun into their weekends. In top markets (Los Angeles, New York, Chicago, Dallas, Miami, and Houston), Pepsi offered 24 live concerts by a top-tier Latino artist, reflecting the unique Latino community and its music culture.

Pepsi's "Sabados de Verano" (Summer Saturdays) music program, a 12-week free music entertainment summer series showcased the hottest Latino acts, including Wysin & Yandel, Alacranes Musical, Belanova, K-Paz, Melina Leon, and Tego Calderon, among others.

"I am pumped to join Pepsi in bringing Sabados de Verano to our Latino communities and neighborhoods to celebrate culture and music," said Tego Calderon, who will be participating in the live concerts. "Music has enriched my life in countless ways, and sharing this with my people is what I live for. I'm happy Latinos across the U.S. will access these music experiences in their own backyards."

Each Sabados de Verano event featured a local DJ who jump-started the events. Attendees had the opportunity to participate in interactive games on-site as well as sample PepsiCo products. The concert series was a success with over 60,000 attendees. Consumer excitement was evident with 623,000 tweets and over 14,000 Facebook RSVPs to the events.

"At Pepsi, we thrive on developing products and programming that connect with our consumers," said Javier Farfan, senior director of cultural branding for PepsiCo Beverages Americas. "We cherish diverse cultures and celebrate the Latino community's love and passion for a variety of music. Sabados de Verano provides a perfect opportunity to gather people for an entertaining family and community summer get-together."

Note: Sonia Scappaticci graduated from Michigan State University with a BA in advertising. While at Michigan State, she was named one of the 25 Most Promising Minority Students in Communication by AAF and Advertising Age. She was nominated by Professor Carrie La Ferle.

Source: Pepsico news release, May 16, 2011, *www.pepsico.com/PressRelease/Pepsi-Brings-Communities-Together-Across-The-US-This-Summer-With-Free-Music-and-05162011.html.*

offensive yesterday may not be considered offensive today. The Odorono ad offended people in 1919, but would it today? By today's standards, that advertisement seems pretty tame. Today's questions of taste center on the use of sexual innuendo, nudity, vulgarity, and violence. What about the Axe ads for male body sprays? Do you find them offensive or in good taste?

An ad can be offensive to the general public even if the targeted audience accepts it, which is the point behind the Axe ads. Brand communicators would be wise to conduct research to gauge the standards of taste for the general population as well as the specific target audience. If they fail to do so, advertisers risk alienating potential consumers. Some might argue that any publicity is good publicity and that offensive advertising calls attention to your product in a memorable way. However, over time, it may damage a brand's precious reputation.

Principle
Good taste is a difficult standard to apply because different things offend different people at different times.

Is Advertising Honest and Transparent? Even though most advertisers try to create messages that communicate fairly and accurately, marketers need to understand what is not considered acceptable so they can avoid unethical and even illegal behavior. Advertising claims are considered to be unethical if they are false, misleading, or deceptive. In the drive to find something to say about a product that will catch attention and motivate the audience to respond, advertisers sometimes stretch the truth. **False advertising**, which is a type of misleading advertising, is simply a message that is untrue. Misleading claims, puffery, comparative advertising, endorsements, and product demonstrations are explained next.

Principle
Advertising claims are unethical if they are false, misleading, or deceptive.

- ***Misleading Claims and Puffery*** The target of the heaviest criticism for being misleading is weight-loss advertising, as well as other back-of-the-magazine, self-improvement advertisements for health and fitness products. In a study of 300 weight-loss ads, the FTC, a regulatory body, found that ads for weight-loss products sometimes make "grossly exaggerated" claims and that dieters need to beware of ads for dietary supplements, meal replacements, patches, creams, wraps, and other products. (The FTC is described more completely later in this chapter.) The study found that 40 percent of the ads made at least one representation that was almost certainly false and that 55 percent made a claim that was very likely false or at least lacked adequate substantiation.[5]

  Misleading claims are not just a problem in the United States. Makeup company L'Oreal accused its rival Christian Dior of misleading consumers with its ad featuring Natalie Portman wearing Christian Dior mascara. It charged that the ad had been digitally retouched and that consumers would unrealistically believe that they, too, could have spectacularly long lashes. Britain's Advertising Standards Authority banned the ads.[6]

  Principle
  Puffery may be legal, but if it turns off the target audience, nothing is gained by using such a strategy.

  Not all exaggerated claims are considered misleading. **Puffery** is defined as "advertising or other sales representations, which praise the item to be sold with subjective opinions, superlatives, or exaggerations, vaguely and generally, stating no specific facts."[7] Campbell Soup, for example, has used the slogan "M'm!, M'm!, Good!," which is vague and can't really be proven or disproven. It's a classic example of puffery, generally deemed to be of little concern to regulators looking for false or misleading claims because it is so innocuous.

  Because obviously exaggerated "puffing" claims are legal, the question of puffery is mainly an ethical one. According to the courts, consumers expect exaggerations and inflated claims in advertising, so reasonable people wouldn't believe that these statements ("puffs") are literal facts. However, empirical evidence on the effectiveness of puffery is mixed. Some research suggests that the public might expect advertisers to be able to prove the truth of superlative claims, and other research indicates that reasonable people do not believe such claims. This is particularly important when advertising to children who might not know the difference between fact and opinion.

  Noted advertising scholar Ivan Preston, a former member of this book's Advisory Board, dedicated his professional life to studying puffery and misleading advertising. Read the tribute to his inspirational work in the " Principled Practice" feature.
- ***Comparative Advertising*** We're used to seeing advertisers take on their competition in an ad—Macintosh versus PC, Dunkin' Donuts versus Starbucks, Campbell's Soup versus Progresso. Although it is perfectly legitimate to compare a marketer's product favorably against a competitor, regulations govern the use of **comparative advertising** if it can be challenged as misleading.

  Advertisers face the common threat that competitors will misrepresent their products. Although no one expects a competitor to be totally objective, advertisers have legal recourse to object to unfair comparisons. Law in the United States permits awards of damages from an advertiser who "misrepresents the nature, characteristics, qualities, or geographic origin in comparative advertising." Recently, a New York court granted Weight Watchers International a temporary restraining order against Jenny Craig, claiming that Jenny Craig's advertising made deceptive claims about its success rate.[8]

  Advertisers who engage in comparative advertising know that research in support of their competitive claims must be impeccable. The Dunkin' Donuts ad compares its coffee to Starbucks and backs up its claim with a national taste test.

  Under the law, companies/plaintiffs are required to prove five elements to win a false-advertising lawsuit about an ad making a comparative claim:

  1. False statements have been made about either product.
  2. The ads actually deceived or had the tendency to deceive a substantial segment of the audience.
  3. The deception was "material" or meaningful. In other words, the plaintiff must show that the false ad claim is likely to influence purchasing decisions.
  4. Falsely advertised goods are sold in interstate commerce.
  5. The suing company has been or likely will be injured as a result of the false statements, either by loss of sales or by loss of goodwill.

A PRINCIPLED PRACTICE

Tribute to Ivan L. Preston: 1931–2011

Herbert Jack Rotfeld, *Auburn University*
Jef I. Richards, *Michigan State University*

Ivan L. Preston

A world-renowned legal scholar who never attended law school, Ivan Preston's work was used in revising part of the Uniform Commercial Code in the 1990s. During a period when he worked at the FTC, he influenced the evidence presented in cases of advertising deception. Pushing the use of survey research over testimony of individual consumers' perception, he conducted the first surveys ever commissioned by the FTC for use in a hearing to establish the proof of consumer perceptions. And from his research on advertising puffery and consumer deception, he became what the *Wall Street Journal* once called the "world's greatest expert on 'pure baloney' in advertising."

Herbert Jack Rotfeld

Explaining his legacy really starts with advertising puffery, the legal term for an age-old advertising practice to claim without evidence that your product is the best on the market.

During the era of the Vietnam War, a former ad agency account executive and then-recent mass communications doctoral graduate, young Professor Preston noted that FTC regulation law for advertising deception properly considered ad claims likely to deceive, even if literally true, if they communicated information that was at variance with the facts by what is implied or even by what the advertisement failed to say.

However, there also existed a vexing exception. When the literal content of a message could be legally designated as puffery, that determination means the statements are considered incapable of causing consumer deception because no one believes what they communicate.

Thus, Professor Preston observed that the FTC's advertising regulation properly dealt with communications as depending on audience perceptions, and he recognized that puffery exists as a perplexing exception. While it was logical that people would not believe certain claims, to universally consider specific literal terms always incapable of deceiving anyone seemed inconsistent at best and, at worst allowed a loophole by which people would be deceived. As he put it years later, "The lawyer told me past court cases established that no one believes advertising puffery claims or what they imply. I wanted to know what was their evidence for that decision."

The proof, he was told, was in an earlier court case. Yet, in reading the reference the lawyers provided, Professor Preston discovered that the legal proof in that case consisted of citation to a still-earlier court case. That is how the common law works. A finding of a prior case does not need to be endlessly retried and proven time and again. However, this earlier case also failed to indicate what research evidence proved no one believes advertising puffery.

Jef I. Richards

Thus, finding the answer he sought became more difficult, tracking citations to earlier and still earlier court cases.

He eventually found that the original "proof" that no one believes puffery or what those literal claims imply a British common law case in 1602 declared it as so obvious that no evidence was needed. The evidence of such uniform consistent consumer disbelief of statements in the superlative did not exist beyond a jurist in an long-distant time saying it was so, with successive cases into the present day citing earlier conclusions.

Over the years, Professor Preston's legal research with applications of communication research to legal questions became a quest, an advocacy. When he started, most other communication researchers didn't bother to understand the law, as most lawyers didn't bother to understand the basic facts of communication research. Yet, in the law, as in mass communication, what you conclude can be based on how you ask the question. Puffery exceptions still exist, but with actual research evidence, it can be constrained.

Courtesy of Dunkin' Brands, Inc.

Dunkin' Donuts hopes to convince coffee drinkers to switch from Starbucks based on results from a national taste test.

In addition to the federal laws, consumers also may rely on state laws governing unfair competition and false ad claims if the consumer is the victim of a false comparative claim.

- ***Endorsements and Demonstrations*** A popular advertising strategy is the use of a spokesperson who endorses a brand. That's a perfectly legal strategy unless the endorser doesn't actually use the product. An **endorsement** or **testimonial** is any advertising message that consumers believe reflects the opinions, beliefs, or experiences of an individual, group, or institution. However, if consumers can reasonably ascertain that a message does not reflect the announcer's opinion, the message isn't an endorsement and may even be misleading.

Consider the billboard of President Obama wearing a Weatherproof-brand jacket during his visit to the Great Wall of China. The company put the image on its website for a time and promoted "the Obama jacket" until the White House asked that they take down the billboard. It claimed the ad was misleading because the company never received approval or an endorsement from the president.[9]

The increasing prominence of digital media raises another ethical dilemma. Is it acceptable for company representatives to pose as consumers or pay bloggers to post endorsements as customer reviews online? The Word of Mouth Marketing Association says no. Its ethics code[10] explicitly prohibits consumers from taking cash from manufacturers, suppliers, or their representatives for making recommendations, reviews, or endorsements, unless full disclosure is provided. Do you think it was ethical that Ford loaned 100 bloggers its new Fiesta[11] to drive and presumably chat about on the Internet? Under what conditions? We'll probably see lots more examples of **blogola**, also referred to as flogging (sponsored conversations), in the future.[12]

Federal regulations require that endorsers be qualified by experience or training to make judgments, and they must actually use the product. If endorsers are comparing competing brands, they must have tried those brands as well. Those who endorse a product improperly may be liable if the government determines there is deception.

Product demonstrations in television advertising also must not mislead consumers. This mandate is especially difficult for advertisements of food products because such factors as hot studio lights and the length of time needed to shoot the commercial can make the product look unappetizing. Think about the problems of shooting ice cream under hot lights. Because milk looks gray on television, advertisers often substitute a mixture of glue and water. The question is whether the demonstration falsely upgrades the consumers' perception of the advertised brand. The FTC evaluates this kind of deception on a case-by-case basis.

Photo: KB4/Newscom

Weatherproof, an apparel company, stirred up controversy with its Time Square billboard showing President Obama wearing what looked to be one of its jackets. Do you think this was a misleading use of a public image?

One technique some advertisers use to sidestep restrictions on demonstrations is to insert disclaimers, or "supers," which are verbal or written words in the ad that indicate exceptions to the advertising claim made. You've probably seen car commercials that start with beauty shots of the product. Suddenly, the message is less clear; for several seconds, five different, often lengthy disclaimers flash on the screen in tiny, eye-straining type, including "See dealers for details and guaranteed claim form" and "Deductibles and restrictions apply."

What Are Some Product-Specific Issues Related to Social Responsibility? Marketers need to consider carefully what they choose to produce and advertise. Some key areas of concern include controversial products, unhealthy or dangerous products such as alcohol and tobacco, and prescription drugs. The decision to produce the product lies with the marketing department and the company's business objectives, but advertising is frequently in the spotlight because of its visibility.

- ***Controversial Products*** Before an agency can create an ad for a client, it must consider the nature of the client company and its mission, marketing objectives, reputation, available resources, competition, and, most importantly, product line. Can the agency and its staff members honestly promote the products being advertised? What would you do if you were a copywriter for an agency that has a political client you don't support? Several agencies have resigned from profitable tobacco advertising accounts because of the medical evidence about the harm cigarettes cause. In cases where the agency works on a controversial account, there are still ethical ways to approach the business.

  Marketing communication reflects the marketing and business ethics of its clients and, because of its visibility, sometimes gets the blame for selling controversial, unsafe, or dangerous products. For example, products that were once considered not suitable to advertise, such as firearms, gambling, hemorrhoid preparations, feminine hygiene products, pantyhose and bras, laxatives, condoms, and remedies for male erectile dysfunctions, have become acceptable, although advertising for them may still be offensive to some people.

  Some products are controversial for political reasons or because of environmental issues. Oil companies, for example, have been criticized for their practices and are constantly trying to prove their role as good corporate citizens. The Shell ad, which comes from Iceland, is an example of a company that is changing its practices to deliver on its social responsibility mission.
- ***Unhealthy or Dangerous Products*** One way to make ethical decisions is to choose the route that minimizes potential harm. Because there has been so much negative publicity about the health effects of eating a steady diet of heavily processed food, food companies, particularly fast-food producers such as McDonald's and Wendy's, have reacted to charges of culpability in the nation's obesity problem. McDonald's slimmed down Ronald McDonald, added healthier choices to its menu, and moved away from using cholesterol-causing saturated fats when making french fries. Disney launched efforts to serve healthier food in its theme parks as an effort to improve the diets of children. Wendy's reduced the amount of trans fats it uses for cooking.[13]

  One of the most heated advertising issues in recent years has been about tobacco advertising. Although Congress passed a law that banned cigarette advertising on television and radio starting in 1971, that did not resolve the issue. Proponents of the ban on cigarette advertising argue that since cigarettes have been shown to cause cancer as well as other illnesses, encouraging tobacco use promotes sickness, injury, or death for the smoker and those inhaling secondhand smoke. They argue that further restricting advertising on those products would result in fewer sales and fewer health problems for America as a whole.

  Opponents of advertising bans counter with the argument that prohibiting truthful, nondeceptive advertising for a legal product is unconstitutional and a violation of their free-speech rights. They feel that censorship is more of a problem than advertising a legal product even if it is unhealthy.

  In recognition of the growing public concerns about cigarette marketing, tobacco companies have voluntarily curbed their advertising and pulled ads from magazines with high levels of youth readership and from most outdoor billboards. Most major tobacco companies also run antismoking ads aimed at teenagers. Philip Morris has virtually stopped advertising and shifted its budget to events and other promotions that reach its customers rather than trying to use advertising to reach new customers.

  In 1996, a government agency established a set of restrictions applicable to tobacco advertisers. Among these were a ban on outdoor ads within 1,000 feet of a school or

Principle

The ethics of selling a controversial or unsafe product lies with the marketing department; however, marketing communication may be criticized because it is the visible face of marketing.

playground and a rule that limited ads to black and white, text only, in magazines with 55 percent readership under the age of 18. The restrictions also stipulated that $150 million be provided to fund antismoking ads targeting children. The case at the opening of this chapter about the antismoking truth® campaign aimed at teens was supported through these efforts.

Banning tobacco advertising is not unique to the United States. Many other countries have even stronger restrictions against such advertising. A near-total advertising ban in the United Kingdom took effect in early 2003, and similar restrictions were launched in the European Union (EU) two years later. Canada and New Zealand have banned tobacco advertising, and Australia and Malaysia have prohibited nearly all forms of it.

The ethics of advertising liquor is another concern. The biggest issue for the spirits industry is charges of advertising to underage drinkers. Liquor executives contend that they follow voluntary advertising guidelines to avoid images and time slots that appeal to kids. That stance has been hard to keep, however, because every major brand is trying to win over young consumers.

The Distilled Spirits Council, a trade organization representing producers and marketers of distilled spirits sold in the United States, offers a model for industry self-regulation. Its Code of Responsible Practices encourages members to follow the guidelines set forth in the code when promoting their products, (available at www.discus.org/responsibility/code).

The beer industry has also been the target of strong criticism. Although it is unlikely that beer advertising will be banned, some companies sensitive to public opinion have initiated proactive programs that educate and discourage underage drinkers.

- ***Prescription Drugs*** In 1997, the government loosened its controls on pharmaceutical advertising. As a result, the amount of prescription drug advertising has skyrocketed. While these print and television ads have proven very successful in terms of increased sales, various consumer groups, government agencies, and insurance companies have been quite critical of them.

Also, some doctors claim that they are being pressured to write prescriptions inappropriately because their patients are influenced by the drug ad claims. Other doctors say they appreciate that

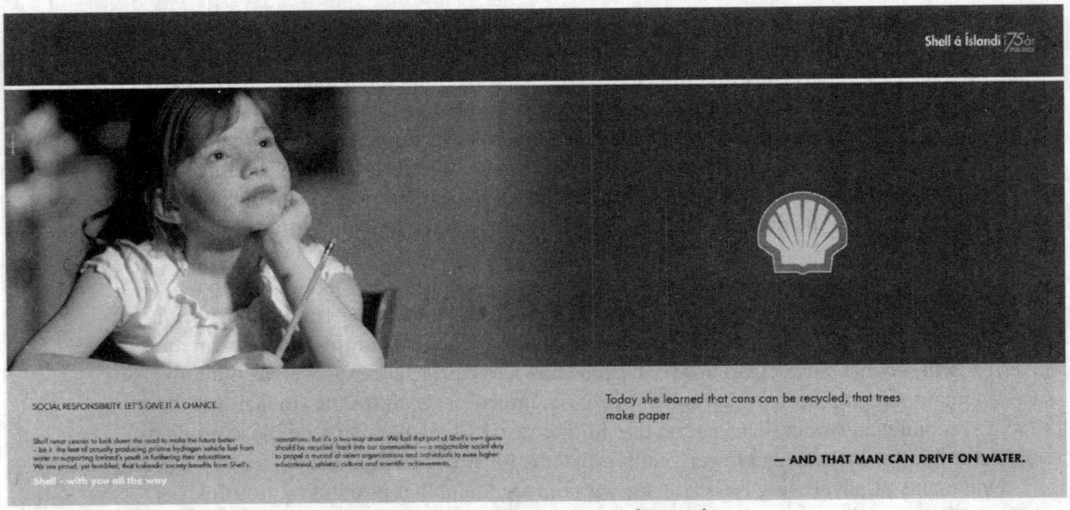

Photo: © Shell International Limited. All rights reserved. Courtesy of HÉR & NÚ;

SHOWCASE

To solve a local crisis in Iceland with its image, Shell used a campaign based on the slogan "Shell—with you all the way." The campaign demonstrated how Shell is involved and "travels" with customers from youth to adulthood, from work to home, from the present to the future—shaping the society that people want to build.

Note: This ad was contributed by Ingvi Logason, principal in HÉR&NÚ, Reykjavik, Iceland. A graduate of Western Florida University, his work was nominated for inclusion in this book by Professor Tom Groth.

Ingvi Jökull Logason CEO and Strategy Director, H:N Marketing Communication, Reykjavík, Iceland

Ronald McDonald is slimmer and more active to help convey the importance of making healthier choices.

Photo: Dennis Jones/Getty Images

the advertising has caused consumers to become more active in managing their own health and more informed about their drug options.

In recent health care reform efforts, some lawmakers targeted the $4.3 billion ad sector because they believe these ads contribute to the high cost of health care.[14] As part of the reform, health insurance companies are required to spend at least 80 percent of the premiums they receive on medical care, not on overhead, advertising, or other costs.[15] For guidelines pertaining to advertising prescription drugs, see the U.S. Food and Drug Administration's website at www.fda.gov/Drugs/ResourcesForYou/Consumers/PrescriptionDrugAdvertising/default.htm.

Communicators' Ethical Responsibilities

By now, you are familiar with many of the ethical and social issues facing marketing communication. How does this involve you? This section will give you a better understanding about what we mean by ethics and provide some decision-making tools as you encounter ethical dilemmas. Let's start by considering a Benetton campaign that challenged personal and professional ethics, as explained by Fred Beard in the "Practical Tips" feature.

Ethics are the "shoulds" and "oughts" of behavior—the "right thing to do." Defining what is right can be challenging. What one person says is right isn't always what others believe appropriate. Ethics and morals are closely related, but they are not synonymous. **Morals** are frameworks for right actions and are more the domain of religion and philosophy. Examples of moral systems are the Ten Commandments from the Judeo-Christian religious tradition or the Buddhists' Eightfold Path. These moral systems provide a framework for behavior.

Although ethics reflect what is right and wrong, the difficulty lies in making choices from equally compelling or competing options, as in the Benetton example—how should you behave when the answer is unclear? We know that doing the right thing is ethical, but it's sometimes hard to know what the right thing is. Sometimes there's no one right answer. Consider, for example, this situation: You are a graphic designer. You want to use a picture you found on the Internet, and you don't want to copy it unethically. How much do you have to change the digital picture before it becomes your own?

Determining what constitutes ethical behavior happens on many levels. Individually, advertisers call on their own moral upbringing. The various marcom industries provide codes of ethics and standards of self-regulation. The government helps regulate marcom practices through legal means.

Practical Tips

Brilliant or Offensive Advertising?

Fred Beard, *University of Oklahoma*

A photo of a priest kissing a nun. An emaciated AIDS victim at the moment of death, attended by his distraught family. An African guerrilla holding an AK-47 and a human leg bone. A dead soldier's bloody uniform.

So began Italian clothing maker Benetton's selfless, noble, and global advertising effort to encourage brotherhood and condemn indifference to human suffering. Or, depending on whom else you ask, so began a cynical and self-serving effort to take advantage of the world's pain and suffering with a purpose no more noble than selling T-shirts and sweaters, with shock and calculated offense being the primary tactics.

When the "United Colors of Benetton" campaign started in 1990, creative director Oliviero Toscani was given free rein. What followed was a steady stream of symbolic, shocking, and often upsetting ads that were only identifiable as Benetton's by a small, green logo. Toscani's 18-year tenure with Benetton ended in 2000, following a firestorm of controversy over the "We, On Death Row" campaign, which was designed to draw attention to the "plight" of 26 convicted murderers in the United States.

Why would an advertiser purposely want to offend people? Benetton certainly isn't alone. The use of "shockvertising" has grown as advertisers have learned that controversy encourages attention and often creates a media buzz far surpassing the reach and frequency of the original media buys. Ethically speaking, though, should advertisers care if they offend people?

The fact is, few people either inside or outside advertising would argue that the presentation of a potentially offensive message is always morally wrong. What questions should we ask to be able to decide for ourselves whether or not an advertising campaign like the "United Colors of Benetton" crosses the line? Here's a start:

- Is it inherently wrong to present words and images that will undoubtedly offend most people if the goal is to draw attention to humanitarian issues and problems?
- Does it make a difference if the goal of widely offensive advertising is solely to sell products?
- Do people have a right not to see ads that offend them? Because some media, such as television and outdoor advertising, are more intrusive than others, does the medium make a difference?
- What do advertising codes of ethics say about audience offense? Are advertisers professionally and morally obligated to follow them?
- To whom do advertisers owe the most responsibility—their own organizations and stakeholders, society, consumers, other advertising professionals?

Considering these questions, where do you come down on the Benetton ads? Should the company have censored them—or let them run? What would you have done if you were the Benetton marketing manager? You can use Google to see examples of Benetton ads.

Photo: Roy Lawe/Alamy

Personal and Professional Ethics

Ethical decisions are usually complex and involve navigating a moral maze of conflicting forces: strategy versus ethics, costs versus ethics, effectiveness versus ethics, and so on. They demand the ability to do what ethicists call "moral reasoning."[16] In the end, if you are a responsible professional making a decision about a strategy or an execution tactic to be used in an advertisement,

A Matter of Practice

Advertising Gets No Respect!

Steve Edwards, *Southern Methodist University*

Why is the profession of advertising ranked just above being a used-car salesman on surveys of ethical practices? Why should you care? Advertising has tremendous power to shape our attitudes about our world and ourselves, inform people of important ideas, and change behavior. Yet advertising students will graduate and get jobs paying less than students in finance, accounting, marketing, or engineering. Why?

Advertising surrounds us and is accessible everywhere and, as with anything that is plentiful, is undervalued. If you have water flowing from the tap, let it flow. But if you were in a desert with a single bottle of water, that same resource becomes precious.

People tend to underestimate the effects of advertising on themselves while overestimating its effects on others. And, while consumers enjoy the information or entertainment advertising provides, they underestimate the knowledge and skills needed to advertise effectively and thus devalue the profession.

Professions are strong to the degree that (1) they are identified and differentiated by their specialized knowledge, (2) they educate new members, and (3) they make the value of their knowledge/work clear to the wider society. Think about why doctors are well respected.

Strengthening the profession of advertising starts with you. Become an advocate for the field. Start by (1) developing an understanding of how advertising affects society both positively and negatively, (2) be able to define the specialized knowledge of advertising that others have not studied, and (3) educate others about the power of the industry.

Specifically, pay attention to the economic versus social effects of advertising. Criticisms of advertising often focus on specific ads that encourage socially undesirable behaviors (overconsumption in general or underage drinking), target impressionable children, or stereotype certain societal groups. Anticonsumerist organizations, such as *Adbusters.org*, promote "buy nothing day" and offer social criticism of advertising using spoof ads. However, people rarely think of the importance of communication messages focused on hygiene, poverty, AIDS, obesity, recycling, alcoholism, literacy, and so on, but it is through advertising that we learn about such things.

It is also through advertising that consumers learn that BMW is "The Ultimate Driving Machine" or that the Toyota Prius "helps save gas and helps the environment." The choices we make as consumers are based on the fundamental values we deem important. And yes, advertising, along with other large societal institutions (e.g., religion or government), helps set or reinforce an agenda for what we as a society value. But it is due in part to advertising that consumers are educated about products in the marketplace and, by making purchase decisions, can force companies to improve products or lower prices to compete.

Advertising is a powerful force and should be respected, but advocates are needed.

Where are you in this debate about the value of advertising? Do you see yourself as an advocate or a critic? If you were at a party, could you defend yourself as a student of advertising—perhaps even an advertising professional?

---

you must be aware of industry standards as well as ethical questions that underlie the core issues we have discussed in this chapter.

More importantly, personal judgment and moral reasoning rest on an intuitive sense of right and wrong, a moral compass that tells you when an idea is misleading, insensitive, too over the top, or too manipulative. And then you need the courage to speak up and tell your colleagues. Does the Benetton advertising pass your personal standards for good advertising? Similarly, the edgy 2013 ad for Mountain Dew that elicited criticism for its perceived racism and making light of violence toward women may have worked for its teenage male audience, but is that a good reason for bringing such criticism to the brand?

Professionals in advertising by and large see themselves as ethical people. However, polls indicate that the public tends to see them differently. In a recent Honesty and Ethics Poll conducted by the Gallup organization, advertising practitioners ranked near the bottom, with nurses, pharmacists, and doctors at the top.[17] Advertising practitioners ranked ahead of telemarketers, lobbyists, members of Congress, and car salesmen. That poll suggests the public is not persuaded that advertising professionals are guided by ethical standards. Read the "A Matter of Practice" feature and begin to think about how you might improve society with your life's work.

Professional Codes of Ethics Industry standards can provide help with a decision about ethical behavior. Many professions write a **code of ethics** to help guide practitioners toward ethical behavior, including the American Association of Advertising Agencies, the Public Relations Society of America, and the Word of Mouth Marketing Association. Professional ethics are often expressed in a code of standards that identifies how professionals in the industry should respond when faced with ethical questions. Codes of ethics can be helpful to guide your actions. However, they are broad statements and are not intended to explain what you should do in every circumstance you encounter.

In an effort to help advertisers build consumer trust and brand loyalty in a global and digital economy, the Institute for Advertising Ethics created eight Principles and Practices for Advertising Ethics, which emphasize the importance of transparency and the need to conduct businesses and relationships with consumers in a fair, honest, and forthright manner[18] (Figure 3.1).

FIGURE 3.1
An advertising code of ethics from the Institute for Advertising Ethics

Principles and Practices for Advertising Ethics

Institute for Advertising Ethics

Principle 1

Advertising, public relations, marketing communications, news, and editorial all share a common objective of truth and high ethical standards in serving the public.

Principle 2

Advertising, public relations, and all marketing communications professionals have an obligation to exercise the highest personal ethics in the creation and dissemination of commercial information to consumers.

Principle 3

Advertisers should clearly distinguish advertising, public relations and corporate communications from news and editorial content and entertainment, both online and offline.

Principle 4

Advertisers should clearly disclose all material conditions, such as payment or receipt of a free product, affecting endorsements in social and traditional channels, as well as the identity of endorsers, all in the interest of full disclosure and transparency.

Principle 5

Advertisers should treat consumers fairly based on the nature of the audience to whom the ads are directed and the nature of the product or service advertised.

Principle 6

Advertisers should never compromise consumers' personal privacy in marketing communications, and their choices as to whether to participate in providing their information should be transparent and easily made.

Principle 7

Advertisers should follow federal, state and local advertising laws, and cooperate with industry self-regulatory programs for the resolution of advertising practices.

Principle 8

Advertisers and their agencies, and online and offline media, should discuss privately potential ethical concerns, and members of the team creating ads should be given permission to express internally their ethical concerns.

Sources: Courtesy of the Institute for Advertising Ethics. Reprinted with permission. An expanded version of the "Principles and Practices for Advertising Ethics with Commentary" is available at www.aaf.org and www.rjionline.org.

The Principles and Practices for Advertising Ethics was the result of a collaboration of the American Advertising Federation, the Reynolds Journalism Institute, and the University of Missouri School of Journalism. Wally Snyder, executive director of the institute, said, "Practicing these high ethics will attract consumers to the advertised product or service."

International Standards and Codes Standards of professional behavior are not found only in the United States or other Western countries. Singapore, for example, has an ad code specifically designed to prevent Western-influenced advertising from impairing Asian family values. Malaysia's requirement that all ads be produced in the country not only keeps that country's advertising aligned with its own standards and cultural values but also cuts back dramatically on the number of foreign ads seen by its public. Advertisers who violate the ethical code of conduct in Brazil can be fined up to $500,000 or imprisoned for up to five years. This punishment would certainly prompt an advertiser to be careful.

In the Netherlands, industry members have encouraged the formation of an "ethical office" to oversee all agencies, advertisers, and media. That office is responsible for reviewing advertisements to ensure that they comply with the Dutch Advertising Code and general ethical principles. In Swedish advertising agencies, an executive known as the "responsible editor" is trained and experienced in marketing law; that editor reviews all advertisements and promotional materials to ensure that they are legally and ethically acceptable.

Why and How Is Brand Communication Regulated?

While it would be ideal if individuals and companies always made socially responsible choices and everyone could agree that those choices resulted in proper actions, sometimes that does not occur and there is a need for regulatory or legal action. The company may decide it is acceptable to advertise certain products, and the government may decide otherwise.

Various systems are in place to monitor the social responsibility of advertising and other brand communication, including laws, government regulatory bodies, professional oversight groups, and industry self-regulation. Figure 3.2 identifies the organizations with oversight responsibility for advertising and groups them in terms of five specific categories: government, media, industry, public or community groups, and the competition. Let's examine each of those systems.

Brand Communication's Legal Environment

Making and enforcing laws are the domain of government. Congress makes laws and regulatory agencies in the executive branch of the federal government enforce the laws related to advertising. The following list summarizes important advertising legislation, most of which shows the growing authority of regulatory bodies, such as the FTC, to regulate advertising:

- ***Pure Food and Drug Act (1906)*** Forbids the manufacture, sale, or transport of adulterated or fraudulently labeled foods and drugs in interstate commerce. Supplanted by the Food, Drug, and Cosmetic Act of 1938; amended by the Food Additives Amendment in 1958 and the Kefauver-Harris Amendment in 1962.
- ***Federal Trade Commission Act (1914)*** Establishes the commission, a body of specialists with broad powers to investigate and to issue cease-and-desist orders to enforce Section 5, which declares that "unfair methods of competition in commerce are unlawful."
- ***Wheeler-Lea Amendment (1938)*** Prohibits unfair and deceptive acts and practices regardless of whether competition is injured; places advertising of foods and drugs under FTC jurisdiction.
- ***Lanham Act (1947)*** Provides protection for trademarks (slogans and brand names) from competitors and also encompasses false advertising.
- ***Magnuson-Moss Warranty/FTC Improvement Act (1975)*** Authorizes the FTC to determine rules concerning consumer warranties and provides for consumer access to means of redress,

FIGURE 3.2
Advertising Review and Regulation

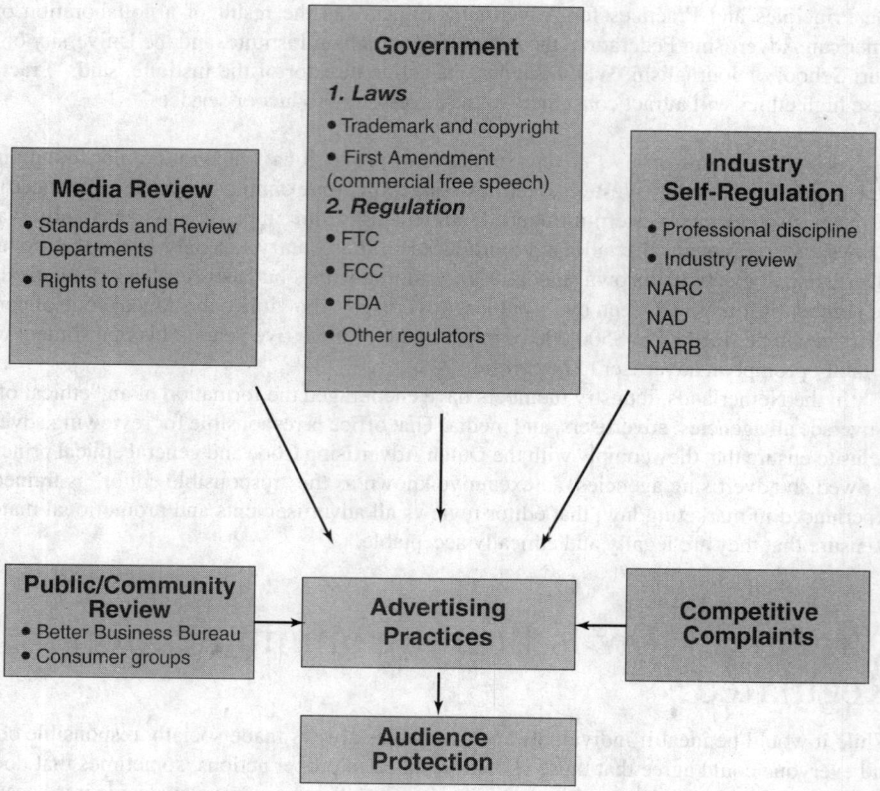

such as the "class-action" suit. Also expands FTC regulatory powers over unfair or deceptive acts or practices and allows it to require restitution for deceptively written warranties costing the consumer more than $5.

- ***FTC Improvement Act (1980)*** Provides the House of Representatives and the Senate jointly with veto power over FTC regulation rules. Enacted to limit the FTC's powers to regulate "unfairness" issues in designing trade regulation rules on advertising.
- ***Telemarketing and Consumer Fraud Act and Abuse Protection Act (1994)*** Specifies that telemarketers may not call anyone who requests not to be contacted. Resulted in the Telemarketing Sales Rules.

In this section, we examine two pivotal areas of case law—trademarks and copyright protection and the First Amendment—as they pertain to advertising and other areas of marketing communication.

Trademark and Copyright Protection A **trademark** is a brand, corporate or store name, or distinctive symbol that identifies the seller's brand and thus differentiates it from the brands of other sellers. A trademark can be registered through the Department of Commerce, which gives the organization exclusive use of the mark, as long as the trademark is maintained as an identification of a specific product. Registered trademarks enjoy more legal protection than those that are not registered. Under the Lanham Trademark Act of 1947, the Patent and Trademark Office of the Department of Commerce protects unique trademarks from infringement by competitors.

Even an audio trademark is protected, as a case in the EU illustrates. A distinctive audio sound based on the noise of a cock crowing and the way it was represented in Dutch had been registered with the EU's trademark office. When this sound trademark was used by a different company, the first company sued for trademark infringement.

A recent trademark issue is protection for **uniform resource locators** (URLs), which are Internet domain names. URLs need to be registered to be protected just like any other trademark.

They are issued on a first-come, first-served basis for any domain name not identical to an existing brand name.

A **copyright** gives an organization the exclusive right to use or reproduce original work, such as an advertisement or package design, for a specified period of time. The Library of Congress controls copyright protection. Copyrighting of coined words, phrases, illustrations, characters, and photographs can offer some protection from other advertisers who borrow too heavily from competitors. Commonly used designs or symbols, however, cannot be copyrighted. Nor can ideas be copyrighted. For a copyright to be obtained, a work must be fixed in a tangible medium. Copyright infringement can occur when a product is used in an ad without proper permission. A sweet example is the maker of Peeps, those marshmallow chicks and bunnies, which sued American Greetings for using pictures of Peeps without authorization.[19]

Brand Communication and the First Amendment The most basic federal law that governs advertising and other forms of marketing communication is the First Amendment to the U.S. Constitution that states that Congress shall make no law "abridging the freedom of speech, or of the press."

How have courts applied the First Amendment to advertising? First Amendment protection extends to **commercial speech**, which is speech that promotes commercial activity. However, that protection is not absolute and is often restricted. The Supreme Court generally applies a different standard to commercial speech than it does to other forms of speech, such as that enjoyed by the press and filmmakers, because the conditions are different for different forms of speech.

Protection of advertising as commercial speech has varied over the years. In 1980, in conjunction with its ruling on *Central Hudson Gas and Electric v. Public Service Commission of New York*, the Supreme Court established a test that determines to what extent the government can restrict advertising. This decision also stipulated the degree to which advertising is considered commercial speech, although a recent 2010 Supreme Court decision enhanced the free speech rights of corporations, particularly for political speech.

A number of cases have attempted to change the common view of advertising as commercial speech. Most notably, the Supreme Court struck down a Massachusetts law that restricted tobacco advertising. Free speech advocates applauded the decision while critics of tobacco companies lamented. Although no one expects advertising to have the same constitutional protection of free speech that is given to individuals, courts throughout the country are narrowing the gap.

The Supreme Court permits some restrictions on commercial speech. For example, the court has held that false or misleading commercial speech can be banned. Even truthful commercial speech can be restricted if the government can prove that the public good demands such restrictions.[20] The courts have also ruled that such acts as the federal ban on junk faxes is valid and that businesses' right to commercial speech does not include printing their advertisements on other people's fax machines.

Essentially, the Supreme Court has ruled that only truthful commercial speech is protected, not misleading or deceptive statements. Because the nation's courts continue to reinterpret how the First Amendment applies in different cases, advertisers need to keep close track of legal developments.

International Laws and Regulations As advertisers, agencies, and media become more global, it will be imperative for the players to understand local laws in the countries in which they operate. Marketing practices, such as pricing and price advertising, vary in their legal and regulatory restrictions.

Some product categories, such as over-the-counter drugs, are particularly difficult to work with because regulations about their marketing and advertising are different in every country. Advertising for certain types of products is banned. Thailand prohibits tobacco ads, as does Hungary. In Hong Kong, outdoor display advertising of tobacco products is banned. Malaysia has banned most forms of tobacco advertising, including print, television, radio, and billboards.

However, these restrictions are fairly ineffective as a result of **indirect advertising** that features a product other than the primary (controversial) product. Examples of these techniques in Malaysia are quite plentiful. Billboards with the Salem, Benson & Hedges, and Winston names dot the landscape, but they're not advertising cigarettes. They're advertising the companies' travel, clothing, and restaurant businesses.

There also are differences in the legal use of various marketing communication tools. A contest or promotion might be successful in one country and illegal in another. Different laws and self-regulatory codes about direct marketing exist in different EU countries. For example, France requires an opt-in clause to a mailing or questionnaire asking permission to add the customer's name to a mailing list.[21] Germany prohibits companies from making unsolicited telephone calls and faxes to consumers. Because of the difficulty in complying with widely varying laws, international advertisers often work with either local agencies or with international agencies that have local affiliates and experts who know the local laws and can identify potential legal problems.

The Regulatory Environment

In addition to specific legislation that affects the practice of marketing communication, there are also government bodies that oversee the application of these laws and establish standards and regulations that marketers must meet. The FTC is the primary body that oversees marketing communication, but a number of other agencies are also involved in regulating the messages sent to consumers, as summarized in the following list:

Specialized Government Agencies That Affect Advertising

Agency	Effect on Advertising
Federal Trade Commission (www.ftc.gov)	Regulates credit, labeling, packaging, warranties, and advertising
Food and Drug Administration (www.fda.gov)	Regulates packaging, labeling, and manufacturing of food and drug products
Federal Communications Commission (www.fcc.gov)	Regulates radio and television stations and networks
U.S. Postal Service (www.usps.gov)	Controls advertising by monitoring materials sent through the mail
Bureau of Alcohol, Tobacco, and Firearms (www.atf.treas.gov)	Division of the U.S. Treasury Department that regulates advertising for alcoholic beverages
U.S. Patent and Trademark Office (www.uspto.gov)	Oversees trademark registration to protect against patent infringement
Library of Congress (www.loc.gov)	Provides controls for copyright protection

In addition to the FTC, the Food and Drug Administration (FDA) and the **Federal Communications Commission** (FCC) are dynamic components of the regulatory environment. Let's look in more depth at their missions and the type of practices they regulate.

FTC Established by Congress in 1914 to oversee business, the FTC is the primary agency governing the advertising industry. Its main focus with respect to advertising is to identify and eliminate ads that deceive or mislead the consumer. Some FTC responsibilities include the following:

- ***Unfairness*** Initiate investigations against companies that engage in unfair competition or deceptive practices.
- ***Deception*** Regulate acts and practices that deceive businesses or consumers and issue cease-and-desist orders where such practices exist. Cease-and-desist orders require that the practice be stopped within 30 days; an order given to one firm is applicable to all firms in the industry.
- ***Violations*** When the FTC finds a violation of the law, such as a deceptive or unfair practice, it mandates (1) a cease-and-desist order, (2) an affirmative disclosure, or (3) corrective advertising.

Specifically, the FTC oversees false advertising and in recent years that oversight has focused on health and weight-loss business practices, 900 telephone numbers, telemarketing, and advertising that targets children and the elderly. The FTC hosts the National Do Not Call Registry to help citizens keep from receiving unwanted telemarketing calls. The FTC monitors the ratings system and the advertising practices of the film, music, and electronic games industries. Periodically, it issues progress reports to Congress on youth-oriented entertainment advertising to make sure that ads for products with potentially objectionable content—primarily violent or sexual content—are not seen on media targeted to youth. The FTC's reports to Congress cover advertising on television and websites as well as print media.

The existence of a regulatory agency such as the FTC influences advertisers' behavior. Although most cases never reach the FTC, advertisers prefer not to risk long legal battles with the agency. Advertisers are also aware that competitors may complain to the FTC about a questionable advertisement. Such a move can cost the offending organization millions of dollars.

The FTC revised its guidelines governing testimonial advertisements, bloggers, and celebrity endorsements in October 2009 for the first time since 1980. These guidelines toughen rules for endorsements and testimonials by requiring that the results touted by endorsers are likely to be typical. The revisions also now cover bloggers who must disclose any free products or other compensation they get in exchange for their endorsements.[22] Updates are available at www.ftc.gov/opa/reporter/advertising/index.shtml.

FDA The FDA is the regulatory division of the U.S. Department of Health and Human Services that oversees package labeling, ingredient listings, and advertising for food and drugs. It also determines the safety and purity of foods and cosmetics. In particular, the FDA is a watchdog for drug advertising, specifically in the controversial area of direct-to-consumer ads for prescription drugs. Its job is first to determine whether drugs are safe and then to see that these drugs are marketed responsibly. Marketing includes promotional materials aimed at doctors as well as consumers.

For pharmaceutical companies, advertising is a commercial free speech issue, and the industry has brought pressure on the FDA to make direct-to-consumer advertising rules for prescription drugs more understandable, simpler, and clearer.

FCC The FCC, formed in 1934 to protect the public interest in broadcast communication, can issue and revoke licenses to radio and television stations. The FCC also has the power to ban messages, including ads, that are deceptive or in poor taste. The agency monitors only advertisements that have been the subject of complaints and works closely with the FTC to eliminate false and deceptive advertising. The FCC takes actions against the media, whereas the FTC is concerned with advertisers and agencies.

Other Regulatory Bodies In addition to the FTC, the FDA, and the FCC, most other federal agencies that regulate advertising are limited to a certain type of advertising, product, or medium. We have already discussed the Patent Office and the Library of Congress and their roles in protecting copyrights and trademarks. Let's now look at other key regulatory agencies:

- ***Bureau of Alcohol, Tobacco, and Firearms*** The Bureau of Alcohol, Tobacco, and Firearms within the Treasury Department regulates deception in advertising and establishes labeling requirements for the liquor industry. This agency's power comes from its authority to issue and revoke annual operating permits for distillers, wine merchants, and brewers. Because there is a danger that public pressure could result in banning all advertisements for alcoholic beverages, the liquor industry strives to maintain tight controls on its advertising.
- ***U.S. Postal Service*** The U.S. Postal Service regulates direct-mail and magazine advertising and has control over the areas of obscenity, lotteries, and fraud. To give you an idea of the magnitude of the U.S. Postal Service's responsibility, *Direct Marketing News* reported that the estimated spending on direct mail in 2012 was $50 billion, even in a period of declining spending on the medium.[23] Consumers who receive advertisements in the mail that they consider sexually offensive can request that no more mail be delivered from that sender. The postmaster general also has the power to withhold mail that promotes lotteries. Fraud can include a number of questionable activities, such as implausible, get-rich-quick schemes.
- ***States' Attorneys General*** The National Association of Attorneys General seeks to regulate advertising at the state level. Members of this organization have successfully brought suits in their respective states against such advertising giants as Coca-Cola, Kraft, and Campbell Soup. More recently, numerous attorneys general have led the way against the tobacco industry and have supported the advertising restrictions discussed earlier.

The Impact of Regulation

In our discussion of issues, we mentioned several that have spurred governmental regulation, such as children's advertising, deception, and claim substantiation. In this section, we discuss these regulations in terms of the government agencies taking responsibility for them.

The FTC and Children's Advertising Developing responsible advertising aimed at children is a critical issue. The FTC and other governmental agencies have gotten involved with the regulation of marketing to children.

After a 1978 study found that the average child viewed more than 20,000 television commercials per year, a heated debate ensued. One side favored regulation because of children's inability to evaluate advertising messages and make purchasing decisions. The other side opposed regulation, arguing that many self-regulatory mechanisms already existed and the proper place for restricting advertising to children was in the home.

In response, the FTC initiated proceedings to study possible regulations of children's television. Despite the FTC's recommendations, the proceedings did not result in new federal regulations until 1990. In the interim, self-regulation in the advertising industry tried to fill this void.

The National Advertising Division (NAD) of the Council of Better Business Bureaus, Inc., set up a group charged with helping advertisers deal with children's advertising in a manner sensitive to children's special needs. The Children's Advertising Review Unit, established in 1974, evaluates advertising directed at children under the age of 12.

In 1990, Congress passed the Children's Television Advertising Practice Act, which placed 10.5-minute-per-hour ceilings for commercials in children's weekend television programming and 12-minute-per-hour limits for weekday programs. The act also set rules requiring that commercial breaks be clearly distinguished from programming, barring the use of program characters to promote products.

Advocates for children's television continue to argue that many stations made little effort to comply with the 1990 act and petitioned the FCC to increase the required number of educational programs to be shown daily. In 1996, broadcasters, children's advocates, and the federal government reached an agreement requiring all television stations to air three hours of children's educational shows a week.

Regulating Deception Ultimately, advertisers want their customers to trust their products and advertising, so many take precautions to ensure that their messages are not deceptive, misleading, or unreasonable. **Deceptive advertising** is intended to mislead consumers by making claims that are false or by failure to make full disclosure of important facts, or both. The current FTC policy on deception contains three basic elements:

1. ***Misleading*** Where there is representation, omission, or practice, there must be a probability that it will mislead the consumer.
2. ***Reasonableness*** The perspective of the "reasonable consumer" is used to judge deception. The FTC tests reasonableness by looking at whether the consumer's interpretation or reaction to an advertisement is reasonable.
3. ***Injurious*** The deception must hold the probability of material injury. Here, "material" is defined as "affecting consumers' choice or behavior regarding the product or service." In other words, the deception is likely to influence consumers' decision making about products and services.

This policy makes deception difficult to prove because the criteria are rather vague and hard to measure. It also creates uncertainty for advertisers who must wait for congressional hearings and court cases to discover what the FTC will permit.

Regulating Substantiation An area of particular concern to the FTC in determining misleading advertisement is **claim substantiation**. The advertiser should have a reasonable basis for making a claim about product performance, or run the risk of an FTC investigation. Food claims, such as those focused on calories or carbohydrates, must be supported by research about nutrition. Even claims in auto advertising, as the Chevy Equinox ad demonstrates, need proof.

Consequently, an advertiser should always have data on file to substantiate any claims it makes in its advertisements. Also, ideally, this research should be conducted by an independent research firm.

The FTC determines the reasonableness of claims on a case-by-case basis. In general, the FTC considers these factors:

- ***Type and Specificity of Claim*** For example, Computer Tutor claims you can learn the basics of using a computer by simply going through its three-CD set.

- ***Type of Product*** FedEx promises a certain delivery time, regardless of weather, mechanical breakdown, and so forth. This product has a great many uncontrollable variables compared to Heinz ketchup, which the company promises will be "thick."
- ***Possible Consequences*** A website that claims it is secure can cause serious damage to its customers if, in fact, it is not.
- ***Degree of Reliance*** Business-to-business customers depend on the many claims made by their vendors. Therefore, if XPEDX (yes, that's how it's spelled), a manufacturer of boxes and other packages, claims in its ad that it can securely deliver any size product, it had better deliver.
- ***Type and Accessibility of Evidence*** The type of evidence could range from testimonials from satisfied customers to complex product testing in multiple laboratories. It could be made available through an 800-number request or online.
- ***What Substantiation Is Reasonable*** What do experts in this area believe is reasonable proof of a claim?

Photo: General Motors LLC. Used with permission

This ad claims the Chevy Equinox is the most fuel efficient car in its category. Note the footnotes that explain how the claim is supported.

Remedies for Deception and Unfair Advertising

Common sources of complaints concerning deceptive or unfair advertising practices are competitors, the public, and the FTC's own monitors. After the FTC determines that an ad is deceptive, the first step in the regulation process is to issue a **consent decree**. The FTC notifies the advertiser of its finding and asks the advertiser to sign a consent decree agreeing to stop the deceptive practice. Most advertisers do sign the decree to avoid the bad publicity.

Duracell was forced to modify one of its ads after Energizer complained that the ad inferred that Duracell CopperTop batteries would last three times longer than other heavy-duty and super-heavy-duty batteries. The ad didn't mention Energizer by name, but Energizer charged the ad was "false and misleading" because consumers would think the comparison was with other alkaline batteries, such as Energizer. In fact, the CopperTop does not last longer than other alkaline batteries. The ad was modified with a disclaimer.[24]

It is important for students of advertising to understand the legal ramifications of deceptive and unfair advertising. Under some circumstances, the FTC holds advertisers and their agencies accountable. Essentially, an agency is liable for deceptive advertising along with the advertiser when the agency is an active participant in the preparation of the ad and knows or has reason to know that it is false or deceptive.

If a complaint seems justified, the commission can follow several courses of action:

- ***Cease-and-Desist Orders*** When an advertiser refuses to sign a consent decree and the FTC determines that the deception is substantial, it issues a **cease-and-desist order**. The process leading to the issuance of a cease-and-desist order is similar to a court trial. An administrative law judge presides. FTC staff attorneys represent the commission, and the accused parties are entitled to representation by their lawyers. If the administrative judge decides in favor of the FTC, the judge issues an order requiring the respondents to cease their unlawful practices. The advertiser can appeal the order to the full five-member commission.
- ***Corrective Advertising*** The FTC may require **corrective advertising** when consumer research determines that an advertising campaign has perpetuated lasting false beliefs. Under this remedy, the FTC orders the offending organization to produce messages for consumers that correct

the false impressions the ad made. The purpose of corrective advertising is not to punish an advertiser but to prevent it from continuing to deceive consumers. The FTC may require a firm to run corrective advertising even if the campaign in question has been discontinued.

A landmark corrective advertising case is *Warner-Lambert v. FTC.* According to the FTC, Warner-Lambert's campaign for Listerine mouthwash, which ran for 50 years, had been deceiving customers, leading them to think that Listerine could prevent or reduce the severity of sore throats and colds. The company was ordered to run a corrective advertising campaign, mostly on television, for 16 months at a cost of $10 million.

Interestingly, after the Warner-Lambert corrective campaign ran its course, 42 percent of Listerine users continued to believe that the mouthwash was being advertised as a remedy for sore throats and colds, and 57 percent of users rated cold and sore throat effectiveness as a key reason for purchasing the brand.[25] These results raised doubts about the effectiveness of corrective advertising to change impressions and have affected recent court decisions.

- ***Consumer Redress*** The Magnuson-Moss Warranty-FTC Improvement Act of 1975 empowers the FTC to obtain consumer redress when a person or a firm engages in deceptive practices. A judge can order any of the following: cancellation or reformation of contracts, refund of money or return of property, payment of damages, and public notification.

Media Review of Advertising

The media attempt to regulate advertising by screening and rejecting ads that violate their standards of truth and good taste. Most networks have a standards and practices department that screens every ad and gives approval before the ad can run. Each individual medium has the discretion to accept or reject a particular ad. For example, some magazines do not accept tobacco and liquor ads, and many magazines and television stations do not show condom ads. The major television networks craft their own standards and guidelines.

The First Amendment gives any publisher the right to refuse to publish anything the company does not want to publish, and this sometimes creates battles between media companies and advertisers. For example, some billboard companies in Utah refused to run billboards for a Wasatch Beer company brand named Polygamy Porter. The brand's slogan "Why have just one!" and headlines such as "Take Some Home for the Wives" were deemed offensive to the state's Mormon population. A similar brouhaha arose when the state's Brighton Ski Resort promoted its four-person lifts with a billboard during the Salt Lake City Olympics that read, "Wife. Wife. Wife. Husband." The billboard company that banned the beer ads received letters both for and against its stand, which indicates the difficulty of such decisions.

Self-Regulation

Rather than wait for laws and regulatory actions, responsible advertisers take the initiative and establish individual ethical standards that anticipate and even go beyond possible complaints. Such a proactive stance helps the creative process and avoids the kinds of disasters that result from violating the law or offending members of society.

Advertisers practice three types of self-regulation: self-discipline, industry self-regulation, and self-regulation by public and community groups.

Self-Discipline An organization such as an advertising agency exercises self-discipline when it develops, uses, and enforces norms within its own practices. Self-discipline starts with the individuals in the agency or organization. It is each person's responsibility to recognize ethical issues and be intentional about their behavior. We hope that this chapter will help you think about making choices that you deem the right thing to do in your career.

Virtually all major advertisers and advertising agencies have in-house ad review procedures, including reviews by agency and client attorneys. These employees help ensure that work is legal. Typically, the attorneys are concerned with how claims are phrased and substantiated. Are the claims verifiable? Is there research and data to prove the truth of the claims? Is there anything in the wording that could be misinterpreted or misleading? Is there anything deceptive in the visual images?

Several U.S. companies (Colgate-Palmolive, General Foods, and AT&T) have their own codes of behavior and criteria that determine whether advertisements are acceptable. Companies without such codes tend to have informal criteria that they apply on an ad-by-ad basis. At a minimum, advertisers and agencies should have every element of a proposed ad evaluated by an in-house committee, lawyers, or both.

Industry Self-Regulation When the development, use, and enforcement of norms comes from the industry, the term used is *industry self-regulation.* In the case of both advertisers and advertising agencies, the most effective attempts at pure self-regulation have come through industry groups, such as the Advertising Review Council and the Better Business Bureau (BBB).

In 1971, several professional advertising associations, in conjunction with the Council of Better Business Bureaus, established the National Advertising Review Council, now known as the Advertising Self-Regulatory Council, which negotiates voluntary withdrawal of national advertising that professionals consider deceptive. NAD of the Council of Better Business Bureaus and the National Advertising Review Board (NARB) are the two operating arms of the Advertising Self-Regulatory Council.[26] None of these is a government agency.

NAD is made up of people from the field of advertising. It evaluates complaints submitted by consumers, consumer groups, industrial organizations, and advertising firms. NAD also does its own industry monitoring. After NAD receives a complaint, it may ask the advertiser in question to substantiate claims made in the advertisement. If that substantiation is deemed inadequate, NAD representatives ask the advertiser to change or withdraw the offending ad. When a satisfactory resolution cannot be found, NAD refers the case to NARB.

NARB is a 50-member regulatory group that represents national advertisers, advertising agencies, and other professional fields. When the advertiser appeals a case to NARB, it faces a review panel of five people: three advertisers, one agency person, and one public representative. This NARB panel reviews the complaint and the NAD staff findings and holds hearings to let the advertiser present its case. If the case remains unresolved after the process, NARB can (1) publicly identify the advertiser and the facts about the case and (2) refer the complaint to the appropriate government agency, usually the FTC. Although neither NAD nor NARB has any real power other than threatening to invite government intervention, these groups have been effective in controlling cases of deception and misleading advertising. Figure 3.3 summarizes the NARB appeal process.

Self-Regulation by Public and Community Groups The advertising industry voluntarily involves nonindustry representatives, such as the BBB or the media, in the development, application, and enforcement of norms. Local and consumer activist groups represent two ways in which self-regulation occurs in this manner:

- ***Local Group*** At the local level, self-regulation has been supported by the BBB (www.bbb.org), functions much like the national regulatory agencies and also provides local businesses with

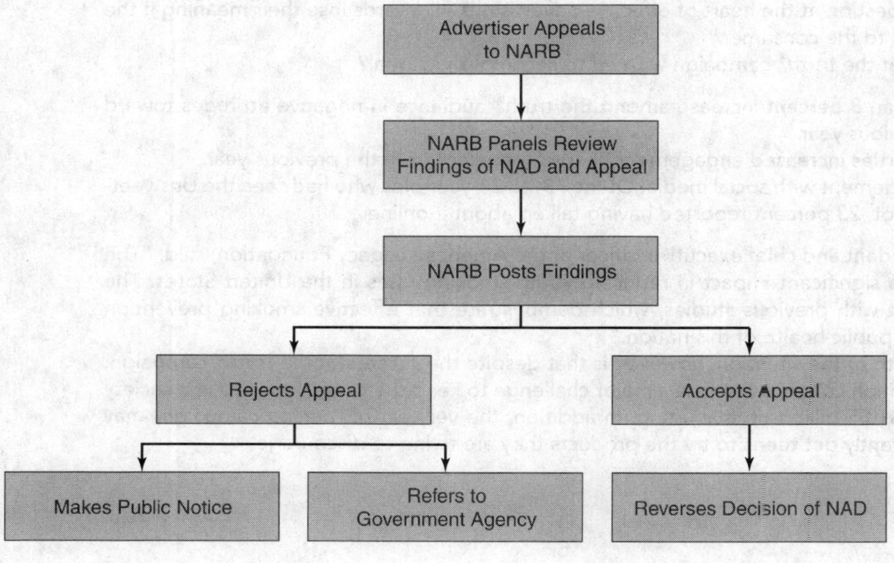

FIGURE 3.3
Consumers or groups submitting a complaint to NAD and NARB go through this process. The ultimate power of NAD and NARB is the threat of passing the claim to the FTC. Usually, cases are settled before that point.

advice concerning the legal aspects of advertising. Approximately 250 local and national bureaus made up of advertisers, agencies, and media have screened hundreds of thousands of advertisements for possible violations of truth and accuracy. Although the BBB has no legal power, it receives and investigates complaints and maintains files on violators. It also assists local law enforcement officials in prosecuting violators. The ease with which the BBB can be accessed on the Internet has prompted businesses to be more careful about complying with its standards.

- ***Consumer Activist Group*** Consumer groups of all kinds monitor advertising practices. The Action for Children's Advertising group follows the practices of advertisers who market to children and will file complaints with industry boards or regulatory agencies about advertisements they consider questionable. The consumer group Public Citizen inspired the FDA to require warnings on print ads for certain types of nicotine products. Groups that are focused on media literacy also review the performance of advertisers. For example, the Cultural Environment Movement is a nonprofit coalition of independent organizations and individuals that focuses on fairness, diversity, and justice in media communication.[27]

Looking Ahead

This chapter asked you to consider the social responsibility dimensions of advertising and marketing communication in terms of ethics and regulation. The next section, Part 2, will introduce you to the basics of brand communication planning with chapters on how marketing communication works, the consumer audience, strategic research, and strategy and planning.

It's a Wrap

The truth® Wins Out in the End

At the beginning of the chapter, we noted that the truth® campaign has won more than 300 creative awards, which is quite impressive. Its winnings include five Effie awards, including a Grand Effie (best of show) award, more than 90 Hatch Awards, 22 Clio Awards, 12 Webby Awards, Emmys, Adweek Media "Ad Campaign of the Decade," and more than a dozen awards for its public relations efficacy.

Remember, though, that winning creative awards doesn't necessarily mean that the campaign was effective. The award-winning innovative approaches and creative accolades mean that the agency gets recognized for its work, but they may fail to address the critical question of effectiveness: Did the campaign work for the client? That's the essential question at the heart of effective advertising. All awards lose their meaning if the message isn't communicated to the consumer.

What is the evidence that the truth® campaign worked to accomplish its goal?

- A tracking study showed an 8 percent increase among the truth® audience in negative attitudes toward big tobacco from the previous year.
- All truth® (Internet) properties increased engagement nearly 20 percent from the previous year.
- The effort increased engagement with social media. Of the 13- to 24-year-olds who had seen the Unsweetened truth® 30-second spot, 23 percent reported having talked about it online.

Dr. Cheryl Healton, president and chief executive officer of the American Legacy Foundation, said, "The truth® campaign has made a significant impact in reducing youth smoking rates in the United States. The study findings are consistent with previous studies, which demonstrate that effective smoking prevention campaigns are critical to the public health of this nation."

The un-sugar-coated truth of the situation, however, is that despite the success of the truth® campaign, the American Legacy Foundation continues to face a major challenge to keep the campaign alive in a society where big tobacco spends $10.5 billion on marketing. In addition, the very act of running campaigns may arouse curiosity and inadvertently get teens to try the products they are trying to discourage.

Logo: Courtesy of truth®

Key Points Summary

1. **What is the social impact of brand communication?** To some extent, advertising creates demands for products; however, the power of advertising to do this is hard to measure. The shape-versus-mirror debate is a central issue in considering advertising's role in society. Critics of advertising tend to believe that it has the power to shape social trends and the way people think and act; advertising professionals tend to believe that it mirrors values rather than sets them. In fact, advertising and society's values are probably interactive, so the answer may simply be that advertising both mirrors and shapes values. Whether or not advertising causes society to become overcommercialized relates to the criticism that buying products appears to be the solution to every problem. Counterarguments emerge from the position that consumers can make intelligent choices about what they need.
2. **What ethical and social responsibilities do communicators bear?** Advertisers have a social responsibility to make good ethical choices. At the root of ethical behavior is the individual decision maker's set of moral values. When faced with a dilemma of equally compelling choices, advertisers can consult their personal values, professional codes of ethics, and international standards of ethical behavior to guide their moral decision making.
3. **Why and how is advertising regulated?** In a complex society, there is usually not one answer to what constitutes "right" behavior. Regulatory agencies help enforce advertising standards. Several governmental bodies help regulate advertising:

    - The FTC is the agency concerned primarily with identifying and eliminating deceptive advertising.
    - The FDA oversees advertising related to food and drugs.
    - The FCC monitors advertising broadcast by radio and television stations.
    - Other regulatory bodies with some advertising oversight include the Bureau of Alcohol, Tobacco, and Firearms; the U.S. Postal Service; the Patent and Trademark Office; the Library of Congress; and the states' attorneys general offices.

    In addition to governmental oversight, advertising is also self-regulated. Individuals working in the field need to act responsibly to make ethical and legal choices. Advertising agencies have in-house ad review procedures and legal staff that monitor the creation of advertising. The industry has a number of bodies that review advertising, such as the Advertising Self-Regulatory Review Council, the National Advertising Division of the Better Business Bureau, and the National Advertising Review Board. Other bodies include the various media review boards, competitors who are concerned about unfair advertising that might harm their brands, and public and community groups that represent either local or special-interest groups.

Key Terms

blogola, p. 98
cease-and-desist order, p. 111
claim substantiation, p. 110
code of ethics, p. 104
commercial speech, p. 107
comparative advertising, p. 96
consent decree, p. 111
copyright, p. 107
corrective advertising, p. 111
cultural imperialism, p. 93
deceptive advertising, p. 110
demand creation, p. 91
endorsement, p. 98
ethics, p. 101
false advertising, p. 95
Federal Communications Commission, p. 108
indirect advertising, p. 107
international advertising, p. 94
marketing imperialism, p. 93
morals, p. 101
puffery, p. 96
social responsibility, p. 90
stereotype, p. 93
testimonial, p. 98
trademark, p. 106
uniform resource locators, p. 106

Review Questions

3-4. Explain the effect of a brand's communication on its audience. Elaborate the role of social responsibility in developing such communication.

✪ 3-5. What do you consider the most pressing ethical issues facing advertisers? Explain.

3-6. Discuss the challenges that international laws and regulations face as a result of indirect marketing.

3-7. In addition to the FTC, what other governmental bodies are involved in regulating advertising practices?

Discussion Questions

✪ 3-8. The Dimento Game Company has a new basketball video game. To promote it, "Slammer" Aston, an NBA star, is signed to do the commercial. Aston is shown in the commercial with the game controls as he speaks these lines: "This is the most challenging court game you've ever tried. It's all here—zones, man-to-man, pick and roll, even the alley-oop. For me, this is the best game off the court." Is Aston's presentation an endorsement? Should the FTC consider a complaint if Dimento uses this strategy? What would you need to know to determine if you are safe from a challenge of misleading advertising?

3-9. Zack Wilson is the advertising manager for the campus newspaper. He is looking over a layout for a promotion for a spring break vacation package. The headline says, "Absolutely the Finest Deal Available This Spring—You'll Have the Best Time Ever If You Join Us in Boca." The newspaper has a solid reputation for not running advertising with questionable claims and promises. Should Zack accept or reject this ad? Take one side of this issue and write a short 1–2 page position paper explaining your viewpoint. In a class discussion determine how many of your classmates agreed or disagreed with your view.

Take-Home Projects

3-10. ***Portfolio Project:*** Check the websites of three big-name companies, such as the following:

- McDonald's (www.mcdonalds.com)
- Avon (www.avon.com)
- Ben & Jerry's (www.benjerry.com)
- Starbucks (www.starbucks.com)
- Body Shop (www.thebodyshop.com)
- Target (www.target.com)

Write a two- to four-page report on their efforts to be socially responsible. How is the company's social responsibility position reflected in its advertising?

✪ 3-11. ***Mini-Case Analysis:*** Imagine that you are now working for Starbucks. What does the company do that provides evidence that it is socially and environmentally responsible? What other ways can you think of for the company to expand these efforts?

TRACE North America Case

Multicultural Ethics and Issues

Multicultural Innovation

Read the TRACE case in the Appendix before coming to class. Then answer the following questions:

3-12. Does the "Hard to Explain, Easy to Experience" campaign communicate its brand message of innovation without using ideas, words, or images that are offensive or insensitive to the target audience?

3-13. Give an example that demonstrates how the TRACE campaign is socially responsible.

3-14. What evidence in this case leads you to believe that the advertising team that created this campaign understood Multicultural Millennials? Can you add any additional insights?

Hands-On Case

Authentically Green?

Increasingly, companies are attempting to align themselves with good causes, such as showing that they're caretakers of the environment. You may be familiar with "Ecomagination," a strategy created by General Electric to drive innovation and growth of earth-friendly environmental solutions. It pledged $1.5 billion investment in research and development of green technologies toward this effort, such as using wind energy, recovering wastewater, and exploring the use of compressed natural gas for vehicles. Read ahead to the opening story in Chapter 15 to find out about Häagen-Dazs's work to solve a mystery of disappearing honeybees. You don't have to look far to see examples of other corporations that are engaged in work to help sustain the environment.

Often criticized for the harm some of the ingredients do to the environment, corporations producing household cleaners are, well, trying to clean up their act.

Recently, the green niche has been a fast-growing segment of the $2.7 billion market for household cleaning products. In 2008, the Clorox Company, a century-old company known for its not-so-environmentally-friendly products, such as bleach, Pine-Sol, and Formula 409, launched a line of ecofriendly products it called Green Works®, in part to take advantage of this opportunity. The products contain 95 percent natural plant and mineral-based biodegradable cleaning ingredients. Packaging can be recycled, and the products are not tested on animals. The Sierra Club even endorsed it. Green Works® products received a seal from the Environmental Protection Agency's program Design for the Environment, which recognizes and promotes green chemistry and the health of humans and the environment.

Sales soared to $100 million. By 2011, though, they fell to $60 million. Do you wonder why? In the Part 1 opener, you read about seven enduring principles of marketing communication. The first of those principles stated that as a marketer, you should build and maintain distinctive brands that your customers love. Capitalizing on social trends can be good business and can connect your company with good causes that make consumers feel good about your brand. It can also backfire if they do not find the marketing to be sincere or the products inferior.

Some critics vented their opinions about Green Works® on blogs and other venues:

- This isn't green; it's greenwashing. How sincere can the Clorox Company be when it sells not only green products but other products that are highly toxic and environmentally unfriendly?
- Green isn't something a company is because it develops a new product line. Rather, its about changing the inside culture of a company.
- Can Green Works® truly claim it's green on its labels when there are no industry standards defining "natural cleaners"?

Do you think Green Works is authentically green?

Consider This

P1-1. After reading about Green Works® in the case and on the Web, do you think this product line is a believable attempt by Clorox to improve the environment? Why or why not?

P1-2. Does Green Works® represent an attempt to mirror a trend in society or create one?

P1-3. Had you been the product manager, would you have put the Clorox name on the Green Works® products, as the company did? Explain your decision.

P1-4. Do you think that green marketing is an enduring movement? Why or why not?

Sources: http://ge.ecomagination.com; www.greenworkscleaners.com; www.environmentalleader.com; "Jack Neff, "Has Green Stopped Giving? Seeds of Consumers Revolt Sprouting Against Some Environmentally Friendly Product Lines," www.adage.com.

PART

2 Principle: Be True to Thy Brand—and Thy Consumer

Part 1 introduced the basics of advertising and brand communication practice. Part 2 focuses on how brand communication works, why and how consumers make the decisions they do, and how a winning strategy—one that reflects how consumers think and feel—can be developed.

No matter how much advertising media and brand communication change, a basic principle is that brands must be true to themselves and to the consumers who buy them. Regina Lewis, explains this principle in her essay below about how true branding works.

Brands Are Built on a Human Foundation

Regina Lewis
Dr. Regina Lewis has been vice president of Global Consumer Insights at InterContinental Hotels Group and vice president and director of the Consumer and Brand Insights Group at Dunkin' Brands, Inc. She is now an associate professor in the Department of Advertising and Public Relations at the University of Alabama.

If there is one thing I have learned in igniting consumer passions across the country for Dunkin' Brands and reigniting consumer passions around the world for Holiday Inn, it is that great brands are "human." Put another way, great brands are not created in a vacuum and then "marketed" successfully. Rather, great brands are built on the basis of knowledge of consumers' deepest values and innermost feelings. Consumer loyalty is built when a brand seeks first to know everything possible about its consumer and then speaks to that consumer with a tone and message that emotionally resonates with them.

For example, consumers who are loyal to Dunkin' Donuts, which has built itself to be a down-to-earth, approachable brand, love the fact that carrying a Dunkin' cup says to others that they, personally, are down-to-earth and approachable. At Dunkin', success did not happen from the "inside out." Success was made possible by the fact that the Dunkin' brand communication team and their agencies worked off of the insight that a very large group of people, because of their "everyday Joe" love of everyday life, wanted an alternative to high-priced, status-oriented coffee brands. These people wanted a "brand for them"—a brand that reflected their personally held value that authenticity trumps bells and whistles.

Another example: At Holiday Inn, the marketing team faced a real challenge because of the large number of similar midscale (mid-price-range) hotel brands on the market. Instead of simply copying others or advertising a tactic like "free Internet," however, the team spoke with consumers around the world to find out how guests really wanted to *feel* when staying in a hotel. They found that travelers are quite weary and just want to feel "at home" on the road—whether on business or with their families. Consumers told us over and over, "I just want to be able to be myself!" So, the successful "Stay You" campaign was launched.

CHAPTER 4 • How Brand Communication Works
CHAPTER 5 • Segmenting and Targeting the Audience
CHAPTER 6 • Strategic Research
CHAPTER 7 • Strategic Planning

When a brand fails to convey a soul or essence that matches personal characteristics that consumers value or when a brand fails to meet emotional needs, it lacks meaning. It blends in with all the other bland brands that lack charisma. On the other hand, when a brand both meets a deep-seated need and becomes a badge that consumers are proud of displaying, it becomes interwoven into consumers' everyday lives.

The Enduring Principles

As I, along with my marketing and advertising agency teams, ensured that Holiday Inn retained its place in the hearts and minds of guests, I heeded the following set of principles:

1. ***Feel*** Because all human decisions involve heed some emotional component, no purely rational advertising approach can offer sustainable advantage. An advertisement must make folks "feel" something!
2. ***Connect*** All advertising must not only contain an emotional component but also get that emotion right. It must nail a way in which folks want to see either their world or themselves.
3. ***Identify*** While all consumers are individuals, we also can identify groups of consumers who think and feel the same way; identifying and understanding these groups is at the root of strategic planning.
4. ***Understand*** To effectively deliver emotion through advertising, we must avoid "group think"; sometimes, the most powerful idea can come from one consumer's story—and the most powerful message can be imagined by one brilliant creative mind that understands the minds of the target audience.
5. ***Smile*** While economic times remain tough, as I write this essay, it is critical to remember that people want to feel happy! Just as songs that made people smile were celebrated during the Great Depression, advertising that makes people smile will always be meaningful when life feels difficult.

These principles will be explained further in the chapters that make up Part 2. Chapter 4 answers the big picture question of "How does advertising and other brand communication work?" Effectiveness factors are spelled out using the Facets Model of Effects. Building on that discussion as a foundation, Chapter 5 introduces the consumer audience and discusses how targeting works. Chapter 6 introduces the basics of research used to gather insights about consumers and the marketplace. Finally, Chapter 7 explains how ideas about how advertising works and insights into how consumers think and behave come together in a strategic plan.

CHAPTER

4 How Brand Communication Works

Courtesy of Chrysler Group LLC

It's a Winner

Campaign:	Company:	Agency:	Award:
Imported from Detroit	*Chrysler*	*Wieden + Kennedy*	*Grand Effie*

CHAPTER KEY POINTS

1. How does brand communication work both as a form of mass communication and interactive communication?
2. How did the idea of advertising effects develop, and what are the problems in traditional approaches to advertising effects?
3. What is the Facets Model of Effects, and how does it explain how brand communication works? What are the key Facets of brand communication effectiveness?

Anatomy of an Award-Winning Campaign for Chrysler

If you were studying biology, you might dissect a frog to see how it is put together, but because you're studying brand communication, you need to study the communication process and examine the innards of an effective campaign. In this chapter, you'll see how brand communication professionals view the components of good brand communication and discover how they work together to have a desired effect on their intended audiences.

Background A good starting place for our study is the Grand Effie–winning "Imported from Detroit" Chrysler campaign created by Wieden + Kennedy (the same agency responsible for Nike's work). This campaign started on the heels of Chrysler's bankruptcy during the recession when not only Chrysler was in crisis but Detroit and American business as a whole were in trouble. Since then, Chrysler has mounted a campaign that contributed to Chrysler's turnaround and the way people think about the Motor City.

Goals *Convince the public that Chrysler is a carmaker with a promising future.*

Objectives *Build loyalty and generate pride in owning Detroit-built Chryslers.*

Procedure for the Analysis

1. Apply communication theory to analyze the source (advertiser and agency), the intended audience (receiver), and the product message (ad or other marketing communication tool).
2. Investigate how brand communication helps consumers (1) see and hear the message (perception), (2) feel something for the brand (emotional or affective response), (3) understand the point of the message (cognitive response), (4) connect positive qualities with the brand (association), (5) believe the message (persuasion), and (6) act in the desired ways (behavior).

Findings Chrysler and its agency Wieden + Kennedy (the source) sought to convince American car buyers, particularly those who buy imports, (the receivers), that they should buy Chrysler 200 and 300 sedans. In the words of Saad Chehab, head of Chrysler brand communications, the message is that "you no longer have to cross oceans to get what you can have from these shores."

The advertising that Wieden + Kennedy created for this campaign included a first-ever two-minute Super Bowl commercial with the tagline "Imported from

Detroit." The $9 million commercial featured rapper Eminem, who was believable because his story matched Detroit's and Chrysler's to some extent. He symbolized "the city's history, its stumble and recovery," according to Chehab. Eminem narrated the commercial with a backdrop of scenes of the Motor City, "a town that's been to hell and back," intercut with beauty shots of the Chrysler 200.

The commercial's theme repeats throughout the long-running campaign: "When it comes to luxury, it's as much about where it comes from as it is who it's for." Chrysler followed up the Super Bowl commercial with other commercials and another Super Bowl commercial the next year: "It's halftime in America," narrated by Clint Eastwood, who said, "Detroit's showing us it can be done." More recent ads urge viewers to "show where you're going without forgetting where you're from."

What is striking about this campaign is that it builds strong emotional connections with the audience. The national campaign was designed to grab people's emotions and heart, according to Aaron Allen, an agency creative director on the Chrysler account. The music, the words, and the images all contribute to the perception that viewers can believe that Chrysler builds luxury cars and turns the import image, as well as Detroit's image, upside down with the tagline "Imported from Detroit."

Supporting the national campaign, regional advertising makes a more rational appeal, giving potential buyers details about the cars' attributes. Wieden + Kennedy extended the "imported" theme by casting dealerships as "embassies" and selling "Imported from Detroit" merchandise.

Turn to the "It's a Wrap" feature at the end of the chapter to learn more about the impact of this award-winning campaign.

Sources: Jeff Bennett, "U.S. Sales Gains Propel Chrysler Earnings," *Wall Street Journal*, July 31, 2012, B5; "Grand Effie Awards 2012 Chrysler: Imported from Detroit," Effie Awards news release, May 23, 2012. www.effie.org; Bradford Wernle, "Chrysler Sets Up Dealers as Embassies for Vehicles 'Imported;' from Detroit," February 14, 2011, www.adage.com and http://www.chrysler.com/en/ifd; Mark Memmott, "Eminem's 'Imported from Detroit' Super Bowl Ad for Chrysler Scores Big," February 8, 2011, www.npr.org.

This chapter will first explain how communication works in brand communication. Then we'll look at various types of consumer responses to messages to identify the key *effects* behind the concept of *effectiveness*, which we organize and present as the Facets Model of Effects. The communication role of brand communication provides a foundation for discussions in the following chapters on consumer behavior, consumer research, and strategic planning. It's our view that you can't make intelligent decisions in those areas unless you understand how communication works in branding.

How Does Brand Communication Work?

Would you hire a doctor who doesn't understand how various parts of the body work? Wouldn't you expect a competent doctor to be able to diagnose ills and know what needs to be done to keep you healthy? Anatomy, chemistry, and biology—these are the fundamentals of medicine. So wouldn't you also expect brand communication professionals to understand the fundamental theories of their field—to know how communication and consumer psychology work as well as how to diagnose problems and keep consumer–brand relationships healthy? That was the challenge Wieden + Kennedy faced in turning around the brand image, as well as the sales levels, of Chrysler.

It begins with communication. At its most basic, brand communication is a message to a consumer about a brand. It gets **attention** and provides information, sometimes even entertainment. It is purposeful in that it seeks to create some kind of response, such as an inquiry, a sale, a visit to a website, or a test drive.

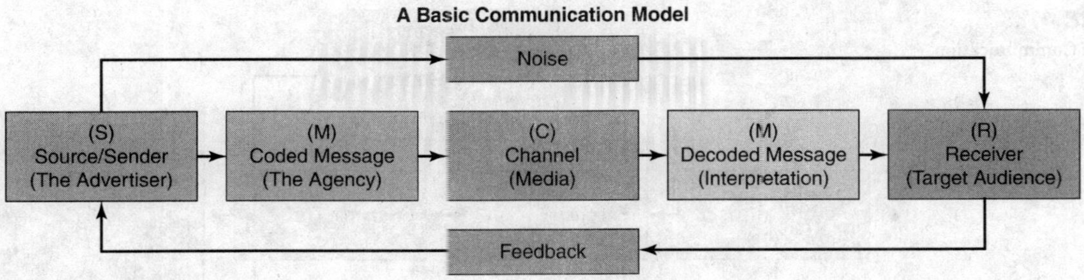

FIGURE 4.1A

A Basic Mass Communication Model

The legendary David Ogilvy would like to see advertising as relevant as a personal conversation.[1] He pretends he is at a dinner party and the woman next to him asks for advice. He explains, "I give her the facts, facts, facts. I try to make it interesting, fascinating, if possible, and personal—I don't write to the crowd."

In reality, however, most traditional advertising is not as personal or as interactive as a conversation because it relies on mass communication. Although other forms of marketing communication, such as personal selling and telemarketing, can deliver the personal contact of a conversation, Ogilvy's comparison ignores the challenge of getting the attention of a largely disinterested audience when using mass media.

So let's look first at how *communication* works in general, and then we'll apply that analysis to mass-media advertising and finally to the broader arena of brand communication, including newer forms of brand-related interaction.

The Mass Communication Foundation

Mass communication is a process, as depicted in the **SMCR model** in Figure 4.1a, that goes back to early work in the 1940s by Shannon and Weaver on the transmission of information.[2]

There are eight key parts to this model. As it has been applied to mass communication, the communication process begins with (1) a **source**, a sender, who (2) **encodes**, or puts it in words and pictures as (3) a **message**. The message is presented through (4) **channels of communication**, such as a newspaper, radio, or television. The message is (5) **decoded**, or interpreted, by the (6) **receiver**, who is the reader, viewer, or listener. The last step is (7) **feedback**, which is obtained by monitoring the response of the receiver to the message. The entire process is complicated by (8) **noise**, things that interrupt the sending and receiving of the message, such as a bad connection or words with unclear meanings. This is sometimes referred to as the SMCR (source → message → channel → receiver) model.

In the chapter-opening Chrysler story, we translated this SMCR model to brand communication where the *source* typically is the marketer (Chrysler) assisted by its agency (Wieden + Kennedy) who encodes the information into various types of marketing communication. In other words, advertising professionals turn the marketer's information (a Detroit-built car from Chrysler, which is as good as imports) into an interesting and attention-getting message (Eminem telling the story of the resurgence of Motor City and Chrysler). The *message,* of course, can be an advertisement or other marketing communication, such as a press release, store banner, brochure, video, or Web page.

Together, Chrysler and its agency determine the *goals* and *objectives* for the message in terms of the effects they want the message to have on the *receiver* (the consumer audience). They also choose the *media* (*channels*), which are the vehicles that deliver the message. In advertising, that tends to be newspapers and magazines in print and radio and television in broadcasting, as well as the Internet and cell phones and other forms of out-of-home vehicles, such as outdoor boards and posters. Other media include the phone, fax, specialty items (mugs and T-shirts), in-store signs, brochures, catalogs, shopping bags, inflatables, and even sidewalks and toilet doors. The end point of the communication process is the *receiver*, the consumers who make up the

FIGURE 4.1B
A Brand Communication Model

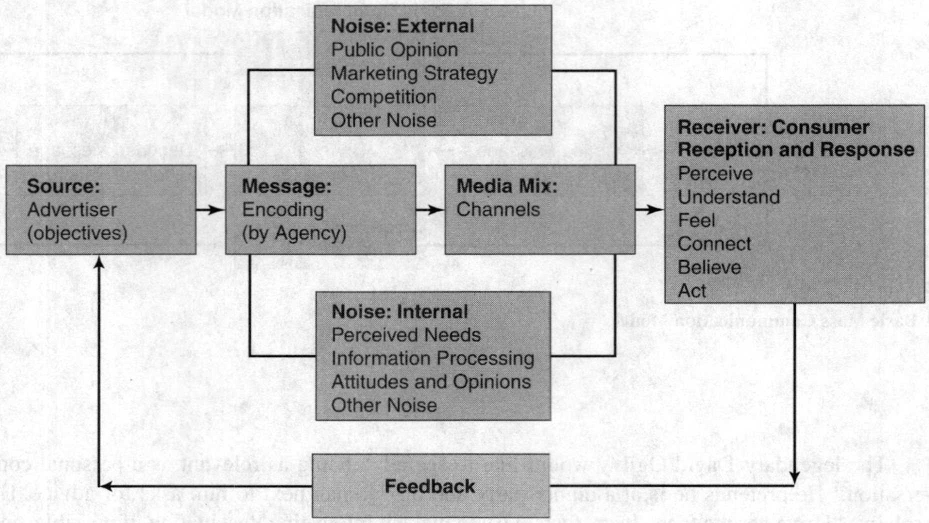

targeted audience. How the consumer responds to (decodes and interprets) the message determines the effectiveness of the brand communication.

If the communication process fails to work and the consumer does not receive the message as intended by the advertiser, then the communication effort is ineffective. The brand communication model shown in Figure 4.1b describes how this communication process works.

External noise, which hinders the consumer's reception of the message, includes technical and socioeconomic trends that affect the reception of the message. Health trends, for example, often harm the reception of fast-food messages. External noise can also be related to media. It can be as simple as bad broadcast or cell phone reception. A more likely cause of noise is **clutter**, which is the multitude of messages all competing to get consumers' attention. It can even include any of the 3,000 or so commercial messages you see in your daily environment.

Internal noise includes personal factors that affect the reception of an advertisement, such as the receiver's needs and wants, language skills, purchase history, information-processing abilities, and other personal factors. If you are too tired to listen or your attention is focused elsewhere, then your fatigue or disinterest creates noise that hinders your reception of the message. In Chrysler's case, the internal noise was the negative impression that many car buyers had of Detroit-built automobiles.

Feedback is the reaction the audience has to a message. It can be obtained through research or through customer-initiated contact with the company, which are important tests of the effectiveness of marketing communication messages. An important thing to remember is that this communication process is not foolproof or even dependable—it's complicated.

Adding Interaction to Brand Communication

Mass communication, as we've been discussing it, is traditionally one-way communication with the message moving from the source to the receiver—from a company to a target audience (see Figures 4.1a and 4.1b). However, **interactive communication** is two-way communication—a dialogue or conversation—and brand communication is moving in that direction with the advent of social media and *word-of-mouth* communication strategies.

The difference between one-way and two-way communication is that in two-way communication, the source and receiver change positions as the message bounces back and forth between them (think ping-pong)—the source becomes the listener, and the receiver becomes the sender. This is different from simply acquiring feedback because in interactive communication, it's not just about the company contacting the consumer—in fact, the consumer may initiate the contact. And they talk to their network of friends spreading the word about their experiences with a product or brand message. If advertisers want to overcome the impersonal nature of mass communication, they need to learn to receive (i.e., *listen to*) as well as send messages to customers. Figure 4.2 is a model of how two-way communication works.

Another way to describe interactive communication is to modify and extend the formula we introduced in Chapter 2, where we described business-to-consumer communication as B → C

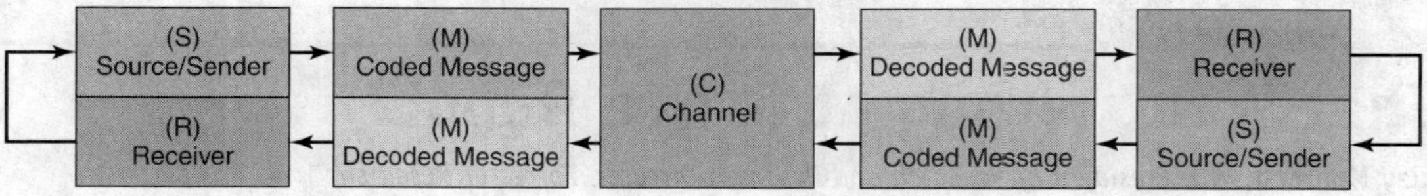

FIGURE 4.2
An Interactive Communication Model
The basic communication model is modified here to show how interactive communication works as a conversation or dialogue including shared communication. Note how the source and receiver change positions as the message bounces back and forth between them.

and business-to-business communication as B → B. With consumer-initiated communication, that formula would turn around (C → B), which means the customer is the sender and the company the receiver.

But communication is more complicated now because of the increasing use of social media and word of mouth, which we represent as B → C^2. We are using C^2 to refer to a network of messages with the communication shared among a network of friends. However, shared communication could also drive the communication as in C^2 → B. In this case, people talk about a brand and then send messages to the company. *Group texts* is a form of shared text messages within a defined group that can be used to share messages to closest friends, such as within brand fan clubs. The point is that the communication situation becomes more complex as it becomes more interactive. Here's a summary that compares one-way and interactive communication:

	Company Initiated	Consumer Initiated
Targeted (one way)	B → C	C → B
Shared (two way)	B → C^2	C^2 → B

Marketers' use of *word of mouth*, *buzz marketing*, and online *social media* are indicators of the need for message integration. The important difference is that consumers are talking to one another in a circle of comments about products and brands. That raises the bar on the need for consistency in company-produced brand communication, whatever the format and medium.

Interactive communication is also making the classic two-step or multistep flow of communication model more relevant. It was developed by Katz and Lazarsfeld in the 1940s as a theory of how persuasion works based on social influence.[3] In their view, people identified as opinion leaders talk to other people and influence the formation of attitudes and behaviors. As Professor Dennis DiPasquale notes, this model helps explain how word of mouth intersects with public relations and new media in brand communication.[4] For example, a report by the Burson-Marsteller agency called "Social Media Check-Up" noted that the *Fortune* Global 100 companies were mentioned a total of 10.4 million times online in one month in 2012. Most of this chatter was on Twitter.[5]

Principle
In interactive communication, there are multiple conversations occurring in a network with people contacting companies as well as talking to one another and companies listening and responding as well as sending messages.

Interactions and Interactive Experiences A final point is that interactive communication is the building block of the customer-brand experience, which can determine the likelihood of repeat business and brand loyalty. Harley Manning, a member of this book's advisory board, asks, "What qualifies as an interaction?" Manning, who is vice president of research and research director at Forrester Research, wrote a book with colleague Kerry Bodine titled *Outside In: The Power of Putting Customers at the Center of Your Business*, in which they explain,

> Here's how we think about interactions: they're reciprocal. Your customer takes an action like visiting your store or website. Your company responds in some way. Maybe an associate walks up to her or the website pops up an invitation to chat. Your customer then responds to your company's response—asking the associate a question or accepting the chat invitation—and so it goes until your customer achieves her goal, or gives up.[6]

The importance of interactions is the point of Manning's "Inside Story" about Office Depot. You can hear Manning and Bodine talk about customer service and the cases in the book at www.outsidein.forrester.com.

The Inside Story

What Went Wrong at Office Depot?

Harley Manning, *Vice President of Research and Research Director, Forrester Research*

When he was president of Office Depot's North American division, Kevin Peters visited stores all over the United States to get a firsthand look at how customers experienced his stores. In some cases it was a painful experience.

He found that high mystery-shopping scores reflected clean floors and fully stocked shelves but not the things customers cared about. These customers are mostly small business owners who want to find the office products they came for, quickly and easily. In other words, they want to get in, buy, and get out.

But Office Depot stores didn't help them do that. They were large, and their signage was cluttered and confusing, making the stores hard for customers to navigate.

Employees were neither as empathetic nor as helpful as they should have been. They had been coached all along to focus on tasks, not on building relationships with customers by listening carefully and responding to their needs.

Wham, bam, thank you customer, and—oh, wait—did you forget to buy something? Sorry, I was so busy stocking the shelves that I missed that part.

Ultimately, Kevin knew that if he wanted to reverse the downward slide in sales, he needed to transform virtually every aspect of his in-store experience. Quickly.

He learned that customer experience goes to the heart of everything you do—how you conduct your business, the way your people behave when they interact with customers and each other. You literally can't afford to ignore any interaction because your customers take it personally each and every time they touch your products and interact with your support people.

Check out Forrester's website at *www.forrester.com.*

This Inside Story was contributed by Harley Manning, a master's graduate of the advertising program at the University of Illinois. He was nominated by the late Kim Rotzell, former dean of the College of Communication.

Photo courtesy of Harley Manning

Other Aspects of Communication

So far, we've been discussing traditional communication based on words and conversations. It's important to recognize, however, that nonverbal communication can be just as powerful as word-based forms. As we mentioned earlier, many commercials are essentially nonverbal, relying on the impact of compelling visuals. Most billboards, packaging, and many posters, as well as ads, rely on the power of visual imagery. With print advertising, most people look at the picture first in their decision about whether to stop and read the ad.

Brand signals include slogans, but they are dominated by logos, imagery, and color. Think about a Coca-Cola can—what comes to mind first? Brand identity operates through systems of *cues* that identify and signal brand personalities and strengths. *Signaling* is particularly important in the clutter and chaos of the Internet, where attention is shortened and recognition happens in an instant.

Cues and signals are used in commercial communication to help structure a consumer's meaning-making process. We create personal brand meanings from formal communication (ads or conversations with friends) but also from brand experiences. Events are an obvious form of experience-based communication, but experiences also include such things as finding the brand in the store, dealing with a sales clerk—or not, using the product, calling tech support, and visiting customer service. A big part of retailing involves managing the shopping experience and making it as painless as possible. Better yet, make it fun and memorable. Navigating a website is another experience that can be challenging or rewarding and colors the impression of the brand.

Brand messages of all types contain layers of meaning. In most cases, particularly with advertising, there are obvious superficial or surface-layer meanings, but there may also be deeper layers of meaning that call for more interpretation (decoding) by the consumer. The "1984" commercial, for example, was obviously a product launch for the new Apple Macintosh. A deeper meaning was the product comparison hinted at through Big Brother, who could be interpreted as representing IBM. **Semiotics** is a research tool used to uncover these layers of meaning.

Logos use cues to help identify a familiar brand, and these visual elements also signal brand personality. What do you think these logos are saying about their brands?

Photo sources Howard Harrison/Alamy; Molly Riley/Reuters Limited; Reproduced with permission of MSD Consumer Car, Inc., a subsidiary of Merck & Co., Inc. All rights reserved. DR. SCHOLL'S is a registered trademark of MSD Consumer Care, Inc.; Dirk Enters/Alamy

What Are the Effects behind Effectiveness?

The most important characteristic of brand communication is that it is purposeful. Ads, for example, are created to have some effect, some impact on the people who read or see their message. We refer to this as **effects**, the idea being that effective brand communication will achieve the marketer's desired impact and the target audience will respond as the marketer intended. This desired impact is formally stated as a set of **objectives**, which are statements of the measurable goals or results that the message is intended to achieve. In other words, the brand message works if it achieves its objectives.

What are the effects that make brand communication effective? Consider your favorite commercials—do they grip you emotionally (think Hallmark)? Do they have a compelling message ("1984")? How about learning something—do you think about things because of something you heard or read in an ad (the Wii campaign that uses demonstrations to launch the new type of television-based game)? Does an ad need to be entertaining to work (Think Eminem's dramatic narration about a city and an industry that's "been to hell and back")?

The theme of this book is that good advertising—and brand communication—is effective when it achieves the advertiser's desired response. For example, the Chrysler campaign wanted to generate pride in Detroit-built Chryslers as well as loyalty and the conviction that Chrysler is a carmaker with a future (even if the U.S. car industry seems to be in serious trouble). Thus, understanding what kinds of effects can be achieved with a marketing communication message is essential to anyone engaged in planning advertising and all other forms of marketing communication.

Principle
The intended consumer response is the message's objective, and the message is effective to the degree that it achieves this desired response.

Traditional Views on Impact When we ask how it works, we are talking about the **impact** that communication has on receivers of the message—that is, how they respond to the message. What are the effects that determine whether an advertisement works? Here are two of the traditional approaches used by professionals to outline the impact of advertising:[7]

- ***AIDA*** The most commonly used explanation of how advertising works is referred to as **AIDA**, which stands for attention, interest, desire, and action. This concept was first expressed around 1900 by an advertising pioneer named St. Elmo Lewis. Because AIDA assumes a predictable set of steps, it also is referred to as a **hierarchy of effects** model.
- ***Think/Feel/Do*** Another relatively simple answer to how advertising works is the **think/feel/do model** developed in the 1970s. Also referred to as the *FCB model* in honor of the agency where it was developed as a strategic planning tool, the idea is that advertising motivates people to think about the message, feel something about the brand, and then do something, such as try it or buy it.[8] That view is supported by recent research by Nyilasy and Reid into what professionals in advertising know and believe about how advertising works. Their in-depth interviews found that "agency practitioners strongly believe that exposure to ads causes changes in human cognition, emotions, and behavior"—or think/feel/do.[9]

One problem with these approaches is that they are based on the concepts of a predictable process that consumers go through in making decisions, beginning with exposure to a brand message.

Principle
Not all purchases begin with a search for information. Some purchases are made out of habit or on impulse.

The assumption is that consumers are engaged in processing information before they make a purchase. In reality, we know that consumers sometimes buy out of *habit*, such as people who are loyal drinkers of Coke or Pepsi. And in other situations, consumers buy on *impulse*, such as when you are standing in line at a checkout counter and pick up a bar of candy. In both situations, you buy first and then think back on the purchase—if you give it any thought at all.

A different approach that attempts to eliminate the idea of predictable linear steps is found in Moriarty's domains model. It is based on the idea that messages have an impact on consumer responses, not in steps but at the same time. The three key effects, or domains, identified in this approach are (1) perception, (2) learning, and (3) persuasion. The idea is that a message can engage consumers' perceptions (attention and interest), engage their thinking (learn), and persuade them (change attitude and behavior), and to some degree that occurs all at the same time.[10]

The Port of Vancouver USA ads are an example of how these effects interact. Even though the ads are in the business-to-business category, the ads get the attention of their audience with curiosity-provoking headlines: the "Vacancy" sign and "Part Specialist, Part Shepherd." The "Vacancy" ad uses explanation to help readers understand ("858 acres to be exact"). It's also persuasive in that it makes the argument that the Port of Vancouver has room to grow and provide space to meet the needs of its customers.

A different approach to analyzing what works in brand communication is presented in Armstrong's *Persuasive Advertising* book, which identifies a set of 194 principles based on research findings over the years. Armstrong has reduced these principles to four categories that drive strategies: information, influence, emotion, and exposure. Other sets of categories describe tactics and media uses.[11]

SHOWCASE

This campaign is aimed at professionals in the transportation industry. These are two in a series of six ads that explain what services the Port of Vancouver USA offers its customers.

This campaign was contributed by Karl Schroeder, formerly a copywriter at Coates Kokes in Portland, Oregon, who now works at Nike. A graduate of the University of Oregon's advertising program, his work was nominated for inclusion in this book by Professor Charles Frazer.

Karl Schroeder, Senior Writer, Coates Kokes, Portland, Oregon

How do we make sense of all of these ideas about how brand communication works? One goal of this book is to organize these effects so they are useful for setting objectives and, ultimately, evaluating effectiveness. But how to do it? That's the question at the heart of this chapter, and we'll answer with our model of how brand communication works, a model that we think you will find to be simple and easy to use in explaining the impact of a brand message.

What Are the Facets of Impact?

Our objective in this chapter is to present our Facets Model of Effects, which does a more complete job than previous models of explaining how advertising creates impact in terms of various types of consumer responses. Ultimately, we are guided by the kind of thinking that Regina Lewis expressed in the Part 2 opener: that consumers are loyal to brands that say something about them as human beings. Effective marketing communication speaks to us about things that we want to know in ways that we like.

The solution to our search for a new model is to build on the effects identified in the think/feel/do approach and add the missing categories, such as perception, association, and persuasion. It is interesting that these missing areas are also related to the three factors that the Ameritest research company uses in evaluating effective commercials: attention, brand linkage, and motivation (see www.ameritest.net).

Thus, we propose a six-factor model that is useful both in setting objectives and in evaluating the effectiveness of brand communication. Our answer to the question of how brand communication works is that effective brand messages create six types of consumer responses—(1) see/hear, (2) feel, (3) think/understand, (4) connect, (5) believe, and (6) act/do—all of which work together to create the response to a brand message. These six consumer responses and the categories of effects to which they belong are represented in Figure 4.3.

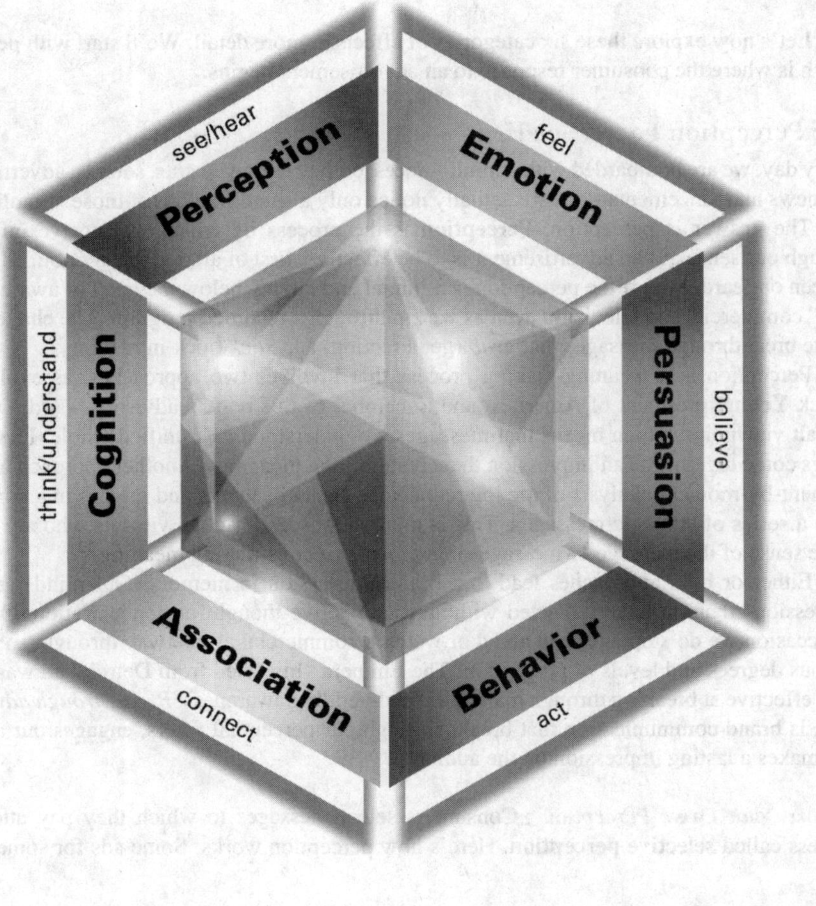

FIGURE 4.3
The Facets Model of Effects

Think of these six effects as facets—polished surfaces like those of a diamond or crystal—that come together to make up a unique consumer response to a brand message. The effects are holistic in the sense that they lead to an impression, or what Preston calls an "integrated perception."[12] An effective message has a diamond-like quality that represents how the message effects work together to create the desired consumer response. The effects can vary in importance with some campaigns more focused on one or several of the facets.

Here is a table to help you analyze impact in terms of the goal the message is trying to achieve and how that will be apparent in the way consumers respond to the message. The final column lists factors that can be measured to determine if you achieved the desired type of impact.

Communication Goal	Consumer Response	Factors That Drive a Response
Perception	See/hear	Exposure, selection and attention, interest, relevance, curiosity, awareness, recognition
Emotion/affect	Feel	Wants and desires, excitement, feelings, liking, resonance
Cognition	Think/understand	Need, cognitive learning, comprehension, differentiation, recall
Association	Connect	Symbolism, conditioned learning, transformation
Persuasion	Believe	Motivation, influence, involvement, engagement, conviction, preference and intention, loyalty, believability and credibility
Behavior	Act/do	Mental rehearsal, trial, buying, contacting, advocating and referrals, prevention

Let's now explore these six categories of effects in more detail. We'll start with perception, which is where the consumer response to an advertisement begins.

The Perception Facet: See/Hear

Principle
Breakthrough messages *grab* (get attention) and *stick* (lock in memory).

Every day, we are bombarded with stimuli—faces, conversations, scents, sounds, advertisements, and news announcements—yet we actually notice only a small fraction of those stimuli. Why?

The answer is perception. **Perception** is the process by which we receive information through our senses. If an advertisement is to be effective, first of all, it must get noticed. It has to be seen or heard, even if the perception is minimal and largely below the level of awareness. We "see" commercials on television even as we zip through a recorded program. The challenge is to create breakthrough messages that *grab* (get attention) and *stick* (lock in memory).

Perception is a meaning-making process that involves two approaches, as explained by Chuck Young, president of Ameritest and a member of this book's advisory board. One is the Gestalt viewpoint, which means that messages are understood as a unified whole. It is the way things come together as an impression that creates brand meanings. Another approach involves a moment-by-moment analysis of the interconnected string of words and images in a commercial or in a series of strategic messages. This is a process used by active viewers who are trying to make sense of the message or messages in a process of constructing meaning.[13]

Principle
Breakthrough advertising breaks through perceptual filters, engages attention, and makes a lasting impression.

Either or both approaches lead to a brand impression in memory. Our minds are full of impressions that we have collected without much active thought or concentration. Of course, on occasion we do stop and read an ad or watch a commercial all the way through, so there are various degrees and levels of perception. The Eminem "Imported from Detroit" ad was particularly effective at breaking through inattention and building awareness. *Breakthrough advertising*, then, is brand communication that breaks through our perceptual filters, engages our attention, and makes a lasting impression on the audience.

Factors That Drive Perception Consumers select messages to which they pay attention, a process called **selective perception.** Here's how perception works: Some ads for some product categories—personal hygiene products, for example—battle for attention because people don't choose to watch them. However, if the message breaks through the disinterest and is selected and attended to, then the consumer may react to it with interest if it is relevant. The result is awareness of the ad or brand, which is filed in memory at least to the point that the consumer recognizes the brand or ad.

The key factors driving perception, then, are exposure, selection and attention, interest, relevance, curiosity, awareness, and recognition. Here is a brief review of these terms and how they relate to impact:

- ***Exposure*** The first test of perception is whether a brand communication message is seen or heard. In advertising, this is called **exposure**, which is an important goal of media planners who try to find the best way to reach consumers with a message.
- ***Selection and Attention*** The next factor that drives perception is **selective attention**, the process by which a receiver of a message chooses to attend to a message. Amid all the clutter in the media environment, selection is a huge problem. The ability to draw attention that brings visibility to a brand is one of advertising's greatest strengths. Advertisements, particularly television commercials, are often designed to be **intrusive**, which means they intrude on people's perception in order to grab attention.
- ***Interest*** A factor in crossing the selection barrier is **interest**, which means the receiver of the message has become mentally engaged in some way with the ad and the product. Ad messages are designed not only to get attention but also to hold the audience's interest long enough for the audience to register the point of the ad. That level of interest and attention is sometimes referred to as **stickiness**, particularly for websites.
- ***Relevance*** One reason people are interested in something is **relevance**, which means that the message, such as the accompanying example for the Peace Corps, connects on some personal level. The Peace Corps launched a national recruiting campaign with the theme "See yourself in someone else." It was designed to address more relevant personal issues for potential volunteers and tell them how the volunteer experience would enrich their lives.
- ***Curiosity*** Another reason people pay attention is curiosity, which results from questioning, wanting to know more, or being intrigued by something. Curiosity also may be a problem for certain types of campaigns, such as antidrug and antismoking efforts, as Professor Carson B. Wagner of Ohio University found out in his research on the government's "Just Say No" campaign. He explains,

> One weekend, my father, who is an advertising executive, and I got into a conversation about how it seemed every time a news story aired about illicit drugs, a small epidemic of drug use would ensue. Of course, there's been a lot of research done about the ways media can encourage

Photo: Courtesy of the Peace Corps

Messages that are personally relevant speak to a consumer's special interests.

drug use, but most of that is about popular media such as movies and music. We'd presume that news programs and antidrug ads that are meant to show illicit drugs in a negative light shouldn't lead people toward drugs. But, as almost any student of communication has learned, media don't tell us what to think; they tell us what to think about.

So, I decided to test the idea on antidrug ads—the most counterintuitive possibility—in a small experiment for my master's thesis. I scoured prior research, but I couldn't find anything suggesting that antidrug ads might lead to drug use. Almost all studies showed that drug attitudes became more negative. But, the psychology-of-curiosity literature suggested something else: If antidrug ads make people think drug use is widespread, they might become curious about experimenting themselves. My study found that the curiosity literature was correct.

Wagner's counterintuitive results were so compelling that he found himself on talk shows and featured in news and wire stories. He also presented his findings to Congress and was featured in an NPR interview in 2013. Since then, a large-scale government-sponsored survey examining the first five years of the government's "Just Say No" campaign uncovered similar relationships between antidrug advertising and drug use. Unfortunately, it doesn't seem to have gotten any better a reception than Wagner's study did. It's hard to convince some experts that even negative attention is still attention.

- ***Awareness*** When you are aware of something, you know that you have seen it or heard it before. In other words, **awareness** results when an advertisement makes an impression—when something registers. New product campaigns, for example, seek to create high levels of brand awareness. Brand reminder ads on billboards and Web pages are also designed to maintain a high level of awareness of familiar brands, as are logos on clothing.
- ***Recognition*** Advertisers are interested in two types of memory: **recognition**, which means people remember seeing the ad, and **recall**, which means they remember what the ad said. Recognition is a measure of perception and is used to determine awareness. Recall is a measure of understanding, which we will talk about in a later section on cognitive effects. Recognition relies on simple visuals that lock into memory, such as logos (Nike's swoosh), as well as colors (IBM's blue), jingles and sounds (Gershwin's "Rhapsody in Blue" for United Airlines), characters and key visuals (Polo's pony and the disbelieving look of the Aflac duck), and slogans (Altoids, "The Curiously Strong Mints"). Memory depends heavily on repetition to anchor an impression in the mind.

IMC Principle
People automatically integrate brand messages and experiences. Synergy occurs when all of the messages work together to create a coherent brand perception.

The Synergy Requirement We mentioned earlier Preston's idea that the end result of effective marketing communication is *an integrated perception*. We call that a brand. In campaigns that use an integrated marketing communication (IMC) approach, marketers coordinate all the marketing communication messages to create **synergy**, which means that individual messages have more impact working jointly to promote a product than they would working on their own.[14] The reason is that people automatically integrate the messages and experiences they have with a brand to create their own personal brand perception. This happens whether or not the marketer plans for integrated communicated. That's just how perception works. Sophisticated managers understand this and try to manage their communication programs so all the messages work together to create Preston's coherent brand perception.

The Subliminal Issue Before we leave the perception category, let's consider the controversial area of subliminal effects. **Subliminal** effects are message cues given below the threshold of perception. In other words, they don't register. As Professor Sheri Broyles explains in the "A Matter of Principle" feature, "By definition, *subliminal* means the stimulus is below your threshold of consciousness. The first thing to know is that if you can see something, then it isn't subliminal." The idea is that subliminal messages are designed to get past your perceptual filters by talking directly to your subconscious. In contrast to the views of most professionals and even professors in advertising, critics who believe in subliminal advertising presume such messages to be intense enough to influence behavior, and they consider it to be unfair manipulation of unaware viewers. Broyles describes the research and thinking about the idea that unseen messages can be communicated in advertising.

A PRINCIPLED PRACTICE

Ice Cubes, Breasts, and Subliminal Ads

Sheri Broyles, *University of North Texas*

For 50 years, people have been looking for secret little subliminal messages carefully hidden in advertising we see every day. It began in 1957 in a movie theater experiment when James Vicary subliminally suggested people "eat popcorn" and "drink Coca-Cola" by projecting those words at 1/3,000th of a second on the screen during a movie. News media at the time widely reported his claims that sales of popcorn and soda increased as a result. Though he later admitted these results were a hoax, it was as if Pandora had let subliminal advertising out of her box. A large majority of people have repeatedly said that they have heard of subliminal advertising (74 to 84 percent), they believe advertisers use this technique (68 to 85 percent), and they think it is effective (68 to 78 percent). Obviously, subliminal advertising continues to be an issue today.

Subliminal also has been misused to mean "suggestive" or "sexual." In the 1970s and 1980s, Wilson Bryan Key popularized this view in his books *Subliminal Seduction*, *Media Sexploitation*, and *The Clam-Plate Orgy*. He suggested that photographs were embedded (i.e., manipulated by airbrushing) with sexual or arousing images in ambiguous portions of the picture. He maintained that products ranging from alcoholic beverages to Ritz crackers used these sexual embeds. Key's self-proclaimed disciple, August Bullock, makes similar statements in his more recent book *The Secret Sales Pitch*.

There's been a continuing debate over the years about whether subliminal advertising actually exists. However, it's impossible to convince devout believers in subliminal advertising that what they *think* they see isn't there. Even more troubling is their assumption that presence implies effectiveness. Their belief is that because subliminal advertising exists—at least in their minds—it must be effective; otherwise, it wouldn't exist. Perhaps the more important question isn't whether subliminal advertising exists but whether it's an effective advertising tool. It should be noted that neither Key nor Bullock offers documentation that subliminal advertising actually works in any of the many examples in their books.

Several studies followed Vicary's theater experiment that explored whether subliminal advertising had an effect on consumers. Many different methodologies were used to test the effectiveness of subliminal stimuli. One 1959 study used early television to test subliminal persuasion. Another used a slide projector to subliminally superimpose a message. Others placed embeds in print ads. Most experiments showed no effect. Either those that did could not be replicated by the researchers or the effect was so weak that it would be canceled out by competing stimuli for the consumer's attention if it were not in a laboratory setting. There is no evidence to suggest that subliminal advertising would persuade real consumers to buy real products.

If subliminal advertising isn't effective, why are we still talking about it 50 years later? While research has repeatedly shown that subliminal advertising doesn't work, the general public hasn't been persuaded, perhaps because they haven't been exposed to the decades of research. Subliminal advertising is like an urban legend or a good conspiracy theory—it's something that people want to believe. However, whether valid or not, it does affect the public's perception of advertising. That, in turn, reduces the credibility of advertisers and their agencies. And that's a concern for everyone in the advertising industry.

By permission of American Association of Advertising Agencies, Inc.

A liquor advertising campaign showed ice cubes with shapes in them and deliberately called attention to these supposedly "subliminal" messages. Of course, they weren't subliminal because you could see the images. The whole campaign was a spoof on Key's theories.

Photo courtesy of Sheri Broyles

The Emotion or Affect Facet: Feel

Do you have favorite brands that you like—and did advertising have anything to do with why you like that brand? Can you remember any ads that you liked and why you liked them? **Affective responses** mirror our feelings about something—anger, love, fear, hate. The term *affective* describes something that stimulates wants, touches the emotions, establishes a mood, creates liking, and elicits feelings. (*Affective* refers to emotional responses; *effective* refers to how well something works.) Charles Young, president of the Ameritest research company and a member of this book's advisory board, makes the point that feelings are emotions that make it into our consciousness[15]—in other words, we are aware of them.

In the Part 2 opener, Lewis emphasized that brands have a "human" quality and the importance of connecting with consumer's innermost feelings. A lesson learned from the recent economic downturn is that positive brand communication is important. She explains, "During tough times, brands that are able to lift the mood through their communications are rewarded." But it's more than just cheery messages; she also notes that certain types of emotional messages have more resonance: "Nostalgic brands that give people a sense of tradition and security tend to thrive."

Feelings and emotions can be positive or negative. Generally, brand communication seeks to wrap a positive halo around a brand and a purchase decision. "Kevin Roberts, CEO of Saatchi & Saatchi, described the passion loyal customers feel for their favorite brands in his books Lovemarks and The Lovemarks Effect. More recently Brian Sheehan, a Saatchi executive who is now a Syracuse University advertising professor and member of this book's Advisory Board, has expanded this idea with the cases in his book, Loveworks: How the World's Top Marketers Make Emotional Connections to Win in the Marketplace."

Courtesy of Nightlife Navigators, University of Florida

SHOWCASE

The "expensive gas" poster from the Nightlife Navigators campaign intends to create a negative feeling about the financial impact of a DUI ticket. This is one of a series of ads about drinking and driving by the Adwerksstudent advertising agency at the University of Florida.

Lisa Yansura, Marketing Coordinator, Gragg Advertising, Kansas City, MO

The importance of positive responses has been institutionalized by Facebook with its famous "likes" button. Retailers are finding success with displays that allow customers to try such things as cosmetics or play with games before committing to a purchase. Entertainment has always had a positive value for commercial messages, and many commercials, such as the "imported from Detroit" campaign, have high entertainment values that drive viewers' positive responses.

Sometimes, however, a brand message arouses different emotions—dislike or anger, for example. Ralph Lauren stumbled into negative territory with its ads promoting the uniforms the firm designed for the U.S. Olympic athletes. When the word got out that the outfits were made in China, angry Americans flooded Twitter and Ralph Lauren's Facebook page with negative comments.

Some ads are designed to make you feel negative about something (smoking, bugs in your home, or a political candidate). Negative messages are often used to alert consumers to problems that need to be solved, usually by applying or using the product being advertised. The "expensive gas" ad delivers a message about the dangers of drinking and driving. In the case of irritating advertising, you may even respond by disliking a brand or an ad, which may be a sign of a failed campaign. Researchers have found that scaring people into action doesn't always work and that too much negativity can frighten people and make them turn against the brand.[16] Have you ever seen an ad that you positively disliked? How did that affect your attitude toward the brand?

Look back at the Facets Model of Effects in Figure 4.3. Notice how *perception* and emotion sit side by side at the top of the model. Although this isn't a linear process model, the perceptual process begins with perception, if a message registers at all. However, emotion is a driving factor because it is so closely related to perception. Erik du Plessis, the CEO of a global advertising research firm, makes the argument in his book *The Advertised Mind* that attention is driven by emotion.[17] He says our emotional responses to a message determine whether we pay attention. The key task of an ad, then, is initially to evoke an emotional response. It's generally thought that people respond to positive communication because they are more likely to like the subject of the message.

A question arises, however, about the power of a negative message, one that aims to generate negative responses, such as dislike and loathing. Negative political advertising, for example, is a huge area for debate. In her research, Marilyn Roberts of Zayed University in the United Arab Emirates asks a key question: "Do negative ads work?" In her work, she has found that "almost in unison political media consultants for major U.S. political parties say, 'Yes!' " And that's the reason "the frequency of attack ads in presidential campaigns has risen steadily over the past decades, regardless of party affiliation." She also points out that "exception is taken by consultants when referring to what they create as 'negative' advertising. Instead, many professionals prefer to use the term *contrast advertising* to underscore the differences between their candidate and his or her opponent."[18] A study during the 2012 presidential primary contest also found that negative advertising was more frequent and vicious than in past primaries.[19]

Factors That Drive Emotion Emotional responses are powerful not only because they drive perception but also because the ad breaks through disinterest. Furthermore, positive emotional responses drive memory as well as attention.

The affective response drivers are wants and desires, excitement, feelings, liking, and resonance. Emotion, then, causes us to "feel" something. A classic commercial that has generated positive responses for more than 40 years is the Coca-Cola "Hilltop" commercial, which shows a multiethnic group of young people singing, "I want to teach the world to sing in perfect harmony." A product of the antiwar, peace movement, Woodstock generation, the 1972 commercial touched nerves, as well as hearts, and continues to get airtime, particularly on holidays. (Check out Coca-Cola's "Hilltop" commercial on YouTube.)

- ***Wants and Desires*** "I want something" implies desire. **Wants** are driven by emotions and based on wishes, longings, and cravings—such as teaching the world to sing, which is a metaphor for peace. Impulse buying is a good example of the motivational power of wants. When you are standing in line at a store and see a display of candy bars, you may want one, but that doesn't mean you need it. It's strictly desire, and desire is driven by emotion. Consider Axe, which pioneered the new category of body spray for men in 2002. Now it boasts an astonishing $150 million in annual sales. Did guys know before 2002 that they would want scented body spray?
- ***Excitement*** A step above interest in terms of intensity of response (see the discussion of perception) is excitement, which means our emotions or passions are aroused. If we are excited about something, we are agitated or energized and more willing to participate or make a commitment.
- ***Feelings*** Our passions and feelings are addressed in a number of ways in brand messages, such as humor, love, fear, or hate. Ads that rely on arousing feelings are referred to as using **emotional appeals**. The idea that emotional appeals may have more impact than rational approaches on both attitudes and behavior was supported by a University of Florida study that analyzed 23,000 consumer responses and found that the emotional response is more powerful than cognition in predicting action.[20]
- ***Liking*** Two important affective responses to a message are liking the brand and liking the ad—and, on the opposite side, there's disliking the brand and the ad. *Liking* means having positive feelings—warmth, pleasure, enjoyment, and love. In brand communication, liking may reflect the personality of the brand or the entertainment power of the execution of the message. The assumption is that if you like the ad, then that positive feeling will transfer to the brand, and if you feel positive about the brand, you will be more likely to buy it. A classic study of advertising testing methods by the Advertising Research Foundation found that liking—both the brand and the ad—was the best predictor of consumer behavior.[21]

  Dislike, on the other hand, can lead to *aversion*, which means people avoid buying a brand because they don't like the ads or what they associate with the brand. Avoidance is also a problem with messages and media—for example, zapping commercials on television.

Principle
A positive response to an ad is important because marketers hope that liking the ad will increase liking the brand.

We don't like to see condom ads, so they aren't often found in the mass media. Negative political ads are an example of a strategy that seems to work by associating the candidate with negative qualities, but most people say they dislike these ads because they seem unfair or mean spirited.

- ***Resonance*** Effective advertisements sometimes create **resonance**, or a feeling that the message "rings true." Like relevance, messages that resonate help the consumer identify with the brand on a personal level. Resonance is stronger than liking because it involves an element of self-identification. These sympathetic vibes amplify the emotional impact by engaging a consumer in a personal connection with a brand.

The Cognition Facet: Think/Understand

How many ads that you have seen on television or noticed in print caused you to stop and think about the brand? Can you recall any instance where you learned something new about a product from an ad? Have you ever seen an ad you liked and then can't remember the name of the advertiser? Although perception and its partner, emotion, are the first effects of a brand message, messages may generate any of the other responses—cognition, association, persuasion, and behavior—nearly at the same time. For this discussion, we'll talk first about cognitive impact.

Cognition refers to how consumers search for and make sense of information as well as how they learn and understand something. It's a rational response to a message that comes from thinking something through. Some call this a left-brain approach, based on the left–right brain ways of thinking that evolved from brain hemisphere research. Right-brain thinking is presumed to be more emotional, creative, and holistic. The American Airlines ad uses the left–right brain metaphor to demonstrate the difference between a cognitive and an emotional message. Traditionally, researchers have studied information processing as a way to understand how consumers think and learn about a product.

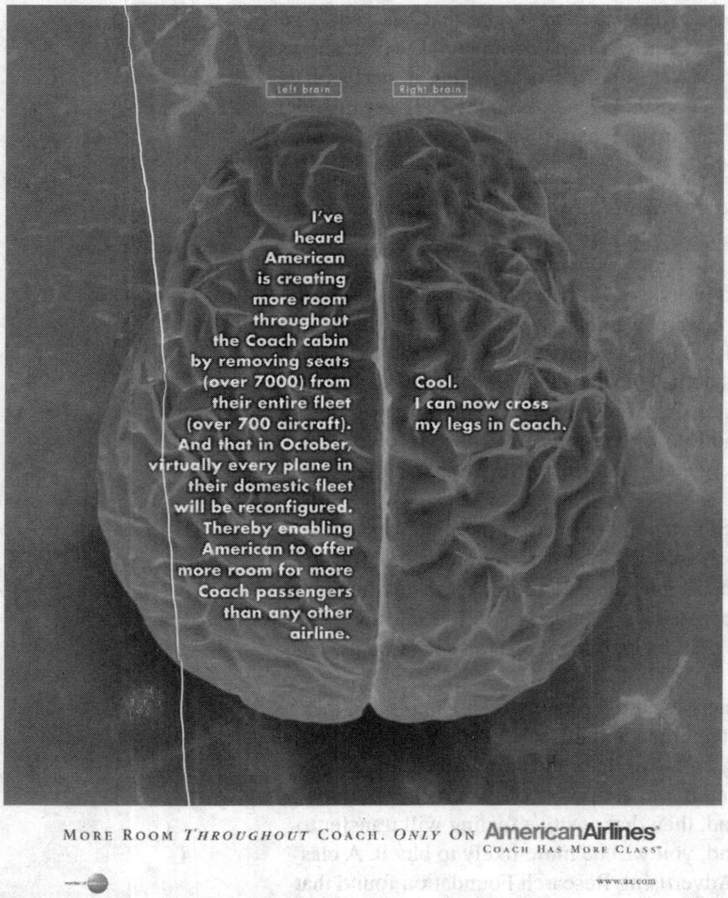

Courtesy: TM Advertising Creative: Bill Oakley

To creatively communicate its new seating in coach, American Airlines used a picture of a brain with the left side representing cognitive thinking and the right brain illustrating an affective response.

The opposite of understanding is confusion and misunderstanding, which is equally of concern to brand communicators. Sometimes the information is too complex, such as the legal texts that are required to accompany pharmaceutical advertising. Critics of children's advertising are concerned that "children under 12 cannot fully recognize and interpret bias and they're not equipped to make rational decisions about it."[22] And sometimes there is brand confusion because too many messages from too many marcom functions are not consistent with one another.

Factors That Drive Cognition Information processing—thinking things through—leads to a cognitive response. A consumer may need to know something in order to make a decision, and the information gathered in response to that need leads to understanding. The information has to be perceived and then filed in memory, but it can be recalled when needed. Advertising and other marketing communication often provide information about products, usually facts about product performance and features, such as size, price, construction, and design. In certain situations, such as the purchase of a big-ticket item (e.g., a computer or a car), consumers search for this kind of information and use it to compare one product with another.

The informative nature of brand communication is particularly important for product categories that are complex (e.g., appliances, cars, insurance, computers, and software) or that involve a high price or high risk (e.g., motorboats, vacations, and medical procedures). It is much less important for purchases bought out of habit, such as a favorite brand of soft drink, or impulse purchases made on the spot in the store. The key drivers of a consumer's cognitive response are need, cognitive learning, comprehension, differentiation, and recall.

Principle
Information processing leads to a cognitive response such as understanding—the information is filed in memory and can be recalled when needed.

- ***Need*** Brand stewards talk a lot about consumer needs and wants. Generally, **needs** are basic biological motivations (see the Imodium), but they may also be something you think about; *wants* tend to be based more on feelings and desires. In other words, when we refer to needs, we are usually talking about a message that describes something lacking in consumers' lives and that often stimulates a cognitive response. Advertisers address consumer needs through informational ads that explain how a product works and what it can do for the user—the benefits it offers to the user. For example, consumers need a virus protection program for their personal computers, but they also may need an explanation of how the program works. Complicating our understanding of needs and wants is the impact of a major event, such as the recent recession. Consider the tug between *want* (a Cadillac Escapade specially designed on GM's website to a customer's order) and *need* (a used car that offers the best value in terms of miles and price)—or a need that's simply postponed because it's of less significance that other, more compelling needs.

Photo: Feature Photo Service/Newscom

Imodium, an antidiarrheal product, uses these artsy toilets-in-a-park to call attention to a basic biological need. The port-o-potties are decorated by some of New York's top artists and located in some of the city's most visited parks.

- ***Cognitive Learning*** Consumers learn about products and brands through two primary routes: cognitive learning and conditioned learning. (We'll talk about conditioned learning in the section on association.) **Cognitive learning** occurs when a presentation of facts, information, and explanations leads to understanding. Consumers who are trying to find information about a product before they buy it are taking the cognitive learning route. This typically applies to large purchases, such as cars, computers, and major appliances. Learning is also a part of new product introductions—in recent years, we have had to learn to use computers, VCRs, the Internet, TiVo, and the iPod, and brand communication is the key tool used by marketers to teach prospective customers about these products and product innovations.
- ***Comprehension*** The process by which people understand, make sense of things, and acquire knowledge is called **comprehension**. Confusion, on the other hand, is the absence of understanding and is usually the result of logic problems. For example, it's difficult for consumers to understand why an outdoor board for the gas-guzzling Hummer would use a green marketing strategy. The headline "Thirst for adventure. Not gas." suggests a gas-efficient Hummer, and the logic doesn't follow from what people commonly know about this vehicle.
- ***Differentiation*** The consumer's ability to separate one brand from another in a product category is called **differentiation**. Distinguishing between competing brands is what happens when consumers understand the explanation of a competitive advantage. In a classic study of effective television commercials, researchers concluded that one of the most important effectiveness factors is a brand-differentiating message.[23]
- ***Recall*** We mentioned earlier that recognition is a measure of perception and that recall is a measure of learning or understanding. When you recall the ad message, you remember not only seeing the ad and, it is hoped, the brand but also the copy points, or the information provided about the brand. To recall information presented in the ad, however, you must have concentrated on it and thought about it either as the information was being presented or afterward. Thinking about it—similar to mentally rehearsing the key points—is a form of information processing that helps anchor ideas in memory and makes recall easier.

Thinking and Feeling Even though this section is on cognitive processing, note that feeling and thinking work together. Psychologist and advertising professor Esther Thorson and her colleagues have developed a *memory model of advertising* to explain how commercials are stored in memory as traces that contain bits and pieces of the commercial's message, including the feelings elicited by the message. Recall of any of those elements—especially feelings—can serve as a cue to activate memory of the commercial.[24]

Principle
In communication perception, emotion comes first, and thought comes second.

A frequent question asked by researchers is this: Which is more important in brand communication—thinking or feeling? Chuck Young, the founder of the Ameritest research company, emphasizes, "In all acts of perception and communication, emotion comes first, and thought comes second."[25] The important role of emotion in directing perception also structures

A Matter of Principle

Thought vs. Feeling

Ann Marie Barry, *Boston College*

Building a brand identity that fits the preferred self-image of the target market is a matter of designing advertising messages so that they are fully in tune with the self-identity of the consumer. To do this, advertisers need to understand basically how the mind functions, beginning with the fundamental relationship between thought and feeling.

Rational thought takes place in the *neocortex*, the most evolved and "highest" part of the brain, but feelings emanate from the *limbic system*, the cerebellum and brain stem, the most primitive part of the brain.

When we see something, the sensory path follows two distinct routes—one through emotion (to the brain's *amygdala*) and the other up to thought (the brain's neocortex). The emotional route is very fast and is geared toward survival, sending reaction signals to other parts of the brain and the rest of the body, well before the neocortex has had the chance to form a conscious thought. Emotion is the first path that perception takes. It is also the fastest, and most significant factor in perception. The whole process might be diagrammed this way:

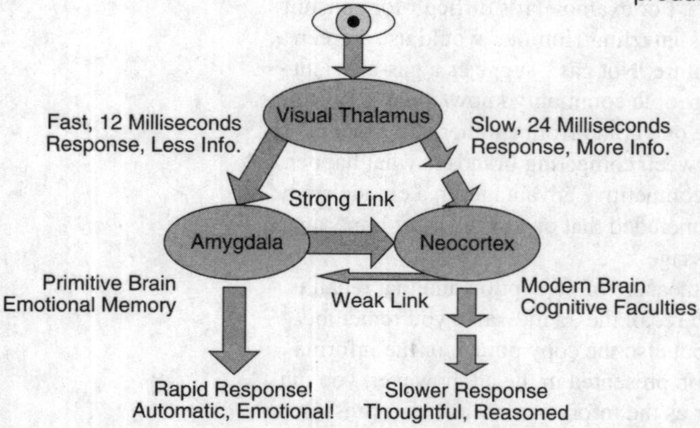

Not only do we feel before we think, but we need to feel in order to think. Unconscious emotional processing sets up thinking by producing a definite attitude. This attitude uses the memory of past experience to prepare thoughts and actions before we are even consciously aware of reacting at all. In fact, most of what we call the *thought process* in making decisions is actually trying to rationalize what we have already concluded through our emotional system. Marketers know that if they can convince us emotionally, we can rationalize away any objections by ourselves.

Descartes professed, "I think therefore I am." Today's neurologists, however, concur that we think because we feel. Advertising images can connect with consumers' self-image on a deep emotional level because neurons come together in the mind as circuits that form mental meaning, in what might best be described as a story. When you buy an Apple computer or an iPod, for example, you buy more than electronics; you buy a message about a product user that confirms you as a person. This is the story implicit in Apple's commercials—that its customers are nonconformist and very hip. It is this attitude that resonates with us emotionally when we think of Apple products and that sets up our rational decision making.

Every brand that we use in effect advertises who we are when we wear it or use it, telling people a little bit about us or just reinforcing how we feel about ourselves (or would like to feel). If the emotional appeal is missing, however, we lose a personal connection with the product or service. If the rational benefit is missing, we may not find enough reason to purchase an item where elements such as price, ease of use, or technological advantages play a major role. For an advertisement to be truly effective, the visual story implicit in it must seamlessly bring together both consumer image and brand image in a perfect integration of both thought and feeling.

our responses to brand messages, particularly those that engage us on a personal level. That, of course, completely contradicts the traditional information-processing–based models of effectiveness.

This view is supported by recent research in the neurosciences, which advertising professor Ann Marie Barry says "acknowledges the primacy of emotions in processing all communication."[26] She explains further that "perception, the process by which we derive meaning from what we see, is an elaborate symphony played first and foremost through the unconscious emotional system." Check out Barry's comments on thinking versus feeling in the "A Matter of Principle" feature.

Although researchers now recognize the significance of emotion in effective brand communication, it is important to note that the two responses of think and feel also work together. As Chuck Young explains his firms' research findings, "Images that made consumers simultaneously both *think and feel* were much more likely to be associated with the brand's current image. These same images also better fit the brand's positioning in the marketplace." And the opposite is also true. He says, "Images that engendered a thought without an emotion—or an emotion without a thought—were not associated in their memories of the brand to any significant degree."[27]

Principle
Communication that makes consumers both think and feel provides better support for a brand image; thought without emotion or emotion without thought makes it difficult to anchor the brand in memory.

The point is that brands live in the heads and hearts of users. A brand may be priced in the middle of the category, but if customers think it's high priced, then that confusing misinformation (the head) muddies the brand impression. It may create a negative feeling (the heart). The communication has to change either the head by doing a better job of explaining the price relative to the competition or the heart by making customers feel better about the value of the brand.

The Association Facet: Connect

What do you think of when you see an ad for Nike, Viagra, or Mountain Dew? The things that come to your mind, such as athletes for Nike, older men for Viagra, and teenage guys having fun for Mountain Dew, are the brands' associations. **Association** is the technique of communicating through symbolism—we might say symbolic meanings are transferred through the process of association. The transfer of meaning connects personal meanings to goods and other symbols, such as celebrities.[28]

Association is the primary tool used in brand communication and guides the process of making symbolic connections between a brand and desirable characteristics as well as people, situations, and lifestyles that cue the brand's image and personality. Chuck Young emphasizes the importance of association in creating brand images in his e-book *Branded Memory.* He defines a brand image as "the set of emotional and experiential association with the brand that is built up over time."[29]

You see association at work in brand communication in the practice of linking a brand with a positive experience, an idea, a personality type, or a lifestyle, such as Axe with cool young men or Coke with a mountaintop experience. The idea is to associate the brand with things that resonate positively with the customer. It's a three-way process: the (1) brand relates to (2) a quality that (3) customers value. Brands take on symbolic meaning through this association process. Professor Ivan Preston, in his *association model of advertising*, believes that you can explain how advertising works by understanding association.[30]

Sometimes associations can be powerful because they are unexpected. The Keebler cookie brand found a sweet spot in its partnership with the American Red Cross by encouraging consumers to donate blood. Keebler provided a much-needed sugary treat to those that did. Sometimes association can backfire as it did in a 2013 ad for Nike that featured Oscar Pistorius with a picture of the double-amputee Olympian blasting from the starting line and a headline that read, "I am the bullet in the chamber." The symbolism was tragically ironic after Pistorius was arrested for the alleged shooting of his girlfriend.

Principle
Brand communication creates brand meaning through symbolism and association. These meanings transform a generic product into a specific brand with a distinctive image and personality.

Factors That Drive Association The goal of association is to use symbolic connections to define the brand and make it distinctive. **Brand linkage** reflects the degree to which the associations and ideas presented in the message, as well as the consumer's interest, are connected to the brand and transform it from a product to a recognizable and memorable brand image. For example, an ad for BisquickHeartSmart mix shows a pancake in the shape of a heart. In this case, the brand name—BisquickHeartSmart—is easily associated with the product use—your heart and healthy pancakes.

Linking a brand with an idea in order to build a brand image can be difficult to the degree it involves cognition. In contrast to Chrysler, for example, GM reported in 2012 that its brand communication wasn't working. The reason: In spite of spending some $4 billion on marketing and communication, "GM hasn't been able to dent the perception that other brands, particularly imports, are better."[31] In contrast, Chrysler linked its brand to the idea that imported cars are better quality with a twist on that idea in its "Imported from Detroit" campaign. At the same time, GM was using such slogans as "Chevy Runs Deep," whatever that means.

The association drivers are symbolism, conditioned learning, and transformation:

- ***Symbolism*** Through association, a brand takes on a *symbolic meaning*, which means the brand stands for certain qualities. It represents something, usually something abstract. Bisquick's pancakes shaped like hearts convey the heart-healthy message symbolically. The Port of Vancouver USA business-to-business ads use symbolism to catch attention and tell a story, such as the vacancy sign in the ad analyzed earlier. Symbolism is also used on the front of Coke's Hug Me vending machine.
- ***Conditioned Learning*** Although advertisements sometimes use a cognitive strategy, they frequently are designed to elicit noncognitive associations through **conditioned learning**, the process by which a group of thoughts and feelings becomes linked to the brand through repetition of the message. Beer advertising directed at a young male audience, for example, often uses images of sporting events, beach parties, and good-looking young women. People also learn by watching others, which is called **social learning**. We learn about fashion by watching how others dress and about manners by watching how other people interact. We connect their appearance and manners to certain situations reflected in the ads.
- ***Transformation*** The result of the brand association process is transformation. **Transformation**, as originally explained by former DDB research director Bill Wells, is what happens when a product takes on meaning and is transformed from a mere product into something special. It becomes differentiated from other products in the category by virtue of its brand-image symbolism and personality cues. BisquickHeartSmart is more than just flour; it rises above the average product in the category and stands out as something unique and healthy. That transformation in a consumer's mind is a perceptual shift created by the associations cued through marcom messages.

Photo: Solent News/Newscom

This vending machine dispenses free cans of Coca Cola after you literally give it a hug. Part of the Open Happiness campaign in Singapore, it links Coke with the warm feeling of a hug in an effort to encourage public displays of affection, which are rare in that country.

Association Networks You probably had a number of associations when we asked you to think about Nike. Athletes come to mind, but so do shoes, engineering, design, the "swoosh" logo, competition, sporting events, and maybe even a fun retail experience if you have ever visited a Nike store. The association process is built on a **network of associations**, called a **knowledge structure**. Solomon, in his book on consumer behavior, describes these networks as spider webs[32] where one thought cues other thoughts. Your thoughts and feelings about the Nike brand are elements linked in your own individual pattern of associative thinking. You might say that these association networks explain how our memories work. Researchers seeking to determine the meaning of a brand will ask people to talk about their associations with a brand and to re-create these association networks in order to understand how a brand's meaning comes together as an impression in people's minds.

The Persuasion Facet: Believe

When you see ads from the "Got Milk?" campaign with celebrities sporting a milk mustache, what do you think is the objective of the advertising? Is it providing information about milk? Is it trying to connect with you on an emotional level through fear, love, envy, hunger, or some other feeling? Is it trying to get you to run down to the store and load up on milk? The real objective of these ads is to change your attitude toward milk. It aims to convince you that milk isn't just for kids and that attractive, interesting adults drink it, too.

Persuasion is the conscious intent on the part of the source to influence or motivate the receiver of a message to believe or do something. Persuasive communication—creating or changing attitudes and creating conviction—are important goals of most brand communication. An **attitude** is a state of mind—a tendency, inclination, or mental readiness to react to a situation in a given way. Since advertising rarely delivers immediate action, *surrogate* effects, such as changing an attitude that leads to a behavior, are often the goal of advertising. Attitudes are the most central factors in persuasion.

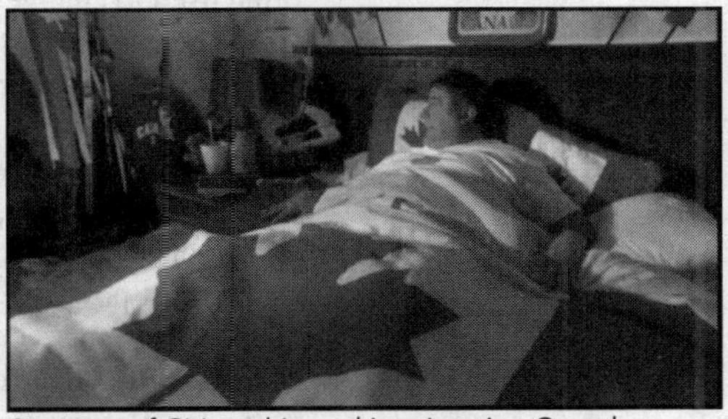

Courtesy of Citizenship and Immigration Canada

An unsuspecting but newly recognized Canadian citizen wakes up to find his bedroom has become a center of Canadian symbols.

Attitudes can be positive, negative, or neutral. Both positive and negative attitudes, particularly those embedded in strong emotions, can motivate people to action—or away from action. A negative attitude toward smoking, for example, may keep teenagers from trying cigarettes, and creating that negative attitude was the objective of the truth® campaign discussed in Chapter 1.

Attitudes are both rational and emotional. The rational element is confirmed by David Ogilvy, who says in his classic little book *Confessions of an Advertising Man*, "Very few advertisements contain enough factual information to sell the product." He was also quoted on the Advertising Hall of Fame website as saying that it needs to be informative to be persuasive.[33]

Rational *information processing* is important for certain types of ads. Consider, for example, the Canadian government's Citizenship Act, which was designed to restore citizenship to thousands of unsuspecting foreigners, many of them Americans, who were forced to renounce their Canadian citizenship when they became citizens of another country. Canada used ads on YouTube titled "Waking Up Canadian" to inform former Canadians about this situation.[34] (Check it out at www.youtube.com/watch?v=eDeDQpIQFD0.)

Principle
Brand communication employs both rational arguments and compelling emotions to create persuasive messages.

When people are convinced of something, their attitudes are expressed as **beliefs**. Sometimes attitude strategies attempt to extinguish beliefs—for example, that getting drunk is a badge of masculinity, overeating is acceptable, or racist and sexist comments are funny. Attitude change strategies often use the tools of logic and reasoning, along with arguments and counterarguments, to intensify the feelings on which beliefs are built.

Persuasion, in other words, is an area where cognitive and affective factors are interrelated—persuasion works both through rational arguments and by touching emotions in such a way that they create a compulsion to act. Negative political advertising, or attack ads, are a good example of how people form opinions at the same time as they process information that is presented within an emotional frame.

Factors That Drive Persuasion Persuasion has many dimensions, but advertisers identify the following factors to explain how persuasion affects consumers: motivation, influence, involvement, engagement, conviction, preference and intention, loyalty, and believability and credibility.

- ***Motivation*** A factor in creating a persuasive message is **motivation**. Underlying motivation is the idea that something, such as hunger or a desire to be beautiful or rich, prompts a person to act in a certain way. How strongly does someone feel about acquiring something or about taking a certain kind of action, such as applying to graduate school or signing up for the Peace Corps? This sets up a state of tension, and the product becomes a tool in achieving that goal and thus reducing the tension. A more current example of the power of motivation cropped up in the development of **carrot mobs**, a technique used by environmentalists to reward companies that support green marketing. It's a reverse boycott that uses positive action—getting large groups of people to shop at eco-friendly stores.

- ***Influence*** If you think you need to lose weight or stop smoking, how much of that decision is based on your own motivations, and how much of your motivation results from messages from others? Some people, known as **opinion leaders**, may be able to influence other peoples' attitudes and convince them of the "right" decision. The idea is that other people—friends, family, teachers, and experts such as doctors—may affect your decision making. Testimonies—from real people, celebrities (the "Got Milk?" campaign), and experts—are often used to change attitudes.

  There's even a social media site that seeks to measure influence. Called Klout, the site estimates users' online influence based on their Facebook, Twitter, Foursquare, Google+, and LinkedIn activities. A +*K* button lets users vote on whether a person identified by Klout as having clout really is influential on a certain topic. In terms of promotional communication, **bandwagon appeals**—messages that suggest that everyone is doing it—are also used to influence people's decisions. Word-of-mouth communication has always been recognized as the most powerful form of persuasion, and that's why strategies that engage influencers are so important.

- ***Involvement*** Advertisers distinguish between products, messages, and media on the basis of the level of involvement they require from the buyer. Earlier when we described reasons people don't always go through serious information processing, such as habit and impulse purchases, we were referring to their level of involvement with the product decision. **Involvement** refers to the degree to which you are engaged in attending to a message and the process you go through in interacting with a product, including responding to a message and making a decision to buy. Some products, such as cosmetics, call for a more involving process than others, say, toothpaste. Products with **high involvement** demand more from consumers who may spend considerable time and effort searching for information and thinking before making decisions. These **considered purchases** include such products as cars, computers, and houses as well as things you care about a lot like expensive clothing.

  Examples of products with **low involvement** are aspirin, paper napkins, envelopes, paper clips, and lettuce. The idea is that with some products, you don't spend much time thinking about them before you buy them. Nor do you pay much attention to their brand messages, which you may ignore or file away without much thought.

  In addition to product categories, some message strategies are more involving than others, such as dramas and humor. Likewise, various types of media are intrinsically more or less involving. Television, for example, is considered to be less involving than print, which demands more concentration from its readers than television does of its viewers—although a gripping television drama can be involving because of the power of the story line.

- ***Engagement*** The idea of **engagement** is that a consumer is more than just interested in something—that he or she is, in the words of the Advertising Research Foundation committee that investigated engagement, "turned on."[35] Participation and engagement cultivates passion and also drives people to be more involved cognitively in a brand experience. Chuck Young explains what goes on in the mind of someone engaged with a promotional message, such as a commercial, as they ask themselves questions such as the following:[34]

  "What's important here?"

  "How does this point fit with that other point?"

  "Where is this going?"

  "How do I feel about this?"

  "How is it relevant to me?"

  Engagement with a brand or message is generally a good thing, but McDonald's had one engaging social media program blow up all over the Web. The plan was to have McDonald's appear on the trend list on Twitter's home page with the **hashtag** #MeetTheFarmers that led to a series of ads with gritty farmers talking about real food born of the earth. But when viewers were led to #McDStories, a site where viewers were encouraged to continue the conversation, the site was overwhelmed with critics commenting about everything from health concerns to the "supersize-me" debate. The anti-McDonald's Twitter storm got all the media attention even if the positive comments were four to five times as frequent. In a matter of minutes, McDonald's social media director took down the #McDStories site.[35] Engagement is such an important concept for the new online media that there are companies, such as sitecore.net, that specialize in measuring it.

- ***Conviction*** Effective persuasion results in **conviction**, which means that consumers agree with a persuasive message and achieve a state of certainty—a belief—about a brand. A factor in conviction is the power of the **argument**, which uses logic, reasons, and proof to make a point and build conviction. Understanding an argument is a complex cognitive process that demands the audience "follow through" on the reasoning to understand the point and reach a conclusion.
- ***Preference and Intention*** When consumers marry belief with a **preference** for or an **intention** to try or buy a product, they are motivated by conviction. Intention can be heightened with reward strategies, such as good deals, sale pricing, and gifts. Good intentions are the motivations behind cause marketing and social responsibility. Hewlett-Packard (HP), for example, promotes its computer recycling program to increase preference for HP products by its customers. According to the company's vice president of global branding and marketing communication, the PC recycling program attracts consumers to HP products because the company assumes responsibility for recycling its old products. That's a benefit for customers and leads to higher customer satisfaction and, thus, loyalty to the HP brand.
- ***Loyalty*** Is there any brand you buy, use, or visit on a regular basis? Do you have a favorite shampoo, restaurant, or beverage? Why is that? What we are referring to when we talk about a "favorite" brand is preference but also **brand loyalty**, which we mentioned in Chapter 2. Loyalty is an attitude (respect or preference), an emotion (liking), and an action (repeat purchases). It is a response to brand communication that crosses over between thinking, feeling, and doing—a response that is built on **customer satisfaction**. If you try a product and like it, then you will be more likely to buy it again. Is there a return policy or guarantee that frees you from risk when you buy something for the first time in case you don't like it? Providing information about warranties, customer service, and technical support for technology products is an important part of preference and loyalty strategies. The idea is to reduce risk and put the customer's mind at ease. Incentives are also used in loyalty programs, such as frequent-flyer or frequent-buyer programs. In addition, social responsibility and cause marketing programs can build trust, respect, and preference that lead to loyalty.
- ***Believability and Credibility*** An important issue in persuasion is **believability**, which refers to the credibility of the arguments in a message. Puffery or unprovable claims, such as the common phrase "9 out of 10 doctors recommend . . . ," can strain believability. Related to believability is **credibility**, which is an indication of the trustworthiness of the source. **Source credibility** means that the person delivering the message, such as an expert, is respected, trusted, and believable. Believability and credibility are the two key ingredients in *trust*, which is essential to brand liking and loyalty. Trust took a hit during the recession as polls showed that people were much less likely to trust business leaders and believe that businesses would do the "right thing."[36]

  Credibility is one of the big advantages of public relations because publicity stories delivered through a supposedly unbiased news medium have higher credibility than advertising, which is seen as self-serving. Using data to support or prove a claim, for example, gives consumers a **reason to believe** the advertising. Advertising can use a credibility strategy to intensify the believability of its message. After the oil spill off the Louisiana coast, BP used advertising to say that the company was committed to cleaning up the mess. The strategy hinges on the company's credibility.

The "A Matter of Practice" feature explains how Chuck Young analyzes the impact of a brand message and identifies the key drivers of a persuasive message.

The Behavior Facet: Act/Do

We introduced loyalty in the previous section on persuasion and noted that it intersects with behavior. Behavior can involve different types of action in addition to trying or buying the

A Matter of Practice

May VW's Force Be with You

Charles Young, *President, Ameritest*

A commercial for Volkswagen's Passat called "The Force" was created by the Deutsch agency and first aired on the 2011 Super Bowl. It was ranked by most commentators as the number one commercial shown during the game.

It opens with a pint-sized Darth Vader in costume marching through the house to Star Wars music. He is seen raising his hands to engage the power of The Force on home appliances and even his dog and a doll—with no effect. When his father returns home in a new Passat, Little Darth rushes outside to use "The Force" on this new machine. As he faces the car, the engine starts, and he jumps back, triumphant at having finally found "The Force." His father is shown looking out the window after pressing the start button on the radio key.

This commercial was analyzed by Steven Sands of Sands Research using brain wave metrics. He found that it was not only the highest-performing ad of that Super Bowl but also one of the strongest commercials he's ever tested in terms of its ability to arouse viewers' brains.

I decided to test the ad using the Ameritest system, which uses information from an analysis of respondent's conscious reactions to a message. It includes classic measures of attention, branding, communication, and motivation.

Consistent with Sands's engagement ranking, we found that this ad is very strong in attracting attention, scoring in the 99th percentile of the thousands of ads we've tested. It's also significantly above the norm in motivation but below average in its brand linkage to Volkswagen.

The drivers of its attention score are its entertainment value, uniqueness, and the likability of the music. The drivers of its motivation score are its believable message and the relatability of the characters and the situation. The soft branding score is because, in part, it stretches brand perceptions, meaning the message has to work harder to achieve good top-of-mind brand scores.

In terms of brand communication, the commercial did communicate the surface meaning that the new Passat is a "fun" car. The subtext, however, was that the new Volkswagen was "surprisingly powerful." This insight led Volkswagen to adopt the tagline "The Power of German Engineering" in the next evolution of this campaign.

See VW's "Force" at *www.youtube.com/watch?v=R55e-uHQna0.*

product—for example, to visit a store, return an inquiry card, call a toll-free number, join an organization, donate to a good cause, or click on a website.

We must distinguish, however, between **direct action**, which represents an immediate response (cut out the order form and send it back by return mail), and **indirect action**, which is a delayed response (recall the message later in the store and select the brand). Advertising almost by definition is characterized by indirect action—we're seldom at the store when we hear, see, or read an ad for the store's products. Mobile advertising, which means that targeted messages are sent to people in the neighborhood through their smart phones, is one way to better link a message and action.

Principle
Advertising has delayed effects in that a consumer may see or hear an advertisement but not act on that message until later when in a store.

The "I Want You" World War I poster by artist James Montgomery Flagg is a classic example of an advertising message that was designed to create action, although visiting a recruiting station would necessarily be indirect or delayed action. This image has been used many times by other organizations to replicate the power of this compelling message.

There is also purposeless action, which became a fad in the 2000s when viral e-mail messages would generate a sudden and conspicuous gathering of people. Called **flash mobs**, these public spectacles included concerts, marriage proposals, and even a worldwide day of pillow fights. Flash mobs demonstrate the power of the Internet and buzz to engage people, involve them in something memorable, and drive them into action—even if the action is largely meaningless. Find "Puttin' on the Ritz" in Moscow on YouTube.

In terms of media use, one behavior that worries marketers is the tendency to avoid brand messages. Ad skipping, which allows viewers to skip the ads in previously recorded television programs, is available through a number of technologies, such as Dish Network's Auto Hop. Millions of television viewers do it, and the industry recognizes the need to develop better or different programming to keep its audience in place.

Factors That Drive the Behavioral Response The behavioral response involving action of some kind is often the most important goal of brand communication, particularly for tools such as sales promotion and direct marketing. Factors that drive a behavioral response include mental rehearsal, trial, buying, contacting, advocating and referrals, and prevention.

Library of Congress, LC-DIG-ppmsc-03521

CLASSIC

A highly effective poster designed to create action, this ad was used during World War I to convince young people to join the military. Most modern advertising is more subtle than this, but the motivation to inspire action is still the same.

- ***Mental Rehearsal*** The **mental rehearsal** of behaviors is made possible by showing visuals of people doing things. As Charles Young explains,[37] one of the functions of brand messages is to create virtual memories, in other words, experiences that we can imagine ourselves doing. Visualization is an imagined action but one that is the predecessor to the behaviors with which the advertiser hopes the consumer will feel comfortable and familiar.
- ***Trial*** The first step in making a purchase is often to try the product. A **trial** is important for new products and expensive products because it lets a customer use the product without initially committing to a purchase. In other words, the risk is reduced. Sales promotion is particularly good at driving trials through special price deals, sampling, and incentive programs that motivate behavior, such as a free gift when you go to a dealer to test drive a new car.
- ***Buying*** The objective of most marketing programs is sales. In advertising, sales is sometimes stimulated by the **call to action** at the end of the ad, along with information on where to purchase the product. From a customer perspective, sales means making a purchase. In customer-focused marketing programs, the goal is to motivate people to try or buy a certain brand. But in some marketing programs, such as those for nonprofit organizations, the marketing program may be designed to encourage the audience to sign up, volunteer, or donate. For many managers, however, sales is the gold standard for effective advertising. They feel that, even if they are funny, memorable, or entertaining, ads are failures if they don't help sell the brand. The problem is that it may be difficult to prove that a brand communication message is the one factor in the marketing mix that delivered the sales. It could be the price, the distribution, the product design and performance, or some combination of the marketing mix elements. Effectiveness programs, such as the London-based Institute of Practitioners Award program, encourage advertisers to use research to prove that it was, in fact, the advertising that actually drove the sales.
- ***Contacting*** Trying and buying may be the marketer's dream response, but other actions also can be important measures of an advertisement's behavioral effectiveness. Responding by making contact with the advertiser can be an important sign of effectiveness. Initiating contact is also valuable, particularly in IMC programs designed to maintain brand relationships

by creating opportunities for customer-initiated dialogue, such as encouraging customers with a complaint, compliment, or suggestion to contact the company.

- ***Advocating and Referrals*** One of the behavioral dimensions of brand loyalty is **advocacy**, or brand fans speaking out on a brand's behalf and referring to it when someone asks for a recommendation. Contacting other people is a valuable response, particularly when a satisfied customer brings in more business for the brand by providing testimonials to friends, family, and colleagues on behalf of the brand. In terms of the impact of **referrals**, when a satisfied customer recommends a favorite brand, this form of word of mouth can be incredibly persuasive, more so than advertising, which is seen as self-serving. Apple Computer's success is credited to its passionate customers who, as evangelists for the brand, spread the word among their friends and coworkers. Social media has intensified the importance of fans advocating on behalf of a brand to their friends.

  This *advocacy level*, which Smith and Cross describe in their book *Customer Bonding*,[38] represents the highest form of a brand relationship. A recommendation to buy a specific brand is the ultimate test of the bond between consumers and their favorite brands. And the opposite—brand aversion—can be disastrous if the dissatisfied customer shares his or her dislike with other people.
- ***Prevention*** In some social action situations, brand messages are designed to deter behaviors, such as clean-air campaigns that hope to reduce car use. This is a complicated process that involves *counterarguing* by presenting negative messages about an unwanted behavior and creating the proper incentives to stimulate the desired behavior. Because the effects are so complicated, the impact of such campaigns is not always clear. Earlier in the discussion of perception, we mentioned the national "Just Say No" campaign, which claims to have had an impact on teenagers' drug use. However, as Carson B. Wagner discovered, sometimes antidrug advertising can boomerang because it calls attention to the unwanted behavior.

The Power of Brand Communication

The six-factor Facets Model of Effects that we've been describing is our answer to the question of how brand communication works. These six factors, when they work together, can create a coherent brand perception. You should remember two things about how this model works: (1) the effects are interdependent, and (2) they are not all equal for all brand communication situations. In terms of impact, we recognize that different product situations call for different strategies. Sometimes more emphasis in a message strategy needs to be placed on emotion or image building than on reasons and facts.

In terms of effects interaction, we suggested in previous discussions that cognitive and emotional responses work together. Consider that memory is a function of both attention (the perception facet) and emotion (the affective facet). As du Plessis explains, "What we pay attention to, we remember."[39] The stronger the emotional hook, the more likely we'll attend to and remember the message. Even informative messages can be made more memorable if they are presented with an emotional story. Furthermore, recent ideas about how memory works suggest that an effective brand message helps consumers remember their best moments with a product, so it brings back emotion-laden brand experiences that encompass both feelings and thoughts.

Strong and Weak Effects

Some professionals believe that sales is the only true indication of message effectiveness. The power of advertising, for example, is determined by its ability to motivate consumers to buy a brand. Some even believe advertising is so powerful that it can motivate people to buy things they don't need, a perception counterargued by the American Association of Advertising Agencies.

Principle
Effects other than sales are important because they lead to long-term brand relationships.

Others, including the authors of this textbook, believe that communication effects include a wide range of consumer responses to a message—responses that may be just as important as sales because they lead to the creation of such things as brand liking and a long-term brand relationship.

This debate over the power of brand communication is analyzed in terms of "strong" and "weak" effects.

This debate is the source of controversy in the analysis of what message effectiveness really represents. The sales-oriented philosophy suggests advertising can move the masses to action. Those who believe in the "strong" theory reason along these lines:

> *Advertising increases people's knowledge and changes people's attitudes, and therefore it is capable of persuading people who had not formerly bought a brand to buy it, at first once and then repeatedly.*

In contrast, those who believe in the "weak" theory of advertising think that advertising has only a limited impact on consumers and is best used to reinforce existing brand perceptions rather than change attitudes:

> *Consumers are not very interested in advertising. The amount of information communicated is limited. Advertising is not strong enough to convert people whose beliefs are different from those in the ad, overcome their resistance, or change their attitudes. Most advertising is more effective at retaining users rather than converting new ones.*

By permission of American Association of Advertising Agencies, Inc.

The "strong effects" view of advertising is parodied in this ad by the American Association of Advertising Agencies, which has created a long-running campaign to explain and defend advertising.

These differences explain why some experts believe that communication effects, such as emotion, knowledge, and persuasion, are merely "surrogate" effects—communication effects that can be measured more easily than sales but are less important to marketing managers. Others believe these communication effects are important in and of themselves because of what they contribute to brand strength.

Complicating the issue is the recognition that the impact of traditional advertising is seldom immediate. In other words, advertising is a victim of **delayed effects**; that is, messages are seen and heard at one time (at home on the television, in the car on the radio, or in the doctor's office in a magazine ad) and may or may not come to mind at a later date when you are in a purchase situation (in a store or in a car looking for a place to eat). Advertisers must keep the delayed effects problem in mind when relying on the "surrogate effects," such as attention, interest, motivation, and memory to bring a message to mind days or weeks later.

Long-term research by retired Syracuse professor John Philip Jones, who worked for many years at the J. Walter Thompson advertising agency, using extensive industry data, proves that there is a link between advertising and consumer behavior and that advertising can trigger sales. However, his research also led him to conclude that only 41 percent of advertising actually works in terms of producing sales.[40]

The problem has always been understanding *how it works* and, in many cases, *how it doesn't work.* The important conclusion to the bigger question about how brand messages work is that we know that advertising (and other marketing communication) does work when it's carefully planned and executed and it can work in a variety of ways. It may not work in every situation, and every ad may not be equally effective, but if it's done right, then brand communication can have impact on consumer responses. That's why the Effie awards and other award shows that recognize effectiveness are so valuable.

If you are interested in reading more about how advertising and other marketing communication work in order to answer questions like that, then see the "Practical Tips" feature by Professor Sheri Broyles at www.pearsonglobaleditions.com/Moriarty and consult some of the fascinating books that have been written about this industry, including Bob Garfield's *The Chaos Scenario: Amid the Ruins of Mass Media the Choice for Business Is Stark: Listen or Perish.*

An excerpt from this provocative book can be found at the end of the interview transcript at www.npr.org/templates/story/story.php?storyid=111623614.

Looking Ahead

This chapter focused on the effects of brand communication. In other words, how does the consumer relate to the brand and respond to the brand message. In many cases, there is little or no connection because the brand, and/or the message, is irrelevant to that particular consumer. Women, for example, are less interested in shaving cream messages than are men, unless it's a product designed specifically for women, which is the strategy used by shaving cream manufacturers to create relevance for women.

The point is that many consumers, particularly young people, are constantly creating and adjusting their self-images. If a brand message connects, it probably does so because it connects with this innate search for personal identity. As Charles Young explains, "The mind of the consumer can be thought of as being continuously engaged in the process of defining the self and orienting it with respect to the outside world." Brand communication is just one small piece in the personal identity puzzle. He explains, "A brand's image is constructed in relationship to the consumer's concept of self."[41] The next chapter is on consumer insight and consumer behavior, which leads to targeting and segmenting the audience for a brand message.

It's a Wrap

Finding Chrysler's Heart and Soul

In this chapter, you've become acquainted with the tools for dissecting a brand communication campaign. You learned about the Facets Model of Effects and applied it to Chrysler's "Imported from Detroit" campaign.

To describe the impact of this turnaround campaign, Chrysler's chief executive, Sergio Marchionne, addressed 700 Chrysler dealers:

> "Those who have lived through difficulties and have seen the dark days of desperation know that the only way to get through them is by finding the values that are important in life; rediscovering a sense of belonging to a project, a community, a nation; embracing hope; looking ahead; and taking your destiny into your own hands. If Chrysler—a company that was practically sentenced to death by the press, the financial world, and the public at large—was able to do it, then there's hope for everyone."

Marchionne offers an excellent insight into effective brand communication, as well as a truth about selling automobiles: It must connect to consumers emotionally.

Indeed, Chrysler was resurrected from the brink of collapse. It repaid the government loans six years early and made a turnaround from millions of dollars in losses in 2008 to an 18 percent revenue gain announced in 2012. Although Chrysler's turnaround cannot be attributed solely to the ad campaign, it played a significant role. The Super Bowl commercial featuring Eminem was the heart of the campaign. It did what ads are supposed to do: It generated a lot of "super buzz" (i.e., a lot of positive attention), and sales skyrocketed, contributing significantly to the company's sales growth. When the Super Bowl commercial ran, marketing researchers noted a dramatic spike in online shopping for the model. To date, the Eminem commercial garnered more than 15 million hits on YouTube, demonstrating the power of communication to attract attention for a brand.

One of the Effie judges declared that this campaign deserved to win the Grand Effie award because it "sold the product, the category, and the city." Another judge said that the campaign, "gave the brand its soul back."

Logo: Courtesy of Chrysler Group LLC

Key Points Summary

1. **How does marketing communication work as a form of both mass communication and interactive communication?** By analyzing advertising as mass communication, we have a model for explaining how commercial messages work. In traditional mass media advertising, consider that the *source* typically is the advertiser assisted by its agency, and the *receiver* is the consumer who responds in some way to the message. The *message* is the advertisement or other marketing communication tool. The *medium* is the vehicle that delivers the message; in advertising, that tends to be newspapers and magazines in print, radio and television in broadcasting, the Internet, and other forms of out-of-home vehicles, such as outdoor boards and posters. In integrated marketing communication, the media are varied and include all points of contact where a consumer receives an impression of the brand. *Noise* is both external and internal. *External noise* in advertising includes consumer trends that affect the reception of the message as well as problems in the brand's marketing mix and clutter in the channel. *Internal noise* includes personal factors that affect the reception of the message. If the communication process fails to work and the consumer does not receive the message as intended by the source, then the communication effort is ineffective. Interactive communication is two way, such as a dialogue or conversation, and the source and receiver change positions as the message bounces back and forth—the source becomes the listener, and the receiver becomes the sender. Interactive also introduces the idea that consumers may initiate the conversation and, furthermore, that brand communication can occur within a network of social communication among friends.
2. **How did the idea of advertising effects develop, and what are the problems in traditional approaches to advertising effects?** The most common explanation of how advertising works is referred to as AIDA, which stands for attention, interest, desire, and action. This model in all of its subsequent forms is described as a hierarchy of effects because it presumes a set of steps that consumers go through in responding to a message. A different approach, referred to as think/feel/do, recognizes that different marketing communication situations generate different patterns of responses. Two problems are inherent in these traditional approaches: (1) the idea of predictable steps and (2) missing effects, particularly those that govern other ways people respond to brand messages.
3. **What is the Facets Model of Effects, and how does it explain how brand communication works? What are the key facets of brand communication effectiveness?** The authors believe that marketing communication works in six key ways: It is designed to help consumers (1) see and hear the message (perception), (2) feel something for the brand (emotional or affective response), (3) understand the point of the message (cognitive response), (4) connect positive qualities with the brand (association), (5) believe the message (persuasion), and (6) act in the desired ways (behavior). All of these work together to create a brand perception and create the desired consumer response.

Key Terms

advocacy, p. 146
affective response, p. 134
AIDA, p. 127
argument, p. 143
association, p. 139
attention, p. 122
attitude, p. 141
awareness, p. 132
bandwagon appeals, p. 142
beliefs, p. 141
believability, p. 143
brand linkage, p. 139
brand loyalty, p. 143
call to action, p. 145
carrot mobs, p. 142
channels of communication, p. 123
clutter, p. 124
cognition, p. 136
cognitive learning, p. 137
comprehension, p. 137
conditioned learning, p. 140
considered purchase, p. 142
conviction, p. 143
credibility, p. 143
customer satisfaction, p. 143
decode, p. 123
delayed effects, p. 147
differentiation, p. 137
direct action, p. 144
effects, p. 127
emotional appeals, p. 135
encode, p. 123
engagement, p. 142
exposure, p. 131
feedback, p. 93
flash mob, p. 144
hashtags, p. 142
hierarchy of effects, p. 127
high involvement, p. 142
impacts, p. 127
indirect action, p. 144
intention, p. 143
interactive communication, p. 124
interest, p. 131
intrusive, p. 131
involvement, p. 142
knowledge structure, p. 140
low involvement, p. 142
mental rehearsal, p. 145
message, p. 123
motivation, p. 141
needs, p. 137
network of associations, p. 140
noise, p. 123
objectives, p. 127
opinion leaders, p. 142
perception, p. 130
persuasion, p. 141
preference, p. 143
reason to believe, p. 143
recall, p. 132
receiver, p. 123
recognition, p. 132
referrals, p. 146
relevance, p. 131

resonance, p. 136
selective attention, p. 131
selective perception, p. 130
semiotics, p. 126
SMCR model, p. 123
social learning, p. 140
source, p. 123
source credibility, p. 143
stickiness, p. 131
subliminal, p. 132
synergy, p. 132
think/feel/do model, p. 127
transformation, p. 140
trial, p. 145
wants, p. 135

Review Questions

4-4. What are the key components of a communication model, and how do they relate to brand communication?

4-5. What is the difference between interactive communication and mass communication?

4-6. In relation to the Facets Model of Effects, discuss the factors driving perception and explain how they are related.

4-7. Explain the difference between recall and recognition. What facet does each represent?

4-8. Can we reflect on the elements of Facets Model of Effects as being interdependent? Would they all have the same effect when applied in any situation?

4-9. What are the effects of advertisements on a brand? How do ads influence consumer behavior and consumer preferences?

Discussion Questions

4-10. This chapter identifies six major categories of effects or consumer responses. Find an ad in this book that you think is effective overall and explain how it works, analyzing the way it cultivates responses in these six categories.

4-11. Eva Proctor is a planner in an agency that handles a liquid detergent brand that competes with Lever's Wisk. Eva is reviewing a history of the Wisk theme "Ring around the Collar." In its day, it was one of the longest-running themes on television, and Wisk's sales share indicated that it was successful. What is confusing Eva is that the Wisk history includes numerous consumer surveys that show consumers found "Ring around the Collar" to be a boring, silly, and irritating advertising theme. Discuss why Wisk was such a popular brand even though its advertising campaign was so disliked?

4-12. You have been asked to participate in a debate in your office about three different views on advertising effects. Your office has the assignment to introduce a new electric car. A copywriter says informing consumers about the product's features is most important in creating effective advertising. An art director argues that creating an emotional bond with consumers is more important. One of the account managers says that the only advertising performance that counts is sales and that the message ought to focus on that. Your client wants to be single-minded and tells you to pick one of these viewpoints to guide the new marketing communication. Develop a position on one side or the other and discuss your point of view.

4-13. You are a team member in the social responsibility department, and your group has been assigned the task of planning and developing an "anti-drug" campaign to educate teenagers about the dangers and consequences of drug addiction.

Discuss the challenges facing and arguments against such campaigns. What would you suggest to avoid any boomerang effects of your advertisements, which will include the display of photos and illustrations about drugs, addicts, and drug paraphernalia?

Take-Home Projects

4-14. *Portfolio Project:* From current magazines, identify one advertisement that has exceptionally high stopping power (attention), one that has exceptionally high pulling power (interest), and one that has exceptionally high locking power (memory). Make photocopies of these ads to turn in. Which of them are mainly information, and which are mainly emotional and focused on feelings? Which are focused on building a brand or creating associations? Do any of them do a great job of creating action? Choose what you believe to be the most effective ad in the collection. Why did you choose this one, and what can you learn from it about effective advertising?

4-15. ***Mini-Case Analysis:*** We discussed some aspects of the "Imported from Detroit" campaign for the Chrysler turnaround in the chapter. Briefly summarize the key decisions behind this campaign. Now apply the facets model to analyze how the campaign worked and explain your conclusions about what did or didn't make this an effective campaign. Write a short analysis (no more than one double-spaced page) that explains your thinking.

TRACE North America Case

Multicultural Communication Effectiveness

Read the TRACE case in the Appendix before coming to class.

4-16. Explain how brand communication works in the case of the "Hard to Explain, Easy to Experience" campaign.

4-17. How could you strengthen the target audience's participation in the campaign?

4-18. Analyze the campaign in terms of the Facets Model of Effects. Based on this model, what might be done to strengthen the campaign's desired effect?

CHAPTER

5 Segmenting and Targeting the Audience

Image courtesy of Ogilvy & Mather: Janet Kestin; Nancy Yonk; Tim Piper; Mike Kirkland; Aviva Groll; Coby Shuman

It's a Winner

Campaign
Dove's Campaign for Real Beauty

Company
Unilever

Agency
Ogilvy & Mather

Award
Grand Effie; Grand Prix, Cannes International Advertising Festival, Ad Age's Best Non-TV Campaigns of the Decade, Festival of Media Awards

CHAPTER KEY POINTS

1. **How does the consumer decision process work?**
2. **What cultural, social, psychological, and behavioral influences affect consumer responses to advertising?**
3. **How does targeting work and how is it different from segmenting?**
4. **What characteristics are used to segment markets and target consumers?**

Dove Audiences Redefine Beauty

So far, you've read a lot about what makes brand communication effective. At the beginning of this book, we said that the most basic and important principle that should guide the practice of marketing communication stressed the importance of understanding your brand. So far, you've seen examples of companies that have done that exceptionally in the opening case stories for each chapter, such as Old Spice and McDonald's, and this chapter's opener, the Dove "Campaign for Real Beauty." As these cases demonstrate, a second fundamental principle of successful communication is the ability to understand how best to connect with the consumer.

Unilever's campaign for Dove, which won a Grand Effie and Festival of Media Award for "branding bravery," showcases great advertising that recognized a truth held by consumers and then connected on a personal level with those consumers. The "Campaign for Real Beauty" touched a nerve and punctured the cultural obsession with stick-thin bodies and Barbie doll images. The Dove campaign was risky because it sought to literally redefine beauty in advertising and to acknowledge a change in the way women see themselves. It could have been a bomb, but it was a winner because it spoke to every woman's need to look and feel her best without promising or reinforcing impossible standards of beauty.

Unilever commissioned research that eventually drove the marketing campaign. Some startling statistics from the study included these findings:

- Only 4 percent of the respondents believed they were beautiful.
- Although 80 percent of women agree that every woman has something about her that is beautiful, they do not see their own beauty.

Here's how the Dove "Campaign for Real Beauty" unfolded.

Dove recognized it needed to reach every woman, and to do that strategically, it placed messages in many different media. The message of the Dove "Campaign for Real Beauty" provided a deliberate contrast with that of the competition in beauty and women's magazines like *Glamour*, *Allure*, and *Vogue*.

Dove didn't ignore broadcast media, however—it even ran an ad during the Super Bowl. Dove established a website (www.campaignforrealbeauty.com), which urges a boost in self-esteem by defying stereotypes that define beautiful as perfect—and skinny. Part of the campaign, a Web video titled *Evolution*, was a viral phenomenon that reached millions. Outdoor and transit advertisements were plastered on billboards and buses to generate public debate.

A similar strategy was used in 2007 to launch Dove's ProAge line, which continued the counterintuitive strategy by celebrating older women with their silver hair, wrinkles, and age spots. Dove scored another viral megahit with "Real Beauty Sketches" in 2013, using a law-enforcement sketch artist to demonstrate that women see themselves as less beautiful than strangers do.

To launch Dove's new Nourishing Oil Care line for hair, Dove Canada extended the celebration of real women in its contemporary "Singin' in the Rain" campaign. Real women blogged about beauty and showcased their beautiful frizz-free hair as they sang and danced in a video shot in the rain. The social media effort was supported by paid media and included a partnership with The Weather Network, where ads reminded viewers that on "rainy days" or "humid days like today," the product worked to keep hair frizz-free.

Although the U.S. culture is one that worships physical perfection, Dove is trying valiantly to broaden that definition. Is the definition of beauty universal? Does this message translate effectively to all women? Look for Professor Tsai's explanation elsewhere in this chapter to discover why the Dove campaign flopped in China. At the end of the chapter, you'll read about the results of the Dove efforts.

Sources: "Singin' in the Rain" Effie Awards published case study, www.effie.org, July 2012; Effie brief supplied by Ogilvy & Mather; "Dove Campaign for Real Beauty Case Study: Innovative Marketing Strategies in the Beauty Industry," June 2005, www.datamonitor.com; Molly Prior, "Most Innovative Ad Campaign: Dove Campaign for Real Beauty," *Women's Wear Daily* 190, no. 122 (December 9, 2005): 36–39; Ann-Christine Diaz, "Book of Tens: Best Non-TV Campaigns of the Decade," December 14, 2009, http://adage.com; Michael Bush, "Unilever Wins Two Awards for Axe, Dove Media Campaigns," April 20, 2009, http://adage.com. www.unilever.com. www.dove.us.

The success of brand communication, such as Dove's "Real Beauty" campaign, hinges on a critical consumer insight that gives direction to the advertising. By recognizing that the cultural obsession with stick-thin models was impacting women's self-image, Dove was able to make the argument that real women were beautiful, too. This chapter explores influences on consumers' behavior, what motivates them as they make purchasing decisions, and how these factors help define groups of people who might profitably be targeted with marketing communication or advertising messages.

Photo by Derek Alexander Hall @white_canvas Used with permission of Nestlé

You have to understand the needs and wants of people to find the right prospect for a message at the right time.

Starting the Conversation

There are more than 315 million people in the United States, not all of whom are in the market for every product and every service. For every brand, some are more likely to be interested than others. How do you find them, and then how do you start the conversation with them? The point is that messages cost money both to send and to receive. Ideally, a brand conversation occurs with customers and prospective customers, and money is not wasted on others who aren't in the market. So how do you find those people?

As Regina Lewis explained in the Part 1 opener, communication begins by knowing everything possible about a brand's consumers, then speaking to them with a tone and message that resonates emotionally with what moves them, like a candy bar when you're sitting on a bench. Then we identify the best prospects by segmenting the market and targeting the most likely audience.

Let's begin with some ideas about consumer decision making that relates to the topics we discussed in Chapter 4.

How Do Consumers Make Brand Decisions?

The traditional view of consumer decision making, which is similar to the classic AIDA-based model of message impact that we discussed in Chapter 4, is based on a linear, information-processing approach. It suggests that most people follow a decision process with fairly predictable steps: (1) *need recognition*—the goal of brand communication at this stage is to activate or stimulate this need; (2) *information search*—marcom messages help the search process by providing information that is easy to find and remember; (3) *evaluation* of alternatives—brand communication helps sort out products on the basis of tangible and intangible features; (4) *purchase decision*—in-store promotions, such as packaging, point-of-purchase displays, price reductions, banners and signs, and coupon displays affect help with this purchase decision; and (5) *postpurchase evaluation*—guarantees, warranties, and easy returns are also important for reducing the fear of a purchase that goes wrong.

This set of steps is hierarchical and suffers from the limitations we discussed in Chapter 4; however, it is useful in analyzing how consumers make decisions about certain types of major purchases, such as your choice of a college or university. But there are other paths to brand decisions.

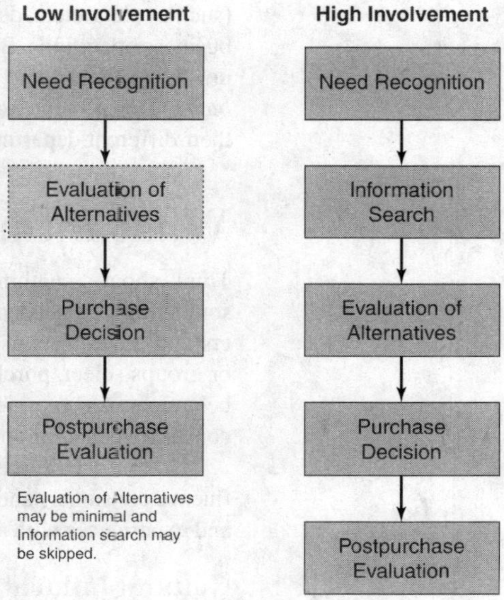

FIGURE 5.1
Low and High Involvement Decisions
The decision processes people use for low- and high-involvement products are quite different. What have you purchased recently that could be considered low- or high-involvement products? How did your decision process compare to these models?

Paths to a Brand Decision

The think/feel/do model of consumer response to a message can also be used to analyze various ways consumers make decisions. The amount of information needed, for example, varies between low-involvement and high-involvement situations and products (see Figure 5.1).

The chart below summarizes six ways consumers make decisions relative to their need for information—note how the first step indicates whether the consumer thinks about the decision first, makes a decision based on feelings (feel), or just buys something without much thought (do).

Path	Goal	Example	Communication Objective
Think/feel/do	Learning, interest	Computer game, CD, DVD	Provide information, emotion
Think/do/feel	Learning, understanding	College, a computer, a vacation	Provide information, arguments
Feel/think/do	Needs	A new suit, a motorcycle	Create desire
Feel/do/think	Wants	Cosmetics, fashion	Establish an emotional appeal
Do/feel/think	Impulse	A candy bar, a soft drink	Create brand familiarity
Do/think/feel	Habit	Cereal, shampoo	Remind of satisfaction

The point is that the path to a decision depends on the type of product and the buying situation. If you're hungry (feeling drives the decision), you grab a candy bar without much information search. If you try a sample product and like it (behavior is the driver), then you may buy the product without much evaluation of alternatives. In other words, not all responses begin with thinking about a product, nor do they follow the same route to a decision.

In business-to-business (B2B) marketing, businesses buy goods and services for two basic reasons: (1) they need ingredients for the products they manufacture, and (2) they need goods (such as computers, desks, and chairs) and services (legal, accounting, and maintenance) for their business operations. Buying decisions are often made by committees on behalf of the people who use the products, and the actual purchase is negotiated by a specialist in that category called a *buyer*. Department stores, for example, have a team of buyers who select the merchandise for their different departments.

What Influences Consumer Decisions?

Think about something you bought last week. How did the purchase process happen? Was it something you needed or just something you wanted? These are the kinds of questions marketers and advertisers ask about their customers. **Consumer behavior** describes how individuals or groups select, purchase, and use products as well as the needs and wants that motivate these behaviors. As we proceed through this chapter, keep asking yourself questions about your own consumer behavior and that of your friends and family.

Before we segment markets and target audiences, let's consider the various factors that influence consumers and their decisions: their cultural affinities, family and friends, personal needs, and experiences with a brand. Figure 5.2 is a general model the influences on consumer behavior.

Cultural Influences

Marketing communication that grabs people's attention, sticks in their minds, and moves them to act often builds on or confronts deep-seated cultural values. **Culture** is made up of tangible

FIGURE 5.2
Influences on Consumer Decision Making

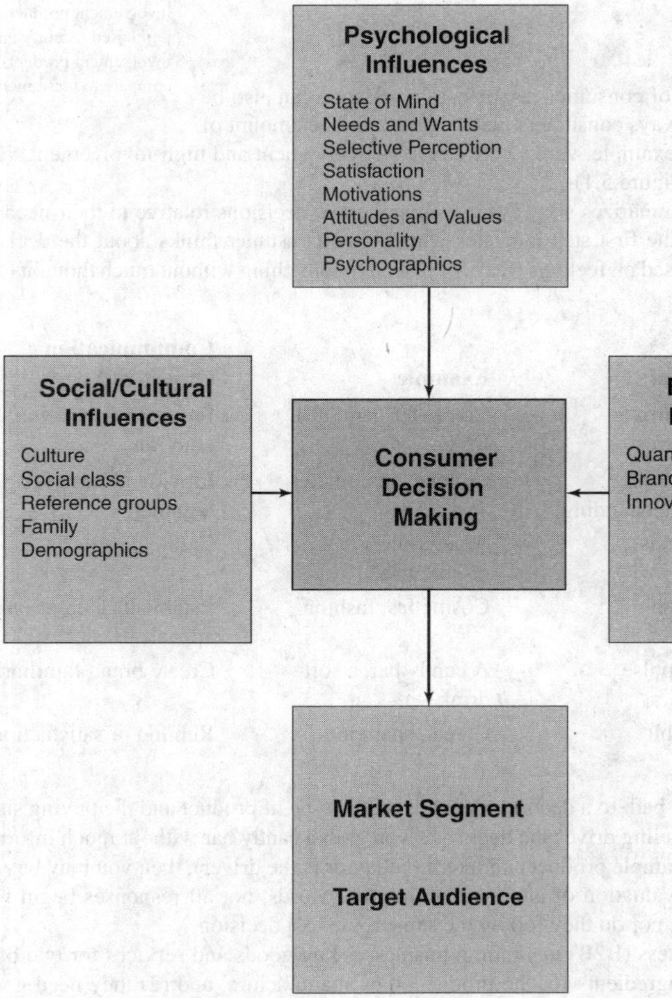

items (art, literature, buildings, furniture, clothing, and music) and intangible concepts (history, knowledge, laws, morals, customs, and even standards of beauty) that together define a group of people or a way of life. Cultural values are learned and passed on from one generation to the next. Culture generally is seen as providing a deep-seated context for marketing communication, but popular culture—what we see on television, sports, fashion, and music, among other areas—is dynamic.

Norms and Values The boundaries each culture establishes for "proper" behavior are **norms**, which are simple rules we learn through social interaction that specify or prohibit certain behaviors. The source of norms is our cultural **values**, which represent our underlying belief systems. In the United States, we value freedom, independence, and individualism; in other countries, particularly some Asian and Latin countries, people value families and groups more than individualism. Of course, there are some universals—most people value good health.

Values are few in number and hard to change. Advertisers strive to understand the underlying **core values** that govern people's attitudes and guide their behavior. A message's primary appeal aims to match the core values of the brand to the core values of the audience. Here are 10 basic core values:

1. A sense of belonging
2. Excitement
3. Fun and enjoyment
4. Warm relationships
5. Self-fulfillment
6. Respect from others
7. A sense of accomplishment
8. Security
9. Self-respect
10. Thrift

Thrift and frugality were hallmarks of the recession of the late 2000s, and a Harris Poll found that Americans tightened their belts, saved more, spent less, and borrowed less. The spendthrift mind-set subsequently moved to Europe as consumers began to scrimp under the pressure of sick economies, increasing unemployment, and austerity budgeting.[1]

Cross-Cultural Factors International or global marketing programs also have to consider multicultural differences that might derail communication. Dutch scholar Geert Hofstede insists that the impact of national culture on consumption patterns is huge and should be accommodated in marketing and advertising strategies. Based on a classic study of 116,000 IBM employees around the world, Hofstede found that the American values of taking initiative, personal competency, and rugged individualism are not universal values and that some cultures prize collective thinking and group norms rather than independence.

Working with Hofstede's research and theories, Marieke de Mooij, a cross-cultural communication researcher and consultant, developed a set of principles for cross-national marketing communication.[2] One conclusion is that there is no one universal model for information processing—in the collectivistic cultures of the south of Europe, people do not search for information in a conscious way as do those in the north of Europe. Instead, information is gathered through social communication with friends and family. Her research also discredited the idea of a universality of emotions finding that both expression and recognition of emotions vary across cultures. Likewise, personality cues are difficult—people in different countries attribute different personality traits to successful global brands. Furthermore, consumers attribute personalities to brands that fit their own cultural values, not the values of the producer.

An example of how difficult it is to manage brand communication across cultures comes from Professor Sunny Tsai, who described in the "A Matter of Principle" feature how the Dove "Real Beauty" campaign was reworked for Taiwanese consumers. The point is that it may be necessary to localize a campaign to appeal to audiences in a different culture.

Corporate Culture The concept of culture applies to B2B marketing as well as business-to-consumer marketing. **Corporate culture** is a term that describes how companies operate.

A Matter of Principle

"There Are No Ugly Women, Only Lazy Ones": Why Dove's Real Beauty Campaign Flopped in Taiwan

Wanhsiu Sunny Tsai, *School of Communication, University of Miami*

Against the cultural backdrop of airbrushed supermodel perfection, Dove's "Campaign for Real Beauty" uses images of "real" women of different ages, races, and body shapes to empower female consumers. The campaign has won major awards and contributed to Dove's double-digit sales growth in North America and Europe.

Dove's international campaigns feature native models and address local beauty myths. For example, its pan-Asian campaign challenged the ideals of fair skin and larger eyes. However, consumer surveys and sales data revealed that women in Chinese societies were unmoved by the message, and Dove had to drop its ad campaign in the pan-Asian market.

As an international scholar, I was intrigued by this unexpected apathy toward the Dove campaign, and I visited Taiwan to conduct in-depth interviews with female consumers there. These women told me they did not think of beauty media as promoting out-of-reach illusions; in fact, they appreciated glamorous images for their entertainment, aesthetic, and even fantasy value. They also expressed a strong desire for self-improvement, reinforced by beauty magazines, television shows, and websites that featured women with common appearance "flaws" being transformed into glamour girls. The step-by-step instructions accompanying these makeovers assured consumers that high standards of beauty could indeed be achieved.

Every participant mentioned a popular Taiwanese saying, "There are no ugly women, only lazy ones." The cultural belief that any woman can be beautiful—if she tries hard enough—rendered Dove's message of embracing one's natural beauty irrelevant to local consumers' desires and concerns. The intended message of challenging beauty stereotypes was lost on many participants, who only wanted to know how the product could *improve* their skin. Lesson learned: cultural differences really can make a difference in how an ad will be received.

Dove eventually found a solution for the Chinese version of its "real women" campaign by partnering with the Chinese version of the "Ugly Betty" program based on the character "Ugly Wudi." Viewers were able to see the connection between Betty/Wudi and beauty and Dove's underlying message in this new version.[3] Check out this version of the campaign at *http://live.wsj.com/video/ugly-betty-inspires-dove-campaign-in-china/6E3A6A3A-DE05-4116-900F-DCEC5A5666C7.html#!6E3A6A3A-DE05-4116-900F-DCEC5A5666C7*

Some are formal with lots of procedures, rigid work hours, and dress codes. Others are more informal in terms of their operations, office rules, and communication. The same patterns exist in the way businesses make purchasing decisions: some rigidly control and monitor purchases, others are loose and easygoing, and purchases may be less controlled or governed more by friendships and handshakes, as in Japan, than by rules. However, Hofstede, in his cross-cultural research on IBM, found that cultural differences were stronger than the legendary IBM corporate culture—he had assumed it would be a standardizing influence.

Social Influences

In addition to the culture in which you were raised, you also are a product of your social environment, which determines your social class or group. Reference groups, family, and friends also are important influences on opinions and consumer behavior and affect many of your habits and biases. For example, the "Inside Story" feature explains how a brand character was developed based on insights into consumer attitudes and opinions about others in the neighborhood.

Social Class The position you and your family occupy within your society is called a **social class**, and it is determined by such factors as income, wealth, education, occupation, family prestige, value of home, and neighborhood. In more rigid societies, such as those of India, people have a difficult time moving out of the class into which they were born. In the United States, although people may move into social classes that differ from their families', the country still

The Inside Story

Scotts Brand Comes Alive as Scott

Trent Walters, *Brand Management Team Leader, The Richards Group, Dallas, Texas*

As The Richards Group looked to develop a new advertising campaign for Scotts, the lawn care and gardening company, there were two key insights that came out of consumer research to drive the campaign.

"OMG, It's alive"

When consumers were reminded that their lawn was a living thing, it was very motivating. They felt a responsibility to care for the grass plants in their yards like they do for their houseplants. No longer could they sit back and do nothing. The lawn is alive and needs to be cared for. And if they didn't do it, who would?

Mike Bales: Writer. Jeff Hopler: Art Director. Used with permission of Scotts Miracle-Gro.

Everyone Has a "Billy" in the Neighborhood

Billy is the guy that exists in every neighborhood who has the perfect lawn. He's the guy who loves to be out working in his yard. If you have any questions on what to do, you turn to ol' Billy. And when you see Billy doing something in his yard, that's your cue that it's probably time for you to do something in yours.

Those two insights were key in developing the new ad campaign for Scotts: "Scott the Scot for Scotts." Scott is basically Billy. He is the guy in his neighborhood who has the healthy lawn. His neighbors know they can turn to him for advice on what to do. Scott reminds them that their lawns are alive and points them back to Scotts' products to feed and care for them.

The campaign was designed to give Scotts a way to bring its brand personality to life. Scott is the embodiment of the Scotts brand personality: "An uncomplicated, optimistic expert." Scott helps the brand communicate in a way that is interesting, engaging, and does not lecture consumers. In addition, his name and his catch phrase, "Feed your lawn. Feed it!" help continuously reinforce the brand name and the activity that Scotts want consumers to regularly engage in.

Photo courtesy of Dennis Murphy

Trent Walters is a graduate of the University of North Texas, where he was selected by the American Advertising Federation as one of its "Most Promising Minority Students." He was nominated by Professor Sheri Broyles.

has a class system consisting of upper, middle, and lower classes. Brand communication assumes that people in one class buy different goods for different reasons than people in other classes.

Reference Groups A **reference group** is a group of people you use as a model for behavior in specific situations. Examples are teachers and religious leaders as well as members of political parties, religious groups, racial or ethnic organizations, hobby-based clubs, and informal

Courtesy of Virginia Commonwealth University. Used with permission.

Graduates of universities and colleges tend to identify themselves by their school affiliation, as this ad for the Virginia Commonwealth University demonstrates. What can you tell about this person's career choice and interests from these bumper stickers?

affiliations, such as fellow workers or students—your peers. The ad for Virginia Commonwealth University uses a reference-group strategy to describe the type of students the school wants to recruit.

Groups of people devoted to a particular brand are called **brand communities**, such as the Harley Owners Group (HOG). To get a sense of how this group operates, check out www.harley-davidson.com/wcm/Content/Pages/Owners/Owners.jsp?locale=en_US. Apple is another company that generates a brand community. One writer described a "Cult of Apple" with "fanboys" and "fangirls" who have Apple stickers on their briefcases, wear Mac- or iPod-related clothing, and sport Mac tattoos. He observes, "It's not a brand, it's a lifestyle."[4] You can check out some of this at www.CultofMac.com. The Internet has had a huge impact on the creation of reference groups in the form of online virtual communities that revolve around interests, hobbies, and brands.

For consumers, reference groups have three functions: (1) provide information, (2) serve as a means of personal comparison, and (3) offer guidance. Ads that feature *typical users* in fun or pleasant surroundings are using a reference strategy. The Dove campaign used a counterargument to say that the stick-thin women in glamor magazines and advertising are stereotypes that don't represent average women.

Sociologist David Reisman describes individuals in terms of their relationships to other people as *inner directed* (individualistic) or *outer directed* (peer group and society). Advertisers are particularly interested in the role of peers in influencing their outer-directed friends' wants and desires. On the other hand, inner-directed people are more likely to try new things first.

Family The family is the most important reference group for many people because of its formative role and the intensity of its relationships. According to the U.S. Census definition, a **family** consists of two or more people who are related by blood, marriage, or adoption and live in the same household. A **household** differs from a family in that it consists of all those who occupy a dwelling whether they are related or not.

In the 21st century—for the first time in U.S. history—one-person households outnumber married couples with children. This reflects a growing trend in America during the past 30 years to marry later in life, divorce, or never get married at all. Marketers and their advertisers have been right on top of this trend. Banks have created special mortgages, builders are providing homes and apartments to meet the needs of single occupants, and food marketers have introduced "single" portions.

Psychological Influences

Personal characteristics also affect how you respond to brands as an individual in terms of both needs and wants as well as motivations.

Needs and Wants In Chapter 4, we described needs and wants as two different types of responses that lead to different reactions to an advertising message. The basic driving forces that motivate us to do something that reflect basic survival, such as choose a motel (shelter) or restaurant (food) when traveling, are called *needs*. Primary needs (biological) include the need for water, food, air, and shelter. In the case of the needs pyramid developed by psychologist Abraham Maslow (see Figure 5.3), these are called physiological and safety needs.

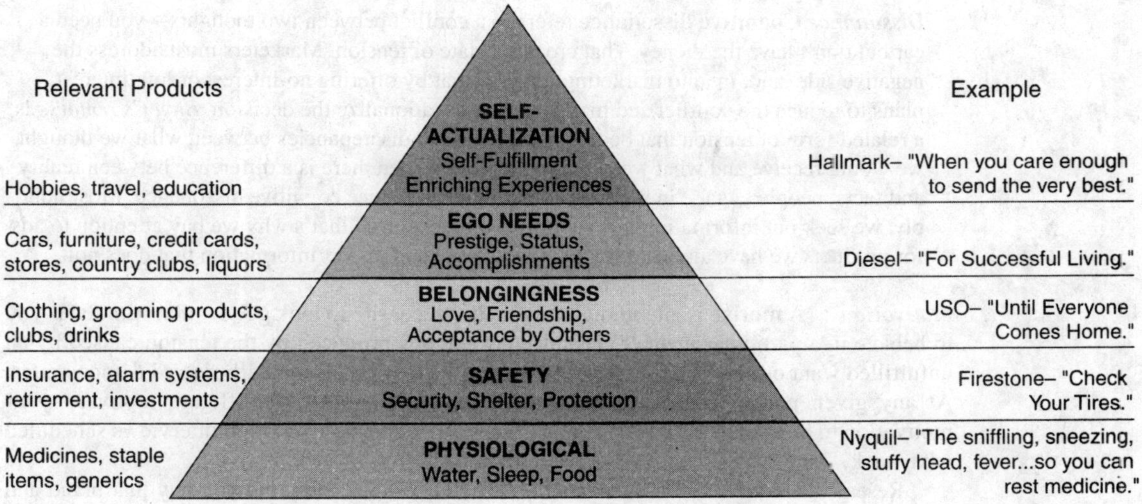

FIGURE 5.3
Maslow's Hierarchy of Needs

Needs we learn in response to our culture and environment are called **acquired needs.** These may include the need for esteem, prestige, affection, power, learning, and, yes, beauty. Because acquired needs are not necessary to your physical survival, they are also called secondary needs. Maslow called them *belonging* (social), *egoistic*, and *self-actualization*. The Dove campaign was directed to self-esteem or self-actualization.

A want occurs when we desire or wish for something—we won't die if we don't get it, but it can still provide a strong motivation to try or buy something new. Research has uncovered the power of new and novel. As account planner Susan Mendelsohn, who is a member of the book's advisory board, explains, "In some cases, we want things just for the sheer fun of newness—think about how many pairs of shoes or the amount of clothes people have."[5]

Principle
An item we need is something we think is essential or necessary for our lives; an item we want is something we desire.

Desire is the driving force behind demand and successful brands focus more on what we want than on what we need. Brian Martin, the founder of Brand Connections, has built a list of 10 desires that successful brands satisfy:[6]

Ten Desires

1. To feel safe and secure
2. To feel comfortable
3. To be cared for and connected to others
4. To be desired by others
5. To be free to do what we want
6. To grow and become more
7. To serve others and give back
8. To be surprised and excited
9. To believe there is a higher purpose
10. To feel that they matter

In his book *Breakthrough Advertising*, Schwartz describes the power of what he calls "mass desire." He explains that mass desire is the public spread of a private want; it can't be created by advertising, but advertising can address it and channel it to connect with a particular brand.[7] The trend toward more gas-efficient cars has led to a demand for hybrid cars such as the Prius. If there weren't a mass desire for this type of vehicle, there would be no market for the Prius. On the other hand, there is also a market for the Cadillac Escalade. Related to needs and wants are satisfaction and dissonance.

- ***Satisfaction*** A feeling of satisfaction is only one possible response to a brand message or brand experience; more troublesome is dissatisfaction or doubt. People can pay attention to a commercial, then buy a product and be disappointed. One of the reasons is that advertising sometimes raises consumers' expectations too high; in other words, it promises more than it can deliver.

- ***Dissonance*** **Cognitive dissonance** refers to a conflict between two thoughts—you need a car but don't have the money. That creates a state of tension. Marketers must address the negative side, and, in auto marketing, they do that by offering no-interest or low-interest plans to reduce the conflict and make it easier to rationalize the decision. *Buyer's remorse* is a related form of tension that occurs when there are discrepancies between what we thought we would receive and what we actually received. When there is a difference between reality and facts, people engage in a variety of activities to reduce cognitive dissonance. Most notably, we seek out information that supports our decisions—that's why we pay attention to ads for products we have already bought—and ignore and distort information that does not.

Motivations A **motive** is an internal force—like the desire to look good—that stimulates you to behave in a particular manner. This driving force is produced by the tension caused by an unfulfilled want or need. People strive to reduce the tension, as the Airborne ad demonstrates. At any given point, you are probably affected by a number of different motives—your motivation to buy a new suit will be much higher if you have several job interviews scheduled next week.

Research into motivation uncovers the "why" questions: Why did you buy that brand and not another? What prompted you to go to that store? Unfortunately, motivations operate largely at an unconscious level. Some of the reasons may be apparent—you go to a restaurant because you are hungry. But what else governs that choice—is it location, interior decoration, a favorite menu item, or the recommendation of a friend?

In our discussion in Chapter 4 of routine or habit approaches to consumer decision making, we noted the lack of conscious thought about many decisions. That is true also for decisions that are driven by emotions and feelings. Ann Marie Barry described the emerging field of neuroscience in Chapter 4. Applying neuroscience to consumer decision making, **neuromarketing**, the new brain-science approach to how people think, provides a deeper understanding of the way low-attention processing actually works and motivates people into unconscious, intuitive decision making. Barry reports that neurological research "reveals that visuals may be processed and form the basis of future action without passing through consciousness at all."[8] These studies are particularly useful in describing how emotion is the driving force behind motivations that can lead to largely unconscious brand decisions and behaviors.

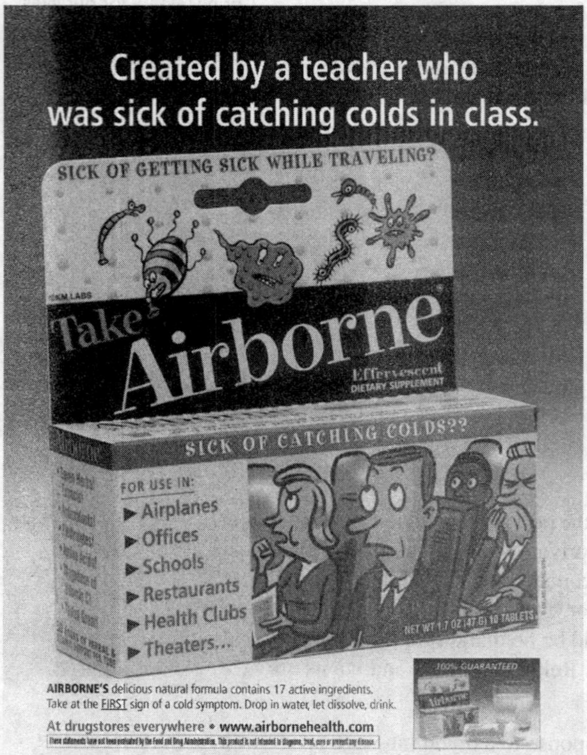

The motivation is obvious for a product that helps you avoid catching a cold when you travel. Do you think it is effective to also feature the motivation of the product's creator?

Influences on B2B Decision Making

Many of the influences that affect consumer buying also are reflected in B2B marketing. We know that B2B decision making generally follows the information path. Emotion may still be important in certain situations (e.g., the buyer wants to impress the boss), but ultimately these decisions are more rational than emotional for the following reasons:

- In organizational buying, many individuals are involved in reviewing the options, often with a buying committee making the final decision.
- Although the business buyer may be motivated by both rational and emotional factors, the use of rational and quantitative criteria dominates most decisions.
- The decision is sometimes made based on a set of specifications to potential suppliers who then bid on the contract. Typically in these purchases, the lowest bid wins.
- Quality is hugely important, and repeat purchases are based on how well the product performs.

The McGraw-Hill ad is a classic that illustrates the information-based factors that business people use in making purchasing decisions—as well as a legendary get-to-the-point business attitude.

How Do We Segment Markets and Target Audiences?

Cost efficiency—and effectiveness—demands that marketers (1) segment the market and (2) target the audience group most likely to respond to brand communication. First, let's discuss **segmenting**, which means dividing the market into groups of people who have similar characteristics in certain key product-related areas. Segmenting does two things: it identifies those people who are in the market, but it also eliminates those who aren't.

There are various ways to segment markets. One way is to divide them by the type of market they represent—either business or consumer—this leads to B2B or *business-to-consumer* marketing strategies. Another way is to refer to markets either as (1) those who shop for and purchase the product (*purchasers or customers*), (2) those who actually use the product (*users*), or (3) *influencers*—people who help the buyer make a brand choice (children, trendsetters, family, and friends). Purchasers and users can have different needs and wants. In the case of children's cereals, parents (the purchasers) often look for nutritional value and a decent price. In contrast, children (the users) may look for a sweet taste and a package with a prize inside.

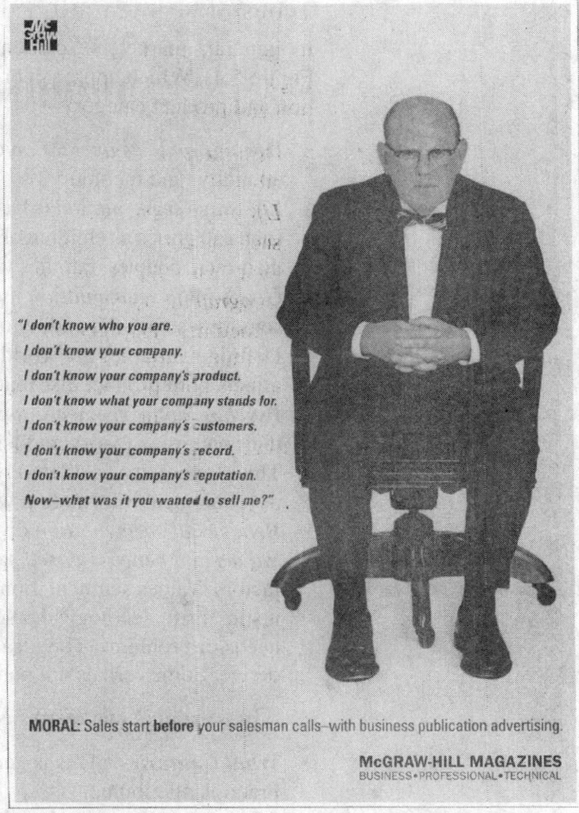

CLASSIC

This ad ran in 1958, but it continues to show up in marketing and communication books as an example of how important it is in B2B marketing to understand the client's business and branding situation.

Segmentation Strategies

Political columnist David Brooks recently asked, "Are people more alike than they are different? In spite of a common history, currency, and national identity, the United States in 2012 "has become more polarized, not less." And he sees this as a worldwide trend. Rather than a convergence of values, "People in different nations, even people within nations, have become less alike in at least as many ways as they have become more unlike."[9] Why is that important to brand communication? Our era, as Brooks put it using a marketing phrase, is "the Segmentation Century." It's not about convergence of values but rather about diverging opinions, interests, and tastes.

At one point in its history, Coca-Cola viewed the U.S. market for its brand as homogeneous and used general appeals—such as "Coke is it!"—for all consumers, which is considered an **undifferentiated strategy**. But even Coke is sold in different types of places, and people hear about Coke through different types of media, particularly in international markets. Therefore, customers now are grouped based on their tastes as well as contact points with the product. Of course, there are also differences in age, such as between a longtime adult Coke drinker and a teenager.

Principle

Segmenting is efficient and cost effective when it identifies those people who are in the market but also eliminates those who aren't.

Consumer differences, as well as product variations, determine how marketers address people in marketing communication and reach them using media. Few examples of homogeneous markets exist in contemporary marketing, so most strategies are based on a **market segmentation** strategy.

By using a segmentation strategy, a company can more precisely match the needs and wants of the customer with its products. That's why Coke and Pepsi introduced product variations to appeal to different consumer segments, such as diet, caffeine-free, diet caffeine-free, and flavored versions of their basic products.

Principle

Buyers may not be the users and users may not be the buyers. Buyers and users often have entirely different needs and wants.

Instead of marketing to a big undifferentiated market, marketers target narrow segments, such as single women in the international traveler category. Although marketing has gone global to reach large markets, at the same time many marketers have moved toward tighter and tighter **niche markets**, which are subsegments of a more general market segment. Individuals in a niche market, such as ecologically minded mothers who won't use disposable diapers, are defined by a distinctive interest or attitude. Niche marketers are companies that pursue market segments of sufficient size to be profitable although not large enough to be of interest to large marketers. Road Scholar, for example, markets to seniors who are interested in educationally oriented travel experiences.

Types of Segmentation

In general, marketers segment their markets using six key consumer characteristics (see Figure 5.4). Which approach or combination of approaches is used varies with the market situation and product category.

- *Demographic segmentation* divides the market using such characteristics as age, gender, ethnicity, and income.
- *Life-stage segmentation* is based on the particular stage in consumers' life cycle, which includes such categories as children or young people living at home, college students, singles living on their own, couples, families with children, empty nesters, and senior singles living alone.
- *Geographic segmentation* uses location as a defining variable because consumers' needs sometimes vary depending on where they live—urban, rural, suburban, North, South. Defining variables are world or global, region, nation, state, city, or ZIP code. Geography affects both product distribution and marketing communication.
- *Psychographic segmentation* is based primarily on studies of how people spend their money, their patterns of work and leisure, their interest and opinions, and their views of themselves. This strategy is considered richer than demographic segmentation because it combines psychological information with lifestyle insights.
- *Behavioral segmentation* divides people into groups based on product and brand usage.
- *Values and benefits-based segmentation* groups people based on tangible and intangible factors. Values segmentation reflects consumers' underlying value system—spiritual, hedonistic, thrifty, ecological, and so forth. Benefit segmentation strategy is based on consumers' needs or problems. The idea is that people buy products for different benefits they hope to derive. Some cereals are purchased for their taste; others for their health benefits.

International marketers need to answer three basic segmentation questions:

- ***What Countries?*** This is generally the easiest to answer because it is driven by where the brand is distributed.
- ***Market Development Level*** Countries, especially developing countries, vary greatly in market infrastructure, literacy levels, economic level, and level of media development. Some countries' standard of living is such that luxury brands, for example, would not find a large enough segment of the population to cover the cost of setting up distribution and supporting the brand with marketing communication and a sales force.
- ***Cultural Cohorts*** A **cultural cohort** is a segment of customers from multiple countries sharing common characteristics that translate into common wants and needs. New mothers are an example. Regardless of their nationality, new mothers want their babies to be happy and healthy. Teenagers are another cohort—teens in Tokyo and New York City may have more in common than a teen and his father in either country.

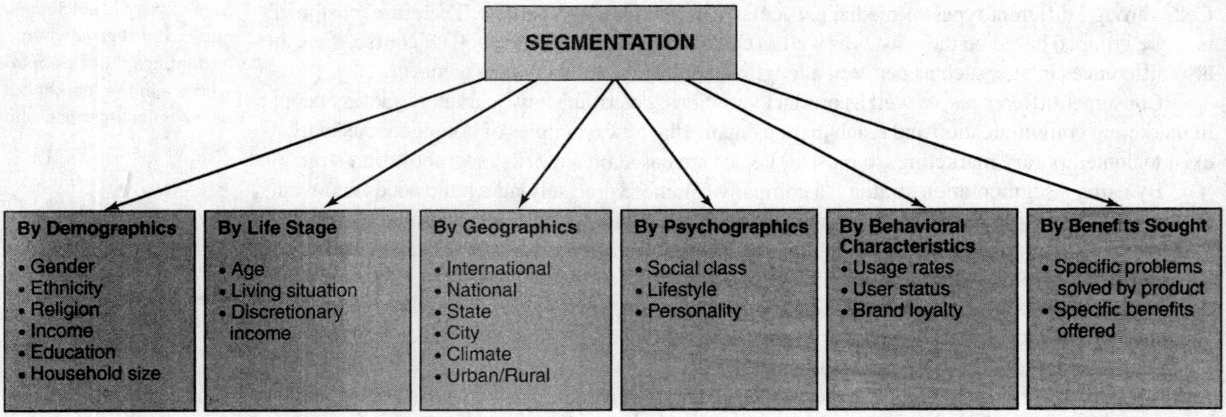

FIGURE 5.4
Market Segmentation Approaches

Targeting the Best Audience

Regardless of whether the marketing communication uses one-way or two-way communication strategies, planners still need some sense of who they are talking to and with. Through **targeting**, the organization can design specific communication strategies to match the audience's needs and wants and position the product in the most relevant way to match their interests.

Consider, for example, how Niman Ranch of Bolinas, California, built a luxury brand for its beef. The obvious target would be upscale consumers who value natural food and are willing to pay more for the best. But instead Niman marketed directly to prestigious chefs whose restaurants featured the brand on their menus. By using an innovative targeting strategy, Niman moved from commodity to a cachet brand bringing huge growth to the little company. With the interest in organic products and local farming, Niman also has knit together a network of hundreds of small-scale, organic farmers that leverages economies of scale while at the same time leaving farmers in control of their local operations.[10]

The target is first described using the segmentation characteristics that separate a group of prospective consumers from others who are not as likely to buy the brand, such as women who buy hair color. Then the descriptive variables are added until an ideal consumer group is identified. Pretend you're launching a new diaper service. What are your brand features, and how important are they to parents: price, materials, ecological sensitiveness, and so forth? In the large market of parents of infants, who cares for the features that are distinctive for your brand? Mothers are primary caretakers of infants, but you know that mothers are not all alike. In order to narrow your target, what makes them different? Some are affluent, while others struggle to get by. Are these important factors for the brand (inexpensive or expensive?), or do factors other than income need to be considered?

You identify the target by starting with the most important characteristic that predicts which consumers are prospective customers—matching the key brand features to the interests and concerns of the market. In the diaper service example, that would be gender—primarily mothers and then age, say, women ages 18 to 35. Then you add other factors, such as income, urban versus rural dwellers, education, or whatever factors come up in research as important predictive variables for your brand.

Principle
Each time you add a variable to a target audience definition, you narrow the size of the target audience as you try to find the largest group to whom you can direct a relevant message and reach with specific media.

As Figure 5.5 illustrates, each time you add a variable, you narrow the market as you come closer to the ideal target audience. The objective is to get the largest group that can be defined in such a way that you can direct a message that will speak to people in that group and that you can reach with specific media. Once these predictor variables have been sorted out, it should be possible to build an estimate of the size of this target market.

A targeting practice that has emerged from political campaigning is called **microtargeting**, which refers to using vast computer data banks of personal information to direct highly tailored messages to narrow slices of a segment. Marketers are also able to profile prospects by carefully analyzing data on their regular customers and then using this information to identify these revealing tendencies and characteristics in a group of prospects. The practice of using data banks that contain collections of personal information is controversial; the privacy issues will be discussed in more detail in Chapter 16.

Another example of microtargeting based on location comes from retailers who use "geofencing"—drawing a perimeter around a location—to reach customers via their cell phones who are in the neighborhood of the store. Promotional texting can be localized to announce a special on umbrellas when a storm is approaching or contact a consumer in aisle 3 with a coupon for a product on aisle 4.[11]

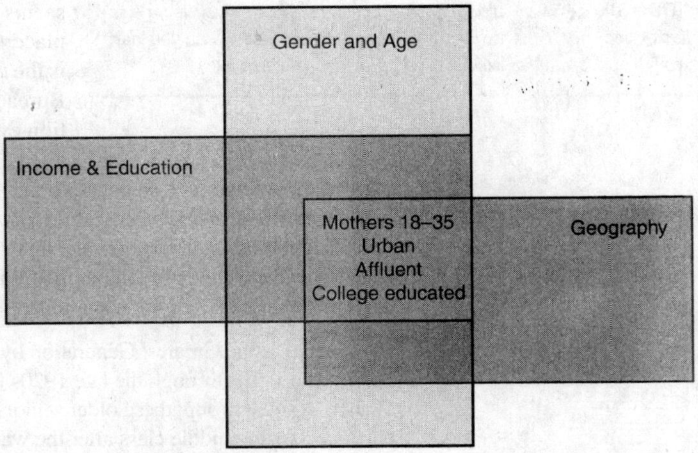

FIGURE 5.5
Narrowing the Target
As descriptors are added to the identification of the target, the number in the middle of the target gets smaller. As this target is defined, the size of the group can be predicted.

Courtesy of The Procter & Gamble Company and Clairol Inc.

CLASSIC

One of advertising's most familiar slogans—"Does she . . . or doesn't she?"—moved women who were tired of being told that there are things ladies don't do, such as color their hair. Legendary copywriter Shirley Polykoff understood these emotions and that it was okay to be a little bit naughty as long as you were nice. In 1967, Time *magazine reported that the number of women who used hair color increased from 15 to 50 percent after this campaign began in 1956. The campaign also appears as number 9 on Advertising Age's list of the Top 100 Campaigns in history. What lesson can you learn from a successful ad like this even if it's 50 years old?*

Profiling Markets and Target Audiences

As our Dove opening story stressed, marketing communication planners need to describe prospective customers using characteristics that help predict the likelihood that they will respond to a brand message and, ultimately, buy the brand. Using these descriptions, profiles are built for typical customers or prospects in order to make the brand communication more personal and relevant. **Profiles** are descriptions of the target audience that read like a description of someone you know. Analyze how Clairol profiled its target in the classic "Does She or Doesn't She" campaign.

Another example of how consumers are profiled comes from Forrester Research, which uses a research approach called "personas." Harley Manning, research director for customer experience and a member of this book's advisory board, describes a persona as "a fictional character that embodies your target customers' key behaviors, attributes, motivations, and goals"—a vivid profile of a type of person. Unlike segmentation descriptions, "personas come to life with first and last names, photographs, and vivid narratives that describe day-in-the-life scenarios." For example, he referred to "Stanley," a person used by J. P. Morgan to model its active, savvy investors. He notes that this type of person won't be satisfied with a simple account summary and instead wants advanced portfolio details.[12]

Targeting and Profiling Using Demographics

The statistical, social, and economic characteristics of a population, including such factors as age, education, occupation, gender and sexual orientation, income, family status, race, religion, and geography, are called **demographics**. Knowing these characteristics helps in message design and media selection for the **target audience**, the market segment that seems most likely to be interested in the product. The first place to start when analyzing and compiling demographics is the country's census data. In the United States, the Census Bureau compiles a huge collection of demographic information every 10 years—the most recent census was in 2010.

Age The most important demographic characteristic used by marcom planners is age. People of different ages have different needs and wants. Age determines product choice. How old are you? What products did you use 5 or 10 years ago that you don't use now? Look ahead 10 years. What products might you be interested in buying in the future that you don't buy now? The following list describes some of the other more common age-related population categories that are used by marketers:

- Referred to as the Greatest Generation by Tom Brokaw in his book by that name, this generation born in the 1910s through the late 1920s lived through the Great Depression and fought World War II. A small group, these older seniors are in their final years. This group opened up college education to the middle class after the war and lived frugal yet financially satisfying, lives.
- Known as the Silent Generation or traditionalists, these people, born from the late 1920s through the war years, are now active seniors. They were described in a national poll as the generation having the most "positive impact" on the American economy for their role in fueling the postwar boom.
- Baby boomers, people born between 1946 and 1962, represent the largest age-related category in the United States. The 79 million baby boomer consumers are now in the final

years of their careers and moving into retirement having made a huge population bulge as they moved through the life cycle. While they were growing up, boomers' numbers affected schools, then the job market, and now retirement programs and health care. This generation has been influenced by significant societal movements and scientific breakthroughs, from the Civil Rights movement to the anti–Vietnam War protests to putting a person on the moon.

- A boomer subgroup called Generation Jones consists of the younger baby boomers who were born from the mid- to late 1950s through the mid-1960s. The "Jones" reference comes from their continuing need to chase the dream of affluence by trying to "keep up with the Joneses."
- Gen X, also known as baby busters, is the group whose 49 million members were born between 1962 and 1981. Now adults, they have been described as independent minded and somewhat cynical and also a generation that is most characterized by growing up in divorced households. They are concerned with their physical health (they grew up during the AIDS outbreak) and financial future (the job market became more difficult just about the time they reached their prime years).
- Sometimes referred to as the Me Generation because of their affluent younger years, those born in the 1970s to early 1990s are characterized as more self-absorbed and narcissistic than their parents, although that changed as they confronted the dot-com bust at the end of the 1990s and subsequent economic problems in the 2000s.
- Generation Y members were born between 1980 and 1996 and are also known as "echo boomers" because they are the children of baby boomers. They are important to marketers because they are next in size to the boomer generation with more than 74 million members. This generation is also described as the Digital Generation or Net Generation because they are seen as more technologically savvy than their older siblings or parents. They are the first generation to grow up with e-mail and cell phones. They are also environmentally conscious and more interested in "right-size" houses than the megamansions of Gen X.
- Millennials, who overlap with Gen Y, include the children and young people born from the late 1980s into the beginning decade of the new century. Also called the iGeneration, these young adults are digital natives and spend considerably more time texting and using social media than even the older Net Generation. This is the generation that most marketers are desperately trying to understand, as they are also most unlike older generations in the ways they communicate and receive and interpret information.

Age is a key factor in media plans because age usually determines what media you watch, listen to, or read. The older the age-group, the more likely they are to use traditional media daily or several times a week, and the more likely they are to read newspapers. Kids ages 8 to 18 spend more than seven and a half hours a day with electronic devices, which include smart phones, computers, televisions, and video games.[13]

Age is driving a fundamental shift in U.S. marketing strategy. Since the 1960s, marketers have focused on reaching young people not only because they are in the formative years of making brand choices but also because the youth market was huge. Now with the boomer bulge moving into retirement, marketers realize that wealth and numbers belong to this active senior market.

Gender and Sexual Orientation An obvious basis for differences in marketing and advertising is gender. Many brands are either masculine or feminine in terms of use as well as brand personality. It is unlikely that men would use a brand of cologne called "White Shoulders." Women account for 85 percent of all consumer purchases in the United States, which makes them an important target for many marketers, and there have been signs since the mid-2000s that the United States is evolving into a matriarchal society.[14] Other studies point to the increasing percentage of women in college,[15] which also may mean eventual changes in income and occupation patterns.

Gender stereotypes have been a problem in advertising for decades, and some believe that may be because the majority of the work has been created by men writing for women. Jessica Shank, a copywriter at Goodby, Silverstein & Partners, concluded, "If most of the work specifically aimed at women were any indication of modern life, we'd all be at home dancing with our mops and fretting about plastic food storage."[16]

During the past decade, lesbian, gay, bisexual, and transgender (LGBT) households have become far more visible in the economy—as consumers, employees, shareholders, entrepreneurs, and business decision makers. Bob Witeck, a member of this book's advisory board and CEO of Washington, D.C.–based Witeck Communications (www.witeck.com), explains that

A Matter of Practice

Same-Sex Marriage: A Boon to the Economy?

Bob Witeck, *President, Witeck Communications, Inc., Washington, D.C.*

In 2012, six states plus Washington, D.C., offered same-sex couples the freedom to marry, while other states appear poised to join them. Several additional states today recognize same-sex marriages performed elsewhere, and another handful of states currently offer civil unions for lesbian and gay couples. All told, consider that 42 percent of America's population currently lives in a state that offers legal marriage or some form of legal protections and recognition for gay couples.

These social, cultural, and political changes are reshaping not only American households but the economy itself. One year following the adoption of marriage equality in New York, New York City itself conducted an economic impact study that totaled up the travel, hospitality, and overall spending on weddings of gay and lesbian couples. They discovered that more than 10 percent, or 8,200, of the marriage licenses issued in the past year were for gay and lesbian couples. These weddings drew more than 201,000 guests from outside the city and booked more than 235,000 hotel rooms. Mayor Michael Bloomberg declared that New York City had earned $259 million of economic benefits from same-sex marriages in its very first year.

Many major corporations and multinational marketers welcome the trend, not just the short-lived wedding and honeymoon boomlet. They see the visibility and economic contributions of gay households as tangible evidence of new market and employment trends, too.

Not surprisingly, more leading corporations, including Starbucks, Nike, and household-friendly General Mills, have taken public positions in support of same-sex marriage. Whether as consumers or potential employees, corporations see these changes mirroring their own competitive objectives—especially since a majority of Americans, by almost all polling studies, now favor treating same-sex couples equally with their heterosexual counterparts.

with nearly 20 years of expertise with this market, he conservatively estimates the buying power for LGBT consumers at $790 billion in 2012—based on a population projection of approximately 6.7 percent of all adults, or roughly 15 million people.[17] He explains how that affects the wedding market in his "A Matter of Practice" feature.

Education, Occupation, and Income Generally, white U.S. consumers attain higher levels of education than blacks and Latinos. According to a 2009 Census Report, U.S. males are falling behind females in higher levels of education. Education tends to correlate with media use. Consumers with lower education are higher users of television, especially cable. Consumers with higher education prefer print media, the Internet, and selected radio and cable stations.

Likewise, education dictates the way promotional messages are written and its level of difficulty. Examine ads in *Fortune* or *Forbes*, and you will find different words, art, and products than you will in *People*. Advertisers don't make value judgments about these statistics. Their objective is to match advertising messages to the characteristics of the target audience.

Most people identify themselves by what they do. In the United States, there has been a gradual trend from blue-collar occupations (e.g., manufacturing) to white-collar occupations (e.g., management and information). There have also been shifts within white-collar work from sales to other areas, such as professional, technical, and administrative positions. The number of service-related jobs continues to increase, especially in health care, education, and legal and business service sectors.

Another key demographic indicator for many advertisers is income, which relates to both education and occupation. You are meaningful to marketers to the extent that you have the resources to buy their products or services or contribute to their causes. The updated census income data reported in 2011[18] showed a shift toward fewer people in the top third (6 percent, or around 7,000 households) and more people in the bottom third of the income distribution (72 percent, or 94,000 households), which reflected the impact of the recession and continued employment. The remaining 21 percent (30,000 households) made up the shrinking middle class. But it's more than the size of the middle class that is worrisome to marketers. Federal Reserve statistics in 2012 showed that the economic crisis fell disproportionately on the middle class.[19]

Although the demand for luxury goods continued to be healthy because of the increasing wealth of the top group, the retail winners for the rest of the population were dollar stores, sales, and low-price retailers, such as Walmart. A single word describes consumers in the postrecession—"cautious"—particularly in mortgages and borrowing for car loans as well as student loans. People are more conscious of debts and afraid that they will get overextended.[20]

European consumers are even more frugal, as many of their countries are in economic trouble and suffering from government austerity programs that have drastically increased unemployment and reduced income levels. In contrast, the middle class in China has been growing dramatically during the 2000s although it is slowing down as the worldwide recession hits Asian markets. However, there has been a huge demand for major products, including everything from digitally controlled water heaters to big-screen televisions and washing machines. This generation is rapidly acquiring the furnishings of a modern **lifestyle** and learning how to use products that their parents never had.[21]

Principle

Income is a key demographic factor because consumers are meaningful to a marketer only if they have the resources needed to buy the product advertised.

Advertisers track trends in income, especially **discretionary income**, which is the amount of money available to spend after paying for taxes and basic necessities, such as food and shelter. Some industries, such as movie theaters, travel, jewelry, and fashion, would be out of business if people didn't have discretionary income. Discretionary income has been found to be a more reliable predictor of spending than income, although it is most vulnerable in times of economic downturn.

Race, Ethnicity, and Immigration Status In the United States, ethnicity is a major factor in segmenting markets. According to the 2011 census update, Latinos (or Hispanics) make up 16.3 percent of the population (up from 12.5 percent in 2000)[22] and have overtaken African Americans at 13 percent as the largest ethnic group. African Americans, however, have seen a dramatic increase of more than 55 percent in their buying power since 2000.[23] Asians are 5 percent. The United States is more multicultural than ever.

Latinos, a category based on language rather than race, are the fastest-growing minority. Because of the size of this market, special brand communication programs are often designed for Hispanic as well as black consumers. Marketers are wise to note that Latinos are not a homogeneous group but rather one with widely varied backgrounds—from Mexico, Central or South America, or Cuba. Others trace their ancestry to Spain. In 2013, Coke, for example, began emphasizing its iconic contour bottle in packaging designed for Latino markets with Mexican backgrounds because soft drinks in Mexico traditionally are sold in glass bottles rather than cans.

Latinos and blacks make up more than half of the births in the U.S. population, according to the Census Bureau, which announced in 2012 that whites now account for only 49.6 percent of all births.[24] The Census Bureau also revealed that minorities accounted for 92 percent of the nation's population growth in the decade that ended in 2010.[25]

The Census Bureau has found that about one in five U.S. residents speaks a language other than English at home—mostly in California, New Mexico, and Texas. In three metro areas—Miami, San Jose, and Los Angeles—more than a third of residents are foreign born. Research also found that of all Hispanics, most (56 percent) were U.S. born.[26]

Media use differences may be based on ethnicity. For example, Latino viewers are more likely to watch commercials in their entirety than non-Hispanic viewers. Also, Latino audiences are more influenced by advertising than other U.S. consumers—they are more likely to base their purchasing decisions on advertisements, and they are less cynical about marketing.

Many marketers are employing multicultural strategies to better serves their customers. McDonald's chief marketing officer reports that 40 percent of the fast-food chain's customers come from the Latino, Asian, and African American markets, and 50 percent of customers under the age of 13 are from those segments. He observes that these ethnic segments are also McDonald's most loyal customers.[27]

Self-identity is also affected by race and ethnicity. This is another reason diversity is so important in advertising—both in the ads themselves but also in the minds of the professionals who create the advertising.

© The Procter Gamble Company. Used by permission

This ad for Tide targets the Hispanic market. The translation is "The salsa is something you dance, not what you wear." If you were on the Tide team, would you recommend continuing to use strategies like this? Why or why not?

Geography In targeting and profiling consumers, a retailer's first strategic concern is geography: Where do my customers live? How far will they drive to come to my store? In large market areas, individual retailers who only have one or two stores try to find media that just reach those within their stores' shopping area (generally a two- to five-mile radius).

Geographic segmentation is a basic strategy because marketers are often tied to locations where their products are sold. Beyond the distribution factor, marketers study the sales patterns of different parts of the country because people residing in different regions need certain products. For example, someone living in the Midwest or the Northeast is more likely to purchase products for removing snow and ice than a Floridian.

Differences also exist between urban areas and suburban or rural areas. Swimming pools that sell well in a residential suburban neighborhood would not be in demand in an urban neighborhood filled with apartment buildings. Another important role for geography is in media planning, where a **designated market area** (DMA) is used in describing media markets. A DMA is identified by the name of the dominant city in that area, and it generally aligns with the reach of local television signals. The Seattle-Tacoma DMA in Washington, for example, covers some 13 counties in the northwestern corner of the state.

Religion One area that connects culture to demographics is religion. In terms of demographics, Christianity is the largest religion both in the United States and in the world. Islam is one of the fastest-growing faiths in the world and may soon overtake Christianity in numbers worldwide. As an indication of that growth, *Mohammad* has become the top male name in England, many European cities, and also in the world.[28] There is also a large percentage of the population, both in the United States and worldwide, that is secular or unaffiliated with any organized religion.

Religion is sometimes an important factor because of product bans. Some religions forbid certain products. Mormons, for example, avoid tea, coffee, caffeinated soft drinks, alcohol, and tobacco. Muslims also avoid alcohol and both Muslims and Jews avoid pork products as well as other food products that aren't certified as *halal* (Muslim) or *kosher* (Jewish). Religions sometimes affect people's choice of clothing and adornment. It depends on the product category, but religion can be a key factor in identifying those who are or are not in the market for a good, service, or idea.

Targeting and Profiling Using Psychographics

Principle
Often, differences in consumer behavior lie in psychographics—consumers' interests and lifestyles—rather than in demographics.

Just as demographics relates to social characteristics, psychographics summarize personal factors. **Psychographics** refers to lifestyle and psychological characteristics, such as activities, values, interests, attitudes, and opinions. Sometimes these complex psychographic factors are more relevant in explaining consumer behavior than are demographics. For example, two families living next door to each other with the same general income, education, and occupational profiles may have radically different buying patterns. One family may be obsessed with recycling, while their neighbors rarely bother to even keep their newspapers separate from their trash. One family is into hiking and other outdoor sports; the other watches sports on television. One is saving money for a European vacation; the other is seriously in debt and can barely cover the monthly bills. The differences lie not in their demographics but in their personalities, interests, and lifestyles.

Advertisers use psychographics to depict fairly complex consumer patterns. Libraries of psychographic measures can be purchased from research firms, or a company and its agency can create its own set of psychographic measures to fit its particular product and market. These psychographic measures can then be used to describe customers (such as heavy users of gourmet coffee), their response to message strategies (taste comparison ads), or their media choices (heavy users of the Internet).

Principle
Strategies that are designed to affect attitudes focus on establishing, changing, reinforcing, or replacing them.

Attitudes An **attitude** is a predisposition that reflects an opinion, emotion, or mental state directed at some object, person, or idea. Advertisers are interested in attitudes because of their impact on motivations. Because attitudes are learned, we can establish them, change them, reinforce them, or replace them with new ones. However, most attitudes are deeply set, reflect basic values, and tend to be resistant to change—you can hold an attitude for years or even decades. Attitudes also vary in direction and strength; that is, an attitude can be positive, negative, or neutral. Attitudes are important to advertisers because they influence how consumers evaluate products, institutions, retail stores, and brand communication.

One trend that depicts changing attitudes is what *Time* magazine editor Richard Stengel called "ethical consumerism," which refers to consumers who buy according to their conscience, whether it be a concern for supporting local businesses and ecology and energy efficiency or boycotting wasteful packaging and sweatshops. The *Time* poll found that 82 percent said they shop local, and 40 percent said they purchased a product "because they liked the social or political values of the company that produced it." Stengel explains, "With global warming on the minds of many consumers, lots of companies are racing to 'outgreen' one another." This results in business practices that build a positive "triple bottom line": profit, planet, and people.[29] Another term is *LOHAS*, which stands for Lifestyles of Health and Sustainability and defines a market segment that responds to "green" marketing strategies.

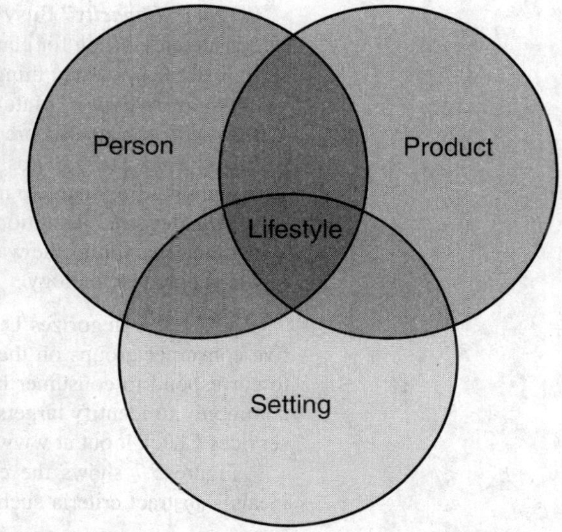

FIGURE 5.6
Lifestyle Components
Products are linked to lifestyles in the way they reflect the interests of people and the settings in which the products are used.

Lifestyles Psychographic analysis looks at lifestyles in terms of patterns of consumption, personal relationships, interests, and leisure activities. Figure 5.6 illustrates the interactions between the person, the product, and the setting in which a product is used and how those three factors create a lifestyle.

Some of the most common lifestyle patterns are described by familiar phrases, such as *yuppies* (young urban professionals) and *yuppie puppies* (their children). These terms are group identifiers, but they also refer to a set of products and the setting within which the products are used. For example, yuppies have been characterized as aspiring to an upscale lifestyle, so products associated with this lifestyle might include Cole Haan shoes, Hermes scarves, and BMW cars.

The DDB advertising agency has been conducting lifestyle research annually in the United States since 1975. The agency surveys 5,000 men and women on nearly 1,000 questions pertaining to such diverse topics as health, financial outlook, raising kids, shopping, religion, hobbies, leisure activities, household chores, politics, even their desired self-image. The survey also asks people about the products they use (from soup to nuts!) and their media habits. This wealth of information makes it possible to paint a vivid, detailed, multidimensional portrait of nearly any consumer segment that might be of interest to a client—and it also lets the agency spot changes and trends in people's lifestyles over time.

An example of the use of the Life Style Survey data to segment an audience comes from the Blood Center of Wisconsin when the center found itself low on donations. The DDB research team was able to describe frequent donors as sociable, doting parents, hard working, information seekers, and community leaders. The communication strategy was refined to appeal to a more professional working people audience, and the center saw a turnaround in its level of donations.

As part of their services to clients, some research firms create lifestyle profiles that collectively reflect a whole culture. We discuss two of these proprietary tools here: the Yankelovich (renamed The Futures Company) MONITOR's MindBase and the VALS System from SRI Consulting Business Intelligence (SRIC-BI).

The MONITOR™ has been tracking consumer values and lifestyles since 1971. Its MindBase® tool uses the MONITOR database to identify groups of people with distinctive attitudes, values, motivations, and lifestyles. (Check this company out at www.thefuturescompany.com.) Although the database can be used to custom design segments for individual clients, MindBase has identified eight general consumer groups:

- ***"I Am Expressive"*** Lives life to the fullest; not afraid to express my personality; active and engaged; "live in the now" attitude; believes that the future is limitless and I can do anything I put my mind to.
- ***"I Am Down to Earth"*** Cruising through life at my own pace; seek satisfaction where I can; hope to enhance my life; I like to try new things; I treat myself to novel things.
- ***"I Am Driven"*** Ambitious with a drive to succeed; self-possessed and resourceful; determined to show the world I'm on top of my game.
- ***"I Am Sophisticated"*** Intelligent, upstanding with an affinity for finer things; high expectations; dedicated to doing a stellar job, but I balance career with enriching experiences.

- ***"I Am at Capacity"*** Busy and looking for control and simplification; a demanding and vocal consumer; looking for convenience, respect, and a helping hand; want to devote more of my time to the important things in life.
- ***"I Measure Twice"*** Mature; like to think I'm on a path to fulfillment; live a healthy, active life; dedicated to a secure and rewarding future.
- ***"I Am Rock Steady"*** Positive attitude; draw energy from home and family; dedicated to an upstanding life; listen to my own instincts for decisions in life and in marketplace.
- ***"I Am Devoted"*** Traditional; rooted in comforts of home; conventional beliefs; spiritual and content; like things the way they've always been; doesn't need novelty for novelty's sake or newfangled technology.

VALS™ categorizes U.S. and Canadian adults age 18 years of age and older into distinctive consumer groups on the basis of an individual's responses to attitude questions validated to correspond to consumer behavior and a proprietary algorithm. Advertisers use VALS most commonly to identify targets, plan strategy, and develop communication for their products and services Check it out at www.strategicbusinessinsights.com/vals.

Figure 5.7 shows the eight VALS groups. "Thinkers" and "Believers" are motivated by ideals—abstract criteria such as tradition, quality, and integrity. "Achievers" and "Strivers" are

FIGURE 5.7
U.S. VALS™ Lifestyle Framework
Psychographic consumer groups identified by VALS research.

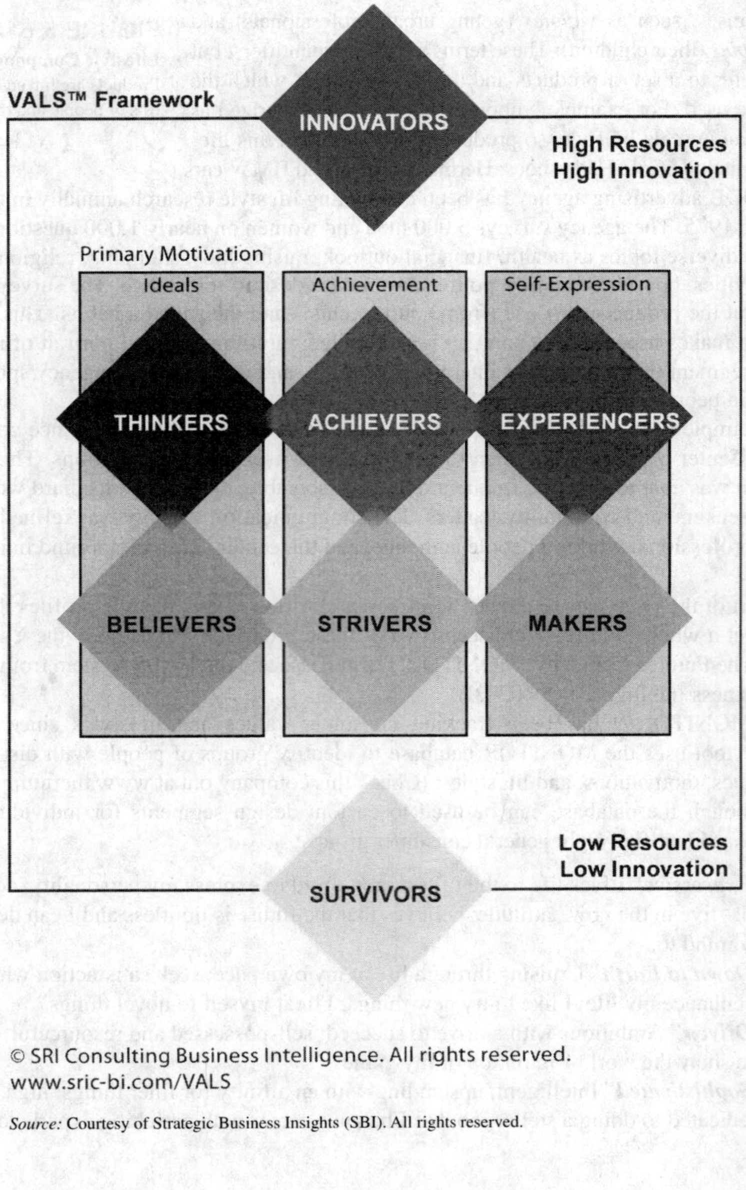

Source: Courtesy of Strategic Business Insights (SBI). All rights reserved.

motivated by achievement, seeking approval from a valued social group. "Experiencers" and "Makers" are motivated by self-expression and make value purchases that enable them to stand out from the crowd or make an impact on the physical world. The VALS groups on the top half of the framework (Innovators) have more resources—a combination of physical, emotional, and psychological resources—than do groups in the lower half (Survivors). You can take the survey yourself and find out your own VALS type at www.strategicbusinessinsights.com/vals/presurvey.shtml.

VALS explains why different consumer groups exhibit different behaviors and why various groups exhibit the same behaviors for different reasons. One application of VALS is creating communication that will connect emotionally with the target through the use of the most appropriate language and images. In addition to the U.S. framework, VALS frameworks are available for Japan, the United Kingdom Venezuela, the Dominican Republic, Nigeria, and China.

Sociodemographic Segments

Age-groups also connect with lifestyles. We've talked about the incredible impact baby boomers have had as a market category, so you can understand their importance as a market segment, but savvy marketers recognize many differences in lifestyles and attitudes among this huge population. Generations X and Y, as well as the echo boomers, are also important demographic segments, but their sociodemographic characteristics may represent more consistent lifestyle differences.

Seniors are also referred to as the *gray market* and divided into two categories: young seniors (ages 60 to 74) who are the *boomer-plus* group, and older seniors (ages 75 and older). Seniors, both younger and older, make up a huge and often wealthy market. As baby boomers move into their retirement years, this senior market will become even larger relative to the rest of the population, although the recession has hurt their wealth profile. Other terms that have been used to describe demographic and lifestyle segments include the following:

- ***Dinkies*** Double-income young couples with no kids
- ***Guppies*** Gay upwardly mobile professionals
- ***Skippies*** School kids with purchasing power
- ***Ruppies*** Retired urban professionals; older consumers with sophisticated tastes and generally affluent lifestyles
- ***Mini-Me*** Infants and toddlers of affluent parents and grandparents who spend large amounts on luxury brands with parents wanting their kids to reflect their taste and style[30]

Trends and Fads **The phenomenon of trends and fads is related to lifestyle and psychographic factors as well as the fascination with choice in a consumer culture. We've seen "acre homes"**

ForceHuman

Courtesy of Michael Dattolico

SHOWCASE

This company is a nonprofit, trying to reverse the momentum at which society is destroying the planet. Since no known external forces can stop momentum we are creating, a new physics force variable. Ultimately, this is a spin on the "green" revolution, focusing on using yourself to power daily activities but also the application of the mind to think differently. The physics reference is embedded in the logo above the "F" as well in the "baggy man's" hair (the symbol for force). The second focus, the momentum of changing preconceptions and minds, is captured in the pushing movement of "baggy man."

Owner of his own design studio, Musion Creative LLC (www.musioncreative.com), Michael Dattolico graduated from the advertising program at the University of Florida and a creative advertising program in England at the University College of Falmouth. His work was nominated for inclusion in this book by Professor Elaine Wagner.

and fancy bathroom retreats as well as low-carb diets, healthy food (oat bran and antioxidants), natural products, fitness fads and personal trainers, hybrid cars, carbon trading, simple life (don't buy things), and local products (don't buy things that use a lot of gas in transportation to get to your local store). Sustainability and green marketing reach a population who are often passionate about the environment. The logo design for ForceHuman was created to reach this group. Michael Dattolico, its designer, explains the reasoning behind the design in the "Showcase" feature.

Young people are particularly involved in trends. For example, the way teenagers dress and talk and the products they buy are driven by a continuing search for coolness. **Trend spotters** are professional researchers hired by advertisers to identify trends that may affect consumer behavior. **Cool hunters** are trend spotters who specialize in identifying trendy fads that appeal to young people. They usually work with panels of young people in key trendsetting locations, such as New York, California, urban streets, and Japan. Loic Bizel, for example, hunts Japanese super-trendy fads as a consultant for many Western companies and designers. Through his website (www.fashioninjapan.com), you can get a taste of those cool ideas and fashion in Japan's streets and life.

Targeting and Profiling Using Behavioral Patterns

Behavioral targeting is a practice used by online marketers who track customers' activities—sites visited and products bought—to predict consumer interest in a product and design personalized brand communication. Google, for example, uses tracking to identify which advertisements to show to its viewers.[31] Another example of behavioral targeting comes from Orbitz, where Mac users were steered to more expensive accommodations than PC users. The *Wall Street Journal* reported that Orbitz's tracking data found that Mac users spend as much as 30 percent more on hotels than did PC users.[32]

Behavior is related to feelings (impulse) or thoughtful search. One area where such behaviors has been investigated is grocery shopping. An observational study by a University of Florida student, Kate Stein, found that grocery shoppers often buy food impulsively and irrationally. (Stein worked with Professor Brian Wansink, director of the Cornell University Food and Brand Lab, and you'll read more about her research experience in the next chapter.) Published as an op-ed piece in the *New York Times*, Stein reported that browsing slowly doesn't necessarily help you pick out the best products. She observed, "The shoppers I studied who took the longest, examining packages, stopping at whatever caught their eye, invariably spent more money." Furthermore, she noticed that these slow and thoughtful shoppers often loaded their shopping carts with unhealthy items that, when questioned, they couldn't give a reason for buying. In other words, the best shoppers use a grocery list, control their instincts, and move quickly through their product selections. For more tips on streamlining your grocery shopping endeavors, check out www.mindlesseating.org.[33]

Brand Usage and Experiences There are two ways to classify **usage**: usage rates and brand relationship. *Usage rate* refers to quantity of purchase: light, medium, or heavy. Heavy users typically buy the most of a product category or a brand's share of the market. An old rule of thumb called the Pareto rule states that 20 percent of the market typically buys 80 percent of the products. That explains why the heavy-user category is so important to marketers and why planners make special efforts to understand this key customer group. Heavy users and brand-loyal buyers are usually a brand's most important customers, and they are the most difficult for competitors to switch away from a brand. **Switchers** are people with low levels of brand loyalty who may be willing to try a new brand. Below is a chart that identifies consumer categories based on product usage.

Principle
In many product categories, 20 percent of the users buy 80 percent of the products.

Quantity	***Brand Relationship***	***Innovation***
Light users	Nonusers	Innovators
Medium users	Ex-users	Early adopters
Heavy users	Regulars	Early majority
	First-timers	Late majority
	Loyal users	Laggards
	Switchers	

Innovation and Adoption Another type of behavior has to do with how willing people are to try something new. Everett Rogers developed the classic system, called the *diffusion of innovation curve*, to identify adoption behaviors for new ideas. This **adoption process** is identified in terms of the speed with which people are willing to try something new, such as *innovators, early adopters, early majority*, *late majority*, and *laggards*.[34] This system reflects the speed of **diffusion** of new ideas. See Figure 5.8 for an interpretation of Rogers' Diffusion of Innovation model.

The innovator category, which is the group of brave souls willing to try something new, represents only about 2.5 percent of the population. Obviously this early-adopter category is an important group for marketers launching new products. They become opinion leaders for their friends. *Risk taking* is a personality characteristic, but it drives behavior in the area of trying a new product. **Perceived risk** is your view of the relationship between what you gain by trying something new and what lose if it doesn't work out—how important is the consequence of not making a good decision? Price is a huge barrier for high-involvement products; personal status and self-image may be a risk barrier for a fashion product.

Who are these people? SRI's research has found that, contrary to popular belief, there is no one innovator or early-adopter group; rather, adoption patterns vary with the product category. Early adopters are in different strata and roles in society and cannot be identified by demographics alone.

An example of a campaign targeting Latino innovators is found in the launch of the Sync technology in Ford's fuel-efficient Focus and Edge cars. Sync allows drivers to control cell phones and MP3 players at the touch of a button or a voice-activated command. An important feature is that the technology could understand various dialects of Spanish. Research found that many Latinos are technologically savvy and use their MP3 players during long commutes, so this was an ideal market to target with this new technology.[35]

Seeking Seekers

Segmenting and targeting works differently in the 21st century. The traditional approach, which involved identifying groups of people and directing messages to them using mass media, is today only one piece of brand communication. This new more complex communication system recognizes the increased importance of word of mouth (C → C), where consumers talk among themselves about brands. Furthermore, companies are much more involved in listening and responding to consumers (C → B→ C), rather than just targeting them. What this means is that we not only need to rethink targeting but also the way consumers interact with brands.

Don Schultz, founder of the IMC program at Northwestern University and a leading thinker on changes in brand communication, notes that consumers have evolved from having little to say

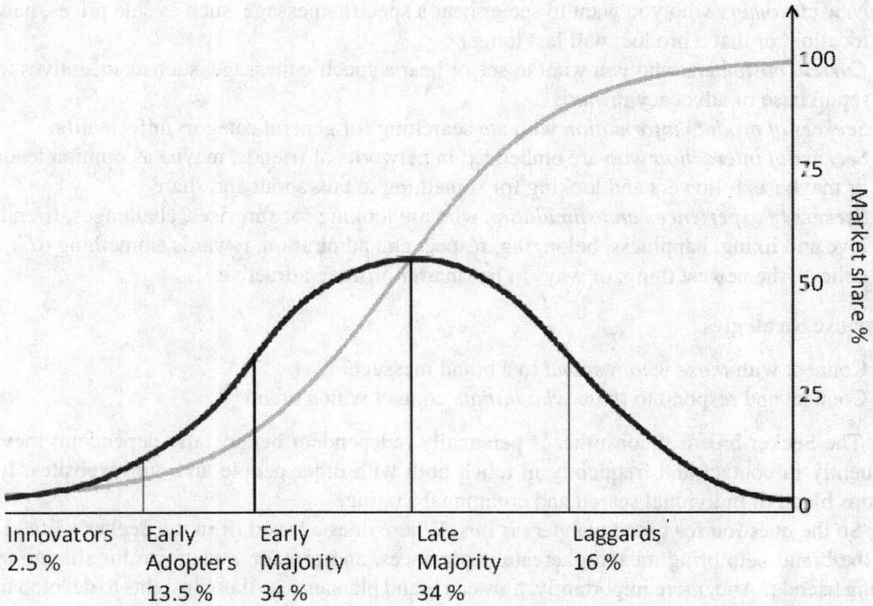

FIGURE 5.8
The Diffusion of Innovation
This version of Rogers's diffusion of innovation model shows the usual bell curve with data estimating the percentage of people in the standard adaption categories; however, it also presents a percentage line that estimates the cumulative effect of successive groups of consumers adopting a new idea until it eventually reaches a saturation level.

Source: Tungsten, http://en.wikipedia.org/wiki/Everett_Rogers. Based on E. Rogers, *Diffusion of Innovations* (London: Free Press, 1962).

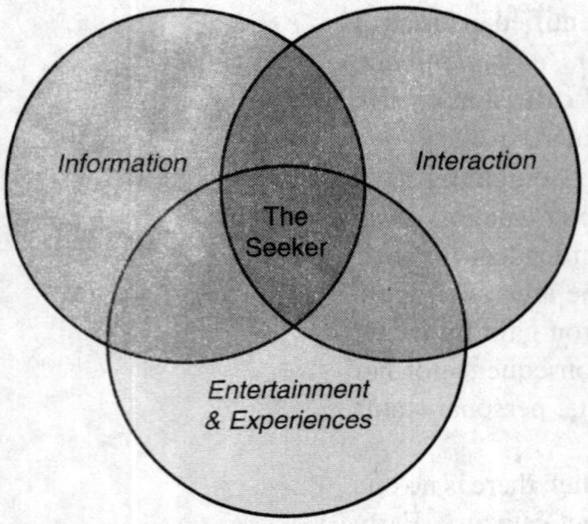

FIGURE 5.9
The Seeker Model

and less control over marketing messages to a new model where customers are much more in control of the system. He explains that as customers got access to information through the Internet, they can find, sort through, evaluate, make decisions, and share their thoughts with like-minded customers all over the world.[36]

This expansion of marketplace communication has, as Schultz argues, changed the dynamics of marketplace power bringing a loss of control by marketers over marketing and marketing communication systems. More importantly, it makes the consumer more important as an agent using the new media to search for things they find relevant and important. We call them *Seekers*—people who search, share, and initiate marketing communication and brand relationships.

On one level, they seek traditional products, services, and ideas using powerful Internet search tools to find things that interest them—information, but also brand meanings and experiences that intersect with their self-esteem. They also are seeking pleasure, personal strokes, fellowship, and positive experiences. So consider that when Seekers go online, they are looking for information and answers—but also sensory stimulation, surprises, challenges, friends, things to like, happiness, belonging, respect and admiration, rewards, something to believe, something to talk about and share, the newest thing, and ways to be smarter or more attractive.

In terms of targeting strategy for this new category of Seeker, there are three types of searching (see Figure 5.9):

1. ***Information*** A search for specific content—Where can I get the lightest notebook computer? How do I return a product and get a refund?
2. ***Interaction*** Friends, fellowship, belonging, respect and admiration, or something to talk about and share.
3. ***Entertainment, experiences, and stimulation*** Surprises, challenges, love and liking, happiness, rewards, something to believe, the newest thing, or ways to be smarter or more attractive.

In terms of expanding segmentation strategies that include Seekers, we can distinguish between two communication behaviors that reflect these new types of brand relationships: *targeting* and *responding*. Within those two basic categories are variations that lead to seven new consumer approaches:

Targeting Strategies

1. *New customers* who you want to see or hear a specific message, such as sale prices, new location, or that a product will last longer
2. *Current customers* who you want to see or hear a specific message, such as incentives to repurchase or advocacy rewards
3. *Seekers of product information* who are searching for general category information
4. *Seekers of interaction* who are embedded in networks of friends, maybe as opinion leaders or maybe as followers and looking for something to talk about and share
5. *Seekers of experiences and stimulation* who are looking for surprises, challenges, friends, love and liking, happiness, belonging, respect and admiration, rewards, something to believe, the newest thing, or ways to be smarter or more attractive

Response Strategies

6. Connect with *those who respond* to a brand message
7. Connect and respond to *those who initiate* contact with a brand

The Seeker breed of consumer is personally independent but socially dependent: they are frequently in contact and frequently in touch both with other people and with websites. It's a curious blend of individual search and communal sharing.

So the question for brand planners is this: Where does a brand fit in the Seeker's life? How can the brand help bring meaning, create experiences, and provide a platform for sharing ideas among friends? And, more importantly, how can brand planners use these insights to develop more effective brand communication? For Seekers, marketing communication is like a video game, and successful marketers will offer exciting, engaging, and even mesmerizing brand experiences.

Looking Ahead

The stuff of consumer insight—needs and wants, thoughts, knowledge, attitudes, and responses—is uncovered through various kinds of research. These findings ultimately lead to brand communication strategies and plans, but before designing strategies we will discuss methods of obtaining consumer insight, which we introduce in the next chapter.

Dove

It's a Wrap

The Beauty of a Campaign

This chapter underscores the importance of understanding the influences that affect consumer responses to advertising. Key to effective customer-focused advertising is staying sensitive to consumers and understanding how they think, act, and feel—and where they'll be able connect with the brand message.

The provocative copy in the Dove "Campaign for Real Beauty" challenges the audience to reconsider how they define beauty and to love their bodies, no matter what their age or shape. The campaign generated a huge buzz. But did it work to sell the product? According to Unilever, the campaign resulted in a 24 percent sales increase during the initial advertising period across the entire Dove brand.

The brand also fared well globally—in some places. When it was launched in the United Kingdom, sales of Dove Firming Lotion reportedly increased by 700 percent in the first seven months after the posters appeared. It generated a substantial press interest, with about 170 editorial pieces written in the first four months after the launch in Great Britain.

However, the Dove message did not resonate with all audiences. Ultimately, Dove created a localized campaign for the Chinese market inspired by the *Ugly Betty* television series when it was found that Chinese women didn't embrace the brand's "Real Beauty" philosophy.

The campaign radically changed the Dove brand image in the United States with its culturally relevant message. More than 8.5 million young people received help from the Dove Self Esteem project since 2005, with a goal of helping 15 million by 2015. More than a million participated in the Dove Self Esteem Program in 26 countries in 2011 alone, according to the Unilever website.

The definition of beauty portrayed in advertising really seems to be changing. When asked about the images in Dove ads, 76 percent said women in the ad are beautiful, and 68 percent said, "It made you think differently about the brand."

Advertising Age named the Dove's "Evolution" Web video, which earned more than 6 million hits and lots of mentions in the national press, as one of its best nontelevision campaigns of the decade. The "Singin' in the Rain" campaign helped Dove become one of the top five hair brands in Canada. Beautiful.

Logo: Courtesy of Ogilvy & Mather

Key Points Summary

1. **How does the consumer decision process work?** The information-driven decision process involves five stages: need recognition, information search, evaluation of alternatives, purchase decision, and postpurchase evaluation. The paths approach to consumer decision making identifies a multitude of different routes that a consumer may take to reach a purchase decision.

2. **What cultural, social, psychological, and behavioral influences affect consumer responses to advertising?** The social and cultural influences on consumer decision making include norms and values, society and subcultures, social class, reference groups, age, gender, family status, education, occupation, income, and race. Psychological influences on consumers include perception, needs and wants, learning, and motivations.

3. **How does targeting work and how is it different from segmenting?** In contrast to segmentation, which involves dividing a market into groups of people who can be identified as being in the market for the product, targeting identifies the group that would be the most responsive to an advertising message about the product. Both segmenting and targeting use social/cultural, psychological, and behavioral characteristics to identify these critical groups of people. But targeting uses this data to build a profile of the ideal person to whom the marketing communication is directed.
4. **What characteristics are used to segment groups of consumers?** Advertisers identify audiences in terms of demographics, psychographics, product-related behavior, and decision making. Demographic profiles of consumers include information on population size, age, gender and sexual orientation, education, occupation, income, family status, race, religion, and geography. Psychographic profiles include information on attitudes (activities, interests, and opinions) and lifestyles. Behavior profiles emphasize brand usage, as well as innovativeness and risk taking, and participation in trends and fads. Quantity of usage is an important characteristic of a profitable market. The relationship the consumer has with the brand in terms of use and loyalty is also important. Finally, the innovativeness of people in the group in terms of their willingness to try something new is another important behavioral characteristic.

Key Terms

acquired needs, p. 161
adoption process, p. 175
attitude, p. 170
brand communities, p. 160
cognitive dissonance, p. 162
consumer behavior, p. 156
cool hunters, p. 174
core values, p. 157
corporate culture, p. 157
cultural cohort, p. 164
culture, p. 156
demographics, p. 166
designated marketing area, p. 170
diffusion, p. 175
discretionary income, p. 169
family, p. 160
household, p. 160
lifestyle, p. 169
market segmentation, p. 163
microtargeting, p. 165
motive, p. 162
neuromarketing, p. 162
niche market, p. 163
norms, p. 157
perceived risk, p. 175
profiles, p. 166
psychographics, p. 170
reference group, p. 159
segmenting, p. 163
social class, p. 158
switchers, p. 174
target audience, p. 166
targeting, p. 165
trend spotters, p. 174
undifferentiated strategy, p. 163
usage, p. 174
values, p. 157

Review Questions

5-4. In what ways does the culture in which you grew up affect your consumer behavior? Describe and explain one purchase you have made recently that reflects your cultural background.

5-5. What is segmentation? List the consumer characteristics that marketers rely on to segment markets.

5-6. Differentiate between buyers and users. Explain, using examples, whether they have the same needs and wants.

✪ 5-7. What are your key demographic and psychographic characteristics? Build a profile of yourself and discuss how each one might be used in planning an advertising campaign targeted to someone like you.

✪ 5-8. What are the key steps in the adoption process, and how do they relate to product purchases? Who do you know who might clarify as an early adopter? As a laggard? Profile those two people and discuss the key characteristics that make them different in their orientation to new ideas or products.

5-9. Analyze the characteristics of demographics, and explain its role in designing the communication messages for a target market.

Discussion Questions

5-10. Analyze the corporate culture at various agencies and clients. Start with the statement on www.ogilvy.com/About/Our-History/Corporate-Culture.aspx for an inside view of how this agency articulates its view of its own corporate culture. Then find at least one other agency or client website that refers to its corporate culture, and compare that statement with Ogilvy's. (Look first at companies whose websites have been mentioned in this chapter or previous chapters.) Discuss where you would prefer to work and why.

5-11. Consider Dove's campaign for Real Beauty that took place in Taiwan, and refer to the popular Taiwanese saying: "There are no ugly women, only lazy ones," to explain the following:

a. Why did this cultural belief challenge Dove's advertising campaign?

b. How did stereotyping lead to Dove dropping its ad campaign in the Pan-Asian market?

5-12. Regarding consumer behavior, complete the following:

a. Describe how you and some of your peers select and purchase products, and the needs that drive these behaviors.

b. Compare your consumer behavior with that of others.

5-13. What age-group category do you and your friends fit into? Gen Y? Millennial? There's always debate about the characteristics of these population groups, yet there are usually some general characteristics that help identify interests, attitudes, and behaviors. So develop a profile that fits yourself and your friends (who are in the same age-group). Try to identify characteristics that generally represent this group.

5-14. Discuss the decision making involved in choosing your college:

a. Interview two classmates and determine what influenced their decision to attend this school.

b. How did you—and the people you interviewed—go about making this decision? Is there a general decision-making process that you can outline? Where are the points of agreement, and where did you and your classmates differ in approaching this decision?

c. Draw up a target audience profile for students attending your college. How does this profile differ from another school in your same market area?

5-15. An international travel and tourism company developed an advertisement to promote a special honeymoon package; the ad will be displayed in all the countries where the company operates.

a. Do you think the advertisement should use the same photos, illustrations, and communication messages across all countries in order to commit to the campaign consistency concept? Why or why not?

b. How can such ads be localized to appeal to different audiences and cultures?

c. What are the advantages of customizing an ad to meet the local taste?

Take-Home Projects

5-16. ***Portfolio Project:*** Choose two VALS™ and two MindBase® categories. Find one print advertisement that appears to be targeted to people in each category. Explain why you think the ad addresses that audience. Do you believe that the categories are mutually exclusive? Can consumers (and ads directed to them) be classified in multiple categories? Why or why not?

5-17. ***Mini-Case Analysis:*** Review the chapter opening and closing story about Dove's "Real Beauty" campaign. How does this campaign reflect a cultural or social insight? What psychological insight helps explain the thinking behind this campaign? From what is presented in this minicase, develop a profile of an individual member of this target audience.

TRACE North America Case

Multicultural Innovation

Read the TRACE case in the Appendix before coming to class.

5-18. From the case study and your own personal experiences in college, what factors do you believe most strongly influence Multicultural Millennials is their decision making?

5-19. What campaigns targeted to African Americans, Chinese American, and Hispanic Americans are you aware of, and do you believe they are successful? Why or why not?

CHAPTER 6

Strategic Research

Photo: Domino's Pizza LLC

It's a Winner

Campaign
Domino's Pizza Turnaround

Company
Domino's

Agency
Crispin Porter + Bogusky

Contributing Agencies
Northstar Research Partners, Lieberman Research Worldwide, Millward Brown, Qualitative Research Centre

Awards
Advertising Research Foundation Grand Ogilvy Award, AdAge's Marketer of the Year Runner-Up

CHAPTER KEY POINTS

1. **What are the basic types of strategic research, and how are they used?**
2. **How do brand communicators use research?**
3. **What are the most common research methods used in brand communication?**

Domino's Cooks Up a Recipe for Success

This is a story about the importance of listening to your consumers, about being honest, and about taking risks—and the role of research in creating positive brand communication. It is the tale about Domino's Pizza Company, which started with one store in 1960 and now boasts more than 10,000 locations. Its growth has not been without challenges, however.

In 2009, pizza makers generally faced a decline in business, as consumers opted for healthier, fresher options or less expensive burgers and sandwiches rather than pizza. Like its competitors, Papa John's and Pizza Hut, Domino's faced a dim outlook. Domino's same-store sales had been flat or down for four years.

The first big chain to base its entire business on delivering food to your home, Domino's discovered through a tracking study it commissioned that "speed" and "best in delivery" didn't matter as much to consumers as it used to. "Taste" counted, and that was a problem. Domino's ranked last in taste among the top three pizza chains.

Domino's researched its customers, asking how they liked the pizza, and were told more than once that it tasted like cardboard with ketchup. Basically, the pizza sucked. It's a finding that was hard to swallow because it is hard to grow a business if consumers don't like the product.

So what were the ingredients that allowed Domino's to turn around consumers' perceptions, enabling it to deliver 400 million pizzas a year, enough for a pizza (and a slice) for every man, woman, and child in the United States?

First, Domino's listened. Domino's employed several primary and secondary research methodologies, including a tracking study, on-the-street intercepts, ethnographies, and focus groups. From this research, Domino's analysts were able to synthesize the information they gathered and identify some key findings that led to a better understanding of its customers as well as the "big idea" for the campaign:

- Customers valued personal relationships, but they perceived Domino's as an impersonal company that provided efficient service. One focus group participant offered her observation: "They just get their food off the back of Sysco trucks." A key insight: Consumers didn't know who Domino's was.

- Skeptical consumers wouldn't believe it if Domino's said the pizza was new and improved. Seemingly every product makes that claim. People needed a reason to believe that a new recipe would taste better.
- Companies never admit they were wrong.

The second ingredient for success: The company needed to be honest and authentic. Before people could believe the new pizza tasted better, the company had to do something that was believable. Dare Domino's to own up that the pizza recipe that had been used for 49 years tasted bad? Unheard of.

After listening to consumers, creating a better pizza recipe, and analyzing the research findings, Domino's and its agency Crispin Porter + Bogusky did the unthinkable. They created a campaign in which they admitted that the pizza tasted bad. Instead of pretending the product was good, the pizza maker opted for transparent communication in its "Pizza Turnaround" campaign.

Shots from focus groups and messages from Domino's CEO and other executives told the story about how bad the original pizza was and how Domino's listened and changed the pizza. Domino's became authentic and human.

Did this gutsy move pay off? Turn to the "It's a Wrap" feature at the end of the chapter to find out.

Sources: "Pizza Turnaround," David Ogilvy Awards published case study, www.thearf.org; "Domino's Bold Ad Strategy: We're No Longer Bad," www.nbcmiami.com; www.dominosbiz.com; "Marketer of the Year Runner-Up: Domino's, October 18, 2010, www.adage.com.

In our previous chapters on how to plan marketing communication that has a real impact on consumers, we noted that marketers such as Domino's need to do brand, market, and consumer research. This research effort becomes the foundation for setting objectives, segmenting the market and targeting the audience, and developing a brand communication plan. This chapter presents some key research concepts that lead to consumer insight, beginning with an explanation of the two most basic categories of research (primary and secondary), the basic types of research tools (quantitative and qualitative), and the most common research methods used in planning marketing communication. We also discuss the challenges facing advertising researchers.

How Do You Get Insights into Consumer Behavior?

Whether you realize it or not, you were engaged in strategic research when you looked for an acceptable college to attend. You conducted market research (what information is available?), strategic research (what factors are most important in making a decision, and how do the schools stack up?), and evaluative research (how will I know I made the best decision?). A brand communication plan goes through similar stages of development with research as the first step.

Principle
Listening is the first step in understanding customers.

In the Part 2 opener, Regina Lewis stressed that an effective brand communication program is totally dependent on consumer insight. Know your customer—and listening—is the first step in understanding customers. What does that mean? It means that brand strategy begins with consumer research—the tools of listening. Consumer research investigates the topics we discussed in the previous chapter on segmentation and targeting, including attitudes, motivations, perceptions, and behaviors. The research findings then led to analysis and insights, which are explanations for why people think and behave as they do. But first we must understand the principles and practices of communication research and how to listen effectively to consumers.

In-house researchers or independent research companies hired from outside the company usually handle a client's market and consumer research. The objective at all stages of the planning process is to answer this question: What do we need to know in order to make an informed decision about consumer behavior? Here are various types of research used in planning advertising and marketing communication, such as the Domino's campaign:

- **Market research**, often used with new product launches, compiles information about the product, the product category, competitors, and other details of the marketing environment, such as the size of the prospective market, that will affect the development of a brand communication strategy. Facebook, which was notorious for launching new products without testing them on users that generated anger and even protests, is more careful now in its product development.[1]
- **Consumer research** identifies people who are in the market for the product in terms of their characteristics, attitudes, interests, and motivations. Ultimately, this information is used to decide who the targeted audience for the advertising should be. In an integrated marketing communication (IMC) plan, the consumer research also acquires information about all the relevant stakeholders and their points of contact with the brand.
- **Brand communication research** focuses on all elements of advertising and other forms of brand communication, including message development research, media planning research, evaluation, and information about competitors' advertising. **IMC research** is similar, except that it is used to assemble information needed in planning the use of a variety of marketing communication tools. IMC is particularly concerned with the interaction of multiple messages from a variety of sources to present the brand consistently.
- **Strategic research** uncovers critical information that becomes the basis for strategic planning decisions for both marketing and marketing communication. In brand communication, this type of research covers all of the factors and steps that lead to the creation of message strategies and media plans. Think of strategic research as collecting all relevant background information needed to make a decision on advertising and marketing communication strategy.

What Are the Basic Types of Research?

New advertising assignments always begin with some kind of informal or formal background research into the marketing situation. This is called *secondary research*, and we'll compare it with *primary research*, which is original research conducted by the company or brand.

Secondary Research Background research that uses available published information about a topic is **secondary research**. When advertising people get new accounts or new assignments, they start by reading everything they can find on the product, company, industry, and competition: sales reports, annual reports, complaint letters, and trade articles about the industry. They are looking for important facts and key insights. This kind of research is called secondary not because it is less important but because it has been collected and published by someone else.

A typical advertising campaign might be influenced, directly or indirectly, by information from many sources, including in-house agencies and outside research suppliers. The use of secondary information—finding information about the pizza market in Domino's case—underscores the importance of reading widely. Here are a few of the more traditional sources of secondary information that are available to advertisers doing backgrounding:

- ***Government Organizations*** Governments, through their various departments, provide an astonishing array of statistics that can greatly enhance advertising and marketing decisions. Many of the statistics come from census records on population size, geographic distribution, age, income, occupation, education, and ethnicity. As we explained in Chapter 5, U.S. Census Bureau demographic information of this kind is fundamental to decision making about brand communication targets and market segmentation. An advertiser cannot aim its advertising at a target audience without knowing that audience's size and major characteristics, such as media habits. In addition to census information, other government agencies generate reports that help advertisers make better decisions, such as the *Survey of Current Business* from the U.S. Department of Commerce (www.bea.gov/scb).
- ***Trade Associations*** Many industries support trade associations—professional organizations whose members all work in the same field—that gather and distribute information of interest to association members, such as the American Frozen Food Institute and the

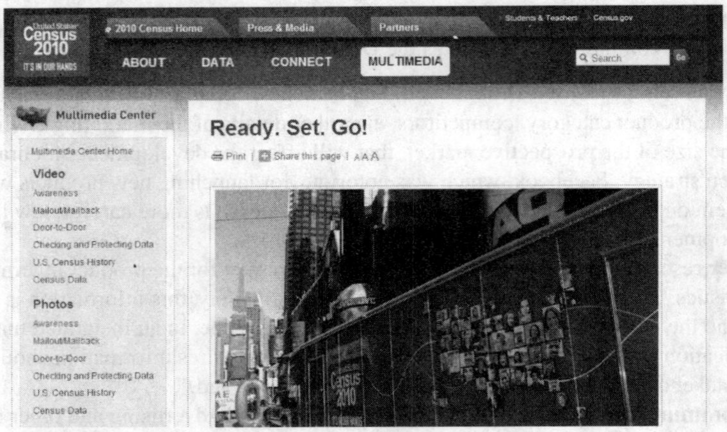

Photo: Courtesy of Perdue Farms Incorporated

Demographic information, such as that available from the U.S. Census Bureau, is fundamental to marketing and communication planning.
Source: www.census.gov/2010census.

Game Manufacturers Council, which are organizations that assist members in conducting their business. The trade associations for marketing communication include, among others, the American Association of Advertising Agencies, which issues reports that help ad agencies monitor their performance and keep tabs on competitors; the American Advertising Federation, which represents a grassroots network of advertisers and agencies; the Radio Advertising Bureau, which publishes *Radio Facts*, an overview of the commercial U.S. radio industry; the Account Planning Group, which conducts seminars and training sessions for account planners; and the Advertising Research Foundation, which conducts, aggregates, and analyzes research findings relevant to the information needs of the advertising industry.

- ***Secondary Research Suppliers*** Because of the overwhelming amount of information available through secondary research, specialized suppliers gather and organize that information around specific topic areas for other interested parties. Some secondary research suppliers are FIND/SVP, Off-the-Shelf Publications, Dialog Information Services, Lexis-Nexis, and Dow Jones's Factiva.
- ***Secondary Information on the Internet*** For any given company, you're bound to find a website where you can learn about the company's history and philosophy of doing business, check out its complete product line, and discover who runs the company. These sites offer credible information for account planners and others involved in market research. Other sources of Internet information are blog sites and chat rooms where you can learn about people's reactions to brands and products. There are also many industry-related sites for marketing that report on research, essays, and best practices:

BrandEra (www.brandera.com) offers information by product category.

MarketPerceptions (http://marketperceptions.com) represents a research company that specializes in health care research. The site has information about its focus group capabilities.

Forrester Research (www.forrester.com) provides industry research into technology markets.

Greenbook.org (www.greenbook.org) is a worldwide directory of marketing research focus group suppliers.

Cluetrain (www.cluetrain.com) publishes new ways to find and share innovative marketing information and ideas.

Primary Research Information that is collected for the first time from original sources is called **primary research.** To obtain primary research, companies and their agencies do their own research.

In Chapter 5, we mentioned the DDB Life Style Survey, which is a form of primary research conducted by an agency. Former DDB strategy director Marty Horn says that "DDB believes that advertising—and all other forms of marketing communication—is really a personal conversation between the brand being advertised and the consumer, and the better we know the consumer with whom we are conversing, the more engaging and persuasive our message will be." The agency's Life Style Survey is an important source of information that lets this conversation happen. Horn explains, "The DDB Life Style Survey helps us get a more 'up close and personal' look at who our clients' customers are than what conventional research alone can provide."

An example of a company that took on its own research is Perdue Farms, which conducted its own consumer research to develop its classic "tough man" campaign.

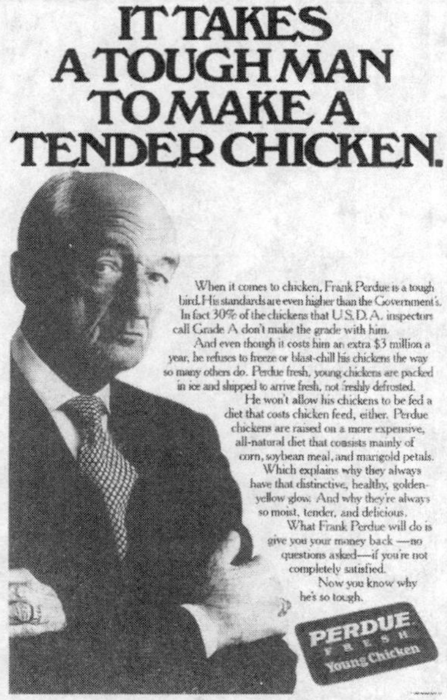

Photo: Image courtesy of Perdue

CLASSIC

"It takes a tough man to make a tender chicken" was the signature line for a long-running campaign that began in 1971 for Perdue Farms. It featured the owner, Frank Perdue, as the plain-spoken farmer who cared about the quality of his chickens. Scali, McCabe, Sloves was the agency behind the campaign that created the first recognizable brand for an unlikely commodity product—chickens. But the reason the campaign was successful wasn't just the iconic, perhaps ironic, "tough man" line but rather Frank Perdue's knowledge of his market. When he decided in the 1960s to eliminate brokers and sell directly to stores, he spent months on the road talking to butchers about what they wanted in chickens and identified 25 quality factors. Then he modified his operations to produce chickens that delivered on those 25 factors—a tough man who was obsessed with tender chickens.

Primary research suppliers (the firms clients and agencies hire) specialize in interviewing, observing, recording, and analyzing the behavior of those who purchase or influence the purchase of a particular good or service. The primary research supplier industry is extremely diverse. Companies range from A.C. Nielsen, the huge international tracker of television viewing habits to several thousand entrepreneurs who conduct focus groups and individual interviews, prepare reports, and provide advice on specific advertising and marketing problems for individual clients.

Many advertising agencies subscribe to large-scale surveys conducted by the Experian Simmons, formerly known as Simmons Market Research Bureau (SMRB), or by GfKMediamark Research & Intelligence (MRI). These two organizations survey large samples of American consumers (approximately 30,000 for each survey) and ask questions about the consumption, possession, or use of a wide range of products, services, and media. The products and services covered in the MRI survey range from toothbrushes and dental floss to diet colas, camping equipment, and theme parks.

Both Simmons National Consumer Study and MRI conduct original research and distribute their findings to their clients. The resulting reports are intended primarily for use in media planning, but because these surveys are so comprehensive, they also can be mined for unique consumer information. Through a computer program called Golddigger, for example, an MRI subscriber can select a consumer target and ask the computer to find all other products and services and all of the media that members of the target segment use. This profile provides a vivid and detailed description of the target as a person—just the information creative teams need to help them envision their audiences. To give you an idea of what the media data look like, check out Figure 6.1 for a sample MRI report of the types of television programs that adults ages 18 to 34 watch.

Basic Research Designs

Primary research can be designed to collect both quantitative and qualitative data. Quantitative data are also collected through experimental research designs, another type of primary research.

Quantitative Research Design Research that delivers numerical data such as number of users and purchases, their attitudes and knowledge, their exposure to ads, and other market-related information is called **quantitative research**. The MRI page is an example of data obtained through quantitative research. It also provides information on reactions to advertising, sometimes called *purchase intent*. Quantitative methods that investigate the responses of large numbers of people are useful in testing ideas to determine if their market is large enough or if most people really say or behave in a certain way.

Principle

Quantitative research is best used to count or predict and to draw conclusions about how much and how often.

Quantitative research is usually designed either to accurately count something, such as **sales levels**, or to predict something, such as attitudes. To be predictive, however, this type of research must follow careful scientific procedures. Two primary characteristics of quantitative research are (1) large sample sizes, typically from 100 to 1,000 people, and (2) random sampling. The most common quantitative research methods include surveys and studies that track such things as sales and opinions.

		Respondent 18–34 1-Person Household				Respondent 18–34 and Married, no children				Respondent 18–34 and Married, Youngest Child <6				Respondent 18–34 and Married Youngest Child 6+			
		A	B	C	D	A	B	C	D	A	B	C	D	A	B	C	D
Base: Adults	***Total U.S. 000***	***000***	***% Down***	***% Across***	***Index***	***000***	***% Down***	***% Across***	***Index***	***000***	***% Down***	***% Across***	***Index***	***000***	***% Down***	***% Across***	***Index***
All Adults	184274	5357	100.0	2.9	100	7559	100.0	4.1	100	18041	100.0	9.8	100	4978	100.0	2.7	100
Program-Types: Average Show																	
Adven/Sci Fi/West-Prime	19969	590	11.0	3.0	102	875	11.6	4.4	107	2303	12.8	11.5	118	694	13.9	3.5	129
Auto Racing-Specials	6590	*226	4.2	3.4	118	*242	3.2	3.7	90	634	3.5	9.6	98	*251	5.0	3.8	141
Awards-Specials	16490	397	7.4	2.4	83	514	6.8	3.1	76	1576	8.7	9.6	98	*451	9.1	2.7	101
Baseball Specials	28019	806	15.0	2.9	99	1128	14.9	4.0	98	2671	14.8	9.5	97	*506	10.2	1.8	67
Basketball-Weekend-College	7377	*222	4.1	3.0	104	*244	3.2	3.3	81	531	2.9	7.2	74	*183	3.7	2.5	92
Basketball Specials-College	17096	529	9.9	3.1	106	694	9.2	4.1	99	1459	8.1	8.5	87	*423	8.5	2.5	92
Basketball Specials-Pro.	32470	1057	19.7	3.3	112	1369	18.1	4.2	103	3128	17.3	9.6	98	886	17.8	2.7	101
Bowling-Weekend	16808	312	5.8	1.9	654	744	9.8	4.4	108	1476	8.2	8.8	90	*386	7.8	2.3	85
Comedy/Variety	26254	930	17.4	3.5	122	1150	15.2	4.4	107	3257	18.1	12.4	127	999	20.1	3.8	141
Daytime Dramas	7621	*192	3.6	2.5	87	*287	3.8	3.8	92	845	4.7	11.1	113	*343	6.9	4.5	167
Daytime Game Shows	7747	*97	1.8	1.3	43	*194	2.6	2.5	61	734	4.1	9.5	97	*235	4.7	3.0	112
Documen/Information-Prime	22514	532	9.9	2.4	81	504	6.7	2.2	55	1739	9.6	7.7	79	*454	9.1	2.0	75
Early Morning News	12226	280	5.2	2.3	79	*429	5.7	3.5	86	1065	5.9	8.7	89	*330	6.6	2.7	100
Early Morning Talk/Info/News	14681	258	4.8	1.8	60	580	7.7	4.0	96	1291	7.2	8.8	90	*268	5.4	1.8	68
Early Eve. Netwk News-M-F	25946	596	11.1	2.3	79	836	11.1	3.2	79	1822	10.1	7.0	72	*594	11.9	2.3	85
Early Eve. Netwk News-Wknd	11338	*197	3.7	1.7	60	*208	2.8	1.8	45	795	4.4	7.0	72	*187	3.8	1.6	61
Entertainment Specials	19630	408	7.6	2.1	71	701	9.3	3.6	87	1719	9.5	8.8	89	*494	9.9	2.5	93
Feature Films-Prime	17232	371	6.9	2.2	74	*538	7.1	3.1	76	1209	6.7	7.0	72	*475	9.5	2.8	102
Football Bowl Games-Specials	13322	369	6.9	2.8	95	*381	5.0	2.9	70	1512	8.4	11.3	116	*245	4.9	1.8	68
Football Pro.-Specials	44804	1471	27.5	3.3	113	1766	23.4	3.9	96	4555	25.2	10.2	104	1104	22.2	2.5	91
General Drama-Prime	19880	581	10.8	2.9	101	571	7.6	2.9	70	2095	11.6	10.5	108	*555	11.1	2.8	103
Golf	5161	*102	1.9	2.0	68	*152	2.0	2.9	72	*324	1.8	6.3	64	*15	.3	.3	11
Late Evening Netwk News Wknd	5146	*146	2.7	2.8	98	*114	1.5	2.2	54	*293	1.6	5.7	58	*104	2.1	2.0	75
Late Night Talk/Variety	9590	313	5.8	3.3	112	*297	3.9	3.1	75	1009	5.6	10.5	107	*198	4.0	2.1	76
News-Specials	14508	234	4.4	1.6	55	510	6.7	3.5	86	1297	7.2	8.9	91	*212	4.3	1.5	54
Pageants-Specials	22025	439	8.2	2.0	69	952	12.6	4.3	105	2503	13.9	11.4	116	547	11.0	2.5	92
Police Docudrama	23575	726	13.6	3.1	106	1179	15.6	5.0	122	2309	12.8	9.8	100	731	14.7	3.1	115
Pvt Det/Susp/Myst/Pol.-Prime	28183	673	12.6	2.4	82	763	10.1	2.7	66	1739	9.6	6.2	63	*493	9.9	1.7	65
Situation Comedies-Prime	19097	598	11.2	3.1	108	919	12.2	4.8	117	2737	15.2	14.3	146	688	13.8	3.6	133
Sports Anthologies-Weekend	4847	*218	4.1	4.5	155	*232	3.1	4.8	117	*403	2.2	8.3	85	*108	2.2	2.2	82
Sunday News/Interview	5809	*70	1.3	1.2	41	*116	1.5	2.0	49	*214	1.2	3.7	38	*97	1.9	1.7	62
Syndicated Adult General	10444	*271	5.1	2.6	89	462	6.1	4.4	108	766	4.2	7.3	75	*221	4.4	2.1	78
Tennis	10033	338	6.3	3.4	116	380	5.0	3.8	92	826	4.5	8.2	84	*105	2.1	1.0	39

FIGURE 6.1

MRI Consumer Media Report

This MRI report breaks down the 18–34 age market into four market segments based on size of household and age of children, if any, and describes their television viewing patterns. Here's a question: Where would you advertise to reach single adults in the 18–34 category? First look at the "Index" column under that category heading and find the two highest percentages. Then, for each high rating, look across to column A and determine the size of that group. As a point of comparison, do the same analysis for the "Married with the Youngest Child over 6" category. How do the two groups differ in the television viewing patterns?

Source: Mediamark Research, Inc. GfkMediamark Research & Intelligence, LLC

One of the biggest problems in using quantitative methods to study consumer decision processes is that consumers are often unable to articulate the reasons they do what they do because their reasons may not fit into answers provided in a survey. Furthermore, most people aren't tuned in to their own thoughts and thinking process so that they are comfortable saying yes or no or checking a space on a rating scale. Respondents also have a tendency to give the answers that they think the researcher wants to hear. These are all reasons why qualitative research has become much more important in brand communication in the last 20 years. It offers the ability to probe and move beyond the sometimes simplistic responses to a survey.

Qualitative Research Design The goal of **qualitative research** methodologies is to provide insight into the underlying reasons and motivations for how and why consumers think, feel, and behave as they do.

Principle
Qualitative research provides insight into underlying reasons and motivations.

For example, when Pepsico/Frito Lay considered changing its target audience for Cheetos from kids to adults, this scary new strategy called for in-depth research into the attitudes and behaviors of this new target. Researchers listened to what Cheetos fan said about the experience of eating the crunchy orange snack and found that these people loved eating Cheetos and licking their fingers. They liked a food that was playful and that gave them permission to not act their age.[2]

Common qualitative research methods include such tools as observation, ethnographic studies, in-depth interviews, and case studies. They trade large sample sizes and scientific predictions for greater depth of insight. These exploratory research tools are useful for probing and gaining explanations and understanding of such questions as these:

- What type of features do customers want?
- What are the motivations that lead to the purchase of a product?
- What do our customers think about our advertising?
- How do consumers relate to the brand? What are their emotional links to the brand?

Qualitative methods often are used early in the process of developing a brand communication plan or message strategy for generating insights as well as questions and hypotheses for additional research. They are also good at confirming hunches, ruling out bad approaches and questionable or confusing ideas, and giving direction to the message strategy. However, because qualitative research is typically done with small groups, researchers cannot project their findings to the larger population. Rather than drawing conclusions, qualitative research is used to answer the question of why and to generate hypotheses that can be tested with quantitative methods.

As Sally Reinman, worldwide market planner at Saatchi & Saatchi, wrote for this book in an earlier edition, qualitative research also can be applied in cross-cultural marketing situations: "As consumers around the world become better informed and more demanding," she said, "advertisers that target different cultures need to find the "commonalities" (or common ground) among consumer groups from these cultures. She used the example of research for Toyota's sport-utility vehicle (SUV), the RAV 4, which showed that consumers in all the targeted countries had three common desires: They all wanted an SUV to have style, safety, and economy.

Experimental Research Design Tightly controlled scientific studies are sometimes used to puzzle out how people think and respond to messages and incentives. **Experimental research** is designed using formal hypothesis-testing techniques that compare different message treatments and how people react to them. The idea is to control for all factors except the one being tested; if there is a change in the results, then the researcher can conclude that the variable being tested caused the difference. Experimental research is used to test marketing factors as well as advertising appeals and executions in such areas as product features and design, price, and various creative ideas.

Do your professors and instructors talk about the research they conduct? Here's an example of one professor's research about cigarette advertising that has practical implications for the tobacco industry and policy makers. It tests the idea that cigarette advertising can prime (or prepare) teens to think that smoking is cool. The "Principled Practice" feature explains how this researcher used experimental studies to determine the impact of advertising on behavior.

Sometimes in experimental research, the measurements are electronically recorded using such instruments as MRI (Magnetic Resonance Imaging) or EEG machines or eye-scan tracking devices. Electrodes can be used to monitor heart rate, pulse, and skin temperature to determine if people have a physical response to a message that they may not be able to put in words.

A PRINCIPLED PRACTICE

Does Advertising Make Smoking Cool?[3]

Cornelia (Connie) Pechmann, *University of California, Irvine*

In 1991, I began a program of research on tobacco-use prevention through advertising and the mass media. I wondered how often people saw advertisements for products shortly before experiencing the products. It occurred to me that advertising exposure and product experience were perhaps most likely to occur concurrently in the case of cigarette advertising and encounters with smokers. In 1991, cigarette advertising on billboards was ubiquitous, and 20 percent of high school seniors smoked daily, so I reasoned that adolescents might see cigarette advertisements and peers smoking concurrently. I also reasoned that encounters with smokers would often be ambiguous.

Looking at the literature, I could find few controlled experiments on cigarette advertising. However, surveys indicated there was a strong association between adolescents' perceptions of smokers and smoking initiation. With the assistance of coauthors, I completed two research projects that documented that cigarette advertisements can prime adolescents' positive beliefs about smokers and thus alter their social encounters with smokers. Specifically, cigarette advertisements serving as primes can favorably bias adolescents' perceptions of peers who smoke and thus increase their intent to smoke. One of our papers on this topic received the Best Paper Award from the *Journal of Consumer Research*. I continue to conduct research in this area.

I am told that my tobacco-related research has been cited by expert witnesses in legal cases such as the federal tobacco case, in legislative hearings, and in U.S. Attorney General meetings. I believe that some academic research should be conducted to inform public policy and that if research is not designed for this purpose, it likely will not have this effect.

Emotional responses, in particular, are hard to verbalize but may be observable using these types of sensors. Hewlett-Packard Company, for example, wired a group of volunteers with electrodes to see how they reacted to photos of people smiling. The study found that there were obvious differences in brain activity in people looking at photos of smiling people, particularly pictures of children smiling. New *computer-vision* software attached to high-resolution cameras is trying to read expressions on faces to determine viewers' responses during such activities as watching a movie trailer or shopping online.[4] And *eye-tracking* technology, a retina-tracking camera hooked up to a computer screen that projects images, has long been used to watch how readers and viewers scan print and video. It is now being used to test shoppers' attention to shelf designs and store layouts.[5]

How Do We Use Research?

Agencies and clients use research to make strategic decisions, as we have just discussed, but agencies rarely *conduct* research. Most research has become so specialized that separate research companies, as well as in-house client research departments, are the most likely research sources. These firms and departments collect and disseminate secondary research data and conduct primary research that ultimately finds its way into brand communication efforts. DDB is one of the few large agencies that still does its own in-house research. Its annual Life Style Survey, which we discussed in Chapter 5, began in 1975 and is the nation's longest-running and largest longitudinal study of consumer attitudes and behaviors. Its 2013 survey found, for example, that the number of stay-at-home dads is increasing and becoming a large enough group to be targeted for products and services traditionally targeted to women.

As markets have become more fragmented and saturated and as consumers have become more demanding, the need for research-based information in advertising planning has increased. Figure 6.2 summarizes the seven ways research is used in marketing communication planning:

1. Market information
2. Consumer insight research
3. Brand information

4. Media research
5. Message development research
6. Advertising or IMC plan
7. Evaluation research

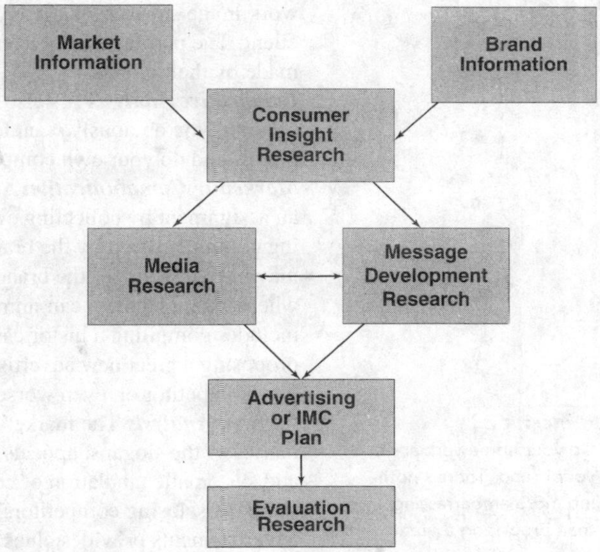

FIGURE 6.2
The Use of Research in Marketing Communication Planning

Market Information

Formal research used by the marketing department for strategic planning is called **marketing research**. It includes surveys, in-depth interviews, observational methods, focus groups (which are like in-depth interviews with a group rather than individuals), and all types of primary and secondary data used to develop a marketing plan and ultimately provide information for a brand communication plan. A subset of marketing research, *market research* is research used to gather information about a particular market, such as size or ethnic makeup.

An example of marketing research comes from Iceland, a country hard hit by the global economic downturn that brought Iceland's economy to its knees in 2009. As explained by Ingvi Logason, a member of this book's advisory board and a principal in his own advertising firm in Reykjavik, "Iceland, with its over-expanded banking sector, was hit worse than any other Westernized country." This recession hit the Icelandic public suddenly and hard—obliterating purchasing power. One of his clients, Icelandic Lamb, had to react quickly to the changed market. Traditionally, lamb consumption was almost exclusively on the prime (and more expensive) parts of the lamb. So how could the industry market less expensive cuts to consumers who were turning to cheaper meat products? Logason used clever probing in focus groups and found that the primary consumer problem was that they didn't know how to prepare these less costly cuts. In other words, lamb had become a luxury item, one that was dropped from the menu in tough times. The solution, of course, was to disseminate ideas with cooking shows and recipes that became viral ads.

Marketing information includes everything a planner can uncover about consumer perceptions of the brand, product category, and competitors' brands. Planners sometimes ride with the sales force and listen to sales pitches, tour manufacturing plants to see how a product is made, and work in a store or restaurant to evaluate employee interaction with customers. In terms of marketing communication, planners test the brand's and its competitors' advertisements, promotions, retail displays, packaging, and other marketing communication efforts.

Brand information includes an assessment of the brand's role and performance in the marketplace—is it a leader, a follower, a challenger, or a subbrand of a bigger and better-known brand? This research also investigates how people perceive brand personalities and images. Here are some common methods used to gather information about a brand and the marketplace:

- ***The Brand Experience*** When an agency gets a new client, the first thing the agency team has to do is learn about the brand through brand research. That means learning where the brand has been in the past in terms of the market, its customers, and competitors, as the Domino's campaign demonstrated. Also important is eliciting the corporate point of view regarding the brand's position within the company's line of products as well as corporate goals and plans for the brand. Another critical area of brand research is the brand's relationships with its customers. Researchers, for example, may go through all of the experiences that a typical consumer has in buying and using the product. If you were taking on a pizza restaurant account, for example, you might

Photo: Courtesy of Icelandic Lamb and Hér & NÚ Advertising

SHOWCASE

To help cooks use less costly cuts of Iceland lamb, Ingvi Logason and his team at H:N Marketing Communications in Ice and created educational ads with great appetite appeal.

Note: This ad was contributed by Ingvi Logason, Principal in H&N, Reykjavik, Iceland, and a member of this book's advisory board. A graduate of Western Florida University, his work was nominated for inclusion in this book by Professor Tom Groth.

work in the store or visit it as a customer. Brand buying is also a form of commitment to the client: The parking lots of agencies that have automotive accounts are usually full of cars made by their clients.

- ***Competitive Analysis*** It's also important to do a competitive analysis. If you handle a soap account, you obviously want to use that brand of soap, but you may also buy the competing brands and do your own comparative test just to add your experiences to your brand analysis.
- ***Marketing Communication Audit*** Either formally or informally, most planners will begin an assignment by collecting every possible piece of advertising and other forms of marketing communication by the brand as well as its competitors and other relevant categories that may have lessons for the brand. Often these pieces are attached to the walls in a "war room" where team members can immerse themselves in messages to stimulate new ideas. This includes compiling a historical collection as well. There's nothing more embarrassing than proposing a great new advertising idea only to find out that it was used a couple of years ago by a competitor or, even worse, by your client.
- ***Content Analysis*** The marketing communication audit might include only informal summaries of the slogans, appeals, and images used most often, or it might include more formal and systematic tabulation of competitors' approaches and strategies, called a **content analysis**. By disclosing competitors' strategies and tactics, analysis of the content of competitive advertisements provides clues about how competitors are thinking and suggests ways to develop new and more effective campaigns. Planners also try to determine what mental territories or positions competitors claim and which are still available and relevant to the brand.

Principle
Do your homework about your brand. There's nothing more embarrassing than proposing a great new advertising idea only to find out that it was used a couple of years ago by a competitor or, even worse, by your client.

The DDB agency regularly conducts "Barriers to Purchase" research,[6] realizing that these barriers often create an opportunity for advertising messages to present information or change perceptions. The American Dairy Association, for example, asked DDB to find out why cheese consumption was declining. Similar to the Icelandic lamb story, the study identified one barrier that was most easily correctable through a marketing communication effort: the absence of simple cheese recipes for home cooks. Ads and the association's website (www.ilovecheese.com) offer many such recipes.

Consumer Insight

A basic principle in this book is that effective marketing communication rests on truly understanding the consumer. As Regina Lewis, a member of this book's advisory board, explained in the Part 2 opener, brands have to be true to the consumers who buy them. Both the creative team members (who create messages) and the media planners (who decide how and when to deliver the messages) need to know as much as they can and in as much depth and detail as possible about their audience. That's the point of the story about selling Icelandic lamb during the recession. To turn the sales pattern around, the agency had to understand how its target market was adapting to the new economic situation.

Researchers often try to uncover the *whys of the buys*, but insight research may also uncover reasons why people don't want to try or buy a product. Lewis explained that Dunkin' Donuts, when she was vice president of consumer and brand insights, found in its consumer research several reasons why its customers were uncomfortable ordering fancy coffee drinks. Mostly, they were intimidated by the whole "barista" thing and the fancy coffee names.

Principle
Insight research is designed to uncover the whys of the buys as well as the why nots.

Collecting Feedback We mentioned earlier that *feedback* can be obtained from customers as a part of interactive customer contact—systematically recording information from customer service, technical service, inbound telemarketing calls, and online sites. Some businesses use the Internet to involve customers in making decisions about product design, distribution, price, and company operations using online surveys, blogs, online communities, and other social media. Travel marketers, for example, have found that social media offer an opportunity to collect meaningful customer feedback on a mass scale; however, they have also found that conversation-oriented customers want to be the ones to start the conversation.[7]

You've probably heard the phrase "This call may be monitored for quality assurance." These recordings are used for training, but they also can be analyzed for marketing intelligence.[8] If customers say they are confused or ask the representative to repeat a phrase, then it could indicate that the sales offer or technical explanation isn't working right. These calls can provide instant feedback about the strength of a brand's offering as well as competitors' offers. Specific questions such as "Where did you hear about this?" are used to monitor brand contact points and media performance.

Monitoring Buzz and Tracking Behavior The Internet has made it easy to track comments about a brand. Many marketers, such as IBM and Microsoft, monitor chats and blogs and also do more general scanning for key words to find out what people are saying about their brands and products. These findings can be incorporated back into other methods, such as focus groups, to verify and explain the sentiments expressed online.[9]

Monitoring buzz also can be used to monitor attitudes. For example, the *Wall Street Journal* followed the conversation on social networks about Twinkies after Hostess announced its bankruptcy. The study found that 25 percent of the comments focused on health issues (obesity), 33 percent were sad (an American icon going away), 35 percent were about unions (bankruptcy to break labor contracts), and 7 percent were jokes.[10] Social media, such as Facebook, can also be used to get consumer responses. Lay's Facebook app, for example, suggested new flavors and asked people to click on an "I'd Eat That" button.[11]

Pinterest, an online bulletin board where people post pictures, articles, and videos, allows users to save images and group them. It's another online tool that can be used unobtrusively to monitor consumer thinking. As Kaila Strong explains, the Pinterest categories are a way to see what content is popular in a niche market. The "Popular" category lets users—and marketers—see the most popular of all pins on the site.[12]

Photo: © American Dairy Association managed by Dairy Management, Inc.

The DDB agency found that a barrier to purchasing cheese was the lack of good recipe ideas using cheese products. The American Dairy Association responded by getting more recipes distributed through advertising and its website.

Neuromarketing To get inside consumers' minds to see what they are really thinking, marketers have turned to neuroscience, which uses highly technical equipment to scan the brain as it processes information and makes decisions. Neuromarketing, which we have mentioned in the previous chapter, is the application of this research technology to consumer behavior. For example, one study by a researcher at the University of California, Los Angeles, mapped how viewers responded to Super Bowl ads below the level of their awareness. In the "Principled Practice" feature at www.pearsonglobaleditions.com/Moriarty, Professor Ann Marie Barry, who wrote in Chapter 4 about brain science and 'thought vs. feeling' also investigates the neuroscience research and its implications for ethics and privacy.

Campbell's Soup used neuromarketing and biometrics to analyze consumer responses to brand communication. As part of a major two-year study and redesign of the labels on its iconic red and white soup cans, Campbell's used neuromarketing techniques to see how consumers reacted to everything from pictures of bowls to the use of a spoon and other graphic cues, such as steam rising from the bowl. The objective was to find ways to help consumers connect on a deeper and more emotional level with the brand. Changes included color coding the different varieties; depict steam to make the soup in the picture look warm; remove the spoon, which consumers said served no purpose; update the look of the bowl; and move the Campbell's logo to the bottom in order to better identify the varieties.[13]

Media Information

Media planning begins with consumer research and questions about media behavior that help with the media selection decision. Media planners often work in conjunction with the information account planners uncover to decide which media formats make the most sense to accomplish the objectives. The goal is to activate consumer interest by reaching them through some medium that engages their interest.

Next, **media research** gathers information about all the possible media and marketing communication tools that might be used in a campaign to deliver a message. Media researchers then match that information to what is known about the target audience. The MRI data shown earlier in Figure 6.1 illustrates the type of information media researchers consult to develop recommendations.

Message Development and Diagnostics

As planners, account managers, and people on the creative team begin to develop a message strategy, they involve themselves in various types of informal and formal message development research. They read all of the relevant secondary information provided by the client and the planners to become better informed about the brand, the company, the competition, the media, and the product category.

Writers and art directors almost always conduct informal research of their own. They may do their own personal observational research and visit retail stores, talk to salespeople, and watch customers buy. In addition to reading, they will look at previous advertising, especially that of competitors, to see what others have done before. This personal research is a source of insight and has a powerful influence on what happens later in the message development process.

The next step after personal backgrounding is to produce and test different "big ideas" both informally within the team and through more formal structured research. Creative development research often uses qualitative methods to predict the idea's effectiveness. Called **concept testing**, it can help evaluate the relative power of various creative approaches. It's a "work-in-progress" type of evaluation. The idea is to test the Big Idea to see if it communicates the strategy behind the message—as well as test various types *executions* of this big idea. These interviews are often conducted online or in malls or other areas where there are lots of people in the target who agree to look at a rough sketch of the idea or ad and respond to it.

Principle
Diagnostic research is used during the creative development of a brand message in order to find problems, make the communication clearer, and strengthen the impact of the execution.

After the Big Idea is agreed on, the creative team will rough out the message in whatever format being used—print, broadcast, or online—at which point the execution will be tested to determine if there are any unexpected problems in the execution. For example, does the brochure catch attention? Does an ad take too long in the beginning to set up the problem? Does the brand get lost in an entertaining story line in a commercial? This diagnostic research is early enough in the creative process that it is still possible to find problems, adjust the Big Idea to make the branding and communication clearer, and make changes in the execution to strengthen the impact.

Another diagnostic technique used to analyze brand meaning is **semiotic analysis**, which is a way to take apart the signs and symbols in a message to uncover layers and types of meanings. The objective is to find deeper meanings in the symbolism that might relate to different groups of consumers. Its focus is on determining the meanings, even if they are not obvious or highly symbolic, that might relate to particular consumer motivations.

For example, the advertising that launched the OnStar Global Positioning System of General Motors used a Batman theme. By looking at this commercial in terms of its signs and symbols, it is possible to determine if the obvious as well as hidden meanings of the message were on strategy. For example, the decision to use a comic book hero as the star created a heroic association for OnStar. However, Batman isn't a superhero but rather more of a common person with a lot of great technology and cool gadgets—remember Jack Nicholson's line as the Joker when he said, "Where does he get all those wonderful toys?" Batman is also ageless, appealing to young people who read comic books and watch movies, as well as older people who remember Batman from their youth. A highly successful effort, this Batman OnStar campaign won a David Ogilvy Research Award.

Evaluation

Concept testing is actually the first level of evaluation. After an advertisement or other type of marcom message has been developed and produced, it can be evaluated for its effectiveness both before and after it runs as part of a campaign. **Pretesting** is research on an execution in its finished stages but before it appears in media—this is the last step where diagnostics can generate change in the message. While creative development research looks at the power of the advertising idea, pretesting looks at the way the idea is presented. The idea can be strong, but the target might hate the execution. This type of test elicits a *go or no-go* decision for a specific advertisement. Sometimes, pretesting will also call into doubt the strength of the advertising idea, forcing the creative team to rethink its strategy.

Ameritest is a research company that specializes in pretesting as well as evaluating the effectiveness of brand messages in print, on television, on radio, and online. Charles Young, president of Ameritest and a member of this book's advisory board, explains how his firm's pretesting methodology diagnoses effectiveness of the execution of a brand message to identify, among other things, the high and low points of attention as well as the emotional structure of the message. These are the moments when the audience is most engaged with the message.

A Matter of Principle

Finding Moments of Truth

Charles E. Young, *President, Ameritest*

The most powerful search engine of all is the human eye, which scans advertising film, television commercials, and Web videos, continuously deciding on an unconscious level whether the visual information streaming toward it is important enough to let into consciousness. Because our conscious minds have limited bandwidth or workspace, much of the imagery that advertisers are trying to communicate to consumers is ignored or deleted by our preconscious eye-brain filters as so much visual spam.

Ameritest's Picture Sorts® is a set of nonverbal research tools that have been developed for the Internet to survey the right-brained scanning and sorting processes involved in visual communication. These tools make use of the power of still photographs to capture an instant of time and store our fleeting emotions.

By sorting a randomized deck of pictures taken from the ad itself—which is like the visual vocabulary of the film—the ad researcher can reconstruct consumers' moment-by-moment attention and emotional response to an ad they just saw. Three different sorting exercises enable the advertiser to perform the equivalent of putting on 3-D glasses to see advertising through the eyes of its target audience.

The Flow of Attention® graph, the first of three measurement dimensions, is like a visual spell-checker that the researcher can use to analyze whether a piece of advertising film or Web video has been put together well according to principles of proper film syntax or good visual grammar. The Flow of Attention graph reveals the hidden structure of audience attention to moving pictures, which, like music, follows a rhythmic beat of cognitive processing. The beat, or focal points of attention, is where the most important information in an ad, like the brand identity, is conveyed.

From the emotional hook at the beginning to the turning points in a story to the surprise ending of a funny commercial, engaging the emotions of consumers is essential to motivating them. The Flow of Emotion® graph not only measures the volume of emotions pumping through ad film but also reveals which of four archetypal dramatic structures is being used in the creative design. Knowing this structure tells the advertiser when the timing is exactly right to first introduce the brand in the ad, which might be at the beginning, somewhere in the middle, or not until the end of a commercial.

The Flow of Meaning® tool shows the researcher where key communication points or brand values are being cued visually. Meaning is created when thought and emotion come together in a few memorable and emotionally charged moments in a commercial when memories are being created. Because there are three distinct memory systems in the mind, branding moments come in three flavors: (1) images that convey concepts or rational ideas go into our knowledge, or semantic, memory system; (2) images that evoke emotions go into our emotion, or episodic, memory system; and (3) images that rehearse or mirror the behavior the advertiser is trying to influence go into our action, or procedural, memory system (where memories of how you ride a bike or play a violin are stored). Taken together, this learn–feel–do imaging process is how the long-term work of advertising is performed, building a brand's image.

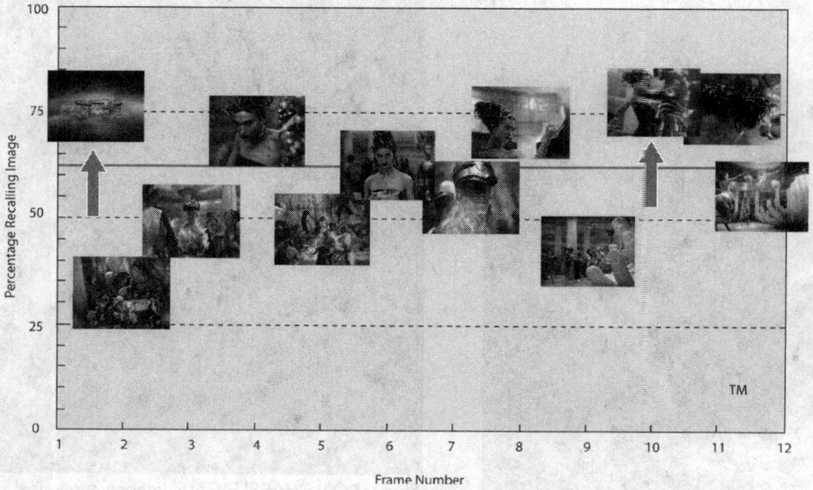

Photo: Courtesy of Unilever PLC and Ameritest/CYResearch Inc. Used with permission

This diagram demonstrates the flow of attention across a commercial for Unilever's Thermasilk. The selected still frames represent those places in the commercial where the attention is high (above the red line) or low (below the red line). Note the highest attention points, which are indicated with the red arrows. In this commercial, that tight shot of the face is the "moment of truth," the most highly attended to frame in this execution.

In advertising, **evaluative research** is done during a campaign and afterward. If it's used during a campaign, the objective is diagnostic: to adjust the brand messages to make them stronger. This is sometimes referred to as **copytesting**. The goal of **posttesting** research is to determine the effectiveness of the ad or campaign.

What Are the Most Common Research Methods?

This section focuses on the types of research used in message development and the research situations where these methods are typically used. Consumer research methodologies are often described in terms of the ways researchers contact their respondents. The contact can be in person, by telephone, by mail, through the Internet or cable television, or by a computer kiosk in a mall or store.

Ways of Contact: Quantitative Methods

Most quantitative research in marketing communication is survey based; however, consumers can also be contacted in malls and other public places where they are invited to participate in experimental research.

Survey Research In a survey, questionnaires are used to obtain information about people's attitudes, knowledge, media use, and exposure to particular messages, and this was an important part of the Domino's rebranding campaign. **Survey research** is a quantitative method that uses structured interviews to ask large numbers of people the same set of questions. The questions can deal with personal characteristics, such as age, income, behavior, or attitudes. The surveys can be conducted in person, by phone, by mail, or online.

An example of a company doing its own survey research is Toyota, which undertook a huge two-year study of ultrarich consumers in the United States to better market its upscale Lexus brand. A team of nine Lexus employees from various departments was designated the "superaffluent team" and sent on the road to interview wealthy car buyers about why they live where they do, what they do for enjoyment, what brands they buy, and how they feel about car makes and models. One surprising finding was that these consumers don't just buy a car—they buy a fleet of cars because they have multiple homes and offices.[14]

Photo: Copyright © Jeff Greenberg/PhotoEdit

Survey research can be conducted in person and is often conducted in malls, supermarket aisles, or other public places.

Photo: RON CHAPPLE\Getty Images, Inc. – Taxi

Phone surveys are commonly used. Often they come from commercial call centers where many people hired by a research company staff a bank of phones. In recent years, the contact is made through electronic dialing, and when respondents answer, the call is transferred to an interviewer.

Incentives are important when doing surveys. As Karl Weiss, president/CEO of the Market Perceptions research company and a member of this book's advisory board, explains, choose an incentive that is appropriate for your audience—perhaps $5 or $10 in cash, a drawing for a Wii or iPhone, or even a summary of the results. Different audiences have different interests, so make your incentive appealing to them. Be careful, however, not to bias your results in the process. If you are studying airline travel behavior and your incentive is a PlayStation, don't be surprised to find that most of those who complete the survey are males under 35 years old. Opinionators are people who sign onto consumer market research survey sites as paid panelists. They are asked their opinions on everything from product design to television commercials or sales promotions.[15]

There are two big questions to consider in designing a survey: how to build a representative sample of people to be interviewed and what method is best to collect the data.

Sampling and Data Collection A technique called sampling is used to find interviewees because, in most cases, it is cost prohibitive to try to interview everyone in the population or target market. Instead, the people interviewed are a representative **sample** of the larger group, a subset of the population that is representative of the entire population. For survey research to be an accurate reflection of the population, those who participate must be *selected at random*, which means that every person who belongs to the population being surveyed has an equal likelihood (probability) of being chosen to participate. Random sampling is the basic requirement of opinion research and polling, which you hear about every time an election comes around.

Principle
Careful scientific procedures are used in survey research to draw a representative sample of a group in order to accurately reflect the population's behavior and attitudes.

For years, phone number lists in phone directories gave researchers the perfect source from which they could draw a **random sample**, which means that each person in the population has an equal chance of being selected. Phone lists have become less reliable in recent years as more people have dropped their landlines in favor of cell phones.

There are a number of market research companies that specialize in creating samples, particularly for online research. They try to identify appropriate groups based on the targeting decisions of a client—for example, certain demographics or usage rates—and then define the locations and size required as well as the methods for reaching these people. This is a method used by Ameritest in doing online tests of commercials.

Online Survey Research Since survey research first began, the way researchers have gone about collecting data from respondents has seen almost constant change as new technologies have made such research more cost efficient. Since the 1950s, research methods that involve personal interaction have moved from door-to-door interviews to phone interviews and now to online surveys. Online surveys now make up half of the $3.3 billion spent on market research.[16] As Weiss explains and as his diagram shows, the Internet has opened up new opportunities for collecting data (see the "A Matter of Practice" feature).

In addition to survey research, the Internet can also be a useful tool for monitoring online behavior. Jason Cormier, co-founder of social-media agency Room 214, explains that marketing communication data can be based on interactions on social networks such as Facebook. We have printed here the screen download, "Take the Survey," from the Billings, Montana, rebranding campaign—it took off with an online survey of more than 1,000 people. In Chapter 18, you'll read about Doha: A New City—a campaign that was launched with online support.

Photo: Courtesy of the Billings Chamber of Commerce

SHOWCASE

A rebranding campaign for Billings began with a broad survey of people involved in the business of supporting the city. For online surveys to work, they need to be supported by an invitation to participate that showcases the easy-to-use message.

The Billings, Montana, "Trailhead" brand identity campaign was provided by John Brewer.

Ways of Contact: Qualitative Methods

Various types of surveys are the most common quantitative research methods, but certain types of surveys both with individuals and groups—can also be used for probing and to gather more insightful responses. In addition, qualitative methods take researchers into homes and stores to watch how consumers behave.

A Matter of Practice

Online Marketing Research

Karl Weiss, *President/CEO, Market Perceptions Inc.*

Remember when survey researchers came to your door with clipboards in hand, asking to come into your home to ask you some questions about a new product idea or some different advertising approaches? Unless you're well over 50 years old, probably not.

Times have changed, and conducting surveys by going door-to-door was replaced by telephone interviewing in the 1960s. Someday you can tell your children, "When I was growing up, marketing researchers used to call people on the phone to do surveys," and that will seem about as foreign a concept to them as door-to-door interviewing does to most people today.

There are many reasons for the current shift from phone to online surveys, but they are largely the same as when door-to-door interviewing switched to phone. It was cheaper, it was faster, and the quality of the data was better. The Internet allows us to gather data so much faster since tens of thousands of requests can be send out via e-mail in a matter of seconds, and it's much less expensive since the data are all captured by computer rather than live interviewers. And while the quality of the data has been the greatest obstacle facing widespread acceptance of online surveying, the continued declines in people participating in telephone surveys has diminished the randomness (and representativeness) of telephone survey data.

So what does this mean for marketing research beyond an evolution in data collection methodology? Gathering data by telephone was an improvement in data randomness by being able to draw a better random sample. It also offered a reduction in cost since conducting surveys by phone is cheaper than going door-to-door, not to mention an improvement in timing. While online surveying has further reduced both the cost of the data collection and even more dramatically the timing to gather the information, it has not been able to maintain the same quality when it comes to the representativeness of the data. With telephone surveying, almost every person in the United States has a phone number, and telephone directories provide a pretty good listing from which to draw a sample, and if you want to do even better, the phone numbers can be randomly generated so that even unlisted numbers are included.

For online surveys, there is no directory of all e-mail addresses in the United States. And even though most people today have an e-mail address, there are significant differences between those who do and those who do not, representing not only the "digital divide" but even differences in how those who have computers with Internet access utilize this technology. Some only text and hardly ever check their e-mail addresses. Some simply have not set up an e-mail address to begin with.

Without a comprehensive directory from which marketing researchers can draw a sample, we cannot know how well our results reflect those of the larger population. And spamming people at random to complete a survey does not go over well in the Internet age, even if such a directory existed. The rules of the game have changed, and marketing research needs to adjust. Participants who do surveys online almost always have signed up to do so, joining an online panel where they get paid to do surveys. People who choose to join an online survey panel may be quite different from those who do not, likely thinking this is a fun way to make a little extra money on the side. Do you belong to a panel? How about your classmates? If there are different motivations for choosing whether to join a panel, those differences in thinking style will be reflected in the data that are gathered, creating a bias in the results.

But it's not all bad news, and researchers do simply need to adapt. Online surveying provides us with many new opportunities—the ability to present images, sounds, videos, and websites to participants for their review prior to answering questions. It's the new world of marketing research, and with the challenges come many new benefits.

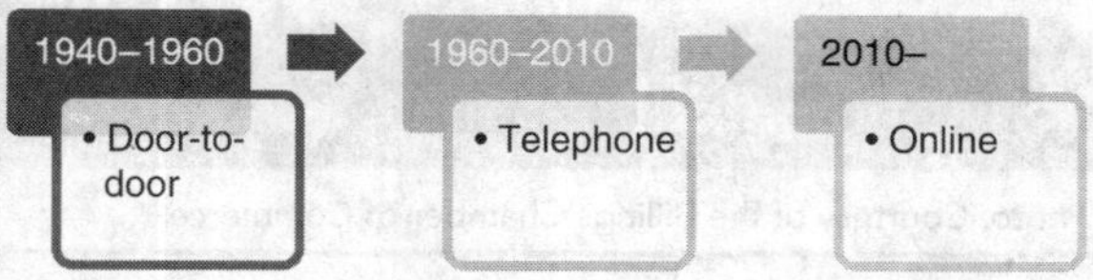

In-Depth Interviews One qualitative method used to survey consumers is the **in-depth interview**, which is conducted one-on-one using **open-ended questions** that require respondents to generate their own answers. The primary difference between an interview and a survey is the interviewer's use of a more flexible and unstructured questionnaire. This is the type of research method used by the Lexus "superaffluent team" we discussed earlier. Interviewers use a discussion guide, which outlines the areas to be covered during the session.

The discussion guides tend to be longer than surveys with questions that are usually very broad. Examples include "What do you like or dislike about this product?" and "What type of television programs do you like to watch?" Interviewers probe by responding to the answer with "Why do you say that?" or "Can you explain in more detail?" Interviews are considered qualitative because they typically use smaller sample sizes than surveys, their results cannot be generalized, and they are not subjected to statistical tests.

Focus Groups Another qualitative method is a **focus group**, which is a group interview of 6 to 10 users and potential users of a product who are gathered around a table to have a discussion about some topic, such as a brand, product category, or marketing communication. The objective is to get participants talking in a conversational format so that researchers can observe the dialogue and interactions among the group. It's a *directed group interview*. A moderator supervises the group, providing direction through a set of carefully developed questions that stimulate conversation and elicit the group members' thoughts and feelings in their own words. Other qualitative tools can also be used with groups, such as asking participants to create posters, diaries, or poems, or to complete exercises in day mapping or memory associations (what comes to mind when you think of something, such as a brand, situation, or location).

Focus groups can be used at any step in the planning process, but they are often used early in information gathering to probe for patterns of thought and behavior that are then tested using quantitative research tools, such as surveys. For example, the Domino's team conducted focus groups with frequent users of pizza, particularly the Domino's brand. Information from focus groups can uncover, as it did in this case, answers to "how" and "why" questions. The Domino's participants said that they didn't like the taste of the pizza but that other features, such as delivery, were good. Focus groups are also useful in testing creative ideas or exploring various alternatives in message strategy development.

A **friendship focus group** takes place in a comfortable setting, usually a private home, where the host has recruited the participants. This approach is designed to break down barriers and save time in getting to more in-depth responses. For example, one study of sensitive and insensitive visuals used in advertising directed to black women found that a self-constructed friendship group was easier to assemble and yielded more honest and candid responses than a more traditional focus group where respondents are recruited by a research company.[17]

The Web is a tool not only for online surveys but also for online focus groups based on the idea of getting a group of brand loyalists together as a password-protected online community.

Photo: © Janine Wiedel Photolibrary/Alamy

In-depth interviews are conducted one-on-one with open-ended questions that permit the interviewee to give thoughtful responses. The informal structure of the questions allows the interviewer to follow up and ask more detailed questions to dig deeper into attitudes and motivations.

Photo: © Marmaduke St. John/Alamy

Focus groups are conducted around a conference table with a researcher serving as the moderator working from a list of prepared discussion questions. The session is usually held in a room with one-way glass so the other team members from the agency and client can observe the way respondents answer the questions.

Online research company Communispace has created some 225 online communities for marketers, including Kraft Foods, Unilever for its Axe brand, and Charles Schwab.

Online focus groups can be a form of **crowdsourcing**, which refers to aggregating the wisdom of large groups of Internet users in a type of digital brainstorming. In a search for "collective intelligence," crowdsourcing collects opinions and ideas from a digital community.

Suggestions and Comments Dialogue creates new ways to listen to customers. In the traditional communication model we described in Chapter 4, customers' responses, or *feedback*, are gathered primarily through research, but in newer approaches to communication, feedback is achieved by monitoring more interactive forms of marketing communication (personal selling, customer service, online marketing, and social media) as well as the customer-initiated dialogue that comes through response devices such as toll-free numbers and e-mail addresses.

Informal feedback has always been available in stores through suggestion boxes and customer satisfaction cards and surveys. Target took that idea online by publishing an ad in the *Wall Street Journal* asking customers to "Tell us what more we can do for you." Some 627 respondents e-mailed suggestions. Target then published the suggestions and the company's responses to them in two-page ads. It was a novel way of eliciting comments, listening to them, and then responding. Starbucks (and many other companies) uses an online suggestion box incorporating the practices of crowdsourcing. MyStarbucks Idea is a website for Starbucks customers to contribute ideas, join the discussion, and vote on the ones they like best. Check it out at http://mystarbucksidea.force.com/ideaHome.

Panels An **expert panel** gathers experts from various fields into a focus group setting. This research tool can stimulate new ways of looking at a brand, product, or customer pattern. More commonly, however, a marketing panel or **consumer research panel** is an ongoing group of carefully selected people interested in a topic or product category. A standing panel can be maintained over time by a marketer as a proprietary source of information or by a research company whose clients provide topics for the panel members' consideration. Panels can gather in person or be contacted by phone, mail, or the Internet. An example of this type of research comes from cool hunters and trend watchers who may use proprietary panels to track fashions and fads.

Observation Research Like anthropologists, observation researchers study the actual behavior of consumers in settings where they live, work, shop, and play, acting as what Professor Shay Sayre refers to as "professional snoops."[18] Direct **observation research** is closer and more personal than most other types of research. Researchers use video, audio, and disposable cameras to record consumers' behavior at home (with consumer consent), in stores, or wherever people buy and use their products.

Lululemon, a women's athletic apparel chain, has built a mini-empire based on an unexpected strategy—it doesn't stock a lot of merchandise and cultivates a sense of scarcity. How does it work? The company doesn't use a lot of standard marketing research techniques, such as focus groups, but its executives spend hours each week observing customers, watching them shop, and listening to their comments and complaints in order to tweak the stores' offerings and merchandising.[19]

A marketer may rely on observation in the aisles of grocery, drug, and discount stores to watch people as they make product selections. Grocery shopping might seem like a mundane, mechanical activity, but look around next time you're in a store and watch how your fellow shoppers make their product choices. An example of this type of experience comes from a *New York Times* article written by Kate Stein, who was at the time of the article a University of Florida undergraduate student. She describes what it's like to participate in observational research.

Cool watchers, researchers who keep tabs on trends, also use observational research when visiting places and events where their target market gathers. The Consumer Behavior Odyssey was a classic observational research project that opened the door for this type of research in marketing. The Odyssey put a team of researchers in a Winnebago on a trip from Los Angeles to Boston in the mid-80s. Along the way, the researchers used a variety of observational techniques to watch and record people behaving as consumers.[20]

A variation on observational research is **participant observation**. In this research method, the observer is a member of the group being studied. For example, research into television-viewing behaviors sometimes uses friendship groups of the researcher who unobtrusively records his or her friends' behavior as part of the viewing session. The idea is that by immersing themselves in the activity, observers have an inside view—perhaps a more empathetic or informed view—of their groups' experiences.

A Day in the Life

A Stopwatch, Code Sheet, and Curiosity

Kate Stein, *University of Florida and Cornell Law School*

I interned as a consumer-behavior researcher in grocery stores for Brian Wansink, director of the Cornell University Food and Brand Lab, and got an eyeful of insight about how people select the products they buy. I observed shoppers in the aisles as they checked the freshness of produce, compared prices, and read package labels.

Collecting data and running studies like these require observing thousands of supermarket customers in situ as they complete their shopping expeditions. The goal is to collect data that will be descriptive of reality without interfering with it. So I'm a participant as well as a researcher.

My observations were made across several different types of grocery stores to obtain data about a wide variety of shopper types and of products available to select. I spent between 5 and 10 hours a day in grocery stores, pacing the tiled floors as I conducted my research. Setting up a study requires creating a detailed map of the grocery store, complete with measurements of the width of the grocery aisles.

To remain unnoticed and observe real behavior, researchers must appear to be supermarket shoppers themselves, blending in with their surroundings as just another innocuous grocery store patron. Using a cart and pretending that your data sheet is a grocery list are two useful measures to enhance the credibility of an undercover researcher.

Much like people watching in an airport, the appeal of observational research is easy to understand. One can feel like a true spy as you attempt to blend in with the surroundings and pose as a neutral participant in an environment where you are actually conducting research.

Observational research requires a sharp eye and a curiosity into the actions of others. Anyone with a natural interest in human nature should find consumer behavior research to be a rewarding pursuit. For more on this study, check out Professor Wansink's website at www.mindlesseating.org.

Ethnographic Research Related to observation, **ethnographic research** involves the researcher in living the lives of the people being studied. Ethnographers have elevated people watching to a science. In ethnographic research, which combines anthropology and marketing, observers immerse themselves in a culture to study the meanings, language, interaction, and behavior of the people in the group.[21] The idea is that people's behavior tells you more than you can ever get in an interview or focus group. This method is particularly good at deriving a picture of a day in the life of a typical consumer. An example comes from a Walgreen's vice president who wore glasses that blurred his vision, taped his thumbs to his palms, and wore shoes containing unpopped popcorn. The exercise was designed to help him and other retail executives understand the difficulties facing elderly shoppers—confusing store layouts, eyesight problems, arthritis, and the inability to reach or stoop.[22]

Principle

Direct observation and ethnographic research methods reveal what people actually do rather than what they say they do, but they also lack the ability to explain *why* these people do what they do.

Major companies like Harley-Davidson and Coca-Cola hire marketing experts trained in social science research to observe and interpret customer behavior. These participant observers then meet with the company's managers, planners, and marketing staff to discuss their impressions. The case of Eight O'Clock coffee is an example of the use of a videotaped ethnographic study. The brand's agency, New York–based Kaplan Thaler, got 14 families in Pittsburgh and Chicago to use video cameras to record their typical mornings in order to identify the various roles that coffee played in their morning rituals.

Direct observation and ethnographic research have the advantage of revealing what people actually do as distinguished from what people say they do. It can yield the correct answer when faulty memory, a desire to impress the interviewer, or simple inattention to details would cause an interview answer to be wrong. The biggest drawback to direct observation is that it shows what is happening but not *why*. Therefore, the results of direct observation often are combined with personal interviews afterward to provide a more complete and more understandable picture of attitudes, motives, and behavior.

The McCann agency has dedicated a $2.5 million research effort to understanding the lives of low-income Latinos from Mexico to Chile.[23] A new division named "Barrio" studies the marketing efforts of its clients, such as Nestlé and Danone. It has transformed conference rooms into "bodegas" (corner grocery shops) and sent employees to live with families amassing some 700 hours of video recordings. The reason is that practical insights into low-income groups are hard to find, yet these people are consumers, too, and marketers need to understand their needs as emerging economies bring new lifestyles to the disadvantaged.

Diaries Sometimes, consumers are asked to record their activities through the use of diaries. These **diaries** are particularly valuable in media research because they tell media planners exactly what programs and ads the consumers watched. If comment lines are provided, then the activities can also be accompanied by thoughts. *Beeper diaries* are used as a way to randomize the recording of activities. Consumers participating in the study are instructed to grab the diary and record what they are doing when the beeper goes off. Diaries are designed to catch the consumer in a more realistic, normal life pattern than you can derive from surveys or interviews that rely on consumers to remember their activities accurately. This can also lead to a helpful reconstruction of a typical day in the life of a consumer.

An example comes from Regina Lewis and Dunkin' Donuts, where she used a young adult diary study to determine when this target audience starts drinking coffee. She recruited 20 people in five cities. From their records, Lewis and her team had hundreds of points of observations. At research centers, the participants were then asked to explain what was going on when they thought about having coffee—what day, what time, why are they thinking about coffee, and so forth. From that research, the team learned that many young adults want "chuggable" coffee, particularly because they want an immediate caffeine hit. As a result, they drink iced coffee because hot coffee is too hot and they can't get their caffeine shot fast enough. Dunkin' responded with "Turbo Ice" coffee with an extra shot of espresso.[24]

Other Qualitative Methods Marketing communication planners are always probing for reasons, feelings, and motivations behind what people say and do. To arrive at useful consumer insights, they use a variety of interesting and novel research methods. In particular, they use stories and pictures. Cognitive psychologists have learned that human beings think more in images than in words. Most research continues to use words to ask questions and obtain answers, but recent experiments with visual-based research opens up new avenues of expression that may be better able to uncover people's deep thoughts.

Researchers use pictures as well as other tools to uncover mental processes that guide consumer behavior. Professor Larry Soley refers to these methods as **projective techniques**, which means they ask respondents to generate impressions rather than respond to more controlled quantitative surveys and rating systems. He describes projective techniques as psychoanalytic.[25]

Professor Gerald Zaltman of the Harvard Business School believes that the conventional wisdom about consumer research, such as using interviews and focus groups that rely on talking to people and grilling them about their tastes and buying habits, is only good for getting back predictable answers. If you ask people what they think about Coke, you'll learn that it is a "high-energy, thirst-quenching, fun-at-the-beach" kind of drink. But that may not be an adequate description of how people really feel about the soft drink.[26]

Word association is a projective technique that asks people to respond with thoughts or other words that come to mind when they are given a stimulus word. The idea is to uncover the **network of associations** in their thought patterns. Brand perceptions are tested this way to map the structure and logic of these association networks. For example, what do you think of when you think of Taco Bell? Wendy's? Arby's? Each restaurant should bring to mind some things in common (fast food, cheap food), but they also have distinct networks of associations based on type of food (Mexican, hamburgers, roast beef), restaurant design, logo and colors, brand characters, healthfulness, and so forth. Each restaurant, then, has a distinctive profile that can be determined from their associations network.

Here is a collection of some of the more imaginative ways qualitative researchers use projective techniques as games to gather insights about people's relationships with the brands they buy:

- *Fill in the blanks* is a form of attitude research in which people literally fill in the blanks in a story or balloons in a cartoon. Perceptions can come to the surface in the words that participants use to describe the action or situations depicted in the visuals.
- *Sentence completion* tests give respondents the beginning of a sentence and ask them to finish it. These are good at eliciting descriptions, causes, results, and the meanings in personal experiences.

- *Purpose-driven games* allow researchers to see how people solve problems and search for information.[27] Games can make the research experience more fun and involving for participants. They also uncover problem-solving strategies that may mirror the participants' approach to information searching or the kinds of problems they deal with in certain product situations.
- *Theater techniques* use games in a theater setting where researchers have people experience a variety of exercises to understand how they think about their brand. Some of these games have people tell stories about products or simulations where they have to convince others to use a brand.
- *Sculpting and movement techniques*, such as positioning the body as a statue, can be a source of insight in brainstorming for creative ideas and new product ideas. Sculpting involves physically putting product users in static positions that reflect how they think about or use a brand. Physical movements, such as dance movements and martial arts, can be added to increase the range of insight.
- *Story elicitation* asks consumers to explain the artifacts of their lives, such as the photos displayed in their homes and the objects they treasure. These stories can provide insights into how and why people use or do things.
- *Artifact creation* is a technique that uses such ideas as life collages, day mapping (tracking someone's activities across a day), and the construction of instruction books as ways to elicit stories that discuss brands and their role in daily life. These projects are also useful later in explaining to others—clients, the creative team, or other agencies—the triggers behind consumer insights.[28]
- *Photo elicitation* is similar to artifact research except it uses visuals to elicit consumer thoughts and opinions. Emotions are elicited by asking consumers what they think people in various photos and situations are feeling. A form of photo-based interviewing, consumers can be asked to look at a set of visuals or instructed to visually record something with a camera, such as a shopping trip. Later in reviewing the visuals, they are asked to explain what they were thinking or doing.
- *Photo sorts*, which is yet another visual technique, asks consumers to sort through a deck of photos and pick out visuals that represent something to them, such as typical users of the product or situations where it might be used. In identifying typical users, they may be asked to sort the photos into specific piles, such as happy, sad, angry, excited, or innovative people.
- *Metaphors* is a tool used by researchers to enrich the language consumers use to talk about brands. (Remember your grammar: A **metaphor** compares one thing to another without using the actual words *like* or *as*.) The Evian ad, for example, uses a strong metaphor to define its product. The insight into how people perceive brands through such connections comes from exploring the link between the two concepts. Metaphor games are used in creativity to elicit new and novel ideas, but they can also be used to analyze cognitive patterns in people's thinking.

These methods can be combined. Zaltman is the creator of ZMET (pronounced ZEE-MET), the Zaltman Metaphor Elicitation Technique, which uses metaphors and visual images to uncover patterns in people's thinking. For a typical session, the respondents find images that they think relate to the product category or brand being studied. Then they make up stories that describe their feelings about the product or brand.[29] For Coca-Cola in Europe, Zaltman asked volunteers to collect at least a dozen pictures that captured their feelings about Coca-Cola. Then they discussed the images in personal interviews. Finally, the volunteers created a summary image—a digital collage of their most important images—and recorded a statement that explained its meaning. The ZMET team found that Coke is not just about feelings of high energy and good times; it also has an element of calm, solitude, and relaxation.[30]

How Do You Choose a Research Method?

Determining the appropriate research method to use is an important planning decision It might help to understand two basic research criteria, validity and reliability, that are derived from what researchers call the "scientific method." **Validity** means that the research actually measures what it says it measures. Any differences that are uncovered by the research, such as different attitudes or purchasing patterns, really reflect differences among individuals, groups, or situations. **Reliability** means that you can run the same test again and get the same answer.

Quantitative researchers, particularly those doing experiments and surveys, are concerned about being faithful to the principles of science. Selecting a sample that truly represents the population, for example, increases the reliability of the research. Poorly worded questions and talking to the

This metaphoric ad equating Evian sparkling water with a mermaid tries to add a touch of originality, as well as meaning, to the Evian brand image.

wrong people can hurt the validity of surveys. The problem with experiments is twofold: (1) Experiments are limited by a small number of people in the experimental group, and (2) they are conducted under artificial conditions.

The information you get from surveys of a broad cross section of a population is limited to your ability to develop good clear questions that everyone can understand and answer. This tight control makes it harder to ask questions around the edges of a topic or elicit unexpected or unusual responses. On the other hand, focus groups and in-depth interviews that permit probing are limited by small numbers and possible problems with the representativeness of the sample.

Generally, quantitative methods are more useful for gathering numerical data (how many do this or believe that?), and qualitative methods are better at uncovering reasons and motives (why do they do or believe?). For these reasons, most researchers use a variety of research methods—quantitative and qualitative and occasionally experimental designs.

Which method should you choose when you conduct research? The answer depends on what questions you need to answer. In many cases, the answer may be multiple methods. As Karl Weiss explains, sometimes the best way is to "triangulate," which means using a number of research methods to come at the research question from different directions.

A note of caution: Sometimes the biggest consumer research projects may not give reliable results. A classic example is the New Coke reformulation introduced in 1985 after some 200,000 consumers participated in blind taste tests. Based on this huge $4 million research effort, Coke managers decided to dump the old Coca-Cola formula, which had been in use since 1886, because researchers concluded that Coke drinkers preferred a new, sweeter taste. The reaction was overwhelming from loyal Coke drinkers who wanted the "Real Thing," an emotional bond that wasn't revealed in the consumer taste-testing research.

Research Trends and Challenges

Marketing communication researchers face a number of challenges: globalization and new media technology are reshaping the industry. Practices are also changing as the industry searches for ways to gain more insightful analyses and move into IMC planning. Let's examine some of these challenges briefly.

Sampling Challenges

We hinted at this problem earlier in the chapter, but with the increasing use of new media and the Internet, research experts are struggling to find ways to find samples that are representative. As Karl Weiss, observes, "I wish I could fully support some mode of data collection but there's just nothing right now that is truly "good."[31] The problem with online samples, for example, is representativeness. Weiss explains, "If you are using an online panel there is no way to ever know if your results have any relationship to the population of interest." As mentioned earlier, he recommends triangulating to increase the effectiveness of the research design, as well as sampling quality, using a variety of methods rather than relying on surveys. He concludes, "This is why the future of research cannot rely on survey data. Future researchers will be part mathematician and part philosopher. It will be a beautiful time."

Global Issues

The key issues that global researchers face include how to manage and communicate global brands in widely different localities and how to shift from studying differences to finding similarities around the world. The biggest problem is cross-cultural communication and how to arrive at an intended message without cultural distortions or insensitivities. Researchers are becoming more involved in puzzling out cultural meanings and testing marketing communication messages for cultural sensitivity in different countries. They struggle to determine how other cultures will interpret the elements of a campaign so that they convey the same brand message across cultures. Cultural differences complicate planning, as account planner Susan Mendelsohn, who is a member of this book's advisory board, discovered in planning for a new analgesic that contained caffeine. In test markets, the agency discovered that perceptions about caffeine vary positively and negatively in different cultures.

IMC Research Challenges

The deluge of data is only complicated by IMC planning, which requires research into many stakeholder groups and contact points. Instead of campaign planning, where messages are tweaked slightly to fit different media, *strategic consistency* in IMC planning suggests that different audiences, as well as media, need different messages. Susan Mendelsohn calls this a more radical trend in planning research and points to "companies that are experimenting with multi-message strategies that fit each vehicle uniquely and yet might be radically different from each other." She cautions that the company needs to be clear about the goals for its brand, recognizing that there might be multiple goals—a set of integrated goals—rather than one big underlying goal, and that suggests multiple measurements of effectiveness as well.

Looking Ahead

Research and analysis that lead to insight into consumer thinking and behavior, form the foundation for brand communication plans and strategic decisions, which will be the topic of the next chapter. The research findings also lead to message strategies, which we introduce in Part 3, and media strategies, which will follow in Part 4.

It's a Wrap

Domino's Gets Its Slice of the (Pizza) Pie

Changing the product is risky business. In 1985, Coca-Cola introduced reformulated New Coke, which bombed, and more recently Tropicana changed the packaging on its orange juice, which consumers lambasted. Would a half-baked strategy bold enough to admit to an awful product work for Domino's? Some critics worried the move could backfire.

But it didn't. During the first full quarter the campaign was active, Domino's rose 14.3 percent in same-store sales, which was a record for the fast-food industry. A taste test of nearly 1,800 consumers confirmed the claims. Domino's beat out both Papa John's and Pizza Hut by a wide margin. Domino's continues to hear that consumer attitudes toward the brand are improving through follow-up quantitative and qualitative research.

The campaign was mentioned in major media outlets and on blogs, and even television personalities took note of the campaign. Steven Colbert tasted a slice on his show and asked, "Is that pizza, or did an angel just give birth in my mouth?"

For listening, for being honest about its product, and for having the courage to make a gutsy campaign, the pizza maker accomplished its business goals and in the process earned the Advertising Research Foundation Grand Ogilvy Award. It also was named AdAge's Marketer of the Year Runner-Up. That's some turnaround.

Logo: courtesy of Domino's Pizza LLC

Key Points Summary

1. **What are the basic types of strategic research, and how are they used?** Secondary research is background research that gathers already published information, and primary research is original research findings collected for the first time from original sources. Quantitative research is statistical and uses numerical data to investigate how people think and behave; qualitative research is exploratory and uses probing techniques to gain insights and identify questions and hypotheses for further quantitative research. Experimental research tests hypotheses using carefully designed experiments.
2. **How do brand communicators use research?** Research is used to (1) develop an analysis of the marketing situation, (2) acquire consumer information and insights for making targeting decisions, (3) identify information about available media to match the media to the target audience, (4) develop message strategies, and (5) evaluate the effectiveness of the brand communication.
3. **What are the most common research methods used in advertising?** Survey research is used to amass quantities of responses from consumers about their attitudes and behaviors. In-depth interviews probe the reasons and motivations consumers give to explain their attitudes and behavior. Focus groups are group interviews that operate like a conversation directed by a researcher. Panels are long-running consumer groups that permit tracking of attitude and behavior changes. Observation research happens in the store or home where researchers watch how consumers behave. Ethnographic research is an anthropological technique that involves the researcher in participating in the day-to-day lives of consumers. Diaries are records of consumers' behavior, particularly their media use. A number of other qualitative methods are used to creatively uncover patterns in the way consumers think and act.

Key Terms

brand communication research, p. 183
concept testing, p. 192
consumer research, p. 183
consumer research panel, p. 198
content analysis, p. 190
copytesting, p. 194
crowdsourcing, p. 198
diaries, p. 200
ethnographic research, p. 199
evaluative research, p. 194
experimental research, p. 187
expert panel, p. 198
focus group, p. 197
friendship focus group, p. 197
IMC research, p. 183
in-depth interview, p. 196
market research, p. 183
marketing research, p. 189
media research, p. 191
metaphor, p. 201
network of associations, p. 200
observation research, p. 198
open-ended questions, p. 196
participant observation, p. 198
posttesting, p. 194
pretesting, p. 192
primary research, p. 184
projective techniques, p. 200
qualitative research, p. 187
quantitative research, p. 185
random sample, p. 195
reliability, p. 201
sales levels, p. 185
sample, p. 195
secondary research, p. 183
semiotic analysis, p. 192
strategic research, p. 183
survey research, p. 194
validity, p. 201
word association, p. 200

Review Questions

6-4. What are the levels of evaluation, and when should each level be conducted?

✪ 6-5. Discuss the difference between primary and secondary research.

6-6. Many marketers feel that qualitative research is superior to quantitative research. Compare the main strengths and weaknesses of qualitative and quantitative research.

6-7. What information can be obtained from market research and consumer research? How would each of these help in developing an advertising campaign?

6-8. Use a current advertising campaign to discuss the seven ways research is used in brand communication.

✪ 6-9. Discuss when each of the following research methods: focus group, in-depth interviews, observational research, ethnographic research, panels, and diaries.

6-10. Explain the difference between validity and reliability and explain how these concepts affect brand communication research.

Discussion Questions

✪ 6-11. Consult the MRI data reproduced on page 186 and do the following analysis. Look first at the four "Index" columns and find the highest viewing category of late evening weekend news and compare that with the highest viewers of early evening weekend news. If you were advertising a new hybrid car, which category and time slot would deliver the greatest *percentage* of viewers who might be in the market? Now analyze the size of the category to determine which of the high viewing categories delivers the greatest *number* of viewers.

6-12. An interview is a research tool used for data collection in a variety of research situations. Although each situation elicits information from respondents, the goals and processes involved in an interview vary considerably, depending on the type of information needed. Discuss the following:

a. The purposes of the interview
b. The relationship between data and theory
c. The roles assumed by the interviewer and the respondent
d. The relevant criteria for assessing the validity and reliability of the information obtained

Take-Home Projects

6-13. ***Portfolio Project:*** Assume you are working for Gerber Baby Foods. You have been asked to identify the relevant trends that are forecasted for U.S. birthrates between 2015 and 2017. Identify Internet sources that would provide that information. Gather as much information as you can from these sites and write a one-page report on the trends you find.

✪ 6-14. ***Mini-Case Analysis:*** What were the key research findings that led to the Domino's rebranding campaign? You have just been assigned to the Domino's team for the next year of the campaign. What research would you want to do before planning the next year's efforts? Identify a list of key research questions that have to be answered before the campaign can move forward.

TRACE North America Case

Multicultural Research

Read the TRACE case in the Appendix before coming to class.

6-15. How did the "Hard to Explain, Easy to Experience" team members use research to better understand the problem they were trying to solve?

6-16. How did the "Hard to Explain, Easy to Experience" team use research to inspire a creative solution to the Trace marketing challenge?

6-17. What other methodologies would you recommend to the team to better understand the success of their program in market?

CHAPTER 7

Strategic Planning

Photo: John Foxx Collection. Imagestate

It's a Winner

Campaign:	Company:	Agency:	Awards:
"Three Little Pigs"	The Guardian Newspaper	*Bartle Bogle Hegarty*	*Yellow Pencil D&AD Design Award for TV & Cinema Advertising, The Grand CLIO Award, The Eurobest Awards, Business Insider's 10 Best Ads of 2012, The British Arrow Craft Awards, TED: Ads Worth Spreading, The Adweek Awards 2012*

CHAPTER KEY POINTS

1. **What is the difference between objectives, strategies, and tactics in strategic planning, and how are the four levels of planning connected?**
2. **What are the key strategic decisions, and why are they central to brand communication planning?**
3. **What is account planning, and how is it used in advertising?**

Re-telling a Tale

"Little Pig! Little Pig! Let us in!"

Surprisingly, it's not the big bad wolf clawing at the door of the third little pig's house. In *The Guardian*'s Three Little Pigs advertisement, a SWAT team is seen banging on the door and arresting the pig, which triggers a chain reaction the world over.

The Guardian had roped in the creative advertising agency Bartle Bogle Hegarty (BBH) to demonstrate that it was fast evolving beyond being a print-only product. The ad showed how the newspaper might cover the story of the Three Little Pigs today. How would it feature the story on the front page, leading the discussion about the story through social media? How might the story end in modern society?

It used this campaign to project its role in open journalism—so readers don't buy a pig in a poke—and also highlight the changing role of news media in general.

With the availability of various social media platforms, such as Twitter and Facebook, a global audience is now connected and given the power to take a big bite out of the pork pie!

The ad subtly shows how every story is newsworthy and how a news organization is ultimately responsible for not just retelling the story, but for bringing together various aspects and details—through objective commentary and an amicable exchange of opinions—to avoid butchering the truth—and portraying the whole picture for readers, who once might have been satisfied with wolfing down whatever's being served to them by one source.

Driven by Alan Rusbridger, *The Guardian*'s editor, the newspaper now publishes its news lists online, ahead of its print publication. The paper's online presence allows bloggers to share their views. Readers are able to use a search tool to find information according to their needs and are encouraged to upload data and share their favorite sources of information.

But for the three little pigs, the fat's in the fire! There's no way a global audience, armed with technology, is likely to buy the traditional "happily ever after" given to the pigs.

But without busting anyone's chops, *The Guardian* shows how it's capable of unraveling a story within a story—homeowner's rights, insurance fraud, and mortgage defaults—all the while giving due credit to the opinions of readers and the truth.

The Guardian's wolfish appetite can be traced back to 1821 when it was published as a weekly until 1836, becoming a daily in 1855, all to meet the demands of an ever-growing audience. In 2011, it was named Newspaper of the Year as a result of its partnership with WikiLeaks. It was also instrumental in breaking the story about phone hacking by other newspapers.

Instead of putting itself in a "pig-arious" position of spoon feeding readers, *The Guardian* built on the fact that it believes in open journalism.

During 2009 and 2010, it launched a series of new digital services. Apps were created for various devices, and the newspaper dubbed itself as being "digital first" in 2011. Since then, the newspaper has continued to expand on the digital front, with new applications and platforms being launched to disseminate news and comments. Digital editions have been created for the US and Australian markets, and editions have been launched for the Kindle, iPad, Android, Blackberry, and Facebook.

The Guardian wanted the ad to convey that it is capable of helping its audience feast on wholesome and honest news, without making pigs out of themselves.

But were the customers actually convinced to buy more copies of *The Guardian*? Did the campaign increase sales for the news organization? Huff and puff to the end of the chapter to see the results.

Sources: www.adweek.com/news/advertising-branding/ad-day-guardian-138652; www.ted.com/initiatives/aws/three_little_pigs.html; creativereview.co.uk/cr-blog/2012/march/guardian; www.theguardian.com (all accessed 21–22/10/2013).

In most cases, there is no one completely right way to do anything in advertising or brand communication, but if you understand how communication works, you may be able to identify the best strategy to accomplish the objectives most efficiently and effectively. This chapter explains the concept of strategic planning as it is used in business, marketing, and brand communication. In addition to targeting the right audience, which we discussed in the previous chapter, key planning decisions include identifying critical problems and opportunities, positioning or repositioning the brand against the competition, and making implementation (tactics) decisions. It also introduces the concept of account planning and explains its critical role in determining the consumer insights that lead to message and media strategies.

What Is Strategic Planning?

So what was the key idea that made the Three Little Pigs campaign so successful? Can you identify a strategy that jumps out at you? What about the Domino's campaign that introduced the previous chapter? How would you describe the strategy that made it a winner?

So what is strategy—and strategic planning? **Strategic planning** is the process of identifying a problem that can be solved with communication (as opposed to marketing mix problems), then coming up with a great idea that solves that problem. Here's the mission of planning: identify a problem, determine **objectives** (what you want to accomplish with a message), decide on **strategies** (how to accomplish the objectives), and implement the **tactics** (specific activities that make the plan come to life). This process occurs within a specified time frame.

We talk a lot about creativity in this book, and we'd like to emphasize that strategic thinking is just as creative as coming up with a Big Idea for a brand communication campaign. Both processes involve searching for ideas to solve problems, whether they are found in marketing situations or communication challenges. Pat Fallon and Fred Senn, cofounders of the legendary agency Fallon Worldwide, explain that principle in their book *Juicing the Orange: How to Turn Creativity into a Powerful Business Advantage.* They have identified seven principles that link creative thinking and strategic planning to business results[1]:

1. ***Always Start from Scratch*** Simplify the problem. You know too much. There's a good chance that you know so much that you can't see how the problem could be solved in a fresh way.
2. ***Demand a Ruthlessly Simple Definition of the Business Problem*** Smart people tend to make things too complicated. Be a relentless reductionist. Einstein said, "Make things as simple as possible, but no simpler."
3. ***Discover a Proprietary Emotion*** The key component of any communication program is a powerful consumer insight that leads to a ruthlessly smart strategy executed brilliantly across all platforms. It all starts with the insight, which is the central truth of what you are going to say and how you are going to operate. Once you find an emotional truth, you can make it proprietary through execution.
4. ***Focus on the Size of the Idea, Not the Size of the Budget*** It's our credo that it's better to outsmart than outspend.
5. ***Seek Out Strategic Risks*** Understand the benefits of prudent risk. Great big ideas in the early stages are often scary ideas. When Darwin taught us about the survival of the fittest, he didn't mean the strongest. He meant that it's the most nimble—the quickest to adapt to a changing environment—who prosper both in nature and in a capitalist economy.
6. ***Collaborate or Perish*** This is more than "getting along"; it is about recognizing that the rules of engagement have changed. We live in an era in which victory goes to the best collaborators. This means teams from different disciplines and different corporate cultures will be working together. Teams that are aligned and motivated can make history.
7. ***Listen Hard to Your Customers (Then Listen Some More)*** Listening is often step number one on the road to understanding. Listening often yields that precious insight that gives you a competitive advantage; something your competitors have overlooked.

In her introduction to Part 2, Regina Lewis identified the key ideas that drove her consumer insight work for Dunkin' Brands and for Holiday Inn. For Dunkin', people loved the "everyday joe" image of Dunkin' and its coffee—a brand with which they could identify. For Holiday Inn, the challenge was to help a traveler feel at home and "stay you." Both created authentic meanings and met emotional needs. This chapter will look at how strategic decisions such as these are made by planners.

Strategic planning occurs in a complex business environment, which, for the sake of simplification in this discussion, includes four levels of plans: the business plan, the marketing plan, the brand communication plan, and plans for specific areas of marketing communication, such as advertising or public relations.

Principle
Coming up with a big problem-solving idea in strategic planning is just as creative as coming up with a Big Idea for a brand communication campaign.

Pat Fallon (top) and Fred Senn were cofounders of Fallon Worldwide, the agency behind NBC, Holiday Inn Express, Travelers Insurance, Sony, and many other major brands.

The Business Plan

Strategic planning is a process that starts with the business plan and then moves to functional areas of the company such as marketing where a marketing plan is developed that outlines objectives, strategies, and tactics for all areas of the marketing mix. A business plan is a snapshot of the company and the environment in which it operates.

External conditions, such as technological changes, have made companies obsolete as Kodak found when the market died for its film. Forays into printers and online photo albums failed to revive the iconic brand, and it moved into bankruptcy in 2012. The recession that began in the United States in 2007 and picked up speed in subsequent years in Europe before moving on to Asia has affected almost every category of business. External facts are the framework in which

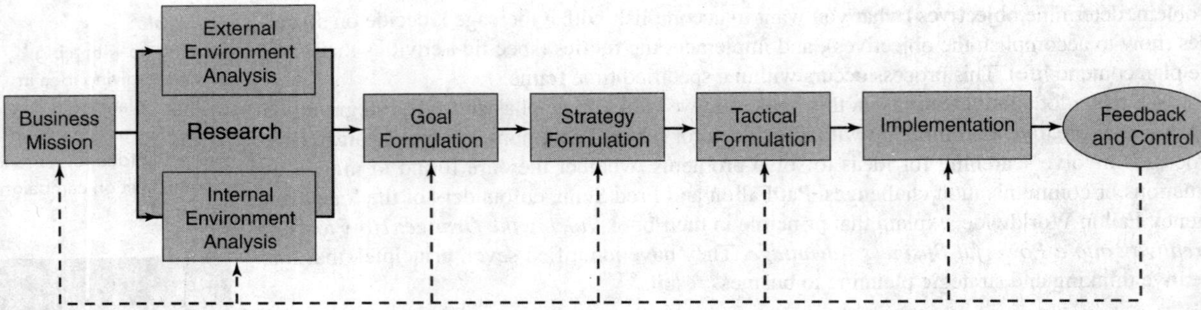

FIGURE 7.1

Steps in the Development of a Business Plan

The business planning process begins with a mission statement and moves through research, goal setting, strategy statements, identifications of tactics, implementation processes, and controls (e.g., meeting the budget and quality standards). The entire process is monitored through feedback.

Source: Philip Kotler, *Marketing Management*, 13th ed. (Upper Saddle River, NJ: Prentice Hall, 2009), 48. Reproduced by permission of Pearson Education, Inc., Upper Saddle River, NJ.

business plans are created and also present the challenges that may become the focus of strategic decision making in companies that either are threatened or see opportunities in such changes.

The business plan directs the operations of the entire company or, in larger companies, a specific division called a **strategic business unit**, which is a line of products with all the offerings under a single brand name. It also is the document given to investors. Figure 7.1 depicts a framework for a business plan.

Mission Statement and Business Philosophy A business plan begins with a description of the business itself—the history of the company, its products, the scope of its offerings, its corporate strengths, and its organizational structure and management team. A **vision statement** may also be used to describe where the business is headed—what senior management sees as the organization's future. A more general direction of the company is expressed in a **mission statement**, which is a concise expression of the broad goals and policies of the business. The mission statement is unique, focused, and differentiating. Tom's of Maine states its mission clearly on its website:

> Through the years, we have been guided by one simple notion—do what is right, for our customers, employees, communities, and environment. We call this Natural Care—a philosophy that guides what we make and all that we do.

The Crocs mission statement is also the first thing seen on its website. It ties its mission to a philosophy it calls "ocean minded," a mind-set that values using recycled and sustainable materials. Crocs celebrated its 10-year anniversary in 2012.

The Crocs mission statement also expresses the company's **business philosophy**, the fundamental principles that guide the operations of the business. For many companies, the philosophy is simply to make a profit, and, of course, that is a central goal for most for-profit companies. There are other companies like Crocs and Tom's of Maine whose business philosophy also reflects a commitment to the belief that what's good for a business should also be good for society.

Principle

Embedding social responsibility principles in the corporate mission, business plans, and operations imbues the brand image with integrity.

A **societal marketing** philosophy describes the operations of companies whose corporate mission reflects their desire to do good. Their commitment is expressed in the way they design products, source their ingredients, manufacture, and market their products. Embedding social responsibility deep in the corporate mission, business plans, and operations not only guides business decisions but also imbues the brand identity with integrity. If a commitment reflects a company's core business strategy as described in its mission statement, as in Dove's "Real Beauty" campaign, it is called **mission marketing.**[2]

Research Chapter 6 identified a number of research tools used in planning business decisions as well as marketing and brand communication programs. In business plans, it is particularly important to look both inside and outside the organization to identify strengths and weaknesses, both corporate and brand. Being able to foresee market changes, business opportunities, and technological breakthroughs determines a company's long-term success. Consider Apple's growth over the last 20 years, which was generated by innovative products, such as the iPod, iPhone, iPad, and the iTune store. The "Principled Practice" feature about antismoking campaigns provides insight about the role research plays in tracking consumer trends.

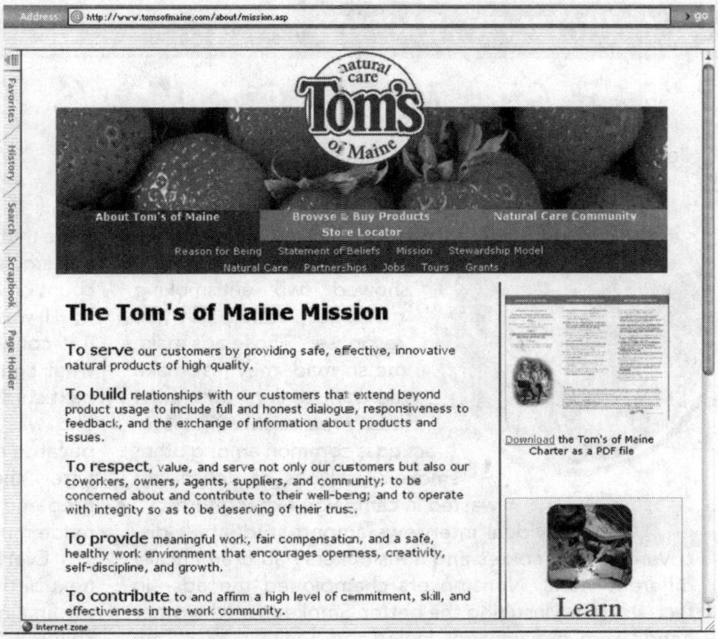

Photo: Courtesy Toms of Maine

This mission statement for Tom's of Maine helps its managers develop specific business objectives and goals. It also guides all of the company's marketing communication efforts.

Goals and Objectives Business **goals**, which are long term and general, such as moving to a global strategy or developing a low-price product or brand for a particular market, provide direction to business plans. Often these plans are stated in terms of 5- or 10-year plans. They outline the financial side of the business.

The objectives for planning at this corporate level tend to focus on maximizing profit and **return on investment** (ROI). ROI is a measurement that shows whether, in general, the costs of conducting the business—the investment—are more than matched by the revenue produced in return. The revenue above and beyond the costs is where **profit** lies. A note about goals and objectives: Both describe things you want to achieve, but goals tend to identify broad directions for the company, and objectives tend to be more specific and measurable.

Strategies, Tactics, and Controls At the business plan level, planning decisions are focused on research and development, operations, and sales and marketing. Strategies are plans that will achieve the organization's goals, as well as objectives. If the goal is to be the biggest maker of bicycles in your part of the country, then strategies might involve buying other bike manufacturers, increasing the number of lines of bikes that you make, or energizing your regional sales staff. The tactics are specific activities that make the strategies come to life, such as designing a new bike for a specific niche market. Implementation consists of the decisions you need to make to actually design that new bike, including personnel (designers and engineers) as well as scheduling and budgeting.

Every company operates with budgets, audits, time sheets, and quality control procedures. These are some of the management tools that keep programs on strategy and that track the effectiveness of strategic decisions and implementation programs. This information feeds back into the planning process and is used to adjust future plans.

The Marketing Plan

A **marketing plan** is developed for a brand or product line—McDonald's, for example, may have a marketing plan for the corporate McDonald's brand, but there may also be marketing plans for individual product lines, such as the breakfast menu or the McCafé line. Marketing plans are evaluated annually. To a large extent, the marketing plan mirrors the corporate business plan, although the strategies are focused on a specific brand rather than the larger organization or corporation. Figure 7.2 illustrates the strategic decisions found in a marketing plan.

We can summarize these decisions in terms of the steps in the process of developing a marketing plan:

Step 1. A **situation analysis** is based on extensive market research that assesses the external and internal environments that affect marketing programs—the company's products and brands as well as the competitive environment, consumer trends, and other marketplace trends that impact on the product category. A set of "what's going on" questions structure this market analysis. Answers to these questions help define the key marketing problem through a **SWOT analysis**,

A PRINCIPLED PRACTICE

"Just Give Me My One Vice"[3]

Joyce M. Wolburg, *Marquette University*

One day I asked my students to bring in samples of magazine ads to critique. One student showed two antismoking messages, which got the response, "Those ads make me so mad, they just make me want to light up a cigarette." I realized that if this reaction is common among other smokers, millions of dollars are wasted in campaign expenditures.

Using individual interviews among students, I discovered that smokers and nonsmokers had dramatically different views. Nonsmokers championed the ads—in fact, the more insulting the better. Smokers, on the other hand, were defiant and denied the health risks. "I am going to die from something someday, so why shouldn't this be my cause of death?" Some smokers also felt a sense of entitlement toward smoking. "All I'm doing is smoking. I'm not doing heavy drugs or robbing banks or murdering people. This is as bad as I get. Let me have my cigarette."

Psychologists have known for decades that when people are told to change their behavior, they are likely to dig in their heels and resist change because their freedom is at stake. My findings fit that theory perfectly. And since smokers took up the habit despite the many messages out there, antismoking messages must not work—or so the logic goes. They knew the health risks—"you would have to be a moron to not know that it kills"—but they didn't find the ads compelling. "There isn't an ad out there that would get me to quit." Most figured they would quit smoking before it harmed their health, but they didn't count on how quickly they would become addicted.

I was convinced that antismoking messages were not connecting with students, and I began to wonder what convinced them to quit and how they did it. My next study found that the most common reason for quitting was a personal health scare; however, some quit because they no longer identified with smokers. Unfortunately, they thought quitting would be easy and weren't prepared for the challenge. Every student I interviewed made multiple attempts before they finally succeeded.

Every student also had a quit date in mind—"by my next birthday, by the time I graduate, by the time I get my first job, by the time I get married, by the time I have children." But they didn't have a plan for how to do it. One of the most common problems was not anticipating the situations that triggered smoking, and going out drinking was the most difficult.

Most students wanted to quit "cold turkey" because they saw it as a badge of honor. However, this strategy worked for only a few. One student beat the odds by meeting regularly with a physician's assistant because it gave him a sense of accountability. "I knew that if I smoked, I would have to tell him."

So, what does it all mean? Smokers won't quit unless they are ready, but campus support should be in place for those who are. Messages should use real examples of what worked and what didn't—not judgmental campaigns with scare tactics.

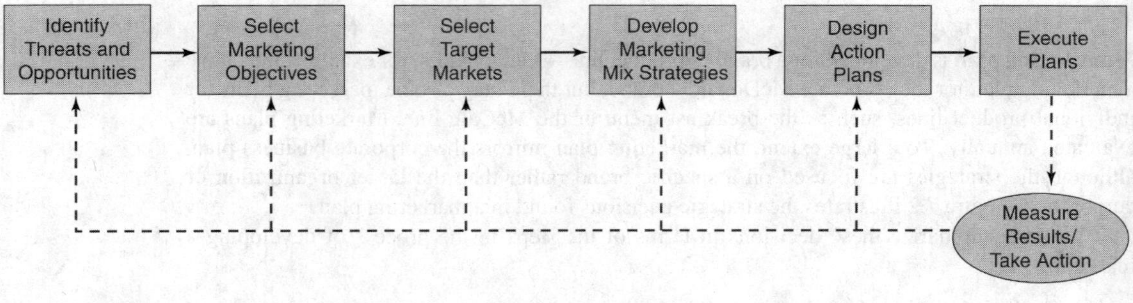

FIGURE 7.2

Steps in the Development of a Marketing Plan

A marketing plan begins with an analysis of the marketing situation in terms of strengths, weaknesses, opportunities, and threats. Setting objectives is the next step. Target markets are selected and marketing strategies are developed, as well as action plans and specific executions of ideas and programs. The plan is evaluated and that information feeds back into the next generation of planning.

which stands for Strengths, Weaknesses, Opportunities, and Threats. Strategic decisions find ways to leverage strengths and opportunities and address weaknesses and threats:

- What is happening with the brand and the category?
- How is it happening?
- Where is it happening?
- When is it happening?
- To whom is it happening?

Principle
SWOT analysis is the process of finding ways to address a brand's weaknesses and threats and leverage its strengths and opportunities.

We could answer those questions for Burger King's Whopper, which is a popular brand with huge customer loyalty, although the fan's passion is largely unrecognized. In order to demonstrate that situation, Burger King's agency, Crispin Porter + Bogusky (CP+B), used a prank—it took over a Burger King in Las Vegas for a single day and videotaped the reactions of customers who ordered Whoppers and then were told the popular sandwich had been removed from the menu. The Whopper's fans reacted with disbelieve. Some freaked out. Their reactions to this "deprivation strategy" were depicted in commercials and on a website where customers were able to watch an 8-minute documentary about the experiment. The "freakout" campaign for the Whooper's 50th anniversary demonstrated the power of consumer demand, but also the power of a strong brand identity. The sales results went through the roof and the Burger King Whooper Freakout campaign won a Grand Effie.

Step 2. Set objectives, which at the marketing level tend to be focused on *sales* and **share of market**, measurements referring to the percentage of the category purchases that are made by the brand's customers. Sales objectives may operate annually, but they may also be quarterly or even weekly. Other objectives deal with specific areas of the marketing mix, such as distribution, where an objective might detail how a company will open a specific new territory or engage channel members in supporting a promotion (see Sunkist ad), and with brand relationship programs, such as frequent-flyer programs that drive loyalty and repeat business (see United Airlines ad).

J. Scott Armstrong, in his book *Persuasive Advertising*, believes that objectives should be designed to have a good return on the brand communication investment. The objective, in other words, is sales and profits (or the equivalent for nonprofits). His point is that logically the effort

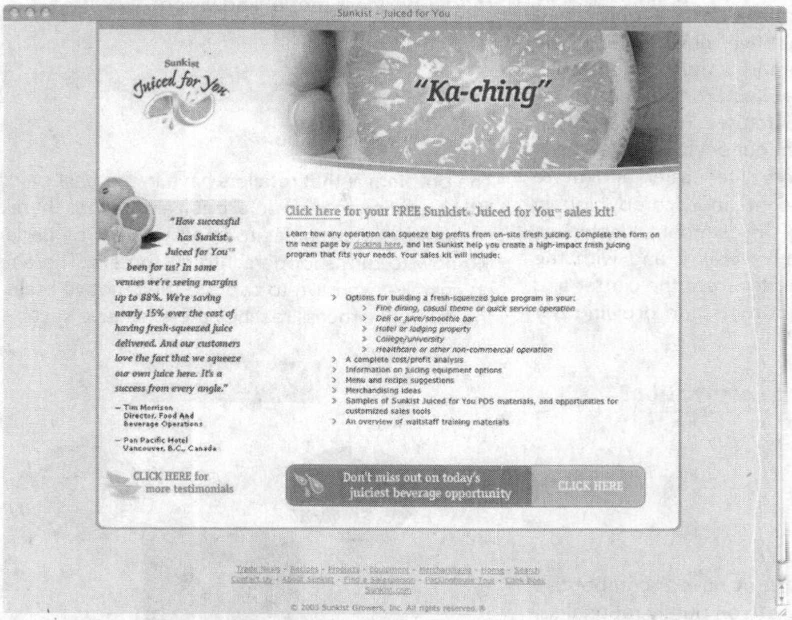

Photo: Reprinted with permission of Sunkist Growers, Inc. Sunkist and design are trademarks of Sunkist Growers, Inc. © 2004 Sherman Oaks, California, U.S.A. All rights reserved

Sunkist's B2B "Ka-ching" ad is addressed to members of the distribution channel and focuses on sales returns and an offer of a free sales kit.

Photo: © Images.com/CORBIS

This United Airlines ad addresses business travelers with a reminder about the quality of the airline's frequent-flyer program.

should not be directed at the competition (i.e., increasing market share) but rather at increasing ROI. He feels that this is a mistake that many marketing and marcom professionals make in writing their objectives.[4]

Step 3. Assess consumer needs and wants relative to the product, segment the market into groups that are likely to respond, and target specific audiences and uncover insights about their thoughts and behaviors.

Step 4. Develop the brand strategy, differentiating and positioning the product relative to the competition.

Step 5. Develop the marketing mix strategy, selecting product design and performance criteria, pricing, distribution, and marketing communication.

Step 6. Implementation of tactical programs that execute the strategic decisions.

This marketing analysis—and the marketing mix strategy derived from it—link the overall strategic business plan with specific marketing programs, including advertising and other IMC areas. For marcom managers, the most important part of the marketing plan is the discussion of the brand strategy, which gives direction to the strategy for all brand communication programs. In addition, the *marketing mix strategy,* which includes decisions about the target market, brand position, product design and performance, pricing, and distribution, as well as marketing communication, are all important in planning brand campaigns. Product design and formulation decisions are

A Matter of Practice

"My SPAR": Letting Our Customers Lead

Daryl Bennewith, *Strategic Planning Director, TBWA Group, Durban, South Africa*

SPAR South Africa is one of the biggest chains of grocery stores in the country. Operating in a highly competitive environment, the brand must constantly evolve. From extensive research we knew that SPAR continued to make consumers' life easier and more convenient and scored high in community involvement. However, were we becoming just another retail brand with the ever-present danger of becoming part of the clutter and just concerned with achieving targets and growing our bottom line?

So Where Could We Fight the Competition?

- Price?
- Quality?
- Freshness?
- Aspiration?
- Range?

In most of these areas, we did not have a competitive advantage and could not compete on purely rational aspects of shopping, and often consumers will perceive an attempt to do so as false. There is nothing unique about low prices! But to be in the game you obviously need to be price competitive.

Where Could We Have an Edge?

- Close connections with the customer
- Our business model and vision
- Service
- Convenience
- Employee's attitude
- Ownership
- Geographic locations

The problem is that retailers have in the past paid far too little attention to shoppers, but it also means there are tremendous opportunities to improve sales by understanding how to turn shoppers into customers. There must be no mistake; we have to capture the emotive brain before the thought process reaches the executive section.

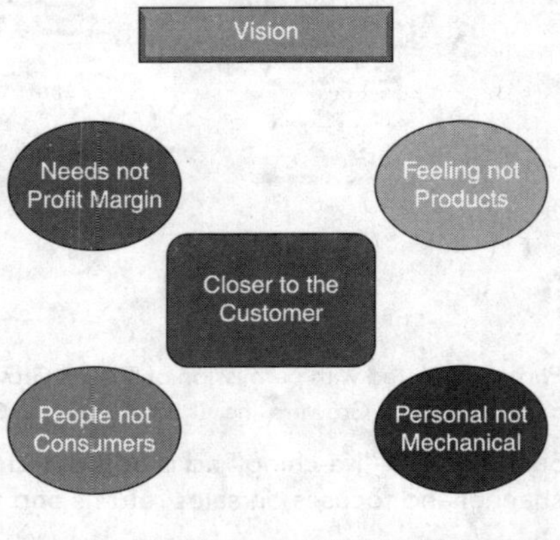

sometimes responses to consumer trends, such as the increase in the number of packaged foods making high-fiber claims (think Fiber One with its expanded line of cereals and snack bars).

The Brand Communication/IMC Plan

Brand communication planning operates with the same concern for objectives, strategies, and tactics found in business and marketing plans. It outlines all of the communication activities needed to deliver on the business and marketing objectives in terms of communication objectives, strategies, tactics, timing, costs, and evaluation. Briefly, here are the marcom planner's goals:

- ***Who?*** Who are you trying to reach, and what insight do you have about how they think, feel, and act? How should they respond to your brand message?
- ***What?*** What do you say to them? What directions from the consumer research are useful to the creative team?
- ***Where?*** How and where will you reach them? What directions from the consumer research are useful to the media team?

In general, a communication plan seeks to match the right audience to the right message and present the message in the right medium to reach that audience. If the marketing goal is to increase loyalty, for example, then the brand communication plan would determine whether to use a frequency club, an advertising campaign, a sales promotion strategy, or all of the above. Such a plan typically includes a variety of marcom messages carried in different media and sometimes targeted to different audiences.

The SPAR story in the "A Matter of Practice" feature lets you see inside the mind of a planner as he works through a series of strategic decisions.

Principle
A brand communication plan seeks to match the right audience to the right message and present the message in the right medium to reach that audience.

How Do We Do This? We Had to Find Something That Made Us Unique

In SPAR's business model, every store is managed and run by the person who owns that store. It is not owned by some noncaring corporate entity. And that means a closer connection to the customer and greater understanding of their needs.

SPAR Planning Model

We need the magic that no other retail chain has. The magic that comes from each SPAR owner being an individual. The magic of SPAR being involved in the community. The magic of feeling at home when you walk in. We need the consumer to feel like SPAR is theirs.

As soon as you perceive something as being yours, your attitude toward that object changes. You know have a vested interest, you establish an emotional bond, and you develop a positive attitude. So could we instill those feeling in the SPAR brand?

"My SPAR" appeals directly to the emotional part of the brain. It will be our competitive positioning; we will have added the "feeling" part to the brain's brand-choice equation.

Our campaign started with a Facebook site (MySPAR) and print campaign where we appealed to people to tell us their unique stories of how SPAR made a difference in their lives. We chose some of the most endearing stories and converted them to television commercials using the actual people in the stories. It was a breakthrough in grocery advertising.

So what "My Spar" and its consumer stories did is turn the rational purchasing decision into an emotional one. It is a position far removed from the corporate face of our competitors.

It puts us one step ahead. And that's a great place to be.

"My Spar gave my little girl with muscular dystrophy the opportunity to shop with a 'baby trolley.' One of her first experiences of walking on her own."

Earlier, we mentioned that there is a difference between a *strategy*, what you want to accomplish, and *tactics*, how you will accomplish it. That's true of brand communication plans as well as marketing and business plans. In the discussion of message effects in Chapter 4, we introduced Armstrong's work on evidence-based principles and the four categories he used for strategies—information, influence, emotion, and exposure. His outline also included two other groups of tactics that are useful in making brand communication plans. He identified general tactics as focused on resistance, acceptance, message, and attention. In other words, tactics are often employed to lower resistance, create acceptance, deliver a message, or grab attention.[5]

Note how these various levels of planning set up a cascade of goals and objectives. We said before that the marketing plan mirrors the corporate business plan and contains many of the same components. But what might be a more general goal at the business level gets transformed into objectives at the marketing level because marketing has the task of designing the strategies that will deliver the business-level goal. And the same thing happens between marketing and brand communication. The strategic decisions and communication objectives are designed to implement the marketing strategies.

As illustrated in Figure 7.4, the business and marketing plans provide direction to the brand communication (IMC) plan as well as to specific plans for specialist areas, such as advertising and other areas of marketing communication.

This section provides a brief overview of brand communication plans, but we will discuss IMC campaign plans in more detail in Chapter 18. Now let's look at one last level of planning.

Plans for Marketing Communication Functions

Advertising, public relations, sales promotion, and other marcom areas all operate with their own plans. Most often these are campaign plans and outline a series of activities to be undertaken during a specified period of time.

They begin with the same strategic decisions found in a marketing or brand communication (IMC) plan, such as a communication situation analysis, SWOTs leading to the identification of the key (communication) problem, communication objectives, identification of a target audience,

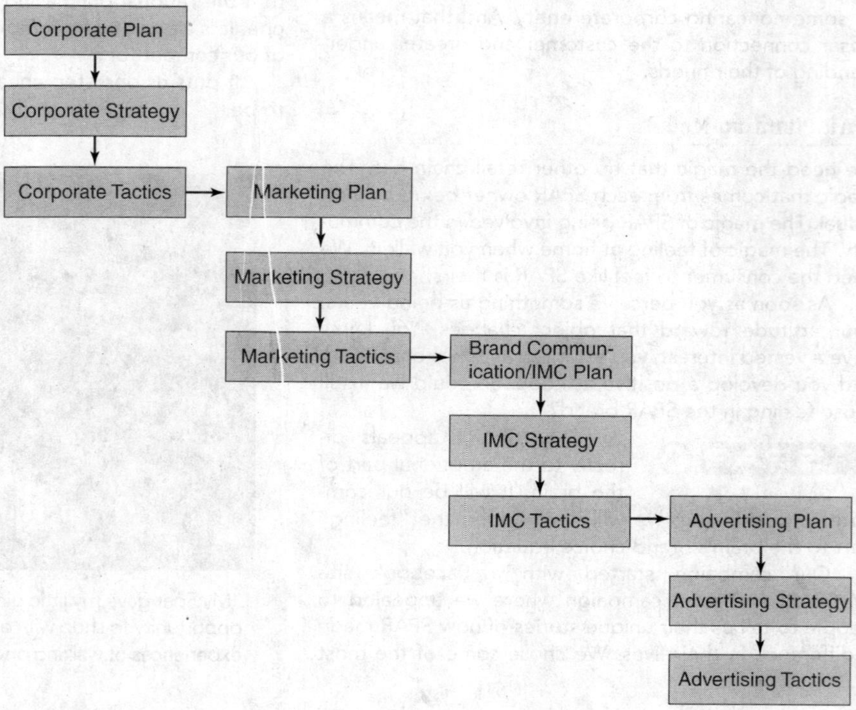

FIGURE 7.4
Cascading Objectives from Top to Bottom
Business planning involves a set of cascading objectives and strategies. Corporate objectives and strategies are achieved through planning at the level of marketing (and other marketing mix areas), and marketing objectives and strategies give direction to brand communication programs and finally to plans for specific marketing communication areas.

communication-based consumer insights, and analysis of the communication dimensions of the brand position.

The tactics section of these plans identifies specific activities that will be undertaken, such as a series of ads in key media scheduled at critical times purchase times (e.g., back-to-school time and holidays). Three key elements—audience insight leading to a Big Idea, message strategy, and media strategy—are at the heart of communication planning and make up the key sections in these functional area plans.

Key Strategic Decisions

Key strategic decisions that guide marcom plans include the analysis and statement of communication objectives, the target audience, brand position, and consumer insights. We'll also discuss brand communication strategy, which refers to the overall direction of the campaign—its focus and approach.

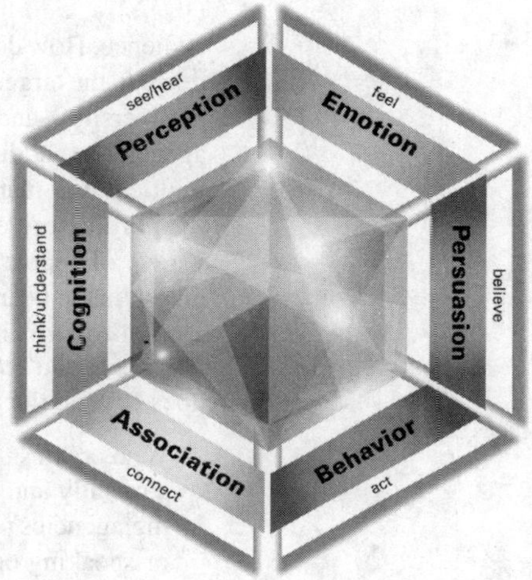

The Communication Objectives

After planners have examined the external and internal environments and defined the critical areas that need to be addressed, they can develop specific communication objectives to be accomplished during a specified time period—formal statements of the goals of the advertising or other marketing communication. They outline what the message is designed to achieve in the long term and how it will be measured.

Remember from Chapter 4 the six categories in the Facets Model of Effects: perception, emotion, cognition, persuasion, association, and behavior. These effects can be used to identify the most common consumer-focused objectives. For example, here are some sample objectives for each category as well as sample ads and campaigns that we have discussed in this or previous chapters:

- ***Perception Objectives*** Grab attention; create awareness; stimulate interest; stimulate recognition of the brand or the message; create brand reminder

  Examples: "1984" ad for Macintosh launch; Burger King's "Whopper Freakout" campaign
- ***Emotion/Affective Objectives*** Touch emotions; cue the psychological appeal; create brand or message liking; stimulate brand loyalty; stimulate desire

  Examples: McDonald's "I'm Lovin' It" campaign; the "My SPAR" campaign
- ***Cognition Objectives*** Deliver information; aid in understanding features, benefits, and brand differences; explain how to do or use something; counterargue; establish brand identity or cue the brand position; stimulate recall of the brand message; stimulate brand loyalty

  Examples: "Imported from Detroit" campaign; "Unsweetened truth" campaign
- ***Association Objectives*** Establish or cue the brand personality or image; create links to symbols and associations; connect to positive brand experiences

  Example: Old Spice and its "hunk on a horse" in the "What It Takes to Be a Man" campaign
- ***Persuasion Objectives*** Stimulate opinion or attitude formation; change or reinforce opinion or attitude; present argument and reasons; counterargue; create conviction or belief; stimulate brand preference or intent to try or buy; reward positive or desired response; stimulate brand loyalty; create buzz or word of mouth; energize opinion leaders; create advocacy and referrals

  Examples: The "Unsweetened truth" campaign; Dove's "Campaign for Real Beauty"
- ***Behavior Objectives*** Stimulate trial, sample, or purchase; generate other types of response (coupon use, attendance, test drive, visit store or dealer, volunteering, sign up, call in, visit website, clicks, attend, participate); create word-of-mouth buzz; create advocacy and referrals

  Examples: Burger King's "Whopper Freakout" campaign; Domino's "Pizza Turnaround"

This review provides a framework for setting objectives for various types of brand communication efforts.

The Target Audience

As we discussed in Chapter 5, segmenting and targeting are important because marketing communication strategy is based on accurately targeting an audience that will be responsive to a particular type of message, one that will deliver the objectives. Market segments are identified in marketing plans, but targeting audiences for messages happens in brand communication plans.

The decision about the target audience (or audiences) is made possible because of a deep knowledge of consumers. In particular, this research-based knowledge identifies what makes specific groups of consumers different from people in other groups. These characteristics also identify how consumers are similar to others in ways that characterize a specific type of viewpoint or lifestyle. A peer-group strategy at the University of Florida addresses the problem of students' driving drunk, which is explained in the "Inside Story" feature.

Diversity and Empathy There is more to targeting than just identifying and profiling a possible audience. How does the target audience relate to the brand, and how do marketing communicators relate to the target audience? Multicultural communication, in particular, demands an appreciation of diversity—and the empathy that results from such an appreciation. To deal with this problem, agencies are adding multicultural specialists as well as creating or buying firms that specialize in multicultural marketing.[6]

Professor Peggy Kreshel defines *diversity* as "the acknowledgment and inclusion of a wide variety of people with differing characteristics, attributes, beliefs, values, and experiences." This notion is the heart of *Madison Avenue and the Color Line* by historian Jason Chambers.

In advertising, diversity tends to be discussed primarily in terms of *representations of gender, race,* and *ethnicity in advertising content*, although, as Kreshel points out below, diversity goes beyond the images used in ads:[7]

> Who creates the ads we see? The industry's troubled, largely unsuccessful efforts to create a racially and ethnically diverse workplace tell part of the story. Minority-owned advertising agencies provide opportunities for diversity but are frequently viewed as being capable of speaking only to minority audiences. Women comprise the majority of the advertising workforce, yet an *Adweek* study a few years ago found only four female creative directors in the top 33 advertising agencies. We can only guess at the impact, knowing that creative directors are chiefly responsible for an agency's output.
>
> Content reflects those who create it and their perceptions of audiences. Advertisers' persistent emphasis on 18- to 34-year-olds, a group they view to be impressionable trendsetters who haven't yet formed brand loyalties, has occurred largely to the exclusion of other demographic groups. This preoccupation shapes our business (which constructs itself as youthful, rebellious, and cutting edge), media (where reality programming, the "entertainmentization" of news, and technological wizardry target 18- to 34-year-olds), and culture (reinforcing our celebration of the young, beautiful, and white).
>
> Similarly, marketers routinely define the Hispanic market primarily as "Spanish speaking." The richness and diversity of the many cultures that comprise that group—from Puerto Rico, to Mexico, to Central and South America—have been lost in the desire to construct a homogeneous market large enough to be economically viable. It is only recently that a conversation about the complexity of the Latino market—a complexity that goes beyond merely language or ethnic predilections—has begun to appear in the trade press.

In recognition of the importance of this diversity issue, the American Advertising Federation (AAF) sponsors multicultural programs such as the Most Promising Minority Students and the AAF Mosaic Awards. The leader of those programs, Constance Cannon Frazier, is on this book's advisory board, and the work of some of the Most Promising Minority Students are featured in this book.

Brand Identity Strategy

A brand identity must be distinctive. In other words, it represents only one particular product within a category, and it needs to be recognizable and, therefore, memorable. Recognizing the brand means that the consumer knows the brand's identification markers—name, logo, colors, typeface, design, and slogan—and can connect those marks with a past brand experience or message.

The Inside Story

Mistake #1: Drinking and Driving Drunk

Lisa Yansura, *Marketing Coordinator, Gragg Advertising, Kansas City Missouri, Formerly Adwerks Director, University of Florida*

Nightlife Navigators, a student-run organization at the University of Florida (UF), is leading the effort to end drunk driving by educating students about safe and affordable late-night transportation options in Gainesville, Florida. Nightlife Navigators is sponsored by the University of Florida's Student Government.

Nightlife Navigators approached Adwerks and asked us to help them launch their new website, *www.nightlifenavigators.com.* The website would include information on local bus routes, taxis, discussion boards, alcohol education, and other services for students. A graphic designer for Student Government created the logo, which looks like a neon bar sign.

On the launch date, Student Government and Nightlife Navigators would be on the UF campus giving out free food and distributing flyers, beverage koozies, and bottle opener key chains. SG representatives would be available to speak with students about the site and transportation options in Gainesville. To create buzz for the event, we ran full-page "Coming Soon" ads in local newspapers. Press releases were also issued to news outlets.

On the day of the event, hundreds of students received information about Nightlife Navigators. Additionally, the two largest newspapers in Gainesville, the *Independent Florida Alligator* and the *Gainesville Sun*, ran front-page stories regarding the event.

After the site launch, Adwerks created ads that would be placed in over 50 restroom ad spaces in local bars and restaurants. Placement in these restaurants and bars was intended to reach students while they were out drinking and in need of a ride home.

The ads featured catchy headlines with various mistakes people tend to make when they're intoxicated, including performing karaoke, calling the wrong girl, going home with someone from the opposing team, and ordering shots for the entire bar. The subhead, found under the humorous images, reads, "At least you didn't drive"—the point being that we all do regrettable things when we drink, but one of the mistakes does not have to be drinking and driving.

Rather than using scare tactics or take a more serious approach as many anti–drunk driving campaigns do, Adwerks decided to take a more humorous approach that students can relate to instead of feeling like they're being lectured to.

Contributors to this campaign included Kelly Jack, who created the logo and the Adwerks team: Account Director Kaely Coon, Senior Account Executives Lisa Yansura and Monica Moreno, Art Directors Larry Rosalez and Klara Cu, and Junior Account Executives Monica Jones and Danielle Dennis.

Photo: Courtesy of Nightlife Navigators, University of Florida

To better understand how a brand can become an integrated perception, we propose an outline of the communication dimensions of branding using the same six effects we presented in the Facets Model in Chapter 4 and explain them into terms of different aspects of brand identity:

Advertiser's Brand Objective	*Consumer's Response*
Create brand identity	See/hear
Cue brand personality, liking	Feel
Cue brand position, leadership	Think/understand
Cue brand image	Connect
Create brand promise, preference	Believe
Inspire brand loyalty	Act/do

Photo: Copyright 1999-2004 American Express Company. All rights reserved. Courtesy of Jerry Seinfeld and Ogilvy & Mather

A commercial for American Express featuring Jerry Seinfeld was designed to create brand liking through association with Seinfeld's personality. It also generated buzz, which extended its impact through the power of word of mouth.

- ***Brand Personality and Liking*** Brand personality—the idea that a brand takes on familiar human characteristics, such as loving (Hallmark, Kodak), competent (IBM), trustworthy (Volvo, Michelin), or sophisticated (Mercedes, Hermes, Rolex)—contributes an affective dimension to the meaning of a brand. Green Giant, for example, built its franchise on the personality of the friendly giant who watches over his valley and makes sure that Green Giant vegetables are fresh, tasty, nutritious, and appealing to kids. Larry Kelley and Donald Jugenheimer explain in their account planning textbook that it is important to measure the way these personality traits are associated with a brand or a competitor's brand. They observe, "Sometimes it is as important to understand what your brand isn't as much as what it is."[8] The point is to profile the brand as if it were a person, someone you like, someone like Jerry Seinfeld, for example.
- ***Brand Position and Leadership*** What does the brand stand for? As Jack Trout explained, "You have to stand for something," and it has to be something that matters to consumers.[9] Kodak is a classic example of a brand with a soul, one deeply embedded in personal pictures and memories. Hallmark's soul is found in the expression of sentiment. Starbucks created the high-end coffeehouse, and eBay owns the world of online auctions. Brand essence is also apparent when a brand dominates or defines its category. Category leadership often comes from being the first brand in the market—and with that comes an ownership position. ESPN, for example, owns sports information, and Silk is *the* soy milk drink. We'll talk more about positioning strategies in the section that follows.
- ***Brand Image*** Understanding brand meaning involves understanding the symbolism and associations that create a brand image, the mental impression that consumers construct for a product. The richness of the brand image determines the quality of the relationship and the strength of the associations and emotional connections that link a customer to a brand. Advertising researchers call this brand linkage.
- ***Brand Promise and Brand Preference*** A brand is sometimes defined as a promise because it establishes an expectation based on familiarity, consistency, and predictability. And believing the brand promise leads to brand preference and intention to buy. That's what has driven McDonald's to its position as a worldwide leader in the fast-food category. You know what to expect when you walk into a McDonald's anywhere in the world—quality fast food at a reasonable price.
- ***Brand Loyalty*** A personal experience with a brand can develop into a brand relationship, which is a connection over time that results in customers preferring the brand—thus brand loyalty—and buying it over and over. People have unique relationships with the brands they buy and use regularly, and this is what makes them brand loyal. The company's attitude toward its customers is another factor in loyalty.

Principle

A brand is an integrated perception that includes fragments of information, feelings, and personal experience, all of which come together to give the brand meaning.

To put all this together, a brand perception is created from different fragments of information, feelings, and personal experiences with a brand. You could say that a brand is an *integrated perception*[10]—in other words, all of these different aspects of brand communication work together to create brand meaning. In the best of all worlds, these meanings would be consistent from one customer to another, but because of the vagaries of personal experience, different people may have different impressions of a brand.

Emotional branding is one way to anchor a brand perception. As we have said, emotion is a powerful tool in marketing communication, and brand liking leads to trust and loyalty. Branding expert John Williams explains, "Research shows that reason and emotions differ in that reason generates conclusions but not necessarily actions, while emotions more frequently lead to actions."[11] Brand liking is a powerful differentiator. The challenge to advertisers is to manage their communication efforts so the fragments fit together to form a coherent and integrated brand impression.

An example of creating a brand meaning that connects with its audience is the classic *Wall Street Journal* campaign that ran for 25 years in advertising trade publications and established the *Journal* as a premier medium for advertising. You can find many of the ads from this campaign at www.aef.com/industry/careers/2026.

Brand Positioning Strategy

Principle
The goal of positioning is to locate a product in the consumer's mind based on its features and advantages relative to its competition.

We mentioned brand positioning in the previous list, but let's look at it in more depth. A **position** is how consumers define the product or brand relative to its competitors.

A classic example of positioning is the campaign for Avis, which used the line "We Try Harder" to describe how it competes against category leader Hertz. The line was not only a good positioning statement but also was named as one of the Top 10 Slogans of the 20th Century. The campaign was described by the fathers of positioning, Jack Trout and Al Ries, in their groundbreaking book *Positioning: The Battle for Your Mind*.[12]

Planners may find themselves engaged in a new product launch, which allows them to develop a positioning strategy from scratch, but in most cases, they are dealing with a brand that has been on the market, and the question is, Is the position working? Is it clear and focused, or does it need to be polished, clarified, or adjusted?

A position is based on two things. First, it is based on a particular feature or attribute—Coke Zero is low calorie but tastes like regular Coke. The feature also can be psychological, such as heritage (Hallmark: quality—"When you care enough to send the very best") or leadership (regular Coke: "It's the real thing."). Second, that feature must be important to the consumer.

In the cola wars, it's also interesting to note Pepsi's efforts at carving out a distinctive position. Probably it's classic effort came in the 1960s with the line "Come Alive! You're in the Pepsi generation." Most of Pepsi's memorable positions have in some way reflected its "cool quotient" and pop-culture relevance, such as "Catch that Pepsi Spirit" in 1979 and "Be Young, Have Fun, Drink Pepsi" in the 1990s. Pepsi undertook a huge study and repositioning effort in 2012 in order to reinvigorate the brand. Its researchers concluded that while Coke represents happiness and moments of joy, Pepsi represents individuality and "the excitement of now," hence the new slogan: "Live for Now."[13]

A position also is based on some notion of comparison. Is the brand more expensive or less; is it a status product or a symbol of frugality; is it sporty, functional, safe, or risky? Walmart's position, for example, is encompassed in its slogan, "Always Low Prices." Positioning, then, is about locking the brand in consumers' minds based on some quality relevant to them where the brand stands out. Compare the positioning strategies of the various arms of the U.S. military as they represent themselves in their ads.

In June 2013, *The Guardian* broke the story that the U.S. administration was holding a secret collection of telephone

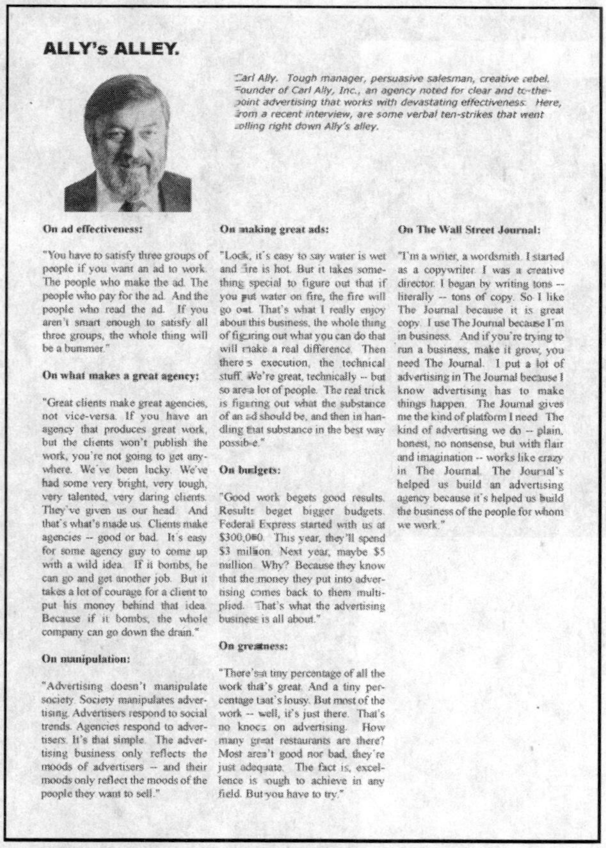

Photo: © Dow Jones & Company, Inc. All rights reserved worldwide

CLASSIC
This ad that features Carl Ally is one in a campaign series that the *Wall Street Journal* placed in advertising trade publications. The long-running campaign began in 1975 and featured leaders in advertising explaining their views on how advertising works and why the *Wall Street Journal* is a good medium in which to advertise.

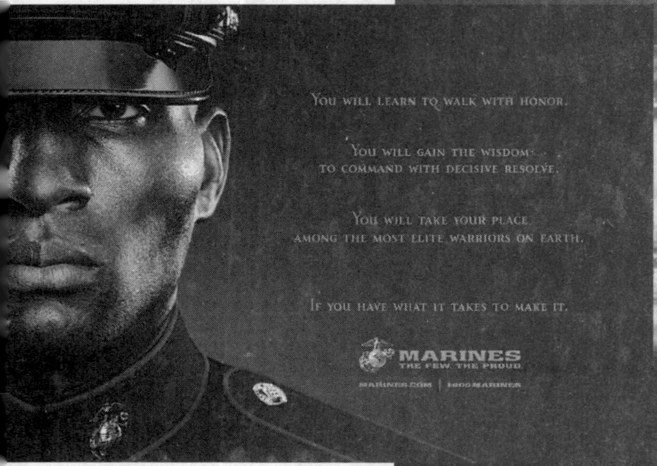

In these four ads for the Navy, Army, Air Force, and Marines, can you perceive a difference in their positioning strategies? How do they communicate their differences in the style, copy, and graphics? Which do you think would be most effective recruiting volunteers from your generation? Why do you think that is so?

Photo sources (listed left to right): Army materials courtesy of the U.S. Government; U.S. Navy materials courtesy of the U.S. Government; Courtesy of the U.S. Marines Corps; Courtesy of the United States Air Force and GSD&M

records. Ultimately, this led to the revelation that the United States was running a surveillance program called Prism. The news had been leaked to *The Guardian* by whistleblower Edward Snowden. The newspaper's involvement in the story resulted in the British government ordering that computer hard drives housing the information were to be destroyed. The offices of the newspaper were visited by representatives of the UK's own surveillance network (GCHQ) and the destruction of the hard drives was supervised by them.

Members of the UK parliament debated whether they considered the newspaper to have endangered the security of the country by publishing extracts from the leaked information. With an ongoing criminal investigation in progress, the newspaper found itself in the role of a witness in the proceedings. Do you think publishing the leaks was a good strategic decision?

Principle
Positioning identifies the features that make a brand different from its competitors and relevant to consumers.

Product Features and Attributes An initial step in crafting a position is to identify the **features** of the brand, as well as those of the competition, to determine where the brand has an advantage over its competitors. A marketer carefully evaluates the product's tangible features (such as size, color, design, price, and ease of use) and other intangible attributes (such as quality, status, value, fashion, and safety) to identify the dimensions of the product that are relevant to its customers and that make it different from its competitors.

An interesting twist on features developed when electric hybrid cars, such as GM's Volt, were introduced to the market. The standard miles-per-gallon (MPG) estimate of fuel efficiency was turned upside down with projections of 230 MPG for Volt and 367 MPG for the Nissan Leaf. Of course, these cars use very little gas as long as they are running on their batteries—gas is used only when the charge runs out. If you only use the car to run around town, theoretically you could get unlimited gas mileage.[14] So what does this changing standard do to traditional car-buying marketing and decision making?

Differentiation and Competitive Advantage Most markets involve a high level of competition. How does a company compete in a crowded market? It uses **product differentiation**, a strategy designed to focus attention on product differences that are important to consumers and that distinguish the company's product from that of its competitors. We refer to products that really are the same (examples include milk, unleaded gas, and over-the-counter drugs) as undifferentiated or **parity products**. For these products, marketers often promote intangible, or psychological, differences, particularly through branding.

The creation of a unique brand image for a product (think Swatch) is the most obvious way to differentiate one product from another. Internet-based Mozilla and Craigslist are small companies but big brands that are strong because they have the support of dedicated users. This strong customer–brand relationship reflects a leadership position—a brand that has defined or created its category. But it's not just hot Internet companies that have achieved this type of leadership—McIlhenny's Tabasco Sauce, which was launched in 1868, created and still owns the hot sauce category.

A technique called **feature analysis** helps structure an assessment of features relative to competitors' products to identify where a brand has an advantage. To conduct a feature analysis, first, make a chart of the product and competitors' products, listing relevant features, as the following table illustrates. Then evaluate how well the product and the competitors' products perform on those features. What are the brand's strong points or weak points? Next, evaluate how important each feature is to the target audience using opinion research. In other words, how much do consumers care about various features (which ones are most important to them), and how do the various brands compare on these features?

How to Do a Feature Analysis

		Product Performance			
Feature	*Importance to Prospect*	*Yours*	*X*	*Y*	*Z*
Price	1	+	–	–	+
Quality	4	–	+	–	+
Style	2	+	–	+	–
Availability	3	–	+	–	–
Durability	5	–	+	+	+

Using the two factors of importance and performance, **competitive advantage** is found where (1) the product has a strong feature (2) in an area that is important to the target and (3) where the competition is weaker. The product in the preceding table would compete well on both price and style against X, on price against competitor Y, and on style against competitor Z. Competitor X seems the most vulnerable on two features, price and style, that consumers rate as the most important decision points.

An example of product turnaround built of a knowledge of competitive advantages, disadvantages, and consumer performance was discussed in the Domino's case in the previous chapter. You may remember that Domino's was rated good on delivery and speed but last on taste, which was the number one feature preferred by consumers. To turn around the brand's position, it had to overcome the taste problem.

Locating the Brand Position Let's return now to the concept of a position to see how it is created. In addition to specific product attributes, a number of factors can be used to locate a position for a brand in consumers' minds, including the following:

Principle
Strong brands are known for one thing—the test is, "What do you think of when you mention the brand's name?"

- ***Superiority Position*** Jack Trout suggests that positioning is always easy if something is faster, fancier, safer, or newer.
- ***Preemptive Position*** Being first in the category often creates category leadership and dominance.
- ***Value Position*** Walmart's "Always Low Prices" is the epitome of offering good value for the money. Hyundai rode that position through the economic downturn and picked up market share faster than its competitors, passing both Honda and Ford to become the fourth-largest automaker in the world.[15]
- ***Psychological Position*** Often brands are designed around nonproduct differences. For psychological positions, consider these examples: Volvo owns the safety position, Coke owns a position of authenticity for colas ("It's the real thing"), and Hallmark owns a quality position ("When you care enough to send the very best").
- ***Benefit Position*** How does the product help the consumer?
- ***Usage Position*** How, where, and when is the product used and who is using it?
- ***Competitor's Strategy*** How can the product go head to head with or move completely away from the competition?
- ***Category Factors*** Is the competition coming from outside the category, and, if so, how does the brand compare to these other categories, and how does that change the analysis of strengths and weaknesses?

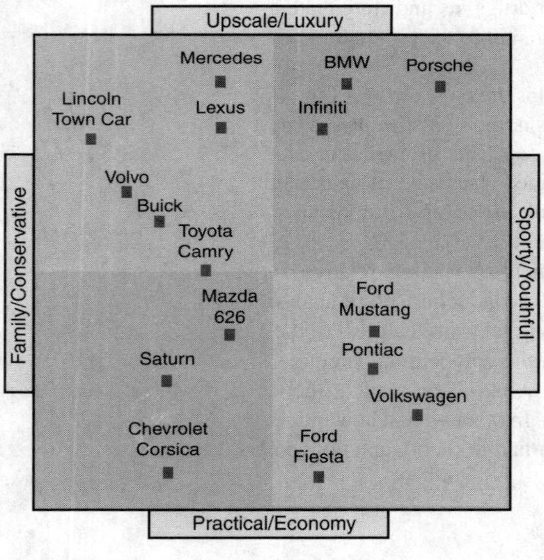

FIGURE 7.5
Perceptual Map
Perceptual maps illustrate the positions occupied by competitors relative to important decision factors. These positions are determined by research into the perceptions of the target market.

As we've mentioned the differences have to be distinctive to the brand as well as important to the consumer. The point is that strong brands become well known for one thing. When you think of Google or eBay, what's the first thing that comes to mind? (Google = search engine; eBay = online auctions.)

James Stengel, former global marketing chief at Procter & Gamble, has developed a new positioning approach that he calls "purpose-based marketing." He points to the company's Pampers brand, which moved from just keeping babies' bottoms dry to a higher purpose—helping moms nurture healthy, happy babies. The company created new programs offering parenting advice and conducted research on infant-related problems, such as sleeping, that led to product redesigns.[16]

There's a reason we talk about "locating" a brand position. Many campaigns are designed to establish the brand's position by giving the right set of cues about these decision factors to help place the brand in the consumer's mind relative to the competition. If a position is a point in a consumer's mind, planners can map that—in fact, the way planners compare positions is by using a technique called a **perceptual map** that plots all of the competitors on a matrix based on the two most important consumer decision factors. Figure 7.5 illustrates how positions can be mapped for automobiles.

Repositioning Positions are difficult to establish and are created over time. Once established, they are difficult to change, as Kodak discovered with its ownership of the film category when the market moved to digital pictures. Category dominance is important, as Al Ries, one of the founders of the positioning concept, argues, but sometimes the category changes, and the brand has to change as well or get left behind. Al and Laura Ries recommend the difficult challenge of **repositioning** when the market changes or new targeting opportunities arise.

A campaign by Coke Zero to change its brand perception illustrates how positions define products in their users mind. How many guys will admit that they are on a diet and drink Coke Zero? Sounds like a girl thing. But Coke knows that 18- to 34- year-old males are a big cola-drinking market, and most of them preferred the taste of regular sugary sodas. Coca-Cola wanted to grow its market by convincing these guys that Coke Zero tastes like Coke. Its agency Crispin Porter + Bogusky overcame the negative perception of a diet drink with an edgy campaign that used self-deprecating humor. The Big Idea was that Coke's legal department wanted to sue Coke Zero for taste infringement. The unconventional message not only changed guys' perception of Coke Zero's taste but also won a Silver Effie for its effectiveness.

We mentioned Kodak earlier, which is a fascinating study in positioning and repositioning, Kodak has always stood for pictures and over the years has owned the moment of capturing an image with a photo: "the Kodak moment." But Kodak also stands for film (think yellow box), and that was the reason for its recent marketplace problems as the camera industry moved to digital formats. Kodak's agency, Ogilvy, developed a repositioning strategy to adapt Kodak's position from "the Moment" to "the gallery"—a place where pictures are kept.

Repositioning, in the view of the Rieses, can work only if the new position is related to the brand's core concept. They worried about Kodak's move and wondered if the link between the Kodak brand and film is too strong to stretch to digital products. In fact, the gallery position didn't work, and the changing environment, as well as public perceptions, were too problematic to overcome. It will be interesting to see if Paula Deen with her fat-laden recipes can effectively change into a healthy food guru for diabetics.[17] (Of course, that may be a moot issue after Dean's supposedly racist comments became an issue in 2013, which led to the loss of her Food Network show.)

The principle in repositioning is to move ahead while at the same time retaining the brand essence. For an effective example, Ries and Ries point to IBM as a company that repositioned itself from a computer manufacturer to a provider of services. Even though the market for mainframe computers has been declining, they observe that the connection with IBM's brand essence is still there in IBM's new position as a global computer service company. An example comes from China, where IBM is marketing an urban-planning tool called Smart City that connects public services and infrastructure projects through information technology. IBM sees China, with its huge public sector and infrastructure projects, as a big market for its services.

The role of brand communication in a repositioning strategy is to relate the product's position to the target market's life experience and associations. A classic example of an effective repositioning campaign that retains the brand essence as it carves out a new location in consumers' minds is 7-Up, which is described in the "A Matter of Principle" feature.

Consumer Insight and Account Planning

The concept of consumer insight, which we introduced in the previous chapter, is the last of our key strategic decisions. It may also be the hardest decision that planners make because it calls for solid research and thoughtful analyses that leads to, in many cases, unexpected conclusions about the direction the brand communication should take.

So when we say **consumer insight**, what are we talking about? Kelley and Jugenheimer define and describe this special kind of insight as follows:

- "Understanding the 'why' we behave the way we do"
- "Seeing and understanding clearly the inner nature of things"

A Matter of Principle

The 7-Up Uncola Story: A Classic in Repositioning

Bill Barre, *Department of Journalism, Central Michigan University*

How do you turn what was originally a medicinal product (intended to cure hangovers) and then a mixer with whisky into a soft drink without changing anything about the product or its packaging?

If you said "magic," you'd be correct. But it's not the kind of magic you might think. This is branding magic. It's called positioning. And it created magical results for 7-Up in 1967, when the company repositioned the brand as the Uncola.

Preceding 1967, during the first 37 years that 7-Up was marketed, consumers didn't think of 7-Up as a soft drink, just as we don't think of club soda and tonic water as soft drinks. In 1967, a soft drink was a cola, and a cola was a soft drink.

Four people were in the room when the term "uncola" was first uttered. Three of them are deceased—Orville Roesch, 7-Up's ad manager; Bill Ross, creative director at JWT; and Bob Taylor, senior art director at JWT. Charlie Martell was the fourth person and just a young writer at JWT at the time of the meeting.

"I remember the meeting to this day," recalls Martell. "We realized that we had to be a lot more specific if we hoped to change people's minds about 7-Up. We had to find a way to pick up that green bottle (7-Up), pick it up mentally in consumers' minds, and move it over to here, where Coke and Pepsi were. And until we did that, anything we did that smacked of soft-drink advertising was going to be rejected by consumers."

The objective was clear, yet getting there proved to be completely perplexing. "They had to find a way to attach the word *cola* to 7-Up. Nobody had ever done that before. This was before the word *positioning* was even used in advertising and marketing," says John Furr, a management supervisor at JWT at the time.

Martell remembers that the strategy meeting started as it always started for 7-Up. "We got to talking about how to get somebody to move this green bottle from here to there. And I think Orville said something like we had to associate ourselves with the colas. And Bill Ross started talking about, 'Well, how about, maybe, we call ourselves the non-cola.' And Orville nodded. Thought that sounded good. And I chimed in with 'Maybe we could call it the uncola.' And everyone nodded and said that was an interesting thought. Didn't blow anybody away at that point. They filed it away in their collective consciousness. Few days later, came back and said, 'Maybe we just got something here.' Uncola—it did everything we had been wanting to do. In one word, it did it all. It positioned 7-Up as a cola, yet not a cola. We said, 'Hey . . . let's make some advertising.'"

Today, the 7-Up Uncola campaign is regarded as perhaps the classic example of brand repositioning—and a classic example of how the right brand positioning can lead to marketing magic.

And how exactly do we do that? What special skills are required for this type of seeing and understanding? Again, from Kelley and Jugenheimer:

- "Looking at things differently and seeing things intuitively"
- "Acute observation, deduction, penetration, and discernment"
- "Looking at relationships in a new and unique way"

As Fallon and Senn outlined in one of their principles at the beginning of this chapter, the key to effective brand communication is finding a central emotional truth about a customer's relationship with a brand. Kelley and Jugenheimer, in their book on account planning, explain, "A true insight into consumer behavior will connect with the consumer at an emotional level." It will elicit a response, such as "that is exactly how I feel."[18]

As Regina Lewis[19] noted, consumer insights and the account planning function responsible for identifying them has transformed marketing research as well as communication planning. She calls for "deep insight into consumer minds and hearts." As we stressed in Chapter 4, it's not just about how people think. In Lewis's view, it's about consumer minds and hearts—their mental and emotional mind-sets."

When the Eight O'Clock coffee brand planners, for example, wanted to know more about its audience to better target its message, it used videotaped observational research to identify key insights into how people relate to coffee. Rather than a rosy sunrise, the tapes showed that it was a struggle to get moving. "In real life," the strategic planner concluded, "people stumble around, trying to get kids out of bed. Coffee is the fuel that gets them dressed, fed, and out the door." On other tapes, it also showed that coffee was the reward for mom after the kids are out the door. "I have my cup of coffee when the kids leave," one mom observed. "It's my first moment to take a breather. And it gives me energy."[20] Notice how many emotional truths emerged from this analysis?

Account Planning

Account planning analyzes the research to uncover consumer insights. Insight—that's what happens when the lightbulb goes off and the planner sees something in a new way. As in the Eight O'Clock coffee example, the planner struck gold by finding out that coffee is the fuel that gets adults, particularly moms, through the morning rush—and it's also the reward for surviving that busy routine. From this insight come clues about how and when to reach the target audience and what to say to her.

Account planning is the research and analysis process used to gain knowledge of the consumer that is expressed as a key consumer insight about how people relate to a brand or product. An **account planner**, then, is a person in an agency who uses a disciplined system to research a brand and its customer relationships to devise advertising (and other marketing communication) message strategies that are effective in addressing consumer needs and wants. Account planning agencies are based in research but focus on deriving meanings about consumers. Hall & Partners, for example, has noted that with the new social media, the walls between private life and public life have been breached. (Check the company out at www.hall-and-partners.com.)

In case you're interested in account planning as a career, here is an actual job description for a vice president for global consumer insights for a major apparel company:

> The role of the VP, Global Consumer Insights, is to create competitive advantage by delivering fact-based consumer/customer understanding and insights that facilitate speed and accuracy of strategic and tactical decision making across all critical parts of the organization—in short, turning data into Insights, and then into Action. The planner will accomplish this by placing consumers first, integrating their "voices" into the planning process, and creating sustaining value at the corporate and brand levels.

As the job description suggests, the account planning function develops the marketing communication strategy with other members of the client and agency team and guides its implementation in the creative work and media planning.

Here's an example from Dunkin' Donuts of how account planning works to uncover, in this case, the barriers to purchasing fancy coffee drinks. This mini-case was provided by Regina Lewis and referred to in the Part 2 opener. A member of this book's advisory board, she was formerly vice president of consumer and brand insights at Dunkin' brands:[21]

> We found through our research that people wanted to try espresso drinks like lattes and cappuccinos, but they were intimidated and thought such fancy coffee drinks were an ordeal to order. Dunkin' Donuts, of course, is known for its coffee and we felt that to be a great coffee player, we had to have an espresso line. But our brand has always been hot regular coffee for average Joe. What we realized was that there was a place in the marketplace for espresso-based drinks for everybody. It doesn't have to be a fancy treat. We learned that a lot of people like the milky steamed beverages, but they were intimidated by whether they would know how to order them.
>
> When we launched our new line, we used the positioning umbrella of the *democratization of espresso*. We dramatically changed the way our customers view a latte and eliminated the whole barista thing. With push-button machines, we created a world where you can get espresso through the drive-through in less than two minutes. We made espresso available for everybody and we also priced our drinks under Starbucks. We launched with a big public relations campaign titled "The Espresso Revolution—a Shot Being Fired in New England."

In contrast to account managers who are seen as the voice of the client, account planners are described as the voice of the consumer. As London's Account Planning Group explains

Principle
The account manager is seen as the voice of the client, and the account planner is seen as the voice of the consumer.

it, "The job is to ensure that an understanding of consumer attitudes and behavior is brought to bear at every stage of communications development via continuous involvement in the process."[22]

Account planners don't design the creative strategy for a brand message because this is usually a team process with the participation of the creative people. Rather, the planner evaluates consumers' relationships with the brand to determine the kind of message to which they might respond. Ultimately, the objective is to help the creative team come up with a better idea—making their creative process easier and faster. Susan Mendelsohn, a leader in the U.S. account planning industry and another member of this book's advisory board, explains the account planner's task as the following:[23]

1. Understand the meaning of the brand.
2. Understand the target audience's relationship to the brand.
3. Articulate communication strategies.
4. Prepare creative briefs based on an understanding of the consumer and brand.
5. Evaluate the effectiveness of the communication in terms of how the target reacts to it (so that planners can keep learning more about consumers and brand communication).

The Consumer Insight Process

Through the process of strategic and critical thinking, the planner interprets consumer research to find a key consumer insight that uncovers the relevance factor—the reason why consumers care about a brand. Consumer insights reveal the inner nature of consumers' thinking, including such things as mind-sets, moods, motivations, desires, aspirations, and motives that trigger their attitudes and actions. This chapter's "Inside Story" feature explained how a university student ad group sorted out significant consumer insights into drunk driving.

Research: Brand Intelligence Insight begins with research. The objective is to puzzle out a key insight that will help move the target audience to respond to the message. **Insight research**, in other words, is basically about asking and listening and then asking more questions to probe deeper into thoughts, opinions, attitudes, desires, and motivations.

Planners use a wide variety of research tools to arrive at insights that lead to an intelligent strategic decision. In a sense, they are social anthropologists who are in touch with cultural and social trends and understand how these trends take on relevance in people's lives. To do that, the account planner is an *integrator* (who brings all of the information together) and a *synthesizer* (who expresses what it all means in one startlingly simple statement).

As Sally Reinman, worldwide market planner at Saatchi & Saatchi, wrote for this book in an earlier edition, research is more than numbers. She explains that research processes used to find insights are more varied than ever before. "To find these commonalities, I work with experts to learn the cultural meaning of codes and symbols that people use to communicate. The experts I work with include cultural and cognitive anthropologists, psychologists, interior decorators, and Indian storytellers." Her point is that anyone and any methodology that "can help me understand consumers and the consumer decision-making process is fair game."

Principle
A great insight identifies the intersections between the interests of the consumer and the features of the brand.

Insights: The Fuel of Big Ideas Advertising is sometimes thought to be *an idea* factory, but account planners look at advertising as *an insight factory*. As Mendelsohn says, "Behind every famously great idea, there is a perhaps less flashy, but immensely powerful insight." Insights are the fuel that fires the ideas. Kelley and Jugenheimer describe this value as a "quality-of-life insight." They explain that it "identifies the intersection of the brand's benefit and the quality of life it provides to the consumer."[24]

Finding the "a-ha" in a stack of research reports, data, and transcripts, which is referred to as **insight mining**, is the greatest challenge for an account planner. The Account Planning Group association describes this process on its website (www.apg.org.uk) as "peering into nooks and crannies without losing sight of the big picture in order to identify a key insight that can transform a client's business."

Mendelsohn describes insight mining as "a deep dive" into the meaning of a brand looking for "major truths." She explains that the planner engages in unearthing the relationship that a target audience has with a brand or product and what role that brand plays in their lives. Understanding the brand/consumer relationship is important because account planners are taking on the position of the agency's *brand steward*. As Abigail Hirschhorn, chief strategic planning officer at DDB, explains, "Our work puts our clients in touch with the souls of their brands."[25]

But how do you get started on finding these elusive insights? The account planning tool kit is made up of questions that lead to useful insights culled from research. Kelley and Jugenheimer recommend seven topics or questions you might ask to begin your search:[26]

- What is the product's reason for being?
- What is the product's history?
- How do consumers use the product?
- How do brand consumers see themselves?
- What are the untapped beliefs about the product?
- What are the barriers to using the product?
- What appears in category and brand advertising for the product?

Here is another set of questions that can lead to useful insights:

- What is a realistic response objective (perception, knowledge, feelings, attitudes, symbolic meanings, behavior) for this target group?
- What are the causes of their lack of response?
- What are the barriers to the desired response?
- What could motivate them to respond in the desired way?
- What is the role of each element in the communication mix to motivate them or remove a barrier?

Here's an example of how data analysis works. Imagine you are working on a cookie account. Here's your brand share information:

	2012 Share (%)	*2013 Share (%)*
Choco Nuts (your brand)	50	40
Sweet 'n Crunchy (your main competitor)	25	30

What's the problem with this situation? Obviously, your brand is losing market share, and your primary competitor is gaining share. As a result, one of your goals might be to use a marketing communication mix to drive higher levels of sales. But that goal is so broad that it would be difficult to determine whether communication is sufficient to solve the problem. Let's dig deeper and consider another set of data about household (HH) purchases in a year:

	2012 HH Purchases	*2013 HH Purchases*
Choco Nuts	4	3
Sweet 'n Crunchy	2.5	3

What problem can you identify here? It looks like your loyal brand users are reducing their purchases at the same time Sweet 'n Crunchy customers are increasing their purchases. It may even be that some of your customers are switching over to Sweet 'n Crunchy. A strategy based on this information might be to convince people that your brand tastes better and to remind your loyal customers of the reasons they have preferred your brand.

When you combine the two pieces of information and think about it, another insight might explain this situation. Perhaps people are simply eating fewer cookies. If that's a problem, then the communication opportunity lies in convincing people to return to eating cookies. That is more of a *category sell* problem (sell cookies) rather than a *competitive sell* (set the brand against the competition). In the Choco Nuts example, it would take more research to know which situation applies here. Here's a summary of these two different strategic approaches:

	Competitive/Brand Sell	*Category Sell*
What?	Challenger brand	Leader brand
Who?	Loyal buyers	Medium/light/lapsed buyers
What effect?	Compare cookie brands	Compare against other snacks
Objective?	Increase share of wallet	Increase total category sales
Message?	"Our cookies are better than theirs"	"Cookies are better than candy or salty snacks"

The important dimensions account planners seek to understand in planning brand strategies include relationship, perceptions, promise, and point of differentiation. Most importantly, planners are looking for clues about the brand's *meaning*, which is usually phrased in terms of the brand essence (core or soul), personality, or image, and how that connects with consumers' lifestyles, as the SeaPort posters illustrate.

The Creative Brief

The outcome of strategic research usually reaches agency creative departments in the form of a strategy document called a **creative brief** or **communication brief**, which explains the consumer insight and summarizes the basic strategy decisions.

Although the exact form of this document differs from agency to agency and from advertiser to advertiser, the brief is an outline of the message strategy that guides the creative team and helps keep its ideas strategically sound. As the planner's main product, it should be clear, logical, and focused. Here is an outline of a typical communication brief:

- ***Problem*** What's the problem that communication can solve? (establish position, reposition, increase loyalty, get people involved, increase liking, and so on)
- ***Target Audience*** To whom do we want to speak? (brand loyal, heavy users, infrequent users, competition's users, and so on)

Photo: Courtesy of SeaPort Airlines

Photo: Courtesy of SeaPort Airlines

SHOWCASE

These posters are for SeaPort Airlines, which serves Seattle, Juneau, Portland, and other West Coast cities. They make a statement about the SeaPort target audience—influential business travelers—and their lifestyle.

These ads were contributed by Karl Schroeder, former copywriter at Coates Kokes in Portland, Oregon. A graduate of the University of Oregon advertising program, he was nominated by Professor Charles Frazer.

- ***Consumer Insights*** What motivates the target? What are the "major truths" about the target's relationship to the product category or brand?
- ***Brand Imperatives*** What are the important features? What's the point of competitive advantage? What's the brand's position relative to the competition? Also, what's the brand essence, personality, and/or image? Ogilvy & Mather says, "What is the unique personality for the brand? People use products, but they have relationships with brands."
- ***Communication Objectives*** What do we want customers to do in response to our messages? (perception, knowledge, feelings, symbolic meanings, attitudes and conviction action)
- ***The Proposition or Selling Idea*** What is the single thought that the communication will bring to life in a provocative way?
- ***Support*** What is the reason to believe the proposition? Ogilvy & Mather explains, "We need to give consumers 'permission to believe'—something that allows them to rationalize, whether to themselves or others, what is in reality an emotionally driven brand decision. The support should be focused on the insight or proposition, the truths that make the brand benefit indisputable."
- ***Creative Direction*** How can we best stimulate the desired response? How can we best say it?
- ***Media Imperatives*** Where and when should we say it?

Source: This outline was compiled from one contributed by Susan Mendelsohn as well as from the creative brief outline developed by the Ogilvy agency and presented on its website (www.ogilvy.com).

The brief is strategic, but it also should be inspirational. It is designed to ignite the creative team and give a spark to their idea process. A good brief doesn't set up limitations and boundaries but rather serves as a springboard. It is the first step in the creative process. Charlie Robertson, an account planner and brand consultant, likens the brief to a fire starter: "The match is the brief, the ignition is the inspiring dialogue [in the briefing], and the flare is the creative."[27]

Looking Ahead

Strategic consistency is the result of carefully researched marketing communication plans. The actual messages that bring the strategy to life are a result of strategic planning but also creative thinking. Part 3 of this book will review the creative side of marketing communication beginning with Chapter 8, which continues the strategy discussion in terms of message strategy.

It's a Wrap

Re-telling a Tale

The Three Little Pigs full advertisement made its debut on February 29 2012. It was initially broadcast on the UK's Channel Four as well as online. Despite the fact that the advertisement was only broadcast in the UK, it quickly gained global coverage and media attention.

According to *The Guardian*'s own research, it generated over 80,000 tweets and over 2 million online viewers. A third of these viewers were in the UK and another third in the US. With two thirds of the viewers being non-UK, the expectation is that the newspaper's global profile has been enhanced.

The Guardian's CMO David Pemsel had invited the newspaper's biggest advertisers and a number of CEOs from media agencies for a meal on the night of February 29, so they could watch the advertisement live. At the same time, the newspaper monitored the live feedback on Twitter and other social media.

What they experienced was extraordinary, but nerve-wracking. Very quickly it became apparent that viewers of the advertisement saw the newspaper as being modern and progressive. It was also seen as being open and international in approach. The hashtags on the newspaper's Twitter accounts all featured these perceptions.

The main point of the exercise was achieved; the advertisement and subsequent feedback had transformed perceptions of the newspaper in an incredibly short period of time. As for sales of the newspaper, the continued long-term decline in sales had not been arrested, but *The Guardian* could report a respectable rise in sales on a monthly basis.

Key Points Summary

1. **What is the difference between objectives, strategies, and tactics in strategic planning, and how are the four levels of planning connected?** Objectives are what you want to accomplish, or goals; strategies are how you will accomplish the objectives, or the design or plan; and tactics are the ways in which you implement the strategies, or the execution. The four-tiered process of strategic planning involves a set of cascading objectives and strategies. Corporate objectives and strategies as spelled out in a business plan are achieved through planning at the level of marketing (and other business areas, such as production), and marketing objectives and strategies give direction to a brand communication or IMC plan, which is implemented through plans for specific marketing communication areas, such as advertising.
2. **What are the key strategic decisions, and in what ways are they central to brand communication planning?** The key strategic decisions are setting communication objectives, targeting the audience, developing a brand strategy, and designing a brand positioning strategy. The objectives determine how the impact of the brand communication is to be measured; the target audience is identified relative that is most likely to respond to the brand messages in ways that will deliver on the objectives; the brand strategy reviews the critical dimensions of branding to either create or refine aspects such as brand identity, image, and personality; and the brand positioning strategy considers whether the brand position location needs to be established, refined, or repositioned. The brand strategy dimensions, including the position, connect with the target audience as expressed in the brand communication to the extent that the consumer thoughts and emotions are understood.
3. **What is account planning, and how is it used in advertising?** Account planning matches the right message to the right audience and identifies the right media to deliver that message. The primary purpose of account planning is to use research to uncover consumer insights and then create a communication brief for the creative team that outlines how the insight gives direction to the message strategy and media strategy.

Key Terms

account planner, p. 227
account planning, p. 227
business philosophy, p. 210
communication brief, p. 230
competitive advantage, p. 224
consumer insight, p. 225
creative brief, p. 230
feature analysis, p. 223
features, p. 223
goals, p. 211
insight mining, p. 228
insight research, p. 228
marketing plan, p. 211
mission marketing, p. 210
mission statement, p. 210
objectives, p. 209
parity products, p. 223
perceptual map, p. 224
position, p. 221
product differentiation, p. 223
profit, p. 211
repositioning, p. 225
return on investment, p. 211
share of market, p. 213
situation analysis, p. 211
societal marketing, p. 210
strategic business unit, p. 210
strategic planning, p. 208
strategies, p. 209
SWOT analysis, p. 211
tactics, p. 209
vision statement, p. 210

Review Questions

7-4. Define strategic planning and explain the elements involved.

7-5. What is a business plan, and what are the stages that constitute its development?

7-6. What is a SWOT analysis, and how does it help in the success and development of a marketing plan?

✪ 7-7. Discuss the cascading concept in planning and setting objectives.

7-8. What are the goals of a brand communication plan?

7-9. What type of strategy should a company follow to stand out in a competitive market?

7-10. What is an insight, and how is it uncovered? What is insight mining?

7-11. What is account planning, and what does the account planner bring to a marketing communication plan?

Discussion Questions

✪ 7-12. The owners of the Vico brand of organic coconut water believe that it is the next big trend in the bottled water category. It uses the clear liquid inside young, green coconuts (not coconut milk, which is derived from pressing the coconut pulp). Healthy and natural, the product is popular in South America and is becoming a niche market in New York City and other cities with South American immigrant populations. Outline a preliminary situation analysis, objectives, targeting, positioning, and branding strategies. In each section, explain what other information you would need to fully develop this plan.

7-13. You have been requested by your marketing manager to analyze an existing product line of shampoos for women—antidandruff, colored hair, and clean and shiny—and to determine the level of competition in the local markt.

Choose an existing local brand and create a system that compares your products with those of competitors. Define the system you should use. List and explain the factors of comparison, the characteristic features of the existing products. Discuss why it is important to know where your products stand compared to those of competitors.

Take-Home Projects

7-14. *Portfolio Project:* Examine the following websites: www.lexus.com, www.infiniti.com, and www.mercedes-benz.com. Based on what you find on these sites, compare the positioning strategies for these top-of-the-line SUV models. Analyze the product features, competitive advantage, and points of differentiation.

✪ 7-15. *Mini-Case Analysis:* Review The Three Little Pigs case that opened and closed this chapter. Assume you are working on this account and have been asked to pull together a presentation for the brand team for the next year of this campaign. What research would you recommend conducting in order to decide if the campaign should be continued or modified? What do you need to find out in order to make this decision?

TRACE North America Case

Planning for Multicultural Communication

Read the TRACE case in the Appendix before coming to class.

7-16. Develop a creative brief based on what you believe an account planner would have developed. Keep it to one page.

7-17. Develop at least three business objectives and strategies, three communications objectives and strategies, and three media objectives and strategies based on the case study.

Hands-On Case

Connecting Heart and Soul

In the opening to Part 2, Regina Lewis, former vice president of insights for both Dunkin' Brands and InterContinental Hotels Group, said, "When a brand fails to convey a soul or essence that matches personal characteristics that consumers value, that brand lacks meaning. . . . On the other hand, when a brand becomes a badge that consumers are proud of displaying, that brand becomes interwoven into consumers' everyday lives."

True enough. In Part 2 of this text, you learned that understanding your audience is key to being able to understand how consumers think and behave.

But what should brand communicators do when they are faced with promoting products and ideas to audiences who are unlike themselves? Most likely, as a professional marketing communicator, most of what you'll be advertising will be to groups of which you're not a part.

Here are vignettes of two Effie award–winning campaigns that effectively reached diverse audiences. Although these are outstanding examples of transcending multicultural boundaries of race and ethnicity, communicators may face other challenges reaching diverse audiences related to sexual orientation, age, geography, and many other factors.

- Everybody knows about Oreo cookies, right? For generations, moms have bought Oreos as treats for their kids and have encouraged them to drink milk with the cookies. Kraft Foods aimed to increase Oreo cookie consumption in Hispanic households and discovered that unlike fully acculturated Hispanics and native-born Americans, immigrants were unfamiliar with the ritual of pairing cookies and milk. Kraft craftily recognized the well-loved Oreo ritual of "twist, lick, and dunk" as something that would need to be taught to immigrants if they were to share in the moments of family fun.

  Kraft also realized that in the less acculturated Hispanic households, parents ask their children to help translate. The big idea of this campaign centered on taking advantage of the kids to transmit the message of the brand to their parents and build on the culturally held value of strong family ties. Kraft brought the idea to life with its message, "To pull apart is to come together" (in Spanish: Separar es Unir). As kids pull the cookie apart, the family comes together to share the silly fun of eating Oreos.

  Seen in a variety of media—television, radio, and consumer magazines—this emotional message resonated with the audience, who responded by consuming more Oreos. Although the sales data are confidential, the campaign exceeded all Kraft performance goals.

- To increase market share of the African American segment, Verizon worked with GlobalHue, the largest multicultural agency, to align the wireless company with something near and dear to the community: gospel music. Verizon sponsored "How Sweet the Sound," a nationwide competition to find the best gospel choir in America. Verizon approached this without a hard sell for its product by simply supporting and organizing the competition and offering substantial cash prizes.

The Verizon experience connects with the community through multiple media involving online, television, radio, newspaper, out-of-home, mobile, direct mail and e-mail. The competition increased Verizon Wireless sales 14 percent in cities where the program was hosted, and this success led Verizon to expand the competition in subsequent years to other cities around the country. GlobalHue was nominated as Multicultural Agency of the Year for its efforts.

Consider This

P2-1. Compare and contrast these two campaigns. What lessons can you learn from these cases that might help you communicate to diverse audiences?

P2-2. Explain how these campaigns work using the facets model. How do these campaigns help communicate brand meaning?

P2-3. Evaluate Kraft's strategy of reaching parents in less acculturated Hispanic households by linking the fun of the Oreo ritual with the valued relationship between parents and their children.

Sources: Laura Wentz, "Agency Hits: African-American Favorites," *AdAge*, January 4, 2010, 16; Effie Briefs—"How Sweet the Sound" and "Through the Voice of a Child," www.effie.org; Cameka Crawford, "Chicago-Based Choir Named 'America's Best Gospel Choir,'" January 10, 2013, www.news.verizonwireless.com.

PART

3 Practice: Developing Breakthrough Ideas in the Digital Age

The new century has created a huge challenge for brand communication creatives who have to develop breakthrough messages that will not get lost in the media explosion of the 21st century. As Professor Karen Mallia explains, we're in a second creative revolution that challenges creative thinkers to reimagine the way they work.

The Second Creative Revolution: Magical Thinking Meets Bits and Bytes

Time was, if you had a clever headline, an arresting visual, and a memorable slogan, ta-da—you had an ad. Not anymore. You've no doubt seen many "ads" in the past few years that aren't really "ads" in the old-school sense: Burger King video games and BK coupons delivered by "unfriending" Facebook friends, mobile apps from MasterCard, and flash mobs in the United Kingdom for T-Mobile.

Now brand communication can be anything from sponsored tweets to a charmingly retro 30-second television spot. Increasingly, campaigns consist of media channels that are layered and interwoven in clever and complex ways. A good example of this is the groundbreaking Old Spice campaign you read about in Chapter 1. Don Draper never imagined scripting, shooting, and airing ads responding to consumer comments for 56 straight hours—which is what the creative team, talent, and production crew did to make that "Responses" campaign.

Welcome to the second creative revolution. The entire process of making brand communication has undergone a massive shift—the likes of which the industry hasn't seen since Bill Bernbach first paired copywriters and art directors into creative teams and launched the first creative revolution.

Coming up with radical brand ideas still calls for strategic and creative thinking, talent in art direction and writing, and the same passion and fearlessness and resilience. But now that creative is married to technology, it also means collaborating with the UX (user experience) designer, programmer, information architect, mobile developer, and countless others that Sterling Cooper never envisioned.

Karen L. Mallia
Karen L. Mallia is a professor at the University of South Carolina, and former copywriter and creative director.

Yet, despite changes bringing more and different talents into creative work and developing new kinds of messages for the latest digital toys, the underlying principles behind making brilliant work hasn't changed much. Many core creative tenets are as true today as they were before we saw color television. It's important to know what truisms to hang on to—and to learn some radical new truths.

CHAPTER 8 • The Creative Side
CHAPTER 9 • Promotional Writing
CHAPTER 10 • Visual Communication

Enduring Creative Truths

- Great creative work starts with fresh insight, which comes from research. Insight comes from understanding people, products, and the relationship between them.
- Great creative work is built on a tight creative strategy, brilliantly executed.
- Great work is relevant—to its audience (not the whole world) and to the brand. It isn't art or stand-up comedy for its own sake.
- Great ideas are critical to great executions. In old-tech parlance, GIGO: Garbage-In-Garbage-Out. Or, more explicitly, "you can't polish a turd." (See hundreds and hundreds of dull or stupid ads, forgettable taglines, and irrelevant celebrities to understand that no amount of hip typography and flashy gimmicks can mask the absence of a strong selling idea.)
- One execution is not an idea. Ideas are big, inspiring, and exciting and can have many iterations and live long lives. A one-off execution is as useless as yesterday's stale slang or moldy Starbucks.
- Every communication is a building block of brand image. Every ad, every video, every tweet, and every line of type either contributes to brand image or undermines it. The look and the voice convey as much as the concept.
- Great ideas often look obvious *after* they're conceived because they are the most perfect solution to the problem. But that doesn't make them easy to come by. What Edison said about inventing is equally valid for brand communication: It's 1 percent inspiration and 99 percent perspiration.

New Creative Truths

- Great work now takes a village—not just one or two geniuses. Creating for digital media requires diverse talents of more than just a writer and art director. Collaboration is key.
- The creative process doesn't flow like a waterfall, from step to step. It's *agile*, meaning that technology must be threaded and embedded throughout the creative process in order to develop great work. Digital is treated like an afterthought.
- In a 24/7 contact world, work is never done. Creative people live in constant beta, especially in a world where consumers can post on your Facebook page and deadlines are tighter.
- Scattershot brand communication is more dangerous than ever (see brand image).

In sum, if you want any career in this business, internalize them all, and you are well on your way. If you want a creative career, beware. While you need to be aware of every new campaign and media idea that others are doing, creative isn't about chasing the next big thing (like the quick-response code). It's grounded in a thorough understanding of the core tenets, great persuasive communication, and fluency with all the tools in your tool kit. Brilliant brand ideas are those that solve the client's problem in an engaging and unexpected way. Simple. (Not!)

CHAPTER

8 The Creative Side

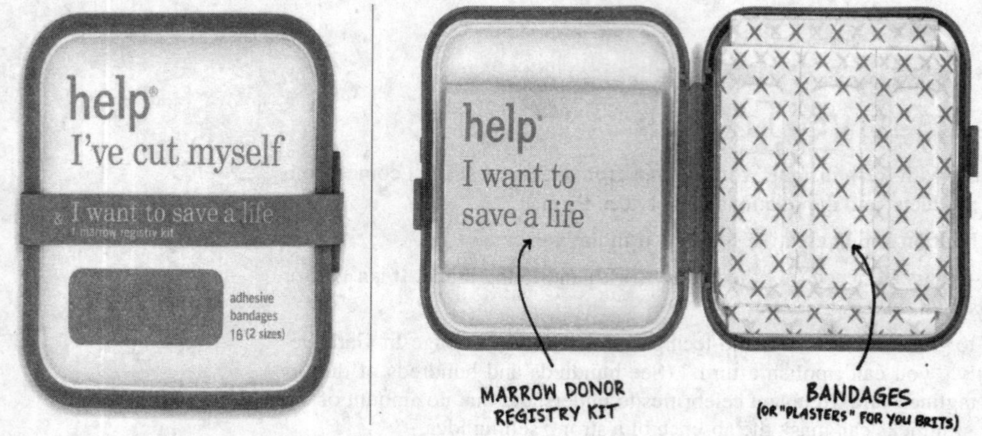

Photo: Courtesy of Graham Douglas

It's a Winner	Campaign	Company	Agency	Awards
	Save a Life	*Help Remedies*	*Droga5*	*Cannes Grand Prix for Good, two Gold Lions*

CHAPTER KEY POINTS

1. How do we explain the science and art of creative strategy as well as the logic and important parts of a creative brief?
2. What are some key message strategy approaches?
3. How is creative thinking defined, and how does it lead to a Big Idea?
4. What characteristics do creative people have in common, and what is their typical creative process?
5. What issues affect the management of creative strategy and its implementation?

A Tale of Brotherly Love and Sharp Thinking

In Chapter 2, you read about the four Ps of marketing (product, price, place, and promotion). Now we're going to switch gears and tell you about some "P" words that are significant to those on the creative side: problem solving, passion, perception, and powerful ideas.

As we discuss in this chapter, creativity isn't just about "ads" any more. A creative idea can begin with product development. And creative problem solving drives brand communication as well. We identify a problem, and we attempt to fix it by communicating a solution.

You'll see in this "Save a Life" case that the product, the message, and the media through which the fix is communicated demonstrate the creative thinking of ad wizard Graham Douglas, who describes himself has having grown up in Fort Worth, Texas, with an identical twin brother, Britton, and an obese beagle named Sam.

The Problem: More than 10,000 Americans need bone marrow transplants each year to help them win the battle against leukemia. Transplants are a last resort for those suffering from blood cancers, and only three of five people will receive the treatment they need because not enough donors have volunteered. How can you convince people to become donors?

The Passion: Graham's twin, Britton, fell ill with leukemia and chemotherapy failed. His hope for survival lay in finding a donor whose bone marrow matched his blood. The process is safe and relatively noninvasive; the risk to the donor is minimal, and bone marrow regenerates. Britton and Graham are identical twins, and Graham could not donate his bone marrow because their blood types were too similar. Inspired by his brother's plight and others in similar situations, Graham worked obsessively for almost a decade to find a creative solution to attract more donors.

The Perception: Graham imagined a simple concept—something that no one had ever done: create and market a product that would help convince people to become donors. He searched for and found a company, Help Remedies, to partner with him. The ingenious product sports an unusual name: "Help I've cut myself & I want to save a life." But it's what's inside that counts: Bandage strips packaged with donor kits that let consumers swab their blood from a cut and send the sample to DKMS, the world's largest bone marrow donor center.

Powerful Ideas: Graham Douglas had already made a name for himself as a copywriter at Droga5 and other agencies with his award-winning work. Now he had to figure out how to grab the attention of potential donors to save lives like those of his brother, Britton.

The resulting "Thank You Sharp Objects" online video demonstrates to viewers how lucky they are when a cat scratches them, a cheese grater nicks their finger, or a cactus falls from the sky cutting their arm. Why? Instead of letting the blood go to waste, consumers can send a sample in to the DKMS registry.

Graham himself stars as a bloody blade. Weird? Yes. Effective? You bet. How powerful? Flip to the end of the chapter to the "It's a Wrap" feature to learn the fate of the campaign and, more importantly, what happened to Britton.

Note: Graham Douglas, one of this book's Ad Stars, shared this story about his award-winning "Save a Life" campaign. His work was nominated for inclusion in this book by Professor Sheri Broyles.

SHOWCASE

Sources: Graham Douglas, personal communication; Emma Brazilian, "Ad of the Day: Help Remedies," March 2, 2012, www.adweek.com; Ann-Christine Diaz, "Graham Douglas, Copywriter, Problem Solver, Droga5," July 9, 2012, www.adage.com; Susan Donaldson James, "Leukemia Patient Nearly Dies; Twin Has Idea to Save Thousands," ABC News, March 1, 2012, http://abcnews.go.com.

Effective advertising is both an art in its creativity and a science in its strategy. This chapter explores how the two dimensions come together as creative strategy—the logic behind the creative message. We also examine a planning tool called a *creative brief*, which provides direction for the execution of the Big Idea and for the evaluation of the creative strategy. We discuss the characteristics of creative people and the process of creative thinking with the aim of showing how you can be a more creative thinker.

Principle
Effective advertising is a product of both science (persuasion and logic) and art (creativity).

Science and Art?

So how would you sell an old-fashioned product like a fountain pen—you know the kind you have to fill with ink? The message magic lies in understanding that writing is a form of personal expression, something that gets lost on a computer. And a pen with the right nib can give an impressive and distinctive flourish to a signature. But mostly, these pens are status symbols, and as a present they are a lasting gift that reminds the user of the giver with every stroke of a pen. In the showroom, the fountain pens are displayed like gems or jewelry. Who would have thought that the lowly fountain pen is so rich in meaning for a certain niche group of fans. So take a moment and pretend you've been asked to handle the brand communication for the Fountain Pen Store. Write down your ideas on what you think would be the most effective sales messages.[1]

Effective marketing communication is a product of both logic and creativity. The message plan, for example, is a rational analysis of a problem and what's needed to solve that problem. As Karen Mallia explained in the Part 3 opening essay, this logic is built on a fresh insight that comes from research. The message itself translates the logic of the planning decisions into a creative idea that is original, attention getting, and memorable. Creative messages, such as the "thank you sharp objects" online video for the Save A Life campaign, bring the strategy to life in an attention getting and memorable way. It grabs attention and sticks in memory.

As we said in Chapter 7, effective advertising is successful because the right media delivers the right message to the right target audience at the right time. In Part 2, we explained how marketing communication works and how it's planned, and in Part 4 we'll consider the media and how a message is delivered. In the next three chapters, we'll concentrate on how the message is created. It's important to keep in mind, however, that like two hands clapping, media and message need to work together to create effective communication. In fact, planning the message usually happens simultaneously with planning the media. Figure 8.1 diagrams this relationship.

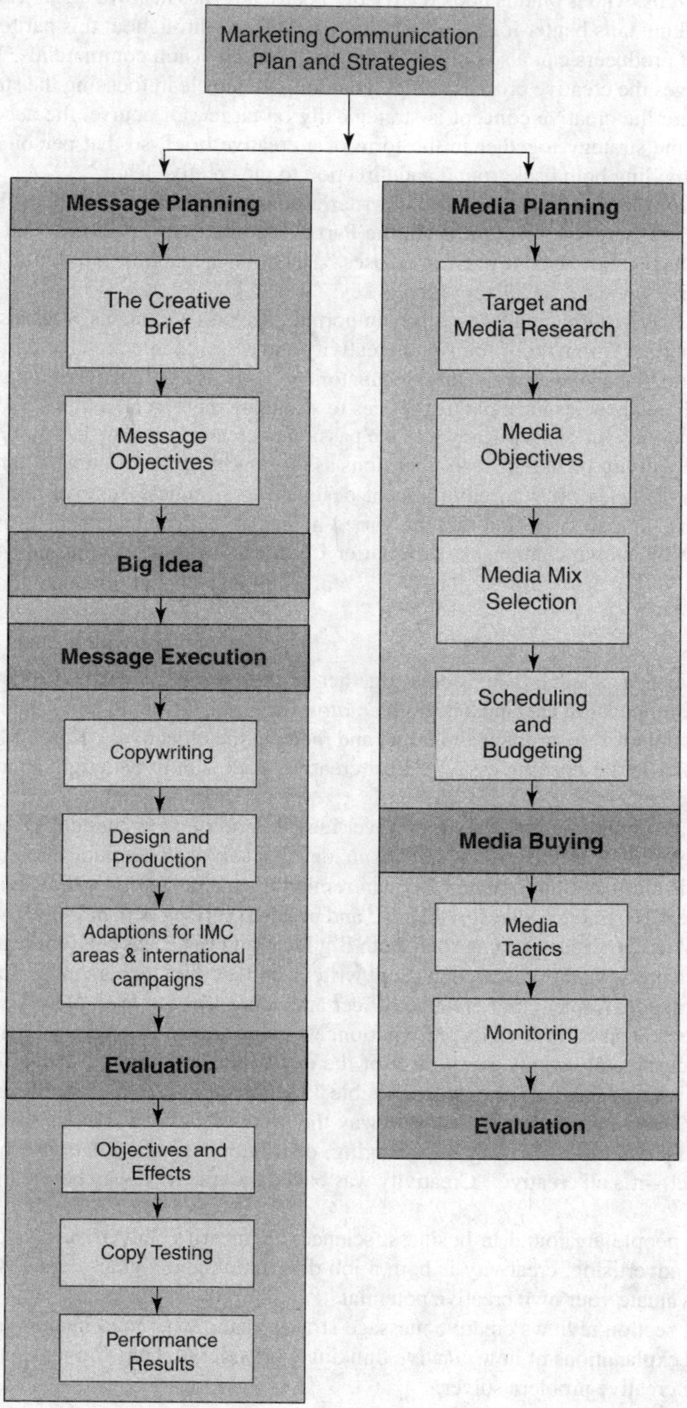

FIGURE 8.1
Media and Message Strategy Work in Parallel

Who Are the Key Players?

All agencies have copywriters and art directors who are responsible for developing the creative concept and crafting the execution of the idea. They often work in teams, are sometimes hired as a team, and may work together successfully for years. Because advertising creativity is a product of teamwork, copywriters and art directors work together to generate concept, word, and picture ideas. Their writing or design specialties come into play in the execution of the idea.

Shawn Couzens and Gary Ennis, for example, were an award-winning creative team at the Grey agency that came up with the idea of wise-cracking talking animals on the tails of Frontier airplanes. Couzens, who is on this book's advisory board, now has his own agency and continues to write the talking tails banter for Frontier, which we refer to throughout this part of the book.

Broadcast producers can also be part of the team for television commercials. The **creative director** manages the creative process and plays an important role in focusing the strategy of ads and making sure the creative concept is strategically on target. Of course, the account planner originally put the strategy together in the form of a creative brief, so that person may also be involved in providing both background and direction to the creative team.

The creative team is expanding beyond writer/art director/creative director, as Karen Mallia said in one of her "new creative truths" in the Part 3 opening essay. She says that "great work now takes a village—not just one or two geniuses." Her point is that this new digital environment "requires diverse talents. . . . Collaboration is key."

The agency environment is particularly important. As Sasser explains, advertising agencies represent the perfect "think tank" to inspire creativity and research into creative thinking. Her research has found that agencies are natural incubators in terms of the three Ps of innovation: *place* (creative boutique agencies have playful offices to stimulate their creative team's ideas), *person* (personality and motivation, also known as the passion to create, stimulate individual creativity), and *process* (creativity includes such dimensions as originality, appropriateness, and artistry).

Although agencies offer an environment designed to stimulate creative thinking, professionals working on their own find that the varied nature of their management assignments and projects create their own challenges, as Jennifer Cunningham describes in her "A Day in the Life" feature.

What Is the Role of Creativity?

Principle
Creative strategy solves problems, and problem solving demands creative thinking. Both Big Ideas and Big Plans call for creative thinking.

The art and science of advertising come together in the phrase *creative strategy*. A winning marketing communication idea must be both *creative* (original, different, novel, and unexpected) and *strategic* (right for the product and target and meeting the objectives). Karen Mallia phrased it this way in her Part 3 opening essay: "Great creative work is built on a tight creative strategy, brilliantly executed."

It's not just about coming up with a novel idea that no one has thought of before; rather, advertising creativity is about coming up with an idea that solves a communication problem in an original way. Professors Stuhlfaut and Berman remind us that creativity is directed at achieving objectives. Creative strategy solves problems,[2] and problem solving demands creative thinking—the mental tool used in figuring things out. Both Big Ideas and Big Plans call for creative thinking.

Media planners, market researchers, copywriters, and art directors are all searching for new ideas. Ty Montague, former chief creative officer and copresident at JWT New York, made this point in a speech at an Effie Awards presentation. Montague noted that "every client I have ever worked with desperately wants every facet of the development of a product and its marketing to be infused with as much creativity as possible."[3] Montague pointed to Apple and its launch of the iPod: "The creativity begins with the way the product looks, works, and feels." And everything else is a creative challenge—packaging, distribution, public relations, the events, the business model—it's all creative. "Creativity was baked into the iPod way before the agency got involved."

Creative people are found in business, science, engineering, advertising, and many other fields. But in advertising, creativity is both a job description and a goal. Figure 8.2 contains a mini-test to evaluate your own creative potential.

The next section reviews creative message strategy and then comes back to an analysis of Big Ideas and explanations of how creative thinking works. It will help you understand how you can be a more creative problem solver.

A Day in the Life

Tweets from the Front Line

Jennifer Cunningham, *Previously Content Manager at Crispin Porter + Bogusky and Currently Account Manager at Disney's Yellow Shoes Creative Group*

As a content manager (account executive) at Crispin Porter + Bogusky's Boulder office, I never know what's in store for me on any given day. What I *do* know is that the days will never be boring. From presenting creative to clients to going on late-night caffeine runs for teams pulling all-nighters—anything goes.

Though tasks vary from day to day, part of my job is to constantly stay up to date on the latest and greatest technologies and trends. Now, I'm no tech expert, but if a client asks for my opinion on brand integration on Twitter, for example, I better know what they're talking about.

And since Twitter is all the rage right now, here's a day in my shoes at CP+B via real-time tweets:

- Parking. Better hustle, have a 9:30 meeting and need some coffee first! (Had a late night last night sending a print ad to the printer—when ads are due, I stay in the office and help make sure everyone has approved it before it goes out.) *9:08*
- Reading all my morning e-mails—my clients are on East Coast time so their workday started 2+ hours ago. *9:19*
- Content team status—this is an informal weekly meeting to ensure everyone knows what's up on the account. *9:32*
- Confirming teams are ready for an 11 A.M. client presentation. Creatives here don't let *any* work out the door unless it's perfect. But sometimes perfection doesn't sync with the client call times. *9:55*
- Writing setup slides for the presentation—this includes recapping our assignment, thoughts on the work, and background info. *10:08*
- Don't have the creative yet—checking in with teams, starting to get a little nervous. *10:30*
- Talked with my creative director—they're making the last few tweaks on the presentation, but they're running 10 to 15 minutes behind. *10:41*
- Calling my client. She's running behind too—starting late will be "just fine." Whew. *10:49*
- Call from another client—the publisher is saying they didn't receive our print ad last night. Asking if we can look into it—oh boy. *10:53*
- E-mailing my print producer to check in with the publisher. *10:55*
- E-mailing my media planner to ensure we won't miss our insertion deadline. *10:56*
- Got the presentation! Looks awesome—have a feeling the clients will love these ideas. *11:10*
- On the call—reinforcing the strategy and schedules as the creatives present ideas. *11:22*
- Recapping the presentation call to make sure the creative teams have clear feedback for revisions and to ensure our clients had the same takeaways from the call. *12:01*
- Hopping on a media call—gathering info for Production, so we can start work once ideas from the presentation are approved. *1:11*
- Reviewing invoices over lunch—have to make sure our billing is accurate and that we stay on budget for projects. *2:03*
- Call with Business Affairs—just finalized legal approvals on scripts and the contracts for celebrity talent for our next television spot. Pretty exciting! *3:15*
- Whew—lost track of time. Re-released the print ad for the publication. Confirmed teams are working on feedback. Put together a postcampaign analysis to see how we met our goals numberwise on our last project. Participated in a brainstorming session for another account—gotta help where you can. *6:08*
- Wrapping up—need to walk my dog at home. *6:31*
- Hopping back on my computer for a couple more e-mails and prep for tomorrow. All in all a pretty good day. *8:15*
- Finishing up this day-in-the-life—hope you enjoyed reading it. Good luck should you pursue a career in advertising! There's never a dull moment. *9:01*

To learn more about Crispin Porter + Bogusky, check out www.cpbgroup.com.

Note: Jennifer Cunningham is a graduate of the advertising program at the University of Colorado. She was a student of Professor Kendra Gale.

The Creative Brief

The **creative brief** (or creative *platform*, *worksheet*, or *blueprint*) is the document prepared by the account planner to summarize the basic marketing and advertising strategy described in Chapter 7. It gives direction to creative team members as they search for a creative concept, or Big Idea. Remember that we make a distinction between creative strategy and creative executions. **Creative strategy**,

Leonardo DaVinci, Albert Einstein, and Georgia O'Keefe excelled in different fields, but all three qualify as creative geniuses.

How Creative Are You?

By Sheri Broyles, *University of North Texas*

Do you ever wonder whether you are creative? Does creativity have anything to do with your personality? Your personality is your own distinctive and consistent pattern of how you think, feel, and act. You may not be a creative genius but still you may have creative abilities that can be nurtured and developed.

A current view of creativity suggests that the area of personality most related to creativity is how open you are to new experiences. According to researchers, how open you are to new experiences can be measured by survey questions that ask if you agree or disagree with statements like the following:

1. "I enjoy working on mind-twister-type puzzles."
2. "Once I find the right way to do something, I stick to it."
3. "As a child I rarely enjoyed games of make-believe."
4. "I enjoy concentrating on a fantasy or daydream and exploring all its possibilities, letting it grow and develop."

Which ones do you believe may predict a creative personality? Explain why. What can you do to expand your talents in those areas?

FIGURE 8.2

The Creative Personality

Source: Sheri J. Broyles, University of North Texas Department of Journalism, P.O. Box 311277, Denton, TX 76203, sbroyles@unt.edu. Also based on R. R. McCrae and P. T. Costa Jr., "Openness to Experience," in *Perspectives in Personality*, vol. 1, ed. R. Hogan and W. H. Jones (Greenwich, CT: JAI Press, 1985), 145–172.

or **message strategy**, is *what* the advertisement says; **execution** is *how* it is said. This chapter focuses on creative strategy, and the two chapters that follow explore the writing, design, and production of advertising executions.

The following outline summarizes the key points in a typical brief:

- *Problem* that can be solved by communication
- *Target audience* and key *insights* into their attitudes and behavior
- *Brand position* and other branding decisions, such as *personality* and *image*
- *Communication objectives* that specify the desired response to the message by the target audience
- *Proposition* or *selling idea* that will motivate the target to respond

- *Media considerations* about where and when the message should be delivered
- *Creative direction* that provides suggestions on how to stimulate the desired consumer response

These aren't creative ideas but may touch on such execution or stylistic direction as the ad's **tone of voice**.

Different agencies use different formats, but most include these basic advertising strategy decisions. The point is that advertising planning—even planning for the creative side—involves a structured, logical approach to analysis. Other agencies may focus more on the intuitive, emotional message effects. The Crispin Porter + Bogusky agency, for example, designs its advertising by looking for what it calls "tension points." Its brief asks planners to consider "What is the psychological, social, categorical, or cultural tension associated with this idea?"

The Road Crew social marketing campaign is an example of creative problem solving for a good cause. The problem was to get young men in Wisconsin small towns who drink and drive to use a ride service. The objective was to reduce the incidence of alcohol-related car crashes by 5 percent. The breakthrough creative concept was to use the idea of a road crew for a group of young partiers who needed a ride on their big night out. The Road Crew campaign planning began with a creative brief:

- ***Why are we advertising at all?*** To create awareness for an evening alternative ride service.
- ***What is the message trying to do?*** Make the new ride service appealing to men in order to reduce the number of alcohol-related crashes.
- ***What are their current attitudes and perceptions?*** "My car is here right now. Why wait? There are few options available anyway. I want to keep the fun going all night long."
- ***What is the main promise we need to communicate?*** It's more fun when you don't have to worry about driving.
- ***What is the key moment to which we tie this message?*** "Bam! The fun stops when I need to think about getting to the next bar or getting home."
- ***What tone of voice should we use?*** The brand character is rugged, cool, and genuine. We need to be a "straight-shooter" buddy on the bar stool next to the target. They do not want to be preached to or told what to do. We need to communicate in a language to which they can relate. (Words like *program* may cause our audience to tune out.)

The creative brief summarizes the key strategic decisions that we identified in Chapter 7, such as message objectives, message targeting, and brand positioning, but they are interpreted in terms of creative strategy. Let's review them here as they apply to the Road Crew campaign.

Message Objectives What do you want the message to accomplish? What message objectives would you specify for the Road Crew campaign, for example, in order to meet the goal of reducing alcohol-related crashes by 5 percent? We introduced the concept of the *Facets Model of Effects* (Figure 8.3) in Chapter 4. Here is a review of some common message objectives that relate to the facets of effectiveness. Do any of them relate to the Road Crew goal of reducing alcohol-related crashes?

- ***See/Hear*** Create attention, awareness, interest, and recognition
- ***Feel*** Touch emotions and create feelings
- ***Think/Understand*** Deliver information, aid understanding, and create recall
- ***Connect*** Establish brand identity and associations and transform a product into a brand with distinctive personality and image
- ***Believe*** Change attitudes, create conviction and preference, and stimulate trust
- ***Act/Do*** Stimulate trial, purchase, repurchase, or some other form of action, such as visiting a store or website

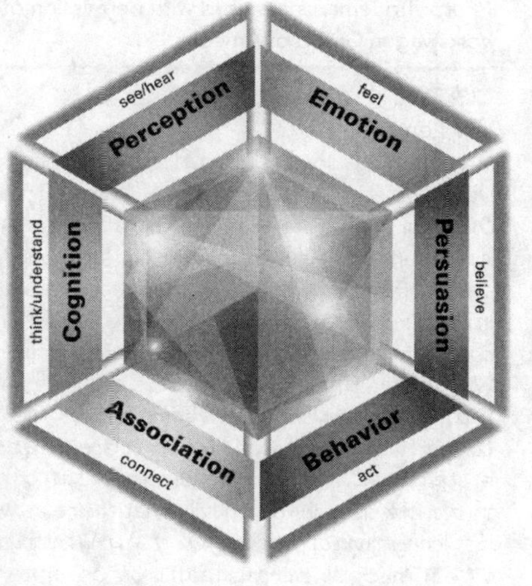

FIGURE 8.3
Facets Model of Effects

We mentioned that the primary goal of the Road Crew campaign was to reduce the number of alcohol-related crashes. Other objectives involved creating awareness of the ride service program and positive attitudes toward it as well as establishing a cost-efficient level of rides in the first year of operations. To accomplish this, the Road Crew team used fund-raising, solicited volunteers, and lined up other community support. The heart of the problem uncovered by the Road Crew research was a gap between *awareness* (don't drink and drive), *attitudes* (risky, scary, and potentially dangerous), and *behavior* (get someone else to drive). The campaign was designed to address this gap and encourage the target audience's behavior to change in accordance with their attitudes and awareness.

Targeting The target decision is particularly important in planning a message strategy. The target audience for the Road Crew campaign was identified as 21- to 34-year-old single men with a high school education and employed in blue-collar jobs. They were the primary target for the ride service because research found that this group is responsible for the most alcohol-related crashes, they kill more people than any other age-group, and they themselves are most likely to die in an alcohol-related crash. What moves this group? Research found that many of these guys tended to worry about driving home drunk as the end of the evening approached and this worry took the edge off an otherwise fun evening. So the ride service made their evening more fun because it reduced their worry.

Photo: Courtesy of Road Crew. Used with permission

The Road Crew creators wanted to create a design in the spirit of the Harley-Davidson motorcycle image, realizing that members of the target audience were all Harley fans.

Branding and Positioning The demands of the brand are also important considerations. Brand positions and brand images are created through message strategies and brought to life through advertising executions. Finding the right position is difficult enough, but figuring out how to communicate that position in an attention-getting message that is consistent across multiple executions and various media is difficult. The classic "Think Small" campaign that launched the VW Beetle is an example of advertising that created a powerful brand at the same time it carved out a unique position in a cluttered automobile market.

Brand communication creates symbols and cues that make brands distinctive, such as characters, colors, slogans, and taglines as well as brand personality cues. The Geico Gecko and Frontier's talking animals are brand-savvy characters that make Mr. Clean, Pillsbury Doughboy, and Jolly Green Giant look way too earnest. The difference is that the new-age characters are ironic and even a little self-depreciating, and they speak to the ad resistance of today's consumers with irony and inner conflict.

The Harley-esque logo for the Road Crew campaign reflected the devil-may-care attitude of Harley riders. The connection with the Harley image made the Road Crew's do-good message more acceptable to the target audience.

Advertising and other forms of marketing communication are critical to create what brand guru Kevin Keller calls *salience*[4]—that is, the brand is visible and has a presence in the marketplace, consumers are aware of it, and the brand is important to its target market. In addition to brand salience—measured as *top-of-mind awareness*—another objective for branding and positioning campaigns is to create trust. We buy familiar brands because we've used them before and trust them to deliver on their promises. The Road Crew program, for example, would be a waste of time if the hard-partying young men in the target audience didn't think to call the limo service and trust it to be there to pick them up when they wanted to leave.

Photo: Trademarks are used with permission of Volkswagen Group of America

CLASSIC

VW Lemon

In an era of big cars and huge tail fins, Volkswagen launched its unimposing little Beetle in the 1960s. Other car ads were in full color with mansions in the background and beautiful people in the foreground. In the classic "Think Small" campaign, the Beetle was shown in black and white with a simple headline, "Lemon," in contrast to the bombastic promises of its competitors. Why "Lemon"? The copy explains that this little car had a quality problem with a chrome strip on its glove compartment, and it needed to be replaced. The ad stated that VW's inspectors found no detail too small to overlook, assuring consumers that their cars would last longer than other cars. *Advertising Age* recognized VW's "Think Small" campaign as number one on its list of the Top 100 advertising campaigns in history.

Message Strategies

Once you have objectives stated, how do you go about translating them into strategies? Remember, there is no one right way to do brand communication—in most cases there are a number of ways to achieve a communication objective. If you were creating the advertising for a hotel, for example, what would you emphasize—speed of check-in, size of the room, hair dryers, or mints on the pillow? Rather than tangible features like these, Sheraton decided to emphasize the emotional side of traveling and show people greeting one another. Since it's a global company, the greetings include hugs, bows, and kisses on both cheeks. The company believes that its customers worldwide like to be welcomed, appreciated, and made to feel at home.

Planners search for the best message design—the approach that makes the most sense given the brand's marketing situation and the target audience's needs and interests. Note the use of the word "design." The idea of design—as in **message design**—is not graphics but rather problem solving. Stanford University, for example, has a design school that was created to ignite creativity and collaboration in solving problems for innovators and entrepreneurs (www.dschool.stanford.edu). This is a wider view of creative problem solving, one that uses anthropological observation as well innovation and teamwork environments.[5]

Which Strategic Approach to Use?

So there are a lot of ways to design a message, but how do you talk about the various strategic approaches that might work? In other words, how do you put strategies into words? First let's review some simple ways to express a strategic approach—head and heart and hard sell or soft sell. Then we'll look at some more complex models that get a little deeper into the complexities of message strategy.

Head and Heart In the Facets Model, the cognitive objectives generally speak to the head, and the affective objectives are more likely to speak to the heart. Sometimes, however, a strategy is designed to inform the mind as it touches the emotions. For example, in a strategy statement for Volkswagen's "Drivers Wanted" campaign, the agency identified both rational and emotional dimensions to the VW brand message:

> VW's rational brand essence: *"The only brand offering the benefits and 'feeling' of German engineering within reach."*
> VW's emotional brand essence: *Exciting; different driving feeling; different way of living; more feeling, fun, alive, connected*

Another way to refer to head and heart strategies are hard-sell and soft-sell approaches. A **hard sell** is an informational message that is designed to touch the mind and create a response based on logic. The assumption is that the target audience wants information and will make a rational product decision. A **soft sell** uses emotional appeals or images to create a response based on attitudes, moods, and feelings. The assumption with soft-sell strategies is that the target audience has little interest in an information search and will respond more favorably to a message that touches their emotions or presents an attractive brand image. A soft-sell strategy can be used for hard products. NAPA Auto Parts ran an emotional ad that showed a dog sitting at a railroad crossing, forcing a truck to brake hard to avoid hitting him as a train bears down on the scene. The slogan puts the heart-stopping visual story into perspective: "NAPA, because there are no unimportant parts."

> ***Principle***
> Hard-sell informational messages lead to rational decisions; soft-sell emotional strategies create responses based on attitudes, moods, and feelings.

But there are also examples of ads designed to stir emotions that didn't work because they are too manipulative or raised inappropriate emotions. It is possible to manipulate emotions in a way that viewers and listeners resent. For example, a billboard for a pest control company located in the heart of downtown that depicted a huge scary bug looming over the sidewalk elicited many complaints from pedestrians as well as drivers.

Sometimes, however, high emotion works. A 30-minute public service announcement designed to teach Welsh teens about the dangers of texting while driving used a strong fear appeal. The commercial features Cassie, a nice girl from a nice family who kills four people on the road because she lost her concentration for a few seconds. It starts with three girls in a car with Cassie, the driver, texting while driving. The next scene is a horrifying slow-motion three-car accident with the girls being thrown around inside the car followed by images of blood, wounds, and the seriously injured girls as well as the horror and fear of the driver who survives with minor injuries. In the other cars, there is a middle-age driver who is motionless and two unconscious adults in the third car with an infant and two-year-old girl who keeps saying, "Mommy, Daddy, wake up." Bob Garfield, *Advertising Age*'s critic, says that usually such graphic displays turn off the audience, but he suspects that this one may force people "to confront the consequences of a few moments of driver inattention"—presumably the death of four people. He explains,

"We can't help but put our stupid selves in Cassie's flip-flops."[6] You can see the video online at www.gwent.police.uk/leadnews.php?a=2172.

Systems of Strategies Head and heart and hard sell or soft sell—all these terms refer to some basic, simple concepts, but creative strategy often is more complex. We'll look at two of approaches that address other aspects of advertising strategy: Frazer's six creative strategies and Taylor's strategy wheel.

University of Washington professor Charles Frazer proposed a set of six creative strategies that address various types of message situations.[7] Although not comprehensive, these terms are useful to identify some common approaches to message strategy:

Frazer's Six Creative Strategies

Strategy	***Description***	***Uses***
Preemptive	Uses a common attribute or benefit, but brand gets there first—forces competition into "me too" positions.	Used for categories with little differentiation or new product categories.
Unique selling proposition	Uses a distinct difference in attributes that creates a meaningful consumer benefit.	Used for categories with high levels of technological improvement and innovations.
Brand image	Uses a claim of superiority or distinction based on extrinsic factors such as psychological differences in the minds of consumers.	Used with homogeneous, low-tech goods with little differentiation.
Positioning	Establishes a place in the consumer's mind relative to the competition.	Used by new entries or small brands that want to challenge the market leader.
Resonance	Uses situations, lifestyles, and emotions with which the target audience can identify.	Used in highly competitive, undifferentiated product categories.
Affective/anomalous (or ambiguous)	Uses an emotional, sometimes even ambiguous message to break through indifference.	Used where competitors are playing it straight and informative.

The preemptive strategy shows up in competitive advertising where one competitor tries to build a position or lay a claim before others enter the market. An example comes from the Coffee Wars between Starbucks and McDonald's that erupted when McDonald's announced its McCafé line of fancy coffees at lower prices. In anticipation of the McCafé advertising blitz, Starbucks began its first-ever branding campaign. Designed with burlap-sack backgrounds that are reminiscent of roasted coffee bags, the ads used hard-hitting headlines like "Starbucks or nothing. Because compromise leaves a really bad aftertaste" and "If your coffee isn't perfect, we'll make it over. If it's still not perfect, you must not be in a Starbucks." The campaign was designed to separate the Starbucks' experience from the mass-market approach of McDonald's and Dunkin' Donuts.

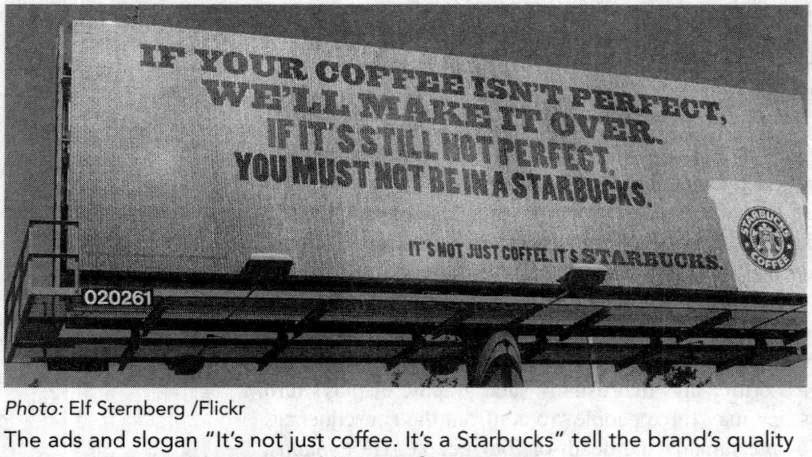

Photo: Elf Sternberg /Flickr

The ads and slogan "It's not just coffee. It's a Starbucks" tell the brand's quality story and counters the McDonald's McCafé campaign.

University of Tennessee professor Ron Taylor developed a process of analysis that divides strategies into the *transmission view*, which is similar to

Six Message Strategies in Six Minutes

Ronald E. Taylor, *University of Tennessee*

It's crunch time. You've got to generate several different message strategies to discuss with your boss for a new business pitch. She's meeting with a regional bottler who plans to add bottled water to her product line. Your boss wants to hear your ideas over lunch. Problem is, this bottled water is no different from all the other brands of bottled water.

You head out to meet your boss, a six-minute trip away from your office. You've got to enter the restaurant with the strategies in your head. You remember a strategy device from your advertising class in college: the six-segment strategy wheel (Figure 8.4). It was designed primarily to generate strategies, to create several to choose from. You remember that it had two broad divisions—transmission and ritual—and three segments under each division. You mentally work your way counterclockwise around the wheel to think about ways to promote the product:

1. *Ration Segment* Ration strategies are based on rational thought and logic. They represent the classic reason-why, product-focused message strategies. You think, "Brand X Water, the economical, convenient, portable beverage."
2. *Acute Need Segment* Acute need, or special need, strategies are based on consumers' unanticipated need for the product or service, like appliance repair or medical surgery, or special occasions, like the need for a tuxedo or dress for a formal occasion. But when do you have an acute need for water? When traditional supplies aren't available! "Stock up on Brand X Water for the hurricane season."
3. *Routine Segment* Routine strategies attempt to routinize everyday behavior. You remember that drinking multiple glasses of water a day is good for you, so you think, "Brand X Water, a great beverage with every meal every day."

You've moved down the left-hand side of the wheel, and the amount of time consumers spend deliberating on choices has been reduced in each segment. Now you are mentally crossing over the vertical line to the ritual, or emotional, side, and the importance of the item and emotional connection will increase as you move up the right-hand side of the wheel—and you're halfway to lunch with the boss:

4. *Sensory Segment* Sensory strategies are based on one of the five senses: sight, touch, hearing, smell, and taste. You think, "Refreshing, clear taste. Brand X Water."
5. *Social Segment* Many social strategies are based on establishing, maintaining, or celebrating relationships with others. You think, "Get noticed. Drink Brand X Water" or "Share Brand X Water with someone you love."
6. *Ego Segment* Ego strategies are based on images that consumers have of themselves. Brands say to consumers, "This is who you are." Active people who eat healthy foods and exercise regularly like reinforcement that they are doing the right thing. You think, "Brand X Water, the bottled water for people who care about their health."

The wheels are turning now. You've arrived at the parking lot and you start combining strategies:

- Serve refreshing (sensory) Brand X water to your family (social) every day (routine).
- Clear refreshment (sensory) in an unbreakable (ration), portable (ration) container.

Your boss is impressed with your ability to generate strategies. Most advertising professionals generate two or three and then do multiple executions within a single strategy. But you are not so limited. In fact, your boss has invited you to lunch again tomorrow to discuss the pitch for a national pizza chain. How many strategies can you generate?

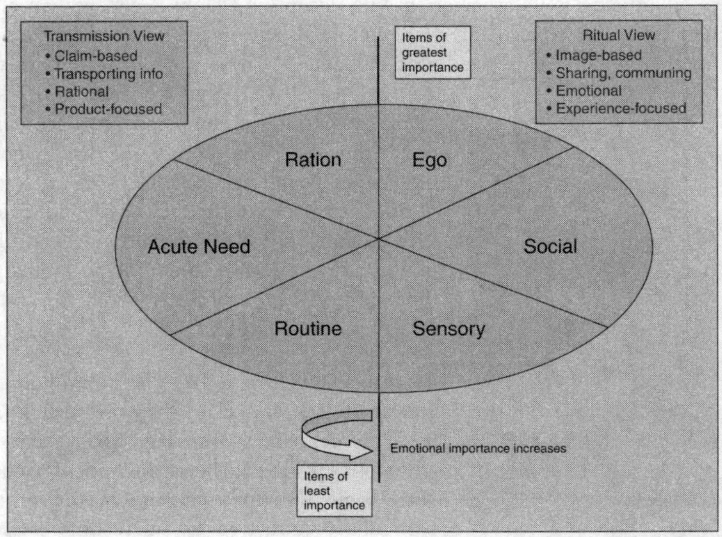

FIGURE 8.4
Taylor's Six-Segment Strategy Wheel

Source: Ronald E. Taylor, University of Tennessee, *http://web.utk.edu/~retaylor/six-seg.htm.*

the more rational "head" strategies, and the *ritual view*, which is similar to the more feeling-based "heart" strategies. He then divides each into three segments: ration (rational), acute need, and routine on the transmission side and ego, social, and sensory on the ritual side.[8] He explains the principles behind this model as well as its application in a problem-solving context, in the following "A Matter of Principle" feature.

Strategic Formats

Even though advertising is a constant search for a new and novel way to express some basic truth, there are also some tried-and-true formats that have worked over the years. We'll talk about these options from a literary, psychological, and sales viewpoint.

Lectures and Dramas Most advertising messages use a combination of two basic literary techniques to reach the head or the heart of the consumer: lectures and dramas.[9] A lecture is instruction usually given verbally—or it could be a demonstration using visuals. The speaker presents evidence (broadly speaking) and uses a technique such as an argument to persuade the audience. The advantages of lectures are many: They are relatively inexpensive to produce and are compact and efficient. A lecture can deliver a dozen selling points in seconds, get right to the point, and make the point explicitly. In advertising, we use the phrase *talking head* to refer to an announcer who delivers a lecture about a product. This can also be a celebrity spokesperson or an authority figure, such as a doctor or scientist.

Drama, however, relies on the viewer to make inferences about the brand. Usually, the drama is in the story that the reader has to construct around the cues in the ad. Through dramas, advertisers tell stories about their products; the characters speak to each other (Frontier's talking animals), not to the audience. Like fairy tales, movies, novels, parables, and myths, advertising dramas are essentially stories about how the world works. They can be funny as well as serious. In Chapter 6, we saw that Domino's big apology campaign for its mediocre pizza created drama, and customers responded dramatically. The Leo Burnett agency built a creative philosophy around "Inherent Drama," which describes the story lines built into the agency's archetypal brand characters, such as the Marlboro Man, Charlie the Tuna, the Jolly Green Giant, and Tony the Tiger.

Political advertising is a particular challenge in terms of how much information versus how much drama. In particular, the issue of negative advertising, which arouses emotions as well as counterarguments, is a topic of research, debate, and criticism. Professor Kathleen Hall Jamieson, who is known for her television commentary on political advertising, says that the danger with negative advertising is its association with deception.[10] John Geer, however, has found in his research that negative advertising is often more issue oriented than positive ads and that attack ads are frequently better supported with evidence.[11] These scholars and their work are reviewed by Marilyn Roberts, who asks,[12] "Does negativity in campaigns hurt the democratic process?" She points out that "whether one views negativity as good, bad, or mixed, politics is about conflict." And she concludes, "As interactive political advertising and blogs play a larger role in contemporary campaigns, the questions and concerns about the rise in negativity will not diminish."

Photo: © 2004 Quaker Oats Company. All rights reserved

The appetite appeal of the trail mix bar is dramatized by an extremely close-up visual that shows all the nuts and raisins larger than life.

Psychological Appeals The psychological appeal of the product to the consumer is also used to describe a message that speaks to attitudes as well as the heart. An **appeal** connects with some emotion that makes the product particularly attractive or interesting, such as security, esteem, fear, sex, and sensory pleasure. Although emotion is at the base of most appeals, in some situations appeals can also have a logical dimension, such as saving money for retirement (relief based on knowledge). Appeals generally pinpoint the anticipated response of the audience to the product and the message. For example, if the price is emphasized in the ad, then the appeal is value, economy, or savings. If the product saves time or effort, then the appeal is convenience. Advertisers use a status appeal to establish something as a high-quality, expensive product. Appetite appeal using mouth-watering visuals is used in food advertising, such as the Quaker Trail Mix Bar ad.

Selling Premises Advertising has developed a number of strategic approaches that speak to the head with a sales message. A **selling premise** states the logic behind the sales offer. A premise is a proposition on which an argument is based or a conclusion is drawn. To have a practical effect on customers, managers must identify the product's **features** (also called **attributes**) in terms of those that are most important to the target audience. A **claim** is a product-focused strategy based on a prediction about how the product will perform. Health claims on food products like cereal or oatmeal, for example, suggest that the food will be good for you. In a Blue Diamond® Almond headline, the nuts were called a "superfood." The copy that followed supported the claim:

> Ounce for ounce Blue Diamond® Almonds have more vitamin E than blueberries, more iron than spinach and 4 × more fiber than broccoli, making them the supersnack of superfoods.

In other words, a rational, prospect-centered selling premise identifies a *reason* that might appeal to potential customers and motivate them to respond. Here is a summary of various types of rational customer-focused selling premises:

- A **benefit** emphasizes what the product can do for the user by translating the product feature or attribute into something that benefits the consumer. For example, a GM electric car ad focuses on the product feature (the car doesn't use gas) and translates it into a benefit: lack of noise (no pistons, valves, or exhaust) and low mileage costs.
- A **promise** is a benefit statement that looks to the future and predicts that something good will happen if you use the product. For example, Dial soap has promised for decades that if you use Dial, you will feel more confident.
- A **reason why** emphasizes the logic behind why you should buy something, although the reason sometimes is implied or assumed. The words *because* and *reasons* call attention to a reason-why statement. For example, a multivitamin headline says, "Multiple Reasons to Take a Multi." The list that follows includes five points: immune health, heart health, bones and teeth, eye health, and energy.
- A **unique selling proposition** (USP) is a benefit statement that is both unique to the product and important to the user. The USP is a promise that consumers will get this unique benefit by using this product only. For example, an ad for a camera states, "This camera is the only one that lets you zoom in and out automatically to follow the action."

Most selling premises demand facts, proof, or explanations to support the sales message. Proof statements that give the rationale, reasoning, and research behind the claim are used to substantiate the premise. The proof, or **substantiation**, needed to make a claim believable is called **support**. In many cases, this calls for research findings. Volvo's longtime crash-safety position, which has been built over the decades, relies on the claim that 9 of 10 Volvos registered in the United States are still on the road.[13] With claims—and particularly with comparisons—the proof is subject to challenge by the competitor as well as industry review boards.

Other Message Approaches In addition to the basic categories of selling premises, some common message formulas emphasize different types of effects. The planner uses these terms as a way to give direction to the creative team and to shape the executions. Here are some common formats:

- A **straightforward message**, which is factual or informational, conveys information without any gimmicks, emotions, or special effects. For example, in an ad for www.women.com, the website advertises, "It's where today's educated, affluent women are finding in-depth coverage on issues they care about."
- A **demonstration** focuses on how to use the product or what it can do for you. For example, an ad for Kellogg's Special K and Smart Start uses cereal bowls to demonstrate how a daily

Photo: Courtesy of Kellogg Company and the Leo Burnett Company. Special K® is a registered trademark of Kellogg Company.

The Kellogg's Smart Start ad uses 28 cereal bowls to demonstrate the amount that Special K and Smart Start equal in weight loss.

regimen of healthy cereal would help a dieter lose six pounds.

- A **comparison** contrasts two or more products to show the superiority of the advertiser's brand. The comparison can be direct, with competitors mentioned, or indirect, with just a reference to "other leading brands." In the comparison approach, as with a demonstration, seeing is believing, so the objective is to show something that builds conviction. When people see two products being compared, they are more likely to believe that one is better than the other.
- In a **problem solution message**, also known as **product-as-hero**, the message begins with a problem and then showcases the product as the solution. The bandage product for a cut makes it easy to do a blood test to save a life as illustrated in this chapter's opening story. A variation is the **problem avoidance message** format, in which the product helps the consumer avoid a problem.
- **Humor** can be a useful creative strategy—using a comedian such as Jerry Seinfeld as the star, for example—because it grabs attention and is memorable. Planners hope people will transfer the warm feelings of being entertained to the product. Recent research however, found that funny commercials don't sell better than unfunny ones and that the funny ads that work best balance the humor with information and relevance.[14]
- The **slice-of-life message** is an elaborate version of a problem solution staged in the form of a drama in which "typical people" talk about a common problem and resolve it.
- In the **spokesperson** (also **spokes-character** or **brand icon**) or **endorser** format, the ad features celebrities whom we like (Michael Jordan), created characters (the Aflac duck or the Geico gecko), experts we respect (the Maytag repairman or doctors), or someone "just like us" whose advice we might seek. An effective spokesperson brings liking and trust and speaks on behalf of the product to build believability. (Note: a recent change in Federal Trade Commission rules now makes endorsers as well as advertisers liable for false or unsubstantiated claims, so spokespersons have to be very careful about what they say about any product they advertise.) The Scotts lawn and garden company created a character—Scott—who we described in Chapter 5. You may remember that he knows everything you need to know about keeping your lawn alive and in good shape.
- **Teasers** are mystery ads that don't identify the product or don't deliver enough information to make sense, but they are designed to arouse curiosity. These are often used to launch a new product. The ads run for a while without the product identification, and then, when curiosity is sufficiently aroused, usually at the point when the product is officially launched, a concluding ad runs with the product identification.

Principle
In the comparison approach, as with a demonstration, seeing is believing, so the objective is to build conviction.

The use of celebrities as spokespersons, endorsers, or brand symbols is an important strategy because it associates the brand positively—or negatively—with a famous person and qualities that make that person a celebrity. Michael Jackson is credited with starting a new era of celebrity advertising when he signed a record-breaking $5 million contract with Pepsi in 1984. More recently, Volvo picked Jeremy Lin, the upstart star of the New York Knicks now with the Houston Rockets of the National Basketball Association (NBA), to be its "brand ambassador." You might wonder why Volvo, which is owned by a Chinese company, picked Lin to promote "sportsmanship and intelligence." That works for Lin, who is the only NBA star with a Harvard degree, and, of course, he's also Chinese.[15]

The luxury bag and luggage company Louis Vuitton is an icon, and its "LV" logo design is an easily identifiable brand logo on its products. But its brand communication is also iconic with a long list of eclectic celebrities. Most recently, it used Angelina Jolie shown floating on a Cambodian boat with a Louis Vuitton bag at her side. A newer campaign features Muhammad Ali and his grandson. Others include soccer great Pele, musician Keith Richards, Russian leader Mikhail Gorbachev, and even Lady Gaga—all iconic individuals on extraordinary journeys.[16]

Before that time, celebrities were often reluctant to appear for a brand because they feared it might tarnish their image. More recently, advertisers have worried about celebrities they have signed who might tarnish the brand's image. In 2013, for example, after being accused of making racist statements, Paula Deen lost her sponsorships with brands such as J.C. Penney, Sears, and Home Depot. The biggest celebrity crashes followed missteps by Lance Armstrong and Tiger Woods. Lance Armstrong, the legendary Tour de France bike racer and founder of nonprofit LiveStrong, was also sponsored by a stable of big marketing names, including Nike, Nissan, and Anheuser-Busch, all of whom were dismayed when he faced doping charges and was stripped of his medals in 2012. One source estimates that golf star Tiger Woods lost between $23 million and $30 million in endorsements with companies such as Accenture and AT&T.[17] Temperamental stars, drug and driving arrests, assaults, and loose tongues are a nightmare for marketers.

Another aspect of celebrity effectiveness is their appeal or influence. There are a number of ways to measure this. An **E score** is a system of ratings for celebrities, athletes, and other newsmakers that measures their appeal. A **Q score** is a measure of the familiarity of a celebrity as well as a company or brand. The Davie Brown Index measures a celebrity's awareness, appeal, and relevance as a brand image. It also evaluates the influence of the celebrity on buying behavior.

But these scores are not just related to conventional celebrities. In social media, anyone can be a celebrity or at least attract a lot of followers. If you have a lot of followers, you may already have been scored in terms of your level of influence and identified as an "influencer." The website Klout is the dominant scorekeeper, but PeerIndex is another rating service for social networks. Scores range from 1 to 100, and the average score is in the high teens. A score in the 40s indicates a strong following.[18] Above that are the people whom marketers want to cultivate as brand advocates.

Matching Messages to Objectives

We talked earlier about message planning, including objectives, and then moved to a discussion of various types of message strategies. Now, let's try to bring those two together. What types of messages deliver which objectives? If it's a credibility problem, for example, you might want to think about a testimonial, a demonstration of proof, a reason why, or even a press release with the built-in believability of a news story. The Facets Model can be helpful in thinking through objectives and their related strategies:

- ***Messages That Get Attention*** To be effective, an advertisement needs to get exposure through the media buy and get attention through the message. Getting consumers' attention requires stopping power. Creative advertising breaks through the old patterns of seeing and saying things—the unexpectedness of the new idea (the Geico Caveman) creates stopping power. Ads that stop the scanning and break through the clutter can also be high in personal relevance, such as the "Save a Life" online video. Intrusiveness is particularly important in cluttered markets. Many clutter-busting ads are intrusive and use loud, bold effects to attract viewer attention—they work by shouting. Others use engaging, captivating ideas, curiosity/ambiguity, or mesmerizing visuals. Curiosity is particularly important for teaser strategies. The SuperCuts "Expired" parking meter guerilla advertising grabbed the attention of people walking by with a funny comment on "expired" haircuts.
- ***Messages That Create Interest*** Getting attention reflects the stopping power of an advertisement; keeping attention reflects the ad's pulling power. An interesting thought keeps readers' or viewers' attention and pulls

PARKING METER GUERILLA ADVERTISING — ***SUPERCUTS***

Photo: Courtesy of SuperCuts, Inc.

SHOWCASE

Mike Latshaw is a copywriter and president of Full Flannel Nudity, a Pittsburgh, Pennsylvania, agency. This campaign, called "Expired," won an Addy in the Pittsburgh Ad Club competition. His client was so happy with the success of the campaign that she gave him and his partner free haircuts for a year!

Note: Latshaw is a graduate of Pennsylvania State University, and his work was nominated by Professor Ron Smith.

them through to the end of the message. One way to intensify interest is through curiosity, such as using a teaser campaign where the message unfolds over time. Ads that open with questions or dubious or ambiguous statements are designed to create curiosity.

- ***Messages That Resonate*** Ads that amplify the emotional impact of a message by engaging a consumer in a personal connection with a brand are said to resonate with the target audience. The women's campaign for Nike, for example, does a good job of speaking to women in a way that addresses their concerns about personal achievement rather than the competitive theme of the more traditional men's campaign. If a woman identifies with this message, then it is said to resonate for her.
- ***Messages That Create Believability*** Advertising sometimes uses a credibility strategy to intensify the believability of a message. Using data to support or prove a claim is critical. The use of brand characters such as Colonel Sanders for KFC, who was a real person and the creator of the famous chicken recipe ("11 herbs and spices"), is designed to give consumers a *reason to believe* in a brand by cementing conviction.
- ***Messages That Are Remembered*** Not only do messages have to *stop* (get attention) and *pull* (create interest), but they also have to *stick* (in memory), which is another important part of the perceptual process. Most advertisements, such as the Smoky the Bear campaign, are carefully designed to ensure that these memory traces are easy to recall. In Chapter 4, we explained that much of advertising's impact lies in its delayed effects; hence, memorability is a huge factor in effectiveness. Ads use catchy headlines, curiosity, and intriguing visuals to make this recall process as easy as possible and lock the message in memory.

  Repetition is used both in media and message strategy to ensure memorability. Jingles are valuable memorability devices because the music allows the advertiser to repeat a phrase or product name without boring the audience. Clever phrases are useful not only because they grab the consumer's attention but also because they can be repeated to intensify memorability. Brand communication uses **slogans** for brands and campaigns, such as "Get Met. It Pays" (MetLife) or Nike's slogan, "Just Do It." **Taglines** are used at the end of an ad to summarize the point of the ad's message in a highly memorable way, such as "Nothing outlasts the Energizer. It keeps going and going and going." In addition to verbal memory devices, many print and interactive messages and most television commercials feature a *key visual*. This visual is a vivid image that the advertiser hopes will linger in the viewer's mind. Color can be a memory cue. Wrigley's Doublemint gum uses green, and Juicy Fruit uses yellow.
- ***Messages That Touch Emotions*** Emotional appeals create feeling-based responses, such as love, fear, anxiety, envy, sexual attraction, happiness and joy, sorrow, safety and security, pride, pleasure, embarrassment, and nostalgia. Appetite appeal uses mouth-watering food shots to elicit feelings of hunger and craving, like the photo in the Quaker Trail Mix Bar print ad. A more general emotional goal is to deliver a message that people like in order to create liking for the brand.
- ***Messages That Inform*** Companies often use news announcements to provide information about new products, to tout reformulated products, or even to let consumers know about new uses for old products. The news angle, which is often delivered by publicity stories, is information focused. Informative ads and brochures that focus on features

Photo: Wrigley, Doublemint and all affiliated designs owned by and used courtesy of the Wm. Wrigley Jr. Company

SHOWCASE

The familiar Doublemint green anchors the brand's identity even when the campaign is aimed at Hispanics and the ads are written en Español.

Note: This ad was contributed by Sonia Montes Scappaticci, who is new business director at Catmandu Branded Entertainment. A graduate of Michigan State University's advertising program, she was also named one of AAF's Most Promising Minority Students. She was nominated by Professor Carrie La Ferle.

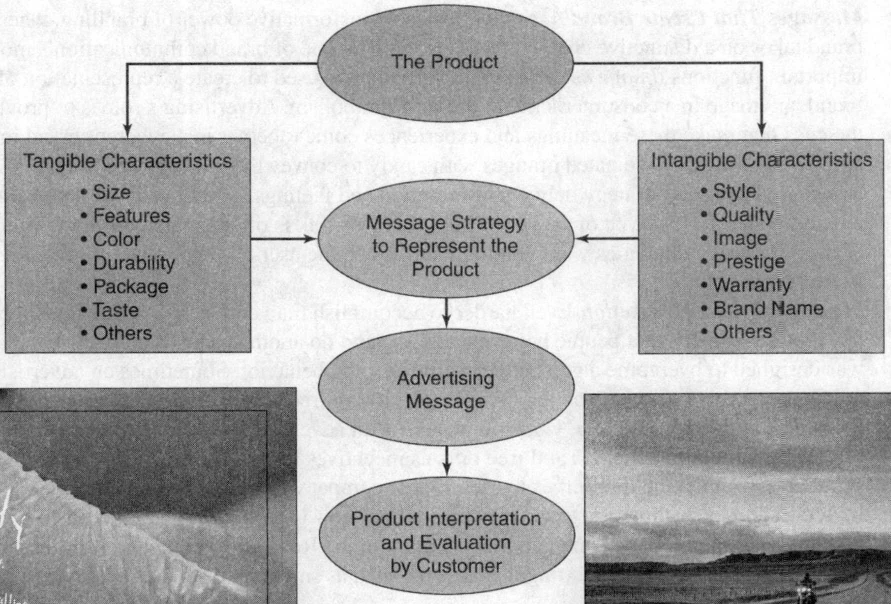

Photo: Reprinted with permission of Sunkist Growers, Inc. Sunkist and design are trademarks of Sunkist Growers, Inc. ©2004 Sherman Oaks, California, U.S.A. All rights reserved

Photo: Courtesy of Harley-Davidson and Carmichael Lynch. All rights reserved

FIGURE 8.5
Tangible and Intangible Product Attributes

The diagram illustrates the characteristics of tangible and intangible features. The Sunkist ad compares its oranges to candy, but in the comparison it identifies tangible product characteristics, such as flavor and color. The Harley-Davidson ad uses intangibles—it associates the Harley brand image with the personality of people who ride on the edge of life.

and attributes seek to create understanding about a product's advantages. Comparison ads are often heavy on information and used to explain a product's point of difference and competitive advantage. Attributes can be both tangible and intangible (see Figure 8.5). The ads for Sunkist oranges and Harley-Davidson focus on tangible and intangible features.

- ***Messages That Teach*** People learn through instruction, so some advertisements are designed to teach, such as demonstrations that show how something works or how to solve a problem. Educational messages are sometimes designed to explain something, such as why it is important to brush your teeth or get involved in local politics. Learning also is strengthened through repetition. That's why repetition is such an important media objective.
- ***Messages That Persuade*** Persuasive messages are designed to affect attitudes and create belief. Strategies that are particularly good are *testimonials* and messages that generate word of mouth about the product. Endorsements by celebrities or experts are used to intensify conviction. Selling premises that focus on how the product will benefit the consumer, state a reason why, or explain a USP are persuasive, particularly if they provide proof or support. Torture tests, comparisons, and before-and-after demonstrations also are used to prove the truth of a claim. Conviction is often built on strong, rational arguments that use such techniques as test results, before-and-after visuals, testimonials by users and experts, and demonstrations to prove something. Celebrities, product placements, and other credibility techniques are used to give the consumer **permission to believe** a claim or selling premise.

- ***Messages That Create Brand Associations*** The transformative power of branding, where the brand takes on a distinctive character and meaning, is one of brand communication's most important functions. *Image advertising*, in particular, is used to create a representation of a brand, an image in a consumer's mind, through symbolism. Advertising's role is to provide the cues that make these meanings and experiences come together in a coherent brand image. The Sunkist ad associated oranges with candy to convey the message of sweetness. An association message strategy delivers information and feelings symbolically by connecting a brand with a certain type of person or lifestyle. This link is often created through visuals. Some advertising strategies want you to identify with the user of the product or see yourself in that situation.

Principle
A message needs to *stop* (get attention), *pull* (create interest), and *stick* (be memorable).

- ***Messages That Drive Action*** Even harder to accomplish than conviction is a change in behavior. It often happens that people believe one thing and do another. The Road Crew campaign was designed to overcome a gap between attitudes and behavior. Sometimes an advertising message can drive people to act by offering something free or at a discounted sales price. Sales promotion, for example, works in tandem with advertising to stimulate immediate action using sampling, coupons, and free gifts as incentives for action. Most ads end with a signature of some kind that serves to identify the company or brand, but it also serves as a **call to action** and gives direction to the consumer about how to respond, such as a toll-free phone number, website URL, or e-mail address. Similar to the Road Crew campaign, another form of action is to discourage or extinguish actions, such as smoking, drug use, or driving drunk.

Ultimately, marketers want loyal customers who purchase and repurchase the product as a matter of habit or preference. **Reminder advertising**, as well as distributing coupons or introducing a continuity program (such as a frequent-flyer program), is designed to keep the brand name in front of customers to encourage their repeat business.

Creative Thinking: So How Do You Do It?

Principle
When advertising gives consumers permission to believe in a product, it establishes the platform for conviction.

Given how much we've been talking about creativity, perhaps a definition might be appropriate. In a research review of creativity in advertising education, Professor Mark Stuhlfaut identified the significant elements, which begin with novelty but include appropriateness as well as authenticity and relevance. Stuhlfaut adds that if it's creative, it is also often generative; in other words, it leads to other new ways of thinking.[19] So **creativity** can be defined as generating novelty and uniqueness that makes something ring true.

Imagine: How Creativity Works is a book by Jonah Lehrer, *Wired* and *New Yorker* contributing writer. His focus is on nurturing creativity in all areas of business, including advertising. The publisher of Ad Age's *Creativity* magazine has written a book called *The Book of Doing*, which is like a coloring book for adults. Her approach to kick-starting imagination is to just jump in, get your hands dirty, and make stuff. Both of these books are inspirational for anyone who values creativity and its most valued product—new ideas—and both advocate the juxtaposition that comes from cross-pollinating ideas from a variety of unrelated disciplines.

Marketing communication and advertising are creative idea businesses. But what do we mean by an idea? An **idea** is a thought or a concept in the mind. It's formed by mentally combining pieces and fragments of thoughts into something that conveys a nugget of meaning. Advertising creatives sometimes use the term **concepting** to refer to the process of coming up with a new idea, such as the "Save a Life" bandage. Big Ideas are also called **creative concepts**.

An example of the evolution of a Big Idea comes from Internet company GoDaddy, which has long got attention with its sexy "GoDaddy Girls," including race car driver Danica Patrick. It's new agency, Deutsch New York, figured it was time for the brand to grow up yet not leave its old strategy totally behind. So for the 2012 Summer Olympics, it introduced the sexy Charlene, who is then joined by a nerdy Carl. The idea is that it's "Charlene on the outside and Carl on the Inside." Charlene attracts customers, and Carl keeps them.[20]

We have tried to define creativity and creative ideas, but to understand what it is, it may be helpful to think about what it isn't. What's the opposite of creative? In advertising, **clichés** are the most obvious examples of generic, nonoriginal, nonnovel ideas. An example of an industry whose advertising is immersed in clichés is hospitals—advertising conventions typically feature skilled doctors and caring nurses working together as teams in new high-tech buildings with amazing technology. In contrast, an innovative campaign for the Akron Children's Hospital uses unscripted commercials featuring patients and their families who talk about how they are coping. The idea is that hospitals are dramatic places, and the challenge was to present the inherent drama in the hospital situation by focusing on real people. When the New York–based DeVito/Verdi agency was hired by the Mount Sinai hospital to also break away from the clichés, the agency drafted a list of commandments: no pictures of doctors, no smiling people, no fancy machinery, no overpromises about medical care, no complicated medical terminology.[21]

To help you understand how creative people think about strategy and advertising ideas, consider the 10 tips offered in the "Practical Tips" box by Professor Tom Groth, whose students consistently win awards. These are suggestions about how professionals approach creative assignments, but they also provide you with a road map for your own personal growth as a creative person.

Big Ideas

What we call a **Big Idea**, or a creative concept, becomes a point of focus for communicating the message strategy. The Marlboro Man with its connotation of western independence and self-reliance is a Big Idea that has been worth millions, maybe billions, of dollars in brand equity over the years. It's ranked number three in *Advertising Age*'s Top 100 advertising campaigns of the century. Other campaigns on the list that we feature in this book include Smokey the Bear, Volkswagen's "Think Small," Nike's "Just Do It," Avis's "We try harder," Clairol's "Does she or doesn't she?," and Apple Computer's "1984."[22]

But Big Ideas can be risky because they are different and, by definition, untested. The "Whopper Freakout" campaign by Crispin Porter + Bogusky described in Chapter 7 was a risky strategy because it was so unexpected. The firm has had trouble with some of its other edgy ideas, such as the creepy Burger King. To be fair, the agency was recognized for its cutting-edge work and named Agency of the Year at the CLIO award show's 50th anniversary in 2009. The agency, however, lost VW as a client because its brassy taglines and quirky situations departed too much from VW's "heritage of tasteful wit." The ads, some of which alienated VW's dealers, featured a lab-coated Helga, a soccer mom who mocked Brooke Shields, and a VW Bug with a heavy Teutonic accent hosting a late-night talk show.[23] Thus, risky is good for edgy Big Ideas, but how far on the edge is a difficult question.

Principle
Big Ideas are risky because they are by definition new, unexpected, and untested.

Photo: Courtesy of Harley-Davidson and Carmichael Lynch. All rights reserved

The Harley-Davidson ad equates the taste of a steak with the throaty roar of a Harley engine.

Practical Tips

Checklist for Killer Ads

Tom Groth, *University of West Florida*

Groth's ✓list for killer ads.

Instructions: 1) Do your ad
2) Go through this list.
3) Redo your ad.
4) Smile.

1. A safe ad is a bad ad.

✓ Your goal isn't to blend in like elevator music. Many advertisers are afraid to "rock the boat."

✓ Safe advertising is liking waving at friends in the dark—you know it but they don't.

✓ If an ad doesn't scare you a bit…it's not much of an ad at all.

2. Make mistakes!

✓ Breakthrough creativity doesn't come from home runs…it comes from strike outs! *Winning* says something worked in the past. Don't be tempted to just repeat what worked before.

✓ Trial and error brings new answers. Trial and error opens doors instead of closing them.

3. What's your brand's "hook?"

"Ina-Gadda-Da-Vida…."
"All Right Now…"
"Keep on rockin me baby…"

You may not know the lyrics—but you know the *hook*!

✓ **Decide exactly one thing in your ad that you want to stick in your prospect's mind?** It can visual, verbal, musical…it's repetitive and is a sticks like glue in the mind.

✓ Many prospects buy what they know and it is just **one thing**—*the hook*! They remember *the hook* and buy *the hook*.

Which battery? ❍ Pink bunny battery or ❍ Coppertop battery
Which tuna? ❍ Charlie the tuna or ❍ Mermaid tuna.

✓ You need a sharp hook to catch the fish.

4. Leave something out.

"She gave you a big kiss for the birthday flowers.
This year make it Diamonds. ………"

This open-ended headline let's the guy figure out its meaning.

✓ **Let the prospect "fill in the blanks."**
This *theatre of the mind* approach works for all media not just radio.
It transforms a passive viewer into an active participant.

5. It's all about problem solving.

"Sales are falling!!! What are you going to do?"
"I'm gaining weight!!! What are you going to do?"

✓ It's all about problem solving—client's problems and prospect problems.

✓ If you can cleverly solve problems you'll never be unemployed.

6. Think "viewers" not "readers."

✓ **Is your promise visual?**
Do you read body copy? If you're under 30 your answer is probably…*rarely*.

✓ **Visuals offer instant gratification.**
Quick—show me! We are a visual culture. Images communicate at light speed and that's about all the time your ad has to get it's message across.

✓ **Become *visually literate*!** Sure you understand the language of visuals but can you speak the language? It takes more than knowledge of the Creative Suite to be visually literate. It's time to learn that foreign language!

✓ **Agencies employ *Art Directors* not *Art Decorators*.** Your goal is **not** to make an ad look good. Your design must immediately make the brand's *significance shine through* as images and words combine in the viewer's mind.

7. Everything communicates.

✓ Does ***everything*** *in your advertisement* support your message? Yes, every last thing talks—your choice of fonts, props, wardrobe, colors, white space, talent, media, music, tone of voice etc...

✓ Choose wisely. Never just stick something into the ad.

✓ You cannot not communicate.

8. You're really different.

What is the answer to this math problem? 1+1=___

Now imagine a math class where everyone in class comes up with a ***different*** answer yet everyone's answer is *right!*

✓ Unlike a math problem *creativity* recognizes that there are an unlimited number of answers to an advertising problem. They all can be *right.* .....or *wrong!*

✓ **There is only one of you.** Use your uniqueness to produce original answers that solve the toughest client and prospect problems.

9. "Good enough isn't good enough."-Jay Chiat

✓ **Work hard.** Resting is somehow very fatiguing.

Where do Big Ideas come from? As advertising legend James Webb Young, a founder of the Young & Rubicam agency, explained in his classic book on creative thinking, *A Technique for Producing Ideas*, an idea is a new or unexpected combination of thoughts. Young said, 'The ability to make new combinations is heightened by an ability to see relationships."[24] An idea, then, is *a thought that comes from placing two previously unrelated concepts together*, as the Harley "Steak for Your Ears" ad for Harley-Davidson demonstrates—a most unexpected juxtaposition.

The name "Road Crew" was the defining element of that campaign's Big Idea. It was supported with a slogan—"Beats driving"—that conveyed the benefit of the program in the language of the target audience. The logo was in the style of the Harley-Davidson logo. The Road Crew planners realized that a Big Idea that reflects the lifestyle of the target audience in appealing language and tone can motivate behavior and change attitudes, and Harley connects with the attitude of the young male audience the campaign wanted to reach.

The ROI of Creativity

A Big Idea is more than just a new thought because in advertising it also has to accomplish something—it has a functional dimension. According to the DDB agency, an effective ad is *relevant* and *original* and has *impact*—which is referred to as *ROI of creativity*. That formula sounds like the way a businessperson would talk metaphorically about creativity in terms of "return on investment."[25] But it has a different meaning here. According to DDB's philosophy, ideas have to be **relevant** and mean something to the target audience. **Original** means one of a kind—an advertising idea is creative when it is novel, fresh, unexpected, and unusual. Because it is novel, it is surprising and gets your attention. To be effective, the idea also must have **impact**, which means it makes an impression on the audience.

But how do you know if your idea is creative? Any idea can seem creative to you if you have never thought of it before, but the essence of a creative idea is that *no one else has thought of it either*. Thus, the first rule is to avoid doing what everyone else is doing. In an industry that prides itself on creativity, **copycat advertising**—that is, using an idea that someone else has originated—is a concern.

Principle

An idea can be creative for you if you have never thought of it before, but to be truly creative, it has to be one that no one else has thought of before.

The importance of originality may be obvious, but why is relevance important to an advertising Big Idea? Consider the award-winning California Milk Board campaign "Got Milk?" The consumer insight is that people drink milk with certain foods, such as cupcakes and cookies. If milk is unavailable to drink with those foods, people are—to say the least—frustrated. Thus, associating these products with milk is a highly relevant idea.

Likewise, why is impact important? We know that many advertisements just wash over the audience. An idea with impact, however, breaks through the clutter, gets attention, and sticks in memory. A *breakthrough ad* has stopping power and that comes from an intriguing idea—a Big Idea that is important, interesting, and relevant to consumers.

Photo: Agency: Goodby, Silverstein & Partners
Photo: Dan Escobar

The idea that some moments, such as when eating cupcakes and cookies, require a glass of milk is the creative concept behind the award-winning "Got Milk?" campaign. The creative concept is expressed in both words and pictures in this ad.

The Creative Leap

We all use different ways of thinking in different situations. For example, the term **divergent thinking** is used to describe a style of thinking that jumps around exploring multiple possibilities rather than using rational thinking to arrive at the "right" or logical conclusion. The heart of creative thinking, divergent thinking uses exploration (playfulness) to search for alternatives. Another term for divergent thinking is **right-brain thinking**, which is intuitive, holistic, artistic, and emotionally expressive thinking in contrast to **left-brain thinking**, which is logical, linear (inductive or deductive), and orderly. How can you become a more creative thinker—someone who uses the right brain for divergent explorations?

First, think about the problem as something that involves a mind shift. Instead of seeing the obvious, a creative idea looks at a problem in a different way, from a different angle. That's referred to as *thinking outside the box.* It doesn't matter how dull the product might appear to be, there is always an opportunity to move it beyond its category limitations through a creative Big Idea.

Second, put the strategy language behind you. Finding the brilliant creative concept entails what advertising giant Otto Kleppner called the *creative leap*[26]—a process of jumping from the rather boring business language in a strategy statement to an original idea. This Big Idea transforms the strategy into something unexpected, original, and interesting. Since the creative leap means moving from the safety of a predictable strategy statement to an unusual idea that hasn't been tried before, this leap is a *creative risk.*

A classic example of out-of-the-box thinking is Michelin's tire advertising, which is driven by the strategic idea that the tire is durable and dependable—language that would make a pretty boring ad. The creative idea, however, comes to life in the long-running campaign that shows a baby sitting in a tire. The visual is reinforced by the slogan "Because so much is riding on your tires." The creative concept "leaps" from the idea of a durable tire to the idea of protecting your family, particularly precious members like tiny children, by surrounding them with the dependability of a Michelin tire.

Dialing Up Your Creativity

How creative are you? You probably know people who are just naturally zany, who come up with crazy, off-the-wall ideas. As Sasser reminds us, "Everyone has some level of internal creativity." Creative advertising people may be weird and unconventional, but they can't be totally eccentric. They still must be purpose driven, meaning they are focused on creating effective advertising that's on strategy.

Coming up with a great idea that is also on strategy is an emotional high. Advertising creatives describe it as one of the biggest emotional roller coasters in the business world. One copywriter explained that when the ideas aren't flowing, you feel like fleeing the country. But when it's a good idea, there's nothing better. It's a real high.

Ingvi Logason, owner of an award-winning agency in Iceland and a member of this book's advisory board, explains how he got the idea for a campaign for SORPA, a recycling center in Iceland. The project was to encourage people who were recycling to minimize the volume of their waste—and, of course, recycle more. "The idea came from the unlikeliest source," he said. After working on the problem for some time, "the idea came to me while channel surfing and stumbling on a specific scene in a film I had seen—*Fargo*," where the murderer is trying to dispose of a body by putting into a tree shredder. Even though it has no correlation with recycling, the shredder, Logason said, "lit my lightbulb." The result was a humorous ad that received the highest likability score ever measured in Iceland and that led to an increase in waste brought in for recycling. According to Logason, "Inspiration for my ideas can almost always be traced to things I have done, experienced, seen, heard, or read." He concludes, "In a creative world it is important to try new things and live life like a discoverer."

Principle
A breakthrough ad has stopping power that comes from an intriguing idea.

Principle
To get a creative idea, you must leap beyond the mundane, formal business language of the strategy statement and see the problem in a novel and unexpected way.

Principle
Getting a great advertising idea that is also on strategy is an emotional high.

Logason's "discoverer" is why we say that curiosity is the most important characteristic of creativity.[27] But what else is important? Research by the Center for Studies in Creativity in Buffalo, New York, has found that most people can sharpen their skills and develop their creative potential by understanding and strengthening certain personal characteristics. Research indicates that creative people tend to be independent, assertive, self-sufficient, persistent, self-disciplined, and curious, with a high tolerance for ambiguity. They are also risk takers with powerful egos that are internally driven. They don't care much about group standards and opinions and typically have inborn skepticism and strong curiosity. Here are a few other characteristics of creative people:

- ***Problem Solving*** Creative problem solvers are alert, watchful, and observant and reach conclusions through intuition rather than through logic.
- ***Playful*** Creative people have fun with ideas; they have a mental playfulness that allows them to make novel associations.
- ***The Ability to Visualize*** Most of the information we accumulate comes through sight, so the ability to manipulate visual images is crucial for good copywriters as well as designers. They can see products, people, and scenes in the mind's eye, and they can visualize a mental picture of the finished ad while it is still in the talking, or idea, stage.
- ***Open to New Experiences*** As we said earlier, one characteristic that identifies creative people is that they are open to new experiences. Over the course of a lifetime, openness to experience may give you many more adventures from which to draw. Those experiences would, in turn, give a novelist more characters to write about, a painter more scenes to paint, and the creative team more angles from which to tackle an advertising problem.[28]
- ***Conceptual Thinking*** It's easy to see how people who are open to experience might develop innovative advertisements and commercials because they are more imaginative.[29] Such imagination led to a famous Nike commercial in which Michael Jordan and Larry Bird play an outlandish game of horse—bouncing the ball off buildings, billboards, and places that are impossible to reach.

Photo: Image provided courtesy of Michelin North America, Inc.

Michelin's dependability and durability surround and protect a car's precious cargo.

The Creative Process: How to Get an Idea

Only in cartoons do lightbulbs appear above our heads from out of nowhere when a good idea strikes. In reality, most people who are good at thinking up new ideas will tell you it is hard work. They read, study, analyze, test and retest, sweat, curse, and worry. Sometimes they give up. The unusual, unexpected, novel idea rarely comes easily—and that's as true in science as it is in advertising.

The creative process can be portrayed as a series of steps. English sociologist Graham Wallas was the first to outline the creative process, but others followed, including Alex Osborn, one of the founders of the BBDO agency and the Creative Education Foundation.[30] Let's summarize this classic approach in the following steps:

Step 1. **Immersion** Read, research, and learn everything you can about the problem.

Step 2. **Ideation** Look at the problem from every angle; develop ideas and generate as many alternatives as possible.

Step 3. **Brainfag** Don't give up if—and when—you hit a blank wall.

Step 4. **Incubation** Try to put your conscious mind to rest to let your subconscious take over.

Step 5. **Illumination** Embrace that unexpected moment when the idea comes, often when your mind is relaxed and you're doing something else.

Step 6. ***Evaluation*** Does it work? Is it on strategy?

Another approach comes from Professor Linda Correll, who developed Creative Aerobics, a four-step idea-generating process.[31] The idea is to go through a structured creative exercise that opens new doors and windows for ideas to enter your mind. To illustrate, think about finding a creative idea for a new brand of oranges. Here's how Creative Aerobics works:

1. ***Facts*** As a left-brain exercise, come up with facts about your product—an orange has seeds, is juicy, has vitamin C.
2. ***New Names*** Create new "names" for the product—a vitamin supplement, a kiss of sunshine.
3. ***Similarities*** Find similarities between dissimilar objects—both Florida sunshine and oranges suggest warmth, freshness, sunshine, the fountain of youth.
4. ***New Definitions*** Like creating a pun, creates new definitions for product-related nouns—peel (face eel, peel out), seed (seed money, bird seed), navel/naval (naval academy, contemplating one's navel), pulp (pulp fiction), C/see/si/sea (C the light).

Correll says that headlines derived from these idea starters might be "Seed money" (the money to buy oranges), "Peel out" (when your store is out of oranges), "Pulp fiction" (a story about an orange), "C the light" (the orange is a low-calorie source of vitamin C).

Brainstorming

As part of the creative process, some agencies use a thinking technique known as **brainstorming** where a group of 6 to 10 people work together to come up with ideas. One person's idea stimulates someone else's, and the combined power of the group associations stimulates far more ideas than any one person could think of alone. The group becomes an idea factory.

An example comes from David Droga, chairman of the award-winning Droga5 agency who explained how his team came up with a tagline for a campaign for athletic-wear brand Puma.[32] After weeks of filling sweaty notebooks with half-baked ideas, the painful process ended with a great line for this very unusual company. You see Puma champions "social" sports and the people who play them, everything from foosball to darts to karaoke to bowling—the kinds of sports you play with a drink in your hand. So what do you call highly competitive people in social sports? And then, at the point of giving up, someone on the team came up with "the after-hours athlete." And a slogan, as well as a position and name for the category, was developed.

The term *brainstorming* was coined by Alex Osborn, founder of the advertising agency BBDO and explained in his classic book *Applied Imagination.* The secret to brainstorming is to remain positive and defer judgment. Negative thinking during a brainstorming session can destroy the informal atmosphere necessary to achieve a novel idea. The role of the brainstorm facilitator is to encourage what the Idea Champions organization calls "the in-the-moment opportunities to spark the ever-mutating, collective genius of the group."[33] Read more about their brainstorming recommendations at www.ideachampions.com.

To stimulate group creativity against a deadline, some agencies have special processes or locations for brainstorming sessions with no distractions and interruptions, such as cell phones and access to e-mail and walls that can be covered with sheets of paper on which to write ideas. Some agencies rent a suite in a hotel and send the creative team there to get away and immerse themselves in the problem. When the GSDM agency was defending its prized Southwest Airlines account, the president ordered a 28-day "war room/death march" that had staffers working around the clock, wearing Rambo-style camouflage, and piling all their trash inside the building to keep any outsiders from rummaging around for clues to their pitch.

The following list builds on our previous discussion of creative thinking. It can also be used as an outline for a brainstorming session.

To create an original and unexpected idea, use the following techniques:

- ***What If?*** To twist the commonplace, ask a crazy *what if* question. For example, what if wild animals could talk? What kind of personalities would they have? That question is the origin of Frontier's talking animals campaign
- ***An Unexpected Association*** In **free association**, you think of a word and then describe everything that comes into your mind when you imagine that word. If you follow a chain of associations, you may come up with an idea that sets up an unexpected juxtaposition with the original word or concept. An ad for Compaq used a visual of a chained butterfly to illustrate the lack of freedom in competitors' computer work stations.

- ***Dramatize the Obvious*** Sometimes the most creative idea is also the most obvious. The "Save a Life" video shows sharp things bringing blood. It's an over-the-top execution, but the idea is pretty simple and obvious.
- ***Catchy Phrasing*** Isuzu used "The 205 Horsepower Primal Scream" for its Rodeo headline.
- ***An Unexpected Twist*** A road crew usually refers to highway construction workers or the behind-the-scenes people on a concert tour, but for the Road Crew campaign, the phrase was twisted to refer to limo drivers who give rides to people who have had too much to drink.
- ***Play on Words*** Under the headline "Happy Camper," an ad for cheese showed a picture of a packed sport-utility vehicle (SUV) with a huge wedge of cheese lashed to the rooftop.
- ***Analogy and Metaphor*** Used to see new patterns or relationships, metaphors, and analogies that by definition set up juxtapositions. Harley-Davidson compared the legendary sound of its motorcycles to the taste of a thick, juicy steak.
- ***Familiar and Strange*** Put the familiar in an unexpected situation: UPS showed a tiny model of its familiar brown truck moving through a computer cord.
- ***A Twisted Cliché*** They may have been great ideas the first time they were used, but phrases such as "the road to success" or "the fast track" become trite when overused. But they can regain their power if twisted into a new context. The "Happy Camper" line was twisted by relating cheese to an SUV.
- ***Twist the Obvious*** Avoid the predictable, such as a picture of a Cadillac on Wall Street or in front of a mansion. Instead, use an SUV on Wall Street ("fast tracker") or a basketball hoop in front of a mansion ("slam dunk").
- ***Exaggeration*** Take a common situation or item and exaggerate it until it becomes funny (an unbreakable kiss with the lovers totally unresponsive to over-the-top attempts to break them apart).

To prevent unoriginal ideas, avoid or work around the following:

- ***The Look-Alike*** Avoid copycat advertising that uses somebody else's great idea. Hundreds of ads for escape products (resorts, travel, liquor, and foods) have used the headline "Paradise Found." It's a play on "paradise lost" but still overused.
- ***The Tasteless*** In an attempt to be cute, a Subaru ad used the headline "Put it where the sun don't shine"—an attempted twist on a cliché, but it doesn't work.

Getting the Big Idea for marketing communication campaigns has always been the province of creative teams in agencies. Recently, however, with the development of new crowdsourcing practices, marketers are finding ways to enlist the collective ideas of thousands to come up with great ideas. Doritos has held "Crash the Super Bowl" competitions that invite consumers to create ads to run during the Super Bowl.

Managing Creative Strategies

We've talked about creative strategy and how it is developed, along with the types of effects advertising creates and the message strategies that deliver on these objectives. Let's now look at three management issues related to creative strategies: extension, adaptation, and evaluation.

Extension: An Idea with Legs

One characteristic of a Big Idea is that it gives *legs* to a campaign. By that, we mean that the idea is strong enough to serve as an umbrella concept for a variety of executions in different media talking to different audiences. It can be endlessly extended. Extendability is a strength of the Chick-fil-A, Geico Gecko, and Frontier's talking animals campaigns. This is what Stuhlfaut was referring to when he explained that creative thinking is *generative*.

Adaptation: Taking an Idea Global

The opportunity for standardizing the campaign across multiple markets exists only if the objectives and strategic position are essentially the same. Otherwise, a creative strategy may call for a little tweaking of the message for a local market or even major revision if there are cultural and market differences.

In the case where the core targeting and positioning strategies remain the same in different markets, it might be possible for the central creative idea to be universal across markets. Although the execution of this idea may vary from market to market, the creative concept works across all types of consumers. Even if the campaign theme, slogan, or visual elements are the same across markets, it is usually desirable to adapt the creative execution to the local market, as we explained in the discussion of cultural differences in Chapter 5.

An example of a difficult adaptation comes from Apple's series of "Mac vs. PC" ads that show a nerdy PC guy who can't keep up with the activities of a laid-back Mac guy. It uses delicate humor and body language to make subtle points about the advantages of the Mac system. In moving the campaign to Japan, Apple's agency TBWA/Chiat/Day wrestled with the fact that in Japanese culture, direct-comparison ads are considered rude. The Japanese version was tweaked to make the Apple more of a home computer and the PC a work tool, so the differences were focused more on place than on person.[34] The point is that cultural differences often require nuanced and subtle changes in ads if they are to be acceptable beyond the country of their origin.

Evaluation: The Go/No-Go Decision

How do you decide if the creative idea is strong enough to justify the expense of creating a campaign based on it? Whether local or global, an important part of managing creative work is evaluation, which happens at several stages in the creative process. Later we'll focus on evaluation of effectiveness, but we'll introduce some basics here to help you understand this important final step in the creative process.

A book on Bill Bernbach and the golden age of advertising, *Nobody's Perfect* by Doris Willens,[35] analyzed the brilliant advertising his creative team at DDB produced during the 1960s. In commenting on the book, positioning guru Al Ries observed that Bernbach was a true creative genius because he had the ability to sort good ideas from bad. Ries concluded, "It's a trait that's extremely rare."[36]

So nobody starts off being a Bernbach, but everyone can learn to be more critical about the brand messages they see. The first question is, Is it on strategy? No matter how much the creative people, client, or account executive may like an idea, if it doesn't communicate the right message or the right product personality to the right audience at the right time, then it is not effective.

However, as Alex Bogusky, formerly chief creative officer at Crispin Porter + Bogusky, says about the firm's over-the-top work (think the Burger King king), "I don't mind spectacular failure or spectacular criticism," he says, because those ideas make headlines, which means everybody's talking about them. "There's so much advertising that nobody knows even exists," he adds. "That's the stuff that I worry about making."[37]

Structural Analysis The Leo Burnett agency has used an approach for analyzing the logic of the creative strategy that goes beyond just evaluating the strategy. The Burnett creative teams have used it to keep the message strategy and creative concept working together. This method, called **structural analysis**, relies on these three steps:

1. Evaluate the *power of the narrative* or story line (heart).
2. Evaluate the *strength of the product claim* (head).
3. Consider *how well the two are integrated*—that is, how the story line brings the claim to life.

Burnett creative teams check to see whether the narrative level is so high that it overpowers the claim or whether the claim is strong but there is no memorable story. Ideally, these two elements will be so seamless that it is hard to tell whether the impact occurs because of the power of the story or the strength of the claim. Such an analysis keeps the rational and emotional sides of an advertisement working together.

Principle
Vampire creativity means the creative storyline overpowers the brand message.

Copytesting A formal method to evaluate the effectiveness of an ad, either in draft form or after it has been executed, is called copytesting. Remember that to evaluate the results, the objectives need to be measurable, which means they can be evaluated to determine the effectiveness of the creative strategy. Copytesting uses a variety of tools to measure and predict the impact of the advertisement, and we discussed some of them in Chapter 6. Chapter 19 explains these tools in more detail.

A particular problem that Big Ideas face is that the message is sometimes so creative that the ad is remembered but not the brand. That's called **vampire creativity**, and it is one reason some advertisers shy away from really novel or entertaining strategies. That's also why it is important to copytest the effectiveness of the ad's creative features while still in the idea stage to determine if there is brand linkage and memorability.

Looking Ahead

This is a brief review of message strategy and creative thinking. The next step in learning about the inner workings of the creative side is to move to the execution of message—both copy and design. We'll talk first about copywriting in Chapter 9 and then visual communication in Chapter 10.

help®
I want to save a life

It's a Wrap

Creating Ideas That Stick

Graham Douglas is on the cutting edge of saving lives. He came up with an idea that pierced the media environment to try to convince enough people to become bone marrow donors to save 10,000 lives a year.

Selling an idea is challenging enough. Convincing people to part with their blood defies their conventional behavior and makes the job seemingly impossible. Yet Douglas invented a product, found a pharmaceutical company that would sell it, and created a bizarre online video to market the bandages/donor combo kit.

The innovative product combined with the compelling story of one brother desperately helping both his blood relative and his unrelated brothers (and sisters) resulted in communication that took on a life of its own. Television reporters from *CBS News*, *ABC News*, *MSNBC*, and *CNN* picked up on the story and multiplied the impact by adding stories they told about people desperate for bone marrow matches. Some of the print/online highlights were the *Wall Street Journal*, *Bloomberg Businessweek*, *Fast Company*, *Good Magazine*, and some big industry publications, such as *Creativity*, *AdWeek*, *Advertising Age*, *Creative Review*, and *Campaign Brief*, also helped educate the public about bone marrow donation. The number of media impressions has surpassed 75 million and continues to grow.

Graham's ability as a superior creative problem solver earned him the honor of the Grand Prix for Good plus two other Gold Lions at Cannes by the age 27. Even better, as a result of receiving a bone marrow donation from a stranger, Britton Douglas, his twin brother, is a healthy, successful Dallas attorney.

Logo: Courtesy of Graham Douglas

Key Points Summary

1. **How do we explain the science and art of creative strategy as well as the logic and important parts of a creative brief?** From the advertising strategy comes the problem statement, the objectives, the target market, and the positioning strategy. The message strategy decisions include the appropriate type of creative strategy, the selling premise, and suggestions about the ad's execution, such as tone of voice.
2. **What are some key message strategy approaches?** Creative strategies are often expressed as appeals to the head, the heart, or both. More complex systems of strategies have been proposed by Frazer and Taylor. Creative strategy formats include lectures, dramas, psychological appeals, and selling strategies. Different formulas have evolved that deliver these strategies and guide the development of executions.
3. **How is creative thinking defined, and how does it lead to a Big Idea?** To be creative, an ad must make a relevant connection with its audience and present a selling idea in an unexpected way. There is both a science (the way a message is persuasive, convincing, and relevant) and an art (the way a message is an unexpected idea). A Big Idea is a

creative concept that makes the message attention getting and memorable.

4. **What characteristics do creative people have in common, and what is their typical creative process?** Creative people tend to be independent, assertive, self-sufficient, persistent, and self-disciplined, with a high tolerance for ambiguity. They are also risk takers with powerful egos that are internally driven. They don't care much about group standards and opinions and typically have inborn skepticism and strong curiosity. They are good problem solvers with an ability to visualize and do conceptual thinking. They are open to new experiences. A typical creative process involves immersing yourself in background research; developing alternatives through ideation; getting past brainfag, where you hit the wall and can't come up with anything; and embracing illumination of the great idea.

5. **What issues affect the management of creative strategy and its implementation?** Those working on the creative side of advertising must do so within the parameters of the business context. Some factors that have an impact on the development of creative strategy and its implementation are extension, adaptation, and evaluation. A concept is extendable if it can serve as an umbrella idea for other communication. A campaign is adaptable if the idea can be used in another context, such as a global application. Evaluation is a critical management issue because it is important to test whether a concept communicates the intended message to the target audience.

Key Terms

appeal, p. 250
attributes, p. 251
benefit, p. 251
Big Idea, p. 257
brainfag, p. 261
brainstorming, p. 262
brand icon, p. 252
call to action, p. 256
claim, p. 251
clichés, p. 256
comparison, p. 252
concepting, p. 256
copycat advertising, p. 259
creative brief, p. 243
creative concept, p. 256
creative director, p. 242
creative strategy, p. 243
creativity, p. 256
demonstration, p. 251
divergent thinking, p. 260
E score, p. 253
endorser, p. 252
execution, p. 244
features, p. 251
free association, p. 262
hard sell, p. 247
humor, p. 252
idea, p. 256
ideation, p. 261
illumination, p. 261
immersion, p. 261
impact, p. 259
incubation, p. 261
left-brain thinking, p. 260
message design, p. 247
message strategy, p. 244
original, p. 259
permission to believe, p. 255
problem avoidance message, p. 252
problem solution message, p. 252
product-as-hero, p. 252
promise, p. 251
Q score, p. 253
reason why, p. 251
relevant, p. 259
reminder advertising, p. 256
right-brain thinking, p. 260
selling premise, p. 251
slice-of-life message, p. 252
slogans, p. 254
soft sell, p. 247
spokes-character, p. 252
spokesperson, p. 252
straightforward message, p. 251
structural analysis, p. 264
substantiation, p. 251
support, p. 251
taglines, p. 254
teaser, p. 252
tone of voice, p. 245
unique selling proposition, p. 251
vampire creativity, p. 264

Review Questions

8-4. What is a creative brief, and who is responsible for its development?

✪ 8-5. How do various strategic approaches deliver on the objectives identified in the Facets Model of Effects?

8-6. Define *hard sell* and *soft sell*, and explain how they differ.

8-7. Explain the importance of originality in preparing creative ideas.

8-8. What are the key points that should be addressed in a communication/creative brief?

8-9. List and describe Frazer's creative strategies, and explain with examples where each should be used.

8-10. Explain how brainstorming is used in advertising.

8-11. List five characteristics of creative people. How do you rate yourself on those factors?

Discussion Questions

8-12. Divide the class into groups of 6 to 10 people and discuss this problem: *Your community wants to encourage people to get out of their cars and use alternative forms of transportation.* Brainstorm for 15 minutes as a group, accumulating every possible idea. How many ideas are generated? Here's how to run this brainstorming group:

- Appoint one member to be the *recorder* who lists all the ideas as they are mentioned.
- Appoint another member to be the *moderator* and suggest techniques described in this chapter as idea starters.
- Identify a *cheerleader* to keep the discussion positive and find gentle ways to discourage critical or negative comments.
- Work for 15 minutes generating as many different creative concepts as your team can come up with, regardless of how crazy or dumb they might initially sound.
- Go back through the list as a group and put an asterisk next to the 5 to 10 ideas that seem to have the most promise.

When all of the groups reconvene in class, each recorder should list the group's best ideas on the blackboard. As a class, pick out the three ideas that seem to have the most potential. Analyze the experience of participating in a brainstorming group and compare the experiences of the different teams.

8-13. You work as a designer in one of the local advertising agencies. Part of your role is to meet with clients, throughout the creative process. to present concepts, clarify project objectives, and discuss any possible changes.

You will be meeting with a new client to discuss a proposal that your agency will handle. Regarding the meeting, complete the following:

a. Prepare a list of questions that you should discuss with your client at the first meeting. These questions will help you understand the project and come up with the best design solution.

b. Develop a creative brief in the form of an Excel spreadsheet or Word document that contains your list of questions and your clients, answers. Explain the logic you used to develop your brief and its essential parts. Why is it useful? Who should keep a copy of the brief and why?

Take-Home Projects

8-14. ***Portfolio Project:*** Find at least two newspaper or magazine advertisements that you believe are bland and unexciting. Rewrite them, first to demonstrate a hard-sell approach and then to demonstrate a soft-sell approach. Explain how your rewrites have improved the original ad. Also explain how the hard-sell and soft-sell appeals work. Which do you believe is the most effective for each ad? If you were a team of professionals working on these accounts, how would you go about evaluating the effectiveness of these two ads? In other words, how would you test your intuitive judgment of which one works best?

8-15. ***Mini-Case Analysis:*** Summarize the creativity aspects of the "Save a Life" effort. What makes this effort and its promotion creative? Brainstorm on an idea for a new commercial that would extend the campaign's theme and develop this new Big Idea as a proposal to present to your instructor.

TRACE North America Case

Creative Multicultural Communication

Read the TRACE case in the Appendix before coming to class.

8-16. What was the Big Idea behind the "Hard to Explain, Easy to Experience" campaign?

8-17. How would you describe the campaign's message strategy?

CHAPTER 9

Promotional Writing

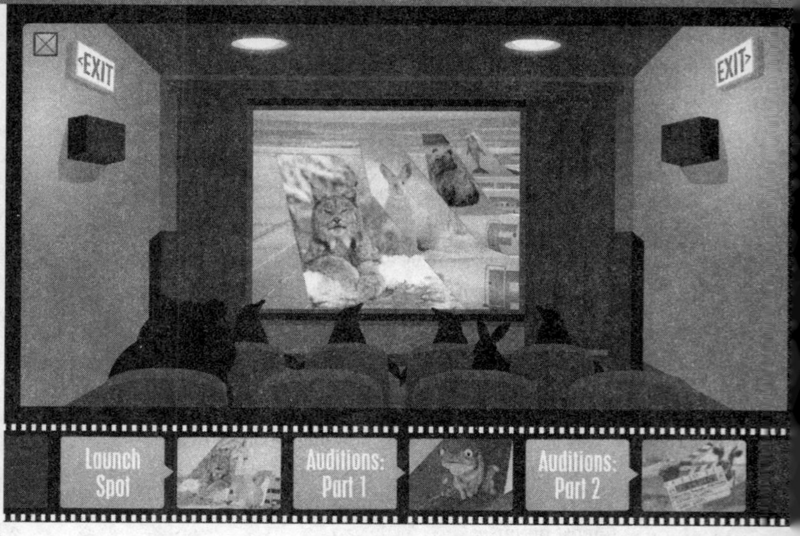

Photos: Courtesy of Frontier Airlines and Grey Worldwide

It's a Winner

Campaigns:
"Frontier's Next Animal," "Flip to Mexico"

Company:
Frontier Airlines

Agency:
AbbaSez; Grey Worldwide

Awards:
Long-running Frontier campaign awards include Gold Effie (for sustained success); Silver Clio, Silver Effie, and Gold Mobius ("Best of show" Nomination) for "Flip to Mexico"

CHAPTER KEY POINTS

1. What are the basic word, language, and writing skills that distinguish brand communication?
2. How is advertising copy written?
3. Which copy elements are essential to print media pieces?
4. How can we characterize the design and tools of radio messages?
5. What are the major elements of television writing?
6. How do writers design Internet messages?

Wildlife Blaze Trails for Frontier

Jack the rabbit, Grizwald the bear, Foxy the fox (for whom Jack has a crush), Flip the dolphin, Larry the lynx, Hector the sea otter, and Sal the cougar. These are some of the irascible, lovable characters that contribute to Frontier's reputation as being a "whole different animal" when it comes to flying.

When low-cost carrier Frontier Airlines started in 1994, it took off with animals emblazoned on the tails of its planes as a way to distinguish Frontier from its competitors. Frontier's distinctive aircraft tails, all of which depict a variety of cifferent wildlife, have made the Frontier brand synonymous with the airline's western heritage. Years of award-winning integrated marketing communications have firmly established the airline with its talking animals on the planes' tails as a favorite of consumers in the Denver market and beyond.

The tale behind the tails reveals how important writing is in the process of promoting products, services, and ideas in all forms of media. In 2003, Shawn Couzens and Gary Ennis, creative directors at Grey Worldwide, brought the tail animals to life by creating a likable cast of characters—each unique in its own way. The humorous campaign broke away from the buttoned-up approach used by most airlines by creating an "episodic sitcom" much like *Modern Family* or *The Big Bang Theory.* As a result, consumers built an emotional attachment to the brand and its spokes-animals. And with each new brand contact, consumers grew connected to the wise-cracking animals as Frontier continued to evolve the campaign. Two campaigns, "Flip to Mexico" and "Frontier's Next Animal," illustrate the critical role of copywriters.

"Flip to Mexico"

In 2006, when rival airline United emerged from bankruptcy with a multi-million-dollar ad campaign, Frontier decided to steal the spotlight by creating a diversion. Couzens said, "We wanted to promote our increased service to Mexico. For years, Flip the Dolphin had been dying to travel to a warm, tropical climate. But we always sent him to the cold, windy city of Chicago. It was a long-running joke in our campaign. Well, Flip had had enough. He decided to offer Frontier an ultimatum: Either they send him to Mexico, or he would quit."

Couzens and Ennis conceptualized the commercials as a news story, which would unfold and evolve in real time. The "Flip to Mexico" campaign featured ads with Flip, fake news spots on Flip's demand that he be allowed to fly to Mexico, staged protests, podcasts, blogs, Flip's anthem on iTunes, and a Flipmobile that was conspicuous around Denver to generate awareness. Fans caught the spirit and started demonstrating on Flip's behalf. The four-week campaign culminated in an ad that played during the Super Bowl announcing that Flip was finally going to Mexico.

"Frontier's Next Animal"

When Frontier added a new plane in 2012, Couzens, now heading his own agency, AbbaSez, said, "We decided to let consumers choose which animal would appear on the tail. The resulting campaign featured 18 different contenders—from a dung beetle to a parrot—all auditioning for the coveted role. The interactive campaign included two hilarious audition reels . . . nine TV spots . . . a robust social media campaign . . . and a detailed microsite, which allowed consumers to vote, view content, learn about the contestants, and share their vote via Facebook or Twitter."

Go to Couzens's website at www.abbasez.com in the *Integrated* and *Viral* sections to listen to the animals make their pitches. As you listen to the clever banter, think about how the entire effort to brand the airline results catches your attention and strategically communicates a specific underlying message that Frontier either now has a route to Mexico or is adding new planes to its fleet and animals to its stable. As you read this chapter, refer to this campaign to see how the characteristics of writing effective copy apply to Frontier's communication efforts.

Then check the "It's a Wrap" feature at the end of the chapter to see the results of Frontier's efforts to involve consumers in the process of building the brand.

Sources: Shawn Couzens, personal communication; Frontier Airlines Web pages: www.frontierairlines.com/who-we-are and www.frontierairlines.com/fun-stuff.

Words and pictures work together to produce a creative concept. However, the idea behind a creative concept in advertising and other brand communication is usually expressed in some attention-getting and memorable phrase, such as "Curiously Strong Mints" for Altoids. Finding these "magic words" is the responsibility of writers who search for the right way to warm up a mood or appeal to the audience. This chapter describes the role of the writer as part of this team and explains the practice of copywriting in various types of advertising media. It also describes the work of writers for other marketing communication areas, such as public relations and direct response.

The Writer's Role in Brand Communication

Advertising copywriting is a major job category, but writers are also important in other areas, such as public relations and direct marketing. All these areas have specialists, but in some agencies and corporate departments, writers are expected to handle all different types of marketing communication. So we'll begin with some general writing considerations, then discuss specific areas in more detail.

The Language of Brand Communication

The most important word selection in marketing communication is the brand or corporate name, and this responsibility can lie with the advertising department, corporate communication, or an outside branding consultant. Low-cost airline JetBlue was originally founded in 1999 as New Air, but its founders realized it needed a more distinctive name. They considered naming it Taxi and painting the planes yellow but backed off because of negative associations with New York

City taxis and questionable service. JetBlue has been a good choice because it states the business (jet = airlines) as well as sky (blue) with its calming connotations.

There is a science to letters and sounds as well as words. Research has determined that letters with a hard edge, like T or K, suggest effectiveness (Kodak, Target, Tide); X and Z relate to science (Xcel, Zantac, Xerox); C, L, R, P, and S are calming or relaxing (Cialis, Lexus, Puffs, Revlon, Silk); and Z means speed (Zippo, Ziplock, Zappos.com). In the erectile dysfunction category, Lilly's drug Cialis is derived from *ciel*, the French word for "sky," and was chosen because it is a smooth, soft sound that connotes a sense of intimacy. In contrast, Pfizer's Viagra evokes the power of Niagara Falls.[1]

Many brand names are made up, but it's not just names that are created by marketing communicators. The "uncola" position was created for 7-Up, and more recently the True Value hardware chain has proclaimed itself "masters of all things hardwarian," a phrase that suggests mastery of a traditional art or skill.

A long-term brand or corporate identity effort, **slogans** have to be catchy and memorable. A distinctive catchphrase that serves as a motto for a campaign, brand, or company, it is used across a variety of marketing communication platforms and over an extended period of time. The award-winning and much-copied "What happens in Las Vegas stays in Las Vegas" is a tourism slogan permanently enshrined on the Madison Avenue Walk of Fame that hints at the pleasures you don't enjoy at home.

The word **tagline** is often used to refer to a slogan, but technically it means a line at the end of an ad that wraps up the creative concept. It's more of a campaign theme than a brand slogan, so it is less enduring than a slogan. For example, online travel company Orbitz used "Take vacation back" as a theme line for a campaign that challenges business-focused folks to reclaim their lost vacation days.

The best slogans have a close link to the brand name: "With a name like Smucker's, it has to be good," "America runs on Dunkin'," and "Ford Tough." "Finger lickin' good" for KFC doesn't use the brand name but still is highly recognizable because it connects with the product (fried chicken) and has been in use since 1952. "Only you can prevent forest fires" is one of the best-remembered slogans of all time even though it was created for a good cause.

That's another characteristic of a good slogan: It is enduring—slogans are rarely changed. A true classic, Maxwell House's "Good to the last drop," has been used since 1915, and Morton Salt's "When it rains, it pours" has been around since 1914. Avis made headlines in 2012 when its new chief marketing officer replaced its hugely successful "We Try Harder" slogan with "It's Your Space." The reason given by the new manager is to find something that is more customer focused. The "We Try Harder" slogan, created by the DDB agency and its legendary copywriter Paula Green, had been used since 1962 and is a classic example of a slogan that communicates a position as well as a brand personality. *Advertising Age* has it on the magazine's list of Top Ten Slogans of the 20th Century.[2] What do you think—how would you go about testing the wisdom of this branding decision?

Of course, slogans also have to be original, as Wisconsinites found out when the official state slogan was changed to "Live Like You Mean It." The state spent some $50,000 on the new slogan and then later discovered that it had been used as the tagline in a Bacardi Rum campaign.[3]

Unfortunately, many corporate slogans fall back into marketing language or clichés and come across as leaden

Photo: Courtesy U.S. Forest Service

CLASSIC

The Smoky Bear campaign by the nonprofit Ad Council is one of the best-remembered campaigns of all time. Its slogan, "Only you can prevent forest fires," is locked into public memory. It was brought back in a new form in the summer of 2012 during the nationwide epidemic of wildfires and rephrased as "Only you can prevent wildfires." Note the burnt-out forest image in Smoky's eye.

("Total quality through excellence," "Excellence through total quality," or "Where quality counts"). Wells Fargo, for example, uses "Together we'll go far," which is not distinctive, could be used by any company, and says nothing about Wells Fargo or its business. Accenture uses "High performance. Delivered." which also is nondistinctive and not very memorable. Consider the distinctiveness and memorability of the following slogans:

TEST YOURSELF

Match the Company with Its Slogan:

1. Together we can prevail	a. Merck
2. Imagination at work*	b. Bristol-Myers Squibb
3. A mind is a terrible thing to waste*	c. Hallmark
4. Know how	d. Swatch
5. A business of caring	e. Hitachi
6. Melts in your mouth, not in your hands*	f. Verizon
7. Always surprising	g. Cigna
8. We deliver for you*	h. FedEx
9. Diamonds are forever*	i. L'Oréal
10. Inspire the next	j. Diesel
11. When you care enough to send the very best*	k. UPS
	l. Canon
12. Where patients come first	m. Chrysler
13. Can you hear me now?*	n. deBeers
14. For successful living	o. U.S. Postal Service
15. Inspiration comes standard	p. M&Ms
16. When it absolutely, positively has to be there overnight*	q. United Negro College Fund
	r. GE
17. Because I'm worth it	
18. What can brown do for you?*	

Answers to Companies: 1.1:b *Bristol-Myers Squibb;* 2:p *GE*;* 3:o *United Negro College Fund*;* 4:k *Canon; Cigna;* 6:n *M&Ms*;* 7:d *Swatch;* 8:m *USPS;** 9:e *Hitachi;* 10:c *Hallmark*;* 11:a *Merck;* 12:f *Verizon*;* 13:i *Diesel;* 14:l *Chrysler;* 15:h *FedEx*;* 16:j *UPS.**

Study the slogans in the matching activity. Which ones did you get, and which ones stumped you? Note the nine slogans identified with an asterisk. They have been recognized by *Adweek* as winning slogans. In your view, why were they selected for this honor, and what makes them different from the others on the list that have not been honored in this way?

One of America's favorite slogan winners, according to *Adweek*, is the "Don't Mess with Texas" antilitter slogan. Created by Austin-based GSD&M for the Texas Department of Transportation, the award-winning social-marketing campaign built around this slogan features billboards, print ads, radio and television spots, and a host of celebrities (Willie Nelson, Stevie Ray Vaughan, Matthew McConaughey, George Foreman, and LeAnn Rimes, among others) who take turns with the tough-talking slogan that captures the spirit and pride of Texans. One billboard, for example, warns, "Keep Your Butts in the Car." The Dontmesswithtexas.org website, where you can see all these ads, including the commercials, also has been featured by *Adweek* as a "Cool Site."

Writers use a number of catchy literary techniques to enhance the memorability of slogans:

- ***Direct Address*** "Have it your way"; "Think small."
- ***A Startling or Unexpected Phrase*** Twists a common phrase to make it unexpected, as in the NYNEX campaign: "If it's out there, it's in here."
- ***Rhyme, Rhythm, Alliteration*** Uses repetition of sounds, as in the *Wall Street Journal*'s slogan, "The daily diary of the American Dream."

- ***Parallel Construction*** Uses repetition of the structure of a sentence or phrase, as in Morton Salt's "When it rains, it pours."
- ***Cue the Product*** Maxwell House's "Good to the last drop"; John Deere's "Nothing runs like a Deere"; Wheaties' "Breakfast of Champions"; "Beef. It's What's for Dinner."
- ***Music*** "In the valley of the Jolly, ho-ho-ho, Green Giant."
- ***Combination*** "It's your land, lend a hand," which is the slogan for Take Pride in America. (rhyme, rhythm, parallel)
- ***Keep Them Short*** "Eat Mor Chikin" for Chick-fil-A.

Writing Styles

Writing in brand communication can be formal or informal, personal or impersonal—and it is uses all possible types of media. We'll discuss three types of promotional writing in this chapter—advertising, public relations, and direct response. All have some things in common, but their stylistics vary tremendously.

Photo: Courtesy of BU AdLab

SHOWCASE

The "Truck Stop" headline for D&A uses a twist to make the repair shop the hero. This ad was designed by students in the Boston University AdLab.

Advertising In almost all situations, advertising has to win its audience, no small task given that it usually competes in a cluttered environment and the audience is generally inattentive and uninterested. For that reason, the copy should be as simple as possible—think "Eat Mor Chikin." Chick-fil-A's single line of copy is succinct and single-minded, meaning that it has a clear focus and conveys only one selling point.

Every word counts because both space and time are expensive. Ineffective or overused words and phrases—such as *interesting*, *very*, *in order to*, *buy now and save*, *introducing*, and *nothing less than*—waste precious space. The challenge of writing verbal diamonds in 140 characters predates Twitter—the average outdoor board copy has always been around eight words.

Principle

Effective copy is succinct, single-minded, and tightly focused.

Ad copy is usually written in a conversational style using real people language. The legendary David Ogilvy, founder of the advertising agency that bears his name, Ogilvy & Mather, explained his view many years ago of advertising as conversation:

> I always pretend that I'm sitting beside a woman at a dinner party, and she asks me for advice about which product she should buy. So then I write down what I would say to her. I give her the facts, facts, facts. I try to make it interesting, fascinating, if possible, and personal—I don't write to the crowd. I try to write from one human being to another. . . . And I try not to bore the poor woman to death, and I try to make it as real and personal as possible.[4]

You can listen to David Ogilvy talking about his views on advertising on YouTube.

Copywriters try to write the way the target audience thinks and talks, often with personal language and direct address. For example, an ad for Trojan condoms makes a pointed argument on a touchy subject for its young, single-target audience. Combining headline with body copy, it reads as a dialogue:

> I didn't use one because I didn't have one with me.
> Get real.
> If you don't have a parachute, don't jump, genius.

Public Relations There are a variety of styles of writing used in public relations because that area uses so many different types of communication tools. Publicity, for example, is designed for news media and uses the basic stylistics of journalism. Corporate publications, such as newsletters and magazines, may be journalistic, but magazines may be more unconventional with features about employees and moving personal stories. Public relations also produces corporate videos and press releases—again, the press releases and video news releases are more like television news, but the corporate videos may function more like films with action and dramatic stories. Public relations departments also produce brochures that can vary from informational to technical, depending on their audience. And, you may be surprised to know that public relations departments also sometimes produce advertisements that may be created as part of a public relations campaign but also as corporate or advocacy point-of-view ads or a form known as *public service advertising*, which is developed in support of a good cause. So public relations writers also need to know the stylistics of advertising writing.

Direct Response There are also a number of media formats used in direct-response writing—everything from direct-mail letters and brochures to online social media and customer service or technical support. For that reason, the writing style can be more or less formal, depending on the target audience. On the other hand, the objective of many direct response efforts is to talk to individual customers or prospects using personalized messages (as much as possible) and direct address. It's about building a positive relationship with customers. Conversational style is more appropriate in the interactive forms that engage consumers one to one.

Strategy and Legal Imperatives

One thing that is common to all forms of brand communication is that it always has an objective and is designed to reach a particular audience. That means even beautiful writing also has to make the strategy sing. As Susan Gunelius, author of *Kick-Ass Copywriting in 10 Easy Steps*, explains, "Copywriting is about creating perceived needs among a specific audience."[5] If it doesn't move the audience and deliver on the objectives, then it's not effective copywriting. And that's true for all areas of promotional writing.

Not only does the writing have to be strategic, but the claims have to be tested and meet basic requirements of truth. The athletic shoe brand, Skechers, wound up paying $50 million to settle charges that its "toning shoes" language was using unfounded claims that the shoes would help consumers tone muscles and lose weight.[6] But sometimes it's hard for a writer to know what to do. Consider the following examples from the cereal market:

- Kellogg's was challenged by the Federal Trade Commission for advertising that children's attentiveness improved nearly 20 percent for those who ate Frosted Mini-Wheats compared to those who skipped breakfast. It's probably true that kids who eat breakfast pay more attention in school, but the commission said the numbers didn't support the claim.[7]
- Kellogg's Cocoa Krispies was challenged for bragging that the sugary cereal "helps support your child's immunity."[8]
- The Food and Drug Administration challenged Cheerios' long-running cholesterol-reduction claims: "You can lower your cholesterol 4 percent in six weeks." The agency allows the more general claim of reduced heart disease but doesn't allow specific rates of risk reduction, which it says is more appropriate for drugs. In defense of the Cheerios claim, General Mills responded that "the clinical study supporting Cheerios' cholesterol-lowering benefit is very strong." General Mills points to 25 years of clinical proof that Cheerios can help lower cholesterol and, therefore, is heart healthy.[9]

So are consumers being led astray by health claims on food packages, websites, and advertising? This is a public relations, as well as an advertising, problem. So what is a writer to do if a marketing director asks for health claims? What kind of support would you like to see before you are comfortable writing this kind of copy?

Types of Brand Communication Writing

We'll start with advertising copywriters because the other marketing communication areas also use advertising as part of their campaigns. Furthermore, many of the advertising writing practices apply to all forms of promotional writing.

The Ad Copywriter

The person who shapes and sculpts the words in advertising is called a **copywriter**. *Copy* is the text of an ad or the words people say in a commercial. Copywriters begin with the strategy and creative brief. Then, working with an art director and perhaps a creative director, the creative team searches for Big Ideas in the form of magic words and powerful visuals that translate the strategy into a message that is attention getting and memorable. A truly great Big Idea will come to life in the interaction between the words and pictures.

Photo: Courtesy of NYNEX

CLASSIC

The NYNEX ads feature puns based on Yellow Pages category headings. This ad, which is directed to media buyers, uses that same creative Big Idea with a visual pun on the heading "Amusement Devices" in the directory

For example, a long-running campaign for the NYNEX Yellow Pages illustrates how words and pictures work together to create a concept with a twist. The outdoor campaign used a visual play on words to illustrate some of the headings in its directory. Each pun makes sense when the visual is married with the heading from the directory, but neither the words nor the pictures would work on their own. One commercial in the series included three train engineers with overalls, caps, and bandannas sitting in rocking chairs in a parlor and having tea to illustrate the "Civil Engineering" category; a picture of a bull sleeping on its back illustrates the category "Bulldozing."

Although advertising is highly visual, words are crucial in four types of advertisements:

1. ***Complex*** If the message is complicated, particularly if it is making an argument, words can be more specific than visuals and can be read over and over until the meaning is clear.
2. ***High Involvement*** If the ad is for a high-involvement product, meaning the consumer spends a lot of time considering it, then the more information, the better. That means using extensive copy.
3. ***Explanation*** Information that needs definition and explanation, like how a new wireless phone works, is best delivered through words.
4. ***Abstract*** If a message tries to convey abstract qualities, such as justice and quality, words tend to communicate these concepts more easily than pictures.

Love of Language A successful copywriter is a savvy marketer and a literary master, sometimes described as a "killer poet." Many copywriters have a background in English or literature. They love words and search for the clever twist, the pun, the powerful description, the punch, the nuance, and the rhyme and rhythm of speech. They use words that whip and batter, plead, sob, cajole, and impress. They know the meanings, derivations, moods, and feelings of words and the reverberations and vibrations they create in a reader's mind.

A classic ad titled "The Wonderful World of Words" expresses this fascination. A house ad for the Marsteller business-to-business agency, it was written by Bill Marsteller, an advertising legend. He also was cofounder of public relations agency Burson-Marsteller. Here is an excerpt from this ad (see the copy from the entire ad on www.pearsonglobaleditions.com/Moriarty):

> Human beings come in all sizes, a variety of colors, in different ages, and with unique, complex and changing personalities.
>
> So do Words.
>
> There are tall, skinny words, and short, fat ones, and strong ones and weak ones, and boy words and girl words.
>
> For instance, title, lattice, latitude, lily, tattle, Illinois, and intellect are all lean and lanky. While these words get their height partly out of t's and l's and i's, other words are tall and skinny without a lot of ascenders and descenders. Take, for example, Abraham, peninsula and ellipsis, all tall.
>
> Here are some nice short-fat words: hog, yogurt, bomb, pot, bon-bon, acne, plump, sop, and slobber.

Real estate agents have also found that certain words affect a house sale. For example, words with selling power include "beautiful," "move-in condition," "landscaping," and "starter home." Words that either stall a sale or lead to lower prices include "motivated," "handyman special," and "good value."[10]

In addition to having an ear for the perfect phrase, copywriters listen to the way people talk and identify the tone of voice that best fits the target audience and the brand. An example comes from an all-copy ad for British Airlines. Set up like a poem with definite rhythm and alliteration, the copy block begins and ends with the airline's initials, but in between it lyrically interprets what "upgrading" to BA means to a passenger:

Be a guest not a passenger. We believe
The way you fly is
just as important
as where you fly.
It's not simply
about getting
a seat, it's about
getting service.
Not just food
but a meal. Not
just something
to watch but
something worth
watching. In short,
it's about upgrading
flying for every
passenger on
every plane. Now
there's an ide**A**.

Source: Courtesy of British Airways plc.

Like poets, copywriters may spend hours, even days, crafting a paragraph. After many revisions, others read the copy and critique it. It then goes back to the writer, who continues to fine-tune it. Copywriters must have thick skins, as there is always someone else reading their work, critiquing it, and asking for changes. Versatility is a common trait of copywriters. They can move from toilet paper to Mack trucks and shift their writing style to match the product and the language of their target audience.

As Professor Karen Mallia writes for this book,[11] copywriters can rejoice because the power of words remains strong even with new visual media. She explains, "The power of words doesn't rest in their volume, but in their clever combination. In fact, the fewer the words, the more important every single one becomes—and the more critical copywriting talent becomes." The skill, she explains, is to "distill a thought down to its most concise, precise, and unexpected expression. That's the reason the craft isn't about to disappear anytime soon, and great copywriters will always be in demand. Think 'Got Milk?' and 'Think different' and see true mastery of the craft. Each tagline is just two words but rich in meaning and power."

How to Write Effective Ad Copy The tighter the writing, the easier it is to understand and the greater its impact. Simple ads avoid being gimmicky, full of clichés, or too cute; they don't try too hard or reach too far to make a point. The following list summarizes some characteristics of effective copy:

- ***Succinct*** Use short, familiar words, short sentences, and short paragraphs.
- ***Specific*** Don't waste time on generalities. The more specific the message, the more attention getting and memorable it is.
- ***Personal*** Directly address your audience whenever possible as "you" rather than "we" or "they."
- ***Single Focus*** Deliver a simple message instead of one that makes too many points. Focus on a single idea and support it.
- ***Conversational*** Use the language of everyday conversation. The copy should sound like two friends talking to each other, so don't shy away from incomplete sentences, thought fragments, and contractions.
- ***Original*** To keep your copy forceful and persuasive, avoid stock advertising phrases, strings of superlatives, brag-and-boast statements, and clichés.
- ***News*** News stories are attention getting if they announce something that is truly newsworthy and important. (In contrast, Post Shredded Wheat ran an ad with the headline "Beware of New" in which it bragged about its original recipe that it had been using for 117 years.)
- ***Magic Phrases*** Phrases that grab and stick add power and memorability. In comparing its paper towels with the cheaper competition, Bounty asked, "Why use more when you can use less?"
- ***Variety*** To add visual appeal in both print and television ads, avoid long blocks of copy in print ads. Instead, break the copy into short paragraphs with subheads. In television commercials, break up monologues with visual changes, such as shots of the product, sound effects, and dialogue. The writer puts these breaks in the script, while the art director designs what they will look like.
- ***Imaginative Description*** Use evocative or figurative language to build a picture in the consumer's mind.

- ***A Story—with Feeling*** Stories are interesting and they have a structure that keeps attention and builds interest. But most importantly, they offer an opportunity to touch emotions. An ad about two brothers, one with cancer and the other who became inspired to become a radiation oncologist, told their story as they confronted the rare cancer and turned to the Memorial Sloan-Kettering Cancer Center to help defeat the illness.

To develop the right **tone of voice**, copywriters write to the target audience. If the copywriter knows someone who fits the audience profile, then he or she may write to that person as if they were in a conversation as the Trojan ad demonstrated. If the writer doesn't know someone, one trick is to go through a photo file, select a picture of the person who fits the description, and write to that person.

As the best example of a tone-of-voice ad, Molson Beer won awards for a commercial it created, called "The Rant," which mirrors the attitude of many Canadians. The commercial starts softly with an average Joe character disassociating himself from Canadian stereotypes. As he talks, he builds up intensity, and at the end he's in a full-blown rant ending with the line "My name is Joe, and I am Canadian" at the top of his voice. The commercial was so successful that it was played at events all around the country. You can watch it (you must watch it, as it's a wonderful piece of brand communication) on YouTube.

Humor is a type of writing that copywriters use to create entertaining, funny ads. The idea is that, if the humor works, the funny copy will lend a positive aura to a brand. It's particularly important to master funny writing if you are trying to reach an audience that's put off by conventional advertising, such as young males.

A great example of humor in sports promotion, for example, is the "It's not crazy, It's Sports" campaign for ESPN. In one commercial, an average-looking guy with the name Michael Jordan walks up to a counter, greets a guy with a Michael Jordan sign in an airport, and claims a restaurant reservation—always faced with the disappointment of people who expect a different Michael Jordan. Check out these commercials on YouTube. The "Practical Tips" feature provides some suggestions on how to use humor in brand communication.

The newest game in choosing a tone of voice is for voice response systems and brand avatars. If you were to talk with eBay or MTV, what would that brand's voice sound like? You get computerized voices when you call most companies, but some organizations have moved away from the easily recognized computer voice to a voice that better reflects the brand's personality. So think about the way a brand sounds to customers as another dimension of styling the tone of voice for a brand or company.

Grammar and Adese Copywriters also are attuned to the niceties of grammar, syntax, and spelling, although sometimes they will play with a word or phrase to create an effect, even if it's grammatically incorrect. The Apple Computer campaign for the Macintosh that used the slogan "Think different" rather than "Think differently" caused a bit of an uproar in Apple's school market. That's why copywriters think carefully about playing loose with the language even if it sounds right.[12]

There are also some things copywriters try to avoid. Meaningless words (*really*, *very*, *a lot*) or words made meaningless by overuse (*free*, *guarantee*, *opportunity*) are to be shunned in business writing and advertising.

Formulaic advertising copy is a problem that is so obvious that comedians parody it. This type of formula writing, called **adese**, violates all the guidelines for writing effective copy that we've been describing. It is full of clichés (as easy as pie), superlatives and puffery (best in class), stock phrases (buy now; free trial offer), and vague generalities (prices too low to advertise). For example, consider this copy; can you hear yourself saying something like this to a friend?

> Now we offer the quality that you've been waiting for—at a price you can afford. So buy now and save.

For more advertising clichés, check this website and vote for your favorite: www.the-top-tens.com/lists/most-overused-advertising-cliches.asp. The pompous overblown phrasing of many corporate statements doesn't work—it doesn't get attention, it's not memorable, and it doesn't

Practical Tips

So You Think You Want to Create a Funny Ad?

Fred Beard, *University of Oklahoma*

These parting words of British actor Sir Donald Wolfit should give anyone thinking of creating a funny ad second thoughts: "Dying is easy, comedy is hard."

Writing a funny, effective ad is especially hard when you consider that the ad must make people laugh at the same time it accomplishes an advertising objective—an increase in attention, recall, favorable attitudes, or an actual purchase. If you're still not deterred, keep in mind that funny ads work best when the following circumstances apply:

1. *Your goal is to attract attention.* Decades of research and the beliefs of advertising creative professionals match up perfectly on this one.
2. *Your goal is to generate awareness and recall of a simple message (think Aflac).* Most advertising creatives agree that humor works best to encourage recall of fairly simple messages, not complex ones.
3. *Your humor is related.* Did you ever laugh at an ad and forget what it was advertising? Creatives will tell you humor is a waste of money if it isn't related to a product's name, uses, benefits, or users.
4. *Your goal is to get the audience to like your brand.* Research shows people often transfer their liking of funny ads to the brand.
5. *You expect the audience to initially disagree with your arguments.* An ad's humor can distract people from arguments they disagree with, encouraging them to lower their perceptual defenses, accept the message, and be persuaded by it.
6. *Your target audience is men, especially young ones.* Creative professionals say younger male audiences respond best to humor, and research confirms men favor more aggressive humor.
7. *Your audience has a low need for cognition (NFC) or a high need for humor (NFH).* People with a low NFC don't enjoy thinking about things—they prefer emotional appeals like humor. People with a high NFH seek out humor. If your audience is low NFC and high NFH, you can't miss.
8. *You have good reasons for using the broadcast media.* By far, the majority of creatives believe humor works best in radio and television ads.
9. *You're advertising a low-involvement/low-risk product or service.* Academic researchers and creative professionals agree that funny ads seem to work best for routine purchases people don't worry about too much.
10. *Your humor is definitely funny.* Research shows if an ad's humor fails, not only will there be no positive outcomes, it could even produce negative responses.

get read. We call it **your-name-here copy** because almost any company can use those words and tack a signature on the end. For example, a broadband company named Covad started off an ad like this:

> Opportunity. Potential. These are terms usually associated with companies that have a lot to prove and little to show for it. But on rare occasion, opportunity can be used to describe a company that has already laid the groundwork, made the investments, and is well down the road to strong growth.

It's all just platitudes and clichés—and any company could use this copy. It isn't attention getting, and it doesn't contribute to a distinctive and memorable brand image. That's always a risk with company-centered copy, which doesn't say much that relates to the customer's needs, wants, and interests.

Another type of adese is **brag-and-boast copy**, which is "we" copy written from the company's point of view with a pompous tone, similar to the Covad ad. Consider a print ad by Buick. The ad starts with the stock opening, "Introducing Buick on the move." The body copy includes superlatives and generalities, such as "Nothing less than the expression of a new philosophy," "It strikes a new balance between luxury and performance—a balance which has been put to the test," and "Manufactured with a degree of precision that is in itself a breakthrough." Because people are so conditioned to screen out advertising, messages that use this predictable style are easy to ignore—or parody if you're a comedian.

There are great writers who, as David Droga, chairman of Droga5, says, "are skilled poets performing on a commercial canvas." Yet there is still adese, clichés, and brag-and-boast copy.

As Droga says, "Writing bad copy is easy, which is why the majority of advertising feels disposable."[13] Our objective here is to help you develop sensitivity to the good—and bad—practices of copywriting.

Public Relations Writing

In public relations, news stories are written for both internal corporate media, such as newsletters and magazines, and for external media, such as newspapers and television stations. News and feature stories may be written and distributed in a ready-to-publish format called a **news release**.

The primary criterion for a news story is newsworthiness. Editors judge news value based on such considerations as *timeliness* (something just happened or is about to happen), *proximity* (a local angle for local media), or *impact* (importance or significance). Announcements of new products, for example, are common publicity stories that are usually first presented internally in corporate publications and then follow in news releases for general media as well as specialized media where the product is relevant for a particular product category (groceries, medical procedures) or audience (mothers of infants, mountain bikers).

For news stories, the traditional journalism "five W" form is followed, which means the release should lead with information that answers questions of who, what, why, when, where, and how. In other words, the first sentence clearly states the facts in such a way that the focus, as well as the importance of the news, is immediately obvious.

Video news releases are distributed to broadcast media with footage that explains the story. University research into global warming, for example, may be accompanied by stories such as Artic research that drew core samples for thousands-year-old ice to determine if there are identifiable changes in the atmospheric markers locked into the ice cores. There is no way local media would be able to develop the video footage on its own, but the university can facilitate the story, recognizing that television reporting is dependent on visual explanations of such complex issues and questions.

Feature stories are less reliant on news and more focused on *human interest*—the story about an employee with an unusual hobby or who accomplished some kind of record. For example, stories about a United flight attendant who held a Guinness world record after a 63-year career appeared in corporate publications as well as national media (*New York Times*, among many others) and local papers in the community where the 84-year-old lived (*Boulder Daily Camera*) and in Hawaii, where he started his career (*Pacific Business News*). Although the formats may differ slightly, news and feature stories are written for and distributed to print and broadcast media as well as the Internet.

Direct-Response Writing

Direct-response messages are often longer and contain more explanation and detail than other forms of marketing communication. That is because if the message doesn't provide enough information and motivate the receiver to respond to it in some way, the message is wasted. To be persuasive, messages must contain clear comparisons or details about relevant decision factors, such as price, style, and convenience.

Because direct-response messages can be individually targeted, the more personalized the message, the better. For example, when a customer orders a book from Amazon.com, the company's system immediately suggests similar books. When one of the airlines sends out promotional offers to its frequent flyers, these messages often show the number of miles traveled in the past year and the number of rewards earned year to date. This is obviously a personalized message and definitely attracts more attention.

Most importantly, the message needs to counter consumers' reluctance to buy. Buying something through direct marketing has elements of risk because there is no salesperson or store to rely on for assistance and information. Most direct-response messages will include copy intended to put the buyer's mind at rest. Guarantees and warranties are important, but other strategies, such as testimonials, are used to reassure buyers about the company's reliability.

Writing for Various Media

Different types of media have different styles, restrictions, and audiences. Writers adjust their presentation to accommodate the stylistics differences of the medium.

Basics of Writing for Print Media

The two categories of copy that print uses are display copy and body copy (or text). **Display copy** includes all elements that readers see in their initial scanning. These elements—headlines, subheads, call-outs, and taglines—usually are set in larger type sizes than body copy and are designed to get attention and to stop the viewer's scanning. **Body copy** includes the elements that are designed to be read and absorbed, such as the text of the ad message and captions.

We have suggested that ad copy should be succinct, but some respected copywriters, such as David Ogilvy and Howard Gossage, were successful in writing long copy ads that intrigued their audiences, building high levels of interest. Gossage, a legendary San Francisco adman, played with humorous ideas as well as words. One ad for Eagle Shirtmakers asked, "Is this your shirt?" A following line said, "If so, Miss Afflerbach will send you your [Eagle logo picture] label." The idea, which is explained in the body copy, is that Eagle makes shirts for various shirtmakers, so you can contact "Miss Afflerbach" for the official logo to add to your shirt. If you're interested in more of Gossage's tongue-in-cheek ads, check a collection compiled by the LA Creative Club at www.lacreativeclub.com/gossage.html or get his book *The Book of Gossage* from the Copy Workshop (www.adbuzz.com/copyworkshop_catalog.pdf).

Photo: Courtesy of the Corporate Angel Network

The most common tools in the print writer's tool kit are listed here:

- ***Headline*** A phrase or a sentence that serves as the opening to the ad. It's usually identified by larger type or a prominent position, and its purpose is to catch attention. In the Corporate Angel Network ad, for example, the headline is "Cancer Patients Fly Free."
- ***Overlines and Underlines*** These are phrases or sentences that either lead into the headline or follow up on the thought in the headline. They are usually set in smaller type than the headline. The purpose of the **overline** is to set the stage, and the purpose of the underline is to elaborate on the idea in the headline and serve as a transition to the body copy. The **underline** leads into the body copy, as demonstrated in the DuPont ad: "Find food that helps prevent osteoporosis."
- ***Body Copy*** The text of the ad. It's usually smaller-sized type and written in paragraphs or multiple lines. Its purpose is to explain the idea or selling point.
- ***Subheads*** Used in longer copy blocks, **subheads** begin a new section of the copy. They are usually bold type or larger than the body copy. Their purpose is to make the logic clear to the reader. They are useful for people who scan copy, and they help them get a sense of what the copy says. The Corporate Angel Network ad uses subheads.
- ***Call-Outs*** **Call-outs** are sentences that float around the visual, usually with a line or arrow pointing to some specific element in the visual that they name and explain. For example, Johnson & Johnson once ran an ad that used call-outs as the main pieces of the body copy. The head read, "How to bathe a mommy." Positioned around a picture of a woman are short paragraphs with arrows pointing to various parts of her body. These call-outs describe the good things the lotion does for feet, hands, makeup removal, moisture absorption, and skin softening.

Photo: Courtesy of DuPont

- ***Captions*** A **caption** is a sentence or short piece of copy that explains what you are looking at in a photo or illustration. Captions aren't used very often in advertising because the visuals are assumed to be self-explanatory; however, readership studies have shown that, after the headline, captions have high readership.
- ***Taglines*** A short phrase that wraps up the key idea or creative concept that usually appears at the end of the body copy. It often refers back to the headline or opening phrase in a commercial. For example, see the line "Need a lift? Just give us a call. We'll do the rest" in the Corporate Angel Network ad.
- ***Call to Action*** This is a line at the end of an ad that encourages people to respond and gives information on how to respond. Both ads—Corporate Angel Network and DuPont—have response information: either an address, a toll-free phone number, an e-mail address, or Web address.

Display Copy The **headline** is a key element in print pieces. It conveys the main message so that people get the point of the message. It's important for another reason. The headline works with the visual to get attention and communicate the creative concept. This clutter-busting idea breaks through the competitive messages both in advertising and in surrounding articles. It comes across best through a picture and words working together, as the DuPont ad illustrates. The headline carries the theme ("To Do List for the Planet") and the underline ("Find food that helps prevent osteoporosis") makes a direct connection with the visual.

People who are scanning may read nothing more, so beyond getting attention, writers want to at least register a point with the reader. The point has to be clear from the headline or the combination of headline and visual. That's particularly true with outdoor boards. In advertising, researchers estimate that only 20 percent of those who read the headline go on to read the body copy, so if they take away anything from the ad, it needs to be clear in the headline.

Principle
Good headlines interrupt readers' scanning and grab their attention.

Headlines are often catchy phrases, but they also have to convey an idea and attract the interest of the audience. Tobler has won Effie awards for a number of years for its clever headlines and visuals. For Tobler's Chocolate Orange, the creative concept showed the chocolate ball being smacked against something hard and splitting into orange-like slices. The headline was "Whack and Unwrap." The next year, the headline was "Smashing Good Taste," which speaks to the candy's British origins and to the quirky combination of chocolate and orange flavors. The headline and visual also tell consumers how to "open" the chocolate orange into slices—by whacking it.

Agencies copytest headlines to make sure they can be understood at a glance and that they communicate exactly the right idea. Split-run tests (two versions of the same execution) in direct-mail pieces have shown that changing the wording of the headline while keeping all other elements constant can double, triple, or quadruple consumer response. That is why experts, such as ad legend David Ogilvy, state that the headline is the most important element.[14] A series of Good Housekeeping Seal of Approval ads use metaphors in the headlines to spark curiosity, such as "The Seal is like a push-up bra," followed by a copy line that explains that "it makes what you have a lot more noticeable."

Because headlines are so important, some general principles guide their development and explain the particular functions they serve:

- ***Target*** A good headline will attract only those who are interested—there is no sense in attracting people who are not in the market. An old axiom is "Use a rifle, not a shotgun." In other words, use the headline to tightly target the right audience. That's true in advertising as well as in other publications.
- ***Stop and Grab*** The headline must work in combination with the visual to stop and grab the reader's attention. An advertisement by Range Rover shows a photo of the car parked at the edge of a rock ledge in Monument Valley with the headline "Lots of people use their Range Rovers just to run down to the corner."
- ***Identify*** In all brand communication, the headline should identify or suggest the company, product, or brand. The Big Idea also should be evident in the headline. That's true in magazine and news releases as well as advertisements.
- ***Change Scanning to Reading*** The headline should lead readers into the body copy or text. For readers to move to the text, they have to stop scanning and start concentrating. This change in mind-set is the reason why only 20 percent of scanners become readers.

Photo: Good Housekeeping

Headlines can be grouped into two general categories: direct action and indirect action. **Direct-action headlines** are straightforward and informative, such as "Keep Your Body Strong," which is one in a series of "Healthy People" posters for Johnson & Johnson. The copy associates the health of your body with the health of nature. It closes with a line that pulls these two thoughts together: "Your body is just like nature. Keep it strong with daily physical activity and bring your planet to balance." Note how this structure of the message is consistent in the "Mind" and "Spirit" posters.

Direct-action headlines are highly targeted, but they may fail to lead the reader into the message if they are not captivating enough. **Indirect-action headlines** are not as selective and may not provide as much information but may be better at drawing the reader into the message and building a brand image.

Here are some common types of direct-action headlines:

- ***Assertion*** An assertion is a headline that states a claim or a promise that will motivate someone to try the product.
- ***Command*** A command headline politely tells the reader to do something.
- ***How-to Heads*** People are rewarded for investigating a product when the message tells them how to use it or how to solve a problem.
- ***News Announcements*** News headlines are used with new-product introductions but also with changes, reformulations, new styles, and new uses. The news value is thought to get attention and motivate people to respond.

Here are some common types of indirect-action headlines:

- ***Puzzles*** Used strictly for their curiosity and provocative power. Puzzling statements, ambiguities, surprises, and questions require the reader to examine the body copy to get the answer or explanation. The intention is to pull readers into the body copy.
- ***Associations*** These headlines use image and lifestyle to get attention and build interest.

A headline for the Motorola Talk About™ two-way radio demonstrates the problem of bad reception: "Help, I Think I Need a Tourniquet!" That headline then draws us into the underline, which makes the point that, if the reception isn't clear, the headline can sound like "Well, I think I'll eat a turnip cake!" This headline, which played with the similar sounds of words, and other curiosity-provoking lines are provocative and compel people to read on to find out the point of the message. Sometimes indirect headlines are called "blind headlines" because they give so little information. A **blind headline** is a gamble. If it is not informative or intriguing enough, the reader may move on without absorbing any product name information, but if it works as an attention getter, it can be effective.

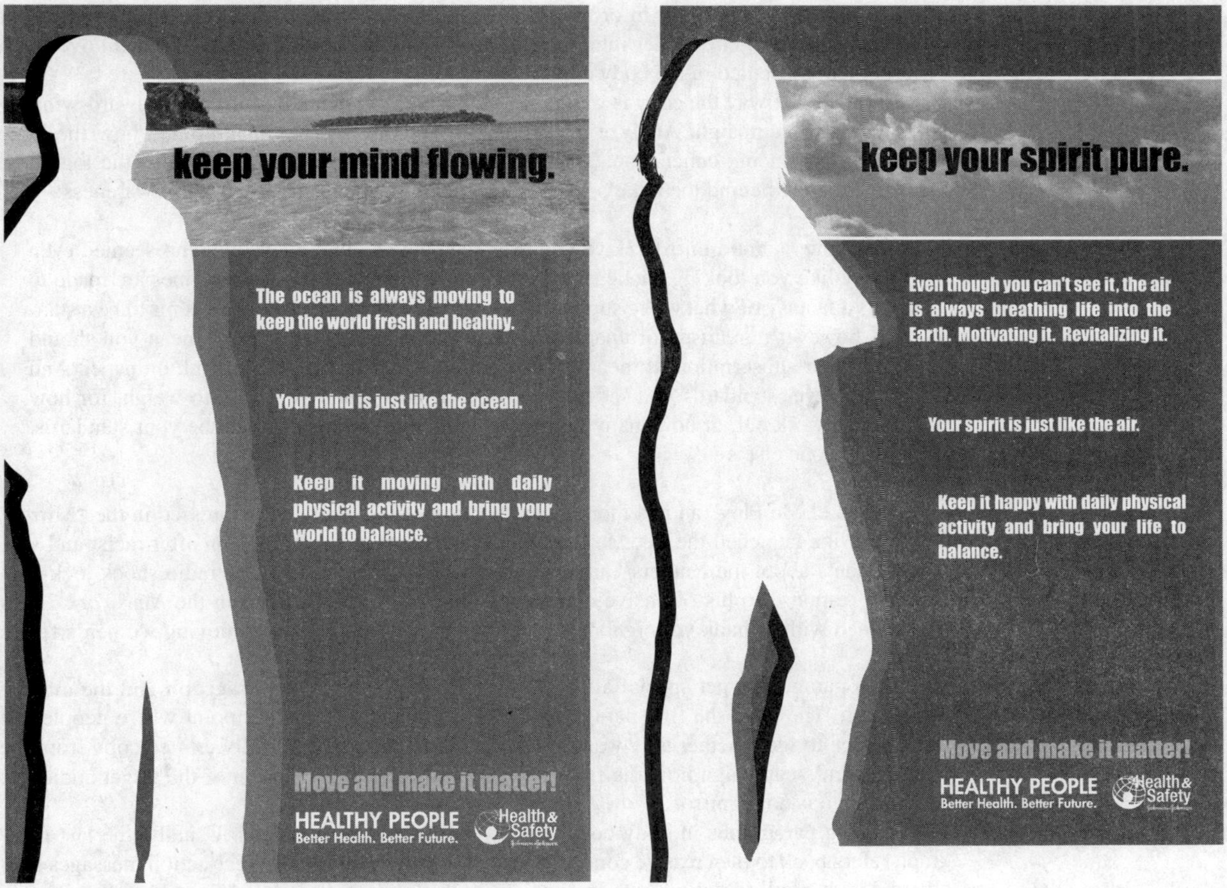

Photo: Courtesy of Johnson & Johnson

SHOWCASE

Michael Dattolico designed a series of posters for Johnson & Johnson to use in promoting its "Healthy People" initiative. These two advise you to keep "your mind flowing" and "your spirit pure."

A graduate of the University of Florida, Dattolico's work was nominated for inclusion in this book by Professor Elaine Wagner.

Next to the headline, captions have the second-highest readership. In addition to their pulling power, captions serve an information function. Visuals do not always say the same thing to every person; for that reason, most visuals can benefit from explanation. That's particularly true in images for news and feature stories. In addition to headlines, writers also craft the subheads that continue to help lure the reader into the body copy. Subheads are considered display copy in that they are usually larger and set in different type (bold or italic) than the body copy. Subheads are sectional headlines and are also used to break up a mass of "gray" type (or type that tends to blur together when one glances at it) into a large block of copy.

As we mentioned earlier, taglines are short, catchy phrases and particularly memorable phrases used at the end of an ad to complete or wrap up the creative idea. An ad from the Nike women's campaign used the headline "You are a nurturer and a provider. You are beautiful and exotic" set in an elegant script. The tagline on the next page used a rough, hand-drawn, graffiti-like image that said, "You are not falling for any of this."

Body Copy The body copy is the text of the message, and its primary role is to maintain the interest of the reader. It provides information, states the argument, summarizes the proof, and provides explanation. It is the information and, in the case of advertising, the persuasive heart of the message. You excite reader interest with the display elements, but you win them over with the argument presented in the body copy.

Consider the way the copy is written for this classic ad that comes from the award-winning Nike women's campaign. Analyze the argument the copywriter is making and how the logic flows to a convincing conclusion. The "A Matter of Principle" feature explains the logic and message strategy behind the Nike's women's campaign, which focuses on self-awareness:

> A magazine is not a mirror. Have you ever seen anyone in a magazine who seemed even vaguely like you looking back? (If you have, turn the page.) Most magazines are made to sell us a fantasy of what we're supposed to be. They reflect what society deems to be a standard, however unrealistic or unattainable that standard is. That doesn't mean you should cancel your subscription. It means you need to remember that it's just ink on paper. And that whatever standards you set for yourself, for how much you want to weigh, for how hard you work out, or how many times you make it to the gym, should be your standards. Not someone else's.

The "Let Me Play" ad is a more recent version of the sentiment expressed in the "Mirror" ad copy. Nike launched the Let Me Play Fund in support of this campaign after racist and sexist comments about the Rutgers University women's basketball team by radio shock jock Don Imus. In response to his offensive comments, Nike ran a full-page ad in the *New York Times* that opened with "Thank you, ignorance" followed by "Thank you for moving women's sports forward."

Two paragraphs get special attention in body copy: the **lead paragraph** and the **closing paragraph**. The lead, the first paragraph of the body copy, is another point where people test the message to see whether they want to read it. Notice in the beautifully crafted copy from the Nike women's campaign how the first lines work to catch the attention of the target audience: "A magazine is not a mirror."

Closing paragraphs in body copy and text serve several functions. Usually, the last paragraph refers back to the creative concept and wraps up the Big Idea. Direct-action messages usually end with a **call to action** with instructions on how to respond. A Schwinn bicycle ad that is headlined "Read poetry. Make peace with all except the motor car" demonstrates a powerful and unexpected ending, one that is targeted to its youthful audience:

> Schwinns are red, Schwinns are blue.
> Schwinns are light and agile too.
> Cars suck. The end.

An example of using a closing to contradict or confuse a point appeared in a 2013 New Balance advertisement that touted its dedication to a Made in America strategy, which it claims is a competitive advantage for its shoes. In small type at the very bottom of the full-page ad, the reader finds this statement: "1 of every 4 shoes we sell in the USA is made or assembled here." One would think this is a small claim for such a big ad.

Print Media Requirements The media in the print category—from newspapers and magazines to outdoor boards and product literature—all use the same copy elements, such as headlines and body copy. However, the way these elements are used varies with the objectives for using the medium. Most newspaper advertising copy, for example, is straightforward and informative. The writing is brief, usually just identifying the merchandise and giving critical information about styles, sizes, and prices.

Magazines offer better-quality ad production, which is important for brand image and high-fashion brand communication. Consumers may clip and file advertising and publicity articles that tie in with the magazine's special interest as reference information. This type of magazine story can be more informative and carry longer copy than do newspaper ads. Publicity writers and copywriters also take care to craft clever phrasing for the headlines and the body copy, which, as in the Nike women's campaign, may read more like poetry.

A Matter of Principle

The Principle of Truth

Jean Grow, *Marquette University*

It wasn't advertising. It was truth. We weren't selling a damn thing. Just the truth. And behind the truth, of course, the message was brought to you by Nike.

—Janet Champ, *Nike*

The creatives who produced early Nike women's advertising (1990–1997) were an amazing trio of women (Janet Champ, copywriter, and Charlotte Moore and Rachel Manganiello, art directors). Their work was grounded in the principle of truth, fueled by creativity, and sustained by nothing less than moxie.

"Nike in 1990 was not the Nike of today," Manganiello said. There was always this "political stuff about big men's sports. And, you know, (it was like we were) just kind of siphoning off money for women. So, in some ways we couldn't be as direct as we sometimes wanted to be." However, being direct and being truthful are not always the same thing. And truth for the Nike women's brand, and for themselves, was what these women aspired to.

Living the principle of truth and trusting their gut is what defined their work ethic and ultimately the women's brand. Moore explained, "I would posit that market research has killed a lot of advertising that was based on effective human dialogue, because it negates faith in intuition. Guts. Living with your eyes open."

To launch the women's brand within the confines of the male parent brand was no easy assignment. The creative team members began with their "gut" and with their "eyes open." They created campaign after campaign that moved the needle, but each time the approval process was a test of their principles, with meetings that were more than tinged with gender bias.

"We were almost always the only women in the room, and they killed the stuff because it scared them," said Champ. "But we always came back. And they let us do what we wanted, as long as we didn't 'sully' the men's brand . . . and as long as women's products kept flying off the shelves, they were happy."

As time went on, their instincts and principles earned them respect. According to Champ, "We told them, pretty much, that we believed in it and they had to run it and trust us, and they sighed, once again. They were soooooo tired of hearing me say that. And they ran it and they were *shocked* at what a nerve it touched."

In trusting their guts—in telling the truth—they created award-winning campaigns and exceeded marketing expectations. "As creative people," Moore said, "we had found our home and our voice, and we'd found the most fertile ground for the brand."

In the end, truth and the willingness to "trust your gut" are what make great brands and create fertile ground for others. When you consider the terrifically truthful Dove campaign, I suggest we owe a debt of gratitude to the women of early Nike women's advertising, who stood for truth nearly 20 years ago. I only wish we would see more truthful work. That, however, might take a truthful acknowledgment that women still make up less than a quarter of all advertising creative departments. In the end, truthful work depends on making a commitment to increasing the number of women in creative departments. To have guts. To live with one's eyes wide open.

This ad from the "Let Me Play" campaign ad reflects Nike's strategy of talking to women about sports in a way that reflects their attitudes and feelings.

Photo:

Directories that provide contact information, such as phone numbers and addresses, often carry display advertising. In writing a directory ad, copywriters advise using a headline that focuses on the service or store personality unless the store's name is a descriptive phrase, such as "Overnight Auto Service" or "The Computer Exchange." Complicated explanations don't work well in the Yellow Pages either because there is little space for such explanations. Putting information that is subject to change in an ad can become a problem because the directory is published only once a year.

Posters and outdoor boards are primarily visual, although the words generally try to catch consumers' attention and lock in an idea, registering a message. One of the most famous billboard campaigns ever was for a little shaving cream company named Burma Shave. The campaign used a series of roadside signs with catchy, cute, and sometimes poetic advertising copy aimed at auto travelers. Some 600 poems were featured in this classic campaign, which ran for nearly 40 years, from 1925 to 1963, until the national interstate system and fast roads made the signs obsolete.[15] (To read more about Burma Shave, go to www.eisnermuseum.org/_burma_shave/signs_of_the_times.html or check the collection at www.sff.net/people/teaston/burma.htm.) On the Burma Shave signs, the product was always a hero:

If you think
she likes
your bristles
walk bare-footed
through some thistles
Burma Shave

My job is
keeping faces clean
And nobody knows
de stubble
I've seen
Burma Shave

More recently, the city of Albuquerque used the Burma Shave format to encourage drivers to reduce their speeds through a construction zone. Today, a construction zone is about the only place where traffic moves slowly enough to use a billboard with rhyming copy:

Through this maze of machines and rubble
Driving fast can cause you trouble
Take care and be alert
So no one on this road gets hurt.

In contrast to the Burma Shave signs, the most important characteristic of writing for outdoor boards is brevity. Usually, a single line serves as both a headline and product identification. Often the phrase is a play on words. A series of black-and-white billboards in the Galveston–Houston area, recruiting priests for the Roman Catholic diocese, features a Roman collar with witty wording, such as "Yes, you will combat evil. No, you don't get to wear a cape." Others are more thoughtful: "Help wanted. Inquire within yourself." The copy must catch attention and be memorable. For example, a billboard for Orkin pest control showed a package wrapped up with the word "Orkin" on the tag. The headline read, "A little something for your ant."

An effective poster is also built around a creative concept that marries the words with the visual. For the Coffee Rush chain, Karl Schroeder created a series of posters to change consumers' perceptions that the shop was merely a drive-through for fast, cheap coffee. Schroeder's team did this by promoting a line of cold drinks with captivating names such as Mango Guava and Wild Berry.

Sometimes called **collateral materials** because they are used in support of a campaign, product literature—brochures, pamphlets, flyers, and other materials—provides details about a product, company, or event. They can be as varied as hang tags in new cars or bumper stickers. Taco Bell's little messages on its tiny taco sauce packages are an example of clever writing in an unexpected place with messages like "Save a bun, eat a taco" and "My other taco is a chalupa."

Typically, product literature is a heavy copy format or at least a format that provides room for explanatory details along with visuals; the body copy may dominate the piece. For a pamphlet with folds, a writer must also consider how the message is conveyed as the piece is unfolded. These pieces can range from a simple three-panel flyer to a glitzy multipage, full-color brochure.

Photo: © 2004 Register-Guard. All rights reserved. Courtesy of Coates Kokes

SHOWCASE

These posters for the Coffee Rush group of small, drive-through coffee shops, told newcomers that Coffee Rush sold more than just "a cup of joe." The copy, which had to be simple to be read by people in a car, was designed to tease people into tasting these fun drinks.

These posters were contributed by Karl Schroeder, a graduate of the University of Oregon. Formerly a copywriter at Coates Kokes in Portland, Oregon, he is now a senior writer/editor at Nike. He was nominated by Professor Charles Frazer, University of Oregon.

Radio Messages and How to Write Them

Ads and announcements that are broadcast on either radio or television are usually 15, 30, or 60 seconds in length, although 10- and 15-second spots may be used for brand reminders or station identification. This short length means that the message must be simple enough for listeners to grasp yet intriguing enough to prevent viewers from switching the station. That's why creativity is important to create clutter-busting messages that break through the surrounding noise and catch the listener's attention.

Radio is pervasive in that it surrounds many of our activities, but it is seldom the listener's center of attention and is usually in the background. Because radio is a transitory medium and listeners are often in the car or doing something else, the ability of the listener to remember facts (such as the name of the organization, addresses, and phone numbers) is difficult. That's why writers repeat the key points of identification information, such as a phone number or address. Radio urges the copywriter to reach into the depths of imagination to create a clutter-busting idea that grabs the listener's attention or a catchy tune that can be repeated without being irritating.

Radio's special advantage, referred to as **theater of the mind**, is that in a narrative format the story is visualized in the listener's imagination. Radio writers imagine they are writing a play that will be performed before an audience whose eyes are closed. The writer has all the theatrical tools of voices, sound effects, and music but no visuals. How the characters look and where the scene is set come from their listeners' imaginations.

As an example of theater of the mind, consider a now-classic commercial written by humorist Stan Freberg for the Radio Advertising Bureau. The spot opens with an announcer explaining that Lake Michigan will be drained and filled with hot chocolate and a 700-foot mountain of whipped cream. The Royal Canadian Air Force will fly overhead and drop a 10-ton maraschino cherry, all to the applause of 25,000 screaming extras. The point is that things that can't be created in real life can be created by radio in the imagination of listeners.

The Radio Advertising Bureau has used the slogan "I saw it on the radio" to illustrate the power of radio's ability to evoke rich images in the listener's mind. Research indicates that the use of imagery in radio leads to high levels of attention and more positive general attitudes toward brand messages.[16] Even though we're talking about imagery, it is produced by a writer's masterful use of the tools of audio.

Tools of Radio Writing In radio advertising, the tools are the audio elements the copywriter uses to craft a commercial: voice, music, and sound effects. The most important element in radio is the human voice, which is heard in songs, spoken dialogue, and announcements. Most commercials use an announcer either as the central voice or at the closing to wrap up the product identification. The voices the writer specifies help listeners "see" the personalities in the brand message. Dialogue uses character voices to convey an image of the speaker: a child, an old man, an executive, and so forth. Writers specify voices for commercials based on the evocative qualities they contribute to the message. Chicago radio announcer Ken Nordine's voice was once described as sounding like warm chocolate; singer Ray Charles was described as having a charcoal voice.

Two of the most famous jingles ever written used children singing about Oscar Mayer meats. The "Bologna Song" used a little child singing: "My bologna has a first name, it's O-S-C-A-R. My bologna has a second name, it's M-A-Y-E-R." The second big hit also used kids singing: "Oh I wish I were an Oscar Mayer Weiner. That is what I'd truly like to be. 'Cause if I were an Oscar Mayer Wiener, everyone would be in love with me."

In radio, speaking style should match the speech of the target audience. Each group has its own way of speaking, its own phrasing. Teenagers don't talk like eight-year-olds or 50-year-olds. Spoken language is different from written language. We talk in short sentences, often in sentence fragments and run-ons. We seldom use complex sentences in speech. We use contractions that would drive an English teacher crazy. Slang can be hard to handle and sound phony, but copy that picks up the nuances of people's speech sounds natural.

Principle
Radio copywriters try to match their dialogue to the conversational style of the target audience.

Music is as important as the voice in radio writing. Similar to movie scriptwriters, radio writers have a sense of the imagery of music and the role it plays in creating dramatic effects. Music can be used behind the dialogue to create mood and establish the setting. Any mood, from that of a circus to a candlelit dinner, can be conveyed through music. The primary use of music is a **jingle**, which is a commercial in song, like the Oscar Mayer songs. Radio writers understand the interplay of catchy phrases and "hummable" music to create little songs that stick in our minds. Anything consumers can sing along with helps them remember and get involved with the message.

Organizations can have a piece of music composed for a commercial or borrow it from previously recorded songs. Numerous music libraries sell *stock music* that is not copyrighted. In addition to customer-made jingles, many *jingle houses* create "syndicated" jingles made up of a piece of music sold to several different local advertisers in different markets around the country.

One of the most famous jingles of all time was the song "I'd Like to Teach the World to Sing" produced for Coca-Cola in 1969 by its agency, McCann-Erickson. A great example of a jingle that was an instant hit worldwide, it later was recorded as a pop song without the Coke reference and sold millions of copies. Called "Hilltop," the television commercial shows young people singing "I'd like to buy the world a Coke" on a hilltop in Italy. Surveys continue to identify it as one of the best commercials of all time. It is still run by Coke on special occasions, and the sheet music continues to sell more than 30 years after the song was first written. You can read more about this famous commercial on www.thecoca-colacompany.com/heritage/cokelore_hilltop.html. Click through to "Hilltop" to hear the commercial.

Sound effects are the icing on the radio message. The sound of seagulls, automobile horns honking, and the cheers of fans at a stadium all create images in our minds to cue the setting and drive the action. The classic Freberg "Lake Michigan" commercial for the Radio Advertising Bureau used **sound effects** to punctuate the imaginary event. The point is that radio can be more powerful than television in creating images in your mind. Sound effects can be original, but more often they are taken from *sound-effects libraries* available on CDs or online.

The Practice of Radio Writing The following guidelines for writing effective radio commercials address the distinctive characteristics of radio messages:

- ***Keep It Personal*** Radio has an advantage over print—the human voice. The copy for radio ads should use conversational language—as if someone is "talking with" the consumer rather than "selling to" the consumer.
- ***Speak to Listeners' Interests*** Radio offers specialized programming to target markets. Listeners mostly tune in to hear music, but talk radio is popular, too. There are shows on health, pets, finance, politics—whatever interests people. Writers design commercials to speak to that audience interest and use the appropriate music and tone of voice.
- ***Wake Up the Inattentive*** Most people who are listening to the radio are doing something else at the same time, such as jogging, driving, or fixing breakfast. Radio messages are designed to break through and capture attention in the first three seconds with sound effects, music, questions, commands, or something unexpected.
- ***Make It Memorable*** To help the listener remember what you are selling, ads should mention the name of the product emphatically and repeat it. An average of three mentions in a 30-second commercial and five mentions in a 60-second commercial are recommended, as long as the repetition is not done in a forced and/or annoying manner. Copywriters use taglines and other key phrases to lock the product in consumers' memories.
- ***Include Call to Action*** The last thing listeners hear is what they tend to remember, so writers make sure the product is it. In radio, that's particularly important since there is no way to show a picture of the product or the label. Those last words communicate the Big Idea in a way that serves as a call to action and reminds listeners of the brand name.
- ***Create Image Transfer*** Radio messages are sometimes designed to link to a television commercial. Called **image transfer**, the visuals from the television version are re-created in a listener's mind by the use of key phrases and ideas from the television commercial.

Writers working on a radio commercial use a standard **radio script** format to write the copy to certain time blocks—all of the words, dialogue, lyrics, sound effects, instructions, and descriptions. The instructions and descriptions are to help the producer tape the commercial so that it sounds exactly as the copywriter imagined. The script format usually has the source of the audio written down the left side, and the content—words an announcer reads, dialogue, and description of the sound effects and music—on the right. The instructions and descriptions—everything that isn't spoken—are typed in all-capital letters. You may also see a script written in paragraph form with the instructions in parentheses.

Television Messages and How to Write Them

Television writers understand that it is the moving image—the action—that makes television so much more engaging than print. The challenge for the writer is to fuse the images with the words to present not only a creative concept but also a story, as the Frontier Airlines commercials do so well.

One of the strengths of television is its ability to reinforce verbal messages with visuals or reinforce visuals with verbal messages. As Ogilvy's Peter Hochstein explains,

> The idea behind a television commercial is unique in advertising. The TV commercial consists of pictures that move to impart facts or evoke emotion, and selling words that are not read but heard. The perfect combination of sight and sound can be an extremely potent selling tool.[17]

Principle
Television's ability to touch our emotions and to show us things—to demonstrate how they look and work—make television highly persuasive.

Viewers watching a program they enjoy often are absorbed to a degree only slightly less than experienced by people watching a movie in a darkened theater. Storytelling is one way that copywriters can present action in a television message more powerfully than in other media. Effective television messages are written to maximize the dramatic aspects of moving images and storytelling, as the "A Matter of Practice" feature explains about "the emotional pivot" in a story.

Dramatic stories with high emotion, as well as demonstrations, are just a few of the techniques used in television advertising. Here are more:

- ***Action*** Good television messages use the effect of action and motion to attract attention and sustain interest. Torture tests, steps, and procedures are all actions that are easier to present on television than in print.
- ***Demonstration*** Seeing is believing. Believability and credibility—the essence of persuasion—are high because we believe what we see with our own eyes.

A Matter of Practice

How the Emotional Pivot Works in a Story

Charles Young, *Founder and CEO, Ameritest*

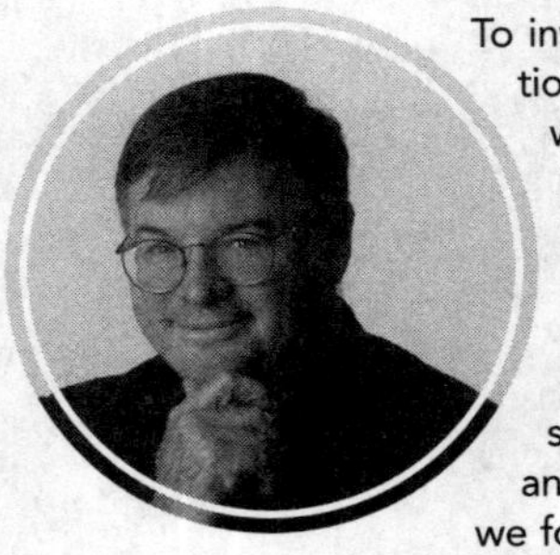

To investigate the power of emotional engagement in a video, we studied the structure of a six-minute film of Susan Boyle, who turned in a surprising 2009 performance on *Britain's Got Talent.* Employing the same research techniques we use to analyze television commercials, we found that this YouTube video is built on a standard dramatic structure that we commonly see in advertising, one that we call an "emotional pivot." (You can watch it on YouTube.)

Good storytellers understand that with a pivot structure, the emotional impact is particularly strong because the valence of the emotion changes from initially negative to positive, which creates the strongest possible contrast between what the audience feels at the beginning of the story and what they feel at the end.

Here's how we identified the emotional pivot in the *Britain's Got Talent* video featuring a rather frumpy Scottish woman named Susan Boyle. Using a photo sort of still frames from the video, we track the flow of emotion throughout the six-minute video. In the graph, you can see strong negative emotions at the beginning of the video shown with strong spikes in the red line. This reflects the entrance onstage of this rather overweight and middle-aged Scottish woman. The rolled eyes and sideway glances of disbelief from the lead judge Simon Cowell reinforce this negative first impression.

Then toward the middle, the green (positive) line begins to rise rapidly, and the red (negative) line fades away as emotions turn, or pivots, on frame 18 as Susan begins to sing. As her beautiful voice fills the room, the judges and the audience are transformed.

Finally, positive emotions rise to a sustained, high volume of intensity for the rest of the video. It ends with the entire studio audience—and even one of the judges—on their feet cheering wildly.

At the pivot point—the boundary between these two states of emotion—lies the most dramatic, brand-creating moment of this piece of film. So in frame 18, when Susan first begins to sing, we are able to pinpoint the actual moment of a birth of a new star—or brand, in advertising terms.

In storytelling, this is the moment when a gap opens up in the mind of an audience—a break between what the audience expected to see and what just happened. The mind of the audience is forced to turn in a new direction. As their personal interpretations of the event are recalculated, audience members build a new mental model of realty to make sense of what they are seeing. Unexpectedly, the ugly duckling just turned into a swan!

Interestingly, when we tested a shorter version of the video with the "negative setup" removed, we found the emotional response to the singing was just as positive, but when we interviewed respondents, it was obvious that something was lost. This shorter version was much less likely to be rated as "unique," "involving," "entertaining," or "inspirational." In other words, changing the narrative to an uninterrupted flow of positive emotions diminished the impact. Ironically, the Susan Boyle story would be different—and she might not be a star—without Simon Cowell's display of cynicism at the beginning.

You can watch this video on YouTube. Search for "Susan Boyle I dreamed a Dream."

Flow of Emotion®

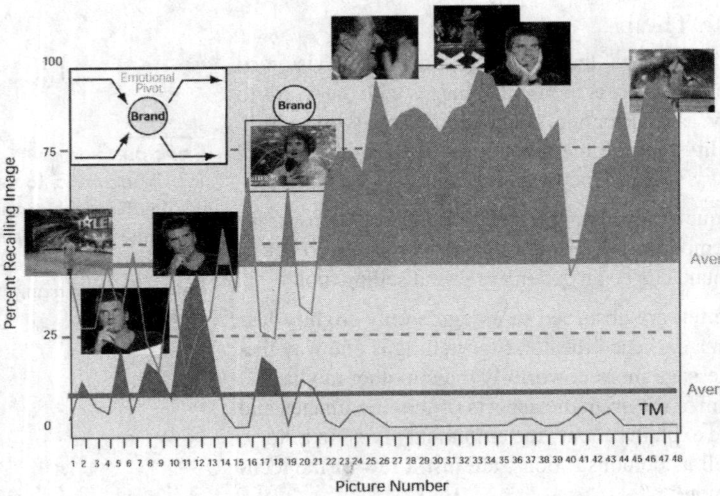

The Susan Boyle story is a classic example of an emotional pivot from negative to positive emotions.

Photo: Young, Charles, *The Birthplace of a Brand*, White Paper, exhibit 1. Reprinted with permission of Charles Young

- ***Storytelling*** Television is our society's master storyteller because of its ability to present a plot and the action that leads to a conclusion in which the product plays a major role.
- ***Emotion*** The ability to touch the feelings of the viewer makes television commercials entertaining, diverting, amusing, and absorbing. Real-life situations with all their humor, anger, fear, pride, jealousy, and love come alive on the screen.

Tools of Television Writing Television writers have two primary tool kits: visual and audio. Both words and pictures are designed to create exactly the right impact. Because of the number of visual and audio elements, as well as the many ways they can be combined, a television message is one of the most complex of all brand communication forms. It is also an ideal form for storytelling.

When we watch a commercial, we are more aware of what we're seeing than anything else. Copywriters keep in mind that visuals and motion, the silent speech of film, should convey as much of the message as possible. Likewise, emotion, which is the effect created by storytelling, is expressed convincingly in facial expressions, gestures, and other body language. Because television is theatrical, many of the copywriter's tools, such as characters, costumes, sets and locations, props, lighting, optical and computerized special effects, and on-screen graphics, are similar to those you would use in a play, television show, or movie.

As in radio, the three audio elements are music, voices, and sound effects, but they are used differently in television commercials because they are connected to a visual image. The writer may have an announcer speak directly to the viewer or engage in a dialogue with another person who may or may not be on camera. The writer writes the words they will say and blocks out on paper how this "talk" happens. A common manipulation of the camera–announcer relationship is the **voice-over**, in which an announcer who is not visible describes some kind of action on the screen. Sometimes a voice is heard **off camera**, which means you can't see the speaker and the voice is coming from the side, behind, or above.

Dialogue, both in radio and on television, is an interesting challenge for writers who try to keep the words natural and the interaction interesting. In the Frontier Airlines talking animals commercials, for example, the repartee between the characters is as important to the message as the words themselves. Note how the dialogue between Jack the Rabbit and Larry the Lynx bounces back and forth in the "Leather Seats" commercial. Also note the brand identity text in the middle.

Music is also important. Sometimes it is background; at other times, the song is the focus of the message. In recognition of the role of music in advertising, Universal Music released a CD called "As Seen on TV: Songs from Commercials," a collection of tunes that have become popular—or resurrected—thanks to their use in television commercials. Included among the 20 songs are "Mr. Roboto" by Styx, "Lust for Life" by Iggy Pop, and "Got to Give It Up" by Marvin Gaye. All of these songs have been used effectively in a television commercial. Clash's "London Calling" song became the theme for a highly successful special event for Jaguar.

Other creative tools that support the story line are the setting, casting, costumes, props, and lighting—all of which the writer must describe in the script. The setting, or **set**, is where the action takes place. It can be something in the studio, from a simple tabletop to a constructed set that represents a storefront or the inside of a home, or it can be a computer creation layered behind the action. Video shot outside the studio is said to be filmed **on location**, which means the entire crew and cast are transported somewhere away from the studio.

For many brand messages, the most important element is the people, who are called **talent**. Finding the right person for each role is called **casting**. People can be cast as follows:

- ***Announcers*** (either onstage or offstage), presenters, or introducers
- ***Spokespersons*** (or "spokes-animals," such as the Frontier talking animals)
- ***Character types*** (old woman, baby, or police officer)
- ***Celebrities,*** such as Michael Phelps and Catherine Zeta-Jones

Costumes and makeup can be an important part of the story depending on the characterizations in the commercial. Of course, historical stories need period costumes, but modern scenes may also require special clothing, such as golf outfits, swimsuits, or cowboy boots. Makeup may be important if you need to change a character from young to old. The writer must specify all of these details in the script. The director usually manipulates the lighting, but the writer might specify

GREY
Famously effective since 1917

Fade in on *Jack the Rabbit* pulling into the gate.

Jack: I'll tell ya Larry, the tarmac never looked better.

He sees his pal *Larry the Lynx* and the two banter throughout . . .

Larry: I'll say.

Jake: New planes, new cities, new leather seats.

Larry: Pretty exciting stuff, huh?

Jake: Hey Larry, what's leather made from?

Larry: Cowhide

Jack: Ohhhh—so *that's* why there are no cows on the tails of our planes.

Larry: It's creepy.

Cut to supers . . .

MUSIC: Frontier music under staged

SUPER: New planes. New cities. New leather seats.

SUPER: A whole different animal. FRONTIER

Cut back to the tarmac for a quick button . . .

The "moment of silence" is ridiculously short . . .

. . . and they quickly turn their attention toward lunch

Larry: Wanna do a moment of silence for cows?

Jack: Sure

SFX: *Slight pause . . .*

Jack: That's enough—wanna grab a burger?

Larry: I'm starving.

Frontier's "Leather Seats" commercial, which is part of the long-running "A Whole Different Animal" campaign, was carefully planned to deliver the brand personality conveyed through its menagerie of high-flying characters.

Source: Courtesy of Frontier Airlines and Grey Worldwide.

special lighting effects in the script. For example, you might read "Intense bright light as though reflected from snow" or "Light flickering on people's faces as if reflecting from a television screen."

Writers might also specify the commercial's **pace**—how fast or slowly the action progresses. Some messages are best developed at a languid pace; others work better when presented at an upbeat, fast pace. Research has found that the pace of television commercials has been steadily getting faster since the mid-20th century. Why do you suppose that might be?

Planning the Television Message Writers must plan how long the message will be, what shots will appear in each scene, what the key visual will be, and where and how to shoot the commercial. Other key decisions the writer must consider are the length, number of scenes, and key frames. The common lengths of television commercials and announcements are 10, 15, 20, 30, and 60 seconds. The 10-, 15-, and 20-second lengths are used for reminders and product or station identification. The 60-second spot, which is common in radio, has almost disappeared in television because of the increasing cost of airtime. The most common length for a television announcement is 30 seconds.

A commercial is planned in **scenes**—segments of action that occur in a single location. A scene may include several shots from different angles. A 30-second commercial usually is planned with four to six scenes, but a fast-paced commercial may have many more. Because television is a visual medium, the message is often developed as a **key visual** that conveys the heart of the concept. The **key frame** is the shot that sticks in the mind and becomes the image viewers remember when they think about the commercial.

A Day in the Life

A Copywriter's View of Television Production

Lara Mann, *Associate Creative Director at mcgarrybowen, Chicago*

As a copywriter at an ad agency, a typical day for me involves a few meetings, a little presenting, a fair amount of concepting, some writing, and more than one trip to the coffee bar. Some of it's challenging. All of it's exciting. But once I've sold a campaign to a client, that's when the real fun begins.

Just between you and me, when I first started out, I didn't even know shooting television was part of my job description. They never covered that in school. Director reels? Location scouting? Huh?

Now that I've been around the block (on a tricycle), I can confidentially tell you that coming up with ideas is only half of a copywriter's job. The members of the creative team have to shepherd their idea through all stages of production to make sure their vision is fully realized—or something like that.

First, we're assigned a producer, who will send us director's reels. We pick a director, pack our bags, and grab the next plane out of town. Once on location, we spend the next few days scouting scenes, casting the talent, selecting wardrobe, finding props, and reviewing the director's shooting boards. These tend to be long days, followed by long nights at the hotel watering hole.

Then the shoot begins. My partner and I will either sit in "video village" along with our client and account team or off to the side with our own little monitor so we can keep track of the action. Should we see an issue (and there are sure to be many), we grab the ear of our producer, who will then tell the line producer, who will then tell the director. This is called the "chain of command" and helps the shoot run smoothly.

After the shoot has wrapped (yes, someone will yell, "That's a wrap!"), we pack up and head back to town, where we will then begin putting the footage together with the help of a talented editor. And so ends another exciting day in the world of advertising.

That's a wrap.

Lara Mann, a graduate of the University of Florida, previously worked for DraftFCB in Chicago before moving to mcgarrybowen. She was nominated by Professor Elaine Wagner.

Writers need to answer many questions when planning a television spot. How much information should there be in the commercial or announcement? Should the action be fast or slow? How intrusive should it be to catch people's attention?

Two documents are used to plan commercials: a television script prepared by the writer and a storyboard drawn by the art director. Similar to a radio script, a **television script** is the written version of the message. It contains all the words, dialogue, lyrics, instructions, and descriptions of the details we've been discussing—sets, costumes, lighting, and so forth. For television, the script is written in two columns, with the audio on the right and the video on the left.

The key to the structure of a television script is the relationship between the audio and the video. The dialogue is typed as usual, but the instructions and labels are generally typed in all-capital letters. The video part of the script includes descriptions of characters, actions, and camera movements. Sometimes the script is in a two-column format with the video instructions on the left and the audio on the right.

A **storyboard**, which is a visual plan or layout of the commercial, is drawn (by hand or on the computer) to show the number of scenes, composition of the shots, and progression of the action. The script information usually appears below the key images. Its purpose is to guide the filming. A **photoboard** uses photographic stills instead of art to illustrate the progression of images. It's created from the still photos or frames from the filming and is used to present to clients. (See the Frontier "Leather Seats" commercial.)

The Internet and How to Write for It

The Internet is more interactive than any other mass medium. Not only do viewers initiate the contact, but they can respond as well. This makes the Internet more like two-way communication, and that's a major point of difference from other advertising forms. As a result, the Internet writer is challenged to attract people to the site and to manage a dialogue-based communication experience. In addition to targeting messages to audiences, organizations have to be prepared to listen and respond to those audiences. Social media writers also master the psychology of influence and understanding how to get people talking,

> ***Principle***
> To write great copy for the Web, copywriters must think of it as an interactive medium and open up opportunities for dialogue with the consumer.

It is true, however, that there are forms of Internet advertising that look like more traditional ads, such as banners (usually across the top or down the side of the page), sidebar ads, and pop-ups. E-mail and video ads, as well as mobile ads on smart phones, all require variations of traditional copywriting techniques. Most of these formats end with a link to the sponsor's website where the user can participate in a more interactive brand experience.

In this complicated, fast-changing medium, there aren't a lot of rules. In fact, marketing communication that uses text messaging and Twitter may even throw out the rules of spelling with vowel-free words. Twitter has its own microsyntax that is moving into popular culture with codes like "LOL," "OMG," and "#," the hashtag sign that means a searchable topic.[18] Internet writers write everything from catchy phrases for banners to copy that works like traditional advertisements, brochures, or catalogs.

Websites The challenge for Internet writers is to understand the user's situation and design messages that fit their needs and interests. However, the Web is an information medium, and users come to it, in some cases, for reference information—formats that look a lot like catalogs or even encyclopedias. Corporate or organizational websites are designed to provide information as well as image cues, so strategies that organize information and package it for easy accessibility are important. **Key words** are used to help *visitors* or *surfers* (rather than readers, listeners, or viewers) search for the site online as well as within the site for the information they need.

Creativity is also valued both to entice visitors and to keep them actively involved with the site. For example, the previously mentioned "Don't Mess with Texas" antilitter website invites visitors into the campaign with testimonials, letters, special events, and involvement programs. It uses colorful animation to create action and spark interest. The language reflects the tough-talking slogan. For example, one section asks, "Who wants to live in a pig sty?" and "Why swim in an ashtray?" Check it out at http://dontmesswithtexas.org.

Banners The most common form of online advertising is a small **banner** containing a little bit of text, images that grab attention, and perhaps motion (**animation**). Banners in this small format have to be creative to stand out amidst the clutter on a typical Web page, and, similar to outdoor advertising, they have to grab the surfer's attention with few words. Effective banners arouse the interest of the visitor, who is often browsing through other information on the computer screen. It is critical to make the site easy to navigate.

Sometimes banners provide brand reminder information only, like a billboard, but they usually also invite viewers to click on the banner to link to an ad or the advertiser's home page. The effectiveness of such efforts is monitored in part by the number of **click-throughs**. One mistake copywriters sometimes make, however, is to forget to include the company name or brand in the banner or ad. Surfers should be able to tell immediately what product or brand the banner is advertising. Effective banner ads satisfy the need for entertainment, information, and context (a link to a product) and often use promotional incentives, such as prizes or gifts, to motivate visitors to click through to the sponsor's website[19] to drive action.

Internet Ads Similar in some ways to traditional advertising, Internet ads are designed to create awareness and interest in a product and build a brand image. In terms of creating interest, good copywriting works well in any medium, including the Internet. The "Ocean Speaks" ads in "The Inside Story" at www.pearsonglobaleditions.com/Moriarty illustrates how the same writing style can transfer from print to the Internet and maintain a consistent brand personality. The objective of this striking campaign for the scuba diving industry was to move people from print to the company's website. Art director Chris Hutchinson explains, "We created a campaign in the literal voice of the ocean. The Ocean irreverently compares itself to the dull world up above and invites people to come down for a visit. Instead of using traditional beauty shots of scuba diving, we commissioned surreal organic underwater scenes."

Copywriting Challenges

As discussed throughout this chapter, the copywriter's job is to find a memorable way to express the creative concept. All of a copywriter's talent will do no good if the audience cannot understand the "magic words." Understanding the words, as well as the creative idea, is particularly complicated in global brand communication.

Writing for a Global Brand

Language affects the presentation of the message. English is more economical than many other languages. This creates a major problem when the space for copy is laid out for English and one-third more space is needed for French or Spanish. However, English does not have the subtlety of other languages, such as Greek, Chinese, or French. Those languages have many different words for situations and emotions that do not translate precisely into English. Standardizing the copy content by translating the appeal into the language of the foreign market is fraught with possible communication blunders. It is rare to find a copywriter who is fluent in both the domestic and foreign language and familiar with the culture of the foreign market.

Headlines in any language often rely on humor, a play on words, or slang. Because these verbal techniques don't cross borders well, writers remove them from the international campaigns unless the meaning or intent can be re-created in other languages. For this reason, international campaigns are not literally translated word by word. Instead, a copywriter usually rewrites them in the second language. An ad for a Rome laundry shows how a poor translation can send the wrong message: "Ladies, leave your clothes here and spend the afternoon having a good time."

The major distinction in cross-cultural communication is between **high-context cultures**, in which the meaning of a message can be best understood when contained within contextual cues, and **low-context cultures**, in which the message can be understood as it stands.[20] In other words, in Japanese a word can have multiple meanings. Listeners or readers will not understand the exact meaning of a word unless they clearly understand the context in which the word is used. In contrast, English is a low-context language—most of its words have clearly defined meanings that are not highly dependent on the words surrounding them. Figure 9.1 lists cultures from the highest to lowest context, with

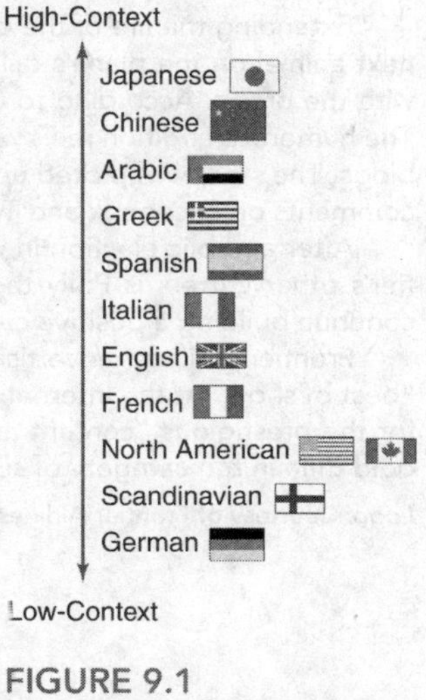

FIGURE 9.1
High- and Low-Context Cultures

Japanese being the highest-context culture. This model helps explain the difficulties of translating brand messages into other languages.

Experience suggests that the most reasonable solution to the language problem is to use bilingual copywriters who understand the full meaning of the English text and can capture the essence of the message in the second language. It takes a brave and trusting international creative director to approve copy that he or she doesn't understand but is assured is right. A **back translation** of the ad copy from the foreign language into the domestic one is always a good idea, but it seldom conveys a complete cultural interpretation.

The most recent announcement on the global stage is the opening up of the Internet to non-Roman letters, such as those used in Chinese, Korean, and Arabic. It's a challenge to develop translations for these languages so that a posting can be read in its original language as well as in Roman letter alphabets, but the technology is making that possible.

Looking Ahead

The most important enduring principle is that in a Big Idea, the meaning emerges from the way the words and images reinforce one another. We've explored the practices and principles of promotional writing. In the next chapter, we'll introduce the role of the art director and explain the important role of visual communication.

FrontierAirlines.com

It's a Wrap

And the Winner Is . . . Frontier

In the process of giving its fledgling airline a brand identity, Frontier Airlines sent an unmistakable message that airline advertising doesn't need to be stuffy. Talking and singing animals broke through the clutter demonstrating an important lesson: You can sell your audience and entertain them simultaneously, but accomplishing the client's business goals is central to success. The communication works not only because it delivers on the brand promise but also because customers like the airline more because of the campaign and are engaged enough with the Frontier brand to follow the stories of its cast of characters—and fly in its planes.

Over time, the animals and their quirky personalities made an emotional connection with would-be travelers. A campaign about sending an animal to a warm weather destination is much more fun and memorable than a plain-vanilla announcement that an airline now has a route to Mexico.

Extending the life of the campaign of these crazy and wild characters by letting consumers vote for the next animal on the plane's tail also brilliantly illustrates how consumers can get involved and stay engaged with the brand. According to Couzens, the results of the most recent campaign surpassed all expectations. The humorous audition reels were featured on ABC.com, GoodMorningAmerica.com, and dozens of popular blogs. The story was picked up by CNN and other networks. And fans of the campaign posted thousands of comments on Facebook and Twitter.

After a public election in which nearly 65,000 votes were cast, the newest animal selected to join Frontier's other critters is Polly the wise-cracking parrot, who will undoubtedly repeat Frontier's messages to continue building a positive customer experience.

Frontier Airlines' advertising has been recognized with a hangar full of awards. It was nominated for "best of show" at the International Mobius awards for two years in a row. Frontier was awarded a Silver Clio for the prestigious "content and contact" category. Frontier won coveted Effie awards as well, including a gold Effie in the category of sustained success.

Logo: Courtesy of Frontier Airlines and Grey Worldwide

Key Points Summary

1. **What are the basic writing concerns of brand communication?** In general, writers of marketing communication care about words and language, particularly in the development of brand names, as well as slogans and taglines. Although advertising, public relations, and direct response writing are different stylistically, all are bound by strategy and legal considerations.
2. **How is advertising copy written?** Words and pictures work together to shape a creative concept; however, it is the clever phrases and "magic words" crafted by copywriters that make ideas understandable and memorable. Copywriters who have an ear for language match the tone of the writing to the target audience. Good copy is succinct and single-minded. Copy that is less effective uses adese to imitate a stereotyped style that parodies advertising.
3. **Which copy elements are essential to print media pieces?** The key elements of a print ad are the headlines and body copy. Headlines target the prospect, draw the reader's attention, identify the product, start the sale, and lure the reader into the body copy. Body copy provides persuasive details, such as support for claims, as well as proof and reasons why.
4. **How can we characterize the design and tools of radio writing?** Radio commercials are personal and play to consumers' interests. However, radio is primarily a background medium. Special techniques, such as repetition, are used to enhance retention. The three audio tools are voice, music, and sound effects.
5. **What are the major elements of television writing?** The elements of television commercials are video and audio tools. Television commercials can be characterized as using action, emotion, and demonstration to create messages that are intriguing as well as intrusive to catch and maintain viewers' attention.
6. **How do writers design Internet messages?** Internet advertising is interactive and involving. Online advertising has primarily focused on websites and banners, although advertisers are using new forms that look more like magazine or television ads. Banners and other forms of online advertising have to stand out amid the clutter on a typical Web page and arouse the viewer's interest. Good writing is still good writing, even online.

Key Terms

adese, p. 277
animation, p. 294
back translation, p. 296
banner, p. 294
blind headline, p. 282
body copy, p. 280
brag-and-boast copy, p. 278
call to action, p. 284
call-outs, p. 280
caption, p. 281
casting, p. 291
click-throughs, p. 295
closing paragraph, p. 284
collateral materials, p. 286
copywriter, p. 275
direct-action headline, p. 282
display copy, p. 280
feature stories, p. 279
headline, p. 281
high-context cultures, p. 295
image transfer, p. 289
indirect-action headline, p. 282
jingle, p. 288
key frame, p. 293
key visual, p. 293
key words, p. 294
lead paragraph, p. 284
low-context cultures, p. 295
news release, p. 279
off camera, p. 291
on location, p. 291
overlines, p. 280
pace, p. 293
photoboard, p. 294
radio script, p. 289
scenes, p. 293
set, p. 291
slogans, p. 271
sound effects, p. 288
storyboard, p. 294
subheads, p. 280
tagline, p. 271
talent, p. 291
television script, p. 294
theater of the mind, p. 287
tone of voice, p. 277
underlines, p. 280
voice-over, p. 291
your-name-here copy, p. 278

Review Questions

9-4. What is the role of language in brand communication, and why is it important?

9-5. Discuss the differences in writing for advertising, public relations, and direct response.

9-6. Describe the various copy elements of a print ad.

9-7. List and explain the techniques used by writers to create effective slogans.

9-8. Enumerate the types of promotional writing, and explain their commonalities and differences.

9-9. One principle of print writing is that the headline catches the reader's eye but the body copy wins the reader's heart and mind. Find an ad that demonstrates that principle and explain how it works.

9-10. Explain the process of copywriting an ad in terms of the team members involved.

9-11. What are the main characteristics of a successful copywriter?

Discussion Questions

9-12. Creative directors say the copy and art must work together to create a concept. Consider all of the ads in this chapter and the preceding chapters and identify one that you believe best demonstrates that principle. Explain what the words contribute and how they work with the visual.

9-13. What do we mean by "tone of voice," and why is it important in advertising? Find a magazine ad that you think has an appropriate tone of voice for its targeted audience (the readers of that particular magazine) and one that doesn't. Discuss your analyses of these two ads.

9-14. Your instructor divides the class into three groups. Two groups are requested to prepare a radio ad for a local orphanage to attract charity donations. The third group, to which you belong, will act as the jury to decide which ad is more effective and successful in meeting the ad objective. As means of evaluating each ad, explain and interpret the creative process, the writing style, production characteristics, the appeal used, and the interplay between emotions and logic for each.

9-15. Critique the following (choose one):

a. Jingles are a popular creative form in radio advertising. Even so, there may be as many jingles that you don't want to hear again as there are ones that you do. Identify one jingle that you really dislike and another one that you like. Analyze why these jingles either work or don't work and present your critique to your class.

b. Surf the Web and find one banner ad that you think works to drive click-throughs and one that doesn't. Print them out and prepare an analysis that compares the two banner ads and explains why you think one is effective and the other is not. Present your critique to your class.

Take-Home Projects

9-16. ***Portfolio Project:*** In the discussion questions at the end of Chapter 6, you were asked to consider the research needed for a new upscale restaurant chain that focuses on fowl—duck, squab, pheasant, and other elegant meals in the poultry category. Now your creative team is being asked to develop the creative package for the restaurant chain. A specialty category, this would be somewhat like a seafood restaurant. You have been asked to develop the creative package to use in launching these new restaurants in their new markets. Develop the following:

- The restaurant's name
- A slogan for the restaurant chain
- A list of five enticing menu items
- A paragraph of copy that can be used in print to describe the restaurant
- The copy for a 30-second commercial to be used in radio.

9-17. ***Mini-Case Analysis:*** Summarize the creative strategy behind Frontier's "Whole Different Animal" position as well as the "Flip to Mexico" and "Frontier's Next Animal" campaigns. Explain how the Big Idea works and how it expressed in the copy. What makes the writing so engaging? Analyze the structure and writing in the "Leather Seats" commercial in Chapter 8. Come up with an idea for another Frontier "one-shot" ad (i.e., like "Leather Seats" an ad that is not part of a campaign) and draft the copy.

TRACE North America Case

Writing for a Multicultural Audience

Read the TRACE case in the Appendix before coming to class.

9-18. The case briefly discusses the tonality (voice) of the communications. Write a one-page direction to the creative team explaining what the tonality should be and giving rationale for your recommendation. Keep in mind the target audience and your client (TRACE).

CHAPTER 10 Visual Communication

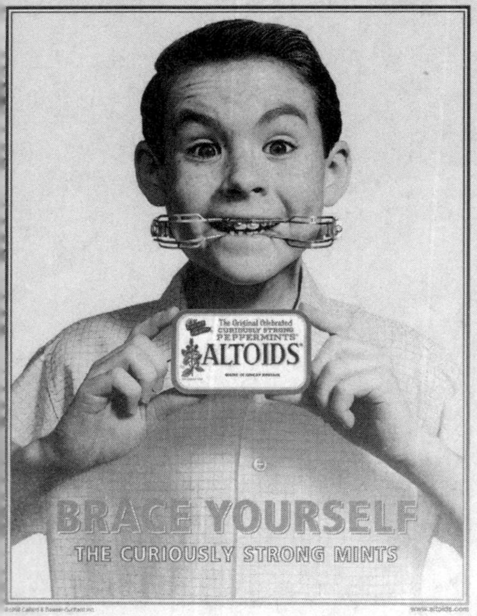

It's a Winner

Campaign:
"Curiously Strong Mints"

Company:
Kraft Foods; Wm. Wrigley Jr. Co. (which became a subsidiary of Mars)

Agencies:
Leo Burnett, Publicis & Hal Riney, BBDO Chicago

Awards:
Two Kelly Awards, including the Grand Prize, two One Show prizes, three Clios, the New York Festival Grand Prix

CHAPTER KEY POINTS

1. What is the role of visual communication in brand communication messages?
2. What is the difference between *layout* and *composition*, and why are those concepts important?
3. How are art and color reproduced in print media?
4. What are the steps in planning and producing video?
5. What are the basic techniques of Web design?

A Strong Mint with a Curious Past Goes Digital

Shortly after the United States fought for its independence from England, Smith Kendon in 1780 created a revolutionary British product designed to relieve intestinal discomfort. Its name: Altoids. Today, we know Altoids as a "curiously strong mint" designed to fight bad breath. The story about how Altoids came to be the top-selling mint in the United States parallels the evolution of its brand personality and demonstrates how established brands can be relevant in the digital world.

Advertising as far back as the 1920s plugged the "curiously strong" mint-flavored lozenges, but Altoids was largely unknown in the United States until Kraft Food purchased it in 1995 and turned its advertising over to the Leo Burnett agency.

Kraft inherited a product that came in a distinctive, Old World–looking red-and-white metal tin emblazoned with the slogan "The Original Celebrated Curiously Strong Peppermints." The Burnett creatives adapted that phrase and captured the brand essence with its campaign's wry and somewhat irreverent slogan: "Curiously Strong."

The campaign tone features a type of amusing, rather British self-deprecation, as if the brand doesn't take itself seriously. That approach struck a nerve with the largely cynical, sometimes sarcastic Generation X and Y males who have been the brand's most loyal fans.

Burnett's memorable ads from this classic campaign have featured a muscle builder with the line "Nice Altoids," a 1950s teenager with oversized braces and the headline "Brace Yourself," and a stern-looking nurse carrying the little red-and-white Altoids tin with the headline "Now This Won't Hurt a Bit." Another ad proclaimed, "No Wonder the British Have Stiff Upper Lips."

Keeping the brand relevant with Gen X and Y requires translating this vibe digitally to engage consumers. Evolution Bureau created a campaign, "Curiously Strong Awards," which invited Facebook users to send their friends 12 different archetypal character awards. The possibilities included the Like-A-Lot, who gives thumbs up to everything; the Oversharer, who offers too much information; or the Friend Tycoon, who "friends" everyone. Within the first week, 160,000 people viewed the introductory music video, and 8,000 fans signed up. The Altoids website also engages consumers with online games like the Great Flying Mintini and Altoids Factory.

Change is an inevitable fact of life. Not only has Altoids come to mean something different to consumers over time, but brand ownership has changed hands, and so have the agencies that manage the marketing communication. How does a brand maintain a consistent personality amid changing ownership and agencies?

The success of a brand's advertising is based on more than the humor of a single campaign—especially as ownership of a brand shifts. Altoids ads have had an iconic look. Altoids's classic print campaign created by the Leo Burnett agency featured an intriguing headline that is only a few words long in all-capital letters and a drop shadow outline. Many of the ads are laid out on a plain, mint green background with a double-ruled border—a great retro look that reflects the package design, which reinforces the brand identity.

When Energy BBDO Chicago took over the account, it dropped the "Curiously Strong" theme, replacing it with "A Slap to the Cerebellum." Steffan Postaer, one of the Leo Burnett creatives whose ideas resulted in Altoids award-winning work, said this of the new campaign: "You can still see the brand's DNA in the language and typography as well as in the tone and manner." It's too soon to know if the approach works for this venerable band.

See for yourself what you think gives a campaign continuity by viewing current advertising at www.energybbdo.com/work.php. Then, in the "It's a Wrap" section at the end of the chapter, see how well the advertising has performed over time for this intense, extreme, and curiously strong mint.

Sources: www.wrigley.com; www.altoids.com; http://godsofadvertising.wordpress.com/2008/03/13/my-altoids-can-beat-up-their-altoids; Rita Chang, "Altoids Pokes Fun at Itself with 'Brainstorm,'" www.adage.com, September 21, 2009, www.evb.com/work/altoids-curiously-strong-awards.

The visual consistency and wry humor in the Altoids campaign go far beyond the ability of words to describe things. The quirky images communicate ideas about the brand personality as well as the feelings and sense of humor of the brand's target market. This chapter is about the visuals used in advertising—how they are designed and what they contribute to the meaning of the ad. First we review some basic ideas about visual impact, both in print and broadcast, and the role of the art director. Then we consider print art production and video production and end with a discussion of the design of Internet advertising.

Why Is Visual Communication Important?

What makes Altoids so visually remarkable? Does the product grab your attention? How does the visual build brand personality? Is it interesting? Do you remember it? The success of Altoids breath mints is primarily a result of the consistent graphic presentation of the brand in its marketing communication. The visual consistency not only is apparent in the design of the package and the ads but also reflects the history of the brand as a quirky old British lozenge.

The Altoids ads use association to create curiosity but also to reflect the meaning of the slogan. "Nice Altoids" builds on a unique connection between the sound of "deltoids" and the brand name. You may also have seen an ad used to launch the Altoids Cinnamon line, which continues to build on the brand position but modifies it slightly to read "curiously hot" rather than "curiously strong." A firewalker tiptoeing across a patch of the little white mints visually reinforces a truth about the product—the Cinnamon Altoids are hot enough to tickle your toes.

Visual Impact

A provocative outdoor board for the Italian women's apparel firm, No-l-ita, certainly got people's attention, but it also raised a furor in Italy because it showed shocking pictures of a naked anorexic woman. The image was shot by Oliviero Toscani, the former photographer/art director for Benetton, who stirred up emotions over his photos for that clothing brand by depicting a dying AIDS victim, death-row inmates, and a nun and priest kissing. In the "Principled Practice" feature, Professor Edoardo Brioschi examines the ethics of this image. The issue was only complicated several years afterward when the woman died.

The No-l-ita outdoor board had good intentions; it was designed to convey an antianorexic message. So what do you think? Should it have run? Should it be taken down?

In effective advertising, both print and television, it's not just the words that need to communicate the message—the visuals communicate as well. And as the No-l-ita outdoor board illustrated, the image can be powerful, even shocking, and may inadvertently splash negative responses all over the brand.

A PRINCIPLED PRACTICE

An Imperative: Respect the Dignity of the Person

Edoardo Teodoro Brioschi, *Università Cattolica del Sacro Cuore, Milan, Italy*

I believe that there exist certain ethical principles that apply to business activities, and those include principles for marketing communication activities. Specifically, I'm concerned about the protection of the dignity of the person. A case in obvious conflict with this principle is the use in an advertisement of an image of a woman suffering from an illness: acute anorexia. This is the case in the "No-Anorexia No-l-ita" campaign for an Italian brand of youth apparel.

The woman we see presented in the ad is, in fact, practically a living skeleton. The message shows the image of a naked woman suffering from anorexia posing with her gaze turned to the observer. (The model is 27-year-old French actress named Isabelle Caro, who is five feet five inches tall and weighs 70 pounds.) Both front and back views of her poses were used on outdoor boards and in the daily press during Milan fashion week as well as in other big cities, such as Rome and Naples.

The advertiser claimed that by presenting the images in this way, it sought to make specific reference to a drama experienced by young women: anorexia: "We want to keep young people informed about this terrible illness so that, by seeing the effects, the young will not take the same risk."

The body that self-regulates the advertising industry in Italy (Istituto di Autodisciplina Pubblicitaria [Italian Self-Regulation Institute]) examined the No-l-ita "No Anorexia" campaign and judged this message to be in conflict with its Code of Self-Regulation. It summoned the advertiser, Flash & Partners, producer of the No-l-ita brand, for a specific hearing to discuss the case.

As a number of experts testified, anorexia is a complex illness. It follows that, whatever the factor causing the pathology, the behavior at risk is not due to ignorance of its effect. Hence, the principle "If you know the results you will avoid them" is not valid. In fact, this pathology unfortunately derives from deep drives, probably including biochemical imbalances, which cannot be overcome or rectified by an advertisement that simply displays its devastating effects.

Therefore, this advertising was banned. In fact, the message in question uses the physical devastation of the naked body of a young woman for commercial purposes—for the purpose of marketing the firm's products—and in so doing, it offends her dignity and debases the personal and social drama caused by this type of pathology.

On this question, there was a more general observation by this jury, the highest judicial organ of the Italian Self-Regulation Institute. It notes that promotional campaigns dealing with such delicate areas as health and prevention call for extreme caution in their conduct, requiring scientific preparation and justifying a preventive screening by the bodies responsible for advertising self-regulation.

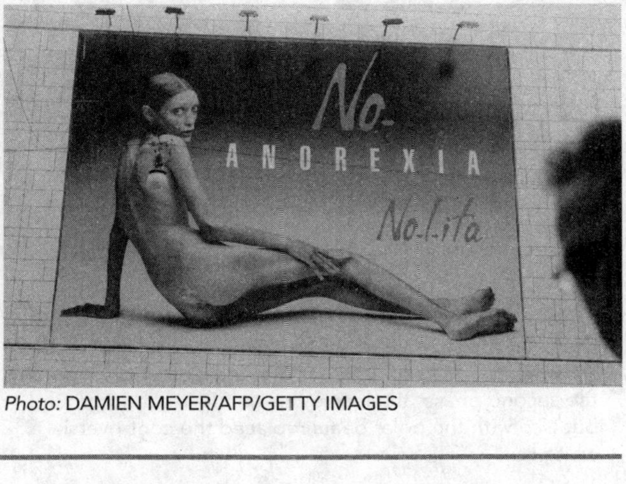

Photo: DAMIEN MEYER/AFP/GETTY IMAGES

Photo: Courtesy of IBM Archives

IBM used a chick and an egg to demonstrate the smallness of a hard disk drive, which, at the time this illustration was created, was about the size of a large coin.

In fact, visuals do some things better than words, such as demonstrate something. How would you demonstrate, for example, the smallness of a computer chip or a new miniature hard drive? In this classic image, IBM did it through a visual analogy—showing its hard disk drive inside half an eggshell next to a newborn chick.

Even radio can evoke mental pictures through suggestive or descriptive language and sound effects. The effective use of visuals in advertising can be related to a number of the effects we have outlined in our Facets Model of Effects:

1. ***Grab Attention*** Generally, visuals are better at getting and keeping attention than words.
2. ***Stick in Memory*** Visuals persist in the mind because people generally remember messages as visual fragments, or key images that are filed easily in their minds, as the Altoids retro look demonstrates.
3. ***Cement Belief*** Seeing is believing, as the IBM chick ad demonstrates. Visuals that demonstrate add credibility to a message.
4. ***Tell Interesting Stories*** Visual storytelling, such as was used in the quirky Altoids ads, is engaging and maintains interest.
5. ***Communicate Quickly*** Pictures tell stories faster than words, as the IBM chick visual illustrates. A picture communicates instantly, while consumers have to decipher verbal/written communication word by word, sentence by sentence, line by line.
6. ***Anchor Associations*** To distinguish undifferentiated products with low inherent interest, advertisers often link the product with visual associations representing lifestyles and types of users, as the "Nice Altoids" ad demonstrates.

Principle
The visual's primary function in an advertisement is to get attention.

In general, print designers have found that a picture in a print layout captures more than twice as many readers as a headline does. Furthermore, the bigger the illustration, the more the message grabs consumers' attention. Layouts with pictures also tend to pull more readers into the body copy; initial attention is more likely to turn to interest with a strong visual. People not only notice visuals but also remember the layouts with pictures more than those composed mostly of type. Both the believability factor and the interest-building impact of a visual story are reasons why visuals are anchored so well in memory.

Coca-Cola's "Artic Home" campaign for polar bears was launched for the holiday season with a dramatic white can showing the bears and the familiar red Coca-Cola logo. In the second phase, the iconic can with its red background but also with the polar bears replaced the controversial white can.

Big Ideas that capture attention can be puzzling, funny, or shocking, like the No-l-ita billboard. A less controversial but also highly discussed visual campaign was created by Coca-Cola on behalf of polar bears whose Artic home was becoming increasingly threatened by global warming. Coke's "Artic Home" campaign raised over $2 million in donations for the World Wildlife Fund. The effort involved a series of limited edition Coca-Cola cans. Interestingly, complaints via social media about the unusual white can led to a return to a more traditional red can, although the polar bears continued to march around the base of both designs. In addition to the highly visible cans, the campaign also featured a beautifully produced IMAX 3-D film of polar bears in their Artic wilderness. You can see the television version at http://vimeo.com/43990022.

Attention, interest, memorability, believability—these factors help explain the impact of visual messages. Karl Schroeder's team at Coates Kokes in Portland, Oregon designed a not-to-be-missed ad that was painted on the wall of a building using the distinctive artwork in the SeaPort Air campaign, which we showcased in Chapter 7.

Courtesy of SeaPort Airlines

SHOWCASE

The distinctive illustration style from the SeaPort Air campaign was used to paint an ad on the side of a multistory building in Tillamook, Oregon.

A graduate of the University of Oregon advertising program, Karl Schroeder worked at Coates Kokes before moving to Nike as senior writer/editor. He was nominated by Professor Charles Frazer.

Brand Image and Position

The story about changing the color on the iconic Coke can reflects the important role marketing communication plays in the creation of brand images. Much of that contribution comes from the visual elements—the symbolic images associated with the brand and the elements that define the brand, such as the trademark and logo. A classic brand symbol, for example, is the target graphic used by the Target store. The association with the brand name is immediately clear, and the brand meaning—that Target is a store where you can go to get what you are looking for—also adds to the identity of the retailer.

A **logo**, which is the imprint used for immediate identification of a brand or company, is an interesting design project because it uses typography, illustration, and layout to create a distinctive and memorable image that identifies the brand. Think of the cursive type used for Coca-Cola, the block letters used for IBM, and the apple with a bite out of it (in both rainbow stripes and white) for Apple computers. An example of the value of a logo came in 2006 when Ford pledged its blue logo, among other properties, to qualify for loans to survive the recession—it was returned in 2012 because of the company's financial recuperation. Also check out the logo designs by Michael Dattolico and the captions, which explain his thinking about the objectives of the designs.

Brand icons are characters associated with a brand, such as Mr. Peanut, Uncle Ben, and Ronald McDonald. If they are effective, they become an enduring symbol of the brand. Initially, the character is designed to reflect the desired brand personality. The Jolly Green Giant is an imaginary and kind friend who encourages kids to eat their vegetables. Over time, however, they may need to be updated as the Betty Crocker image has been a number of times. The trade magazine *Adweek* celebrates brand icons and annually inducts winners into its Madison Avenue Advertising Walk of Fame event every fall. Check these out at www.adweek.com.

Package design is another area where brand image is front and center. Sometimes the brand link is in the shape of the packaging, as in the distinctive grandmotherly Mrs. Butterworth syrup bottles (see an example at www.mrsbutterworthsyrup.com). It may also be in the stylistics as we have shown with Celestial Seasonings tea boxes (see Chapter 2). During the Great Recession, a number of manufacturers found that new packaging with retro designs appealed to consumers—Ritz crackers, Oreo cookies, and Corn Flakes brands, among others.

The package design also accommodates strategic elements with positioning statements, flags that reference current campaigns, recipes, and pricing announcements, as well as economic and popular culture events. The classic association between

BGB LANDSCAPING

eMotion TECHNOLOGIES | LLC

Photo: Courtesy of Michael Dattolico

SHOWCASE

BGB is a pretty standard landscaping company, but we wanted to give it a more Zen-like quality—clean, concise, a strong Asian influence in the circle, a groomed almost-bonsai tree, and the color red. Brought together, these elements offer a soothing company image to combat some of the negatives associated with landscaping (hard work and hassles!). eMotion is a start-up company creating a product that utilizes the motion of a musical instrument and translates that into audible note variations. We wanted to capture both the "motion" of the musical notes in the logo and the emotion that all music embodies. The concept of the product captures a more fluid, rhythmic pairing of both the audible elements and movement of performance.

Note: A graduate of the University of Florida advertising program, Michael Dattolico was nominated by Professor Elaine Wagner.

Photo: Courtesy of General Mills

CLASSIC

Wheaties were first introduced in 1924, but it wasn't until 10 years later that the company realized the power of associating the health benefits of the brand with athletic performance. The connection was made on the box featuring New York Yankees slugger Lou Gehrig. The famous "Breakfast of Champions" boxes have showcased all kinds of winners, from Michael Jordan, with his record 18 boxes, to Tiger Woods and many Olympic stars, such as swimmer Michael Phelps and volleyball champion Misty May-Treanor.

Wheaties and sports figures brings to life the brand's famous slogan, "Breakfast of Champions." See the parade of Wheaties stars on www.wheaties.com.

A brand position is often thought to be tied to words, such as the Avis "We Try Harder" slogan. Laura Ries, daughter of legendary Al Ries, one of the creators of the positioning concept, argues that one of the best ways to nail down a position is with a visual. She points to the universal recognition of the pink ribbon for the Komen Foundation, the contour bottle for Coke, the Swoosh for Nike, and the Clydesdales for Budweiser—the King of Beers. Her ideas on how visuals play a more important role in marketing than words is explained in her iBook *Visual Hammer.* She explains that visuals are powerful "because they hold emotional power that sticks."[1]

Visual Storytelling

In visual storytelling, such as seen in the Altoid ads, the images set up a narrative that has to be constructed by the reader or viewer. Visual storytelling is important even for abstract concepts such as "empowered," "inspired," and "inventive," which were the focus of commercials in the PBS "Be More Inspired" campaign. In the "Be more empowered" commercial, a goldfish makes its escape from its little round bowl in an apartment and jumps from a puddle to a bottle to a river where it works its way upstream accompanying giant salmon that are leaping up waterfalls in their annual migration.

In another commercial in the series titled "Be more inspired," a composer agonizes over the right notes and eventually hits a point of total frustration. As he looks out the window, he sees a group of birds sitting on a set of five power and telephone wires that are conveniently aligned to look like a music staff. From the bird's positions, he crafts a tune that becomes the theme for his composition. PBS used these clever little visual stories to present itself as a creative force that inspires people to use their imaginations.

The point is that art directors design images that tell stories and create brand impressions. An example of a simple story told totally through the visuals is the Best of Show award for a One-Show competition that showcased a British campaign for Volkswagen. It featured a gently humorous 30-second commercial built around the low price of the VW Polo. Bob Barrie, when he was president of The One Club, an association for people in the creative side of advertising, explained that it was possibly the quietest, most understated television spot entered in the show. The idea was simple: A woman sits at her kitchen table. Her scanning of the newspaper—and her hiccups—stop abruptly as she discovers an ad for the VW Polo with its "surprisingly ordinary" price.[2]

Our ethics discussions in this book often focus on the appropriateness of an image and the story it tells about the brand. For example, an ad for Vaseline Intensive Care Lotion shows a conference room with a speaker and a group of businesspeople—both men and women—paying careful attention to the presentation. In the foreground is a happy woman in a business suit with her back to the speaker and her colleagues. Her legs are up on the table, and she's caressing them. Unfortunately, she's also a black woman. The headline reads, "Nothing keeps you from handling your business." So does Vaseline Intensive Care want us to know that if black women use their product, they become totally clueless in a business meeting? The point is that what appears to the creative team to be a dynamite visual may, on reflection, send a number of contrary messages

Emotion and Visual Persuasion

We've talked about visual impact and the power of visual storytelling, but both come together in persuasive messages that are designed to touch the emotions and "move" the consumer to respond favorably to the brand. We know from Chapter 4 that emotion is a powerful factor in determining the persuasive effect of brand communication. We also know that emotional responses can be linked to moving visual images—moving, as in touch the emotions. Research by Professor Karen Mallia suggests that images are not only moving but also becoming increasingly more dramatic and controversial, such as a trend toward using religious imagery, including nuns and priests in compromising positions.

In many situations, emotion is the key driver of a prospect being "turned on" to a message. In the "A Matter of Principle" feature, Professor Joe Tougas explores why emotionally loaded visuals are particularly useful in certain types of environmental messages—and maybe overlooked in other equally deserving causes.

Principle

The power of visual storytelling enhances persuasive messages because visuals touch the emotions and move the consumer to respond favorably to the brand.

A Matter of Principle

Save the Pandas! Save the Baby Seals! Save the Eagles! Save the Toads?

Joe Tougas, *Evergreen State College*

Messages about the importance of ecological preservation are often accompanied by stunning images of animals endangered by human activities. The images are carefully chosen to tug at our heartstrings—baby seals with large dark eyes, a panda mother with her pup, and a majestic eagle soaring in total freedom.

By combining the image with the verbal message, the author intends to motivate the viewer to very specific actions—sending a check to the sponsoring organization, calling members of Congress in support of a piece of environmental legislation, and so on. Such campaigns have been very effective in protecting endangered species and habitats.

The animals used in these campaigns tend to be "charismatic species" that most people find beautiful to look at or that easily trigger human emotions of sympathy or love. But does that mean that those species are more deserving of protection than the ugly or slimy ones—the toads and slugs of this world?

Changes in the climate and atmosphere have created a worldwide crisis for amphibians. Many species of toads and frogs are severely endangered. Are there reasons that people should care just as much about those ugly animals as we do about the beautiful ones?

The practice of using emotionally appealing images to promote a complex message illustrates a very general problem in communication strategy. When an organization decides to appeal to aesthetic values rather than moral, scientific, or political values, they are, in effect, choosing to persuade people to *do the right thing for the wrong reasons.*

Such an approach can be very successful but comes with a danger: Once we have saved the eagles, we may feel justified in ignoring or undervaluing other species that are just as endangered and just as much at the mercy of human activities but that don't excite the same tender feelings.

Principle
The emotional hook of a visual engages the attention of a viewer and contributes to the depth of the memory traces left behind by the brand message.

Emotion is a "hook" that helps engage the attention of a viewer and contributes to the depth of the memory traces left behind by the brand message. The stronger the feelings elicited by a message, the more likely the viewer will find meaning in a message and link that meaningful experience to a brand. A visual can be the cue that turns on this brand linkage process.

As Charles Young, president of Ameritest and a member of this book's advisory board, explains, "It is the meaning of the emotions evoked by a particular string of images that is critical to the strategic brand-building process."[3] The Ameritest methodology is designed to identify those moments in a brand message that resonate emotionally for viewers—both negatively and positively. The Ameritest work over the years has determined a magnifier effect for emotionally engaging visuals that results in higher levels of liking. Emotional resonance delivered through visual content is particularly impactful. As the Ameritest researchers concluded in a study that identified this magnifier effect, prospects would be turned on to a brand more strongly when advertising is enhanced by emotional engagement with the surrounding context.[4]

What Is Art Direction?

The person most responsible for creating visual impact, as well as the visual brand identification elements, is the art director. The art director is in charge of the visual look of the brand message, both in print and on television, and how it communicates mood, product qualities, and

The Inside Story

Large or Small, Which Would You Choose? The Good, Bad and Ugly, Exposed

Amy Niswonger, *President, Ninth Cloud Creative & Little Frog Prints*

Having worked at both a boutique advertising/design firm as well as a large corporate design powerhouse, I can confidently say there are benefits to both. As a fresh new graduate, I was torn, which direction is right for me?

The smaller advertising firms certainly do have their benefits. As a young designer, I was able to wear multiple hats. I created ads, brochures, logos, billboards, and full marketing campaigns. Looking at my portfolio, I can confidently say, "That's my work." Stretched on a daily basis by my colleagues and creative director, I was entrusted to get the job done efficiently and effectively. I would be challenged to create unique successful solutions for my clients. Actively involved in a client-facing role, I pitched my ideas and backed up my concepts with research and reasoning. This was challenging but very rewarding. Now, for the "bad and ugly," so to speak. The downside was that my clients were local, and some were regional but on a much smaller scale than if I had opted for a large design firm.

On the flip side, working at a corporate design firm also has its ups and downs. Huge international clients are in my personal portfolio. I am able to walk into many national retail stores and see projects that I contributed to. It's a great feeling of accomplishment. However, the downside is that I worked on a team that "did that," so only a tiny portion of the design is my own personal blood, sweat, and tears. Working on the same client for months at a time, I was sometimes overwhelmed by the level of detail that sometimes consumed my entire day, week, or even month.

Regardless, whichever direction is right for you, there are numerous benefits to both. You need to be happy in whatever direction you choose. At both positions, I had a sense of purpose, a responsibility to make my clients shine whether it be a diamond in the rough or a Fortune 500 company. I was there to make it happen. The end result is "all good" because, let's face it, our job is to redesign the bad and the ugly.

Amy Niswonger is a creative director and professor who owns her own design studio. A graphic design and marketing graduate of Miami University in Oxford, Ohio, she was named a Most Promising Minority Student by the American Advertising Federation (AAF). She was nominated by Connie Frazier, AAF chief operating officer.

psychological appeals. The art director and copywriter team usually work together to come up with the Big Idea, but the art director is responsible for bringing the visual side of the idea to life.

Specifically, art directors make decisions about whether to use art or photography in print and film or animation in television and what type of artistic style to use. They are trained in graphic design, including art, photography, typography, the use of color, and computer design software. Although art directors generally design the ad, they may not create the finished art. If they need an illustration, they hire an artist. Newspaper and Web advertising visuals are often **clip art** or **click art**, images from collections of copyright-free art that anyone who buys the clip-art service can use.

In addition to advertising, art directors may also be involved in designing a brand or corporate logo as well as packages, merchandising materials, store or corporate office interiors, and other aspects of a brand's visual presentation, such as shopping bags, delivery trucks, and uniforms. Graphic designer Amy Niswonger explains in "The Inside Story" feature how she views the working environment of graphic designers.

Photo: FedEx service marks used by permission. Provided courtesy of Frito-Lay North America, Inc.; Courtesy of NBCUniversal Media, LLC

The Designer's Tool Kit

One of the most difficult problems that art directors—and those who work on the creative side of advertising—face is to transform a creative concept into words and pictures. During the brainstorming process, both copywriters and art directors are engaged in **visualization**, which means they are imagining what the finished ad might look like. The art director, however, is responsible for translating the advertising Big Idea into a visual story. To do this, the art director relies on a tool kit that consists of illustrations or animation, photos or film shots, color, type, design principles, layout (print), and composition (photography, video, or film), among other visual elements.

Visual symbols are also fun and challenging for designers. Check out the following logos and see if you can find a symbolic message in designs with which you are probably very familiar. (FedEx has a white arrow between the E and X; there are two folks enjoying chips and a bowl of dip in the middle of Tostitos; the peacock logo with its full spectrum of colors serves as a metaphor for NBC and its range of programming and technological capabilities.)

Principle
For credibility, photography is a good medium.

Illustrations and Photos When art directors use the word *art*, they usually mean photographs and illustrations, each of which serves different purposes in ads. For instance, photography has an authenticity that makes it powerful. Most people feel that pictures don't lie (even though they can be altered). For credibility, then, photography is a good medium.

The decision to use a photograph or an illustration is usually determined by the advertising strategy and its need for either realism or fanciful images. Generally, a photograph is more realistic, and an illustration (or animation in television) is more fanciful, as the Sony illustration shows. Illustrations, by definition, eliminate many of the details you see in a photograph, which can make it easier to understand their meaning since what remains are the "highlights" of the image. This ease of perception can simplify the visual message because it can focus attention on key details of the image. Illustrations also use artistic techniques to intensify meanings and moods, making illustrations ideal for fantasy (think about comic books and animated films). Photos convey a "seeing is believing" credibility. Photographs, of course, can also evoke fanciful images. For example, the Maxell "500 Plays" ad uses visual symbolism to represent a blast of sound.

It is also possible to manipulate a photograph and turn it into art, a technique that brought recognition to Andy Warhol, among others. This practice has become popular with the advent of the Internet and the availability of easy-to-find digital images, some of which are copyrighted. That technique was used to create a political poster in 2008 and, at the same time, a legal nightmare for the artist, Shepard Fairey. Initially, Fairey claimed he found the original Obama photo using a Google Image search. The problem is that the iconic portrait with its social realism style was eventually found to have been constructed from a copyright-protected image taken by Mannie Garcia while on assignment for the Associated Press (AP), which claims ownership of the image and demanded credit as well as compensation. Garcia also believes he owns the copyright and supports Fairey's use of the image. Fairey claimed his use of the image follows the legal definition of fair use and doesn't infringe on AP's copyright.[5] Eventually, he admitted that he had used

Photo: © flab/Alamy

Photo: Courtesy of the Estate of Steve Steigman

CLASSIC

The experience of being "blown away" by a blast of sound, like sitting in front of a jet engine, was depicted in this Maxell ad from the 1970s, a campaign used through the 1980s. It became a pop culture iconic image and imitated in countless parodies, including the 2010 movie Jackass 3D.

Photo: Used by permission of Sony Electronics, Inc.

CLASSIC

Sony's "Full-Color Sound" campaign used the Big Idea that sound relates to colors. This campaign by Milt Glaser is one of the few signed by the art director. The original is in the permanent collection of the Metropolitan Museum of Art.

the AP image as a reference and was sentenced to two years of probation and 300 hours of community service.[6] Dilemmas like this face everyone who finds images online and wants to reuse them in marketing communication projects.

Another issue involving digitized images in a global environment revolves around the ability of software programs, such as Photoshop, to manipulate specific content within a photo. Microsoft fell into a hole in 2009 when its website in Poland used a clumsy Photoshop application to turn a black man white. The original image had been used on Microsoft's U.S. website and featured diverse genders and people of many colors. However, on the Polish website, where, presumably, there are fewer people of color, the artist chose to paste a white man's head on the body of a black man. Microsoft has apologized, of course, but the fiasco ran wild on news sites and blogs.[7]

Color In addition to photos and illustrations, another important visual element that art directors manipulate is color. Color attracts attention, provides realism, establishes moods, and builds brand identity. Art directors know that print ads with color, particularly those in newspapers, get more attention than ads without color. Most ads—print, broadcast, and Internet—are in full color, especially when art directors use photographs.

Color is particularly important in branding. An example comes from Pepsi's rivalry with Coke in China. Coke, until recently, has always used a red can and logo, and Pepsi traditionally

Photo: Mannie Garcia/AP Photo

Photo: Shepard Fairey

Recognized as one of the most important political images of recent years, the Obama "Hope" poster raises questions about fair use of manipulated images.

uses a blue can. For the Beijing 2008 Olympics, Pepsi, which was an official Olympics sponsor, brought out a red can. The marketer defended itself, saying the new can was more appealing to Chinese consumers and mirrors the color of the country's flag. Critics wonder if the dueling cans will just cause confusion among Chinese consumers who are slowly building loyalty to these Western brands.[8]

In print, designers also use **spot color**, in which a second color in addition to black (a black-and-white photo or illustration with an accent color) is used to highlight important elements. The use of spot color is highly attention getting, particularly in newspaper ads. The ACG ad uses red spot color to accent the product and key words.

Color also can help an ad convey a mood. Warm colors, such as red, yellow, and orange, convey happiness. Pastels are soft and often bring a friendly tone to a print ad. Earth tones are natural and no-nonsense. Cool colors, such as blue and green, are aloof, calm, serene, reflective, and intellectual. Yellow and red have the most attention-getting power. Red may symbolize alarm and danger as well as warmth. Black communicates high drama and can express power and elegance. Note that these color associations are culturally determined, and uses like these are common in Western countries but may not be effective in other cultures. White, for example, is the color of death in many Asian countries.

The use of black and white is also an important design choice because it lends dignity and sophistication to the visual, even if it's a boot, as the Dunham ad demonstrates. A historical effect can be created by shooting in black and white or by using a sepia tone, which can make the images look like old prints that have been weathered by time. When realism is important to convey in an ad, full-color photographs may be essential. Some products and ad illustrations just don't look right in black and white—pizza, flower gardens, and nail polish, for instance.

Typography Not only do art directors carefully choose colors, but they also specify the ad's **typography**—the appearance of the ad's printed matter. In most cases, good typesetting does not call attention to itself because its primary role is functional—to convey the words of the message. Type or lettering, however, also has an aesthetic role, and the type selection can, in a subtle or not-so-subtle way, contribute to the impact and mood of the message, as the ACG boot ad demonstrates.

Principle

Type has a functional role in the way it presents the letters in words so they can be easily read, but it also has an aesthetic role and can contribute to the meaning of the message through its design.

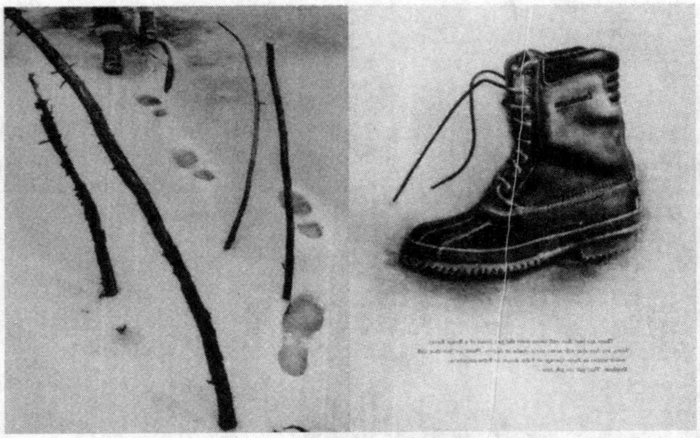

Photo: Courtesy of New Balance Athletic Shoe, Inc.

The layout for the Dunham boot ad shown here speaks in a quiet voice about the beauty of nature. Even though it's a boot ad, it projects an elegance that reflects an appreciation for nature and a serene outdoor scene (footprints in the snow). The ACG "Air Krakatoa" ad with an asymmetrical layout uses spot color effectively in the copy. Note how the layout "shouts," in contrast to the soft tone of voice of the Dunham boot ad.

Photo: Courtesy of Nike

Ad designers choose from among thousands of typefaces to find the right one for the ad's message. Designers are familiar with type classifications, but it is also important for managers and other people on the creative team to have some working knowledge of typography to understand what designers are talking about and to critique the typography and make suggestions. Here are some of the many of the decisions an art director makes in designing type:

- The specific typeface, or **font**
- The way capitalization is handled, such as all caps, small caps, or lowercase
- Typeface variations that come from manipulating the shape of the letterform
- The edges of the type block and its column width
- The size in which the type is set (vertical height)
- **Legibility**, or how easy it is to perceive the letters

Generally, logos are designed to last for a long time, but sometimes brands change the design and typography in an attempt to modernize the look or match the mood of the country. An example comes from the Great Recession period, when a number of major brands, such as Kraft and Walmart, among others, moved from their all-cap presentations to lowercase. The idea was to make their logos look softer and less stiff.[9]

Design Principles, Layout, and Styles

The arrangement of the pieces in a print ad or video shot is called a layout, and it is governed by basic principles of design. The design has both functional and aesthetic needs—the functional side makes the visual message easy to perceive, and the aesthetic side makes it attractive and pleasing to the eye.

These design principles guide the eye by creating a visual path that helps the viewer scan the elements. For example, dominant elements that are colorful or high in contrast (big versus small light versus dark) catch the viewer's attention first. How all of the elements come together is a function of the unity and balance of the design. Direction or movement is the way the elements are positioned to lead the eye through the arrangement. Simplicity is also a design principle, one that is in opposition to visual clutter. In general, the fewer the elements, the stronger the impact, an idea expressed in the phrase "less is more." Another saying is KISS, which stands for "Keep

It Simple, Stupid." The Frontier "Caribou" ad is a powerful image because of its use of a simple horizontal photo across a two-page spread and the way the composition of the photograph directs the eye to the Frontier plane.

Principle

Design is usually improved by simplifying the number of elements. Less is more.

Let's look at how these design principles are used in print layout and in the composition of a picture or photograph. For print messages, once art directors have chosen the images and typographic elements, they manipulate all of the visual elements on paper to produce a layout. A **layout** is a plan that imposes order and at the same time creates an arrangement that is aesthetically pleasing.

Different layouts can convey entirely different feelings about a product. For example, look at the two ads for work boots. The ACG "Air Krakatoa" boot ad screams "waterproof!," signaling the boots' ability to stand up to the most serious weather conditions. In contrast, the ad for the Dunham boot looks like a work of fine art. The difference between the two campaigns clearly lies with the visual impact that comes from the layouts as well as the imagery.

Here are some common types of layouts an art director might use and these apply to brochures and magazines as well as advertisements:

- ***Picture Window*** A common layout format is one with a single, dominant visual that occupies about 60 to 70 percent of the ad's space. Underneath it is a headline and copy block. The logo or signature signs off the message at the bottom. The Altoids ads are of this style.
- ***All Art*** The art fills the frame of the ad and the copy is embedded in the picture. The Frontier "Caribou" ad is an example.
- ***Panel or Grid*** This layout uses a number of visuals of matched or proportional sizes. If the ad has multiple panels all of the same size, the layout can look like a windowpane or comic strip panel. The Dunham boot ad uses two side-by-side panels.

Photo: © 2007 Frontier Airlines. Used with permission. Courtesy of Grey Worldwide

Sometimes the most powerful images are the simplest in structure—just a wide horizontal landscape with a swimming caribou leaving a trail in the water and a plane flying above. Notice how the antlers point to the Frontier plane with a caribou on its tail. The whole composition is designed to pull your eye to the right and then up.

- ***Dominant Type or All Copy*** Occasionally, you will see layouts that emphasize the type rather than the art or even an all-copy advertisement in which the headline is treated as type art, such as the ACG ad. A copy-dominant ad may have art, but it is either embedded in the copy or placed in a subordinate position, such as at the bottom of the layout.
- ***Circus*** This layout combines lots of elements—art, type, and color—to deliberately create a busy, jumbled image. This is typical of some discount store ads or ads for local retailers, such as tire companies.
- ***Nonlinear*** This contemporary style of layout can be read starting at any point in the image. In other words, the direction of viewing is not ordered, as in the "What a Ride" ad for Schwinn. This style of ad layout works for young people who are more accustomed to nonlinear forms.

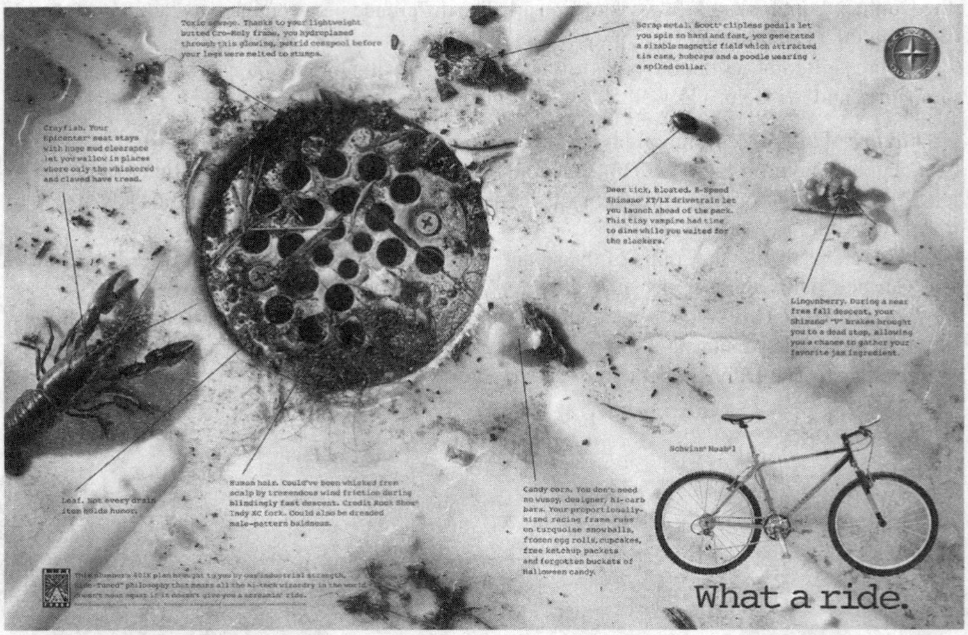

Photo: Schwinn is a division of Pacific Cycle, LCC. © 2004 Pacific Cycle, LCC. All Rights Reserved

This ad for Schwinn bicycles uses a plumbing drain motif to convey the industrial-strength features of the bike. It is a nonlinear design in that it doesn't matter where you start reading and what you read next. The text is carried in call-outs that point to different visual elements in the layout.

These layout categories are functional, but there are also stylistic categories that designers will sometimes use to refer to their approach. For designers working with a layout problem that calls for a historical feeling, they might use design aesthetics from such periods as art nouveau, art deco, or modern or moderne. These are all international styles popular in the late 19th century into the early to mid-20th century. Art nouveau uses flowing, curved lines reminiscent of vines and flowers. It was followed by art deco, which is much more linear and symmetrical. Modern design added an industrial, streamlined, and architectural quality to the elegance of art deco.

Other styles include postmodern, which is an eclectic primarily architectural design style that incorporates assemblages of elements from previous periods. Since then, we've seen the psychedelic art of the 1960s with its hippie images, followed by pop art, which turned everyday items, such as Andy Warhol's Campbell's Soup cans, into art.

Grunge design, which appeared in the 1990s, was a rejection of the niceties of traditional design. The Schwinn nonlinear layout is similar in style to grunge. Its most recent incarnation is a contemporary style studied by graphic designer Nikki Arnell, who coined the term "Beautiful Messy" for this artfully hand-drawn design style that seems to reflect the Millennial personality and style. The point of understanding these historical styles is that art directors often use them to communicate certain types of messages. There's nothing that says counterculture, for example, like a design in the psychedelic style.

A Matter of Practice

The Beautiful Messy

Nikki Arnell, *Arkansas State University*

As with all forms of communication, a designer must know the audience and then problem solve to correctly deliver the message in a memorable way. All visual communication should relate to the target audience's comfortable visual genre, from typefaces to image crops to white space. Visual communication is much more than legibility of the written word on a page. Eloquence and application of visual vocabulary must contribute to the emotional comprehension of a communication. This is the specialty of the graphic designer and art director.

And a new audience has entered the consumer stage, challenging this goal of communication at the emotional level. The Millennials (born late 1970s to late 1990s) is the largest generation the United States has ever known. Growing up in the "Decade of the Child," Millennials have been told since birth that they could be anything they wanted to be. Arrogance is simply a new kind of confidence. Yet it may be a surprise that this is not an overly violent group. There has been a *decrease* in teen arrests, drug use, drunk-driving deaths, pregnancy, abortions, and high school dropouts.

This is surprising when one considers the amount of violence the Millennials have known as normal. Pre–9-11 are like the days of innocence, if even remembered. Shootings on suburban school campuses are not strange. There was never a world without AIDS. The distrust of governments and religious institutions is assumed. Gen X experienced these things and rebelled with sarcasm and anger. The difference between Gen X and Gen Y is a subtle evolution, but its impact can be seen. Millennials are more optimistic but not unaware. They do not reject. They calmly *rewrite* the rules with their confidence, and they don't need to ask for permission to do so.

From a design viewpoint, this is the cause of a new obviously handmade, *beautifully messy* style that has become common in the aftermath of aggressive post-modernist deconstructionist design. The public is less concerned with what is said and more with *why* it is said.

The details of handmade elements and the process of their execution living comfortably in and with the digital world draw attention to the originator of the message, which allows the audience to witness idiosyncratic thoughts of this "individual" in the mass-produced, digital world where it is less expected. The inconspicuously handmade style invites conversation, and it seems the goal is to create an intimate experience of the content. In this way, even everyday design interaction becomes a proclaimed gift encouraging dialogue.

This is a step beyond the sterile message delivery of modern design's universal monologue. Like postmodernism's deconstructive style and often sarcastic tone, this obviously handmade style further brings back the transparency of maker/process in order to undermine and deconstruct the frame of reference. It is not to say that the superclean corporate sheen of modern is replaced by the deconstructive aggressive magnificent chaos of either postmodern, or what I call "Beautiful Messy." True to our pluralistic culture, the styles coexist.

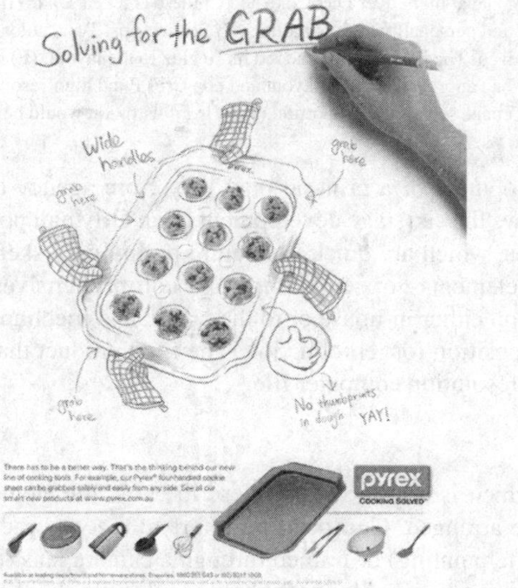

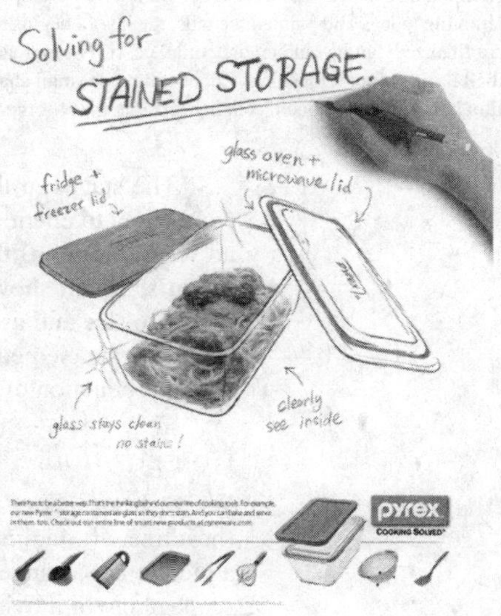

Photo: Courtesy of World Kitchens

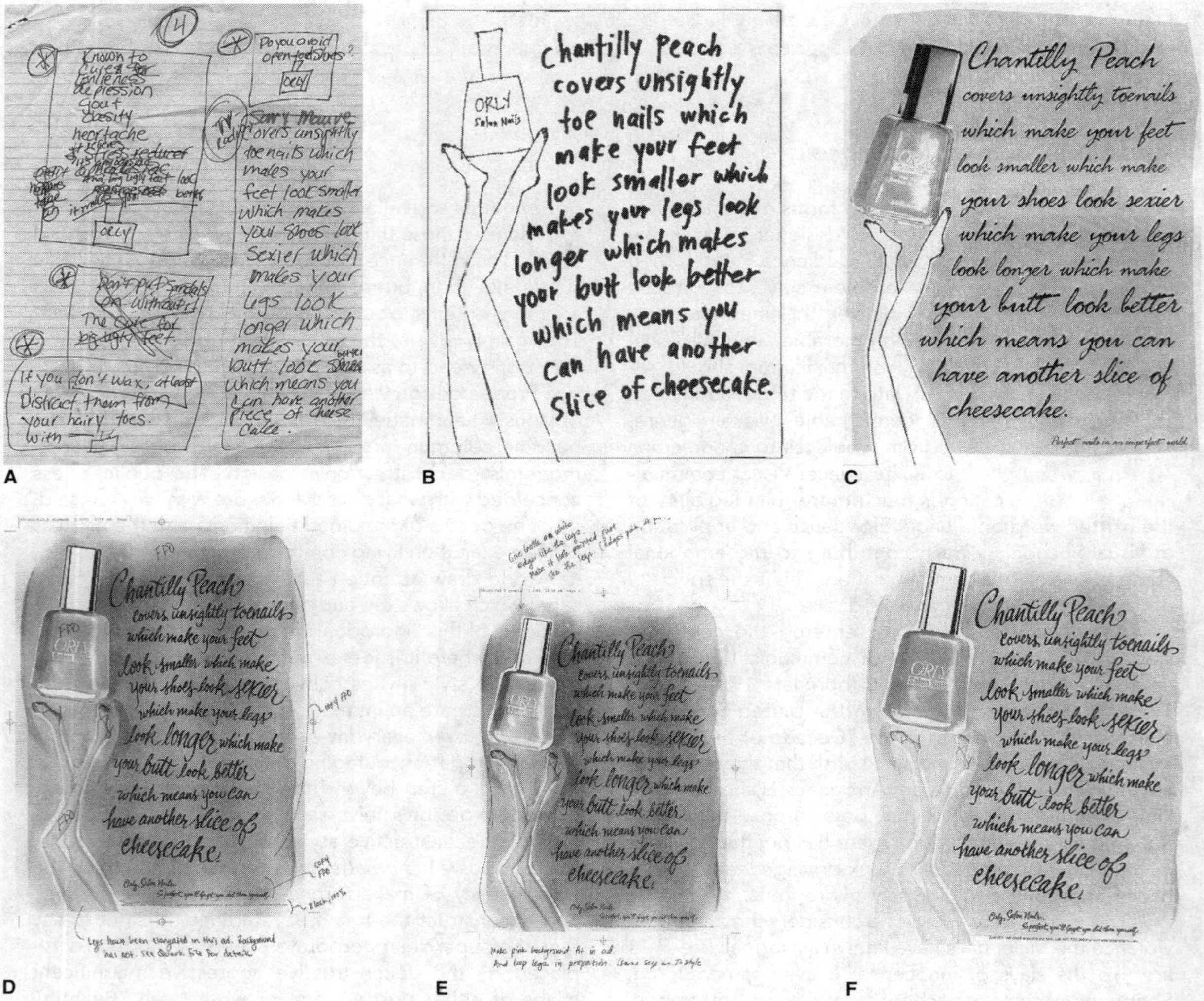

FIGURE 10.1

Orly "Chantilly Peach" Creative Process

(A) Thumbnail sketches. These ideas for Orly were developed by the creative team late at night over Diet Coke and Chinese chicken salad. (B) Rough layout. Transitioning to legs and painted toenails, the layout begins to give some glamour and personality to the product. (C) Semicomps. Type, color, and tagline are still not finalized, but layout is more complete. (D) Comprehensives. Tagline approved. The illustrator has added more glitz to the layout. (E) Mechanicals. The digital file before retouching. Client still made small changes at this stage but had approved the ad's layout and copy. (F) Final high-resolution film. The film house had to retouch, creating separate files for the legs and background image so that the proportion of the leg illustration would be correct.

The stages in the normal development of a print ad may vary from agency to agency or from client to client. Figure 10.1 shows the six-stage development of an Orly nail polish ad. This ad went through **thumbnail sketches**, which are quick, miniature preliminary sketches; **rough layouts**, which show where design elements go; **semicomps** and **comprehensives**, which are drawn to size and used for presentation either in-house or to the client; and **mechanicals**, which assemble the elements in their final position for reproduction. The final product that is used for actual production of the ad is a high-resolution computer file.

Composition

We've been talking about layout, which is a term used to describe how the elements in print (headline, art, tagline, and so on) are arranged. **Composition** refers to the way the elements in a picture are arranged (think a still-life painting) or framed through a camera lens (think a landscape photo or movie scene). Photographers and **videographers** (people who shoot a scene using a video camera) handle composition in two ways: (1) They may be able to place or arrange the elements in front of their cameras, and (2) they may have to compose the image by manipulating their own point of view if the elements can't be moved. In other words, they move around to find the most aesthetic way to frame an image that isn't movable, such as a scene or landscape, as well as to catch different lighting situations, such as bright sun and shade or shadow.

Similar to the way layouts are developed by using sketches, video images are also drawn and presented as **storyboards**, which are sketches of the scenes and key shots in a commercial. The art director imagines the characters and setting as well as how the characters act and move in the scene. The art director sketches in a few key frames the visual idea for a scene and how it is to be shot and how one scene links to the scenes that follow. In addition, the storyboard sketches also reflect the position and movement of the cameras recording the scene, a description of which is spelled out both in the script and on the storyboard.

Environmental Design

Think about the last time you went to a sit-down restaurant versus your experiences in fast-food places. What's the difference in the way these spaces are designed both inside and outside? Think about the colors and surfaces and types of furniture. What do these design features say about the personality of the restaurant? How is a sit-down restaurant different in its design from a fast-food place?

Environmental design is entirely different from the usual marketing communication pieces. Remember we said in Chapter 2 that everything communicates, and that includes the design of the environment in which goods and services are offered for sale. Physical decisions about space and color and texture can communicate just as quickly as posters and signs.

The architectural design and interior ambiance of a store also contribute to its brand personality. If you have been in a Polo store or Polo section in a department store, you might remember some of the details of the environment that make the space different from, say, a Sears department, not to mention a Nike or a Patagonia store. Nike stores have even been described as retail theater with displays and spaces that showcase not only the shoes and apparel but also the sports with which they are associated.

What Do You Need to Know about Production?

Art directors need to understand print media requirements and the technical side of production because these factors affect both the look of the printed piece and its cost. Marketing communication managers also need to understand some of these basics in order to critique ideas and evaluate them in terms of cost and feasibility.

Print Media Requirements

Different media put different demands on the design and production of advertising. Newspapers and directories, for example, are printed at high speed on an inexpensive, rough-surfaced, spongy paper called **newsprint** that quickly absorbs ink on contact. Newsprint is not a great surface for reproducing fine details, especially color photographs and delicate typefaces. Most newspapers offer color to advertisers, but because of the limitations of the printing process, the color may not be perfectly in **registration** (i.e., all of the color inks may not be aligned exactly, creating a somewhat blurred image). For that reason, ads such as the Oklahoma City ads are specifically designed for high-contrast, black-and-white printing. These work well for both newspaper and directory ads.

Magazines have traditionally led the way in graphic print production because their glossy paper is a higher grade than newsprint. Excellent photographic and color reproduction is the big difference between newspapers and magazines. Magazine advertisements are also able to take advantage of more creative, attention-getting devices, such as pop-up visuals, scent strips, and computer chips that play melodies when the pages are opened. An Altoids ad

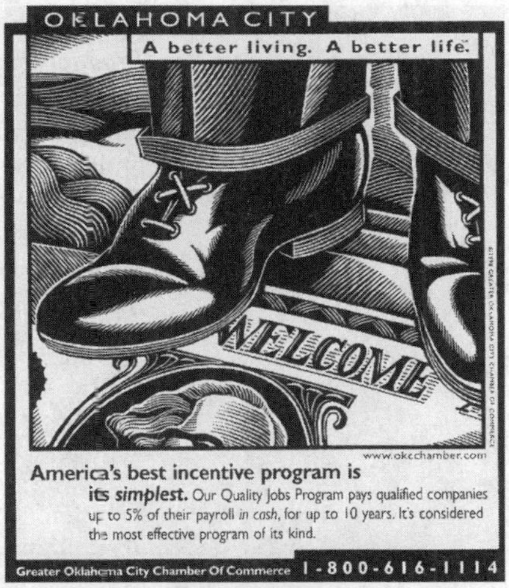

Photo: Courtesy Greater Oklahoma City Chamber

High-contrast graphics are the key to good reproduction in a newspaper. The art in these ads simulates an old wood engraving.

that launched Altoids chewing gum, for example, ran in magazines with a novel print production technique. It showed a box of Altoids chewing gum on one page and a singed logo burnt onto the cartoon on the opposite page.

The key to an effective poster or outdoor board is a dominant visual with minimal copy. Because billboards must make a quick and lasting impression from far away, their layout should be compact with a simple visual path. The Institute for Outdoor Advertising recommends these tips for designers:

- ***Graphics*** Make the illustration an eye-stopper.
- ***Size*** Images in billboards are huge—a 25-foot-long pencil or a 43-foot pointing finger. The product or the brand label can be hundreds of times larger than life.
- ***Colors*** Use bold, bright colors. The greatest impact is created by maximum contrast between two colors, such as dark colors against white or yellow.[10]
- ***Figure/Ground*** Make the relationship between foreground and background as obvious as possible. A picture of a soft drink against a jungle background is hard to perceive when viewed from a moving vehicle at a distance. The background should never compete with the subject.
- ***Typography*** Use simple, clean, uncluttered type that is easy to read at a distance by an audience in motion. The industry's legibility research recommends avoiding all-capital letters, fanciful ornamental letters, and script and cursive fonts.
- ***Product Identification*** Focus attention on the product by reproducing the label or package at a huge size.
- ***Extensions*** Extend the frame of the billboard to expand the scale and break away from the limits of the long rectangle.
- ***Shape*** For visual impact, create the illusion of 3-D effects by playing with horizons, vanishing lines, and dimensional boxes. Inflatables create a better 3-D effect than most billboards can, even with superior graphics. Made of a heavyweight, stitched nylon, inflatables can be freestanding, or they can be added to outdoor boards as an extension.

FIGURE 10.2
Line Art and Halftone Art
An example of a figure reproduced as line art (left) and as a halftone (right).

- ***Motion*** Add motors to boards to make pieces and parts move. Disk-like wheels and glittery things that flicker in the wind create the appearance of motion, color change, and images that squeeze, wave, or pour. Use revolving panels, called *kinetic boards*, for messages that change.

Print Art Reproduction

In general, there are two types of printed images: line art and halftones. A drawing or illustration is called **line art** because the image is solid lines on white background, as in the Oklahoma City ads. Photographs, which are referred to as **continuous tones** or **halftones**, are much more complicated to reproduce because they have a range of gray tones between the black and white, as shown in Figure 10.2.

Printers create the illusion of shades of gray in converting photos to halftones by shooting the original photograph through a fine **screen**, which converts the image to a pattern of dots that gives the illusion of shades of gray—dark areas are large dots that fill the screen and light areas are tiny dots surrounded by **white space**. The quality of the image depends on how fine the screen is: Newspapers use a coarse screen, usually 65 lines per inch (called a 65-line screen), whereas magazines use fine screens, which may be from 120 up to 200 or 300 lines per inch.

Screens are also used to create **tint blocks**, which can either be shades of gray in black-and-white printing or shades of color. A block of color can be printed solid, or it can be screened to create a shade. These shades are expressed as a range of percentages, from 100 percent (solid) down to 10 percent (very faint). Figure 10.3 gives examples of screens in color. A similar process is used with computer images, which are presented in pixels and measured in pixels per centimeter or inch (PPCM or PPI). Quality photos, for example, are generally presented in 300 PPI.

It would be impossible to set up a printing press with a separate ink roller for every hue and value in a color photo. How, then, are these colors reproduced?

Full-color images are reproduced using four distinctive shades of ink called **process colors**, in order to produce **four-color printing**. These colors are *magenta* (a shade of pinkish purple), *cyan* (a shade of bright blue), *yellow*, and *black*. Printing inks are transparent, so when one ink overlaps another, a third color is created, and that's how the full range of colors is created. For example, red and blue create purple, yellow and blue create green, and yellow and red create orange. The black is used for type and, in four-color printing, adds depth to the shadows and dark tones in an image.

The process printers use to reduce the original color image to four halftone negatives is called **color separation**. Figure 10.4 illustrates the process of color separation.

Digitization If an ad is going to run in a number of publications, there has to be some way to distribute a reproducible, duplicate of the ad to all of them. The duplicate material for **offset printing** is a slick proof of the original mechanical. More recently, **digitization** of images has been used to distribute reproducible images. This is also how computers now handle the color reproduction process. These digitized images can be transmitted electronically to printers across a city for local editions of national newspapers or by satellite for regional editions of magazines

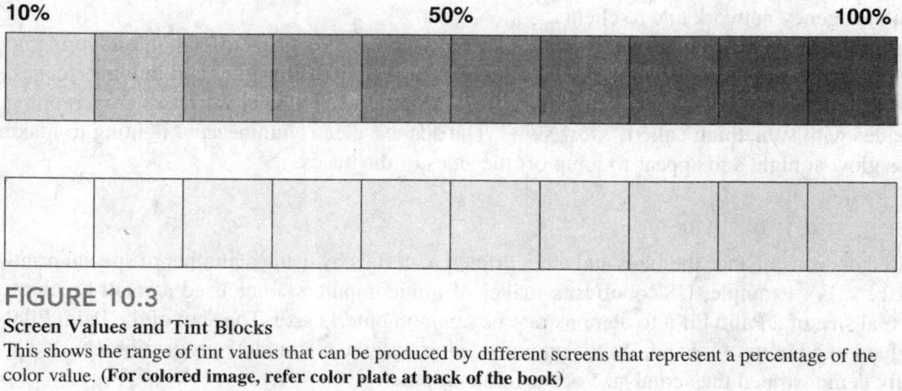

FIGURE 10.3
Screen Values and Tint Blocks
This shows the range of tint values that can be produced by different screens that represent a percentage of the color value. **(For colored image, refer color plate at back of the book)**

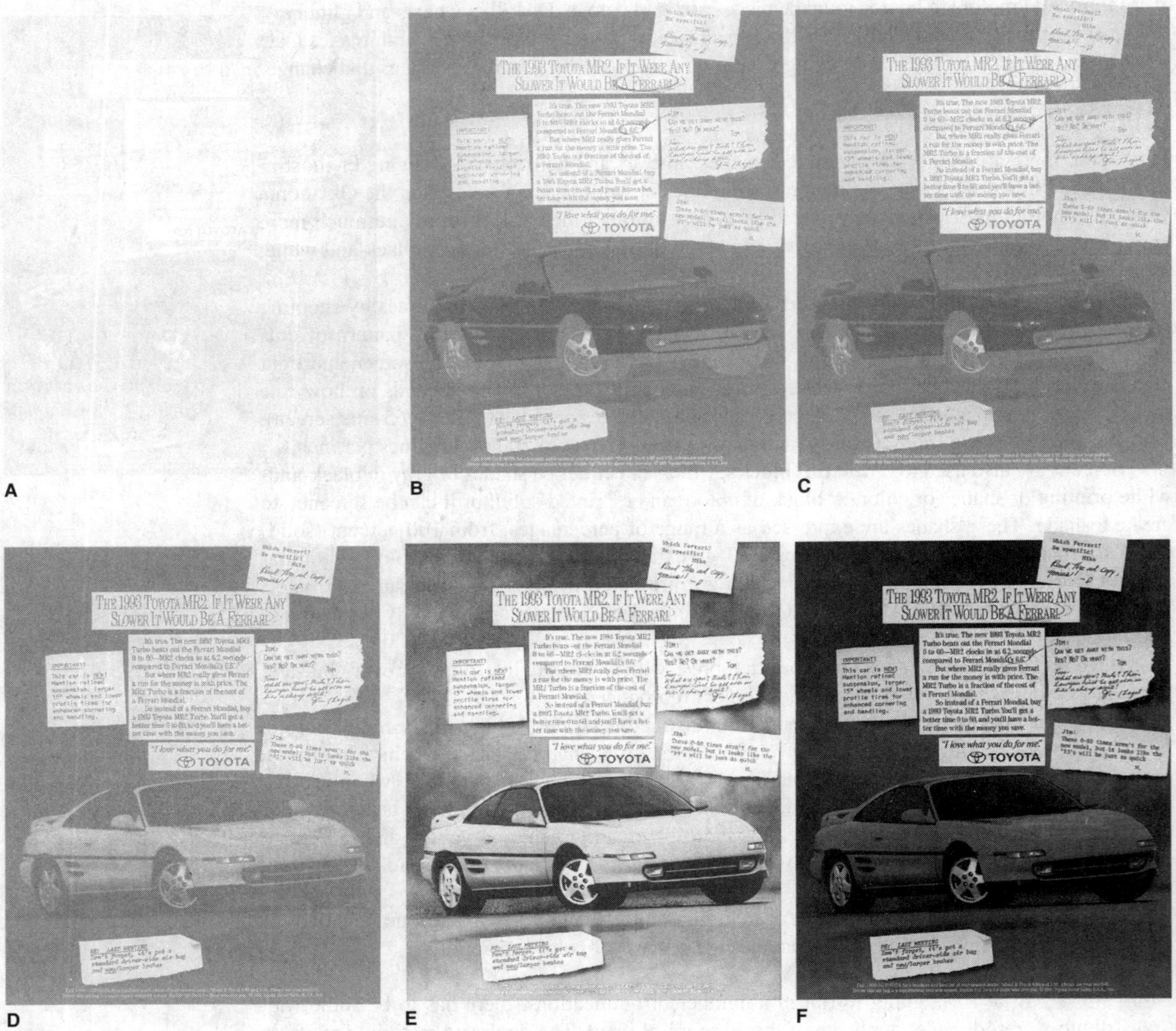

FIGURE 10.4

The Color Separation Process

These six photos illustrate the process of creating four-color separations: (A) Yellow plate. (B) Magenta plate. (C) Yellow and magenta combined plate. (D) Cyan plate. (*Note:* After cyan is added, there would also be combined plates showing cyan added first to yellow, then to magenta, then to the combined yellow and magenta plates. These steps were left out to simplify the presentation.) (E) Black plate. (F) Finished art with all four process colors combined. **(For colored image, refer color plate at back of the book)**

and newspapers, such as *USA Today*. Agencies also use this method for transmitting ad proofs within the agency network and to clients.

Digitization makes it possible to create some spectacular effects in out-of-home advertising. Some outdoor boards have become digital screens complete with changing and moving images. A new technique in transit advertising comes from Atlanta, where the city's buses are wrapping their sides with something called "glow skin." The ads use electroluminescent lighting to make the ads glow at night and appear to jump off the sides of the buses.

Binding and Finishing

Art directors can enhance their ads and other printed materials by using a number of special printing effects. For example, USRobotics, a maker of minicomputers, once used a small brochure the actual size of a Palm Pilot to demonstrate its minicomputer's size. The shot of the Palm Pilot was glued to a photo of a hand. As the ad unfolded, it became a complete product brochure that visually demonstrated the actual size of the minicomputer.

Other mechanical techniques include the following:

- ***Die Cutting*** A sharp-edged stamp, or die, is used to cut out unusual shapes. A common **die-cut** shape you're familiar with is the tab on a file folder.
- ***Embossing or Debossing*** The application of pressure to create a raised surface (**embossing**) or depressed image (**debossing**) in paper.
- ***Foil Stamping*** The process of **foil stamping** involves molding a thin metallic coating (silver or gold) to the surface of an image.
- ***Tip-Ins*** A **tip-in** is a separate, preprinted ad provided by the advertiser that is glued into a publication as the publication is being assembled or bound. Perfume manufacturers, for example, tip in samples that are either scratch-and-sniff or scented strips that release a fragrance when pulled apart.

3D Printing

The latest printing technology innovation, which began making headlines in 2013, is 3D printing, which doesn't mean images appear to jump off the page; rather, 3D imaging processes are used to manufacture objects, such as iPad stands, jewelry, machine parts, or weapons and ammunition. A printer that looks like your desktop computer printer extrudes materials—plastics, even metal to a specified size and shape. Experts predict a new Industrial Revolution from this developing technology.

What Does an Art Director Need to Know about Video Production?

Where does an art director start when putting together a video for a commercial, a video news release, or some other kind of corporate film or video? Obviously, the first consideration is the nature of the image. The art director can arrange for filming on a constructed set or in a real location. The image is composed through the lens of the camera, just as it is for still images, but the difference—and the challenge—lies in the way the moving image takes shape. That's true for movies but also for commercials and commercial videos used for a variety of promotional purposes, such as the "Artic Home" video created by Coke in support of polar bears and the Wildlife Fund.

In addition to actual filming, another option is to use **stock footage**—previously recorded images, either video, still slides, or moving film. Typical stock footage files are shots from a satellite, historical scenes such as World War II battles, or a car crash. Animation, stop motion, and 3-D are other film production techniques that can be used instead of using stock footage or live filming.

Working within the framework of the creative strategy, art directors also create the look of the video or commercial. The look of the award-winning "Cat Herders" commercial that the Fallon agency created for Electronic Data Systems (EDS) was a parody of the American West, much like a John Ford movie, with horses, craggy-faced cowboys who acted as cat wranglers, and stampeding animals (the cats). Find it on YouTube.

Dogs got their day in a 2012 pre–Super Bowl teaser ad for Volkswagen. Following up on the previous year's winner, "The Force," with its pint-sized Darth Vader, the dozen dogs barked a canine version of the *Star Wars* theme.

Photo: © 2004 Electronic Data Systems. All rights reserved. Used with permission. Courtesy of Fallon Worldwide

The Fallon agency was given the impossible task of creating a commercial that illustrated the EDS positioning statement: "EDS thrives on defeating complexity." It translated that language into a popular phrase used in the Silicone Valley culture—"It's like herding cats." To bring that idea to life, the Fallon team filmed a team of rugged cowboys herding thousands of cats.

The canine stars in this "bark side" show were picked not just for their voices but also for their resemblance to *Star Wars* characters. You just have to see this one, too—check it out at YouTube.

Other graphic elements, such as words, product logos, and still photos, are digitized or computer generated right on the screen. A **crawl** is a set of computer-generated letters that appear to be moving across the bottom of the screen. All of these effects are designed or specified by the art director.

The big change has been the move from film to digital images. Some movies, such as the *Dark Knight* series are still recorded on film, but the trend in 21st-century moviemaking, as well as advertising, is to use digital technology. Sophisticated computer graphics systems, such as those used in the early days of digital filming to create the *Star Wars* and *Matrix* special effects, pioneered the making of artistic film and video. More recently, Keanu Reeves takes you on a tour of this gee-whiz technology and its directors, such as Martin Scorsese and Steven Soderbergh, in the *Side by Side* documentary.[11]

Computer graphic artists brag that they can do anything with an image. They can look at any object from any angle or even from the inside out. Computer graphics specialists use computer software to create, multiply, and manipulate video images. That's how 50 cats can be made to look like hundreds in the EDS "Herding Cats" commercial. One creative video technique is called **morphing**, in which one object gradually changes into another. Photographs of real objects can change into art or animation and then return to life. And sometimes the real life becomes art, as in the 3-D movie *Hugo,* where the characters look like animation.

Filming and Editing

Most local retail commercials are simple and inexpensive, and they are typically shot and taped at the local station. The sales representative for the station may work with the advertiser to write the script, and the station's director handles the taping of the commercial.

Creating a national television commercial is more complex and requires a number of people with specialized skills. The ad agency crew usually includes the copywriter and art director, as well as the producer, who oversees the production and is responsible for the budget, among other things. The director, who is the person responsible for filming the commercial, is usually someone from outside the agency. This person takes the art director's storyboard and makes it come to life.

The producer and director make up the core of the production team. The commercial's effectiveness depends on their shared vision of the final commercial and the director's ability to bring it to life as the art director imagined it. In the case of the "Cat Herders" commercial, the director was chosen by the agency because of his skill at coaxing naturally humorous performances from nonprofessional actors. In this commercial, he worked with real wranglers on their semiscripted testimonials about their work with kitties.

The following list summarizes the responsibilities of broadcast production personnel:

Who Does What in Broadcast Production?

Copywriter	Writes the script, whether it contains dialogue, narrative, lyrics, announcements, descriptions, or no words at all.
Art Director	In television, develops the storyboard and establishes the look of the commercial, whether realistic, stylized, or fanciful.
***Producer** (can be an agency staff member)*	Takes charge of the production, handles the bidding and all production arrangements, finds the specialists, arranges for casting talent, and makes sure the expenses and bids come in under budget.
Director	Has responsibility for the actual filming or taping, including how long the scene runs, who does what, how lines are spoken, and how characters are played; in television, determines how the camera is set up and records the flow of action.
Composer	Writes original music and sometimes the lyrics as well.
Arranger	Orchestrates music for the various instruments and voices to make it fit a scene or copy line. The copywriter usually writes the lyrics or at least gives the arranger some idea of what the words should convey.
Editor	Puts everything together toward the end of the filming or taping process; evaluates how to assemble scenes and which audio elements work best with the dialogue and footage.

The Process of Producing Videos

Originally, film was shot on 35-mm film or videotape and then digitized, after which the editor transferred the image to videotape for dissemination, a process called **film-to-tape transfer**. Digital technology has changed the process. With modern filmmaking, images are recorded on hard drives, eliminating the use of film or videotape. Art directors work closely with editors who assemble the shots and cut the film or digital images to create the right pacing and sequence of images as outlined in the storyboard.

Filming Techniques Obviously, the "Cat Herders" commercial was a product of computer graphics magic. The Big Idea for the ad created some real filming challenges. In the spot, the metaphor of herding cats meant that the cats had to swim across a river, but was that even possible? Here's how it was done: The trainers taught a few cats that weren't adverse to water to swim by starting them out in one-quarter inch of water in a child's swimming pool and then gradually adding water to the pool until it was deep enough for the cats to swim. The "river" was actually a small pool warmed by a portable heater—the art director described it as "a little kitty Jacuzzi." Multiple copies of the swimming kitties were made and manipulated using computer graphics until an entire herd was created. And that's how this famous scene came about.

Animation is another filming technique that is often used in commercials. The technique of **animation** traditionally meant drawing images on film and then recording the images one frame at a time. Cartoon figures, for example, were sketched and then resketched for the next frame with a slight change to indicate a small progression in the movement of an arm or a leg or a facial expression. Animation is traditionally shot at 16 drawings per second. Low-budget animation uses fewer drawings, so the motion looks jerky. The introduction of computers has accelerated the process and eliminated the tedious handwork.

Animation is similar to illustration in print in that it abstracts images and adds a touch of fantasy and/or mood to the image. As Karl Schroeder, a copywriter with Coates Kokes in Portland, Oregon, explains about a project his team worked on for a recycling center, "What was nice about it, when you consider that the spots needed to appeal to *everyone* who recycles in the area, was that it [animation] got us away from casting racially ambiguous, hard-to-pin-an-age-on talent."

Animation effects can also be used to combine animated characters, such as the little green Geico Gecko, with live-action figures or even with other animated characters. The famous Aflac duck was created as a collaboration between Warner Brothers and the Aflac agency, the Kaplan Thaler Group in New York. More advanced techniques, similar to those used in movies like *Avatar*, *Up*, and the *Shrek* series, create lifelike images and movement. A technique called "mental ray" was used in a Levi Strauss ad featuring 600 stampeding buffalo. Mental ray is so good that it not only created lifelike images but even added realistic hair on the animals.[12]

A particular type of animation is **stop motion**, a technique used to film inanimate objects like the Pillsbury Doughboy, which is a puppet. The little character is moved a bit at a time and filmed frame by frame. Karl Schroeder describes how he and his art director settled on the stop-motion technique for two commercials that changed residential recycling behavior in his community. He says that in developing a concept for commercials, he'll usually think of live-action film first. When he does consider animation, it's usually achieved with computer graphics or illustrations. But for these two recycling spots, here's how the stop-action effects were created:

> Both spots have three layers. All of the foreground elements, from the glass bottles to the yellow bins, are actual objects. The animator painstakingly moved each item frame by frame. Furthermore, each frame was shot twice. Normally you'd only need to shoot each frame once. But because we were shooting in front of a green screen and because we were using glass bottles (which reflect), we had to shoot each frame twice, one in front of the green screen and the second in front of a "natural background." So now with two sets of images (as if all this weren't enough work), next up was to clip out the bottles that had the alien green reflection (from the green screen) and drop in the bottles that sported the natural reflections from the other shots, again frame by frame.
>
> The next layer is more straightforward, featuring the house and yard. The third layer has the sky and clouds (which move if you look closely). Since the plastic bag spot didn't have glass, it was a little simpler but otherwise followed the same process. Lastly, we

didn't want the logo, tag, and info to be tacked on at the end against a black background. Instead, we integrated the information by animating it against a tight shot of our yellow bin. The effect is much less jarring and better unites the "business" with the rest of the spot.

The same technique is used in **claymation**, which involves creating characters from clay and then photographing them one frame at a time. Both have been popular with art directors who create advertising where fantasy effects are desired, although new computer effects also are simplifying these techniques.

3-D is a type of film production that creates the illusion of depth using a special motion picture camera and projection hardware. Viewers also have to wear special glasses. The 3-D technique has been around for many years, but only with the big success of the movie Avatar did it achieve wide popularity, but it's slow moving to television and commercials. ESPN launched a 3-D Channel in 2010 for the World Cup broadcast and persuaded major advertisers, such as Procter & Gamble and Sony, to experiment with 3-D spots on the new channel.

Music and Action Specifying the music is usually done as part of the copywriting; however, matching the music to the action is an art director or producer's responsibility. In some cases, as in high-production song-and-dance numbers, the music is the commercial. Other times, it is used to get attention, set a mood, and lock the commercial into memory.

For example, a JanSport commercial for its Live Wire Euphonic Pack, a backpack with built-in earphones and volume controls, cries out for a musical demonstration. The unlikely song picked for the spot, which targets the MTV crowd, was "Do-Re-Mi" from the 1965 *Sound of Music* musical. You might wonder why the creative team at the DDB Seattle agency would choose such a retro piece. Actually, the rendition is not from the early recording but rather from an ethereal, techno-pop version. The stick-in-the-head lyrics match the action on screen in a contemporary version of the classic story boy meets girl, boy loses girl, boy finds girl.[13]

The Television Production Process

For the bigger national commercials, the steps in the television production process fall into four categories: message design, preproduction, the shoot, and postproduction. Figure 10.5 shows the steps in the process.

Preproduction The producer and staff first develop a set of **production notes**, describing in detail every aspect of the production. These notes are important for finding talent and locations, building sets, and getting bids and estimates from specialists. In the "Cat Herders" commercial, finding the talent was critical. Some 50 felines and their trainers were involved in the filming. Surprisingly, different cats have different skills—some were able to appear to be asleep or motionless on cue, while others excelled as runners or specialized in water scenes.

Once the bids for production have been approved, the creative team and the producer, director, and other key players hold a **preproduction** meeting to outline every step of the production process and anticipate every problem that may arise. Then the work begins. The talent agency begins casting the roles, while the production team finds a location and arranges site use with owners, police, and other officials. If sets are needed, they have to be built. Finding the props is a test of ingenuity, and the prop person may wind up visiting hardware stores, secondhand stores, and maybe even the local dump. Costumes must be made, located, or bought.

The Shoot The director shoots the commercial scene by scene but not necessarily in the order set down in the script. Each scene is shot, called a **take**, and after all the scenes in the storyboard have been shot, they are assembled through editing.

Photo: Images Courtesy Metro, www.oregonmetro.gov

SHOWCASE

Karl Schroeder says he really hadn't considered stop motion before but it was perfect for this assignment for Metro Recycling and arguably the only solution for this recycling concept. Everything was shot in a studio and composited in the computer.

A graduate of the University of Oregon advertising program, Karl Schroeder worked at Coates Kokes, Portland, Oregon, before moving to Nike as senior writer/editor. He was nominated by Professor Charles Frazer.

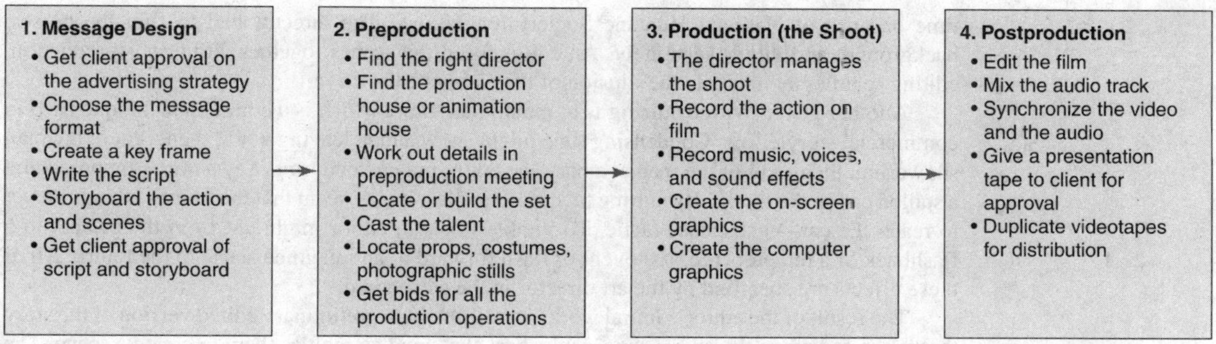

FIGURE 10.5
Video Production Process
In general, there are four steps in the production of a video after agreement is obtained on the message strategy.

If the director films the commercial on videotape, it is played back immediately to determine what needs correcting. Film, however, has to be processed before the director can review it. These processed scenes are called **dailies**—although dailies can now be available instantaneously with digital filming. **Rushes** are rough versions of the commercial assembled from **cuts** of the raw film footage. The director and the agency creative team, as well as the client representative, view them immediately after the shoot to make sure everything's been filmed as planned.

The film crew includes a number of technicians, all of whom report to the director. For both film and video recording, the camera operators are the key technicians. Other technicians include—and you've probably seen these terms in movie credits—the **gaffer**, who is the chief electrician, and the **grip**, who moves props and sets and lays tracks for the dolly on which the camera is mounted. The script clerk checks the dialogue and other script details and times the scenes. A set is a busy crowded place that appears, at times, to be total confusion and chaos.

The audio director records the audio either at the time of the shoot or, in the case of more high-end productions, separately in a sound studio. If the sound is being recorded at the time of shooting, a **mixer**, who operates the recording equipment, and a *mic* or *boom* person, who sets up the microphones, handle the recording on the set. In the studio, audio is usually recorded after the film is shot, so the audio has to be synchronized with the footage. Directors often wait to see exactly how the action appears before they write and record the audio track. However, if the art director has decided to set the commercial to music, then the music on the audio track may be recorded before the shoot, as in the "Do-Re-Mi" audio track, and the filming done to the music.

In some rare cases, an entire commercial is shot as one continuous action rather than individual shots edited together in postproduction. Probably the most interesting use of this approach is "Cog," an award-winning commercial for the Honda Accord that shows the assembly of pieces of the car piece by piece. It begins with a rolling transmission bearing and moves through valves, brake pedals, tires, the hood, and so forth until the car drives away at the end of the commercial. It's tempting to think it was created through computer animation, but the Honda "Cog" commercial was filmed in real time without any special effects. It took 606 takes for the whole thing to work—that's 606 run-throughs of the sequence! One of the most talked-about spots ever made, the publicity given to the commercial was probably even more valuable than an advertising buy. The "Cog" commercial won a Grand Clio (a creative award show) as well as a Gold Lion at the Cannes Advertising Festival. Altogether, it picked up no fewer than 20 awards from various British and international organizations. The spot can be seen at www.ebaumsworld.com/flash/play/734.[14]

Postproduction For film and video, much of the work happens after the shoot in **postproduction**—when the commercial begins to emerge from the hands and mind of the editor. The objective of editing is to assemble the various pieces of film into a sequence that follows the storyboard. Editors manipulate the audio and video images, creating realistic 3-D images and combining real-life and computer-generated images. The postproduction process is hugely important in video because so many digital effects are being added to the raw film after the shoot. In the "Cat Herders" commercial, Fallon could not film the cats and horses at the same time because of National Humane Society regulations. The director had to film the horses, background, and kitties separately. An editor fused the scenes together during postproduction, editing seamlessly to create the illusion of the elaborate cat drive.

Another goal of **video editing** is to manipulate time, which is a common technique used in commercial storytelling. Condensing time might show a man leaving work, then a cut of the man showering, then a cut of the man at a bar. The editor may extend time. Say a train is approaching a stalled car on the tracks. By cutting to various angles, it may seem that the train is taking forever to reach the car—a suspense tactic. To jumble time, an editor might cut from the present to a flashback of a remembered past event or flash forward to an imagined scene in the future. All of these effects are specified by the art director in the storyboard.

The result of the editor's initial work is a **rough cut**, a preliminary edited version of the story that is created when the editor chooses the best shots and assembles them to create a scene. The editor then joins the scenes together—in contemporary film production, all this happens digitally. After the revision and re-editing have been completed, the editor makes an **interlock**, which means the audio and film have been assembled together. The final version with the sound and film mixed together is called an **answer print**. The answer print is the final version printed onto a piece of film. For the commercial to air on hundreds of stations around the country, the agency makes duplicate copies—a process called **dubbing**. The dubbed copies are called **release prints**.

Web Design Considerations

Visuals are just as important on websites and Internet ads as they are in print ads and outdoor boards. Photos on company websites are particularly important in terms of what they say about the corporate or brand image. Since websites are often created on the cheap, viewers may find themselves looking at product images that are fuzzy or confusing.

An article in the *Wall Street Journal*, for example, showed a baking company's unappetizing photos with a brownie baking pan that could be used as a roasting pan showing hunks of meat—prompting a customer wrote in asking what connected brownies and bloody meat. Such photo flubs can eat into sales as well as hurt the company's image. As the founder of ProPoint Graphics, a presentation design firm explained, "The images you use should reinforce your brand and message because in the end it the pictures that your clients will remember."[15]

Web design includes creating ads that run on the Web as well as the website itself. Banner ads are designed more like outdoor boards than conventional print ads because their small space puts intense requirements on the designer to make the ad communicate quickly and succinctly and yet attract attention and curiosity to elicit a click-through response. You can check out banner ads online at http://thelongestlistofthelongeststuffatthelongestdomainnameatlonglast.com/banner.html.

Designers know that Web pages, particularly the first screen, should follow the same layout rules as posters: The graphics should be eye catching without demanding too much downloading time; type should be simple, using one or two typefaces and avoiding all caps and letterspacing, which can distort words. Because there is often a lot to read, organizing the information is critical. In terms of legibility, black type on a high-contrast background usually is best; all of the design elements—type and graphics—should be big enough to see on the smallest screen.

What makes Web design different from print designs is the opportunity to use motion, animation, and interactive navigation. While attention getting, these can also be irritating. Professor Mallia reminds us that online ads can succeed or fail because of their design as well as their copy. She explains, "Visual tactics like rollovers and motion often annoy more than attract." She also points out that copy is important in Web design: "Experts find it's the copy that often gets the click-through—because it offers something the reader wants to *read* more about." So even in the highly visual online world, it's still important for the art and copy to work together to attract attention and build interest.

Usually, the illustrations are created by artists, but sometimes for low-budget projects, the illustrations and photos are obtained from clip-art services or, rather, click art, such as that provided by www.dreamstime.com or www.1StopPictures.com. Actually, any image can be scanned and manipulated to create a Web image, which is causing copyright problems for artists and others who originally created the images, as explained with the Obama "Hope" story earlier in the chapter. Because of the magic of digitizing, Web pages can combine elements and design styles from many different media: print, still photography, film, animation, sound, and games.

The combination of interactive navigation, live streaming video, online radio, and 360-degree camera angles creates Web pages that may be more complex than anything you see on television, which is why ease of use is a factor in website design.

Web designers use a completely different toolbox than other types of art directors. Animation effects, as well as sophisticated navigation paths, are designed using software programs such as Flash, Silverlight, Director, Blender, and Squeak and nonlinear editing tools such as Premier, FinalCut, and AfterEffects. It's such a rapidly changing design world that it's difficult to keep track of the most recent innovations in Web design software. The use of animation effects and streaming video has made websites look more like television and film.

For more examples of excellence in website design and reviews of the top websites, check out the following websites:

www.webaward.org
www.worldbestwebsites.com
www.100bestwebsites.org
www.topsiteslinks.com
www.webbyawards.com
www.clioawards.com
www.oneclub.com

Action and Interaction

Web advertisers are continuing to find ways to bring dramatic action to the small screen to make the imagery more engaging. For example, Ford used a banner on the Yahoo! home page with the familiar Ford oval and a bunch of little black birds on a wire. Then three of the birds flew down to the middle of the page and started pecking at what looked like birdseed, uncovering an image of the new Explorer. The link read, "Click to uncover the next territory." Those who did click probably expected a pop-up image, but instead the page shook, the birds scattered, and a big red Ford Explorer drove up to the front of the screen, replacing most of the content. It was a surprising, highly involving, and effective announcement of the vehicle.

Because users can create their own paths through the website, designers have to make sure that their sites have clear **navigation**. Users should be able to move through the site easily, find the information they want, and respond. Navigation problems can really turn off viewers. Eye-tracking research (studies that use a camera to follow eye movement when looking at a page or screen) has found that if the navigation is cluttered or unclear, viewers will give up and move on to some other site.[16] Ideally, users who visit a site regularly should be able to customize the site to fit their own interests and navigation patterns.

Online video has also expanded the avenues for action on the small screen on mini-computers, tablets, and cell phones. Web video is becoming a new business opportunity for businesses that want to use videos to display their products. The secret is to plan these videos specifically for a small screen and not just try to use regular television or film images because the screen is just a fraction of the size of a television and a lot of the detail in an image can get lost.[17]

If a site is well designed, people may want to interact with the organization sponsoring the site. For example, Texture/Media, a Boulder, Colorado, Web design firm, created a seven-episode series over five months that detailed the journey of two men attempting to climb the MeruSharksfin summit in India for client Marmot Mountain Works. Called ClimbMeru.com, it chronicled the team's training and trip and hosted contest giveaways that helped gather information about Marmot's customers. Texture/Media's objective with its award-winning websites is to make the consumer a participant in its brand stories.

Looking Ahead

This chapter has focused on the impact of visuals and how to use them effectively in brand communication. To summarize, in most marketing communication media, the power to get attention lies primarily with the visual. Ideally, the visuals work with the words to present the creative concept. The excitement and drama in a television commercial is created through moving images, but it is an intriguing idea that grabs attention and remains in memory. This is particularly so for larger-impact formats, such as posters and outdoor boards.

This is the last chapter in Part 3 of our discussion on the design of the message. We introduced creative thinking and the creation of creative briefs and then discussed copywriting. In this chapter, we have provided you with a brief introduction to art direction and design. Next we discuss how messages are delivered—both to and from the target audience and other key stakeholders.

It's a Wrap

ALTOIDS®

Keeping the Altoids Brand in Mint Condition

As a product's owners change hands, the new owners are smart to recognize the value of the brand's heritage. The Altoids campaign has a strong, consistent look strengthened by the continuing presence of the distinctive Altoids tin. Repetition of the look and tone in all forms of media, including digital applications, is the key to brand recognition.

The brand is recognizable because it builds on the principle that the more times viewers see an ad with a consistent format, the more likely they are to remember the product. Another lesson to be learned from the curiously strong mint: Even though campaigns change, sometimes brands have accrued valuable equity in the previous work that needs to be maintained and protected.

The classic "Curiously Strong Mints" campaign is one of the most awarded and successful campaigns. The advertising has garnered multiple awards, including a long string of Kelly Awards for magazine advertising, One Show creative prizes, and multiple Clios. It won an international effectiveness award when it received the New York Festival's Grand Prix award. The Magazine Publishers of America bestowed its $100,000 Grand Prize Kelly Award for outstanding magazine advertising for the Altoids "Burn Through" campaign, which launched Altoids gum.

The low-cost, edgy print campaign has been a business builder. The brand had virtually no presence in 1995 when Kraft bought it, but by 2000 it dominated the extreme mint market with a 25 percent share. Altoids now is the number-one-selling mint in the United States. Whether current efforts build on this success remains to be seen.

What makes Altoids advertising a winner? The memorability and extendibility of a curiously strong idea.

Key Points Summary

1. **What is the role of visual communication in marketing communication messages?** Visual communication is important in brand communication because it creates impact—it grabs attention, maintains interest, creates believability, and sticks in memory. It also tells stories, delivers emotion, and creates brand images.
2. **What is the difference between *layout* and *composition*, and why are those concepts important?** A layout is an arrangement of all of a print piece's elements. It gives the reader a visual order to the information in the layout; at the same time, it is aesthetically pleasing and makes a visual statement for the brand. Principles that designers use in layout include direction, dominance, unity, white space, contrast, balance, and proportion. Composition is the way the elements in a picture are arranged, either through placement or by manipulating the photographer's viewpoint.
3. **How are art and color reproduced in print media?** Illustrations are treated as line art, and photographs are

reproduced through the halftone process by using screens to break down the image into a dot pattern. Full-color photos are converted to four halftone images, each one printed with a different process color—magenta, cyan, yellow, and black—through the process of color separation.

4. **What are the steps in planning and producing video?** Videos are planned using scripts and storyboards. Television commercials are shot live, shot on film or videotape, or created digitally. Videos can also be created by hand or digitally using animation, claymation, or stop action. There are four stages to the production of videos: message design (scripts and storyboards), preproduction, the shoot, and postproduction.

5. **What are the basic techniques of Web design?** Online brand communication can include ads and banners, but the entire website can also be seen as a promotional message. Art on Web pages can be illustrations or photographs, still images as well as moving ones, and may involve unexpected effects, such as 360-degree images. When designers plan a Web page, they need to consider navigation—how people will move through the site. They also need to consider how to incorporate elements that allow for interaction between the consumer and the company that operates the site.

Key Terms

animation, p. 323
answer print, p. 326
claymation, p. 324
click art, p. 309
clip art, p. 309
color separation, p. 319
composition, p. 316
comprehensives, p. 316
continuous tone, p. 319
crawl, p. 322
cut, p. 325
dailies, p. 325
debossing, p. 321
die-cut, p. 321
digitization, p. 319
dubbing, p. 326
embossing, p. 321
film-to-tape transfer, p. 323
foil stamping, p. 321
font, p. 282
four-color printing, p. 319
gaffer, p. 325
grip, p. 325
halftones, p. 319
interlock, p. 326
layout, p. 313
legibility, p. 312
line art, p. 319
logo, p. 305
mechanicals, p. 316
mixer, p. 325
morphing, p. 322
navigation, p. 327
newsprint, p. 317
offset printing, p. 319
postproduction, p. 325
preproduction, p. 324
process colors, p. 319
production notes, p. 324
registration, p. 317
release prints, p. 326
rough cut, p. 326
rough layouts, p. 316
rushes, p. 325
screen, p. 319
semicomps, p. 316
spot color, p. 311
stock footage, p. 321
stop motion, p. 323
storyboards, p. 317
take, p. 324
thumbnail sketches, p. 316
tint blocks, p. 319
tip-in, p. 321
typography, p. 311
video editing, p. 326
videographer, p. 316
visualization, p. 309
white space, p. 319

Review Questions

10-4. In terms of impact, explain why visual communication is a critical part of an advertisement.

10-5. What is the role of a logo in brand positioning?

10-6. With regard to the Facets Model, list and describe the effects of visuals in an advertisement.

✪ 10-7. List the design principles and explain each one.

✪ 10-8. What's the difference between line art and halftones?

10-9. In an ad, would a photo be more credible than an illustration? Why or why not?

10-10. Explain the following video terms:
- Stock footage
- Crawl
- Morphing
- Animation
- Stop motion
- Claymation

10-11. Explain how an emotional appeal can create successful visual advertising.

10-12. Draw up a list of guidelines to use in designing a website.

Discussion Questions

10-13. One of the challenges for designers is to demonstrate a product whose main feature cannot be seen by the consumer. Suppose you are an art director on an account that sells shower and bath mats with a new patented system that ensures that the mat will not slide (the mat's underside is covered with tiny almost microscopic suction cups that gently grip the tub's surface). Brainstorm some ways to demonstrate this feature in a television commercial. Find a way that will satisfy the demands of originality, relevance, and impact.

10-14. Choose one of the following design critique problems:

a. ***Print:*** What principles are most important in the design of a magazine ad? Collect two sample ads: one you consider a good example of effective design and one that you think is not effective. Critique the two ads and explain your evaluation based on what you know about how design principles work in layouts. Make suggestions for how the less effective ad could be improved.

b. ***Television:*** Find a television commercial that you thought was creative and entertaining. Then find one that you think is much less creative and entertaining. Analyze how the two commercials work to catch and hold your attention. How do the visuals work? What might be done to make the second commercial more attention getting? You can also use online sources to find commercials, such as www.adcritic.com.

10-15. You have been asked to design a print ad for a women's apparel company that operates locally.

Choose a local existing brand and develop an outline that includes all types of information that you will need your client to provide you with; also include and describe the types of photos and illustrations you will be using.

In order to convince your client with your initial draft and get him to sign off on the advertisement you designed and send it for publishing, you need to explain to him the impact of your design on his target market and how it would grab attention and induce consumers to purchase his products.

10-16. You have a new client who has a new hand lotion for men, one that is designed to help men whose hands take a beating in their jobs. One of your colleagues, a photographer, believes that the only way to visualize the product and its use in an ad is through photography. Another colleague, an artist, argues that there are times when art is a much better way to illustrate a product than photography and that this production is a good example. Analyze the differences between using an illustration and using a photograph. What are their roles, and how do they create different types of effects? Are there certain product categories where you would want to use an illustration instead of a photograph and vice versa? Which would work best for this new product? Develop a quick presentation for your class that explains which approach you would use for this assignment.

Take-Home Projects

10-17. ***Portfolio Project:*** Select a product that is advertised primarily through print. Examples of such products are business-to-business and industrial products, school supplies, many over-the-counter drugs, and some food items. Your objective is to develop a 30-second television spot for this product. Develop a creative brief (see Chapter 8) to summarize the ad's strategy. Brainstorm about ways to develop a creative idea for the commercial. Then write a script and develop a storyboard to present your idea for this product. In the script, include all the key decisions a producer and director would make.

10-18. ***Mini-Case Analysis:*** Summarize the creative strategy behind Altoid's "Curiously Strong Mints" campaign. Explain the critical elements of both the copy and the visuals. The brand management team has proposed developing a new (sugar-free) line of cough drops. How would you adjust this strategy to appeal to this new market? Design a launch ad that presents your copy ideas and a new visual. Accompany the ad with a statement that explains your thinking.

TRACE North America Case

Designing Multicultural Visual Communication

Read the TRACE case in the Appendix before coming to class.

10-19. Write a design memo that describes the "look" of the "Hard to Explain, Easy to Experience" campaign. What elements would you make mandatory (e.g., typeface, colors, and so on), and which would you allow individual campuses to personalize in their own colors?

Hands-On Case

Creative Coffee Wars Brewing

How many ads do you think you see in a day? Estimates vary wildly, running from a few hundred to several thousand. Although there seems to be no authoritative answer, you can safely assume it's a lot. Advertising is ubiquitous. It's everywhere, from logos on golf balls to product placements on television. You see it on T-shirts and in magazines and even on the sides of buildings and in video games. In this message-filled world, it's a challenge to stand out from the competition. But some manage to stand out with outstanding creative.

In Part 3, we said that coming up with radical brand ideas calls for strategic and creative thinking, and McDonald's recent campaign to promote its McCafé coffee proves our point. Starting with a great concept and using the advertising tools of words and pictures, McDonald's launched its premium coffee in Seattle, Starbucks's hometown. The strategy involved recognizing a core value of Washingtonians, their affinity for the unpretentious, to challenge the coffee elitism represented by its arch-competitor.

Expanding this simple idea, McDonald's agency, DDB West, labeled McCafé's coffee "unsnobby" and created a campaign that touched the hearts and minds of consumers. It created memorable traditional outdoor transit signs and billboards proclaiming, "Large is the new grande." Another example, an outdoor tease, featured coffee beans scattered across the board. The outdoor reveal later showed the iconic "M" formed from the coffee beans and simple copy: "now serving espresso." No more fancy names or knowledge of foreign languages required.

McDonald's Web microsite also played a part in the campaign. It invited visitors to get involved with the unsnobby theme by sending a coffee intervention in the form of a personalized Mad-lib type of message to a friend. People could also play a game of HotShot Pinball on its site. While there, why not peruse the coffee menu? The site is simply a couple of engaging activities and a list of drinks. Need it be any more elaborate if the message is about a simple drink?

One element of the campaign included a 12-foot-tall inflatable coffee confessional housing McDonald's version of Dr. Phil, the Unsnobby Advisor, who dispensed advice in the form of "unsnobby" personal interventions.

Starbuck's lovers' reaction to the coffee clash? Some bloggers claim the website was a waste of time. Others complained the campaign was anti-intellectual. Can people who like jazz and speak a foreign language still like McCafé, or are they, as McDonald's suggests, all snobby Starbucksonians?

In all, the campaign succeeded in getting people in the heart of Starbucks country to try McDonald's McCafé, overdelivering the trial goal by 173 percent. The campaign has since been rolled out nationwide with promising results. MarketWatch described the McCafé line as a cash cow for McDonald's.

The coffee wars may be just heating up. Starbucks posted a 7 percent jump in same-store sales during the same period and attributed the results to the success of some new products and new stores in Asia, Europe, and the United States.

Consider This

P3-1. It's easy to see how McDonald's used words and pictures in some of its traditional advertising, like billboards. How are words and pictures used effectively on the www.unsnobby.com website?

P3-2. How does the McDonald's campaign make a relevant connection with its audience and sell its coffee in an unexpected way?

P3-3. How could you extend the concept of unsnobby coffee to use it for a variety of executions in different media?

P3-4. Compare and contrast this campaign with Starbucks's approach. What is the Big Idea of both campaigns? Why and how do they work?

Sources: Angela Moore, "Battle of the Beverages," April 21, 2010; Kevin Helliker, "Starbucks' Traffic Grows, Fueling Increase in Sales," *Wall Street Journal,* April 22, 2010, B2; www.marketwatch.com; Effie Briefs, "Unsnobby Coffee," www.effie.org; www.unsnobbycoffee.com.

PART

4 Principle: Media in a World of Change

We talked about creating messages in Part 3. In Part 4, we turn to the delivery of messages. We'll explore how companies use media to accomplish their objectives, but we'll also look at how consumers use media to serve their own needs.

Push, Touch, Click, and Turn the Media World Upside Down

Note that people consume media, as well as products and services, so media consumers are those folks who watch television and read publications, search for something on the Internet, and use their cell phones to check for a store's location or hours. They push buttons, touch screens, click on links, and turn pages—electronic pages as well as paper. They are consumers of media, but their fingers are always in control of the media relationship.

The media world has seen incredible changes from the dominance of traditional mass media to new hybrid forms with traditional media adding interactive and digital platforms, from marketers' control of media placement to sharing control of media use with consumers, and from media targeting messages to media engaging with consumers. To explore this dynamic media environment, our book's advisory board members Larry Kelley and David Rittenhouse share their thoughts on how the media world is evolving.

Larry Kelley
Larry Kelley is executive vice president and chief planning officer at Fogarty Klein Monroe (FKM) and professor of advertising in the Jack J. Valenti School of Communication at the University of Houston.

Morphing and Converging Media

A major change is the blurring that media have gone through as traditional media forms morph into digital formats and new functions. Kelley describes it this way: "Media convergence is more than just providing content in a variety of forms. It is about the convergence of content, branding, and consumer engagement." *Convergence* is the definitive word in 21st-century media. He explains,

> Brands are now media, and media are now brands. It used to be that brands did something and that media said something. Now media and brands do something, say something, and engage with consumers. For example, Red Bull provides an energy drink, but it also publishes a magazine and engages with consumers through a variety of events. *Better Homes and Gardens* started as a magazine. Now it provides a variety of content. It is now a brand of real estate agents. And it engages consumers through a variety of digital and physical sponsorships and events.

CHAPTER 11 • Media Basics
CHAPTER 12 • Paid Media
CHAPTER 13 • Owned, Interactive, and Earned Media
CHAPTER 14 • Media Planning and Negotiation

From Message Conduits to Consumer Connections

David Rittenhouse
David Rittenhouse is managing director at Neo@Ogilvy, the media arm of Ogilvy, where he plays a leading role in the agency's digital and demand generation media practice.

In his book on media, Kelley says that media are the conduits through which brand information is presented to audiences. But, he says, his push-based approach has been modified by the digital revolution and now includes dialogue. In this new world, media actually make two-way communication possible—people to companies, companies to people, and people to people.

And so we need ways to describe new patterns of media use. Rittenhouse refers to "established" channels, such as broadcast, out of home, print, and even online search and display, in contrast to "emergent" channels, such as social, mobile, and online video. In this complex multimedia environment, we have traditional targeted media and messages, but we also see consumer-generated media and messages.

But it's more complex and interesting than planning across platforms. Rittenhouse describes media as physical/digital—in other words, digital layers are being added to physical content. So planners spread media activities across media but also dive into them. This is being fueled by the rapid proliferation of smart phones and tablets through which consumers can access supplemental digital content or tap straight into an e-commerce environment from just about any physical marketing communication, from a print ad in a magazine to product packaging to an in-store display.

Kelley also points out that consumer engagement may be just as important as the delivery of a message using traditional push media. Media are all about connections—hooking up brands with people and people with information about brands. And the connection, if it's successful, will have high levels of experiential or emotional engagement.

The question then is, How do these media users connect with a brand while using media they choose and media they use to connect with others, including brands? The point is that people come in contact with a brand message in many different ways.

Multimedia, Multiplatform, and Multiuse

Yes, media consumers have always chosen television programs to watch, radio stations to listen to, and magazines to read, but in this environment they may also be doing those activities on a computer or on a smart phone, and sometimes they're doing all of those activities at the same time they're texting a friend or playing a video game. Rittenhouse describes this as coviewing, using multiple media channels simultaneously.

CHAPTER

11 Media Basics

Photo: © Corbis

It's a Winner

Campaign:	Company:	Agencies:	Awards:
"Lottery of Life"	*Save the Children Sweden*	*Lowe Brindfors*	*UN Department of Public Information (UNDPI) Gold Award, Cannes Lions International Festival of Creativity, 2010 (Bronze Lion) for Charities, Public Health & Safety, Public Awareness Messages*

CHAPTER KEY POINTS

1. How do media work in marketing communication, and how is the industry organized?
2. What are the key strategic media concepts and how would you describe them?
3. Why and how is the media landscape changing?

Lottery of Life

The Swedish advertising agency Lowe Brindfors hit the nail on the head when it created the new ad campaign for Save the Children Sweden in 2010, drawing people in by asking them to support the one person who means the most to them—themselves!

This was the birth of the Lottery of Life.

It's very easy to be overwhelmed by the constant bombardment of ads, and consumers often reach the point of compassion overload due to repetitive charity advertisements—a point that was not overlooked by the agency.

Traditionally, charity advertisements have sought to tug at the heartstrings of viewers. They try to trigger feelings of empathy and pity. This sets them apart from most ads, which aim to do the opposite—heighten the viewer's sense of self.

During a period when the world was coping with a financial crisis and charities were struggling to procure funds, Save the Children Sweden decided to take a risk and rolled the dice.

The billboard displays managed to hook viewers in immediately by allowing them to put themselves in two places at once, and feel the difference through a stark visual contrast. Putting a spin on how a Swede would likely perceive life, the agency uses one feature to help the audience become familiar with the scenes and at the same time note the disparity between the two situations instantly: successfully creating motion through still imagery.

The sentiment portrayed on the billboards was supported by a video, which featured flashing images of conflict, poverty, and hunger. The narration accompanying the visuals empathized with the viewer by acknowledging that the number of advertisements that a viewer is subjected to have the potential to overwhelm and exhaust. Turning charity advertising on its head, the narration asked viewers to think of themselves. In this instance, how would a Swede cope and feel if he or she had not been one of the 0.08 percent of the global population to be born in Sweden? The video received over 250,000 hits, which meant that there was a huge jump in Web traffic on the Save the Children Sweden website. The video was also circulated in the media.

An innovative aspect, was offering the audience a chance to virtually spin the wheel of life. Since they would have less than a 1 percent chance of being born in Sweden, the lottery wheel would inevitably conjure thought-provoking images and feelings for the audience.

Each time participants spun the wheel, they were shown an image of a baby and a list of development statistics related to that country of birth. These highlighted issues such as literacy, poverty, child labor, and marriage. Most important, the "new born child" had the name of the person who spun the wheel and an appeal was made to the spinner to help his or her newly born self.

The purpose of the campaign was to illustrate the role chance plays in one being born into a particular predicament. For the first time, rather than focusing on negative and harrowing images of the plight of children, audience members were immersed in the concept of their own struggle for survival, had randomness and chance not determined their birth in affluent Sweden.

Participants were also given options to get a detailed look at their "new country of birth" by clicking on links to Wikipedia, Flickr, Google Maps, and YouTube, and were encouraged to share their experiences using social media platforms.

Most important, the campaign became viral. By collecting enough support from others, participants could get a chance to win a field trip to their "new homeland" and get a firsthand experience of their new realities.

You will find out more about the marketing effects of the Save the Children Sweden campaign, and how it won the jackpot, at the end of the chapter in the "It's a Wrap" section.

Sources: www.savethechildren.se; www.whydev.org/the-lottery-of-life-is-it-just-chance; theinspirationroom.com/daily/2011/lottery-of-life; www.unric.org/en/latest-news/26567-swedish-lottery-of-life-campaign-wins-un-award-for-public-service-advertising (all accessed 22–24/10/2013).

The lesson concerning media brought out by the Save the Children Sweden campaign is that smart marketing requires creative thinking on how to connect with the audience in a complex media environment. Among other creative ideas, read how Axe has made use of branded entertainment in "The Inside Story: The Animated Axe Effect in *City Hunters*" later in this chapter. This chapter explains the media side of marketing communication—the backstory of the selection of the different ways to deliver a message.

What Do We Mean by Media?

Principle
All marketing communication messages, other than personal conversations, are carried by some form of media.

All marketing communication messages—other than face-to-face conversations—are carried by some form of media. When we talk about **media**, we are referring to *the way messages are delivered* to target audiences and, increasingly, back to companies as well as among audience members themselves. Media make up the *channel* step in the communication model, conveying the message and connecting source and receiver—that is, the company or brand and its customers.

It's helpful to remember that the basis for most media historically was as a way to present news to the public—and advertising made presenting the news possible because it supported the costs of producing and distributing print or broadcast media. Of course, some revenue is derived from subscriptions, but in the United States the bulk of the media revenue comes from advertising. As a result, over the years, the word *media* has been associated with advertising, leading many to think that media are used only or primarily for advertising. Nothing could be further from the truth!

We know from the communication model presented in Chapter 4 that messages move through *channels of communication.* So in this sense, media *deliver* messages. In traditional mass media, this is a one-way process from the source (the advertiser) to the receiver (consumers). In another sense, media are *interactive* because they offer opportunities for dialogue and two-way conversation. The media of marketing communication deliver messages to and from customers and move messages back and forth through channels. This expands the concept of delivery to include receiving and listening as well as delivering messages. Interactive communication is a hallmark of IMC programs that aim to build brand relationships, which is why this expanded view of media is so important to IMC planners.

For example, you may remember that in Chapter 6 we introduced the Icelandic lamb case study. In it, Ingvi Logason and his Reykjavik agency redefined the meaning of "advertising media." He explained, "We created 'advertising' in the form of a series of traditional cooking shows designed to teach new and traditional recipes, but the shows would be only 40 to 90 seconds long. The execution of the campaign was ten cooking-show 'ads' that we strategically ran on various stations followed by viral distribution of the same micro-cooking shows through Facebook." Logason explained, "Sometimes the new way to present a message demonstrates creativity in the use of media as much as it does in the design of the message. The nature of creative ideas has changed with the development of new, more engaging media."

Media also offer opportunities for *engagement*, a media buzzword that refers to the captivating quality of media that the audience finds engrossing. Certainly, this can apply to television commercials and cinema advertising, but it can also be applied to print and Internet ads—anything on which readers concentrate for some length of time. Media experts describe engagement as the closeness of fit between the interests of viewers and the relevance of the media content.[1] This is how media open the door of the critical "perception" step in the Facets Model of Effects that we introduced in Chapter 4. The principle of engagement is illustrated in sports marketing, such as ads and other events surrounding the Olympic Games, which are described in the "A Matter of Principle" feature.

A Matter of Principle

The Engagement Strategy behind Sports Advertising

John Sweeney, *University of North Carolina*

The top 50 advertisers invested over $5.68 billion in sports advertising in 2011. It is significant to note that the amount of spending on sports increased every year during the Great Recession.

Sports deliver a mass audience but also a passionate one. By associating with the emotional involvement of fans, a brand can win greater impact than traditional media where the viewers have little or no loyalty.

The entire strategy that a brand brings to be part of sports also gives an insight into why this category has grown so prosperous. Let's look at a few years of McDonald's and its sponsorship of the Olympic Games, which began as a top or global partner at the 1998 Nagano Olympics. A partnership that now has been officially extended to the year 2020.

The Olympics are the world's most popular event with the Games being broadcast to 220 countries. Over 6.5 million tickets were sold to attend Beijing in 2008. It is one of the few opportunities in media for a company like McDonald's to involve not only the United States but also—without hyperbole—the entire planet. And that is clearly valuable for a company with 33,000 locations in 119 countries.

McDonald's, as a partner for the 2012 London Summer Olympics, did far more than run commercials. Most companies use sponsorships in all aspects of their business, including bringing customers to the competitions and increasing company morale by involving employees. Here are a few McDonalds' programs used in London:

- The McDonald's "Champions of Play" program brought up to 200 children from around the world to the London Olympic Games with a guardian. They played with Olympic athletes, toured the Olympic Village, and saw London cultural sites. Each of the 200 won a local promotional event. Olympic medal winner and mom Dana Torres served as the global ambassador for the program.
- McDonald's built four new Olympic restaurants at the Olympics, including the largest freestanding McDonald's in the world. It served the first Happy Meals including fruit, vegetable, and dairy options. These restaurants were staffed by 2,000 of the top-performing restaurant staff from countries across the globe.

This is just the beginning of how McDonald's leveraged its partnership with the Olympics. Every Olympic event brings new strategic uses that can involve tremendous innovation. For the 2008 Beijing Olympics, McDonald's created a global alternate reality game that was available in seven languages.

In a world of too many television channels with programming that gathers only modest interest, sports can deliver passionate involvement in a way that goes beyond a jingle or a catchphrase. That's why so many companies continue to invest in the leagues and events that we follow in sports.

IMC and Media

In IMC programs, media are also *contact points* in that they *connect* a brand with the audience and ultimately *touch* their emotions as well as *engage* their minds. The difference between delivery and connection is significant. To deliver means "to take something to a person or place"; to connect means "to join together." Delivery is the first step in connecting: It opens the door to touching a customer in a meaningful way with a brand message. As a result of the digital revolution, the connection aspect has become even more important. This is not just semantics; the word *connection* changes the perspective of media planning. "Deliver" is a one-way concept; "connect" is a partnership. Laura Bright, a media professor at Texas Christian University, explains that "brand messages are now brand conversations."[3]

Principle
IMC plans are multiplatform, multichannel, and multitargeted.

All marketing communication areas, such as advertising, promotions, public relations, direct marketing, and events and sponsorships use a variety of media to deliver messages to customers. IMC plans are *multiplatform* (use a variety of marcom areas), *multichannel* (use a variety of media), and *multitargeted* (engage a variety of stakeholders).

Effectiveness depends on coordinating all these efforts around some central concept, such as the brand position or, in the case of a campaign, the Big Idea. Kelley and Jugenheimer, who are authors of books on media and account planning, explain, "If all of these channels fail to deliver on the Big Idea you will have gaps in your communication plan, which will lead to a fragmented effort or a waste of money and resources."[4]

To get a picture of the scope of media, consider the following list, which represents not only the breadth of media but also the emphasis that media teachers place on various types of media, starting at the top with Internet advertising:[5]

Internet advertising	Billboards	Transit
Digital media	Newspapers	Direct mail
Television	Out-of-home	Radio online
Social networks	Branded entertainment	Cable online
Cable	Digital billboards	Digital transit
Alternative media	Mobile advertising	Digital in-store
Guerilla marketing	Television syndication	Movie theater advertising
Search engine advertising	Newspapers online	Satellite radio
Broadcast/cable product placement	Television online	Ambient media
Radio	In-store/point-of-purchase ads	Music product placement

Beyond conventional mass media like those listed here, IMC connection media also include personal experiences with events, salespeople, and customer service as well as word-of-mouth messages from people who influence us—all of which may become imbued with emotions leading to strong personal feelings about a brand.

The Media Industry

The recession, combined with the explosion of online media, seriously hurt traditional media. Even though they still dominate in terms of dollars, all traditional media saw decreases in their ad revenues. This was partly because of an overall decline in media advertising but also because marketers were increasingly turning to the Internet for visibility at less cost. *Advertising Age* reported at the end of 2009, at the height of the recession, that 11 of the top 100 media firms had filed for bankruptcy during the year with print companies dominating the list.[6] Newspapers were the biggest losers because of the shift of classified advertising to online sites and the ease with which readers could get news online. Many major papers closed; others were reduced in size, staff, and news coverage. Magazines suffered as well. Revenues for broadcast were down with traditional radio companies seeing red ink; however, the television sector was one of the first to rebound. In 2013, for the first time, industry executives at the Cannes annual advertising awards in France predicted that the ad market was recovering in the United States.

In spite of the recession, traditional mass media advertising, according to Kantar Media, continues to be a huge industry with $144 billion spent on advertising in measured media at the end of 2011.[7] Media research organization Nielsen also monitors advertising expenditures and provided the data used in Figure 11.1, which compares the size of the "ad spend" in the major media categories. Television continues to dominate media budgets, but that's partially because television costs are higher than other media. Keep in mind, however, that even though it may seem expensive, television can be cost effective because it reaches a huge audience. On the other hand, although the Internet seems to be a minor player in terms of spending, that's partially because of the difficulty of measuring its impact and revenues. But it's also due to the Internet's much lower costs. New forms of unmeasured media are an exciting growth area but one that's even harder to track and represent in charts like this, which reports the size of traditional paid (and measured) media.

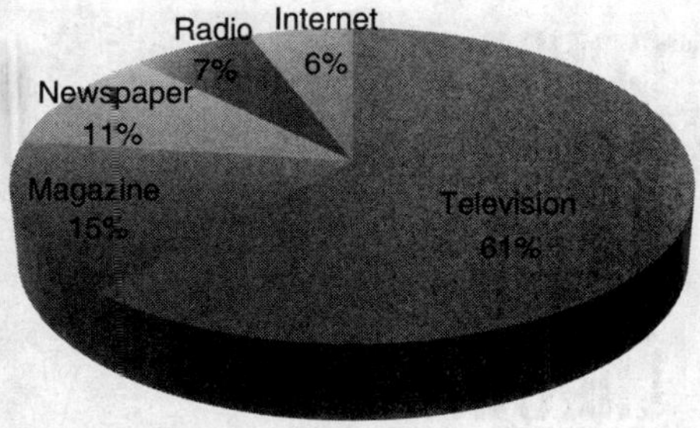

FIGURE 11.1
The Media Landscape

Source: Acapted from data in "Report: TV Continues to Hold the Lion's Share of Ad Dollars and Consumers' Media Time," May 8, 2012, Nielsen, http://blog.nielsen.com/nielsenwire.

Media Types and Terms

The plural noun *media* is an umbrella term for all types of print, broadcast, out-of-home, and Internet communication. The singular noun *medium* refers to each specific type (e.g., television is a medium). A **media vehicle** is a specific television program (*60 Minutes, The Simpsons*), newspaper (*Washington Post, Chicago Tribune, El Nuevo Herald*), magazine (*Woman's Day, GQ*), or radio station or program (NPR's *All Things Considered*, Rush Limbaugh's talk show).

When a company "buys media," it is really buying access to the audiences of media vehicles. The form that those "buys" take is "space" (print, outdoor boards, Internet) and "time" (radio and television). In addition to this basic media language, there are other ways to sort out the media landscape.

Size and Profile of Audience Media, particularly those used in advertising, are referred to as **mass media**, the communication channels through which messages are sent to large, diverse audiences. A mass medium reaches many people simultaneously, and it uses some technological system or device to reach them (as opposed to personal communication). In contrast, the new computer-based media of the digital revolution are essentially personal, and messages are individually delivered.

The size of the audience is the reason why we refer to radio and television as **broadcasting media**—they cast their audio and visual signals broadly to reach mass audiences. In contrast, **niche media** are communication channels through which messages are sent to niche segments—identifiable groups of people with a distinct common interest, such as the Hispanic market. *Advertising Age* and *Adweek*, for example, are a subsegment of the more general business magazine category. They reach the professional advertising industry niche. The distinction between mass and niche is not based necessarily on size. The *AARP Magazine*, for example, which targets baby boomers age 50 and over, is a niche publication, yet it is the world's largest-circulation magazine.[8]

Another term that you'll see in media plans and that we used in describing Figure 11.1 is **measured media**, which refers to the ability of media planners to analyze the cost of a media buy relative to the size of the medium's audience. Kantar/TNS is a media reporting service that tracks spending. The following categories identify the primary types of measured media:

- ***Television*** Network, cable, syndication, spot (local), Spanish language
- ***Magazines*** Consumer, business-to-business, Sunday, local, Spanish language
- ***Radio*** Network, national spot, local

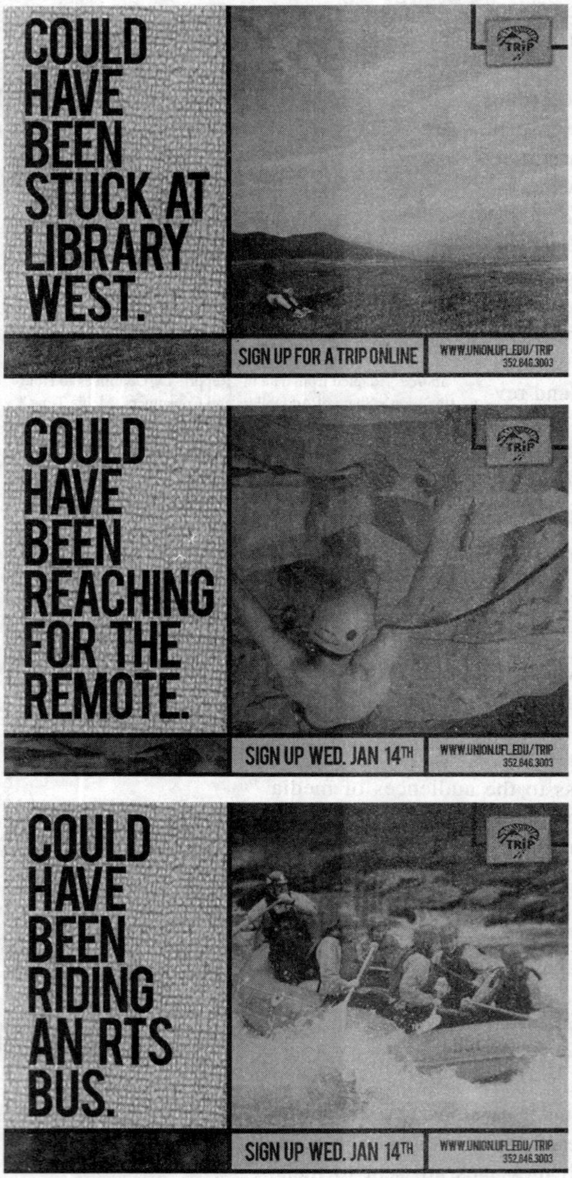

Photo: Brooke Johnson, Writer Travis Damon, Artwork; Courtesy of Philip Erwin

SHOWCASE

TRIP, the Travel and Recreation Program at the University of Florida, is a student-run organization that plans and leads adventure and leisure trips for students and members of the Gainesville community. The student Adwerks agency created the "Could Have Been" campaign with beautiful images from past trips. Playful headlines provided a sarcastic but humorous tone that spoke to the primary target of college students.

Lisa Yansura, director and account supervisor at Adwerks, contributed this campaign on behalf of her University of Florida team: Kaely Coon, Jody Revels, Wendy Casorr, Becky Lazarus, Travis Damon, and Alli Schnur. Yansura is now marketing coordinator, Gragg Advertising, Kansas City, Missouri.

- ***Newspapers*** National, local, Spanish language
- ***Outdoor***
- ***Freestanding inserts*** Distributed primarily in newspapers

Metrics are available for traditional media either from the medium itself or from external auditing agencies, but these figures are much harder to find for new and nontraditional media because the auditing procedures for these new media have yet to be developed.

Note that this traditional way of looking at consumers is based on seeing them as media audiences. Chapter 5 described consumers in other ways based on their personal characteristics and behaviors. Media planners also move away from the target audience mind-set and describe the audience as people. For example, Bright describes targets in terms of their relationship to the brand: Strangers, Prospects, Customers, and Fans.[9]

Targeted and Interactive Conduits Another category refers to the way the media transmit messages. Most mass media are defined by their audiences, and when they are used in brand communication, it is because they allow messages to be conveyed to people who fit certain demographic or psychographic categories. If you want to reach young men who like sports, for example, then you might advertise in *Sports Illustrated* or on ESPN because their audiences match the profile of your target. In the Part 4 opening essay, Larry Kelley described these media as *conduits* because they deliver messages aimed at specific targets.

The placement of the message is an important factor in targeted media plans. For example, an example of tight targeting through specialized local media comes from the University of Florida, where the university's student advertising agency, Adwerks, developed a campaign for the university's student travel program based on posters and flyers that were designed to reach the student audience. The Adwerks team's objective was to increase sign-ups in order to meet the required number of participants. If trips that were close to full didn't reach a certain level of sign-ups, then there was the potential for unhappy participants, creating a negative image for the program.

The Internet, mail, and telephone are called **addressable media** because they are used to send brand messages to specific addresses, both geographic and electronic. They are particularly helpful in keeping in touch with current customers or with brand communities.

Online social media and the phone are examples of **interactive media**, which allow conversations between companies and customers as well as between and among consumers. These messages are two way in that they are carried to and from companies and consumer—and require that both sides in the dialogue listen as well as speak.

Corporate versus Consumer Use of Media So far, we have been discussing media primarily from the viewpoint of companies and their brands. In the Part 4 opening essay, we mentioned that consumers, as well as companies, *use* media—and they use media for specific purposes. For example, companies want to reach certain targets in order to accomplish such objectives as building brand awareness, presenting brand information, and persuading people in the target market to change their attitudes. But just as important is the fact that consumers use media for their own purposes. You may remember that we ended our discussion of the consumer by describing Seekers, who look for information, entertainment, and interaction. That's how they use media, and it affects how companies use media to communicate with them.

In other words, mass media may be good for delivering brand messages, but interactive media may be more useful for engaging consumers in a brand-related conversation, assuming that the conversation is relevant to their interests.

Paid, Owned, and Earned Media Recently, the media industry has begun separating media into three types of channels: **paid, owned, and earned media**. We'll use those categories to do a brief review of the variety of types of media available to brand communication planners. All of these will be discussed in more detail in this chapter and in the two that follow, but here is an outline of these categories and the media included in them:

Paid, Owned, and Earned Media Categories

- PAID MEDIA are the traditional measured media, such as print and broadcast, where ad placements—both time and space—are bought by the company or organization. These "established" or "legacy" media channels are distinctive in that the advertising spending on them, as well as the size of their audiences, is tracked by media research services:
  - ***Print*** Newspapers, magazines, inserts, directories
  - ***Broadcast*** Radio, television, movie trailers
  - ***Place based*** Billboards, transit, kiosks painted buildings and cars, movie trailers, event and sponsorship ads, stadium and aerial ads
  - ***Online*** Banner and display ads, search advertising
- OWNED MEDIA are channels that are controlled by the organization and that carry branded content, such as websites, direct-mail e-mail address lists, Facebook sites, blogs, public relations publications, and catalogs, among other forms. In addition, we also include communication platforms that rely on one-on-one communication, such as personal sales or customer service:
  - ***Corporate media*** Stationery, signage, environmental design, delivery trucks, staff appearance, bags
  - ***Branded media*** Films (video or online) and webisodes, video games, books, events, apps, licensing and naming rights
  - ***Retail*** Packaging, merchandising materials
  - ***Promotions and public relations*** Literature and publications, annual reports, premiums and gifts, sales kits, training materials:

    Video *Corporate and promotional videos—DVDs and streaming*
    Publications *Magazines, newsletters, annual reports, brochures*
    Publicity *Print, video, and online news releases; fact kits, photos and other graphics*
    Events *Displays and exhibits, speakers, information kits*
    Brand reminders *Premiums, gifts*
    Out-of-home (OOH) *Sign spinners and flash mobs.*

  Some owned media also open up the opportunity for interactivity:
  - ***Corporate interactive media*** Kiosks, digital installations
  - ***Direct response*** Mail, phone, online, catalogs,
  - ***Personal contact*** Personal sales, customer service—customer comment cards and surveys
  - ***Interactive public relations and promotions*** Sampling, events, informational and media tours, news conferences, speeches, trade shows, guerilla marketing
  - ***Digital marketing*** E-mail, websites and e-commerce, online catalogs, blogs, paid posts, social media accounts
  - ***Mobile marketing***

- **Earned media** are channels where brand communication is spread by outsiders, such as social media users or news media that carry publicity stories where the brand may be mentioned.
  - ***Publicity*** Hits and mentions in news media
  - ***Word of mouth*** E-mail, texting, buzz and viral communication, business-to-consumer-to-consumer influence
  - ***Social media*** Facebook, Twitter, LinkedIn
  - ***Interest sharing*** YouTube, Pinterest, Tumblr, Instagram, social games

We'll use this three-part classification system here but also use it to organize the media discussions in Chapter 12 and Chapter 13. The chart below summarizes these three media categories and how media professionals use them to make sense of the changing media landscape where media forms are converging, blurring, and changing their shapes. So instead of looking at media forms, paid, owned, and earned media are based on media functions.

Evaluating Paid, Owned, and Earned Media Use

Channel	Examples	Objective	Advantages	Limitations
Paid media: *Brand pays to buy space or time*	• Display and classified ads • Ads in out-of-home media • Ads on search sites	• Reach prospects	• Message control • Scale; can generate broad reach • Good brand reminder • Measurable	• Clutter • Lack of credibility • Low response rates • Indirect action
Owned media: *A channel created and controlled by the brand*	• Website • Blogs, Facebook page, Twitter account • Sponsored programs and events • Brand publications; literature	• Reach customers • Reach niche • Build brand relationships	• Message control • Cost efficiency	• Credibility • Difficult to scale up • Harder to measure
Earned media: *Consumers and mass media control the mentions and comments about the brand*	• Word of mouth • Viral communication • Social media • Publicity hits and mentions • Customer service	• Lets customers initiate contact • Engage in dialogue • Brand listens and responds	• Credible • Most engaging • Most persuasive	• Little brand control • Sometimes negative • Hard to measure

The Evolution of Media Forms and Functions

People in our contemporary society live in a world of media-delivered news, information, and entertainment that traditionally has been supported by advertising. Over several hundred years, media have evolved from print, to radio, then to television, and now to the Internet. Newspapers, magazines, and posters provided the visual dimension of communication; radio added an audio dimension. Television enabled messages to be heard and seen with moving images.

Today, we have the Internet, which has basically combined television and the personal computer, thus providing the added dimension of interactivity. But more than that, the Internet has opened up unimagined new forms of social communication, and these new social media have also created new outlets for brand communication. We can summarize these changes in technology as eras:

- ***The print era*** Ink and print images reproduced as newspapers, magazines, and posters.
- ***The broadcast era*** Visual and audio information in the form of radio and television programs originally transmitted through airwaves but now also distributed by cable and satellite.

- ***The digital era*** Electronic information transmitted through the Internet but, like broadcasting, now also distributed through cable and satellite. Saw the birth of corporate websites and e-commerce.
- ***The social media era*** Social networks connecting friends and contacts. Also where users can become publishers and generate their own content, some of which may be brand related.

Former advertising executive and now publisher Bruce Bendinger observed, "The printing press turned us into readers; the Xerox turned us into publishers; television turned us into viewers; the Internet is turning us into broadcasters." The "Gangnam Style" phenomenon in 2012 illustrates how a YouTube video by South Korean performer Park Jae-sang, or Psy, became the most-watched video of all time. The quirky song and dance was not only shared by South Koreans but also became a massive global hit with some 7 million to 10 million viewers every day.[10]

It's useful to remember that this digital era is quite recent. The first website went online in 1991; the social networking sites of MySpace and Facebook went online in 2003 and 2004, respectively; and Twitter arrived only in 2006. In contrast, the first newspaper ad appeared in the early 1700s, the first radio station went on the air in 1897, and television became popular in the United States in the 1940s and 1950s.

The point is that media have been and continue to be changing in form and function. This change is occurring rapidly, so it's difficult to keep up—or to predict where we will be in five years or even a year. The media scene will probably never be settled, and it's certainly dynamic.

Adaptation Every technological advance has threatened the older media whose managers feared their medium was on the edge of extinction. In fact, the media adjusted to their new circumstances by emphasizing what they do best—newspapers and magazines deliver information in depth, radio delivers music and other programs tailored to listeners' tastes, and television brings entertainment to the living room. The new media take on some of the characteristics and roles of the old at the same time that they add to the richness of the communication experience. Television, for example, has news shows and advertising that sound a lot like radio news programs, and both radio and television use news formats—and advertising—that they adopted from print.

Principle
Every technological advance has threatened older media, and every new medium is launched in the footprints of its predecessor media.

A more dramatic shift, however, is occurring in the 21st century as computers and the Internet personalize media and bring changes unlike any ever encountered in the history of media. Internet-based communication can do everything that the traditional media identified as their distinctive features and offers most of the communication dimensions of its media ancestors, but it also adds an interactive dimension.

The only "medium" that is even more multidimensional and interactive than the Internet is personal selling, which also is a lot more expensive for commercial communication. A salesperson can not only show, tell, and interact but, most importantly, also instantly create customized content. Internet sites can quasi-create content by compiling customer mega-data from which information can be computed and patterns recognized, such as creating a selection of customer preferences (Amazon's suggested books) or providing predetermined answers to frequently asked questions.

In an interesting turnaround, print stories and ads can now carry **QR codes** that let readers scan them to access additional information and websites via their smart phones. The media are learning from each other. QR is short for "quick response" and is represented by a complex pattern that represents a unique location based on geographic coordinates and other data. Like bar codes, they can be electronically scanned. However, you don't need a special reader; they can be scanned by smart phones.

Photo: Kraay Family Farm, Home of the Lacombe Corn Maze Inc.

A Canadian family claimed a Guinness World Record for the largest QR code that it created as a corn maze. The 15-acre corn maze includes this seven-acre QR code design.

Convergence Although new media tend to launch themselves by adapting the forms of the media that preceded them, the older media also adapt by adopting some of the advances of new media. Nearly every media vehicle, for example, now has one or more (most have more) websites—and that creates the **convergence** that Kelley described in the Part 4 opening essay.

This makes it very difficult to categorize media. Is the *New York Times*'s website a newspaper? And now both the *New York Times* and the

FIGURE 11.2
The Digital Overlap
With traditional media, such as print and broadcasting, adding online forms, the distinction between traditional and digital is less important. The same promotional story can run in print, on television, and in online newspapers and streaming video.

Wall Street Journal appear as online newspapers and also as online videos. They are no longer "print," but these new forms do carry news. So what do you call them? Media scholar Don Jugenheimer notes that "newspapers have websites, advertisements can be transmitted by e-mail, and television programs can be downloaded into iPods."[11] Furthermore, catalogs and radio are online, video is on computers, and cell phones and books are electronic.

Figure 11.2 diagrams this overlap of functions as print and broadcast media evolve into new digital forms. The point is that the old traditional form continues—there are still newspapers and magazines and television programs that their audiences enjoy. And as we noted before, they continue to dominate ad spending. At the same time, there are new digital forms that may do some of what a traditional medium does but also may open the door to new and expanded uses. For example, you can click on a link in an online news story and find additional background or related stories.

Although we discuss convergence primarily as shape-shifting where traditional media take on characteristics of new electronic media, there's actually more to it than that. Larry Kelley observes that promotional areas such as advertising and public relations are morphing together in integrated brand planning. Brand stewards and planners on both the corporate and the agency side are working together to broaden the communication dimensions of brand relationships—brand stewards bring conversations inside the company through corporate Facebook and Twitter accounts. At the same time, agency planners create the communication efforts that drive the dialogue to those sites. Finally, Kelley insists that "media convergence is more than just providing content in a variety of forms; it is about the convergence of content, branding, and consumer engagement."[12] The brand, the message, and the media are all interwoven in contemporary media strategies.

The Contemporary Media Landscape There have always been evolution and changes in the shape and forms of media; however, the speed of change has increased, as has the number of media available for use in brand communication, and that has created pressure for more coordination and integration. As Kelley says, "Everything is multiplatform." There's also been change in delivery systems from hardware—computers, hard drives, and dedicated machines, like game consoles—to "cloud marketing," where all the marketing efforts, programs, and even products live on the Internet and can be downloaded to personal devices such as smart phones and tablets. Video games are moving in that direction and will leave game consoles behind.

The modern media landscape includes up to 200 television channels in some markets, a huge number of special-interest publications, millions of websites, and new and novel media forms that weren't even imagined 20 years ago, such as ads on conveyer belts at airports or brands stamped into the sand at the beach.

Media experts Kelley, Jugenheimer, and Sheehan describe what has happened.[13] "We have certainly seen the rise of new kinds of media over the past decade. The Internet has led the way with a wide variety of media such as search-engine marketing, rich media, and streaming audio and video. Other media channels have come into play, including the iPod, cell phones, videogames, and satellite radio."

Kelley and colleagues also looked at existing media and how they have extended and adapted themselves to the lives of new media consumers. Point-of-sale media, for example, have been transformed "with opportunities appearing in seemingly every venue. Malls now have digital signs that show television commercials. In some major markets, buses contain television sets that are programmed to show a retail ad within a block or two of the retail establishment."

And it's not just these new forms that add complexity to the media landscape. Kelley and colleagues continue: "Ads are popping up in elevators, inside fortune cookies, and even on celebrity and wannabe-celebrity body parts." As an example of the creative use of novel media, consider the Jeep trailer that Michael Dattolico designed as a painted brand image for one of his clients.

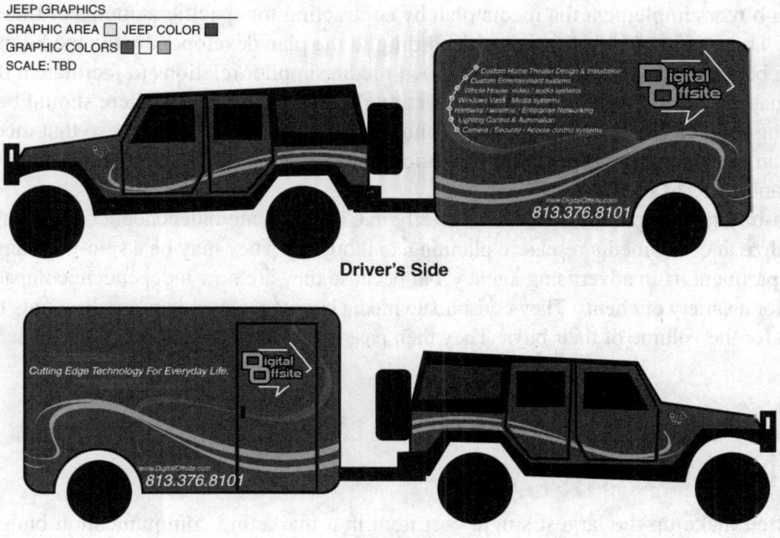

Photo: Courtesy of Digital Offsite

SHOWCASE

The Jeep graphics designed by Michael Dattolico for a technology client turned a vehicle into a moving billboard.

Mike Dattolico graduated from the advertising program at the University of Florida and was nominated by Professor Elaine Wagner.

Key Media Players

In terms of jobs and career opportunities in media, there are professionals who both sell and buy media. It is important that you understand the difference. First let's look at the professionals who sell space or time in media:

- **Media salespeople** also known as **media reps** (short for media representatives), work for a specific vehicle, such as a magazine or local television station, with the objective of building the best possible argument to convince media planners to use the medium they represent. Currently, media conglomerates dominate media sales. CBS, for example, created a coordinated ad-selling division, called CBS RIOT, which stands for "radio, Internet, outdoor, and television." The new division was designed to serve primarily local markets and offers **cross-media** (also called **multichannel**) integrated deals. Disney reorganized its ad sales to deliver a similar cross-media ad sales program for its kids' media properties.
- Media **brokers** are people (or companies) who sell space (in print) and time (in broadcast) for a variety of media. If an agency wants to buy space in all of the major newspapers in the West, for example, the agency's buyer could contract with a media rep firm whose sales reps and brokers handle national sales for all those newspapers. This allows the media buyer to place a complex buy with one order.

On the buying side, media planners, buyers, and researchers work primarily for agencies, although they can also be found working for marketers who handle their own media work in-house. Their challenge is to determine the best way to deliver a message, which is called **media planning**. The job functions are as follows:

- **Media researchers** compile audience measurement data, media costs, and availability data for the various media options being considered by the planners.
- **Media planners** develop the strategic decisions outlined in the media plan, such as where to advertise geographically, when to advertise, and which type of media to use to reach specific types of audiences.

- **Media buyers** implement the media plan by contracting for specific amounts of time or space. They spend the media budget according to the plan developed by the media planner. Media buyers are expected to maintain good media supplier relations to facilitate a flow of information within the fast-changing media marketplace. This means there should be close working relationships between planners and buyers as well as media reps so that media planners can tap this source of media information to better forecast media changes, including price and patterns of coverage.
- **Media-buying companies**, mentioned briefly in Chapter 1, are independent companies that specialize in doing media research, planning, and buying. They may be a spin-off from the media department in an advertising agency, but because they are now independent companies, they work for a variety of clients. They consolidate media buying to get maximum discounts from the media for the volume of their buys. They then pass on some of this saving to their clients.

What Are the Fundamentals of Media Strategy?

Media often make up the largest single cost item in a marketing communication budget, especially for consumer goods and services. Procter & Gamble, for example, spent $9.3 billion on advertising in 2011, although its total promotional spending approached $13.7 billion.[14] (This later figures includes such marketing communication activities as sampling, direct mail, events, sales aids, and displays, among other programs.)

The Media Plan

Principle
The goal of media planning is to maximize impact while minimizing cost.

The challenge that marketing communicators face is how to manage all of the media opportunities and yet maximize the efficiency of budgets that are inevitably too small to do everything the firm would like to do to reach every current and potential customer. All of this decision making comes together in a **media plan**, which identifies the best media to use to deliver brand communication messages efficiently to a targeted audience. This is sometimes referred to as **connection planning** in that brand stewards working with media planners are trying to find ways to connect their brands to consumers' interests and lives, particularly to their customers, who, if they are happy with the brand experience, may become loyal to and advocate for the brand. The goal is to balance message impact and cost—maximizing impact while minimizing cost—at the same time building an enduring brand relationship.

The media plan is a subsection within a marcom plan and has its own objectives, strategies, and tactics. It is also developed in tandem with message planning, the topic of Chapter 8. Figure 11.3 shows these relationships but this time with an emphasis on media planning. We'll introduce some of the basic media planning concepts here but will explain these activities in much more detail in Chapter 14.

Key Strategic Media Concepts

This section is about the language of media. You will need to be familiar with these basic components in media strategy and planning to understand the review of media forms discussed in this chapter and the chapters that follow.

Media Mix In most cases, a media plan will include more than one medium and therefore is called a *media mix*. This **media mix** is the way various types of media are strategically combined to create a certain kind of impact. For example, the classic campaign with the dancing silhouettes that launched the iPod used posters and magazine ads to create awareness of the new product, followed by television advertising that showed how to use the product and billboards that reminded people to look for it in stores. (Check out these distinctive commercials with their day-glo colors and hot music on YouTube.)

Because of the breadth of IMC plans, the term **multiplatform** has become popular to describe multichannel and multimarketing communication areas. In other words, in IMC plans, you will find, in addition to traditional measured media advertising, a variety of other tools being used, such as events and sponsorships, social media (such as Facebook and Twitter), branded entertainment (such as films or video games in which the brand is the hero), product placement, and guerilla marketing in addition to sales staff and channel promotions, training programs, publicity, and customer service.

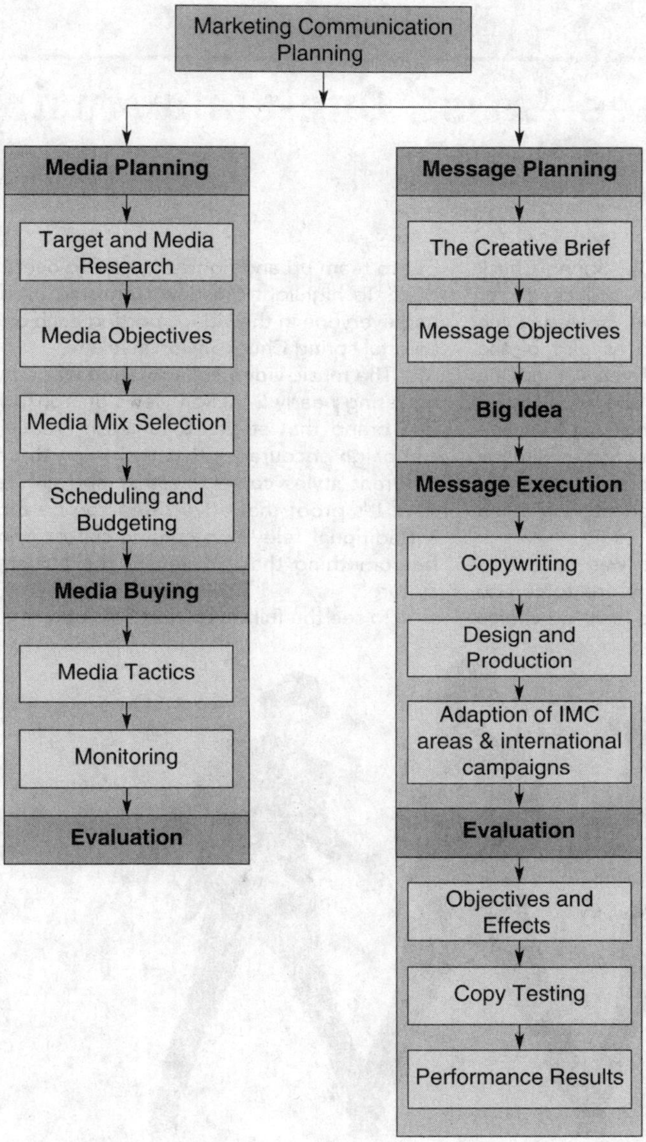

FIGURE 11.3
Brand Communication Planning
Media and message planning activities are interrelated and work in parallel.

Targets and Audiences One of the biggest challenges in developing a media plan is matching the advertiser's target audience with the audience of a particular medium. The same terms that we used to describe target audiences in Chapter 5 can be used to describe media audiences.

Principle
Media planners match the target audience with the audience of a particular medium.

A major study by the Newspaper Association of America, for example, grouped media audiences into four useful categories by generation: traditionalists (born before 1946), baby boomers (born 1946–1964), Gen X (born 1965–1976), and Gen Y (born 1977–1994).[15] Since this study, Millennials (born in the late 1990s into the first decade of 2000) have been commonly added to the list of media audiences categorized by generation. Dramatic differences are seen in the media experiences of these audience groups:

- Traditionalists grew up with newspapers, magazines, and radio (little or no television, no cell phone, no computers, no Internet).
- Boomers, who are in their 50s and 60s, always had those three types of media but also grew up with television (but still no cell phones, computers, or Internet).
- Gen Xers, who are now in their 30s and 40s, grew up not only with the media of the preceding generations but also with tape recorders, Walkman portable radios, video games, VCRs, and cable television (still no cell phones, computers, or Internet).

The Inside Story

"Warrior—A Three-Artist, One-Song Music Video for Converse"

Diego Contreras, *Art Director, Anomaly*

To launch the 2012 Spring Chuck Taylor Colors collection for Converse, we created a fun music video as part of the ongoing "Three Artists One Song" collaboration series by our agency, Anomaly. We enlisted Mark Foster, Kimbra, and A-Trak to collaborate and write a new upbeat song called "Warrior."

Our concept for the music video was an underground *luchalibre* world where fighters are forced to fight for their own freedom. Our artists have no choice but to team up and fight together to overthrow the evil boss. To highlight the new Converse product line, we had everyone in the video sporting each one of the new colorful spring Chuck Taylor sneakers.

The music video collaboration was a huge success, amassing nearly 2 million views on YouTube. Converse is a brand that strives to unleash creativity. And this campaign encourages that by having three artists with different styles come together and create something new. It's proof that advertising can be more than just a traditional television commercial or print ad. It can be something that is relevant the target and today's culture.

To see the full video, visit YouTube.

Photo: Art Director: Diego Contreras; Copywriter: Dave Ramirez; Creative Directors: Ian Toombs and Sheena Brady; Agency: Anomaly

The "Connectivity Chain" image featured the three artists Mark Foster, Kimbra, and A-trak connected by Chuck Taylors to promote their Converse music video collaboration for "Warrior."

Diego Contreras graduated from Southern Methodist University with a degree in advertising. He and his work were nominated for inclusion in this book by Professors Glenn Griffin and Patty Alvey. Check out his work at www.thisisdiego.net.

- Gen Yers, who are twenty-somethings, had all the above media, but also grew up with the computer, as well as satellite television, the Internet, CDs, and cell phones (finally, we have a generation that grew up with computers and cell phones).
- Millennials, the most recent generation, have grown up with DVDs, TiVo, satellite radio, iPods, smart phones and, more recently, have witnessed the introduction of iPads, Facebook, and Twitter. To illustrate how to reach this market with nontraditional media, Diego Contreras in his "The Inside Story," explains his work as art director on a YouTube video for Converse that featured a new song written by a three-artist collaborative team.

The media planners' challenge is to know which media best reach which audiences, whatever their ages. In a classic example of targeting, the market for the launch of the iPod, for example, was a technologically sophisticated young adult. The target market also needed to have enough discretionary income to buy the product. That audience profile led initially to a target of innovators, people who are into cool gadgets and who love music. Now where do you find those people? One place to start was with posters in subways and other urban sites. The campaign also used outdoor boards, print media, and television commercials in ways that would generate buzz. A key strategy was to get people talking about this new gadget. Eventually, the price dropped, and the market widened to include both college and high school students after the initial launch.

The Basis for the Buy

Decisions about which media to use are based on the profile of the audience that reads, views, listens, or visits a medium. Media sales reps provide their own data, but research by account planners and media researchers also uncovers media use patterns that help make these decisions.

Media planners use a variety of terms to identify and measure audiences. The terms are easy to confuse, so let's explain some here before we begin talking about specific characteristics of traditional media forms in the following chapters:

- ***Exposure*** Media impact begins with **exposure**. We know from the discussion in Chapter 4 that the first step in making an impression is perception—you have to be exposed to a message before any other effect is possible. Exposure is similar to circulation for television in that it's a rough estimate of the number of households watching a program. However, just because the television is on doesn't mean you are paying any attention to the program, let alone the advertising that surrounds it.

  Media exposure is related to the idea of corporate and consumer *control* of media. A sporting good manufacturer may want to expose young sports-minded men to its products, but all that company can do is put the message in media that are presumed to be read or viewed by that market. When there were a limited number of media opportunities, media planners could pretty much assume that they would be able to place their message in the right place to reach the right audience. It's not so easy today.

  In other words, companies may control the media buy, but they don't control what their target sees. In this cluttered media environment, consumers control what they read and watch, and media analysts recognize that with hundreds, maybe thousands, of media choices, control of media exposure now lies with the consumer. Exposure, in other words, doesn't equate to readership or viewership. At the most basic level of media planning, however, media planners still must estimate the number of exposures delivered by a media mix in putting together alternative versions of a media plan.

Principle
Exposure doesn't equate to readership or viewership; just because the television is on doesn't mean anyone is paying attention to it.

- ***Impressions*** An **impression** is one person's opportunity to be exposed one time to an ad in a specific vehicle. Impressions can be added up as a measure of the size of the audience either for one medium (one insertion in print) or for a combination of vehicles in a media mix.
- ***Circulation*** Impressions are different from **circulation** because impressions (at least in print) estimate the readership or the opportunity to be exposed (delivery to the household or a newsstand purchase) rather than just the circulation, which refers to copies sold.
- ***Gross Impressions*** Circulation doesn't tell you much about the actual exposure of a print ad. A magazine may have a circulation of 1 million, but it might be read on average by 2.5 people per issue. This means impressions for that issue would be 2.5 million. If the ad ran in three consecutive issues, then the estimate of total impressions, called

gross impressions, would be 7.5 million. Similarly, the number of viewers watching a program might be greater than the number of households reached since there may be more than one viewer watching and the commercial may be repeated several times in a program. Media planners add up all those watching and reading and multiply that times the number of placements to estimate gross impressions for a media plan.

- ***Ratings*** Gross impression figures become very large and difficult to work with, which is why the broadcasting industry uses **ratings** (percentage of exposure), which is an easier measurement to work with because it converts the raw figure to a percentage of households. When you read about a television show having a rating of 20.0, that means that 20 percent, or one-fifth, of all the households with televisions were tuned in to that program. Note that 1 rating point equals 1 percent of the nation's estimated 1,114,000 television homes; that's why planners describe this program as having 20 **rating points**, or percentage points. A 20 rating is actually a huge figure since the fragmentation of cable has diversified television watching and made it very difficult to get 20 percent of the households tuned to any one program.
- ***Share*** A better estimate of impressions might also be found in a program's **share of audience**, which refers to the percent of viewers based on the number of sets turned on. The share figure is always larger than the rating since the base is smaller. For example, the 2012 Super Bowl, which at the time was declared the "most-watched television program ever," got a rating of 47 (47 percent of all households with television), but its share was 71, which means that 71 percent of all televisions turned on were tuned to the Super Bowl. The total audience was 111.3 million viewers.[16]

Principle
The goal of most media plans is to reach as many people in the target audience as often as the budget allows.

Reach and Frequency The goal of most media plans is to reach as many people in the target audience as often as the budget allows. **Reach** is the percentage of the media audience exposed at least once to the advertiser's message during a specific time frame. When we say that a particular media vehicle, such as the Super Bowl, has a wide reach, we mean that a lot of people are watching the program. When we say that it has a narrow reach, such as the *El Nuevo Herald*, we mean that a small percentage of the newspaper audience is reading that publication. The idea for the iPod launch was not only to reach everyone who likes music but specifically to target technologically sophisticated people who are also opinion leaders (whose thoughts on innovations like the iPod would influence many others).

Equally as important as reach is **frequency**, which refers to the number of times a person is exposed to the advertisement. There's a rule of thumb that you have to hear or see something three times before it makes an impact. That's the reason frequency of repetition is so important in many advertising campaigns. Different media have different patterns of frequency. Radio commercials, for example, typically achieve high levels of frequency because they can be repeated over and over to achieve impact. Frequency is more difficult to accomplish with a monthly magazine because its publication—and an ad's appearance in it—is much more infrequent than a radio broadcast.

Most media plans state both reach and frequency objectives, and the media mix is designed to accomplish both of those goals. You may remember the discussion in Chapter 6 of the lamb market in Iceland. The objective was to reposition lamb to meet the budget concerns of recession-stressed consumers. Let's revisit that case with more information about the campaign's media plan, which demonstrates how different media are chosen based on consumer use and the ability of the various media to deliver either reach or frequency.

You may remember that focus groups were used by the H:N Marketing Communication agency in Reykjavik, Iceland, to uncover key consumer insights about lamb—principally that consumers were not buying pricey prime lamb cuts and didn't know how to cook the more budget-priced cuts. Other information uncovered in that research was useful in identifying key media characteristics of the target market. In particular, Ingvi Logason's research found the following:

- The target group members are the largest consumers of television in the country.
- Close to 100 percent of the target group has high-speed Internet access and are frequent users of the Internet at work and at home.

- Iceland most likely has the highest penetration of Facebook users in the world: 94 percent of the population in the age-group of 25- to 40-year-olds (the lamb industry's target group) have Facebook accounts.

Logason explained that his agency created "an interactive media plan that would connect with our target group in settings where they could be engaged in the ads. We would connect with them on their leisure time where they worked, at home, and in social settings." The plan used both television and Facebook. He explains, "The strength of self-dissemination and friend referrals on Facebook made sure the ad recipes traveled far and wide with the recommendation that the person posting the recipe liked it. A strong connection was created between viral ads, the Lamb industry's website, and a Facebook group interested in lamb."

Traditional media, such as television, were also used, but the interactive media "allowed us to focus on reach in the television media buy while we were able to obtain high frequency through viral media." Additional activities included sponsoring television cooking shows, placing the product in television shows (cooking and other), and gathering various lamb recipes already online and linking them to the Facebook site. Logason reported that media measurements showed that the unorthodox media mix reached its target for both reach (mostly through television) and frequency (mostly through viral activities).

Intrusiveness Because of the high level of commercial message clutter, companies in the past have valued all of the help they can get in attracting attention to their messages. **Intrusiveness**—the ability of a medium to grab attention by being disruptive or unexpected—is the primary strategy for countering clutter. Kelley, in the Part 4 opener, pointed out that in the new media world, engagement will replace interruption. But still, most media use intrusiveness to some degree as a way to grab the attention of inattentive media consumers.

Media, as well as messages, vary in their degree of intrusiveness. The most intrusive medium is personal selling because the sales representative's presence demands attention. Likewise, a phone call is also demanding, and a loud voice or sound on television can be irritating. The least intrusive media are print media because users choose when and to what extent to use these media and attend to them. Generally, the more intrusive a medium, the more it can be personalized but the more costly it is to use, which is why personal selling is so much more costly than mass media. Admittedly, the word *intrusive* has negative connotations. If a message is too disruptive or irritating, it may not help build a positive brand relationship.

Principle
The more intrusive a medium, the more it can be personalized but the more costly it is to use.

There are ways to minimize the irritation level of intrusiveness. One is to choose media whose target audience is intrinsically interested in the product category. Research has shown that one of the benefits of specialized magazines is that readers enjoy learning about new products from the advertising. To have visibility without being intrusive is one of the reasons why product placements and events are popular. Giving customers opt-in or opt-out options for receiving brand information digitally means that when messages are sent, they are not unexpected and therefore are less likely to be seen as intrusive.

Changing Patterns of Media Use

Marketing communication media are in an incredible state of flux, partially because of the introduction of the computer and the Internet but also because of the way people choose to spend their time. Bright identifies three factors driving these changes: (1) demassification and the trend to narrowcasting; (2) changes in media consumption, particularly multitasking, and (3) media models are redefining consumer-centric.[17]

Consumer Use of Media

Consumers' use of media is changing as fast as the technology. It used to be that most American audiences were involved with three television networks, a newspaper, and one or two magazines. The modern media landscape includes up to 200 television channels in some markets, a huge number of special-interest publications, millions of websites, and new electronic media, such as Kindle, iPad, and Twitter, that hadn't even been imagined five years ago. Here are other trends:

Principle
Entertainment is as much of a driving force for modern digital media as news was for traditional media.

- ***Consumer Control*** Rather than controlling media choices, consumers are much more in control of their own media and designing their own media landscapes—from video games to Twitter. The people formerly known as "audiences" are creating their own content, a practice we have referred to as *consumer-generated content*, such as the homemade videos and commercials seen on YouTube and personalized audio listening courtesy of the iPod and other MP3 players. Entertainment has become as much of a driving force for modern digital media as news was for traditional media.
- ***Media-Driven Lives*** A major change in consumer media use is the increase in media-driven lives. In their youthful days, the traditionalists' and baby boomers' lives were dominated by work and family activities. In contrast, more recent generations spend more time with media of all kinds, and those channels are more intertwined with their family, work, and leisure time.
- ***Media Multitasking*** People not only spend more time with media but also use more than one medium at a time. There are a lot of screens in our lives—media users may sit at a computer searching for a information, or they may be playing a video game at the same they are listening to an iPod and texting on their cell phones. David Rittenhouse, a member of this board's advisory board, explains the importance of multi-screen viewing in the Matter of Practice Feature.

A Matter of Practice

Connected Viewers + Multiscreen Marketers

David Rittenhouse, *Worldwide Media Director, Ogilvy*

As a student of the present day, the following scenario may sound very familiar to you because it is common behavior for your generation.

You are watching television and have your smart phone or tablet out, simultaneously texting someone watching the same program or searching for whether something you just saw on television is true. Or visiting a web site mentioned in the show or a commercial.

But this media multitasking[18] is a relatively new phenomenon, and so are the devices that enable it—smart phones and tablets. At the time of writing this, the iPhone has been out for five years and the iPad just two.

So is television becoming a background medium? Definitely not. The research we have right now indicates that the new behavior augments or supplements television viewing but does not replace it.

Studies being conducted by groups like the Interactive Advertising Bureau and the Pew Research Center are trying to get a better read on who is doing what, but some initial exploratory and descriptive research have identified a few insights.

First is that connected viewing behavior correlates positively with a few things, including age (younger people are more likely to do it), the number of screens in the household (those with more screens have higher incidence), and level of income and education.

What we are talking about is not confined to the domain of early adopters. More than half of adults who own mobile phones use them while watching television. And they are doing it even while with other people, as cultural resistance to using a mobile phone in a social setting has fallen.

The challenges for marketers resulting from this new consumer behavior are divided attention and complexity in campaign design. But the opportunity is to enable very active brand experiences for consumers via a "linked media" or "hypermedia" strategy.

More research is still needed to describe in further detail what people are doing (shopping? social media?) and how different behaviors correlate to different television programming (drama, sports, reality, comedies) and devices (smart phone, tablet).

Marketers and their agencies will no doubt be doing more experiments, too, to learn how new media products in this space work for them (such as coviewing apps like Viggle and Into Now) and understand how to pair these channels for maximum marketing impact.

At this point, it does not look like there is any going back to more passive, single-screen television experiences. Instead, it seems that audiences are increasingly expecting that content can be moved around from one device to another. And that they will have more choice and control than ever, thanks to their connected devices.

- ***Social Media*** Traditionally, most media involved a solitary experience, such as reading a paper or listening to radio, but another transformation is the creation of truly social media. First there were blogs, then MySpace and Facebook, then Twitter—all of which made personal space public. The immediacy and intimacy of a phone conversation has exploded into millions of interactions via Twitter. (Think about this: If you can send 1 million tweets, are you broadcasting? You probably don't know the 1 million recipients—so has Twitter become a form of mass media?)

Probably the biggest change is found in the increase in *interactive media*. We've always had interactivity in personal selling and direct marketing by telephone, but technological changes have forced traditional media to change their forms. The Wii game-playing platform, for example, turned televisions into game consoles. New technology has brought methods and devices for readers and viewers to participate in the creation of the message and initiate brand contact and to respond to advertisers. New mainly interactive media forms, such as social media (Facebook and Twitter), have opened up entirely new dimensions of interactivity that challenge brand stewards to keep up with their possibilities. We'll discuss this exciting new interactive world in Chapter 13.

Alternative Media Forms

If you want a fun and exciting career area, consider any of the myriad types of alternative or nontraditional media. We use the term *nontraditional media* to refer to media platforms and forms of contact other than traditional advertising media, For example, Olympian Nick Symmonds auctioned the right on eBay to tattoo a Twitter address tag—@HansonDodge—on his shoulder. The winner was Milwaukee, Wisconsin–based advertising agency Hanson Dodge Creative. A new form of transit advertising in New York City is the face of MetroCards, the cards that regular riders of subways and buses use to pay their fare, which have been redesigned to allow space for small reminder brand ads.[19] And then there's the corn maze QR code we mentioned earlier.

The point is that there are also other ways to present promotional messages besides traditional marketing communication. We'll briefly introduce a few of these media platforms, such as product placement, branded entertainment, word-of-mouth marketing, and guerilla marketing. Melissa Lerner, a specialist in new-media planning with Posterscope, a pioneering out-of-home media company, describes nontraditional media in the "A Matter of Principle" feature as a creative opportunity for innovative thinkers.

The search for nontraditional media—that is, new innovative ways to reach target audiences—is particularly important for advertisers trying to reach the elusive youth market since teens are often the first to experiment with new media forms. In some ways, this search for innovative ways to deliver messages is just as creative as the message concepts developed on the creative side of advertising. That's why one of the principles of this book is that the media side can be just as creative as the creative side of advertising.

Product Placement Technological trends, as well as the changing patterns of consumer media use, also affect media planning. For example, because of the difficulty of reaching targeted audiences with traditional media, such as television, brands are increasingly showing up in movies, video games, and television programs—a practice known as *product placement.*

We have been exposed for years to **product placement**, in which a brand appears in a television program, in a movie, or even in print as a prop. With product placement, a company pays to have verbal or visual brand exposure in some other entertainment form. George Clooney's movie *Up in the Air*, for example, prominently features American Airlines and Hilton Hotels. Media analysts estimate that Apple Computer and Pontiac each received over $25,000 in media value through placements in the television series *24*.[20] The 2013 Superman movie, *Man of Steel*, raked in more than $160 million in product placement, including tie-ins with Pepsi-Cola, Burger King, Duracell, PerfectMatch.com, and Quaker State.

Product placement has become important because it isn't as intrusive as conventional advertising, and audiences can't zap the ads, as they can for television advertising using the remote control or a DVR. At the same time, it may make the product a star—or at least be

A Matter of Principle

Creative Use of Out-of-Home and Nontraditional Media

Melissa Lerner, *Vice President, Director, Client Delivery and Data, Posterscope*

As our society becomes increasingly mobile, out-of-home (OOH) nontraditional media helps advertisers make an impact on audiences at different times and locations throughout the day. Innovative media not only reach people while they are on the go but also allow advertisers to intercept particular consumers via highly targeted messaging.

Nontraditional media include innovative emerging media and digital enhancements; place-based, branded environments; and guerilla executions. These new formats are often used in conjunction with traditional outdoor media. New technologies allow for consumer interaction in the outdoor environment.

Advertisers have recognized that successful OOH is no longer passive. The shift from advertising "at" consumers to engaging "with" consumers is affording OOH platforms with unprecedented growth opportunities.

There is nothing better than working on a nontraditional media concept that comes to fruition and generates exciting public relations and buzz within a marketplace.

Melissa Lerner earned a BS in business and economics from Lehigh University.

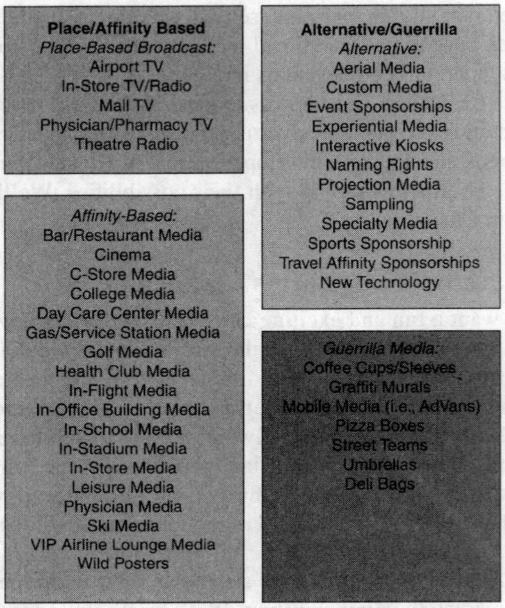

FIGURE 11.4

Nontraditional Media

New media specialist Melissa Lerner says, "clients are demanding more unique plans and ideas than ever before because impact and engagement help to become trendsetters in their respective industries." She describes these as exciting "never done before" campaigns.

associated with a star. Sometimes the product placement is subtle, as when a particular brand of aspirin is shown in a medicine chest or a character drinks a particular brand of beverage. In other cases, the brand is front and center. That happened with the prominent role of a BMW Z28, which became a star in the James Bond movie *The World Is Not Enough.* The movie placement, in fact, was the car's launch vehicle.

Television programs have also gotten into the product placement game. Both the Coca-Cola brand and the Ford Motor brand have been embedded into the successful talent show *American Idol*, and the Target bull's-eye has been seen as part of the action sets and props on *Survivor*.

The greatest advantage of product placement is that it demonstrates product use in a natural setting ("natural" depending on the movie or program) by people who are celebrities. It's unexpected and, if it's an obvious use, may catch the audience when their resistance to advertising messages may be dialed down. It's also good for engaging the affections of other stakeholders, such as employees and dealers, particularly if the placement is supported with its own campaign.

The biggest problem is that the placement may not be noticed. There is so much going on in most movies that, unless you can overtly call attention to the product, its appearance may not register.

A reverse product placement strategy was used by the watch brand Omega that appeared in the James Bond *Skyfall* movie starring Daniel Craig. To extend the association between the movie and the watch, which was a little hard to see despite Craig's glances at his timepiece, a frame from the movie showing Craig on top of a London building looking out over the city's rooftops was used in a two-page Omega magazine advertisement in upscale magazines.

A more serious problem occurs when there is not a match between the product and the movie or its audience. Another concern is that advertisers have no idea whether the movie will be a success or a failure as they negotiate a contract for the placement. If the movie is a dud, what does that do to the brand's image?

Another problem is an ethical one—when is a product placement inappropriate? For example, some pharmaceutical marketers have found that a product "plug" can be a way around the FDA's requirements on the disclosure of side effects. Public policy critics warn that it's not just drugs; the problem exists for weapons, alcohol, tobacco, and gambling, among other product categories that raise social concerns. Product placement has been called "stealth advertising" by the Writers Guild of America, which argued that "millions of viewers are sometimes being sold products without their knowledge . . . and sold in violation of governmental regulations."[21] What do you think? Should there be more controls over product placement?

Branded Entertainment Because media are being used more for entertainment, marketers are increasing their efforts to design **branded entertainment**. Similar to product placement, the use of the media of entertainment to engage consumers with brands is also referred to as **advertainment** or **branded media**, a topic will explore in more depth in Chapter 13.

An example of branded entertainment is described in "The Inside Story" feature, which explains how an animated program was created for the male-grooming brand Axe. It took almost three years and more than 100 people in four different continents to produce the program titled *City Hunters*. The creative team was composed of award-winning screenwriters, novelists, and creatives under the direction of the Catmandu Branded Entertaiment company. The integrated launch campaign was a 360-degree promotional effort, and the show included the following:

- ***Launch Parties*** Celebrities and models depicted the show's characters.
- ***Website*** A dedicated website featured all of the show's information.
- ***Text Messaging*** Mating game tips were sent by the show's main character.
- ***Interactive Billboards*** Consumers could text a message that would change the image in the billboards.
- ***In-Store Video Trailers*** Special displays and flat screens were used to promote the show.
- ***Sweepstakes*** Prizes such as iPods were given aeay with a complete City Hunters season, merchandising, and so on.

Search and Mobile Marketing In Chapter 4, we introduced the Seeker model, which recognizes that consumers are in control of not only their information search but also how they want to be connected with an organization or brand. Because some 97 percent of consumers use computers to search for product and store information, marketing strategies are designed to assist in this process. Most (90 percent) of the search is done through search engines such as Google, Yahoo!, and Bing; however, consumers also use Internet directory listings and do comparison shopping on review sites like Angie's List. Mobile search using cell phones is one of the fastest-growing media forms.[22]

For many companies, this means their communication programs have added *responding*, as well as *targeting*, to their brand communication strategies. Another new practice that responds to this increase in consumer control over the contact point is **search marketing**, which refers to the placement of online ads near topics of interest that people search for on their computers, tablets, or smart phones. These searches provide opportunities for highly targeted ads related specifically to the user's interests. *Search-engine advertising* is driven by these key words that consumers use in their search for information or entertainment.

The Inside Story

The Animated Axe Effect in *City Hunters*

Sonia Scappaticci, *New Business Director, Catmandu Branded Entertainment*

Branded entertainment has become something of a buzzword. Perhaps because global marketers are beginning to understand that the 30-second spot is not the whole answer to creating brand positioning and value.

Unilever's Axe brand has consistently created adventurous advertising that has helped position it as the world's top male-grooming brand. When Unilever launched into the branded entertainment realm in Latin America, it was very specific in its goal: to create a television show for the Axe brand that was fresh, attractive, and relevant and, most important of all, would help the brand's positioning to go even further. It had to be unlike anything ever seen before. The objective was not high ratings at any cost but rather creating a show that would be watched by the right target and that would live up to the Axe brand standards.

The result was *City Hunters*, an animated show that launched on Fox in Latin America. Because Axe is about the mating game, the show had to be created in a universe where sensuality and seduction were always in the air. Character designs where commissioned to legendary Italian comic artist Milo Manara, famous for his sexy female drawings. It is the story of a master, an apprentice, and a secret society called the "X Lodge," whose members are experts in the art of seduction. The main characters are Dr. Lynch, a retired bon vivant rumored to have been one of the inventors of the original Axe fragrance in the 1970s, and Axel, a street-smart young man who doesn't have trouble meeting women—just understanding them. According to the story, "The Axe Effect" is the compilation of more than 2,000 years of the study of women.

Until not so long ago, it would have been unimaginable to believe a network was going to pay the advertiser in order to coproduce a branded entertainment show. However, when we approached Fox with the *City Hunters* project, it was an instant match. For starters, the show was an animation, enabling it to be easily adaptable to different markets. Second, the format of the show made sense. The series of 10 short films could be aired in sets of two as a regular half-hour show but could also be broadcast individually if needed.

In terms of results, *City Hunters* premiered as a weekly show in Argentina, where it was first aired, as Fox's number one show of the year (male viewers ages 18 to 24), reaching similar ratings as hit shows like *24* and *Nip/Tuck*. It was then aired in all of Latin America to similar top rating results. There are thousands of blog postings about the show. We also received a lot of media coverage from consumer magazines that index heavy with our target market, like *Rolling Stone* and *Playboy*. However, most importantly, the special-edition *City Hunters* packaging was a success and sold out immediately, even though it was priced higher that the regular product.

Note: Sonia Scappaticci graduated from Michigan State University (MSU) with a BA in advertising. While at MSU, she was named one of the 25 Most Promising Minority Students in Communication by AAF and Advertising Age. *She was nominated by Professor Carrie La Ferle.*

There are also innovations in how cell phones are used by consumers as well as by marketers who what to send messages to them. The phone is the classic example of how media are shape-shifting as media functions converge. Telephones, of course, started as a hardwired home and office device connected by phone lines. With the development of satellite-based and broadband telecommunication, the cell phone has become the all-purpose personal communication tool. And that means it has become an attractive medium for brand communication.

Mobile marketing is an exciting new platform for location-based messages that, among other uses, can reach consumers with a promotional message when they are in the neighborhood of a store. Both search and mobile marketing will be discussed in more detail in Chapter 13.

Word of Mouth Since we recognize the power of personal communication in decision making, creative folks are challenged to come up with exciting new ways to generate buzz and convey brand messages through **word of mouth**. Buzz is important because it means that people are talking about a brand, and when it gets passed rapidly through a network of friends, we call that **viral communication**. This buzz may be the most important factor in consumer decision making because the recommendations of others are highly persuasive—more so than any advertisement.

Given the engaging work of its agency, Crispin Porter + Bogusky, Burger King is often lauded as the "king of buzz." Tia Lang, interactive director at BK, says, "Social media is very important in today's environment and we think generating buzz is a positive result in and of itself." She explained, "We have done some innovative campaigns that have helped lead to 20 consecutive quarters of positive sales."[23] Word of mouth and its importance to brand communication will also be discussed in Chapter 13.

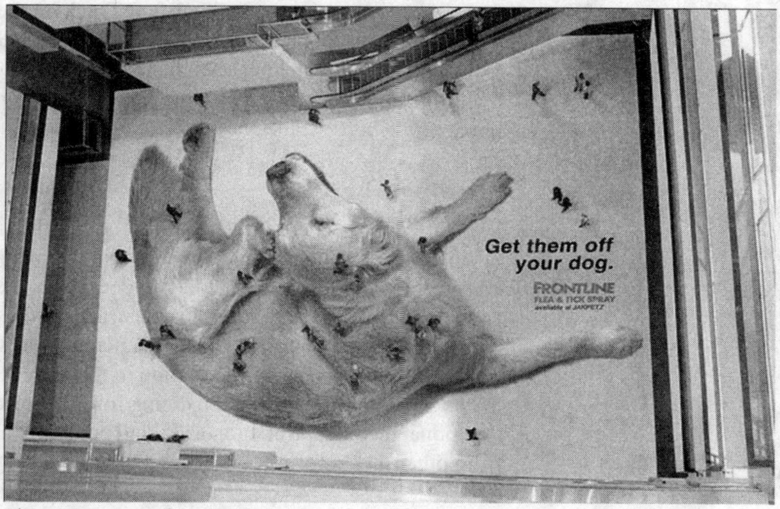

Photo: Courtesy of Merial Limited

People become fleas when walking across this giant picture of a scratching dog as seen from above in a multilevel shopping mall.

Guerilla Marketing Exciting and involving personal experiences are designed to reach people on the street and in public places through a practice known as **guerilla marketing**, which is a really hot area of alternative marketing communication. At its most basic, people are employed in places with a lot of foot traffic—streets, malls, and plazas—to hand out sales materials, such as coupons, samples, or other leaflets. This place-based strategy can also create unexpected personal encounters with a brand, such as a giant picture of a scratching dog on the floor of a mall. Effective guerilla marketing uses surprise and curiosity to catch attention and create excitement as well as buzz about a brand.

The idea is to use creative ways to reach people where they live, work, and walk to create a personal connection and a high level of impact. If it works, the encounter gets talked about, creating a buzz moment. Sears used computer-equipped Segways on Michigan Avenue in Chicago to launch its online layaway program. Microsoft used a team of "wire dancers" hung on a giant billboard on the side of a building for a Windows launch.

Guerilla marketing is so much fun it inspires creative people to come up with great ideas. For example, how do you advertise a rubber bumper protector for a car? See the "Showcase"

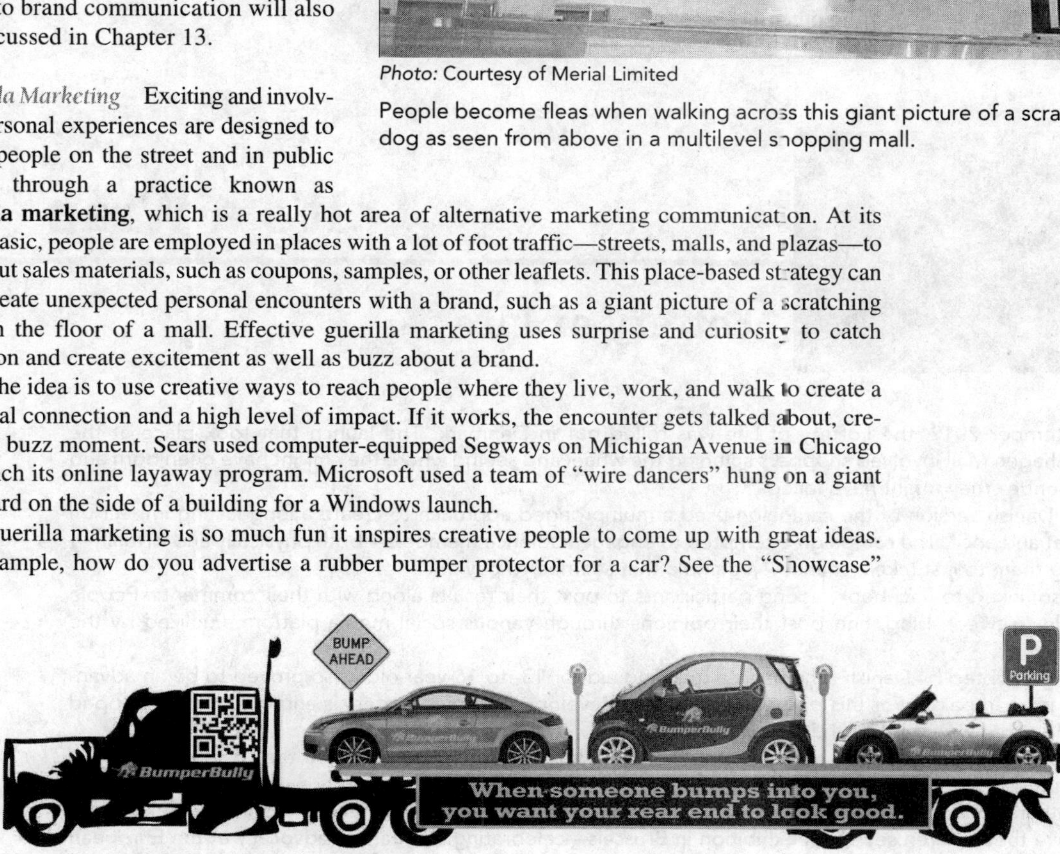

Photo: Courtesy of REM LLC; Professor Tom Fauls

SHOWCASE

The BumpTruck was the idea of Mike Patrick and Mike McGuinness, students in a Portfolio class at Boston University. A guerilla marketing campaign for the rubber bumper protector BumperBully, it features three small cars mounted on a tractor-trailer designed to simulate a city street. The front and rear cars are firmly secured, but the car in the middle is loosely secured and designed to move several inches forward and backward to lightly bump the other cars as the truck accelerates and decelerates. Each car is fitted with a BumperBully, so no damage is done. A QR code on the cab links to the BumperBully website, while a #Bumptruckhashtag stimulates conversation about the brand and its novel product.

Note: Mike Patrick and Mike McGuinness are graduate students at Boston University in the master's program in advertising. Their work on this account was submitted by the late Professor Tom Fauls.

feature for an example of how a BumpTruck on the streets of Boston can demonstrate the effectiveness of what some might see as a humdrum automotive product.

More about matching wits than matching budgets, guerilla marketing has limited reach but high impact. Sometimes a guerilla marketing campaign will generate publicity that extends the impact.

Looking Ahead

We started and ended this chapter by noting that the media environment is going through lots of shifts. This is the most creative time in the history of commercial media. We talk about new, converging, and emerging media—older media are converging with new media, and new forms are being created faster than we can learn how to use them. This chapter also introduced the fundamentals and key concepts of media planning as well as the strategic decisions made by media planners. With this brief introduction to the basics of marketing communication media as well as the new, nontraditional, and changing forms of media, we turn in the next chapter to a review of traditional media—print, broadcast, and outdoor—and the characteristics that make them different from other media forms.

It's a Wrap

Lottery of Life

In September 2012, the Lottery of Life was rolled out in Denmark. The launch that took place at the Copenhagen Mall involved shoppers spinning the wheel and seeing where they might have been born and the challenges they might have faced.

The Danish version of the campaign used a multipronged approach to create a long-lasting impact on the target audience. The campaign attempted to engage audience members—both physically and virtually—by asking them to just take a chance—a gamble that seemed to pay off.

It also linked to Facebook, asking participants to post their results along with their comments. People were able to tweet, blog, and post their opinions through various social media platforms utilized by the campaign.

Being adopted by Danish schools as a teaching aid for 13- to 16-year-olds also proved to be an advantage for the campaign. For this purpose, the charity developed learning materials and guides that mapped the online game with parts of the school curriculum.

Following its roll out, the Lottery of Life campaign has also been used by Save the Children in various other countries, including the UK and Canada.

Another significant initiative was to directly involve the European Parliament in the campaign. In June 2012, Save the Children set up an exhibition in Brussels—celebrating 20 years of advocacy at the European Parliament—giving members of the European Parliament the opportunity to spin the wheel themselves and discover what their lives may have been like had they been born somewhere else on the globe.

Key Points Summary

1. **How do media work in marketing communication and how is the industry organized?** Media send and return messages to and from the company or brand and its customers—in other words, they make connections. Media deliver messages and also offer opportunities for interaction; they also touch emotions, engage minds, and build brand relationships. Media have evolved technologically from print to broadcasting and now the Internet. Marketing communication is evolving to include more Internet-based media. Types of media include mass and niche media as well as addressable, interactive, and measured media. Key players both sell and buy media space and time; they include media salespeople and reps, media researchers, media planners, and media buyers.
2. **How would you describe the key strategic media concepts?** A media plan, which is prepared by a media planner, is a document that identifies the media to be used to deliver an advertising message to a targeted audience both locally and nationally. A media mix is the way various types of media are strategically combined in an advertising plan. Reach is the percentage of the media audience exposed at least once to the advertiser's message during a specific time frame, and frequency is the number of times a person is exposed to the advertisement.
3. **Why and how is the media landscape changing?** Media use is changing with consumers spending a lot more time with media and multitasking more as they are engaged with media. Media forms are also changing with new ways to reach people being included in marketing communication plans, such as product placement, branded entertainment, search and mobile marketing, word-of-mouth marketing, and guerilla marketing.

Key Terms

addressable media, p. 340
advertainment, p. 355
branded entertainment, p. 355
branded media, p. 355
broadcasting media, p. 339
brokers, p. 345
circulation, p. 349
connection planning, p. 346
convergence, p. 343
cross-media, p. 345
earned media, p. 342
exposure, p. 349
frequency, p. 350
gross impressions, p. 350
guerilla marketing, p. 357
impression, p. 349
interactive media, p. 340
intrusiveness, p. 351
mass media, p. 339
measured media, p. 339
media, p. 336
media buyers, p. 346
media-buying companies, p. 346
media mix, p. 346
media plan, p. 346
media planners, p. 345
media planning, p. 345
media reps, p. 345
media researchers, p. 345
media salespeople, p. 345
media vehicle, p. 339
mobile marketing, p. 356
multichannel, p. 345
multiplatform, p. 346
niche media, p. 339
owned media, p. 341
paid media, p. 341
paid, owned, and earned media, p. 341
product placement, p. 353
QR codes, p. 343
ratings, p. 350
rating points, p. 350
reach, p. 350
search marketing, p. 355
share of audience, p. 350
social media, p. 353
viral communication, p. 356
word of mouth, p. 356

Review Questions

11-4. What is media, and how does it work?

11-5. In what circumstances would mass media be preferable to niche media for advertising?

11-6. What is a media mix, and how does the mix differ for an IMC campaign?

11-7. Is interactive media different from addressable media? Explain, providing examples.

11-8. What is media planning, and what is its main objective?

11-9. In what ways are consumer media patterns changing, and how does that affect marketing communication?

Discussion Questions

11-10. What is the difference in perspective between how companies and how consumers use media? Give an example from your own experience where these two perspectives either align or are at odds.

11-11. Are OOH and nontraditional media more effective than traditional media? Explain.

11-12. You have been asked to help your family's restaurants rethink their media planning, which includes two upscale Italian restaurants and a small chain of five grilled panini sandwich shops. Is there any difference in how they might use traditional advertising versus the new online forms of brand communication? What media mix would you recommend for each type of restaurant? Explain the thinking behind your recommendations.

Take-Home Projects

11-13. *Portfolio Project:* Collect three promotional messages from three different types of media. Analyze what you believe to be the target for each piece. Now analyze the medium in which each message appears. Research what you can about that media form to determine its audience. Compare your analysis of the targeting with the reach of the medium. Do you think they match? Explain why or why not.

11-14. *Mini-Case Analysis:* Reread the Save the Children Sweden story at the beginning of this chapter. What was the problem this brand faced, and how did that affect the organisation's media planning? What were the objectives of both the initial campaign and its follow-up? What was the "big idea" that drove the second campaign, and how did that affect the media mix? Do you think the effort was driven by reach or frequency? Considering all of the new media reviewed in this chapter, what other media might Save the Children Sweden use in the next year of this campaign?

TRACE North America Case

Multicultural Media

Read the TRACE case in the Appendix before coming to class.

11-15. Which medium do you believe would be most impactful in the "Hard to Explain, Easy to Experience" campaign? Why?

11-16. What target market insights led to the development of the "Hard to Explain, Easy to Experience" media plan?

CHAPTER

12 Paid Media

Photo: Courtesy of Aflac Incorporated

It's a Winner

Title
"The Search for the New Aflac Duck Voice"

Client
American Family Life Assurance Company (Aflac)

Agency
The Kaplan Thaler Group

Contributing Agencies
Digitas, MediaVest, Paine PR

Awards
Bronze Effie; Cannes Lion Winner

CHAPTER KEY POINTS

1. What should marketers know to make effective decisions about advertising in published media, such as newspapers and magazines?
2. How do radio and television work as marketing communication media?
3. What factors do media planners consider when making place-based (out-of-home) media advertising decisions?
4. How do marketers use movies and other video formats, such as video games, for brand communication?
5. How does online advertising work?

The Art of Laying an Egg and Making It Golden

What do an *Advertising* Age reporter, National Football League (NFL) player Dhani Jones, an Elvis impersonator, a civil engineer who wears duck costumes, a more than 90-year-old woman, actor Eddie Deezen, and three parrots have in common? Read on to find out.

In 1999, not many people knew about American Family Life Assurance Co. (Aflac), nor were they likely to be familiar with its primary service: supplemental workplace medical insurance, a type of insurance that is used by people to help cover the many loopholes and deductibles in their primary insurance coverage. In fact, the company had only a 10 percent brand awareness in a sea of competitors, including Geico, Allstate, Nationwide, and Met Life, to name a few.

Enter the Duck in 2000, and things began to go swimmingly for Aflac. The long-running Aflac campaign featuring the quacking duck was the brainchild of New York's Kaplan Thaler Group. Almost all ads feature a white duck desperately screaming "Aflac!" at unsuspecting people who presumably need supplemental insurance. Alas, the duck's audience never quite seems to hear him. Ideal for television commercials, most of the ads contain a fair amount of slapstick, usually at the expense of the duck, whose memorable, exasperated-sounding voice originated with former *Saturday Night Live* cast member Gilbert Gottfried.

The campaign has been enormously successful, with brand awareness soaring to 94 percent in only three years. *Ad Age* has named a commercial featuring the duck as one of the most recalled ads in the country, and online voters enshrined the icon on Madison Avenue's Advertising Walk of Fame.

The spokesfowl is not without his problems, however. Actually, it was the voice behind the duck that laid an egg becoming a marketing disaster for Aflac, when Gottfried tweeted some insensitive comments following the earthquake and tsunami in Japan in 2011. Japan is home to 75 percent of Aflac's business. Aflac fired Gottfried immediately.

Not wanting to leave its icon speechless, Aflac moved to find a new voice for the duck. Within 24 hours of the Twitter incident, Aflac hatched a plan to invite the public to audition with its version of *American Idol.* Contestants flocked to the opportunity to compete for the unique job of being the duck's voice. More than 12,500 potential quackers tried out in six different cities across the United States and in online auditions, which brings us back to the question posed at the beginning of this case study: What do all those people have in common? They all auditioned to be *The Voice*.

This campaign, which developed from an unplanned incident, offers an opportunity to examine how traditional and interactive media have become inexorably intertwined and critical to the success of brands. To be heard, the duck must appear in some kind of video or broadcast medium. Video can be online, but still, at its heart, it needs to be video to work. Once the personality is established, the duck, because of "image transfer," can move to print and online, which, of course, he's done memorably. Furthermore, this campaign shows how quick and responsive brand managers must be to protect their brand reputation.

Turn to the "It's a Wrap" section at the end of the chapter to learn more about how this effective campaign got consumers to know more about Aflac than quack.

Sources: Rupal Parekh, "Hear the Voice of the New Aflac Spokesduck," April 26, 2011, www.adage.com; Maureen Morrison, "Aflac Goes on Duck Hunt to Find New SpokesQuacker," March 27, 2011, www.adage.com; Rupal Parekh, "Quacksmack: Ad Age's Rupal Parekh Tries Out to Be the Aflac Duck," April 10, 2011, www.adage.com; "The Search for the New Aflac Duck Voice," Effie Awards published case study, www.effie.org; "Aflac Case Study," September 10, 2012, www.kaplanthaler.com.

The Aflac campaign has been successful because of its use of television to dramatize a funny situation where the Aflac duck tries to get the attention of people needing supplemental insurance. Television is a traditional medium for advertising messages—in fact, it's the dominant medium in terms of budget. However, the media world is huge and diverse. To organize this complex media environment, we are using the paid, owned, and earned categories that we mentioned in the previous chapter. This scheme moves the discussion from *channels*—many of which are changing their shapes and no longer true to their original forms—to *functions*.

This paid, owned, and earned approach also recognizes that media are interactive, not just targeted. Furthermore, it is inclusive and opens the door to discussions of media that are used in all the marketing communication areas, not just in advertising. To understand media planning in an IMC program, then, you need to have a broad understanding of all the various types of media used in brand communication.

This chapter will review the paid media category; in Chapter 13, we'll review owned and earned categories of media with a special focus on interactive media. So let's start first with a review in this chapter of the traditional advertising media industries, sometimes called *legacy media*, which dominate the paid media category.

Traditional Paid Media of Advertising

What we are calling traditional advertising media includes print, broadcast, out-of-home, and online media as well as other nontraditional or alternative forms. Those are the major groups of the paid media category used in brand communication, and they usually demand a big share of the brand communication budget. They also play a huge role in creating brand visibility.

There are also specific media tools from the marketing communication areas of public relations, promotions, sales, and merchandising that are traditional in the sense that they've been around for a long time and are widely used. We'll introduce them in this chapter as well.

To review, paid media are used primarily in advertising. Advertisers pay a fee to media in order to present brand messages in their various vehicles—usually space and time in print, broadcast, out of home, or online. Paid media can provide wide reach, as in television audiences, or they can be tightly targeted, as in outdoor boards or magazines directed to small niche audiences.

Although the advertiser controls the size and timing of the message placement, there is no control over whether readers or viewers will notice the ad. All that's guaranteed is that the audience was exposed in some way to the message. There also tends to be lots of *clutter*—think of all the ads in a magazine or in a television program. This can lead to avoidance by the media user—turning the page, leaving the room when television ads come on, changing channels, or zipping through television ads.

Published Print Media

Print media vehicles include newspapers, magazines, brochures, and other printed surfaces, such as posters and outdoor boards. Although it is true that magazines and newspapers especially have expanded their message delivery online, billions of dollars are still spent on traditional print media.

In terms of impact, print media generally provide more information, rich imagery, and a longer message life than broadcast media. It's an information-rich environment, so, in terms of our Facets of Effects Model, print media are often used to generate cognitive responses. If you want someone to read and understand something new, then a magazine ad or brochure is useful because readers can take as much time as they need.

Consumers also find that reading a print publication is more flexible than watching or listening to broadcast because they can stop and reread, read sections out of order, or move through the publication at their own speed and on their own time. They can also save it and reread. Because the print message format is less fleeting than broadcast and more concrete, people tend to spend more time with print and absorb its messages more carefully. Print can be highly engaging when targeted toward audiences that have a special interest in the publication's content, such as women and women's magazines.

Principle
Print media generally provide more information, rich imagery, and a longer message life than other media forms.

Principle
A basic principle of newspaper publishing is that people read newspapers as much for the ads as they do for the news stories.

Published Media: Newspapers

Newspapers' primary function is to carry news, which means that marketers with news to announce, such as a special sale or new product, may find newspapers to be a comfortable

The Inside Story

Tsunami Disaster: The Inherent Value of Newspapers and Their Ads

Masaru Ariga, *Media Marketing Director, Dentsu, Tokyo, Japan*

The catastrophic earthquake and tsunami that hit northern Japan in 2012 and a series of nuclear-related anxieties that followed have apparently changed Japanese people's value system and behavior.

Inevitably, changes in the minds of consumers affect marketing. At Dentsu, an analysis was made of the changes in people's minds before and after the earthquake, using "J-READ," a large-sample consumer database that enables time-series analysis.

Comparison with the 2010 and 2011 data indicates heightened concerns in areas such as energy, disaster prevention, and philanthropic activities. Undoubtedly, these are consequences of the Tohoku region earthquake.

This uplift of "disaster-related" awareness is seen more among those who are older, living in eastern Japan (which is closer to the epicenter), and women. This heightened interest was seen among housewives, conceivably because they found themselves in situations in which they needed to be concerned with such critical daily issues as food safety.

The Tohoku disaster also affected the way people perceive media. People experienced extreme states of mind when accurate and timely information was desperately needed. Analysis was made of the relations between the level of disaster-related awareness and people's evaluation of various media. Interestingly, only the perception of newspapers showed differences.

Those with high disaster-related awareness read newspapers longer and tended to better evaluate newspapers as a source of information. The evaluation of other media showed no such change. Having gone through situations where credible information was an absolute necessity, it may be that people came to realize the unique inherent value of newspapers.

Although attributes such as "can gain knowledge," "contents are credible," and "contains local information" were highly evaluated among all people, those with strong disaster-related awareness tended to also give higher evaluations to attributes such as "daily necessity," "usefulness in everyday life," "can track development in society," and "gain topics for conversation."

Likewise, those with higher consciousness tended to give higher evaluations to newspaper advertising. Interestingly, attributes for which there were wider gaps among people tended to gain high scores. Specifically, people in general highly evaluated "can understand what companies think," "get a feeling of familiarity with companies," and "ads are reliable." Those with higher consciousness were giving even higher ratings for these three particular attributes. These three attributes may represent the intrinsic value of newspaper advertising, which happened to be highlighted as a result of the social anxiety caused by the earthquake.

Marshall McLuhan once said, "The medium is the message." The fact that the value of newspaper ads extends beyond being a source of information about products and services to creating a positive impact on the evaluation of the companies themselves has implications for the strategic role that newspaper advertising can play in a marketing mix.

Note: Masaru Ariga was in the first graduating class in 1992 from the IMC Master's program at Northwestern University; his undergraduate degree was from Waseda University in Tokyo.

environment. Studies have consistently found that people consider many ads—that is, commercial information—to be news, too, and they read newspapers as much for the local ads as they do for the news stories. In fact, as Ariga found after the Japanese disaster, newspapers and their ads became of even more value.

With more than 6,400 national and local papers in the United States, newspapers remain an important but primarily local medium. However, big dailies in the 500 largest markets account for only 1,400 of those papers, which means that most newspapers are small, and many of them are rural and suburban weeklies.

The problem with the major daily newspapers is that readership has been declining for years as readers have moved online. The problem is particularly worrisome among young people. Complicating the readership problem, the recession of the late 2000s brought double-digit-percentage declines in advertising that caused a rash of newspaper closures. At $24 billion, advertising spending in 2011 was less than half the 2005 level of nearly $50 billion.[1]

Principle
Readership is always larger than circulation because a newspaper is often read by more than one person.

Other sources of revenue besides advertising include reader subscriptions and single-copy sales at newsstands. **Circulation** is the primary way newspapers' reach is measured and compared with the reach of other media. Readership is always larger than circulation because a newspaper is often read by more than one person.

The primary characteristic of circulation is geography—whether the publication is national, regional, or local. The *Wall Street Journal* and *USA Today* are national newspapers and have the two highest circulations. Both have gone through major redesign programs to update their looks and appeal more to younger audiences. *USA Today* has been a design leader since it was launched, and now it's challenging the industry to keep up with its colorful design and format that better incorporates opportunities for advertisers to participate in print sponsorships.[2] The online *USA Today* page also has been redesigned to better fit on a tablet.

On the local level, they are followed by the *New York Times*, *Los Angeles Times*, *San Jose Mercury News*, and the *Washington Post*. Advertisers trying to reach a local market use newspapers because most newspapers (other than *USA Today* and the *Wall Street Journal*) are identified by the geography of the city or region they serve. The *New York Times* serves the New York region, but it also has a national circulation, particularly for its Sunday edition. Local papers are struggling to survive, but their readers still value them for their coverage of local politics, education, crime, sports stories, local events, church news, and local people features.

Decreasing subscriptions, however, have been a problem as readers have migrated to online versions and dropped their print subscriptions. In spite of the difficult times since 2008, some analysts see change in the fortunes of local

WEEKEND
USA TODAY 09.14.12
NFL WEEK 2
Preview of all Sunday's matchups
New features
30TH ANNIVERSARY SPECIAL SECTION
WILL WE BE THE FIRST MARTIANS?
Obama's lead poses test for Romney
GOP says economy will tighten race
AT&T. The nation's largest 4G network.
Welcome to USA TODAY — again

The *USA Today* redesign is more colorful and offers new opportunities for advertising print sponsorships. To reach a more digitally oriented audience, *USA Today* redesigned its online presence to reflect the horizontal layout stylistics of a website page that fits on a tablet, such as the iPad.

newspapers beginning in 2013. Paul Gillin, in a "Newspaper Death Watch" blog, predicted a rise in newspaper revenue in 2013, ironically because of the growth in online advertising.[3]

We can't ignore the impact of the digital revolution on newspapers with devoted readers wondering if their cup-of-coffee-and-morning-newspaper ritual is coming to an end. Major papers that have died include the *Rocky Mountain News*, the *Cincinnati Post*, the *Albuquerque Tribune*, and the *Oakland Tribune*, among others. In 2009, Seattle's daily paper, *The Post Intelligencer*, converted to an all-digital operation. The New Orleans *Times-Picayune* made headlines in 2012 as it tried to figure out a survival plan after seeing ad revenue drop more than 50 percent since 2005 at the same time publishing costs increased dramatically. The paper's solution was to experiment with a three-day-a-week publishing schedule—the rest of the daily coverage would appear online. The demise of newspapers, should that happen, also impacts the profession of journalism and the coverage of local politics and community issues.

Gannett Newspapers, which owns 82 newspapers, including *USA Today*, and 23 broadcast television stations, is experimenting with structural change within its organization to cut costs. It is building a central newsroom creating a single national news desk that would serve all its newspapers and television stations.[4]

Industry Structure Newspapers can be categorized according to their publication frequency, such as dailies, weeklies, and Sunday editions. Retailers like to place ads and press releases in daily newspapers because their **lead time** (the advance time needed to produce a publication) is short—just a few days. Food stores, for example, can change offers and pricing quickly depending on product availability.

Although newspapers go to a mass audience, they offer some **market selectivity**, which allows them to target specific consumer groups. Examples of market selectivity are special-interest newspapers (e.g., for coin collectors); ethnic editions, such as Spanish-language papers; special-interest sections (business, sports, and lifestyle); and special editions delivered to particular ZIP codes or zones. Newspapers' special interest groups also include religious denominations, political affiliations, labor unions, and professional and fraternal organizations. For example, *Stars & Stripes* is the newspaper read by millions of military personnel. The *Wall Street Journal* and the *Financial Times* are considered specialty newspapers because they concentrate on financial news.

Newspaper Advertising Newspaper formats come in two typical sizes: broadsheet and tabloid. The broadsheet format—think any large metropolitan or national paper, such as the *New York Times* or *USA Today*—is typically 11 to 12 inches wide and 20 or more inches long. Tabloids are smaller and typically measure around 11 by 17 inches. Tabloids are popular in urban areas where readers may read them on buses or subways.

Newspaper advertising is sold based on the size of the ad space and the newspaper's circulation. The charges are published on a **rate card**, which is a list of the costs for advertising space and the discounts given to local advertisers and advertisers who make volume buys. National advertisers pay a higher rate.

Most advertising sales are handled locally by the sales staff of the newspaper. Some chains centralize the sale of national advertising in their papers. There are also newspaper representatives (called "reps") who may sell space for many different newspapers. This saves an advertiser or its agency from the need to make a multitude of buys to run a national or regional campaign in newspapers. The system is known as **one-order, one-bill**. The Newspaper National Network (www.nnrlp.com) is a partnership of newspaper companies that place ads in newspapers across the country. Google has also gotten into this business, allowing advertisers to buy ads in daily newspapers through its website.

Until the 1980s, national advertisers shied away from using newspapers not only because of the buying problem but also because each paper had its own peculiar size guidelines for ads, making it difficult to prepare one ad that would fit every newspaper. In the early 1980s, the American Newspaper Publishers Association and the Newspaper Advertising Bureau introduced the **standard advertising unit** system to solve this problem. The latest version of the standard advertising unit makes it possible for newspapers to offer advertisers a great deal of choice within a standard format. An advertiser can select one of the 56 standard ad sizes and be assured that its ad will work in every newspaper in the country.

Another alternative that allows national advertisers to pay the local rate is cooperative (co-op) advertising with a local retailer. **Co-op advertising** is an arrangement between the advertiser and the retailer whereby the retailer buys the ad and the manufacturer pays half—or a portion depending on the amount of space the manufacturer's brand occupies.

Types of Newspaper Advertising Three types of advertising are found within the local newspaper: retail/display, classified, and two types of inserts (magazine supplements and preprints). Most of these are found online as well as in the print form of the newspaper:

- ***Display*** The dominant form of newspaper advertising is **display advertising**. Display ads can be any size and can be placed anywhere in the newspaper except the editorial page. Display ads can even be found in the classified section. Display advertising is further divided into two subcategories: *local (retail)* and *national (brand)*. The Aflac ads are examples of national display for the *New York Times*. Advertisers who don't care where their display ads run in the newspaper pay the **run-of-paper rate (ROP)**. If they want more choice over the placement, they can pay the **preferred-position rate**, which lets them select sections in which the ad will appear.
- ***Classified*** Two types of **classified advertising** include advertising by individuals to sell their personal goods and advertising by local businesses. These ads are arranged according to their interest to readers, such as "Help Wanted" and "Real Estate for Sale." Classified ads have represented approximately 40 percent of total newspaper advertising revenue in the past, but local online services, such as Craigslist, have almost destroyed newspaper classified advertising. That has created a huge bottom-line problem for local newspapers.
- ***Supplements*** Newspaper **supplements** are magazine-style publications inserted into a newspaper, especially in the Sunday edition, that are either syndicated nationally or prepared locally. Syndicated supplements, such as *Parade* and *USA Weekend*, are provided by an independent publisher that sells its publications to newspapers. These supplements also carry national advertising.

This is an example of business-to-business newspaper display ad for Aflac that ran in the *New York Times*. It addresses business managers with a message about making the supplemental insurance available to their employees.

Source: Courtesy of Aflac Incorporated

- ***Preprints*** **Preprints** are a type of supplement, **freestanding inserts (FSI)** are advertisements, such as the grocery or department store ads, that are inserted into the newspaper. Also called **circulars**, these preprinted advertisements, which range in size from a single page to more than 30 pages, are often printed elsewhere and then delivered to the newspaper. Newspapers charge the advertiser a fee for inserting a supplement. Next to local ads, preprints are the second largest revenue stream with estimates of up to 70 percent of the Sunday newspaper revenues coming from preprints. Preprints, however, are threatened not only by a shift to online digital formats but also by a Postal Service rate cut that will make it cheaper to mail certain types of national retail preprints.[5]

Self promotion, or **house ads**, is the type of advertising used by newspapers—and other media—to promote themselves. House ads in newspapers are usually set up in advance to help fill the layout where there is space left after the news stories and other ads have been placed. But newspapers may also use other media forms to promote themselves. London's *Guardian*, for example, used a two-minute commercial created by ad agency Bartle Bogle Hegarty based on retelling the *Three Little Pigs* as a modern news story. The highly creative television spot began with the Big Bad Wolf's death, then moved to a fast-paced accumulation of facts and speculation leading viewers through a fascinating introduction to the basics of news coverage. In addition to promoting the *Guardian*, the spot also drove a broader discussion of professional news coverage versus citizen journalism.[6]

Published Media: Magazines

Most American adults read at least one magazine per month, and they spend more time with magazines that with other print media. Similar to other mass media, magazines were hurt by the recession but seem to be slowly bouncing back. Ad spending in magazines was estimated to be $18.3 billion in 2012, which is up from $17.5 billion in 2010.[7]

The more than 6,000 magazines published in the United States appeal to every possible interest. Most magazines aim at niche markets with a focus on a particular hobby, sport, age-group, business category, or profession. These special-interest publications generally have small circulations, but there are exceptions. The number-one magazine in terms of circulation is *AARP, The Magazine*, which is sent free to anyone over age 50.

Principle
People spend more time with magazines because the ads and articles usually are more relevant to their interests.

Color and quality of reproduction are the biggest strengths of magazines. They allow the advertiser's products and brand image to be presented in a format superior to the quality of newspapers. In general, media planners know that people tend to pay more attention to magazine advertising and stories than to television because they are concentrating more on the medium and the messages are generally more relevant to their interests. Readers also spend more time reading a magazine than they do reading a newspaper, so there is a better opportunity to provide in-depth information.

The Magazine Industry The magazine industry hasn't suffered as much from the recession and changing media environment as newspapers, although, like most print media, it has been threatened by the digital revolution and the Great Recession. A number of well-respected magazines have disappeared, but one of the most surprising was the announcement in 2012 that *Newsweek* would no longer appear in print, only online.[8] Despite the high risks associated with the magazine business, new publications continue to emerge, especially those that target business markets and growing market niches.

Magazine revenues come from advertising, subscriptions, and single-copy sales. According to the Magazine Publishers Association, advertising contributes 55 percent of magazine revenue and circulation is 45 percent (subscriptions 32 percent; single-copy sales 13 percent).[9] Some publications, such as *People*, are more dependent on single-copy sales, which tend to be impulse buys. The reliance on single-copy sales was a problem during the recession.

Traditional delivery, called **controlled circulation**, is through newsstand purchases or home delivery via mail. These are measured media, and their circulation or sales can be determined. **Nontraditional delivery**, referred to as **uncontrolled circulation**, means that the magazine is distributed free to specific audiences. In addition to mail, other nontraditional delivery methods include hanging bagged copies on doorknobs, inserting magazines in newspapers (such as *Parade* magazine), delivering through professionals' offices (doctors and dentists), direct delivery (company magazines or those found on airplanes), and electronic delivery, which is being used by organizational and membership publications, such as university alumni magazines.

Meredith, the giant publisher of magazines such as *Better Homes & Gardens* and *Ladies Home Journal*, is searching for new revenue with custom publishing and multiplatform offerings for major marketers who are also its advertisers. For Kraft Foods, Meredith publishes Spanish-language magazines, designs Kraft's website, and coordinates weekly e-mail blasts that feature recipe ideas. It also built Kraft's iFood Assistant, an app for cell phones that includes recipes, how-to videos, and shopping lists.[10]

Sophisticated database management lets publishers combine the information available from subscriber lists with other public and private lists to create complete consumer profiles for advertisers. These databases, combined with new technologies, have made personalized publishing a reality. For example, **selective binding** combines information on subscribers kept in a database with a computer program to produce magazines that include special sections for subscribers based on their demographic profiles. **Ink-jet imaging** allows a magazine such as *U.S. News & World Report* to personalize its renewal form so that each issue contains a renewal card already filled out with the subscriber's name, address, and so on. Personalized messages can be printed directly on ads or on inserts ("Mr. Jones—check out our new mutual fund today").

Satellite transmission, along with computerized editing technology, allows magazines to print regional editions with regional advertising. This technology also permits publishers to close pages (stop accepting new material) just hours before press time (instead of days or weeks, as in the past) so that advertisers can drop up-to-the-minute information in their ads.

Principle

If you want to start a successful magazine, create a special-interest publication aimed at a narrow or niche audience.

Types of Magazines The focus of audience interest is the main factor used when classifying magazines. The two main types of audiences that magazines target are consumer and business audiences. Consumer magazine advertising is directed at people who buy products for personal consumption. Examples are *Sports Illustrated*, *Time*, and *People*, which are general-interest publications.

Business magazines target business readers; they include the following types of publications:

- *Trade magazines* aimed at retailers, wholesalers, and other distributors; *Chain Store Age* is an example.
- *Industrial magazines* aimed at manufacturers; *Concrete Construction* is an example.
- *Professional magazines* aimed at physicians, lawyers, and other professionals; *National Law Review* targets lawyers, and *MediaWeek* targets advertising media planners and buyers.
- *Farm magazines* aimed at those working in agriculture; *Farm Journal* and *Feed and Grain* are examples.
- *Corporate publications* are produced by companies for their customers and other stakeholders; airline magazines are good examples.

Business magazines are also classified as vertical or horizontal publications. A **vertical publication** presents stories and information about an entire industry. *Women's Wear Daily*, for example, discusses the production, marketing, and distribution of women's fashions. A **horizontal publication** deals with a business function that cuts across industries, such as *Direct Marketing*.

In terms of vehicle selection, a number of factors influence how media planners fit magazines into their media mix:

- ***Geography*** The area covered may be as small as a city (*Los Angeles Magazine* and *Boston Magazine*) or as large as several contiguous states (the southwestern edition of *Southern Living Magazine*). Geographic editions help encourage local retail

Photo: © Kevin Britland/Alamy

Advertisers look at the audience, geographic coverage, demographics, and editorial diversity of magazines as criteria for using them in a media plan.

support by listing the names of local distributors in the advertisements. Most national magazines also offer a zone edition that carries different ads and perhaps different stories, depending on the region of the country.

- ***Demographics*** Demographic editions group subscribers according to age, income, occupation, and other classifications. Some magazines for example, publish a special "ZIP" edition for upper-income homes sent to subscribers who live in specific ZIP codes and who typically share common demographic traits, based primarily on income. *Time* sends special editions to students, business executives, doctors, and business managers.
- ***Editorial Content*** Each magazine emphasizes a certain type of editorial content. The most widely used categories are general editorial (*Reader's Digest*), women's (*Family Circle*), shelter (*House Beautiful*), business (*Forbes*), and special interest (*Ski*). *Ladies Home Journal* is experimenting with user generated content by acquiring much of the content from posts on the magazine's website, its Facebook page, and other digital channels.[11]
- ***Physical Characteristics*** Media planners and buyers need to know the physical characteristics of a magazine because ads containing various elements of words and pictures require a different amount of space. The most common magazine page sizes are 8½ by 11 inches and 6 by 9 inches (*Reader's Digest*).

Media planners look for readership patterns that match their target audience and positioning strategy. *Ladies Home Journal* is one of the six magazines in the "women's service" category, which includes *Good Housekeeping*, *Woman's Day*, *Redbook*, *Better Homes and Gardens*, and *Family Circle*. Their positions are different relative to their readership. *Ladies Home Journal*, for example, reaches a "very mature" category whose average age is 56. In contrast, *Woman's Day* reaches a slightly younger audience (average age of 51) that could be characterized as mothers. It maintains a delicate balance as "the magazine my mother (and grandmother) depended on," without seeming old-fashioned. Going directly against competitor *Cosmopolitan*, *Glamour* is trying to reposition its audience (average 34 years) to younger women—Millennials or Generation Y—with a campaign called "Generation Glamour."[12]

The patterns in the male magazine category are equally competitive and complex ranging from what one *New York Times* writer describes as dudes to dandies—or, rather, lad magazines—(*Maxim*) to fashion (*GQ*). *Esquire*, which was close to closing in 2009, is back to health with its "Man at his best" position and mix of well-written, general-interest articles. One aspect of its revival is its more Web-like design with marginalia, small laughs, and in jokes.[13]

Magazine Advertising Advertising in magazines is generally highly targeted because most magazines are designed to reach consumers through their special interests. Magazine advertising benefits from much higher production values than in newspapers and that makes them good for brand-image advertising, although the format is also good for long messages since readers spend more time reading magazines than newspapers.

The emphasis on graphics encourages creativity, good design, and interesting production techniques, such as the see-through graphics in the Specialized Bike advertising. The graphic elements are separated and printed on the front and back of a page. When you look at the ad, you see people in the foreground going about their business, but in the background a faint image shows a daredevil bike rider jumping from one building to another or riding on a handrail going down the middle of a set of steps.

Like newspapers, magazine ad costs are based on the size of the ad and the circulation of the magazine. Although the format may vary from magazine to magazine, all magazines share some format characteristics. For example, the *back cover* and *inside front cover* are the most costly for advertisers because they have the highest level of exposure compared to all the other pages in a magazine. The *inside back cover* is also a premium position.

Normally, the largest unit of ad space that magazines sell is the **double-page spread**, in which an ad runs across two facing pages. A double-page ad must jump the **gutter**, the white space running between the inside edges of the pages, meaning that no headline words can run through the gutter and that body text is on one side or the other of the gutter. A page without outside margins, in which the ad's ink extends to the very edge of the page, is called a **bleed**. Magazines sometimes offer more than two connected pages (four is the most common number) that fold in on themselves. This kind of ad is called a **gatefold**. The use of multiple pages that provide photo essays is an extension of the gatefold concept.

SHOWCASE

Contributed by Aaron Stern, who worked on this ad for Specialized Bikes when he was at Goodby, Silverstein and Partners in San Francisco, the ad shows a creative use of the "see-through" capability of print.

Note: A graduate of the University of Colorado, Stern is a freelance creative director working in New York City. He was nominated by Professor Brett Robbs.

Source: Specialized Bicycles, Inc; © 2007 Specialized Bicycle Components.

Another popular format is a special advertising page or section that looks like regular editorial pages but is identified by the word "advertisement" at the top. Called **advertorials**, the content is usually an article about a company, product, or brand that is written by the corporation's publicity department. The idea is to mimic the editorial look in order to acquire the credibility of the publication's articles. Multiple-page photo-essay ads are more common in magazines such as *Fortune* and *BusinessWeek*; these magazines may present, for example, a 20-page special section for businesses in a foreign country.

Finally, a single page or double page can be broken into a variety of units called *fractional page space* (e.g., vertical half page, horizontal half page, half-page double spread, and checkerboard in which an ad is located in the upper left and the lower right of a double-page spread).

Published Media: Directories

Directories are books like the Yellow Pages that list the names of people or companies, their phone numbers, and their addresses. In addition to this information, many directories publish advertising from marketers who want to reach the people who use the directory. Corporations, associations, and other organizations, such as nonprofits, also publish directories either in print or online that include members as well as other stakeholders. These are often provided as a service to members as part of an organizational communication program. Directory advertising is designed to get attention, communicate key information about the organization, reinforce the company's brand image and position, and drive behavior.

One of the biggest advantages of advertising in directories is that if people have taken the initiative to look for a business or service, then the listing is reaching an audience already in the market for something and ready to take action. Directory advertising doesn't have to create a need because it is a number-one shopping aid, as reflected in the classic Yellow Pages slogan, "Let Your Fingers Do the Walking."

That's why directory advertising's biggest advantage is **directional advertising**: It tells people where to go to get the product or service they want. It's also the backbone of local marketing. If you are going to move across town and you want to rent a truck, you will consult the local phone book, although Angie's List is becoming equally important as an online source for local service providers. As the "A Matter of Principle" feature explains, directory advertising is the main medium that prospects consult once they have decided to buy something they need or want.

Principle
The principle behind directory advertising is that it is directional—it tells people who already are in the target market where to go to get the product or service they want.

The key difference between directory advertising and brand-image advertising is this: Directory advertising reaches prospects, people who already know they have a need for the product or service, whereas brand-image advertising seeks to create a need as well as an attractive personality for a brand. Almost 90 percent of those who consult the Yellow Pages follow up with some kind of action.

The biggest change for this medium is the advent of online directory information as well as the decline in landline phones because of the increase in cell phones. Directories are

A Matter of Principle

Directories: The Medium You Trust the Most

Joel Davis, *San Diego State University*

Which advertising medium satisfies all four of the following criteria? It is specifically designed to reach consumers when they are thinking about a purchase; it is a medium in which consumers voluntarily seek out ads; its monthly reach exceeds the monthly reach of search engines; and it is the most frequently mentioned medium when consumers are asked by the Forrester media research company, "Which media do you trust a lot?"

The answer is the Yellow Pages—both print and online.

The Yellow Pages continue to connect sellers with consumers in its traditional print format. However, as both consumers and media change, the Yellow Pages have expanded their reach through a variety of approaches. Online yellow pages, such as Yellowpages.com and Superpages (www.superpages.com), reach a broad online population, while other, more narrowly focused approaches reach additional consumers:

- AT&T Interactive's partnership with Yahoo! allows Yahoo!'s Yahoo! Local division to use advertiser content from www.yellowpages.com.
- Superpages's new Twitter channel allows users to receive addresses and phone numbers via tweets.

Regardless of how the Yellow Pages reaches a consumer, the majority of Yellow Pages usage is motivated by consumers' needs, which in turn are the results of commonly and infrequently occurring life events.

There are two types of commonly occurring events: anticipated and unanticipated. Anticipated events are those that occur without surprise in the normal course of daily activities. These events may occur frequently, such as having a car's oil changed or ordering office supplies, or they may occur less frequently, such as the decision to build a fence or order flowers.

Unanticipated events are those that take you by surprise, for example, the need to repair a roof or respond to flood damage. Yellow Pages usage increases whenever one of these events occurs. The relationship between these events and Yellow Pages usage is reflected in the most commonly used headings, which typically relate to these types of events. The most frequently referenced headings include restaurants, physicians, pizza, auto parts and dealers, and plumbing contractors.

Infrequently occurring events also motivate Yellow Pages usage. In any given year, many individuals and families undergo a major life event, such as marriage, birth of children, or change in jobs. Regardless of the nature of the event, the presence of the event itself causes a need for assistance or information, and the Yellow Pages are one source of information individuals turn to in an attempt to satisfy problems that arise as a result of a life-related event. Yellow Pages usage more than doubles when these events occur: child getting married, birth of a child, youngest child leaves home, personal marriage, separation, or divorce. Given that these events occur only once (or a few times) in an individual's life, the Yellow Pages provide an opportunity to reach consumers who have an immediate need to satisfy but who have not yet developed strong loyalty to businesses or services that can be used to satisfy their need.

expensive to print, so it is becoming harder for phone companies to justify the costs of community-wide distribution of the residential books. Some directory providers are using an "opt-in" program for those customers who prefer the book to the computer, but the Yellow Pages and business White Pages are still in business, although U.S. spending on Yellow Pages advertising has been on a steep slide. At one time, AT&T's Yellow Pages was the dominant player in an industry with many competing books. By 2012, there were only two major players left—AT&T and Dex.[14]

Broadcast Media: Radio

The reason advertisers like radio is that it is as close as we can come to a universal medium. Most every American listens to radio in some form either over the air or streaming from Internet-based services, such as Pandora or Spotify. Virtually every household in the United States (99 percent) has at least one radio, and most have multiple sets. And almost everybody listens to radio at some time during the day.

Media research firm Arbitron says radio's audience continues to increase. Weekly listening has grown in the 2000s from 224 to 242 million[15] in spite of the economic downtown and the new patterns of electronic listening. In spite of its popularity, however, the $17.4 billion radio advertising industry isn't growing much in revenue.[16] Radio's biggest advantage is that it is tightly targeted based on musical tastes (for example, rock, country, and classical) and special interests (for example, religion, Spanish language, and talk shows).

Principle
Media planners use radio for tight targeting of narrow, highly segmented markets.

Broadcast media messages—both radio and television—are fleeting, which means they may capture attention for a few seconds and then disappear, in contrast to print messages, which can be revisited and reread. Radio is a talk-, news-, or music-driven medium where advertisements can also engage the imagination to create stories in the mind. In terms of our Facets of Effects Model, broadcast media are often more entertaining, using drama and emotion with audio to attract attention and engage the feelings of the audience. If done right, radio can engage the imagination more than other media because it relies on the listener's mind to fill in the visual element. Garrison Keillor's *Prairie Home Companion* is an example of radio stories.

Principle
Radio advertising has the power to engage the imagination and communicate on a more personal level than other forms of media.

The radio listening experience is unlike that of any other media, creating both challenges and opportunities for radio advertisers. It can be a more intimate experience because we tend to listen to it alone, particularly for people wearing headphones. In cars, where many people listen to radio, it offers advertisers something close to a captive audience. And it's relatively inexpensive both to produce commercials and to buy airtime. Check out the Radio Ranch website at www.radio-ranch.com for a look behind the scenes of radio commercial production.

The Radio Industry The United States has more than 10,000 commercial stations, and most of them, except for the new Internet stations, have a limited geographical reach. In recent years, the radio industry's growth has been slow, although advertising spending is bouncing back after being badly hit by the recession. A $20 billion industry in 2007, it saw two good years in 2011 and 2012, when it climbed back to $17.3 billion.

Radio is tightly targeted based on special interests (religion, Spanish language, and talk shows) and musical tastes. In other words, radio is a highly segmented advertising medium. About 85 percent of the radio stations are focused on music. Program formats offered in a typical market are based on music styles and special interests, including hard rock, gospel, country and western, top-40 hits, soft rock, golden oldies, and nonmusic programs, such as talk radio and advice, from car repair to finances to dating. Talk radio host Rush Limbaugh is generally acknowledged to have the largest audience with estimates of his audience ranging from 14 million to 25 million.[17]

Traditional radio stations are found on the AM/FM dial, and most serve local markets. Other options for radio listeners include public radio, cable and satellite radio, low-powered stations, and Web radio. Stations with a broadcast range of approximately 25 miles are considered local stations. Regional stations may cover an entire state or several states. In addition to digital forms, which we'll discuss in Chapter 13, radio stations in the United States broadcast signals in several formats:

- ***Cable Radio*** Launched in 1990, **cable radio** technology uses cable television receivers to deliver static-free music via wires plugged into cable subscribers' stereos. The thinking behind cable radio is that cable television needs new revenue and that consumers are fed up with commercials on radio. The service typically is commercial free with a monthly subscription fee.

- ***Satellite Radio*** **Satellite radio** can deliver your favorite radio stations, regardless of where you are in the continental United States. Sirius and XM satellite radio introduced their systems in 2002. The two companies merged in 2007 as Sirius XM Radio and had some 18 million subscribers in 2009. For a monthly fee, the system allows you to access more than 100 channels.
- ***Low-Power FM*** If you're a college student, you probably have a **low-power FM** station on your campus. These nonprofit, noncommercial stations serve a small market, with a reach of three to five miles.
- ***Web Radio*** Web radio provides audio files downloaded or streaming through a website called **netcasting**, which makes it possible to broadcast radio (and television) online. If the receiver is an iPod or other type of portable media player, the reception is called **podcasting**. Podcasting is possible because of the convergence of three technologies: an audio source (the radio station or music source, such as Spotify or Pandora), a Web connection, and a portable media player or cell phone.
- ***Public Radio Stations*** **Public radio** stations are usually affiliates of National Public Radio (NPR) and carry much of the same programming, although they have to buy or subscribe to the NPR services. For that reason, some local public radio stations might carry a full range of NPR programming, while others that are less well funded may carry only a partial list of NPR programs. Public radio stations are considered noncommercial in that they rely on listener support for most of their funding. In recent years, however, they have slowly expanded their corporate *sponsorship* messages or **underwriting**, which has increased along with the audience size because public radio is one of the few media that can deliver an audience of well-educated, affluent consumers.

Radio Advertising The first radio commercials hit the air in 1922 in New York and advertised a real estate firm. These early ads were highly successful for many of the same reasons that keep radio popular today with advertisers. Media planners use radio to deliver a high level of frequency because radio commercials, particularly **jingles**, which are commercials set to music, lend themselves to repetition.

There are three types of radio buys: network, spot, and syndicated. Local advertising revenues account for approximately 75 percent. Network revenues are by far the smallest category, accounting for approximately 5 percent of total radio revenues. National spot advertising makes up the remainder. **Radio networks** are groups of affiliated stations. The network system produces programs and distributes them to their **affiliates** who contract with the system. Some of the networks include ABC Radio, Clear Channel Communications, CNN Radio Network, the Fox Sports and Fox News networks, and others that deliver special-interest programming, such as talk radio. Let's review the categories of national radio buys:

- ***Network Radio Advertising*** Network advertising can be bought from national networks that distribute programming and advertising to their affiliates. A radio network is a group of local affiliates connected to one or more national networks through telephone wires and satellites. The five major radio

Arbitron is one of several major audience-rating services in the advertising industry. It estimates the size of radio audiences for more than 250 U.S. markets.

Source: Courtesy of Arbitron, Inc.

networks are Westwood One, CBS, ABC, Unistar, and Clear Channel. The largest network by far is Clear Channel, with more than 1,200 stations. Many advertisers view network radio as a viable national advertising medium, especially for food and beverages, automobiles, and over-the-counter drugs.

- ***Spot Radio Advertising—Both Local and National*** Spot advertising lets an advertiser place an advertisement with an individual station rather than through a network. Thanks to the flexibility it offers the advertiser, **spot radio advertising** makes up nearly 80 percent of all radio advertising. In large cities, 40 or more radio stations may be available. Local stations also offer flexibility through their willingness to run unusual ads, allow last-minute changes, and negotiate rates. Buying spot radio and coping with its nonstandardized rate structures can be cumbersome, however. Although networks broadcast blocks of prerecorded national advertisements, they may also allow local affiliates open time to sell spot advertisements locally. (National media plans sometimes buy spots at the local level rather than through the network, so it is possible to have a national spot buy that only reaches certain markets.)
- ***Syndicated Radio Advertising*** This is the original type of radio programming that plays on a large number of affiliated stations, such as the *Paul Harvey* show, which is broadcast on some 1,200 stations. Program **syndication** has benefited network radio because it offers advertisers a variety of high-quality, specialized, and usually original programs. Both networks and private firms offer syndication. A local talk show may become popular enough to be "taken into syndication." Advertisers value syndicated programming because of the high level of loyalty of its audience.

Advertisers considering radio are most concerned with the number of people listening to a particular station at a given time. Radio audiences are grouped by the time of day when they are most likely to be listening, and the assumption is that different groups listen at different times of the day. The typical radio programming day is divided into five segments called **dayparts** as follows:

Morning Drive Time: 6–10 A.M.

Midday: 10 A.M.–3 P.M.

Evening Drive Time: 3–7 P.M.

Evening: 7 P.M.–midnight

Late Night: midnight–6 A.M.

The **morning drive time** segment is the period when the most listeners are tuned in to radio. This drive-time audience is getting ready for work or commuting to work, and radio is the best medium to reach them.

Broadcast Media: Television

Television has become a mainstay of society with, on average, some 280 million sets in use in the United States. Television approaches the universality of radio with 98 percent of American households having one or more television sets. In over half of U.S. households, the television is on "most" of the time. The U.S. television audience, however, is highly fragmented, tuning in to 100 or more different channels, plus online and alternative media, such as game consoles. Nielsen Media Research estimates that the average U.S. household has the set on more than five hours a day.[18]

Principle
Television's dramatic impact comes from its moving images as well as its emotional power.

Television is primarily an entertainment medium with its drama and emotional impact as well as its moving images. In-home theaters with their large-screen televisions are popular with viewers from all income levels, as McNiven and Krugman explain in the "A Matter of Practice" feature.

But it's not just big screens. Through the magic of *video streaming*, programs can also be seen on computers, tablets, an even smart phones. Television's use expanded with the introduction of the Wii, which makes the home television screen a facilitator in exercise programs as well as games. As computers begin to use television screens to project their content, this cross-channel merger will open up entirely new uses for home televisions. MTV producers are

A Matter of Practice

People Really Enjoy Their Large-Screen Televisions

Michael McNiven, *Managing Director and Portfolio Manager for Cumberland Advisors, formerly Assistant Professor, Rowan University* and Dean Krugman, *Professor, University of Georgia*

Televisions with screens of 40 inches or more are commonly referred to as large-screen televisions. The larger sets with a rectangular 16 by 9 aspect ratio—used on movie screens and in DVDs—are rapidly replacing the traditional 14 by 3 box-shaped screen. The large sets are a viable and high-quality television innovation that continues to gain prominence in the television marketplace. Annual total sales exceed 30 million sets per year, and there is no indication that the tremendous growth of large-screen television adoption will decline. Projected worldwide unit sales for large-screen televisions in 2010 was close to 61 million units.

Larger wide-screen televisions, coupled with digital reception, represent a significant change from the past in how television fare is delivered to viewers. The combination of digital programming, wider screens, and larger television displays marks a historic and pivotal entrance into the new era of the 21st-century television industry. People report that the changes in television dramatically improve the viewing process.

Large-screen owners are more likely to be married, have teenagers and older children in the home, live with more people, and earn more money. Family entertainment is a major reason for purchasing the sets, which produces a larger, fuller family experience. In addition, large-screen owners are more likely to view event programming (such as sports and movies) and to play video games, which has become a family and/or multiplayer activity.

The large-screen television experience is found by consumers to be enjoyable and easy to watch and to approximate a theater-like atmosphere. Lifelike pictures and compelling sound often help viewers feel like they are being transported to the location of the content. In most cases, large-screen televisions are part of a cluster of television technologies, including such items as video games, DVRs, and cable/satellite distribution.

The synergies of the home television cluster provide dramatically enhanced viewing and entertainment experiences. The increased viewing experience has a social component. In addition to more family viewing, larger-screen televisions are used for friend and visitor entertaining, providing an important social component.

Source: Courtesy of Michael McNiven; Dean M. Krugman, Professor Emeritus

experimenting with ways to put viewers in the director's set and let them control the camera and send singers into goofy scenarios.[19]

The economic model of broadcast television is generally based on an advertising-supported approach, at least for the traditional networks. The model relies on producing programs that attract a large audience advertisers want to reach. Advertising, plus revenue from the programs that are syndicated after they go off air, has supported network television since its beginnings, although that model is in serious trouble with the development of cable and the splintering of the viewing audience.

In this day of fragmented audiences, television is beholden to organizations like the NFL that can demand big fees for their programs. Football is one of the few programs that still draw huge audiences who watch the shows live, which explains why Fox, CBS, and NBC made a $28 billion deal with the NFL. The *Wall Street Journal* called this "the League That Runs TV."[20]

Television advertising is embedded in programming, so most of the attention in media buying, as well as in the measurement of television advertising's effectiveness, is focused on the performance of various shows and how they engage their audiences. During the golden age of television in the 1950s and 1960s, the three networks virtually controlled the evening viewing experience, but that dominance has shrunk in recent years with the rapid increase in the number of cable channels. The following table shows **prime time** viewing over the years as well as the drastic drop in percentage of adults watching the leading shows during those years.

Years	Top Show (Percentage of Audience)
1952–1953	67 *I Love Lucy* (CBS)
1962–1963	36 *The Beverly Hillbillies* (CBS)
1972–1973	33 *All in the Family* (CBS)
1982–1883	26 *60 Minutes* (CBS)
1992–1993	22 *60 Minutes* (CBS)
2002–2003	16 *CSI* (CBS)
2007–2008	16 *American Idol* (Fox)
2008–2009	9.8 *American Idol* (Fox)
2009–2010	9.1 *American Idol* (Fox)
2010–2011	8.8 *American Idol* (Fox)
2011–2012	8.0 *Sunday Night Football* (NBC)

Source: Adapted from James Poniewozik, "Here's to the Death of Broadcast," Time, March 26, 2009, 62; Sergio Ibarr, "Fox Wins 5th Straight Season in Key 18–49 Demo," July 18, 2009, www.tvweek.com; Nellie Andreeva, "Full 2009–2001 TV Season Series Rankings," Deadline Hollywood, May 27, 2010, www.deadline.com; Nellie Andreeva, "Full 2010–2011 TV Season Series Rankings," Deadline Hollywood, May 27, 2011, www.deadline.com; Bill Garman, "Complete List of 2011–12 Season TV Show Ratings," May 24, 2012, www.tybythenumbers.zap2it.com.

Structure of the Industry To better understand how television works, let's first consider its structure and programming options. The main types of television delivery systems include network, subscription (cable and satellite), pay programming, local and public television, and syndication.

Principle
Cable programming has fragmented the television audience and makes it difficult for advertisers to reach a large, mass audience.

As with radio, a **broadcast network** is a distribution system that provides television content to its affiliated stations. Currently, there are four national, over-the-air television networks in the United States: the American Broadcasting Company (ABC), the Columbia Broadcasting System (CBS), the National Broadcasting Company (NBC), and Fox Broadcasting, the new entry. The big three networks' hold on the viewing audience dropped from 75 percent in 1987 to less than 30 percent. When Fox is included, networks still only capture less than half of the audience because of the rise of hundreds of cable stations, which have fragmented the audience. The networks suffered in the recession except for Fox, which in 2010 made more money than the evening newscasts of NBC, ABC, and CBS combined.[21]

Network Television **Network television** dominates the television landscape with its $9.15 billion in advertising revenue. With some 150 affiliates, the networks sell commercial time to national advertisers for placement on programs that play throughout the network. Some time is left open for affiliates to fill with local advertising. Affiliates pay their respective networks 30 percent of the fees they charge local advertisers. In turn, affiliates receive a percentage of the advertising revenue (12 to 25 percent) paid to the national network. Advertising is the primary source of affiliate revenues. In addition to local affiliates, **independent stations** not affiliated with networks are found in local markets.

Costs for local advertising vary, depending on the size of the market and the demand for the programs carried. Most advertisers are local retailers, primarily department stores or discount stores, financial institutions, automobile dealers, restaurants, and supermarkets. National advertisers sometimes buy local advertising on a city-by-city or station-by-station basis, using **spot buys**. They do this to align the buy with their product distribution, to "heavy-up" a national schedule to meet competitive activities, or to launch a new product in selected cities.

Other forms of television service include the following:

- ***Subscription Television*** **Subscription television** is a delivery system that carries the television signal to subscribers either by cable or satellite. People sign up for television service and pay a monthly fee.
- ***Cable Television*** **Cable television,** a form of subscription television, is a $9.8 billion national network of channels that provide highly targeted special-interest programming. (Notice how that figure compares with network television's $9.15 billion.[22]) The impact of cable programming has been to fragment the audience and make it difficult to reach a large,

mass audience. Cable has become a significant threat to the financial health of the networks. Viewing time for cable also has increased as the quality of the programming has improved and advertisers have found that "narrowcasting," which uses cable's special-interest programs to reach more tightly targeted audiences, can be even more efficient than mass broadcasting. Cable programming comes from independent cable networks; these networks include such channels as Cable News Network (CNN), the Disney Channel, the Entertainment and Sports Programming Network (ESPN), and many others.

- ***Satellite Television*** **Satellite television** is similar to cable in that it's a competing delivery system. Direct broadcast television services became available in the United States in the 1990s. Dish Network and DirecTV provide the equipment, including the satellite dish, to access some 250 national and local channels. In addition to cable channels, satellite television also carries **superstations**, for example, WTBS-Atlanta, WGN-Chicago, and WWOR-New York. Satellite television is particularly useful for people who live in rural areas without local or over-the-air service. Satellite television has the potential to be a highly targeted medium in that it controls the delivery of programming and can target individual homes with *addressable ads*.
- ***On-Demand Programming*** **On-demand programming** is available to subscribers for an additional monthly fee. This type of programming offers movies, specials, and sports under such plans as Home Box Office, Showtime, and The Movie Channel. Pay networks do not currently sell advertising time.
- ***Online Video*** Traditional forms of network television are challenged by their online counterparts. *Netcasting* works for television as well as radio. The television network or station broadcasts programs, many times these are previously run episodes of hit shows, online to a computer, tablet, or other type of portable media player.
- ***Public Television*** Although many people still consider **public television** to be commercial free, the Federal Communications Commission allows the approximately 350 Public Broadcasting System (PBS) stations some leeway in airing commercial messages, called program underwriting. PBS is an attractive medium for advertisers, however, because it reaches affluent, well-educated households. PBS has a refined image and PBS advertisers are viewed as good corporate citizens because of their support for noncommercial television. The Federal Communications Commission, however, says these messages should not ask for a purchase or make price or quality comparisons, which is why many placements are **program sponsorships**. Some PBS stations accept the same ads that appear on paid programming; however, most PBS spots are created specifically for public stations. Some PBS stations will not accept any commercial corporate advertising, but they do accept noncommercial ads that are "value neutral"—in other words, ads that make no attempt to sell a product or service.
- ***Syndication*** An important revenue stream for networks and cable channels, such as HBO, that produce original programming is syndication. As in radio programming, television syndication refers to content providers that sell their programs to independent firms and other cable channels to replay as reruns. Some of the most popular first-run programs, such as *House* and *Law & Order*, are valuable properties and move quickly into syndication.

Principle
If you want to reach an otherwise difficult-to-reach target—the well-educated, affluent household—one way to do it is to underwrite public television programming.

Television Advertising The first television commercial aired in 1941 when Bulova bought time on a New York station before a Major League Baseball game between the Phillies and Dodgers.[23] Television is used for advertising because it works like the movies—it tells stories, engages the emotions, creates fantasies, and can have great visual impact. Because it's an action medium, it is also good for demonstrating how things work. It brings brand images to life and adds personality to a brand. An example of the dramatic, emotional power of television comes from one of the greatest commercials of all time. Called "Iron Eyes Cody," the Ad Council's public service announcement was created as part of an environmental campaign. It shows a Native American paddling a canoe through a river ruined by trash. A close-up shows a tear from his eye.

The first decision in using television is determining the ad's length, which is usually 10, 15, 30, or 60 seconds. The most common length is 30 seconds; for most advertisers, the 60-second spot is considered too expensive. The 10- and 15-second ad is like a billboard and simply announces that a program is "brought to you by [the advertiser]."

CLASSIC

The "crying Indian" image from this famous commercial communicated a strong ecology message. The Indian, played by Iron Eyes Cody, paddled his canoe up a filthy stream and sheds a tear as people in a speeding car throw trash out the window. To read about this "Keep America Beautiful" campaign, go to www.adcouncil.org and choose "Historic Campaigns" from the list on the left, then scan down to the "Pollution: Keep America Beautiful" heading. © 1971. Courtesy of Keep America Beautiful, Inc. (www.kab.org).

Long-form ads, which are of various lengths, are seen on late-night television when the cost of broadcast time is much lower than at other times of day. High-end jeweler Cartier, for example, ran a cinematic three-minute ad in a **roadblock**—meaning that the ad ran on the Big 3 networks of ABC, CBS, and NBC at exactly the same time. *Advertising Age* speculated that this would start a trend and increase demand for these long-form ads.[24]

Late-night **infomercials**, which can be program length, have been the venue for direct-response television with its promise of how-to-do-it tools, vegetable cutters, and fitness equipment as well as get-rich investing. Tony Horton's brutal P90X fitness routine that has Sheryl Crow, former NFL quarterback Kurt Warner, and Representative Paul Ryan as fans has built its $400 million empire on television infomercials and exercise DVDs.[25]

A second decision is time availability. Similar to radio dayparts, television programs are slotted into some common categories. The price of a commercial is based on the rating of the surrounding program (note the rating is for the program, not the commercial). The price is also based on the daypart during which the commercial is shown. The following table shows the Television Standard Dayparts. The most expensive time block is prime time.

Standard Television Dayparts

Early morning	M–F 7–9 A.M.
Daytime	M–F 9 A.M.–4:30 P.M.
Early fringe	M–F 4:30–7:30 P.M.
Prime access	M–F 7:30–8 P.M.
	M–S 8–11 P.M.
	Su 7–11 P.M.
Late news	M–Su 11–11:30 P.M.
Late night	M–Su 11:30 P.M.–1 A.M.
Saturday morning	Sa 8 A.M.–1 P.M.
Weekend afternoon	Sa–Su 1 P.M.–7 P.M.

Note: All times are Eastern Standard Time.

Although these time slots are important to media planners, they are vulnerable to consumers who not only change channels but also change viewing times using time shifting and zipping and zapping. Avoidance of advertising is easy to do with your handy remote control as follows:

- **Time-shifting** using a **DVR**, such as TiVo, allows users to record favorite television shows and watch them whenever they like. The technology makes it possible to record the programming, letting users pause, do instant replays, and begin watching programs even before the recording has finished.
- With DVR-recorded programs, consumers can **zip** past (fast-forward through) commercials completely or **zap** them by changing to another channel. These practices are forcing advertisers to rethink the design of their ads, recognizing that they only have a few moments win the attention of button-happy viewers.

Advertisers and television executives are alarmed over the increasing popularity of time-shifting and zipping and zapping. It calls into question audience measurement numbers: If 20 percent of the audience is recording *American Idol* on Tuesday night only to watch it Saturday morning commercial free, then is the Monday night streaming accurate? The DVR industry estimates that viewers zip past about 6 percent of television commercials—an estimated waste of some $5 billion in ad spending—and predicts that about 16 percent will suffer that fate.[26] A Nielsen study, however, found that viewers are not zipping through commercials as much as advertisers feared. To further understand this pattern, TiVo

Principle

The television audience has become very good at avoiding commercials unless the ads are intrusive or highly engaging.

has also announced that it is considering a service that will provide second-by-second data about which programs the company's subscribers are watching and which commercials they are skipping.

The ad-skipping debate continues in a battle between satellite television networks and networks over the ad-skipping AutoHop feature available on Dish, a practice that is well established on home DVR systems, such as TiVo. The difference is that the skipping is being offered as a feature by Dish, which the networks say represents copyright infringement.[27]

In addition to choosing the length and time slot, a third decision determines the actual type of a television commercial in terms of whether it's a network participation, local spot, or sponsorship. Public serve announcements are another type of commercial.

DVR technology poses a challenge for advertisers since it enables consumers to bypass commercials.

Source: TiVo's trademarks and copyrighted material are used by Pearson Education, Inc. under license.

- ***Participations** (network)* Most commercials are sold as **participations**, where network advertisers pay for commercial time during one or more programs. The advertiser can buy any time that is available. This approach, which is the most common one used in network advertising today, provides a great deal more flexibility in market coverage, target audiences, scheduling, and budgeting. One problem that media buyers must negotiate is the fact that the "time avails" (available time slots) for the most popular programs are often bought up by the largest advertisers or media-buying agencies, leaving fewer good time slots for small advertisers.
- ***Spot Announcements** (local)* The second form a television commercial can take is the **spot announcement**. Spot announcements are slots that appear in the breaks between programs, which local affiliates sell to advertisers who want to show their ads locally. Commercials are sold on a station-by-station basis to local, regional, and national advertisers. However, local buyers dominate spot television.
- ***Sponsorships*** In program **sponsorships**, the advertiser assumes the total financial responsibility for producing the program and providing the accompanying commercials. The *Hallmark Hall of Fame* program is an example of a sponsored program. Sponsorships represent less than 10 percent of network advertising. Sponsorship can have a powerful effect on the viewing public, especially because the advertiser can control the content and quality of the program as well as the placement and length of commercials. However, the costs of producing and sponsoring a 30- or 60-minute program make this option too expensive for most advertisers. Several advertisers can produce a program jointly as an alternative to single sponsorship. This plan is quite common with sporting events, where each sponsor receives a 15-minute segment.
- ***Public Service Announcements*** **Public service announcements** (PSAs) are spots created by agencies that donate their time and services on behalf of some good cause. PSAs are distributed to stations for local play based on the station's time availability. If time is available, PSAs run for free on radio and television stations. Check out the Ad Council's website (www.adcouncil.org) for a collection of these types of spots. The Iron Eyes Cody spot is an example of an Ad Council PSA.

Target Audiences and Viewers Targeting occurs by matching the programs with information about their viewership. For example, Comedy Central knows that its most important demographic is young men who see humor and comedy as essential to how they define themselves. Ralph Lauren announced for the first time it would be a PBS television program sponsor when it signed on for the award-winning Downton Abbey. The Masterpiece Theater show's upscale setting and its tweedy jackets align perfectly with the Ralph Lauren brand image.[28]

Principle

Television advertising is tied to television programming, and the ad's effectiveness is determined by the popularity of the television program.

Some programs are media stars and reach huge audiences—the Super Bowl is a good example. For three straight years, it broke records, with the 2012 Super Bowl recognized as the most-watched program ever at 111.3 million viewers.[29] Other programs reach small but select audiences, such as the *NewsHour* on PBS. An overlooked television audience is the 50-plus boomer crowd. As younger viewers move to online venues, these older folks stay loyal to their televisions, remote controls, and shows like *60 Minutes, NCIS*, and *Blue Bloods*.[30]

The Latino market is another audience group that is increasing in size and importance. Served primarily by Spanish-language programing through cable networks such as Univision, a new development is the partnership between ABC and Univision, which will create a 24-hour cable news channel that will broadcast in English. It will offer a blend of hard news and lifestyle programming along with an accompanying website.[31]

New Television Technology New technology is having an impact on programming options as well as on distribution patterns and systems. Innovations, such as high-definition and interactive television, expand advertising opportunities:

- **High-definition television** (HDTV) is a type of television that delivers movie-quality, high-resolution images. All over-the-air stations broadcast their programming in an HDTV format. It's been a struggle, however, getting enough HDTV programming broadcast to build demand on the consumer side. As stations upgraded their equipment and moved to HDTV in 2009, the increased availability of HDTV programming made it necessary for consumers to upgrade to HDTV sets.
- **Interactive television** means you're watching your favorite program and a commercial comes on for a product that interests you. A button pops up on the screen that you can click with your remote, and you are asked questions about whether you want more information or a coupon or to give some other response. The technology requires that advertisers give their ads to a DVR service, such as TiVo, where codes are embedded. When the ad airs, the DVR boxes pick up the coding and turn on the interactive component for that subscriber. Axe used it to show young men how to use its body spray. The ad featured a motocross champion performing a motorbike stunt. While doing a backflip, the star ripped off his shirt and sprayed Axe from armpit to armpit. Viewers were then asked to go to a different channel to learn the move. Other features included videos and Web pages that can be navigated by using the remote control.
- **Addressable television** uses a type of television that makes it possible for individual homes to receive targeted and personalized advertising. The ability to address ads to different homes through cable and other subscription services is becoming more feasible, particularly for local video-on-demand programming. Cablevision provides viewers with a remote control they can use to request samples or promotional offers to be sent to their homes.
- **3-D television** is coming to living rooms largely because of the popularity and innovations developed for 3-D movies. 3-D sets, as well as set-top boxes, are being tested by Japanese and Korean electronics rivals; Sony and ESPN are particularly focused on this new market.[32] British Sky Broadcasting is proposing a special 3-D television channel that will provide content for these new sets. In the United States, several Super Bowl ads have been filmed in 3-D.
- **Streaming video** is a process by which video programs—television, movies, YouTube creations, even video games—are sent to computers and other electronic devices, such as smart phones and tablets. This practice has created a nightmare for television measurement services that have been scrambling to estimate program viewing in these new media formats. In 2013, the ratings firm Nielsen announced that it had developed the technology to begin measuring viewership on these new broadband-enabled devices.

Movie Advertising

Movie theaters, particularly the large chain theaters, sell time at the beginning of their film showings for commercials, called **trailers**. Most of these trailers are previews advertising upcoming films, but some are national commercials for brands, ads for local businesses, PSAs, or other forms of sponsored programs.

Targeting is possible based on the appeal of the film, as the Cinema Advertising council argues in its "Movies" ad. Some films are for children (and their parents); others draw an audience that is heavily female; and action films, such as the *Matrix* series, draw more males. DVD,

Blu-ray, NetFlix, and other video distribution systems also place ads before their movies. The targeting strategy is the same as that for trailers, where the ad is matched to the film's audience.

The cost of placing a trailer is based on the number of theaters showing the spot and their estimated monthly attendance. Generally, the cost of a trailer in a first-run theater is about the same as the cost of a 30-second television spot in prime time. The reason trailers are valued by marketers is that they play to a captive audience with their attention on the screen, not reading or talking to other people. The attention level is higher for these ads than for almost any other form of commercials. But the captive audience dimension is also the biggest disadvantage of movie advertising because people resent the intrusion. They feel they paid for the ticket, so they shouldn't have to pay with their time and attention to watch commercials.

Movie giant Screenvision now offers a 20-minute preshow called *The Limelight* as a mobile app that lets viewers watch trailers, search for showtimes, and earn points toward free movie tickets and concession snacks. They can also play video games during the preshow, all of which is designed to engage viewers and create a more receptive environment for movie promotions.[33]

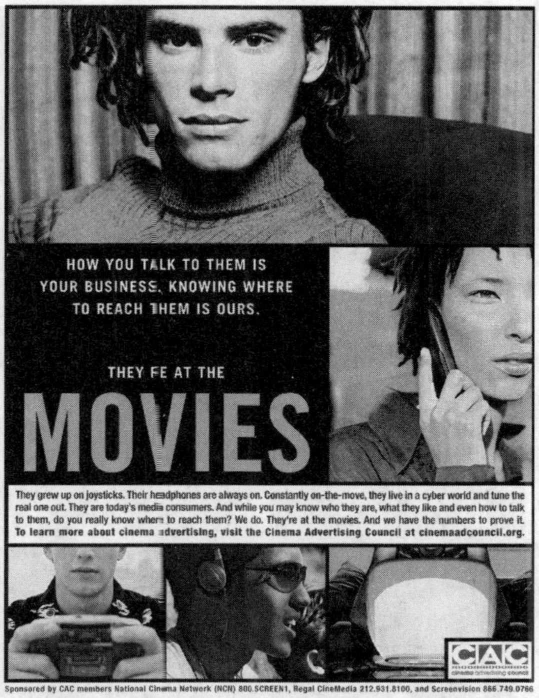

Photo: © Cinema Advertising Council. All rights reserved

The Cinema Advertising Council is an organization devoted to advertising in movies. This ad was placed in *Advertising Age* to reach media buyers and remind them of the power of cinema advertising to target particular groups of moviegoers.

Video Game Advertising

Marketers and media planners have been frustrated trying to reach young people with traditional ads on mainstream media. That has led to an increased focus on unusual media that are clearly the province of young people, such as video games. Now a global multi-billion-dollar industry, the video game business is developing as a major new medium for advertisers to target 12- to 34-year-old males, although girls are getting into the act as well, and Wii is bringing in an older adult audience of both men and women with its sports and exercise programs. The iPad made the video game market mobile. Video games offer opportunities for advertising but also for product placement.

Marketing communication opportunities are mined both by creating online games and by placing products within games. For example, games feature paid product placements for Puma athletic shoes, Nokia mobile phones, and Skittles candies, among others. Volkswagen of America bought a placement on Sony Computer Entertainment's *Gran Turismo 3* car-racing game. These questions remain: How are game players responding to ads in games, and when does it make sense to incorporate branded content in games? Are some brands more acceptable or appropriate than others?

A little bit of history: One of the first computer games, Pac-Man, was developed in 1980 and released for Atari in 1982. Adapted from an arcade game, the movement of the little round yellow big-mouth icon, which traveled a maze gobbling up cookies, was controlled with a joystick. Pac-Man had a spin-off breakfast cereal. Here's another piece of advertising trivia: In 1983, at age seven, Christian Bale of *Dark Knight* fame acted in a Pac-Man cereal commercial. You can find and watch this classic 1980s song-and-dance extravaganza on YouTube.

Place-Based Media

What we call **out-of-home media** or place-based media includes everything from billboards to hot-air balloons. That means ads on public spaces, including buses, posters on building walls (barn roofs in the old days), telephone and shopping kiosks, painted and wrapped cars and semis, taxi signs and mobile billboards, transit shelters and rail platforms, airport and bus terminal displays, hotel and shopping mall displays, in-store merchandising signs, grocery store carts, shopping bags, public restroom walls, skywriting, in-store clocks, and aisle displays.

Principle
Out-of-home advertising is situational in that it targets people at specific locations.

Even tall, highly visible grain silos have been recycled into huge Coke cans in Emporia, Kansas; a 50-foot fiddle in Green Island, Iowa; and a beer can in Longmont, Colorado. And don't

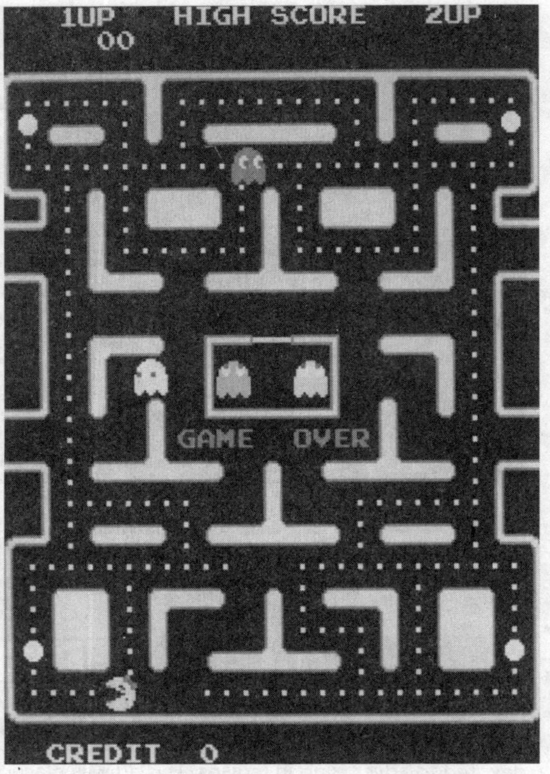

You can still play Pac-Man on the game's website at www.namcogames.com. Do you think there might be a market for an updated version of this classic maze game?

forget blimps and airplanes towing messages over your favorite stadium as well as inflatables that weave and wave in the wind at grand openings and other special events. Figure 12.1 is a depiction of the breadth of the outdoor and place-based media world.

Although total spending on out-of-home media is hard to determine because of the industry's diversity, this category is second only to the Internet as the fastest-growing marketing communication industry. Why is it such a growth area? Out-of-home advertising's defining characteristic is that it is situational or **place-based media**: It can target specific people with specific messages at a time and place when they may be most interested. A sign at the telephone kiosk reminds you to call for reservations at your favorite restaurant, a sign on the rail platform suggests that you enjoy a candy bar while riding the train, and a bus card reminds you to listen to the news on a particular radio station. As mass media have decreased in impact, place-based forms, such as outdoor, have become more attractive to many advertisers.

Outdoor Advertising Of the nearly $6 billion spent on outdoor advertising, billboard ads accounted for approximately 60 percent; street furniture, such as signs on benches, and transit ads brought in the rest. **Outdoor advertising** refers to billboards along streets and highways as well as posters in other public locations. The Outdoor Advertising Association sponsors the OBIE awards for outstanding outdoor boards, such as those for the Cheyenne Mountain Zoo.

An advertiser uses outdoor boards for two primary reasons. First, for national advertisers, this medium can provide brand reminders to the target audience. A second use is directional; billboards are a primary medium when the board is close to or gives information about a company's location. The travel and tourism industries are major users of billboards directing travelers to hotels, restaurants, resorts, gas stations, and other services.

In terms of size and format, there are two traditional kinds of billboards: printed poster panels and painted bulletins, as well as digital LED boards:

- *Printed posters* are created by the advertiser or agency, printed, and shipped to an outdoor advertising company. The prepasted posters, such as those for the Cheyenne Mountain Zoo, are then applied in sections to the poster panel's face on location, much like applying wallpaper. They come in two sizes based on the number of sheets of paper used to make the image: 8 sheet (5 by 11 feet) and 30 sheet (12 by 25 feet).

FIGURE 12.1
Outdoor and Non-Traditional Chart

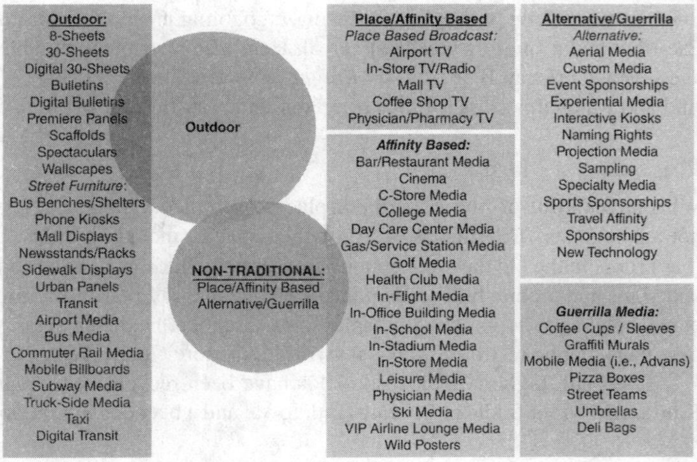

SHOWCASE

Melissa Lerner, vice president at Posterscope, an out-of-home media company, developed this chart to illustrate the connections among outdoor, place-based media, and nontraditional, or alternative, media.

Source: Courtesy of Melissa Lerner

Because of their size and graphics, billboards can make a dramatic statement, such as this OBIE award-winning out-of-home campaign for the Cheyenne Mountain Zoo in Colorado Springs, Colorado.

Source: Sukle Advertising and Design for Cheyenne Mountain Zoo. Courtesy of the Outdoor Advertising Association of America.

- **Painted outdoor bulletins**, differ from posters in that they are normally created on site and vary in size or shape, although their standard size is 14 by 48 feet. However, posters can be painted on the sides of buildings, on roofs, and even natural structures, such as the side of a mountain. Designers can add **extensions** to painted billboards to expand the scale and break away from the limits of the long rectangle. These embellishments are sometimes called **cut-outs** because they present an irregular shape.
- *Digital and LED boards* are brightly lit plastic signs with electronic messaging. These signs come in a variety of sizes, colors, and brightness. **Digital displays** use wireless technology, which allows them to be quickly changed to reflect an advertising situation (a tire company could advertise all-weather tires during snowy conditions) or the presence of a target audience member. Lerner says that "investments in digital pays off." She explains,

Until recently, the outdoor landscape was dominated by large roadside billboards. OOH [out of home] is now experiencing a paradigm shift as static ad displays are being converted to digital units, and in the process becoming much more lucrative for media operators. For advertisers the conversion to digital, in addition to digital's lower production costs and shorter lead times, provides greater *availability*, *scalability*, and *flexibility* on content, as illustrated in Figure 12.2.

FIGURE 12.2

Melissa Lerner explains the ins and outs of using digital out-of-home media.

Digital OOH		
Availability	**Scalability**	**Flexibility**
High demand units now offer multiple faces, providing greater opportunity for advertisers seeking prime real-estate, however, this come with a lower share of voice as total exposure decreases as the space is shared	Operators and advertisers can develop OOH networks for custom coverage taking advantage of lower production costs and shorter lead times to optimize messaging across a custom network	Advertisers can now employ artwork in range of formats, durations, and dayparts to optimize engagements and deployment ot existing assets to reinforce impact, exposure, and drive efficiencies

> The key to the Digital Network is moving beyond a static single message or animated message rotated among others to developing a true communication channel, controlling the content (owned, earned, and paid), its distribution, and consequently the depth and breadth of audience connection.

Advertisers can purchase any number of units (75, 50, or 25 showings daily are common quantities). Boards are usually rented for 30-day periods, with longer periods possible. Painted bulletins are bought on an individual basis, usually for one, two, or three years.

Practical Tips

Outdoor: An Effective Brand Communication Medium

James Maskulka, *Lehigh University*

In a recent campaign, the outdoor industry proclaimed, "Outdoor is not a medium. It's a large." In the contemporary view of outdoor, it is not just complementary but an integral part of a multiplatform advertising campaign and a viable alternative for establishing a brand's image, in addition to building brand awareness. Here are some tips on how to plan for and use outdoor advertising for maximum effectiveness:

1. *Frequency of Exposure* The successful execution of a transformational advertising strategy to build brand image requires frequent exposure over an extended time period—a primary benefit of outdoor.
2. *Brand Image Touch-Up* "Great brands may live forever," according to famous adman Leo Burnett, but even great brands may need image updating. This is the area where outdoor may have its greatest relevance to branding. Shifting a brand's image in response to changing consumer lifestyles guarantees that the brand remains relevant. The dynamic imagery of outdoor is an important tool in brand touch-ups.
3. *The Power of the Visual* Certain brand advertisers, such as those handling fashion and food, use visually driven creative as the brand's raison d'être. The campaigns must have consistent production values from market to market, a benefit offered by national outdoor campaigns.
4. *A Friend in the Neighborhood* Rather than building a brand on attributes and differentiation, brands with strong philosophies and attitudes build on relationships with consumers. Outdoor delivers consistent exposure of brand personality cues to targeted customers who relate to the brand.
5. *Brand Image Buildup* The 30-day posting period is long enough so that these exposures can be seen as repositories of long-term brand image leading to favorable consumer attitude accumulation. It's like making a deposit in a bank and watching your wealth grow.
6. *Speaking the Language of Consumers* Brands increasingly serve as a form of consumer communication shorthand. The compact information of outdoor advertising matches consumers' limited processing time. To illustrate, a billboard combined with a vinyl-wrapped car and reinforced by a transit ad or a taxi poster reaches the time-starved consumer with much less investment in personal processing time.
7. *Clarity of Focus* Usually, the shorter the outdoor ad copy, the more effective the message. The outdoor message imposes a creative and disciplined brand communication lexicon that ensures ongoing reinforcement of the brand message.
8. *A Gigantic Canvas* Successful outdoor advertisers see billboards as "a gigantic canvas" on which the brand advertiser can create "mega art"[34] that links the brand with relevant icons and symbols. Some of the most important slogans and images in advertising have been captured on billboards.

Source: Adapted from "Outdoor Advertising: The Brand Communication Medium," Outdoor Advertising Association of America (OAAA) special report, November 1999; the original can be found at www.oaa.org; Herbert Graf, "Outdoor as the Segue between Mass & Class," *Brandweek*, July 20, 1999, 19.

Source: Courtesy of James Maskulka

The cost of outdoor advertising is based on the percent of population in a specified geographical area exposed to the ad in one day. This is typically based on a traffic count—that is, the number of vehicles passing a particular location during a specified period of time, called a **showing**. If an advertiser purchases a "100 showing," the basic standard unit is the number of poster boards in each market that will expose the message to 100 percent of the market population every day. If three posters in a community of 100,000 people achieve a daily exposure to 75,000 people, the result is a 75 showing. Conversely, in a small town with a population of 1,200 and one main street, one board may produce a 100 showing. As you can see, the number of boards required for a 100 showing varies with the size of the city.

Because of the very short time consumers are normally exposed to a traditional billboard message (typically, three to five seconds), the message must be short and the visual must be very attention getting. No more than 8 to 10 words is the norm. The "Practical Tips" box identifies key features of outdoor media and provides suggestions on how to design effective attention-getting messages for this "gigantic canvas."

New and Novel Forms Innovation is important for the out-of-home industry with some boards now equipped to run mini-movies and ads electronically. The job search company Monster.com has been successful with trailers that replay as electronic signboard messages in public spaces—another example of media convergence with video appearing as out-of-home media. Some digitally enhanced outdoor boards can be hooked up to the Web. Lerner explains, "At Out-of-Home communication agencies, we often plan new media concepts and generate exciting PR and buzz. Creative thinking is necessary to brainstorm and plan 'never-been-done before' campaigns."

In the Philippines, a green growing plant billboard has been created that protects the environment as it displays simple brand images, such as the iconic shape of a Coke bottle.[35] Another experiment in New York City's Herald Square used an electromagnetic dot display, a modern version of the old train station signs that flipped over to announce changes. This real-time display changes based on movements of passersby. If you jump, your dot matrix reflection will also jump.[36]

Another example of an unusual billboard with immense attention-getting power featured two live players on wires playing a game of (vertical) soccer in the Adidas "Football Challenge" outdoor board that captivated audiences in Japan. This follows the famous Microsoft Windows launch with "wire dancers" on a giant outdoor board.

Posters and Kiosks Posters are posted on bulletin boards, the sides of buildings, and even vehicles. In London, daily hand-lettered posters have been used for centuries to announce newspaper headlines. The walls of the subway or Tube stations in London are lined with posters advertising all kinds of products but particularly theater shows. The iPod was launched in London (and other places) with walls of posters that Tube riders encountered coming up or down the escalators. The walls were papered with the distinctive silhouetted images against their neon backgrounds. The repetition of the images created a strong billboarding effect.

"Wire dancers" on an oversized billboard brought the Microsoft logo to life for the launch of the Vista operating system—an example of a highly engaging use of outdoor advertising.

Empty storefronts in prime downtown locations and major thoroughfares have become the latest venue for posting posters. With their large expanse of window space, abandoned retail stores have become a frugal way to deliver a big message during the recession. Landlords may charge as little as $500 a month in comparison to comparable spots on a billboard that might cost $50,000.[37]

Special structures called **kiosks** are designed for public posting of notices and posters. Kiosks are typically located in places where people walk, such as a many-sided structure in a mall or near a public walkway, or where people wait. The location has a lot to do with the design of the message. Some out-of-home media serve the same function as the kiosk, such as the ad-carrying bus shelter.

Transit Advertising Transit advertising is mainly an urban mass advertising form that places ads on vehicles such as buses and taxis that circulate through the community as moving billboards. Transit advertising also includes the posters seen in bus shelters and train, airport, and subway stations. Most of these posters must be designed for quick impressions, although people who are waiting on subway platforms or bus shelters often study these posters, so here they can present a more involved or complicated message than a billboard can. More recently, these walls have become the site for large-scale interactive digital advertising, such as the display along 60 feet of a corridor at New York's Columbus Circle station.

Another type of transit advertising is naming rights; by that, we mean that stations, for a fee, may carry the designation of a nearby business, such as Times Square Station at 42nd Street in New York, which refers to the *New York Times*. More recently, Barclays Center was added to the name of the Atlantic Avenue station in Brooklyn, which advertises both the new arena a block away and the giant international financial services company.[38]

There are two types of transit advertising: interior and exterior. **Interior transit advertising** is seen by people riding inside buses, subway cars, and taxis. These are primarily posters or car cards, sometimes with coupons or other forms of tear-off information that can be taken away. These can be designed like outdoor boards with simple messages, but because the riders are largely a captive audience, interior posters often carry more complex messages.

Exterior transit advertising is mounted on the side, rear, and top exteriors of these vehicles so pedestrians and people in nearby cars see it. Even windows can be covered with see-through silk screen images that carry commercial messages. Wraps started in 1993, when PepsiCo paid Seattle in return for permission to wrap six city buses with its logo.

Exterior transit advertising is reminder advertising; it is a frequency medium that lets advertisers get their names in front of a local audience who drive a regular route at critical times such as rush hour. *Painted vehicles* make up another type of transit advertising. More recently, recession-weary drivers have been tempted to sign up to have their cars and trucks wrapped with ads. Some of these use striking graphics, such as the brand-image designs on the sides of many trucks, both long haul and delivery.

This effect, which surrounds the entire car in a brand message for Tropicana, is called a train or bus wrap. They can be used for either interior or exterior advertising.

Source: TROPICANA is a registered trademark of PepsiCo, Inc. Used with permission.

Event Advertising and Sponsorships Ads at events are another type of out-of-home media. Think about the panels of ads in most stadiums—some are electronic, but many are printed posters. Ads also appear all over cars at races as well as on their driver's outfits. Companies pay huge fees as sponsors in order to get their logos in prominent positions. We'll discuss events and sponsorships in more detail in Chapter 17.

Online Advertising

Internet advertising can be delivered to a website as a traditional display ad, just like those you see in a magazine, or it can be presented in a number of other formats, such as banner ads across the top or bottom of a Web page. Although the percentage of most marketing communication budgets spent on Internet advertising is still relatively small, it is growing fast. In 2009, for example, the United Kingdom became the first major economy in which marketers spent more on Internet ads than they did on traditional television advertising.[39] In the United States, online advertising spending overtook print in 2012.[40]

The greatest percentage of Internet advertising is found on a small group of large, established sites that operate as electronic publishers, such as www.nytimes.com, www.wsj.com, and www.espn.com, as well as on major search engines and service providers, such as Google and Yahoo!. These media and search organizations have established reputations, and they know how to sell advertising, so they have been pioneers in the development of Internet advertising.

Social media sites, such as Facebook, also accept advertising, and Facebook has a section on its site about how to create Facebook advertising (www.facebook.com/advertising). In 2013, Twitter announced that it was beginning to offer advertising space.

With over a billion users, Facebook has a lot of viewers whom advertisers would like to reach. The Facebook philosophy, however, seeks to protect its user experience of friends and conversations. To be true to its mission, it prizes subtle advertising and advocates using such ad forms as *sponsored stories* that look like Facebook posts. This philosophy tends to create tension with big advertisers as well as criticism.

The problem is that advertisers like GM would like a bigger presence on Facebook pages and that, as well as the inability to prove advertising effectiveness, has been a big factor in marketer and investor reluctance to promote Facebook as an advertising platform. In response to the effectiveness issue, Facebook suggests measurement should focus not on "clicks" but rather on brand advertising image and relationship building.[41]

To capture more advertising dollars from its huge trail of user data, Facebook has created Facebook Exchange (FBX), which provides local sales links to targeted customers. Using behavior targeting, FBX retargets consumers who have made previous purchases or shown purchase intention on the Web.[42]

Google has been the most successful at attracting advertising, even during the recession, leading in search engine advertising, display advertising, and mobile advertising.[43] Google also dominates the search ad industry and sells display ads, along with search ads, for thousands of sites. Google and Yahoo! bring in about $88 in revenue per person for its search engine users, while Facebook only makes about $15 per user, which helps explain Facebook's difficulty selling itself as an advertising medium.[44]

Digital media have benefited from innovations in interactivity that we call **rich media**, which means viewers are able to participate in the ads or manipulate them by clicking or rolling over parts of the image. Viewers can also download streaming video or brand-related apps. Tablets, particularly the iPad, have taken advantage of the rich-media technology. An example comes from Gatorade ads aimed at teens with a nutrition message.

Although online advertising continues to be a hot topic at industry seminars, there are some critics who question its effectiveness. Michael Wolff, who blogs on Technology Review, says that people's behavior on the Web and how they interact with advertising is different from traditional media. He charges that "the character of those ads themselves and their inability to command real attention, has meant a marked decline in advertising's impact."[45] So it's safe to say that the word is still out on the effectiveness of online advertising.

Cell Phone Advertising

In addition to being essential communication, information, and entertainment tools in most people lives, cell phones also open up new avenues for commercial communication. Phones, for example, can be used for paid ads, which on cell phones usually look like small banners tucked into the corner of a Web page or spread across the top or bottom of the screen. At two inches wide and one-third of an inch tall, cell phone display ads are a challenge for ad designers. Mobile advertisers have found that context—the website or game—is particularly important for this medium, as intrusive ads seeking to attract attention have little room to work their magic on the small screen.

The Inside Story

Indian Villagers Advertise on Mobile Phones

Elisabeth Loeck, *University of Nebraska–Lincoln*

People in remote Rampur-Mathura village are using mobile phones to learn news about their community. Now local businesses are starting to use the network for advertising.

In the 20-kilometer radius that the news service reaches, Sunil Saxena, the program's founder, said that most people do not have access to television and cannot read newspapers. Mobile phones are the first device they can use to actually communicate information in a language they can understand. The trick will be figuring out how to make the service pay for itself. Advertising may be an answer.

Two reporters file audio stories from the community, which are distributed to 250 subscribers via their mobile phones. It costs 20,000 rupees a month to transmit the stories, but subscribers pay just 10 rupees a month for the service.

The network began running advertisements from local businesses in March 2010. In July, it began to charge 20 rupees a month for the exposure.

Kismet Ali and Lallan Idrieshia, mobile phone merchants in the village, used the network to advertise and saw an increase of 50 new customers from the exposure.

Saxena believe that their experiment with advertising proves that local businesses can be persuaded to use mobile phones as an advertising medium. If they can attract enough subscribers, they say, they may in turn attract enough advertisers to support the network.

Note: In the summer of 2012, journalism and advertising students from the University of Nebraska–Lincoln, traveled to India. Many had never traveled abroad before, and all came from different social and economic backgrounds. The project's goal was to tell stories about life in these rural villages of India.

Source: Courtesy of Elisabeth Loeck

Website Advertising

Small ads on other Web pages that lure visitors to switch pages are called **banner ads**. Visitors can click on them to move to the advertised website, such as the one featured here in a series of animated banner ads for Zippo lighters. Banner ads are easy to create and are usually placed on a website featuring complementary products or related topics.

Display ads, like those in print, are larger than banners and include text and images in their designs. The design of other forms of display Internet advertising is constantly changing as the industry advances. Here are some common, as well as novel, formats:

- **Skyscrapers** are the extra-long, skinny ads running down the right or left side of a website. The financial site CBSMarketWatch.com, for instance, regularly runs this kind of ad. Response rates for skyscrapers, which began to be used aggressively by more companies in the early 2000s, can be 10 times higher than for traditional banner ads.
- **Pop-ups** and **pop-behinds** burst open on the computer screen either in front of or behind the opening page of the website. Companies like Volvo and GlaxoSmith-Kline (for its Oxy acne medicine) use these forms to present games and product information. However, they are seen as intrusive and annoying, so some Internet advertisers have moved away from this format, and some computer software programs block them.
- **Micro-sites** or **mini-sites** are small websites that are the offspring of a parent website, such as the TDI Diesel site on the corporate VW site. For marketing purposes, the micro-site may cover particular products, campaigns, events, or promotions. Micro-sites tend to be more tightly focused than their parent sites and may be transitory because the reason for the site might have a time frame and expire. Another variation allows advertisers to market their products on other branded websites without sending people away from the site they're visiting. General Motors, for example, has used a mini-site on the Shell Oil

site, which the viewer can access and enlarge later. This type of advertising generally gets a higher click rate than banners or display ads; the portal About.com estimates that 5 percent of the people who see the sites click on them.

- **Superstitials** are thought of as the "Internet's commercial" and are designed to work like television ads. When you go from one page on a website to another, a 20-second animation appears in a window.
- **Widgets** are tiny computer programs that allow people to create and insert professional-looking content into their personal websites and also onto their television screens. They include news notes, calculators, weather feeds, stock tickers, clocks, book or music covers, or other Web gadgets that can be a brand-name promotional offer. It's a way to get a nonintrusive brand reminder ad on the desktop, website, or blog. Widgets also refer to mini-applications that pull content from some other place on the Web and add it to your site. In addition to getting onto cell phone screens and social media pages, they also can monitor contacts when someone clicks on the feature. Most recently, Yahoo! has created television widgets that allow access to content from new televisions by pushing a remote control button. The founder of Widgetbox.com classifies widgets as (1) self-expression tools (photos, clips, and games), (2) revenue generators on blogs (eBay categories and favorite DVDs or CDs from Amazon.com), and (3) site enhancement devices (news updates and discussion forums). A fourth type is a marketing communication message.

This series of banners for the Zippo lighter develops a message as the banners unfold. The message is a takeoff on the blackouts that urban areas sometimes experience in the summer when the use of electricity is high. Do think this series of banners would entice people to check out the Zippo website?

Source: Courtesy of Zippo

Principle

The click-through rate nearly doubles when motion and an interactive element are added to a banner ad—or to any form of online advertising.

As advertisers have searched for more effective ways to motivate site visitors to stay longer, they have used animation to become more entertaining with games and contests, interviews with celebrities, and even musical performances. Originally, Internet ads were jazzed up using relatively simple animation techniques to make elements move. New technologies provide even more active components. Research generally finds that the click-through rate nearly doubles when motion and an interactive element are added to a banner ad—and that's true for display ads as well. An example is an animated and interactive Chevrolet Volt display ad that invites viewers to click on a key word to explore different features of the car.

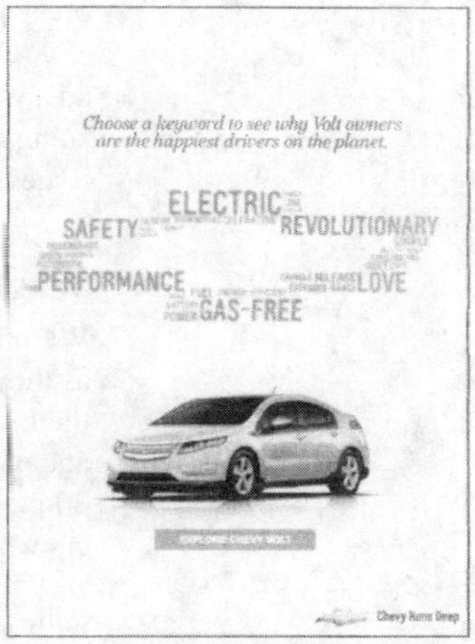

This online display ad for Volt uses a "cloud" of animated features to catch attention and dramatize the electric car's benefits.

Source: General Motors

Click-Throughs The measure of the success of an online ad or banner is the number of times viewers click on the link to check out the advertiser or the message. These clicks usually take viewers to the website of the advertiser or to some other special interesting feature.

Although banner ads were very popular when they first appeared and continue to be a major part of online advertising, the overall **click-through** rate has dropped to less than 1 percent. The most successful banner ads achieve 5 to 7 percent click-through and can help build brand awareness even if they don't deliver a high level of response.

The difference in click-through response lies in the creativity and attention-getting power of the banner ad and where it is placed. The more related and relevant a site is to the brand, the more likely it will generate a higher level of click-throughs. Entertainment helps, too—for a collection of funny banners, check out www.valleyofthegeeks.com. Note the banner ads at the top of this site.

Principle
The more relevant a website is to the brand, the more likely an ad will generate a higher level of click-throughs.

Pay-per-click is a type of online advertising that is driven by consumer search. The advertiser pays when a viewer clicks on an accompanying ad that takes them to the advertiser's site. Similar to search advertising, pay-per-click relies on key words that relate to a brand or product and bring the Seeker (see Chapter 5) to the search. Each time a Seeker clicks on your ad, you pay the negotiated click-through price.[46]

Online Video Ads Website visitors or viewers watching video downloads also confront a variety of online video ads. Because there are some 30 formats available, advertisers who want to use video are struggling to find the best platform for their ads. The most common are in a *pre-roll* format, which forces viewers to watch a video ad before viewing video clips. Other formats include interactive video ads that drop down over the screen and allow viewers to click for more information and videos that allow viewers to click on hot spots or buttons within the video to learn more about a product.

The lack of standardization means that agencies have higher production costs as they try to adapt to different delivery systems. A recent study led by the giant Paris-based agency Publicis with Microsoft, Yahoo!, CBS, and Hulu, the website portal for streaming television programming, as partners, tested a number of these formats and concluded that the best way to deliver video ads is through an *ad selector*, a feature that offers a group of ads and invites viewers to choose one. The test found that consumers are more likely to watch and remember video ads if they are able to pick the ones they watch.[47]

Online Classified Ads A small part of the online advertising world is classified advertising, whether through local media websites or Craigslist. Classifieds are still used by local advertisers and organizations in newspapers but even more so on online sites. Previously the golden goose for local newspapers, the move to online "want ads" has been a big reason why local newspapers are in trouble financially. Craigslist is a community exchange for people who either want to sell something or are looking for something. Its business model is to operate as a public service. It doesn't accept advertising but does charge for real estate listings and open-job postings.

Craigslist does have a problem with spammers who have automated the mass posting of ads, which has caused grief for customers and led to lawsuits by Craigslist. The company is also suing a San Francisco company that runs a look-alike, "parasite" site called Craigsup. Other legal issues focus on its adult category, which carries explicit sexual service ads.[48]

Search Advertising

We introduced the concept of Seekers in Chapter 5. They become a potent force in marketing as they go online to search for information. People do hundreds of millions of searches a day on their computers, smart phones, tablets, and other electronic devices. Estimates for the percentage of Internet advertising that goes to sites connected with search advertising range from 50 to 80 percent, which indicates how important the search function is for consumers and the marketers who are trying to reach them.[49]

The reason why the consumer search function is so important is that it provides the marketer with an opportunity to position a brand message adjoining the list of sites (articles, blogs, and Wikipedia entries) that is compiled in response to a **key word** by search engines. This practice is called **search advertising** or **search marketing**.

With a credit card and a few minutes, a small business owner can set up a link between his or her brand and a key word or key terms, such as "chocolate éclairs" or "real estate staging." It's the ultimate in brand linkage and interest association. Because consumers initiate the search, the adjoining ads are not perceived to be as intrusive as other forms of advertising. In 2013, the Federal Trade Commission expressed concern that search engines would often bring up content that might not be identified as paid advertisements and laid out guidelines to help visitors more clearly distinguish ads from other types of information.

A benefit of online consumer searches is that they leave a trail of clues about products, features, and advertising approaches. This behavior can be mined for insights that lead to new products. AOL uses massive amounts of tracking data to tell what Web search topics are most likely to attract audiences.

Search providers, such as Google, MSN, Bing, and Yahoo!, auction off positions that let advertisers' ads be seen next to specific search results. This has brought a fountain of money to Google over the years. These related ads are priced based on the number of consumer clicks on the ad, with rates averaging around 50 cents per click. To explore how this works, "google" the term "AdWords," and you will find dozens of sites by experts who help businesses construct their search marketing campaigns. Microsoft's Bing.com and Google's "Goggles' also offer visual searches that display search results as pictures rather than words. You can search for pink tennis shoes or titanium tennis rackets and get a response in pictures.

Principle
Search marketing is important because it allows ads to be positioned on sites that are associated with key words, which are topics of interest to the consumer doing the search. It is the ultimate in brand linkage and interest association.

A recent development is Google's foray into *real-time search*, which not only produces the usual search results but also lets Google supplement the results with updates posted each second on social media, such as Facebook and Twitter.[50] This mix of search and social media will only increase the speed with which brand messages spread and will challenge the ability of companies to monitor their brands' online presence.

The practice of maximizing the link between topics and brand-related websites is called **search optimization**. Companies try to affect their search engine rankings in order to drive more traffic to their websites. They want their ads to appear as close to the top of the list as possible in order to have maximum visibility. An important first step for marketers in creating a viable website is getting it registered with popular search engines so that it shows up early on the list provided by the search engine.

Another type of consumer search using smart phones is based on a **quick-response code**, which is a type of two-dimensional bar code that uses a scannable matrix design of square dots. You see them in ads and articles, on packages, and the sides of buildings—even as a design in corn maze (Chapter 11)—and anywhere a company wants to post this code as a scannable link to its website. The point is that this is just one more way consumers can search for information using their mobile phones.

Online Advertising Sales

Selling online advertising space is complicated. Major sites, such as MSNB.com and History .com, sell ads on their pages charging premium prices because they are on high-traffic sites. They can cost from $10 to $50 per thousand viewings, depending on the visibility of the position.[51] Advertisers and their media buyers get access to Internet sites through providers such as DoubleClick, an Internet advertising service owned by Google that places more than 60 billion online ads per month. DoubleClick provides reports on the placement and performance of these ads to both publishers and advertisers and also helps create ads and widgets.

Middlemen companies act as brokers for online ad space that they aggregate across different sites and package as single buys, in effect setting up an ad network. These ad networkers offer less well designed sites and positions and may sell space for less than a dollar per thousand viewers. They are criticized for flooding the Internet with cheap and sometimes tacky ads. Data-mining companies like Blue Kai and eXelate Media collect data on how visitors move around among sites and then sell access to advertising on groups of sites that attract similar visitors. This is similar to how local newspaper advertising can be purchased through group contracts and makes buying much more efficient.[52]

Google, Microsoft, and AOL have gotten into the ad sales business by setting up ad exchanges that allow advertisers to bid directly on available ad space on large groups of websites. In effect, they are cutting out the middlemen. Other big websites, such as ESPN, Turner Broadcasting, and *Forbes* magazine, have stopped doing business with the ad networks in order to gain better control over the quality of the content on their sites. The Online Publishers Association, which represents major publishers of Web content, reported on a study that found that ads on portals, as well as ads bought from ad brokers, were significantly less effective than the ads that the premium sites offer. The idea is that the portals and ad networkers' ads may be cheaper, but they appear in formats that are less interesting and thus are less likely to connect with visitors.[53]

Google, once the guru of search advertising, has been making a big hit in the $12.1 billion display ad market, as has Facebook. Yahoo! dominated the business for years, but its share of the market slipped as both Google and Facebook increased. Google found that its display-ad spending grew twice as fast as its search advertising. Here are the numbers:[54]

	Yahoo!	**Google**	**Facebook**
2008	18.4 %	2.4 %	2.8 %
2011	13.1 %	8.3 %	16.3 %

Yahoo's share dropped to 13.1 percent in 2011 from 18.4 percent in 2008. At the same time, Google rose to 8.3 percent from 2.4 percent.

Digital Issues for Traditional Media

Print media, as well as broadcast, have been struggling with competition from online media as well as decisions on how to support online versions of their own publications, particularly since tablets have made online print versions much more readable. Some newspapers and magazines have "bundled" subscriptions that include print, digital, and apps for smart phones and tablets. Others offer separate subscription rates for print, digital, and/or app packages.

Another problem is Google's practice of displaying media headlines without any charges—either to the media company or to the viewer. Google receives online advertising revenue at the same time print media advertising is in a steady decline. Slate.com, an online current affairs magazine, headlined this problem as "How Google Ate the Newspaper Industry."[55] But it's a problem that affects magazines and broadcast media (think YouTube) as well as newspapers.

Looking Ahead

This chapter has provided an overview of paid advertising in traditional, as well as new media. But, in truth, traditional media hardly exist any more. An interview on public radio's NPR headlined, "In a 24/7 World, What Is a Magazine?" began with this line: "It's hard to know what a magazine is these days." Is it paper? Is it a website? Martin Sorrell, head of WPP, the world's largest communication company (125 firms including Ogilvy & Mather and JWT advertising agencies), asks, "How do you define a newspaper or a magazine?" He observes, "I doubt free-to-air television or, in particular, newspapers and magazines, will ever be the same again."[56] This is one of the key points of change that Kelley pointed out in his essay in the Part 4 opener. He observes that all media, including the traditional ones, will have some type of digital and interactive component and this will only make media selection more challenging.

Not only are these traditional media formats changing, but so are the ads that appear in them. CBS promoted its fall season with ads in the magazine *Entertainment Weekly* that contained video clips of its new programs. Similar to musical greeting cards, the technology used a flexible, thin plastic screen that was activated when the two-page ad was opened. The videos also included a Pepsi Max ad inside the CBS ad. An executive at Time Warner, publisher of *EW*, observed, "It we can efficiently put video into magazines, think about the possibilities it would open up."[57]

So let's move on to the exciting and equally fast-changing world of digital media, which are generating even more new opportunities for marketing communication. The next chapter will review the dynamic world of owned and earned media with its strong communication formats.

It's a Wrap

Aflac's Flap Ducks Disaster

He might not have a vocabulary beyond the word he knows best, "Aflac," but the duck has a voice that is essential to the brand awareness. The Kaplan Thaler Group succeeded in creating a campaign that led to a 94 percent awareness of Aflac and an increase of 55 percent in U.S. sales during the first three years of the campaign, followed by double-digit growth in the following years. This campaign earned two gold Effies for the duck who successfully communicated the brand personality as well as the honor of being voted one of the best-known brand icons.

When the duck's voice was silenced, the company and agency moved with lightning speed to restore it with a multiplatform communication effort, asking America to "answer the duck's call" at the aptly named Quackaflac.com website or the audition sites in six cities.

Aflac posted the job on Monster.com. When an existing media buy could not be canceled, Aflac ran a modified 2006 Aflac TV spot, "Silent Movie," featuring a silent duck who drove viewers to the Facebook page for more information and a chance to see a "Search for My Voice" video.

Finding this a golden-egg opportunity, the effort became news on CNN and CBS, in *Fortune*, *Newsweek*, and the *New York Times*; and on late-night entertainment shows, including Leno, Fallon, and Letterman. The search generated more than 70,000 media stories and 900 million media impressions. The efforts doubled positive brand and character social sentiment in six weeks, according to the agency.

Not only did the campaign create positive news for Aflac, but it appears to have influenced sales. At the peak of the campaign, direct sales leads increased 80 percent. In the words of CNN's Wolf Blitzer, Aflac was able to "turn a gaffe into a gift."

And one lucky duck, Dan McKeague, was plucked from obscurity to be the winner of *American Idol* of the insurance industry and arguably the world's most famous quacker.

Logo: Courtesy of Aflac Incorporated

Key Points Summary

1. **What should marketers know to make effective decisions about advertising in newspapers and magazines?** Newspapers are great for announcements of news. They also provide local market coverage with some geographic flexibility, plus an interaction with national news and the ability to reach shoppers who see the paper as a credible source. Magazines reach special-interest audiences who have a high level of receptivity to the message. People read them slowly, and they have long life and great image reproduction. However, magazines require long lead times, have a low level of immediacy and limited flexibility, and generally do not reach a broad mass market.
2. **How do radio and television work as marketing communication media?** The traditional radio stations are found on AM and FM and serve primarily local markets. AM and FM are only the beginning of the radio listener's options, which also include public radio, cable and satellite radio, low-powered stations, and Web radio. Radio dramas engage the imagination, but radio is primarily a music-driven medium, which serves audiences defined by their musical tastes. Listeners can have a very intimate relationship with radio and can be quite loyal to their favorite stations, but radio also serves as background.

   Television is useful as a marketing communication medium because it works like a movie with story, action, emotions, and visual impact. Television audiences are fragmented, often irritated by advertising, and prone to avoidance. Audiences are measured in terms of ratings and share. Television's greatest advantage is that it is pervasive and cost efficient when reaching a large number of viewers. Because of the special-interest aspect of cable programming, it is good at reaching more narrowly targeted audiences.
3. **What factors do marketers consider when making place-based or out-of-home media decisions?**

Out-of-home media includes everything from billboards to hot-air balloons. A common out-of-home medium is outdoor advertising, which refers to billboards along streets and highways as well as posters. Outdoor is a high-impact and directional medium; it's also effective for brand reminders and relatively inexpensive with a long life. Other forms of out-of-home media include on-premise signs, posters, and transit advertising.

4. **How do marketers use movies and other formats, such as video games, for brand communication?** Movie theaters sell time for advertisements before their films. Marketing communication messages are also carried on discs, such as DVDs and Blu-ray, as well as in lobbies and other public spaces. Video games, whether played on dedicated consoles or computers or downloaded for small-screens, such as smart phones, can carry advertising. Usually, the ads appear as banners at the top or bottom of the opening screen.
5. **How does online advertising work?** Online ads can be display ads, similar to those in print, or they can be banners across the top or bottom or on the sides. All of these can be animated, and display ads can also include videos. Online classified ads have also become a big business. Search advertising means that ads appear on sites that appear when a user searches for a topic using a key word. Since this is directed by consumer searches, the advertising can be highly targeted to their interest.

Key Terms

addressable television, p. 382
advertorials, p. 372
affiliates, p. 375
banner ads, p. 390
bleed, p. 371
broadcast network, p. 378
cable radio, p. 374
cable television, p. 378
circulars, p. 369
circulation, p. 366
classified advertising, p. 368
click-through, p. 391
controlled circulation, p. 369
co-op advertising, p. 367
cutouts, p. 385
dayparts, p. 376
digital displays, p. 385
directional advertising, p. 373
display advertising, p. 368
double-page spread, p. 371
DVR, p. 380
extensions, p. 385
exterior transit advertising, p. 388
freestanding inserts, p. 369
gatefold, p. 371
gutter, p. 371
high-definition television, p. 382
horizontal publication, p. 370
house ads, p. 369
independent stations, p. 378
infomercials, p. 380
ink-jet imaging, p. 370
interactive television, p. 382
interior transit advertising, p. 388
jingles, p. 375
key word, p. 392
kiosks, p. 388
lead time, p. 367
low-power FM, p. 375
market selectivity, p. 367
micro-sites, p. 390
mini-sites, p. 390
morning drive time, p. 376
netcasting, p. 375
network television, p. 378
nontraditional delivery, p. 369
on-demand programming, p. 379
one-order, one-bill, p. 367
outdoor advertising, p. 384
out-of-home media, p. 383
painted outdoor bulletins, p. 385
participations, p. 381
place-based media, p. 384
podcasting, p. 375
pop-behinds, p. 390
pop-ups, p. 390
preferred-position rate, p. 368
preprints, p. 369
prime time, p. 378
public radio, p. 375
program sponsorships, p. 379
public service announcements, p. 381
public television, p. 379
quick-response code, p. 363
radio networks, p. 375
rate card, p. 367
rich media, p. 389
roadblock, p. 380
run-of-paper rate, p. 368
satellite radio, p. 375
satellite television, p. 379
satellite transmission, p. 370
search advertising, p. 392
search marketing, p. 392
search optimization, p. 393
selective binding, p. 370
showing, p. 387
skyscrapers, p. 390
sponsorships, p. 381
spot announcement, p. 381
spot buys, p. 378
spot radio advertising, p. 376
standard advertising unit, p. 367
streaming video, p. 382
subscription television, p. 378
superstations, p. 379
superstitials, p. 391
supplements, p. 368
syndication, p. 376
3-D television, p. 382
time-shifting, p. 380
trailers, p. 382
uncontrolled circulation, p. 369
underwriting, p. 375
vertical publication, p. 370
widgets, p. 391
zap, p. 380
zip, p. 380

Review Questions

12-4. Describe paid media and list its major categories.

12-5. Explain how newspaper readership is determined and measured and how readership differs from circulation.

12-6. Which type of paid media has the best impact on an audience? Why?

12-7. What is directory advertising, and to what level is it considered effective?

12-8. What is outdoor advertising, and what are its advantages?

12-9. How can television be used most effectively, and what are the advantages and limitations of advertising on television?

12-10. What are trailers, and how are they used as an advertising form?

12-11. Explain the ways in which painted outdoor bulletins are different from posters.

12-12. What is a website, and how does it differ from other forms of advertising?

12-13. Define and describe a banner ad. Some experts say the effectiveness of banner ads is declining. Why would that be?

Discussion Questions

12-14. You are the media planner for an agency handling a small chain of upscale furniture outlets in a medium-sized metro market that concentrates most of its advertising in the Sunday supplement of the local newspaper. The client also schedules display ads in the daily editions for special sales. Six months ago a new, high-style metropolitan lifestyle magazine approached you about advertising for your client. You deferred a decision by saying you'd see what reader acceptance would be. Now the magazine has shown some steady increases. If you were to include the magazine on the ad schedule, you'd have to reduce the newspaper advertising somewhat. What would be your recommendation to the furniture store owner?

12-15. You work in the HR department as Talent Acquisition Specialist in an oil and gas company that has international operations. The company is involved in multiple projects and applies short-term contracting as a normal practice due to the nature of its projects, which have a specific start and end date. Considering cost savings and poaching the best professionals with the least budget, answer the following:

a. How would you use paid media to help you save on your hiring costs and meet your objectives?

b. Which paid media channels would you use to attract professionals? How would you use them?

12-16. You are a major agency media director who has just finished a presentation to a prospective client in convenience food marketing where you recommend increasing the use of local radio and television advertising in spot markets. During the question-and-answer period, a client representative says, "We know that network television viewers' loyalty is nothing like it was 10 or even five years ago because so many people now turn to cable, VCRs, and the Web. There are smaller audiences per program each year, yet television time costs continue to rise. Do you still believe we should consider commercial television as a primary medium for our company's advertising?" Another member of the client team questions whether broadcast is effective given the clutter on both radio and television with long commercial pods. "Why shouldn't we decrease our use of broadcast advertising?" How would you answer? Develop an argument either in support of increasing or decreasing the use of broadcast advertising for this client.

Take-Home Projects

12-17. ***Portfolio Project:*** You have been asked by the director of your school's student union to make a chart of all the traditional media serving your market to use in promoting the center's 50th-anniversary events. Develop a profile for each medium giving the key characteristics, such as type of programming (for broadcast), the type of audience reached, the products commonly advertised, and the appropriateness of this medium as an advertising vehicle for the center's special celebration. At the end of your media analysis, identify the top three that you would recommend and explain why.

12-18. ***Mini-Case Analysis:*** Aflac has been an award-winning campaign for years. How important do you think the "voice of the brand" is? Why not have multiple quacking ducks? Explain how its media use has contributed to its success. In particular, describe how the media mix has evolved. If you were a member of the team planning the next year's campaign, what other media might be useful?

TRACE North America Case

Multicultural Advertising Media

Read the TRACE case in the Appendix before coming to class.

12-19. In what ways do traditional advertising media contribute to the "Hard to Explain, Easy to Experience" campaign? Why?

12-20. How can online advertising be used in support of this campaign?

CHAPTER

13 Owned, Interactive, and Earned Media

Photo: Sozaijiten

It's a Winner

Title:	Client:	Agency:	Awards:
"Unleash Deadly"	*adidas*	*Starcom MediaVest Group (SMG)*	*Gold in the Best Sport Brand category and Silver in the Best Sport Marketing Campaign at Middle East Sports Industry Awards 2013 (SPIA), Silver at the Effies MENA 2012*

CHAPTER KEY POINTS

1. What do we mean by owned media that organizations control and manage?
2. What are the interactive owned media that are also managed by organizations, and why is that interactive element important?
3. What are earned media, and how do organizations relate to brand discussions that are beyond their control?
4. How does multiplatform brand communication work, and why is it important?

Unleash Deadly

On the eve of the UEFA Champions League, 2012, adidas kicked off its campaign "Unleash Deadly" to promote the Predator Lethal Zones, a new version of its iconic Predator football boots. If the hype was to be believed, this was the most advanced football boot ever made—featuring five zones: First Touch, Pass, Dribble, Drive, and Sweet Spot. The campaign utilized an integrated platform to get the ball rolling. For five weeks, a white pair of Predators, each with a different zone highlighted, was sent to some of the world's top footballers—Xavi (Barcelona), Robin Van Persie (Manchester United), Kaká (then Real Madrid, now AC Milan), Nani (Manchester United), Samir Nasri (Manchester City), and Angel Di María (Real Madrid).

Videos of the players testing the boots were released, while the players themselves posted photos on various social media networks—Facebook, Instagram, and Twitter. A digital hub was created on the adidas website that contained short clips of the footballers—wearing the boots—taking on challenges sent in by fans, comments posted by viewers, and the players' insights and feedback. This was coupled with the science behind engineering each of the zones, illustrated using videos and slow-motion graphics. Ultimately, the campaign proved to be a clean sweep for adidas.

And with the tempo in place, the campaign was spearheaded by SMG in UAE and the broader Middle East, geared toward young Arab football players. The agency was successful in its communication and strategizing—presenting a consistent brand image, using an effective multimedia approach, and appealing to the local football fans.

Coinciding with the UEFA Championship, SMG's version of the campaign was called "Every Touch Counts"—designed to highlight the five "Lethal Zones" of the boot. Although the global footballers used in the original ads were well known across the Middle East, an integral part of the ongoing campaign was to provide role models from the region itself.

For the UAE Arabian Gulf League's 2013–2014 season, new ambassadors were chosen, all of whom endorse the Predator boot: Al Jazira's midfielder Khamis Esmail, Al Wahda's striker Sebastian Tagliabue, and Al Ahil Club's striker Edinaldo Batista Libânio, popularly known as Grafite—all key players in the league and the official faces of adidas on the pitches across the region.

For the Middle East, the approach was unique. Khamis Esmail was there to endorse the latest version of adidas' Nitrocharge boot. Sebastian Tagliabue champions the company's lightest and fastest boot, the F50 Adizero, and Edinaldo Batista Libânio took on the Predator Lethal Zones.

Currently, adidas has more than 150 stores across the Middle East—85 brand stores and 65 concept stores. Around 14 brand stores and 2 Originals Concept Stores have been established across UAE. The flagship brand store in the Abu Dhabi Mall doubled in size in August 2013 from 2080 to 4042 square feet.

To see the results of this campaign, run to the "It's a Wrap" feature at the end of the chapter.

Sources: www.adidas.com/middle-east/; mena.starcomww.com/press-release/adidas-wins-big-at-middle-east-sports-industry-awards-2013; cargocollective.com/arnaubosch/Adidas-Football-Predator-2012 (all accessed 24/10/2013).

In the UAE in particular, one tried and tested method of engaging the youth market is by sponsoring films on TV and sports coverage. This approach targets a youth market beyond that of sports participants. SMG combined music, social media, and dance to create an emotional connection between the adidas brand and the target market. This part of the campaign, entitled "All In," was primarily designed to increase footfall in adidas stores across the Middle East. The campaign also sought to connect the brand's clothing and footwear with street fashion.

In this chapter, we will discuss media owned and controlled by the brand, as well as a number of interactive media forms, including those set up by the organization, such as personal sales and consumer service, but also digital platforms, such as the Internet, e-mail, and blogs. The newest entry into the digital landscape is social media, which connects people in a network of personal, online, word-of-mouth communication. It's a dynamic and fast-changing media environment that challenges communication planners to not only keep up but also get ahead of the technological changes that are driving innovation and making this such a creative area of marketing communication.

Beyond Paid Media

In this chapter, we'll review a wide variety of media forms and organize them into three categories: owned, interactive, and earned. Owned media are created and controlled by the organization. The interactive owned media include two forms—media programs designed by the organization to unlock two-way communication between the brand and consumers and social media, such as Facebook and Twitter.

The third category is called earned media. Historically, this has been a public relations concept and refers to mentions in the news media. However, in this day of digital media, the concept of earned mentions has been expanded to include comments in social media. So we'll talk about social media both as a type of interactive owned corporate medium in the sense that a company can have a Facebook page that creates a profile for a brand, similar to any user, and as an interactive earned medium where users engage in conversations that can be monitored for brand mentions.

Owned Media: We Own It; We Control It

Principle
Effective brand communication marshals a constellation of contact points to strategically present a consistent brand image.

Owned brand messages are delivered from a company to consumers through channels controlled by the company. These media represent a constellation of contact points that can be strategically designed to present a consistent brand image.

The biggest advantage of owned media is control, but there are other reasons to consider using this category of media. They are versatile and can be created for diverse audiences, contact points, and time frames. They can be used to address various objectives, but one of the most important is loyalty and the development of consumer–brand relationships. A limitation of owned media is that, although you may own the publication or website, you have little or no control over consumer exposure to it. In other words, supplemental efforts are needed to drive traffic and get your audience to come to you. For that reason, some online programs, such as websites, are supported with offline traditional advertising.

The sections that follow are not inclusive; rather, we compiled a variety of different ideas to inspire you to think broadly about brand communication opportunities.

Corporate Presence Media

By corporate media, we are talking about things you might not think of as media, such as the design of a building or a delivery truck. But in IMC planning, we recognize that these are important contact points that create the visual face of an organization or brand. How they present the brand image sends an important message.

Environmental Design What a building looks like—both inside and outside—may reflect the image of the company and make a brand statement. The point is that design, decor, and physical appearance send messages about the style and personality of the brand. Patagonia, for example, uses visual merchandising in its stores—rough wood surfaces, textiles, large outdoor posters, and lighting—to tell its story about its passion for the environment and ecologically sensitive outdoor sports. Other buildings merit recognition for their *visual branding*. The highly recognized Chrysler building in New York City, for example, is a classic skyscraper with its dramatic art-deco crown and spire. It often appears as a logo or graphic image that represents New York.

It's not only the exteriors that speak to corporate image; the interiors of buildings and public spaces also convey messages. For example, graphic designer Amy Niswonger has been following the redesign of McDonald's interiors and explains how that relates to brand image. "McDonald's is updating its image from kiddy classic to a destination for all ages. In the past few years, the company has achieved success both in updating its look and feel and expanding its target market without losing core customers." She asks how changing such a well-known look—the Golden Arches with the red-and-yellow color scheme and plastic interiors—can be accepted by customers. Her answer is that McDonald's immense brand equity makes it possible to update its interior design without taking a hit to its brand persona and hence to its market share.

Signage A form of out-of-home media, retail and corporate signs are owned rather than paid. **On-premise signs** that identify stores have been with us throughout recorded history and are today the most ubiquitous form of brand communication. In this complex environment, an effective sign may be relatively simple, like McDonald's giant "M," or more complex, like those found on the strip in Las Vegas with their large illuminated and animated visual extravaganzas. Some on-premise signs also act like billboards. American Eagle Outfitters, for example, has used a 15,000-square-foot sign above its Broadway store in New York City. The sign was designed with 12 panels to operate 18 hours a day.

On the opposite end of the **signage** continuum are inexpensive forms, such as yard signs, bumper stickers, and buttons—the media of political campaigns. Yard signs are temporary and are used mainly by real estate agents and politicians. Although they may be tacky, yard signs are public statements and perform an important function as either a reminder or a motivation for action.

SHOWCASE

Designer Amy Niswonger analyzes McDonald's new environmental design and concludes that "the customer inherently understand that the Big Mac is still the Big Mac; it's just served now in a hipper, cooler location."

Amy Niswonger is a graphic designer and professor who owns her own design studio. A graphic design and marketing graduate of Miami University. Oxford, Ohio, she was named Most Promising Minority Student by the American Advertising Federation (AAF). She was nominated by Connie Frazier, AAF chief operating officer.

Out-of-home advertising, such as this on-premise sign from Las Vegas, is a highly creative medium as well as the second-fastest-growing medium after the Internet. Every building, every store, needs a sign.

Appearance You probably wouldn't list a uniform or a delivery truck as a communication media, but what comes to your mind when you think of a brown truck? "What can brown do for you?"—UPS used that slogan to illustrate the power of a distinctive truck design that represents what UPS does best: deliver packages. So trucks can deliver messages as well as packages and products. That's why many companies with their own fleet of trucks use unique designs and insist that drivers keep the trucks clean and run them through car washes frequently.

The appearance, attitude, and conduct of staff, who in many businesses are the front line of customer contact, send other types of message—both positive and negative. That's why most companies have *training programs* for new employees. Training is reinforced by ongoing *employee relations* programs, usually run by either public relations or human resources. These programs keep staff informed and, to the degree they are critical to the success of promotional campaigns, on strategy in both their formal and their informal stakeholder communication.

Branded Media

To take advantage of the value-added power of branding, companies find endless opportunities in media tools that bear the brand's name. The use of the media of entertainment, for example, to engage consumers with brands is referred to as **branded entertainment**. The goal is to associate the brand with a fun, entertaining experience that creates positive feelings for the brand.

Principle
Branded entertainment associates the brand with a fun experience that creates positive feelings for the brand.

Film, Fun, and Games Promotional video networks run sponsored programs and commercials, such as the channels you see in grocery stores, doctor's offices, and truck stops, that distribute commercials by video or satellites to in-store televisions. McDonald's is creating its own M Channel with exclusive news, informational, and entertainment content that will play in McDonald's stores nationwide. The news and sportscasts can be localized with local newscasters taping the programs.[1]

Marketers, such as General Electric and Pepsi, are experimenting with short video clips—both live action and animated—that can be watched free on the video-on-demand service available to Time Warner cable customers. The shorts can also be seen on the General Electric website (www.ge.com/imaginationtheater) as well as on sites like Google Video and YouTube. Toyota has developed a YouTube-based "car configurator" with tutorial videos for new Prius owners. The site also lets prospective owners use a miles-per-gallon calculator and adjust the color of the car.

In some cases, companies may produce films for the Internet where the brand is integrated into the story line, such as an award-winning and groundbreaking series of eight mini-films for BMW titled "The Hire." The various films, all of which were by different well-known directors (Guy Ritchie, John Woo, Ang Lee, and Tony Scott, among others), starred Clive Owen as the driver and the BMW as the hero in a high-action escapades. Similar to television programs with recurring episodes in a developing story, these **webisodes** created a new form of Web advertising.

Branded games, in addition to product placement and ads, can showcase a brand name—an actual video game that is designed around a brand experience. The game is created and owned by the company. Nissan created the GT Academy, where drivers can compete in digital driving games in real Nissan sports cars. A multiplatform experience, the winners get to participate in a reality show format (think *Hunger Games*) with drivers competing live against each other in driving performance.[2]

Principle
Naming rights deliver high visibility for a brand and an association with an important gathering point, such as sports arenas and public buildings.

In addition to films, other media carrying the brand name of a sponsor include events such as lecture series and exhibits. Samsonite has produced high-quality photographic desk diaries. Nestlé created a "Milkybar Kid to the Rescue" mass-market paperback for the children's market.

Naming Rights Another high-visibility area of branded media is **naming rights** for events and buildings. The objective is brand visibility; the benefit to the organization or municipality is a hefty payment.

Naming rights dominate football bowl games (e.g., the Discover Orange Bowl and the Chick-Fil-A Bowl) and sports arenas, such as Citi Field in New York, where the Mets play, and

CenturyLink Field (formerly Qwest Field) in Seattle, which hosts both the Seattle Seahawks of the National Football League and the Seattle Sounders soccer team. Heinz Field in Pittsburgh and Coors Field in Denver connect their towns with local companies, which makes a logical fit for the brand. Other names were not so well matched and encountered backlash, as when Candlestick Park in San Francisco was renamed 3Com Park, much to the dismay of local fans, and then became Monster Park after Monster Cable bought the 3Com rights.

Universities name buildings, as well as classrooms, conference rooms, and academic programs, after alumni and local leaders who give sizable donations. One of the most ironic examples comes from Harvard Law School, where the bathrooms in its Wasserstein Hall were named after benefactors. The Falik Men's Room was the gift of a bequest by William Falik, a lawyer and real estate developer with a sense of humor.[3]

The Media of Retail

The retail store is a world of promotion. Packages proclaim brand identities and merchandising materials attract attention and deliver motivating sales messages.

Principle

A package is the last ad a customer sees before making a purchase decision.

Packaging A package is both a container and a communication vehicle. In particular, it is the last ad a customer sees before making the decision to buy a brand, as the Pepperidge Farm shelf photo illustrates.

In an attempt to win over undecided consumers at the point of purchase, many manufacturers create innovative, eye-catching packages. Even if you can't afford a big advertising budget, you've got a chance to grab shopper attention if your product has a compelling image on the shelf Although the industry has never developed a standard for measuring impressions from a shelf, advertisers are aware of the **billboarding** effect of a massed set of packages, a practice that Pepperidge Farm uses to good effect. Once on the shelf at home or in the office, the package is a constant brand reminder.

Packages can also deliver customer benefits. For example, recipes for Quaker Oats's famous Oatmeal Cookies, Nestlé's Tollhouse Cookies, Chex Party Mix, and Campbell's Green Bean Bake all started as promotional recipes on the product's packaging and turned into longtime favorites in homemakers' recipe boxes. There is even a website for these classic recipes (www.backofthebox.com) that features more than 1,500 recipes found on packages.

Sometimes, the package itself is the focus of the advertising, particularly if there is a new size or innovation, such as Coca-Cola's introduction of a new bottle made from plant materials that is more compostable than plastic.[4] Some packages, such as CD covers, can be artwork in and of themselves. The "A Matter of Principle" feature explains the principle of culturally specific design as it is used in promotional communication.

Merchandising Materials Merchandising materials are the media used in promotions for a store, product, or event. Manufacturers often provide brand-related window banners, posters, and freestanding displays. In addition to posters and banners, other media used by retailers include **shelf talkers** (signs attached to a shelf that give brand information and also can invite the consumer take away some piece of information, such as a recipe or coupon). **Point-of-sale** materials, also called **point-of-purchase** materials, call attention to brands and provide a special reason to buy. Other store-based media include end-of-aisle displays, display cartons, banners, signs, and mechanical product and sample dispensers.

In terms of store-based merchandising, think about all the different materials in a Starbucks or McDonald's that carry the brand logo and maybe even other information—tray liners, table tents, coffee cups and sleeves, napkins, and coasters. Posters, signs, or other art are usually on the walls—sometimes art may be a part of the store's environmental design, but signs may also be used to announce special promotions. Bags and sacks—grocery bags, shopping bags, and other retail bags—are important brand reminders.

Pepperidge Farm, with its distinctive brand image, dominates cookie shelves because of the billboarding power of its consistent design across all the brand's variations.

A Matter of Principle

Using Chinese Folk Arts in Promotional Designs

Qing Ma, *Shejiang University City College, Hangzhou, China*

The formation of the colors of Chinese folk arts is based on traditional Chinese philosophy, which focuses on inner experience of lifelike lingering charm and adorns serene, natural, simple, and deep artistic conception.

Many famous graphic designers in China tend to add indigenous elements, such as the elements of traditional Chinese ink painting and Confucianism, in their design works in order to give the advertisements natural and unrestrained artistic scenes.

The CD cover illustrates the theme of traditional Chinese instruments illustrated with high-quality bamboo. The design features a green bamboo shoot on the spine of the cover and bamboo drawings as a design feature with bamboo texture as background. In addition to colors, the freehand brushwork in traditional Chinese painting attracts the attention of Chinese customers.

"Red" has special meanings in the Chinese Lunar New Year. It means wealth, prosperity, and good luck when people celebrate the Spring Festival. For instance, the television animation advertisement "The Dance of Dragon" made by the Coca-Cola company uses the traditional Chinese figurine of an auspicious boy who is called "A Fu"; the figurine is usually made of clay and decorated with red color.

The red color and the traditional Chinese elements of fortune altogether set the tone for a happy new year in a Chinese northeastern village. The happy atmosphere made by the red color and lovely images caters to the taste and psychology of Chinese customers.

Another classic example of successful advertising by using appropriate designs is an advertisement for Hanfang, a Chinese health care company. A special blue background, which is usually used for making traditional Chinese blue printed cloth, is decorated with the patterns of some Chinese medicine and natural brushwork.

Photo: Courtesy of Qing Ma

The CD cover with its bamboo theme was screen printed with an illustration that brings a feeling of classical delicacy. The CD cover won an award at the Taiwan Straits bamboo arts competition for universities.

Principle
The objective of point-of-sale materials is to increase brand visibility, but they also bring together all the elements of a sale, including the consumer, the product, and often price deals.

Even the stuffers that you find when you open up a pizza box delivered to your home are part of the merchandising program.

Department stores will sometimes have theme or seasonal promotions where they bring together related products and create settings in which to display them, such as beach parties or graduation celebrations. All these props and supporting signage become theme-related media for the merchandising event.

The objective may be to increase brand visibility, but merchandising programs are effective because they bring together all the elements of a sale—the consumer, the product, and money, often a price deal—at the same time. That's particularly important to motivate impulse buys.

The Owned Media of Public Relations and Promotions

We mentioned promotions related to retail marketing, but there are a variety of promotional media that are used both in public relations and sales promotion programs. Here are a few of them.

Videos and Publications DVDs, flash drives, podcasts, and online video can be used to distribute corporate videos and films for public relations and promotional programs. Costing $1,000 to $2,000 per minute to make, videos are not inexpensive. However, they are an ideal tool for distributing in-depth information about a company or program. Some companies have taken stock of the YouTube phenomenon and are using online video to reduce costs and draw attention to messages on corporate websites. Monsanto, for example, posted video clips of testimonials from farmers using Monsanto products on its site, hoping to attract customers, employees, and policymakers.

Companies produce huge amounts of publications and literature of various kinds. Corporate publications include books, magazines, newsletters, special reports, annual reports, catalogs, and collateral materials, such as brochures. They may be sent to key stakeholders as part of a corporate communication program. High-quality brochures are often produced for new car lines or high-end real estate developments.

Consider books, for example. They can be used as promotional tools and corporate reputation builders. A number of advertising and marketing communication agencies have published corporate history books, for example, that focus on the thoughts of their founders and the philosophies of their agencies: Crispin Porter + Bogusky and *Hoopla*, Leo Burnett's *Leo*, DDB's *Bill Bernbach Said*, and Ogilvy and Mather's *Ogilvy on Advertising*, among others.

But it's not just marcom agencies that produce books. A bank in Brazil presented 120 reasons why people should be customers of Banco Bradesco—one reason per page. The book is at the center of the bank's customer acquisition program.[5] Traditionally, books have been printed, but with the advent of simplified electronic publication, e-books are now being produced for tablets as well as Nook and Kindle readers.

Publicity Media Publicity, which will be discussed in more detail in Chapter 15, is designed to encourage news media coverage. Press releases and video news releases (VNRs) are prepared news stories and features sent to print and television news media. Public relations offices assemble **press kits** that contain such pieces as news releases, fact sheets, histories, maps, photos, artwork, and position papers, among other collateral materials designed for different audiences and prepared, perhaps, in different languages. We think of press kits as being printed, but the pieces may also be on DVDs, flash drives, or online. Note that publicity is used to support all types of brand communication programs anywhere mass-media coverage is useful to get information to the public.

From Hoopla by Crispin Porter + Bogusky, Written by Warren Berger, Published by powerHouse Books

Brand Reminders and Rewards A **premium** is a tangible reward for a particular act, usually purchasing or repurchasing a product. Common premiums that reward behaviors are the matchbooks and mints given away in restaurants. Events use T-shirts as well as an endless list of freebies, such as cups, caps, stuffed animals, and other souvenirs, most of which carry the brand's logo. These are rewards, but they are also brand reminders.

Premiums and prizes also recognize relationships. If you work on a Habitat for Humanity work site, for example, you may receive a T-shirt or a cap or maybe an energy bar. Premiums are also used as incentives to add value to a product or event. Examples of value-added premiums are the toys in Cracker Jacks or an iPod given for taking a real estate tour.

Similar to premiums, corporate communication and public relations programs, as well as high-end sales programs, may use gifts. Industry data, for example, may be given to a B2B prospect on a logo-decorated flash drive. Executive gifts, which are usually high-end expensive items, are used as special recognition for good B2B customers and sales contest winners. Sales programs often use competitions to increase excitement among the sales staff. The prizes can include big-ticket rewards, such as trips to resorts, beaches, and islands.

Place-BasedMedia We described out-of-home or place-based advertising in Chapter 12. Another type is street-based media, which create unexpected personal encounters with a brand, such as painted messages on streets.

In our discussion of *guerilla marketing* in Chapter 11, we mentioned that people on the street convey brand messages. People can be employed in places with a lot of foot traffic to hand out sales materials, such as coupons or samples. **Sign spinners**, or "human directionals,"

This painted stairway at the Denver Pavillions, an entertainment complex in downtown Denver, is an example of street-based guerilla marketing. It is also a captive ad because it is unavoidable for people walking up the stairs.

Photo: Courtesy of T-Mobile Limited

An example of a flash mob employed as a street marketing technique is the T-Mobile "Dance" video, which created a spectacle in London's Liverpool Station.

are hired by local businesses to stand on street corners with signs and banners that promote their stores or special marketing events. To get drivers' attention, they may appear in costumes or do little dance routines. For some, there is an art form in sign spinning, similar to break dancing, which calls for athletic prowess and dramatic moves in an involved choreography.

Another form of human media is the **flash mob**, which began as rehearsed groups of performers who show up in unexpected places and put on concerts and dances. Some of these are for fun, but some are commercial. One of the first commercial uses of this crowd-based concept was the T-Mobile "Dance," where unassuming people walking through London's Liverpool Street Station seem to spontaneously break out in a 400-personal highly choreographed dance routine. Check out the flash mob and the making of it on YouTube. More recently, T-Mobile livened up the holidays with a flash mob in Chicago. You can find it on YouTube also.

Owned but Interactive: Let's Talk

Interactive media are those forms that invite users to participate in or respond personally to the message. Some of these are similar to owned media in that the organization pretty much controls them, but the media format, such as e-mail and Twitter, allows the organization to initiate communication with consumers, customers, and other stakeholders. Engagement beyond just

Principle
With interactive media, engagement is the goal.

exposure is the goal when organizations use interactive media. Some media, such as texting, are just naturally more interactive and thus more engaging than owned media.

There are also experiments with traditional media, such as television, that make it possible for viewers to interact with television messages through a set-top box or computer-accessible television. Television, however, is not just limited to viewing programs but has become the center of the digital living room with viewers enjoying new experiences, such as games and exercise via their Wii players and other video games that now can be seen on the television screen.

Corporate Interactive Media

A useful and sometimes exciting type of owned but interactive medium is the digital display, which invites viewers to interact with data represented graphically on a screen in front of them on kiosks in public places and lobby walls. Interactive electronic **kiosks** with LCD touch-screen computers, databases of information, full graphics, maps, product photos, and online access are moving into the aisles in many stores—and malls—where they provide information about more products than the store can ever stock on its shelves. New kiosk advances add cameras, which, using facial-identity software, can estimate the user's age and gender, making it possible to do more customized responses.[6] Viewers can sometimes order merchandise directly from these kiosks.

Information that used to be provided in brochures, directories, and other publications can now be seen on **electronic walls** or **digital installations** in buildings, particularly in lobbies. Touch screens driven by extensive computer databases make these media forms interactive as users check out maps and calendars and delve into corporate history and product lines.

Direct-Response Media

Principle

Direct-response media are designed to generate a transaction without a sales person by motivating a customer to take action and place an order.

We mentioned ordering directly from a kiosk. That's actually a type of direct marketing. The first marketing communication area to recognize the value of interactivity in brand communication was **direct-response marketing** (also called **direct advertising**). The traditional media of direct response have been mail (letters, flyers, and catalogs), phone, and now online messages, all of which have some kind of response device built into the message delivery.

Most direct-response programs are designed to generate transactions. The goal is to motivate customers to take action and place an order. Advances in digital technology made it possible to personalize messages and target tightly to prospects who are known to be interested. Even some advertising in print and television carries offers and reply forms to generate a sale.

The big technological changes that made personalized communication possible was online media combined with databases of consumer information. Such advances made it possible to target prospects based on their past behavior (what they bought and what sites they visited).

Technological innovations bring all kinds of new media into direct-response brand communication. Wi-Fi connected billboards can be interactive and create one-on-one brand communication opportunities. Tablet and smart phone users can interact with companies via electronic posters and quick-response (QR) codes, say at bus stops, that offer users free Internet access to download apps, games, video ads, or coupons and may even lead to on-the-spot product sales. The Beneful dog food brand is using a 64-foot installation that, when it detects a passerby, presents a virtual dog that runs up to play a virtual game of chase or fetch. Viewers can customize the dog. The point is to demonstrate how the brand is associated with playing with a dog in real time, if not real life.[7]

Personal Contact Media

Employees and other stakeholders can deliver brand messages. When a friend, family member, or someone you respect tells you something about a brand, you are likely to believe it. That includes employees who are often asked for their advice or opinions on a product or brand. **Employee communication programs** are designed to help employees convey strategic information in these critical personal conversations. Other important avenues for personal communication in business are found in sales and customer service operations.

Personal Sales In addition to conversation with employees, word-of-mouth communication can occur in more structured selling situations. Retail sales employees, for example, use personal communication to relay information about a product and give reasons to buy it. These reasons can be personalized to match the person and his or her interests. Salespeople in stores are trained to answer product questions and help customers find things.

In B2B marketing, sales reps often work from a scripted sales message to make sure they hit on the right selling points and convey the most important strategic information. They also are provided with sales kits that contain product specifications, photos, diagrams, and other information useful in decision making by business customers. More recently, all these data are available online and may be given to the prospect on a DVD or flash drive.

Similarly to press kits, **sales kits** are packets of information prepared to support personal sales efforts. A sales rep who covers a region or several states, for example, will carry along all the information needed to make a pitch to a prospective customer. Sales kits can contain a variety of materials, but they also include such materials as selling strategies, presentation materials, information about the customer, profiles of the customer's market, and pricing charts. They can appear in print, on flash drives, or online. The Sunkist site featured in Chapter 7 is an example of how an online sales kit promotes a brand to channel members.

Similarly, media sales reps in advertising will have **media kits** that include profile information about the people who watch, listen, or read the medium, along with numbers describing audience size and geographical coverage.

Training Materials Another category of assembled information appears as **training materials** used to train B2B sales reps or other employees. Employee training materials may contain information about new projects or products or special promotions with presentation visuals, exercises, and background data. They can be in print, but most professional training sessions use PowerPoint slides, and the materials may be distributed online or on a flash drive.

Customer Service Another environment where personal communication is critical is in **customer service** or **tech support** in the technology industries. Effective communication can cement customer satisfaction or dissatisfaction. What makes customer service different from other forms of commercial media is that customers can initiate the dialogue either in person or by phone or online. If it's a positive experience, customer service can strengthen the brand relationship; if it's negative, it can lead to or increase customer dissatisfaction with the product, brand, and company. Customer service is the front line of consumer attitude change about a brand experience.

Principle
If it's a positive experience, customer service can strengthen the brand relationship; if it's negative, it can lead to or increase customer dissatisfaction.

Traditional media used to elicit customer feedback are shoppers' surveys and comment cards. **Mystery shoppers**, a proactive form of customer service, are used to personally analyze and report on the shopping experience in a store. More recently, customer service is being driven by social media and cell phones.

Customer service is a specific department that handles questions and complaints, but it also refers to a company's attitude toward customers during these interactions. How the company behaves in solving a problem and the way the interaction is handled send some of the most impactful brand messages that customers receive.

General Motors, for example, set up special call centers with technical specialists who can help owners navigate through its MyLink and Cue systems. The call centers are fitted out with replicas of the cars and their "infotainment" center consoles. The tech support folks move from their cubicles to the consoles to walk customers through their problems. Mercedes-Benz uses a system that can link a driver's cell phone directly to its customer center for live help or to send a how-to video loaded onto YouTube.[8]

If the interactive experience in either sales or customer service is positive, it can strengthen the customer's long-term relationship with the brand; if it is negative, it can weaken or even destroy a customer's brand relationship. Because customers have so many choices of brands and shopping outlets, how a company treats customers can be the major reason for choosing one over the others. Why has Southwest Airlines been so successful when competitors have faced bankruptcy? The primary reason is customer service.

Principle
Brand communication planners don't manage customer service, but they can monitor the messages being sent and identify potential problems.

Brand communication planners don't "manage" customer service in most companies, but they can monitor the messages that are being sent at this critical touch point and identify problems that might be undercutting a brand's communication strategy.

The importance of customer service as a contact point that delivers positive (or negative) brand experiences is reflected in a campaign by online retailer Zappos.com that demonstrates to customers how its customer service representatives make it easy to order or return merchandise. Called "zappets," the puppetlike characters in the ads are based on actual Zappos.com employees, whom the company calls its "customer loyalty team." You can meet zappets at this blog site: http://blogs.zappos.com/blogs/inside-zappos/2010/03/09/meet-zappets.

Interactive Promotional Media

We mentioned *events* earlier when we discussed owned media, saying that these media can be interactive environments used by both public relations and sales promotion to involve people personally in positive brand experiences. These brand-sponsored gatherings connect people who are customers, prospective customers, employees, suppliers, or other types of stakeholders.

An interesting variation on interactive advertising is "live" or performance-based commercials found in rural areas, such as India and Africa, where traveling performers present live infomercials from mobile stages to a large and growing population of international brand-focused customers.

Promotional efforts also involve campaigns for good causes. Mary Nichols, founder of Portland, Oregon-base Karmic Marketing, explained in the Inside Story feature how she helped a small nonprofit in Portland increase its donations. Farmers Ending Hunger (FEH) lines up farmers to donate crops to the Oregon Food Bank and then organizes transportation for the crops. Obviously, there's little money for advertising, so that's why Nichol's specialty—digital marketing—made sense for this tiny one-person organization. Her work for FEH received the People's Choice Award by SoMe, a national organization that honors the best social media projects and campaigns in the United States.

Speeches, Conferences, and Tours From the public relations side, speeches and informational tours are events that can generate questions and answers about an organization's programs, policies, and actions. An informational **tour** involves stakeholders in personally engaging situations. A grand opening for a new airport or concert hall, for example, may include tours with trained guides to explain the building's functions and design.

We won't spend a lot of time with news relations because that is covered in more detail in Chapter 15, but there are interactive publicity media that we should call to your attention. **News conferences**, for example, are designed as interactive experiences for the news media. Press representatives are invited to hear a spokesperson present information on some newsworthy topic or event and answer media questions. **Media tours** are a conference on wheels for media representatives that involve an itinerary and a traveling spokesperson. They may tour a location associated with a news topic, such as a new office or manufacturing plan that has achieved an award for its energy efficiency.

In addition to events, other types of promotional media engage people in interactive experiences. **Sampling**, for example, is a way for the consumer to try a product or service before buying it. The food-sampling tables at stores like Costco, for example, are staffed by people who prepare the food samples and provide information about the product and how to buy it as well as answer consumer questions.

Trade Shows, Displays, and Exhibits A **trade show** is a promotional event where B2B companies within the same industry gather to present and sell their merchandise, demonstrate their products, and take orders. Displays and exhibits along with product literature and signage are the media used in these sales and meeting events. Booths are spaces that are designed to showcase the product and allow salespersons to speak personally to attendees.

A conference sponsored by an organization may be a named brand event. Apple's new product announcements, particularly when Steve Jobs was alive and the headliner, were highly

The Inside Story

Farmers Ending Hunger

Mary Nichols, *Founder and Chief Community Builder, Karmic Marketing*

Oregon—the state that wins awards for healthy lifestyles and fit people—has some other statistics that aren't so wonderful. Oregon is the number-one state in the country for food insecurity for children, it's the third-hungriest state in the nation, and one in five Oregonians are on food stamps.

When I was asked to help with the organization's marketing, the first thing I did was create a set of realistic objectives that included building awareness, getting more donations, and building relationships with current and new donors through social media. We also wanted to increase the Facebook fan base, gather data on donors from our online donation program, create an email list database, and upgrade the website to better describe Farmers Ending Hunger (FEH) and our Adopt-an-Acre program.

Adopt-an-Acre was the Big Idea that demonstrated how far donations go in addressing the food crisis. Adopting one acre (a $250 contribution), for example, feeds pancakes to 2,300 families of four; adopting two acres ($500) feeds fresh vegetables for one day to 1,000 families.

To help FEH with its lack of visibility, we created a new easy-to-use website (*www.farmersendinghunger.com*). A CRM (customer relationship management) system was integrated into the site to capture donor information as well as set up recurring monthly donations.

We started cross promoting other like-minded organizations and supporters in all of our Facebook posts. We realized that not all target donors were on Facebook, so we also sought personal contact at the biggest farmers' markets in Portland.

At the markets, we got other vendors to donate vegetables and we created a "Build your own Mr. Potato Head" as a children's activity. While the kids were occupied, we told their parents about FEH and encouraged them to donate. We took photos of the kids who wanted to be photographed and encouraged parents to go to our Facebook page, "like" it, and download the photos.

We also attended the Nike Farmers' Market, earning approval to be on the Nike Global Giving website, where all employee donations are matched by the company.

Recognition, such as the *Portland Monthly* "Light a Fire," Willamette Week Give Guide, and the SoMe award, earned media stories. In terms of quantifiable results, we increased Facebook followers by more than 310 percent, added 1,500 email subscribers (versus none a year ago), earned 45 media feature stories, and, best of all, saw an increase of more than 48 percent in donations versus the previous year.

This organization inspires me—and I like to think I helped a little in dealing with the hunger crisis in Oregon.

anticipated by the computer and new technology markets. In addition to the event itself, there are usually myriad types of media used to publicize and support the event—name tags, programs, publicity materials, bags, and all kinds of take-home **tchotchkes** (samples, trinkets, and souvenirs), to name just a few.

Displays and exhibits may be important parts of sales promotions, events, and public relations programs. Displays include signage and booths, racks, and holders for promotional literature. A model of a new condominium complex, complete with a literature rack offering brochures about its development, is an example of a display. Exhibits tend to be larger than displays; they may have moving parts, sound, or video and usually are staffed by company representatives who deliver personal sales messages and demonstrate the product.

Owned Digital Media

We discussed how digital and online communication changed direct-response marketing, but that's true in all areas of brand communication. Let's review the evolution of this technology and how its various formats are used in corporate-owned brand communication.

E-Mail A product of an earlier time in online communication, e-mail evolved from the days when we used to log on and off our computers and check messages in bursts. Some users still operate that way, but with newer technologies, many users are always online, and messages are constantly streaming into their personal media. That has changed the function as well as the speed of online connections. In addition to speed, one of the attractive features of using e-mail for brand communication is that it is inexpensive. All it takes is a list of e-mail addresses and an Internet connection. Constant Contact is an e-mail service provider that distributes group e-mails and handles the back end of correspondence with prospective customers.

An example of a branded e-mail effort is the announcement by Amazon of the Kindle Fire, which featured a contest to win the new device. Amazon users received e-mails with the announcement, photos, product specifications, and contest information.

This interactive capability has grown exponentially when mobile phones, called **smart phones**, began to act like mini-computers. The constant stream of information means that the in-box is now a river and that we can dip into it whenever we feel like it. What's different from earlier online media is constant connection—contact with this river of information can be made through mobile phones, not just at a desk through a computer, as people fly through their daily activities.

Websites You're familiar with these terms, but let's review how the Internet is shaping brand communication. A company's **website** is a communication tool that blurs the distinction between marketing communication forms, such as advertising, direct marketing, and public relations. It is the online face the organization presents to the world. In some cases, it looks like an online corporate brochure, or it may function as an online catalog or shopping site for **e-commerce**. Amazon.com and eBay are two good examples of Internet-based e-commerce. Websites can also support promotional efforts, such as Guitar Hero's invitation to users to vote for their favorite smash hits.

Principle

A website's critical function is to support an organization's identity and reinforce the brand image and position.

E-commerce ventures are all over the Web, but they serve an important consumer need in certain situations. For example, the Web reaches people with specific interests. In fact, the Internet is the ultimate niche medium in that people turn to it to find out about any topic that interests them.

For example, pungent Australian delicacy Vegemite and its similar uniquely flavored British spread, Marmite, are hard to find by Aussies and Brits living away from home. Both depend on websites to reach homesick fans. Marmite flaunts its distinctive taste with "love it" and "hate it" pages on Facebook and Twitter with humorous copy that reads, "Eat Marmite? You'd rather rip the wings off live chickens."[9]

The website can also be an information resource with a searchable library of stories and data about products, product categories, and related topics. In all cases, however, a critical function of a website is to create and support an organization's identity and reinforce the brand image and position.

Forrester Research has developed methods for evaluating the brand-building function of websites. The company tracks effectiveness of website performance not only in terms of making a brand promise but also in terms of also delivering easy-to-find and easy-to-use information. Harley Manning, a Forrester vice president and member of this book's advisory board, reported that his company's research has found that "on average sites did a better job of making the brand promise than they did of meeting customer needs."

SHOWCASE

The website for Guitar Hero: Smash Hits used a music awards theme with visitors voting for what they consider to be the best of Guitar Hero's music.

Diego Contreras graduated from Southern Methodist University with a degree in creative advertising and business. He and his digital design work were nominated by Professors Glenn Griffin and Patty Alvey.

Manning explains how this research is used in the "A Matter of Practice" feature. (Check Forrester's website at www.forrester.com.)

Whether or not the website is effective depends on several factors—one is **stickiness**, and the other is its ease of **navigation**. A "sticky" website is one that is engaging—it encourages visitors to "stick around" instead of bouncing to another site because it is interesting and offers meaningful interactivity. The interest level is determined by what's "above the fold," to use a newspaper metaphor. Decisions about whether to leave or stay and investigate the site's content depends on what's visible without scrolling downward. Research has shown that 75 percent of the content "below the fold"—that you have to scroll down to see—goes unnoticed.[10]

To increase its stickiness—in this case, its value to its customers—Campbell's Soup redesigned its cooking site based on consumer research that indicated cooks were interested in budget meals and recipes that move beyond the casserole. Within the site, www.CampbellsKitchen.com, visitors can search for dinner options by mood or flavor, such as chocolaty or cheesy, as well as standard menu categories. The site also has a seven-day meal planning tool and a section about recipe substitutions and healthy alternatives.

A Matter of Practice

How Web Sites Build Brands (or Don't)

Harley Manning, *Vice President and Research Director, Customer Experience, Forrester Research, Inc.*

The brand is at or near the top of the priority list for companies doing business on the Web. In one Forrester survey, decision makers at 148 companies rated building the brand as the second most important goal for their business-to-consumer sites. The same group said that when considering new content and features for their sites, building the brand was as important as supporting customer goals.

So if online brand building is so important, how can companies make sure that their websites build their brands? To answer that question, we started by interviewing brand strategists at seven of the largest interactive agencies. We also talked to marketers at two companies that we respect for their brand management expertise: Johnson & Johnson and Procter & Gamble.

We found broad agreement that websites serve two equally critical functions: They are both a communication medium and a delivery channel. In other words, consumers expect sites to not just make the brand promise but also to keep that promise by providing value in the form of detailed product information that's easy to find and use.

As a result of our initial research, we created a methodology that grades how well sites make the brand promise and keep the brand promise. Our approach is a type of heuristic evaluation, sometimes referred to as an expert review. Standard heuristic evaluations date from the late 1990s and depend on three factors: detailed user descriptions, relevant user goals, and a valid set of rules (or heuristics) that identify known types of user experience flaws. We stuck with that approach to gauge how well the sites served consumers (i.e., kept the brand promise).

To measure how well sites make the brand promise, we created a variation on the standard expert review methodology. Instead of starting with user descriptions and goals, we begin by identifying the *brand attributes of the site* we intend to grade. We do this by looking at their annual reports and the public statements made by their executives. Then we collect above-the-line collateral ranging from annual reports to magazine ads to television commercials. This preparation lets us check sites for cross-channel consistency of logos, colors, typography, and layout as well as consistency with intended brand attributes, such as "reliable" or "innovative" (two of the most common).

We've been using this methodology since 2005. During that time, we've spotted a number of interesting trends. For one, websites on average do a poor job of building either major aspect of brands online: in an analysis of 278 reviews, we found that only 7 percent of sites passed both halves of our test, a percentage that is actually declining over time.

We also found that, on average, sites did a better job of making the brand promise than they did of meeting customer needs. A total of 121 sites passed our tests for making the brand promise, but only 30 did an adequate job of serving customers' goals. For example, sites from companies as diverse as Nike, Edward Jones, BP, and Coca-Cola excel at online copy and imagery but fall flat on user experience basics like providing the right content or making that content easy to read via easily legible text.

The VW "Truth & Dare" website for its Jetta TDI diesel models (http://tdi.vw.com) uses video clips and interactive tools to debunk myths about diesel, such as diesel is dirty or diesel cars don't start in the cold. In "diesel decaf," for example, testers place coffee filters on the exhaust pipes of various cars and then make coffee using them. Of course, the VW diesel filter is so clean there is no residue in the coffee—a great idea for a demonstration. The site also features a blog forum and tools to compare the VW TDI brands against competitors, such as a Savings Calculator, which compares fuel efficiency and carbon emissions.[11] (To see the "coffee filter" test, check http://green.autoblog.com/2009/05/04/vw-launches-tdi-truth-and-dare-with-coffee-filter-test.)

Some people may find a marketer's website after doing a search using a search engine; others may come across the website address in some other communication, such as an ad or brochure, often with QR codes that link cell phone users directly to the website. But another way is to encounter a link on a related site usually in the form of an ad with enough impact to entice the visitor to leave the original site and move to this new one. Internet strategists are keenly aware of the difficulty of enticing people to click-through to a different website.

Blogs Some 100 million digital essayists worldwide create Web **blogs** to talk about things that interest them. Historically, bloggers used their blogs for creative expression and opinion pieces for a generally anonymous audience. Some are interested in making money, and others are into news or politics. These personal publishing sites also contain links to related sites the bloggers consider relevant. Although these sound like one-way communication tools, most blogs also invite comments that are shared with other readers stimulating conversations, if not debates, among them. Bloggers often have higher levels of credibility than ads or corporate websites.

Corporations use blogs to engage stakeholders of all kinds. Home Depot, for example, uses its "Apron Blog" on Facebook with how-to information and design ideas as well as to showcase the local community service projects conducted by employees.[12]

Corporate blogs are a way to keep employees and other stakeholders informed, but employees may also be encouraged to have personal blogs. Microsoft has several hundred staffers blogging on personal sites. Sales staffs have found that blogs are changing the sales process by making more experiences with a product available to prospects and keeping customers current with fast-changing technological trends.

A problem with blogs is that they are sometimes criticized as "stealth advertisers." **Paid posts**, where bloggers plug a product in return for cash or freebies from the company, have caught the attention of the Federal Trade Commission. On a blog for parents, for example, a blogger promoted a $135 embroidered baby carrier. The blogger admits that the manufacturer sent the carrier free to the blogger. These endorsements are being addressed by new advertising guidelines that require bloggers to post "clear and conspicuous" disclosures that they have received compensation or freebies.[13]

Socialtizing We've been talking in this section about media owned or controlled by a company or organization and used to generate interactions with its stakeholders. This last topic, social media, refers to the use of the media of social marketing as a promotional tool. Let's call it **socialtizing**—it's a hybrid between advertising and corporate-driven social chatter.

Facebook and Twitter, which you probably know well, are sites that allow users to share personal information with friends. But a Facebook site can also be set up by a company to feature a brand with a brand profile just like any other member. Some 11 million businesses have Facebook pages.[14]

Facebook marketers hope to make friends with interested consumers who visit their sites. Walmart has a corporate site with 21 million followers, but it also encourages its 3,500 local stores to set up individual Facebook pages through its My Local Walmart program.[15]

Likewise, marketers can create a company account on Twitter, one that monitors brand references using a service that tracks news in real time as it searches, filters, and summarizes the huge flood of information appearing on Twitter every second. Marketers can also post brand-related videos on film and video-sharing sites, such as YouTube and Hulu. The Geico Gecko's self-portraits, for example, appeared on YouTube.

Principle
The reason to use social media is to get people talking about a brand.

Socialtizing provides information, but more importantly, it gets people talking about a brand and sharing their thoughts and experiences with a network of friends. The **network effect** describes the success of Facebook—"the more users a site attracts, the more others will want to use it, which creates a natural monopoly and a magnet for advertisers."[16] Services like Off-the-Wall software by Resource Interactive make it possible for companies to sell directly from their Facebook walls, which expands a social media presence into e-commerce. (See more at www.resource.com).

To successfully place a brand within a communication environment like Facebook, planners have to think strategically about the unique voice of the brand. *National Geographic*, for example, has a huge number of fans. But what should *National Geographic* sound like online? What should it say—or not say? The company's mission is "to inspire people to care about the planet," and that's what drives its social media strategy. So *National Geographic*'s message strategy is to stay authentic by focusing on discussion topics that relate to and support its mission.[17]

The point is that every brand has a personality—caring and committed, off-the-wall zany, or badass—and that needs to come through in online posts. Some brands use one person who knows exactly how to speak in the persona of the brand; others use a team of employees who know how to match dialogue to the brand personality. In all cases, these people need to "stay on brand" as they explore the give-and-take of social communication.

Photo: Courtesy of GEICO

Using time-lapse video, the Geico Gecko has a YouTube film where he supposedly takes a picture of himself every day for two years. The images show different postures, expressions, and costumes and project the wacky personality of this well-known brand character.

Grey Poupon used its elitist image to target Facebook fans with a sophistication test that lets them have their profiles checked to see whether they qualify as a taste leader to be a Grey Poupon user. The test looks at such factors as proper use of grammar on their Facebook pages, taste in art and restaurants, and books and movies selected to see if the fans qualify for membership in Grey Poupon's "Society of Good Taste."[18]

Experts recommend that a company have a plan for being present regularly on its social media sites—once or twice a day—and that the interactions be authentic and relevant both to the brand and to its followers. Posts across various social media should be unique for each outlet because the sites are used in different ways by people with different interests. Scheduling and planning posts can be managed through tools, such as Hootsuite and Tweetdeck, that help manage all the social media outlets in a coordinated way.[19]

Research on Facebook usage provides interesting insights about how best to post on the social media site. For example, weekends are better than weekdays and posts at 8 A.M. and before and after lunch are more likely to be shared.[20] Facebook itself provides ideas about how to increase engagement (comments, likes, and sharing) on its site. It suggests that although touchy-feely conversations are okay, there are stronger responses from posts on topics relevant to the brand. Facebook finds that photos and videos generate the most sharing, which is more meaningful because it taps into the friend-of-a-fan network.[21]

Marketers use these new social media tools to promote brands, engage customers, and create brand relationships—and most of these efforts are cheap compared to other forms of marketing

Principle
Organizations use social media to engage customers and create relationships as well as reach a network of people.

communication. They are not only a point of connection—a digital touch point—but they also engage a "social web," a network of people connected through the social media site. Social media sites open up a new environment of conversation-based marketing communication, creating opportunities for entirely different forms of nearly instantaneous customer engagement with a brand.

The movie *Hunger Games*, for example, was aggressively promoted through social networks, saving its Lionsgate marketing firm millions of dollars in conventional movie advertising. The art of movie promotion is increasingly moving to the Web. A Lionsgate executive predicted that movie studios will buy fewer television ads and use more online promotion. He explained, "When they see something they like, they go online to tell their friends about it."[22]

Given that social media generates individual posts, are the numbers of people reached through social media worth an organization's time? In an ideal world, Brandon Bornancin of Resource Interactive estimates that the average Facebook user has 130 friends, and if a brand has 100,000 fans on its e-commerce site, then a brand post potentially can be shared with 13 million Facebook users. That's a lot of reach for one click.[23]

Mobile Marketing

Cell phones have become the medium of choice for many marketers. Not only can they run ads on them, but they can also send messages to people in their target market. **Mobile marketing** makes the cell phone a personal point-of-sale device with a strategy designed to contact people on the run. The "A Matter of Practice" features explains why this is such an attractive medium for advertisers.

Our Mobile Future

Mobile messaging will continue to evolve. The tipping point for computer-based Internet advertising came in 2004 when broadband access in homes passed 50 percent. The same is happening with mobile. Faster speeds allow for better viewing of mobile video content, streaming movies, television, and advertising and bring mobile interactions closer to reality. But faster speeds will come at a cost. All major U.S. wireless carriers will have high-speed broadband networks by 2014, and new larger-screen mobile tablets and phones, while improving viewer experiences, will gobble up larger swaths of expensive bandwidth.

The future of mobile devices is in their role of connecting users with products, services, and media in an unprecedented way. With branded mobile websites or apps, mobile users can access product information and make transactions anywhere and anytime. Mobile users can compare product prices in stores with offerings online, which not only creates a new shopping experience for consumers but also intensifies the competition among different outlets, thus transforming the retailing business fundamentally. Mobile devices can serve as a bridge between the users and conventional advertising media. For example, mobile users can scan a QR code or key in a ** number from a magazine or billboard to access digital content right on their mobile device.

Texting, for example, is a way marketers can contact customers and customers can contact companies. A real estate agent can send a text messages to a client about a new listing as soon as it comes online, media can run instant polls, and organizations can text their members with announcements. The last example involves **group text messaging** software, which moves individualized communication into a form of mass communication.

But mobile marketing involves more than phone calls and text messages. The Mobile Marketing Association defines *mobile marketing* as the use of wireless media, primarily cellular phones and personal digital assistants, such as RIM's BlackBerry. (Personal digital assistants evolved from early handheld digital tools that were used to keep track of schedules, contact lists, and personal reminder notes.)

The explosion in brand communication possibilities came with the introduction of the iPhone. Smart phones are high-end cell phones with computing and photographic capabilities that can access the Internet and do all of the old telephone functions.

As *Ad Age* says, "It is a computer, a camera, a map, a compass, and, for a growing number, a wallet."[24] From a marketing perspective, they can be used to check reviews, comparison shop, and even buy things.

Communication planners are interested in smart phones because they can be used in highly targeted mobile marketing strategies to deliver personal ads to folks on the go. A successful example comes from Starbucks, which uses a mobile ad campaign to promote its green-tea natural

A Matter of Practice

Your Mobile Future

Michael Hanley, *Ball State University*
Hairong Li, *Michigan State University*

How "mobile" will your lifestyle be in the future? Mobile phones have become the most ubiquitous personal communication device in history and a key delivery channel for advertising and IMC. How ubiquitous? There are more than 7 billion people on Earth, and by 2013 there will be nearly as many mobile subscriptions as there are people. Half of all global Internet users access the Web through their mobile devices.

By 2015, U.S. mobile marketing, advertising, and promotions could grow to several billion dollars and rival spending for television and the Internet. This explosive growth has prompted mobile marketing experts to label mobile phones the "Fourth Screen" of marketing, after movies, television, and computers. And for good reason: The mobile device is the first wireless medium where traditional mass media—television, radio, print, Internet, and cinema—can all be read and viewed.

Are the growth estimates for mobile advertising and promotions hype or reality? Or both? To know, it's important to understand the scope of mobile users in the United States.

By mid-2012, there were more U.S. mobile subscriptions than Americans. Wireless saturation, as measured by the number of mobile subscriptions, has easily topped 100 percent (some people have more than one subscription). With the continued fragmenting of consumer media into smaller user-selected niches and the continued drop in advertising revenues by many traditional media segments, mobile devices have become an ideal platform for the delivery of personalized marketing messages.

But how will the future be different for a mobile-focused society? And how will that impact marketers as they try to target smaller more mobile micro-audiences?

The mobile phone is now the communication device that most people say they could not live without. Always on, always available, always in touch—mobile devices provide a one-stop gateway to the information and entertainment we crave As the sophistication of mobile apps, services and websites evolves, we may become better shoppers and more healthy and be able to stay more constantly in touch with our friends and family.

For advertisers and marketers, the mobile channel offers several message delivery options:

- Text messaging
- Internet
- Mobile Internet—branded mobile-only Internet sites
- MMS, messages with video, audio, and images
- Search—key words, images, and sound
- Games
- Music
- Location services, like Foursquare
- Photo- and video-sharing sites, like Pinterest and Mobli
- Video and audio streaming
- Mobile television, free and subscription
- Social networks—a growing number of Facebook and Twitter users access through mobile device

energy booster Refreshers beverages to its customers who are interested in this product. Using short messages and informative imagery, as well as a coupon, the ads link to a store locator to find the nearest location.[25]

Mobile marketers have found several important uses for smart phones with search advertising claiming 49 percent of the advertising spending. Banner ads are next with 33 percent, followed by messaging at 12 percent and video ads at 6 percent, totaling $2.6 million in 2012.[26]

A great example of what can be done with mobile advertising is Google, which won the Mobile Grand Prix award at Cannes with an ad that re-created the iconic "Hilltop" ad for Coca-Cola for the small screen. In addition to presenting "I want to buy the world a Coke," the mobile ad also lets viewers send a free Coke to friends anywhere in the world distributed via certain wired Coke vending machines. Essentially a B2B ad, Google is selling the creative capabilities of mobile advertising. To watch this fascinating ad, check it out at http //bit.ly/Lz4Rar.[27]

Another device in the mobile marketing space is the iPad, which energized the tablet market. It is a wireless tablet hybrid that has some of the capabilities of smart phones but also combines some of the features of a laptop or notebook computer as well as an e-reader (books, newspapers, and magazines), a video viewer, and a video game player.

Marketers are finding gold in **branded apps** for cell phones, which are generally free but prominently linked to a brand. For example, REI has an app for snow reports. Apps that help travelers navigate their journeys lead in usage.

Apps that showcase the brand in a fun way are particularly popular. Zippo has a free virtual lighter for iPhones that looks and acts like a real lighter. You can jerk the phone to open or close the Zippo, and a little button lets you light it with a simple flick. The point is strictly brand identification, but there is a bit of utility in using a cell phone for that Zippo moment in concerts when people hold up their lights—in this case, images of a Zippo on their iPhones. It's almost a toy, but the engagement with the brand has made the Zippo app one of the more popular ones.

Other apps offer more utility. Banks, for example, let you check balances, pay bills, make transfers, and locate branches—and with the GPS navigation capability in some smart phones, the app can even plot a route. Kraft's app iFood Assistant, which is one of the few that comes with a price tag, provides recipes, cooking instruction videos, meal shopping lists, and store locators. Most new media provide apps that carry news feeds, some with a video. Even small stores can use apps for in-store customers that let them view merchandise or bypass the cash register and pay for their products on their mobile phones.

Although cell phone advertising is sometimes seen as an invasion of privacy, that puzzles marketers because it is an opt-in channel of communication. As in other forms of advertising, the way to be less intrusive is to be more relevant and offer **opt-in** options.

Principle
Through its geotargeting capability, mobile marketing can reach willing customers in the area with product and promotional news and announcements.

But mobile marketing can do more than point to a store's location. It can also use of wireless communication (WiFi) combined with GPS locational devices to reach nearby customers with its *geotargeting* capabilities. A form of "push marketing," these opt-in devices increase engagement between brands and their fans.

If a cell phone user, for example, registers with a favorite store, then that store can contact the user when he or she is in the neighborhood. These calls can announce special deals or invite the customer in for a taste test or some other type of promotion. The phones can also be used to contact a store. Pizza Hut's and Papa John's customers, for example, can use their smart phones to place orders, and by dragging and dropping toppings onto virtual pizzas, they can create their own personal pizza. Domino's features a simulated photographic version on its website that can be customized.[28]

Mobile marketing involves more than just cell phones, it also includes laptop computers and even portable game consoles as vehicles that can deliver content and encourage direct response within a cross-media communication program. Mobile marketing delivers instant messaging, video messages and downloads, and banner ads on these mobile devices.

Earned Interactive Media: Let's Listen

By "earned," we mean media that carry mentions or stories about a brand, through either publicity, social media, personal contact, or word of mouth. The term "earned media" has been used in public relations to distinguish between paid advertising messages and unpaid brand mentions in the news media. It's only in recent years that the word "earned" has also been used to describe the way social media and word of mouth convey comments about brands.

Principle
Earned media with their collection of brand mentions and comments give a reading on brand reputation, that is, what people say about the brand.

The various media in the earned category carry conversations, complaints and criticisms, praise, and questions—all of which can and should be monitored by brand stewards. Most importantly, they all impact the **brand reputation**, which is determined by what others say about the brand. That's a critical concept in IMC, and media strategies are particularly important in determining the strength of the brand's reputation as well as a positive impression.

Earned Publicity

We mentioned publicity in the section on owned media when we discussed news releases and press kits prepared by an organization for the news media. However, publicity also is an important type of earned media. In publicity, media-relations specialists seek to persuade media editors to carry stories about an organization or brand. These experts have no control over the media but can only hope that their stories are newsworthy and interesting enough to receive coverage.

The result is a **hit** when a story or significant parts of it appear in the media. At another level, reporters may **mention** a company or brand in a story they are researching and writing. Since mentions can be either positive or negative, public relations specialists who monitor media coverage can only hope the mentions are positive. If they are negative, they may (should) prompt a strategic response by the organization.

Because hits and mentions are not determined by the brand, they are seen as having higher levels of credibility than advertising and other forms of owned media. The reason is that publicity relies on what we call an **implied third-party endorsement**—communication that is not initiated by the company. The medium and its reputation for credibility, which is based on its perceived objectivity, create a halo of respect for the message.

Principle
When news media run a story or give a positive mention to a brand, it creates a halo of respect for the message because of the perceived objectivity of the medium.

Word of Mouth

Interactivity starts with personal communication, and that's why **word of mouth** has caught the attention of brand communication planners. The point is that the closer the medium is to a dialogue or the more users can generate or manipulate the content, the more the brand communication moves away from traditional advertiser-controlled one-way advertising. In the previous section, we talked about interactive media that organizations use to initiate interaction. In this section, we'll talk about the core of interactivity—personal conversation—and why it is important in brand communication.

Principle
The more interactive a medium and the closer it is to a dialogue, the more personal and persuasive the communication experience.

A study of media use by the BIGresearch firm, which polled 15,000 consumers, found that the most influential form of communication is word of mouth. The finding was supported by other research that has found word of mouth to be the most important influence on consumer decision making—considerably more important than traditional media advertising.[29]

Rather than top down, word-of-mouth brand messages flow side to side, creating a network of shared brand experiences and impressions that interconnect within extended communication networks—both personal and professional. In other words, friends (and business colleagues) talk to friends, and each person has his or her own network of contacts through which messages can spread.

Buzz and Viral Communication Brand communication planners have developed a growing respect for media that generate **buzz**—a cycle of word-of-mouth interactions, either personal or online, within a network of friends. The idea is to get people talking about a brand because we recognize that the most important factor in consumer decision making, next to personal experience with the brand, is the opinions of others.

One research finding is that buzz is best generated by disrupting common patterns of thinking—in other words, the idea needs to be new and surprising.[30] A study found that whether the information generates buzz depends on whether it's "interesting." But in face-to-face communication, the topics are more conversational and not as focused on "interesting" ideas. The authors suggest that being interesting is more important for certain types of social media, but in personal conversation, the focus is more on top-of-mind personal experiences.[31] In other words, marketers should match the medium with the message in a word-of-mouth strategy—interesting idea for face-to-face communication and experiential for social media.

The term **viral communication** describes the way a message spreads on the Internet through interconnected networks of acquaintances. The spread of messages depends totally on consumers creating buzz through their own e-mails and social media chatter. Remember the numbers we quoted earlier from Bornancin of Resource Interactive—how one click to 1,000,000 Facebook friends who have 130 people in their network can lead to 13 million impressions? That's a great example of the power of viral communication.

A video that captured a lot of attention worldwide and went viral showed tiny advertising banners on flies

Photo: Courtesy of Eichborn AG and Jung von Matt/Neckar GmbH

Flies are the most unlikely of all media, but they were enlisted by a German publisher as a form of flying banners at the annual Frankfurt Book Fair.

that flitted around with their miniscule billboards at the annual Frankfurt Book Fair—probably the ultimate in guerilla marketing. This Big Media Idea came from the German agency Jung von Matt. Check it out at on YouTube.

B2C2C Influence Some media plans are specifically designed to reach influential or early adopters whose opinions are valued by others. These strategies focus on finding the right individuals to deliver a message—that is, the best-connected people at the hub of an extended social network who will like a brand or brand message and promote it among the people they know.

Who are these people? It takes sophisticated sociographic networking mapping to find them, but generally they are described as community or fashion leaders, well-known experts, or people you turn to for advice.[32] This word-of-mouth marketing strategy is known as **brand advocacy** or **customer referral**. The idea is not just to create buzz but also to connect with influential, high-quality contacts who will spread the brand's story.

Japanese marketing communication giant Dentsu expresses this idea in its **B2C2C** concept, which we mentioned briefly in Chapter 1. On its face, it looks like a traditional model for top-down communication, but it goes beyond that. An expansion and modification of the traditional business-to-consumer marketing concept, the Dentsu B2C2C strategy proposes that a marcom message may emanate from a business and then move to key customers and influencers who then talk about it with other consumers in the target market.

The important part of this model of word-of-mouth influence is the C2C aspect. Because of the interactive network, messages move back and forth between and among consumers. The messages may even recirculate back from consumers to key influential customers who are in touch with the business or maybe directly back to the business.

Principle

A B2C2C strategy is designed to move a message from a business to key influential customers who then talk about it with other consumers—and messages may use the same route to come back to the business.

The point is that this model identifies not only how messages circulate but also how influential people in the network make their opinions known and spread their influence. In Chapter 4, we talked about how influence moves through steps in the persuasion process. This B2C2C model illustrates the important role of a **brand advocate**—that key customer or stakeholder—who has positive things to share about a brand within a circle of friends and contacts. These are critical earned mentions, and that's why organizations track social media conversations to identify these important interactions.

Social Media Mentions

We introduced social media earlier as a platform an organization can use to insert its brands into friendship-based communication networks. However, at its core, social media is online word of mouth that allows users to express themselves, interact with friends, publish their own content on the Internet, and refer to brands and products they like. Social networks, such as Facebook and MySpace, link friends or others who share interests; LinkedIn connects business contacts.

But mostly, social media are about friends. That's why on Facebook, when you are invited to connect with someone, you are asked to "friend" them. Users, including brands and brand fans, can create posts on their own Facebook site, but they can also post them on their friends' "walls" as well as to other content sites.

Hairong Li, a Michigan State University professor and contributor to this book, explains how certain characteristics of social media—personal content, user engagement, social relationships, and group dynamics—create social engagement that helps individuals, particularly young people, develop a sense of self. Li explains that "sharing experience with others is integral to how we construct a coherent yet often fragmented sense of self in a networked society." Li explains that social media are all about relationships:

> Think about your friends in Facebook or MySpace. Some of them are people you first met in person and then continued that relationship online, and some are people with whom you are acquainted only online. Whether you've ever met them in person, some online acquaintances are close friends, some are merely random friends, and the rest are probably in between. Your relationships with these friends will affect how you respond to ads in social media. For example, a close friend of yours may post a comment about a new product she just bought and how she likes it. Wouldn't that make you think about the product after reading her comment?[33]

Digital conversations among friends create opportunities for researchers to get raw, unfiltered brand impressions from consumers. But how to monitor these conversations? The Burson-Marsteller agency monitors earned media as it tracks the mentions of Global Fortune 100 companies on social media. In a sample month, the firm's Social Media Check-Up found that there are more than 10 million mentions of these 100 companies. The companies with the most mentions were HP, Ford, Sony, AT&T Samsung, Toyota, Honda, Walmart, BP, and Verizon. The Check-Up discovered that only 70 percent of the companies respond to comments and posts. On average, more than 6,000 people were talking about each brand. On Twitter, however, 79 percent of the companies also had accounts and were attempting to engage users with retweets.[34]

Twitter or Microblogs The concept of a blog with diary and essay postings was reinvented in miniature by Twitter, which permits posts of fewer than 140 characters. These mini-posts, called **tweets**, invite users to share their daily doings and immediate thoughts with *followers* of the **microblog**. Generally, the followers are people known to the tweeter, although in the case of fans, they may approach the size and scale of a large mass audience. Actor Ashton Kutcher, for example, became the first to collect 1 million followers on Twitter, narrowly beating CNN's breaking-news feed in a widely publicized race.[35]

Twitter posts are searchable based on their **hashtags**, which operate like key words. **Tagging** by inserting a hash symbol (#) before a word in a tweet makes that word a category or topic that can be tracked. People tweeting about a brand or company will tag their post with the hash symbol plus the company name. Brand stewards can follow the tag to see the stream of related mentions.

A hashtag backfire occurred after the Republican National Convention in 2012 when the Romney campaign used the #areyoubetteroff tag to try to generate response to Romney's clarion call in his speech. Unfortunately for the campaign planners, the tweets were five times more likely to be "yes" than "no." The point is that brands can't assume that sponsored hashtags will generate the desired response.[36]

Twitter has become the medium of choice for complaints. Customers can spend many minutes on the phone waiting to talk to customer service—or get lost in the menu options; however, Twitter messages are quick and easy. CitiBank, for example has a Twitter address of @askCiti where customers can bypass the call center and get more immediate attention through the bank's social media operation. Plugged-in companies follow these tweets and are quick to respond—often with a telephone call, which beats waiting in a phone queue for a customer service person to answer.[37]

Advertising messages also can appear on Twitter as part of a user's stream of messages. A growing group of tweeters have signed up to allow advertisers to send commercial messages under their name. Sometimes the ads are testimonials embedded in a person's regular stream of tweets (e.g., where to go to find M&Ms that can be customized or custom-label bottles of wine); others turn over their stream to an ad broker that inserts messages for brands and organizations, such as the Make a Wish Foundation.

A number of start-up companies are trying to match up brands and topics with influencers who are important within a topical community. As you can imagine, this is a controversial practice, particularly if the commercial message is unacknowledged.

Reviews and Comments Movie reviews in newspapers have been around for years, but the development of social media has seen reviews pop up all over the Web. Amazon features customer-contributed reviews of its books and other products. A secondary industry has even built up around paid reviews by ordinary people for e-commerce sites. An article on this practice observed that "consumer reviews are powerful because, unlike old-style advertising and marketing, they offer the illusion of truth."[38]

Angie's List has institutionalized the concept of local reviews by compiling trusted reviews of local businesses—dentists, plumbers, landscapers, and so on. A national network of local websites, users subscribe to access the list. But the important dimension of Angie's List is that these service providers are reviewed and graded by consumers. The reviews are checked by staff and then compiled and posted on the list. Yelp is another social review and local search service. Advertisers can get preferred search position and extra listing space.

Another type of mention is the comments section that follows at the end of stories and blogs in the online news media. If it's a business-related topic, these comments are also important to monitor by brand stewards.

The Media of Sharing

Some may find it hard to believe that people talk about brands online, but they do. **Fan pages** exist for many brands where communities of people, usually loyal users, focus on or follow a favorite brand. Pepsi has some 8 million Facebook followers who contribute user-generated marketing materials, such as photos of Pepsi in interesting settings. Pepsi fans also get to see behind-the-scene clips from commercials and other videos.[39]

Fans also share negative experiences and complaints on some fan sites as well good brand experiences. There are even hate sites for some brands where critics gather to complain.

Proctor & Gamble has set up an office in Silicon Valley to develop social networking sites for its many brands. Its Pringles fan page has more than 2.8 million global fans.[40] These advertisers use video clips, quizzes, downloadable gifts like ring tones and icons, and, of course, links to their own websites. Brand personalities, such as the Geico Gecko, are particularly useful as a featured character on Facebook. Check out his page at www.facebook.com/pages/The-Geico-Gecko/167996161475.

Online Communities Fans are an example of an online **virtual community** organized around a topic, brand, or shared interest. such as the smart USA website, which is the official social networking site for "smart USA Insiders," the fans of smart cars.

Brand communities are also ways to develop loyalty and strong brand relationships in partnership with the brand. The Harley Owner's Group (HOGs) is probably the best-known brand community and one of the biggest, with more than 1 million members. In addition to local groups, the HOG community is supported with its own website, www.hog.com.

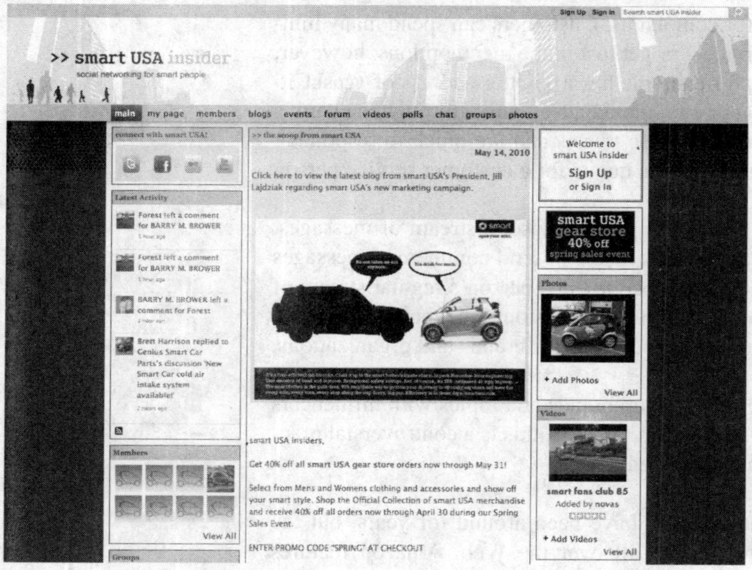

Photo: Courtesy of Daimler and smart USA

The smart USA Insider site enables owners and enthusiasts of the smart car in the United States to interact and stay connected with the smart brand and each other. The site allows members to create personal profiles and blogs and post videos and photos, participate in forum discussions, join groups, and list events. The site also gives members access to exclusive updates directly from smart USA, including occasional blog posts from the smart USA president. Check out the "smart USA insider" website at www.smartusainsider.com and develop a profile of who you think might be a candidate for membership.

Social media are international and sites based on sharing are particularly important in Asian cultures. For example, Babytree is a Chinese-language site for parents of infants with 50 percent of the Chinese Internet-using moms visiting the parent site. Rather than being an information site, Babytree functions more like a Facebook for parents where a network of moms try to help themselves and each other, which is an interesting cultural difference from the U.S-based BabyCenter.[41]

Other sites that engage communities include *Flickr*, which is an online image and video management website; *YouTube*, the giant video posting service; and *Tumblr*, which is a blog-hosting platform where millions of users post their blogs that get reposted as "tumblogs." *Instagram* is a photo-sharing social network that is known for its photo-editing capabilities. *Google+* invites viewers to share games and streaming images as well as photos, hangouts, and events. *SoundCloud* is a Facebook app that lets users share sounds—voices, musics, or other audio forms.

Pinterest, which is the third most popular social site after Facebook and Twitter,[42] allows users to pin images, videos, and other things that they find interesting to their pinboards. It's a sharing site in that images can be "repinned" and passed along to friends. But Pinterest offers more than personal online bulletin boards. An example of using Pinterest to make a point comes from England, where a video by Confused.com, a site known for price comparisons, posted a film of a woman in really tall heels who struggles to drive her car wearing ultra-high heels. It ends with contest information for viewers on how to win a pair of designer folding flat driving pumps by posting a picture of preposterous footwear.[43]

Marketers can join these online communities by buying ads or by posting images or blogs. Adidas, for example, sponsored an official soccer blog on Tumblr and was one of the first to advertise on the site.

Social games are the most popular type of shared-interest app on Facebook, which inspired Google+ to jump into this market. Facebook players spend, on average, about 45 minutes with a game. The Facebook-based "Farmville," created by online game marketer Zynga, was one of the first truly social games with a dedicated community of players who spend money on game currency they can use to buy virtual products. They also engage in business as they buy and sell things. Brands can enter into the game in various ways, but usually they participate by buying a location from which they, too, can do business.

"Farmville" was followed by "Words with Friends," another Zynga entry in the casual-game category but one that is a hit on mobile phones. Some of these online video games charge for a download, but many bring in revenue from selling ads and sponsorships or selling products within the game. The next change will see "cloud" games that live on the Internet and are streamed to computers or handheld devices.

Social media relationships offer opportunities for brand messages, particularly as people serve as viral marketing agents. Professor Li points out that "you may have already seen some movie trailers and album posters on the pages of your friends. These trailers and posters may actually represent **user-generated ads**, that is, content of commercial nature that is created or posted on the pages of users in social media that promotes a product, service, or cause." That was true for Psy, the South Korean musician and dancer who posted his "gangnam style" video to YouTube, where it was announced in 2013 that he became the first YouTube user to generate 1 billion views.

Crowdsourcing We mentioned **crowdsourcing** in Chapter 6 as a tool used by researchers for extended focus groups. That's also how the online encyclopedia Wikipedia was developed by mobilizing a digital crowd to provide collective intelligence. In marketing, crowdsourcing can be used by shoppers to discover and select products as well as generate ideas for new products.

Slim Jim was an early user of crowdsourcing to engage its fans, who were invited to come up with a new name for the brand's community manger—resulting in "The Sultan of Snap." Fans are asked to decide what online projects the Sultan will take on as well as give feedback on videos and proposed and existing products.

Fab.com is a pioneer in crowdsourced online retailing that promotes flash sales of whimsical, limited-edition items. The sites' users have suggested and promoted such things as candy-colored typewriters, funny T-shirts, knitted hats for beards, and wild socks—bumblebee striped, neon orange, and polka dots of all colors. Its fans even posted weird sock images on Pinterest and tagged them on Tumbler blogs.[44]

The site started by inviting design aficionados and influencers—found on design-related Facebook sites—to sign up. The strategy was to build an e-commerce design site through word of mouth. It tracked the ripple effect of sharing and discovered that each person who joined typically invited three friends to join as well. The site managers are devoted to metrics and continually chart customer sharing and orders.

Earned and Interactive Media Considerations

The opportunities brought to brand communication by word of mouth and social media are exciting; however, there are some things to think about in deploying media strategies in these new areas, such as dealing with negative communication and fake messages as well as estimating the true price of digital media messages.

Dealing with Negatives and Fakes An unhappy customer is more than just one person's bad experience, particularly in retailing, because of the power of word of mouth. People share these experiences, and those conversations get passed on. Research has found that although 6 percent of unhappy shoppers will contact the store with their complaints, 31 percent will tell other people about the unhappy experience. Furthermore, half of the people in the study reported that they have avoided a store because of someone else's negative experience. The study concluded that if 100 people have a bad experience, a retailer stands to lose between 32 and 36 current or potential customers.[45]

It's important for marketers to intervene in some way to turn the negative impression into a positive one. Tom Duncan, formerly a brand manager at a processed-meat company, described his company's policy of sending a letter from the president to anyone with a complaint. Most people were so impressed that the company cared at the executive level that they said they would return as brand customers.[46] This was before the days of social media, but it does illustrate the importance of proactive strategies to deal with customer dissatisfaction.

Another problem is fake sites that can damage brand reputation. The Internet in most Western countries is a wide-open system with little policing. That means that fake Facebook pages gather likes, fake Tweets gather followers, and false reviews bedevil consumer websites. Phony likes and paid reviews damage trust even if some brand supporter is behind the effort to puff up the brand's positive mentions, and they also undermine the credibility of the site, whether Facebook or Craigslist.[47]

Cheap but Not Free We used a chart in Chapter 11 that showed the relative percent of brand communication media budgets dedicated to the Internet. If you remember, it was a tiny part of the pie chart. The reason is that the charges for the use of digital media, particularly in the owned, interactive, and earned categories, are relatively low compared to media budget busters like television. At the same time, they don't have the reach that mass media like television have.

But that doesn't mean they are free. Most of the digital media demand resources, such as staffing, hardware and software systems, maintenance and operational support, and, perhaps, fees. In all cases, Internet marketers must budget for the brand monitoring systems that cull mentions from the Internet. These listening systems also need metrics to track volume and determine the level of the impact.

A word of caution: Social media open up opportunities for those valuable referrals where one friend talks to another about a brand. It's hard to know, however, how much that happens. IBM, for example, tried to track these referrals from Facebook, Twitter, and YouTube on 2012's Black Friday (the day after Thanksgiving) and found that, even though online sales increased 21 percent, just 0.34 percent came from referrals on social media. It may just be the difficulty of tracking referrals, but there's also reason to wonder about the value of buzz online.[48]

Multiplatform Brand Communication

We've been talking about a mix of media that we've categorized first as owned and then as earned. You probably noticed that platforms, such as public relations and promotions but particularly interactive, were found in both of those big categories. The reason is that media forms are constantly changing shape and moving across what used to be commonly understood categories. Television was television, print was print, and digital was digital. It wasn't that long ago that we would plan a television campaign or an out-of-home campaign with a message strategy dominated by the strengths of a primary medium. But no longer. Owned and earned just aren't nice and neat like media categories were in the simpler eras of media planning. It's a messy business.

Now we talk about how various media function and how these functions are interrelated and can be used to extend each other's reach and impact. We use the word **platforms**—to talk about big functions, such as public relations, promotions, direct marketing—and big packages of media, such as print, broadcast, social media, viral media, search media, and mobile media. They are all platforms. **Multiplatform** media planning is complicated because sometimes the same types of media—paid, owned, and earned—are used in these different platforms.

One of the biggest differences in 21st-century media is that media planning now operates not only across a variety of media but also across a multitude of platforms and marcom areas. The multiplatform use of blogs, linked social networks, and online communities (sports and celebrity fans and brand communities), as well as traditional media to engage customers and other stakeholders, is designed to engage them personally and build brand relationships.

So let's end this chapter by talking about this bigger picture of media, particularly viral media and social media programs that are examples of more comprehensive approaches to paid, owned, and earned media planning. We'll put these in perspective with a closing note about multiplatform marketing.

Viral Marketing

Viral marketing combines the marketing perspective with social media to create brand-focused viral communication strategies and campaigns. Designed to deliver a groundswell of opinion, buzz, or marketplace demand for a product, **viral marketing** initiates online communication to circulate a brand message among and between family, friends, and other contacts. It's word-of-mouth advertising on steroids.

Depending on public interest in the topic, this practice can distribute a message to an ever-widening network, and messages can flash across the Internet like wildfire. You may remember "The Diet Coke/Mentos Experiment" that resulted in a geyser of e-mails that exploded again and again around the Internet? That viral message was watched by millions, and Mentos's sales rose 15 percent. Check out the YouTube version of this story.

Viral video technology has made it possible for interesting videos from a variety of sources (ads, films, and YouTube) to be sent from one friend to another in a vast network of personal connections. Rhett & Link is a team of YouTubers who created a microsite, www.ilovelocalcommercials.com, to promote themselves as ad creators. Check out the site to see their self-promotion as well as some of their creations, all of which have been distributed as viral videos.

One of the first viral hits was Burger King's "Subservient Chicken," which helped launch the BK Broiler Chicken Sandwich. The silly costumed chicken would respond to commands to do things like tap dance or do exercises. It attracted millions of viewers who then shared the site with millions of their friends. Praised as possibly the most popular marketing website of its time, the site by Crispin Porter + Bogusky quickly registered half a billion hits in the first couple of weeks as well as a big increase in sales of BK's chicken sandwiches. The strategy was to liven up BK's advertising, which was seen as boring, and give BK a more edgy and fun image. See the site and the story behind its complicated execution at www.barbariangroup.com/portfolio/burger_king_subservient_chicken or www.cpbgroup.com/awards/subservientchicken.html.

Photo: Amy Graves/WireImage for BWR Public Relations/Getty Images

With the line "Get chicken just the way you like it," Burger King's agency, Crispin Porter + Bogusky, launched the "Subservient Chicken" interactive video website for Burger King. Play with the "Subservient Chicken" and see if you think it is captivating. Why would it have been so popular at the time it was introduced?

More recently, a character named Uncle Drew brought Pepsi Mix raves for its YouTube video that shows National Basketball Association star Kyrie Irving disguised as a sweatshirt-wearing, potbellied elderly man named "Uncle Drew," who is watching his nephew play a pickup basketball game. To replace an injured player, Uncle Drew joins in and stuns watchers with his crossover dribbles, over-the-shoulder dunks, and three-pointers. The video also shows the behind-the-scenes story about how Irving was transformed into the old guy. Check it out on YouTube or on Twitter.

But viral communication has a dark side, too. A worry for planners is that viral messages can also spread negative stories or even be used to organize a boycott against a brand. As Simon Clift, Unilever's chief marketing officer, explains, "No matter how big your advertising spending, small groups of consumers on a tiny budget might hijack the conversation."[49] Negative word of mouth moves like a flash flood through the Internet. It probably moves even faster than the fun stuff and can do immense damage to a brand's reputation.

In an ironic turn, the legendary Alex Bogusky, who retired from his former agency, Crispin Porter + Bogusky, became a supporter of the Center for Science in the Public Interest's campaign against sugary soft drinks. He created a parody four-minute animated film featuring a white polar bear family that looks a lot like the Coca-Cola bears. Shown guzzling soda and suffering the ill effects of too much sugar, the bears eventually dump their sodas. Designed as a viral video, the film drives viewers to a website, www.therealbears.org, where they get "the

Unhappy Truth about Soda." Viewers are invited to share the video: "Facebook it. Tweet it. Pin it. Google+ it. Email the link to your friends and relatives. . . . Sharing is the only means we have to make sure the unhappy truth about soda gets out to the world."[50]

Social Media Marketing

Principle
Conversation-based social media through such sites as Facebook and Twitter is word-of-mouth advertising on steroids.

Similar to viral marketing, **social media marketing** mixes different kinds of media together in a strategy to drive consumer interaction and build widespread brand visibility and awareness. Brands can sometimes instigate the viral process, but there's no guarantee the word will spread, and the brand can certainly not control it.

Named by *Fortune* magazine as a one of its Top 10 Social Media Stars, Starbucks, for example, makes creative use of its Facebook page, where you will find nearly 30 million fans talking about the company online and posting favorite photos of their lives with Starbucks. In addition to posts that mention the company, you'll also find deals and contests as well as discussions of Starbucks's community service activities. Users can manage their Starbucks account and send gifts to friends. But what really makes the site different is its willingness to display complaints from unhappy customers and create a brand relationship program around their negative experiences. Check it out at www.facebook.com/Starbucks.

Principle
Marketers who use social media recognize the value in conversations and customer relationship–building communication.

The reason social networking sites are so attractive to marketers is that they engage the power of friendship-based influence. Because of these relationships, network members are more likely to respond to messages on the sites, including ads, if they are effective at becoming part of the social context. Social media also are good with local campaigns, particularly for small businesses. A limitation is that social media's posts and conversations may not convert prospects to customers as well as a more directly associated tool, such as search marketing.

Another aspect of social media and viral communication is that, for better or worse, these media mentions and viral videos can live forever. A well-liked YouTube video can be watched for years and, likewise, a negative story, such as Bogusky's "The Unhappy Truth" video parody can be found online forever.

Integration of Platforms

In the Part 4 opening essay, Larry Kelley said that people come in contact with a brand message in many different ways—"everything is multiplatform." What that means is that brand communication is more diverse and complex than ever before. Not only do brand messages move from one medium to another, but they start in one form, say print or television, and wind up as a YouTube video that you can watch on your cell phone.

The Old Spice "Man Your Man Could Smell Like" called attention to this shifting of platforms with a 30-second commercial featuring Isaiah Mustafa that moved from a television commercial on the 2010 Super Bowl to video-sharing websites where it received more than 41 million viewers and won a Grand Prix at Cannes.

Another example of a multiplatform program comes from H&R Block, the tax preparation company that reached into the online tax filing space with a campaign that used a Facebook page as well as a dedicated digital television spot, blogs, a YouTube channel, apps, and widgets. An army of 1,000 tweeters respond to the "Ask a Tax Advisor" buttons on the Block website and answer questions directly and "listen" in on topics being discussed on community forums. Realizing the growing importance of online services, the company hopes to maintain its presence with digital filers and to support its stores and encourage filers to consult with its staff of professional tax experts both online and in stores.[51]

But we haven't seen anything yet. A *New York Times* article described new media forms, such as Internet-connected glasses and wearable computers, not to mention voice-activated assistants like the iPhone's Siri or Microsoft's experiments with gesture-recognition computer programs. The idea is that computer-accessible instant information will become ubiquitous, and the computers that drive these new media forms will be able to do much more than search on command.[52]

Although these technological fantasies will open up unexplored and new opportunities for brand communication, we shouldn't fail to note that the media we have are also changing their shapes, and that, too, opens up new opportunities. In the "A Matter of Principle" feature, David Rittenhouse, a member of this book's advisory board, looks into the future to see even more changes as the shape-shifting continues with old media, such as print and broadcasting, morphing into new types of digital forms.

A Matter of Principle

Advertising at the Intersection of Digital and Physical Media

David Rittenhouse, *Worldwide Media Director, Ogilvy*

Did you happen to watch the Academy Awards on broadcast television? Or the Super Bowl? Did you notice how many commercials had a call to action that involved responding via social media channels like Twitter or Facebook?

Have you read an issue of *Vanity Fair* or *Wired* lately and thought about checking out the feature content that's available only in the tablet replica edition?

Have you saved a special offer coupon or gift card to your iPhone's passbook rather than keeping the printed or hard card?

If you have done any of these things, you have participated in a new space, one created by interconnecting media products delivered to you in the forms of both Atoms and Bits.

Many advertisers and their agencies, broadcasters, publishers, as well as a number of data service companies are all experimenting in this area to "smash together" different digital and physical media forms that give the consumer more choice and control.

Why?

For one, to create new experiences for consumers as a way of differentiating their products. But also, perhaps just as importantly, because it enables completely new customer relationship and selling functions to be placed directly in ads.

Here are some example types, the kinds of things being tested in the marketplace right now by brands with media-forward advertising approaches:

- Fashion apparel retailers can make their advertising posters "shoppable." That is, a consumer with a smart phone and the retailer's app can scan a product on a poster, choose their size and color, and order it right where they are. This reimagines omnichannel retailing, which until now assumed that customers purchased either in a store or on the Web from home or work.
- An auto manufacturer can let tablet magazine viewers "take the car for a spin" by showing the product in 360-degree panoramic view when viewed in landscape mode. The consumer can swipe to see the car from every angle. Then, turning the device to portrait mode, they are shown a configurator in which they can style the car any way they like it or even book a test drive with a local dealer.
- A quick-serve restaurant advertiser can make a 30-second television spot with a Twitter hashtag in the title card at the end, encouraging people to join a conversation about its product online. By using the hashtag in their tweets, consumers share some of the brand or commercial content with their social network. Later the brand can remarket directly on Twitter to people who have demonstrated an interest by joining the conversation.

These examples help illustrate the idea, but there are many more directions still unexplored. Digital augmentations and response paths built out from nondigital media are only beginning to see their potential.

There are some hurdles, as there always are. One big one is the proprietary standards that are rife within the smart phone and tablet space. As companies like Apple, Amazon, Google, and others continue to vertically integrate their devices and content services to work only within their ecosystems, things will get more complicated for advertisers, who may find producing for all of them burdensome.

Caveats aside, this is a very exciting space and one to watch closely. For new people coming into the advertising media field, there is still a lot to be done and plenty of opportunities for them to make their mark.

Looking Ahead

This chapter has described the important developments in owned, interactive, and earned media. These new categories and new forms of media are changing the face of brand communication. Digital media, in particular, are bringing new forms of media, as well as communication, to brand message strategies. This is the most exciting time to be a student in this field because the changes are happening at the fingertips of young people.

The next chapter will pull all of these media channels and platforms together to explain how media planning and buying are managed but also changing to meet the demands of this dynamic industry.

It's a Wrap

Unleash Deadly

2011 saw the launch of adidas' biggest marketing campaign—"All In"—that combined an intoxicating mix of film, sports entertainment, music, graffiti art, hip-hop, and social media. This gave adidas an instant global appeal.

In 2012, SMG partnered with two key Pan Arab TV channels (MBC2 and Fox Movies) to launch the "All In" campaign, and subsequently "Unleash Deadly," in UAE and the Middle East, focusing on the Arab youth.

The adidas campaign, as an integral part of reinforcing the brand across the Middle East, was meant to integrate the brand name, slogans, and products into broader entertainment and increase the market reach. The global initiative—primarily celebrity driven—was successful in achieving these objectives by building an emotional link between the consumer and the brand.

In Saudi Arabia, adidas enjoys a market share of 58 percent compared to Nike's 30 percent. The same results were seen in UAE—adidas with 24 percent compared to Nike's 11 percent. During the campaigns in 2012, the footfall in adidas stores increased beyond the projected 10 percent to 22 percent, and sales increased by 7.4 percent. This contributed to an even bigger lead over main rival Nike.

Key Points Summary

1. **What do we mean by owned media that organizations control and manage?** Owned media deliver brand messages through channels owned by the organization, such as (1) *corporate media*, which includes environmental design, signage, and appearances; (2) *branded media*, which include films and video games and using brand names on events and buildings; (3) *retail media*, such as packaging and merchandising materials; and (4) *public relations and promotional media*, which include videos and publications, publicity media, brand reminders and rewards, and place-based media.
2. **What are the interactive owned media that are also managed by organizations, and why is that interactive element important?** Certain media that are owned are also interactive in that they permit the organization to interact with customers and other stakeholders, often in personal conversations or information exchanges initiated by customers. For example, (1) *corporate media* that are interactive include digital displays on kiosks or electronic walls; (2) *direct response* is the original interactive form of marketing, and its interactions are delivered via mail, phone, or digital forms; (3) personal contact includes personal sales and customer service; (4) interactive promotional media include speeches, conferences, tours, trade shows, events, displays, and exhibits; (5) digital media, of course, are interactive but some of them allow more control by the organization, such as e-mail, websites, blogs, and social media accounts for Facebook and Twitter; and (6) *mobile marketing* uses cell phones to deliver highly targeted messages to people on the go.
3. **What are earned media, and how do organizations relate to brand discussions that are beyond their control?** Earned media are those that carry brand mentions or stories. Traditionally, earned referred to (1) *publicity* hits and mentions in news media; (2) *word-of-mouth* is another foundational area and includes buzz and viral communication as well as influential comments; (3) social media generate brand mentions on Facebook and Twitter as well as review

sites; (4) the media of sharing describes communities as well as brand fan pages and social games; and (5) viral communication is the ultimate in online social communication spread through a network of friends.

4. **How does multiplatform brand communication work, and why is it important?** Media forms are constantly changing shape and moving across what used to be commonly understood formats. Media categories don't hold, and media mixes are messy. So we talk about functions (owned and earned) and marcom areas (corporate presence, public relations, promotions, and direct marketing, to name a few) and big packages of media (social media, viral media, search media, and mobile media). They are all platforms. Media planning now operates not only across a variety of media but also across a multitude of platforms and marcom areas.

Key Terms

B2C2C, p. 420
billboarding, p. 403
blogs, p. 414
brand advocacy, p. 420
brand advocate, p. 420
branded apps, p. 418
branded entertainment, p. 402
brand reputation, p. 418
buzz, p. 419
crowdsourcing, p. 423
customer referral, p. 420
customer service, p. 409
digital installations, p. 408
direct advertising, p. 408
direct-response marketing, p. 408
e-commerce, p. 412
electronic walls, p. 408
employee communication programs, p. 408
fan pages, p. 422
flash mobs, p. 407
group text messaging, p. 416
hashtags, p. 421
hit, p. 419
implied third-party endorsement, p. 419
kiosks, p. 408
media kits, p. 409
media tours, p. 410
mention, p. 389
microblog, p. 421
mobile marketing, p. 416
multiplatform, p. 424
mystery shoppers, p. 409
naming rights, p. 402
navigation, p. 413
network effect, p. 414
news conferences, p. 410
on-premise signs, p. 401
opt-in, p. 418
paid posts, p. 414
platforms, p. 424
point-of-purchase, p. 403
point-of-sale, p. 403
premium, p. 406
press kits, p. 405
sales kits, p. 409
sampling, p. 410
shelf talkers, p. 403
signage, p. 401
sign spinners, p. 406
smart phones, p. 412
social games, p. 423
social media marketing, p. 426
socialtizing, p. 414
stickiness, p. 413
tagging, p. 421
tchotchkes, p. 411
tech support, p. 409
texting, p. 416
tour, p. 410
trade show, p. 410
training materials, p. 409
tweets, p. 421
Twitter, p. 399
user-generated ads, p. 423
viral communication, p. 419
viral marketing, p. 425
viral video, p. 425
virtual community, p. 392
webisodes, p. 402
website, p. 412
word of mouth, p. 419

Review Questions

13-4. What is meant by corporate communication? Is it an important element for every organization?

13-5. What are branded media, and why are they important?

13-6. Explain how packaging is an effective advertising tool that drives purchase decisions and brand recall.

13-7. Explain how customer experience has a great impact on brand image.

13-8. Describe the relationship between the brand communication department and the customer service department.

13-9. What is mobile marketing? Why is it important?

13-10. Explain the importance of a website in building a brand image.

Discussion Questions

13-11. Does your school have a naming rights program? Where do you see it operating on campus? Can you find out how much revenue was or is produced by this program? How does the association help or hinder the school or academic program's image?

13-12. This chapter used the Geico Gecko YouTube photos as an example of expressing a brand personality online. Find another brand that uses YouTube to create a brand personality. Critique its effectiveness.

13-13. Your small agency works for a local retailer (pick one from your community) that wants to make the most effective use of its tool kit of owned media. The retailer has very little money to use on advertising. Your agency team agrees that there might be more the firm could do to strengthen the media it controls. Brainstorm among yourselves and come up with a list of at least five ideas for making better use of these opportunities.

13-14. You are the media planner for a cosmetics company introducing a new line of makeup for teenage girls. Your research indicates that the social media might be an effective medium for creating awareness about your new product line. How do you design a brand communication strategy that will reach your target market successfully using owned and earned forms of social media? What other media would you recommend using as part of this campaign and why?

13-15. You work in a telecommunication company as an assistant manager to the head of the Digital Marketing Department. Your manager requests you to draft the content of a PowerPoint presentation—which he will be presenting for the company VP—discussing the importance of combining paid, owned, and earned media efforts to achieve successful marketing results for the company's prepaid mobile services.

Your document should include all elements of the media mix and contain the following:

a. Each media type, give examples, explain its role, benefits and challenges

b. The advantages of creating such media mix

c. Discussion of the success criteria for evaluating the media mix

Take-Home Projects

13-16. ***Portfolio Project:*** Collect online mentions for three major media outlets. Choose from such media as the *New York Times* (www.nytimes.com), the *Wall Street Journal* (http://online.wsj.com/home-page), FOX News (www.foxnews.com), ABC News (http://abcnews.go.com), the *Washington Post* (www.washingtonpost.com), *USA Today* (www.usatoday.com), MSNBC (www.msnbc.msn.com), AOL (www.aol.com), Yahoo! (www.yahoo.com), NPR (www.npr.org), and PBS (www.pbs.org). What is being said about each one? From what you find, develop a brand reputation profile for each.

13-17. ***Mini-Case Analysis:*** SMG's campaigns were deemed to be successful, and they managed to significantly increase adidas' market leadership and share.

- What made the campaigns effective in delivering their message?
- What elements contributed to a change in the perceptions surrounding the adidas brand?
- This was a high-budget campaign. How did it achieve success? What did this case teach you?

TRACE North America Case

Multicultural and Multiplatform Communication

Read the TRACE case in the Appendix before coming to class.

13-18. Develop an idea that you believe would reach the TRACE target market of Multicultural Millennials (ages 18–29) for these media types:

a. Owned media

b. Owned but interactive media

c. Earned interactive media

d. Multiplatform brand communication

CHAPTER 14

Media Planning and Negotiation

Photo: Courtesy of H:N Marketing Communications

It's a Winner

Title:
"Mottu Mars" Mustache March

Client:
Icelandic Cancer Society

Agency:
H:N Marketing Communication, Reykjavik

Awards:
Icelandic ARA (most effective campaign of the year), Icelandic AAA (most interesting television ad of the year, public interest category)

CHAPTER KEY POINTS

1. **What is a media plan, and what is the role of media research in developing media plans?**
2. **What are the four steps in media planning, and why are they important?**
3. **What are the responsibilities of media buyers?**

A Hair-Raising Story about Men's Cancer

Want to know how growing a mustache can help save lives? Read on to learn how a campaign convinced a third of Iceland's male population to grow a mustache and grabbed their attention for an important cause.

Cancer is the cause of roughly one in every four deaths in the United States, with similar numbers in most of the Western European world. In Iceland, huge strides had been made over the last 10 years educating women about the dangers of breast cancer and the importance of self-examination in between scheduled searches at the doctor's office. But when the talk turned to men and cancer, butt cheeks stiffened and mouths shut—male-related cancer was taboo. Everybody, especially males, avoided talking about cancer like the plague.

Past fund-raisers and awareness campaigns had been largely ineffective. As a result, the Icelandic Cancer Society needed and challenged our agency to come up with a knockout punch in the fight against male cancer. We took the challenge and set out from day one to create the largest and most effective awareness campaign ever created in Iceland, establishing the following campaign objectives:

1. Raise money from individuals to use in the fight against male cancer.
2. Smash the taboo and break the silence—raise awareness of male cancer closer to the level set by the social awareness and discussion acceptance of female cancer.
3. Enlighten men on the importance of self-examination and understanding what to do.
4. Move the whole nation to participation (male cancer is not only an old man thing); do one of the following: give money, raise money on our website, sport a mustache, or do self-examination/get examination if needed.

To get people involved, we decided on an approach that took male humor to a place it had never been before. Being outrageously funny was a matter of life and death.

The starting point was to marry the long-held dream of every self-respecting man to grow and sport a mustache with a fully integrated (from media standpoint) advertising campaign. We aimed to create a campaign that literally broke every rule in the book. We would get people talking, sharing, touching their body, laughing, poking, fondling their balls, viewing, searching, raising money, giving money, and growing mustaches all for the fight against cancer. The goal of the project was to make men comfortable enough with their own bodies that they would perform self-examinations to detect male-related cancer and seek medical assistance if needed. To reach the goal, the campaign aimed to do the following:

- Encourage men to sport a mustache in March, giving visual support for the fight against cancer and starting conversations
- Set up a website where you could show your mustache and raise money through donors/sponsors
- Create hilarious ads that would raise awareness, raise conversation, be shared online, and support mustache wearers relying heavily on television ads with light print
- Follow up with strong public relations tactics, including interviews with cancer survivors, getting celebrity television and radio hosts to be screened for cancer at their doctor's office, working with anchormen on television sport shows to grow a mustache during March, and reporting on who was leading the online fund-raiser
- Start the social media discussion by arming interested people with information and outrageously funny material to share online, stimulating more conversations where people shared personal and sometime outrageous things

March became Mustache March with ads and public relations tactics generating online and face-to-face conversations. On Facebook, women urged other women to kiss only men with mustaches. People posted their mustache story on YouTube. Everybody talked about organs they usually never talked about, or, for that matter, admitted that they touched.

It was fun; it was sexy; it was—to be blunt—ballsy. Did it work to achieve the campaign goals? Go to the "It's a Wrap" feature at the end of the chapter to see.

Note: This chapter-opening story was contributed by Ingvi Logason, Principal, H:N Advertising, Reykjavik, Iceland, and a member of this book's advisory board.

As H:N knows, media planning is a problem-solving process. The problem: How can media choices help meet the marketing and advertising objectives? The ultimate goal is to engage the target audience with the right message in the best possible way at the best possible time in the most efficient way possible. In this chapter, we review how a media plan is developed—how media planners set objectives and develop media strategies. We then explore the media-buying function and explain how media buyers execute the plan.

How Are Media Plans Created?

Media planners are in the connection business. Their work connects brand messages with customers and other stakeholders, as the Iceland cancer case illustrates. They identify and activate the points of contact where brand messages touch consumers and engage their interest. The Iceland cancer campaign was multiplatform and multimedia, including traditional media, particularly print and outdoor, but also websites, Internet videos, social media and viral marketing, a theatrical play, and party hosting. Note that this media plan involved a lot more than advertising, which supports the point we made in Chapter 11 that all forms of marketing communication use media.

Engagement-making connections that resonate with the audience is the hallmark of effective marketing communication. Think about the Dove "Real Women" campaign in Chapter 5.

But how do you find those points of engagement—the media that connect with the audience in a personal way as they go about their lives and talk to their friends?

Media Engagement Research

Some people believe media decisions are the hub in the advertising wheel because media costs are often the biggest element in the marketing communication budget. And if the right media aren't in play, then it's like whistling in the dark because, no matter how great the message, nobody sees or hears it.

Media Sources Before planning can begin, media researchers gather all the information they can find on the media that might be used to engage the audience. Figure 14.1 and the list below illustrate the wide range of media information sources and the critical role media research plays in the overall advertising planning process:

- ***Client Information*** The client is a good source for various types of information media planners use in their work, such as demographic profiles of current customers (both light and heavy users), response to previous promotions, product sales and distribution patterns, and, most importantly, the budget or how much can be spent on media. Geographical differences in category and brand sales also affect how the media budget is allocated. With consumer goods and services especially, rates of consumption can differ greatly from one region to another.
- ***Market Research*** Independently gathered information about markets and product categories is another valuable tool for media planners. Mediamark Research, Inc. (MRI), Scarborough (local markets), and Mendelsohn (affluent markets) are research companies that provide this service. This information is usually organized by product category (detergents, cereals, snacks, and so on) and cross tabulated by audience groups and their consumption patterns. Accessible online for a fee, this wealth of information can be searched and compared across thousands of categories, brands, and audience groups. Although the reports may seem intimidating, they are not that difficult to use. Figure 14.2 is a page from an MRI report showing how to read MRI data. Media planners use MRI data to check which groups, based on demographics and lifestyles, are high and low in category use as well as where they live and what media they use.
- ***Competitive Advertising Expenditures*** In highly competitive product categories, such as packaged goods and consumer services, marketers track how much competing brands spend on media compared to how much they are spending on their particular brand. This is called **share of voice**. In other words, marketers want to know which, if any, competing brands have louder voices (i.e., are spending more) than they do. For example, if the total

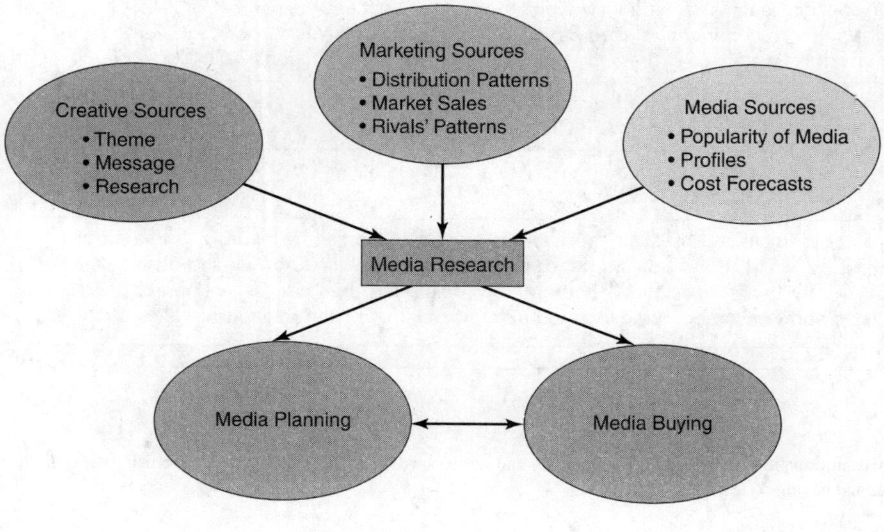

FIGURE 14.1
The Central Role of Media Research
Media planners look for data from creative, marketing, and media sources. All of this information is used in both media planning and buying.

How to Read an MRI CrossTab

The CrossTab format is a standard research display format that allows multiple variables of related data to be grouped together. Below is a screen capture of an MEMRI[2] CrossTab, complete with explanations of key numbers. Please note that all the numbers are based on the 2004 Spring MRI study, and that the projected numbers (000) are expressed in thousands.

Unit labels: these describe each one of the variables in the stacked format — e.g.: the top number in each cell is the unweighted count, and the bottom number in each cell is the index.

Base counts: in the MRI Spring 2004 study weighted to Population (000), there were 25,639 MRI respondents, and they represent 211,845,000 adults (18+) in the 48 contiguous United States

		All	A 18-34	A 35-54
All	Unwgtd	25639	6654	10787
	(000)	211845	66588	84359
	Horz %	100.00	31.43	39.82
	Vert %	100.00	100.00	100.00
	Index	100	100	100
Energy Drinks: Red Bull: All users: Drank in Last 6 Months	Unwgtd	1149	638	424
	(000)	10126	6341	3260
	Horz %	100.00	62.62	32.19
	Vert %	4.78	9.52	3.86
	Index	100	199	81

Unweighted Count: 424 MRI Respondents, Adults age 35–54, who drank Red Bull in last six months.

Projected Count (000): projected to the full population, 3,260,000 Adults 35–54, who said they drank Red Bull in last six months.

Index: people who are 18–34 are 99% more likely to drink Red Bull in the last six months, than the A 18+ population. (9.52%/4.78% = 199)

Vertical Percent: out of all people 35–54, only 3.86% said they drank Red Bull in the last six months.

Horizontal Percent: out of all people 18+ who drank Red Bull in the last six months, 32.19% were 35–54

How the Numbers are Derived

Unwgtd=424	The number of MRI respondents who meet the qualifications specified (in this case, A 35–54 who drank Red Bull in the last six months).
(000)=3,260	After applying each respondent's weight, the "(000)" value is the number of thousands of adults in the 48 contiguous United States represented by the MRI respondents who met the qualifications specified. Expressed in terms of individuals, this means 3,260,000 people.
Horz %=32.19	The percent calculated by dividing the "(000)" value in the cell by the "(000)" value in the base column=3260/10126=32.19%.
Vert %=3.86	The percent calculated by dividing the "(000)" value in the cell by the "(000)" value in the base row=3260/84359=3.86%.
Index=199	The percent calculated by dividing either the horz % in the cell by the horz % in the base row (62.62/31.43) or by dividing the vert % in the cell by the vert % in the base column (9.52/4.78). Either calculation generates the same result, because, when the horz % numbers and vert % numbers are expressed in terms of "(000)", the relationship is identical.

FIGURE 14.2
How to Read MRI CrossTabs
The MRI market research service provides information on 4,090 product categories and services, 6,000 brands, and category advertising expenditures as well as customer lifestyle characteristics and buying-style psychographics.

Source: Courtesy of Mediamark Research Inc.

spent on airline advertising last year was $200 million, and $50 million of that was spent by United Airlines, United Airlines' share of voice would be 25 percent (50 divided by 200 = 25 percent). Most agencies recommend that a brand's share of voice be at least as high as its share of market. For a new brand, obviously its share of voice needs to be more than its share of market if it wants to grow.

- ***Media Kits*** The various media and their respective media vehicles provide media kits, which contain information about the size and makeup of their audiences. Although media-supplied information is useful, keep in mind that this is an "inside job"—that is, the information is assembled to make the best possible case for advertising in that particular medium and media vehicle. For that reason, outside research sources, such as media rep companies and the Nielsen reports, are also used. As discussed in previous chapters, Nielsen Media Research audits national and local television, and Arbitron measures radio. Other services, such as the Alliance for Audited Media (formerly known as Audit Bureau of Circulations), Simmons, and MRI, monitor print audiences, and Media Metrix measures Internet audiences. All of these companies provide extensive information on viewers, listeners, and readers in terms of the size of the audience and their profiles.
- ***Media Coverage Area*** One type of media-related information about markets is the broadcast coverage area for television. Called a **designated marketing area** (DMA), the coverage area is referred to by the name of the largest city in the area. This is a national market analysis system, and every county in the United States has been assigned to a DMA. The assignment of a county to a DMA is determined by which city provides the majority of the county households' television programming. Most DMAs include counties within a 50- to 60-mile radius of a major city center. Even though this system is based on television broadcast signals, it is universally used in doing individual market planning.
- ***Consumer Behavior Reports*** We mentioned some of the consumer research sources in Chapter 5 that are used in developing segmentation and targeting strategies. They are also useful in planning media strategies. For example, media planners use such services as the Claritas PRIZM system, Nielsen's ClusterPlus system, and supermarket scanner data to locate the target audience within media markets.

The importance of media research stems not only from the large amount of money that's on the line but also from the sheer volume of data and information that media planners must gather, sort, and analyze before media planning can begin. Media research begins with collections of data about the readership and viewership of various media. Here's a quick summary of the key concepts and standard sources of the data.

Newspaper Readership Nearly half of all adults receive home delivery of a Sunday or weekday newspaper; delivery levels are highest in small- and medium-size cities and lowest in rural locations and larger metropolitan areas. Historically, newspaper reading tends to be highest among older people and people with a higher educational and income level. It is lowest among people in their late teens and early 20s and among lower-education and lower-income groups.

Newspaper readership tends to be selective, with a greater percentage reading specific sections rather than the whole paper. Business and professional newspapers, such as *Ad Age*, have particularly high readership levels. Newspapers measure their audiences in two ways: circulation and readership. Readership is always a larger number than circulation because when a paper is delivered to a home or office, it is often read by more than one person. This type of information facilitates the media planner's ability to match a certain newspaper's readership with the target audience. Agencies obtain objective measures of newspaper circulation and readership by subscribing to one or both of the following auditing companies:

- ***Alliance for Audited Media*** The Alliance for Audited Media is an independent auditing group that represents advertisers, agencies, and publishers. This group verifies statements about newspaper *circulation* and provides a detailed analysis of the newspaper by state, town, and county. Its members include only paid-circulation newspapers and magazines.
- ***Simmons-Scarborough*** Simmons-Scarborough Syndicated Research Associates provides a syndicated study that annually measures *readership* profiles in approximately 70 of the nation's largest cities. The study covers readership of a single issue and the estimated unduplicated readers for a series of issues.

Magazine Readership Magazine rates are based on the **guaranteed circulation** that a publisher promises to provide. Magazine circulation is the number of copies of an issue sold, not the readership of the publication (called "readers per copy"). A single copy of a magazine might be read by one person or by several people, depending on its content. *Time* magazine turned the industry upside down when it announced in 2007 that it would trim its rate base (average circulation level) by almost 20 percent to 3.25 million from 4 million. (In 2011, it continued to hold circulation at 3.3 million.[1]) More importantly, it also offered advertisers a figure for its *total audience*, which it estimates at 19.5 million.

Several companies attempt to verify the circulation of magazines, along with the demographic and psychographic characteristics of specific readers. As with newspapers, the Alliance for Audited Media is responsible for verifying circulation numbers. Created in 1914, this group audits subscriptions as well as newsstand sales and also checks the number of delinquent subscribers and rates of renewal. MediaMark, which provides a service called MRI, is the industry leader in magazine readership measurement. MRI measures readership for many popular national and regional magazines (along with other media). Reports are issued to subscribers twice a year and cover readership by demographics, psychographics, and product use. The Simmons Market Research Bureau provides psychographic data on who reads which magazines and which products these readers buy and consume. Other research companies, such as Starch and Gallup and Robinson, provide information about magazine audience size and behavior.

One problem with these measurement services is the limited scope of their services. MRI, for example, measures only about 210 magazines. That leaves media buyers in the dark regarding who is actually seeing their ads in magazines not covered by MRI's research. Without the services of an objective (outside) measurement company, advertisers must rely on the data from the magazines themselves, which may be biased.

One interesting change in magazine measurement is the move, which is supported by the MPA, to quantify the "experience" of reading the magazine rather than just the circulation and readers per copy. A major study to pilot test this concept found that the more engaged people were in the magazine experience, the more impact the advertising had.[2]

The Radio Audience The radio industry and independent research firms provide several measures for advertisers, including a station's **coverage**, which is similar to circulation for print media. This is simply the number of homes in a geographic area that can pick up the station clearly, whether those homes are actually tuned in or not. A better measure is station or program **ratings**, which measures the percent of homes actually tuned in to the particular station. Factors such as competing programs, types of programs, and time of day or night influence the circulation figure.

The Arbitron Ratings Company estimates the size of radio audiences for more than 250 markets in the United States. Arbitron has been using a seven-day, self-administered diary. A new technology Arbitron is rolling out called the Portable People Meter is a pager-size device that detects codes embedded in the audio programming regardless of where the device—whether traditional radio, computer, or cell phone—is located. The device has been found to be quite effective at predicting audience interest, even leading to some major format changes such as when WRFF in Philadelphia switched from a Spanish-language talk show format to alternative rock after new data revealed that rock music was more popular with the WRFF audience.

The Television Audience A great number of advertisers consider television their primary medium. Can television deliver a target audience to advertisers effectively? What do we really know about how audiences watch television? Is it a background distraction? Do we switch from channel to channel without watching any single show? Or do we carefully and intelligently select what we watch on television?

Television viewers are sometimes irritated by the intrusiveness of advertising and are not reluctant to switch channels or zip through commercials on prerecorded programs. Clutter is part of the problem advertisers face, and the audience has become very good at avoidance, unless the ads are intrusive or highly engaging. The Super Bowl is one of the few programs where viewers actually watch commercials.

A. C. Nielsen is the research company that dominates the television measurement industry. We introduced some of these measurement concepts in Chapter 11, but let's look at them again in the context of television research. **Exposure** is television's equivalent to circulation. Exposure measures households with sets turned on, a population referred to as **households using television** (HUT). But a HUT figure doesn't tell you if anyone is watching the program. Remember from Chapter 11 that we defined an **impression** as one person's opportunity to be exposed one time to the advertising in a program. Like print, the impressions from television—the number of viewers exposed to a program—might be greater than the number of households reached since there may be more than one viewer watching and the commercial may be repeated several times in a program or during a time period. We add all of these impressions up and call them **gross impressions**.

For television programs, the exposure is estimated in terms of number of viewers. The 2012 Super Bowl was watched by 111 million people, making it the most watched telecast ever,[3] surpassing the viewership of the 1983 *M*A*S*H* final episode, which has been heralded as the largest. Following those programs, the 1996 Dallas–Pittsburgh Super Bowl game drew 97 million viewers, and the 2007 Super Bowl featuring the Chicago Bears and Indianapolis Colts, attracted some 93 million viewers.

Other forms of television viewing measurement, which we talked about in Chapter 11, include ratings and share. Ratings (percentage of exposure) are used because gross impression figures are so large. A rating of 10 means that 10 percent of HUT were tuned to the program carrying a brand's ad. Since one rating point equals 1 percent of the 114 million homes in the United States, a 10 rating would be around 11 million households.

Another way to look at viewership is in terms of the share of the audience, which is based on the number of televisions turned on. The share is larger than a rating because the base figure (televisions turned on) is smaller than HUT. A rating of 10 for a Sunday night program might, for example, be a share of 20, which means that 20 percent, or one-fifth, of the 11 million televisions turned on were tuned to the program carrying the brand's ad.

Independent rating firms, such as A. C. Nielsen, provide the most commonly used measures of national and local television audiences. Nielsen periodically samples a portion of the television viewing audience, estimates the size and characteristics of the audiences watching specific shows, and then makes these data available, for a fee, to advertisers and ad agencies, which use them in their media planning.

Nielsen's calculations are based on audience data from about 5,000 measurement instruments, called **people meters**, which record what television shows are being watched, the number of households that are watching, and which family members are viewing. The recording is done automatically; household members indicate their presence by pressing a button. These are placed in randomly selected households in the 210 television markets in the United States. The company also uses viewer diaries mailed out during the **sweeps** period, which are quarterly periods when more extensive audience data and demographics are gathered. About 1 million diaries are returned each year.

Nielsen continues to add people meters in its top markets to track local viewing patterns. Meters are used only to determine what show is being watched, not the specific demographics of who is watching it. Demographic data come from diaries. A new locally based meter system would allow Nielsen to identify the age, race, and sex of viewers on a nightly basis. Note that these ratings are based on programs and are not measures of specific advertisements.

One interesting finding from an analysis of ratings is that even in this age of DVRs, the lead-in show does matter. Fox's *American Idol*, for example, has been a strong lead-in to other Fox shows, such as *Fringe*. Another finding during the recent recession is the power of ethnic media. For example, the number-one television station in Los Angeles isn't one of the networks; rather, it's the Spanish-language KMEX.

Something not measured by all of these metrics is the dedication of a program's superfans. When NBC proposed dropping *Chuck*, fans launched a campaign on Facebook, Twitter, and television blogs in defense of their favorite program. Realizing the significance of the attachment, Subway jumped in as an ally. To demonstrate the marketing power of ChuckTV net, a consumer-generated campaign called "Finale & Footlong" urged fans to buy foot-long sandwiches from Subway to eat as they watched the season finale. The effort was successful, and NBC announced it would renew the show, although the always cancellation-challenged show did eventually reach its end with the 2011–2012 season.[4]

Outdoor Viewership Outdoor advertising reaches people as they travel by a sign's site. The advertiser is interested in the percentage of the population of the total market (based on car or pedestrian counts) who, within a 24-hour period, are exposed one or more boards carrying the brand message.

Traditionally outdoor boards have been purchased and measured in terms of **showings**, which are estimates of the percentages of the population who had the opportunity to see the sign. These showings are usually stated as 25, 50, or 100 percent. The number of signs carrying the brand message is determined by the percentage of the audience that the media planner hopes to reach. A 50 showing, for example, means that 50 percent of the market's population was exposed to one or more of the outdoor brand messages in one day. Media plans still may refer to showings for outdoor media buys; however, the planners may convert this figure to something equivalent to rating points in order to make it easier to compare the weight of the various media buys.

Online Audiences Media planners are interested in estimates of the number of visits to a website, how much time was spent on the site, and new and repeat visitors as well as supplemental information, such as more sophisticated analytics that are provided by ad-buying services and the sites themselves. Google and Yahoo! have built impressive models and ad-buying programs to help media planners. For ads and banners, data are collected about the number of click-throughs that moved the user from the ad to the advertisers' site.

Various types of software programs are available that can be integrated into the advertiser's information technology system that collect these types of usage data, which are then transmitted to companies that specialize in providing these measurement systems. Nielsen and comScore have digital ratings program, as do Google, Microsoft, and Facebook. These systems record activity, but less is known about demographics, so the data are not as useful as planners might like.

Key Steps in Media Planning

The **media plan** is a written document that summarizes the objectives and strategies that guide how media dollars will be spent, primarily on the paid advertising media. The goal of a media plan is to find the most effective and efficient ways to deliver messages to a targeted audience. Media plans are designed to answer the following questions: (1) who (target audience), (2) what for (objectives), (3) where (the media vehicles used), (4) where (geography), (5) when (time frame), (6) how big (media weight), and (7) at what cost (cost efficiency). The first three are media objectives, and the second group represents media strategies.

When IMC planners develop a media plan, they also take into consideration the media of all the marketing communication functions as well as consumer and target audience *contact points*. Contact points include exposure to traditional mass media as well as word of mouth, place-based media, in-store brand exposures, and the new, interactive media. We'll mention the IMC dimension of media planning throughout this chapter but will discuss it in more depth in Chapter 18.

Media planning is more than just choosing favorite media from a long list of media options. Traditional **measured media** are chosen on the basis of such metrics as gross rating points and cost per thousand, which are explained later in this chapter, but the new media lack similar metrics and are characterized more by such considerations as the quality of the brand experience, involvement, and personal impact. Old-line advertising media planners are intent on buying reach and frequency, but the problem is that many of their clients are looking for more effective outcomes, such as engaging experiences and brand-building relationships. Thus, the framework for making media-planning decisions is changing along with the list of media options.

The four basic steps in media planning are targeting, setting media objectives, developing media strategies, and analyzing the metrics of a media plan.

Step 1: Target Audience

A key strategic decision, one that follows from the campaign plan, is identifying an audience for the brand message. In traditional media planning, based on targeting, the challenge is to select

A Day in the Life

What Do I *Do* as a Media Planner?

Heather Beck, *formerly Senior Media Planner, Melamed Riley Advertising, Cleveland, Ohio, and now photographer, Beck Impressions Photography*

People often ask me what it is that I *do* all day at work. There are 12 media planners in my office, and each of us would have a different answer to that question. But here's a general outline of a week's worth of work.

Monday morning there is a conference call involving everyone who works on an account. The client shares information such as sales numbers from the past week, as well as budget changes or which markets are going to run a test campaign. The agency shares results from market research and the status of current projects. During the next couple of hours I do *media research*—requesting and researching information from media sources for new projects.

It's lunchtime now! Once or twice a week, media reps either bring in a deli tray for the office or take us out for a lunch meeting to pitch their media products. It is the job of the media planner to do *media analysis*, by which I mean analyzing all the options and determining what is best for the client. So we don't let a nice lunch or fancy gift basket sway our judgment.

After lunch, I return phone calls and reply to e-mails. I spend the rest of the day gathering and organizing any information I have received and analyzing the data—that's when I do *media planning*. Actually, I do this all week long.

The rest of the week is similar. Tuesday morning conference calls are split up so that groups can talk specifics about their projects with their counterparts on the client side. This is the time to share detailed feedback. What works best in one market might not work well in another so these results are essential in tailoring the media plans.

On Wednesday mornings, the agency has informal status meetings or conference calls on Thursday—this is a good time to check in with clients and do *evaluations* of our media plans. Then the day is spent finalizing projects.

Fridays are when all of the agency players on an account put their projects together and determine the best way to do *presentations* of the results to clients. Another typical Friday task is to do *media buying*—that is, place the planned media buys for the following week or month.

This is a generalized example of a typical week in the life of a media planner. Some days you might work until midnight, and other days you'll take long lunch breaks. It might seem like the same thing day to day, but the actual projects vary enough to keep it interesting and challenging. And if you need a break, you can always catch up on the latest issues of *Media Week* or *Ad Age*.

Note: A graduate of the advertising program at Middle Tennessee State University, Heather Beck worked as a media planner at Cleveland-based Melamed Riley Advertising before starting Beck Impressions Photography.

---

media vehicles (1) that are compatible with the creative executions and (2) whose audiences best match those of the brand's target audience. In other words, does the group of people who read this magazine, watch this television program, or see these posters include a high proportion of the advertiser's ideal target audience? If so, then these media vehicles may be a good choice for the campaign, depending on other strategic factors, such as timing and cost.

The composition of households is particularly important in media planning where many of the decisions are based on reaching households who subscribe or view programs rather than individuals. That's because the media vehicles generally report their data and compute their impact (readers, users, or viewers) based on household estimates. So it's important to match the demographics with the household characteristics given for the media vehicle.

Media planners, for example, are unlikely to run ads for women's products on the Super Bowl, which is skewed 56 percent male; instead, they buy time on the Oscars, which has a much higher percentage of female viewers. However, in 2010, Dove used the Super Bowl to launch its Men+Care personal care products.[5] These are the kinds of decisions that make media planning both fun and challenging.

The breadth of the target, as defined in the marketing communication plan, determines whether the media planner will be using a broad mass-media approach or a tightly targeted and highly focused approach. The tighter the focus, the easier it is to find appropriate media to deliver a relevant and focused message that connects with audience interests and engages them personally in a brand conversation.

Principle
The tighter the focus on a target market, the easier it is to find appropriate media to deliver a relevant message.

As you can imagine, every media vehicle's audience is different and therefore varies regarding what percentage of its audience is in the brand's target audience. For example, Mercury Marine, which makes outboard boat motors, targets households that own one or more boats. It prefers to advertise in magazines where it can feature beautiful illustrations of its products as well as room to explain the many benefits of its motors. Should it advertise in *Time* or *Boating* magazine? *Time* magazine reaches 4 million households, of which 280,000 have boats; in comparison, *Boating* has only 200,000 household subscribers. If you said *Time*, you're not being very cost efficient. This is because even though *Time* reaches 80,000 more boat-owning households, it also reaches 3.7 million households that don't own boats. Mercury would have to pay to reach all readers, even those not in its target audience. By advertising in *Boating*, it can pretty well assume that subscribers either own a boat or at least are interested in boating.

The *Boating* story is an example of tight targeting to a *niche market*. In fact, the Internet is the ultimate niche medium in that people turn to it to find out about any topic that interests them. The "A Matter of Practice" feature explains how Toyota used online communication to reach a specific do-it-yourself target audience.

In addition to information compiled by the team's media researchers, consumer insight research also is used to identify and analyze the target audience's media use patterns. Industry research helps. For example, research has determined a major shift in media use with online media taking over from traditional media forms as the beginning spot in the search process. In a 2011 study, 86 percent of consumers say search engines are very important in the buying process with Google and Bing the first stop for 58 percent. Another 24 percent visited company sites, and 18 percent started with social media.[6] But even though search begins online—and that's true for B2B as well as consumer purchases—researchers say most customers still make purchase decisions using a combination of old media, new media, and old-fashioned conversations.[7]

A problem is that most consumers don't really know what influences them. (Just ask some of your friends how much advertising impacts what they buy. Most will probably say that "it doesn't" or "just a little.") For the launch of the Audi A3, the McKinley + Silver media team knew it needed an in-depth understanding of young males to develop a media plan that would work for this difficult-to-reach group. From research, they found that they typically don't read or watch traditional media. They're busy and skeptical about commercial messages. The team came up with a profile of the target, which they described as "intelligent, independent, and innovative" and heavy users of new media. This target audience for this product category is made up of opinion leaders who influence their peers and who are not as interested in buying an entry-level car as they are in getting "what's next."[8]

A note about the changing dynamics of media planning: This traditional approach to media that we've been describing is based on *exposures*, but newer approaches, particularly those coming from an IMC perspective, focus on *moments* when a message becomes a relevant brand experience. IMC planners have talked about consumer-based **moments of truth** for years, but now that concept is making its way into media planning. Procter & Gamble used the term FMOT, which refers to **first moment of truth**—the initial point of contact with a brand, say, is on a shelf; the second moment of truth is later when the product is used. But more recently, planners are focusing on what Google has called the **zero moment of truth**—the point when consumers search for information online or share brand experiences in a discussion with a friend. That moment typically precedes the first moment, hence the zero designation. As observed on a blog by the Location3 digital marketing agency, although advertising has always "exposed people to products before they see them in person, the Internet provides more in-depth communication about products."[9]

So you can see how this shifts the focus away from traditional targeting of households. Modern views of planning find ways to engage personally with consumers as individuals rather than as a member of a household at important moments when they are forming brand impressions.

We also have mentioned in previous chapters that in interactive communication, the targeting concept expands to include consumer initiation of messages to friends as well as to the brand organization. All of these new ways of looking at consumers are shifting the concept of targeting and have implications for how media planners look at their media opportunities. We'll say more about these changing perspectives as we continue to explain these more traditional approaches to media planning.

A Matter of Practice

Toyota Taps the Do-It-Yourself Community

Brian Sheehan, *Syracuse University*

The emergence of the Internet has created innumerable online communities where like-minded people gather around their interests and passions. One such online community is the "do-it-yourself" crowd. These are people with an insatiable desire to know how things work: how they can install their own plumbing, rebuild their own computer, and fix their own car. For the launch of Toyota's new V-8 Tundra truck, Toyota realized that many of the full-sized truck buyers are the kind of people who want to do things for themselves and put their truck to the test. Many of them use their big trucks to haul big loads, trailers, or boats.

Toyota and its agency, Saatchi & Saatchi, saw an opportunity to match this audience with their media objective of connecting in-market truck buyers with credible, objective content about their cars. They did it by creating a unique partnership with HowStuffWorks.com (HSW). HSW is true to its name: It explains how everything works. Just put in your subject, and it will give you a detailed description of its inner workings. HSW does it so well that they are able to rely on organic search to get to their audience, and their content consistently ends up in the top 10 search results.

Toyota's agreement with HSW was a comprehensive package. There were the usual display ads tied to relevant content. For example, when someone typed in "How to Tow a Boat," HSW would give the answer while displaying an ad about Tundra's powerful, high-torque engine. There were 131 towing-related categories alone! If "How to Brake While Towing" was typed, the ad would be about the truck's huge rotors, which gave better braking performance. In addition, HSW created over 100 pieces of specific Toyota-branded content per month for articles relating to Tundra as well as Toyota's Prius and Venza.

By tapping into a tight community with relevant, targeted advertising and content, Toyota was able to garner terrific online metrics and improve its image. After the campaign launched, display ad click-throughs, search engine traffic to Toyota.com, and time spent on the Toyota site all increased. In fact, traffic to the site was up 50 percent, and brand favorability shot up 40 percent.

The online space is noted for its fragmentation. Increasingly, the Internet is dividing into communities of people who congregate around specialized websites and blogs and insulated social networks. The marketers who succeed online will be the ones, like Toyota, who know how to embed their communications relevantly and seamlessly within the communities most disposed to using their products.

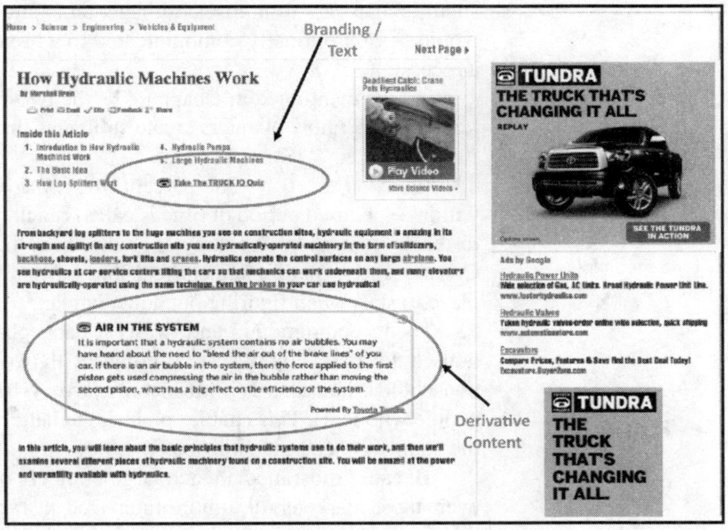

Actual Article and Served Ad

Photo: Courtesy of HowStuffWorks.com and Toyota Motor Sales

Step 2: Communication and Media Objectives

Although creative decisions are sometimes made before media planning, this is changing. With the increasing variety of media options available, smart clients and agencies are having up-front cross-functional planning meetings that include creatives, media planners, and account executives. The point is that the media and message strategies are interdependent, and decisions in one area affect decisions in the other.

Marketing communication objectives, as you will recall, describe what a company wants target audiences to think, feel, and, most importantly, do. **Media objectives** describe what a company wants to accomplish regarding the delivery of its brand messages and their impact on the target audience.

The communication objectives provide guidance to media planners. For example, why would brands want to spend some $3 million to advertise on the Super Bowl unless the buy fits with its brand communication objectives? Pepsi, a longtime Super Bowl advertiser, pulled out in 2010, deciding that expensive brand reminder ads in front of an audience that already knows the brand don't make sense. (Pepsi has advertised in subsequent years.) On the other hand, brands that are building their images, launching new products, or want to use messages to shape public perceptions on a mass scale—the Super Bowl reaches some 100 million viewers—might see the investment as a good one. Two advertisers illustrate reasons corporations might want to make the investment. Hyundai, for example, wanted to change its image from a maker of small, cheap cars to a upscale image, and Career Builder believed that its job search services would be appropriately communicated to a broad population as the United States comes out of a recession.[10]

As we mentioned in Chapter 11, the two basic media objectives are reach and frequency. Let's consider how planners create strategies that deliver on those objectives.

Principle
Reach is the first place to start when setting objectives for a media plan.

The Reach Objective The percent of people exposed to a brand message one or more times within a specified period of time is called **reach**. A campaign's success is due in part to its ability to reach as many of the targeted audience as possible within a stated budget and time period. Consequently, many planners feel that reach is the most important objective and that it's the place to start when figuring out a media plan.

Using demographic and lifestyle data, planners can focus on reaching specific types of households (e.g., empty nesters, homes with two or more children under age 18, or single-parent households, households with incomes over $100,000) or individuals (males ages 25 to 49 or people who rent). This enables planners to better match media profiles with the characteristics of the campaign's target audience.

Because most media reach large numbers of people who are not in the target market, however, most marketers are more interested in **targeted reach**, which is the percentage of a vehicle's audience that matches the brand's target market. An estimate of targeted reach can be developed assuming that the brand's target market can be identified in the vehicle's audience profile. Targeted reach is particularly important to calculate in order to estimate the amount of **wasted reach**, which is the number of people in the vehicle's audience who are neither customers nor prospects. We mentioned this problem in our discussion of network television, which is particularly susceptible to this criticism because of its mass audience.

Assessing the media for target audience opportunities is a major challenge for media planners. The evening news on television, for example, reaches a broad mass-market audience; if your target is women ages 25 to 49, then you have to consider the *targeted reach* of that news program. Obviously, both men and women watch news, so you know that your audience would probably be half or less of that, especially since you are targeting a specific age-group. Maybe the evening news isn't a good option to reach this target because there would be so much waste. The outdoors, as the *Court TV* posters illustrate, is a location-bound medium, and posters are particularly good at targeting a specified population.

Principle
It's less about reach than about finding the appropriate way to connect.

Given the newer views of consumers not as targets but as participants in brand conversations, you can imagine that media planners are revising their views of reach as well. It's less about reach than about finding the appropriate way to connect. Susan Mendelsohn, a member of this book's advisory board, describes in her "A Matter of Practice" feature what she calls vertical and horizontal reach, reflecting the difference between traditional mass media and online social media.

A Matter of Practice

Horizontal and Vertical Reach

Susan Mendelsohn, *President, Susan Mendelsohn Consultants*

What's more important in the current advertising climate—traditional vertical advertising or horizontal social media reach?

Vertical advertising relies mainly on television, print, and radio to get the majority of its messages to potential consumers. Using this top-down model, advertisers attempt to motivate people to buy products by force-feeding messages and expecting the consumer to react. More recently, traditional vertical advertising has incorporated feedback loops so that consumers can have some say in how they respond to messaging and products, but consumers are not equal partners, and their input is minimal.

Enter the age of horizontal brand communication, where messages are targeted only to people who want them and advertisers encourage active participation of consumers via all forms of social media. Here, individual consumers become part of the advertiser's strategy to spread its message. Consumers feel empowered to make choices and shape the products and brands they use. Through the use of social media such as blogs, Twitter, and Facebook and the rise of smart phones, consumers are shaping the way information and products are being created, disseminated, and attended to.

In our fast-paced, information-overload world, successful advertisers need to incorporate both far-reaching vertical messaging and loyalty-building horizontal messaging in their communication plans. Both types of advertising approaches have advantages and disadvantages unique to themselves. Vertical advertising quickly and reliably gets its message out to mass audiences, even to those disinterested parties. The advertisers remain sovereign and have control over what is being said. Horizontal advertising requires that advertisers give up control in order to have the end user become part of the communication plan by passing information along. Using the horizontal paradigm, advertisers have become adept at listening and responding to consumers, although it can take much longer to build momentum for a product/message and requires more work to keep a dialogue going (unless the message is fortunate enough to go viral—a rare occurrence).

Both vertical and horizontal advertising play a significant role in the marketing mix. With the advent of consumer's use of technology in making purchases and affiliation decisions, vertical loop advertising can no longer exist in isolation but must embrace horizontal advertising to maximize message and brand effectiveness. One complements the other, and both are important.

The Frequency Objective As we explained in Chapter 11, **frequency** refers to the repetition of message exposure. You should keep in mind that the frequency number for a media buy is actually the average number of exposure opportunities of those reached.

Because frequency is an *average*, it can be misleading. The range of frequency is often large: Some people see a particular brand message once, while others may see it 10 times within a given period. **Average frequency**, then, can give the planner a distorted idea of the plan's performance because all of those people reached vary in the number of times they have the opportunity to be exposed to a message.

Suppose that a media mix includes four magazines and that each magazine carries one ad a week for four weeks. The total number of message insertions would be 16 (4 magazines $\times$ 1 insertion a week $\times$ 4 weeks $=$ 16 total insertions). It is possible that a small percentage of the target audience could be exposed to all 16 insertions. It is also possible that some of the target would not have the opportunity to be exposed to any of the insertions. In this case, the frequency ranges from 0 to 16. Thus, because the average frequency equals 8, you can see how misleading this average frequency number can be.

For this reason, planners often use a **frequency distribution** model that shows the percentage of audience reached at each level of repetition. A **frequency quintile distribution analysis** divides an audience into five groups, each containing 20 percent of the audience. Employing media-usage modeling, it is then possible to estimate the average frequency for each quintile, as shown in the following table. For example, this table shows that the bottom 20 percent has an average frequency of 1, whereas the top 20 percent has an average frequency of 10. In this hypothetical distribution, the average frequency is 6.

Quintile	Frequency (Average Number of Exposure Opportunities)
Top 20% of universe	10
20%	7
20%	5
20%	3
Bottom 20%	1

If the media planner feels it is necessary that 80 percent of those reached should have an average frequency of 8, then a more intensive media plan would be needed to raise the overall number of exposures, in other words, to shift the average from 6 to 8.

Effective Frequency Because of the proliferation of information and clutter, there should be a threshold, or minimum frequency level, that produces some type of effect, such as a request for more brand information, a change in attitude toward the brand, or the most desired effect—purchase of the brand.

Principle
Effective frequency means you add frequency to reach until you get to the level where people respond.

A standard rule of thumb is that it takes 3 to 10 exposures to have an effect on an audience. Obviously, this frequency range is extremely wide. The "right" frequency number is determined by several factors, including level of brand awareness, level of competitive "noise," content of the message, and sophistication of the target audience. Because so many different things can impact a response (i.e., an effect), audience response research is necessary. If the desired effect/response is not achieved, you may need to increase frequency of exposure or change the message. Research diagnostics, such as tracking studies, provide direction. The principle of **effective frequency** is that you add frequency to reach until you get to the level where people respond.

Media Waste In the discussion of targeted reach, we mentioned waste as a result of targeting too wide of a target market. Actually, there are two sides to waste—both reach and frequency. The goal of media planning is to maximize media efficiency, which is to eliminate excessive overlap or too much frequency. Efficiency is achieved, therefore, by reducing **media waste**. Media professionals use their own experience, as well as audience research and computer models, to identify media efficiency. The point is that when additional media weight ceases to increase the response, it produces waste.

Writing Media Objectives Given this discussion of the relationship between reach and frequency, it should be clear that usable media objectives would focus on those dimensions ideally including both factors. Here are some examples of media objectives:

1. Reach 60 percent of target audience with a frequency of 4 within each four-week period in which the advertising runs.
2. Reach a maximum percentage of target audience a minimum of five times within the first six months of advertising.
3. Reach 30 percent of the target audiences where they have an opportunity to interact with the brand and users of the brand.
4. Reach category thought leaders and influencers in a way that will motivate them to initiate measurable word of mouth and other positive brand messages.

The first of these objectives is the most common. It recognizes that you can seldom ever reach 100 percent of your target audience. It also acknowledges that a certain level of frequency will be necessary for the brand messages to been seen, heard, or read. The second objective would be for a product where the message is more complex; through research (and judgment), it has been decided that prospects need to be exposed to the message at least five times to be effective. In this case, frequency is more important than reach. Put another way, it is more important to reach a small portion of the audience five or more times and have them respond than it is to reach a major portion fewer than five times and have little or no response.

Objectives 3 and 4 deal directly with impact. To achieve these objectives, media buyers will have to find media vehicles and contact points, such as events and sponsorships, where interaction with the brand and its users is possible as opposed to using more passive media, such as traditional mass media. Note that objective 4 is not measurable as stated.

Step 3: Media Strategies

Strategic thinking in media involves a set of decision factors and tools that help identify the best way to deliver the brand message. Regardless of whether a company spends a few hundred dollars on one medium or millions of dollars on a variety of media, the goal is still the same: to reach the right people at the right time with the right message. It's good to remember that there are always multiple ways to reach an objective; the difficult decision is which way is the best? Specific **media strategies** are based on analyzing and comparing various ways to accomplish the media objectives and then selecting the approach that is estimated to be the most effective alternative.

Media Mix Selection As you probably noted from our review of media in Chapter 12 and Chapter 13, media planners have a tremendous variety of media from which to choose, including all the owned and earned media as well as paid advertising. Traditional media planning, however, is a process of selecting advertising media to reach a certain audience and accomplish reach and frequency objectives is based on matching the advantages and limitations of the available media to the needs of the campaign strategy.

Most brands use a variety of targeted media vehicles, called a **media mix**, to reach current and potential customers. ESPN, for example, uses television, magazines, radio, and the Internet as well as original programming on its own ESPN channel to promote its programs. Media mixes are used for a number of reasons. We mentioned earlier that you can rarely generate an acceptable reach level with just one media vehicle, so a reason for using a mix is to reach people not reached by the first or most important medium. Using a variety of media vehicles distributes the message more widely because different media tend to have different audience profiles. Of course, these different audience groups should generally fit within the brand's target market.

Some people even reject certain media: Television advertising, for example, is considered intrusive, and Internet advertising is irritating to some people. Other reasons for spreading the plan across different media include adding exposure in less expensive media and using media that have some attractive characteristics that enhance the creative message.

Still, the reason for choosing a particular medium or a set of media vehicles depends on the media objectives matched with the strengths of particular media. What media will best deliver what effects—and can you reinforce and extend those effects with a mix of media? If audience reach is an objective, then television still reaches the largest audience; if frequency is important, then radio may be the best media vehicle to use. Print and television are considered more trustworthy, so they might be used by a media planner for a campaign that seeks to establish credibility for a brand or believability for a product claim

The choice of media in the media mix is based on an analysis of their strengths and limitations and how those factors relate to a specific marketing situation. Figure 14.3 summarizes the various media we discussed in Chapter 12 and Chapter 13 in terms of their strengths.

An analysis of one industry's media mix choices presents an interesting argument about the logic of the media mix. The telecom industry (AT&T, Verizon, and Sprint) was critiqued by BIG Research and a team of media researchers from Northwestern University. Based on consumer research and a customized analytical model, the team was able to develop an idealized set of media allocations. In comparison to actual expenditures, the team concluded that the industry overspends on television at the expense of others, such as the Internet, radio, magazines, and outdoor. In particular, the consumer-based research determined an underuse of the Internet based on amount of time, its ability to influence purchase, and its lower costs.[11]

Part of the problem is that in the past, media plans have been dominated by one medium—a television-based campaign, for example. With media fragmentation and the diversity of consumer media use, these kinds of campaigns are rarely found anymore. Almost all are integrated with a wide variety of media, including social media and other online vehicles. As Laura Bright, media professor at Texas Christian University, explained, these "silo-driven campaigns" have given way to integrated campaigns focused on brand experiences rather than specific types of media forms.[12] But even as we say that most media plans are multiplatform, another approach is to focus primarily on online media. The reason is that in order to connect with young markets,

FIGURE 14.3
Guide to Media Evaluation and Selection

	Strengths	*Limitations*
PAID MEDIA		
Print Advertising	• *Newspapers*: good for news announcements and comparison shopping; has positive consumer attitudes; good for reaching educated and affluent consumers; good for local market coverage; flexible in geography & scheduling	• *Newspapers*: short life span; clutter; limited reach for certain groups; poor production values
	• *Magazines*: High production values; targets consumers' interests—specializedaudiences; receptive audience; long life span; format encourages creativity & good design; good for brand image messages; good for complex or in-depth messages	• *Magazines*: Long lead times—limited flexibility; lack of immediacy; high cost; may have limited distribution
	• *Directories*: Directional—tells where to find something in the local market; provides shopping information; trusted; inexpensive; good ROI; flexible in size, colors, formats but hard to change or update; long life	• *Directories*: Lack of flexibility in timing—can be a long time before a change can be made; competitive clutter and look-alike ads; low production quality
Broadcast Ads	• *Radio*: Pervasive; in most every home and car; reaches specialized target audiences in local market; reaches them at critical apertures (morning and evening drive time); can be timed to match consumer purchase cycles; offers high frequency; music (jingles) can be repeated more easily than other forms of advertising; good for reminder messages: flexible, easy to change; good for local tie-ins and promos; mental imagery can be highly engaging; audience less likely to switch channels when ads come on • *National Television*: Pervasive; in almost every home; high level of reach; reaches a broad mass national audience although can be targeted by programs; high impact: has audio, video, motion; good for demonstration or drama; impresses other stakeholders, such as suppliers and franchisees • *Spot Television*: Good for local & regional markets; good to "heavy up" in certain cities or regions where sales are higher or where strategy calls for increased emphasis	• *Radio*: Listener inattentiveness; may just be on in the background; lack of visuals; clutter; may have buying difficulties for local buys; lack of control: talk show content is unpredictable and may be critical • *TV*: Clutter—cable offers a large number of channels; high production costs; wasted reach; inflexible—can't easily make last-minute changes; intrusiveness—audience resistance to advertising leads to avoidance and zipping and zapping
Place-Based Ads	• *Outdoor*: Good for local markets; directional; brand image and reminder; high-impact—larger than life; less expensive; long life; place-based message for nearby businesses • *Posters & Kiosks*: *Posters* can be dramatic and attention getting; sometimes in captive audience locations; *kiosks* are good for geographic messages; flexible and easy to update • *Transit*: *Interior* Good for captive audience; can present explanations; tear-offs & take-aways; *Exterior*: good for area markets; brand reminders	• Traffic moves quickly; can't handle complex messages—designs must be simple; may be easy to miss (depending on location); cluttered; some criticize outdoor ads as "polluting" the landscape; • *Posters & Kiosks*: often cluttered environment; can't be complex message • *Transit*: low reach; hard to target; *Exterior Transit*: lacks the size advantage of other outdoor media

	Strengths	*Limitations*
	• *Movie Trailers*: Captive audience; not highly targeted; less need for intrusiveness because captive audience; high impact if quality production values • *Event and sponsorship ads*: High intensity environment; local targeting unless televised; positive association with event	• *Movie Trailers*: Audience resistance is high—hates being a captive audience; expensive; needs high-value production • *Event and sponsorship ads*: easy to ignore
Online Ads	• Good for hard-to-reach audiences, such as young males; inexpensive; particularly pay-per-click programs; with search marketing can be targeted based on viewer interest; generates dialog; good messages can create buzz and go viral; can collect user information and track online behavior; engaging—high user involvement; real time	• Online ads should be consistent with other brand messages; cluttered; viewers may not notice ad or resent ad in social space; hard to measure impact
OWNED MEDIA		
Corporate Face	• Building design & interiors reflect organizational image; also bags, trucks & staff appearance; on-premise and other signs provide identification, directions	• Hard to change; hard to measure impact
Branded Media	• *Events, video games, films,* books, apps, etc., that carry brand name make brand visible in positive environment; can engage consumers in positive experiences—builds good will; *Branded apps* give something useful to user; widgets are reminders • *Naming rights* connect places to brand	• Hard to measure impact • Hard to measure impact or tie visibility to ROI
Retail Media	• *Package* delivers last message before purchase; billboard effect from multiple shelf facings; can reinforce brand image • Merchandising gets attention; increases in-store brand visibility; can tie in with special promotion	• Not easily changed; cluttered environment; hard to measure impressions; limited space for brand message • Can add clutter to store environment; retailer may not use them
PR & Promo Media	• *Publications* are under control of company; publications can be high quality, or inexpensive and quick to produce • *Videos* can present in-depth info, demonstrations, and tours • *Info and Press Kits* can be custom assembled for event or audience • *Speakers*, and books can tell corporate story; speakers can explain and present a point-of-view • *Publicity* materials provide information to media • *Premiums and Gifts*: provide brand reminders, reward behavior and reinforce relationships • *Training materials and Sales Kits*: teach employees and sales personal about brand and focus them on message strategy • OOH: sign spinners, flash mobs	• Quality *publications, videos, books, gifts, speakers* can have high cost per contact; limited reach; also hard to change • Inexpensive *premiums* can be seen as cheap trinkets' limited reach • *Publicity materials* may not reach or be used by news media • *Premiums* can be seen as cheap; limited reach; executive gifts are expensive • Sales force and employees may not follow the program; high cost per contact

(*continued*)

FIGURE 14.3

Guide to Media Evaluation and Selection (*continued*)

	Strengths	*Limitations*
OWNED & INTERACTIVE		
Corporate Interactive	• *Electronic installations* (walls) and *Kiosks* allow users to find things and interact with information databases	• High cost per contact; hard to change
Direct Response	• *Direct-response* generates sales without intermediary; media can be mail, phone, print, broadcast, and online; can engage attention; can be personalized; builds in feedback • *Catalogs* can be highly targeted; trusted; attention getting; good visual sales tool; can provide in-depth information; convenient shopping	• *Direct*: Inexpensive per contact but low response rates; resistance to mail, email and intrusive forms such as phone calls; depends on accurate database
Personal Contact	• *Personal sales* is more persuasive than mass media because one-on-one; sales messages can be tailored to consumer; personalized reason-to-buy; sales kits and scripts keep sales message strategically focused • *Customer service* delivers customer-initiated messages; high impact; adequacy of response leads to customer satisfaction or dissatisfaction with brand experience; represents the company's attitude to its customers; positive customer service can strengthen brand relationship; feedback through customer service, comment cards, & surveys can be used for on-going customer research	• *Personal sales* is expensive per sales contact; sales persons need training; may not be strategically connected with marketing • Customer service is expensive per contact; representatives need training; the department may not be connected with marketing strategies; poor customer service leads to increased negative attitudes by customers
Interactive PR & Promos	• *News conferences and media tours* invite media to hear about—or see—something in person and respond with questions; the source's responses to the questions affect the credibility of the event • *Promotions*: Sampling, events, tours, and trade shows involve customers with a positive brand experience at a purchase point of contact; events create a sense of brand excitement	• If topic is not seen as newsworthy, media may not show up • Reach is small; hard to calculate ROI
Digital Marketing	• *E-mail and texting* can be used to generate one-to-one communication • *Website* can provide in-depth content; can function as an online catalog and generate e-commerce; can be animated; may use streaming video; good for visual display; can demonstrate; inexpensive; flexible; easy to change • *Blogs* and mini-blogs (Twitter posts) are more personal; can stimulate responses • *Social Media Accounts*: Can establish brand profile on Facebook; can tweet Twitter messages to followers; fan pages create brand community; used to engage customers and strengthen brand relationships; entry into online communication networks; uses friendship-based patterns of influence	• Can be irritating, intrusive • *Website* may not match brand image; hard to track impact; navigation may be difficult; have to promote offline and online; keywords must be effective for search • *Blogs* may be seen as disguised advertising • *Social media* users have to find FB & Twitter feeds; consumer may resent commercial use of social media; hard to measure impact

	Strengths	*Limitations*
Mobile Marketing	• *Mobile Marketing*: Can reach customers in the area of a store of promotion via a cell phone	• Reach is small; hard to calculate ROI; needs opt-in
EARNED INTERACTIVE		
Publicity	• *Hits* when a story is used by media; usually a positive impact; the story's impact increases because of its appearance in a credible 3rd party medium • *Mentions* when a brand appears in a story; can be positive or negative	• Hard to monitor for brand depictions and impact; no control over media use of stories or comments in media investigations; hits and mentions can be counted but hard to know about impact on reader
Word of Mouth	• *Personal conversation*; also WoM using online media such as e-mail and texting on cell phones • *Buzz* happens when people talking to one another spread the word about something; *viral* because it spreads through a web of interconnecting networks; posts that are "liked" can circulate rapidly within network; crowdsourcing lets fans generate and share brand-related ideas. • *B2C2C* generates influence by engaging thought and fashion leaders who become brand advocates	• Hard to measure impact; hard to monitor comments for brand or category mentions; organization can only initiate, can't control content or impact • Hard to control; hard to evaluate ROI
Social Media Mentions	• *Social media*, such as Facebook, Twitter, LinkedIn, connect friends and family in conversational settings; energized word-of-mouth; brand mentions happen in a natural conversational setting	• Hard to monitor, particularly Facebook comments; hard to evaluate ROI; mentions can be negative
Media of Sharing	• Online virtual communities–brand fan clubs–gather around a mutual topic to share images and experiences; social games are played through apps • Crowdsourcing mobilizes a digital crowd to provide collective intelligence	• Sponsored brand fan clubs can be seen as corporate tools but unsponsored fan clubs are under no brand control and can generate negative or erroneous information; hard to measure impact

brands may find that the best way to reach this elusive group is through social or mobile media. Juicy Fruit, for example, created a "Sweet Talk" campaign that was launched as an app and supported on the brand's Facebook page.[13]

Media choices are sometimes designed to deliver the strategy of using one medium to deliver an audience to another medium or marketing communication tool. For example, mass media have frequently been used to promote special events and sales promotions. Likewise, mass media have been used to promote packaging, such as the famous Coca-Cola glass bottle. In 2013, Coke found that the bottles appealed to two different audiences with two radically different appeals and two entirely different sets of media usage—one is an older senior audience who respond to nostalgic messages and are heavy users of traditional media, and the other is a young audience for whom the glass bottles have a "cool" factor and are best reached through online and social media.

The emergence of the Internet has intensified what you might call a two-step media platform. Print and broadcast, which are basically informative and awareness-building media forms, are often used to drive traffic to a brand's website, which is more interactive and experiential. The Frontier "Web" ad is an example of this use.

Geographical Strategies Another factor planners use in analyzing the target audience is geography. Are potential customers found all over the country, therefore calling for a national campaign, and

Photo: © 2007 Frontier Airlines. Used with permission. Courtesy of Grey Worldwide

This ad demonstrates the use of a creative print ad to drive traffic to a website.

does the client have the budget to afford such an extensive media plan? In most cases, the media plan will identify special regions or DMAs to be emphasized with a **heavy-up schedule**, which means that proportionately more of the budget is spent in those areas. The company's sales coverage area (i.e., geography) is a major factor used to make this decision. There's no sense advertising in areas where the product isn't available. Most national or regional marketers divide their market geographically. The amount of sales produced in each geographic market will vary, and marketers try to match advertising investments with the amount of forecasted sales or the sales potential.

To determine which geographical areas have the highest (and lowest) rate of consumption for a particular product category, marketers compute a **category development index** (CDI) for each market in which they are interested. Then they calculate a **brand development index** (BDI), which estimates the strength of their brand in the various geographical areas. If General Mills were to bring out a new line of grits, for example, it wouldn't advertise nationally because most grits are consumed in the South.

A CDI is calculated for product categories. It is an index number showing the relative consumption rate of a product in a particular DMA or region as compared to the total universe (national or regional). A BDI is an index of the consumption rate of a brand in a particular market. The CDI tells you where the category is strong and weak, and the BDI tells you where your brand is strong and weak. CDI data can be found in industry and government sources, and BDI information is available through such services as Simmons and Scarborough as well as company data.

Principle
The CDI tells where the category is strong and weak, and the BDI tells where the brand is strong and weak.

Different strategies are used to deal with these levels, and they have implications for the media mix and schedule. Planners typically don't make heavy allocations in weak sales areas unless strong marketing signals indicate significant growth potential. Conversely, strong sales markets may not receive proportional increases in advertising unless clear evidence suggests that company sales can go much higher with greater advertising investment. When there is a lot of competitive activity, a heavy-up strategy may be used to defend the brand's market share.

An example of geography affecting a media plan is found in local outdoor advertising. Local advertising is, by definition, geographic. But in the case of Bertucci's outdoor, the billboard's location is both near the restaurant and the baseball stadium.

Another change resulting from the digital revolution is that media plans are deemphasizing national campaigns and focusing on local connection points. Actually, we've had local media strategies all along, but media planners are looking at local marketing in the same way

Photo: Courtesy of BU AdLab

SHOWCASE

A billboard located at Kenmore Square above the Bertucci's restaurant is just two blocks from Fenway Park. Developed by the Boston University AdLab group, this billboard illustrates a message delivered at the right time and the right place.

they are looking at consumers as initiators of brand contact rather than just targets. In a study of media planners' views of the changing dynamics of their field, Bright found that search advertising and mobile marketing are driving this trend.[14] Google has found that almost three-fourths of all online activity is related to local content, meaning that, for marketers, "local is no longer just a nice add-on option" and "more and more marketing is moving to the local level."[15] The term for this new emphasis on local marketing is **SoLoMo** (which stands for the convergence of social with local and mobile marketing), described as "the perfect storm of popular technologies and platforms that promises to deliver information you want where you are, usually via social apps."[16]

Scheduling Strategies When should a potential customer be exposed to a brand message? Scheduling strategies are designed to identify the best times for consumers to come in contact with a brand message.

For many product categories, prospective customers have one or more ideal times or places at which they are most receptive to receiving and paying attention to a brand message. This ideal time/place is called an **aperture** and becomes an important factor in scheduling media placements. The goal is to know when the target is most likely to be involved and tuned in. Movies and restaurants advertise on Thursdays and Fridays, knowing these are the days when potential customers are planning for the coming weekend. Jewelry stores run special ads before Christmas, Valentine's Day, and Mother's Day. Ads for sporting goods, beer, and soft drinks pop up at athletic venues because sports fans are thinking about those products as they watch the game. Finding the right aperture is even more important with the new considerations of moments, brand engagements, and consumer connections.

Regardless of whether a company spends a few hundred dollars on one medium or millions of dollars on a variety of media, the goal is still the same: to reach the right people at the right time with the right message. If advertising budgets were unlimited, most companies would advertise every day. Not even the largest advertisers are in this position, so media planners manipulate schedules in various ways to create the strongest possible impact given the budget. Three scheduling strategies involve timing, duration of exposure, and continuity of exposure:

Principle
Advertising is most effective when it reaches the right people at the right time and place with the right message—in other words, finding the right aperture.

- ***Timing Strategies: When to Advertise?*** Timing decisions relate to factors such as seasonality, holidays, days of the week, and time of day. These decisions are driven by how often the product is bought and whether it is used more in some months than in others. Timing also encompasses the consumers' best aperture and competitors' advertising schedules. Another consideration is **lead time**, or the amount of time allowed before the beginning of the sales period to reach people when they are just beginning to think about seasonal buying. Back-to-school advertising is an example. Advertising typically starts in July or early August for a school calendar that begins in late August or September. Lead time also refers to the production time needed to get the advertisement into the medium. There is a long lead time for magazines, but it is shorter for local media, such as newspapers and radio.

- ***Duration: How Long?*** For how many weeks or months of the year should the advertising run? If there is a need to cover most of the weeks, advertising will be spread rather thin. If the amount of time to cover is limited, advertising can be concentrated more heavily. Message scheduling is driven by use cycles. For products that are consumed year-round, such as fast food and movies, advertising is spread throughout the year. In general, if you cannot cover the whole year, you should heavy up the schedule in higher-purchase periods. For example, movie marketers do most of their newspaper advertising on the weekends, when most people go to movies.

  Another question is, How much is enough? At what point does the message make its point? If the advertising period is too short or there are too few repetitions, then the message may have little or no impact. If the period is too long, then ads may suffer from **wearout**, which means the audience gets tired of them and stops paying attention.
- ***Continuity: How Often?*** **Continuity** refers to the way the advertising is spread over the length of a campaign. A **continuous strategy** spreads the advertising evenly over the campaign period. Two other methods to consider, pulsing and flighting, are shown in Figure 14.4.

A **pulsing strategy** is used to intensify advertising before a buying aperture and then to reduce advertising to lower levels until the aperture reopens. The pulse pattern has peaks and valleys, also called *bursts*. Fast-food companies such as McDonald's and Burger King often use pulsing patterns as they increase media weight during special promotional periods. Although the competition for daily customers suggests continuous advertising, they will greatly intensify activity to accommodate special events, such as new menu items, merchandise premiums, and contests. Pulsed schedules cover most of the year but still provide periodic intensity.

After a media schedule has been worked out in terms of what media will run when and for how long, these decisions are plotted on a **media flowchart**. Across the top is the calendar for the period of the campaign and down the side is the list of media to be used in this campaign. Bars are then drawn across the calendar that identify the exact timing of the use of various media. When the chart is complete, strategies such as pulsing and flighting are easy to observe. You can also see where reminder advertising in less expensive media (in-store signs, for example) may fill in between bursts and pulsing in more expensive media, such as television.

A **flighting strategy** is the most severe type of continuity adjustment. It is characterized by alternating periods of intense advertising activity and periods of no advertising, called a *hiatus*. This on-and-off schedule allows for a longer campaign. The hope in using non-advertising periods is that the consumers will remember the brand and its advertising for some time after the ads have stopped. Figure 14.4 illustrates this awareness change. If the flighting strategy works, there will be a **carryover effect** of past advertising, which means consumers will remember the product across the gap until the next advertising period begins. The critical decision involves analyzing the *decay* level, the rate at which memory of the advertising is forgotten.

FIGURE 14.4
The Strategies of Pulsing and Flighting

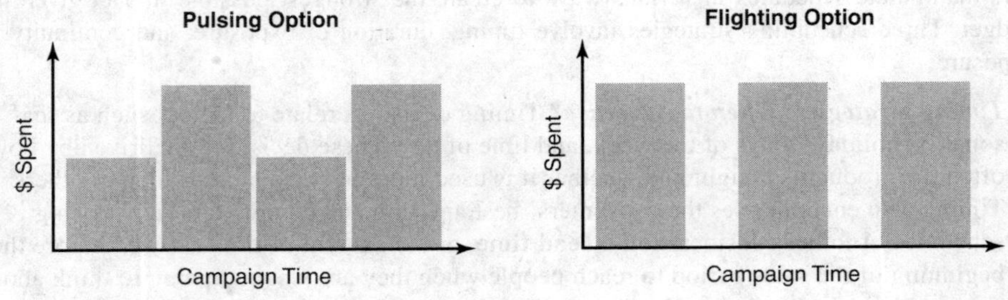

Photo: MIKE CLARKE/AFP/Getty Images

This photo illustrates how transit advertising—in this case a panel on the top of a taxi—can be used to heavy up in a geographical area. The media plan would give direction to the decisions about the size of the sign and the duration of its appearance.

Size, Position, and Media Weighting Strategies In addition to selecting the media mix, a media planner works with the creative team to determine the appropriate size and length of the message for each medium. This question of scope and scale applies to all media—even transit advertising, as the taxicab ad illustrates.

Media planners often use decision criterion called **weighting** to help them decide how much to budget (we have referred to this as "heavy up") in each DMA or region and for each target audience when there is more than one. For example, if a media planner is advertising disposable contact lenses, there might be two target segments to consider: consumers who need help with their eyesight and the eye doctors who make the recommendations. You may recall the discussion in Chapter 2 of push and pull strategies, which is also relevant here. If the strategy is to encourage the consumer to ask the doctor about the product, the planner might recommend putting more emphasis on consumer publications to execute a **pull strategy** rather than focusing on professional journals for eye doctors, which would represent a **push strategy**. A weighting strategy might be to put 60 percent of the budget on consumers and 40 percent on doctors.

In the case of DMAs, weak markets may be given more than their share of media weight in the hopes of strengthening the brands in these markets, a practice known as *investment spending*. On the other hand, if competition is extremely heavy in a brand's strong markets, the strategy may be to give them more than their proportional share of media dollars to defend against competitors. Weighting strategies are also used in terms of seasonality, geography, audience segments, and the level of brand development by DMA.

Step 4: Media Metrics and Analytics

Like every other aspect of marketing communication, media plans are driven by questions of accountability. And because media decisions are based on measurable factors, identifiable costs, and budget limitations, media planners are engrossed in calculating the impact and efficiency of their media recommendations. With millions of dollars at stake, clients want data to justify media recommendations.

Impact: Gross Rating Points and Targeted Rating Points Among the most important tools media planners use in designing a media mix is a calculation of a media schedule's gross rating points and targeted rating points. As we've suggested, reach and frequency are interrelated concepts that, when combined, generate an estimate called gross rating points. **Gross rating points** (GRPs) indicate the weight, or efficiency, of a media plan. The more GRPs in a plan, the more "weight" the media buy is said to deliver.

To find a plan's GRPs, you multiply each media vehicle's rating by the number of ads inserted into each media vehicle during the designated time period and add up the total for the vehicles.

Once the media vehicles that produce the GRPs have been identified, computer programs can be used to break down the GRPs into reach and frequency (R&F) numbers. These R&F models are based on consumer media use research and produce data showing to what extent audiences, viewers, and readers overlap.

To illustrate how GRPs are determined and the difference in R&F from one media plan to another (using the same budget), look at the two media mixes that follow. Both are for a simple television media plan for a pizza brand. As you will remember from Chapter 12, a *rating point* is 1 percent of a defined media universe (country, region, DMA, or some other target audience description) of households unless otherwise specified. *Insertions* are the number of ads placed in each media vehicle/program within a given period of time (generally four weeks). For example, consider the data below: If the plan delivered a household rating of 6 with eight insertions, the program *Survivor* would achieve an estimated 48 GRPs.

Using the same budget, the two different media mixes produce different GRP totals. A good media planner will look at several different mixes of programs that reach the target audience, figure the GRPs for each, and then break this calculation into R&F estimates for each plan. Because ratings are in percentages, the GRPs in both the plans in these tables indicate that they reach more than 100 percent. Of course, this is impossible, just as it's impossible to eat 156 percent of a pie. This is why these numbers are called *gross* rating points; they include exposure duplication. Nevertheless, knowing the GRPs of different plans is helpful in choosing which plan delivers more for the money budgeted.

How would computer models calculate reach and frequency numbers based on achieving 208 GRPs in plan A? The media mix model would estimate something close to the following: R = 35, F = 6.9. (Even though reach is a percent, industry practice is to not use the percent sign for reach numbers.) For plan B, where the number of GRPs is 176, the estimated R&F would be R = 55, F = 3.2.

Calculating GRPs for Plan A (R = 35; F = 6.9)

Program	*Household Rating*	*Insertions*	*GRPs*
Survivor	6	8	48
NCIS	7	8	56
American Idol	9	8	72
Homeland	4	8	32
		Total	208

Calculating GRPs for Plan B (R = 55; F = 3.2)

Program	*Household Rating*	*Insertions*	*GRPs*
Survivor	6	8	48
America's Got Talent	7	8	56
The Big Bang Theory	5	8	40
Monday Night Football	4	8	32
		Total	176

How do you decide which is best? If a brand has a tightly targeted audience and wants to use repetition to create a strong brand presence, then plan A might be a wise choice because it has a higher frequency (6.9 vs. 3.2). If, however, a brand has a fairly simple message where frequency is less important, a planner would probably choose plan B because it has significantly higher reach. The reason for the higher reach (55 vs. 35) with plan B, even though it has fewer GRPs, is that plan B has a much more diverse set of programs that attract a more diverse audience than plan A. But because plan B has a higher reach, it also has a lower frequency.

Principle

Reach and frequency are interrelated: When reach increases, frequency decreases and vice versa, within the constraints of the advertising budget.

It is important to remember that GRPs are a combination of R × F. When R increases, F decreases and vice versa. Once experienced planners are given budgets, they generally have a good feel for how many GRPs those budgets will buy. The planning challenge is to decide whether to find a media mix with more reach or more frequency. This depends, of course, on media objectives.

The two media mixes shown previously are based on household rating points. For products that have a mass-market appeal, households are often used in targeting. However, for more specialized products, such as tennis racquets, sports cars, and all-natural food products, target audiences can be more narrowly defined. For example, let's say that those consuming the most natural food products are females, ages 25 to 49, with a college degree; in addition, we know that they participate in at least one outdoor sport. This would be the target audience for most brands in this category. Therefore, when developing a media plan for a natural food brand, a media planner would be interested not so much in a media vehicle's total audience but in the percentage of the audience that can be defined as being in the campaign's target audience. Those not in the target are called waste coverage.

Since the total audience obviously includes waste coverage, the estimate of **targeted rating points** (TRPs) adjusts the calculation to exclude the waste coverage so that it more accurately reflects the percentage of the target audience watching a program. Because the waste coverage is eliminated, the TRPs are lower than the total audience GRPs. TRPs are, like R&F, determined by media usage research data, which is available from syndicated research services like MRI and from the major media vehicles themselves.

To illustrate the difference between household GRPs and TRPs, we'll use media plan A, shown previously. As shown below, the first column is household rating points, while the new second column shows targeted rating points, or the percent of homes reached that include a female, age 25 to 49, with a college degree and an affinity for at least one outdoor sport. The insertions remain the same, but the TRPs are greatly reduced, as you can see when you multiply targeted ratings by insertions. When the 80 TRPs are compared to the 208 household GRPs, you can see that 128 GRPs (208 − 80 = 128) were of little or no value to a natural food brand. The less waste, the more efficient the media plan.

Calculating TRPs for Plan A

Program	*Household Rating*	*Targeted Rating*	*Insertions TRPs*	*Total TRPs*
Survivor	6	3	8	24
NCIS	7	3	8	24
American Idol	9	1	8	8
Homeland	4	3	8	24
				Total 80

Another reason to tightly describe a target audience, especially in terms of lifestyle, is to take advantage of the many media vehicles—magazines, television programs and channels, and special events—that connect with various types of lifestyles. Examples of media that offer special interest topics are *Runners World*, which features topics of interest to runners; *This Old House*, the television program that describes home improvement and remodeling; *Self* magazine, which focuses on health and fitness; and *Budget Travel* for those looking for interesting but economical trips and vacations.

As important as ratings have been in traditional media plans, this computation may not be as important with individual contact media used by social and mobile advertising. It's the nature of the engagement rather than the breadth of the exposure that determines the effectiveness of the media impact.

And new media plans also are substituting GRPs with something called **total audience impressions**, which are designed to better estimate the impact of an integrated campaign—including digital impressions as well as those delivered by measured media. Total audience impressions are derived from impression management efforts in public relations. Sophisticated programs are offered by companies such as comScore that provide validated impression reporting as well as comprehensive audience figures.[17] These new methods attempt to do a better job of estimating the impact of multiplatform campaigns.

Cost Efficiency As mentioned earlier, one way to compare budgets with the competition is called *share of voice*. It sets the budget relative to your brand's and your competitors' market share. For example, if your client has a 40 percent share of the market, then you may decide to spend at a 40 percent share of voice in order to maintain your brand's competitive position. To calculate this budget level, you need to find the total ad spending in your category as well as the share of market owned by your brand and your key competitors.[18] For example, if the category ad spending totals $10 million and you want your share of voice to be 40 percent, then you would need to spend $4 million ($10 million × 0.40 = $4 million).

At the end of the planning process, after the media mix has been determined, the media planner will prepare a pie chart showing *media allocations*, a term that refers to allocating the budget among the various media chosen. The pie chart shows the amount being spent on each medium as a proportion of the total media budget. The pie chart visualizes the media mix and the relative importance, atleast in terms of the budget, of each vehicle in the mix.

Although much of the discussion in this book has been focused on measured advertising media and their objectives, it's useful to note that the other IMC disciplines are also concerned about proving their efficiency. Public relations, for example, has established metrics comparable to those used in evaluating advertising media. The "A Matter of Practice" feature explains how important it is to integrate not only media planning but also evaluations of efficiency comparing these other areas with advertising media planning. The author also explains the concept of *earned media*, in contrast to purchased (and measured) media.

Cost Per Thousand, Targeted Cost Per Thousand, and Cost Per Point Advertisers don't make decisions about the media mix solely in terms of targeting, geography, and schedule considerations.

A Matter of Practice

Integrating Advertising and Public Relations Media Planning

Clarke Caywood, *Medill Graduate School, Northwestern University*

Ask advertising directors in a company or agency what profitable target media they have chosen for message delivery for their new corporate or product/service brand strategy, and they will probably give a list of traditional mass-media advertising vehicles.

Then ask the public relations director in the same company or agency what the targeted media will be for the same program, and it will often be a list of news and feature story outlets.

In an integrated approach to media planning, the communication leaders should be targeting the same media to reach similar readers, viewers, and listeners. If not, the C-Suite—chief executive officer, chief financial officer, and chief marketing officer—in the client company would want to know why not.

These newer models of media planning seem to be aligned with the growth of the large holding companies that contain advertising, direct database marketing, e-commerce, public relations, and, now, media-buying agencies where coordination and cross-functional planning are essential.

In the IMC program at Medill, we define integrated media planning as "coordinated research, planning, securing, and evaluation of all purchased and earned media." *Earned media* are used by marketing and public relations practitioners to differentiate paid media about a product, service, or company (advertising, promotions, direct mail, Web ads, and so on) from positive or negative broadcast, print, and Internet media articles and simple mentions about the product, service, or company. The term *earned* is used to avoid the term *free*, which accurately suggests the company does not pay the media for the placement, but it does not address the fact that the publication of such stories requires hours of effort or years of experience by public relations professionals to persuade journalists to cover the product, service, or company for the benefit of their readers or viewers.

Just as selecting media for advertising has become a science and management art, the field of selection and analysis of earned media (including print, broadcast, and blogs) for public relations is now more of a science. Today, the existence of far richer database systems assists media managers who want to know which reporters, quoted experts, trade books, new publications, broadcasts, bloggers, and more are the most "profitable" targets for public relations messages. In other words, when we refer to *media planning*, we mean coordinating and jointly planning the earned media of public relations along with advertising and other purchased media.

Using the new built-in media metric systems, public relations directors can calculate return on investment on advertising versus public relations. With public relations, they can read and judge a range of positive, neutral, or negative messages as well as share-of-mind measures of media impact, advertising equivalency estimates, and other effectiveness indicators (see www.biz360.com).

Now, when the chief marketing officer and other C-Suite officers ask the integrated agency directors of advertising, public relations, or IMC if the media are fully planned to reach targeted audiences, they can answer affirmatively.

Sometimes the decision comes down to cold, hard cash. The advertiser wants prospects, not just readers, viewers, or listeners; therefore, they compare the cost of each proposed media vehicle with the specific vehicle's ability to deliver the target audience. The cheapest vehicle may not deliver the highest percent of the target audience, and the highest priced vehicle may deliver exactly the right target audience, so the selection process is a balancing act between cost and reach.

The process of measuring a target audience's size against the cost of reaching that audience is based on calculations of efficiency as measured by two commonly used metrics: cost per thousand and cost per point.

The term **cost per thousand** (CPM) is industry shorthand for the cost of getting 1,000 impressions. CPM is best used when comparing the cost of vehicles within the same medium (comparing one magazine with another or one television program with another). This is because different media have different levels of impact. To be more precise and to determine the efficiency of a potential media buy, planners often look at the **targeted cost per thousand** (TCPM).

To calculate a CPM for a broadcast commercial, you need only two figures: the cost of an ad and the estimated audience reached by the vehicle. Multiply the cost of the ad by 1,000 and divide that number by the size of the broadcast audience. You multiply the cost of the ad by 1,000 to calculate a "cost per thousand."

In the case of print, CPMs are based on circulation or number of readers. *Time* magazine has a circulation of 4 million but claims a readership of 19.5 million. The difference between circulation and readership is due to what is called **pass-along readership**. In the case of *Time*, this means each issue is read by about five people. As you would suspect, media vehicles prefer that agencies use readership rather than circulation for figuring CPM because this produces a much lower CPM. Here are the procedures for calculating both CPM and targeted CPM:

- ***Calculating CPM*** In the following example, CPM is calculated based on *Time* readership and the price of a one-page, four-color ad, $240,000. Remember, you want to know what it costs to reach 1,000 readers:

$$\text{CPM} = \frac{\text{Cost of ad} \times 1{,}000}{\text{Readership}}$$

$$\text{CPM} = \frac{\$240{,}000 \times 1{,}000}{19{,}500{,}000} = \$12.31 \text{ CPM}$$

- ***Calculating TCPM*** To figure the TCPM, you first determine how many of *Time*'s readers are in your target audience. For the sake of discussion, we'll say that only 5 million of *Time*'s readers fall into our target audience profile. As you can see from the following calculation, the TCPM greatly increases. This is because you still have to pay to reach all the readers, even though only about one-fourth of them are of value to you:

$$\text{TCPM} = \frac{\text{Cost of ad} \times 1{,}000}{\text{Readers in target audience}}$$

$$\text{TCPM} = \frac{\$240{,}000 \times 1{,}000}{5{,}000{,}000} = \$48.00 \text{ TCPM}$$

- ***Calculating Cost Per Point*** Now we'll look at how to determine **cost per point** (CPP), which estimates the cost of reaching 1 million households based on a program's rating points. Divide the cost of running one commercial by the rating of the program in which the commercial will appear. If a 30-second spot on *NCIS* costs $320,000 and it has a rating of 8, then the cost per rating point would be $40,000:

$$\text{CPP} = \frac{\$320{,}000}{8 \text{ rating}} = \$40{,}000 \text{ CPP}$$

- ***Calculating Targeted Cost Per Point*** To figure the **targeted cost per point** (TCPP), the rating points based on the target audience you want to reach, determine what percentage of the audience is your target. In the case of *NCIS*, we will estimate that half of the audience is our target. Thus, the overall rating of 8 is reduced to 4 (50% × 8 = 4 rating). Now we divide the one-time cost of $320,000 by 4 and find the TCPP is $80,000:

$$\text{TCPP} = \frac{\$320{,}000}{4 \text{ target rating}} = \$80{,}000 \text{ TCPP}$$

We can do this calculation to compare several different programs and identify those with lower costs.

CPMs have a wide range. A media planner may calculate a CPM of $56 to reach some 44 million viewers of the Super Bowl. In contrast, in the real estate example given earlier, iMapp .com might charge a CPM of $125 to reach a small but select group of realtors. iMapp is twice as expensive as the Super Bowl ad (not in real dollars but in CPM), but the higher CPM is justified because of the tight targeting. Media planners are constantly balancing cost with audience characteristics to decide if the media vehicle makes sense given the target audience size and characteristics.

Media Optimization In our earlier discussion of media mix strategy, we looked at the efficiency of various media plans. Tools that help estimate the most optimum use of various media plans using computer models involve calculating the weight of a media schedule and optimizing the schedule for the greatest impact. These **optimization** techniques enable marketers to determine the relative impact of a media mix on product sales and optimize the efficiency of the media mix.

Generally, the models can create an unlimited number of media combinations and then simulate the response produced by each. For example, during the 2012 election, President Obama's media strategists married data about viewing habits with personal information about voters the campaign wanted to reach in a program called "The Optimizer." This allowed the campaign to direct messages with a high level of efficiency. The analytics department created a new set of ratings based on a model of targeted voters as opposed to broader media audience categories. After rating their likelihood to support the candidate, the strategists then worked backward to figure out how best to reach these individuals, whether online or through traditional media. It also identified voters who were unlikely to be reached by traditional campaign buys, including undecided voters who did not regularly watch news sources. Therefore, the campaign surprisingly bought more *TV Land*, the cable network that shows reruns, as well as late-night television than might have been expected.[19]

Using optimization models, the media planner can make intelligent decisions, given factors such as budget, timing, and so forth. Optimization services include CPM Advisors (www.cpmadvisors .com), Aggregate Knowledge (www.aggregateknowledge.com), and Telmar (www.telmar.com).

The issue of media optimization, however, is bigger than just numbers and estimates of efficiency. It also involves questions of media overload and consumer irritation.

How Do Media Buying and Negotiation Work?

So far in this chapter, you've read about media plans and the key steps you would take to develop a media plan, and you looked at some important big picture issues related to media planning. As you recall, the media plan is a recommendation that the client must approve before any further steps are taken. In fact, planning is only the first stage in advertising media operations. Once the plan directions are set, media buyers convert objectives and strategies into tactical decisions. They select specific media vehicles and negotiate with media companies for the time and space in media. A media buyer has distinct responsibilities, as outlined in Figure 14.5.

Media-Buying Basics

Media buying is a complicated process. The American Association of Advertising Agencies lists no fewer than 21 elements of a media buy for traditional media. The most important one, however, is matching the media vehicle to the strategic needs of the message and the brand. In addition to media selection, however, media negotiation makes the media plan come to life in a cost-effective way. In this section, we examine the most important buyer activities: providing information to media planners, selecting the media vehicles, negotiating costs, and monitoring the media performance and billing.

Principle
Media buyers should be consulted early in planning as they are a good source of information on changes in media.

Provide Inside Information Media buyers are important information sources for media planners. They are close enough to day-to-day changes in media popularity and pricing to be an important source of inside current information. For example, a newspaper buyer discovers that a key newspaper's delivery staff is going on strike, or a magazine buyer's source reveals that the new editor of a publication is going to change the editorial focus dramatically. All of these things

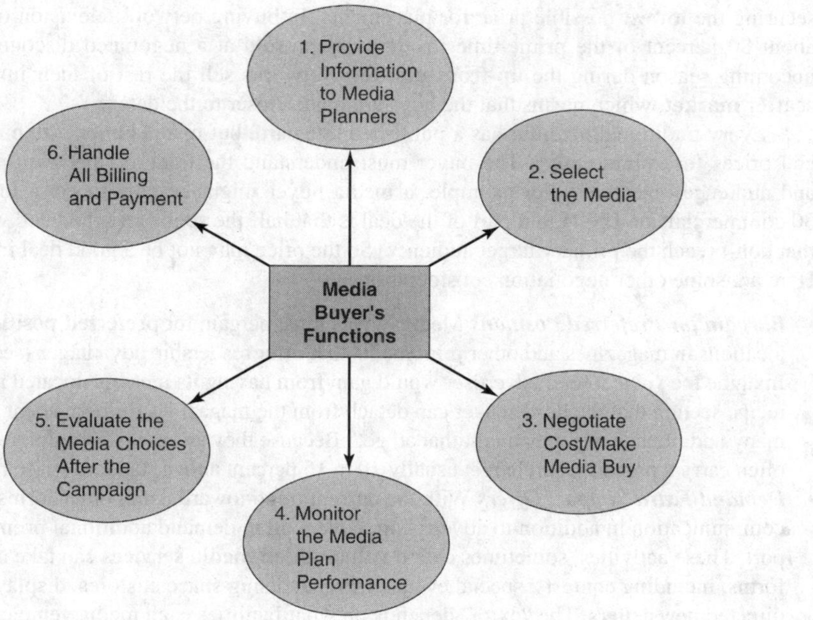

FIGURE 14.5
The Functions of a Media Buyer

can influence the strategy and tactics of current and future advertising plans.

Select Media Vehicles The media planner determines the media mix, but the buyer is responsible for choosing the specific media vehicles. A *Mediaweek* article, for example, identifies patterns in media buyers' decision making. In terms of programs, *American Idol* has been the most-watched show on television since 2007, even though its numbers started dropping in 2009. More than 20 million watched the show in 2012, although the show lost nearly a quarter of its audience during the season.[20]

Online media buying is usually handled through ad networks and the big portals. AOL, Yahoo!, Google, and Microsoft are four of the five biggest online ad networks, and the Microsoft Media Network is the fastest-growing service.[21] Online vehicles are also offering **programmatic buying**, which means that algorithms are used to target individual viewers, not just aggregated audiences based on their digital tracking data.[22]

Armed with the media plan directives, the buyer seeks answers to a number of difficult questions as various media vehicles are considered. Does the vehicle have the right audience profile? Will the program's current popularity increase, stabilize, or decline? How well does the magazine's editorial format fit the brand and the message strategy (see the V8 example). The answers to those questions bear directly on the campaign's success.

Photo: © 2004 Campbell Soup Company. All Rights Reserved

The physical characteristics of a magazine can affect its ability to deliver the desired message. For example, this V8 ad, which appeared in *Reader's Digest*, uses simple visuals and minimal copy to accommodate the smaller page size. *Reader's Digest* may not be the best choice for a complex ad.

Negotiate Costs Just as a person buying a car often negotiates for the best price, so does a media buyer negotiate for the best prices. The key questions are whether the desired vehicles are available and whether a satisfactory schedule and rates can be negotiated. Aside from finding the aperture of target audiences, nothing is more crucial in media buying than securing the lowest possible price for placements. In buying network television time, typically about 80 percent of the prime-time inventory is presold at a negotiated discount rate for the upcoming season during the **up-front market**. Networks sell the rest of their inventory in the **scatter market**, which means that the buys are made closer to the date.[23]

Every traditional medium has a published rate card, but media buyers often negotiate special prices for volume buys. The buyer must understand the trade-off between price received and audience objectives. For example, a media buyer might be able to get a lower price for 30 commercials on ESPN, but part of the deal is that half the spots are scheduled with programs that don't reach the primary target audience. So the price may not be a good deal in the long run. Here are some other negotiation considerations:

- ***Bargain for Preferred Positions*** Media buyers must bargain for **preferred positions**, the locations in magazines and other print media that offer readership advantages (see Chapter 12). Imagine the value a food advertiser would gain from having its message located in a special recipe section that the homemaker can detach from the magazines for permanent use. How many additional exposures might that ad get? Because they are so visible, preferred positions often carry a premium surcharge, usually 10 to 15 percent above standard space rates.
- ***Demand Extra Support Offers*** With the current trend toward using other forms of marketing communication in addition to advertising, buyers often demand additional promotional support. These activities, sometimes called **value-added media services** can take any number of forms, including contests, special events, merchandising space at stores, displays, and trade-directed newsletters. The "extra" depends on what facilities each media vehicle has and how hard the buyer can bargain.

Monitor Performance A media buyer's responsibility to a campaign does not end with the signing of space and time contracts. The media buyer is responsible for tracking the performance of the media plan as it is implemented and afterward as part of the campaign evaluation. Buys are made in advance, based on forecasted audience levels. What happens if unforeseen events affect scheduling? What if newspapers go on strike, magazines fold, or a television show is canceled? Buyers must fix these problems.

Facebook, for example, faced a user revolt in 2013 by activist women who insisted the social media site should do a better job of finding and removing sites that glorify violence and abuse of women. The protests led a group of advertisers to withdraw their ads from Facebook.

Underperformance and schedule problems are facts of life. Poorly performing vehicles must be replaced, or costs must be modified. Buyers also check the publication issues to verify whether advertisements have been placed correctly. Buyers also make every attempt to get current audience research to ensure that schedules are performing according to forecast. Media buyers are even found out "riding the boards," which means they check the location of the outdoor boards to verify that the client is receiving the outdoor exposure specified in the plan. Here are other responsibilities of media buyers:

- ***Postcampaign Evaluation*** Once a campaign is completed, the planner's duty is to compare the plan's expectations and forecasts with what actually happened. Did the plan actually achieve GRP, reach, frequency, and CPM objectives? Did the newspaper and magazine placements run in the positions expected? Such analysis is instrumental in providing guidance for future media plans.
- ***Monitor Billing and Payment*** Bills from the various media come in continuously. Ultimately, it is the responsibility of the advertiser to make these payments. However, the agency is contractually obligated to pay the invoice on behalf of the client. Keeping track of the invoices and paying the bills are the responsibility of the media buyer in conjunction with the accounting department.

So far, we've focused on buying for traditional media, but another complexity is the growth of online media, most of which call for entirely different media-buying techniques. The basis for the buy includes such new measures as click-throughs, and the data are monitored through services such as Nielsen Net Ratings and comScore. Google provides analytic data for search users (which includes visits to a site) as well as new or repeat viewers and time spent on the site. The "Practical Tips" feature provides additional ideas on how to buy interactive media.

In addition to negotiating, bargaining, buying, and monitoring the execution of a media plan, media buyers also have to deal with situations that crop up and complicate the planning. In effect,

Practical Tips

Interactive Media Buying

Glenda Alvarado, *University of South Carolina*

Early 20th-century retail tycoon John Wanamaker is thought to have said, "I am convinced that about one-half the money I spend for advertising is wasted, but I have never been able to decide which half."

Advertising executives have struggled with this adage for years, inherently understanding that he was probably right, but there wasn't much that could be done about it. Traditional media buys are locked in a few days ahead of time and deciding which piece of the puzzle convinced a consumer to make a purchase is almost impossible.

Not so with digital and interactive media! All elements are adaptable at a moment's notice. A headline can be altered, an offer can be changed, and the location of the advertisement can me moved—all with the click of a mouse.

Digital and interactive media buys are usually made through an Adserving company. Media executives can set limits on how many times a person is exposed to a message and receive regular updates on how each placement is performing. Detailed information on which sites are pulling consumers to a company, which version of an message is getting more hits, and what the return on investment for each ad has been are available in an Excel spreadsheet on a weekly, daily, or even hourly basis, if need be.

If the campaign goals or key performance indicators are not being met. buyers can negotiate with the placement company to gain better responses. This is known as optimization and allows poor-performing advertising dollars to be more effectively allocated.

they are also troubleshooters. Buyers deal with the temporary snags in scheduling and in the reproduction of advertising messages that are sometimes unavoidable. Buyers must be alert for missed positions or errors in handling the message presentation and ensure that the advertiser is compensated appropriately when they occur. A policy of compensating for such errors is called "making good on the contract," known as **make goods**. Here are some of the common problems they may run into:

- ***Program Preemptions*** Special programs or news events sometimes interrupt regular programming and the scheduled commercials. In the case of long-term **program preemptions**, such as war coverage, buyers may have difficulty finding suitable replacements before the schedule ends.
- ***Missed Closings*** Magazines and newspapers have clearly set production deadlines, called **closings**, for each issue. Sometimes the advertising materials do not arrive in time. If the publication is responsible, it will make good. If the fault lies with the client or the agency, the publication makes no restitution.
- ***Technical Problems*** Technical difficulties are responsible for numerous goofs, glitches, and foul-ups that haunt the advertiser's schedule. **Bleed-throughs** (the printing on the back side of the page is visible and conflicts with the client's ad on the front side) and **out-of-register color** (full-color printing is made from four-color plates, which sometimes are not perfectly aligned) for newspapers, torn billboard posters, broken film, and tapes out of alignment are typical problems.

The media buyer's life got even more complicated in 2010 with the live broadcast of the Academy Awards where E! Entertainment and Google worked feverishly to make real-time placements that would match the drama playing out onstage. The E! online channel was able to alter its Oscar-related ads within minutes to reflect not just the winners but also the content of the speeches, the onstage events, what the presenters were wearing, and other features of the coverage.[24]

Multichannel Buying (and Selling)

It should be clear from this review of media buyers' responsibilities that this is a challenging job. Tom Carey, a retired Omnicom executive, observes that "service to clients is much about knitting together the multiple media choices and getting different companies—media, promotion, event marketing, public relations, etc.—to work together."[25]

A number of media services are available on the media side to help make buying for complicated media plans easier. General Electric and its media arm, NBC Universal, for example, promote their media opportunities using a multichannel plan that includes broadcast, cable, and the Internet as well as original programming on its own channels. But the difference is that the media deals are packaged around a cause, such as the environment or wellness. Campbell Soup, for example sponsored health segments on NBC's *The Today Show* as well as Dr. Nancy Snyderman's MSNBC health program. The idea is to match the media use of the target audience in all its complexity.

Newspapers have long offered simplified buys through such companies as Nationwide Newspapers, which can handle classified and display advertising in more than 21,000 newspapers. The Newspaper National Network is a trade association representing some 9,000 newspapers that also handles ad placement. In the digital world, DoubleClick's DART for Advertisers service helps advertisers manage online display and search marketing campaigns across online channels. All of these services not only place ads but also provide performance data to help optimize a buy as well as report on the effectiveness of a marketer's specific plan.

On the other side of that coin is the *cross-media buy*, which is made easier by media companies that sell combinations of media vehicles in a single buy. This approach makes it easier to buy media across all of these platforms with a single deal rather than six phone calls. These **multichannel** deals are a result of media convergence. As content moves across these various forms of new media, so does advertising. Giant media groups, such as Viacom and Disney, are packaging "deals" based on the interests of the target audience. ESPN, for example, serves the sports market and can provide media integration that includes television, magazines, radio, and the Internet. The media conglomerate Disney created a one-stop buying opportunity for advertisers targeting kids. To create this opportunity, Disney reorganized its ad sales staff to create one sales force for its various properties that reach children—two cable networks (Disney Channel and Toon Disney), kids' programming on ABC, Radio Disney, *Disney.com*, and *Disney Adventures* magazine.

Global Media Buying

Advertising practitioners can debate global theories of advertising, but one fact is inescapable: A true global medium does not currently exist, which means that global media plans have to piece together worldwide coverage using a variety of media tools. Television can transmit the Olympics around the globe, but no one network controls this global transmission. An advertiser seeking global exposure, therefore, must deal with different networks and different vehicles in different countries.

The definition of global media buying varies widely, but everyone agrees that few marketers are doing it yet. However, many are thinking about it, especially computer and other information technology companies that are being pursued by media such as AT&T. Today, the growth area is media buys across a single region. As media become more global, however, some marketers are beginning to make the leap across regions. About 60 percent of ad buys on CNN International are regional, and 40 percent are global.

Satellite transmission now brings advertising into many homes, but its availability is not universal because of the *footprint* (coverage area of the satellite), technical limitations, and regulations of transmission by various governments. Satellites beam signals to more than one country in Europe, the Asian subcontinent, North America, and the Pacific, but they are regional, not global, in coverage. Despite its regional limitation, satellite transmission is still an enormous factor in the changing face of international advertising. Star TV, with an audience spanning 38 countries, including Egypt, India, Japan, and Indonesia and Russia's Asian provinces, reaches a market of some 2.7 billion people. It is closely followed by CNN and ESPN. Sky Channel, a U.K.-based network, offers satellite service to most of Europe, giving advertisers the opportunity to deliver a unified message across the continent.

Photo: © Newsies Media/Alamy

CNN International illustrates an opportunity for marketers to obtain coverage across the globe.

The North American, European, Asian, and Latin American markets are becoming saturated with cable television companies offering an increasing number of international networks. Such broadcasters include the hugely successful Latin American networks of Univision and Televisa, whose broadcasts can be seen in nearly every Spanish-speaking market, including the United States. One of Univision's most popular programs, *SabadoGiganta*, is seen by tens of millions of viewers in 16 countries.

In Europe, the rise of buying "centrals" came about with the emergence of the European Union and the continuing globalization of trade and advertising. *Buying centrals* are media organizations that buy across several European countries. Their growth also began with the development of commercial broadcasting and the expansion of media choices. These firms have flourished in an environment of flexible and negotiated rates, low inflation, and a fragmented advertising market. The buying centrals have nearly three-fourths of the media market in France, nine-tenths in Spain, and about two-fifths in Britain, Holland, Italy, and Scandinavia.

The important thing, however, is to be able to consider cultural implications in media use. For that reason, media planning and buying companies are also specializing or buying companies that know specific cultures, such as the Hispanic market in the United States and the Chinese market in Asia. Zenithoptimedia, for example, is a global media-buying company that has created ZO Multicultural, a multicultural unit that helps clients trying to reach ethnic markets.

Media Planning and Buying Trends

Advertising experts have been proclaiming the demise of mass-media advertising for a number of years. It reached a high buzz level when Bob Garfield, an *Advertising Age* columnist, got industry-wide attention with his book *The Chaos Scenario*, in which he speculated about the media landscape in coming years when over-the-air network television is gone and everyone accesses their news, entertainment, and advertising any way they wish: television, phone, camera, laptop, game console, or MP3 player. His concept of "listenomics" emphasizes the importance of consumer-in-charge media choices.[26]

The truth is that the media landscape is dynamic and changing so fast that it's hard to keep track of how the media business is practiced. All of these changes create new ways of operation and new opportunities for innovative media planners and buyers.

Unbundled Media Planning and Buying

We mentioned before the growth of media-buying services, such as the media megashop Starcom-MediaVest, as separate companies that specialize in media buying. This was a shift in the way the media industry is organized, a change referred to as **unbundling media services**. This happens when an agency transforms its media department into a separate profit center, apart from the agency, that allows the media group to work for clients who may be competitors to some of those handled by the agency. Because these media-buying companies control the money, they have become a powerful force in the advertising industry, leading to a tug-of-war over control of planning.

Some of these media companies are now offering **consolidated services**, which means bringing the planning and buying functions back together. To take advantage of this consolidation argument, some media companies are also adding special planning teams for other related areas such as events, product placement, Internet, and guerilla marketing programs. At this point, these big media companies begin to look more like traditional agencies.

Online Media Buying

A bigger threat to agencies than media-buying services comes from Google and Yahoo!, which, although not ad agencies, are making inroads into media buying and selling. Google is using its website to sell ads primarily to small advertisers and publishers who find its automated advertising network, Google Adworks, to be a cost-effective way to connect with one another. Agencies are trying to figure out if Google and Yahoo! are friends or enemies and what their move into online media buying will do to the revenue stream. Google, however, is betting that its expertise in search advertising, which matches ads to user interests, will give it an advantage over traditional ad media services.

New Forms of Media Research

As we mentioned earlier, one challenge media planners face is the lack of reliable audience research and measurement metrics for the new media. The traditional "measured" media with their CPMs were at least somewhat predictable in level of impact. But the metrics for online media—hits and clicks—don't really tell us much about impact. Comparing TRPs and clicks is like comparing apples and oranges.

Search advertising on the Internet is also complicating things because, if it's successful, it steals viewers away from the original site. Does ESPN benefit when viewers leave its site to click on the banner ad for StubHub Ticket Center? As one critic observed, search advertising may make sense as a form of direct marketing, but it is a nightmare for content publishers who sell advertising on their pages. In such a situation, how do you evaluate efficiency of the publisher's site? Of the search advertising? If one is a winner, doesn't that automatically mean the other is a loser?

Viral marketing is equally difficult to measure, although YouTube is developing analytic data to help media planners assess the impact of the video-sharing site. Other companies, such as Visible Measures, Unruly Media, and Millward Brown's Link, provide viral monitoring services that assess the impact not only of YouTube but also of multiple online platforms. As such services mature, marketers will become smarter about selecting marketing communication messages with the most viral video potential.[27]

Another problem is that media research is based on each medium as a silo—separate studies for separate media. Most of the research services are unable to tell you much about the effectiveness of multiplatform media programs.

Looking Ahead

That point leads to the next part of the book in which we review specific areas of marketing communication, such as public relations, direct response, sales promotion, and sponsorships—all of which are important aspects of multiplatform IMC programs. We'll end with a discussion of evaluation and wrap up the effectiveness theme that is so important in today's brand communication.

It's a Wrap

Having a Ball and Saving Lives

A mustache is the epitome of manhood—sexy and fun—and a fitting visual to grab attention for the fight against male-related cancer waged by the Icelandic Cancer Society.

The results were phenomenal. More than 9 out of 10 who experienced the campaign often said they were motivated to take action. More than 80 percent of the nation took part in Mustache March by giving money and/or spreading the conversation as a direct action of seeing the campaign. Slightly less than 40 percent of all grown men sported a dead-sexy mustache in the month of March (making Iceland look like an Eastern European country for a month). The campaign raised roughly $1.80 per inhabitant in Iceland, equivalent to U.S. charity raising $575,104,017. The Mustache March website was the fifth-most-visited site in all Iceland during the campaign.

Measured public relations media exposure was off the charts for the month with more than 13 prime-time television news stories. Countless television shows mentioned and/or had themes related to mustaches and cancer. More than 60 articles about the campaign appeared in major newspapers, resulting in lots of buzz. Mustache March measured 20 times the size of the next topic online in social media and regular online media, completely dominating the online forums for a whole month.

But the biggest success was that 87 percent of all men said they would now talk freely about cancer and were more likely to seek a doctor's examination. And during the campaign month, more than 20 persons claimed that the campaign significantly affected their lives in a positive way since it motivated their doctor's visit where they were diagnosed with cancer and were receiving treatment.

Photo: Courtesy of H:N Marketing Communications

Key Points Summary

1. **What is a media plan, and what is the role of media research in developing media plans?** A media plan identifies how a brand can connect with its customers and other stakeholders in effective ways that resonate with the target audience. Media researchers gather, sort, and analyze the data used by media planners in making their planning decisions.
2. **What are the four steps in media planning, and why are they important?** Step 1 identifies the media use patterns of the target audience and the times and places where they would be more receptive to brand messages. Step 2 states the media objectives in terms of reach and frequency. This step includes selecting the most appropriate media and developing a media mix that reaches the target audience in various ways. Step 3 is to develop media strategies that fine-tune the plan in terms of the reach/frequency relationship, geography, scheduling and timing, size and position in a media vehicle, and the way media vehicles are weighted in terms of their impact for this audience and brand situation. Step 4 is to use media metrics to analyze and predict the effectiveness (impact) and cost efficiency of the plan.
3. **What are the responsibilities of media buyers?** Media buyers have inside information about the media industries that they feed back into the planning. Their responsibilities as buyers include providing information to media planners, selecting media vehicles, negotiating rates, monitoring the media plan's performance, evaluating the effectiveness of the media buy, and handling billing and payments.

Key Terms

aperture, p. 453
average frequency, p. 445
bleed-throughs, p. 463
brand development index, p. 452
carryover effect, p. 454
category development index, p. 452
closings, p. 463
consolidated services, p. 465
continuity, p. 454
continuous strategy, p. 454
cost per point, p. 459
cost per thousand, p. 459
coverage, p. 438
designated marketing area, p. 437
effective frequency, p. 446
exposure, p. 439
flighting strategy, p. 454
frequency, p. 445
frequency distribution, p. 445
frequency quintile distribution analysis, p. 445
gross impressions, p. 439
gross rating points, p. 455
guaranteed circulation, p. 438
heavy-up schedule, p. 452
households using television, p. 439
impression, p. 439
lead time, p. 453
make goods, p. 463
measured media, p. 440
media flowchart, p. 454
media mix, p. 447
media objectives, p. 444
media plan, p. 440
media strategy, p. 447
media waste, p. 446
moments of truth, p. 442
multichannel, p. 464
optimization, p. 460
out-of-register color, p. 463
pass-along readership, p. 459
people meters, p. 439
preferred positions, p. 462
program preemptions, p. 463
programmatic buying, p. 461
pull strategy, p. 455
pulsing strategy, p. 454
push strategy, p. 455
ratings, p. 438
reach, p. 444
scatter market, p. 462
share of voice, p. 435
showings, p. 440
SoLoMo, p. 453
sweeps, p. 439
targeted cost per point, p. 459
targeted cost per thousand, p. 459
targeted rating points, p. 457
targeted reach, p. 444
total audience impressions, p. 457
unbundling media services, p. 465
up-front market, p. 462
value-added media services, p. 462
wasted reach, p. 444
wearout, p. 454
weighting, p. 455
zero moment of truth, p. 442

Review Questions

14-4. List and describe the media sources that media planning depends on.

14-5. What is aperture, and how is it used in media planning?

14-6. What is a media plan, and what is the role of a media planner?

14-7. What is the most important objective in a media plan? Explain with examples.

14-8. Explain what is meant by frequency, and describe what media planners can do to avoid its misleading nature.

14-9. What drives the need for creating and using a specific media mix?

14-10. What do media buyers do?

Discussion Questions

14-11. You have just begun a new job as a media planner for a new automobile model from General Motors. The media planning sequence will begin in four months, and your media director asks you what data and information you need from the media research department. What sources should you request? How would you use each of these sources in the planning function?

14-12. Consider the launch of the new smart TV OLED by Samsung Gulf Electronics in 2013. The media strategy is to reach spouses and couples in the Gulf market. With regard to this strategy, answer the following:

a. Define the main elements of a media plan.

b. Using these elements, create a media plan for Samsung to meet its media objective.

Take-Home Projects

14-13. *Portfolio Project:* You have been asked to develop a media plan for a new reality show that you have created. Focus on the Internet as a primary medium for this launch. Go to both www.google.com/adsense and http://searchmarketing.yahoo.com. Indicate how you would use the information provided by these sites in developing your media plan for this new reality television show.

14-14. *Mini-Case Analysis:* Outline the key decisions in the Icelandic men's cancer campaign. What were the media strategies that contributed to the success of this campaign? Using your analysis as a model, develop a proposal for a media plan for next year's follow-up campaign.

TRACE North America Case

Planning and Buying Multicultural Media

Read the TRACE case in the Appendix before coming to class.

14-15. What media would you recommend to reach the TRACE target market of Multicultural Millennials (ages 18 to 29)?

14-16. Based on TRACE's $100 million advertising budget, draw your own pie chart indicating the media you would select with a dollar figure attached to each medium.

Hands-On Case

Making Milk Cool

"Got milk?" got consumer's attention. The campaign originated in 1993 to turn around a 15-year decline in milk consumption in California, and it did. Sponsored by the California Milk Processor Board (CMPB), the campaign urged consumers to buy more milk to pair with food like peanut butter and cookies by having them imagine what life would be like without enough milk. The campaign worked, winning a slew of major awards, including its recognition by *Advertising Age* as a Top 100 Advertising Campaign. More importantly, sales increased. But one segment of the audience, teens, showed a troubling trend.

Research conducted by CMPB and its agency, Goodby, Silverstein & Partners (GSP), indicated that teens didn't think milk was so cool. In fact, 15 years of studies showed that teens' per capita consumption of milk dipped consistently. As kids age, they become more independent and tend to ignore Mom's advice to "drink milk." Other drinks like pop and sports drinks increasingly quench their thirst and absorb their money.

There's a significant amount spent marketing to the teen demographic. Packaged Facts, a market research firm, estimated that marketing products to teens exceeds $200 billion. More important than the potential profit to be made by increasing teen consumption is this: If milk promotes good health, shouldn't teens be drinking it? Great idea, but it's hard to reach teens.

GSP accepted the challenge to connect to California teens in an attempt to shift their attitudes of milk from uncool to cool. The objectives of the campaign were to engage teens to connect with and talk about milk, improve the image of milk, and ultimately get them to drink more of the white liquid.

How GSP connected with the teens offers a lesson in creative thinking in the brave new media world we described in the Part 4 opener. Blogs with teens revealed the importance of connecting online with teens and the influence of pop culture on their identities. This research also revealed that teens believed milk has lots of health- and self-image–related benefits, such as better teeth and stronger muscles.

The Big Idea? GSP created a rock band called White Gold and delivered the milk message using "bizarre and random" humor. Looking at media as a way to engage consumers rather than interrupt their lives was key to the campaign's success. Thinking like a band promoter and not like traditional advertisers, the agency produced musical magic, delivering the milk message through White Gold and the Calcium Twins. The band recorded an album and entered teens' digital social life through MySpace, Facebook, and Buzznet and on iTunes. Songs like "The Best I Can Give is 2%" deliver the important benefits-of-milk message. Television commercials featuring the band ran during shows like *American Idol*, *The Office*, and *Gossip Girl*. The band's website, WhiteGoldisWhiteGold.com, housed reviews, band history, discographies, and a music video. Poster-like full-page ads ran in *Rolling Stone*, *Seventeen*, and *Spin*. Hulu, Blinkx, and YouTube fed fans' online video viewing habits. The milk message was delivered to teens in ways they found palatable.

The new media world requires fresh thinking. Did the teens connect with the campaign's objectives? You bet they did. About 1.5 million views of White Gold music videos and an equal number website views occurred in the first six months of the campaign. More than half of California teens were aware of White Gold, and nearly nine out of 10 said that White Gold is "a fun and interesting way to learn about milk." White Gold–aware teens rated milk far higher than unaware teens, suggesting that White Gold successfully delivered the message to make milk cool.

Consider This

P4-1. What advice about media would you give to someone who wanted to market to teens?

P4-2. Describe the brand experience. How did this campaign combine the use of digital and traditional media? Was it effective?

P4-3. In what ways were the media choices for this campaign creative?

P4-4. Imagine you had this account. What would you plan for the next campaign? What media would you use?

Sources: Erik Sass, "Teen Market Grows to $208 Billion by 2011," June 27, 2007, www.mediapost.com; "White Gold Phenomenon Explodes on TV & Online," April 8, 2008, www.marketwire.com; Stuart Elliott, "California's Dairy Industry Takes Old Question to New Extreme," March 25, 2010, www.nytimes.com; Effie Briefs, "White Gold," www.effie.org; www.gotmilk.com.

PART

5 Principle: IMC and Total Communication

Hundreds of different communication activities deliver brand messages both formally through planned communication programs and informally through other activities. This part provides a framework for you to understand how all of these programs and tools work together to engage target audiences with consistent, persuasive messages that get people talking about a brand.

In this part, we describe a collection of key marketing communication tools whose activities need to be coordinated as part of an integrated brand communication program. To help you understand how this works to deliver effective brand communication, consider what Professor Tom Duncan, one of the early leaders in IMC education, has to say about IMC.

Tom Duncan
Tom Duncan is the founder of the IMC Master's Program and Director Emeritus, University of Colorado. He also established IMC as a master's program and MBA option at the Daniels School of Business at the University of Denver.

Building Brands, Brand Relationships, and Brand Equity

Because marketing communication functions have become so sophisticated and the media so fragmented, brand message clutter has significantly increased, making if more difficult and costly to manage brand communication. Companies are finding it increasingly difficult to reach prospects and retain current customers. Add to this all of the emerging communication technologies that have empowered customers, facilitating their ability to talk about brands to each other as well as "talking back" to companies.

These changes have resulted in customers becoming more business savvy and at the same time having greater brand expectations than ever before. As these changes take place, competition

CHAPTER 15 • Public Relations
CHAPTER 16 • Direct Response
CHAPTER 17 • Promotions
CHAPTER 18 • The Principles and Practice of IMC
CHAPTER 19 • Evaluating IMC Effectiveness

becomes more intense, and top management demands more and more accountability and results from marketing communication expenditures.

The old marketplace motto "caveat emptor" (let the buyer beware) has become almost obsolete. Today, a more accurate axiom is "let the company beware." Recognizing this new marketing environment, smart companies have intensified their efforts to integrate their marketing communication and all other brand messages because this is the most cost-effective way to build brand relationships and brand equity.

Originally, IMC was about creating "one voice, one look" across all messages in a campaign. So the print ad "looked like" the television commercial, and the billboard matched the website. We now know that a more effective approach to IMC has moved from this narrow "execution" focus to a much broader focus on branding and customer brand perceptions. Rather than just using advertising to sell products, companies now want to use everything that sends a message to create a coherent brand presence that leads to long-term brand relationships.

Although IMC has been around for 25 years, few understand the breadth—and depth—of this communication focus. It's not just advertising, and it's not just marketing communication; rather, it's everything a brand says and does. IMC involves the entire organization.

IMC is a commonsense ongoing process for managing brand perceptions and experiences as well as customer expectations about the brand. IMC planning delivers the brand essence (position, personality, and image) in all marketing communication but also at all brand contact points. It engages all stakeholders in meaningful and often interactive brand experiences. When these best practices are applied, they lead to solid brand relationships, and that leads to enhanced brand equity.

The chapters in this part introduce you to the basic marketing communication tools used in addition to advertising. These include public relations, direct-response marketing, and promotions. We tie everything up with a chapter on IMC, which reviews basic IMC principles and practices, as well as the big picture of total brand communication. The last chapter focuses on how these various tools evaluate effectiveness.

CHAPTER

15 Public Relations

Photo: © HDIP, Inc.

It's a Winner

Campaign: *"Häagen-Dazs Loves Honey Bees"*

Corporation: *Häagen-Dazs*

Agencies: *Goodby, Silverstein & Partners, Ketchum*

Awards: *PRSA Silver Anvil Award; Gold Effie Winner; Festival of Media, Media Responsibility Award; Cannes Lions PR Lion; PRWeek Award for Cause-Related Campaign of the Year, Silver SABRE (Superior Achievement in Branding and Reputation) Award*

CHAPTER KEY POINTS

1. **What is public relations?**
2. **What are the different types of public relations programs?**
3. **What key decisions do public relations practitioners make when they create plans?**
4. **What are the most common types of public relations tools?**
5. **Why is measuring the results of public relations efforts important, and how should that be done?**

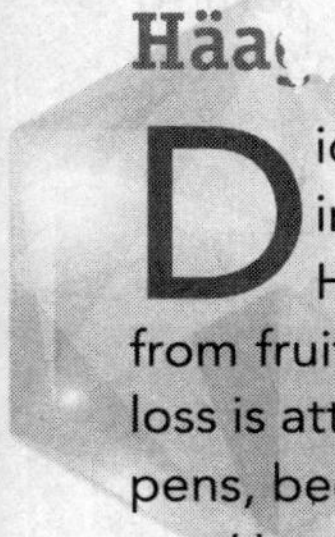

Häagen-Dazs Creates a Buzz about Bees

Did you know that honeybee colonies are disappearing at an alarming rate in the United States, putting much of our natural food supply at risk? Honeybees help pollinate about a third of every bite that Americans eat—from fruits to nuts. The cause of the crisis is not entirely known, but some of this loss is attributed to colony collapse disorder, or "CCD." When this condition happens, bees mysteriously abandon their hives.

How does this crisis relate to Häagen-Dazs? This premium ice cream uses only all-natural ingredients, and bee pollination is essential for ingredients in nearly half of its flavors. It's in the best interest of the company, as well as the bees, to resolve the problem. This is the story about how a company used public relations to build brand integrity.

Faced with a need to ramp up sales and inject zip into the Häagen-Dazs brand (whose main competitor is funkier, socially conscious Ben & Jerry's), the client asked its ad agency, Goodby, Silverstein & Partners, and the public relations firm Ketchum to accomplish these objectives with no increase in budget. In such a situation, it made sense to generate a buzz that could extend the impact of its message beyond the limited media budget for advertising. What Häagen-Dazs discovered was a problem more important than the brand.

Summarizing the situation, three factors led to the big idea for the campaign: a brand known for its all-natural ingredients, consumers who are increasingly concerned about sustainability and environmental issues, and a critical issue. The idea centered on a simple equation: ½ of Häagen-Dazs ice cream flavors + ⅓ of what we eat − honeybees = a bigger-than-ice-cream problem.

To help find a solution, Häagen-Dazs's ad agency, Goodby, Silverstein & Partners, and public relations firm Ketchum created the "Häagen-Dazs Loves Honey Bees" program. Häagen-Dazs kicked off its multifaceted efforts to help solve the honeybee mystery by giving substantial research grants to scientists at Penn State University and the University of California, Davis. An expert advisory "Bee Board," comprised of scientists and beekeepers, served as sources for news media. Häagen-Dazs created *advertorials*, advertising that looks like editorial matter in newspapers or magazines, about the bee problem, which ran in key magazines, such as *National Geographic* and *Gourmet*. Häagen-Dazs even created a new flavor, Vanilla Honey Bee, and earmarked the profits for CCD research.

Other components of the program spread the message to its audience. The www.helpthehoneybees.com site educated consumers about the crisis and invited their involvement. The online presence allowed consumers to purchase T-shirts and even send "bee-mail" to friends. Häagen-Dazs funded a six-minute documentary about CCD that is available on the Serious Eats website (www.seriouseats.com). A "Bee Dance" video was launched on YouTube. Häagen-Dazs encouraged consumer involvement by distributing more than a million free bee-friendly seeds in HD loves HB packets.

Although the bee problem was the center of the communication, selling a brand was still important. Häagen-Dazs hopes that when you crave premium ice cream, you'll choose its Vanilla Honey Bee or Dulce de Leche over Ben & Jerry's Cherry Garcia or Phish Food flavors, partly because it's a brand that cares.

Was this public relations effort to be socially responsible successful? Turn to the "It's a Wrap" feature at the end of the chapter to see how Häagen-Dazs measured the effectiveness of these efforts.

Sources: "Häagen-Dazs Loves Honey Bees," Effie Awards Brief of Effectiveness, www.nyama.org and www.helpthehoneybees.com; Michael Bush, "Häagen-Dazs Saves the Honeybees," May 8, 2009, www.adage.com; Gavin O'Malley, "Viewers Swarm to Häagen-Dazs Bee-Friendly Viral Video," August 21, 2008, www.mediapost.com; Juliana Barbassa, "Food Companies Target Honey Bee Health Problems," December 1, 2008, www.nytimes.com; "Häagen-Dazs Brand Boosts Image and Sales with 'Häagen-Dazs Loves Honey Bees' Campaign," www.ketchum.com; "Häagen-Dazs: Honey, Let's Lick the Problem," www.prsa.org; "Häagen-Dazs 'Help the Honey Bees' Case Study," www.goodbysilverstein.com.

When you read about Häagen-Dazs's efforts to help the honeybees, did it make you feel good about the brand? Would it make you feel good enough to buy a pint of Caramel Cone or Cookies n' Creme? You don't have to think hard to discover lots of other corporations and organizations trying to make their audiences feel good about their brands and gain the goodwill of the public, which is one objective of public relations. We focus our discussion in this chapter on the role of public relations in an organization, exploring how goodwill can be developed effectively in a marketing communication program. You'll find out about the types of public relations programs, planning, and tools and also about gauging their effectiveness.

What Is Public Relations?

Public relations is a fundamental communication discipline covering a wide range of functions that help an organization connect with the people it touches. Those functions include internal relations, publicity, advertising, press agentry, public affairs, lobbying, issues management, investor relations, and development.

Public relations is used to generate goodwill for an organization. That mission is as broad in scope as the definition suggests: "**Public relations** is the management function that establishes and maintains mutually beneficial relationships between an organization and the publics on whom its success or failure depends."[1] A field that is rapidly evolving and growing, public relations is increasingly used to build and maintain reciprocal relationships through dialogue and two-way communication in our networked society.

Public relations focuses on all the relationships an organization has with its various publics. By **publics**, we mean all the groups of people with which a company or organization interacts: employees, members, customers, local communities, shareholders, other institutions, and society at large. Another term for this is **stakeholders**, which refers more specifically to people who have a stake, financial or otherwise, in a company or organization. The "Häagen-Dazs Loves Honey Bees" campaign reaches multiple publics, including consumers, stockholders in Nestlé (the parent company), employees, scientists, and, in this case, even members of Congress.

Public relations is practiced by a wide range of organizations—companies, governments, trade and professional associations, nonprofit organizations, the travel and tourism industry, educational systems, labor unions, politicians, organized sports, and the media. Most organizations have in-house public relations departments that handle the organizations' public relations work, although many also hire outside public relations agencies. Public relations is a dynamic, global profession. The Bureau of Labor Statistics projects that public relations specialists will see significant growth in employment opportunities over the next decade, particularly in light of the growing impact of social media.[2]

On one level, public relations is a tactical function in that public relations staff produce a variety of communication tools to achieve corporate image objectives. On a higher level, it is a management function that monitors public opinion and advises senior corporate executives on how to achieve positive relationships with various audiences (publics) to effectively manage the organization's image and reputation. Its publics may be external (customers, the news media, the investment community, the general public, and government bodies) and internal (shareholders and employees).

Public Opinion

Public relations programs are built on an understanding of public opinion on issues critical to the organization, such as the company's impact on the environment and its local community or workers' rights and how a company deals with its employees. **Public opinion**, the term describing what a group of people thinks, expresses beliefs based on experiences with people, events, institutions, or products.

Principle
Public relations is the conscience of the company, with the objective of creating trust and maintaining the organization's integrity.

The public relations strategist researches the answers to two primary questions about public opinion to design effective public relations programs. First, which publics are most important to the organization, now and in the future? Second, what do these publics think? Public opinion is sometimes confused with mass opinion. Public opinion differs from mass opinion in that public opinion examines specific subgroups rather than a more general mass audience. Particular emphasis falls on understanding the role for each of the publics of **opinion leaders**, important people who influence the opinions of others.

Reputation: Goodwill, Trust, and Integrity

Public **goodwill** is the greatest asset any organization can have. A well-informed public with a positive attitude toward an organization is critical to the organization's survival—and that is why creating goodwill is the primary goal of most public relations programs.

Sometimes a totally unexpected crisis can threaten an organization's respect and trust. After Hurricane Sandy hit the East Coast of the United States, New York City Mayor Michael Bloomberg first announced that the New York City Marathon would take place a few days later as scheduled. He later reversed his decision after a Facebook page called "Cancel the 2012 NYC Marathon" gathered 30,000 likes in 24 hours and sponsors, including ING US and Timex, got caught in the deluge of criticism by those who thought that continuing to hold the marathon showed poor taste and a lack of caring for those still suffering from the widespread storm damage.[3]

Beyond responding to immediate issues, a public relations program that is tuned to creating goodwill operates as the conscience of the organization. Creating goodwill demands that both public relations professionals and the clients they represent act with integrity. Howard Rubenstein, an elder

Photo: Courtesy of Pepsi-Cola North America, Inc.

Pepsi invites customers to submit ideas about good causes that need support, which are listed on the campaign's website and then voted on by visitors to the site.

statesman in public relations, has a paperweight in his office at his agency to remind him, "If you tell the truth, you don't have to remember anything."[4] He said, "Corporate executives ask me, 'How do I prevent bad things from happening to me—like bad publicity, bad headlines?' And my answer always is, 'Well, you don't prevent these things by deception. You need to look at the substance of your situation and say, 'How do I make things right?'"'[5]

To underscore the importance of acting with integrity as a prerequisite for creating goodwill, public relations organizations have created codes of ethics, which encourage ethical behavior of industry members. The Public Relations Society of America's *Code of Professional Ethics* spells out core values of conduct, such as truth, accuracy, fairness, and responsibility to the public. It also includes specific provisions regarding the free flow of information, fair competition, disclosure of information, protection of confidential and private information, and avoidance of conflicts of interest.[6] Other industry organizations, such as the International Association of Business Communicators and the Council of Public Relations Firms, offer similar guidelines.

A reputation for integrity involves more than image. Image is a perception based on messages delivered by advertising and other marketing communication tools. Reputation, however, is based on an organization's actual behavior. Image mirrors what a company says about itself, but reputation reflects what other people say about the company.[7]

Principle
Reputation is earned based on what you do, not on what you say about yourself.

The value of a good reputation is difficult to measure. Although considered a soft asset, one that is not usually included in a company's financial statement, it can be significant in determining company and brand value. The lack of a good reputation can be devastatingly costly, as British Petroleum discovered after weeks, even months, of trying to deal with an oil leak in the Gulf of Mexico and its decision to reimburse businesses harmed by the spill.

How Public Relations Contributes to Brand Perception

Public relations, like advertising, contributes significantly to brand perceptions. In integrated programs, advertising and public relations aim at selected targets with different but complementary messages. Advertising and public relations specialists share a joint responsibility to promote a brand, and at times their efforts converge. For example, the release of Nike's sneaker in the Jordan Brand line, the Super.Fly, involved advertising as well as a coast-to-coast road trip with a tricked-out semi-truck that stopped at basketball courts and events across the country.[8]

To understand public relations better, let's consider how the role of public relations differs from advertising. Advertisers create the consumer awareness and motivation that deliver sales for a brand, and they do this by designing ads, preparing written messages, and buying time or space. The goal of public relations specialists is to communicate with various stakeholders, manage the organization's image and reputation, create positive public attitudes, and build strong relationships between the organization and its constituents.

Ultimately, the difference between advertising and public relations is that public relations takes a longer, broader view of the importance of image and reputation as a corporate competitive asset and addresses more target audiences. Public relations and advertising also differ in how they use the media, the level of control they have over message delivery, and their perceived credibility. Here are some specific differences between public relations and advertising:

- ***Media use*** In contrast to buying advertising time and space, public relations people seek to persuade media gatekeepers to carry stories about their company. **Gatekeepers** include writers, producers, editors, talk-show coordinators, and newscasters. Although public relations has a distinguished tradition, people often mistake it for **publicity**, which refers to getting news media coverage. Publicity, however, is focused on the news media and their audiences, which is just one aspect of public relations, and it carries no direct media costs. Even when public relations uses paid-for media like advertising, the message focuses on the organization, with little or no attempt to sell a brand or product line.
- ***Control*** In the case of news stories, the public relations strategist is at the mercy of the media gatekeeper. There is no guarantee that all or even part of a story will appear. Public relations writers write the story, send it to the media, and cross their fingers that this story will appear. In fact, there is the real risk that a story may be rewritten or reorganized by an editor so that it no longer means what the strategist intended. In contrast, advertising runs exactly as the client who paid for it has approved and it runs as scheduled. Corporations cannot control messages generated by consumers and communicated through social media.

A Matter of Practice

Content Management as a Career in Public Relations

Clarke Caywood, *Northwestern University*

An emerging trend suggests that those with skills in public relations and journalism have new career opportunities. Internet search engine trend spotter Technorati reports that those who can bring journalism-style content and credibility represent 18 percent of the professional bloggers on the subjects of business and technology. Corporate bloggers make up another 8 percent of the blogosphere. It also comes as no surprise that employers seek employees skilled in blogging, Twitter, Facebook, LinkedIn, Avatar sites, and even newspapers, magazines, and broadcast. This paves the way for new career paths for those who can combine public relations and journalism as modern content managers and providers.

Identifying "who will provide content" as the number of traditional news organizations declines is a contemporary topic that is argued by surviving members of the press, by researchers in the automated delivery of journalism, and by investors in new media systems. If a precipitous decline in the numbers of traditional news hunters and gatherers means a relative decline in content, then new sources for news content, information, and even entertainment content will have to be developed, staffed, and supported.

Journalists and public relations practitioners have always experimented in new media. Both fields have served the public and their audiences with useful content and often credible communication standards. These new public relations journalists are poised to contribute content to a wide range of organizations from hospitals, to nongovernmental organizations, to churches, to government and politics to the largest potential content provider—business.

All institutions are loved, abhorred, or not noticed by one stakeholder group or another at some point in time. Who will speak credibly about the missions of our social, economic, political, and governmental organizations? It seems reasonable to suggest that the students from journalism/advertising/public relations programs with their long tradition of credibility and content development through journalistic knowledge and skills can provide an educated and trained source of institutional creditability and content.

Caywood is author of *The Handbook of Strategic Public Relations and Integrated Marketing Communications* (2012).

Public relations specialists can play a significant part in online reputation management. See the "A Matter of Practice" feature for information about what contributor and Northwestern University Professor Clarke Caywood sees as an emerging opportunity for employment in the public relations field.

- ***Credibility*** The public tends to trust the media more than they do advertisers. This consumer tendency to confer legitimacy on information simply because it appears in the news is called the **implied third-party endorsement** factor. Thomas Harris, in his book *Value-Added Public Relations*, observes that today's sophisticated and skeptical consumers know when they are being informed and when they are being "sold to." He explains, "PR closes the marketing credibility gap because it is the one marketing communication tool devoted to providing information, not salesmanship."[9]

Different Types of Public Relations Programs

The word *relations* in *public relations* refers to relationships with various stakeholders. In fact, the main subspecialties in the field—public affairs, media relations, employee relations, and financial relations—call attention to important relationships with such groups as the general public, media, employees, and the financial community. Figure 15.1 outlines the various publics, partners, or stakeholders, for a multinational company. The term **relationship marketing** introduces a point of view in marketing planning that evolved from public relations.[10]

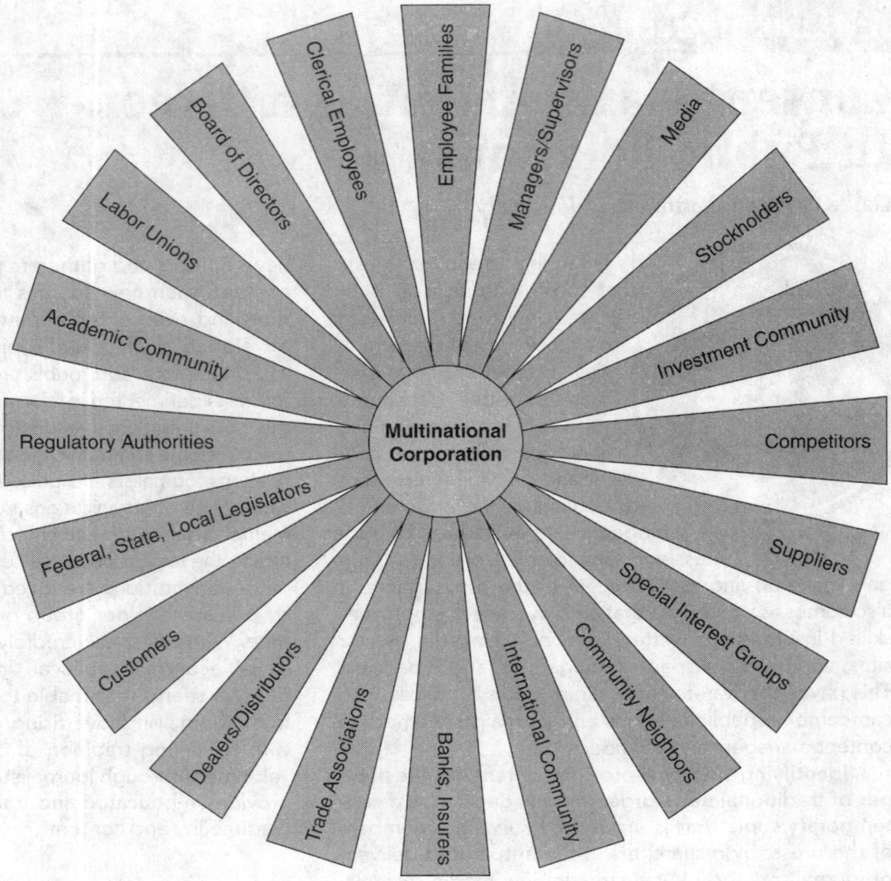

FIGURE 15.1
Twenty Key Publics
Of the 20 key publics of a typical multinational corporation, relationship management programs focus on the media, employees, the financial community, government, and the general public.

Source: Fraser P. Seitel, *The Practice of Public Relations*, 11th ed. (Upper Saddle River, NJ: Prentice Hall, 2011), 10. Printed and electronically reproduced by permission of Pearson Education, Inc., Upper Saddle River, NJ.

An example of a relationship-building program involving several types of partners was found in a contest sponsored jointly by Target and *Fast Company* magazine's technology blog. The objective was to help Target make the best use of its multichannel tools, such as the retailer's website, mobile marketing, and the in-store shopping experience. The winning entry came from a team at the TBWA/Chiat/Day agency who proposed an app named Divvy, which was designed to improve social shopping by making it possible for several people to maintain a shopping list, divide a bill, and get receipts.

Aspects of Public Relations That Focus on Relationships

The key publics addressed by relationship programs in public relations are the media, employees, members, shareholders and others in the financial community, government, and the general public. Here are the specialty areas that focus on these relationship programs:

- ***Media relations*** The area that focuses on developing media contacts—that is, knowing who in the media might be interested in the organization's story—is called **media relations**. When you say *public relations*, most people immediately think about publicity, which indicates the importance of this media function. The organization initiates publicity and provides pertinent information to the media. A successful relationship between a public relations person and editors and producers is built on a public relations person's reputation for honesty, accuracy, and professionalism. Once this reputation is tarnished or lost, the public relations person cannot function effectively as a liaison between a company and the media.
- ***Employee relations*** Programs that communicate information to employees are called **employee relations**. This function may belong to public relations, although it may also be the responsibility of human resources. A related program is called **internal marketing**, which deals with communication efforts aimed at informing employees about marketing programs and encouraging their support.

- ***Financial relations*** All the communication efforts aimed at the financial community, such as press releases sent to business publications, meetings with investors and analysts, and the annual report that the federal government requires of publicly held companies are referred to as **financial relations**.
- ***Public affairs*** Corporate communication programs with government and with the public on issues related to government and regulation are called **public affairs**. For example, a company building a new plant may need to gain the approval of government health and public safety regulators. Public affairs also includes **lobbying**, which occurs when a company provides information to legislators to get their support and vote on a particular bill. It also includes communication efforts with consumer or activist groups that seek to influence government policies. **Issue management** is another term for this function. In addition to government relations, public affairs programs also monitor public opinion about issues central to the organization's interest and develop programs to communicate to and with the public about these issues.
- ***Recruitment*** Public relations professionals are sometimes involved in employee recruitment, working with human resources and also membership recruitment for organizations. This may involve preparing ads, websites, and literature on the company or organization as well as arranging events.
- ***Fund-raising*** The practice of raising money by collecting donations is called **fund-raising (or development)**. It is used by nonprofit organizations, such as museums, hospitals, and emergency groups such as the Red Cross, and directed to potential donors. Professional fund-raisers know how to make the initial contacts that inspire other people to participate, how to use other marketing communication tools such as advertising, and how to make the best use of special events and public recognition. Sometimes fund-raising is called **strategic philanthropy**.
- ***Cause marketing*** When companies, such as Häagen-Dazs, associate themselves with a good cause by providing assistance and financial support, the practice is called **cause marketing**. This topic, along with the related areas of cause marketing and mission marketing, will be discussed in more detail in Chapter 18. The pink ribbon associated with breast cancer awareness, which is described in the opening case of Chapter 17, is another example of cause marketing.

Aspects of Public Relations That Focus on Particular Functions

Other areas of public relations, such as corporate reputation management, crisis management, marketing public relations, and public communication campaigns, are distinctive because of their unique functions rather than their target audience:

- ***Corporate Reputation Management*** The area that focuses on an organization's image and reputation is called **corporate relations**. The overriding goal of **reputation management** in a corporate relations program is to strengthen the trust that stakeholders have in an organization. Public relations expert Fraser Seitel offers advice about the importance of managing corporate image in *The Practice of Public Relations:*

  > Most organizations today understand that corporate image is a fragile commodity, and to improve that image they must operate with the "implicit trust" of the public. That means that for a corporation in the 21st century, winning favorable public opinion isn't an option—it's a necessity, essential for continued long-term success.[11]

  Since corporate reputation is a perception, it is earned through deeds, not created by advertising. Check out the website for Starbucks to learn about its efforts to do good works in the community and environment—examples of **corporate social responsibility**, or companies working to create positive perceptions. Cause marketing, which we just mentioned, is another way corporations demonstrate their social responsibility.

  John Paluszek, senior counsel at Ketchum, an expert in the area of public relations corporate social responsibility, says, "One of the great growth areas for PR is corporate social responsibility/sustainable development/corporate citizenship."[12] Many examples confirm this trend of doing well by doing good. Bill Gates's philanthropic efforts boosted public opinion of Microsoft and generated goodwill for his corporation in the process, and General Electric's "Ecomagination" campaign helps raise awareness of sustainability issues (http://ge.ecomagination.com).

Photo: © Dave and Les Jacobs/AGE Fotostock

General Electric demonstrates its commitment to meet environmental challenges using green technology while spurring economic growth.

- ***Crisis management*** There is no greater test for an organization than how it deals with a crisis. The key to **crisis management** is to anticipate the possibility of a disaster and plan how to deal with the bad news and all the affected publics. Toyota's recall of defective cars in 2010, cyanide-laced Tylenol (a classic case from 1982), and the 2010 BP Deepwater Horizon oil disaster are all examples of crises that public relations professionals would handle or at least consult with the corporations' top executives. Sometimes the stars of the campaign cause the crisis. Remember the story of the voice behind the Aflac Duck in the opening case to Chapter 12? Lance Armstrong's doping scandal caused a crisis for the brands like Nike, Trek, and RadioShack, who had hired him as a spokesperson. It also cost Armstrong an estimated $30 million in potential earnings.[13] He eventually lost his seven Tour de France titles and is banned from cycling for life.

  Preparing for a potential crisis helps organizations weather the storm. By analyzing the potential for emerging crises and identifying resources to cope with them, an organization can be ready to respond quickly and meaningfully.[14] A quick response is essential. Public relations experts believe unnecessary damage was done in 2013 to the reputation of both Paula Deen (charges of racist comments) and Asiana Airlines (San Francisco plane crash) when they delayed responding to criticisms.

  Effective crisis plans can help to both avoid crises and ease the damage if one occurs. A plan outlines who contacts the various stakeholders who might be affected (employees, customers, suppliers, civic and community leaders, and government agencies), who speaks to the news media, and who sets up and runs an on-site disaster management center. One example of crisis preparation is a contingency plan to educate consumers and reassure them that it's safe to eat pork should fears of the swine flu pandemic rise.
- ***Public communication campaigns*** Used as a way to change public opinion, **public communication campaigns** also discourage socially harmful behaviors, such as driving in areas with high levels of air pollution. Sometimes they are engaged in countermarketing as they try to argue against other advertising messages. For example, the truth® campaign featured in the opening case for Chapter 3 was designed to counter big tobacco companies' advertising that may appeal to teenagers.
- ***Marketing public relations*** One area where advertising and public relations overlap is fast-growing field of **marketing public relations**. Tom Harris, author of *The Marketer's Guide to Public Relations*, defines marketing public relations as the process of planning and delivering programs that encourage sales and contribute to customer satisfaction by providing communication that addresses the needs and wants of consumers.

  Marketing public relations is different from a more general public relations approach in its consumer, brand, and sales focus. However, the need to establish a credibility platform is similar in both; that's what public relations brings to marketing and is the greatest strength of public relations in an integrated marketing communication program. In other words, marketing public relations supports marketing's product and sales focus by increasing the brand's credibility with consumers.

  An example of marketing public relations is a public relations push engaged in by some school districts to recruit students and the state funding that accompanies higher enrollments. The Washington, D.C., and Denver public school districts are two examples of public schools hoping to communicate a positive image, attract more students, and convince voters to support school levies and bond issues.[15]

This review of different types of public relations programs should give you a sense of the breadth of the activities as well as the variety of career opportunities in this field. The short exercise below might help you decide if public relations is the career for you.

TEST YOURSELF: WOULD YOU LIKE TO WORK IN PUBLIC RELATIONS?

Here's a list of 10 skills needed for public relations managers and specialists:

1. A knowledge of the role public relations and public affairs play in supporting business goals both locally and globally
2. The ability to understand the "big picture" of communication and how to integrate all communication functions effectively
3. The know-how to leverage traditional and social media to control key messages
4. An aptitude for information technology and the determination to stay current with emerging trends in such areas as mobile, social content creation/curation, and search engine optimization
5. The versatility to work with a range of challenges and people and a knack for discerning which opponents to take seriously
6. Strong verbal and written communication skills
7. A talent for synthesizing, filtering, and validating information and the ability to apply analytics to help sort data
8. Strong organizational skills for multitasking and managing time
9. An ability to work with teams both face to face and remotely
10. The resilience to bounce back from disappointment or failure

Sources: Doug Pinkham, "What It Takes to Work in Public Affairs and Public Relations," *Public Relations Quarterly*, Spring 2004, 15, www.prsa.org; Anik Hanson, "10 Skills PR Professionals Will Need in 2020," June 2012, www.prdaily.com; "Top 7 Skills Needed for a Public Relations Career," www.prcrossing.com.

What Key Decisions Guide Public Relations Plans?

Planning for a public relations campaign is similar to planning an advertising or IMC campaign. The plan should complement the marketing and marcom strategies so that the organization communicates with one clear voice to its various publics. The plan also identifies the various key publics and the public relations activities that public relations people use to address the interests of its various publics. In addition to identifying key targets, public relations plans also specify the objectives that give direction to the public relations program or campaign. Assessing the effectiveness of the campaign in achieving its objectives is important, just as it is for advertising campaigns.

Research and SWOT Analysis

Research is used by an organization, as well as outside public relations agencies, throughout the planning and implementation of a public relations plan. It's also used afterward to determine if the effort was successful and if the organization is spending its money wisely on the public relations efforts.

The public relations effort may also begin with a more formal type of background research, called a **communication audit**, to assess the internal and external public relations environment that affects the organization's audiences, objectives, competitors, and past results. An annual audit or a campaign-specific audit can be used to ensure that a program is on track and performing as intended. Often **benchmarking** is used to identify baselines from previous audits or audits of other related companies and industries so there is a point of comparison. A **gap analysis**, which measures the differences in perceptions and attitudes between groups or between the organization and its publics, may be part of the analysis.

Practitioners categorize publics so that they can develop effective public relations plans to address issues. They consider **latent publics** as those who are unaware of their connection to an organization regarding some particular problem. **Aware publics** are those who recognize the connections between the problem and themselves and others but who do not communicate about it. **Active publics** are those who communicate and organize to do something about the issue or situation.[16] The "Häagen-Dazs Loves Honey Bees" campaign seeks active publics and lets them know about the company's efforts. It also wants to transform latent and aware publics into active publics who will connect Häagen-Dazs's brand with efforts to save honey bees.

Since public opinion is so central to public relations programs, companies often use ongoing research to monitor opinions and attitudes. One such example is the use of companies that monitor voting behavior, such as Gallup, CNN, and Google. Statistician and author Nate Silver evaluated polling results from the 2012 presidential election and noted that some of the most accurate pollsters were those who conducted their surveys online. Some telephone pollsters who called cell numbers as well as landlines also performed well. Those that relied on using landlines only were less accurate.[17]

As in marketing or advertising planning, a public relations plan begins with background research leading to a situation analysis, or SWOT analysis, that evaluates a company's strengths, weaknesses, opportunities, and threats. This analysis reflects a general understanding of the difficulty of changing people's attitudes about issues such as corporations and their role in protecting the environment. Understanding the nature of the problem makes it easier to determine the appropriate communication objectives and the target stakeholder audiences, or publics, who will be addressed by the public relations efforts. In public relations planning, the situation analysis can include such topics as changes in public opinion, industry and consumer trends, economic trends, governmental regulations and oversight programs, and corporate strategies that affect a company's relationships with stakeholders.

Targeting

As in other marketing communication areas, it is important to understand the target audience before designing the campaign. Research is conducted to identify the appropriate publics to which to address the public relations message. Häagen-Dazs tapped into an audience motivated by environmental causes to support research to solve the problem of the disappearing honey bees. The "Häagen-Dazs Loves Honey Bees" campaign formed a natural connection between the premium ice cream and the bees that help create natural ingredients, and research about the bees' dilemma provided a key insight that resonated with consumers.

Objectives and Strategies

Principle
Before changing behavior, a communication program may need to change beliefs, attitudes, and feelings.

A variety of objectives guides a public relations plan, and the organization can use myriad strategies to carry out the plan. Public relations objectives are designed by public relations planners to make changes in the public's knowledge, attitudes, and behaviors related to a company, brand, or organization. Usually, these objectives focus on creating credibility, delivering information, and building positive images, trust, and corporate goodwill. The "Matter of Practice" feature illustrates the thinking behind an image campaign for the University of Colorado–Denver.

A company may also seek to change behavior, but that is a difficult task. Before changing behavior, a communication effort may need to change people's beliefs, attitudes, and feelings. In many public relations efforts, these communication effects are easier to accomplish and measure than behavior change. Typical public relations objectives include the following:

- Creating a corporate or organization brand
- Shaping or redefining a corporate reputation
- Positioning or repositioning a company or brand
- Moving a brand to a new market or a global market
- Launching a new product or brand
- Disseminating news about a brand, company, or organization
- Providing product or brand news and information
- Changing stakeholder attitudes, opinions, or behaviors about a brand or company

A Matter of Practice

Mudo City: A Successful Brand Expansion

Rania Deeb, Business Consultant, UAE

In the early 1960s, two young entrepreneurs—Mustafa Taviloğlu and Doğan Gürün—unveiled a small shop called Mudo with products such as gifts, records, and hand-painted t-shirts. Mudo is now a Turkish retail giant working toward global recognition with the continuous efforts of its founders. As a marketing attempt during its early years, Mudo displayed billboards on boats across the Bosphorus, and it was noted to be the first company in Turkey to use such an advertising channel.

Taviloğlu found inspiration for the famous Mudo clothing line during one of his trips to Paris. This led to the creation of the Mudo Collection brand, at a time when Turkey had no exclusive clothing brand for young people.

Mudo introduced the boutique concept in Turkey in the 1990s, and the small store increased its product range and evolved toward the "Mudo" concept—a new significant brand that offers everything needed for the home and daily life. This continued to develop in the same direction in the following years.

Mudo's next objective—opening larger stores that could offer a range of products under one roof—was achieved by surveying the needs of the population at large. A few Mudo City stores were established throughout Turkey.

Its marketing strategy brought Mudo to the Middle East's most prestigious retail address, The Dubai Mall. This exposed them to a larger consumer base—a young, trendy, and affluent crowd in the Middle East, the Asian subcontinent, and the CIS countries.

The continuous search for innovative approaches to meet the needs and wants of its customers, and considering customer satisfaction among its first priorities, created a brand image for Mudo City that can be described as successful.

Some of the key factors driving its effective expansion include the creation of a brand that mirrors the values of its society, urban locales, products that fulfill target-market needs, an online presence, and a credible image in terms of quality, design, and reasonable pricing. Mudo is aware of the importance of its customers and is constantly evolving to provide the best products to meet its customer's expectations.

Mudo also sponsors several social campaigns and events in the fields of sports, the arts, and other social matters, which supports the company's vision—to meet the ever-changing demands of its audience and take into account global changes in terms of societal and technological innovations.

Sources: 1. Mudo, "About Us," 2013, www.mudo.com.tr/kurumsal/about-us-46; 2. Asadel, "Mudo City," 2013, www.asadelgroup.com/brands/mudo-city/; 3. Middle East Content Portal, "Mudo City Company Profile," 2013, www.tcf-me.com/client_portal/1052874154/company_profile; 4. "Mudo," 2013, http://s3-ap-southeast-1.amazonaws.com/tcfweb-live/system/clipping_files/17437/original/Mudo%20City%202012-5-27%20Wain%20ME-Feature.jpg?1338452860, 5. Yelp, "Mudo City - Bakırköy - Istanbul," 2013, www.yelp.com/biz/mudo-city-istanbul-7; 6. "Dubai Gets Taste of Turkish Delight from Mudo City," *The National*, 2013, www.thenational.ae/business/industry-insights/retail/dubai-gets-taste-of-turkish-delight-from-mudo-city.

- Creating stronger brand relationships with key stakeholders, such as employees, shareholders and the financial community, government, members (for associations), and the media
- Creating high levels of customer (member) satisfaction
- Creating excitement in the marketplace
- Creating buzz (word of mouth)
- Involving people with the brand, company, or organization through events and other participatory activities
- Associating brands and companies with good causes

Change Agent Strategies Changing the attitudes that drive behavior is central to public relations programs. **Change agent** programs can be internal strategies focused on employees (sometimes called internal marketing) or external and focused on other publics, such as customers and other stakeholders. Regardless of the reason for change, "communication with principal stakeholders ranks high in the hierarchy of factors that predict success. Communication is second only to the main stakeholders' participation in the process."[18]

Involvement Strategies Public relations uses participation to intensify stakeholder involvement with a company or brand. Involvement can create interest and a feeling of excitement, but, more importantly, it can also drive loyalty. Getting people to participate in an action plan is one way

Photo: AP Photo/Clark County

Mojave Max is a desert tortoise used as a mascot for a desert conservation program in Nevada.

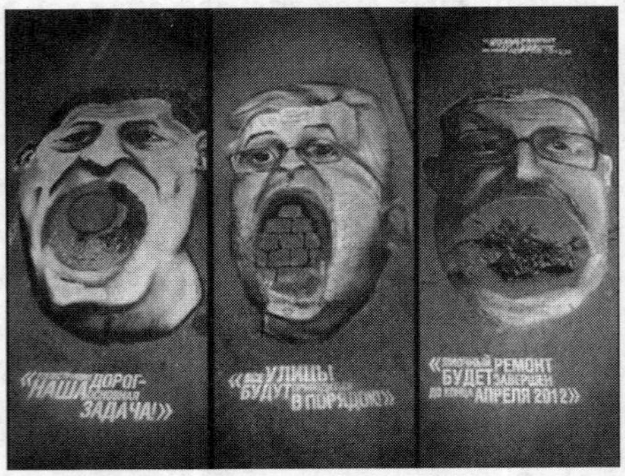

Photo: Make the politicians work. Courtesy of Voskhod Advertising Agency.

Getting roads fixed is apparently a universal problem. This public relations stunt on the streets of Yekaterinburg, Russia's fourth-largest city, reminded the pictured politicians about the pothole problems. It garnered lots of attention and resulted in action that fixed the holes.

to drive behavior change. For example, Pizza Hut's "Book It" effort is an incentive program used by schools to offer free pizzas to reward students for reading.

The Big Idea

Creative ideas are just as important in public relations as in advertising—and for the same reason: to get attention. The Clark County Desert Conservation Program in Nevada wanted to promote desert environments and threats to ecology. Mojave Max, a desert tortoise that is at least 50 years old, became the group's mascot and announces the arrival of spring, just like Punxsutawney Phil does in the East. Who would have thought you could make a media star of a tortoise? The 15-pound Max has become the poster reptile for desert ecology and attracts the attention of children as well as adults.

Public relations stunts designed to get publicity are also part of the promotional arsenal. Janet Jackson's big exposure during the 2004 Super Bowl halftime show is an example of a stunt that got lots of visibility for the performer. Critics say the overexposure was in poor taste, but the stunt has been talked about for years. Jackson also gathered twice the number of U.S. press mentions as the Super Bowl commercials did that year.[19] Other examples: Denny's gave away 2 million free Grand Slam breakfasts after running a 30-second ad that aired during the Super Bowl in 2009 in an effort to reacquaint customers with its brand,[20] and Duracell brought disaster relief in the form of charging stations to Battery Park in Lower Manhattan after Hurricane Sandy washed away people's ability to use their e-mail and social media accounts.[21]

Flash mob marketing is another version of a publicity stunt. You can see these spectacular flash mobs break out at venues across the world that are captured on video and uploaded on YouTube.

Sometimes public relations stunts generate negative publicity, such as the attempt by Pizza Hut, which offered a lifetime of free pizza to someone at one of the 2012 presidential debates brave enough to ask either candidate which topping he preferred. When the media caught wind of the dare, they were outraged by the mockery of the political system, and Pizza Hut was forced to withdraw the offer.[22] Was this effective public relations? Is any publicity good publicity?

Figure 15.2 illustrates that various public relations tactics are controlled, semicontrolled, or uncontrolled messages. They all play a role in a communication campaign plan. The model identifies perception, emotion, cognition, persuasion, association, and behavior as categories of effects that might need to be measured in an evaluation program.

What Are Common Public Relations Tools?

Public relations uses a variety of marketing communication tools just as advertising does. Advertising is particularly useful in corporate image and reputation programs. Direct marketing is sometimes useful in sending out corporate books and DVDs. The Internet is important because the corporate website is one of the primary ways to disseminate information about an organization. Public relations activities, such as publicity and special mailings of DVDs, can help drive traffic to the corporate website. Sales promotion is used in support of public relations activities, such as special events. In some cases, it's hard to know whether an event is a sales promotion or public relations effort. But it's not just the use of these tools that makes public relations a viable function of brand communication; it's also the fact that public relations can contribute valuable effects, such as credibility.

A study conducted by *Advertising Age* and the Council of Public Relations Firms asked marketers in what roles they considered public relations effective. They responded that raising awareness was most effective (83 percent), followed by providing credibility (67 percent),

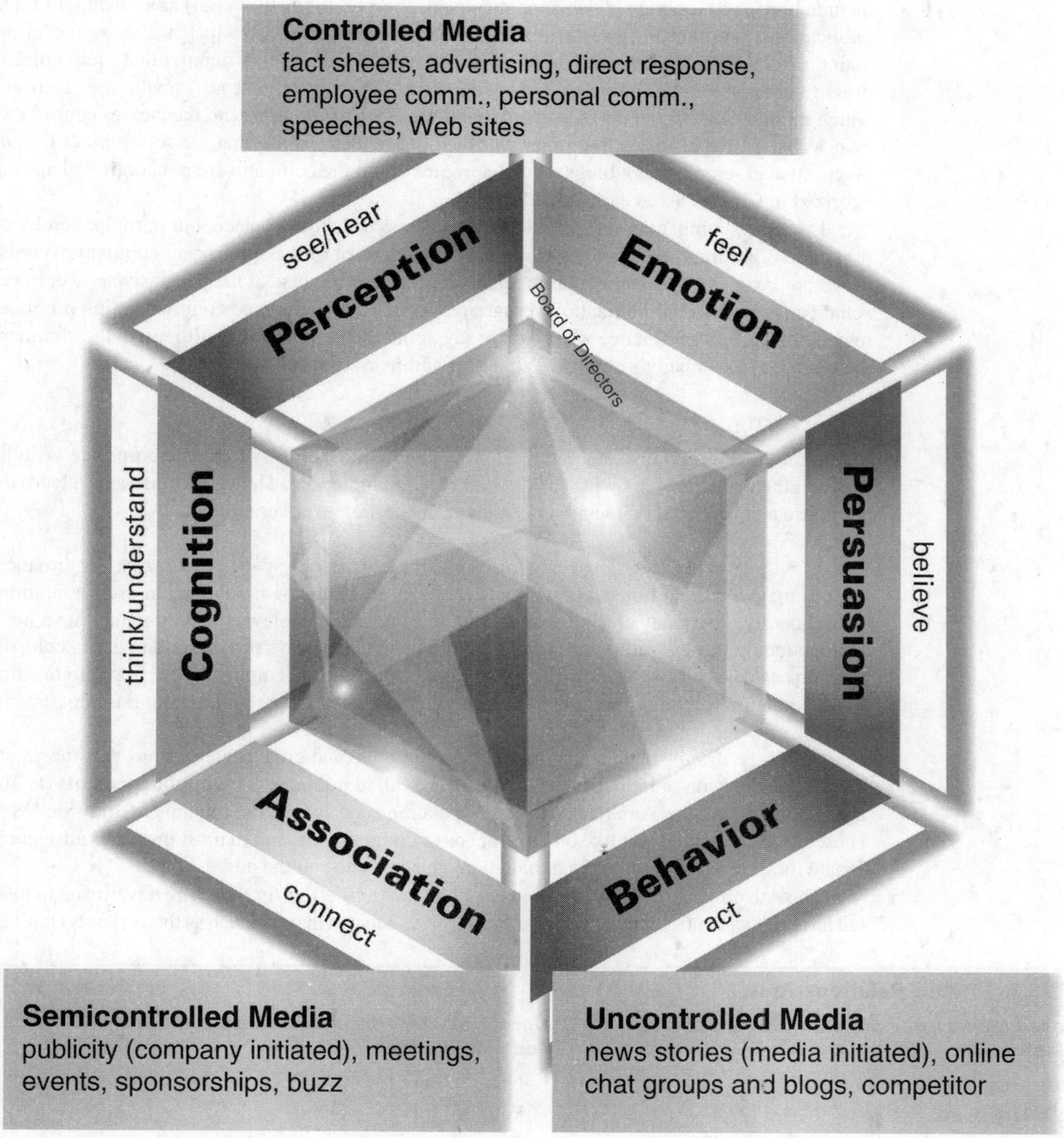

FIGURE 15.2
Communication Campaign Plan
This variation of the Facets of Effects Model shows that even in public relations, the media and messages must work together to deliver communications objectives.

reaching influencers (63 percent), educating consumers (61 percent), prompting trial use of products (28 percent), persuading skeptics (22 percent), and driving sales (22 percent).[23] They also indicated that the most important contribution to marketing programs is in providing media contacts (67 percent).

The same study suggested that public relations and advertising need to merge or at least find common ground as the media fragments and consumers gain more control of their time and media habits. Messages aimed at reaching mass audiences in the shifting media environment are less effective, and new opportunities are emerging for public relations, publicity, and product placements to be integral parts of integrated marketing communication programs. One way that advertising and public relations have worked together is in the Ad Council's work, such as the classic Smokey Bear campaign.

The public relations practitioner has many tools, which we can divide into two categories: controlled media and uncontrolled media. **Controlled media**, which we discussed in Chapter 13, include house ads, public service announcements, corporate (institutional) advertising, in-house publications, and visual presentations. The sponsoring organizations pay for these media and maintain total control over how and when the message is delivered. **Uncontrolled media** include press releases, press conferences, and media tours. The most recent new media are electronic, which might be categorized as **semicontrolled media**. Corporations and businesses control their own websites, for example, but other websites (particularly those that are set up by critics and disgruntled ex-employees), blogs, and chat rooms about the company are not controlled and categorized in Chapter 13 as earned media.

Likewise, companies set special events and sponsorships in place, but participation by the press and other important publics is not under the control of the sponsoring company. Word of mouth, or buzz, is important to public relations programs because of the persuasive power of personal conversation. Public relations programs, particularly employee communication programs, may be designed to influence what people say about the company, but ultimately the comments are outside the company's control. Table 15.1 summarizes these tools.

Advertising

Public relations programs sometimes employ advertising as a way to create corporate visibility or strengthen relationships with various stakeholder audiences. The primary uses of advertising are house ads, public service announcements, and corporate advertising.

House Ads An organization (or a medium, such as a newspaper, magazine, or broadcast station) may prepare a **house ad**, which is an ad for use in its own publication or programming. Consequently, no money changes hands. For instance, a local television station may run a house ad announcing its new fall programming within its evening news program; likewise, a company may run an ad advocating a point of view or promoting a special employee benefit program within its corporate magazine. These house ads are often managed by the public relations department.

Public Service Announcements The ads for charitable and civic organizations that run free of charge on television or radio or in print media are called **public service announcements** (PSAs). The United Way, the American Heart Association, and local arts councils all rely on PSAs. These ads are prepared just like other print ads or commercials, and in most instances ad agencies donate their expertise and media donate time and space to run the ads.

The Advertising Council represents a public relations effort for the entire advertising industry and has produced most of the PSAs you see on television and in print, such as the "Friends Don't Let

Table 15.1 Public Relations Tools

Controlled Media (company controls the use and placement)	*Uncontrolled Media (media controls the use and placement)*
• House ads	• News release (print, audio, video, e-mail, faxes)
• Public service ads	• Features (pitch letters)
• Corporate, institutional, advocacy advertising	• Fillers, historical pieces, profiles
• Publications: brochures, flyers, magazines, newsletters	• The press conference and media advisory (media kits, fact sheets, background info)
• Annual reports	• Media tours
• Speakers	• Bylined articles, op-ed pieces, letters to the editor
• Photographs	• Talk and interview shows
• Films, videos, CD-ROMs	• Public service announcements
• Displays, exhibits	
• Staged events	
• Books	
Semicontrolled Media (some aspects are controlled or initiated by the company, but other aspects aren't)	
• Electronic communication (websites, chat rooms)	
• Special events and sponsorships	
• Word of mouth (buzz)	
• Weblogs (blogs)	

Friends Drive Drunk" campaign, the "Keep America Beautiful" antilitter campaign, and the more recent "I Am an American" campaign that was developed following the tragic terrorist attacks of September 11, 2001. The classic United Negro College Fund campaign has become one of the best-recognized Advertising Council PSAs with its slogan, "A Mind Is a Terrible Thing to Waste" (see the "Classic" feature).

Getting donated time and space is not easy. The PSA directors at various media receive a barrage of public service campaigns every week on different issues, and they must choose which ones to run. There is no guarantee which markets will see the campaign elements, and there is no guarantee that the same people will see the print and television versions of a campaign. Some PSA campaigns do not get any airtime or print placements.

Professor Herb Rotfeld recognizes that many campaigns have produced effective PSAs to help address social ills in the "A Principled Practice" feature. Yet he questions whether these campaigns alone can solve the social problems they seek to address, especially considering their dependency on the generosity of media outlets to offer free time and space. PSAs can help make people aware of social problems, but they may not eliminate them.

UNCF
A mind is a terrible thing to waste®

Photo: Courtesy of UNCF

CLASSIC

PSAs for the United Negro College Fund have helped raise more than $2.2 billion to fund college educations for more than 350,000 minority students since 1972.

Corporate Advertising With **corporate advertising**, a company focuses on its **corporate image** or viewpoint. There is less emphasis on selling a particular product unless it is tied to a good cause. For that reason, the ad or other campaign materials may originate in the public relations department rather than the advertising department.

A PRINCIPLED PRACTICE

The Social Impact of Public Service Advertising

Herbert Jack Rotfeld, *Auburn University*

Government and public agencies concerned about date rape, drunk driving, road rage, unsafe sexual practices, underage cigarette smoking, illegal drug use, and even littering all expect advertising to reduce the incidence of these not-infrequent socially undesirable activities. Yet no one asks whether mass media advertising *can* persuade anyone to change their "problem" behaviors. The power of advertising is presumed, and people behind most public service advertising campaigns see advertising itself as the solution.

The Advertising Council, which is dedicated to using the great resources of the advertising industry to serve the public interest, is the largest producer of public service mass communication campaigns in the United States. Free public service work from anyone is admirable, and the Advertising Council's dedication to public service is a wonderful credit to business groups supporting it. But many Advertising Council campaigns finish their efforts with few people ever knowing they existed, running their entire span with few target consumers ever seeing the commercials. Since the Advertising Council and other groups depend on time or space donated by the media for public service announcements, they take the placements they can get for free. No one is in a position to make certain the free media placements reach the intended audience.

There are examples of successful communication efforts that are locally targeted and carefully planned and that appeal to the values of a closely defined audience. Over the long term, some campaigns can change the public agenda, increasing public awareness and changing general perceptions of issues previously ignored. But in most cases, advertising can't do anything to help solve the problem. Instead, for a variety of reasons, the people involved with public health issues acquire a misplaced trust in the power of advertising to change the world.

Advertising is not magic.

Maybe, sometimes, in some ways, it can do some good with some people, but that weak collection of "maybes" is not a valid basis for all the faith it gets from people wanting to serve social goals. And for the deep-seated problems behind many social ills, mass-media advertising is a very weak tool.

Yet despite these intrinsic limitations and inherent problems, many people feel that they are doing "something" by advertising. And generating conversation might be a step in helping the general public recognize the problem. But it would be misplaced trust in the power of mass communication to think that advertising alone is the solution.

Photo: © HDIP, Inc.

Demonstrating its corporate responsibility, Häagen-Dazs ice cream has donated more than $700,000 to support honeybee research since 2008.

An example of corporate advertising that is tied to a socially redeeming program is Target's goal to give $1 billion for education by the end of 2015. Recognizing that education is the top social concern of Target's "guests" and critical to economic and national security, the company gives more than $4 million every single week to communities it serves,[24] and education is the centerpiece of this funding.

Corporate advertising by Häagen-Dazs has resulted in an association between its name and solving the plight of the disappearing honeybee colonies.

Corporate identity advertising is another type of advertising that firms use to enhance or maintain their reputation among specific audiences or to establish a level of awareness of the company's name and the nature of its business. "The Johnson & Johnson Campaign for Nursing's Future" celebrates the profession and helps recruit and retain nurses in one of its initiatives. Companies that have changed their names, such as Accenture (formerly Andersen Consulting), have also used corporate identity advertising.

Sometimes companies deliver point-of-view messages called **advocacy advertising**. For example, the previously mentioned "Ecomagination" campaign of General Electric shows that the company wants to be a caretaker of the environment and is creating products in line with that philosophy. Another example comes from Procter & Gamble. Following the 1989 *Exxon Valdez* oil spill Procter & Gamble recognized that many animals are injured or killed by the 24 million gallons of oil that typically pollute North American waters each year. In response, it created a campaign for Dawn liquid dishwashing detergent. The soap, known to be tough on grease yet gentle, connects naturally with the advocacy effort to rescue birds and marine mammals harmed by oil spills. Dawn's "Everyday Wildlife Champions" campaign aims to inspire people to get involved.[25] Dawn urges consumers to go to www.dawnsaveswildlife.com to enter numbers printed on the back of bottles, which triggers a $1 donation from Procter & Gamble to wildlife groups. Consumers can also volunteer to help wildlife causes via Facebook.

Dawn's environmental cause-related campaign proved particularly timely in light of the massive BP oil spill in the Gulf of Mexico in 2010. Donating more than 12,000 bottles of Dawn to animal rescuers on the Gulf coast, Procter & Gamble enhanced its reputation and built goodwill based on its long-standing marketing relationship between wildlife rescue organizations and the brand.[26]

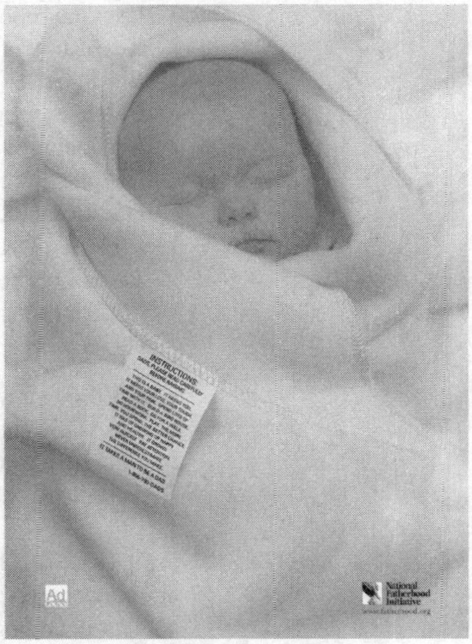

Photo: National Fatherhood Initiative

The Advertising Council has sponsored a number of public communication campaigns in support of good causes. The participating agencies donate their time and talent, and media donate the time and space to run the PSAs. This one is for new dads and encourages them to learn more about parenting.

Publicity

Moving away from controlled messages, consider the various tools and techniques used by media relations specialists to get publicity in the news media on behalf of a company or brand. Human footwear maker Teva created sandals for an Asian elephant with foot problems. The result was an article and photo that ran as a news items. Public relations expert Tom Harris calls this type of media coverage "an endorsement that money can't buy."[27]

Media relations is often seen as the most important core competency for public relations professionals. Media relations specialists know media that would be interested in stories about their companies. They also develop personal contacts with reporters and editors who write regularly on topics related to their organization's industry. In addition to personal contact, the primary tool used in media relations is the news release, along with press conferences and media tours.

News Releases The **news release** is the primary medium used to deliver public relations messages to the various external media. Although the company distributing the news release controls its original form and content, the media decide what to present and how to present it. What the public finally sees, then, is not necessarily what the originating company had in mind, so this form of publicity offers less control to the originating company.

The decision to use any part of a news release is based on an editor's judgment of its news value. **News value** is based on such considerations as

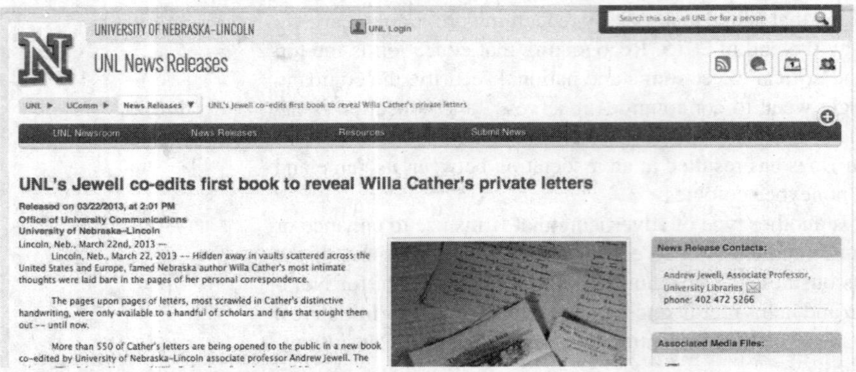

UNL's Jewell co-edits first book to reveal Willa Cather's private letters

Released on 03/22/2013, at 2:01 PM
Office of University Communications
University of Nebraska–Lincoln
Lincoln, Neb., March 22nd, 2013 —

Lincoln, Neb., March 22, 2013 -- Hidden away in vaults scattered across the United States and Europe, famed Nebraska author Willa Cather's most intimate thoughts were laid bare in the pages of her personal correspondence.

The pages upon pages of letters, most scrawled in Cather's distinctive handwriting, were only available to a handful of scholars and fans that sought them out -- until now.

More than 550 of Cather's letters are being opened to the public in a new book co-edited by University of Nebraska-Lincoln associate professor Andrew Jewell. The

News Release Contacts:
Andrew Jewell, Associate Professor, University Libraries
phone: 402 472 5266

Associated Media Files:

Photo: Courtesy of University of Nebraska - Lincoln

This piece from the University of Nebraska-Lincoln shows a typical news release format. It includes contact information at the top and a headline that summarizes the point of the news release.

timeliness (something just happened or is about to happen), proximity (a local angle), impact (importance or significance), or human interest.

News releases must be written differently for each medium, accommodating space and time limitations. Traditional journalism form is followed, which means the 5W format is standard—in other words, the release should lead with answers to questions of who, what, why, when, where, and how. The more carefully the news release is planned and written, the better the chance it has of being accepted and published as written. Note the tight and simple writing style in the news release from the University of Nebraska–Lincoln. News releases can be accompanied in the digital age with associated media files, such as short videos, to help communicate the news.

The news release can be delivered in a number of ways—in person, by local delivery service, by mail, by fax, or by e-mail. Sometimes a company is hired that specializes in distribution, such as the U.S. Newswire. Originally, these companies sent news releases by mail or delivery services, but today news releases are more likely to be distributed electronically through satellite and Web-based networks. PR Newswire, U.S. Newswire, and BusinessWire are services that provide targeted distribution to special-interest media outlets or handle mass distribution of news releases, photos, graphics, video, audio, and other materials. If your organization decides to use e-mail, here is a set of guidelines for delivery:[28]

- Use one reporter's name and address per "to" line.
- Keep subject line header simple.
- Boldface "FOR IMMEDIATE RELEASE" on the first line above the date.
- Catch attention with a good headline.
- Limit length (shorter than print's 500-word limit).
- Use the 5W format.
- Do not include attachments.
- Link to a URL where other background information and photos are posted.
- Remember readability and use short paragraphs, bullets, numbers, and lists to keep it scannable.
- Put contact information below the text.
- Close with conventional end signs such as "30" or "######."

Video news releases contain video footage for a television newscast. They are effective because they show target audiences the message in two different video environments: first as part of a news report and then reused later in an advertisement. Of course, there is no guarantee that such a release will be used.

Pitch Letters Ideas for **feature stories**, which are human interest stories rather than hard news announcements, have to be "sold" to editors. This is done using a **pitch letter** that outlines the subject in an engaging way and sells a story idea. Companies use this form to feature interesting research breakthroughs, employees, or corporate causes. Not only is the distribution of news releases moving online, but so are the letters pitching editors with story ideas.

Press Conferences A **press conference**—an event at which a company spokesperson makes a statement to media representatives—is one of the riskiest public relations activities because the media may not see the company's announcement as being real news. Companies often worry about whether the press will show up for a press conference. Will they ask the right questions, or will they ask questions the company cannot or does not want to answer?

To encourage reporters to cover press conferences, companies may issue a **media kit**, usually a folder that provides all important background information to members of the press, either before or when they arrive at the press conference. The risk in offering media kits (also called press kits) is that they give reporters all of the necessary information so that the press conference itself becomes unnecessary.

Media Tours A **media tour** is a press conference on wheels. The traveling spokesperson makes announcements and speeches, holds press conferences to explain a promotional effort, and offers interviews.

Publications

Organizations may provide employees and other publics with pamphlets, booklets, annual reports, books, bulletins, newsletters, inserts and enclosures, and position papers. The Securities and Exchange Commission requires that each publicly held company publish an **annual report**. A company's annual report is targeted to investors and may be the single most important document the company distributes. Millions of dollars are spent on the editing and design of annual reports. These reports are especially important to stockholders and potential investors.

Some companies publish material in print or online, often called **collateral material**, to support their marketing public relations efforts. Corporate publications, marketing, and sales promotion departments and their agencies also produce training materials and sales kits to support particular campaigns. Think about the high-quality brochures and booklets you can pick up at car dealerships when you go in to look at new cars. Another example, Owens Corning Fiberglass Insulation offers information on home insulation projects as an integral part of its promotion effort.

Zines provide another outlet for businesses. At the eZineArticles.com website, contributors write their own content and publish it online, making it available for others to publish on their own sites as well. The site doesn't like overtly promotional content, but a company can provide a service piece related to its business—any kind of "how-to" piece is welcome. For example, if you have a client that does faux painting, a general article on the art of faux painting and how to use it as a design element can also carry a short bio and link to your client's site.

Other Tools

In addition to advertising, publicity, and publications, public relations practitioners have various other types of materials and activities in their professional tool kits.

DVDs, CDs, Podcasts, Books, and Online Video DVDs and podcasts have become major public relations tools for many companies. Corporate books have also become popular with the advent of simplified electronic publication. Costing $1,000 to $2,000 per minute to make, videos are not inexpensive. However, they are an ideal tool for distributing in-depth information about a company or program.

Speakers and Photos Many companies have a **speakers' bureau** of articulate people who will talk about topics at the public's request. Organizations as varied as Apple Computer, Harvard University, and the Children's Hospital in Houston, Texas, all have speakers' bureaus that can arrange presentations to local groups and classes.

Photo: Courtesy of Karl Schroeder

Deloitte is a big international management consulting firm that created its own university to educate its staff about the company's complex products and services. At the entrance to this building is a giant wall of touch screens stitched together electronically to create a huge informational canvas. At this wall, staff members can learn about such things as current events (using the content stream), the firms' major players (using the family tree app), the key offices (using the globe app) as well as what staff are currently at Deloitte University (the content stream). The wall's background is dynamic and changes to reflect time of day, weather, or seasons. Schroeder says that as viewers interact with the screens, the wall paints a picture of an innovative, forward-thinking company.

SHOWCASE

Note: This interactive project was contributed by Karl Schroeder as a member of a team of programmers and designers at the Downstream design and technology company. Formerly a copywriter at Coates Kokes in Portland, Oregon, now works at Nike. A graduate of the University of Oregon advertising program, his work was nominated for inclusion in this book by Professor Charles Frazer.

Displays and Exhibits Displays and exhibits, along with special events and tours, may be important parts of both sales promotion and public relations programs. Displays include signage and booths, racks, and holders for promotional literature. Exhibits tend to be larger than displays; they may have moving parts, sound, or video and usually are staffed by a company representative. Booth exhibits are important at trade shows, where some companies may take orders for much of their annual sales.

Some brand communication tools, such as sales promotions, events, exhibits and displays, and brand clubs, are inherently more involving, particularly the ones that allow customers to have personal interaction with the brand. The Deloitte University "wall" is an example of a large interactive, digital touch screen that greets the firms' staff members who attend classes at the consulting firm's own university.

Special Events and Tours Some companies stage events to get maximum publicity and generate positive attitudes toward the sponsors by celebrating milestones, such as key anniversaries and introductions of new products. A classic special event is the annual Macy's Thanksgiving Day parade, a tradition started in 1924. The event attracts more than 3.5 million people to watch it in New York City and more than 50 million viewers on television.[29] Corporate sponsorship of various sporting events like golf tournaments and car races has evolved into a favorite public relations tactic.

Thomas Harris, cofounder of Golin/Harris Communications, considers that the late Steve Jobs was one of the world's greatest public relations people. When Jobs took the stage to announce the Apple iPhone, the product launch generated an estimated $400 million in free publicity. According to Harris, by the time the iPhone went on sale six months later, it had already been the subject of 11,000 print articles and had generated 69 million hits on Google for what bloggers were calling the "Jesus phone." Jobs repeated the feat with the announcement of Apple's iPad and iPhone releases, generating lots of buzz for its products. Whether Jobs's successors can match his ability to sell remains to be seen.

Events can also be important for internal communication. Learning objectives and employee buy-in for a new campaign are often accomplished through meetings, seminars, and workshops sponsored by a company, typically in conjunction with training materials and other publications. To facilitate internal marketing, **town hall forums** are sometimes used. Forums provide management with an opportunity to make a presentation on some major project, initiative, or issue and invite employees to discuss it.

In addition to media tours, tours of all kinds are used in public relations programs, such as plant tours and trips by delegates and representatives. You are probably familiar with one form—the campus tour used by colleges in recruiting new students. Realizing the importance of these events, some colleges are hiring consulting companies to train the volunteer guides in appearance, presentation, and more relaxed "walks" designed to give a better sense of what makes a school distinctive.

Photo: Paul Sakuma\ APWide World Photos

In one of his classic performances, the late Steve Jobs unveils the iPad, generating lots of buzz for the new Apple iPad.

Online Communication

Public relations practitioner and author Fraser Seitel says, "While it is irrefutable that the Internet and social media have changed communication forever with newfound immediacy and pervasiveness, it isn't the case that the Internet has replaced human relationships as the essence of societal communications. Nor have the new techniques replaced human relationships as the essence of the practice of public relations."[30] E-mail, **intranets** (which connect people within an organization), **extranets** (which connect people in one business with its business partners), Internet advertising and promotions, and websites and social media, such as blogs, Facebook, and Twitter, have opened up avenues for public relations activities.

Jason Cormier, cofounder of social media agency Room 214, points out in the "A Matter of Practice" feature that social media can be a useful tool in public relations because it stimulates word of mouth. We know from in Chapters 4 and 13 that word of mouth is one of the most powerful communication tools available to marketing communicators and particularly to public relations campaigns.

External Communication Corporate websites have become an important part of corporate communication, which allow for communication directly between organizations and audiences. These sites can present information about the company and open up avenues of interactivity for stakeholders to contact the company and receive responses. Website newsrooms distribute a company's press releases to the media and other interested stakeholders.

A Matter of Practice

Engaging Word of Mouth through Online Influencers

Jason Cormier, *Cofounder and Managing Partner, Room214.com*

A key to understanding social media is found in one of the oldest yet most effective forms of marketing, word of mouth. We exercise word-of-mouth marketing every time we refer a friend, family member, or coworker to something we like (or dislike). This could be a restaurant, movie, product, service, or brand.

For most of history, word-of-mouth marketing has been limited in terms of how it is seeded and spread. Social media enables marketers to guide and prioritize who gets the word first, providing a powerful channel by which to help others spread information about something or someone.

How? One way is through a host of self-publishing tools that have enabled a new wave of user-generated content. For marketers, that means more data that can be applied to research for online advertising, as well as to the emerging field of influencer marketing. Identifying and persuading influencers has been a longtime public relations objective.

Social media agencies, such as Room 214, typically access a range of online monitoring and Web-based business intelligence tools for gaining new insights about online conversations. From blog and Twitter posts to online forums and mainstream media sites, marketers can gauge the volume of conversation around any given topic they choose. For example, language and semantic clustering tools are used to automate the identification of key themes and emerging topics within these online conversations.

Other features include the ability to identify authoritative sources (called **key influencers** or mavens) and conduct sentiment analysis to determine if the tone within conversations is positive, negative, or neutral.

In addition to paid advertising within social networks, the realm of *online influencer*, or **maven marketing**, has quickly emerged. A popular form of this is blogger outreach, involving a process by which influential bloggers are contacted in the hope that they will write about the topic being pitched. For example, online savings program SmartyPig.com implemented a highly effective blogger outreach campaign, reaching out to influential bloggers in the financial community to solicit feedback about a product launch while also making them aware of something new and relevant to their audience. Unlike traditional public relations, the "pitch" to a blogger must take on an entirely different tone to be effective. If the communication is not relevant and authentic to the blogger's audience and to the blogger, respectively, the response will likely be nonexistent or negative.

In SmartyPig's case, a great deal of product loyalty and online visibility was earned from the very start of their business. Their success in this area has led to additional entry points into mainstream media, including coverage in the *Wall Street Journal* and other major industry trade publications. They have also been able to leverage online relationships to help build leadership and participation within social networks. (They were the first in the banking industry to use Facebook Connect technology.)

Bloggers are but one subset of online influencers. While the segmentation, outreach, and tracking of influencers support a broad range of social media and word-of-mouth tactics, the most important thing to stay grounded in is that social media is only a component (not a replacement for of an overall marketing mix—one that is most effective when public relations and advertising are smartly integrated.

In addition to websites, the Internet has become the favorite tool of media relations professionals as well as journalists. Furthermore, most press releases are now distributed online by sending them either directly to reporters or to such services as PR Newswire, which then handles mass distribution online to appropriate publications.

Internal Communication E-mail is a great way for people at separate work sites to communicate. You can get a fast reply if people on the other end are checking their mail regularly. It is also an inexpensive form of internal communication. Internal company e-mail may have its public relations downside, however: It can be used in court. Some of the most damaging evidence the federal government presented against Microsoft in its antitrust suit in 1998 came from e-mail messages exchanged within the company.

Internal company networks have great benefits. Intranets and corporate portals (an extensive collection of databases and links that are important to people working in a company) encourage communication among employees in general and permit them to share data, such as customer records and client information. Some companies urge employees to set up personal home pages as part of the company portal, which allows them to customize the material they receive and set up their own links to crucial corporate information, such as competitor news, product information, and case histories.

Web Challenges The Internet presents at least as many challenges to public relations professionals as it does opportunities. Search engine optimization is a major issue for online experts who continually try to improve the process of key word searching that leads interested Web users to their sites.[31]

Although the Internet makes it possible to present the company's image and story without going through the editing of a gatekeeper, it is much harder to control what is said about the company on the Internet. According to Parry Aftab, a lawyer specializing in computer-related issues, "It used to be that you could control the information because you'd have one spokesman who represented the company. Now where you have thousands of employees who have access to an e-mail site, you have thousands of spokesmen."[32] All employees have "an inside view" of their company, whether sanctioned by the public relations department or not.

Gossip and rumors can spread around the world within hours. Angry customers and disgruntled former employees know this and have used the Internet to voice their complaints. A number of these people have set up websites, such as the Official Internet AntiNike website www.alt.destroy.microsft, I Hate McDonald's, Toys R Us Sucks, GTE Sucks, Why America Online Sucks, Packard Bell Is Evil, and BallySucks. As a defense against this negative press, some companies are registering domain names that might cause them trouble. For example, JP Morgan Chase bank owns IHateChase.com, ChaseStinks.com, and ChaseSucks.com but not Chasebanksucks.com, which is an active website critical of the company.

When Motrin posted an online ad on a Saturday about mothers who carried their babies in slings suggesting that this fashion caused back pain, outraged mommy bloggers and tweeters wasted no time calling for boycotts. Makers of Motrin responded by the end of the weekend with an apology and removed the ad.[33]

Some companies monitor the Internet to see what is being said about them so they can respond to protect their reputations. Thousands of companies have hired eWatch, a firm that provides Web monitoring services, to collect such information.

How should organizations respond to negative information on the Internet or social media? Entrepreneur and venture capitalist Mark Suster warned about the dangers of overreacting. His advice: If you make a major mistake, own it early. If negative information is posted and you believe your company is in the right, see if the story "gets much reverberation." If it's not picked up repeatedly in the media, social or otherwise, resist the temptation to respond because the response itself might make people aware of the issue unnecessarily.[34]

Looking Ahead

This is the first in a set of chapters that focuses on specific marketing communication areas. In this chapter, we reviewed the practice of public relations as well as its specialty areas, planning practices, and tools. As you've seen throughout this chapter, businesses and organizations have many ways to reach their publics and build positive images and reputations for their brands. It's critical to find a way to break through the media clutter for public relations as well as advertising messages. The next chapter will look at direct-response practices.

It's a Wrap

Häagen-Dazs loves Honey Bees™

Just Bee-Cause

As noted at the beginning of this chapter, the crisis of the honeybees is bigger than ice cream—it affects a significant part of the food chain. The work Häagen-Dazs has done to illuminate the problem and work toward a solution demonstrates that profits are only one measure of a brand's success. Acting socially responsible is part of the formula for good business.

Christine Chen, deputy director of communication strategy at Goodby, Silverstein & Partners, said the campaign was successful in part because the honeybee issue was a natural fit with Häagen-Dazs.

Although the bee crisis continues, more resources are focused on solving the mystery. Häagen-Dazs, along with other bee-involved brands, such as Burt's Bees, were invited to testify before the House Agricultural Subcommittee, and they successfully convinced congressional members to allocate funding for the CCD issue.

The investment in the problem paid good dividends for the brand as well. The honeybee buzz had a positive impact on sales. Unaided brand awareness of Häagen-Dazs rose from 29 to 36 percent. It created lots of publicity. It generated 277 million impressions, which is the number of people who may have seen something in the media about the crisis, through more than 1,000 different news placements. The campaign achieved 125 million impressions—the yearlong goal—during the campaign's first week. The viral "Bee Dance" video on YouTube received more than a million hits in the first month, proving, once again, the power of the Internet.

"Häagen-Dazs Loves Honey Bees" won a swarm of awards for this campaign, including a PRSA Silver Anvil, a Gold Effie, a Festival of Media Media Responsibility Award, a Cannes Lions PR Lion, a PRWeek Award for Cause-Related Campaign of the Year, and a Silver SABRE (Superior Achievement in Branding and Reputation) Award.

Lesson learned: Acting socially responsibility is good business.

Photo: © HDIP, Inc.

Key Points Summary

1. **What is public relations?** Public relations is a management function that communicates to and with various publics to manage an organization's brand image and reputation. Public relations professionals perform a wide range of functions that help an organization connect with the people it touches. Those functions include internal relations, publicity, advertising, press agentry, public affairs, lobbying, issues management, investor relations, and development.
2. **What are the different types of public relations programs?** In addition to the key areas of government, media, employee, and investor relations, public relations programs also include corporate relations and reputation management, crisis management, marketing public relations, and public communication campaigns.
3. **What key decisions do public relations practitioners make when they create plans?** Planning for a public relations campaign begins with a SWOT, or situation analysis, that is used as background to identify the target audience and develop objectives and strategies. Research is needed when planning a public relations program and evaluating its effectiveness.
4. **What are the most common types of public relations tools?** Uncontrolled media tools include the news story that results from a news release or news conference. Controlled media are tools that the company uses to originate and control content. Some examples of these are house ads, corporate advertising, and public service ads. Semi-controlled tools are controlled in that the company is able to initiate use of the tool but uncontrolled in that content is

contributed by others. A few examples include electronic communication (websites and chat rooms), word of mouth (buzz), and social media, such as blogs, Facebook, and Twitter.

5. **Why is measuring the results of public relations efforts important, and how should that be done?** The evaluation effort is made to determine how well a public relations program meets its objectives. Public relations evaluation usually focuses on outputs and outcomes and may include relationship management and excellence. The impact of a public relations program is difficult to measure, and evaluation standards are evolving with the development and use of digital media.

Key Terms

active publics, p. 482
advocacy advertising, p. 489
annual report, p. 491
aware publics, p. 482
benchmarking, p. 481
cause marketing, p. 479
change agent, p. 483
collateral material, p. 491
communication audit, p. 481
controlled media, p. 485
corporate advertising, p. 487
corporate identity advertising, p. 489
corporate image, p. 487
corporate relations, p. 479
corporate social responsibility, p. 479
crisis management, p. 480
employee relations, p. 478
extranets, p. 492
feature stories, p. 490
financial relations, p. 479
fund-raising (or development), p. 479
gap analysis, p. 481
gatekeepers, p. 476
goodwill, p. 475
house ad, p. 486
implied third-party endorsement, p. 477
internal marketing, p. 478
intranets, p. 492
issue management, p. 479
key influencers, p. 493
latent publics, p. 481
lobbying, p. 479
marketing public relations, p. 480
maven marketing, p. 493
media kit, p. 490
media relations, p. 478
media tour, p. 491
news release, p. 489
news value, p. 489
opinion leaders, p. 475
pitch letter, p. 490
press conference, p. 490
public affairs, p. 479
public communication campaigns, p. 480
public opinion, p. 475
public relations, p. 474
public service announcements, p. 486
publicity, p. 476
publics, p. 474
relationship marketing, p. 477
reputation management, p. 479
semicontrolled media, p. 486
speakers' bureau, p. 491
stakeholders, p. 474
strategic philanthropy, p. 479
town hall forums, p. 492
uncontrolled media, p. 486
video news releases, p. 490

Review Questions

15-4. What is meant by public relations, and how is it useful for organizations?

✪15-5. Compare and contrast the practice of advertising and the practice of public relations.

✪15-6. In analyzing public relations tools, compare the use of controlled and uncontrolled media. Explain the difference between the two categories.

15-7. Explain the differences between advertising and public relations.

15-8. List the essential skills that PR managers should posses.

Discussion Questions

15-9. What is the difference between corporate communications and public relations? How are they connected?

15-10. In October 2012, Felix Baumgartner, sponsored by Red Bull, leapt from the edge of space. It wasn't just Felix who broke the record for the highest free fall, but Red Bull made the jump too.

After Felix had landed successfully, Red Bull provided the facts on social media channels, but we didn't see any self-congratulatory posts or any brand placements or overt messages where Felix landed.

a. Explain how this jump was a successful public relations stunt to attract a crowd and draw attention to the brand.

b. Analyze the reasons behind the success of this PR campaign as the ultimate publicity stunt in the communication industry.

Take-Home Projects

15-11. ***Portfolio Project:*** Identify a local organization that might benefit from a public relations plan. Study the organization's situation, identify a problem that can be addressed with public relations, and outline a plan to help the organization. Prepare your proposal in a three-page (maximum) paper.

15-12. ***Mini-Case Analysis:*** Study Häagen-Dazs's efforts to solve the problem of the disappearing honeybee colonies on its website. Look at the corporate social responsibility program on Ben & Jerry's website. Compare and contrast their efforts to be good corporate citizens.

TRACE North America Case

Multicultural Public Relations

Read the TRACE case in the Appendix before coming to class.

15-13. Reviewing the public relation tools in this chapter, identify at least two tools you could use effectively on a national basis to increase the impact of the "Hard to Explain, Easy to Experience" campaign.

CHAPTER

16 Direct Response

Photo: © 2007 GEICO. All rights reserved. Used with permission. Courtesy of The Martin Agency

It's a Winner	**Campaign:**	**Organization:**	**Agency:**	**Awards:**
	"The Gecko"	*Geico*	*The Martin Agency, Richmond, Virginia*	*DMA Echo, Silver Addys*

CHAPTER KEY POINTS

1. How does the direct-response marketing process work and who are the key p ayers?
2. What are the primary tools and media available to direct-response programs?
3. How are databases used in direct marketing?
4. What are the trends and challenges facing direct-response marketing?

The Gecko and His Pals Go Direct for Geico

What would it take to motivate you to buy car insurance from the Government Employees Insurance Company when so many companies aggressively vie for your dollar? The company's not-so-catchy-sounding name alone probably won't do it.

This case study demonstrates how direct marketing can successfully employ spokes-creatures to replace a sales force. It's so successful that Government Employees Insurance Company (aka Geico), a subsidiary of Warren Buffett's Berkshire Hathaway corporation, is the leading direct-response auto insurer in a category dominated by major brands, such as Allstate and State Farm

First, Geico identified that its biggest marketing challenge is to generate inquiries for rate quotes and to motivate people to call or go online to find out how they can save money, which is reflected in its long-standing brand promise, "15 minutes could save you 15 percent or more on car insurance."

Then it needed get everyone's attention and convince them to buy Geico. And this feat was miraculously accomplished by a small, green lizard; a caveman; and some of their outlandish friends.

Realizing that nearly everyone needs car insurance, Geico created some memorable spokes-creatures, starting with its now famous Gecko, who evolved from his humble beginnings to sell a heck of a lot of car insurance, and in the process became such an endearing mascot that it was elected to favorite advertising icon status by half a million people.

The Gecko was hatched from an idea in 1999 as ad honchos at The Martin Agency labored over what to do with an account they had for Geico. One member of the creative team noted that customers often mispronounced "Geico" as "Gecko," and someone drew a doodle of the little guy.

The Gecko tells fundamental truths about the human condition in goofy ways. The oddball humor caught on with the audience, although Ted Ward, vice president and chief marketing officer for marketing at Geico, admits he didn't immediately fall in love with the little guy. Ward said, "I quickly became much more fond of him as we sold more policies. I'm a big fan of anything that makes our phone ring or website click. He really has helped us brandwise."

Ted Ward described the business: "We have essentially a direct-to-consumer business model. We try to strip out costs to deliver the lowest price—which includes having very few agents in a process by having a superior technology model, which back in the '70s was direct mail; in the '80s and '90s, a telephone; and in the last 10 years, the online delivery of rates."

It's not just Geico's endearing icon that makes the campaign work. Geico uses the Gecko strategically to accomplish the work that its rival auto insurers do by hiring an army of sales middlemen.

You may have noticed that Geico doesn't just stick with the Gecko in all of its commercials. Geico has a number of other campaigns promoting its insurance running concurrently. The reason has much to do with the size of the market, which includes just about anyone who drives a car. Realizing that one creative approach will not appeal to everyone, Geico uses a diverse approach to reach a wide audience.

That means the Gecko appeals to some, while the indignant Cavemen capture others' attention, and customer testimonials with celebrities like Little Richard reach even others. Another twist is a campaign dubbed "Rhetorical Questions" that doesn't feature any of the company's mascots. Instead, commercials ask rhetorical questions, such as "Did *The Waltons* take way too long to say goodnight?" More recently Caleb the Camel has become a viral hit for Geico.

The concept is simple: different strokes for different folks. The different creative approaches are Geico-ized by using a common humorous tone.

If it's true that imitation is the sincerest form of flattery, you can see the effect Geico's advertising has had on the industry. State Farm, Allstate, and Progressive have followed Geico's strategy, adding their own humor, high action, and other attention-getting techniques to make you remember their brand when it comes time to buy auto insurance.

Just how successful are the Gecko and his pals' efforts to sell insurance? Turn to the "It's a Wrap": feature at the end of the chapter to find out.

Sources: Geico.com; Stuart Elliott, "Choosing to Break Up Monotony with Variety," March 15, 2012, www.nytimes.com; Stuart Elliott, "Geico Uses Many Campaigns to Stand Out in a Crowd, July 7, 2011, www.nytimes.com; Gary Strauss, "Except for Discounteres, Insurers' Funny Ads Not Paying Off," July 26, 2012, www.usatoday.com; Theresa Howard, "Gecko Scores Well in *USA Today* Ad Track," *USA Today*, July 16, 2006; Suzanne Vranica, "Geico's Gecko Shook Up Insurance Ads," *Wall Street Journal*, January 2, 2007, B1; Stuart Elliott, "Geico's Lizard Offers a New Message of Reassurance," *New York Times*, February 19, 2009; Mya Frazier, "Geico Ad Chief Builds Insurer into Master Marketer," June 19, 2006, www.adage.com; Elena Malykhina, "Geico Answers Its Own Questions," December 28, 2009, www.adweek.com; Leslie Scism and Erik Holm, "Geico Spends Nearly $1 Billion on Ads as Car Insurers Battle," *Wall Street Journal*, June 25, 2012.

Marketers use direct marketing in every consumer and business-to-business (B2B) category. IBM, Xerox, and other manufacturers selling office products use direct-response brand communication, as do almost all banks and insurance companies. Airlines, hotels, and cruise lines use it. Packaged-goods marketers such as General Foods, Colgate, and Bristol Myers; household product marketers such as Black and Decker; and automotive companies use it. Direct marketing shows up in membership drives, fund-raising, and solicitation for donations by nonprofit organizations such as the Sierra Club and Audubon Society and by political associations, so it is also used by other marcom tools, such as public relations.

In this chapter, we will discuss the practice and process of direct-response brand communication, the key players, the tools and media of direct response, and the principles of integrating direct marketing into the total brand communication effort.

What Is Direct-Response Brand Communication?

As the Internet and mobile communication devices have become more pervasive and sophisticated, marketers are shifting more of their marcom budgets into some form of **direct-response brand communication** (DBC). Because this type of messaging is specifically designed to motivate an immediate response, it is sometimes also called direct-response marketing. And because DBC is designed to generate immediate responses, this means it is also easy to tell quickly if the messages are meeting their objectives. In other words, unlike mass-media advertising and public relations, the effects of DBC are more immediate and more easily measured.

The Direct Marketing Association is the professional association for this type of brand communication. We'll define **direct-response marketing** as a multichannel system of marketing that uses a variety of media to connect sellers and customers who deal with each other directly rather than through an intermediary, such as a wholesaler or retailer.

There are two pieces to the direct-marketing business: First, direct marketing relies on communication that is sent in some form directly to the consumer, and, second, the response (sales, sign-up, or request for information) comes directly back to the source.

As noted in Figure 16.1, direct marketing includes a strong focus on market research to guide strategy and database development to better target customers and prospects and invite them to interact with a company. Using an interactive communication model, the contact is designed to elicit an immediate response, usually a sale, as well as invite customers to contact a company. It also helps marcom planners listen to what their customers are saying as they respond.

The most important function of direct marketing is that it opens up the door for interactivity—and why is that important? In the Part 5 opener, Duncan said that the best practices of IMC engage stakeholders in meaningful and often interactive brand experiences. Interactivity—two-way communication—is considered to be the heart of DBC and drives its ability to create engaging, relation-building contacts. If marketing is a conversation with consumers about a brand, then one of the most intimate marcom tools in the toolkit is DBC.

Principle
Direct marketing may have higher costs per impression than mass media, but it is less expensive in the long run because its messages are tightly targeted to reach prime prospects.

Some marketers see direct response as more limiting than brand or image advertising because it doesn't reach as many people or, if it does, the traditional cost of reaching each individual is higher per impression. Proponents justify the higher costs by noting that the objective is action rather than recall or attitude change and action is the most desired, if not the hardest, impact to achieve. Today the higher cost argument is weak. This is because the Internet and mobile media dramatically reduce the cost of message delivery—the media cost (although there may still be a cost for producing these messages).

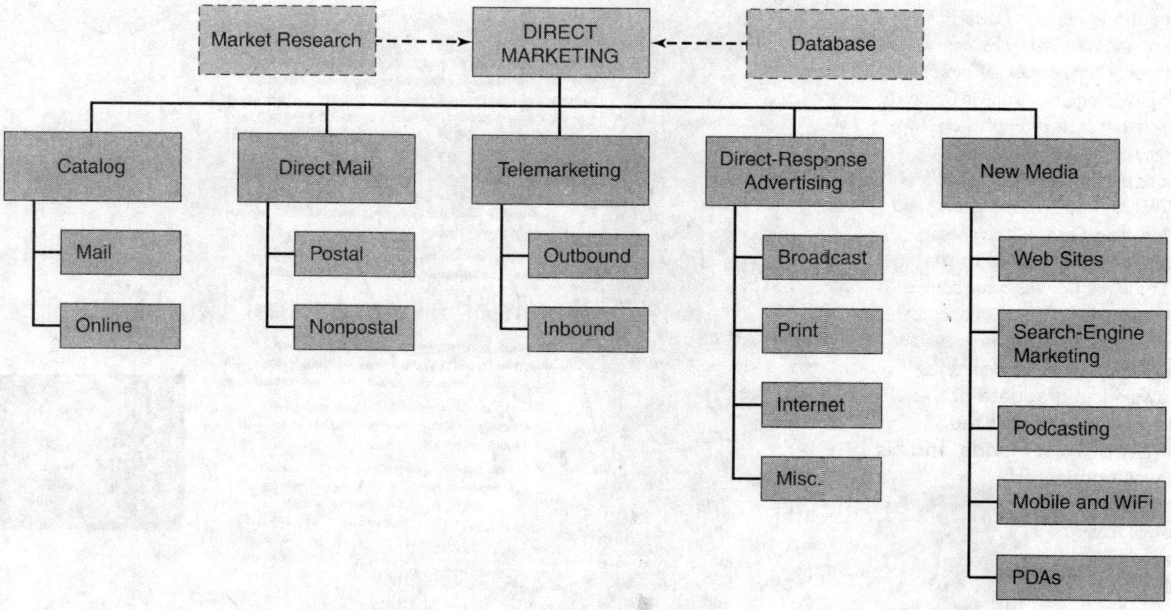

FIGURE 16.1
The Direct-Marketing Industry
The direct-marketing industry begins with research and database development. Its main tools are catalogs, direct mail, telemarketing, direct-response advertising, the Internet, and other new media.

Who Are the Key Players?

The four main players in direct-response marketing communication are (1) marketers who use direct response to sell products or services; (2) agencies that specialize in direct-response communication; (3) phone, mail, or Internet media that deliver messages; and (4) consumers who are the recipients of the information and sometimes initiators of the contact.

Marketers Traditionally, the types of companies that have made the greatest use of direct marketing have been book and record clubs, publishers, insurance companies, sellers of collectibles, gardening firms, and e-marketers, such as Amazon.com. Even computer companies, such as Dell, have built their business platform on marketing computers directly to consumers rather than through dealers.

This is also true for Geico. And now Google is designing a distribution system for its Android mobile operating system that gives multiple mobile-device makers access to early release versions of Android. Then Google will shift from working with only one hardware maker at a time to multiple Android-powered devices that Google can sell directly to consumers.[1]

Why don't all companies sell directly? For one thing, their retailers might retaliate if a manufacturer started experimenting with direct sales. Furthermore, it takes a lot of effort and infrastructure to set up a direct-marketing business. Rather than an army of sales reps, direct-marketing companies employ an army of people in fulfillment who take the order, match the product to customer specifications, handle the money, and arrange for shipping. And finally some consumers just enjoy going shopping—trying on clothes and test driving cars just aren't the same in digital communication.

Direct marketing can contribute to the brand impression. If the contact is irritating or intrusive, the message response may be negative. It if the messages are well done and targeted to appropriate audiences, then they may be appreciated, particularly if the recipient has opted in and is willing to be contacted. Skilled direct marketers, supported by research findings, have discovered that the appearance of a direct-response message—the character and personality communicated by the graphics—can enhance or destroy not only the brand image but also the credibility of the product information. The Crane & Company "Banknote" brochure is an example of the power of good design to enhance corporate image, even in B2B marketing.

SHOWCASE

This beautifully designed B2B brochure was created by Peter Stasiowski when he was art director at Gargan Communications in Dalton, Massachusetts. It promotes the durability of Crane & Company's banknote paper. You're looking at the cover (which wraps front to back) and an inside page. Crane is the primary provider of banknote paper to the U.S. Mint. The impact of the piece comes from the unity of creative concept, the product itself, the selling premise, and the well-designed visual elements.

Stasiowski is a graduate of the advertising program at the University of West Florida, and his work was nominated for inclusion in this book by Professor Tom Groth.

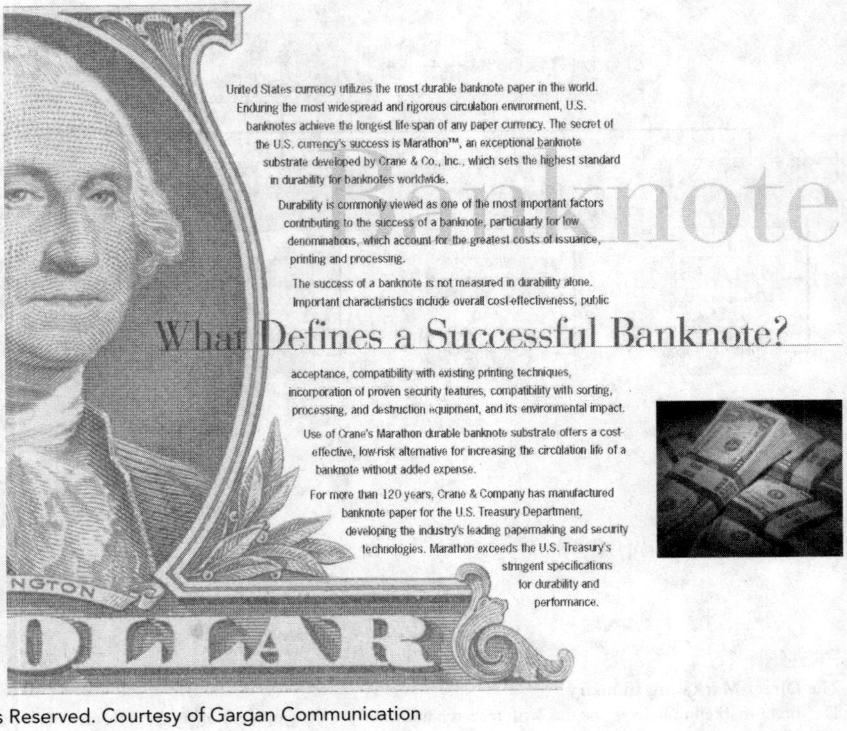

Photo: © 2004 Crane & Co., Inc. All Rights Reserved. Courtesy of Gargan Communication

Agencies and Media Companies The four types of firms in direct-response advertising include advertising agencies, independent direct-marketing agencies, service firms, and fulfillment houses:

- ***Advertising Agencies*** Most major agencies whose main business is mass-media advertising either have a department that specializes in direct response or own a separate direct-response company. Even if there isn't a special division or department, the staff of the agency may still be involved in producing direct-marketing pieces.
- ***Direct-Marketing Agencies*** Independent direct-marketing agencies create the DBC messages, arrange for their delivery to a target audience, and evaluate the results.
- ***Service Firms*** Service firms specialize in supplying printing, mailing, list brokering, and data management.
- ***Fulfillment Houses*** This business is responsible for making sure consumers receive whatever they request in a timely manner, be it a catalog, additional information, or the product itself.

In terms of media, there are also thousands of telemarketing and Web marketing firms that handle contact with consumers, as well as a variety of other more traditional media companies. One of the most active direct-mail media organizations, for example, is the U.S. Postal Service. We'll discuss these tools later in the section on DBC media.

Customers and Prospects Although some people might dislike the intrusiveness of direct response, many appreciate the convenience. It is a method of purchasing goods in a society that is finding itself with more disposable income but with less time to spend it. A new generation of consumers armed with push-button phones and a billfold full of credit cards likes to shop from home. This push-button shopper is joined by an even larger group of mouse-clicking shoppers. Although there is some risk in ordering a product you can't see, touch, feel, or try out, more and more consumers are confident and willing to take a chance buying online. To help reduce risk, many customers check out brands and goods in regular retail stores, then buy online. Also, numerous websites have been created that publish consumer reviews of online companies.

What Is Included in the DBC Process?

As outlined in Figure 16.2, there are five basic steps in traditional direct marketing: (1) the establishment of objectives and strategic decisions (research helps marketers target, segment, prospect, and set objectives); (2) the communication of an offer (the message) by the seller through the appropriate medium; (3) response, or customer orders; (4) fulfillment, or filling orders and handling exchanges and returns; and (5) relationship building through maintenance of the company's database and customer service.

Objectives and Strategies The common thread that runs through all types of direct response is that of action. Syracuse University Professor John Philip Jones points to direct advertising as being more effective than general advertising and says advertisers have a lot to learn from direct marketers.[2]

DBC planning begins by delineating the specific objectives. Direct marketing can be used to (1) provide in-depth product information, (2) drive traffic to a store or website, (3) develop leads for or follow-up sales contacts or other direct-response efforts (**lead generation**, also called **prospecting**), (4) drive a response, (5) retain or strengthen customer relationships, and (6) test offers to predict their effectiveness.

The most typical DBC objective is to create sales (or some other action) by convincing customers to order products, make payments, or take action, such as visiting a dealer, returning a response card, or visiting a website. **Conversion rates** are the percentage of contacts who actually take action, and this is the most important metric used in evaluating DBC programs. Relationship building is also important because direct marketers seldom make a profit on the first sale to a new customer; profit comes from subsequent sales.

Principle
Relationship building is critical because direct marketers seldom make a profit on the first sales to a new customer; profit comes from subsequent sales.

Nonprofits also are big users of direct-response marketing practices, using them to generate donations, memberships, and volunteers. UNICEF, for example, used a creative mailer for its child-soldier campaign. The challenge was to communicate the idea that Africa has the world's highest

FIGURE 16.2
The Direct-Response Process
The direct marketer's challenge is to manage the five steps in the DBC process not only so their messages generate purchases but also so they build a long-term relationship with consumers.

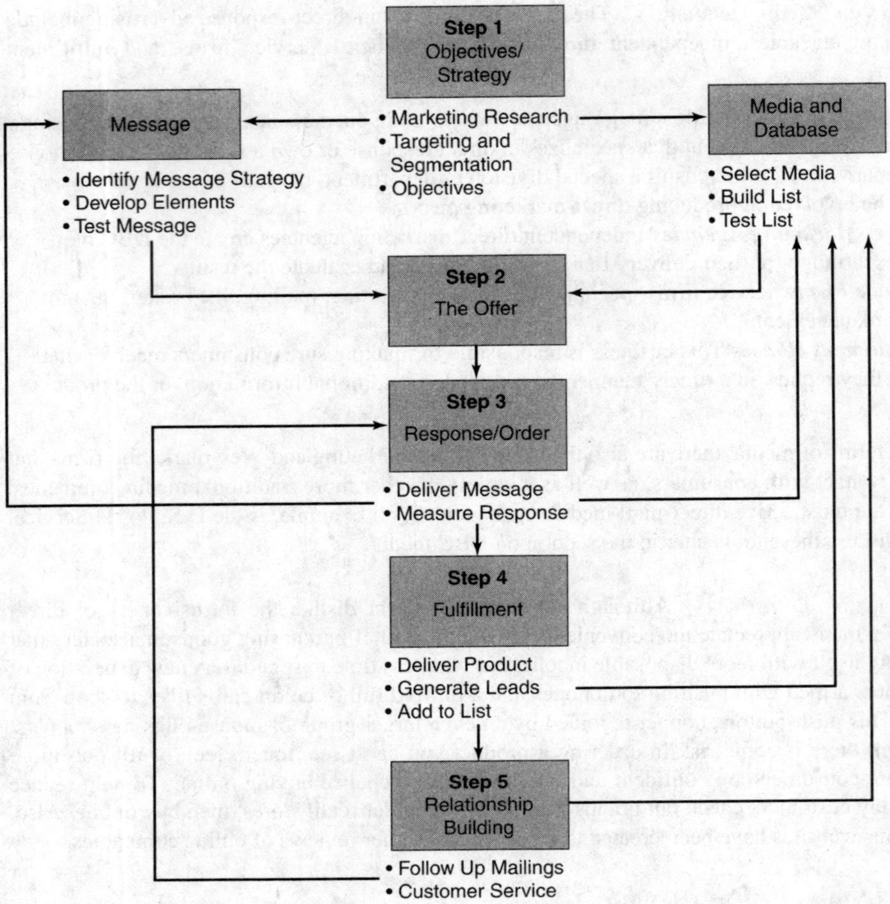

number of child soldiers fighting in wars they don't believe in for causes they don't understand. UNICEF's goal is to save these kids from war and give them an opportunity to rejoin society. The Y&R Johannesburg agency in South Africa took on this challenge and developed a direct-response program that was sent to UNICEF supporter lists as well as potential corporate sponsors.

Direct marketers make these basic objectives more specific by spelling out such factors as timing, amount of increase, and the acquisition of information about consumers' specific behavior, such as where they see the product. For example, a local Ford dealership might expect its direct-marketing program to increase showroom traffic by 60 percent in the next 90 days, but one objective also might be to test the effectiveness of a booth at a local shopping center.

Targeting One of the most important decisions made in direct marketing is selecting those who are to receive the offer. As we have said, for those DBC messages conveyed via catalog, phone calls, and mail, the cost per thousand (CPM) is high. Therefore, if the DBC effort is to have a positive return on investment, it is critical that the target prospects have a higher-than-average interest in the brand offer.

Principle
The best customer prospects of direct marketers are current customers.

The best customer prospects of direct marketers are current customers. If someone has bought from a company several times before, they are much more likely to buy again from that company than someone who has never bought from that company. In other words, current customers have already been sold on the brand, so it is much easier (i.e., less costly) to motivate them to buy again.

Principle
The more *recently* customers have bought from a company, the more *frequently* they have bought, and the more they have *spent* all increase the odds that they will buy again.

Direct marketers have identified three criteria that help them predict who is most likely to repurchase: **recency, frequency, and monetary**. The more recently customers bought from a company, the more likely they are to buy again. The more frequently customers have bought from a company, the more likely they are to buy again. Finally, the more money customers have spent buying from a company, the more likely they are to buy again. Computer models are used

Photo: Courtesy of UNICEF

This direct-mail piece from the UNICEF campaign appears to contain a packet of toy soldiers, but when opened, they turn out to be figures of children doing normal childhood activities such as playing soccer and riding bikes. The message on the package, which is also the campaign theme, is "Turn Soldiers Back into Children." Do you think this is an effective public service piece?

to do ongoing analyses of customers' buying behaviors and to produce lists, using these criteria, of who the company can best afford to send more catalogs, e-mails, and promotional letters. Similar to media planning, this modeling is also called **optimization**.

For acquiring new customers, a targeting strategy is to *profile current customers* and then look for potential customers who have similar profiles from databases of customer information. For example, if Wendy's finds that a high percentage of its customers in a college town are graduate students, then it should try to find mailing lists of graduate students to mail promotional coupons to because this target audience has a higher probability of responding than the average person.

The Offer and Response All direct-marketing messages contain an **offer**, typically consisting of a description of the product, terms of sale, and payment, delivery, and warranty information. In its offer, a successful DBC campaign must communicate benefits to buyers by answering the enduring question, "What's in it for me?" Also, many DBC offers include an incentive for responding quickly because marketers know that the longer people think about responding, the less likely they will respond.

All of the variables that are intended to satisfy the needs of the consumer are considered part of the offer. These variables include the price, the cost of shipping and handling, optional features, future obligations, availability of credit, extra incentives, time and quality limits, and guarantees or warranties. The offer is supported by a message strategy, a media strategy, and the database. Because DBC messages are tightly targeted, they are often longer and personalized and contain sufficient information to help a consumer make a purchase decision. They also try to reduce the risk, particularly with guarantees and warranties.

A DBC message should reflect whether the offer is a one-step offer or two-step offer. Because a **one-step offer** asks for a direct sale response, it must include a mechanism for responding to the offer. A **two-step offer** is designed to gather leads, answer consumer questions, set up appointments, and drive customers to a website or retail store.

Generating a response is the third step in the direct-marketing process (see Figure 16.2). To maximize the response/order rate, the DBC message must make it as easy as possible for customers to respond. One way to do this is to offer a variety of ways in which to respond—online, mail, phone, and fax. Also, if phone is one channel, then the more hours the phone lines are open, the better. When customers respond online, it is important that the company immediately acknowledge the response, thanking the customer for the order and advising when the product will arrive. The types of customer service offered, such as toll-free telephone numbers for product support, free limited-time trials, and acceptance of several different credit cards, are important techniques for overcoming customer resistance to responding. To create urgency, the direct-marketing message may also include a promotional device, such as a gift or limited-time-only price deal.

Fulfillment and Customer Follow-Up The next step in the direct-marketing process is called **fulfillment**, which is responding to customers' responses by getting the product to those who order it. Fulfillment includes all of the back-end activities of processing the transaction, including delivering the product, receiving payment, and providing customers with tracking numbers so they can track the delivery of their orders. The most critical aspect of successful direct marketing, however, is maintaining a positive customer relationship.

Relationship Building Direct marketers use a database to track customer interactions and transactions, the final step in Figure 16.2. Measuring and evaluating consumer behavior helps the direct marketer not only understand how the customers have responded to direct-marketing messages but also predict their future behavior and build a relationship.

Principle
Because direct-marketing messages are constantly being measured, it is good practice to learn what works and to modify succeeding campaigns based on those results.

Direct marketing is not a "shot-in-the-dark" approach. Direct-marketing professionals continually evaluate and accurately measure the effectiveness of various offers in a single campaign. By employing such measurement tools as tracking printed codes on mail-in responses that identify different offers and using different telephone numbers for each commercial (by time slot, station, or length), the direct-marketing professional can clearly identify those offers that yield the best results and modify the campaign to take advantage of them. Because of this constant evaluation, there is an emphasis in direct marketing on learning what is most effective and employing that information in succeeding efforts. Such accurate measurements and adjustments are largely responsible for DBC's success.

What Are the Primary Tools and Media of DBC?

Principle
Marketers use new media forms to talk directly with rather than at customers and other stakeholders, creating higher levels of customer engagement.

As you know from your own observations and from reading the previous chapters, most brand messages have been carried by mass media as "one-way" messages that talk "at" customers and prospects. Although these messages are cost efficient (i.e., have a lower CPM), they are not as effective as messages that are more interactive and have the potential to create higher levels of customer engagement. We'll review a number of the tools and media used in direct-response brand communication, but we'll start first with personal sales.

Personal Sales

Personal sales is the original and most effective—and also most expensive—form of direct marketing. Salespersons are found in stores, they knock on the doors of homes, and they also make calls on business prospects. Personal sales are also found in home parties, which are sponsored by such companies as Mary Kay and Tupperware. These are the original form of social networking sales.

Fuller Brush, for example, is a 100-year-old cleaning products company known in its heyday for its small army of door-to-door salespeople. The Fuller Brush Man was a business icon, one that left its mark on popular culture with mentions in songs and appearances in movies and television shows. But times change, and it's now facing bankruptcy, although its products will continue to be distributed online and through select retailers, such as HomeDepot.[3] But its real contribution to business history lies with its personal communication strategy that was memorialized in its "Ask the Fuller Brush Man" positioning strategy.

Avon is one of the biggest direct-sales companies with its millions of sales representatives and some $11 billion in revenue.[4] A new Avon little-sister brand is Mark, a college program for direct sales on campus. The Mark college coeds roam dormitories and sorority houses selling Mark beauty products and fashion accessories. In early 2010, there were more than 40,000 Mark Girls signed up in North America. The new organization combines personal sales with an e-boutique, iPhone app, and Facebook e-shop.[5]

But nothing in the direct-selling industry can compare with Holly Chen, a tiny Taiwanese woman who is megastar for Amway. One of the most prolific salespeople on Earth, Holly Chen, motivates her multilevel commission-based network of thousands of salespeople with her personal story. Speaking in Mandarin, she tells her Amway followers that "the most powerful weapon is to move somebody emotionally." She demonstrates by talking about her late mother, a powerful personal story that moves her—and her audience—to tears. Amway's $10 billion in sales reflects its strong position in Latin America and Asia, where the personal sales opportunities are attractive to moonlighters and self-starters. Amway's long-controversial business method, which is sometimes criticized as a pyramid scheme, is turning to social media to link distributors and customers as well as to turn these networked groups into a shadow sales force with commissions for referrals.[6]

Beyond personal sales, direct marketing employs five primary tools to achieve its objectives: (1) direct-response advertising, (2) direct mail, (3) catalogs, (4), telemarketing, and (5) online e-marketing. What is typical of all of these forms is that they offer an opportunity for in-depth information. Copywriter and professor Karen Mallia, who wrote the Part 3 opener, observes that "direct marketers have known for years that people considering expensive or complex products want information, and people will be persuaded when that information is delivered in copy that sells while it tells."

Photo: Courtesy of Fuller Brush Company

CLASSIC

"Dear Fuller Brush Man, I have a hard time reaching into the shower to clean it. What do you have that will make this job easier?"
—Sara from NC.

The popular "Ask the Fuller Brush Man" feature, which draws on a 100 years of door-to-door sales, answers consumer cleaning questions as an important feature on the company's website.

Source: www.fuller.com/index.php/faq/

Direct-Response Advertising Media

In addition to direct mail, catalogs, and telemarketing, direct marketers use a variety of traditional and nontraditional media, including mass-media advertising, the Internet, and digital forms of media such as cell phones, smart phones, BlackBerries (personal digital assistants), and social media, such as Facebook and Twitter.

Print Media Advertising Ads in the mass media are less directly targeted than are direct mail and catalog, but they can still provide the opportunity for a direct response. Ads in newspapers and magazines can carry a coupon, an order form, an address, or a toll-free or 900 telephone number. The response may be either to purchase something or tc ask for more information. In many cases the desired response is an inquiry that becomes a sales lead for field representatives.

A classic example of the power of direct-response advertising is the "97-Pound Weakling" ads for the Charles Atlas body building mail-order courses that featured a cartoon telling the story of a scrawny guy who decides to bulk up after a well-built lifeguard kicks sand in his face and steals his girlfriend. The business was launched in 1928 when Atlas partnered with adman Charles Roman to promote the Charles Atlas exercise system and correspondence course. The campaign created a multi-million-dollar business and the "97-pound weakling" who turned into a "he-man" became a pop-culture icon.

Broadcast Media Advertising A direct-response commercial on radio or television can provide the necessary information (usually a simple, easy-to-remember toll-free phone number or Web address) for the consumer to request information or even make a purchase. Radio's big advantage is its highly targeted audience. In contrast, television is a good medium for direct marketers who are advertising a broadly targeted product or one that needs to be demonstrated.

Direct-response advertising on television used to be the province of late-night television with pitches for Vegematics and screwdrivers guaranteed to last a lifetime. As more national marketers, such as Geico, move into the medium, the direct-response commercial is becoming more general in appeal, selling clothes and entertainment as well as insurance and financial services.

Direct-response television also makes good use of **infomercials** that blur the lines between retail and direct response. Infomercials have been around since the emergence of the cable industry and have become a multibillion-dollar industry. An infomercial is typically 30 or 60 minutes long and tends to be played during non–prime-time periods. The Salton-Maxim Juiceman infomercial took the company from $18 million to $52 million in sales overnight and made a marketing superstar of George Foreman. The Salton commercial made Juiceman the brand to buy, whether direct from television or from a local department store or mass merchant.

Today, the infomercial is viewed as a viable medium because (1) consumers now have confidence in infomercials and the products they sell; (2) with the involvement of upscale advertisers, the quality of infomercial production and supportive research has improved; (3) consumers can be better segmented and infomercials are coordinated with respect to these audiences; and (4) infomercials can easily be introduced into foreign markets. Marketers are more likely to use the infomercial format if their product needs to be demonstrated, is not readily available through retail outlets, and has a relatively high profit margin.

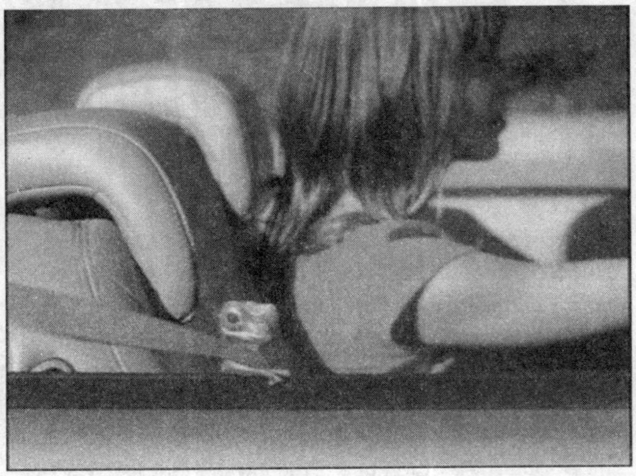

Photo: © 2004 GEICO. All rights reserved. Used with permission. Courtesy of The Martin Agency

A leading direct-response auto insurer, Geico uses its Gecko character as a spokes-creature to sell its products on television as well as in print.

Cable television lends itself to direct response because the medium is more tightly targeted to particular interests. QVC and the Home Shopping Network reach more than 70 million households and service their calls with huge phone banks.

Direct Mail

Of those organizations that use direct marketing, **direct mail** is the most popular method. Anyone with a mailing address has received direct mail. Advertising mail represented more than 63 percent of all mail received by households, according to the U.S. Postal Service's *Household Diary Study*.[7]

A direct-mail piece is a print advertising message for a product or service that is delivered by mail. It may be as simple as a single-page letter or as complex as a three-dimensional package consisting of a letter, a brochure, a sample, a premium, and an order card with a return envelope. A well-designed envelope is critical in grabbing the attention of consumers and persuading them to open the piece.

With the advances in digital printing, it is now possible to personalize not only the address and salutation on the letter but also other parts of the information as well as the offer. Called **variable data campaigns**, these marketing messages can be highly targeted, even unique to the recipient.

The following guidelines can be helpful for putting together direct-mail pieces:

- Get the attention of the targeted prospect as the envelope comes from the mailbox.

Photo: Courtesy of the Billings Chamber of Commerce

SHOWCASE

This envelope is used by the Billings Chamber of Commerce/Convention & Visitors Bureau to send information about visitor, tourism, and relocation opportunities. It reinforces a new brand identity campaign and carries the campaign's "Trailhead" logo and slogan as well as the "explore" graphics.

The Billings, Montana, "Trailhead" brand identity campaign was provided by John Brewer, president and CEO of the Billings Chamber of Commerce/ Convention & Visitors Bureau. A graduate of the University of West Florida, Brewer was nominated by Professor Tom Groth.

- Create a need for the product, show what it looks like, and demonstrate how it is used.
- Answer questions, as a good salesperson does, and reassure the buyer.
- Provide critical information about product use.
- Inspire confidence, minimize risk, and establish that the company is reputable.
- Make the sale by explaining how to buy, how to order, where to call, and how to pay for the purchase.
- Use an incentive to encourage a fast response.

Most direct mail is sent using a third-class bulk mail permit, which requires a minimum of 200 identical pieces. Third class is cheaper than first class, but it takes longer for delivery. Estimates of nondelivery of third-class mail run as high as 8 percent. The response rate for direct mail can vary from 0.1 to 50 percent, but it's typically in the 2 to 3 percent range. The primary variables are the offer and target audience. Offers mailed to current customers generally have a higher response rate than those sent to noncustomers.

Because of the high level of nonresponse, direct mail is also a fairly costly tool in terms of CPM. It can be cost efficient, however, because it can be designed to reach a highly targeted audience with an offer of interest. It also is much easier to calculate the actual payout rate—at what point do the returns on the investment begin to exceed the costs? That's why it is considered so much more accountable than other forms of marketing communication.

Direct-Mail Message Design How the direct-mail piece looks is as important as what it says. The most critical decision made by the target is whether to read the mailing or throw it away, and that decision is based on the attractiveness and attention-getting power of the outer envelope. A mailing for Krispy Kreme got attention when it created a coupon mailer in the shape of a box of doughnuts. Attached to the mailer was an offer to buy a box of a dozen and get another dozen free. Instead of the usual 2 to 3 percent response rate, Krispy Kreme got an 11 percent response. The envelope should spark curiosity through a creative idea, as the Billings mailer for its "Trailhead" campaign illustrates. Ideas about using direct mail creatively are offered in the "Inside Story" feature.

The functions of a direct-mail message are similar to the steps in the sales process. The message must move the reader through the entire process, from generating interest to creating

The Inside Story

Thinking outside the Mailbox

Michael Dattolico, *Musion Creative, LLC*

The most creative way to get people's attention with direct mail is to go back to the basics. A synergistic message and visual can go a long way toward achieving your result. Here's an example of an effective direct-mail campaign.

The client, Microflex, Inc., has proven to be an innovative leader in U.S. metal part manufacturing since 1975. Recently, it individually branded its automotive division, emphasizing the company's specialization in automotive parts.

The majority of Microflex's marketing efforts focused on introducing this new branding (i.e., division of the company) and offering specific distinction over the competition and the company's dedication to the automotive industry.

The objective of this campaign was to introduce and reinforce awareness of the company's automotive specialization to current clients and to emphasize its experience and new facility dedicated to automotive parts. Although this was originally intended for current clients, forethought was put in to make this a stand-alone piece for future leads gathered through Internet sales or trade show follow-ups.

After doing market research, it was clear how to make this new division stand above the competition. The company focused on establishing its experience (although Microflex was newly branding this individually, the company still had the years of experience to back it up) and emphasizing its capabilities. Further research showed a distinct breakdown of capabilities among the competition, so it was easy to follow this as a guide and focus on Microflex's superior design, testing and development, manufacturing, and support.

At the agency, we used an attention-getting format—a double gatefold (which means both the inside front cover and the inside back cover fold out)—to draw the viewer to some dramatic visual cues as well as anticipate the flow of information to the viewer. We also viewed the dramatic opening of the brochure as an emphasis on the new chapter in the company's history: opening its doors on a 120,000-square-foot manufacturing facility dedicated to the automotive division.

The intense visuals, the folding path that leads readers through to the major content, and targeted copy focusing on establishing the company's new dedication to the automotive industry as well as the selling points above the competition all made this a powerful, effective direct-mail piece.

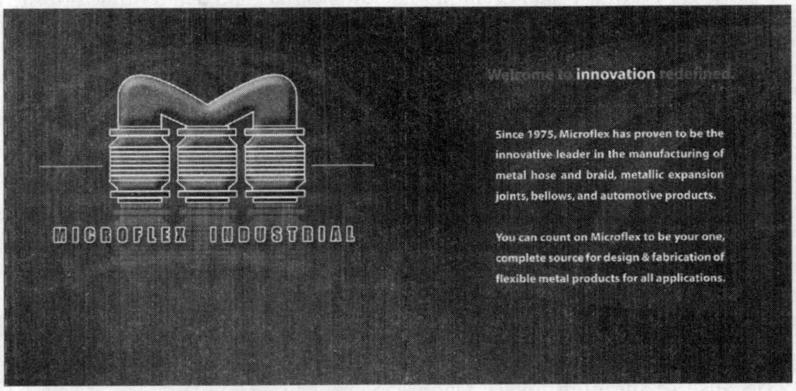

Photo: Courtesy of Michael Dattolico

Owner of his own design studio, Musion Creative, LLC (*www.musioncreative.com*), Michael Dattolico graduated from the advertising program at the University of Florida, where he was a student of Professor Elaine Wagner, and from a creative advertising program in England at University College Falmouth.

conviction and inducing a sale. It's all done with a complex package of printed pieces. Most direct-mail pieces follow a fairly conventional format. They usually consist of an outer envelope, a letter, a brochure, supplemental flyers or folders, and a reply card with a return envelope. These can be one-page flyers, multipanel folders, multipage brochures, or spectacular **broadsheets** that fold out like maps big enough to cover the top of a table.

Historically, the letter has been the most difficult element in a direct-mail package to develop and therefore the focus of much research. Over the years, many techniques have proven effective in getting consumers to read a direct-mail letter, flyer, or brochure. Here are some hints for writing an effective direct-response letter:

1. ***Get Attention*** To grab attention or generate curiosity, use pictures and headlines that tout the product's benefits.
2. ***Be Relevant*** Send the right message to the right person.
3. ***Personalize*** Use a personalized salutation. If the individual's name is not available, the salutation should at least be personalized to the topic, such as "Dear Cat Lover."
4. ***Use a Strong Lead-In*** Begin the letter with a brief yet compelling or surprising statement. For example, "Dear Friend: I could really kick myself!"
5. ***The Offer*** Make the offer as early in the body of the letter as possible and dramatize it.
6. ***The Letter*** Explain the details of the offer and use testimonials or evidence that clearly describes benefits to the customer to create conviction.
7. ***Drive to Website*** Use short pieces and drive interested prospects to the website for details.
8. ***The Closing*** End by repeating the offer and stating additional incentives or guarantees and a clear call to action.
9. ***Test, Test, Test*** Check every single element—small changes can boost conversion rates dramatically.

One advantage of direct mail is that it has a tactile quality that is missing in most other forms of marketing communication. An insurance company once sent out a mailing that contained one leather glove. A message accompanying the glove invited recipients to call the insurance agency if they would like to have the matching glove and hear a little more about the company's insurance policies.

Test, Test, Test The secret behind effective direct mail is scale—in other words, enough pieces are sent using various strategies (e.g., phrasing, visuals, or offers) to determine what increases the response and what doesn't. Smile Train, an organization that pays for cleft-palate operations in poor countries, raises millions of dollars with its very sophisticated approach to direct-response analytics.[8] It uses direct mail, as well as direct-response advertising and other promotional strategies, to help some 600,000 people who could never afford this type of surgery.

Issues: Trees, Water, and Waste Critics of direct mail cite its environmental impact. Production of direct mail uses an estimated 100 million trees and 28 billion gallons of water annually. And untold millions of dollars are spent for disposal and recycling. In Colorado alone, recycling experts estimate that junk mail accounts for more than 340 million pounds of trash annually.

Is there a need for an aggressive ban on direct mail? Consider local mailings. What would be the impact of such a ban on your local pizza restaurant, video store, or hair salon, which might rely on direct-mail offers? How do such businesses announce their presence in the market? Does the waste and irritation factor of "junk mail" justify a ban on this form of marketing communication? On the other side of the debate, might banning direct mail infringe on an organization's right to commercial free speech? What's fair, what's right, and what's a responsible marketer to do?

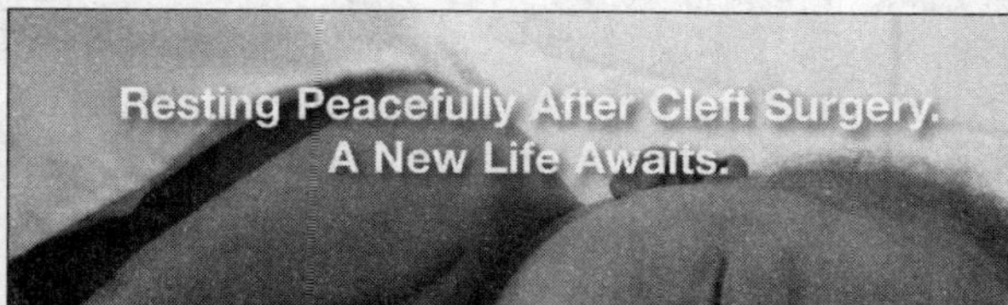

Photo: Courtesy of Smile Train

The organization sends out more than 100 million letters a year and generates, in addition to donations, reams of data about which appeals and visuals generate the most money as well as information about which ZIP codes have the best responses.

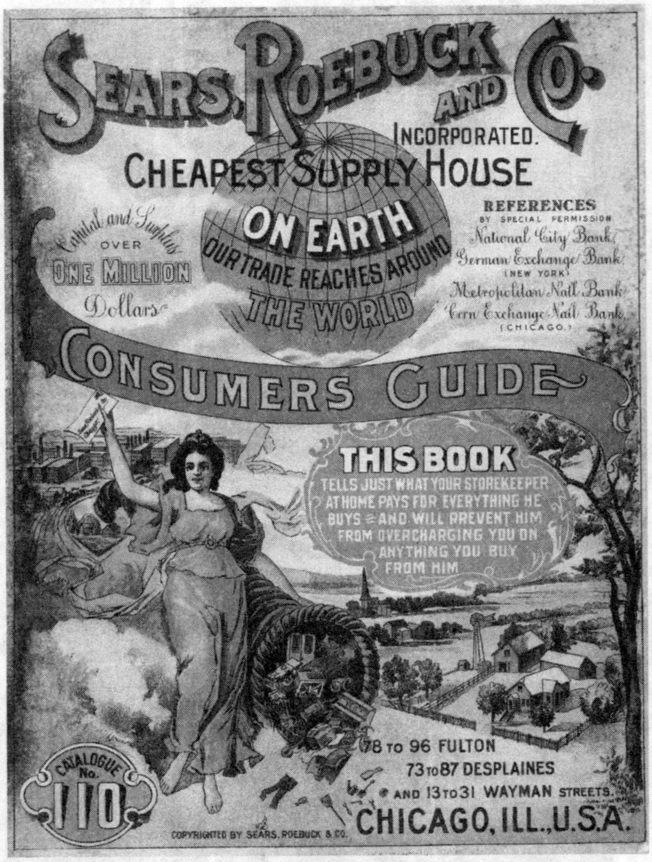

Photo: © Bettmann/CORBIS All Rights Reserved.

CLASSIC

For most of its life, the Sears catalog was sent to homes via the U.S. Postal Service and shoppers could order directly from the "Wish Book" with their merchandise also delivered to them by mail. Some surprising offerings included the Sears Motor buggy from 1909 to 1912, and from 1908 to 1940, Sears sold some 75,000 mail-order homes from its catalogs.

Catalogs

Catalogs have been effective direct-response marketers for as long as there has been mail. The famous Sears catalogs began in 1888 with a line of watches and jewelry. In 1894, the offerings were expanded to include sewing machines, bicycles, saddles, musical instruments, and a host of new items. In 1896, the slogan "Cheapest Supply House on Earth" was added to the cover. For more on the history of this iconic direct-response vehicle, visit www.searsarchives.com.

A **catalog** is a multipage direct-mail publication (in print) that shows a variety of merchandise. Following the explosion of digital media, however, catalogs have also evolved into easy-to-use online publications.

The growth in the 21st century is in specialty catalogs, which are aimed at niche markets. There are catalogs for every hobby and for more general interests. Duluth Trading Company, for example, sells tough work clothes, and Soft Surroundings sells upscale women's clothing and home accessories. One of the most interesting catalogs is the Neiman Marcus Christmas Book, which features highly expensive fantasy gifts, such as a $250,000 two-seater plane complete with flying lessons, a $10 million Zeppelin, or a $10 million stable of racehorses.

The traditional catalogs all have a variety of brands and products, but there are also brand catalogs whose merchandise is all from the sponsoring brand. J. Crew, for example, features J. Crew–branded clothing. Marriott invites travelers to purchase its bed, bath, and room decor products from a catalog that is available in its rooms.

Another factor in the effectiveness of catalogs is the nature of the interactions between customers and the company, whether over the phone or on the Internet. Lands' End has been a model of customer care that leads not just to brand loyalty but also to brand love. Lands' End has been recognized for doing things like marshaling a corps of some 200 employee volunteers who respond to customer mail. The company has even been known to replace products before the customers discover they are faulty. Jeanne Bliss, chief customer officer at Lands' End who helped create this culture of customer care, explains that this high-touch approach has won Lands' End a lot of love, a point she writes about in her book *I Love You More Than My Dog*.[9]

Some catalog retailers have their own stores, such as Williams-Sonoma and Tiffany's. Banana Republic, which began as a catalog marketer and then moved into retailing, is now launching its first catalog since 1988. Many large retailers are now multichannel, using catalogs, websites, and stores. Some marketers, such as L.L. Bean, have also seen their catalog mailings drive business to their websites. Bean expects that its online sales will soon overtake its catalog business, but it will still send out catalogs as a way to generate online sales.

A number of marketers are using video or CD catalogs because these provide more information about their products. Car companies, for example, use online catalogs or CDs. The message can be interactive and feature animated illustrations. The catalog presents graphic descriptions and detailed text on the current models, including complete specifications. With some, you can even custom design your dream car. We just saw the Microflex direct-mail design by Michael Dattolico. Here is an example of CD design for that same client.

Telemarketing

Before telemarketing calls were greatly limited by government-supported do-not-call lists, more direct-marketing dollars were spent on **telemarketing** phone calls than on any other DBC medium. That's because telemarketing is a form of personal sales but a lot less expensive. An in-person sales call may cost anywhere from \$50 to \$1,000 after factoring in time and transportation. In comparison, a telephone call ranges from \$2 to \$15 per call. That is still expensive if you compare it to the CPM of an advertisement placed in any one of the mass media (\$10 to \$50 per thousand); however, the returns are much higher than those generated by mass advertising because they are intrusive, personalized, and interactive. The caller also can respond to buyers' objections and make a persuasive sales argument.

A typical telemarketing campaign usually involves hiring a telemarketing company to make a certain number of calls using a prepared script. These callers work in **call centers**, which are rooms with large banks of phones and computers. Most calls are made from databases of prospects who were previously qualified on some factor, such as an interest in a related product or a particular profile of demographics and psychographics. Occasionally a **cold call** is used, which means the call center staff are calling random numbers, but this practice has a much lower response rate.

There are two types of telemarketing: inbound and outbound. An **inbound telemarketing** call is initiated by a customer. The consumer can be responding to an ad, catalog, e-mail, or fax. L.L. Bean's telephone representatives are trained to handle inbound calls in such a helpful manner that the company often features their friendly approach in its catalogs. Calls originating from the firm are outgoing or **outbound telemarketing** or outgoing telemarketing. These calls typically generate the most consumer resistance because they are uninvited, intrusive, and unexpected.

Photo: Courtesy of Microflex

SHOWCASE

This is a CD cover designed by Michael Dattolico for his client Microflex, a B2B company in the automotive industry.

Owner of his own design studio, Musion Creative, LLC (www.musioncreative.com), Michael Dattolico graduated from the advertising program at the University of Florida, where he was a student of Professor Elaine Wagner, and from a creative advertising program in England at University College Falmouth.

Telemarketing Message Design The key point to remember about telemarketing messages is that they need to be simple enough to be delivered over the telephone. If the product requires a visual demonstration or a complicated explanation, then the message might be better delivered by direct mail. The message also must be compelling. People resent intrusive telephone calls, so there must be a strong initial benefit or reason-why statement to convince prospects to continue listening. The message also must be short; most people won't stay on the telephone longer than two to three minutes for a sales call.

Issues: Intrusion and Fraud Telemarketing has its drawbacks. Perhaps the most universally despised telemarketing tool is **predictive dialing**. Predictive dialing technology makes it possible for telemarketing companies to call anyone—even those with unlisted numbers. Special computerized dialing programs use random dialing. This explains why, from time to time, when you answer your phone you simply hear an empty line; the predictive dialer has called your number before a call agent is free. Many people consider these calls a nuisance, and they can

Photo: Ulrich Baumgarten via Getty Images

Call centers are large rooms with multiple stations for staff who make the calls (outbound) or answer calls from people placing orders (inbound).

even be alarming because burglars have been known to call a house to see if anyone's home before they attempt a break-in.

Telemarketing's reputation also has been tarnished by fraudulent behavior, such as promising a product or service in exchange for an advance payment, convincing consumers they need some kind of financial or credit protection that they don't really need, or enticing consumers to buy something by promising them prizes that are later discovered to be worthless. In response to these telemarketing abuses, the Federal Trade Commission (FTC) enacted the Telemarketing Sales Rule in 1995 to protect consumers. This rule prohibits telemarketers from calling before 8 A.M. or after 9 P.M., imposes strict informational disclosure requirements, prohibits misrepresentative or misleading statements, and provides for specific payment collection procedures. More recently, FTC regulations have required telemarketing firms to identify themselves on caller ID.

The most serious restriction on telemarketing—a program that consumers love—is implemented by state and national "do-not-call" lists. The national Do Not Call Registry had 31.6 million sign-ups even before it took effect in 2003 and grew to more than 149 million by 2007. Telemarketing companies responded by challenging the legality of these lists in court based on what they believe to be an illegal restriction on commercial free speech. In late 2004, however, the U.S. Supreme Court let stand a lower-court ruling that the industry's free speech rights were not violated by the do-not-call list.

The do-not-call lists do not restrict companies from calling their own customers, and they allow nonprofits to continue calling and market research firms to continue conducting phone surveys. Telemarketers subscribe to the database and check the list at least monthly for numbers they need to delete. The subscription cost is $62 for each area code with a $17,000 maximum for a national list.

Some phone companies offer their customers a service called "Privacy Manager" that screens out sales calls. For customers who have caller ID, numbers that register as "unavailable" or "unknown" are intercepted by a recorded message that asks callers to identify themselves. If the caller does so, the call rings through.

The Internet and New Forms of Direct Response

Much Internet advertising is simply direct marketing in electronic form: E-mails are just another kind of "letter," and search engine advertising is direct copy at its tightest. Direct marketers saw the Internet's potential early. Because of its interactive dimension, the Web is moving direct marketers much closer to one-to-one marketing, and social media are accelerating that trend; as a *Wall Street Journal* special edition on direct selling explained, "Conversations about purchasing products can be turned into a buying experience at an accelerated level with a mobile device and an appropriate app."[10]

Actually, direct marketing—particularly catalog marketing—is the model for e-commerce. Amazon.com is the leader of the pack, but other companies that sell merchandise direct include Columbia House Online (www.columbiahouse.com), eBags (www.eBags.com), and CDNow (www.cdnow.com).

Photo: Courtesy of Title Nine

Note how the catalog and web page work to build the brand for Title Nine through a consistent visual look and brand personality.

Online catalogs cross the line between e-commerce and direct marketing. Amazon.com's website, for example, contains complete information about the product offerings, such as book reviews, as well as a way to place an order, pay for it, and contact customer service if there is a problem. The website operates like a direct-mail catalog but interactivity makes it even more useful than a print version can be. Customers can make inquiries, and the company can use its databases to personalize customer communication. An example of a company that sells its sport fashions in print catalogs, as well as online catalogs, is Title Nine, which also has a chain of retail stores.

The technology of the Internet also has produced dramatic changes in the direct-mail industry. At a most basic level, the Internet has facilitated the ease in producing and distributing traditional direct mail by e-mail. E-mail marketing software and advertising assistance is available from such companies as Constant Contact (www.constantcontact.com), which even provides e-mail templates. Services such as Constant Contact and MailNow offer a streamlined process that allows users to point and click their way through a series of predesigned e-mailer templates priced and sorted by industry as well as select mailing lists and various mail media (postcards, letters, flyers, or newsletters). Customers can customize the mailer with their logo and other proprietary images or copy.

Another feature of Internet direct marketing is greater sampling opportunities. Online music stores now have hundreds of thousands of music clips for shoppers to listen to before making a purchase. Eddie Bauer lets site visitors "try on" clothes in a virtual dressing room. It also sends them e-mail messages offering special prices on items based on their past purchasing patterns.

Today, the use of extensive database information and innovative e-mail technology, combined with creative marketing strategies, has brought the benefits of highly personalized, inexpensive messages to far-reaching mass campaigns. E-mail marketing is developing and becoming more strategic as new technologies are developed. Three basic types of e-mail campaigns are used in marketing communication:

- Addressable to current customers
- Addressable to prospects
- Unsolicited and often unwanted, or spam

An option in the "addressable" category is one that is still evolving, and that is the idea of sending automated direct-marketing messages via GPS-enabled mobile devices, such as iPhones. Various innovations are being tested to make these geomarketing techniques useful without becoming a privacy issue.[11]

Well-known corporate brands such as BMW are using e-mail as a DBC tool. In one campaign, the company invited existing and prospective customers to view a collection of Web movies about new BMW models. Another campaign notified BMW owners of a new section at BMW.com reserved strictly for their use. Called the "Owner's Circle," the section allows owners to obtain special services and set up profiles that track maintenance items specific to their cars. Shortly after the mailing, enrollment in the Owner's Circle doubled, and participation in BMW's financial services program tripled.

The most exciting advances in Internet direct response, however, are found in the areas of mobile marketing and social media. With mobile phones, marketers are also able to meet people "where they are," or, as a *Wall Street Journal*[12] special supplement on direct selling explains, business owners can "meet their customers wherever their habits take them and integrate into that behavior."

Social selling, also known as *network marketing*, utilizes the reach and persuasiveness of social media and its endless and continuous conversations. Business are finding opportunities in this need to connect and share. Network marketing has always been used in word-of-mouth campaigns enlisting friendship groups. The difference is that with social media, that network can include 150 Facebook fans and 200 Twitter followers. The network can grow exponentially as messages zing through cyberspace. According to a *Wall Street Journal* special report on social selling, network marketing "is the only model that truly connects online social selling and offline social purchasing."[13]

Issue: Spam Although e-mail marketing has enjoyed increased success, the practice has received intense criticism for generating too much unwanted e-mail, otherwise known as **spam**. The FTC has determined that 90 percent of all spam involving business and investment opportunities contains false or misleading information. The problem also exists with nearly half of the messages promoting health products and travel and leisure. This is why Congress passed the CAN-SPAM Act in 2003. The problem is so big that some industry experts estimate that more than half of all e-mail messages are spam.

Retailers can be seen as spammers. The *Wall Street Journal* reported that in 2011, the nation's top 100 e-commerce retailers sent customers an average of 177 e-mails each. Although there's nothing wrong with online sales directed to consumers, the problem comes with large numbers of unwanted messages, which can be seen by recipients as spam. For example, Nieman Marcus, a particularly aggressive e-mailer, has sent some 500 emails to consumers on its lists. Retailers are beginning to recognize that the sheer volume is turning off customers. The solution to retail spam is to better target the messages and send them less frequently.[14]

Twitter has filed complaints in federal court against companies and individuals who it claims violate the antispam provisions in its user agreement. Specifically, Twitter prohibits users from spamming others as well as from creating multiple accounts in order to send questionable tweets. Charges against two individuals claim they duped people into clicking on questionable links.[15]

Amazon has filed lawsuits in U.S. and Canadian courts to stop e-mail spammers it says have been fraudulently using its identity to send out spam, a practice known as **spoofing**. Facebook has been plagued with spam and began offering its users a complimentary six-month subscription to McAfee's Internet Security Suite, which railroads spam as well as viruses.[16] One of the largest e-mail marketers, OptInRealBig, has been sued by the State of New York for allegedly sending misleading and fraudulent e-mail solicitations. Microsoft also sued the company for bombarding its Explorer service with spam.

Critics would like to see the government close down the bulk e-mail operations. There are technological problems to controlling these practices, however, and spammers have proven creative in finding ways to get through filters. It's become a worldwide problem as spammers from outside the United States have helped to double the volume of unwanted e-mail. A register of spammers known as *Rokso*, or Register of Known Spam Operations, has been created. It's a kind of "most wanted" list maintained by Internet hosts and service providers like AOL, whose computers strain to handle the huge amounts of e-mail and are quick to kick off known spammers. An antispam website called Spamhaus.org also tracks spam senders, and Congress has various proposals for regulating spam.

Is spam cost effective? Spammers solicit business from sources like AOL's profiles where people indicate their interests and activities. A spammer might send out 100,000 e-mails and get only two to five clients, which seems like a totally unacceptable number of responses. But a spammer who charges $300 to send out 100,000 messages or $900 for a million might make $14,000 to $15,000 on those few responses. That's not a bad return when you consider the cost of getting into the business—a computer and an Internet connection.

Here are some of the ways consumers can reduce the amount of unwanted direct mail or spam they receive:

- If you enter a contest or order an item by mail, you may wind up on a mailing list. To protect your contact information, check the "opt-out" box and write "No mailing lists" beside your contact information.
- Use the "Contact Us" link on retailers' websites to ask to be taken off mailing lists.
- Check the "Privacy" link at the bottom of a company's home page for directions on removing your name from its mailing lists.
- The Mail Preference Service of DMA permits you to register for $5 to get off mailing lists (www.dmaconsumers.org/cgi/offmailing).
- To get off credit card solicitation lists, call 888-5-OPT-OUT. A recorded message will ask for your contact information, but that's just confirmation. This service already has your contact information; providing it by phone confirms your identity so your request can be processed.
- To register for the federal do-not-call list, go to www.donotcall.gov and sign up. That will cut down on unwanted phone calls from marketers.
- To reduce the amount of spam you receive, register at e-MPS, which is DMA's e-mail Preference Service (http://dmaconsumers.org/consumers/optoutform_emps.shtml).

You might note that in most cases, if you have a relationship with a company—which means you've ordered something within the past 12 months—you won't be deleted from those lists. Blanket requests to end unsolicited calls or mail may not apply to charities and politicians because of First Amendment issues. Nonprofit organizations do a lot of solicitations by mail.

Permission Marketing Because spam is a huge problem for legitimate e-mail marketers, they are now using an approach called **permission marketing**. It attempts to address the spam problem by asking potential consumers for their permission to send them e-mail. Solutions to the problem usually incorporate one of two permission-marketing strategies for consumers to control their inclusion on lists. **Opt in** means that all bulk mailers have to get your permission before sending a promotion. Legitimate direct marketers use this permission form, which is tougher for spammers to abuse and more sensitive to consumer rage when they do. **Opt out** means that e-mailers can send the first e-mail but must give recipients the means to refuse any further e-mails from that business. These options give customers control over the amount and type of e-mail messages they receive, and companies reduce wasted resources on marketing to uninterested individuals. The concept at the heart of permission marketing is that every customer who opts in to a campaign is a qualified lead.

Principle
Opt-in and opt-out strategies make e-mail campaigns more acceptable because customers give permission to marketers to contact them. At the heart of permission marketing is the idea that every customer who opts in to a campaign is a qualified lead.

Databases: The Foundation of DBC

Looking back, you'll note that both Figure 16.1 and Figure 16.2 begin with databases. Why is that so? Direct marketers use **databases** to keep track of current customers and identify prospective customers. They are also a segmentation tool to communicate relevant offers to specific groups of customers and prospects. Another benefit for companies that keep track of their customers' online behavior is that they are better able to personalize their DBC messages. Big Data, a term that became popular in 2013, refers to using huge computer data storage capabilities combined with analytic software to do highly strategic targeting.

A database is at the heart of direct marketing and of the practice of **behavioral targeting**, which means that individuals are targeted based on what they have done in the past—products they've bought, shows they've watched, sites they've visited, and so forth.

For example, consider how Carnival Cruise Lines uses databases to manage its customer relationships. Information is gathered at check-in when customers get their Sail & Sign card, which serves as money on the cruise (it also allows Carnival to track its customers' purchases and activities). New customers receive a standard card but returning passengers get a gold card that triggers "Welcome back" messages from staff. Frequent cruisers get a platinum card and automatic membership in the

Concierge Club with perks such as priority embarking and debarking, dining times, and spa reservations. These data are then used to target follow-up e-mail and direct-mail offers.

The authors of a set of books that focus on one-to-one marketing defined data-driven communication as a strategy that delivers customer-focused objectives by treating different customers differently. Through the use of databases, they describe the *learning relationship* that results from customer dialogue. Here is how this data-driven relationship works:[17]

> If you're my customer and I get you to talk to me, I remember what you tell me, and I get smarter and smarter about you. I know something about you competitors don't know. So I can do things for you my competitors can't do, because they don't know you as well as I do. Before long, you can get something from me you can't get anywhere else, for any price. At the very least you'd have to start all over somewhere else, but starting over is more costly than staying with us.

An example of using a database to identify good customers and treat them differently comes from a direct-response campaign designed by Wisconsin-based Carlson Marketing that segmented customers by usage. By analyzing its database, a large multinational packaged goods company was able to send a premium quality direct-mail piece with a unique shape to the top 15 percent of the company's 200 million customers. The middle-tier customers—55 percent of the customer base—received a more modest flat mail piece, and the bottom group received cost-effective e-mails.

Databases Drive a Circular Process

Principle

DBC is a continuous process, beginning and ending with a database of prospect and customer information.

A database is important at both the beginning of the direct-marketing process and the end of the process where it captures and updates information for the next interaction. It's a circular process. If an important objective is to build relationship programs, then the information gathered through customer interaction feeds back into the process and becomes an input for the next round of communication efforts.

DBC is possible because of innovations in computer technology that have helped companies keep up with their customers. People move, have children, marry, divorce, remarry, change jobs, age, and retire and change their purchase behavior through all of these changes. The purpose of the database is to produce up-to-date information on customers and prospects as well as their interactions with the company. According to the DMA, a good marketing database has these primary objectives:

- Record names of customers, expires (names no longer valid), and prospects
- Store and analyze responses
- Store and analyze purchasing performance
- Continue direct communication with customers

These objectives also set up categories of data that need to be collected, stored, and manipulated in order to develop direct-response strategies. According to Forrester Research, which has a program called Personal Identity Management, there are four categories of data being collected by marketers:[18]

1. *Individual identity data* include name, Social Security number, driver's license number, and IP (Internet Protocol) address that identifies the user's computer.
2. *Behavioral data* include transaction data, Internet browsing history, and location information from mobile devices.
3. *Derived data*, such as credit scores and personas, are computed or compiled by modeling and profiling.
4. *Self-identified data* consist of information provided by the user, such as purchase intent, "likes," product opinions, and personal profiles from professional and social media.

The goal is for a marketer to know its customers better in order to direct relevant messages and offers to them. Messages targeted on behavior are more than twice as effective as more general advertising in converting website visitors to buyers.[19]

The database management process illustrated in Figure 16.3 begins with an initial information collection point. This could be the completion of a warranty card, entering a contest or sweepstakes, opting in on a website, or filling out a card at a trade show, to name a few. The second stage is to enter the data into the computer to merge it with other information already in the file or added at the same time. Stage 3 allows the marketer to assess the data and determine the relevant level of detail. In stage 4, the direct marketer can create clusters of characteristics and behaviors representing valuable consumer segments or target markets (audiences). Stage 5 applies the database to the specific marketing problems or strategies. An example might be sending coupons to a particular

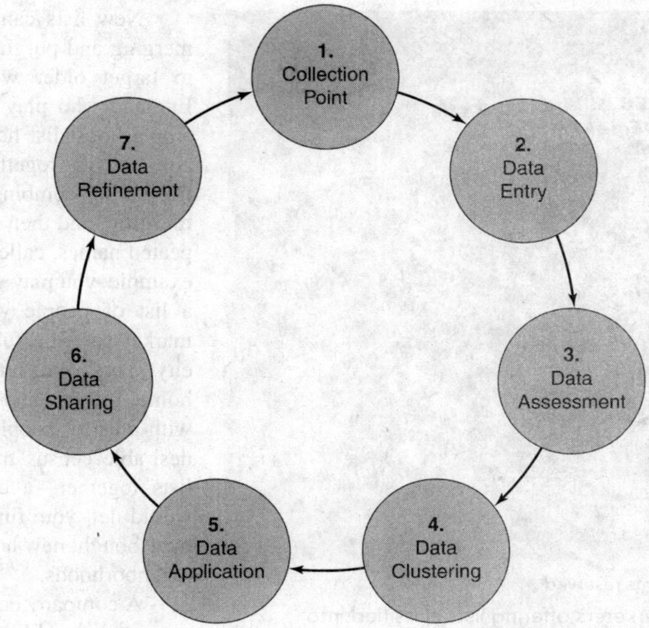

FIGURE 16.3
The Database Marketing Process
Using database marketing, planners can continually improve the effectiveness of their marketing communication campaigns. Results feed back into planning for a continual loop of improvement.

customer segment. In stage 6, the direct marketer makes decisions about data sharing and partnerships. A manufacturer may decide that his retail outlets could use the data. Finally, the database goes through a refinement process that includes corrections, updates, additions, and deletions.

Lists

Customer and prospect lists that contain contact information (addresses, phone numbers, and e-mail and other online addresses) are used by all areas of direct marketing. Direct-mail lists that match market segments identified in the marketing communication plan can be purchased or rented from list brokers who maintain and sell thousands of lists tied to demographic, psychographic, and geographic breakdowns. They have further classified their data on such characteristics as hobbes, affiliations, and personal influence, such as the Response Alliance database of decision makers. Geography is a common classification; American households can be broken down by their postal carrier routes. For instance, one company has identified 160 ZIP codes it calls "Black Enterprise" clusters, inhabited by "upscale, white-collar, black families" in major urban fringe areas.

Marketers own their own lists or rent lists based on customer characteristics, such as geography, age, gender, and personal interests (sailboat owners, college students). There are three types of lists:

- A **house list** is made up of the marketer's own customers or members, which is its most important target market and the most valuable list. These lists are compiled when stores offer credit plans, service plans, special sale announcements, and contests that require customers to sign up. Some stores, such as Radio Shack, fill in customers' names and addresses at the cash register.
- A **response list** is made up of people or households who have responded to some type of direct-response offer. The more similar the product to which they responded is to the marketer's product, the more valuable the list because these people should be similar to the company's current customers. For example, if you sell pet food for dogs, you might like a list of people who have responded to a magazine ad for a pet (dog) identification collar. Two important criteria are obvious from such a list: These people are very likely have a pet (dog), and they are open to buying from a catalog, mail offer, or website.
- A **compiled list** is a list of some specific category, such as sports car owners, new home buyers, graduating seniors, new mothers, association members, or subscribers to a magazine, book club, or record club. Luxury car manufacturers are always interested in lists of people who belong to country clubs, own a yacht, or travel first class because these people obviously like and can afford such luxuries. Lists of decision makers related to particular industries are extremely important in B2B marketing.

Photo:

This is a postcard mailed to B2B direct marketers offering lists classified into 47 different types of buying characteristics. It separates prospects in terms of 47 "buying influence selectors" that include such factors as job function, industry, and decision-making patterns.

New lists can be created by merging and purging. If you want to target older women in New England who play tennis, for example, most list houses would be able to put together a database for you by combining lists, called **merging**, and then deleting the repeated names, called **purging**. For example, you may want to develop a list of people who are in the market for fine furniture in your city. You could buy a list of new home buyers and combine that with a list of people who live in a desirable census tract. These two lists together—a compiled list—would let you find people who have bought new homes in upscale neighborhoods.

A company can hire database management firms whose sole purpose is to collect, analyze, categorize, and market an enormous variety of detail about customers. Companies such as National Decision Systems and Donnelly Marketing Information Systems are only a few of the firms that provide these **relational databases**—that is, databases that contain information useful in profiling and segmenting as well as contact information. Donnelly, for example, developed Hispanic Portraits, a database of households that segments the U.S. Hispanic population into 18 cluster groups.

Services such as Prodigy and Melissa DATA provide users with online buying services, remember purchases, and, over time, can build a purchase profile of each user. This kind of information is valuable to marketers, resellers, and their agencies. It's also of concern to consumer activists and consumers who worry about privacy.

Nintendo uses the 2 million names in its database when it introduces more powerful versions of its video game system. The names and addresses are gathered from a list of subscribers to its magazine, *Nintendo Power*. The company believes that many of its current customers will want to trade up systems, and this direct communication makes it possible for Nintendo to speak directly to its most important target market about new systems as they become available. Nintendo began its database in 1988 and credits database marketing with helping it maintain its huge share of the $6 billion to $7 billion video game market.

Data Mining

The practice of sifting through and sorting information captured in a company's database to target customers and maintain a relationship with them is called **data mining**. Such information includes profiles based on demographics, lifestyle, and behavior as well as basic contact information.

As a result, marketing departments are spending more of their budgets on hardware and software that let them better manage activities like online marketing and social media guided by data tracking and the analytics of tight targeting. And vendors like IBM are shifting their B2B marketing efforts from the traditional information technology officers to chief marketing officers.[20]

How is data mining used? Marketers collect information about their customers to better target customers who might really be interested in their offers. This is called *behavioral targeting,* to which we referred earlier in this chapter and in Chapter 5. Instead of sending mass e-mails (spam) to everyone on a list, marketers can send information to people who are really interested in their product or service based on their past purchases and other product-related actions.

Data mining is also used to spot trends and patterns—frequent flyers may also be buyers of international phone cards, for example. Using the practice discussed earlier called *prospecting*, data mining can be used to profile prospects based on key characteristics of current customers. If a grocery store that uses a loyalty card to track its customers' purchases notices that the young families in its customer pool live in certain neighborhoods, then it can target family-oriented promotions to those particular neighborhoods rather than spraying them across its entire geographical market.

Issue: Privacy

One of the unexpected facts about life with social media is that your friends and associates can share information about you on all their online social networks. Say you have a party and some of the people attending post notes, photos, and tweets online. And then you start hearing from people you didn't invite. Even your friendly cell phone can tell tales about your comings and goings as it tracks your locations as well as your apps, your calls, and the sites you visit. It's a new life in the "Nothing's Private Anymore" universe.

To deal with the public distribution of private messages, a new mobile application called Pair is designed let you share secret little notes with a special friend that aren't spread across the social networks like Facebook and Twitter. It combines the fuzzy feeling of being connected to someone you care about without the public sharing of personal thoughts.[21]

Marketing and Privacy Privacy is a huge concern for all direct marketers, not just those engaged in e-commerce, and it has generated fierce debate among consumer privacy advocates, marketing and advertising associations, and federal regulators. Companies are increasing the amount of data they collect on their customers in order to do better *behavioral targeting*—sometimes with their permission and knowledge but often without customers even being aware of the practice.

The lack of privacy on social media is an issue, particularly when it's combined with the gathering of marketing information. Larry Ellison, president of Oracle, explains the implications: "Now we can track not only what products you're buying, but what you're saying about those products. We know who your friends are. We know what you're saying to your friends. We know your friends' friends." His point is that when a company launches a product, it's easy to look at a Twitter or Facebook feed and find out what you and other users are saying about the product.[22] That may sound like good research being used to collect useful insights, but privacy activists see huge problems with these practices.

This unknown tracking is the problem with "cookies," little files installed on user's Web browsers without users' knowledge, to track their online behavior. Privacy is not just a concern in the United States. Officials in the European Union have debated the issue and created a set of recommendations for data collection but especially addressing the use of cookies.[23] And the use of cookies is increasing as the number of data trackers collecting information of consumers has increased. Research at the University of California, Berkeley, found that 100 of the most popular sites had 6,485 cookies. Most of these are installed by third-party trackers, not the websites themselves. DoubleClick, Google's ad service, was the most prevalent tracker.[24]

David Rittenhouse, a member of this book's advisory board and an expert in digital marketing, observed that "a huge ad tech industry is dependent on consumers and lawmakers not getting too excited about data collection and privacy." He continues, "at this moment, in my opinion, consumers have *no idea* how much data is being collected on them from their Web browsing."[25]

For example, a study in 2011 found that an average visit to a Web page triggered 56 instances of data collection. The rise in the number of companies collecting data and the increase in the amount of data collected, according to the *Wall Street Journal*, "is testament to the power of the $31 billion online-advertising business, which increasingly relies on data about users' Web surfing behavior to target advertisements."[26]

And what about marketing to kids? The original 1998 Children's Online Privacy Protection Act hasn't kept up with technology. The old rules required parents to give permission on how data were collected from children. But it's possible with some iPhone games for kids to join social networks that collect data without parental permission. The *Wall Street Journal* found in 2010 that popular children's websites had more data-gathering technology than websites aimed at adults. The FTC proposed new rules in 2012 to close some of these loopholes.[27] It updated its rules about privacy, taking into account the growing use of kids' smart phone apps and social networks.[28]

From its beginning, Facebook has promised users that their personal data would be kept private. However, its trillion-member user base is its most valuable asset, so the company has been in a quandary trying to figure out how to make information available to marketers without violating its covenant with its users. In 2012, it began studying the links between Facebook ads and members' shopping habits as part of an effort to prove the effectiveness of its ad business.[29] Most companies on the Web have a privacy policy, but you can find Facebook's statement at www.facebook.com/about/privacy.

Facebook's privacy-versus-personalization dilemma is a red flag for all e-marketers. A legal studies and business ethics professor explained the issues: "Companies are trying to figure out the relationship of privacy to users while also trying to provide personalization and customization of their services."[30] A social media site, ShareThis.com, makes privacy a big issue on its site. Its privacy policy is worth studying. You can find it at http://sharethis.com/privacy#sthash.uTOSevCC.

Many browsers come with a "do not track" option, particularly Mozilla's Firefox, Apple's Safari, and Microsoft's Internet Explorer. Microsoft's latest version of its Internet Explorer, which came packaged with Windows 10, comes with the "do not track" option turned on making the whole privacy issue much more public for its users who have to opt in and customize their preferences.[31]

Google got in trouble with the FTC in 2012 when it was demonstrated that Google bypassed these privacy settings for users of Apple's Safari and presented personalized Web ads through its DoubleClick ad network, which customizes ads based on sites users have visited. Pleading that it was unintentional, Google was still fined $22.5 million.[32]

To be fair, many customers appreciate relevance in the brand messages they receive. Although many customers are willing to give permission to marketers to collect personal data, concerns arise if there is any thought that a company is "spying" on them or collecting personal information without permission. The TRUSTe organization warns that companies ignore these privacy-related concerns at their own peril and do potential damage to their brands if their customers lose confidence in the brand's privacy practices. TRUSTe and the Harris Interactive research organization found that 90 percent of adults worry about their online privacy—so it's a major issue for consumers as well as regulators.[33]

Photo: Courtesy of TRUSTe

Companies can earn their customers' trust by displaying the TRUSTe seal on their websites.

Privacy is particularly an issue with data mining. D'Souza and Phelps call it the "privacy paradox,"[34] meaning that you can't do narrow targeting without collecting personal information. That may make direct-response targeting more efficient with consumers getting fewer unwanted contacts, but at what point is efficiency of targeting compromised by privacy concerns? What is the impact of privacy concerns on consumers' purchasing behavior? Research by D'Souza and Phelps found that privacy concerns do matter and that privacy policies and marketing strategies are interdependent. This issue is discussed in the "A Principled Practice" feature.

Regulation Ultimately, these concerns translate to regulation or, maybe, self-regulation. Senators John McCain and John Kerry introduced bipartisan "privacy bill of rights" legislation in 2011. The FTC, which is the government agency most involved in consumer data oversight, published a report, "Protecting Consumer Privacy in an Era of Rapid Change," in 2012.[35] The agency doesn't have the authority to write new privacy rules but hopes to spur the industry to regulate itself. Action items include the following:

- ***Do Not Track:*** Control data collection as well as data use.
- ***Mobile Tracking:*** Asks the mobile industry to improve privacy protections and use disclosures.

A PRINCIPLED PRACTICE

Privacy: *Use but Don't Abuse Consumer Information*

Joseph E. Phelps, *University of Alabama*
Jimmy Peltier, *University of Wisconsin, Whitewater*
George R. Milne, *University of Massachusetts, Amherst*

In your advertising and marketing communication classes (including this one), you will be encouraged to collect and examine all of the information that is available in order to develop the consumer insights necessary to select the optimal audience and then develop and deliver messages that will move this audience to respond in the desired way.

To accomplish this task, marketing professionals are collecting and using more individual-level consumer information than ever before. Information such as names, addresses, demographic characteristics, lifestyle interests, shopping preferences, and purchase histories have been collected for many years. New information channels have emerged that provide marketers with the ability to capture more information and to capture that information in real time. For example, marketers can easily track online behaviors and use that information to deliver behavioral-based marketing communication.

Radio-frequency identification and video surveillance allow for the tracking of product and customer in-store movements. GPS-based functions in mobile devices also provide location-tracking abilities. Marketers have the ability to capture, store, and analyze tremendous amounts of consumer information.

This information helps marketers to better understand and cater to the wants and needs of their customers and to more effectively identify and communicate with prospective customers. However, because marketers have the ability to piece together personally identifying information from multiple sources, consumers have a real concern regarding their "digital dossier" and how their information dossiers are generated, utilized, and shared, particularly if there is a potential for their information to be used with negative personal and financial consequences.

As you become a marketing communicator, these consumer concerns should be important to you for multiple reasons, each of which revolves around your responsibilities to practice in the best interests of your customers, society, and the ongoing success of the organization for which you work. You need to understand consumer privacy concerns and privacy regulations because you will have the ethical and, in many cases, legal responsibility to thoughtfully protect consumers' personal information while using these data effectively. Your responsibility to the long-term success of your company is critical, and consumer privacy concerns represent an important yet too often ignored factor influencing the potential long-term success. Developing and maintaining long-term customer relationships require organizations to consider the negative impact that privacy concerns have on trust.

Thus, careful consideration of the amount and types of information collected and how that information will be used is critical. It is also essential to make sure that consumers are aware when information is being collected, what is being collected, and how that information will be used. This transparency is difficult to accomplish with emerging media that collect data in ways that are often invisible to the consumer. No one said the job would be easy.

Balancing the use of individual-level consumer information with consumer privacy is, however, a necessary task for which there are legal, ethical, and bottom-line business ramifications. You need consumer information to create great marketing communication, to direct it to the proper audience, and to build long-term relationships. Be sure to treat that information with the respect and protection it deserves.

- ***Data Brokers:*** Creating legislation to make these businesses and their practices more transparent.
- ***Self-Regulation Codes:*** The FTC will work with the Department of Commerce to create specific codes of conduct for different business sectors.

Photo: Courtesy of the Future of Privacy Forum

Like the recycling symbol, this "i" will help people understand why they got the ad or online message. When they click on the symbol, the copy explains that the marketer used their Internet surfing behavior to identify their interests.

In terms of self-regulation, the Digital Advertising Alliance, a consortium of organizations in the advertising and marketing industries, has created the AdChoices program, which includes a code of conduct—Self-Regulatory Program for Online Behavioral Advertising—as well as training and certification programs that encourage companies to commit to the code of conduct.

In an attempt to avert regulation, the direct-marketing industry has developed an icon—a stylized "i"—to use on ads and other online messages that use behavioral targeting.[36] The TRUSTe organization also authorizes companies to use its privacy seal when they are certified as following FTC guidelines and the Digital Advertising Alliance code of conduct.

DBC Trends and Challenges

Direct marketing speaks in the voice of the brand, and, as Duncan noted in his comments in the Part 5 opener, the brand voice needs to be true to the brand. In other words, direct marketing offers a great opportunity to convey the essence and personality of a brand in a one-on-one conversation with a customer or prospect. So what needs to be done to develop and protect this brand voice? Planning an integrated approach is critical, and keeping the message consistent across international borders is also important.

Integrated Direct Marketing

Historically, direct marketing is the first area of marketing communication that adopted an integrated marketing approach. In fact, some people refer to DBC as **integrated direct marketing**. As technology has provided more and better ways to interact with customers, the challenge to direct marketers has been to integrate direct mail, catalogs, telemarketing, websites, e-mail, text messaging, and instant messaging with other marketing communication, such as advertising—and to do so with a consistent brand voice that reflects the brand strategy.

Principle

Direct marketing conveys the essence and personality of a brand in a one-on-one conversation with a customer or prospect.

Two reasons integration plays so well in the direct-response market is because of its emphasis on the customer and its measurability. The coordination problem is a challenge due to the deluge of data bombarding customers from many different channels. The only way to manage the information is to focus it around customer needs and interests. By using databases, companies can become more sensitive to customer wants and needs and less likely to bother them with unwanted commercial messages.

Linking the Channels Instead of treating each medium separately, as some advertising agencies tend to do, DBC companies seek to achieve precise, synchronized use of the right media at the right time, with a measurable return on dollars spent. Here's an example: Say you do a direct-mail campaign, which generates a 2 percent average response. If you include a toll-free 800 number in your mailing as an alternative to the standard mail-in reply—with well-trained, knowledgeable people handling those incoming calls with a carefully thought-out script—you can achieve a 3 to 4 percent response rate. If you follow up your mailing with a phone call within 24 to 72 hours after your prospect receives the mailing, you can generate a response two to eight times as high as the base rate of 2 percent. So, by adding your 800 number, you bring the response rate from 2 percent to 3 or 4 percent. By following up with phone calls, you bring your total response rate as high as 5 to18 percent.

The principle behind integration is that not all people respond the same way to direct-response messages. One person may carefully fill out the order form. Someone else may immediately call the 800 number. Most people, if a DBC message grabs them, tend to put it in the pending pile. That pile grows and grows and then gets tossed out at the end of the month. But if a phone call or e-mail follows the direct-mail piece, the marketer may get the wavering consumer off the fence. Hewlett-Packard, AT&T, Citibank, and IBM have all used integrated direct marketing as a multimedia effort to improve their direct-marketing response rates.

Safeway Stores has become interested in integrated direct marketing. Safeway has signed up manufacturers such as the Quaker Oats Company and Stouffer Food Corp. (owned by Nestlé) for a database marketing program that provides trade dollars in exchange for quality customer data. The program exemplifies the convergence of two trends: grocers looking for manufacturers to supplement their own shrinking marketing budgets and manufacturers eager to allocate new field-marketing support dollars are working more closely as partners. A number of manufacturers whose products are carried in Safeway stores fund Safeway's quarterly mailings in exchange for in-store support and sales data.

A common problem with IDM is that direct-marketing messages and advertising messages often do not reinforce each other as well as they should because the two functions—advertising and direct marketing, which often are handled by different agencies—don't talk to one another. This will change, however, as clients demand more coordination of their marketing communication programs. The Geico campaign is a good example of how advertising and direct pieces can present a consistent brand message. The point is that direct marketing can add impact to an IMC campaign and increase its efficiency.

Principle
One-on-one communication leads to a strengthened customer relationship and, ultimately, increased brand loyalty.

Creating Loyalty One of the best practices noted by Duncan in the Part 5 opener is the development of solid customer–brand relationships. When effective, one-on-one communication

Photo: © 2009 GEICO. Reprinted with permission from GEICO. All rights reserved

More than just a lighthearted lizard, the Gecko is smart enough to deliver a reassuring message to jittery consumers in an economic downturn that Geico is financially stable, even mentioning investment giant and corporate owner Warren Buffett and his Berkshire Hathaway company in this two-sided flyer.

leads to a customer retention strategy that ultimately increases brand loyalty. Direct response is a highly targeted form of marketing communication that lets planners focus on their best customers and inform, encourage, or reward them for their brand loyalty. Frequent-flyer and -buyer programs are examples of database-driven reward programs that help keep customers loyal.

Perhaps the most ambitious attempt to create consumer loyalty is through a concept called **lifetime customer value**, which is an estimate of how much purchase volume companies can expect to get over time from various target markets. To put it formally, lifetime customer value is the financial contribution through sales volume of an individual customer or customer segment over a length of time. The calculation is based on known consumption habits plus future consumption expectations. The estimate of the contribution is defined as return on investment, or revenue gains as a function of marketing costs. In simpler terms, by knowing your consumers' past behavior, you can decide how much you want to spend to get them to purchase and then repurchase your product, and you can track your investment by measuring the response.

Consumer resistance to direct marketing must be considered in efforts to build loyalty. Changing consumers' attitudes about direct marketing has not been easy because consumers resent companies that know too much about them. If the company can demonstrate that it is acting in the consumer's best interest rather than just trolling for dollars, it might gain and maintain consumers' loyalty. Saks Fifth Avenue, for example, identified the customers who account for half of all sales and offered the group exclusive benefits through a program called Saks First. The benefits include fashion newsletters and a first crack at all sales.

The most important goal, however, is supporting brand building, and some marketers have been concerned that DBC's emphasis on accountability and on driving sales has made it less focused on the brand presence.

Global Considerations in DBC

The direct-marketing industry is growing fast in many Far Eastern and European countries—in some places, even faster than in the United States. The global trend is fueled by the same technological forces driving the growth of direct marketing in this country: the increasing use of computer databases, credit cards, toll-free phone numbers, and the Internet, along with the search for more convenient ways to shop. The growth may be even greater in B2B marketing than in consumer marketing.

Direct marketing is particularly important in countries that have tight restrictions on advertising and other forms of marketing communication. However, these countries often have restrictions on direct marketing as well. Privacy issues are even more intense in some countries than in the United States. In some countries, lists are not available, or they may be of poor quality. Databases can be more freely transferred between European countries than they can between the United States and European countries.

Some countries have instituted outright bans on direct marketing, although these restrictions seem to be loosening up. China lifted its national ban on direct sales, such as Amway and Avon, in late 2005. The ban had been in place since 1998 because of a series of scandals and frauds.

Governmental regulation of the U.S. Postal Service may also place limitations on the use of direct mail. For example, language and characters are a problem, particularly for American companies that may not understand that the letter *e* isn't the same as *é*, *è*, *ê*, or *ë* in an address. Computers and typesetting systems have to accommodate these differences. The format of the address has to be exactly correct in some countries, such as Germany, where the Deutsche Post has strict rules about correct address formats. In Hungary, the street name is in the third line of the address, whereas it is on the second line along with the postal code in Germany. Presorted mail in a wrong format may result in charges to the end user that significantly raise the cost of the mailing.

Looking Ahead

Direct-response marketing communication is an important tool in the IMC tool kit because it is uniquely designed to deliver interactivity. DBC is also important because of its ability to track effectiveness. In the next chapter, let's consider the various ways people are engaged in brand experiences through promotions.

It's a Wrap

The Gecko and Pals Deliver Direct Response

In this chapter, we identified many benefits of using direct-response marketing. It can reach a large, diverse audience efficiently to generate customers for auto insurance. Geico's aggressive effort to blanket the nation with an array of campaigns, including the Gecko, the Cavemen, the customer/celebrity testimonials, Caleb the Camel and "Rhetorical Questions," teaches an important brand communication lesson about direct marketing. It demonstrates how effective direct-response advertising and a little bit of humor can sell a product to a wide-ranging and varied audience, even in a tough economy.

In lieu of a sales force, direct advertising does the job on billboards, the Internet, and many television shows. According to one report, Geico spent more than any other car insurer in 2011, nearly $1 billion to promote its products. Geico and rivals Progressive, State Farm, and Allstate are among the 20 most-advertised brands, amazingly spending more than Coca-Cola, Budweiser, and Home Depot.

The Gecko and the Caveman have earned their way into the hearts of consumers, winning many awards, including the Direct Marketing Association's Echo award. The Caveman joined the Gecko as a favorite brand icon, having been elected to the Madison Avenue Advertising Walk of Fame. According to the Geico website, "The Caveman, still perturbed with Geico for its 'So easy, a caveman could do it' slogan, did not attend the award ceremony."

Photo: © 2007 GEICO. All rights reserved. Used with permission. Courtesy of The Martin Agency.

Key Points Summary

1. **How does direct-response marketing work?** Direct marketing always involves a one-on-one relationship with the prospect. It is personal and interactive and uses various media to effect a measurable response. The four main players in direct marketing are the marketers, the agencies, the media that deliver the message, and the consumers. The process involves setting objectives and strategies, targeting, deciding on the offer, developing a message and media strategy, facilitating the response or order, filling the order, and evaluating the direct-marketing effort.
2. **What are the primary tools and media available to direct-response programs?** Direct-response media include direct mail, catalogs, telemarketing, direct-response advertising in print and broadcast media, and the Internet and other new forms of media.
3. **How are databases used in direct marketing?** Direct-marketing communication has benefited from the development and maintenance of a database of customer names, addresses, telephone numbers, and demographic and psychographic characteristics. Advertisers use this information to target their campaigns to consumers who, based on demographics, are likely to buy their products.
4. **What are the trends and challenges facing direct-response communication?** Direct-response brand communication (DBC) has been an innovator in the use of integrated strategies, particularly those that link the various channels used in DBC campaigns. A challenge has been to create brand loyalty and respectful long-term brand relationships using DBC tools. Another challenge is global marketing because of the different legal requirements in various countries.

Key Terms

behavioral targeting, p. 517
broadsheets, p. 510
call centers, p. 513
catalog, p. 512
cold call, p. 513
compiled list, p. 519
conversion rates, p. 503
data mining, p. 520
databases, p. 517
direct mail, p. 508
direct-response marketing, p. 501
direct-response brand communication, p. 500
fulfillment, p. 506
house list, p. 519
inbound telemarketing, p. 513
infomercial, p. 508
integrated direct marketing, p. 524
lead generation, p. 503
lifetime customer value, p. 526
merging, p. 520
offer, p. 505
one-step offer, p. 505
opt in, p. 517
opt out, p. 517
optimization, p. 505
outbound telemarketing, p. 513
permission marketing, p. 517
predictive dialing, p. 513
prospecting, p. 503
purging, p. 520
recency, frequency, and monetary, p. 504
relational databases, p. 520
response list, p. 519
spam, p. 516
spoofing, p. 516
telemarketing, p. 513
two-step offer, p. 505
variable data campaigns, p. 508

Review Questions

16-4. In which situations should a marketer consider direct-response marketing as superior to other promotional tools?

16-5. Define DRM, and explain how it is supported by the use of a database.

16-6. Discuss the importance of individualized messages in direct-response marketing.

16-7. Discuss the difference between direct-response marketing messages addressed to customers and those targeting prospects.

16-8. What is a database, and how do direct marketers use it?

16-9. If you are using data mining to develop a prospecting program for a client, what would you be trying to accomplish?

16-10. Explain the privacy issues that involve direct-response communication.

16-11. What is the objective of data-driven relationship programs?

16-12. What does RFM stand for, and how is this concept used in targeting?

16-13. Discuss permission marketing and what strategies can be used to overcome the problems of spam?

16-14. How is integrated direct marketing used in an IMC program?

16-15. What is a loyalty program, and how does lifetime customer value enter into the planning for such a program?

Discussion Questions

16-16. You have been appointed as the marketing manager in a company that sells electronic components in the B2B industry. Specify what would be your best marketing tool to boost sales and explain your reasoning.

16-17. Kali Johnson, a recent college graduate, is interviewing with a large garden product firm that relies on television for its direct-response advertising. "Your portfolio looks very good. I'm sure you can write," the interviewer says, "but let me ask you what is it about our copy that makes it more important than copy written for Ford, Pepsi, or Pampers?" What can she say that will help convince the interviewer she understands the special demands of direct-response writing?

✪16-18. One of the smaller, privately owned bookstores on campus is considering a direct-response service to cut down on its severe in-store traffic problems at the beginning of each semester. What ideas do you have for setting up some type of direct-response program to take the pressure off store traffic?

16-19. Define 7 methods of direct-response marketing. Choose one method and discuss its merits in creating revenues for a company's business.

✪16-20. How does the recent fervor surrounding personal privacy affect direct marketing—specifically, telemarketing, and e-mail advertising? You are designing a direct-marketing campaign for a local record store that employs telemarketing and e-mail advertising, but your client is concerned because of privacy issues. Argue either for or against the use of these tools in this situation.

Take-Home Projects

16-21. ***Portfolio Project:*** Check out a set of three catalogs and their companion websites in a particular category (such as www.llbean.com, www.eddiebauer.com, or www.landsend.com). In what ways are they similar and different?

Pick one of the brands:

- Identify what direct-marketing strategies the company employs. Which do you think are the most successful? Why? What are the least effective?
- Analyze the brand image as presented in the catalog and online. Develop a proposal to make the brand image more distinctive and yet consistent across the two media formats.

16-22. ***Mini-Case Analysis:*** Explain how Geico operates as a direct-to-consumer insurer in the auto insurance market. Why would you think humor would be an effective creative strategy in this situation? You may also remember that we have suggested that being single-minded is a wise strategy. Why, then, does Geico use different approaches? If you were on the Geico team and had been asked to submit ideas for the next year's campaign, what would you recommend? Develop and explain an idea that you think would continue the unusual strategy Geico is using.

TRACE North America Case

Multicultural Direct-Response Communication

Read the TRACE case in the Appendix before coming to class.

16-23. What is the chief advantage of direct marketing with this target audience? What is the main disadvantage?

16-24. Create at least five direct-response materials that you feel will make this campaign more effective.

CHAPTER

17 Promotions

Photo: Created by Burson-Marstellar, LLC d/b/a Proof Integrated Communications. Copyright, 2012 by Susan G. Komen.

It's a Winner	Campaign:	Organization:	Agency:	Awards:
	"I am Susan G. Komen for the cure."	*Susan G. Komen for the Cure*	*Burson-Marsteller's Proof*	*Multiple Halo Awards for Cause Marketing*

CHAPTER KEY POINTS

1. **What are the current trends and practices in planning promotions?**
2. **What are the tools of consumer promotion, and how are they used?**
3. **What are the types and purposes of trade promotions?**
4. **How do multiplatform promotions—sponsorships and events, loyalty programs, and partnership programs—work?**
5. **What are the critical promotional practices in integration?**

The Power of Pink

Although you might not initially consider pink a fall color, think again. Everywhere you look in National Breast Cancer Awareness Month (October), you see pink. The National Football League's pink football equipment and pink-trimmed uniforms, Delta Airlines' pink plane, Panera Bread's Pink Ribbon Bagels, Avon's Pink Products, Yoplaits' pink yogurt lids, KitchenAid's pink blenders, NASCAR's pink racecars, OtterBox's pink smart phone covers—you get the point.

Inspired by the success of red ribbons in raising awareness of AIDS, proponents of breast cancer awareness started using a pink ribbon as the symbol for its cause, which has evolved into one of the most successful charity promotional campaign ideas ever. The Susan G. Komen Foundation for the Cure, dedicated to educating women about breast cancer and finding a cure, was the first to distribute pink ribbons in 1991 in New York City to breast cancer survivor participants in its "Race for the Cure." Other groups with similar goals quickly adopted the pink ribbon.

The following year, leaders at the National Breast Cancer Awareness Month adopted the pink ribbon as its symbol. In 1993, Evelyn Lauder, a vice president of the Estée Lauder Companies, founded the Breast Cancer Research Institute and used the pink ribbon as its symbol as well.

What makes this campaign idea remarkable from a branding and IMC perspective is the number of companies that have found synergy in joining an important cause as they promote their products. A *New York Times* reporter described the pinking of America as "multi-billion-dollar business, a marketing, merchandising and fund-raising opportunity that is almost unrivaled in scope." Behind this effort is a fascinating story of a brilliant marketing insight and sustained work to communicate the important cancer message.

Nancy G. Brinker, the founder and CEO of Susan G. Komen for the Cure Foundation, rebranded the disease from hopeless to hopeful, in memory of her sister, who had died of breast cancer. Drawing on her career as a sales trainee at Neiman Marcus, she made the message about cancer more optimistic, convincing people that there is hope for surviving the disease. That hope depended on educating women to get mammograms and investing in research about breast cancer. An annual event, "Race for the Cure," helps spread the positive message. Brinker replicated the message across the country by enlisting 121 affiliates to replicate the event, Komen's biggest revenue producer.

To fund the efforts to educate women and produce a cure, Brinker successfully enlisted a multitude of companies who found synergy in cobranding their products with a good cause, especially during October. She recognized the power of pink—to help companies associate their brand with a good cause. Companies generate goodwill for their brands and income to support the cause.

The ads featured on the opening page of this case study tell the stories of cancer survivors and the foundation. Much of the advertising in cause marketing features not only the charity but its partnering companies as well.

In 2012, Komen expected to raise $50 million in revenue from its promotions with 216 corporate partnerships. Is pink the color of success? Find out at the end of this chapter in the "It's a Wrap" feature.

Sources: Sam Borden, "A New Twist to N.F.L. Breast Cancer Awareness: A Pink Tutu," October 5, 2012, www.nytimes.com; Natasha Singer, "Welcome, Fans, to the Pinking of America," October 15, 2011, www.nytimes.com; Deborah Sweeney, "5 Companies Going above and beyond for Breast Cancer Awareness Month," October 11, 2012, www.forbes.com; "OtterBox Promotes Strength in Numbers during Breast Cancer Awareness Month," October 4, 2012, http://markets.onnytimes.com; Pink Ribbon, www.wikipedia.org.

The Komen Foundation's "Pink Ribbon" campaign is an example of an award-winning promotional idea that captivates supporters and sponsors and involves them personally in building a successful breast cancer research organization. Sales promotion is about the fun, creative, and exciting ideas that the promotion industry uses to spur action and build strong brand relationships. In this chapter, we will explain the difference between consumer and trade promotions as well as other programs, such as loyalty programs, tie-ins, and sponsorships, that integrate advertising, public relations, and promotion efforts. First, let's discuss the concept and basic principles of sales promotion.

Why Sales Promotion?

When a marketer increases the value of its product or brand by offering an extra incentive to purchase it, the marketer is creating a **sales promotion**, which is the subject of this chapter. In most cases, the objective of sales promotion is to encourage action by adding to the value of the brand. Also called *marketing at retail*, sales promotion works with other aspects of the marketing mix to motivate consumer action and maximize the marketing investment.[1] For example, Macy's created a springtime Brazil-focused campaign as a merchandising event. The "Brazil: A Magical Journey" promotion saluted Brazil's culture, fabrics, and designs as it brought big, bright colors into "O Mercado," Brazilian-themed markets inside Macy's stores.[2]

The professional sales promotion industry, with annual revenues of about $12 billion, is estimated to include some 8,000 companies representing advertising and large marketing firms that specialize in sales promotion, such as Carlson Marketing. The Promotion Marketing Association is the professional organization that includes not only the professional companies but also marketers who use sales promotion. Founded in 1911, the organization promotes excellence in promotion marketing and showcases such practices in its Reggie Awards program.

Although the breadth of the industry has exploded with the new opportunities provided by the Internet, a simple definition identifies the key elements of promotion marketing as follows: "The media and non-media marketing pressure applied for a predetermined, limited period of time at the level of consumer, retailer, or wholesaler in order to stimulate trial, increase consumer demand, or improve product availability."[3]

Let's examine this definition. First, it acknowledges that consumers are an important target for promotions, but so are other stakeholders, such as the company's sales representatives and members of the trade (wholesalers and retailers). Second, media are carriers of a message that motivates the target (see the Chevy billboards), and the media can be nontraditional or even human, such as sales staff. Third, the definition recognizes that sales promotion is a set of techniques that prompts members of three target audiences—consumers, sales representatives, and the trade (distributors, retailers, and dealers)—to take action, preferably immediate action.

Simply put, sales promotion affects demand by offering an incentive to act, usually in the form of a price reduction, but it also may offer additional amounts of the product, cash, prizes and gifts, premiums, special events, and so on. An example of a promotional incentive was a $1 million offer by Netflix to consumers who could offer ideas for improving its movie recommendation software. Promotions may also just contribute to a fun brand relationship-building experience, as Frontier Airlines' favorite animal contest you read about in Chapter 9 illustrates.

Principle
Sales promotion is primarily designed to affect demand by motivating people to act.

Why Is Sales Promotion Growing?

Over the years, advertising and sales promotion have been battling for their share of the marketing communication budget. In many marketing-savvy companies, sales promotion budgets are larger than advertising budgets. Until the 1980s, advertising was the dominant player in the marketing communication arena. But during the 1980s, more marketers found themselves driving immediate bottom-line responses through the use of sales promotion.

Accountability In terms of the need for accountability for marketing communication efforts, most U.S. companies focus on immediate profits, a drive that sales promotion satisfies. Because the benefits of advertising are often more apparent in the long term, companies invest more

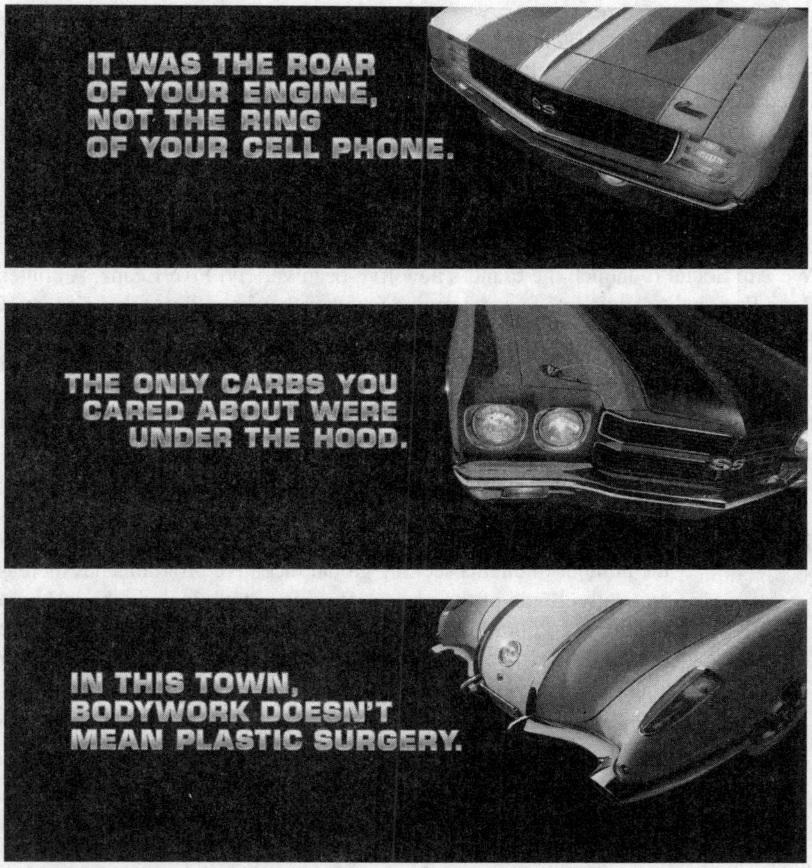

Photo: Courtesy of General Motors Media Archive

These three billboards are from a series of billboards that celebrate the history of GM's iconic Chevy brand. The billboards, with their dramatic images and quirky headlines celebrate an earlier era of car fanatics, are posted during the annual classic car event in Detroit. Their purpose is more event sponsorship and brand recognition than traditional advertising.

money in sales promotion when they want quick results. Product managers are under pressure to generate quarterly (or even monthly or weekly) sales increases. Arlene Gerwin, a marketing expert who consults on promotional planning, explains, "Sales promotions deliver more immediate consumer response and a quicker payback than advertising."[4] Hence, the pressure for short-term profits leads to bigger sales promotion budgets.

Another aspect of accountability is result driven. Sales promotions are relatively easy to evaluate in terms of their impact on sales and whether a sales promotion strategy has accomplished its objectives. Because promotions operate in a finite time frame and deliver action, in Gerwin's view, it is relatively easy and quick to evaluate their success because there is usually an immediate response of some kind.

It also is easier to compute a return on investment (ROI) for promotions than for advertising. This process, known as **payout planning**, means that the results derived from a promotion can be estimated and compared with the projected costs of the effort. If the promotion doesn't deliver more than it costs, then it is not a good idea, at least financially. Admittedly, there may be other reasons for conducting a promotion, but usually the go/no-go decision is based on the effort's ROI.

For example, Moonfruit, a company that helps small businesses build do-it-yourself websites, gave away 10 MacBook Pros as part of a birthday celebration. To be eligible, participants had to send a creative tweet, an idea that exploded on Twitter, brought lots of people to the company's website, and generated tons of publicity. If handled through a traditional advertising campaign, the exposure would have cost far more than the price of 10 MacBook Pros.[5] (Check out Moonfruit at www.moonfruit.com.)

Media Shifts Advertisers also cite other economic reasons for the shift. Traditional media costs have escalated to the point where alternative types of media must be considered. As the networks have raised their advertising prices, their share of prime-time television viewers has dropped. The proliferation of digital media and competition for audiences' attention also factor in the need for accountability. Advertisers, therefore, are exploring marketing communication forms that cost less and produce immediate, tangible results. Sales promotion can deliver these results, particularly if these programs take advantage of the efficiencies and impact of social media.

An example is the Heinz "personalized bean" social media promotion designed by U.K. based We Are Social to launch the brand's new five-bean variety, Five Beanz. A contest based on a "Bean Personality" quiz lets fans determine whether they're a Pinto, Red Kidney, Cannellini, Haricot, or Borlotti, which then enters them in a drawing. Winners were drawn every hour during the 12-day campaign for 1,440 fans who received their favorite bean engraved with their name. This isn't the first personalized promotion by We Are Social for Heinz. Previously, Heinz fans could send sick friends Heinz soups whose labels were customized with their names and get-well messages.[6]

Global incentive programs are also experiencing explosive growth, and much of that relates either to IMC or changes in global media. The international product manager for one promotional company indicates that the number of clients seeking global incentive programs has increased dramatically. Some of the reasons for this growth include the interest of multinational corporations in aligning all units with corporate goals, increasing bottom-line efficiency, and taking advantage of the rise of the Internet.[7]

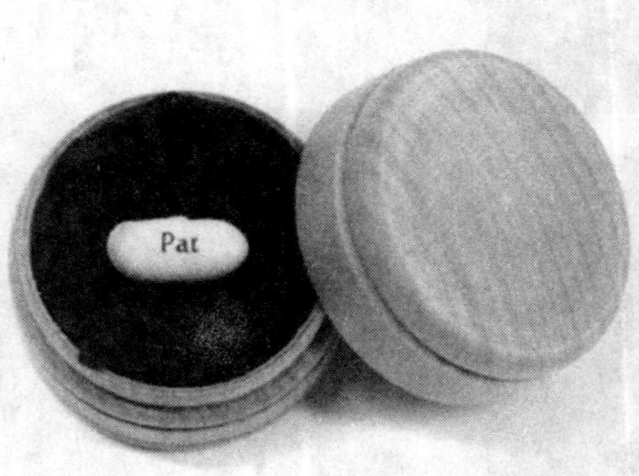

Photo: Courtesy of H.J. Heinz Company

Advertising Age extolled the unique prize in a drawing for Heinz—adorable little beans engraved with the names of winners—as the "cutest social media campaign." The contest was for the launch of the Heinz Five Beanz line.

Marketplace Changes Other reasons for the move to sales promotion match changes in the marketplace, such as these:

- ***Consumer Behavior*** Shoppers today are better educated, more selective, and less loyal to brand names than in the past, which means they are more likely to switch brands.
- ***Pricing*** Consumers have come to expect constant short-term price reductions, such as coupons, sales, and price promotions.
- ***Market Share*** In most industries, the battle is for market share rather than general product growth. Sales promotion encourages people to switch products, increasing market share.

- ***Parity Products*** Sales promotion is often the most effective strategy for increasing sales of a parity product when the products in the category are largely undifferentiated. When products are similar, promotions become the tiebreaker in the consumer's decision making.
- ***The Power of the Retailer*** Dominant retailers, such as Safeway, Walmart, Toys "R" Us, and Home Depot, demand a variety of promotional incentives before allowing products into their stores.

From the consumers' perspective, sales promotion reduces the risk associated with a purchase by giving them something of *added value*, such as a coupon, rebate, or discounted price. Promotions typically offer the consumer added value, or "more for less," as a Southwest Airlines promotion illustrates. Developed in conjunction with Alamo, the promotion promised those who fly Southwest and rent vehicles from Alamo that they could earn double Rapid Rewards credit toward a free flight—for a limited time, of course.

Principle
Sales promotion reduces the risk of trying a new product by giving something of added value to motivate action.

Sales Promotion Planning

Similar to advertising and other marcom areas, sales promotions are developed with a plan, sometimes called a creative brief. This summarizes the usual planning decisions, such as SWOTs, brand positioning strategy, promotional objectives, targeting and consumer insights, budget, scheduling, and timing.

An example comes from the launch of Via, Starbucks' instant coffee. To demonstrate that the instant product tastes like its regular brew, the company promoted a "taste challenge" that took place at Starbucks stores on the launch weekend. Customers were able to sample a cup of brewed coffee and a cup of Via to see if they could tell the difference. The event was promoted with television commercials and on social marketing sites.

Promotion Objectives As part of an integrated program, sales promotion has different functions than other marcom tools. Marketing consultant Gerwin explains, "The objective of advertising is quite different from that of sales promotion. Advertising is usually viewed as a longer-term investment. Over time, advertising builds brand equity by establishing a consistent image or feeling for a brand." In contrast, she explains, "sales promotions are more immediate, involving a finite time period." In return for taking action, "sales promotions offer the consumer something more tangible."[8]

A number of reasons exist for using promotions, and these can easily be translated into objectives. Many of the reasons focus on using promotions in a new product launch and how that can deliver trial. Promotions can offer consumers an immediate inducement to try or buy a product, often simply by making the product more valuable. Sales promotions can make consumers more brand aware and generate trial as well as persuade them to buy the product again once they've tried it. It can push the product through the distribution channel by generating positive brand experiences among resellers and buyers in many places along the channel-and-purchase continuum. It's also good at building traffic for a retailer. J.C. Penney, for example, has used free back-to-school haircuts for kids as part of its back-to-school promotion, which is a key selling period for the family retailer.[9]

In addition to helping introduce a new product and create brand awareness, promotions can build a brand over time by reinforcing advertising images and messages. Promotions can create an affinity between brands and buyers by creating brand involvement and positive experiences that people associate with the brand, as the "Pink Ribbon" case illustrates. When used for brand building, the primary objective in most marketing communication programs is to build brand awareness as well as drive behavior. That's also true for nonprofits, such as the Susan G. Komen Foundation, whose campaigns are designed to generate contributions, corporate sponsorships, and participation in events.

The Oreo "Daily Twist" campaign, which celebrated the iconic brand's 100th birthday, showcased a group of

Photo: Brain Ach/Ap Images for Oreo

The Oreo "Daily Twist" campaign used ideas contributed by Oreo fans and created live, one a day, from a glass booth on Times Square. The 100 ads were beamed each day to the more than 27.9 million people who "like" Oreo on Facebook as well as to fans on Pinterest, Twitter, and Oreo.com.

creatives from the Draftfcb and 360i agencies working in a glass box in Times Square. Sort of a crowdsourcing experiment, the creative team created 100 daily ads based on ideas suggested by and voted on by consumers through social media. The theme was a "Daily Twist," which was a play on the "twist, lick, and dunk" ritual dear to Oreo fans.[10]

Promotions are not effective in achieving all marketing objectives. For example, promotions cannot do much to change negative attitudes toward a product, overcome product problems, or reposition a brand. Brand building, however, is an interesting challenge to promotion, so let's look at it in more depth.

The Issue of Brand Building For years, a heated debate has focused on sales promotion and brand building. Advertisers claim that the strength of advertising is creating and maintaining brand image, and sales promotion's price deals actually negate all their hard work by diverting the emphasis from the brand to the price. The result, sales promotion critics complain, is a brand-insensitive consumer. Consider McDonald's, which has long based its image on everyday value, one of the four pillars of McDonald's marketing mantra: quality, service, cleanliness, and value. Advertisers contend that price promotions, like a 99-cent Big Mac, damage more than the company's bottom line because the price promotion undercuts the value pillar. In other words, if value is central to McDonald's pricing, then it wouldn't need to offer special sale prices. On the other hand, in difficult economic times, the special-price strategy may also convey the message that companies are sensitive to customers' needs and adjusting its prices in order to be supportive.

Procter & Gamble's division manager of advertising and sales promotion explains it this way: "Too many marketers no longer adhere to the fundamental premise of brand building, which is that [brand] franchises aren't built by cutting price but rather by offering superior quality at a reasonable price and clearly communicating that value to consumers." The price-cutting promotions began in the 1970s fostering a buy-only-on-sale orientation that some branding experts believe has caused long-term brand building to suffer. Critics point to a general decline in consumer brand loyalty as just one negative result of price-based promotions.

The problem is that brand building is a long and time-consuming process of establishing the brand's core values. Promotion, whether a sale price, premium, coupon, or some other incentive, is inherently short term, so the promotion can undermine the brand's established values if not handled carefully. Analyst Doug Brookes says that even in economic downturns, promotion strategies can be designed to balance both long-term brand building and short-term price promotion with the help of predictive analytic techniques that optimize ROI.[11]

Sales promotion experts argue that their practices can help to build brand image. First, they refer to many cereal brands, rental car companies, airlines, and hotels that have used a variety of well-planned sales promotion strategies (e.g., loyalty programs) to enhance their brand images. An example comes from a classic promotional ad for Eagle Shirtmakers. Second, they acknowledge that continuous promotion—particularly continuous price promotion—does not work well with brand building, except for discount marketers, whose image is built on the notion of sale prices, although even Walmart is rethinking its "always low prices" positioning strategy.

According to one industry expert, the solution is to make advertising more accountable and promotion more brand focused. In other words, the advertising and promotion need to work more closely together, and, in particular, short-term campaigns shouldn't be at odds with one another. More integration is needed when planning marketing communication programs.

The Primary Sales Promotion Targets The most common sales promotion strategies target three audiences: consumer, trade, and sales force. The first two—customer sales and trade support—have direct implications for advertising and marketing communication.

The third category, sales force promotions, are also important in building trade support. These include two general sets of promotional activities directed at the firm's salespeople to motivate them to increase their sales levels. The first set of activities includes programs that better prepare salespeople to do their jobs, such as sales manuals, training programs, sales presentations, and supportive materials (training films, slides, videos, and visual aids). The second set of activities deals with incentives for retailers to use as in-store promotions and other programs, such as contests, that motivate salespeople to work harder.

Photo: Courtesy of Phillips-Van Heusen Corporation

CLASSIC

San Francisco adman Howard Gossage was known for his sense of humor and tongue-in-the-cheek promotional ideas. This ad for Eagle Shirtmakers featured what you might call a premium—a handkerchief made from the shirt fabric, which also made it a sample. The wry copy is in classic Gossage ad-writing style.

Estimating Performance Because promotions are so focused on action, it makes sense that sales volume is the primary measure of their effectiveness. After all, they are called *sales promotions*. Response rate—consumers calling the company or sending back a card—is also important to sales promotion. So are redemption rates, which are the rates at which people redeem coupons, refunds, and rebates. These rates are used to evaluate the effectiveness of promotional programs. All of these will be discussed in more detail in Chapter 19.

An important dimension of sales promotion effectiveness is payout planning. The goal of creating a payout plan is to produce promotions that increase sales and profits. Needless to say, a promotion should not cost the company more money than it brings in.

An example of poor payout planning comes from Hoover, a company owned by Maytag at the time, and an ill-fated U.K. promotion. It was a simple offer: Customers in Great Britain and Ireland were offered two free airline tickets to the United States or continental Europe when they purchased at least $150 worth of Hoover products. Hoover planned to use the commissions it made from land arrangements, such as hotel reservations and car rentals, to help pay for the airline tickets. How did the promotion turn into a catastrophe? Unfortunately, the commissions were less than anticipated, and the ticket demand was far greater. Maytag's travel agents began attaching unreasonable demands to the free tickets, expensive extras, inconvenient airports, and undesirable departure dates to discourage acceptance of the offer. All these strategies turned happy winners into complaining customers. In the aftermath, Hoover fired three top executives and set up a $30 million fund to pay for the airline tickets.

The trade press is full of stories about poorly designed or performing promotions. Such failures hurt companies' reputations, waste money, and sometimes even hurt consumers. For

Photo: Maria Dryfhout/Shutterstock

The "Bacon Barter" stunt was designed to prove the value of Oscar Mayer's Butcher Thick Cut Bacon. In this stunt, the bacon barterer, Josh Sankey, substituted bacon for hard, cold cash and traded his way across the country receiving not only housing and food but also New York Jets tickets (six bacon bricks) and an invitation to a Hamptons wedding (one bacon brick).

example, Burger King once had to recall 400,000 toy boats given away with kids' meals after reports that children had been stuck with metal pins that came off the boats too easily. That recall came a week after McDonald's recalled a Happy Meal "Scooter Bug" toy. In 1999, the fast-food industry reeled from the deaths of two infants who suffocated from containers used in a Pokémon promotion. About 25 million of those toys were recalled.

Promotional Big Ideas

From the planning document, promotional planners develop their ideas—in fact, a Big Idea, like the breast cancer Pink Ribbon, is just as important for sales promotion as it is for advertising. In many cases, the promotion is part of a bigger IMC plan, and one of the requirements is that the promotion's Big Idea should support the campaign's creative idea. For example, Frontier's long-running position that we described in the Chapter 9 opening story as "a different kind of animal" was reflected in a short-term promotional campaign to choose a favorite animal from the spokes-animals on the planes' tails.

The challenge is to come up with exciting, interesting promotional ideas that are involving and capture the attention of the target market—and that includes consumers as well as trade partners in the industry—at the same time remaining true to the brand strategy. One of the wackiest promotional stunts recently was a "Bacon Barter" for Oscar Mayer. The stunt was the idea of digital agency 360i, which put bacon-loving Josh Sankey on the road—penniless except for a trailer full of 3,000 pounds of bacon. On his cross-country trek, he bartered bacon for housing, food, and drink. His adventure was tracked on Facebook and Twitter. Check out his photo album at www.bing.com/images/search?q=Bacon+Barter&qpvt=Bacon+Barter&FORM=IGRE.

Consumer Promotions

Principle
Consumer promotions provide an incentive so that consumers will look for a particular brand.

Although trade promotion claims the greatest percent of the promotion budget, we'll start with consumer promotions because these are familiar to most people. Consumer sales promotions are directed at the ultimate user of the good or service. They are intended to provide an incentive so that when consumers go into a store, they will look for a particular brand. The primary strengths of consumer sales promotions are their variety and flexibility as well as their accountability.

Tools of Consumer Promotions

A product manager can use and combine many promotion techniques to meet almost any objective. Sales promotion works for all kinds of businesses, including movies. Here's a summary of the most common types of consumer promotions:

- ***Price Deals*** A popular sales promotion technique is a **price deal**, a temporary price reduction, a sale price, or even freebies. *Giveaways* of some books, usually those that are in the public domain, such as Jane Austen's *Pride and Prejudice*, were used by Amazon.com to promote its Kindle e-reader.[12] Amazon also sometimes gives away limited numbers of certain new titles to spark interest in a new book. The Billings, Montana, "Trailhead" branding campaign that we discussed in Chapter 7 also used a giveaway to build excitement for the new brand identity.

  Freebies can be a killer if the company doesn't adequately predict the consumer response. That happened to KFC when it introduced its new grilled chicken. In what it thought was a great idea, the KFC promotion team got Oprah to announce a deal for freebie meals. Unfortunately, KFC wasn't prepared for the enormous response, and its stores ran out of food, angering millions of customers. Next, it tried to make good on its giveaway with downloadable coupons from its website, but because of problems online, many customers gave up on that offer as well. Even with all the bad press, the KFC president found a silver lining: "There's no one in America right now who doesn't know we're selling grilled chicken," he said.[13]

The four common price deals include the following:

1. A *cents-off deal* is a reduction in the normal price charged for a good or service (e.g., "was $1,000, now $500," or "50 percent off") announced at the point of sale or through mass or direct advertising.
2. *Prize-pack deals* provide the consumer with something extra through the package itself—a prize in a cereal box, for instance.
3. *Bonus packs* contain additional amounts of the product free when consumers purchase the standard size at the regular price. For example, Purina Dog Food may offer 25 percent more dog food in the bag.
4. *Banded packs* are more units of a product sold at a lower price than if they were bought at the regular single-unit price. Sometimes the products are physically packaged together, such as bar soap and six-packs of soft drinks.

One result of price deals can be price wars, such as when Walmart and Amazon.com took turns reducing hardback book prices in late 2009 as Walmart tried to steal Amazon's position as the number-one bookseller. Sales of new releases that normally sell for $28 to $29 were offered by Walmart.com for $20. Amazon matched that price, and Walmart responded with a $9 price. Authors were particularly concerned that the price war would reset the price point for new hardbacks.[14] A similar issue arose in 2010 when Apple led a group of publishers in opposing Amazon's pricing and staying firm on e-book prices that were closer to print book pricing, a strategy that came unglued in 2013 when a federal judge found Apple guilty of conspiring to fix prices.

- ***Refunds and Rebates*** A **refund** or **rebate** is a marketer's offer to return a certain amount of money to the consumer who purchases the product. Sometimes, the refund is a check for a certain amount of money; at other times, it may be a coupon to encourage repeat use.
- ***Sampling*** Allowing the consumer to try the product or service is called **sampling**. Advertisers can distribute samples to consumers in numerous ways. Sampling tables, particularly for food products, can be set up in stores. Small samples of products can show up with newspapers and on house doorknobs, in doctors' and dentists' offices, and, most commonly, through the mail. An interesting offer by Millstone Coffee involved an empty coffee bag delivered with a newspaper in the newspaper's plastic bag that could be taken to the store and filled with a half-pound Millstone sample of their choice. Advertisers can design ads with coupons for free samples, place samples in special packages, or distribute samples at special in-store displays. Product samples influence consumers more than other types of in-store promotions, according to one survey.

Sampling is not just an in-store activity. Consider car rentals. A *Washington Post* columnist took automakers to task for selling low-budget, stripped-down models to car rental companies. His point was that car rentals are an unrecognized sampling opportunity and that if the experience is uncomfortable or the performance is underwhelming, then the carmaker has suffered a possibly fatal hit to its brand experience. His point: It would make more sense for an automobile manufacturer to display the best samples of its cars in the rental market, even if that means selling them to rental car companies at a loss.[15]

Photo: Courtesy of the Billings Chamber of Commerce/ Convention and Visitors' Bureau

SHOWCASE

The Billings "Trailhead" campaign used weekly drawings with the winners receiving caps as well as dinner and two nights at the Crowne Plaza Hotel for the grand prize winner.

John Brewer, president and CEO of the Billings Chamber of Commerce/ Convention and Visitors Bureau, graduated from the University of West Florida. He was nominated for inclusion in this book by Professor Tom Groth.

Sampling has also become a mainstay of interactive promotions on the Internet. Some companies sample their products on their Web page.[16] Recently, Dove enticed customers with free samples of its new Dove Body Nourishers and Dove Ultimate Clear deodorant; however, most farm out the efforts to online companies that specialize in handling sample offers and fulfillment. Some of these online sampling companies are Freesampleclub.com, Startsampling.com, Freesamples.com, and Sampleville.com. In addition, freebie portals, such as Amazingfreebies.com, Nojunkfree.com, and Freesite.com, have endless offers for gratis goodies.

- ***Premiums*** A **premium** is a tangible reward for a desired behavior, such as buying a product. Premiums are either free or low in price. The two general types of premiums are direct and mail. Direct premiums award the incentive immediately, at the time of purchase. The four variations of direct premiums are (1) store premiums, given to customers at the retail site; (2) in-pack premiums, inserted in the package at the factory; (3) on-pack premiums, placed on the outside of the package at the factory; and (4) container premiums, in which the package is the premium. Mail premiums require the customer to take some action before receiving the premium. A **self-liquidator** premium usually requires that a payment be mailed in along with some proof of purchase before the customer receives the premium. The payment is sufficient to cover the cost of the premium. Another type of mail premium requires the customer to save coupons or special labels attached to the product that can be redeemed for merchandise.
- ***Coupons*** The two general types of **coupons** that provide a discount on the price of a product are retailer and manufacturer coupons. Coupons have always been popular, but with the recent Great Recession, research found that 40 percent of U.S consumers used coupons, a 10 percent increase from the previous year. The study estimated that shoppers save some $3 billion with coupons.[17]

Retailer-sponsored coupons can be redeemed only at the specified retail outlet. The Old Navy "human coupon" is an example of a retail promotion. *Manufacturer-sponsored* coupons can be redeemed at any outlet distributing the product, such as the McDonald's McCafé brochure, which was filled with coupons for the new coffee offerings. They are distributed directly (direct mail or door-to-door), through media (newspaper and magazine ads or freestanding inserts), in or on the package itself, or through the retailer (co-op advertising). Manufacturers pay retailers a fee for handling their coupons.

More recently, social sites such as Groupon.com, LivingSocial.com, Google Offers, and Foursquare offer daily deals that may appear in the local newspaper but may also be promoted through e-mail alerts or posts on Facebook or Twitter. The deal is offered as a voucher with a deep discount for the item or service. Groupon, for example, sends coupon e-mails to consumers who have signed up for special deals, such as discounts for restaurants, car rentals, personal shoppers, and other services. Constant Contact, an online direct-marketing company serving small businesses, has also entered coupon-based deal marketing. Amazon.com has set up its own local deals site, AmazonLocal, where it sells $10 gift cards for $5.

These instant deals have brought new life to local coupon strategies used by small business owners, although these local businesses have found it difficult to predict the traffic and return business lured by the deals.[19] But it's not just small business that use daily deals. Starbucks had success driving up business when it used a daily deal on Living social that allowed people to redeem a $5 voucher for $10 of products. In less than 24 hours, 1.5 million people signed up for the coupon.[20]

- ***Contests and Sweepstakes*** Contest and sweepstake promotions create excitement by promising "something for nothing" and offering impressive prizes. **Contests** require participants to compete for a prize or prizes

Photo: Courtesy of Gap, Inc.

When Old Navy hit 5 million fans on Facebook, it celebrated with a coupon for 30 percent off.[18] But to make the coupon idea come alive, Old Navy's agency, Crispin Porter + Bogusky, created a 120- by 60-foot "human coupon" using hundreds of Facebook friends and fans. The coupon is a scannable bar code of 88 placards held above their heads by the participants. Check it out at http://creativity-online.com/news/old-navy-celebrates-5-million-fans-with-human-coupon/237694.

based on some sort of skill or ability. **Sweepstakes** require only that participants submit their names to be included in a drawing or other chance selection. In keeping with a society that is in love with cell phones, sweepstakes are now offered via mobile marketing. Both *Redbook* and Procter & Gamble's Max Factor brand have sponsored such promotions. A **game** is a type of sweepstakes. It differs from a one-shot drawing type of sweepstake because the time frame is longer, so it establishes continuity by requiring customers to return several times to acquire additional pieces (such as bingo-type games) or to improve their chances of winning.

Sweepstakes, contests, and games are effective promotional tools for driving people to marketers' Internet sites. As part of the Coke Zero campaign (see Chapter 7), Crispin Porter + Bogusky created the Department of Fannovation and invited NCAA fans to submit ways to improve the fan experience. Fans downloaded a brief to submit for a chance to win $10,000 and a trip to the basketball finals. The results from Internet sweepstakes, contests, and games can be huge because of the multiplier effect of interaction and social media.

- ***Specialties*** **Specialty advertising** presents the brand's name on something that is given away in an attempt to remind consumers about the brand. Items include calendars, pens and pencils, T-shirts, mouse pads, tote bags, and water bottles, among many others. The ideal specialty item is one that is kept out in the open where other people can see it, such as a coffee mug. The Advertising Specialty Institute is the trade group behind the $19 billion industry. The group believes that almost anything can be a brand reminder—not only the ubiquitous, cups, caps, calendars, and candidates buttons but also flip-flops that leave a company's logo on the sand at a beach, "space pens" that write underwater, USB drives that come in every shape and size, and accessories for iPads, iPhones, and e-book readers.[21]

Another type of freebie is the **swag** given to people who attend events. Gifts bags with low-cost promotional knickknacks are often given to conference and trade show attendees. Many of the items represent the local city or exhibitors' products. The Academy Awards is known for its high-end gift bags filled with expensive and desirable branded items.

Promotional Media The types of sales promotions we just listed can be delivered in various media, including print, broadcast, and online. Direct mail has dominated the delivery of special promotions, but much of that has moved online. The Internet in particular is useful for distributing coupons, inviting participation in games and sweepstakes, and even in sampling.

In-store promotions using posters, shelf talkers, displays, and other types of signage are particularly effective at reaching people who are making a purchase decision. Although women are the most likely target for these materials, research into the purchasing behavior of dads who do the shopping have found that they are also responsive. In fact, a study by eMarker reported that "dads often rely on old-fangled marketing channels to inform their grocery decisions." In-store promotions were the most important information source cited by dads as influential in their decisions.[22]

Internet promotion is one of the hot areas of sales promotions. The "Bunny" promo for Frontier was delivered to Frontier's Early Returns members by e-mail. Many advertising campaigns include a campaign-dedicated website, such as a "microsite" designed as a tie-in. The Cheetos campaign we described in Chapter 6, for example, was supported with an online website, Orangeunderground.com, which displayed the work of a social network of practical jokers committing Random Acts of Cheetos—in other words, using Cheetos to turn things orange.

Coupons can be delivered via the Internet. Several sites have been designed for this. Catalina's ValuePage website (www.valupage.com) allows users to print coupons they can use at 7,000 supermarkets. The coupon is printed with

Photo: Courtesy of Frontier Airlines and Grey Worldwide

This is an example of an e-mail price promotion sent to Frontier's frequent flyers. Even though it's promoting a sale price, it's still faithful to the Frontier image and "different kind of animal" campaign theme.

Photo: Richie Buxo/Splash News/Newcom

A comprehensive promotional campaign supported the Green Giant "One Giant Pledge" effort to encourage families, particularly children, to eat one more vegetable a day.

a bar code and is used with the shopper's store card. If a product were to offer coupons this way, the site could link the shopper's Internet information with store card information, which the brand manager could use in determining the effectiveness of the coupon strategy.

Promotional Campaigns Special promotions are usually approached as a campaign because they involve a variety of media and reach many stakeholders; they also have a limited time frame. Promotional planners are continually looking for new ways to engage consumers. In particular, the Internet has opened up new opportunities, with viral media driving a high level of social interaction that reinforces the involvement dimension of promotions.

Big Ideas are critical to effective promotional campaigns. An example is the Green Giant "One Giant Pledge" campaign, which urged families to pledge to eat one more vegetable per day for 30 days. A giant-sized Green Giant appeared, via augmented reality, in New York City's Grand Central Terminal and interacted with visitors who were rewarded with a fist bump or high-five when they took the pledge. Veggie jugglers, stilt walks, and other entertainers added to the excitement. The One Giant Pledge campaign kicked off with a television spot, but the hub of the campaign was the Green Giant's Facebook page. Young visitors can create personalized pledges, setting their own goals, and uploading photos as well as the "Proof of Pledge." Pledges were also randomly selected as "veggie art" to be featured on the Facebook page. The site had other tools, including a 30-day pledge calendar, a tool for making a postcard of a child getting a Green Giant fist bump, downloadable "ho, ho, ho" ringtones, and personalized text messages to kids with notes of encouragement.[23]

How Are Consumer Promotions Used?

Although an action response is the goal of most sales promotions, some programs, such as the Frontier Airlines "favorite animal" campaign, are designed to build awareness first but always with action as the ultimate goal. Consumers get to choose the animal they like best to represent Frontier, but in the long run, the airline wants consumers to book flights online. What better way to get them to the site than generating Web traffic via an entertaining contest?

To demonstrate the strategy behind the use of these promotional tools in a new product launch, let's suppose we are introducing a new corn chip named King Corn. Promotion is particularly useful to launch the corn chip because it has a number of tools designed to encourage trial, but it can also be used later in the brand's life to maintain or increase its share of market and to remind and reward loyal customers. Promotions, in other words, deliver on a number of elements in our Facets Model of Effects and drive a specific set of objectives.

Awareness Our first challenge is to create awareness of this brand, which is the real strength of advertising and, you may remember from Chapter 5, the first step in consumer decision making. However, sometimes awareness can be increased when advertising is combined with an appropriate promotion to call attention to the brand name to get people to try the product. Awareness-building promotion ideas for this new corn chip might include colorful point-of-purchase displays, sponsorship of a King Corn team, or a special event that will attract people in the target market.

Trial Creating awareness will take the product only so far, however. Consumers must also perceive King Corn as offering some clear benefit compared to the competition. Sales promotion does this by arranging for experiences, such as special events where people can try the product or see it demonstrated. Trial is one of the most important objectives of promotion, but it is essential to get the right people, the targeted audience, involved with the product. Sales promotion has other tools that lead to trial, such as sampling. An effective way to get people to try King Corn is to give away free samples at events, in stores, or through direct mail to the home. Sampling is an effective strategy for introducing a new or modified product or for dislodging an entrenched market leader by enticing potential users to try the product. As a general rule of thumb, retailers and manufacturers maintain that sampling can boost sales volume as much as 10 times when used with a product demonstration and 10 to 15 percent thereafter. Sampling is generally most effective when reinforced on the spot with product coupons. Most consumers like sampling because they do not lose money if they do not like the product. To be successful. the product sampled must virtually sell itself with a simple trial experience.

Another way sales promotion can motivate people to try a new product like King Corn is to offer a price deal—you try this product, and we will give it to you cheaper than the usual price. These price deals are usually offered through coupons, refunds, rebates, or premiums. Refunds and rebates are effective because they encourage consumers to purchase a product before a deadline. In addition, refunds stimulate sales without the high cost and waste associated with coupons.

Coupons mainly encourage trial, induce brand switching, and reward repeat business. The main advantage of the manufacturer's coupon, such as those that run in consumer magazines, is that it allows the advertiser to lower prices without relying on cooperation from the retailer to distribute them. Announcements for cents-off deals include the package itself and signs near the product or elsewhere in the store. Advertising for these deals include sales, flyers, and newspaper and broadcast ads.

Maintain or Increase Market Share In addition to encouraging trial of a new product, another purpose of price deals is to convince prospective users to switch from an established competing brand, such as Cheetos in the King Corn case. Later, after the King Corn brand is established, a price deal can be used to reward loyal users and encourage their repeat business. Price deals are particularly effective in those situations where price is an important factor in brand choice or if consumers are not brand loyal.

To maintain a brand's presence, increase its market share, or counter competitive actions, marketers use promotional tools such as coupons, premiums, special events, and contests and sweepstakes. The Blue Bunny brochure was used as a Sunday newspaper supplement. It features the entire Indulge line of low-carb and low-fat products as well as coupons to encourage trial.

In addition to serving as a reward for buying a product, premiums can enhance an advertising campaign or a brand's image. Characters like the Campbell's Soup Kids, Tony the Tiger, Cap'n Crunch, and Ronald McDonald are used on premiums, such as soup or cereal bowls, to reinforce the consumer's association of the brand with the character. Cereal manufacturers are among the biggest users of in-pack premiums as reminder devices.

Brand Reminder In addition to new product launches, promotions are also used in the reminder stage. This means that you change advertising copy to remind customers about the positive experience they had with the product and use sales promotion to reinforce their loyalty with coupons, rebates, and other rewards. After the initial purchase, you want the customer to remember the brand and repeat the purchase, so specialty items, such as a King Corn snack bowl, can serve as a brand reminder. Specialty advertising serves as a reminder to the consumer to consider the product. Specialties also build relationships, such as items given away as New Year or thank-you gifts (the calendar hanging in the kitchen). Advertisers use specialty items to thank customers for patronage, to reinforce established products or services, and to generate sales leads.

Photo: © 2004 Wells' Dairy, Inc. All rights reserved

Coupons are used in special promotions such as this one designed to increase sales of Tyson Any'tizers and its range of sauces.

Trade Promotions

Consumer awareness and desire mean nothing unless King Corn is available where the consumer thinks it should be. Somehow the trade must be convinced that the product will move off the shelves. Marketers know they

Principle
Consumer promotion is of little use if the product isn't available where the consumer can find it.

must engage the trade in the program if their consumer promotions are to be effective. In such programs, *trade* refers to all the people involved in the distribution channel, including buyers, brokers, distributors, wholesalers, dealers, franchisees, and retailers.

Trade promotions are usually directed at distribution channel members, a practice that is sometimes referred to as **channel marketing**. It can also be used in any kind of situation where one business is promoting its services to another, which also includes personal sales and materials used in sales presentations.

An example comes from Kuni Automotive, a small group of auto dealerships that was pitching the smart car company to get dealerships in Portland, Seattle, and Denver. Karl Schroeder, copywriter at the Coates Kokes agency in Portland, explained the Big Idea behind the sales presentation kit his team designed to win the dealerships. Kuni "needed something that would stand out and give them instant name recognition with the people at smart." The idea was to send a set of kits before sending the official paperwork proposal. "They were all shrink wrapped. They came with scissors, glue, colors, points of interest for each city, smart cars, dealership buildings, and even customers ready to buy." Kuni was successful in winning two smart centers in Portland and Denver with this promotion.

Typically, companies spend more than half of their total promotion budget on promotions directed at the trade, which is to say that although consumer promotion is highly visible, trade promotion is equally important as a marketing communication strategy. Let's look at the types of trade promotion.

Types of Trade Promotion

Trade advertising directed at wholesalers and retailers provides trade members with information about the new product and its selling points. In addition, trade promotion techniques, especially price discounts, point-of-purchase displays, and advertising allowances, motivate retailers to provide shelf space for products and consumer promotions. Resellers, the intermediaries in the distribution channel, employ millions of people, including salespeople in retail and those in wholesaling, who help distribute the products manufacturers make. The King Corn manufacturer in our fictional example will be more encouraged that the product is acceptable if resellers are willing to carry and help promote it. Many promotional devices designed to motivate resellers to engage in certain sales activities are available to the manufacturer. Here are the most common types of trade promotion tools:

- ***Retailer (Dealer) Kits*** Materials that support retailers' selling efforts or that help representatives make sales calls on prospective retailing customers are often designed as sales kits. The Kuni Automotive kits are good examples of this type of promotional sales materials. Sales kits contain supporting information, such as detailed product specifications, how-to display information, and ad slicks—print ads that are ready to be sent to the local print media as soon as the retailer or dealer adds identification, location, promotion price, or other information.
- ***Trade Incentives and Deals*** Similar to consumer price deals, a manufacturer may reward a reseller financially for purchase of a certain level of a product or support of a promotion. These promotional efforts can take the form of special displays, extra purchases, superior store locations, or greater local promotion. In return, retailers can receive special allowances, such as discounts, free goods, gifts, or cash from the manufacturer. The most common types of **trade deals** are buying allowances for increasing purchases and advertising allowances, which include deals on cooperative advertising and display allowances, or deals for agreeing to use promotional displays.
- ***Contests*** As in the case of consumer sales promotion, advertisers can develop contests and sweepstakes to motivate resellers. Sweepstakes are a random drawing, and contestants are required only to provide their names and contact information to enter. Contests are far more common than sweepstakes, mainly because resellers find it easy to tie contest prizes to the sale of the sponsor's product. A sales quota is set, for example, and the retailer or person who exceeds the quota by the largest percentage wins the contest.
- ***Point-of-Purchase Promotions*** According to the Point-of-Purchase Advertising International (POPAI) association, the marketing-at-retail industry includes three forms:

manufacturer-designed displays distributed to retailers who sell their products. These materials create excitement for the stores, and the signs and displays can help differentiate stores from those of competitors.[24] These are referred to as **point-of-purchase materials**. Although point-of-purchase formats vary by industry, they can include special racks, display cartons, banners, signs, price cards, and mechanical product dispensers, among other tools.

- ***Trade Shows and Exhibits*** The **trade show** is a place where companies within the same industries gather to present and sell their merchandise and to demonstrate their products. Exhibits are the spaces that are designed to showcase the product. Karl Schroeder, senior copywriter at Nike, previously worked at Downstream, a design and technology firm as a writer and content strategist. One of his projects involved an interactive trade show booth with an iPad-based game, which he explains in his "Inside Story."

The Inside Story

Explore. Discover. FEI and the World of Images

Karl Schroeder, *Senior Copywriter and Editor at Nike*

FEI is one of the top two manufacturers in the world for ultrasophisticated electron microscopes. The company wanted an exhibit that projected the image of a world-class imaging company. The structural design included three bays with products for demonstration and trial. The images produced by the microscopes are beautiful as well as authentic and meaningful to users from different types of markets.

The interactive booth included an iPad experience based on a game challenging scientists to participate in building an image library. Visitors received online invitations to participate in creating the most beautiful image. The game also challenged them to try to stump fellow scientists.

Each image could be transferred to a card, and visitors could take these cards to an interactive panel to discover what's behind the image—What industry? Which device? What is the image? Who produced the image? The game created a competitive element with posted scores, and the cards, which looked like abstract art, became takeaways.

The insight that led to the iPad-based game was that scientists like to either see—or show off—how smart they are.

My experience on projects like this as a writer/content strategist was incredible. I worked in a team made up of a myself, a sketch-up designer/architect, a lead designer, and an interactive designer. Being immersed in a truly multidisciplinary team was an awesome experience.

SYSTEM DESIGN
PERSPECTIVE VIEW

CARD GAME INTERACTIVE
INITIAL DESIGN EXPLORATION

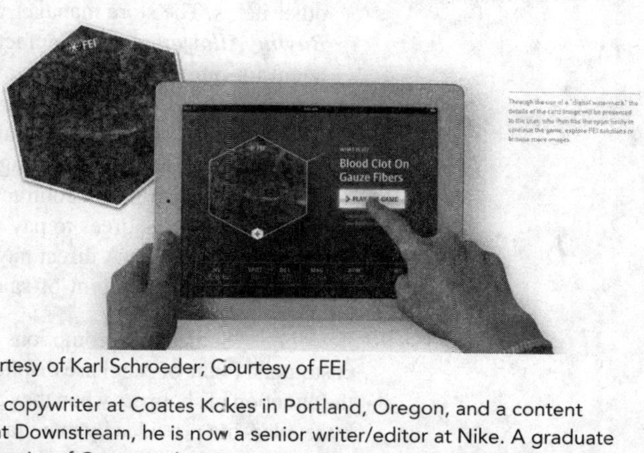

Photo: Courtesy of Karl Schroeder; Courtesy of FEI

Formerly a copywriter at Coates Kokes in Portland, Oregon, and a content strategist at Downstream, he is now a senior writer/editor at Nike. A graduate of the University of Oregon advertising program, his work was nominated for inclusion in this book by Professor Charles Frazer.

How Is Trade Promotion Used?

The ultimate gauge of a successful trade promotion is whether sales increase. Trade promotions are primarily designed to get the cooperation of people in the distribution channel and to encourage their promotion of the product to consumers. Trade promotion brings resellers to that point of conviction. There are two primary roles for a trade promotion:

1. ***Trade Support*** To stimulate in-store merchandising or other trade support (e.g., feature pricing, superior store location, or shelf space)
2. ***Excitement*** To create a high level of excitement about the product among those responsible for its sale

In addition, trade promotion is also used to accomplish other marketing objectives, such as manipulating levels of inventory held by wholesalers and retailers and expanding product distribution to new areas of the country or new classes of trade.

Principle
Consumer and trade promotions interact through complementing push and pull strategies.

Demand: Push and Pull Strategies As explained in Chapter 2, manufacturers hope to see their trade partners push a product. To understand the role of trade promotion, consider how sales promotion is used in push and pull strategies. Consumer and trade promotions interact through complementing push and pull strategies. If people really want to try King Corn based on what they have heard in advertising and publicity stories, they will ask their local retailers for it, which is called a *pull strategy*; that is, by asking for it, they will pull the product through the distribution channel. By conducting a contest in conjunction with sampling within the store, for example, you can increase demand at the store and at same time increase trial.

However, you might use a *push strategy* to push the product through the channel by convincing (motivating or rewarding) members of the distribution network to carry King Corn. For example, we want grocery stores not only to carry them but also to allocate good shelf space in the crowded chip aisle. Here are the most common types of incentives and trade deals used with retailers as part of a push strategy:

- ***Bonuses*** A monetary bonus, also called *push money* or *spiffs,* is paid to a salesperson based on units the salesperson sells over a period of time. For example, an air-conditioner manufacturer might give salespeople a $50 bonus for the sale of one model and $75 for a fancier model within a certain time frame. At the end of the sales period, each salesperson sends in evidence of total sales to the manufacturer and receives a check for the bonus amount.
- ***Dealer Loader*** These are premiums, comparable to a consumer premium, that a manufacturer gives to a retailer for buying a certain amount of a product. A loader trade promotion rewards retailers for buying the product. Budweiser offered store managers a free trip to the Super Bowl if they sold a certain amount of beer in a specified period of time. Display loaders reward retailers by giving them the display after the promotion ends. For example, Dr. Pepper built a store display for the Fourth of July holiday that included a gas grill, picnic table, basket, and other items. The store manager was awarded these items after the promotion ended.
- ***Buying Allowances*** A manufacturer pays a reseller a set amount of money or offers a discount for purchasing a certain amount of the product during a specified time period.
- ***Advertising Allowances*** The manufacturer pays the wholesaler or retailer a certain amount of money to advertise the manufacturer's product. This allowance can be a flat dollar amount, or it can be a percentage of gross purchases during a specified time period.
- ***Co-Op Advertising*** In a contractual arrangement between the manufacturer and the resellers, the manufacturer agrees to pay a part or all of the retailers' advertising expenses.
- ***Display Allowance*** A direct payment of cash or goods is given to the retailer if the retailer agrees to set up the point-of-sale display.

Attention Some trade promotions are designed to get the attention of both trade members and their customers. Point-of-purchase displays, a promotional tool we mentioned earlier, are designed to get the attention of shoppers when they are in the store and to stimulate impulse purchases. They are used by retailers but provided by manufacturers. As we have moved to a self-service retail environment in which fewer and fewer customers expect help from sales clerks, the importance of point-of-purchase materials continues to increase. POPAI has found that the point-of-purchase forms that have the greatest impact on sales are displays that tie in with entertainment, sports, or charities.

In the "Practical Tips" feature, marketing consultant Arlene Gerwin explains how best to plan effective point-of-purchase promotions.

Practical Tips

Planning Point-of-Purchase Promotions

Arlene Gerwin, *Marketing Consultant and President, Bolder Insights*

Ever since retail establishments came into existence, there has been some form of point-of-purchase (PoP) promotion—carefully hand-painted signs announcing a sale can be seen in photos of 19th-century country general store windows. Inside the store, special displays of merchandise sometimes promoted seasonal prices or special deals.

Point-of-purchase promotions, also referred to as marketing-at-retail promotions, usually fall under the definition of marketing tactics; however objectives, strategies, and tactics are as important in planning PoP promotions as they are in the development of the overall marketing plan:

- *SMART Plans* Effective PoP promotions support the marketing plan and deliver on its strategies by being Strategic, Measurable, Actionable, Realistic, and Timely—that is, SMART.
- *Objectives* The most successful PoP promotions are developed against a clear set of objectives, such as countering competitive actions. A PoP campaign should be long range and strategic.
- *Big Idea* The best PoP promotions develop from campaignable, ownable "Big Ideas" that extend over a minimum of one year or more and should be in line with the overall marketing objectives. Many times, PoP promotions creatively echo the advertising campaign.
- *Brand Fit* When the promotion becomes intricately intertwined with the brand or service, it enhances the brand image.
- *Bridge* PoP displays serve as a bridge linking trade and consumer promotions. The most powerful offers are delivered directly to consumers in the retail environment, but they need retailer support to be strategically placed. Trade and consumer promotions should work in tandem often with a push–pull strategy—trade for push and consumer for pull.
- *Timing* PoP promotions should consider the consumer product-use cycle and not artificially inflate sales volume at the expense of short-term sales spikes.
- *Co-promotions* Two brands that share PoP materials and link their products in a single promotion can make the shoppers' task easier if they have similar target audiences and consumer usage patterns. Co-promotions may also be delivered via electronic media, many times in the store.
- *Realistic Tactics* The specific tools in a PoP promotional plan should be affordable, on strategy, and produced on time. This is crucial for seasonal or specific holiday promotions.
- *Detailed Budgeting* Avoid Murphy's Promotions Law: Designs that look great on paper often present unanticipated production complications, not to mention the unpredictability of natural disasters and ill-timed strikes. Whenever possible, test a prototype of the display in stores to work out the kinks before production.
- *ROI* Because PoP promotions are planned across a finite time period and their costs can be predicted, planners can evaluate the promotion's ROI and estimate the payback.
- *Flexibility* Use contingency planning and have an arsenal of tactics waiting in the wings in case of unplanned complications.

In addition to getting attention in crowded aisles and promoting impulse purchases, marketers design point-of-purchase efforts to complement other promotional campaigns. As part of getting attention, retailers appreciate point-of-purchase ideas that build store ambience. Club Med designed a floor display for travel agents that featured a beach chair with a surfboard on one side and a pair of skis on the other to show that Club Med has both snow and sun destinations. Advertisers must design point-of-purchase displays that appeal to both end users and the trade. Retailers, who put a premium on their precious store space, will use a point of purchase only if they are convinced that it will generate greater sales.

Motivation Most trade promotions are designed to, in some way, motivate trade members to cooperate with the manufacturer's promotion. Incentives such as contests and trade deals are used. If conducted properly with a highly motivating incentive or prize, contests can spur short-term sales and improve the relationship between the manufacturer and the reseller. They encourage a higher quantity of purchases and create enthusiasm among trade members who are involved with the promotion. Trade incentive programs are used to stimulate frequency and quantity of purchase and encourage cooperation with a promotion.

Information We mentioned trade shows earlier. Trade shows, which are an information-rich environment, display products and provide an opportunity to sample and demonstrate products, particularly for trade buyers, the people who buy for stores. The food industry has thousands of trade shows for various product categories, and the manufacturer of King Corn would want to sponsor an exhibit featuring the new corn chip at the appropriate food shows. Trade shows also permit companies to gather information about their competition. In an environment where all the companies are attempting to give a clear picture of their products to potential customers, competitors can easily compare quality, features, prices, and technology.

Multiplatform Promotions

So far, we have looked at consumer sales promotions and trade promotions. But marketers have more promotion techniques at their disposal. In this section, we focus on sponsorships, event marketing, loyalty programs, and co-marketing or partnership promotions. Many of these promotion techniques, such as sponsorships and event marketing, cross over to other areas of marketing and blur the lines between promotions, advertising, and public relations. The Wheaties box is a classic example of connecting a brand to athletes who bring alive its "Breakfast of Champions" slogan.

Sponsorships and Event Marketing

Sponsorships occur when companies support an event, say, a sporting event, concert, or charity, either financially or by donating supplies and services. **Event marketing** means building a product's marketing program around a sponsored event, such as the Olympics or a golf tournament. Both are used because they generate excitement for both the consumer and trade audiences. Major sponsorships typically can cost a lot of money. Sponsors for major golf tournaments, for example, are expected to invest between $6 million and $8 million.

Sponsorships include sports (events, athletes, and teams); entertainment tours and attractions; festivals, fairs, and other annual events; cause marketing (associating with an event that supports a social cause); and support for the arts (orchestras, museums, and so on). For example, Red Bull, a company with strong worldwide brand recognition particularly for extreme sports events, sponsored Felix's Baumgartner's out-of-this world skydive from the edge of space. The impact? It captivated 8 million who watched the live video, then buzzed about what they saw.[25] Cause marketing sponsorship is a growth area with spending at around $1.6 billion in 2009, and it has been found by a Chicago research firm to be growing faster than sports and arts sponsorships.[26] That kind of impact is what has made the Komen "Pink Ribbon" such a powerful symbol for brand sponsors.

Photo: AP Photo/General Mills

CLASSIC

Olympians have graced the Wheaties "breakfast of Champions" box since 1958 when pole-vaulter Bob Richards was the first athlete to be featured on the box.

Michael Phelps is a more contemporary example, but you can see a long history of champions online—just enter seach for: *classic Wheaties* boxes.

It's not just big sponsorships that interest brand stewards. Some brands, for example, are finding ways to participate in games played on mobile phones without annoying players. Kiip, for example, offers rewards to players who reach certain milestones. Tap.Me lets players choose in-game tools and rewards sponsored by brands.[27]

Companies undertake sponsorships to build brand associations and increase the perceived value of the brand in the consumer's mind. The important thing is that the event must project the right image for the brand. That's particularly important in troubled economic times when companies with budget problems find it hard to justify spending money on glitzy events. Companies that use sponsorships focus their efforts on supporting causes and events that matter most to employees and customers. Unilever signed on as sponsor for the *Today Show*'s food and recipe website, called Cooking School. The idea is to feature Unilever's brands, such as Bertolli, Country Crock, and Ragu. Although the most common sponsorships are around events, particularly sporting events, brands can also sponsor product-related websites that are particularly effective at creating sales or recruiting people. The 2BLIKEu.com network is a consumer products social network that lets companies sponsor product pages.

Hundreds of companies sponsor NASCAR cars both to reach the sport's expanding fan base and to link their brand to a winning car and driver. Sponsors shell out in excess of $650 million to get NASCAR's top 35 cars in the

Nextel Cup Series to put their logos on the car. The investment pays. Marketing analysts estimate that Dale Earnhardt Jr. earns the equivalent of $150 million in televised exposure time for his sponsor Budweiser, quite a bargain considering that Anheuser-Busch (and other sponsors) spends much less on the sponsorships.

Just think about sponsorships associated with football bowl games and other sporting events. The first bowl to have a sponsor, the Sunkist Fiesta Bowl, led the way in 1986, followed by the Tostitos Fiesta Bowl, the Outback Bowl, the Meineke Car Care Bowl, and others. A twist on the sports sponsorship concept comes from convenience store chain 7-Eleven, which made a deal with the Chicago White Sox that their games would start at 7:11. Of course, when the club lost the 7-Eleven sponsorship, it also got a new start time—7:10.

The importance of sponsorships is growing worldwide. Mengniu Milk, a Mongolian milk company, raised its profile by backing the National Basketball Association in China. Beyond exposure, these events give corporations the opportunity to build their image and reputation by associating with an activity that audiences enjoy.[28]

Event Marketing

The term *event marketing* describes the practice of linking a brand to an event, such as the Jose Cuervo beach volleyball tournament. Marketers use related promotional events, such as a tour or the appearance of the product or its spokesperson at a mall or sporting event, to gain the attention and participation of people in the target audience who attend the event. The event showcases the brand, often with sampling, coupons, other incentives, and attention-getting stunts. To be successful, the event must match the brand to the target market's lifestyle.

An innovative example of street-based promotional events comes from New York City, which has closed parts of Broadway to create pedestrian plazas. In addition to civic activities,

A Matter of Practice

Active Engagement through Event Sponsorships

James Pokrywczynski, *Marquette University*

Can you remember the title sponsor of the last concert you attended? Can you name one sponsor of the last summer festival or sports event you attended? If your answer to either question is "I dunno," that's okay, because event and sports sponsors have a variety of goals for sponsorship beyond recall.

Event marketing, which connects a sponsor with attendees of events like concerts, art exhibits, city and ethnic festivals, and sports (either as participants or viewers), is an increasingly important component in integrated marketing communication. Over $25 billion is spent annually in the United States. Tactics range from more active engagement with attendees, such as distributing free samples or logoed merchandise, supplying tickets and hospitality tents on-site for loyal customers or employees, to more passive efforts, such as signage on-site, logos on tickets or in event ads, and media mentions. Goals of event marketing include building brand and top-of-mind awareness, enhancing brand attitudes, and, in some instances, generating sales.

Sponsorship has moved beyond slapping a name on an event and hoping for the best. Events, sponsors, and especially sports teams have utilized social media to enhance the engagement with participants and extend the impact of sponsorships. According to a 2011 *Sports Business Journal* study, game-day use of social media is highest for college football and basketball fans, with almost half using before, during, or after games. Pro sports leagues are not far behind.

As of mid-2012, pro basketball's Miami Heat has almost 6 million Facebook "likes," baseball's New York Yankees has 5.7 million, and pro football's Dallas Cowboys corralled 4.8 million. These numbers are key given a study of baseball's Milwaukee Brewers fans that shows higher Facebook usage is correlated with both higher ticket-buying rates and projected merchandise buying. The 2011 Women's World Cup soccer final set a record for tweets per second (7,196), according to Twitter. The 2012 London Olympic Games are touted as the first "social media Olympics," as more sponsors provided interactive experiences around their brand's role in the Games. These results mirror evidence in event marketing, where promotions on LinkedIn, Facebook, and Twitter for a PRSA conference on health produced measurable, positive results related to attendance.

Of course, Twitter and other social media offer dangers when players and participants offer negative comments. A spring 2012 tweet from Miami Marlins manager Ozzie Guillen that enraged local Cubans to protest outside the ballpark led Guillen to later say, "Stop following me . . . Twitter is stupid."

companies can rent these spaces for commercial events, such as when the Bravo Network's *Top Chef* cooking competition held a promotion there or when Glidden Paint set up large paint can and product literature displays and a team of young men and women in bright-colored T-shirts handed out paint chips and advice on colors and decorating.[29]

Nintendo and Target paired up to set up Wii exercise kiosks that offered Target customers an opportunity to sample the new Wii Fit Plus Experience game. The kiosks were placed in front of stores and in parking lots for January weekends, creating a *sampling event* at a time when people are falling off their New Year's resolutions and looking for fitness ideas.

Events can also be used to build goodwill, as a holiday promotion by Yahoo! demonstrated. The online firm sent employees to airports to pay for airline customers' baggage fees. The stunt was described as "one small act of kindness," but it reinforced Yahoo!'s brand promise: "Yahoo! makes your life easier."

Business-to-business promotions also use events to reach trade audiences, which can include the sales staff, distributors, retailers, and franchisees. These stakeholders are invited to participate in the event as a reward for their support, and that's one of the big reasons why brands participate in the Super Bowl.

The granddaddy of all events is the Super Bowl, which is also an "Ad Bowl," as there is as much interest in the advertising as in the game. The ads are the most expensive on television; prices can top $4 million for a 30-second commercial—and that's just the cost of the time. Don't forget that generally there is a significant budget tied up in the production of the commercials because they have to be highly professional in order to justify the costs. (For another trend affecting costs, see the "A Matter of Principle" feature.) The reason these costs make sense is because they

A Matter of Principle

The Underdog Wins the Super Bowl Ad Championship

Bonnie Drewniany, *Associate Professor, University of South Carolina*

Special effects. Expensive celebrities. Exotic locations. These are just some of the tactics advertising agencies use in the hopes of winning the Super Bowl advertising championship, the number-one spot in the *USA Today* Ad Meter. Once dominated by major agencies, the championship title has recently gone to the underdog: the average Joe (and Jane). And rather than spend upwards of $1 million dollars as the big agencies do, the winners spend a few thousand dollars or less to create their winning commercials.

It all began in 2007 when Doritos sponsored its first Crash the Super Bowl competition. A commercial created by a 22-year-old for less than $13 was the fourth most popular spot in the 2007 Ad Meter. The commercial, which shows a dorky guy trying to impress a woman while he's driving and munching on Doritos, beat out ads that cost upwards of $1 million to produce.

Two years later, two unemployed brothers from Indiana created a Doritos commercial that won the ultimate coup: the number-one spot in the Ad Meter and a $1 million prize. The ad features a man trying to predict if he will get free Doritos chips for the office. He gets the answer he wants by throwing a snow globe at the vending machine. Impressed, a colleague uses the globe to predict if he'll get a raise. Not the best aim, the unlucky man hits his boss in a rather painful spot. "Promotion?" the first guy quips as he munches on a Doritos chip, "Not in your future."

A newly engaged couple won the 2011 Ad Meter and used part of the $1 million prize money on their wedding. Their commercial features a man, standing behind a storm door, taunting his girlfriend's pug with a Doritos chip. The pug beats the man at his own game by knocking over the door, pinning the man to the floor.

Two consumer-generated Doritos commercials came out on top in 2012. The *USA Today* panel's favorite spot features a man who sees his Great Dane burying the collar of a missing cat. To buy his silence, the dog slips his owner a bag of Doritos with a note "You didn't see nuthin." Another spot, "Sling Baby," won the *USA Today*/Facebook online poll. Here, a grandmother uses a baby swing to catapult a baby to grab a bag of Doritos from an obnoxious boy.

Notice how none of these commercials used expensive celebrities or elaborate special effects? It's the idea that counts. Tell an engaging story that resonates with viewers, make your brand central to your message, and who knows? You may be the next underdog to win the Super Bowl advertising championship.

also reach huge audience. The 2012 game, which featured the New York Giants beating the New England Patriots, broke all audience records, becoming the most watched program in history.

It's not just the commercials, however, that get the attention of marketers. Brands buy a Super Bowl spot to participate in all the frenzy that surrounds the event—both before with pre-event teasers, during the game, and in the postgame coverage. The television spots are the opportunity for wide-ranging promotional campaigns that involve publicity, point-of-purchase displays, video clips, websites and social media, search engine ads, and relationship programs with important partners, such as retailers and shareholders. YouTube, for example, gets involved by sponsoring a Super Bowl Ad Blitz channel where viewers can vote for their favorite spots. Viewers are known to rewatch spots online on YouTube, AOL, Yahoo!, and other sites. They also pass along favorite commercials to friends and family.

The "A Matter of Principle" feature makes the point that even in big-event advertising, it's still the Big Idea that counts. Check out Super Bowl commercials on www.superbowl-ads.com and www.youtube.com/superbowl. MSNBC has collected the 10 best of them at www.msnbc.msn.com/id/16691199 and the 10 worst at www.msnbc.msn.com/id/16790823.

Ambush Marketing **Ambush marketing** is the term given to promotional stunts used at events, such as the Olympics and the soccer and rugby World Cups, by companies that are not official sponsors. Ambush marketing typically occurs when one brand is trying to undermine the presence of a competitor that is sponsoring an event. If it can create enough confusion, it can reduce the return on the official sponsor's investment at the same time it can pick up additional visibility through publicity.

Did you watch the 2012 Olympics in London? Did you notice the beautiful neon shoes on 400 track-and-field athletes? They were the brainchild of Martin Lotti, Nike's global creative director for the Olympics.[30] Of course, Nike wasn't an official London 2012 sponsor; Adidas was. So how did all those Nike FlyKnit Volts get on all those feet? Because the shoes' styling belonged to Nike and the decision to wear them was the athlete's choice, the spectators saw a highly recognizable incandescent blur whizzing down the track. And the shoes were also in London stores for everyone to recognize and anyone to buy.

Dutch brewer Bavaria has a long-running track record as an ambush brand. At the 2010 World Cup, 36 Dutch women were kicked out of their country's soccer game against Denmark. Why? They were accused of wearing orange minidresses to promote the unlicensed Dutch Bavaria beer at the World Cup event. American firm Anheuser-Busch, maker of Budweiser beer, was one of the official sponsors of the World Cup; Bavaria was not. FIFA, the organizer of the event, said that ambush marketing was not permitted. This was not the first time Bavaria was accused of being involved in ambush marketing. In a 2006 World Cup match, Dutch fans were forced to take off the orange lederhosen given to them by Bavaria. The idea of fans removing their pants in itself was potentially amusing, and the ambush tactic again detracted from the official sponsor Anheuser-Busch.

Other Promotional Support Advertisers use blimps, balloons, inflatables, and skywriting planes to capture attention and create an aura of excitement at events. Everybody has probably heard of the Goodyear blimp, but other companies sponsor dirigibles as well. MetLife, which uses characters from the popular "Peanuts" comic strip in its advertising, has two blimps, *Snoopy I* and *Snoopy II*, that connect with the corporate campaign to provide brand reminder messages. Inflatables—giant models of products, characters, and packages—are used at all kinds of events, including grand openings, sporting events, parades, trade shows, beaches, malls, and other places where they can make an impression for a new product rollout. A giant inflatable, such as Spider-Man on a building, demands attention and provides an entertaining and highly memorable product presentation.

Photo: Courtesy of Nike, Inc.

Nike's FlyKnit shoe, the Volt, and its vivid neon-green-highlighter-yellow color was designed based on focus group research with amateur and professional athletes who universally loved the style and color. The high-style shoes with the glorious color became an iconic image of the 2012 Olympic Games.

Photo: Eric Risberg\APWide World Photos

To help promote the opening of the movie *Spider-Man*, inflatables like this one were placed along buildings in major cities throughout the world.

Loyalty Programs

Another type of program that crosses the line between advertising and promotion is frequency, or loyalty, programs. A **loyalty program**, also called a **continuity program** or **frequency program** (such as airline frequent-flyer programs), is a promotion to increase customer retention. Marketers typically design loyalty programs to keep and reward customers for their continued patronage, which is why they are called *continuity programs*. Typically, the higher the purchase level, the greater the benefits.

Today, loyalty programs are synonymous with the word *frequent.* The frequent-flyer club, first created by United Airlines and American Airlines in 1981, is the model for a modern continuity program. These programs offer a variety of rewards, including seat upgrades, free tickets, and premiums based on the number of frequent-flyer miles accumulated. Although the frequent-flyer programs were originally established to create customer loyalty, they have turned into a rewards program. For example, people can earn miles through credit card purchases. Continuity programs work in competitive markets in which the consumer has difficulty perceiving real differences between brands. TGI Friday's, for example, has used a "Frequent Fridays" program with several million members. The key to creating a successful loyalty program is offering memorable incentives that consumers want.

Marketers like membership programs because they also generate information for customer databases. The enrollment application at TGI Friday's, for example, captures name, address, telephone number, birth date, and average visit frequency. The database can also record the restaurant locations, date, time, purchase amount, and items ordered on each visit. Marketers can then use this information to more specifically target customers with promotions and advertising materials.

Partnership Programs

Another promotion tool that crosses the lines is the partnership program. **Co-marketing** involves manufacturers developing marketing communication programs with their main retail accounts instead of for them. If done right, these partnerships strengthen relationships between manufacturers and retailers. Co-marketing programs are usually based on the lifestyles and purchasing habits of consumers who live in the area of a particular retailer. The partnership means that the advertising and sales promotions build equity for both the manufacturer and the retailer. For example, Procter & Gamble and Walmart might develop a spring cleaning promotion directed at Walmart shoppers that features Procter & Gamble cleaning products sold at reduced prices or with premium incentives.

An interesting experience with an electronic-coupon partnership between Kroger and Procter & Gamble ended after a tug-of-war about the click-through of customers to each others' website. Procter & Gamble got a lot of clicks, more so than did Kroger. Kroger, of course, was unhappy when its viewers would move to the P&GeSaver.com site rather than staying with Kroger.com.[31] So who is the dominant player in this distribution channel—the manufacturer or the retailer? Kroger finally decided it didn't need to compete with Procter & Gamble via a coupon website.

Co-branding When two companies come together to offer a product, the effort is called **co-branding**. An example of cobranding is when American Airlines puts its logo on a Citibank Visa card and awards AAdvantage points to Citibank Visa card users. Both companies are equally present in the product's design and promotion, and both get to build on the other company's brand equity.

Licensing With **licensing**, legally protected brand identity items, such as logos, symbols, and brand characters, must be licensed—that is, a legal contract gives another company the right to use the brand identity element. In brand licensing, a company with an established brand "rents" that brand to other companies, allowing them to use its logo on their products and in their advertising and promotional events. Fashion marketers such as Gucci, Yves St. Laurent, and Pierre Cardin have licensed their brand names and logos for use on everything from fashion accessories to sunglasses, ties, linens, and luggage, and they do this because it makes them money and extends their brand visibility. The PGA Tour is a golf brand that has become recognizable through an elaborate, integrated marketing campaign. Charles Schwab, the financial investment house, has used the PGA Tour logo as a part of its advertising. This lets the company associate its brand with a golf event that has a lot of interest and positive associations for the target audiences.

Photo: © 1995-2004, PGA TOUR, Inc. All rights reserved

The PGA licenses the use of its logo to other advertisers who want to associate themselves with the PGA Tour event and pros.

Tie-Ins and Cross Promotions Another type of cooperative marketing program is a **tie-in promotion** or **cross promotion**, which is an effective strategy for marketers using associations between complementary brands to make one plus one equal three. For example, Doritos may develop a tie-in promotion with Pace salsa in which bottles of salsa are displayed next to the Doritos section in the chip aisle (and vice versa). The intent is to spur impulse sales of both products. Ads are also designed to tie the two products together, and the sponsoring companies share the cost of the advertising.

The biggest cross promotions are arranged around movies and other entertainment events. The Aflac duck became a passenger in a commercial for the Pixar movie *Up* who is shown hitching a ride on the balloon-borne house. The voice-over on the Pixar-created commercial explained that Aflac "can help keep your dreams afloat," which reflected Aflac's position as a friend who provides support in a time of need.[32]

But cross promotions are not only used by packaged goods. Billings, Montana, for example used a promotion in its "Trailhead" rebranding campaign with Pepsi-Cola. A half a million special Pepsi cans with the campaign logo and slogan offered $5.00 off a "Trailhead" cap when visitors brought the can to the chamber of commerce. The promotion also was supported with a point-of-purchase poster in stores where Pepsi was sold.

Tie-ins and cross promotions succeed because brands can leverage similar strengths to achieve a bigger impact in the marketplace. Typically, marketers align themselves with partners that provide numerous complementary elements, including common target audiences, purchase cycle patterns, distribution channels, retailer penetration, and demographics, to drive their products and promotions through retail channels and into the minds of consumers.

Photo: Courtesy of the Billings Chamber of Commerce/ Convention and Visitors' Bureau

SHOWCASE

As another element in the Billings, Montana, rebranding campaign that we discussed earlier, a cross promotion enlisted Pepsi-Cola to sponsor special cans with a premium offer on a "Trailhead" cap.

John Brewer, president and CEO of the Billings Chamber of Commerce/ Convention and Visitors Bureau, graduated from the University of West Florida. Nominated for inclusion in this book by Professor Tom Groth, he contributed a case study on the "Trailhead" campaign, which we feature in Chapter 18.

Photo: Andrew Hoxey Photography

Should beer manufacturers be allowed to "borrow" school colors in local marketing of their products? That was the question when Bud Light's "Fan Cans" hit the stores in limited markets during the college football season. What do you think? If you were brand manager for Bud Light and your promotion manager presented this idea, how would you decide what to do?

An interesting although questionable promotion was Bud Light's use of "Fan Cans" in college colors. It raised questions about licensing and rogue "tie-in" strategies that aren't sanctioned by the schools. In the fall of 2009, Anheuser-Busch had a great idea to tie in with the start of the college football season by issuing Bud Light in cans with collegiate colors, some 27 different color combinations to be exact. "Show your true colors with Bud Light," the promotional materials announced. Retailers reported that Bud Light's "Fan Can" promotion seemed to be a hit among football fans in those cities where wholesalers chose to participate. Several problems surfaced with this promotion. Some universities complained that the colored cans infringed on the schools' trademark licensing. Anheuser-Busch agreed not to offer the promotion in areas where the schools protested. Others complained that it promoted drinking among students, many of whom were underage. A Federal Trade Commission senior attorney, Janet Evans, followed up on that complaint expressing "grave concern" about its impact on underage drinking.[33]

The company responded that it takes the problem of underage drinking very seriously. Anheuser-Busch's vice president of corporate social responsibility explained that these cans were being made available only in communities where purchasers must be age 21 or older to drink. Anheuser-Busch stood by its rights to sell Bud Light using colors associated with universities—and to sell these cans to college fans. Furthermore, there are lots of fans who are not underage and think the game-day promotion is cool.

Sales Promotion and Integration

Similar to direct-response and other marcom tools that we discuss in this book, promotions are strategically designed to work within a mix of brand messages and experiences to build brand strength and presence. Marketing consultant Gerwin explains, "When all the marketing tasks are driven by a common strategy and shared objectives, the company communicates with the consumer in a single voice with a consistent creative approach. For publicly held companies, this ultimately translates into building shareholder value and increasing the stock price."[34]

An example of a multiplatform promotion that demonstrates how a variety of media and tools can work together was the Voyeur Project for HBO that won a Grand Prix at the Cannes Film Festival. The idea for the promotional campaign was to project a massive film on the wall of a building in New York showing the illusion of looking inside eight fictional apartments. Each apartment and its inhabitants depicted a different story, which reinforced HBO's position as "the greatest storyteller in the world."

It was also an event—street teams passed out invitations to the showings, which were held at different times on a street in New York. Street viewers could hold up their invitations and see clues about the story lines, and they also could interact through mobile messaging. Viewers at home could go online and zoom in on the various stories, or they could go to HBO On Demand and see the film *The Watcher*, which tied in with one of the story lines about an assassin murdering an FBI agent.

Created by BBDO and a team of partner agencies, other content about the story lines was found online on Web mini-sites as well as in photo and video clips on social media platforms, such as Flickr and YouTube. It was an event, an outdoor advertising experience, an online experience, and it involved many bloggers who followed the stories and commented to their digital communities. See the film at www.youtube.com/watch?v=EwkQpzgFaqs.

Looking Ahead

As you've read in this chapter, promotions can successfully deliver sales to a company, but they must be well planned and executed if they are to enhance the brand's reputation. The next chapter will wrap up our discussion of IMC and will reinforce the idea that all the tools, media formats, and communication platforms that we have presented in this book must work together to create a consistent and coherent brand image.

It's a Wrap

Positively Pink

The pink ribbon campaign is arguably one of the most successful promotion efforts ever by co-branding a good cause with other brands. As you've read in this chapter, marketers can employ a variety of promotional techniques, and the pink ribbon campaign demonstrates the effectiveness of product tie-ins. Products and brands, such as Avon and Yoplait, that fit naturally with a cause, such as breast cancer awareness and research, can mutually benefit both the sponsors and the charity.

Since its inception, the Susan G. Komen Foundation has raised more than $2 billion for breast cancer research, education, and services. In 2010 alone, Komen generated $420 million and funded an estimated $141 million on public health education, $75 million to finance medical research, and $67 million to pay for breast cancer screening and treatment. But is it good business for the partners?

Apparently. Yoplait, for instance, donates 10 cents for each pink yogurt lid to Komen, and since 1999, it has given more than $22 million. That's a lot of yogurt. New Balance's "Lace Up for the Cure" promotion donates 5 percent of retail sales of some of its pink shoes, guaranteeing Komen a minimum of $500,000 per year.

So there is potential to profit financially from such partnerships. What is harder to gauge is the value of the goodwill that product tie-in promotions create.

Tom Wyatt, president of Old Navy, which produced pink Komen logo T-shirts, said that 5 percent of the purchase price goes to Komen. He says he does not expect big revenue for the shirts, but the association with the world's largest breast cancer charity will generate abundant goodwill for the Old Navy brand plus several million dollars for the Komen cause.

Over time, Komen's work to improve women's chances to understand and survive breast cancer has garnered many awards, including many Halo Awards for Cause Marketing. As the pink ribbon campaign matures, it will be interesting to see how messaging develops so that the partnering companies messages do not get lost in the pink dust.

Logo: Courtesy of Susan G. Komen

Key Points Summary

1. **What are the current trends and practices in planning promotions?** Sales promotion offers an "extra incentive" to take action. It gives the product or service additional value and motivates people to respond. Sales promotion is growing rapidly for many reasons. It offers the manager short-term bottom-line results, it is accountable, it is less expensive than advertising, it speaks to the current needs of the consumer who wants to receive more value from products, and it responds to marketplace changes. In brand building, promotions can reinforce advertising images and messages and encourage or remind consumers to buy the brand again. They can be used to push or pull a product through the distribution channel by creating positive brand experiences. Effective promotional plans are based on Big Ideas.
2. **How are various consumer promotions used?** Sales promotions directed at consumers include price deals, coupons, contests and sweepstakes, refunds, premiums, specialty advertising, continuity programs, and sampling. Their purpose is to pull the product through the distribution channel.

3. **What are the types and purposes of trade promotions?** Sales promotions directed at the trade include point-of-purchase displays, retailer merchandising kits, trade shows, and price deals, such as discounts, bonuses, and advertising allowances. These are used to push the product through the channel.
4. **How do multiplatform promotions—sponsorships and events, loyalty programs, and partnership programs—work?** Sponsorship is used to increase the perceived value of a brand by associating it with a cause or celebrity. Internet promotions can be used to drive people to a sponsor's Web page. Licensing "rents" an established brand to other companies to use on their products. Loyalty programs are designed to increase customer retention. Partnership programs, such as co-branding and co-marketing programs, are designed to build stronger relationships between manufacturers and retailers and between two brands that market related products to a similar target audience.
5. **What are the critical promotional practices in integration?** Promotions offer an incentive to action and stimulate trial, which is important in launching a new product. Interactive promotions are more involved. Sales promotions are used with advertising to provide immediate behavioral action.

Key Terms

ambush marketing, p. 551
channel marketing, p. 544
cobranding, p. 552
comarketing, p. 552
contests, p. 540
continuity program, p. 552
coupons, p. 540
cross promotion, p. 553
event marketing, p. 548
frequency program, p. 552
game, p. 541
licensing, p. 552
loyalty program, p. 552
payout planning, p. 534
point-of-purchase materials, p. 545
premium, p. 540
price deal, p. 538
rebate, p. 539
refund, p. 539
sales promotion, p. 532
sampling, p. 539
self-liquidator, p. 540
specialty advertising, p. 541
sponsorships, p. 548
swag, p. 541
sweepstakes, p. 541
tie-in promotion, p. 553
trade deal, p. 544
trade show, p. 545

Review Questions

17-4. What is the main objective behind creating a sales promotion?

17-5. What are the common types of trade promotion tools?

17-6. Explain the three audiences for sales promotion and the two primary categories used to reach those audiences.

17-7. What are the primary objectives that consumer promotions can deliver?

17-8. Elaborate, with examples, the main roles of a trade promotion.

17-9. Define sponsorship and event marketing, and explain why companies use this approach.

17-10. Explain why advertisers distribute product samples.

17-11. Why are sponsorships and events used by marketers?

17-12. Define loyalty programs and explain why they are useful.

17-13. How and when are partnership promotions used?

Discussion Questions

17-14. You have been named promotion manager for Maybelline, a well-known brand of cosmetics. You know the brand has been successful in using sales promotion plans lately, but you are concerned about how to use promotions successfully without harming the brand. How is sales promotion weak in building and maintaining a brand, and how can it be used to strengthen a well-known brand? What kind of promotions would you suggest for maintaining and strengthening this brand franchise?

17-15. You have been assigned as the marketing manager for a newly opened pizza restaurant. Considering that promotion is a useful way to introduce your brand, what would be your objectives to expand and maintain your brand existence and how would you practically fulfill such objectives?

Take-Home Projects

17-16. ***Portfolio Project:*** Select a print ad for a national marketer. Redesign the ad, including the use of a consumer sales promotion. Now design a second version, orienting the ad to a trade audience. Write a one-paragraph explanation for each ad that summarizes the objectives and strategy you are proposing.

17-17. ***Mini-Case Analysis:*** Why do you think the Susan G. Komen "Pink" campaign has been so successful over the years? What lessons might you learn about promotional planning from this case? If you were on the "Pink" team, what would you do next to continue the momentum? Come up with a big idea for a new promotion for the next year and explain how it would work and what it would accomplish.

TRACE North America Case

Multicultural Promotions

Read the TRACE case in the Appendix before coming to class.

17-18. Which promotional efforts in the case do you believe will be most successful? Develop at least two new promotional efforts to strengthen this campaign.

17-19. Create at least three promotional ideas that you feel will make this campaign more effective. Explain how they would work in a one-page proposal for each. Include sketches of your idea, if appropriate.

CHAPTER

18 The Principles and Practice of IMC

Photo: © MIXA Co., Ltd/PAL

It's a Winner

Campaign: *"I'm Amazing"*
Company: *McDonald's Restaurants HK*
Agencies: *DDB Group HK*
Awards: *Kam Fan Awards 2012—Gold for Outdoor Advertising, Best-Integrated Media Campaign, Ambien, and Best Use of Branded Content, Product Placement, Experiential, Sponsorship, Stunts, and Events; Grand EFFIE; Gold, 2013 Cannes—Silver Lion (Media)*

CHAPTER KEY POINTS

1. What are the eight key IMC concepts, and why are they important?
2. How would you outline the key parts of an IMC campaign plan?
3. Which strategic decisions underlie effective international marketing communication?
4. What do we mean by 360° communication programs?

I'm Amazing

In the summer of 2012, McDonald's Restaurant, Hong Kong (HK), launched their "I'm Amazing" campaign. The key concept behind this integrated marketing campaign—conceptualized by the DDB Group—was to collaborate with parents and children from all over the country to create a McDonald's outlet, which would likely feature in their wildest of dreams. No mean feat, particularly since it would be designed by children for children. This was part of McDonald's HK's initiative to re-connect with families, harness childrens' passion and creativity, and transform their ideas into reality. For the parents, it was to show them just how talented their children are and what they could achieve.

To avoid biting off more than it could chew, the agency made use of a multimedia and interactive approach when serving up the idea to the children. Initial work to start the design process was carried out in collaboration with one of Hong Kong's top schools. The campaign promised to use the 20 most popular designs, selected online by Hong Kong residents, in creating a one-of-a-kind outlet. After the campaign ended, the designs created were sold at an auction to raise funds for charities.

The campaign cooked up a storm by putting out one simple question—If a children were given the chance to build a McDonald's restaurant of their dreams, what would it look like? McDonald's launched an interactive website (imamazing.hk), inviting both parents and children to participate in designing the McDonald's hub of their dreams. Participants could use the online colouring system feature, or upload an image or video onto the website. They could also compete simply by submitting their designs at a McDonald's counter anywhere in the country. Using the feedback and votes from the website visitors, each design was rated. At the opening event held at Mega Box—a shopping centre in Hong Kong's Kowloon Bay—children were able to draw their own designs on a canvas on one of the walls.

To drive Web traffic—for entries, comments, and votes—a series of 30- and 60-second teasers was designed for TV. In addition, the campaign was supported by online banner ads and packets of direct-marketing materials, which were sent straight to schools in the country.

Within the first 10 days alone, the website racked up some 45,000 hits, with nearly 800 submissions. Parents received regular updates and tips about creativity on the website and could track the campaign on Facebook.

Marketing Director at McDonald's HK, noted Hong Kong is a very busy and crowded place, which makes daily life quite stressful. To cater for other target groups and to help increase their market share, another campaign was launched, focusing on good food at affordable prices—masterminded by the DDB Group, Hong Kong. The concept of a "moment of happiness" fit chimed well with the overall image of the corporation. The campaign—TV, radio, print, social media, and outdoor advertising—was fronted by 30-second TV commercials. Other components included redesigning a double-decker bus that would run on the Cross Harbour Tunnel Route. When passengers swiped their Octopus Cards, instead of hearing the usual "beep" sound, they heard laughter. The "Happy Bus" was also fitted with optical illusion games. Disortion mirrors were placed at bus stops across Hong Kong as a part of the integrated strategy.

Find out how effective McDonald's effort to get a bigger piece of the pie from its fast-food competitors was in the "It's a Wrap" feature at the end of the chapter.

Sources: "McDonald's & DDB HK Awarded the Most Effective Campaign at 2013 HK4As EFFIE Awards," www.campaignbrief.com/asia/2013/05/the-hk4as-the-association-of.html; "DDB Group Hong Kong Scoop the Grand Kam Fan at This Year's Kam Fan Awards," www.campaignbrief.com/asia/2012/12/ddb-group-hong-kong-was.html; "DDB Group Hong Kong Launches 'i'm Amazing' Campaign for McDonald's," www.ddbchina.com/ddblog/2012/07/ddb-group-hong-kong-launches-im-amazing-campaign-for-mcdonalds-1.html; "McDonalds Hong Kong - I'm Amazing!" www.mauricemoynihan.com/68079/562006/gallery/mcdonalds-im-amazing) (all accessed 24–25/10/2013).

The McDonald's HK case is about an award-winning integrated campaign, illustrating how marketers tackle decision-making and brand communication in a highly competitive market. This chapter will review the fundamentals of IMC principles—describing the formalities of planning for the campaign to introduction to the challenges of handling an IMC campaign.

Key IMC Concepts

Integrated marketing communication is an important business concept as well as a set of principles and practices. It has been a major theme in this book, and we will use this chapter to summarize the basic principles and review the practices of IMC. We'll begin with the key concepts that separate IMC plans and programs from more traditional advertising.

Stakeholders and Brand Relationships

We start with stakeholders because a customer focus is critical in most IMC strategies. Although we say "customer," we are really referring to all the stakeholders who impact on that customer relationship. Relationship marketing, a concept that originated with public relations, shifts the focus from the objective of a one-time purchase to the maintenance of long-term involvement from and by all of the firm's critical stakeholders, whether employees, distributors, channel members, agencies, investors, government agencies, the media, or community.

Principle
Interactive communication is the glue that joins brands and their stakeholders in respectful long-term relationships.

Interactive and respectful communication is the link that connects brands and their key stakeholders and the glue that joins them in respectful long-term relationships. The possibility of authentic two-way communication has exploded with the development of digital technology and social media.

All stakeholders are critical in relationship marketing because they are communicators who can send either positive or negative messages about the brand. It is important to keep in contact with them, but it's even more important to set up relationship programs that invite two-way communication and let them initiate messages.

Relevant messages delivered through media that drive positive experiences create value for consumers. This value adds up over time and emerges as loyalty—the ultimate goal of relationship marketing programs. Brand relationships are indicators of **brand value**—what a brand is worth both to the company and to its customers. Positive relationships underlie the financial value of a brand as well as its perceived value to customers. Negative impact, however, can come from mishandling the type and amount of messages directed to stakeholders, as the "A Matter of Principle" feature explains.

Principle
Brand relationships drive brand value.

It's important to remember that although we talk about stakeholders as if they were independent groups, in fact stakeholders may overlap. Employees, for example, are often customers as well as shareholders, and they often live in communities where the company is in business. It's important that a brand not say one thing to one stakeholder group and something opposite or contradictory to another—particularly not in this time of instant Internet communication.

Principle
Stakeholders overlap, and so do their messages.

The growth of **permission marketing**, a practice that invites consumers to sign up for messages, self-selecting themselves into a brand's target market, mirrors the shift from one-way to two-way communication. That's important as brands become more involved in social communication where online technology permits contacts that move beyond the frequently intrusive and unwanted forms of mass-media advertising.

Total Communication

Media planning includes all the traditional as well as nontraditional media, but it is well to remember that in **360° communication** planning, there are other message delivery points in the

Principle
Receiving and responding to messages is as important as sending them.

A Matter of Principle

When Is Too Many Too Much?

Tom Duncan, *University of Colorado and University of Denver*

The question advertisers have to ask themselves when approving a plan that involves nontraditional media is whether they are using this tool effectively and with respect for consumers. Are advertisers trying to find every possible contact point they can identify, or are they creating logical associations that consumers will appreciate?

The fact is that we are inundated with commercial messages from advertising of all sorts in all kinds of unexpected places that we routinely encounter. Message clutter is overwhelming every aspect of our daily lives.

Think about something as noncommercial as attending a symphony. You may find a new car in the lobby as well as promotional signs for any number of products—not to mention the symphony itself, which is promoting concerts and season subscriptions. Of course, there are ads in the program, but there may also be ads in the bathrooms and around the snack counter you visit at intermission. When you leave, you'll probably see more posters in windows adjoining the concert hall. You might even find a flyer tucked under the windshield wiper on your car.

There is a difference between "buying eyeballs" and delivering messages in a context that will intersect with a target audience's interests. Wilson Sporting Goods, for example, sponsors Tennis Camps by furnishing practice balls and making racquets available that participants can try for free. Even though the camp may be surrounded by Wilson, the message is relevant and the brand experiences are positive.

The point is that the less relevant the messages, the more irritating they become. Why is this a problem? The tipping point in impact is when the percentage of irrelevant messages is so high that people respond by tuning out *all* commercial messages—the relevant along with the irrelevant.

One reason TiVo became popular is because viewers can time-shift programs and zip through commercials. In what ways will consumers create defense mechanisms to protect themselves from nontraditional media that assault them in unwanted ways in inappropriate times?

How many messages can we surround them with before they rebel?

way a company does business. A **total communication** program monitors all these sources of brand messages. And remember, contemporary brand communication includes two-way as well as targeted strategies—receiving and responding to messages is as important as sending them.

Principle
Every part of the marketing mix—not just marketing communication—sends a message.

Older views of IMC focused primarily on coordinating marketing communication, but as we mentioned in Chapter 2, we also believe that the marketing mix delivers messages. DeLozier's marketing communication book, as long ago as 1976, treated all the marketing mix variables as communication variables.[1] How the product is designed and how it performs, where the brand is sold, and at what price—all of these marketing decisions send messages about the brand's position, quality, and image.

Principle
Integrating the marcom tools is futile if contrary and more powerful messages are sent by other brand actions.

For example, upscale hotel brands are targeting the Chinese market, but not just with advertising and other forms of marketing communication. Recognizing that even environmental details send messages, these new hotels appeal to affluent Asian travelers by adding gardens and teahouses in the hotels' lobbies.[2] Integrating the marcom tools is futile if contrary and more powerful messages are being sent by other brand actions.

Principle
Everything a brand does, but also what it doesn't do, can send a message. You can't NOT communicate.

Furthermore, consider that everything a brand does—and sometimes what it doesn't do—can send a message. You can't *not* communicate. Unintentional messages can arise from carelessly delivered brand experiences. For example, a long wait on a customer service help line or the inability of a company representative to answer a product safety question sends the message that the company doesn't value a customer's time or safety. Those messages can be more powerful—in a negative way—than anything said in the advertising. That's why it's necessary to monitor all marketing elements from a communication perspective.

Moving from Channels to Contact Points

The concept of **contact points** has redefined and broadened our understanding of media as a message delivery system. Contact points are the various ways a consumer comes in contact with a brand. As we proposed in Part 4, this view of media moves from traditional advertising media (print, broadcast, and outdoor) and the media of various marketing communication functions (press releases, events, promotional materials, and sponsorships) to experiential contacts that in previous advertising-dominated media plans weren't generally considered to be media, such as word of mouth and customer service.

These opportunities are found in a huge variety of vehicles including everything from television to T-shirts and tweets on Twitter. The list is endless and can be identified only by studying the lives of customers to spot the points where they come in contact with a brand—or an opportunity for a brand experience or brand conversation. Every one of these varied vehicles can deliver a brand message, either positive or negative, whether planned and managed or not.

Principle
IMC planning is designed to maximize and leverage the good contact points and minimize the bad ones.

Contact point management, then, is the way marketing communication planners develop systems of message delivery—both to and from all key stakeholders. The objective is to maximize and leverage the good contact points and minimize the bad ones.

Principle
Touch points are contact points that touch our emotions.

We also call them brand **touch points** because of the impact these personal experiences can have on stakeholder feelings about a brand. Consumers may receive information and impressions from a brand at a contact point, but a touch point is a brand experience that delivers a message that also touches emotions leading to positive and negative judgments. It has more emotional impact than a regular contact point. A *critical touch point*, then, is one that connects the brand and customer on an emotional level and leads to a yes-or-no decision about a purchase decision or a brand relationship.[3]

Sometimes referred to as experiential marketing, touch-point strategies and programs use events and store design, among other means, to engage consumers in a personal and involving way. Some would argue that every brand contact is an experience; however, in experiential marketing, the goal is to intensify active involvement beyond the more passive activity of reading, viewing, and listening to traditional media. The idea is to connect with consumers in ways that create higher levels of emotional engagement that lead to brand liking as well as lasting bonds with a brand.

Message Synergy

When you combine stakeholders and contact points—all the messages delivered through all possible media to all key stakeholders—you have a bundle of messages. How do you manage all the meanings and points where inconsistency or confusion might arise? And why does that matter?

The point is that brand communication is not about single messages but rather about the impact of various impressions and brand meanings that evolve as the messages interact and reinforce one another. Remember the principle of synergy that proposes that $2 + 2 = 5$. In other words, messages that reinforce one another have a multiplier effect that not only cements a brand impression but also polishes and magnifies it. If you hear good things (or bad things) about a brand in advertising (but also in comments from friends) and what you hear corresponds to your experience with the brand, then you are likely to become not just a customer but also a loyalist, perhaps even a brand fan.

Principle
Synergy happens when all the messages work together to create a coherent brand perception.

At every point of contact with every stakeholder, the essence of the brand should be the same. Drivers, for example, look at cars and car safety differently, and so do car manufacturers, their suppliers and investors, and local community leaders. But the essence of a brand like Volvo must be consistent on its safety position. Strategic consistency drives synergy, and synergy drives the brand impression. Therefore, brand stewards and IMC planners are insistent on **strategic consistency**—the core or essence of the brand is clear in every message if they are tailored to the particular interests of various stakeholders.

Principle
Strategic consistency drives synergy.

Principle
A brand is a unified vision (the art) and a complex system of message delivery and exchange (the science).

An example of a brand meaning that speaks to a specific stakeholder group is the classic *Wall Street Journal* campaign that has run for more than 30 years in advertising trade publications. It showcases the ideas of great creative leaders of advertising and connects them to a specific media vehicle—the *Wall Street Journal*. You can find many of the ads from this campaign at www.aef.com/industry/careers/2026.

A Brand Is an Integrated Perception

Message synergy is the basis for seeing a brand as an integrated perception. People automatically integrate brand messages and experiences—it's a natural process in perception. And that happens whether or not brand stewards try to manage the process. What do you think of when you think of Volvo, Mountain Dew, and Apple? Your impression will probably contain ideas about the brand's position in the market as well as images of the people you see using it and the messages you've heard articulated in media and mentions by people you know. How that stew of information and images comes together as an **integrated perception** is just the way we make sense of things, and that's how a brand impression is created. Perceptual integration works only if the pieces fit together.

Photo: Copyright © Dow Jones & Company, Inc.

CLASSIC
This ad that features Carl Ally is one in a series by the *Wall Street Journal* that features leaders in advertising explaining their views on how advertising works and why the *Wall Street Journal* is a good advertising medium.

Unified Brand Vision

There is an art and a science to IMC management. A successful brand is the product of both science—a complex system of planned and managed activities—and art—a vision of the essence of the brand in which all the pieces and parts fit together perfectly in a coherent brand perception.[4] The vision of the brand steward and how that unified vision is communicated to all the agents involved in the complex system of brand communication determines the effectiveness of a brand communication program.

In other words, marketing communicators are managing a multiplicity of brand activities and programs that are interrelated and that work well only to the extent that they work together. When they work together with a single **unified vision** of the brand, like a great symphony, the pieces and parts fit together perfectly, generating meaning and creating something of value.

Internal Integration

Brand management involves creating and monitoring a complex set of philosophies and activities. You can't

Principle
You can't be integrated externally if you are not integrated internally.

be integrated externally if you are not integrated internally. A core brand strategy—a shared vision—drives the entire organization. **Cross-functional management** across department lines delivers unity of vision, which is the foundation for the consumer's integrated brand perception.

Brand Integrity

Principle
Integration leads to brand integrity.

At the root of it all, if you look in the dictionary, you'll see that the word *integration* has the same Latin root as *integrity*. So you might conclude that an integrated brand is one that has **brand integrity**. It is more believable because what it says and does matches what others say about it. In other words, its brand reputation is supported by word-of-mouth comments, media stories, and testimonies from satisfied users. Being a good corporate citizen also adds trust to brand relationships and embellishes a brand's reputation.

Crisis communication is always a test of brand and corporate integrity, as the Carnival Cruise ship line found in 2013 when its disabled *Triumph* ship ad to be towed back to port from its Caribbean route. Cell phones and social media were filled with words and pictures about overflowing toilets, nasty smells, and a lack of food. The company made an effort to redeem itself with customers and the cruise ship public by providing full refunds, discounts of future trips, and a $500 bonus to its suffering passengers.

This review of IMC's basic concepts also identifies a set of basic principles. We'll show how these principles are applied to IMC campaign planning and program management in the sections that follow. So to summarize, here are 14 principles that guide IMC:

1. Interactive communication is the glue that joins brands and their stakeholders in respectful long-term relationships.
2. Brand relationships drive brand value.
3. Stakeholders overlap; so do their messages.
4. Receiving messages is as important as sending them.
5. Every part of the marketing mix sends a message.
6. Integrating the marcom tools is futile if contrary and more powerful messages are sent by other brand actions.
7. Everything a brand does (and sometimes what it doesn't do) can send a message. You can't *not* communicate.
8. IMC planning is designed to maximize and leverage the good contact points and minimize the bad ones.
9. Touch points are contact points that touch our emotions.
10. Synergy happens when all the messages work together to create a coherent brand perception.
11. Strategic consistency drives synergy.
12. A brand is a unified vision (the art) and a complex system of message delivery and exchange (the science).
13. You can't be integrated externally if you are not integrated internally.
14. Integration leads to brand integrity.

IMC Campaign Planning

One principle you have learned is that in marketing communication campaigns, a key objective is to create consistency among all the marcom tools and platforms. That's essentially a tactical approach, one focused on orchestrating consistent brand messages. In the Part 5 opener, Duncan referred to this approach as a "one-voice, one-look" strategy, which has always been a critical goal for campaigns. We now recognize, however, that although it's important to have strategic consistency based on the brand essence, there may be different message strategies for different audiences.

Stan Richards, founder of the Dallas-based Richards Group, explains the process his agency goes through in planning an integrated campaign. It's also the creative brief for what he calls **spherical branding**, which means that no matter what your angle of vision, the brand always looks the same:[5] We call this *360° planning*. Both refer to looking at a brand from all directions and points of view. Richards's brief outline is a good starting point for building a complete campaign plan:

- ***Three-Part Positioning*** Target audience? Competitors? Most meaningful brand benefit?
- ***Brand Personality*** Five to six words that define the brand's personality.
- ***Affiliation*** What club do you join when you adopt a brand?
- ***Brand Vision*** A statement of the brand's "highest calling."

What Is a Campaign Plan?

An IMC campaign is a complex set of interlocking, coordinated activities that has a beginning and an end. An IMC campaign plan is more complex than a traditional advertising plan because of the variety of marcom areas and stakeholders involved. An IMC plan outlines the objectives and strategies for a series of different but related marketing communication efforts that appear in different media, use different marketing communication tools, and convey different but complementary brand-consistent messages to a variety of stakeholders.

An IMC plan follows the same basic outline as an advertising plan. The difference, however, lies with the scope of the plan and the variety of activities involved in the effort. The more tools used, the harder it is to coordinate their efforts and maintain consistency across a variety of messages. The objective in IMC planning is to make the most effective and consistent use of all marketing communication functions and to influence or control the impact of other communication elements. Here is a typical outline:

Principle
The more tools used, the harder it is to coordinate their efforts and maintain consistency across a variety of messages.

I. Situation Analysis
- Background research
- SWOTs: strengths, weaknesses, opportunities, threats
- Key communication problem(s) to be solved

II. Key Strategic Campaign Decisions
- Objectives
- Targeting and engaging stakeholders
- Brand positioning strategy

III. Marcom Mix
- Platforms and objectives
- Synergy

IV. Message Strategy
- Key consumer and brand relationship insights
- Message direction
- Strategic consistency

V. IMC Media and Contact Points
- Multimedia and multichannel
- Multiplatform
- Contact points, touch points, and critical touch points

VI. Management and Campaign Controls
- Budgeting
- Evaluation of effectiveness

This outline is useful as a guide for a planning document, but, more importantly, it identifies the key strategic decisions that guide various sections of an IMC campaign plan. Before we look at these strategic planning decisions in more detail, read the "A Matter of Practice" story.

Situation Analysis

The first step in developing an IMC plan, just as in a marketing plan, is not planning but *backgrounding*—researching and reviewing the current state of the business and gathering all pertinent information. After the research is compiled, planners try to make sense of the findings,

A Matter of Practice

Doha: A New City

Rania Deeb, *Business Consultant, UAE*

Being different is what Doha is all about, and this is exactly the positioning that the brand identity campaign strived toward.

Qatar is a small peninsula with a total area of about 11,500 km of flat, featureless terrain, with sand dunes in the south and a rocky desert in the north. It is hot and dry, surrounded by a shallow, hyper-saline, semi-enclosed sea. Its population exceeds 1.7 million, and 85 percent of the people are expatriates.

It was only a few years ago when Doha was referred to as a "sleepy town" and was rated by a travel guidebook as the most boring city on earth. However, the city succeeded in reconstructing itself into a whole new and different destination, reinventing and rebranding but remaining true to its roots. The entire rebranding effort was encapsulated on an online portal.

Qatar's development progressed at an unprecedented pace. It took only a couple of years for the country to go from being one of the poorest countries to becoming the richest country on earth, with remarkable economic growth over the past decade. The tremendous economic boom, which Doha has been witness to, has been supported largely by an influx of expatriate workers. The country has become the main attraction for the external workforce in the last five years.

The demographic structure of Doha and the dominating population of non-Qatari residents compared to the locals threatens its national identity, but at the same time offers great potential for creating Doha's new identity as a globalized urbanism.

The main aspects that personify the rebranding of the country can be easily identified within the city: It's the architecture and the urbanization itself that creates "Dohaization." Knowledge-based urban development is the first aspect, and the balanced combination of local and global urbanism is the second. Doha is considered as the most advanced city in the Middle East to have adopted a knowledge economy as a conceptual base for its 2030 vision, and making Doha a vibrant science and technology hub and attracting and retaining highly skilled employees are part of its strategic plan.

The plan to create a world-class set of cultural facilities made an impressive start with the opening of the Museum of Islamic Art in Doha, which perfectly fits the purpose of the new brand. The objective behind opening national museums is to support the creation of a distinct national identity linked to the past and at the same time to preserve a changing lifestyle; both purposes were deemed necessary for creating the new city.

Along with its mission to create a unique presence and differentiate itself from other Gulf cities, the overall construction of the new city had to meet the demands of the region and be relevant to the community and roots on the one hand and meet global standards on the other in order to reserve a place on the global stage and brand itself as a global city that attracts people from all over the world.

Sources: 1. Lusail: Qatar's Future City, 2013, available at http://www.lusail.com/English/Pages/English_Home.aspx. [Accessed 06 November 2013]; 2. *Constructing a New Urbanity Brand amid Gulf and Middle Eastern Cities.* | *Ali A. Alraouf - Academia.edu.* available at: http://www.academia.edu/1879733/DOHAIZATION._Constructing_a_New_Urbanity_Brand_amid_Gulf_and_Middle_Eastern_Cities. [Accessed 09 November 2013]; 3. An *Alchemy of Architecture, People and Places.: The State of Arab Cities, The Case of Qatar. Prof. Ali A. Alraouf*, available at: http://analchemyofarchitecture.blogspot.ae/2013/09/the-state-of-arab-cities-case-of-qatar.html. [Accessed 09 November 2013]; 4. There is no heritage in Qatar': Orientalism, colonialism and other problematic histories, available at: http://www.tandfonline.com/doi/full/10.1080/00438243.2013.852069. [Accessed 10 November 2013]; 5. *In Doha*, available at: http://indoha.wordpress.com/ [Accessed 09 November 2013]; 6. *Doha International Airport | Home*, available at: http://www.dohaairport.com/en/home.html. [Accessed 08 November 2013].

a process sometimes referred to as a **situation analysis**. The goal for both advertising and IMC planning is to identify a problem that can be solved with communication. As Fallon and Senn explained in their "Juicing the Orange" list, you have to start by simplifying the problem (see Chapter 7). The information collection will probably be huge, but the problem statement zeros in on the most relevant concerns.

SWOT Analysis The primary tool used to make sense of the information gathered and identify a key problem related to a brand or product is a **SWOT analysis**. The strengths and weaknesses are *internally focused*, and the opportunities and threats lie in the *external* marketing environment. In strategic planning, the idea is to *leverage* the strengths and opportunities and *address* the weaknesses and threats, which is how the key problems and opportunities are identified:[6]

- The *strengths* of a business are its positive traits, conditions, and good situations. For instance, being in a category leader is a strength. Planners ask how they can leverage this strength in the brand's communication.
- The *weaknesses* of a business are traits, conditions, and situations that are perceived as negatives. Losing market share is a weakness. If this is an important weakness, then planners ask how they can or should address it with communication. Avis found a positive in a negative in its classic campaign when it positioned itself as number two, so "we try harder."
- An *opportunity* is an area in which the company could develop an advantage over its competition. Often, one company's weakness is another company's opportunity. Planners strive to identify these opportunities and leverage them in the brand's communication. This is a huge strategy for political campaign advertising.
- A *threat* is a trend or development in the environment that will erode business unless the company takes action. Competition and economic downturns are common threats. Communication planners ask themselves how they can address a threat if it is a critical factor affecting the success of the brand. McDonald's has promoted its healthy menu items to counter the perception of burgers as unhealthy choices.

For the launch of Coke Zero, the strength of the brand lies with the Coca-Cola tradition as "the real thing." The opportunity existed to transfer that Coke magic to a calorie-free version of the flagship brand. The weakness is the association of diet drinks with women when Coke saw an opportunity in marketing to men. The threat lies with the perception that "diet drinks" have an unpleasant taste; the opportunity was to explain that Coke Zero tastes like regular Coke.

Key Communication Problem(s) The key word in the title of this section is *analysis*, or making sense of all the data collected and figuring out what the information means for the future success of the brand. Planners must analyze the market situation for communication problems that affect the successful marketing of a product as well as opportunities the advertising can create or exploit. Analyzing the SWOTs as well as the directions from the client and identifying key problems that can be solved with a brand message are at the heart of strategic thinking. An example of locating a timing opportunity is illustrated by Special K's "2-Week Challenge," which capitalized on consumers' goals to lose weight after the holidays.

IMC can solve only message-related problems such as image, attitude, perception, and knowledge or information. It cannot solve problems related to price, availability, or quality, although it can address the perception of these marketing mix factors. For example, a message can speak to the perception that the price is too high by focusing on a value strategy, or it can portray a product with limited distribution as exclusive. In other words, promotional messages can affect the way consumers perceive price, availability, and quality. The marketer's basic assumption—and success criteria—however, is that a campaign works if it creates the desired brand impression, influences people to respond, and separates the brand from the competition.

Principle
A campaign works if it creates the desired brand impression, influences people to respond, and separates the brand from its competition.

Campaign Strategy

Once the situation has been analyzed and the key problem or problems identified, planners decide a general statement of strategy—in other words, what is this campaign all about? The general strategy that guides a campaign can be described in several ways. For example, a strategy can focus on branding, positioning, countering the competition, or creating category dominance.

Photo: Nadine Laubacher

The message strategy for the launch of Coke Zero used self-deprecating humor with a Big Idea that the Coca-Cola legal department wanted to sue Coke Zero for taste infringement.

In the case of McDonalds, the "I'm Amazing" campaign was designed to separate the brand from other fast-food restaurants and, at the same time, to stake a claim in a distinctive brand vision.

Maybe the strategy is designed to change consumers' perception of the brand's price or price–value relationship. The strategy may also seek to increase the size of the market, or what marketers call **share of wallet**, the amount customers spend on the brand. Other marketing efforts might involve launching a new brand or a brand extension or moving the brand into a new market.

Another common focus is the role and importance of the brand's competitive position and how to respond to competitor's messages. During the recession, for example, a number of major brands, such as Dunkin' Donuts, Burger King, and Campbell's Soup, developed highly competitive advertising. Domino's Pizza, for example, used an aggressive campaign comparing its oven-baked sandwiches as tasting better than Subway's hoagies. This is a strategy often seen in economic downturns, which analysts describe as "a dogfight" for market share.[7]

The important thing to remember, as marketing professor Julie Ruth explains,[8] is that planners have to first analyze the situation to arrive at a great strategy before racing ahead to think about tactics. So what's the difference between strategy and tactics? The decision to expand the market (strategy) by increasing share of wallet (objective) is implemented through promotional tactics ("buy four and get one free").

The situation analysis is the first step in developing the IMC campaign strategy. There are a number of related strategic decisions that follow from the situation analysis, and we'll discuss three of them here: *objectives*, *targeting*, and *brand position*.

Objectives Given the huge amounts of money spent on brand communication, it is important for marketers to know what to expect from a campaign. Although a rule of thumb for advertising is that it should be single minded, we also know from Chapter 4 that multiple effects are often needed to create the desired impact, and that's particularly true in IMC planning. Some messages may use an emotional strategy while others are informational, but sometimes the message needs to speak to both the head and the heart. We mentioned in the discussion of the Coke Zero launch that customers needed to understand that the taste of Coke Zero was similar to regular Coke but that the message had to do it with a style and attitude that twenty-something males would like and find believable.

Although some objectives are tightly focused on one particular effect, others, such as brand loyalty, call for a more complex set of effects. To create brand loyalty, for example, a campaign must have both cognitive (rational) and affective (emotional) effects, and it must move people to repeat buying. That's one reason brand loyalty is considered a type of long-term impact developed over time from many experiences that a consumer has with a brand and brand messages.

Note also that communication objectives may be important, even if they aren't focused directly on a sale. For example, Expedia.com, a travel consulting company, uses its campaigns as a way to draw attention to itself, create name recognition, and create understanding of the products and services it sells. The idea is that after brand awareness and understanding are created, the selling can start.

We cannot overstate the importance of writing focused and measurable objectives. Every campaign must be guided by specific, clear, and measurable objectives. We say **measurable objectives** because that's how the effectiveness of a campaign is determined. A measurable objective has a starting baseline and a goal—the distance between those two points is what is measured. The starting point can be a **benchmark**, which means the planner uses a comparable effort, such as a similar product or prior brand campaign, to predict a logical goal. A measurable objective includes five requirements:

1. A *specific effect* that can be measured
2. A *time frame*
3. A *baseline* (where we are or where we begin)
4. The *goal* (a realistic estimate of the change the campaign can create; benchmarking is used to justify the projected goal)
5. *Percentage change* (subtract the baseline from the goal; divide the difference by the baseline)

A hypothetical objective, then, would read like this: "The goal of this campaign is to move the target's awareness of Coke Zero's taste similarity with regular Coke from 18 to 23 percent within 12 months, an increase of 28 percent."

Targeting and Engaging Stakeholders We introduced the concept of stakeholders in the IMC introduction in Chapter 2, but let's look a little deeper into this concept. The target in an IMC plan includes more than just consumers. As a reminder, the term *stakeholder* refers to any group of people who have a stake in the success of a company or brand. These potential audiences include all those who might influence the purchase of products and the success of a company's marketing program, as the table below shows. Employees are particularly important, and their support or *buy-in* for marketing communication programs is managed through an activity called **internal marketing**.

Based on research into consumers and customers as well as the involvement of other stakeholders, the targeting or engagement strategy identifies the most important audience groups. Research by account planners will help to flesh out the interests of these folks and provide critical insights. Account planning, with its strong emphasis on insights, has moved beyond its original advertising orientation and has become much more useful in IMC campaign planning. Jon Steel,

Types of Stakeholder Audiences

Corporate Level

Employees

Investors, financial community (analysts, brokers, and the financial press)

Government bodies and agencies

Regulatory bodies

Business partners

Marketing Level

Consumers

Customers

Competitors

Market segments

Distributors, dealers, retailers, and others in the distribution channel

Suppliers and vendors, including agencies

Marcom Level

Target audiences

Target stakeholders

Employees

Trade audiences

Local community

Media (general, special interest, trade)

Consumer activist groups

General public

Opinion leaders

author of a book on advertising and account planning, says that planning works best as it is integrated into the entire communication mix.[9] Insights into consumer, customer, and stakeholder relationships with the brand identify specific groups who might respond to brand messages. From this, a list of primary and secondary targets is built, along with profiles of typical members of this group.

As we mentioned in our list of principles, an important thing to remember is that people don't simply line up in one box or another. The fact of overlapping membership complicates message strategy and demands that there be a certain core level of consistency and integrity in all brand messages both from a company but also within stakeholder conversations.

Brand Strategy Message consistency has to have a heart, core, soul, or DNA—a central concept around which various messages can be unified. We refer to this as *brand essence*, and it describes what makes the brand different and distinctive from all other brands in its product category. It tells consumers precisely what the brand stands for—what it means in the marketplace. It is the admission ticket to enter the minds of consumers in the battle for the mental marketplace.[10]

Red Bull is the energy drink; Coke Zero is the diet cola that tastes the same as the original cola. In some cases, perhaps most, the central core is the brand position—the statements about the core concept of Red Bull and Coke Zero are based on their positions. An example of a brand vision that reflects a core value comes from global marketer, IBM, which expressed its support for world peace and world trade in this classic 1938 ad.

Photo: Courtesy of IBM Archives

CLASSIC

IBM used this "World Peace" ad to demonstrate its commitment to world trade and the international marketing of its products in this ad campaign that ran on the eve of World War II.

There are times, however, when the brand position is adjusted for different markets. For example, if a brand is moving into a new country and represents a category of product that is new or unknown, then the campaign strategy would need to be based on launching a category as well as a brand. In other markets, where the brand is well known, the brand strategy may be much more competitive, and the position is determined by the need to separate itself from other similar brands. Starbucks moving into India is an example of a new brand in a new category. Most of the world knows Starbucks, but coffee and the coffee shop environment may call for different kind of message strategy, particularly in a solidly tea-based society.

Effective IMC plans lead to profitable long-term brand relationships. That's another dimension of the strategic decisions about the most profitable stakeholders to engage in brand communication. How do you engage them the first time, and how does the brand conversation continue and evolve? What are the links and connections in the relationship that must be built and protected?

The IMC Mix

The decision about which marcom tools to use in a campaign is based on an analysis of their strengths and weaknesses as well as consumer insights to determine how these functions can best be employed to meet the campaign's objectives. As we explained in Chapter 7, certain tools are better at delivering specific objectives. You use public relations, for example, to announce something that is newsworthy, whereas you use sales promotion to drive immediate action. Therefore, an IMC plan operates with a set of interrelated objectives that specify the strategies for all of the different tools. Each area has a set of objectives. The following list presents the main IMC areas in terms of their primary effects:

- ***Advertising*** Reach wide audience through mass media; acquire new customers; establish brand image and personality; define brand position; identify points of differentiation and competitive advantage; counter competition,; deliver brand reminders.
- ***Public Relations*** Announce news; affect attitudes and opinions; maximize credibility and likability; create and improve stakeholder relationships.
- ***Consumer Sales Promotion*** Stimulate behavior; generate immediate response; intensify needs, wants, and motivations; reward behavior; stimulate involvement and relevance; create pull through the channel; provide brand reminder.
- ***Trade Sales Promotion*** Build industry acceptance; push through the channel; motivate cooperation; energize sales force, dealers, distributors.
- ***Point of Purchase*** Increase immediate sales; attract attention at decision point; create interest; stimulate urgency; encourage trial and impulse purchasing.
- ***Direct Marketing*** Stimulate sales; create personal interest and relevance; provide in-depth information; create acceptance, conviction.
- ***Sponsorship and Events*** Build awareness; create brand experience, participation, interaction, involvement; create excitement.
- ***Packaging*** Increase sales; attract attention at selection point; deliver product information; create brand reminder.
- ***Specialties*** Reinforce brand identity; continuous brand reminder; reinforce satisfaction; encourage repeat purchase; reward loyal customers.
- ***Guerilla Marketing*** Intercept prospects where they work, live, and visit: create curiosity and excitement; provide opportunity for involvement; stimulate buzz.
- ***Customer Service*** Answer questions; solve customer problems; record complaints and compliments; turn bad customer experiences into positive experiences; listen to consumer perceptions and record feedback; notify appropriate departments of complaints and compliments; test-market communication strategies and copy points.

As you look over the list, think about what's required to launch a new product. In that situation, which tools would you select as the most appropriate? That's the type of thinking planners use at this point to initially decide which marcom tools would be most useful in meeting the campaign's objectives. Sometimes there might be a lead area, such as an event. The other areas provide support—for example, advertising, public relations, and direct marketing may be needed to get the word out; promotional materials are useful to reward people for getting involved; and specialties provide reminders. Other times, the campaign operates with a basket of tools—all of them important in their own way.

In times past, these functional areas were often little empires with their own ideas and programs. Sometimes the programs conflicted—a special promotion might be planned at the same time as an event or big advertising campaign but with an entirely different theme. We refer to this approach as **silos**, which means they operated on their own with little concern for what the other areas were doing. They were jealous of their budgets and protective of their responsibilities. IMC has sought to break down the walls between these functional areas and coordinate their activities with brand-focused planning. The result has been more consistency and synergy in message strategies.

Message Strategy

Chapter 8 explored the ins and outs of message strategy—how much to focus on rational or emotional messages, what message formats to use, and how to get a Big Idea that gets attention and sticks in memory. Those deliberations and their conclusions are written into the campaign plan. The message strategies are also matched to the different targeted stakeholders based on insights into what moves them.

Good Big Ideas are valued because they may be enduring, such as the Frontier talking animals. Furthermore, they lend themselves to extendability, which means they "have legs." By that we

A Matter of Practice

A Campaign with Legs (and Flippers)

Shawn Couzens, Conceptual Engineer, AbbaSez and *Gary Ennis, Freelance Creative Director/Art Director, both former Creative Directors, Grey Advertising*

When Frontier has something to sell—whether it's a new city, a website, or the frequent-flyer program—we let the animals deliver the message in a fun, humorous way. Certain characters are better suited for certain messages than others.

Flip, for example, is the lovable loser who never gets a break. For years, he's been dying to fly to a warm, tropical climate, such as Florida. But instead, he always gets sent to Chicago. This has been a recurring theme in several commercials. So, when Frontier expanded its service to Mexico, this was the perfect opportunity to build on Flip's story line—hence, "Flip to Mexico."

The point is that the campaign has always been episodic, like a situation comedy. With 10-plus television spots a year, we needed a structure that allowed us to build on the characters and their story lines.

If our base-brand campaign were a sitcom, then *Flip to Mexico* would be a spin-off. The idea was to blanket a city with the "news" that Flip would quit unless he went to Mexico—and he needed the public's help to get there. We wanted the community to be an active participant in the story. To facilitate this, we launched a series of mock newscasts covering Flip's evolving story line. We hired "activists" to hold placards and distribute leaflets, and we created an elaborate underground website with lots of interactive content. We even involved real Frontier employees, like CEO Jeff Potter, to help blur the line between reality and fiction. Consumers enjoyed the interplay, and they happily rallied for Flip. The story really captivated the city of Denver. It was all over the news. And it deepened the bond between Frontier and the community at a time when other airlines were trying to eat into Frontier's home turf.

But it's no longer about just television, print, and radio. An idea has to perform across multiple platforms, and new media are a big part of that. Brands will have to find other ways to connect with consumers—like podcasts, interactive websites, YouTube contests, branded entertainment, product placement, long-format digital content, and more. Some brands are creating their own television shows or Web channels with original programming. The media landscape will continue to change. What won't change is the need for talented writers and art directors who can think outside the parameters of traditional media and make the brand story relevant and entertaining across all of these different media and formats.

A campaign is an evolving story, so you can't rest on your awards. When you launch a successful campaign and everyone likes it, you've set the creative bar pretty high. Everyone's waiting to see what you'll do next. Your job is to keep surprising them, keep raising the bar—because if you don't do it, someone else will.

There's a saying in the industry, "You're only as good as your last ad." It's kind of true. One week, you're being praised for an ad or campaign. But the next week, you have a new creative brief in your hand, and you have to prove yourself all over again.

mean that the idea is strong enough to serve as an umbrella concept for a variety of executions or mini-campaigns. The "A Matter of Practice" feature explains how Frontier's animals can be endlessly extended.

Message strategy decisions support the overall campaign objectives and direction that we discussed earlier. For example, the campaign strategy might involve the long-term use of a celebrity spokesperson who becomes the face of the brand. This creates positive associations for the brand, and, to the extent that the celebrity is a superstar, the reputation of a winner is associated with the brand image.

Photo: Copyright 1999–2004 American Express Company. All rights reserved. Courtesy of Jerry Seinfeld and Ogilvy & Mather

An online mini-film commercial for American Express featuring Jerry Seinfeld was designed to entertain and create brand liking. It also generated buzz, which extended its impact through the power of word of mouth.

For example, golf's Tiger Woods was one of the athletes whom Nike (as well as other brands, such as Accenture) signed as a spokesperson. The strategy disintegrated when Woods was caught up in a sex scandal. That event moved him from one of the most respected celebrity endorsers to a flawed figure with questionable integrity. His sponsors, including Nike and Accenture, among others, had to decide how to relate their brands not only to his longtime dominance of golf but also to his loss of honor. It's not just the brand images that were threatened by Tiger's infidelities; economists estimate the loss to shareholders of his nine corporate sponsors as close to $12 billion.[11] And the same problem erupted with the legendary Tour de France winner Lance Armstrong, whose seven medals were taken away after officials determined that he had been actively blood doping during those competitions. Another big hit to the Armstrong reputation and image—as well as his to his well-respected Livestrong cancer research foundation—was Nike's announcement that it would no longer use Armstrong as a celebrity figure in its advertising.

Another example of the strategic use of a celebrity, one that worked better than the Woods and Armstrong examples, was an American Express four-minute humorous online commercial featuring comedian Jerry Seinfeld and an animated Superman. The strategy was to use a favorite comedian and a favorite hero to create *brand liking*. The two sidekicks play the role of neurotic New Yorkers complaining about such earthshaking topics as the amount of mayonnaise on their tuna sandwiches. They also relate the benefits of using an American Express card. The message is soft sell and embedded in a gag, which makes the commercial feel more like cinema than advertising. Seinfeld jokes that it isn't going to be interrupted by a commercial because it is a commercial.[12]

As we mentioned earlier, strategic consistency comes from the creative theme and the consistent presentation of the brand position and personality, even when different stakeholders groups receive different types of messages and interact with the brand in different ways. Consistency is a standard built into a carefully designed multiplatform and multimedia plan.

In most cases, the drive for brand consistency is a strategic need, but at other times it reflects cost efficiency. IMC programs can be more effective because of their repetition, and this reinforcement creates more cost-efficient campaigns as well as more effective message strategies. Managers have learned that using multiple tools and channels in a consistent way is more profitable and builds longer-lasting customer relationships than relying on uncoordinated tools doing their own thing.

IMC Media and Contact Points

When most people think about media, they think about traditional mass media and advertising. Media planning in an IMC context does more than just deliver targeted messages; media also involve, engage, and connect consumers to the brand and to one another. We presented the connection role of media in Part 4. Melissa Lerner, vice president of Posterscope, an out-of-home media company, summarizes the various roles that media play in a comprehensive IMC media plan.

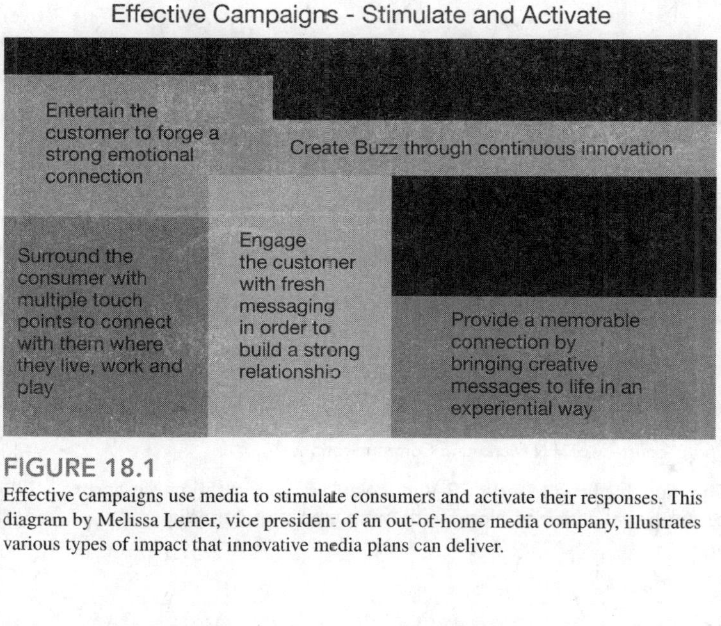

FIGURE 18.1

Effective campaigns use media to stimulate consumers and activate their responses. This diagram by Melissa Lerner, vice president of an out-of-home media company, illustrates various types of impact that innovative media plans can deliver.

Multichannel and Multiplatform On one level, media planning involves using media as planners have done for years—by employing all different types of traditional media, a practice identified as *multichannel* or *multimedia*. As DePaul University marketing professor Steve Kelly explains, "IMC tries to tie it all together. IMC is the goal of most marketers, but multichannel is what they actually do."[13]

We described media plans in Chapter 14, and all the information described in that document (e.g., media objectives, media selection and media mix, scheduling, and budgeting) appears in an IMC campaign plan.

When IMC planners think about media, they think about message delivery systems, and that includes all of the media used in all the various marketing communication functions. We reviewed many of these in Chapter 13 under the title *multiplatform*. Direct response, for example, can appear in traditional media (print, with return forms to get more information about a brand or place an order, or infomercials on television) but also in letters mailed directly to the home or office, telemarketing (phone calls to the home or office), and in digital forms, such as e-mail and Twitter. And Facebook makes it possible to order directly from that site.

For example, consider a Honda CR-V campaign in Iceland. The agency's owner, Ingvi Logason, described his agency's multimedia and multiplatform approach:[14]

> The media emphasis had been on print with support from TV and the Internet. We shifted the emphasis to a 360° integrated approach where we focused, among other things, on media with large reach at the expense of high frequency. TV and interactive Web banners were at the forefront of the campaign with support from newspaper, radio, and event marketing. We also extended the traditional media with sponsorship of some big sports and cultural events that tied in with the car owners' lifestyles.

An example of IMC multimedia planning comes from *The Today Show*, which launched a new recipe website and mobile application in sponsorship with Unilever. The "Cooking School" website contains previously aired segments of "Today's Kitchen" and streaming video webisodes as well as recipes, cooking tips, and promotions for Unilever brands such as Bertolli, Country Crock, Hellmann's, and Ragu. The recipes can be downloaded at home or to a mobile device. A smart phone app allows users to compile recipes and build shopping lists. The "Cooking School" partnership links mobile, online, and broadcast media.[15]

Contact Point Management Another distinctive feature of IMC media plans is its emphasis on every important contact point. These can include a variety of experiential media as well as conventional media. Think about all the ways you come in contact with a brand message when you fly on an airline—reservations, check-in, baggage checking, the gate, the cabin attendants' and officer's messages over the loudspeaker, the seats and food and other cabin features, departure and arrival times, deplaning, baggage again, not to mention customer service when you miss a plane or a bag gets lost.

Photo: courtesy of H:N Marketing Communications

The launch of the Honda CR-V in Iceland used digital media and promotional activities along with more traditional media.

Here's a case study of how one agency's "ContactPoint Management" works: Tokyo-based Dentsu, which is the world's largest individual agency, has a strong IMC orientation, which shows up in the way Dentsu planners create IMC media plans. Dentsu's ContactPoint Management is a section in its IMC 2.0 model that identifies a wide diversity of contact points. Let's take a closer look at Dentsu's approach to IMC media planning.[16]

The objective of Dentsu's ContactPoint Management planning is to select the most effective contact points required to achieve the desired communication goals and to implement optimum integrated communication programs that eliminate waste. ContactPoint Management focuses on two strategies that are critical in delivering effective integrated communication:

1. *Identify the value contact points*, that is, the emotion-driving points at which or during which consumers come in contact with a brand.
2. *Move away from the traditional B2C model*, in which business targets a consumer with a message, *to a more interactive B2C2C model*, in which a business talks to consumers—particularly influential people, such as fashion leaders, who talk to other consumers. This approach uses mass media to stimulate interconsumer communications, or word of mouth, which delivers messages more persuasively.

Media selection recognizes that (1) contact points that work well must differ depending on the communication goal and (2) contact point effectiveness will differ from product category to product category and from target to target.

An example of how Dentsu manages a full set of brand contact points comes from an automotive campaign where two target audiences have been identified as a father (male, 50s) and a daughter (female, 20s). The communication objective is to position the new subcompact car model as "fun driving for grown men" and "a small cute model for young women."

The various contact points considered are evaluated and ranked using a proprietary contact point planning system called VALCON (Value Contact Point Tracer). Dentsu planners also have access to hundreds of media-related databases with vast volumes of contact point information to consult in this process. The final decisions about media usage are based on the roles and effects of the various media.

For the new subcompact, contact points were evaluated based on three objectives: their ability to launch a new product (recognition, build awareness), arouse interest (evaluation), and make the target feel like buying (intention, attitude). Here are the results by points assigned to various options:

	Father	**Both**		**Daughter**
Awareness	1. Newspaper			1. Train poster
	2. Out-of-home ads			2. Television ad
		3. Direct mail	4.	3. Magazine ad
Interest	1. Car on display at event	3. Car on streets	1.	
		4. Television ad	2.	3. Automaker's website
		2. Catalog	5.	
		5. Newspaper insert	8.	4. Cars owned by friends
Intention	3. Car magazine story	2. Catalog	1.	
		1. Car on display	2.	
		6. Test drive	3.	
				4. Television ad

As you can see, the plan calls for contact points that reach both audiences (television ads, catalogs, street media, newspaper inserts, and direct mail). Newspaper ads, out-of-home ads, the car on display at the dealer's showroom, and car magazine stories were added or emphasized for the "father" audience. For the "daughter" audience, magazine ads, a website, transit ads, radio ads, family word of mouth, and television ads were added. Here is how this complex media plan is diagrammed in terms of its effects.

	Recognition	***Evaluation***	***Attitude***
Father	Newspaper and out-of-home ads, car display at dealer		Car magazine stories
Both	Television ads, catalogs, street media, newspaper inserts, direct mail	Television ads, friends word of mouth	Catalog, car display at dealer, test drive
Daughter	Magazine and transit ads, website	Radio ads, family word of mouth	Television ads

Cross-Media Integration Media selection also considers message needs. Here is where media planning and message planning intersect. Brand reminders, for example, are often found in television commercials and in out-of-home media. More complex information-laden messages are more likely to be found in magazines, direct mail, or publicity releases. If you want to stimulate immediate action, you might use daily newspapers, radio, or sales promotion.

The chief marketing officer at a digital media company reminds planners that "brand advertising is about telling a story, not just directing traffic." He calls for refocusing on media basics: "Interactivity has given us new options to tell a story, social media have given us tools to make it spread, and digital more broadly has forced advertisers to consider utility to the user." But he insists, "The basics persist—find paths to the consumers where you can get scale, buy attention, and repeat."[17]

The challenge is to create **cross-media integration**, which means the various media work together to create coherent brand communication. In traditional media, this synergistic effect is sometimes called *image transfer* and refers to the way radio, in particular, reinforces and re-creates the message in a listener's mind that was originally delivered by other media, particularly television.

An example of cross-media integration comes from the revitalization campaign for the *Atlantic Monthly* magazine. To reinforce its position as an intellectual leader, the campaign used the slogan "Think. Again." To bring that idea to life, the campaign presented 14 of *Atlantic*'s most thought-provoking questions as 14 huge neon signs placed around New York. At night, the creative team taped interviews with viewers as they wondered about the brightly lit messages. These videos, which showcased the personal, profound, and sometimes hilarious responses, were housed on a website and used as a hub for a debate of these great issues. So it was out-of-home marketing that created an event that turned into videos that enlivened a website (see http://vimeo.com/52209849). In this case, to quote media scholar Marshall McLuhan, the media became the message. Was it successful? The magazine saw a double-digit increase in readership, and the number of visitors to TheAtlantic.com increased by 27 percent over the previous year.

Management and Campaign Controls

In order to manage IMC, whether of a campaign or a program, a manager must keep up with an incredibly complex set of tasks. Sometimes the brand manager is able to keep track of everything, but another approach is to hire a consulting firm that specializes in managing big projects. The "Inside Story" feature describes how one consultant with a marketing communication background views his job.

In addition to keeping track of everything, all campaigns are designed to operate within a certain set of parameters, such as budgets, schedules, and evaluation. These controls keep the activities on track, on budget, and on strategy.

Budgeting and Scheduling How much should an organization spend on a campaign? What a difficult decision that is. It depends on the organization, the area it serves (local or international), the time frame (a couple of weeks or months or a year), the stakeholders to be reached, as well as its need for big, expensive media, such as television. In fact, all budgeting is dependent on a time frame or schedule.

A $50,000 budget will only stretch so far and probably will not be enough to cover the costs of television advertising in most markets. Microsoft, for example, used a $300 million ad blitz to launch its Windows 7 operating system in 2009, and the launch of Windows 8 in 2012 called for an even more massive budget of $400 million.[18] The budget determines how many stakeholders can be targeted, how many media and platforms the campaign can support, and the length of time the campaign can run.

Determining the total appropriation allocated to a campaign is not an easy task. Typically, a dollar amount is budgeted for marketing communication during the annual budget planning process. For major campaigns, the company or organization will decide on the overall budget level and apportion that out to campaigns and marcom programs as well as to various agencies and suppliers involved with the campaign or campaigns.

The big budgeting question at the marketing, as well as marcom mix, level is, How much do we need to spend? Let's examine five common budgeting methods used to answer that question:

- ***Historical Method*** Historical information is the source for this common budgeting method. A budget may simply be based on last year's budget, with a percentage increase for inflation or some other marketplace factor. This method, although easy to calculate, has little to do with reaching brand communication objectives.

The Inside Story

What in the World Is Marketing Portfolio Management?

Eric Foss, *Director of Consulting Services, North America, Pcubed*

"Consulting services" in my title refers to the professional services my company, Pcubed, provides our clients including a broad range of consulting services focusing on portfolio, program, and project management—hence the name, Pcubed.

My "marketing portfolio" focus is not unlike some IMC concepts that integrate advertising and marketing campaigns, programs, and activities—and then ties them to objectives of a specific program (e.g., a new product launch) or an organization (as with my retail client).

The goal remains consistent: *create the collaboration, transparency, and delivery rigor necessary to select the optimal mix of marketing and messaging initiatives that are aligned to marketing strategies.*

We focus on establishing collaboration and visibility not only to help drive effective marketing management but also to ensure that money spent on messaging and marketing is optimized to best achieve our objectives. This foundation is necessary to measure effectiveness and return on investment.

I have worked across industries (e.g., aerospace and defense, technology, health care, and retail). I led a team on a major computer software firm's North American launch. A few years back, I partnered with the chief marketing officer and his team of vice presidents in the Dallas retail world to put together a marketing portfolio and help them more effectively identify and execute marketing programs.

Here's what the portfolio management concept means in practice:

- Creating a collaborative and dynamic decision-making model
- Aligning marketing programs to long-term marketing strategies and goals
- Integrating marketing activities with operations
- Balancing the independent needs of a broad group of stakeholders
- Maintaining visibility and oversight of a fast-moving portfolio of marketing initiatives, activities, and messaging
- Managing and measuring marking and communication impact in the field
- Linking marketing spend to tangible outcomes

As a management consultant partnering with marketing leadership, the challenge is tailoring these concepts to fit the unique needs of an organization's marketing culture.

Eric Foss graduated from the Department of Advertising at Michigan State University. He was nominated to appear in this book by Professor Sandra Moriarty.

- ***Objective-Task Method*** The **objective-task method** looks at the objectives for each activity and determines the cost of accomplishing each objective. For example, what will it cost to make 50 percent of the people in the market aware of this product or to extend a six-month plan to a year? This method's advantage is that it develops the budget from the ground up so that objectives are the starting point.
- ***Percentage-of-Sales Method*** The **percentage-of-sales method** compares the total brand sales with the total advertising (or marketing communication) budget during the previous year or the average of several years to compute a percentage. This technique can also be used across an industry to compare the expenditures of different product categories on advertising and marketing communication. For example, if a company had sales of $5 million last year and an advertising budget of $1 million, then the *ratio* of advertising to sales would be 20 percent. If the marketing manager predicts *sales* of $6 million for next year, then the ad budget would be $1.2 million. How can we calculate the percentage of sales and apply it to a budget? Follow these two steps:

1. $\frac{\text{Past advertising dollars}}{\text{Past sales}} = \text{\% of sales}$
2. % of sales × Next year's sales forecast = New advertising budget

An example of this approach comes from Procter & Gamble. To illustrate the growth of Procter & Gamble's marketing spending in recent years, in 2012 a chart of all-inclusive marketing costs pegged outlays at around 16.5 percent of sales the previous year, or around \$13.7 billion. In comparison, only \$9.3 billion of that amount was for advertising spending, which incorporates only media and agency costs. Using the broader measure, Procter & Gamble's marketing as a *percent of sales* grew about a point from 15.5 to 16.5 percent, more than rebounding from a deep recession-related dip in 2009.[19]

- ***Competitive Budgets*** This method uses competitors' budgets as benchmarks and relates the amount invested in advertising to the product's share of market. This suggests that the advertiser's share-of-advertising voice—that is, the advertiser's media presence—affects the share of attention the brand will receive, and that, in turn, affects the market share the brand can obtain. Here's a depiction of these relationships:

$$\text{Share of media voice} = \text{Share of consumer mind} = \text{market share}$$

Keep in mind that the relationships depicted here are only a guide for budgeting. The actual relationship between *share-of-media voice* (an indication of advertising expenditures) and **share of mind** or share of market depends to a great extent on factors such as the creativity of the message and the amount of clutter in the marketplace.

- ***All You Can Afford*** When a company allocates whatever is left over to marketing communication, it is using the "all-you-can-afford" budgeting method. It's really not a method but rather a philosophy about advertising. Companies using this approach, such as high-tech start-ups driven by product innovation, don't value advertising as a strategic imperative. For example, a company that allocates a large amount of its budget to research and has a superior product may find that the amount spent on advertising is less important.

Evaluation Advertising and other marketing communication agencies are creating tools and techniques to help marketers evaluate the efficiency and effectiveness of their marketing communication expenditures. The Interpublic Group, for example, a large marketing communication holding company, has created the Marketing Accountability Partnership to determine what marketers' dollars accomplish or how they can be better used.[20] The issue of accountability is made more complicated by the growing use of global marketing. Chapter 19 will explore this topic in more depth.

Photo: Courtesy of Procter & Gamble Company. All rights reserved

Charmin continues to emphasize softness in its international marketing. This cuddly bear was used in a campaign in Mexico. Note that it is largely a nonverbal execution, which is easier to use for global campaigns than those with a lot of words.

International IMC Campaigns

Agencies involved with international campaigns need an international organizational structure as well. Organization depends on whether the client company as well as its agencies are following a **standardization** or a **localization** strategy. Some firms and their agencies exercise tight control, while others allow more local autonomy. All these approaches fall into three groups: tight central international control, centralized resources with moderate control, or a match of the client's organization—if the client is highly centralized, then the agency account structure will be highly centralized.

Strategic Decisions The problem of managing brand consistency limits most objectives to awareness and recall, two effective yet easily attainable marketing communication measures, although more specific objectives may be needed in individual markets. For example, a brand may be well known in one market, so its primary objective, then, is reminder. At the same time, it may be newly launched in another country, so the objectives there are awareness building and trial.

Positioning is one of the key strategic elements that brands usually try to keep consistent from country to country. Research is conducted to identify the problems and opportunities facing the product and its positioning strategy in each of its international markets, as the Charmin commercial illustrates. Particularly important is a good understanding of consumer buying motives in each market. This is almost impossible to develop without locally based consumer research. If analysis reveals that consumers' buying behavior and the competitive environment are the same across international markets, it may be possible to use standardized positioning throughout.

The international consulting firm Accenture faced a strategic problem when Tiger Woods, the brand's longtime celebrity spokesperson, faced allegations of extramarital affairs. Much of Accenture's brand communication appears as images in airports, so the problem was to find universal imagery that continued to reflect the Accenture brand position. After testing a number of ideas, the decision was to use animals, such as an elephant, in unexpected and challenging situations. For example, one of the electronic displays shows an elephant balancing on a surfboard with text that reads, "Who says you can't be big and nimble?"[21]

Photo: Courtesy of Accenture

Accenture's replacement campaign for its well-known celebrity, Tiger Woods, used animals that are less likely to make unfortunate headlines. Accenture's slogan "High Performance. Delivered." continued to be used in the new campaign depicting animals in challenging but semihumorous situations.

Setting the Budget All the budgeting techniques apply in foreign markets. When preparing a single plan for multiple markets, many companies use an objective-task budgeting approach that entails a separate budget for each foreign market. (Remember that this approach looks at the objectives for each activity and determines the cost of accomplishing each objective.) This technique adds some flexibility to localize campaigns as needed. However, local practices also may affect the budget decision. Most notably, the exchange rate from country to country may affect not only the amount of money spent in a particular market but also the timing of the expenditures. The cost of television time in Tokyo is approximately twice what it is on U.S. networks, and, rather than being sold during an up-front market every spring, Japanese television time is wholesaled several times during the year.

Central Control versus Local Adaptation As noted previously, some marketers develop centralized global campaigns; others develop local campaigns in every major market. Most companies are somewhere in the middle. How are global campaigns created? International brand communication campaigns have two basic starting points: (1) success in one country and (2) a centrally conceived strategy. Planning approaches also include variations on the central campaign and bottom-up creativity:

- ***Local Initiative*** A successful campaign, conceived for national application, is modified for use in other countries. Wrigley, Marlboro, IBM, Waterman, Seiko, Philips, Ford, and many other companies have taken successful campaigns from one country and transplanted them around the world, a practice called *search and reapply*. When a local campaign is found to be successful, that campaign is taken to one or two countries that are similar to see how well the campaign works in these areas. If it is successful, use of the campaign is expanded and can eventually become the brand's primary international campaign. What is interesting about this strategy is that it provides additional motivation for local agencies. While all local agencies want to do a good job to keep their local business, it is a major ego boost—not to mention the additional financial awards—when a local campaign is taken beyond its original country's borders.

The Honda CR-V in Iceland is an example. As Logason explains, "Because of the effectiveness of the original campaign—both the insights behind the strategy and the idea of ownership of the 4 × 4 concept, which was so successful in Iceland—the campaign caught the eye of the global office, and it has been distributed and showcased globally to dealers in other markets as an example of strong, clever positioning."

- ***Centrally Conceived Campaigns*** The second approach, a centrally conceived campaign, was pioneered by Coca-Cola and is now used increasingly in global strategies. Microsoft uses a centralized strategy for its Xbox video game system; since it was a new brand, a consistent marketing strategy was deemed to be essential. Although the centralization concept is simple, its application can be difficult. A work team, task force, or action group (the names vary) assembles from around the world to present, debate, modify (if necessary), and agree on a basic strategy as the foundation for the campaign. Cost is a huge factor. If the same photography and artwork can be used universally, this can save thousands of dollars over each local variation.
- ***Variations on Central Campaigns*** Variations on the centrally conceived campaign also exist. For example, BBDO's many local agencies were used to adapt the creative ideas for all the markets served by DaimlerChrysler (now Chrysler after the company split). The office that develops the approved campaign would be designated the **lead agency** and would develop all the necessary elements of the campaign and prepare a standards manual for use in other countries. Because photography, artwork, television production, and color printing are costly, developing these items in one location and then overlaying new copy or rerecording the voice track in the local language saves money. However, because some countries, such as Malaysia, require that all campaign materials be locally produced, this approach gives direction to the message but still allows for local requirements to be met.
- ***Bottom-Up Creativity*** Sometimes a competition may be used to find the best new idea. For example, to extend McDonald's "I'm Lovin' It" campaign, McDonald's global chief marketing officer held a contest among McDonald's ad agencies all over the world. One winner, which became part of the international pool of ads, came from China, which is developing a lively creative advertising industry that produces edgy, breakthrough ads for young people. McDonald's strategy was not just to do the creative work in the United States but rather to "Let the best ideas win."

Executing an International Campaign The execution of a global campaign is usually more complex than a national plan. The creative may need to be reshot with local models and settings as well as language translation. Language is always a problem for a campaign that is dependent on words rather than visuals as the primary meaning carrier. A team of language experts may be needed to adjust the terms and carry over the meanings in the different languages. The Pepsi slogan "Come Alive," for example, was translated in Taiwan as "Pepsi will bring your ancestors back from the dead." KFC's "Finger Lickin' Good" slogan translated into Chinese as "Eat Your Fingers Off."

Product names can even be a problem. In Canada, Mercedes-Benz found that its GST model name is also the familiar initials of a tax commonly referred to in English as the "gouge and screw tax."

Government approval of television commercials can be difficult to secure in some countries. As advertisers move into international and global advertising, they also face many of the same ethical issues that advertisers deal with in the United States, such as the representation of women and advertising to children, but they may also have to deal with questions about the Americanization or westernization of local cultures.[22] An example comes from a Nike ad used in China that showed LeBron James teaching moves to martial arts masters. Chinese officials banned it because they consider it insulting to national dignity.

But it's not just government bans that can trouble message strategies. Social responsibility is taken seriously in some countries, and, with the Internet and e-mail, consumer concerns can create a huge issue. For example, an ad by fashion house Dolce & Gabbana showed a bare-chested man pinning a glamorous woman to the ground while his buddies looked on. Consumers in Spain, Italy, and the United States complained that it trivialized violence against women, and the many e-mail complaints led the company to drop the ad.

The IMC Factor in International Campaigns To create a coherent brand impression on a global level requires both horizontal and vertical coordination. The vertical effort represents the coordination of the key planning decisions, such as targeting, positioning, objectives, strategies, and tactics, across all the various tools used in the communication program. The horizontal level requires coordination across all countries and regions involved in the plan.

Principle
Global brand communication needs integration horizontally (across countries) and vertically through all the key strategic decisions.

Because of this complexity, it takes a dedicated manager to ensure that all the various marketing communication activities stay consistent to the brand and campaign strategy. Because of the complexity, IMC planners use planning grids to plot strategic coordination of messages across countries and across marcom programs. The table below illustrates how such a grid might be constructed. The messages are plotted indicating how they may vary locally for different cultures as well as what brand elements are used, such as position or personality, to maintain consistency. Some companies sell not just one brand but a portfolio of subbrands or brand extensions, and the challenge is to maintain brand consistency across these different product lines in different countries. There may also be differences in the message strategy for different stakeholder groups. For each country, the planner describes the following brand message variations:

- Country-specific changes
- Audience-specific changes
- Brand consistency elements (the unchangeables)

Marcom Tool	*Country A*	*Country B*	*Country C*	*Country D*
Advertising				
Direct response				
Public relations				
Etc.				

Managing 360° Communication Programs

Tom Duncan, one of the architects of IMC, explains that IMC practice originally focused on creating "one voice, one look" campaigns, but companies broadened that focus as they realized the need for greater consistency for all aspects of brand communication that lead to customer relationships.[23] That ongoing, multichannel, multiplatform, multistakeholder approach to the practice of IMC is possible only if there is an organizational commitment to integrated communication programs.

A lesson you may have learned from our previous discussions is that IMC is a way of managing a brand with a singular vision of what the brand stands for. Unlike a short-term campaign approach, this is a philosophy that delivers total communication over the life of a brand. We are calling this *360-degree communication* because a unifying brand vision surrounds all the brand's interactions with all its stakeholders—a vision that must be shared by everyone involved with the brand. As Duncan said in the Part 5 opener, "It's not just advertising. . . it's everything a brand says and does." And that includes being a good corporate citizen.

Principle
360-degree communication is driven by a unifying brand vision that surrounds all the brand's interactions with all its stakeholders—a vision that must be shared by everyone involved with the brand.

Cause and Mission Marketing

Concern for social issues is increasingly important for for-profit companies because they want to be seen as socially responsible—and being a good citizen in actions as well as words is important in building and maintaining a positive brand reputation.

Adopting a good cause and helping in its fund-raising and other community-oriented efforts is called **cause marketing**. For example, Target has donated a huge amount of money to its local communities as part of its community-caring effort. Another example of undergirding a program with a good cause is the website for Process for Progress, a credit card processing company, that donates part of its profits to nonprofit organizations.

Carol Cone, founder of the Cone agency, which specializes in cause marketing, calls these efforts *passion branding* because they link brands to causes for which people feel passion

Photo: Courtesy of Michael Dattolico

SHOWCASE

A website powered by good intentions of the Process for Progress site, which explains how the credit card processing company donates 15 percent of its profits to a good cause.

Owner of his own design studio, Musion Creative, LLC (www.musioncreative.com), Michael Dattolico graduated from the advertising program at the University of Florida, where he was a student of Professor Elaine Wagner.

(check out this agency at www.coneinc.com). The Cone agency was behind the "Red" campaign, which supports women's heart health, as well as Yoplait's "Save Lids to Save Lives" and Avon's "Breast Cancer Crusade." Being a good corporate citizen is good for the bottom line. An article in *Advertising Age* explained the bottom-line importance of such strategies as "Companies do well by doing good."[24]

Professor Scott Hamula explains that "in addition to operating with a sense of social responsibility, marketers engage in philanthropy through cause marketing."[25] The primary goals, he says, are "to help communities and nonprofit organizations while generating goodwill, positive word-of-mouth, and the hope that people will look more favorably on these brands when making their next purchase decision."

If a commitment reflects a company's core business strategy, as in Dove's "Real Women" campaign and Avon's support of breast cancer research, it is called **mission marketing.**[26] Mission marketing links a company's mission and core values to a cause that connects with its customers' interests. It is more of a commitment than cause marketing because it reflects a long-term brand-building perspective, and the mission becomes a point of passion for all stakeholders as well as the focal point for integrating all the company's marketing communication.

Mission marketing also contributes to synergy through what we identified earlier as brand integrity**.** The **integration triangle** identifies three key aspects of brand communication that must work together to create integration as well as integrity: (1) what the company or brand says about itself (*say*), (2) how the company or brand performs (*do*), (3) and what other people say about it (*confirm*). Figure 18.2 shows these relationships. The point is that a brand fails as an integrated perception if there are gaps between what the brand says in its planned messages, what it does, and what others say about it.

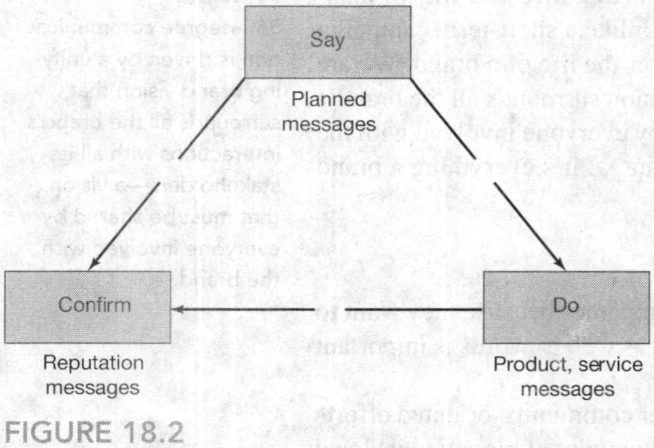

FIGURE 18.2

Integration Triangle

The "say-do-confirm" Integration Triangle explains how planned brand messages (say) are either reinforced of undercut by messages deliver by the product or service marketing mix (how well the brand and company perform). Reputation messages (what others say) are the ultimate test of the brand's integrity. When there are gaps between the say, do, and confirm messages, then integration has failed.

Internal Integration

The problem of departmental *silos* with each marcom function going its own way is a barrier to integrated planning both at the marketer level and within agencies. The solution according to Tom Duncan is cross-functional management with a team of functional area representatives who coordinate their activities.[27] The Association of National Advertisers describes this organizational structure as "a team of colleagues who have the responsibility vision, understanding, and commitment to engage in a media-agnostic planning process."[28]

Another concern is coordinating all the agencies involved in creating the various brand messages. Maurice Levy, CEO of the Paris-based Publicis Groupe holding company, has criticized the way the agencies in his group coordinate their work on behalf of a brand. He contends that the giant company has suffered from a "silo mentality" that hurts clients. He asks, "How do we stop confusing clients with contradictory points of view coming from teams each defending their little piece of turf—to the detriment of the client's interests?"[29] Check out the Publicis website at www.publicisgroupe.com to see how complex this problem can be for a large international agency.

The importance of the need for a shared vision was evident when the new chief executive at Ford realized that what the troubled car company needed after the auto meltdown of the late 2000s was a unifying vision. To rally the troops, he had a motivating vision printed on laminated, wallet-size cards and given to the thousands of Ford employees. It proclaimed, "One Ford . . . One Team . . . One Plan . . . One Goal." The statement conveyed a strategy for returning Ford to its leadership position and undergirded the launch of the Ford Focus, the firm's first truly global car.[30]

To implement such a management effort, a cross-functional brand-focused team is created involving members from all of the relevant parts of a company that interact with customers, with other stakeholders, and with outside agencies. Its members represent all of the areas and tools that control contact points and brand interactions. This cross-functional team operates with a singular brand vision as it plans marketing communication, monitors its impact, and tracks consumer response.

Who is in charge of planning all of these brand-building opportunities? One is the marketing and communication manager on the client side, such as Peter Stasiowski, who was featured in Chapter 2. But marketing communication managers work in partnership with agency managers

A Matter of Principle

Who's the Integrator Here, Anyway?

Ed Chambliss, *Vice President and Team Leader, The Phelps Group*

I love smaller clients. I'm talking about clients who have little to no marketing department. Those clients who recognize the importance of integrated marketing communication (IMC) but don't know how to actually make it happen. They come to us and say, "Here—you be the integrator." That's because most smaller clients are smart enough to know they don't know everything, and that's why you hire a specialist—in this case, a specialist in IMC.

Over time, however, smaller clients become larger clients. And larger clients need in-house marketing departments, and marketing departments need marketing directors, and marketing directors need to be the integrators because, well, that's their job.

Which leaves a lot of marketing directors wondering, "If I'm the integrator, why should I hire an IMC agency? Why don't I just hire a bunch of agencies that are each 'best in breed' and then I'll integrate all of them myself?" It's a fair question and one that should be answered with other questions. To start, does the marketing director really know how to be an integrator? That is, do they have the formal training in how to create an organization and processes that can orchestrate all of the brand touch points, both outbound and inbound, across multiple suppliers? Or do they merely believe that integration sounds like a great idea and think they can make it happen?

Chances are, the marketing director isn't one of the handful of trained IMC specialists out there. More likely, they're a specialist in one particular area of marketing communication who has been promoted into the "integrator" position. For these clients, hiring an IMC agency is a shortcut to integration. An IMC agency can advise the marketing director about how to best integrate the internal organization while doing all of the external heavy lifting that true integration requires.

If the marketing director is trained in IMC, then they'll already be asking these questions: "Are the 'best of breed' agencies I want to hire used to working in an integrated fashion? Or am I going to spend all of my time trying to get them to understand that the overall puzzle is more important than just their one piece?"

This is where an IMC agency shines again. Whether a client hires us to do everything or just one particular type of work, they know that we understand the bigger picture. As one of my IMC-trained clients (who, by the way, hires us only for online work) says, "You guys get it. You understand the big picture. With other agencies, it's like explaining color to a blind man."

In the end, integration needs to happen, so a smart marketing director will assemble the team that has the best possible chance of making it a reality. If it works, the marketing director can take all of the credit. But if integration doesn't happen, there's no credit to take, only blame.

For more about The Phelps Agency, check out *www.thephelpsgroup.com*.

Chambliss graduated from the University of Colorado–Boulder with a master's degree in integrated marketing communication. He was nominated by Professor Tom Duncan.

who also provide guidance about such things as IMC strategies. Ed Chambliss, in his "A Matter of Principle" feature, discusses how this partnership works as well as the qualifications needed to be an IMC manager, whether on the client side or the agency side. Check the website at the end of the feature for more information on The Phelps Group, a true IMC-focused agency.

An Organizational Case Study An example of the organizational structure behind an IMC program comes from the Tokyo-based Dentsu agency, which has provided total communication service to its clients for decades.[31] But until the 2000s, the agency was able to do multimedia coordination only at a one-voice, one-look level. New technology and a new management philosophy, however, created a new way of doing business.

To truly operate with an IMC orientation, Dentsu underwent a total reorganization and designed a comprehensive new IMC tool kit. Now the giant agency's employees have sophisticated tools to actually deliver on that total communication promise with a more advanced approach that Dentsu calls IMC 2.0. It defines IMC 2.0 as "an ongoing systematic process for creatively planning, production, and evaluating brand communication that creates customer relationships, builds strong brands, and increases sales and profits."[32]

To engineer this turnaround, it first held an IMC audit, conducted by Professor Tom Duncan, to determine the agency's IMC strengths and weakness internally as well as in the eyes of key clients. Then it created an IMC Development Division with the mission of undertaking the IMC research-and-development arm. That division has some 90 to 100 staff members dedicated to basic research into IMC processes. The agency also created an IMC online site with more than 250 planning tools, models, and processes that can be used in IMC 2.0 projects. This portal also provides access to case studies, training modules, articles, and research on IMC. It registers more than 2,000 unique visits a day from Dentsu employees.

An IMC Planning Center with 350 people from a variety of media and marcom areas was established. The staff members assigned to this department are given intensive IMC training so that they have the skills to work in cross-functional IMC teams on client projects brought to them by various account groups. The agency's Brand Creation Center, an existing brand consulting group, was also integrated into the IMC Planning Center. Finally, each of Dentsu's 22 account groups has 5 to 10 embedded account planners who are trained in IMC practices. These planners help educate clients on the goals of IMC and establish a common language for planning.

It's a work in progress—and one complicated by the worldwide recession—but Dentsu's IMC executives and managers believed that the investment in reorganization was justified. The effort didn't come cheap: Dentsu initially dedicated some 600 of its 4,500 employees to IMC development and client services.

Looking Ahead

We're near the end of this book. If you have any interest in working in marketing or marketing communication, what have you learned about integrated marketing communication that might help you in your career?

The industry is definitely moving in that direction. A study by the Association of National Advertisers, for example, found that 74 percent of its members said they were using IMC for most or all of their brands. The association's CEO sees that as a call for "Renaissance Marketers" who understand the essentials of IMC. He describes them as "a new breed of holistic professionals who are system thinkers, customer-centric believers, innovators, and dreamers."[33] So there's definitely a job opportunity here—does that sound like you?

Maybe you're even thinking about starting a business or going to graduate school and becoming a consultant. If so, it's important to understand that the concept of advertising has broadened to include almost everything that sends a brand message. If you go to work in marketing or marketing communication, you may be asked to help plan an IMC campaign or develop an IMC program. This chapter is your guide to IMC thinking and management practices.

This chapter started with IMC principles and then reviewed the development of IMC campaigns and the management of IMC programs. The objective is to drive consistency through all brand messages and experiences. It's cost-effective as well as more effective communication. The next chapter will wrap up this marketing communication journey with a discussion of evaluation—the last and most important step in proving the effectiveness of IMC programs and campaigns.

It's a Wrap

I'm Amazing

The store chosen to incorporate the children's designs was the Mega Box McDonald's store in Kowloon Bay. The organizers selected 22 of the most unique designs and then brought in interior decorators and fabricators to recreate the designs sent in by the children.

In Hong Kong, McDonald's must continue to innovate and work to keep up its pace in the fast-food business. According to South China Research, the total number of restaurant receipts in Hong Kong increased annually by 4.4 percent for each of the past 4 years. The Hong Kong restaurant sector is estimated to be worth around US$12 billion per year. The share of total receipts for fast-food restaurants also increased from 16.5 percent to 17.4 percent.

The main players in the fast-food market are Café de Coral, Fairwood, and Tsui Wah. All of these companies have consolidated and gained market share. Fast-food outlets are incredibly popular among Hong Kong diners. International chains like McDonald's, KFC, and Pizza Hut have to compete with these large local fast-food outlets (especially Café De Coral, Maxim's, and Fairwood). Café De Coral alone is believed to have a fast-food market share in excess of 20 percent. They service around 20 million customers a month and are very popular as far as the 19–29 age groups are concerned.

An integrated marketing campaign seems to be working in McDonald's favor, as the burger giant has some 235 outlets (including 84 McCafe outlets), which compares favorably with Maxim's 339, Café de Coral's 151, and Fairwood's 105. McDonald's dwarfs Pizza Hut with just 43 and KFC with 59.

Key Points Summary

1. **What are the eight key IMC concepts, and why are they important?**
   a. IMC campaigns focus on *stakeholders.* The objective is to engage them in a meaningful relationship as well as target them for brand communication.
   b. IMC is built on a philosophy of *total communication* as a way to develop campaigns that maximize consistency among all the marcom tools. It is a philosophy that monitors and manages all brand messages with all stakeholders at all contact points—not just the traditional marketing communication.
   c. In IMC, traditional advertising channels are expanded to include *contact points* that represent all the ways a consumer and other stakeholders come in contact with a brand. All of these deliver messages and should be monitored if not controlled.
   d. *Message synergy* develops when all the messages from all contact points work together to present a coherent brand presence.
   e. Because people automatically integrate all the brand messages they receive, we refer to the way these diverse impressions come together as an *integrated brand perception.*
   f. Brand impressions are integrated on the basis of some core concept or brand essence, which is communicated throughout the organization as a *unified brand vision.*
   g. *Internal integration* means you can't be integrated externally unless you are integrated internally. In addition to a brand vision, that calls for an organization that creates and monitors all brand messages.
   h. *Brand integrity* means that what a brand says and does matches what other people say about it.
2. **How would you outline the six key parts of an IMC campaign plan, and what's included in them?**
   a. *Situation analysis* includes the background research, the SWOTs, and identification of the key communication problem(s).

b. The *key strategic decisions* are objectives, targeting and engaging stakeholders, and the brand positioning strategy.

c. The *marketing communication mix* includes selection of the platforms based on the objectives they can accomplish and how they lead to message synergy.

d. The *message strategy* includes key consumer and brand relationship insights, overall message direction, and strategic consistency.

e. *IMC media* consider multimedia, multichannel, and multiplatform *contact points*.

f. The *management* of IMC campaigns uses *controls*, such as budgeting and evaluation.

3. **Which strategic decisions underlie effective international marketing communication?** Marketing begins with a local brand, expands to a regional brand, and, finally, goes global. Advertising and marketing communication follow the same path. The biggest strategic decision involves how much of the marketing communication strategy is globalized or localized. Ultimately, such campaigns should be centrally controlled and centrally conceived. There should also be local applications and approval. In international as in all IMC campaigns, the challenge is to create brand consistency in all messages and customer experiences with the brand.

4. **What do we mean by 360° communication programs?** Integration is both a way to develop campaigns that maximize consistency among all the marcom tools and a philosophy that monitors and manages all brand messages with all stakeholders at all contact points—not just the traditional marketing communication. The latter delivers total brand communication with a consistent vision for the life of the brand. 360° communication means that everything communicates—messages are delivered by every element of the marketing mix as well as every marcom message and brand experience.

Key Terms

benchmark, p. 569
brand integrity, p. 564
brand value, p. 561
cause marketing, p. 581
contact points, p. 562
cross-functional management, p. 564
cross-media integration, p. 576
integrated perception, p. 563
integration triangle, p. 582
internal marketing, p. 569
lead agency, p. 580
localization, p. 578
measurable objectives, p. 569
mission marketing, p. 582
objective-task method, p. 577
percentage-of-sales method, p. 577
permission marketing, p. 561
share of mind, p. 578
share of wallet, p. 568
silos, p. 571
situation analysis, p. 567
spherical branding, p. 564
standardization, p. 578
strategic consistency, p. 563
SWOT analysis, p. 567
360° communication, p. 561
total communication, p. 562
touch points, p. 562
unified vision, p. 563

Review Questions

18-4. Explain the difference between planning an IMC campaign and planning a 360° total communication program.

18-5. What do we mean when we say that media planning in an IMC campaign plan moves from channels to contact points?

18-6. Why is a brand an integrated perception?

18-7. What is the role of stakeholders in an IMC campaign?

18-8. What is a contact point, and how is it managed?

18-9. What is message synergy, and why is it important? Explain with examples.

18-10. What is a campaign plan? How does it differ from the traditional advertising plan?

18-11. How can you identify a campaign's statement of strategy?

Discussion Questions

18-12. Choose a restaurant in your community and develop a campaign plan. What types of people does it target? Would you recommend that its advertising focus on price or image? What is (or should be) its image? Which media or marcom area should it use?

✪ 18-13. You have gotten a new assignment to be on a launch team for an upscale pen made in Switzerland under the brand name of Pinnacle. Its primary advantage is that it has an extremely long-lasting cartridge, one that is guaranteed to last for at least five years. The pen is available in a variety of forms, including roller ball and felt tip, and a variety of widths, from fine to wide stroke. Analyze the globalization or localization options for launching this pen first in Europe and then globally. What would your recommendation be on standardizing the brand communication?

18-14. The head of the Marketing Department, whom you report to, asks you to prepare a theoretical marketing plan form that will be used during his next team meeting and will describe all the strategic decisions related to the new product launch campaign.

List the sections that should constitute your outline and explain each.

18-15. Luna Pizza is a regional producer of frozen pizza. Its only major competitor is Brutus Bros. The following is a brief excerpt from Luna's situation analysis for the next fiscal year. Estimate the next year's advertising budgets for Luna under each of the following circumstances:

a. Luna follows an historical method by spending 40 cents per unit sold in advertising, with a 5 percent increase for inflation.

b. Luna follows a fixed percentage of projected sales method, using 7 percent.

c. Luna follows a share-of-voice method. Brutus, the primary competitive pizza brand, is expected to use 6 percent of sales for its advertising budget in the next year.

	Actual Last Year	**Estimated Next Year**
Units sold	120,000	185,000
$ sales	420,000	580,000
Brutus $ sales	630,000	830,000

Take-Home Projects

18-16. ***Portfolio Project:*** Compare the brand positioning and customer-focused content of three of the following corporate sites: www.accenture.com, www.ibm.com, www.nielsen.com, www.forrester.com, and www.strategicbusinessinsights.com. Analyze the three sites you selected in terms of their brand vision and position as well as their commitment to a customer focus philosophy. What would you recommend to improve their online brand presence?

18-17. ***Mini-Case Analysis:*** How has McDonald's HK built its reputation? Who does it target? What is its brand essence or core brand concept? Explain how its "I'm Amazing" campaign brings the brand's vision to life. What might you suggest to continue to improve the impact of this series of campaigns?

TRACE North America Case

Multicultural IMC

Read the TRACE case in the Appendix before coming to class.

18-18. How could you increase the consistency of the "Hard to Explain, Easy to Experience" campaign so that the overall impact was greater?

18-19. If you wanted to go global with this campaign, what would you need to learn about each new market before you ran the campaign?

CHAPTER 19

Evaluating IMC Effectiveness

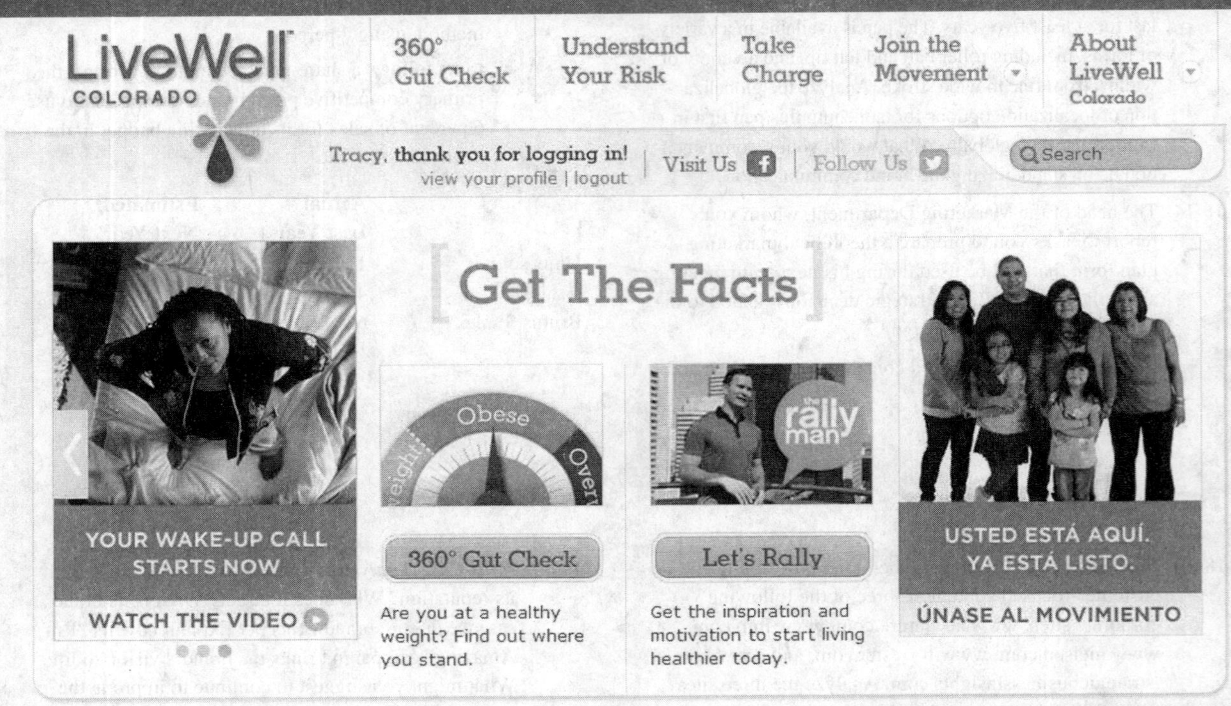

Photo: Courtesy of LiveWell Colorado

It's a Winner

Campaign
LiveWell Colorado Awakening Campaign

Company
LiveWell Colorado

Agency
Launch Advertising

Contributing Agencies
Rabble + Rauser, GroundFloor Media

Awards
Telly Award, Webby Award, "Best Website Award" from PR News, PR News Nonprofit Campaign Award, The Platinum MarCom Award (Association of Marketing & Communication Professionals), and the Gold Davy Award (International Academy of the Visual Arts)

CHAPTER KEY POINTS

1. Why is it important to evaluate brand communication effectiveness?
2. What role do campaign objectives play in the measurement of campaign success?
3. What are the key ways in which campaign evaluation is conducted?
4. What are some key challenges faced in evaluating IMC effectiveness?

Gut-Checking Obesity

One would think being labeled as leanest state in the country that Colorado might be content to sit around and rest on its laurels. Not so. Recognizing that Colorado is not immune to the growing health crisis of obesity, nonprofit LiveWell Colorado is committed to reducing obesity in Colorado by promoting healthy eating and active living. Its communication campaign literaly provides a textbook example about planning and evaluating the effectiveness of its work. Here's a brief summary of the case.

Situation Analysis

More than half (58 percent) of Colorado adults are overweight or obese, and the number is growing at an alarming rate. About a quarter (23 percent) of Colorado children ages 2 to 14 are overweight or obese. As an economic result, Colorado spent more than $1.6 billion on obesity-related medical costs in 2009 alone. LiveWell Colorado was created to take a leadership role in tackling the complex problem of obesity and realizing the vision of all Coloradans embracing a healthier lifestyle supported by initial funding from the Colorado Health Foundation, Kaiser Permanente, and the Kresge Foundation and in partnership with the Colorado Department of Public Health and Environment.

Analysis of initial research including surveys from 1,100 Colorado residents and nine focus groups with 100 mothers revealed that Coloradans had difficulty identifying obesity, especially when it came to their own weight and lifestyle. Participants typically underestimated what it means to be obese or even overweight. In short, many didn't realize their own weight was something they personally needed to address because they didn't think obesity applied to them—it was someone else's problem.

Key Strategic Campaign Decisions

To dispel these misperceptions and motivate healthy behavior changes, LiveWell Colorado kicked off an unprecedented, statewide advertising and community engagement campaign. A key insight driving the campaign was the need to communicate the surprising commonness of the problem and to awaken Colorado residents to the realization that the new normal isn't healthy for them or their families. The campaign needed to engage consumers to make a personal connection to the obesity issue.

Message Strategy

The "culture change" campaign included the country's first ads aimed at destigmatizing obesity and presenting the surprising commonness of the problem. The advertising illustrated that overweight and obese people look like everyday Coloradans and emphasized the issue is not about vanity or labeling but rather about long-term health. Television ads' call to action encouraged viewers to go to www.livewellcolorado.org to find out if they are at risk for an obesity-related disease and engage in their own "gut check." The interactive website lets visitors "Get the Facts. Get Your Stats. Get Inspired."

Media and Marcom Strategy

In addition to the interactive website, key media choices focused on statewide television and cable, Hispanic television and radio, a website, social media, events and community outreach. Community outreach, events, and social media components supported the advertising messages. Viva Streets, Denver's first "ciclovia," closed some neighborhood streets to cars and opened them up to walkers and bicycles to showcase the potential of city streets in getting people active within communities.

As we have been saying throughout this book, a key component of successful advertising and integrated marketing communications is evaluating the effectiveness of the communication. Did the effort achieve the goals? In this chapter, you will read about many ways to gauge effectiveness. At the end of the chapter, in the "It's a Wrap" feature, you will discover how LiveWell Colorado measured the effectiveness of this campaign and the extent to which it was successful.

Sources: Tracy Faigin Boyle, vice president of marketing and communications, LiveWell Colorado, and Karl Weiss, president, market perceptions and health care research and a member of this book's advisory board, contributed to this case study (http://movement.livewellcolorado.org).

Note: This chapter was contributed by Regina Lewis, Associate Professor, University of Alabama.

By this point, you should understand the potential power of brand communication. We've emphasized that effective campaigns do more than win awards for creativity. They also work hard to achieve the campaign's communication and marketing goals. As you will see in this chapter, there are many ways to evaluate the effectiveness of various aspects of an IMC program. Companies evaluate the impact of the program's message, the performance of its individual IMC components, the power of the media that delivered the message, and the extent to which the IMC campaign's components worked in harmony to create changes in people's attitudes and behaviors. This chapter discusses the establishment of campaign objectives (against which campaign success can be evaluated) and examines the many types of effectiveness measurement that are possible.

Brand Communication Impact: Did It Work?

What makes an IMC campaign effective? The fact that people like it, or the fact that it moves people to take some kind of action? Or something else altogether? You'll recall from our chapter-opening LiveWell case that a key goal of that campaign was to destigmatize obesity. Another goal was to change the attitude among Coloradans that the new normal wasn't healthy.

First Things First: The Campaign Objectives

Typically, a brand communication campaign has multiple objectives; for example, one (attitudinal) objective may be to change brand perceptions, and another (behavioral) objective may be to make people engage in some way with the brand. If we think about the LiveWell introductory case, we recall that the LiveWell IMC program was launched with a goal of making people aware of the obesity problem as well as a goal of engaging them to make a personal connection to it.

Regardless of the number of objectives a company sets for a campaign, it is critical that such stated objectives be established up front because they provide the all-important framework for evaluating whether a campaign was a success. Setting objectives—and establishing specific measures that will demonstrate success—make campaign evaluation possible. If, for example, Dunkin' Donuts stated that an objective of an IMC program was a 10 percent improvement in customers' perceptions of drive-through service quality, at least one way in which its campaign would be evaluated would be automatically established. In using social media, in particular, clear campaign goals must be set. According to Jason Falls, founder of Social Media Explorer LLC, these goals can range from online community building to changes in public sentiment. But whatever the goals, they must be clear and specific and provide ways to measure the success of your social marketing efforts.[1]

Principle

Campaign objectives and campaign evaluation work hand in hand. In the absence of solid campaign objectives, evaluation becomes a much murkier task.

A Matter of Practice

Can You Really Predict the Impact of Advertising on Sales?

Charles Young, *President, Ameritest*

We know from years of collecting and comparing ads that every player in the fast-moving quick-service restaurant (QSR) category puts strong and weak ads on air each year—and that includes giants like McDonald's and Burger King. But how can you predict which ones will be effective or ineffective?

Our research company, Ameritest, constantly monitors commercials as they air and we track ad quality using a proprietary system of metrics and analysis tools. From such data, we are able to measure, diagnose, and predict advertising effectiveness.

Importantly, in validating our commercial metrics, we recently asked the question, Can we predict the sales that McDonald's reports to Wall Street? This is an important driver of the company's stock price.

In the QSR category, we collect data on all new television commercials during their first week of airing. For the five years from January 2007 to January 2012, we tested 1,292 QSR commercials—338 McDonald's ads and 954 competitive ads from 17 other major QSR brands. This validation to sales analysis, the largest ever conducted by a pretesting company—is based on 129,000 online consumer interviews—100 per commercial used in our standard analysis of all the commercials.

During this same time period, we collected the public sales figures that McDonald's reported to Wall Street for 62 consecutive months. The sales figures used included the change in same-store sales versus year ago for U.S. sales.

To evaluate advertising quality, we looked at measures of executional quality and strategic message communication. Executional quality is a composite of three performance measures: attention-getting power, branding, and motivational impact. These measures were compared to competitive norms for this time period. Message communication was a variable that described which of nine possible strategic messages (taste, healthy, enjoyable place, and so on) were conveyed by each ad.

In building our sales validation model, we also included a sales momentum variable to describe other McDonald's marketing efforts (store remodels, menu changes) and a variable for the economic recession. Together, these two macroeconomic variables explained 22 percent of McDonald's sales growth.

When we added in the variable for advertising quality—combining executional impact and message communication—the predictive power of our sales validation model improved to 46 percent.

Given that our model did not even include advertising media spend data or other variables in the marketing mix, such as relative pricing, and so on, this finding is highly significant. It shows that a quarter of McDonald's sales growth—and its stock price—can be explained by the quality of its advertising creative.

So macroeconomic variables explain roughly a quarter of sales growth, ad quality explains a quarter, and ad spending yet another quarter, leaving all other variables to explain the rest. Clearly, advertising is the major force driving the growth of the McDonald's business.

This confirms not only that McDonald's ads generally are high in ad quality but also that television advertising has been a good investment for McDonald's over that five-year period.

The Campaign Purpose: Brand Building

To begin thinking about measuring IMC effectiveness, let's consider just one IMC component—advertising. Many executives believe that advertising works only if it produces sales. Syracuse University Professor Emeritus John Philip Jones, who has written many books and articles on the topic, estimates that of the $500 billion spent annually on advertising globally, only 41 percent—less than half—produces sales.[2] Jones contends that "advertising must generate an immediate jolt to sales before it can be expected to produce any further effect."[3]

Simon Broadbent, another leading figure in effectiveness research and originally a proponent of sales impact, however, came to realize that "long and deep" effects of advertising, or its brand-building effects, also are important.[4] Many other experts agree with this view, and it is the perspective supported by this text. A couple of reasons why we support Broadbent's view are as follows.

Principle
Brand communication can be deemed successful when set objectives—attitudinal, behavioral, or both—have been met.

First, determining advertising's impact on sales can be very difficult because of the impact of other environmental factors. Consider Amazon.com. If sales increase in a major northeastern city that is receiving holiday advertising, can this truly be attributed to the advertising? Or could the sales gains be a result of horrible winter weather that is causing people to shop from their homes? It is extremely difficult to gauge the impact of different factors that may have contributed to revenue.

Second, sales simply are not the only reason brands advertise; rather, one of the major objectives of advertising is to create higher levels of brand awareness among consumers. An article in *Business 2.0* reported that an ad for the Six Flags amusement park was a smash success in viewer surveys—but that it must be deemed ineffective, regardless, because attendance at the company's 31 theme parks fell after the campaign instead of increasing. Is this appropriate? Probably not. Perhaps the only reason people didn't come to the parks was an increase in gas prices. And if brand awareness increases demonstrated were in keeping with Six Flags campaign objectives, then the campaign was successful.

It's our view that marketers intend their messages to accomplish a variety of goals. The goal of a nonprofit campaign may be to inform donors of how their donations are being spent, put another way, to make donors more knowledgeable (and, hopefully, more engaged). The goal of a packaged good team may be to build a brand relationship. And the goal of a hotel company campaign may be to recruit new members for its frequent-traveler program. All of these point to ways in which advertisements may serve campaign objectives—and, therefore, be effective—that are not reflected in sales numbers alone.

All of this said, are marketers pleased when great advertising contributes to sales increases? Of course. Charles Young, a member of this book's advisory board, describes a situation in the Matter of Practice feature in which advertising has played an important role in sales for McDonald's.

The classic campaign for Avis also is an example of one that works on both levels. People like it, and it drove the company to record sales levels.

Because campaigns often have multiple objectives and because there are so many ways of measurement available in the IMC tool kit, there are multiple ways to assess the effectiveness of marketing communication campaigns. We discuss many of the more common ways of gauging

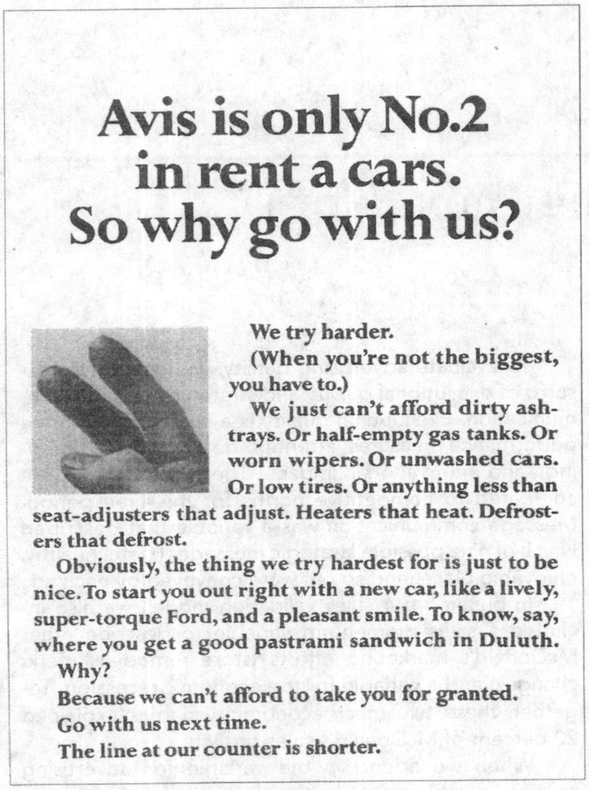

Photo: Courtesy of Avis Rent A Car System, LLC.

CLASSIC

According to *Advertising Age*, the Avis "We Try Harder" campaign was one of the top 10 in advertising history. It was the ultimate simple idea that conveyed a great idea that was truthful and believable. The strategy—to state strongly a self-effacing underdog position—also tapped into people's sympathy for underdogs. The copy defined what it means to try harder (and what a leader in the car rental business should be providing)—clean ashtrays, full gas tanks, wipers that work, washed cars, heaters and defrosters that work—and the lines at the counter are shorter. It also subtly suggested the problems you might find with number one—Hertz. Created by the legendary Doyle Dane Bernbach agency in 1962 when Avis's market share was only 11 percent, the campaign drove a turnaround for the company. Four years later, Avis's market share was 35 percent, and the campaign got credit for a 300 percent increase in business.

campaign success in this chapter. That said, we also encourage all future marketers to know that new ways of measuring effectiveness always are possible.

Why Evaluation Matters

As was mentioned in Chapter 6, some evaluation of brand communication is informal and based on the judgment of experienced managers, and there always is a need for this. The important thing to recognize—very early in campaign planning stages—is that there also will be a need for multiple, formal evaluation mechanisms. As Professor Mark Stuhlfaut explains, evaluation should be "planned in" to any campaign. This is not an onerous task in the case where solid campaign objectives have been written, as evaluation can and should flow directly from those goals. But the inclusion of a "campaign evaluation phase" on the program time line is mandatory.

Principle
If you can't measure it, you can't manage it.

Structured evaluation not only determines the success of a campaign from an objective perspective but also provides valuable feedback as brands plan campaigns for the future. Professor Stuhlfaut's "A Matter of Principle" feature builds on the idea of a cycle beginning and ending with research.

Principle
The sheer costs of brand communication demand that it be evaluated so that its effectiveness can be understood.

From the business perspective, formal evaluation of brand communication is a must. Why? The first reason is that the stakes in making an advertising misstep are high. By the time an average 30-second commercial is ready for national television, it has cost hundreds of thousands

A Matter of Principle

Completing the Cycle

Mark Stuhlfaut, *Associate Professor, University of Kentucky*

So you've analyzed the market up and down, honed a strategic position, spent months creating the most attractive image, produced hard-hitting materials, placed ads in all the right media, stretched the budget, made sure everyone in your marketing chain is on message, and launched a tightly integrated communication campaign. It's time to sit back and enjoy the afterglow, right?

Not quite. You're job isn't finished until you've properly evaluated the results. Why? There are three very good reasons: (1) You need to find out what worked in the campaign, what didn't, and what could have worked better to solve any problems now; (2) a comprehensive evaluation provides valuable information that will serve as input for the next planning cycle; and (3) managers of marketing communication need to responsibly demonstrate the effectiveness of their efforts to clients and corporate management—you owe it to them to prove that their investment of resources in your programs and their trust in you were worth it.

Where do you start? A good beginning is to go back to the campaign's goals to see if they were met, which brings back the importance of having clear, measurable, and attainable objective statements.

What standards should you employ to know if you've succeeded? Sales data? They're one indicator, but too many intervening factors make tying marketing communication to sales figures difficult and not very meaningful. Therefore, other measures, such as the levels of awareness, comprehension, importance, and brand preference, are more useful for communication managers to determine whether the campaign was effective.

A thorough review takes more than a few quick surveys. Sure, you'll want to conduct quantitative and qualitative research to get feedback from consumers or customers. But you should also contact all the key stakeholders in the market—such as company sales personnel, distributors, dealers, editors, broadcasters, consultants, and other friendly third parties—to see if their communication needs were satisfied by the campaign. Include these important people in your evaluation, and you'll not only gain helpful information, you'll build strong relationships for the future.

The best evaluation techniques aren't something you add on to a campaign; they're something you build in to every phase of the process. Assess alternative positions early in the campaign's development. Compare different concepts in the rough layout stage. The earlier you test, the cheaper it is, and the better chance you have to get it right.

It's easy to say you don't have the time or the money to evaluate the campaign's elements. But consider the cost of not getting it right. The effort made to evaluate the effectiveness of the campaign before and after launch will pay off in the long run.

of dollars in production costs. If it is run nationally, its sponsor can invest several million dollars in airtime alone. The second reason is that advertising optimization—reducing risk by testing, tracking brand performance, and making changes where possible to increase the effectiveness of communication—ensures future success.

As this chapter is being written, experts in the IMC business are putting evaluation skills at the very top of the list of skills that will be needed in the communication industry over upcoming years. According to *Advertising Age*, a group of 75 ad industry leaders who recently met in New York City to brainstorm about the future of their field concluded that "the next-generation advertising exec will be a data geek with the soul of an artist, the business acumen of Warren Buffett and the storytelling skills of Don Draper."[5] This is due to the power that big data will bring to IMC decision making.

How Evaluation Fits into the Stages of Brand Communication Testing

A complete understanding of the strength of your brand communication is accomplished through testing, monitoring and measurement through testing, monitoring, and measurement, as depicted in Figure 19.1, which illustrates how IMC planning is circular with evaluation being both a last step of one planning effort and the first step of the next effort.

In Chapter 6, we discussed message development testing; more specifically, we discussed how **concept testing**, **semiotic testing**, and **pretesting** are used to make a campaign as strong as possible before it "goes live" in the marketplace. Ideally, the results of preliminary testing should be available before large sums of money are invested in finished work or in media buys. We also discussed the monitoring of buzz and the tracking of behavior while a campaign is running. Here, our focus will be on measurement—how we evaluate actual effects and results after a campaign effort has been completed.

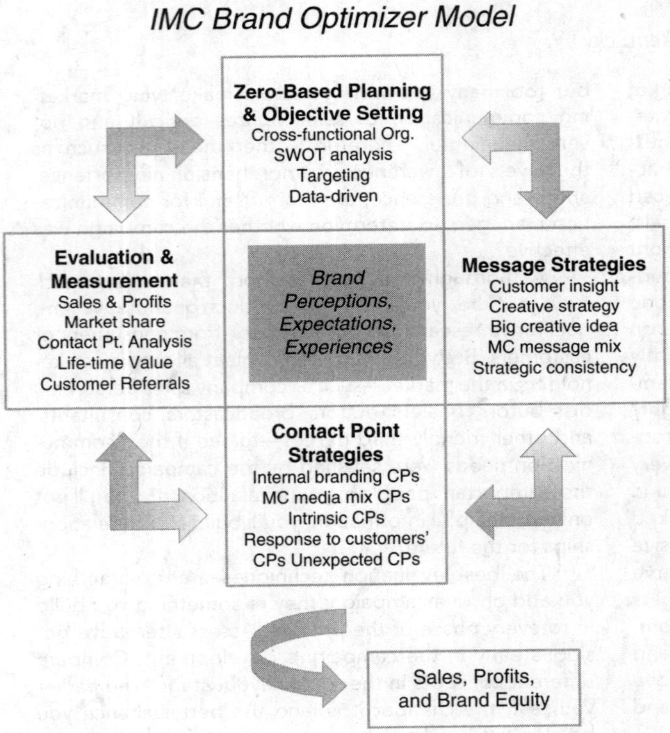

FIGURE 19.1
IMC Brand Optimizer Model

This IMC model created by Professor Tom Duncan illustrates that evaluation is a circular process—IMC plans start by gathering information and move through the various steps in the planning process to come back to the last step in the process, which is again gathering information. This time, however, information is gathered to determine what worked and what didn't. That information feeds back into the process, and the organization learns from the results.

Evaluating the IMC Message

Once a campaign is over, how do we find out whether brand communication was effective? How do we know whether the messaging "worked"? Questions about impact are critical and must be addressed. If they are not and there is no proof that a campaign worked, companies may be tempted to make the mistake of cutting communication spending that is driving their business. Put another way: In the absence of proof that IMC efforts have made a brand stronger, brand managers who are under pressure to cut spending could put a stop to the very IMC efforts that are allowing them to remain competitive. Also, in a scenario in which an IMC program is not having positive effects on attitudes or behaviors, brand managers need to know this so that they can improve on their campaigns moving forward.

As we discussed earlier in this chapter, any attempt to measure the impact of brand messaging by looking only at sales numbers poses challenges. Therefore, the impact of brand messaging typically is measured in terms of its communication effects—the mental responses to a message (such as increased awareness or a change in brand perceptions) that serve as **surrogate measures** for sales impact. Positive postcampaign changes in measures such as brand awareness, knowledge of what a brand offers, liking of a brand, and intent to purchase a brand suggest that an advertising message or some other form of brand communication is making a positive contribution to an eventual brand purchase. Many other measures for which we hope to see increases as a result of brand communication also are important and will be included in our discussion below.

When campaigns don't work, a very important role of postcampaign message testing involves understanding what went wrong. Some messages confuse the audience. Others might fail to get people's attention, and still others might fail to resonate with consumers. In these situations, campaign message evaluation must bring the issues to light. In some cases, brand messages lack credibility and can even have a negative impact. For example, when a 2007 publicity release for the "God of War" video game actually featured a deceased goat, animal rights groups were incensed.[6] Other consumers likely were offended as well. Again, a brand manager must know not only that this has happened but also exactly why and how. Solid campaign evaluation measurements tell us precisely what a campaign has and has not accomplished.

Table 19.1 groups key message effectiveness measures and then matches them to the types of research questions that are used to determine effectiveness. We use the word "ad" throughout the table, but the questions are relevant for all IMC tools used in a given campaign.

Table 19.1 Effectiveness Research Questions

Effect	*Research Questions*
Perception	
Awareness/noticed	Which ads do you remember seeing? Which ads were noted?
Attention	What caught your attention? Did the ad stand out among the other ads and content around it? What stood out in the ad?
Recognition (aided)	Have you seen this ad/this campaign? Sort elements into piles of remember/don't remember.
Relevance	How important is the product message to you? Does it speak to your interests and aspirations?
Emotional/affective	What emotions did the ad stimulate? How did it make you feel?
Liking/disliking	Do you like this brand? This story? The characters (and other ad elements)? What did you like or dislike about the brand? The ad?
Desire	Do you want this product or brand?
Cognition	
Interest	Did you read/watch most of it? How much? Did it engage your interest or curiosity? Where did your interest shift away from the ad?
Comprehension/ confusion	What thoughts came to you? Do you understand how it works? Is there anything in the ad you don't understand? Do the claims/product attributes/benefits make sense? Do you have a need for this brand or can it fulfill a need for you?
Recall (unaided)	What happened in the commercial? What is the main message? What is the point of the ad?
Brand recall/linkage	What brand is being advertised in this ad? [In open-ended responses, was the brand named?]
Differentiation	What's the difference between Brand X and Y?
Association	When you think of this brand, what (products, qualities, attributes, people, lifestyles, etc.) do you connect with it? Do you link this brand to positive experiences?
Personality/image	What is the personality of the brand? Of whom does it remind you? Do you like this person/ brand personality? What is the brand image? What does it symbolize or stand for?
Self-identification	Can you see yourself or your friends using this brand? Do you connect personally with the brand image?

(Continued)

Effect	*Research Questions*
Persuasion	
Intention	Do you want to try or buy this product/brand? Would you put it on your shopping list?
Argument/ counterargument	What are your reasons for buying it? Or for not buying it—or its competing brand(s)? How does it compare to competitors' brand(s)? Did you argue back to the ad?
Believability/conviction	Do you believe the reasons, claims, or proof statements? Are you convinced the message is true? The brand is best?
Trust	Do you have confidence in the brand?
Behavior	How many people buy, try, call, send, click, visit, attend, inquire, volunteer, donate, advocate, or whatever the desired action? What is the rate of change?

Experts in Message Evaluation

Many research companies, in addition to some large agency research departments, specialize in measuring the various dimensions of effectiveness described in Table 19.1. The most successful of these companies have conducted so many tests that they have developed **norms** for common product and service categories. Put another way: After a campaign runs, these companies can look at a client's changes in key measures (e.g., increases in brand awareness or intention to purchase) and compare them to changes achieved by other campaigns of comparable budget. Norms allow brand and agency leaders to determine whether a particular campaign message has performed above or below the category average in terms of "moving the needle" on items such as those listed in Table 19.1.

Most large measurement companies also have developed diagnostic methods that identify the strong and weak aspects of an IMC campaign. This is important because, as we have discussed above, understanding what worked and what did not work is what makes us able to make campaigns better over time.

Below is a list of a few of the more prominent communication evaluation companies and the types of tests and measurements they provide. Of course, new entrants (often working with new technology) and mergers cause this list of firms to change quite frequently:

- ***Ameritest*** Brand linkage, attention, motivation, communication, flow of attention and emotion through the commercial
- ***Ipsos ASI*** Recall, attention, brand linkage, persuasion (brand switch, purchase probability), communication
- ***Millward Brown*** Branding, enjoyment, involvement, understanding, ad flow, brand integration, feelings about ad, main standout idea, likes/dislikes, impressions, persuasion, new news, believability, relevance
- ***TNS Global*** Brand choice, brand power (in the mind and in the market), motivations driving brand choice
- ***GfK*** Advertising planning, advertising optimization (testing of communication across channels), monitoring of ongoing effectiveness of brand communication
- ***Sapient*** Advanced analytics, storytelling across digital channels

Also, major online companies, such as Google, provide myriad tools for campaign evaluation that include everything from straightforward analytic tools that measure site traffic or key word search results to more complex tools that allow marketers to create experiments. In such experiments, for example, a campaign might appear to some consumers but not to others so that its impact on consumer attitudes may be clearly assessed. Companies such as MetrixLab use a tagging technology to know how many times people are exposed to a campaign and then measure how heavily exposed consumers and lightly exposed consumers differ in their intent to try a brand.

Message Evaluation Techniques

Now that we understand the broad role of campaign evaluation—through which we learn not only whether an IMC campaign met its objectives but also how it may have failed to deliver results—we can examine the most common research techniques used. Different types of measurement are required because brand managers are likely to set different objectives for different types of campaign messages. For example, LiveWell expected its television ads to drive website usage, and it expected its neighborhood events to arm people with the knowledge that they could become active within their communities. To begin, we'll expand on the role of communication tracking research, which initially was mentioned in Chapter 6.

Photo: © 2004 John West Foods Ltd. All rights reserved. Used with permission

A beautifully done image for John West, a British beer, uses a simple photograph of the top of a can. It takes on new meaning when the can's rings are associated with the rings in water from a fishing bobber. The question is do people get the association and understand the larger meaning of "Relax with a Can of John West."

Tracking Studies Communication *tracking studies* are conducted from the time a campaign is launched until after it has concluded and involve the collection of information from random samples of consumers who live in markets where they were exposed to a campaign. Companies differ in their exact time lines for data collection; in a best-practice scenario, however, information is collected from consumers two weeks after a campaign is launched, six weeks after a campaign is launched, and then at regular intervals between that point and the point at which the campaign concludes. The reason why tracking studies are relevant to this chapter's campaign evaluation discussion is that those measures collected at the conclusion of a campaign cycle are analyzed particularly closely by brand managers. It is through analyzing these measures that brand managers not only determine campaign impact but also determine whether the campaign's core message has the staying power to be used for another cycle.

Of the research questions listed in Table 19.1, those focusing on campaign recall, recognition, comprehension and relevance are staples of communication tracking surveys. It is imperative that consumers understand the message because they may become disengaged if they have to puzzle out the meaning. An example of a billboard that likely would require testing is that for a British beer brand John West, which is given a dramatic touch by making the rings on top of the can look like rings of rippling water cast from a fishing bobber.

Tracking surveys also include specific questions about how consumers perceive the personality of the brand (has the campaign reinforced the personality the brand team seeks to build?), self-identification with the brand (do consumers feel the brand is "a brand for me"?), purchase intent, and purchase rate. If a campaign did not cause consumers to feel increased affinity with the brand and/or increase their likelihood of buying it, IMC campaign effectiveness is certain to come under question. At its most basic level, a brand tracker includes the components shown in Figure 19.2.

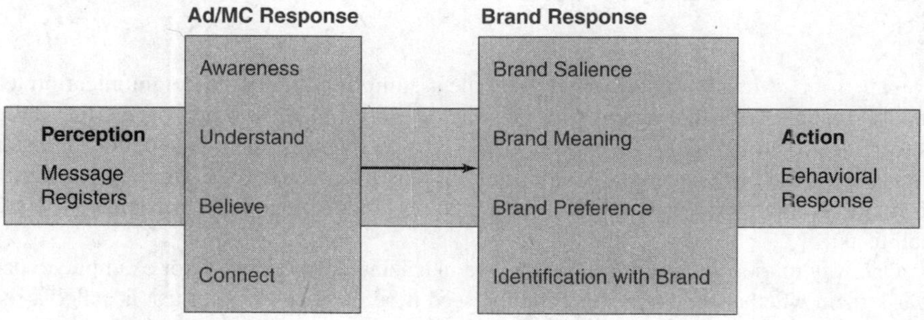

FIGURE 19.2
Tracking Brand Response

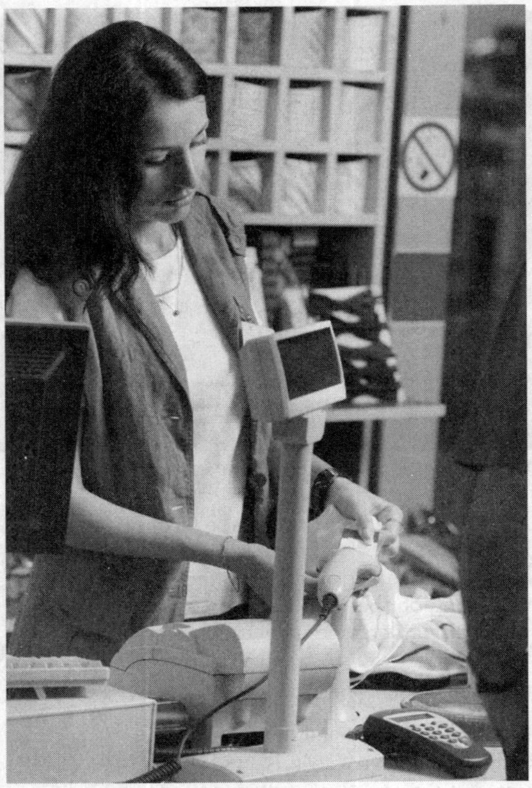

Photo: Dmitry Kalinovsky/Shutterstock

Scanner research reads the information from a shopper's identification card and records that along with product information. Many retail outlets use electronic scanners to track sales among various consumer groups.

Scanner Analysis Still another common component of post-test evaluation is **scanner research**. Many retail outlets, especially drug, discount, and food stores, use electronic scanners to tally up purchases and collect consumer buying information. When you shop at your local Safeway, for example, each product you buy has an electronic bar code that conveys the brand name, the product code, and its price. If you are a member of Safeway's frequent-buyer program and have a membership card that entitles you to special promotional offers, the store can track your purchases.

Scanner research is also used to see what type of sales spikes are created when certain ads and promotions are used in a given market. Both the chain and the manufacturers of the brands are interested in this data. The regional Safeway system may decide to establish a consumer panel so it can track sales among various consumer groups. In this instance, you would be asked to join a panel, which might contain hundreds of other customers. You would complete a fairly extensive questionnaire and be assigned an ID number. You might receive a premium or a discount on purchases for your participation. Each time you make a purchase, you also submit your ID number. Therefore, if Safeway runs a two-page newspaper ad, it can track actual sales to determine to what extent the ad worked. Various manufacturers who sell products to Safeway can do the same kind of testing. The panel questionnaire also contains a list of media that each member reported using, so media performance can also be evaluated.

Single-Source Research Using scanner data and the cooperation of local cable networks, researchers are closer to showing a causal relationship between IMC programs and sales because of **single-source research**. Single-source research companies, such as A. C. Nielsen, arrange to have test commercials delivered to a select group of households within a market to compare changes in behavior to a control group of households. The purchasing behavior of each group of households is collected by scanners in local stores. Because brand communication is the only manipulated variable, the method permits a fairly clear reading of cause and effect. Data collected in this way are known as **single-source data** because brand communication exposure and brand purchasing data come from the same household source.

Syracuse University Professor Emeritus John Philip Jones, who spent many years at J. Walter Thompson, has used single-source data from the firm combined with Nielsen television viewing data to prove that advertising can cause an immediate impact on sales. His research has found that the strongest campaigns can triple sales, while the weakest campaigns can actually cause sales to fall by more than 50 percent.[7]

Although fairly expensive, single-source research can produce dependable results. Brand communication is received under natural conditions in the home, and the resulting purchases are actual purchases made by consumers. One drawback is that single-source research is better for short-term immediate sales effects and doesn't capture very well other brand-building effects.

Memory Tests Memory tests are based on the assumption that brand communication leaves a mental residue with the person who has been exposed to it; in other words, the audience has learned something. One way to measure IMC effectiveness, then, is to contact consumers who were exposed to the campaign and find out what they remember. Memory tests fall into two major groups that you may remember reading about previously: recognition tests and recall tests.

One way to measure memory is to show a magazine advertisement, for example, to people and ask them whether they remember having seen it before. This kind of test is called a **recognition test**. In a **recall test**, respondents who have read the magazine are asked to report what they remember from the ad about the brand. In tests, the interviewer may go through a deck of cards containing brand names. If the respondent says, "Yes, I remember seeing an advertisement for that brand," the interviewer asks the interviewees to describe everything they can remember about the ad. Obviously, recall is a more rigorous test than a recognition test.

Similarly, new television commercials often are run during the Super Bowl. The next evening, interviewers may make thousands of random phone calls until they have contacted about 200 people who were watching the program at the exact time the commercial appeared. The interviewer then asks a series of questions, such as the following:

- Do you remember seeing a commercial for any SUVs?
- ***If No*** Do you remember seeing a commercial for the Jeep Wrangler? (memory prompt)
- ***If Yes to Either of the Above*** What did the commercial say about the product? What did the commercial show? What did the commercial look like? What ideas were brought out?

Photo: © 2004 Pacific Life Insurance Company

Pacific Life used an image of a leaping whale to reflect its image of a confident insurance company that excels in its market. Is it effective? Does it work?

The first type of question is called an **unaided recall** question because the particular brand is not mentioned. The second question is an example of **aided recall**, in which the specific brand name is mentioned. The answers to the third set of questions are written down verbatim. The test requires that the respondent link a specific brand name—or at least a specific product category—to a specific commercial. This type of test sometimes is called a **brand linkage test**. The long-running Pacific Life campaign is a good example of a visual that could serve as a strong brand message.

When this method was used to measure impact of the LiveWell campaign described in our opening case, researchers found that 53 percent of moms recalled the campaign unprompted and that 63 percent recalled it when prompted. Of all the respondents who recalled the campaign, almost half (48 percent) said it changed their image of the obesity problem in Colorado. These test results are strong indications of the campaign's success.

Inquiry Tests A form of action response, **inquiry tests** measure the number of responses to an advertisement or other form of brand communication. The response can be a call to a toll-free number, an e-mail or website visit, a coupon return, a visit to a dealer, an entry in a contest, or a call to a salesperson. Inquiry tests are the primary measurement tool for direct-response communication, but they also are used to evaluate advertisements and sales promotions when the inquiry is built into the message design. Inquiry tests also may be used to evaluate the effectiveness of alternative advertisements using a split-run technique in magazines, where there are two versions of the magazine printed, one with ad A and the other with ad B. The ad (or direct-mail piece) that pulls the most responses is deemed to be the most effective.

Evaluating the Performance of Various IMC Tools

As we know from Chapter 18, IMC synergy exists when all campaign components work together to create a solid and understandable brand meaning. And the overarching campaign impact is strongest when the right mix of IMC tools is used. Therefore, before overarching campaign synergy is measured, evaluation usually is conducted on a tool-by-tool basis. In other words, brand managers determine whether each element of the IMC mix (e.g., public relations efforts or a website) individually achieved its desired objectives. They may employ internal data, or they may examine results from an outside research organization, such as Gallup-Robinson or

Millward Brown. Either way, as was mentioned earlier in this chapter, the important thing to remember in planning an evaluation program is that brand managers must think about evaluation up front, and specific objectives must be set for every IMC tool used in the mix.

Advertising may be the most visible IMC tool; however, other brand communication tools, such as sales promotions and online messages, may be better at achieving the objective of getting people to respond with an immediate purchase. Public relations can be particularly strong at building credibility. Whatever its objective, each IMC tool that is employed in a campaign must be evaluated to understand whether it has achieved its goals. And most IMC tools have their own metrics through which their performance is measured at a campaign's close.

In an integrated plan, we must use the best tool to accomplish a desired effect and then measure success in achieving that effect accordingly. In Table 19.2, the main effects are located in the first column, with a collection of surrogate measures identified in the second column (this list is not inclusive, it's just a sample). The last column lists the communication tool or tools that may be most appropriate for achieving the objective. Below, we explain in more detail how a few IMC tools are measured in terms of their effectiveness.

Advertising

How do you describe effective advertising? You've been watching it for most of your life. An examination of Table 19.2 shows that advertising has the potential to be particularly effective in accomplishing a number of objectives, such as increased brand awareness and improved brand image. It also can be a useful tool for providing brand reminders to the customer and encouraging repurchases.

The most common **post-testing**, or campaign evaluation, technique used to evaluate advertising is the tracking study, which is described earlier in this chapter. Whether a campaign runs for six weeks or six months, the measures taken at its close—and for several weeks beyond—are closely scrutinized

Table 19.2 Message Effectiveness Factors

Key Message Effects	*Surrogate Measures*	*Communication Tools*
Perception	Exposure	Advertising media; public relations, point-of-purchase; digital
	Attention	Advertising; sales promotion, packaging; Point-of-purchase
	Interest	Advertising; sales promotion; public relations, direct; point-of-purchase; digital
	Relevance	Advertising; public relations; direct; point-of-purchase; digital
	Recognition	Advertising; public relations, packaging; point-of-purchase; specialties
Emotional/Affective	Emotions and liking	Advertising; sales promotion, packaging; point-of-purchase; digital
	Appeals	Advertising; public relations; sales; events/sponsorships
	Resonate	Advertising; public relations; events/sponsorships
Cognition	Understanding	Advertising; public relations; sales; direct; digital
	Recall	Advertising; sales promotion; public relations, point-of-purchase, specialties
		Advertising; public relations; packaging
Association	Brand image	Advertising; public relations; events/sponsorships; digital
Persuasion	Attitudes	Advertising; public relations; direct; digital
	Preference/intention	Advertising; public relations; sales; sales promotion; digital
	Credibility	Public relations
	Conviction	Public relations; sales; direct
	Motivation	Advertising; public relations; sales; sales promotion; digital
Behavior	Trial	Sales promotion; sales; direct, point-of-purchase; digital
	Purchase	Sales promotion; sales; direct; digital
	Repeat purchase	Advertising; sales promotion; sales; direct, specialties; digital

by company and agency leaders to determine whether the campaign can be deemed a success. Communication tracking studies represent very large investments on the part of marketers; that said, given the cost of creating advertising, thorough campaign evaluation represents money well spent.

Public Relations

Public relations practitioners typically track the impact of a public relations campaign in terms of successful **output** (e.g., how many news releases led to stories or mentions in news stories) and **outcome** (attitudinal or behavioral change due to the impact of materials produced). Put another way: To get a comprehensive picture of the impact of public relations, practitioners have evaluated process (what goes out) and outcome (effect on the target audience).

Output evaluation might be conducted by asking questions such as these: How many placements (news releases that ran in the media) did we get? How many times did our spokesperson appear on talk shows? How much airplay did our public service announcements receive, or how much and what kind of buzz are tweets generating? The results are presented in terms of counts of minutes, mentions, or retweeting.

Outcomes, on the other hand, usually are measured in terms of changes in public opinion and relationship tracking. Ongoing public opinion tracking studies ask these questions: Has there been a change in audience knowledge, attitudes, or behavior? Can we associate behavioral change (e.g., product trial, repeat purchase, voting, or joining) with the public relations effort?

The search for methods to tie public relations activities to bottom-line business measures, such as return on investment (ROI), is like the quest for the Holy Grail. Public relations practitioners would like to demonstrate ROI because this would provide even more support for the importance of public relations effects. A surrogate ROI measure can be based on shareholder value, which can be seen as a company or brand's reputation capital. For example, research conducted on companies with the most effective employee communication programs has determined that they provide a much higher total return to shareholders. In addition, Web-based analytical tools are making it possible to connect earned media results to online business goals, such as the generation of website traffic, sales leads, revenue, and donations for nonprofit organizations.[8]

Although some still argue that not all the value of public relations programs is measurable,[9] others claim that it is possible to increase the use of metrics to determine the impact a public relations campaign is having on consumer engagement—especially in the digital arena. According to Lee Odden, CEO of Top Rank Online Marketing, "Linking, bookmarking, blogging, referring, clicking, friending, connecting, subscribing, submitting inquiry forms and buying all are engagement measures at various points in the customer relationship.[10] Mark Story, of the Securities and Exchange Commission, says that engagement can be measured by time spent on a website or comments made on blogs; he also has stated, however, that successful online engagement created by public relations depends on the target audience. Others agree with this latter view. But again, we come back to the fact that objectives and the metrics for measuring success must be established up front; only then are public relations professionals truly capable of campaign evaluation.

Consumer, Trade, and Point-of-Purchase Promotions

Sales promotion managers for packaged goods and other products that use distribution channels need to evaluate both the impact of consumer (or end-user) promotions and promotions targeted at retailers and other channel members. You will recall that sales promotion is a set of techniques that prompts consumers, sales representatives, and the trade to take immediate action. At the most basic level of evaluation, managers require proof of promotion execution, such as copies of store ads and pictures of in-store displays. One responsibility of the sales force is to conduct store checks to verify that stores are doing what they promised. At the most important level of promotion evaluation, however, the behaviors and types of involvement that promotions are designed to create must be measured.

Promotions that contain a response device, such as coupons, have a built-in evaluation measure. Beyond response and redemption rates, however, brand managers often also measure consumer awareness of promotions, sales force participation in promotions, and

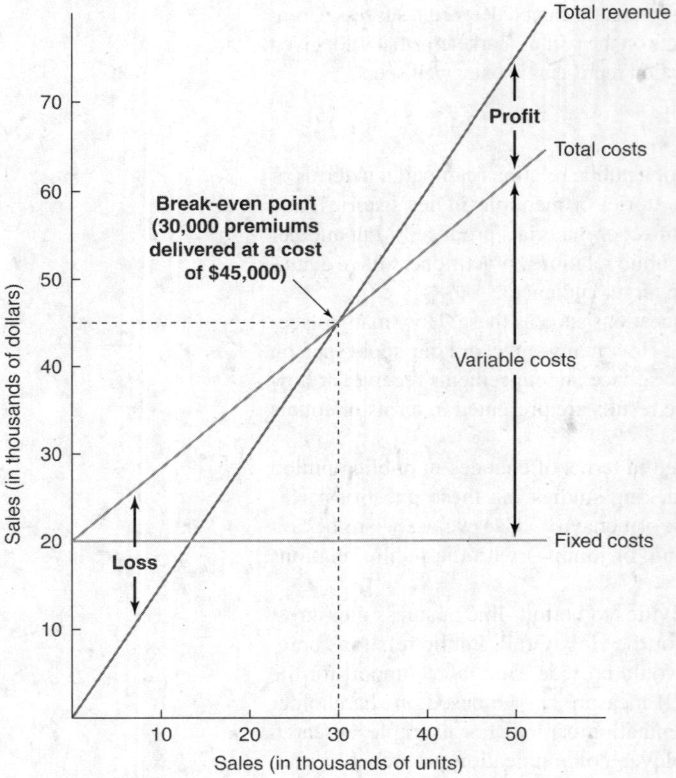

FIGURE 19.3

A Sales Promotion Break-Even Analysis

At the break-even point, where 30,000 premiums are delivered at a cost of $45,000, the sales revenues exactly cover but do not exceed, total costs. Below and to the left of the break-even point (in the portion of the diagram marked off by dashed lines), the promotion operates at a loss. Above and to the right of the break-even point, as more premiums are sold and sales revenues climb, the promotion makes a profit.

various appropriate forms of online consumer reaction. What is measured depends on promotional objectives.

Overall, the efficiency of a sales promotion can be evaluated in terms of its financial returns more easily than can the impact of advertising. We compare the costs of a promotion, called a **payout analysis,** to the forecasted sales generated by the promotion. A **break-even analysis** seeks to determine the point at which the total cost of a promotion exceeds the total revenues generated, identifying the point where the promotion was not productive. Figure 19.3 depicts this analysis.

Direct Marketing The primary objective of direct-marketing communication is to drive a transaction or generate some other type of immediate behavioral response, such as a donation or visit to a dealer. What makes this marketing communication tool so attractive to marketers is that response is so easily measurable. Some advertisements request direct response via a toll-free number, a mail-in coupon, a website or e-mail address, or an offer embedded in the body copy. Instead of depending on consumers' memories, measures of a message's persuasive abilities, or some other indirect indication of effectiveness, the advertiser simply counts the number of viewers or readers who either buy a product or take some other action (e.g., request additional information). In this way, direct marketing mechanisms are the easiest IMC tools to evaluate in terms of message efficiency and in terms of return on marketing investment.

Evaluation of Digital IMC Components Many IMC efforts, whether advertising, public relations or other campaign elements, are conducted not only offline but also online. Some digital performance indicators are website traffic volume, such as **page views** or the simple number of visitors to a site. Banner advertising and other ads are evaluated using **click-through rates,** as mentioned in Chapter 12; however, one thing the industry has learned is that this form of advertising is decreasing in effectiveness. Pop-up banners, in particular, can get more attention, but they are also seen as more irritating.

Instead of click-through rates, some advertisers use a **cost-per-lead** metric that records how well a click-through generates prospects, an attempt to get at ROI. A more important metric, however, is **conversion rate,** which is the percentage of people who complete a desired action, such as playing a game, signing up for a newsletter, or buying something. Of course, online sales also are an important measure of digital effectiveness.

The most important thing to understand in considering evaluation of online efforts is that while websites used to be the primary digital properties for connecting with targets and the place where the most digital interaction was happening, that no longer is true. Today, digital communication is multichannel (e.g., desktop, mobile, tablet, outdoor display) and multiplatform (social sharing, paid digital media like banners, e-mail, consumer reviews, video sharing, music, games, and much more). According to Melissa Read, director of marketing analysis and strategy at Sapient, "We think of this world and the experience consumers have with it as an **ecosystem** of digital properties. The consumer journey in discovering, considering and purchasing products from brands happens inside and outside of this ecosystem, as it also includes offline touch points, such as the in-store experience and **experiential marketing.**"[11]

The Inside Story

The Best and Worst Website Designs

Harley Manning, *Research Director at Forrester Research*

Over the years, Forrester has graded the quality of user experience on over 1,600 websites with a technique called **heuristic evaluation**. Today, variations on this methodology are used by virtually every interactive design agency and testing lab to judge the effectiveness of sites.

To identify some of the best and worst examples of Web design each year, we grade sites in each of four industries. Most recently, we graded the sites of the four largest auto insurers, discount retailers, online travel agencies, and tablet manufacturers. When we published the results, we kicked up quite a storm because we named names. Here are some key results from Forrester's research into the best and worst of site design in 2011:

- Overall user experience was mediocre. Out of 16 sites, only Orbitz earned a passing score. The most common flaws included lack of essential content that shoppers need to make a purchase decision—a killer flaw that frustrates potential customers *and* hurts the business.
- The auto insurer category had the highest average score. Even the lowest-scoring sites (a tie between Allstate and State Farm) had merit. But it's interesting to note that both Geico and Progressive, with their heavier emphasis on direct-to-consumer business, scored much higher.
- The tablet manufacturer sites we graded had the lowest average score. What's significant here is the spread between best and worst: While Apple and Motorola had surprisingly weak but not awful sites, BlackBerry and Samsung—which had the lowest score by far across all four categories—put themselves at a competitive disadvantage with notably poor design.

There are some important takeaways from this study for anyone involved in site creation. Two stand out. The first is that it's critical to start with a detailed understanding of the target customers' needs, goals, and context—for example, how much they know about the products or services on offer and how anxious they are about the purchase process. Had the designers of the Expedia, Orbitz, and Travelocity sites followed that advice, they wouldn't have buried details about room cancellation policies, and the designers of the BlackBerry and Samsung sites wouldn't have left out battery life estimates for their tablet computers.

The second is that it's critical for creatives working in digital media to add user-centered design skills to their arsenal. That's because you cannot frustrate and annoy customers into liking your brand. Yet sites seem determined to do just that, with barely legible typography and extra steps in navigation that make it hard to find and compare products. The bottom line: Good usability is half the battle of selling in digital media.

Check out Forrester's website at *www.forrester.com*.

The information was contributed by Harley Manning, a master's graduate of the advertising program at the University of Illinois. He was nominated by the late Kim Rotzell, advertising professor and former dean of the College of Communication.

When she says "experiential marketing," Read is referring to all of the other ways that consumers experience a brand.

What all of this means is that in addition to evaluating digital efforts through looking at conversion rates (e.g., the rate of shift from information seeking to trial usage) and sales, experts are now evaluating digital campaign components in terms of their ability to generate awareness and consideration—measures that used to be applied only to traditional media—as well. Consumers no longer see themselves as bouncing back and forth between traditional and digital worlds as they make commitments to brands, so we must attempt to understand myriad influences that digital efforts may be having on the way they think and feel, as the Inside Story explains.

Evaluating the Performance of Media Vehicles

Brand communication has little chance to be effective if no one sees it. Analyzing the effectiveness of the media plan is yet another important part of campaign evaluation. Did the plan actually achieve reach and frequency objectives? Did the newspaper and magazine placements run in the positions expected and produce the intended GRP and cost-per-thousand levels? In other words, did brand managers get what they paid for?

Media Optimization

When a brand manager optimizes the mix of IMC tools used, the resulting brand perception becomes stronger. One of the biggest challenges in media planning is media efficiency—getting the most for the money invested. As we explained in Chapter 14, media planners operate with computer models of **media optimization** that are used in making decisions about media selection, scheduling, and weights (amount of budget). Models are always theoretical, so one important benefit of campaign evaluation is that the actual performance of a plan can be compared with the results projected by the media planner's model. The goal of media optimization is to optimize the budget—to get the most impact possible with the least expenditure of money. When we compare actual media reach and frequency, for example, with projections, our findings allow us to fine-tune our spending for the future to be as efficient as possible.

Evaluating Exposure

For major campaigns, agencies do postbuy analyses, which involve checking the media plan against the performance of each media vehicle. As mentioned above, a critical question is whether campaign reach and frequency objectives were obtained.

Verifying the audience measurement estimates is a challenge. Media planners are working sometimes with millions of dollars, and they can't afford to get it wrong. For print, services such as the Alliance for Audited Media (formerly known as Audit Bureau of Circulations), Experian Simmons (formerly known as SMRB), and MediaMark provide data. Likewise for broadcast, Arbitron and A. C. Nielsen provide audience monitoring. Media planners use these estimates up front to develop a media plan, and media buyers use them later to verify the accumulated impact of the media buy after the campaign has run. As we use the word "impact," however, an important point must be clarified: When impact is judged by media audience measures, those numbers must be viewed with caution. The simple fact that audience members have been exposed to marketing communication does not mean they have paid attention to it—and media professionals must always keep this top of mind.

As media choices and thus, their jobs, become more and more complex, media planners are being asked to prove the wisdom of their recommendations in areas where the data they use are sometimes suspect or unreliable, particularly if there are problems with the media measurement companies' formulas and reporting systems. Nielsen, for example, has been subject to much questioning of its television ratings. Online measurement systems certainly remain imperfect even though media agencies such as MindShare have made vast progress in recent years.

Photo: Courtesy of J. Walter Thompson, London. "Anti-Aggressive Driving Campaign," 1996

This outdoor board from the United Kingdom attracted attention because of its interesting visual but also because of its challenging idea. Research based on traffic counts finds it difficult to account for the emotional impact of messages like these.

Vehicle-by-Vehicle Evaluation

To better understand the obstacles encountered in media evaluation, let's first look at a few areas where media performance is hard to estimate: out-of-home media, digital media, and alternative media. Then we will review some traditional media evaluation techniques.

Out-of-Home Media As you would expect, accurately evaluating the mobile audience for outdoor advertising is challenging. Traffic counts can be reviewed, but the problem is that traffic does not equal exposure. Just because a car drove by a board doesn't mean that the driver and/or passengers actually saw it.

To address this issue, Traffic Audit Bureau for Media Measurement, Inc., has created the TAB visibility research program, which uses eye-tracking technology to determine how a billboard's format and angle to the road affect the likelihood that it will be noticed. TAB out-of-home measures even take into account the speed limits of roads on which signs are placed. So, while outdoor advertising continues to present measurement challenges, progress is being made to better understand its impact. In particular, evaluation experts are seeking to move beyond traffic counts to understand the emotional impact of billboards such as the "road rage" billboard shown on the previous page.

Digital Media Until recently, the measures of effectiveness used to evaluate offline campaigns did not seem to transfer well to the online world. Put another way: It used to be the case that digital tracking was tough and offline tracking was stronger in showing the relationship between IMC spend and results. Today, however, this has changed. Web-analytic firms are developing much more sophisticated evaluation programs. As Melissa Read of Sapient said, "We have people who study digital analytics and are experts at telling stories about the consumer journey with both offline and online data."[12] That said, some obstacles to establishing clear measures of digital media effectiveness do remain and will be discussed later in this chapter.

Alternative Media Alternative media programs, such as word of mouth, social media, and guerilla marketing campaigns, are even harder to evaluate, and media planners continue to search for reliable indicators of exposure numbers and buzz from these new sources that equate to the performance measures for traditional media. Research company Millward Brown designed a metric for online word of mouth to track and analyze sentiments expressed on social networks, blogs, and chat rooms.[13] Procter & Gamble created TREMOR, which develops buzz campaigns and also is used to design analysis techniques to track measurable business results for word-of-mouth campaigns. Another interesting experiment was conducted by Boston University college students and the Mullen ad agency using Twitter to get near-instantaneous feedback on how viewers were reacting to Super Bowl ads. This project was designed "to use a new medium to comment on an old medium," according to Mullen's chief creative officer.[14] However, as with mobile media, obstacles to clear measurement of alternative media effectiveness remain.

Newspaper Readership Measurement For newspapers and other traditional media, assessment is more straightforward. As we introduced in Chapter 12, newspapers measure their audiences in two ways: **circulation**, or number of subscribers, and **readership**, or number of readers. These same measurements are re-visited in post-campaign evaluation. Agencies obtain objective measures of newspaper circulation and readership by subscribing to one or both of the following auditing companies: The Alliance for Audited Media, an independent auditing group, and Scarborough Research, which provides local data for almost 80 of the nation's largest cities.

Magazine Readership Measurement As also was mentioned in Chapter 12, magazine rates are based on the **guaranteed circulation** that a publisher promises to provide, as well as figures for their **total audience**, or total number of readers.

Post-campaign evaluation requires verification of the circulation of magazines, along with the demographic and psychographic characteristics of specific readers. As for newspapers, the Alliance for Audited Media is responsible for verifying magazine circulation numbers. MRI verifies readership for many popular national and regional magazines (along with other media), and also covers readership by demographics, psychographics, and product use. Experian Simmons provides psychographic data on who has read which magazines and which products these readers buy and consume. Still other research companies, such as Gallup and Robinson, provide information about magazine audience size and behavior.

Measuring the Broadcast Audience A station's **coverage**, which is similar to circulation for print media, and station or program **ratings**, as delivered by Arbitron, certainly is revisited post-campaign by marketers to ensure that the radio medium delivered. For television, A. C. Nielsen data help advertisers understand the audience that a campaign actually delivered. Again, ratings, along with *shares*, *households using televisions* and *gross impressions* are re-visited so that a comparison of anticipated and actual audience delivery can be conducted

In the next section, now that we have discussed some details of how the performances of individual IMC tools and media are gauged, we will examine key challenges involved in overall IMC campaign evaluation. Some key concerns revolve around how results from traditional and new media can be integrated and how their combination affects the results of the overarching campaign.

IMC Campaign Evaluation Challenges

As we have discussed, most IMC campaigns use a variety of tools and media to reach and motivate customers to respond. The major challenge in overall program evaluation is to pull everything together and look at the big picture of campaign performance (components' synergistic performance) rather than the individual pieces and parts.

As companies move from an evaluation mind-set that only considers measures such as impressions to one that looks closely at conversion rates and consumer engagement, they are getting closer to a true measure of overarching campaign success. These better metrics, when combined with important metrics collected in ongoing brand tracking studies, should give marketers a more complete picture of campaign performance. That said, exactly which metrics companies choose to combine for evaluation and how those metrics are weighted with regard to their individual importance differs from brand to brand and remain an area of intense debate.

Measuring ROI

Advertisers continue to improve how they measure **brand communication ROI**, which compares the costs of creating and running communication versus the revenue it generates; however, since the dollar impact of communication is difficult to measure, so is this cost-to-sales ratio. ROI is easier to calculate for direct marketing and sales promotions (because the impact of these tools can be isolated and verified) than for the campaign overall.

One question related to ROI is this: How much spending is too much? That is, how do you determine whether you are overadvertising or underadvertising? The best way to answer this question is to use **test marketing**; in this approach, a campaign is launched in several different but matched (similar) cities at different levels of media activity. Then a comparison of the campaign results (sales or other kinds of trackable responses) in the different markets helps brand managers determine the appropriate levels and types of media spending.

Even though test marketing helps brand managers to assess ROI, however, time is a factor as well. We mentioned in the beginning of this chapter that there is a debate about advertising's ability to impact short-term sales results as well as long-term branding.

University of Southern California professor Gerard Tellis reminds us that advertising not only has **instantaneous effects** (consumer responds immediately) but also **carryover effects** (delayed impact).[15] Any evaluation of campaign effectiveness, therefore, needs to be able to track both types of effects over time. And so, even when test markets are established, brand analysts face a challenge in determining just how long they continue to compare results in markets after the campaign has concluded. This means that ROI measures can remain subjective.

The Synergy Problem

Another challenge with evaluating campaigns—particularly IMC campaigns—is estimating the impact of synergy. Intuitively, we know that multichannel communication with messages that reinforce and build on one another will have more impact than will single messages from single sources; however, this can be difficult to prove. As Bob Liodice, CEO of the Association of National Advertisers, observes, "There is no single, consistent set of metrics that transcends discipline-centric measurements."[16]

If the campaign planning is well integrated, which means that each specialty area cooperates with all others in message design, delivery, and timing, then there should be a **synergistic effect**.

This means that the overall results are greater than the sum of the individual functional areas if used separately.

A number of studies have attempted to evaluate IMC impact by comparing campaigns that use two or three tools to see what is gained when more message sources are added to the mix. For example, a study by the Radio Ad Effectiveness Lab reported that recall of advertising is enhanced when a mix of radio and Internet ads are used rather than just website advertising alone.[17] A study published in the *Journal of Advertising Research* developed a multidimensional approach based on evaluation of four factors including unified and consistent communication, strategic consistency in targeting (different messages for different audiences), database communication, and relationship programs.[18] Such studies of both the platforms and the components of IMC are beginning to tease out the effects of synergy, but they are a long way from perfect evaluation of the effects of a total communication program.

The most common way of measuring a campaign's total impact is the brand tracking approach mentioned previously. As various ingredients in the campaign are added and taken away, changes in tracking study results can show the effects and help identify what combinations of marketing communication tools and media work best for a brand. In other words, the brand manager looks at tracking study results over time, as tools and media used vary, and asks, Has the brand become stronger on critical dimensions of the image, such as personality and positioning cues, because of the campaign?

A final complication in evaluating the synergy of programs is the need to consider other messages and contact points beyond the brand communication campaign. Brand experiences, such as those involved with customer service and word of mouth, may be even more important than the planned communication campaign. The "A Principled Practice" feature by Professor Keith Murray demonstrates how these unconventional message effects can have important impact on the brand.

According to Murray in his analysis of the impact on the United airlines brand by one unfortunate brand experience with a broken guitar, three points are dramatized:

1. Key management decisions count for a lot. Crafting and fostering a superb product—in the case of United, creating a great customer service and experience—involves the provision of a real, tangible, palpable reality that the customer can and does detect and enjoy. No amount of promotion hype can compensate for an inferior product offering.
2. Social media is not to be ignored or taken lightly by the firm. Social media messages, which are inherently powerful to begin with in conveying useful information to current and prospective customers, take on an even greater influence in the absence of competing counterpart information from the firm itself through mass media and other paid sources. To disregard the impact of social media is to make a huge management error.
3. Managing the brand involves more than just having a good promotion strategy. Guarding the brand as well as the image of the firm generally involves an integrated management strategy whereby promotion decisions are called on to (1) support sound management and product-related practices (e.g., offer good customer service to begin with and attentive customer service in its absence) and (2) deploy a comprehensive range of promotion strategies—including fostering favorable social media (and responding to it when it happens), not just ignoring the negative messages that come along. The most successful carriers strive to manage their media exposures as much as they pay attention to their service operations. Evidence of this can be amply seen by the volume of negative clips posted by patrons of struggling, relatively unprofitable carriers compared to hardly any negative postings for the more exemplary ones (e.g., Southwest).

Digital Challenges

There are several challenges marketers face when capturing the success of digital marketing communication efforts. First and foremost, marketers often want to skip straight to digital measurement without having a clear sense of their business objectives. At its core, digital IMC is about connecting with a target audience and getting them to do something valuable. So marketers must remind themselves to start their digital measurement planning with the desire business outcomes in mind.

A PRINCIPLED PRACTICE

Can a Broken Guitar Really Hurt United?

Keith Murray, *Professor, College of Business, Bryant University*

It's been a YouTube hit and made the e-mail rounds for a long time—the "United Breaks Guitars" video. It's the story of a musician who made a trip on United Airlines (UA) and was compelled to "check" his Taylor guitar as baggage—which is how UA came to be vulnerable to the charge that, in the handling of it, they damaged the instrument. When asked to make it right—to pay for fixing the Taylor guitar—UA declined.

The musician, Dave Carroll, responded by writing a ballad about the experience and posting it on YouTube and the Internet. A lot of people viewed the clip; it's catchy and tells the story in an amusing way. People have sent it to their friends, and friends have sent it to their friends, which has led now to literally millions of people seeing it. You can see the video and a CBS report about the incident on YouTube.

So was UA smart to ignore this incident? In other words, did UA really "save" the $1,200 it would have taken to fix the guitar in the first place?

It seems clear that UA might have been shortsighted. If you "do the numbers," you come to the conclusion that UA may have paid a much higher price than it realized.

The following table shows how much money might have been—and is still being—lost by UA from 8 million people (in 2010) seeing the YouTube clip and deciding *against* using UA. It gives various levels of impact from 1 to 10 percent. It also compares the percent of this lost revenue against UA's sales revenue in 2008.

What the calculations show is compelling. If only 1 percent of those who learned of the broken Taylor guitar were affected by the story, then UA only lost somewhere between $30 million and $60 million. However, if the negative influence is higher, then UA could arguably have forgone as much as half a *billion* dollars, or about 3 percent of its annual sales. In any case, all of these figures stand in stark contrast to the $1,200 asked for by Mr. Carroll in the first place.

This gets to the real point of the story: If UA (or any company) has a flawed system to handle and remedy customer complaints—in other words, if UA has customer service "issues" that produce unsatisfactory results for customers—then it can pay a very high price for its poor service. And the damage is exponential because the average person tells about 10 people about a bad brand experience—all of which has a chilling effect on patronage by those who hear such tales of woe.

These numbers show the huge impact of failure to pay attention to customer complaints and service system problems. Can one little broken Taylor guitar—and all the other little failures each day—affect a mammoth company like United Airlines? You bet.

Number of $500 Trips Not Taken in a Year	*Percent of Viewers Influenced by YouTube Videos to Not Patronize UA in a 12-Month Period*			
	1%	2%	5%	10%
One trip	$30 million	$60 million	$150 million	$300 million
% 2008 revenue	0.15	0.31	0.78	1.56
Two trips	$60 million	$120 million	$300 million	$600 million
% 2008 revenue	0.31	0.63	1.56	3.13

Second, marketers must develop the right digital **key performance indicators**, which tell us whether or not digital communications are driving the business toward success. A measure of success can be direct, such as a product purchase. Or it can be indirect, such as viewing a product podcast (this suggests that product purchase will happen eventually). Either way, success indicators must be succinctly defined.

Finally, digital communication evaluation must be phrased in a way and in a language that broader business leaders can understand. Due to the range of digital properties that can be measured and the range of key performance indicators that can be captured, reporting communication performance can become quite complex quickly. So digital evaluation experts must keep returning to the business objectives that were set initially and communicate in those terms. According to Melissa Read of Sapient, "Reporting to executive-level audiences is not about showing clicks or views or time spent on digital properties; rather, it is about helping them understand how these things contributed to the broader business goals that they care about—like product sales, customer retention, cross-sell and up-sell."[19]

International Challenges

International brand communication is difficult to evaluate because of market differences (e.g., language, laws, and cultural norms) and the acceptability of various research tools in different countries. There also may be incompatibilities among various measurement systems and data analysis techniques that make it difficult to compare the data from one market to similar data from another market. An international communication program definitely should focus, at least initially, on pretesting because unfamiliarity with different cultures, languages, and consumer behaviors can result in major miscalculations.

After a campaign has concluded, international evaluation is critical yet difficult. One of the things that complicates international campaign evaluation is that countries may have had very different starting points (precampaign measurements) with regard to brand awareness and affinity. So, while the campaign can be analyzed in terms of global impact, analysis still must be conducted on a country-by-country level as well. Also, consumers in different countries approach rating scales differently; in parts of Asia, for example, consumers may feel that to give a brand low ratings on a 1-to-7 scale is less than respectful, so ratings that are reported are inflated.

A final challenge in international IMC evaluation lies in the fundamental communication challenges that all multinational companies experience. Getting managers across countries "on the same page" as to how evaluation measures can and should be interpreted is not an easy task.

Back to the Big Picture: Did the Campaign Work?

The ultimate measure of campaign performance is the answer to one seemingly simple question: Did the campaign achieve the objectives that were set at the very beginning of the planning process? Because a planning process can be imperfect, this question is not always so simple.

The Vail Resorts's Colorado Pass Club launch is an example of how a model of effects can be developed for a specific campaign and used to drive not only the planning of the effort but also the evaluation of its effectiveness. One of the goals of a successful ski season is to lock in revenue as early as possible. In advance of the 2009–2010 season, when tasked with the objectives of keeping recent pass holders loyal as well as bringing in competitive pass holders, Vail Resorts introduced its innovative Colorado Pass Club (CPC) and marketed it in unique ways.

The CPC program included biweekly e-mails full of promotions, offers, and discounts exclusively for pass holders and promotions that ranged from dining and ticket events to discounted lodging and gear. Many efforts were supported by radio spots and a special CPC website.

What were the results? The number of total season passes sold for the ski season represented a 12 percent increase, and this increase was generated despite a historically low snowfall and a struggling economy. Pass holders loved the brand relationship-building efforts, and so did Vail Resorts.

Connecting the Dots: Tying Measurement Back to Objectives

Competent brand communication managers return to the campaign objectives—all of the various desired effects that were stated up front—and then adequately and realistically measure the campaign's performance against those objectives. Here's an example that demonstrates how evaluation methods should be matched to the original campaign objectives.

Effie award winner UPS wanted to reposition itself by broadening its package delivery image.[20] Although UPS owned ground delivery, it lost out to Federal Express in the overnight and international package market. UPS knew from its customer research that to break out of the "brown and ground" perception, the company had to overcome the inertia of shipping managers who use UPS for ground packages and FedEx for overnight and international. The company also had to shift the perception of senior executives from a company that handles packages to a strategic partner in systems planning. From these insights came three sets of objectives that focused on breaking through awareness, breaking the inertia trance, and breaking the relevance trance. Here's how the campaign performed on those objectives. Notice the mix of perception, image, and behavioral measures. Also, note the important fact that measurement of success was made possible by the presence of baseline and benchmark measures that had been collected in the past; in the absence of such data, it is very difficult for a brand manager or agency to point to significant increases or "wins."

Objective 1: Breaking through Awareness

- Awareness of the Brown campaign outpaced *all* past UPS advertising measured in the 10-plus-year history of its brand tracking study.
- Among those aware of the campaign, correct brand linkage to UPS was 95 to 98 percent across all audiences (compared to a historical average of 20 to 40 percent for past UPS advertising).
- "What Can BROWN Do for You?" has taken hold in popular culture. For instance, the tagline was mentioned in both *Saturday Night Live* and *Trading Spaces* shows.

Objective 2: Breaking the Inertia Trance

- With shipping decision makers, the brand showed steady and significant gains in key measures like "Helps my operation run more smoothly," "Dynamic and energetic," and "Offers a broad range of services."
- International shipping profitability increased 150 percent, and overnight volume spiked by 9.1 percent after the campaign ran. The targeted companies' total package volume increased by 4.39 percent.
- From the start of the campaign in March to the year-end, annual ground shipping revenue grew by $300 million.
- The campaign was a hit in terms of response with a 10.5 percent response rate and an ROI of 1:3.5. In other words, every dollar spent on the campaign generated $3.5 dollars in revenue.

Objective 3: Breaking the Relevance Trance

- For the first time in the 10-plus-year history of the brand tracking study, UPS leads FedEx in all image measures among senior-level decision makers. All significant brand image measures continued upward.
- Among senior decision makers, the biggest gains were in key measures like "For people like me," "Acts as a strategic partner to my company," "Helps in distribution and supply chain operations," and "Provides global competitive advantage."
- At the start of the campaign, annual nonpackage (supply chain) revenue was approximately $1.4 billion. By the end of the year, nonpackage revenue had almost doubled to $2.7 billion. This unquestionably represents IMC program success.

Bringing It All Together

Beyond connecting the objectives and the measurements, advertisers continue to search for methods that will bring all the metrics together and efficiently and effectively evaluate brand communication effectiveness. A Florida agency, Zimmerman Advertising, has positioned itself specifically on that issue. Through its "Brandtailing" program, it measures all of its initiatives based on ROI success but also promises to deliver long-term brand building as well as short-term sales.

The leading global public relations and communications firm Burson-Marsteller uses what it calls and "Evidence-Based Approach to Communications." According to its website, this approach is designed as a "scientific approach to communications, driven by data at the beginning, the middle and the end." Also, the site states that "by using Evidence-based tools for benchmarking at the beginning of a program and measuring effectiveness at the end, clients can demonstrate a positive communications ROI."[21] This certainly meshes with what we have presented as true, "best-practice" IMC throughout this chapter.

Photo: © JGI/Jamie Grill/Blend Images/Corbis

Evaluation doesn't just happen at the end of a campaign or after the ad is run. It has to be planned into the campaign from the very beginning, as this planning meeting illustrates.

Ultimately, the goal is to arrive at holistic, cross-functional metrics that are relevant for integrated communication, a task undertaken by Dell Computers and its agency DDB. Given Dell's direct-marketing business model, the company had extensive call and order data in its database. DDB helped organize the collection of detailed marcom information, which made it possible to begin linking orders to specific marcom activities. This new marcom ROI tracking system made it possible for Dell to recognize a 3 percent gain in the efficiency of its marketing communication. As the metrics system became more sophisticated, it also began to move from a reporting and metrics evaluation engine to a strategic tool providing deeper insights into consumer behavior.[22]

Many pieces are still missing in the evaluation of complex IMC programs. Research think tanks are struggling to find better ways to measure consumers' emotional connections to brands and brands' relationships with their customers[23] and how those connections and relationships are affected by various types of marketing communication messages. But let's end with an inspirational video called "Life Lessons from an Ad Man." It's a little old, but Rory Sutherland makes a good point about having fun even as you contemplate how marketing communication creates intangible value for brands. See it at www.ted.com.

It's a Wrap

Results of Colorado's Gut Check

In the beginning of the chapter, you read about LiveWell Colorado's Awakening Campaign, a major communication effort aimed at engaging residents in healthier lifestyles. Now you'll find out about its effectiveness.

Within one year following the official campaign launch, LiveWell Colorado exceeded 500,000 "gut checks" calculated on the LiveWell Colorado website and attracted more than 100,000 website visitors—a 540 percent increase compared to traffic prior to the campaign. The Facebook page attracted more than 16,000 fans, an increase of 13,000 before the campaign, and LiveWell Colorado successfully launched a LiveWell Moms ambassador program that has since connected more than 800 moms from across the state to advocate for healthier living. To date, the Awakening Campaign has received numerous accolades, including a Telly Award and "Best Website" award from PR News Nonprofit.

More importantly, attitudes have shifted. A campaign assessment/research effort included many of the same questions asked in the prior year to test the effectiveness of LiveWell Colorado's educational outreach, obesity awareness, and any resulting behavioral change for Coloradans. Again, 1,100 people from diverse backgrounds throughout Colorado were surveyed. This was the first known rigorous analysis of changes in knowledge and attitudes following a statewide public education campaign targeting obesity.

The Results? Coloradans gained a better understanding of obesity from before the campaign's implementation. Obesity is less someone else's issue, and many more people have faced a reality check that they have work to do. Perceptions of one's own weight status as being overweight increased nine points, from 46 to 55 percent (now more consistent with Colorado's actual rate of 55 percent obese and overweight adults).

The "Awakening" campaign suggests that educational campaigns are a potentially useful means to increase public understanding of obesity as a personal health issue and, ultimately, to facilitate behavior change toward improved prevention of obesity.

Logo: Courtesy of LiveWell Colorado.

Key Points Summary

1. **Why is it important to evaluate brand communication effectiveness?** Marketing communication evaluation is used to test, monitor, measure, and diagnose the effectiveness of IMC messages. Without campaign evaluation, marketers cannot know whether IMC efforts had any impact; they also do not know how to improve on their current campaign.
2. **What role do campaign objectives play in the measurement of campaign success?** Campaign objectives set the stage for measurement. Based on objectives, companies can determine exactly what to measure and which tools to use to evaluate campaign success.
3. **What are the key ways in which campaign evaluation is conducted?** Campaign evaluation is conducted using tracking studies, scanner analyses and single-source research, among other methods. Campaign research also is conducted for various IMC tools (e.g., digital) specifically and to understand the wisdom of media choices.
4. **What are some key challenges faced in evaluating IMC effectiveness?** Key challenges relate to difficulties in assessing monetary return on campaign investment. Also, building communication programs that span many types of traditional and digital media, not to mention different cultures, requires special team-building skills and analytical talents.

Key Terms

aided recall, p. 599
brand communication ROI, p. 606
brand linkage test, p. 599
break-even analysis, p. 602
carryover effects, p. 606
circulation, p. 605
click-through rates, p. 602
concept testing, p. 564
conversion rate, p. 602
cost-per-lead, p. 602
coverage, p. 605
(digital) ecosystem, p. 602
experiential marketing, p. 602
gross impressions, p. 606
guaranteed circulation, p. 605
heuristic evaluation, p. 603
households using television (HUT), p. 606
inquiry tests, p. 599
instantaneous effects, p. 606
key performance indicators, p. 608
media optimization, p. 604
norms, p. 596
outcome, p. 601
output, p. 601
page views, p. 602
payout analysis, p. 602
post-testing, p. 600
pretesting, p. 594
ratings, p. 605
readership, p. 605
recall test, p. 598
recognition test, p. 598
scanner research, p. 598
semiotic testing, p. 564
single-source data, p. 598
single-source research, p. 598
surrogate measures, p. 594
synergistic effect, p. 606
test marketing, p. 606
total audience, p. 605
tracking studies, p. 597
unaided recall, p. 599

Review Questions

19-4. Why is the setting of campaign objectives important?

19-5. What is the difference between attitudinal and behavioral brand communication?

19-6. How would you evaluate an IMC campaign? When would it be considered as successful?

19-7. What is media optimization, and how do we evaluate how close we are to achieving it?

19-8. What are the stages of planning in a marketing campaign?

19-9. What are the two categories of evaluating an ad communication? How do they differ?

Discussion Questions

19-10. Most clients want a quick and easy answer to the question of whether an IMC program works. Advertising professionals, however, tend to believe that a sales-only approach to evaluation is not appropriate. Why do they feel that way? If you were helping an agency prepare for a presentation on its campaign results, what would you suggest the agency say to explain away the idea that you can evaluate a campaign with a single sales measure?

19-11. McDonald's Arabia recently announced the launch of its newest chicken sandwich range—the first collection of spicy chicken products. The introduction of such a new flavor emphasizes its ongoing commitment to respond to the preferences of its customers. As a marketer, explain the best communication tools required to create perception to this new flavor profile.

19-12. Explore the websites of two IMC evaluation companies, such as Ameritest (www.Ameritest.net), Ipsos ASI (www.ipsos.com), Millward Brown (www.millwardbrown.com) or Sapient (www.sapient.com), and compare the services they offer. If you were looking for a company to evaluate a campaign for recall, which one would you prefer? Why? What about if you were looking for a company to evaluate a campaign for digital impact? Why?

Take-Home Projects

19-13. ***Portfolio Project:*** Put together a portfolio of 10 ads for a set of product categories targeted to a college audience. Set up a focus group with participants recruited from among your friends and ask them to look at the ads. In a test of unaided awareness, ask them to list the ads they remember. Identify the top-performing ad and the bottom ad in this awareness test. Now ask the focus group participants to analyze the headline, the visual, and the brand identification of each ad. How do the two ads compare in terms of their ability to get attention and lock the brand in memory?

19-14. ***Mini-Case Analysis:*** Reread the chapter opening story about LiveWell. Explain what is meant when we say the point of this campaign is to build a brand relationship. How did this campaign succeed in that objective? How was effectiveness determined? If you were on the marketing team and were asked to develop a broader set of evaluation tools, what would you recommend and why?

TRACE North America Case

Evaluating Campaign Effectiveness

Read the TRACE case in the Appendix before coming to class.

19-15. If you worked for TRACE, how would you pretest this campaign prior to using it across the country?

19-16. What methods would you use to conduct concurrent and posttesting of the campaign?

19-17. If you worked for TRACE, how would you evaluate the success of the "Hard to Explain, Easy to Experience" campaign in market year to year?

Hands-On Case

The Company You Keep

Marketing communicators try to create coherent brand messages that lead to long-term brand relationships. In Part 5, you learned about tools that help deliver effective brand communication. Public relations, direct response, promotions, retail, business-to-business (BB), and nonprofit marketing communication—as well as everything related to the brand beyond these tools—is important because these tools help build brand meaning by cultivating relationships with their prospects and current customers.

Celebrity spokespeople can be used to enhance the credibility of a brand. William Shatner and Priceline.com; Michael Jordan and Nike, Hanes, and Wheaties; and Bill Cosby and Jell-O are some classic examples. Endorsers are especially effective when the famous person has a direct connection with the product. Michael Jordan can sell Nike sneakers because he could play basketball like few others. The connection is believable, and just maybe if we use that brand, we'll be a little better at the game ourselves.

Celebrity endorsers can have a positive impact on a brand. They can also cause it great harm. Kobe Bryant promoted McDonald's and Sprite before he was charged with sexual assault. Michael Vick had a relationship with Nike until he was convicted of conducting dogfights. Michael Phelps had a little problem with pot. Martha Stewart went to jail. Tiger Woods lost endorsements after his extramarital affairs were exposed. And the list goes on.

When celebrity spokespeople behave badly, how does that harm the relationship between consumers and the brand? No one wants their brand to be tarnished by negative associations such as those related to Lance Armstrong's confession of doping.

The scandal cost cyclist Lance Armstrong much more than his seven Tour de France titles and a ban from the sport. He lost the backing of his sponsors who couldn't risk being associated with negative public opinion. Reviewing Lance Armstrong endorsements in light of his well-publicized scandal can be instructive about what marketing communicators should do when a spokesperson misbehaves.

Clearly, clients have an investment to protect. Nike, Radio Shack, Anheuser-Busch, Trek, Easton-Bell Sports, 24-Hour Fitness, Honey Stinger, Oakley, and other sponsors distanced their brands from the sullied cyclist by ending their contracts with him. Armstrong even had to give up his position as chairman of the charity he created to support people with cancer, Livestrong. Bloomberg reported that the financial blow to Armstrong would cost him as much as $200 million in future earnings.

Can Armstrong's reputation be salvaged, and can he make a marketing comeback? Kobe Bryant and Tiger Woods were eventually able to maintain their relationships with Nike. The future is not clear for Armstrong.

Many public relations experts recommend that crises can be managed by coming clean—confessing and asking for public forgiveness. In an attempt to "control the narrative" of his life during an interview with Oprah Winfrey, the disgraced cyclist admitted to cheating by using performance-enhancing drugs. However, some observers did not find his confession convincing enough to forgive the cyclist.

Is there a difference between athletes who can make marketing comebacks, such as Bryant and Woods, and Armstrong, who some predict can't regain his reputation? Bryant and Woods had personal flaws for which they repented; Armstrong's downfall goes to the heart of the sport, a culture that accepted widespread doping. Ironically, Lance Armstrong, someone who did so much to build the sport, is the cause of much of its downfall as well as his own. According to industry estimates, beyond the cost to Armstrong, professional cycling stands to lose between $300 million and $400 million a year in sponsorships.

Would a brand with any credibility want to associate with a spokesperson with such a past as Armstrong's?

Consider This

P5-1. What effect can spokespeople have on brands and their relationship to consumers? Is any publicity good publicity?

P5-2. Do you think Lance Armstrong can make a marketing comeback? Explain.

P5-3. How can studies of sales data and social media be used to help gauge the effectiveness of brands and their celebrity endorsers?

P5-4. What advice would you give to a client such as Champion Sports if the brand decided it needed a celebrity strategy?

Sources: "Armstrong Scandal Sullies Cycling for Many Sponsors," October 22, 2012, www.adage.com; "The Implosion of Lance Armstrong's Endorsement Empire" October 19, 2012, www.adage.com; "How Will Sponsors React to Lance Armstrong Confessional?," January 17, 2013, www.adage.com; "Lance Armstrong Blew His Last Chance, Experts Say," January 19, 2013; Jason Gay, "What Lance Wants from Oprah," January 10, 2013, www.wsj.com; Aaron Lazare, "What Lance Armstrong Needs to Learn from Other Sports Apologies," January 20, 2013, www.wsj.com; Mason Levinson, Eben Novy-Williams, and Alex Duff, "Armstrong Faces $200 Million Salary Loss with Reputation Hit," October 24, 2012, www.bloomberg.com.

APPENDIX

TRACE*
2012 American Advertising Federation Competition

The following case was written by Phil Willet, assistant professor of advertising at the College of Journalism and Mass Communications at the University of Nebraska–Lincoln. Professor Willet is the faculty adviser to the National Student Advertising Competition team and winner of the 2012 American Advertising Federation National Student Advertising Competition. The competition is the oldest and largest advertising competition in the United States.

Trace North America: Multicultural Innovation

Hard to Explain, Easy to Experience

To Be Understood and Appreciated by the Target Audience, TRACE Has to Be Experienced

The challenge for the 2012 NSAC is to develop a fully integrated marketing campaign to help TRACE build awareness and lasting favorability among African American, Hispanic, and Chinese Millennial consumers in the United States. The campaign should focus on the TRACE innovation theme and ultimately lead to increased market share across this multicultural target.

The Problem

The demographic landscape of the United States is changing. Now more than ever, larger populations of multicultural individuals are present and fully integrated into all parts of American society. As such, building a market share in the African American, Hispanic, and Chinese Millennial markets is absolutely necessary. TRACE recognizes the need to connect with these audiences and will do so by generating increased awareness about its innovative brand.

Research

What we learned about Multicultural Millennials

Foundation

"People don't buy what you do, people buy why you do it."

This quote, from former advertiser Simon Sinek, is relevant to our challenge of increasing brand awareness in the Multicultural Millennial market. Naturally, our first step was to discover exactly *why* TRACE makes vehicles.

---

*TRACE CAR CO. is a fictitious brand created by the author. This case is based the actual case created by the University of Nebraska–Lincoln for the 2012 American Advertising Federation National Student Advertising Competition.

Brand Promise

The TRACE brand aspires to provide customers with innovative ideas for the joy of everyday driving. The target audience expresses its aspiration to make daily life vital and energetic by adding spice or edge and TRACE delivers innovative ideas to its customers.

TRACE lives, breathes, and implements innovation into every aspect of its company. *For customers to buy TRACE, they have to "buy" that TRACE is innovative.*

The target demographic must believe that TRACE adheres to its brand promise. The foundation of our research and the communication model was to observe how the target market relates to innovation and its importance in their lives.

Objectives and Methods

The University of Nebraska–Lincoln research team conducted 311 quantitative surveys, 35 video interviews, 30 written interviews, 10 dealership interviews, 5 test drive interviews, and 4 multicultural focus groups to find out the following:

1. What does innovation mean to Millennial Hispanics, Chinese, and African Americans?
2. What are the similarities and differences between these target markets?
3. How do the target markets want to see themselves in advertising?
4. What factors influence the car buying process?
5. How do the target markets feel about TRACE and its main competitors?

Research Insights

Chinese American

- Place heavy emphasis on education, work, and family
- Are sensitive to prestige
- Favor luxury auto advertising

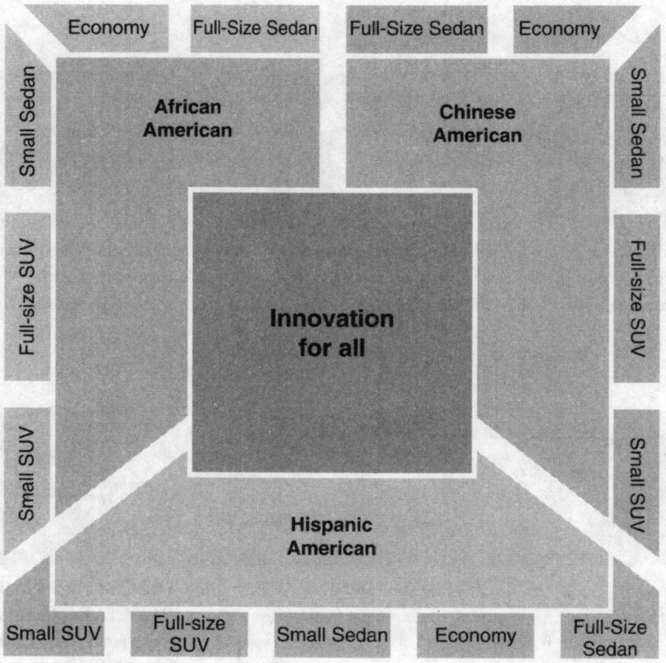

ABOVE: **This model demonstrates the parallels between TRACE, the target markets, and innovation. At the core of the model is innovation, surrounded by the three target markets. This layer represents what the audiences associate with innovation. We connected their associations to TRACE's five core models, composing the outer layer. This gave us a basis for positioning each model for the three markets.**

Hispanic American

- Focus on technological aspects of vehicles
- View features as more important than brand image
- Favor commercials that are especially creative or humorous

African American

- Female spouse or family member makes most purchasing decisions
- Loyal to brands they have grown up with
- Favor humorous advertising

Key Combined Insights on the Target Audiences:

- They have strong bonds with family. Family is *key* for big purchase decisions, typically accompanying the target markets to the dealership.
- They want to see themselves in advertising more often, being portrayed in a positive and professional light.
- They are youthful, price conscious consumers.
- Decisions rely *heavily* on brand experience.
- They associate with others based on interests more often than ethnicity.

Strategy:

What we want to say and reason to believe

Our Proposition: To be understood and appreciated by the target audience, TRACE has to be experienced.

Reason to Believe: Once the target markets know more about TRACE and its innovative features, they will realize that it is the intelligent choice. Features that the targets find innovative include Brake Override Technology, Vehicle Dynamic Control, and Continuously Variable Transmission. Once the markets experience these innovations, they will find them valuable in their purchasing decisions. *Driving a TRACE can't be explained; it must be experienced.*

"Ever since having so much space in my new TRACE, I have been inspired to make some changes."
—Alisha, 21

Alisha drags chair across classroom, away from group of students. Other students look confused.

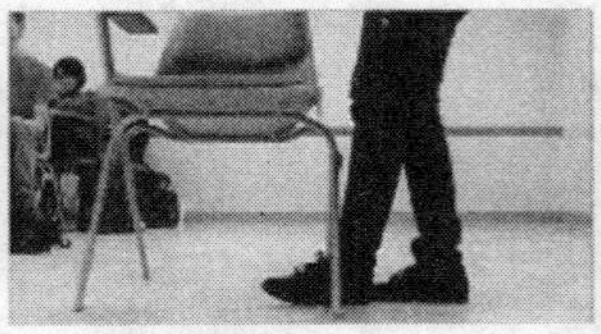

Closeup of desk chair as it is moved across the floor. "SCREEECH!"

Classmates have confused expressions while Alisha looks relaxed in her moved desk.

Panning of TRACE.
MUSIC: Countdown-Beyoncé
VOICEOVER: "The new TRACE is big on space but small on price. It's innovation that's . . ."

Wide shot of the TRACE: ". . . but easy to experience."

TRACE Logo including the "Hard To Explain, Easy To Experience" and "Innovation for All" tags.
MUSIC: fade out
Alisha looks relaxed in her moved seat. ". . . hard to explain . . ."

Creative Executions

The television spots pair a vehicle and its features with a specific demographic in the target audience. A character in each of the spots has experienced a TRACE feature and has been inspired to make changes in their life to reflect these innovations.

Because TRACE is an innovative company, we wanted our print campaign to share that spirit of innovation. We created ads that feature members of the target market and use new tactics, which include foldout pages and peel-off stickers. The creative format will drive home our idea that TRACE's innovations are hard to explain but easy to experience.

Promotions and Public Relations

In addition to the print and television, the "Hard to Explain, Easy to Experience" creative team created point-of-purchase dealership displays, interactive walkways, in-window outdoor displays with the ability to post to Facebook Timeline, out-of-home theater displays, and elevator wraps. Public relation efforts included post-recycled playgrounds with an innovation playground Web application and multicultural scholarships.

Media

Our $100MM media plan will go a long way in helping us reach multicultural Millennials.

Objectives

- Nationwide: Maintain 70 percent reach with an average frequency of 3 throughout the year
- Spot Markets: Achieve 85 percent reach with an average frequency of 4 during targeted months
- Generate buzz through outdoor, digital, and traditional advertising integration

Strategies

- Pulse media by maintaining a yearlong national presence with extra emphasis placed in strategic areas at strategic times. TRACE sales data from 2010 and 2011 was also used in these decisions.

In-Window Outdoor

In-window outdoor technology creates an interactive storefront display to allow consumers to interact with TRACE's history and its Facebook Timeline page. Individual screens reflect real-time footage of people interacting with TRACE vehicles correlating to a specific year in TRACE history. The selected year determines what is reflected in the window. For example, if they select the year 1934, a black-and-white display of a TRACE from that year will appear. Consumers can then take photos of themselves with the vehicles and share it to their own Facebook Timeline profiles.

- April–May to launch campaign and coincide with May's typically high car demand
- August–September to coincide with the launch of new models and higher-than-average car demand
- December because it historically ranks first or second in car-buying volume for TRACE
- March because it historically ranks first or second in car-buying volume for TRACE and to finish the campaign on a strong note
- Target the top 10 markets in population for each of the three segments (total of 16 markets with the overlap)

Tactics

Media buys are based on each of the target audiences' media usage and lifestyle. While some vehicles are geared toward one of the target markets, others can be used for all three.

Overview

The April 2013–March 2014 "Hard to Explain, Easy to Experience" campaign will use an optimized combination of traditional and nontraditional media to maximize our reach to three target markets as well as generate buzz around the TRACE brand.

Evaluation

We will explore several tactics to measure the effectiveness of our campaign.

Concurrent and posttesting will be conducted to reaffirm the achievement of our objectives during the campaign. Concurrent testing will take place at three-month intervals during the campaign to measure the level of effectiveness. Concurrent testing will include tracking studies of telephone interviews, e-mail interviews, surveys, and product audits. Surveys will accompany these methods to provide a view of the campaign's effectiveness.

In order to keep a better idea of the target market's foot traffic into TRACE dealerships, each dealership will keep a database on all multicultural Millennials that enter a dealership and express interest in the cars.

Posttesting will occur directly after the complete run of the campaign and will measure several factors, including recognition, recall, attitudes, awareness, and sales. Recognition tests will prove most valuable for evaluating brand awareness and lasting favorability among the target market.

Summary

The success of the "Hard to Explain, Easy to Experience" campaign will be determined by its primary goal of driving multiculturals to the dealership to experience TRACE's innovation. The car-buying process is a major and somewhat complicated decision. We believe the better educated the consumer, the more likely TRACE can fulfill its brand promise of "Innovation for all."

University of Nebraska-Lincoln NSAC 2012 Agency

Account Services: Hans Christensen, Account Supervisor; Kevin McCaskill, Account Supervisor; Calvin Drey, Account Planner/Project Manager/PR; Michelle Pineda, Account Coordinator/Project Manager/PR; Paul Henderson, Account Planner; Chelsey Wahlstrom, Account Planner/PR; Zee Chiweshe, Account Planner/PR; Jana Schneider, Account Planner/PR; Ashley Turner, Account Planner.

Media Services: Sara Smits, Media Director; Bingjie Zhao, Media Planner; Tayler Thomas, Account Planner/Media Planner/PR; Megan Homolka, Copywriter/Media Planner.

Creative: Landon Stahmer, Creative Director; Rance Ristau, Project Manager; Nolan Gauthier, Copywriter; Tim Obermueller, Copywriter; Russell Troxel, Copywriter; Dana Oltman, Art Director; Dennis Bukowski, Art Director; Maddie Jager, Art Director; Dylan McCaugherty, Interactive Designer/Writer; Abby Meyer, Film.

Glossary

3-D television *(p. 382)* Television programs that have been filmed using technology that creates the illusion of depth, which is the third dimension—the other two being width and height.

A

Account executive *(p. 43)* A person who acts as a liaison between the client and the agency.

Account management *(p. 54)* People and processes at an ad agency that facilitate the relationship between the agency and the client.

Account planner *(p. 227)* The person responsible for the strategy and its implementation in the creative work.

Account planning *(pp. 55, 227)* A process of using research to gain information about the brand in its marketplace, the consumer's perspective, or both, and to use that research to contribute directly to advertising development.

Account services *(p. 54)* The account management function of an agency, which acts as a liaison between the client and the agency.

Acquired needs *(p. 161)* A driving force learned from culture, society, and the environment.

Active publics *(p. 482)* Those people who communicate and organize to do something about an issue or situation.

Added value *(p. 70)* A marketing activity, such as advertising, makes a product more appealing or useful.

Addressable media *(p. 340)* Media, such as mail, the Internet, and the telephone, that carry messages to identifiable customers or prospects.

Addressable television *(p. 382)* Television technology that permits the signal to be personalized to a home.

Adese *(p. 277)* Formula writing that uses clichés, generalities, stock phrases, and superlatives.

Adoption process *(p. 175)* Buying behavior that reflects the speed with which people are willing to try something new.

Advertainment *(p. 355)* A form of persuasive advertising in which the commercials look like TV shows or short films, and provide entertainment as opposed to high levels of information.

Advertisement *(p. 37)* A notice about a product (good, service, or idea) that is designed to get the attention of a target audience.

Advertiser *(p. 48)* A person or organization that initiates the advertising process.

Advertising *(p. 36)* Paid nonpersonal communication from an identified sponsor using mass media to persuade or influence an audience.

Advertising agency *(p. 50)* An organization that provides a variety of professional services to its client who is the advertiser of a product.

Advertorials *(p. 372)* An advertising page or special segment that looks like regular editorial pages but is identified by the word "advertisement" at the top; the content is often about a company, product, or brand and written by the organization's public relations department.

Advocacy *(p. 146)* A type of advertising that communicates a viewpoint.

Advocacy advertising *(p. 489)* A type of corporate advertising that involves creating advertisements and purchasing space to deliver a specific, targeted message.

Affective response *(p. 134)* A response caused by or expressing feelings and emotions.

Affiliates *(p. 375)* A station that contracts with a national network to carry network-originated programming during part of its schedule.

Agency networks *(p. 54)* Large conglomerations of agencies under a central ownership.

Agency-of-record (AOR) *(p. 50)* An advertising agency that manages the business between a company and the agencies it has contracts with.

AIDA *(p. 127)* A hierarchy of effects identified as Attention, Interest, Desire, and Action.

Aided recall *(p. 599)* When one can remember an idea after seeing a cue.

Ambush marketing *(p. 551)* In event marketing, a competitor advertises in such a way that it steals visibility from the designated sponsor.

Animation *(pp. 294, 323)* A film or video technique in which objects or drawings are filmed one frame at a time.

Annual report *(p. 491)* A financial document legally required of all publicly held companies.

Answer print *(p. 326)* The finished version of the commercial, with the audio and video recorded together.

Aperture *(p. 453)* The ideal moment for exposing consumers to an advertising message.

Appeal *(p. 250)* An advertising approach that connects with some need, want, or emotion that makes the product message attractive, attention getting, or interesting.

Argument *(p. 143)* A cognitive strategy that uses logic, reasons, and proof to build convictions.

Art director *(p. 44)* The person who is primarily responsible for the visual image of the advertisement.

Association *(p. 139)* The process used to link a product with a positive experience, personality, or lifestyle.

Attention *(p. 122)* Concentrating the mind on a thought or idea.

Attitude *(pp. 141, 170)* A learned predisposition that we hold toward an object, person, or idea.

Attributes *(p. 251)* A distinctive feature of a product.

Average frequency *(p. 445)* The average number of times an audience has an opportunity to be exposed to a media vehicle or vehicles in a specified time span.

Aware publics *(p. 482)* Those people who recognize the connection between a problem and themselves or others but do not communicate about it.

Awareness *(p. 132)* The degree to which a message has made an impression on the viewer or reader.

B

B2C2C *(p. 420)* A model of communication that begins with messages from a business (B) directed to key influential consumers (C) who then communicate with other consumers (C).

Back translation *(p. 296)* The practice of translating ad copy into a second language and then translating that version back into the original language to check the accuracy of the translation.

Bandwagon appeals *(p. 142)* The idea that people respond to popular causes and ideas and want to join up or adopt a trendy viewpoint.

Banner ad *(p. 390)* Small, often rectangular-shaped graphic that appears at the top of a Web page.

Behavioral targeting *(p. 517)* The practice of identifying groups of people who might be in the market for a product based on their actions—particularly the patterns of their online behavior.

Beliefs *(p. 141)* A term related to a person's cognitive processing—how they arrive at a position, viewpoint, or decision based on their knowledge, attitudes, and opinions.

Believability *(p. 143)* The extent to which a marketing communication message is accepted as true.

Benchmarking *(p. 481)* Comparing a result against some other known result from a comparable effort.

Benefit *(p. 251)* Statement about what the product can do for the user.

Big Idea *(p. 257)* A creative idea that expresses an original advertising thought.

Billboarding *(p. 403)* The practice of massing a set of packages with a consistent design to create visual impact on a shelf.

Bleed *(p. 371)* A full-page ad with no outside margins—the printed area extends to the edge of the page.

Bleed throughs *(p. 463)* In printed communication, the image on one side of a sheet of paper can be seen on the other usually because the ink has thoroughly saturated the paper.

Blind headline *(p. 282)* An indirect headline that gives little information.

Blog *(p. 414)* A personal diary-like Web page.

Blogola *(p. 98)* Company representatives who pose as consumers or paid bloggers who post endorsements as customer reviews online without the sponsorship being made known to readers, also known as flogging.

Body copy *(p. 280)* The text of the message.

Brag-and-boast copy *(p. 278)* Self-important copy that focuses on the company rather than the consumer.

Brainfag *(p. 261)* In creative thinking, this is the point where concentration ceases to produce ideas because of mental fatigue and the mind closes down.

Brainstorming *(p. 262)* A creative thinking technique using free association in a group environment to stimulate inspiration.

Brand *(p. 72)* A name, term, design, or symbol that identifies the goods, services, institution, or idea sold by a marketer.

Brand advertising *(p. 39)* An advertising strategy that focuses on creating an image or perception of a brand.

Brand advocacy *(p. 420)* A word-of-mouth strategy that uses customer referrals to create buzz and connect with influential contacts who will spread information about the brand.

Brand advocate *(p. 420)* A key customer or stakeholder who communicates positive information within a circle of friends or contacts.

Brand communication *(p. 64)* All the various marketing communication messages and brand experiences that create and maintain a coherent brand concept or image.

Brand communication research *(p. 183)* Research that focuses on messages and targets, including the brand's marketplace and communication environment, as well as message development research, media planning research, evaluation, and competitive information.

Brand communication ROI *(p. 606)* An evaluation technique that compares the costs of creating and running brand communication versus the revenue it generates.

Brand communities *(p. 160)* Groups of people devoted to a particular brand, such as the Harley Owners Group (HOG) for Harley-Davidson.

Brand concept *(p. 75)* The impressions created by a brand's tangible and intangible features – in other words what the brand stands for.

Brand development index (BDI) *(p. 452)* A numerical technique used to indicate a brand's sales within a particular market relative to all other markets where the brand is sold.

Brand equity *(p. 80)* The value associated with a brand; the reputation that the brand name or symbol connotes.

Brand extension *(p. 81)* Use of an established brand name with a related line of products.

Brand icon *(p. 252)* A character used to represent the brand.

Brand identity *(p. 75)* Unique characteristics of a product within a product category.

Brand image *(pp. 40, 78)* A special meaning or mental representation created for a product by giving it a distinctive name and identity.

Brand integrity *(p. 564)* A brand is more believable because what it says and does matches what others say about it.

Brand licensing *(p. 81)* A partner company rents the brand name and transfers some of its brand equity to another product.

Brand linkage *(p. 139)* The extent to which an advertising message is connected to the brand and locked into the memory of people who see the message.

Brand linkage test *(p. 599)* A research method that asks viewers to link a specific brand or product category to a specific commercial.

Brand loyalty *(pp. 80, 143)* The degree of attachment that a customer has to a particular brand as expressed by repeat sales.

Brand management *(p. 72)* An organizational structure that places a manager or management team in charge of a brand's total marketing efforts.

Brand name *(p. 44)* The part of the brand that can be spoken, such as words, letters, or numbers.

Brand personality *(p. 78)* The image projected by a brand that often resembles characteristics of people.

Brand position *(p. 78)* The location a brand occupies in consumers' minds relative to its competitors.

Brand promise *(p. 78)* Communication that sets expectations for what a customer believes will happen when the product is used.

Brand relationship *(p. 80)* Communication aimed at delivering reminders about familiar brands and building trust.

Brand reputation *(p. 418)* What other people say and think about a brand.

Brand steward *(p. 81)* A person who manages a brand's marketing and communication.

Brand transformation *(p. 75)* A brand's meaning is more valuable than the products, goods, or services it represents.

Brand value *(pp. 80, 561)* Enhanced meaning of a brand that adds worth to products and services.

Branded apps *(p. 418)* A software program mounted on a cell phone, computer, or social networking page that contains information sponsored by or related to a brand.

Branded entertainment *(p. 402)* Programs, such as the Hallmark Hall of Fame, that are sponsored by a particular brand.

Branded media *(p. 355)* This refers to forms of entertainment media that are owned by an organization and used to create high levels of engagement with a brand.

Branding *(p. 72)* The process of creating a unique identity for a product.

Break-even analysis *(p. 602)* A type of payout plan that seeks to determine the point at which the total cost of the promotion exceeds the total revenues, identifying the point where the effort cannot break even.

Broadcasting media *(p. 339)* Media, such as radio, television, and interactive media, which transmit sounds or images electronically.

Broadcast network *(p. 378)* A national group of affiliated stations through which programming and advertising are distributed.

Broadsheets *(p. 510)* A newspaper with a page size eight columns wide and 22 inches deep.

Brokers *(p. 345)* People or companies who sell space (in print) or time (in broadcast) for a variety of media.

Business-to-business (B2B) advertising *(p. 39)* Targets other businesses.

Business-to-business (B2B) market *(p. 66)* Organizations that have products for use in conducting their business.

Business philosophy *(p. 210)* The fundamental principles that guide the operations of the business.

Buzz *(pp. 41, 419)* Gossip created by people over a popular interest in something.

C

Cable radio *(p. 374)* A technology that uses cable television receivers to deliver static-free music via wires plugged into cable subscribers' audio systems.

Cable television *(p. 378)* A form of subscription television in which the signals are carried to households by a cable.

Call centers *(p. 513)* Facilities with banks of phones and representatives who call prospects (outbound) or answer customer calls (inbound).

Call to action *(pp. 145, 256, 284)* A concluding line that tells people how to buy the product.

Call-out *(p. 280)* A block of text separate from the main display copy and headline where the idea is presented.

Campaign *(p. 39)* A comprehensive advertising plan for a series of different but related ads that appear in different media across a specified time period.

Captions *(p. 281)* Text that explains what is happening in a corresponding photo or illustration.

Carrot mob *(p. 142)* A technique used by environmentalists to reward companies that support green marketing.

Carryover effect *(pp. 454, 606)* A measure of residual effect (awareness or recall) of the advertising message some time after the advertising period has ended.

Casting *(p. 291)* Finding the right person for the role.

Catalog *(p. 512)* A multipage direct-mail publication that shows a variety of merchandise.

Category development index (CDI) *(p. 452)* A numerical technique that indicates the relative consumption rate in a particular market for a particular product category.

Cause marketing *(pp. 79, 479, 581)* Sponsoring a good cause in the hope that the association will result in positive public opinion about the company.

Cease-and-desist order *(p. 111)* An FTC remedy for false or deceptive advertising that requires an advertiser to stop its unlawful practices.

Change agent *(p. 483)* Programs and individuals whose goal it is to change the attitudes that drive behavior.

Channel markets *(p. 67)* The members of a distribution chain, including resellers or intermediaries.

Channel marketing *(pp. 67, 544)* Advertising and promotion efforts directed at members of the distribution channel.

Channel of communication *(p. 123)* The media through which an advertisement is presented.

Channel of distribution *(p. 66)* People and organizations involved in moving products from producers to consumers.

Channels *(p. 51)* Media or companies such as local newspaper or radio stations that transmit communication messages from the advertiser to the audience and from consumers back to companies.

Circulars *(p. 369)* Preprinted advertisements ranging in size from a single page to more than 60 pages that are often printed elsewhere and supplied to a newspaper where it is inserted between sections.

Circulation *(p. 366)* The number of copies sold.

Claim *(p. 251)* A statement about the product's performance.

Claim substantiation *(p. 110)* The reasonable basis for making an assertion about product performance.

Classified advertising *(pp. 43, 368)* Commercial messages arranged in the newspaper according to the interests of readers.

Claymation *(p. 324)* A stop-motion animation technique in which figures sculpted from clay are filmed one frame at a time.

Clichés *(p. 256)* Generic, nonoriginal, non-novel ideas.

Click art *(p. 309)* See Clip art.

Click-through *(pp. 295, 391)* The act of clicking on a button on a website that takes the viewer to a different website.

Click-through rates *(p. 602)* A method of measuring the effectiveness of online advertising by dividing the number of times the ad was presented on a website by the number of times it was clicked on by viewers.

Clip art *(p. 309)* Generic, copyright-free art that can be used by anyone who buys the book or service.

Closing *(p. 463)* Represents the last date to send an ad to production.

Closing paragraph *(p. 284)* The last paragraph of body copy in an ad that sums up the selling message, usually ending with a call to action.

Clutter *(p. 124)* The excessive number of messages delivered to a target audience.

Cobranding *(pp. 81, 552)* A product offered by two companies with both companies' brands present.

Comarketing *(p. 552)* Programs through which manufacturers partner with retailers in joint promotions.

Code of ethics *(p. 104)* The rules and standards for a system of socially responsible professional practice.

Cognition *(p. 136)* How consumers respond to information, learn, and understand.

Cognitive dissonance *(p. 162)* A tendency to justify the discrepancy between what you receive and what you expected to receive.

Cognitive learning *(p. 137)* When advertisers want people to know something new after watching or hearing a message.

Cold call *(p. 513)* Contacts that are made to leads that have not been qualified as interested; also includes cold calls made by telemarketers to random phone numbers.

Collateral materials *(pp. 286, 491)* Brochures and other forms of product literature used in support of an advertising, public relations, or sales promotion effort.

Color separation *(p. 319)* The process of splitting a color image into four images recorded on negatives; each negative represents one of the four process colors.

360° communication *(p. 561)* The practice of looking a brand from all directions and all points of view using a brand vision that surrounds all the brand's interactions with all its stakeholders.

Commercial speech *(p. 107)* Our legal right to say what we want to promote commercial activity, as defined by the First Amendment.

Commission system *(p. 43)* The procedures through which advertising agencies are paid a commission for placing ads—buying time and space—on behalf of their clients.

Communication audit *(p. 481)* A type of background research that assesses the internal and external PR environment that affects the organization's audience, objectives, competitors, and past results.

Communication brief *(p. 230)* A strategy document that explains the consumer insight and summarizes the message and media strategy.

Comparative advertising *(p. 96)* A message strategy that explicitly or implicitly compares the features of two or more brands.

Comparison *(p. 252)* An advertising strategy that compares two or more brands.

Competitive advantage *(pp. 68, 224)* Features or benefits of a product that let it outperform its competitors.

Compiled list *(p. 519)* In database marketing, a list that is created by merging several lists and purging duplicate entries.

Composition *(p. 316)* The art of arranging the way the elements in a photograph are positioned.

Comprehension *(p. 137)* The process by which people understand, make sense of things, and acquire knowledge.

Comprehensives *(p. 316)* A layout that looks as much like the final printed ad as possible.

Concept testing *(pp. 192, 594)* When a simple statement of an idea is tried out on people who are representative of the target audience in order to get their reactions to the Big Idea.

Concepting *(p. 256)* Creating a big idea.

Conditioned learning *(p. 140)* Learning through association by connecting a stimulus to a reward through repeated exposure to a stimulus that eventually leads to the reward.

Connection planning *(p. 346)* Another way to refer to media planning but in this approach the emphasis is on engagement and two-way communication opportunities.

Consent decree *(p. 111)* A formal FTC agreement with an advertiser that obligates the advertiser to stop its deceptive practices.

Considered purchase *(p. 142)* Buying something after gathering and evaluating information.

Consolidated services *(p. 465)* Company action of bringing planning and buying functions together.

Consumer behavior *(p. 156)* The process of an individual or group selecting, purchasing, using, or disposing of products, services, ideas, or experiences to satisfy needs and desires.

Consumer-generated advertising *(p. 57)* Advertising created by consumers for a brand.

Consumer insight *(p. 225)* Planning conclusions and decisions about why people behave as they do based on solid consumer research and thoughtful analyses of the findings.

Consumer market *(p. 66)* Selling products to a general (non-business) audience.

Consumer research *(p. 183)* A type of market research that identifies people who are in the market for a product.

Consumer research panel *(p. 198)* Information provided by an ongoing group of carefully selected people interested in a particular topic or product category.

Contact points *(p. 562)* The media, as well as other places and ways, where a consumer engages in a brand experience.

Content analysis *(p. 190)* Research that analyzes articles, news stories, and other printed materials for themes and positive or negative mentions of a brand or company.

Contest *(p. 540)* A form of promotion that requires participants to compete for a prize or prizes based on some sort of skill or ability.

Continuity *(p. 454)* Even, continuous advertising over the time span of the advertising campaign.

Continuity program *(p. 552)* A program designed to encourage loyalty and repeat purchases.

Continuous strategy *(p. 454)* A media strategy that spreads the advertising evenly over a period.

Continuous tone *(p. 319)* Photographs are images that have a range of tones from white to black and all the shades of gray in between.

Controlled circulation *(p. 369)* Publications that are distributed, usually free, to selected individuals.

Controlled media *(p. 485)* Media that the direct marketer either owns or has delivered through carefully controlled criteria by a contracted company.

Convergence *(p. 343)* Because of the digitization of media forms, specialized media, such as newspapers and television, are becoming more alike in their content and how they are delivered online.

Conversion rates *(pp. 503, 602)* In sales, changing a prospect into a customer.

Conviction *(p. 143)* A particularly strong belief that has been anchored firmly in one's attitudes.

Cool hunters *(p. 174)* People who specialize in spotting trends.

Co-op advertising *(p. 367)* Also called cooperative advertising; an arrangement between a retailer and manufacturer in which the manufacturer reimburses the retailer for all or part of the retailer's advertising costs.

Copycat advertising *(p. 259)* Using some other brand's creative idea.

Copyright *(p. 107)* The owner or creator of certain types of original works have the sole right to reproduce and distribute the work.

Copytesting *(p. 194)* Evaluating the effectiveness of an ad, either in a draft form or after it has been used.

Copywriter *(pp. 44, 275)* The person who writes the text for an ad.

Core values *(p. 157)* Underlying values that govern a person's (or a brand's) attitudes and behavior.

Corporate advertising *(pp. 39, 487)* A type of advertising used by firms to build awareness of a company, its products, and the nature of its business.

Corporate culture *(p. 157)* The values and attitudes that shape the behavior of an organization and its employees.

Corporate identity advertising *(p. 489)* Promotional method aimed at enhancing or maintaining a company's reputation in the marketplace.

Corporate image *(p. 487)* A perception of a company that its stakeholders create in their minds from messages and experiences with the company.

Corporate relations *(p. 479)* Relations between a corporation and the public involving an organization's image and reputation.

Corporate social responsibility *(p. 479)* Programs designed to create a platform of good citizenship for corporations and other organizations.

Corrective advertising *(p. 111)* An FTC directive that requires an advertiser to run truthful ads to counter deceptive ads.

Cost per lead *(p. 602)* Record of how well a click-through generates prospects.

Cost per point (CPP) *(p. 459)* A method of comparing alternative media vehicles on the basis of what it costs to deliver 1,000 readers, viewers, or listeners; the cost of an advertising unit (30-second TV or radio spot, for example) per 1,000 impressions.

Cost per thousand (CPM) *(p. 459)* The cost of exposing each 1,000 members of the target audience to the advertising message.

Coupons *(p. 540)* Legal certificates offered by manufacturers and retailers that grant specified savings on selected products when presented for redemption at the point-of-purchase.

Coverage *(pp. 438, 605)* The degree to which a particular advertising medium delivers audiences within a specific geographical area.

Crawl *(p. 322)* Computer-generated letters that move across the bottom of the screen.

Creative boutique *(p. 54)* An advertising agency that specializes in the creative side of advertising.

Creative brief *(pp. 230, 243)* The document that outlines the key strategy decisions and details the key execution elements.

Creative concept *(p. 256)* A Big Idea that is original, supports the ad strategy, and dramatizes the selling point.

Creative director *(p. 242)* The person responsible for managing the work of the creative team.

Creative strategy *(p. 243)* The determination of the right message for a particular target audience, a message approach that delivers the advertising objectives.

Credibility *(p. 143)* The believability or reliability of a source of information.

Crisis management *(p. 480)* Management of people and events during times of great danger or trouble.

Cross-functional management *(p. 564)* A practice that uses teams to coordinate activities that involve different areas in and outside a company.

Cross-media *(p. 345)* See Multichannel.

Cross-media integration *(p. 576)* The practice of using a variety of media and messages that work together to create a coherent brand impression.

Cross promotion *(p. 553)* A type of cooperative marketing program in which marketers use associations between complementary brands to create a joint promotional program.

Crowdsourcing *(pp. 198, 423)* Aggregating the wisdom of Internet users in a type of digital brainstorming that collects opinions and ideas from a digital community.

Cultural cohort *(p. 164)* A segment of customers from multiple countries who share common characteristics that translate into common wants and needs.

Cultural imperialism *(p. 93)* Imposing a foreign culture on a local culture; usually referred to as the impact of Western culture, products, and lifestyles on a more traditional culture.

Culture *(p. 156)* The complex whole of tangible items, intangible concepts, and social behaviors that define a group of people or a way of life.

Customer referral *(p. 420)* A form of brand advocacy, this practice seeks to involve satisfied customers in spreading the message about a brand.

Customer satisfaction *(p. 143)* The degree to which there is a match between the customer's expectations about a product and the product's actual performance.

Customer service *(pp. 70, 409)* The process of managing customers' interactive experiences with a brand, particularly those experiences based on complaints or requests for information or service.

Cut *(p. 325)* An abrupt transition from one shot to another.

Cutouts *(p. 385)* Irregularly shaped extensions added to the top, bottom, or sides of standard outdoor boards.

D

Dailies *(p. 325)* Processed scenes on film that a director reviews to determine what needs correcting.

Data mining *(p. 520)* Shifting through and sorting a company's computer database records to target customers and maintain relationships with them.

Databases *(p. 517)* Lists of consumers with information that helps target and segment those who are highly likely to be in the market for a certain product.

Daypart *(p. 376)* The way the broadcast schedule is divided into time segments during a day.

Debossing *(p. 321)* A depressed image created on paper by applying heat and pressure.

Deceptive advertising *(p. 110)* Advertising that misleads consumers by making claims that are false or by failure to fully disclose important information.

Decode *(p. 123)* The interpretation of a message by a receiver.

Delayed effects *(p. 147)* An advertisement's impact occurs at a later time (than its time of delivery).

Demand creation *(p. 91)* An external message creates a want or need.

Demographics *(p. 166)* Human traits such as age, income, race, and gender.

Demonstration *(p. 251)* An advertising strategy that shows how the product works.

Designated marketing area (DMA) *(pp. 170, 437)* Households in each major U.S. metropolitan area, or TV or radio broadcast coverage area.

Diaries *(p. 200)* In advertising research, consumers record their consumption activities, including media use.

Die-cut *(p. 321)* Using a sharp-edged stamp to cut irregular shapes in printed materials.

Differentiation *(p. 137)* An advertising strategy that calls to the consumer's attention the features that make a product unique or better than the competition.

Diffusion *(p. 175)* Adoption of new ideas based on Everett Rogers' Diffusion of Innovations theory.

(digital) ecosystem *(p. 602)* All the digital experiences consumers have with a brand.

Digital displays *(p. 385)* Outdoor advertising that uses digital technology to create an image.

Digital installations *(p. 408)* These are touch-screen formats, such as kiosks and electronic walls, that carry promotional messages and organizational content.

Digitization *(p. 319)* Converting art into computer-readable images.

Direct action *(p. 144)* Immediate response to advertising, such as completing an order form and sending it back by return mail.

Direct advertising *(p. 408)* A form of direct marketing, this is an advertising platform that delivers messages directly to a receiver without an intermediary such as traditional media or sales staff.

Direct-response brand communication *(p. 500)* A type of promotional message that motivates an immediate response usually leading to a purchase without the intermediary impact of a retailer or sales representative.

Direct mail *(p. 508)* A type of direct marketing that sends the offer to a prospective customer by mail.

Direct marketing (DM) *(p. 70)* A type of marketing that uses media to contact a prospect directly and elicit a response without the intervention of a retailer or personal sales.

Direct-action headline *(p. 282)* A headline that is straightforward and informative and leads to some kind of action.

Direct-response advertising *(p. 39)* A type of marketing communication that achieves an action-oriented objective as a result of the advertising message.

Direct-response marketing *(pp. 408, 501)* A multi-channel form of marketing that connects sellers and customers directly rather than through an intermediary, such as a retailer.

Directional advertising *(p. 373)* Tells people where to go to find goods and services.

Discretionary income *(p. 169)* The money available for spending after taxes and necessities are covered.

Display advertising *(p. 368)* Sponsored messages that can be of any size and location within the newspaper, except the editorial page.

Display copy *(p. 280)* Type set in larger sizes that is used to attract the reader's attention.

Distribution *(p. 69)* In marketing, the channel of distribution describes the route a product takes moving from its manufacturer to the customer.

Distribution chain *(p. 66)* The companies involved in moving a product from the manufacturer to the customer.

Divergent thinking *(p. 260)* In creative thinking, people trying to come up with a creative idea are advised to move away from logical thinking (inductive, deductive) and look for unexpected ideas by making mental jumps and creative leaps.

Double-page spread *(p. 371)* An advertisement that crosses two facing pages in a magazine.

DVR *(p. 380)* A digital video recorder that allows users to record television shows and watch them whenever they like, a practice called time-shifting.

Dubbing *(p. 326)* The process of making duplicate copies of a videotape.

E

E-commerce *(p. 412)* Selling goods and services through electronic means, usually over the Internet.

Earned media *(p. 342)* Free publicity generated through promotional efforts other than paid media, often resulting from public relations or social media.

Effective frequency *(p. 446)* A planning concept that determines a range (minimum and maximum) of repeat exposures for a message.

E score *(p. 253)* A system of ratings for celebrities, athletes, and other newsmakers that measures their appeal.

Effects *(p. 127)* The type of impact delivered by an advertisement or other marketing communication.

Electronic walls *(p. 408)* A digital installation that is often found in lobbies and carries corporate information accessed through touch screens.

Embossing *(p. 321)* The application of pressure to create a raised surface image on paper.

Emotional appeals *(p. 135)* Message strategies that seek to arouse our feelings.

Employee communication programs *(p. 408)* Information and training programs for employees that help them deliver brand messages strategically.

Employee relations *(p. 478)* Relations between the company and its workers.

Encode *(p. 123)* The creation of a message in words and pictures by a source.

Endorsement *(p. 98)* Any advertising message that consumers reasonably believe reflects the opinions, beliefs, or experiences of an individual, group, or institution.

Endorser *(p. 252)* A person who testifies on behalf of the product (goods, service, or idea).

Engagement *(p. 142)* Advertisement that gets and holds the attention of its audience.

Ethics *(p. 101)* A set of moral principles that guide our actions.

Ethnographic research *(p. 199)* A form of anthropological research that studies the way people live their lives.

Evaluative research *(p. 194)* Research that determines how well the ad or campaign achieved its goals.

Event marketing *(p. 548)* Creating a promotion program around a sponsored event.

Execution *(p. 244)* The different variations used to represent the message of a campaign.

Experiential marketing *(p. 602)* Marketing strategies and events that connect a brand and a prospective customer in a personal and involving way.

Experimental research *(p. 187)* Scientific research in which an investigator controls most of the key variables in order to study the impact of manipulating one or more—changing the product's price or the type of appeal in an ad, for example.

Expert panel *(p. 198)* A type of research that involves obtaining the opinions from a group of people who are recognized as experts in the area being studied.

Exposure *(pp. 131, 349, 439)* The opportunity for a reader, viewer, or listener to see or hear an advertisement.

Extensions *(p. 385)* Embellishments to painted billboards that expand the scale and break away from the standard rectangle limitations.

Exterior transit advertising *(p. 388)* Advertising posters that are mounted on the sides, rear, and tops of vehicles.

Extranets *(p. 492)* Networked systems of electronic communication that allow employees to be in contact with each other in one business with its business partners.

F

False advertising *(p. 95)* Advertising that is misleading or simply untrue.

Family *(p. 160)* Two or more people who are related by blood, marriage, or adoption and live in the same household.

Fan pages *(p. 422)* Chat rooms and other websites where brand loyalists share stories about a favorite brand.

Fast-moving consumer goods (fmcg) *(p. 66)* European term for package goods.

Feature analysis *(p. 223)* A comparison of your product's features against those of competing products.

Feature story *(pp. 279, 490)* In the media, these are human-interest stories, in contrast to hard news.

Features *(pp. 223, 251)* A product attribute or characteristic.

Federal Communications Commission (FCC) *(p. 108)* A U.S. government agency that regulates broadcast media and can eliminate ads that are deceptive or offensive.

Fee system *(p. 56)* A compensation tool for advertisers requiring that client and agency agree on an hourly fee or rate or negotiate a charge for a specific project.

Film-to-tape transfer *(p. 323)* A procedure by which film is shot, processed, and then transferred to videotape.

Financial relations *(p. 479)* Communications with the financial community.

Flash mob *(pp. 144, 407)* A sudden and conspicuous gathering of people in public places generated by viral e-mail messages, tele-communications or social media.

Flighting strategy *(p. 454)* An advertising scheduling pattern characterized by a period of intensified activity called a flight, followed by a period of no advertising called a hiatus.

Focus groups *(p. 197)* A group interview led by a moderator.

Four Ps *(p. 65)* The marketing mix, which includes the product (design and performance), price (value), place (distribution), and promotion (marketing communication).

Four-color printing *(p. 319)* A printing process that replicates the full color of a photograph although it only uses four colors of ink.

Free association *(p. 262)* Getting a new idea by creating a juxtaposition between two seemingly unrelated thoughts—usually done by describing everything that comes into your mind when you are given a word to think about.

Free standing insert (FSI) *(p. 369)* Preprinted advertisement placed loosely in the newspaper.

Frequency *(pp. 350, 445)* The number of times an audience has an opportunity to be exposed to a media vehicle or vehicles in a specified time span.

Frequency distribution *(p. 445)* A media planning term describing exactly how many times each person is exposed to a message by percentage of the population (reach).

Frequency program *(p. 552)* A type of continuity program designed to encourage repeat purchases.

Frequency quintile distribution analysis *(p. 445)* A media planning analysis technique that divides a target audience into five equal-sized groups, each containing 20 percent of the audience, and establishes an average frequency of exposure for each of these segments (also called quintile analysis).

Friendship focus groups *(p. 197)* Group interviews with people who know one another and have been recruited by the person who hosts the session, which is usually held in that *person*'s home.

Fulfillment *(p. 506)* The back-end operations of direct marketing, which include receiving the order, assembling the merchandise, shipping, and handling returns and exchanges.

Full-service agency *(p. 53)* An agency that provides clients with the primary planning and advertising services.

Fund-raising (or development) *(p. 479)* The practice of raising money by collecting donations, sometimes called development or strategic philanthropy.

G

Gaffer *(p. 325)* Chief electrician on a film shoot.

Game *(p. 541)* A type of promotional sweepstakes that encourages customers to return to a business several times in order to increase the chances of winning.

Gap analysis *(p. 481)* A research technique that measures the differences in perceptions and attitudes between groups or between them and the organization.

Gatefold *(p. 371)* Four or more connected pages that fold in on themselves.

Gatekeepers *(p. 476)* Individuals who have direct relations with the public such as writers, producers, editors, talk-show coordinators, and newscasters.

Global brand *(p. 82)* One that is marketed with the same name, design, and creative strategy in most or all of the major regional market blocs.

Goals *(p. 211)* Long-term business directions and decisions that can be measured and evaluated.

Goodwill *(pp. 81, 475)* A positive attitude about a company among the general public.

Grip *(p. 325)* Individual who moves the props and sets on a film shoot.

Gross impressions *(pp. 350, 606, 439)* The sum of the audiences of all the media vehicles used within a designated time span.

Gross rating points (GRPs) *(p. 455)* The sum of the total exposure potential of a series of media vehicles expressed as a percentage of the audience population.

Group text messaging *(p. 416)* Software that makes it possible to deliver individualized online communication through a mass distribution system.

Guaranteed circulation *(p. 438, 605)* Publications such as magazines guarantee to their advertisers that a certain number of copies will be sold or distributed to subscribers.

Guerrilla marketing *(p. 357)* A form of unconventional marketing, such as chalk messages on a sidewalk, that is often associated with staged events.

Gutter *(p. 371)* The white space, or inside margins, where two facing magazine pages join.

H

Halftones *(p. 319)* (Continuous tone): Image with a continuous range of shades from light to dark.

Hard sell *(p. 247)* A rational, informational message that emphasizes a strong argument and calls for action.

Hashtags *(pp. 142, 421)* Mashed-together phrases marked with a hash symbol (the pound sign) that indicates what topic the Twitter tweet addresses.

Headline *(p. 281)* The title of an ad; it is display copy set in large type to get the reader's attention.

Heavy-up schedule *(p. 452)* In media planning, a schedule can be designed that spends proportionately more of the budget in certain key ways, such as season or geography.

Heuristic evaluation *(p. 603)* A process of discovery leading to the evaluation of the effectiveness of user experiences.

Hierarchy of effects *(p. 127)* A set of consumer responses that moves from the least serious, involved, or complex up through the most serious, involved, or complex.

High involvement *(p. 142)* Perceiving a product or information as important and personally relevant.

High-context culture *(p. 295)* The meaning of a message is dependent on context cues.

High-definition television (HDTV) *(p. 382)* A type of television set that delivers movie quality, high-resolution images.

Hits *(p. 419)* The number of times a website is visited.

Holding companies *(p. 54)* One or more advertising agency networks, as well as other types of marketing communication agencies and marketing services consulting firms.

Horizontal publication *(p. 370)* Publications directed at people who hold similar jobs.

House ad *(pp. 369, 486)* An ad by an organization that is used in its own publication or programming.

House list *(p. 519)* A compilation of a company's past customers or members.

Household *(p. 160)* All those people who occupy one living unit, whether they are related or not.

Households using television (HUT) *(pp. 439, 606)* A measure of households using TV.

Humor *(p. 252)* An advertising message strategy that tries to be funny to attract an audience, build a positive brand connection, and lock the product in memory.

I

Idea *(p. 256)* A thought or product of thinking.

Ideation *(p. 261)* The process of creating an idea.

Illumination *(p. 261)* The point when a new idea strikes.

Image transfer *(p. 289)* When the presentation in one medium stimulates the listener or viewer to think about the presentation of the product in another medium.

IMC research *(p. 183)* Research used to plan and evaluate the performance and synergy of all marketing communication tools.

Immersion *(p. 261)* Gathering information and concentrating your focus on a problem.

Impact *(pp. 127, 259)* The effect of the message on the audience.

Implied third-party endorsement *(pp. 419, 477)* When the media endorse a product and the public finds it credible.

Impression *(pp. 349, 439)* In media planning, one person's opportunity to be exposed to an advertising message.

In-depth interview *(p. 196)* One-on-one interview using open-ended questions.

In-house agency *(p. 53)* An agency within an advertiser's organization that performs all the tasks an outside agency would provide for the advertiser.

Inbound telemarketing *(p. 513)* Incoming calls initiated by the customer.

Incubation *(p. 261)* A step in the ideation process, when you turn your attention elsewhere and let your subconscious play with a problem.

Independent stations *(p. 378)* Local stations unaffiliated with a national network.

Indirect action *(p. 144)* Delayed response to advertising such as recalling the message and later in the store selecting the brand.

Indirect advertising *(p. 107)* Advertising that features a related product or idea instead of the primary (controversial) product.

Indirect-action headlines *(p. 282)* Headlines that aim to capture attention although they might not provide much information.

Infomercial *(pp. 380, 508)* Infomercials are extended TV commercials that use the techniques of direct response communication to make an offer to viewers who are prospects for the brand.

Ingredient branding *(p. 81)* Acknowledging a supplier's brand as an important product feature.

Ink-jet imaging *(p. 370)* A printing process that allows a mailer, such as a magazine to personalize its content for the reader.

Instantaneous effects *(p. 606)* Immediate responses to advertising and other marketing communication, as opposed to delayed or carryover impact.

Interactive media *(p. 340)* Media that offer the opportunity for two-way communication.

Inquiry tests *(p. 599)* Evaluation that measures the number of responses to a message.

Insight mining *(p. 228)* Finding some nugget of truth in a stack of research findings that lead to a key understanding of how consumers feel, think, or behave.

Insight research *(p. 228)* Intelligence about consumer behaviors, thoughts, opinions, attitudes, desires and beliefs that come from asking probing questions and carefully listening and analyzing the answers.

Institutional advertising *(p. 39)* A type of corporate advertising that focus on establishing a corporate identity or viewpoint.

Institutional markets *(p. 66)* Usually a nonprofit organization, such as hospitals, government agencies, or schools, that buy products to use in delivering their services.

Integration *(p. 71)* In marketing communication, integration means every message is focused and works together to present a coherent impression of a brand.

Integrated direct marketing (IDM) *(p. 524)* A method of achieving precise, synchronized use of a tightly targeted medium at the right time, with a measurable return on dollars spent. Also known as integrated relationship marketing.

Integrated marketing communication (IMC) *(pp. 48, 71)* The practice of unifying all marketing communication efforts so they send a consistent brand message to target audiences.

Integrated perception *(p. 563)* The process of synergy creates a coherent brand impression—a perception of a brand—from a multitude of messages, mentions, and personal experiences.

Integration triangle *(p. 582)* Three key aspects of brand communication include: 1. what a company or brand says about itself (say), 2. how the company or brand performs (Do), and 3. what other people say about it (confirm).

Intention *(p. 143)* A preference that motivates consumers to want to try or buy a brand.

Interactive communication *(p. 124)* Personal conversations between two people.

Interactive television *(p. 382)* A television with computer capabilities.

Interest *(p. 131)* Activities that engage the consumer.

Interior transit advertising *(p. 388)* Advertising posters that are mounted inside vehicles such as buses, subway cars, and taxis.

Interlock *(p. 326)* A version of the commercial with the audio and video timed together, although the two are recorded separately.

Internal marketing *(pp. 478, 569)* Providing information about marketing activity and promoting it internally to employees.

International advertising *(p. 94)* Advertising designed to promote the same product in a number of countries.

International brand *(p. 82)* A brand or product that is available in most parts of the world.

Intranets *(p. 492)* Networked systems of electronic communication that allow employees to be in touch with one another from various locations.

Intrusive *(p. 131)* Marketing communication messages that intrude on people's perception in order to grab attention.

Intrusiveness *(p. 351)* Techniques used by messages and media to grab attention by being disruptive or unexpected.

Involvement *(p. 142)* The intensity of the consumer's interest in a product.

Issue management *(p. 479)* The practice of advising companies and senior management on how public opinion is coalescing around certain issues.

J

Jingles *(pp. 288, 375)* Commercials set to music.

K

Key frame *(p. 293)* An image from a commercial that sticks in the mind and becomes the visual that viewers remember when they think about the commercial.

Key influencers *(p. 493)* Persons of knowledge or authority who serve as opinion leaders within a social network.

Key performance indicators *(p. 608)* Identifying the most reliable factors that drive effectiveness and business success.

Key visual *(p. 293)* Image that conveys the heart of the concept.

Key words *(pp. 392, 294)* A word or phrase typed into a search engine to finds websites relevant to a certain topic.

Kiosks *(pp. 388, 408)* Multisided bulletin board structures designed for public posting of messages.

Knowledge structure *(p. 140)* See Network of associations.

L

Latent publics *(p. 481)* Those people who are unaware of their connection to an organization regarding a problem.

Layout *(p. 313)* A drawing that shows where all the elements in the ad are to be positioned.

Lead agency *(p. 580)* In international marketing, the agency that develops the campaign.

Lead generation *(pp. 70, 503)* The identification of prospective customers.

Lead paragraph *(p. 284)* The first line or paragraph of the body copy that is used to stimulate the reader's interest.

Lead time *(pp. 367, 453)* Production time; also time preceding a seasonal event.

Leads *(p. 70)* The identification of potential customers, or prospects.

Left-brain thinking *(p. 260)* Logical, linear, and orderly thought; inductive or deductive.

Legibility *(p. 312)* How easy or difficult a type is to read.

Licensing *(p. 552)* The practice whereby a company with an established brand "rents" it to another company.

Lifestyle *(p. 169)* The pattern of living that reflects how people allocate their time, energy, and money.

Lifetime customer value (LCV) *(p. 526)* An estimate of the revenue coming from a particular customer (or type of customer) over the lifetime of the relationship.

Line art *(p. 319)* Art in which all elements are solid, with no intermediate shades or tones.

Lobbying *(p. 479)* A form of public affairs involving corporations, activist groups, and consumer groups who provide information to legislators in order to get their support and to get them to vote a certain way on a particular bill.

Local advertising *(p. 39)* Advertising targeted to consumers who live within the local shopping area of a store.

Local brand *(p. 82)* A brand that is marketed in one specific country.

Localization *(p. 578)* A strategy in international advertising that adapts the message to local cultures.

Logo *(pp. 77, 305)* A distinctive brand mark that is legally protected.

Low-context cultures *(p. 295)* The meaning of a message is obvious without needing a sense of the cultural context.

Low involvement *(p. 142)* Perceiving a product or information as unimportant.

Low-power FM (LPFM) *(p. 375)* Nonprofit, noncommercial stations that serve a small area market, such as a college campus.

Loyalty program *(p. 552)* A program designed to increase customer retention by rewarding customers for their patronage.

M

Make goods *(p. 463)* Compensation that media give to advertisers in the form of additional message units. These are commonly used in situations involving production errors by the medium and preemption of the advertiser's programming.

Market *(p. 66)* An area of the country or a group of buyers.

Market research *(p. 183)* A type of marketing research that investigates the product and category, as well as consumers who are or might be customers for the product.

Market segmentation *(pp. 46, 163)* The process of dividing a market into distinct groups of buyers who might require separate products or marketing mixes.

Market selectivity *(p. 367)* When the medium targets specific consumer groups.

Marketer *(p. 66)* The company or organization behind the product.

Marketing *(p. 65)* Business activities that direct the exchange of goods and services between producers and consumers.

Marketing communication (marcom) *(pp. 40, 64)* The element in the marketing mix that communicates the key marketing messages to target audiences.

Marketing imperialism *(p. 93)* Marketing practices that result in imposing foreign cultural values on a local culture with different values and traditions.

Marketing mix *(p. 65)* A blend of four main activities: designing, pricing, distributing, and communicating about the product.

Marketing plan *(p. 211)* A written document that proposes strategies for using the elements of the marketing mix to achieve objectives.

Marketing public relations (MPR) *(p. 480)* A type of public relations that supports marketing's product and sales focus by increasing the brand's and company's credibility with consumers.

Marketing research *(p. 189)* Research that investigates all elements of the marketing mix.

Marketing services *(p. 50)* This includes a variety of suppliers hired by marketers, such as researchers and various types of marketing communication agencies.

Mass media *(pp. 51, 339)* Communication channels, such as newspapers or television, used to send messages to large, diverse audiences.

Maven marketing *(p. 493)* People who are considered expert or knowledgeable about some topic.

Measured media *(pp. 339, 440)* Media used in advertising that are evaluated by auditing companies that track performance data, such as circulation, readership, and viewership.

Measurable objectives *(p. 569)* The effectiveness of brand communication is determined by how well it meets its objectives which must be specific, clear, and measurable in terms of a starting baseline and a goal.

Mechanicals *(p. 316)* A finished pasteup with every element perfectly positioned that is photographed to make printing plates for offset printing.

Media *(pp. 51, 336)* The channels of communication that carry the ad message to target audiences.

Media buyer *(p. 346)* Specialists who implement the media plan by contracting with various media for placement of an advertisement.

Media-buying services *(p. 54)* These are companies that specialize in buying media for clients or other agencies.

Media flowchart *(p. 454)* A planning document that shows how the media plan will run in terms of the scheduling of the various media used.

Media kit *(pp. 409, 490)* Also called a press kit, a packet or folder that contains all the important information for members of the press.

Media mix *(pp. 346, 447)* Selecting the best combination of media vehicles, nontraditional media, and marketing communication tools to reach the targeted stakeholder audiences.

Media objective *(p. 444)* Goals or tasks a media plan should accomplish.

Media optimization *(p. 604)* The best use of various communication methods to promote the company.

Media plan *(pp. 346, 440)* A decision process leading to the use of advertising time and space to assist in the achievement of marketing objectives.

Media planners *(p. 345)* Media specialists who develop the strategic decisions outlined in the media plan.

Media planning *(p. 345)* The way advertisers identify and select media options based on research into the audience profiles of various media.

Media relations *(p. 478)* Relationships with media contacts.

Media reps *(p. 345)* Media salespeople who sell media time and space for a variety of media outlets.

Media research *(p. 191)* The process of gathering information about all the possible media and marketing communication tools available to be used in a marketing communication plan.

Media researchers *(p. 345)* The specialists who gather information about media audiences and performance.

Media salespeople *(p. 345)* People who work for a specific medium and call on media planners and buyers in agencies to sell space or time in that medium.

Media strategy *(p. 447)* The decisions media planners make to deliver the most effective media mix that will reach the target audience and satisfy the media objectives.

Media tour *(pp. 410, 491)* A traveling press conference in which the company's spokes-person travels to different cities and meets with the local media.

Media vehicle *(pp. 51, 339)* A single program, magazine, or radio station.

Media-buying companies *(p. 346)* An offshoot of the media-buying function in full-service agencies, these companies become free-standing agencies that specialize in buying media for clients and other agencies.

Media waste *(p. 446)* Wasted efforts in media buying come from targeting too wide of a target market (reach) or buying too many exposures (frequency).

Mental rehearsal *(p. 145)* Visualization of imagined actions that is the predecessor to the behaviors with which the advertiser hopes the consumer will feel comfortable and familiar.

Merging *(p. 520)* The process of combining two or more lists of data.

Message *(p. 123)* The words, pictures, and ideas that create meaning in an advertisement.

Message design *(p. 247)* The communication approach that makes the most sense given the brand's marketing situation and the target audience's needs and interests.

Message strategy *(p. 244)* The determination of the right message for a particular target audience that delivers the advertising objectives.

Metaphors *(p. 201)* A figure of speech in which a term or phrase from one object is associated with something entirely different to create an implicit comparison.

Microblog *(p. 421)* A small blog—Twitter, for example.

Micro-sites *(p. 390)* Small websites that are offspring of a parent website.

Microtargeting *(p. 165)* The practice of using vast databases of personal information to predict attitudes and behavior of selected groups.

Mini-sites *(p. 390)* Smaller websites that exist on a marketing partner's site permitting viewers to click on the minisite for additional information without leaving the original website.

Mission marketing *(pp. 210, 582)* Linking the mission of the company to a good cause and committing support to it for the long term.

Mission statement *(p. 210)* A business platform that articulates the organization's philosophy, as well as its goals and values.

Mixer *(p. 325)* The individual who operates the recording equipment during a film shoot.

Mobile marketing *(pp. 356, 416)* The use of wireless communication to reach people on the move with a location-based message.

Morals *(p. 101)* The framework for separating right from wrong and identifying good behavior.

Moments of truth *(p. 442)* The moments in time when a message is particularly relevant to a consumer and becomes an engaging media experience.

Morning drive time *(p. 376)* On radio the day part that reaches people when they are commuting to work.

Morphing *(p. 322)* A video technique in which one object gradually changes into another.

Motivation *(p. 141)* An unobservable inner force that stimulates and compels a behavioral response.

Motive *(p. 162)* An internal force—like the desire to look good—that stimulates you to behave in a particular manner.

Multichannel *(pp. 345, 464)* An advertising plan that uses several different forms of media, such as TV, print, radio, and online.

Multiplatform *(pp. 346, 424)* In IMC planning, multiple functional areas and tools, such as public relations and sales promotion, are used to deliver messages and create brand interactions, a practice referred to as multiplatform communication.

Mystery shoppers *(p. 409)* A proactive form of customer service, unidentified shoppers are asked to personally analyze and report on their experiences shopping in a store.

N

Naming rights *(p. 402)* The practice of allowing brand names to be associated with buildings and events in order to create brand visibility.

Navigation *(pp. 327, 413)* The action of a user moving through a website.

Needs *(p. 137)* Basic forces that motivate you to do or to want something.

Network of associations *(pp. 140, 200)* The linked set of brand perceptions that represent a person's unique way of creating meaning.

Network effect *(p. 414)* The impact of shared information through an online communication network creates a multiplier effect.

Network television *(p. 378)* Television networks are central broadcasting companies with affiliated stations in local markets that run programming provided by the network.

Neuromarketing *(p. 162)* The brain-science approach investigating how consumers think.

News conferences *(p. 410)* Presentations by an organization of news announcements through a meeting where reporters are also invited to ask questions.

News release *(p. 279)* Primary medium used to deliver public relations messages to the media.

News value *(p. 489)* The quality of information that makes it of interest to news editors based on such considerations as timeliness, proximity, impact, or human interest.

Newsprint *(p. 317)* An inexpensive paper with a rough surface, used for printing newspapers.

Niche market *(p. 163)* Subsegments of the general market which have distinctive traits that may provide a special combination of benefits.

Niche media *(p. 339)* Communication channels used to reach audience segments defined by a specialized interest, such as ethnicity or profession.

Noise *(p. 123)* Anything that interferes with or distorts the advertising message's delivery to the target audience.

Nonprofit advertising *(p. 39)* Advertising programs used by nonprofit organizations, such as charities, associations, and hospitals.

Nontraditional delivery *(p. 369)* Delivery of magazines to readers through such methods as door hangers or newspapers.

Norms *(pp. 157, 596)* Simple rules that each culture establishes to guide behavior.

O

Objective *(pp. 127, 209)* The goal or task an individual or business wants to accomplish.

Objective-task method *(p. 577)* Budgeting approach based on costs of reaching an objective.

Observation research *(p. 198)* Qualitative research method that takes researchers into natural settings where they record people's behavior.

Off camera *(p. 291)* In television, a voice that is coming from an unseen speaker.

Offer *(p. 505)* A direct marketing tool that provides potential customers with an item's information, description, terms of sale, and often an incentive for quick action in buying.

Offset printing *(p. 319)* A printing process that prints an image from a smooth-surface chemically treated printing plate.

On location *(p. 291)* Commercials shot outside the studio.

On-demand programming *(p. 379)* A form of subscription television that allows subscribers to receive special programming for a fee.

One-order, one-bill *(p. 367)* When media companies buy newspaper advertising space for national advertisers and handle the rate negotiation and billing.

On-premise signs *(p. 401)* Signage that identifies stores.

One-step offer *(p. 505)* A message that asks for a direct sales response and has a mechanism for responding to the offer.

Open-ended questions *(p. 196)* A qualitative research method that asks respondents to generate their own answers.

Opinion leaders *(pp. 142, 475)* Important people who influence others.

Opt in (Opt out) *(pp. 418, 517)* In e-mail advertising (and direct mail) consumers agree to be included or not included in the list.

Optimization *(pp. 460, 505)* Computer modeling that helps media planners determine the relative impact and efficiency of various media mixes.

Original *(p. 259)* Unique and the first of it's kind.

Out-of-home media *(p. 383)* All advertising that is displayed outside the home, from billboards, to blimps, to in-store aisle displays.

Out-of-register color *(p. 463)* When the four colors used in full-color printing are not perfectly aligned with the image.

Outbound telemarketing *(p. 513)* Telemarketing sales calls initiated by the company.

Outcome *(p. 601)* Evaluation techniques that determine the effect of communication on the target audience.

Outdoor advertising *(p. 384)* Advertising on billboards along streets and highways.

Output *(p. 601)* In public relations evaluation, the number of press releases and contacts that led to stories or mentions in news stories.

Overlines *(p. 280)* Text used to set the stage and lead into the headline of copy.

Owned media *(p. 341)* Media channels controlled by the organization and that are used to carry branded content.

P

Pace *(p. 293)* How fast or slowly the action progresses in a commercial.

Package goods *(p. 66)* Products sold for personal or household use.

Page views *(p. 602)* The number of times a website is visited.

Paid media *(p. 341)* Traditional measured media used in advertising where ad placements—both time and space—are bought by an agency on behalf of a client.

Paid posts *(p. 414)* The practice of using bloggers who plug a product in return for incentives such as cash or freebies.

Painted outdoor bulletins *(p. 385)* A type of advertisement that is normally created on-site and is not restricted to billboards as the attachment.

Parity products *(pp. 75, 223)* Products that really are the same, such as milk, unleaded gas and over-the-counter drugs; also known as undifferentiated products.

Participant observation *(p. 198)* A research method in which the observer is a member of the group being studied.

Participations *(p. 381)* An arrangement in which a television advertiser buys commercial time from a network.

Pass-along readership *(p. 459)* The view that a magazine, although only bought by one consumer, may actually be read by several; difference between circulation and readership.

Payout analysis *(p. 602)* A comparison of the cost of a promotion against the forecasted sales generated by the promotion.

Payout planning *(p. 534)* A way to evaluate the effectiveness of a sales promotion in terms of its financial returns by comparing the costs of the promotion to the forecasted sales of the promotion.

People meters *(p. 439)* Boxes on a TV set that record viewing behaviors.

Perceived risk *(p. 175)* The relationship between what you gain by making a certain decision and what you have to lose.

Percentage-of-sales method *(p. 577)* A budgeting technique based in the relationship between the cost of advertising and total sales.

Perception *(p. 130)* The process by which we receive information through our five senses and acknowledge and assign meaning to this information.

Perceptual map *(p. 224)* An analytical technique that plots the mental positions held by consumers of a set of competitors on a matrix.

Performance incentive *(p. 56)* A form of agency compensation that pays agencies on their ability to develop marketing communication that achieves certain goals agreed upon with the client.

Permission marketing *(pp. 517, 561)* A method of direct marketing in which the consumer controls the process, agrees to receive communication from the company, and consciously signs up.

Permission to believe *(p. 255)* Credibility building techniques that increase consumers' conviction in making decisions.

Personal sales *(p. 70)* Face-to-face contact between the marketer and a prospective customer.

Personal selling *(p. 70)* Face-to-face contact between the marketer and a prospective customer that intends to create and repeat sales.

Persuasion *(p. 141)* Trying to establish, reinforce, or change an attitude, touch an emotion, or anchor a conviction firmly in the potential customer's belief structure.

Photoboards *(p. 294)* A mockup of a television commercial that uses still photos for the frames.

Pitch letter *(p. 490)* A letter to a media outlet that outlines a possible story idea that the PR person would like to provide.

Place-based media *(p. 384)* Out-of-home media that carry ads and other promotional messages in public spaces.

Platforms *(p. 424)* Functions or areas of marketing communication such as public relations or direct marketing.

Podcasting *(p. 375)* The practice of using audio shows broadcast from the Web to be downloaded to an MP3 player.

Point of differentiation *(p. 68)* The way a product is unique from its competitors.

Point-of-purchase *(p. 403)* Also called point-of-sale, these are materials that call attention to a brand in a store and provide a special reason to buy.

Point-of-purchase (PoP) materials *(p. 545)* In-store merchandising materials that use such promotional materials as aisle displays, shelf signs, and window posters to feature a brand and its promotional offer.

Point-of-sale *(p. 403)* see Point-of-purchase

Pop-ups and pop-behind *(p. 390)* Types of ads that burst open on the computer screen either in front of or behind the opening page of a website.

Position *(p. 221)* A brand location in the consumer's mind relative to competing brands based on the relative strengths of the brand and its competitors.

Positioning *(p. 46)* The way in which consumers perceive a product in the marketplace.

Posttesting *(p. 194)* Research conducted after a message or campaign has run that seeks to determine the effectiveness of the communication effort.

Post-testing research *(p. 600)* A type of research that uses a number of methods to evaluate the effectiveness of a program after it has been implemented.

Postproduction *(p. 325)* In TV production, assembling and editing the film after the film has been shot.

Predictive dialing *(p. 513)* Technology that allows telemarketing companies to call anyone by using a trial and error dialing program.

Press kits *(p. 405)* Packets of information provided to reporters that contain such materials as press releases, fact sheets, histories, maps, photos, and other corporate information.

Preference *(p. 143)* Favorable positive impression of a product that leads to an intention to try or buy it.

Preferred positions *(p. 462)* Sections or pages of print media that are in high demand by advertisers because they have a special appeal to the target audience.

Preferred-position rate *(p. 368)* Charges by media for space or time that are in high demand because they have a special appeal to the target audience.

Premium *(pp. 406, 540)* A tangible reward received for performing a particular act, such as purchasing a product or visiting the point-of-purchase.

Preprints *(p. 369)* Advertising circulars furnished by a retailer for distribution as a free-standing insert in newspapers.

Preproduction *(p. 324)* The process of outlining every step and decision to be made in the production process in a set of production notes that are compiled from a preproduction meeting with the creative team, producer and other key participants.

Press conference *(p. 490)* A public gathering of media people for the purpose of establishing a company's position or making a statement.

Pretesting *(pp. 192, 594)* Evaluative research of finished or nearly finished ads that leads to a go/no-go decision.

Price copy *(p. 69)* A term used to designate advertising copy devoted to information about the price and the associated conditions of a particular product.

Price deal *(p. 538)* A temporary reduction in the price of a product.

Primary research *(p. 184)* Information that is collected from original sources.

Prime time *(p. 378)* Programming on TV that runs between the hours of 8 p.m. and 11 p.m.

Profit *(p. 211)* Revenue above and beyond costs; what has been gained after the costs are met.

Pro bono *(p. 39)* Situation in which all services, time, and space are donated.

Problem avoidance message *(p. 252)* A message strategy that positions the brand as a way to avoid a problem.

Problem solution message *(p. 252)* A message strategy that sets up a problem that the use of the product can solve.

Process colors *(p. 319)* Four basic inks—magenta, cyan, yellow, and black—that are mixed to produce a full range of colors found in four-color printing.

Product differentiation *(pp. 46, 223)* A competitive marketing strategy that tries to create a competitive difference through real or perceived product attributes.

Product placement *(p. 353)* The use of a brand name product in a television show, movie, or event.

Product-as-hero *(p. 252)* A form of the problem-solution message strategy.

Production notes *(p. 324)* A document that describes in detail of every aspect of a commercial's production.

Profiles *(p. 166)* A composite description of a target audience using personality and lifestyle characteristics.

Program preemptions *(p. 463)* Interruptions in local or network programming caused by special events.

Programmatic buying *(p. 461)* Media buying based on huge amounts of behavior tracking data and the algorithms that permit targeting individuals, not just aggregated audiences.

Projective techniques *(p. 200)* A psychoanalytic research technique that asks respondents to generate impressions to gather insights about consumers and brands.

Promise *(p. 251)* Found in a benefit statement, it is something that will happen if you use the product.

Prospecting *(p. 503)* In database marketing, this is the process of identifying prospects based on how well they match certain user characteristics.

Prospects *(p. 70)* Potential customers who are likely to buy the product or brand.

Psychographics *(p. 170)* All psychological variables that combine to share our inner selves and help explain consumer behavior.

Psychological pricing *(p. 69)* A strategy that tries to manipulate the customer's purchasing judgment.

Public affairs *(p. 479)* Relations between a corporation, the public, and government involving public issues relating to government and regulation.

Public communication campaigns *(p. 480)* Social issue campaigns undertaken by nonprofit organizations as a conscious effort to influence the thoughts or actions of the public.

Public opinion *(p. 475)* People's beliefs, based on their conceptions or evaluations of something, rather than on fact.

Public radio *(p. 375)* A network of radio stations that use public broadcasting material usually provided by National Public Radio (NPR).

Public relations *(p. 474)* A management function enabling organizations to achieve effective relationships with various publics in order to manage the image and reputation of the organization.

Public service advertising *(p. 39)* A type of advertising that is developed for a good cause usually pro bono.

public service announcements (PSAs) *(pp. 39, 381, 486)* A type of public relations advertising that deals with public welfare issues and typically is run free of charge.

Public television *(p. 379)* Broadcast TV stations that generally function based on donations rather than commercial advertising.

Publicity *(p. 476)* Information that catches public interest and is relayed through the news media.

Publics *(p. 474)* All groups of people with which a company or organization interacts.

Puffery *(p. 96)* Advertising or other sales representation that praises a product or service using subjective opinions, superlatives, and similar techniques that are not based on objective fact.

Pull strategy *(pp. 70, 455)* A strategy that directs marketing efforts at the consumer and attempts to pull the product through the channel.

Pulsing strategy *(p. 454)* An advertising scheduling pattern in which time and space are scheduled on a continuous but uneven basis; lower levels are followed by bursts or peak periods of intensified activity.

Purging *(p. 520)* The process of deleting duplicative information after lists of data are combined.

Push strategy *(pp. 70, 455)* A strategy that directs marketing efforts at resellers, where success depends on the ability of these intermediaries to market the product, which they often do with advertising.

Q

Qualitative research *(p. 187)* Research that seeks to understand how people think and behave and why.

Quantitative research *(p. 185)* Research that uses statistics to describe consumers.

Q score *(p. 253)* A measure of the familiarity of a celebrity, as well as a company or brand.

QR codes *(p. 343)* Short for "quick response," this refers to a complex graphic pattern that represents a data that can be electronically scanned and that links to website addresses and geographic coordinates.

R

Radio network *(p. 375)* A group of local affiliates providing simultaneous programming via connection to one or more of the national networks through AT&T telephone wires.

Radio script *(p. 289)* A written version of a radio commercial used to produce the commercial.

Random sample *(p. 195)* The type of research sample requiring that each person in the population being studied has an equal chance of being selected to be in the sample.

Rate card *(p. 367)* A list of the charges for advertising space.

Ratings, Rating Points *(p. 350)* Percentage of population or households tuned to a program.

Readership *(p. 605)* The number of readers of print media.

Reach *(pp. 350, 444)* The percentage of different homes or people exposed to a media vehicle or vehicles at least once during a specific period of time. It is the percentage of unduplicated audience.

Reason to believe *(p. 143)* Supporting or proving an advertising claim intensifies believability.

Reason why *(p. 251)* A statement that explains why the feature will benefit the user.

Rebate *(p. 539)* A sales promotion that allows the customer to recover part of the product's cost from the manufacturer in the form of cash.

Recall *(p. 132)* People remember seeing an ad and what the ad said.

Recall test *(p. 598)* A test that evaluates the memorability of an advertisement by contacting members of the advertisement's audience and asking them what they remember about it.

Receiver *(p. 123)* The audience for an advertisement.

Recency, frequency, and monetary (RFM) *(p. 504)* The three criteria that help direct marketers predict who among the customer base is likely to be repeat buyers.

Recognition *(p. 132)* An ability to remember having seen something before.

Recognition test *(p. 598)* A test that evaluates the memorability of an advertisement by contacting members of the audience, showing them the ad, and asking whether they remember having seen it before.

Reference group *(p. 159)* A group of people that a person uses as a guide for behavior in specific situations.

Referrals *(p. 146)* When a satisfied customer recommends a favorite brand.

Refund *(p. 539)* An offer by the marketer to return a certain amount of money to the consumer who purchases the product.

Regional brand *(p. 82)* A brand that is available throughout a regional trading block.

Registration *(p. 317)* The way the various color inks align in four-color printing.

Relational database *(p. 520)* Databases used for profiling and segmenting potential customers as well as providing contact information.

Relationship marketing *(pp. 82, 477)* The ongoing process of identifying and maintaining contact with high-value customers.

Release prints *(p. 326)* Duplicate copies of a commercial that are ready for distribution.

Relevance *(p. 131)* The message connects with the audience on a personal level.

Relevant *(p. 259)* Ideas that mean something to the target audience.

Reliability *(p. 201)* In research, reliability means you can run the same test over again and get the same results.

Reminder advertising *(p. 256)* An advertising strategy that keeps the brand name in front of consumers.

Repositioning *(p. 225)* Developing a new position for the product as the marketing environment changes.

Reputation management *(p. 479)* The trust stakeholders have in an organization.

Reseller *(p. 67)* Intermediaries in the distribution channel, typical wholesalers, retailers, and distributors who buy products from manufacturers and then resell them to the ultimate user.

Resonance *(p. 136)* A message that rings true because the consumer connects with it on a personal level.

Response list *(p. 519)* In direct marketing, a list that is compiled of people who respond to a direct-mail offer.

Retail advertising *(p. 39)* A type of advertising used by local merchants who sell directly to consumers.

Retainer *(p. 56)* Agency monthly compensation based on an estimate of the projected work and its costs.

Return on investment (ROI) *(pp. 82, 211)* Return on investment means that the costs of conducting the business should be more than matched by the revenue produced in return.

Right-brain thinking *(p. 260)* A type of divergent thinking that is intuitive, holistic, artistic, and emotionally expressive.

Rich media *(p. 389)* Digital media with multiple formats that allows viewer participation in the presentation of the content.

Roadblock *(p. 380)* Running a television commercial on all the networks at exactly the same time.

Rough cut *(p. 326)* A preliminary edited version of the commercial.

Rough layouts *(p. 316)* A layout drawn to size but without attention to artistic and copy details.

Run-of-paper (ROP) rate *(p. 368)* In newspaper advertising, a rate based on a location that is at the discretion of the publisher.

Rushes *(p. 325)* Rough versions of the commercial assembled from unedited footage.

S

Sales kits *(p. 409)* Packets of information used by media representatives and other types of sales personnel.

Sales promotion *(p. 532)* Marketing activities that add value to the product for a limited period of time to stimulate consumer purchasing and dealer effectiveness.

Sample *(p. 195)* In research, a subset of the population that is representative of the key characteristics of the larger group.

Sampling *(pp. 410, 539)* Allowing the consumer to experience the product at no cost.

Satellite radio *(p. 375)* Subscription radio programming delivered by satellite to receivers anywhere in the continental United States.

Satellite television *(p. 379)* Subscription television programming delivered by satellite to locations with satellite dishes.

Satellite transmission *(p. 370)* A delivery system for television programming that uses satellite transmission to satellite dishes that competes with network television.

Scanner research *(p. 598)* Research that tracks consumer purchases and compares the marketing communication received by the consumer's household.

Scatter market *(p. 462)* Most prime-time television advertising is presold; however the remaining inventory is sold during a period, called the scatter market, which is closer to the date of program's scheduled run.

Scenes *(p. 293)* Commercials are planned with segments of action that occur in a single location.

Screen *(p. 319)* Used to convert continuous tone art to halftone by shooting the image through a fine screen that breaks the image into a dot pattern.

Search advertising *(p. 392)* Advertising that adjoins key-word content on websites.

Search marketing *(pp. 355, 392)* Marketing communication strategies designed to aid consumers in their search for information.

Search optimization *(p. 393)* The practice of maximizing the link between topics that consumers search for and a brand-related website.

Secondary research *(p. 183)* Information that already has been compiled and published.

Segmenting *(p. 163)* Dividing the market into groups of people who have similar characteristics in certain key product related areas.

Selective attention *(p. 131)* The process by which a receiver of a message chooses to attend to the message.

Selective binding *(p. 370)* A database-driven publishing technique that combines information on subscribers with a printing program in order to present special ads, content, and promotional sections based on subscribers demographic profiles.

Selective perception *(p. 130)* The process of screening out information that doesn't interest us and retaining information that does.

Self-liquidator *(p. 540)* A type of mail premium that requires a payment sufficient to cover the cost of the item.

Selling premise *(p. 251)* The sales logic behind an advertising message.

Semicomps *(p. 316)* A layout drawn to size that depicts the art and display type; body copy is simply ruled in.

Semicontrolled media *(p. 486)* Media, such as the Internet, whose messages can be controlled by an organization in some ways, but that also contains totally uncontrolled messages.

Semiotic analysis *(p. 192)* A qualitative research method designed to uncover layers and types of meaning.

Semiotics *(p. 126)* A qualitative research method designed to uncover layers and types of meanings.

Set *(p. 291)* A constructed setting in which the action of a commercial takes place.

Share of audience *(p. 350)* The percent of viewers based on number of sets turned on.

Share of market *(pp. 66, 213)* The percentage of the total market in a product category that buys a particular brand.

Share of mind *(p. 578)* The extent to which a brand is well known in its category.

Share of voice *(p. 435)* One brand's percentage of advertising messages in a medium compared to all messages for that product or service.

Share of wallet *(p. 568)* The amount customers spend on the brand.

Shelf talkers *(p. 403)* Signs or coupons attached to a shelf that customers can take away for information or discounts.

Showing *(pp. 387, 440)* The percentage of the market population exposed to an outdoor board during a specific time.

Signage *(p. 401)* A type of out-of-home media, retail and corporate signs are owned by the organization.

Sign spinners *(p. 406)* A form of "human directional," these are people who hold signs and banners that promote stores or special marketing events.

Silos *(p. 571)* Programs and departments that operate on their own with little coordination with other promotional efforts.

Single source data *(p. 598)* Data collected using single-source research, which combines scanner data and cable viewing data to determine the relationship between television advertising and sales.

Single-source research *(p. 598)* A test that is run after an ad campaign is introduced that shows a causal relationship between marketing communication and sales.

Situation analysis *(pp. 211, 567)* The first section in a campaign plan that summarizes all the relevant background information and research and analyzes its significance.

Skyscrapers *(p. 390)* Extra-long narrow ads that run down the right or left side of a website.

Slice-of-life message *(p. 252)* A type of problem-solution ad in which "typical people" talk about a common problem.

Slogans *(pp. 254, 271)* Frequently repeated phrases that provide continuity to an advertising campaign.

Smart phones *(p. 412)* High-end cell phones, such as the BlackBerry or iPhone, with computing and photographic capabilities that can access the Internet, as well as perform traditional telephone functions.

SMCR model *(p. 123)* A communication model that identifies the Source, Message, Channel, and Receiver.

Social class *(p. 158)* A way to categorize people on the basis of their values, attitudes, lifestyles, and behavior.

Social games *(p. 423)* Like a computer game except it's played with friends—an example is FarmVille and Second Life.

Social learning *(p. 140)* People learn by watching others.

Social media *(p. 353)* Interactions between people via electronic communication that enable users to create and share content and network in virtual communities.

Social media marketing *(p. 426)* Marketing strategies that take advantage of the interactivity found on social media, such as Facebook and My Life.

Social responsibility *(p. 90)* A corporate philosophy based on ethical values.

Societal marketing *(p. 210)* A business philosophy that describes companies whose operations are based on the idea of socially responsible business.

Socialtizing *(p. 414)* This is the practice of using social marketing media as a promotional tool.

Soft sell *(p. 247)* An emotional message that uses mood, ambiguity, and suspense to create a response based on feelings and attitudes.

SoLoMo *(p. 453)* An emphasis on local marketing, which takes advantage of the convergence of social, local, and mobile marketing.

Sound effects *(p. 288)* Lifelike imitations of sounds.

Source *(p. 123)* The sender of a message, the advertiser.

Source credibility *(p. 143)* Belief in a message one hears from a source one finds most reliable.

Spam *(p. 516)* Blasting millions of unsolicited e-mail ads.

Speakers' bureau *(p. 491)* A public relations tool that identifies a group of articulate people who can talk about an organization.

Specialty advertising *(p. 541)* Free gifts or rewards requiring no purchase and carrying a reminder advertising message.

Spherical branding *(p. 564)* A form of 360° degree planning that means that no matter what your angle of vision, the brand always looks the same.

Spokes-character *(p. 252)* A created or imaginary character who acts as a spokesperson.

Spokesperson *(p. 252)* A message strategy that uses an endorser, usually someone the target audience likes or respects, to deliver a message on behalf of the brand.

Sponsorships (cause or event) *(pp. 381, 548)* An arrangement in which a company contributes to the expenses of a cause or event to increase the perceived value of the sponsor's brand in the mind of the consumer.

Spoofing *(p. 516)* A practice used by e-mail spammers who assume the identity of a company or organization to send fraudulent spam e-mails.

Spot announcements *(p. 381)* Ads shown during the breaks between programs.

Spot buy *(p. 378)* Broadcast advertising bought on a city-by-city basis rather than through a national buy.

Spot color *(p. 311)* The use of an accent color to call attention to an element in an ad layout.

Spot radio advertising *(p. 376)* A form of advertising in which an ad is placed with an individual station rather than through a network.

Stakeholders *(pp. 65, 474)* Groups of people with a common interest who have a stake in a company and who can have an impact on its success.

Standard advertising unit (SAU) *(p. 367)* A standardized system of advertising sizes in newspapers.

Standardization *(p. 578)* In international advertising, the use of campaigns that vary little across different cultures.

Stereotype *(p. 93)* The process of positioning a group of people in an unvarying pattern that lacks individuality and often reflects popular misconceptions.

Stickiness *(pp. 131, 413)* Ad messages that hold the audience's interest long enough for the audience to register the point of the ad; also refers to the amount of time a viewer spends on a website.

Stock footage *(p. 321)* Previously recorded film, video, or still slides that are incorporated into a commercial.

Stop motion *(p. 323)* An animation technique in which inanimate objects are filmed one frame at a time, creating the illusion of movement.

Storyboard *(pp. 294, 317)* A series of frames sketched to illustrate how the story line will develop.

Straightforward message *(p. 251)* A factual message that focuses on delivering information.

Strategic business unit (SBU) *(p. 210)* A division of a company focused on a line of products or all the offerings under a single brand name.

Strategic consistency *(p. 563)* Messages vary with the interest of the stakeholder but the brand strategy remains the same, projecting a coherent image and position.

Strategic philanthropy *(p. 479)* Philanthropy involves contributions of time, resources, or money to a good cause—it's strategic when it is aligned with an organization or brand's mission.

Strategic planning *(p. 208)* The process of determining objectives, deciding on strategies, and implementing the tactics.

Strategic research *(p. 183)* All research that leads to the creation of an ad.

Strategy *(pp. 38, 209)* The design or plan by which objectives are accomplished.

Streaming video *(p. 382)* Moving images transmitted online.

Structural analysis *(p. 264)* Developed by the Leo Burnett agency, this method evaluates the power of the narrative or story line, evaluates the strength of the product or claim, and considers how well the two aspects are integrated.

Subheads *(p. 280)* Sectional headlines that are used to break up a mass of "gray" type in a large block of copy.

Subliminal *(p. 132)* Refers to messages transmitted below the threshold of normal perception so that the receiver is not consciously aware of having seen it.

Subscription television *(p. 378)* Television service provided to people who sign up for it and pay a monthly fee.

Substantiation *(p. 251)* Providing support for a claim, usually through research.

Superstations *(p. 379)* Independent but high-power television stations.

Superstitials *(p. 391)* Short Internet commercials that appear when you go from one page on a website to another.

Supplements *(p. 368)* Syndicated or local full-color advertising inserts that appear in newspapers throughout the week.

Supply chain *(p. 66)* The network of suppliers who produce components and ingredients used by a manufacturer to make its products.

Support *(p. 251)* The proof, or substantiation needed to make a claim believable.

Survey research *(p. 194)* Research using structured interview forms that ask large numbers of people exactly the same questions.

Sweeps *(p. 439)* In television programming, these are quarterly periods when more extensive audience data are gathered.

Sweepstakes *(p. 541)* Contests that require only that the participant supply his or her name to participate in a random drawing.

Switchers *(p. 174)* Television viewers who change channels.

SWOT analysis *(pp. 211, 567)* An analysis of a company or brand's strengths, weaknesses, opportunities, and threats.

Syndication *(p. 376)* This is where local stations purchase television or radio shows that are reruns or original programs to fill open hours.

Synergy *(p. 132)* The principle that when all the pieces work together, the whole is greater than the sum of its parts.

synergistic effect *(p. 606)* Evaluation that seeks to determine if the sum of the individual promotional efforts is greater than if the areas are used separately.

Surrogate measures *(p. 594)* Mental responses to a message that may predict eventual sales impact.

Swag *(p. 541)* A type of freebie—gifts and promotional knickknacks—given to people who attend events as brand reminders.

T

Tactic *(p. 209)* The specific techniques selected to reflect the strategy.

Tagging *(p. 421)* In Twitter, a technique of marking a keyword by inserting a hash symbol (#).

Taglines *(pp. 254, 271)* Clever phrases used at the end of an advertisement to summarize the ad's message.

Take *(p. 324)* Each scene shot for a commercial, sometimes done repeatedly for the same scene.

Talent *(p. 291)* People who appear in television commercials.

Target audience *(p. 166)* A segment of a target market to whom promotional messages are aimed.

Targeted cost per point *(p. 459)* The practice of estimating the rating points specifically for the target audience specified in the plan.

Targeted cost per thousand (TCPM) *(p. 459)* The cost to expose 1,000 likely consumers of a product to an ad message.

Targeted rating point (TRP) *(p. 457)* The practice of adjusting a television program's rating points to more accurately reflect the percentage of the target audience watching the program.

Targeted reach *(p. 444)* The practice of identifying key characteristics of the target population to better match media audience profiles.

Tchotchkes *(p. 411)* Brand reminder materials give-aways, such as samples, trinkets, and souvenirs.

Teaser *(p. 252)* A message strategy that creates curiosity as the message unfolds in small pieces over time.

Tech support *(p. 409)* A form of customer support, this is the practice of hiring people who can provide assistance to customers in solving problems using technology.

Telemarketing *(p. 513)* A type of marketing that uses the telephone to make a personal sales contact.

Test marketing *(p. 606)* An evaluation method that launches a campaign is several different (but matched or similar) markets but with different levels of media activity or different message alternatives.

Television script *(p. 294)* The written version of a television commercial specifying all the video and audio information.

Testimonial *(p. 98)* See "endorsement."

Texting *(p. 416)* Text messaging, or texting, refers to the practice of sending a brief message between mobile phones or other computer devices connected to a phone network.

Theater of the mind *(p. 287)* In radio advertising, the story is visualized in the listener's imagination.

Think/feel/do model *(p. 127)* A model of advertising effects that focuses on the cognitive, emotional, and behavioral responses to a message.

Thumbnail sketches *(p. 316)* Small preliminary sketches of various layout ideas.

Tie-in promotion *(p. 553)* Preprinted ads that are provided by the advertiser to be glued into the binding of a magazine.

Time-shifting *(p. 380)* Using digital video recorders (DVRs) to record television programming for playback at some other time.

Tint blocks *(p. 319)* A screen process that creates shades of gray or colors in blocks.

Tip-ins *(p. 321)* Preprinted ads that are provided by the advertiser to be glued into the binding of a magazine.

Tone of voice *(pp. 245, 277)* Ad copy is written as a conversation or an announcement and the voices carry emotional cues.

Total audience *(p. 605)* In magazine research, this is a technique used to determine the total number of readers.

Total audience impressions *(p. 457)* Rather than using GRPS (gross rating points), media planners use total audience impressions which better estimate the total impact of an integrated campaign, including impressions from digital and new media, as well as measured media.

Total communication *(p. 562)* The practice of monitoring and managing all sources of brand communication.

Touch points *(p. 562)* The contact points where customers interact with the brand and receive brand messages.

Tour *(p. 410)* Tours of a facility, building, or some other space are used to provide engaging informational experiences for stakeholders.

Town hall forums *(p. 492)* Meetings within an organization as part of an internal marketing program to inform employees and encourage their support.

Tracking studies *(p. 597)* Studies that follow the purchase of a brand or the purchases of a specific consumer group over time.

Trade deal *(p. 544)* An arrangement in which the retailer agrees to give the manufacturer's product a special promotional effort in return for product discounts, goods, or cash.

Trade show *(pp. 410, 545)* A gathering of companies within a specific industry to display their products.

Trademark *(pp. 77, 106)* When a brand name or brand mark is legally protected through registration with the Patent and Trademark Office of the Department of Commerce.

Traffic department *(p. 53)* People within an agency who are responsible for keeping track of project elements and keeping the work on deadline.

Trailers *(p. 382)* Advertisements shown in movie theaters before the feature.

Training materials *(p. 409)* Information assembled to use in training sessions for sales representatives and other employees and stakeholders.

Transformation *(p. 140)* Creating meaning for a brand that makes it a special product, one that is differentiated within its category by its image.

Trend spotters *(p. 174)* Researchers who specialize in identifying trends and fads that may affect consumer attitudes and behavior.

Trial *(p. 145)* Trying a product is usually the first step in making a purchase.

Tweets *(p. 421)* A short comment of 140 characters made by Twitter users.

Twitter *(p. 399)* An online social networking site that makes it possible for users to share "tweets," short messages limited to 140 characters.

Two-step offer *(p. 505)* A message that is designed to gather leads, answer consumer questions, or set up appointments.

Typography *(p. 311)* The use of type both to convey words and to contribute aesthetically to the message.

U

Unaided recall or recognition *(p. 599)* When one can remember an idea all by oneself.

Unbundling media services *(p. 465)* Media departments that separate themselves from agencies becoming separate companies.

Uncontrolled circulation *(p. 369)* Publications that are distributed free usually in racks in high-traffic areas.

Uncontrolled media *(p. 486)* Media that include the press release, the press conference, and media tours.

Underlines *(p. 280)* Text used to elaborate on the idea in the headline and serve as a transition into the body copy.

Underwriting *(p. 375)* In public broadcasting, a sponsor contributes funds to pay for the cost of the programming.

Undifferentiated strategy *(p. 163)* A view of the market that assumes all consumers are basically the same.

Uniform resource locators (URLs) *(p. 106)* Internet domain names that are registered and protected.

Unique selling proposition (USP) *(p. 251)* A benefit statement about a feature that is both unique to the product and important to the user.

Unified vision *(p. 563)* A vision of what the brand stand for that is shared by all stakeholders.

Up-front market *(p. 462)* Most prime-time television advertising is pre-sold with negotiated discount rates for the upcoming season.

Usage *(p. 174)* Categorizing consumers in terms of how much of the product they buy.

User-generated ads *(p. 423)* Promotional copy on personal websites developed by the site's owner to promote a product, service, viewpoint, or cause.

User-generated content *(p. 51)* (see consumer-generated advertising).

V

Validity *(p. 201)* The research results actually measure what they say they measure

Value added, value-added media services *(p. 462)* A marketing or advertising activity that makes a product—or a media buy—more valuable.

Value billing *(p. 56)* A practice by marketers of paying agencies for creative and strategic ideas, rather than for executions and media placement.

Values *(p. 157)* The source of norms; values are not tied to specific objects or behavior, are internal, and guide behavior.

Vampire creativity *(p. 264)* Big ideas that are so powerful that they are remembered but not the brand.

Variable data campaigns *(p. 508)* A direct-mail piece featuring messages that are personalized through the use of digital technology.

Vertical publications *(p. 370)* Publications targeted at people working in the same industry.

Video editing *(p. 326)* Processing of recorded videotape to improve its final presentation; may include time manipulation and sound additions.

Video news releases (VNRs) *(p. 490)* Contain video footage that can be used during a television newscast.

Videographer *(p. 316)* Person who shoots images with a video camera.

Viral communication *(pp. 356, 419)* Word-of-mouth, or buzz, that gets passed rapidly through a network of friends.

Viral marketing *(pp. 84, 425)* A strategy used primarily in Web marketing that relies on consumers to pass on messages about a product.

Viral video *(p. 425)* The practice of sending interesting videos digitally from a variety of sources, such as ads or YouTube, to friends and colleagues in a vast network of personal connections.

virtual community *(p. 392)* An online group of people interested in a particular topic or brand.

Vision statement *(p. 210)* A statement that communicates what the company or organization aspires to become.

Visualization *(p. 309)* Imagining what the finished copy will look like.

Voice-over *(p. 291)* A technique used in commercials in which an off-camera announcer talks about the on-camera scene.

W

Wants *(p. 135)* Motivations based on desires and feelings.

Wasted reach *(p. 444)* Advertising directed at a disinterested audience that is not in the targeted audience.

Wearout *(p. 454)* The point where the advertising gets tired and there is no response or a lower level of response than at the advertising's launch.

Website *(p. 412)* Sometimes called a "home page," this is the online presence of a person or organization.

Webisode *(p. 402)* Web advertisements that are similar to TV programs with a developing storyline.

Weighting *(p. 455)* In media planning decision criteria are used to determine the relative amount of budget allocated to each medium.

White space *(p. 319)* Areas in a layout that aren't used for type or art.

Widgets *(p. 391)* Tiny computer programs that allow people to create and insert professional-looking content into their personal websites, as well as their computers, and other electronic media screens.

Word association *(p. 200)* A projective research technique that asks people to respond with the thoughts or other words that come to mind when they are given a stimulus word.

Word of mouth *(pp. 37, 356, 419)* Free advertising that comes from people talking about a product.

word-of-mouth communication *(p. 83)* Messages delivered by friends, family members, or other important people who influence your opinions and impressions.

Y

Your-name-here copy *(p. 278)* Pompous writing used in corporate communication that contains generic claims that do not differentiate the company.

Z

Zap *(p. 380)* Changing channels when a television commercial comes on.

Zero moment of truth *(p. 442)* The point in the consumer buying cycle when consmers search for information online or share brand experiences with a friend.

Zip *(p. 380)* Fast forwarding past commercials in a previously recorded program.

Endnotes

CHAPTER 1

[1] Ad Age Staff, "More Bigwigs Weigh in on What to Do in a Downturn," *Advertising Age*, April 13, 2008, http://adage.com/print?article_id=135947.
[2] Stephanie Reese, "Advertisers Will Spend $500 Billion in 2011," September 6, 2011, eMarketer, www.emarketer.com; Plunkett Research, Ltd. "Advertising & Branding Industry Overview," downloaded May 22, 2012, www.plunkettreseearch.com.
[3] "$262M Spent on Ads Debating Health-Care Reform—after Bill Passed," *Advertising Age*, March 22, 2012, http://adage.com.
[4] David Bell, "Inspiration for Advertising Ethics: An Interview with David Bell," American Academy of Advertising, Myrtle Beach, SC, March 15, 2012.
[5] Stephen Fox, *The Mirror Makers: A History of American Advertising and Its Creators* (New York: Vintage Books, 1985); "Advertising History Timeline," *Advertising Age*, 2005.
[6] Bill Bernbach interview, *Printer's Ink*, January 2, 1953, 21.
[7] Maureen Morrison, "Agency of the Year McGarryBowen Proves Solid and Reliable Beat Fast and Furious," *Advertising Age*, January 23, 2012, http://adage.com.
[8] Parekh Rupal, "Agency of the Year: Crispin Porter & Bogusky," *Advertising Age*, January 19, 2009, http://adage.com.
[9] "Pay-for-Performance Starts to Gain Steam," *Advertising Age*, January 29, 2012, http://adage.com.
[10] "ANA: Two-Thirds of Global Marketers to Change Agency Compensation," May 9, 2012, *Advertising Age*, http://adage.com.
[11] Jeremy Mullman and Natalie Zmuda, "Coke Pushes Pay-for-Performance Model, *Advertising Age*, April 27, 2009, http://adage.com.
[12] John Galvin, "The World on a String," *Point*, February 2005, 13–18.
[13] Suzanne Vranica, "CareerBuilder Offers Ad Bounty," *Wall Street Journal*, May 13, 2009, B5.
[14] Suzanne Vranica, "Washington PR Firm Buys Advertising Agency," *Wall Street Journal*, February 16, 2012, B5.
[15] "ANA Survey: 52% of Marketers Will Ask Agencies to Lower Internal Costs," *Advertising Age*, April 2, 2012, http://adage.com.
[16] "Proof That Advertising Works," *Toro Magazine*, July 28, 2010, www.toromagazine.com.

CHAPTER 2

[1] Tom Duncan and Sandra Moriarty, *Driving Brand Value: Using Integrated Marketing to Manage Profitable Stakeholder Relationships* (New York: McGraw-Hill, 1998).
[2] Anupreeta Das and Emily Glazer, "Beauty Brands, Waiting for Suitors," *Wall Street Journal*, August 3, 2012, B1.
[3] Thomas Hazlett, "The iPhone turns five," *Wall Street Journal*, June 27, 2012, A17.
[4] John Bussey, "The Innovator's Enigma," *Wall Street Journal*, October 5, 2012, B1.
[5] Theresa Howard, "Food Marketers Turn to Value with Dollar-per-Meal Strategy," *USA Today*, May 19, 2009, 21.
[6] Stu Woo, "Under Fire, Netflix Rewinds DVD Plan," *Wall Street Journal*, October 22, 2011, www.wsj.com; Eric Rardin, "Marketing Tactics Gone Bad—The Netflix Fiasco, frogloop (blog), October 24, 2011, www.frogloop.com.
[7] Giep Franzen, "The Complex World of Organization Branding," *Advertising and IMC Principles and Practice*, 9th ed. (Upper Saddle River, NJ: Prentice Hall, 2012).
[8] Tom Duncan and Frank Mulhern, eds., *A White Paper on the Status, Scope and Future of IMC,* University of Denver, March 2004, 10.
[9] Giep Franzen and Sandra Moriarty, *The Science and Art of Branding* (Armonk, NY: M. E. Sharpe, 2009), 5); "The World's Top 20 Brands," *Chicago Tribune*, May 22, 2012, www.chicagotribune.com; "2012 BrandZ Top 100," Millward Brown, May 22, 2012, www.millwardbrown.com.
[10] Ben Moger-Williams, "Adventures in Translation," November 21, 2008, http://benmojo.blogspot.com/2008/11/chinese-coke-tasty-happy.html; "Branding in Chinese, the Coca-Cola Story," Csymbolf (Shan Associates), http://csymbol.com.
[11] Sandra Moriarty and Giep Franzen, "The I in IMC: How Science and Art Are Integrated in Branding," *International Journal of Integrated Marketing Communication* 1, no. 1 (Spring 2009): 29.
[12] David Murdico, "Does Your Brand's Personality Come through in Social Media?," *Advertising Age*, May 31, 2012, www.adage.com.
[13] Suzanne Vranica and Jens Hansegard, "IKEA Discloses an $11 Billion Secret," *Wall Street Journal*, August 10, 2012, B1.
[14] "2012 Brandz Top 100," Millward Brown, May 22, 2012, www.millwardbrown.com.
[15] John Galvin, "The World on a String," *Point*, February 2005, 13–18.
[16] Melissa Korn, "General Mills Profit Climbs on Higher Prices," *Wall Street Journal*, June 29, 2011, www.online.wsj.com; Emily York, "General Mills Sees Profits Climb 49%," *Advertising Age*, December 17, 2009, www.adage.com
[17] Joe Mandese, "Simultaneous Research Study Reveals Consumers Buzz Most over Word-of-Mouth, Not Ads," *MediaPost Publications*, January 19, 2007, http://publications.mediapost.com.
[18] Steve Knox, "Why Effective Word-of-Mouth Disrupts Schemas," *Advertising Age*, January 25, 2010, www.adage.com.
[19] Michael Bush, "What's the Next Marketing Platform? How to Measure Success? Ad Age's Media Mavens Answer the Big Questions," *Advertising Age*, December 9, 2009, www.adage.com.

CHAPTER 3

[1] Bob Liodice, "10 Companies with Social Responsibility at the Core," *Advertising Age*, April 19, 2010, www.adage.com.
[2] Harris Poll, "Majorities of Americans Lay at Least Some Blame for Economic Crisis on Media and Advertising Agencies for Causing People to Buy What They Couldn't Afford," *Harris Interactive*, April 15, 2009, www.harrisinteractive.com.
[3] Charles Goodrum and Helen Dalrymple, *Advertising in America: The First 200 Years* (New York: Harry N. Abrams, 1990).
[4] Anna Mehler Paperny, "Virgin Ads Too Sexy for Calgary, Mississauga Transit," *The Globe and Mail*, January 8, 2010, www.theglobeandmail.com.
[5] Herbert Rotfeld, "Desires versus the Reality of Self-Regulation," *Journal of Consumer Affairs* 37 (Winter 2003): 424–427; Nanci Hellmich, "Weight-Loss Deception Found Ads for Many of Those Pills, Patches, Creams, and Wraps Are Grossly Exaggerated," *USA Today*, September 17, 2002.
[6] Suzan Clarke, "Agency Bans Dior Mascara Ad Featuring Natalie Portman," *ABC News*, October 25, 2012, www.abcnrews.go.com.
[7] Herbert J. Rotfeld and Kim B. Rotzoll, "Is Advertising Puffery Believed?," *Journal of Advertising* 9, no. 3 (1980): 45.
[8] Noreen O'Leary, "Weight Watchers Wins 1st Round vs. Jenny Craig, *Adweek*, January 21, 2010, www.adweek.com.

[9] Stephanie Clifford, "Coat Maker Transforms Obama Photo into Ad," *New York Times*, January 6, 2010, www.nytimes.com.
[10] Word of Mouth Marketing Association, "Ethics Code," September 21, 2009, www.womma.org/ethics/code.
[11] Eric Tegler, "Ford Is Counting on Army of 100 Bloggers to Launch New Fiesta," *Advertising Age*, April 20, 2009, http://adage.com.
[12] Josh Bernoff, "When and How to Pay a Blogger," *Advertising Age*, May 26, 2009, http://adage.com.
[13] Bruce Horovitz, "Wendy's Will Be 1st Fast Foodie with Healthier Oil," *USA Today*, June 8, 2006.
[14] Theresa Howard, "Push Is On to End Prescription Drug Ads Targeting Consumers," *USA Today*, August 10, 2009, www.usatoday.com.
[15] Jeffrey Young, "Health Care Reform Rebates for Health Insurance Costs Rolling In," *Huffington Post*, July 16, 2012, www.huffingtonpost.com.
[16] Philip Patterson and Lee Wilkins, *Media Ethics: Issues and Cases*, 6th ed. (Boston: McGraw-Hill, 2008).
[17] "Honesty/Ethics in Professions, Nov. 28–Dec. 1, 2011," 2012, www.gallup.com.
[18] Institute for Advertising Ethics, "Principles and Practices," March 17, 2011, www.rjionline.org/institute-for-advertising-ethics.
[19] Tom Spalding, "Peeps Maker Sues Greeting Card Firm," *USA Today*, October 7, 2009, www.usatoday.com.
[20] Chris Adams, "Looser Lip for Food and Drug Companies?," *Wall Street Journal*, September 17, 2002, A4.
[21] "Database and Internet Solutions," January 31, 2010, www.dbt.co.uk.
[22] Federal Trade Commission, "FTC Publishes Final Guides Governing Endorsements, Testimonials," October 5, 2010, www.ftc.gov/opa/2009/10/endortest.shtm.
[23] Joe Ryan, "North American Advertising Spend to Increase in 2012," *Direct Marketing News*, March 14, 2012.
[24] Jack Neff, "Duracell Agrees to Modify Robo-War Duck Ad," *Advertising Age*, February 6, 2002, www.adage.com; Daniel Golden and Suzanne Vranica, "Duracell's Duck Ad Will Carry Disclaimer," *Wall Street Journal*, February 7, 2002, B7.
[25] John J. Burnett, "Gays: Feelings about Advertising and Media Used," *Journal of Advertising Research*, January–February 2000, 75–86.
[26] Maureen Morrison, "NARC Nixed as Industry Opts for Name Change," *Advertising Age*, April 23, 2012, www.adage.com.
[27] Roy F. Fox, "Hucksters Hook Captive Youngsters," *Mizzou*, Summer 2002, 22–27.

CHAPTER 4

[1] Ennis Higgins, "Conversations with David Ogilvy," in *The Art of Writing Advertising* (Chicago: Advertising Publications, 1965).
[2] Claude E. Shannon and Warren Weaver, *The Mathematical Theory of Communication* (Urbana: University of Illinois Press, 1949).
[3] Elihu Katz and Paul Lazarsfeld, *Personal Influence* (New York: Free Press, 1955).
[4] Dennis DiPasquale, personal communication, June 7, 2012.
[5] "Burson-Marsteller Global Social Media Check-Up 2012," July 17, 2012, www.businesswire.com.
[6] Harley Manning and Kerry Bodine, *Outside In: The Power of Putting Customers at the Center of Your Business* (Cambridge MA: Forrester Research, 2012), 22.
[7] Demetrios Vakratsas and Tim Ambler, "Advertising Effects: A Taxonomy and Review of Concepts, Methods, and Results from the Academic Literature," Marketing Science Institute Working Paper (Cambridge, MA: Marketing Science Institute, 1996), 96–120; Thomas Barry and Daniel Howard, "A Review and Critique of the Hierarchy of Effects in Advertising," *International Journal of Advertising* 9, no. 2 (1990): 429–435; Michael Ray, "Communication and the Hierarchy of Effects," in *New Models for Mass Communication Research*, ed. P. Clarke (Beverly Hills, CA: Sage, 1973), 147–175; Thomas Barry, "The Development of the Hierarchy of Effects: An Historical Perspective," *Current Research and Issues in Advertising* 10, nos. 1–2 (1987): 251–295.
[8] Ray, "Communication and the Hierarchy of Effects"; Richard Vaughn, "How Advertising Works: A Planning Model," *Journal of Advertising Research* 20, no. 5 (1980): 27–33; "How Advertising Works: A Planning Model Revisited," *Journal of Advertising Research* 26, no. 1 (1986): 57–66.
[9] Gergely Nyilasy and Leonard Reid, "Agency Practitioner Theories of How Advertising Works," *Journal of Advertising* 38, no. 3 (Fall 2009): 86.
[10] Sandra Moriarty, "Beyond the Hierarchy of Effects: A Conceptual Model," *Current Issues and Research in Advertising* 1 (1983): 45–56.
[11] J. Scott Armstrong, *Persuasive Advertising: Evidence-Based Principles* (New York: Palgrave Macmillan, 2010), 25.
[12] Ivan Preston, "The Association Model of the Advertising Communication Process," *Journal of Advertising* 11, no. 2 (1982): 3–24.
[13] Charles Young, "The Essence of An Ad," Ameritest Research Reports, 2011, www.ameritest.net.
[14] Tom Duncan and Sandra Moriarty, *Driving Brand Value: Using Integrated Marketing to Manage Profitable Stakeholder Relationships* (New York: McGraw-Hill, 1997).
[15] Young, "The Essence of An Ad."
[16] Katie Ford, "Top 5 Takeaways from Cause Marketing Forum," June 4, 2012, www.causemarketingforum.com.
[17] Erik du Plessis, *The Advertised Mind* (London: Kogan Page, 2005), 4.
[18] Marilyn Roberts, "Does Negative Political Advertising Help or Hinder Citizens?," in *Advertising & IMC Practices and Principles*, 9th ed. (Upper Saddle River NJ: Prentice Hall, 2012), 117.
[19] T. W. Farnam, "Study: Negative Campaign Ads Much More Frequent, Vicious Than in Primaries Past," *Washington Post*, February 20, 2012, www.washingtonpost.com.
[20] Jon D. Morris, Chongmoo Woo, James Geason, and Jooyoung Kim, "The Power of Affect: Predicting Intention," *Journal of Advertising Research*, May/June 2002, 7–17.
[21] Russell I. Haley and Allan L. Baldinger, "The Copy Research Validity Project," *Journal of Advertising Research*, April/May 1991, 11–32.
[22] Mark Bittman, "The Right to Sell Kids Junk," *New York Times*, March 27, 2012, www.nytimes.com.
[23] David Stewart and David Furse, *Television Advertising: A Study of 1000 Commercials* (Lexington, MA: Lexington Books, 1986).
[24] Thomas J. Page Jr., Esther Thorson, and Maria Papas Heide, "The Memory Impact of Commercials Varying in Emotional Appeal and Product Involvement," in *Emotion in Advertising*, ed. Stuart J. Agrees, Julie A. Edell, and Tony M. Dubitsky (New York: Quorum Books, 1990), 255–281.
[25] Charles E. Young, "Co-Creativity," Ameritest Reports, 2007, www.ameritest.net, 1.
[26] Ann Marie Barry, "Perception Theory," in *The Handbook of Visual Communication*, ed. Ken Smith, Sandra Moriarty, Gretchen Barbatsis, and Keith Kenney (Mahwah, NJ: Lawrence Erlbaum Associates, 2005), 23–62.
[27] Charles E. Young, *Branded Memory*, (Ideas in Flight, Seattle, 2011): 62.
[28] Gerard Tellis, *Effective Advertising: Understanding When, How, and Why Advertising Works* (Thousand Oaks, CA: Sage, 2004), 183–184; Grant McCracken, "Culture and Consumption: A Theoretical Account of the Structure and Movement of the Cultural Meaning of Consumer Goods," *Journal of Consumer Research* 13 (June 1986): 71–84.
[29] Young, *Branded Memory*, 52.
[30] Preston, "The Association Model of the Advertising Communication Process"; Ivan Preston and Esther Thorson, "Challenges to the Use of Hierarchy Models in Predicting Advertising Effectiveness," in *Proceedings of the 1983 American Academy of Advertising Conference*, ed. Donald Jugenheimer (Lawrence: University Press of Kansas, 1983), 27–33.
[31] Tom Krisher, "GM's Ads Aren't Getting the Job Done," *Boulder Daily Camera*, August 1, 2012, 11A.
[32] Michael Solomon, *Consumer Behavior*, 8th ed. (Upper Saddle River, NJ: Prentice Hall, 2004), 109.
[33] David Ogilvy, *Confessions of an Advertising Man* (New York: Dell, 1963), 119; American Advertising Federation Advertising Hall of Fame, www.advertisinghalloffame.org/members.
[34] Young, "The Essence of An Ad," 2.
[35] Keith O'Brien, "Supersize," *New York Times Magazine*, May 4, 2012, 44–48, 78, 81.
[36] "Davos Man Needs His Image Polishing," *The Economist*, January 25, 2011, www.economist.com.
[37] Charles Young, "Imaging the Four Types of Brand Memory Tags in Restaurant Advertising,

2007," Ameritest/CY Research, 2008, www.ameritest.net, 15.
[38] Richard Cross and Janet Smith, *Customer Bonding: Pathway to Lasting Customer Loyalty* (Lincolnwood, IL: NTC, 1995), 54–55.
[39] Erik du Plessis, *The Advertised Mind: Ground-Breaking Insights into How Our Brains Respond to Advertising* (London: Millward Brown, 2005), 4.
[40] John Philip Jones, *When Ads Work: New Proof That Advertising Triggers Sales*, 2nd ed. (New York: Lexington Books, 2007); Louise Marsland, "How Much Advertising Actually Works?," SAMRA Convention 2006 News, www.bizcommunity.com.
[41] Young, *Branded Memory*, 4.

CHAPTER 5

[1] Sam Schechner, "European Consumers Tighten Their Belts," *Wall Street Journal*, August 6, 2012, A14; "Consumers Are Saving More and Spending and Borrowing Less," Harris Poll news release, June 26, 2009, www.harrisinteractive.com.
[2] Marieke deMooij, "How Advertising Works Cross-Culturally," in *Advertising Principles and Practices*, 8th ed., ed. Sandra Moriarty, Nancy Mitchell, and William Wells (Upper Saddle River, NJ: Pearson Prentice Hall, 2009), 549.
[3] Michael Bush, "Dove Finds Perfect Match in China's 'Ugly Betty,'" *Advertising Age*, May 26, 2009, www.adage.com.
[4] Dave Taylor, "The Odd World of the Cult of Apple," *Boulder Daily Camera*, January 7, 2009, 9.
[5] Susan Mendelsohn, private e-mail, September 20, 2009.
[6] Brian Martin, "Remember to Give Them What They Want (It's Really Very Simple)," *Advertising Age*, February 3, 2010, www.adage.com.
[7] Eugene Schwartz, *Breakthrough Advertising* (Stamford, CT: Bottom Line Books, 2004), 4.
[8] Ann Marie Barry, "Perception Theory," in *The Handbook of Visual Communication,* ed. Ken Smith, Sandra Moriarty, Gretchen Barbatsis, and Keith Kenney (Mahwah, NJ: Lawrence Erlbaum Associates, 2005), 23–62.
[9] David Brooks, "The Segmentation Century," *New York Times*, May 31, 2012, www.nytimes.com.
[10] Bryan Walsh, "America's Food Crisis and How to Fix It," *Time*, August 31, 2009, 31–37; Paul Kaihla, "Sexing Up a Piece of Meat," *Business 2.0*, April 2006, 72–74 www.time.com/time/health/article/0,8599,1917458,00.html.
[11] Dana Mattioli and Miguel Bustillo, "Can Texting Save Stores?," *Wall Street Journal*, May 9, 2012, B1.
[12] Harley Manning and Kerry Bodine, *Outside In: The Power of Putting Customers at the Center of Your Business* (Cambridge, MA: Forrester Research, 2012), 124.
[13] Tamar Lewin, "If Your Kids Are Awake, They're Probably Online," *New York Times,* January 20, 2010, www.nytimes.com.
[14] MCorp Consulting, "Insights and Influence in 140 Characters of Less . . .," *Touchpoint Insights*, October 2009, http://blog.mcorpconsulting.com; Mickey Meeco, "What Do Women Want? Just Ask," *New York Times*, October 29, 2006, 29.
[15] "Graduate Degree Attainment of the U.S. Population," U.S. Census Bureau, July 2009, www.cgsnet.org; Aimeee Heckel, "Layoffs Hit Men Hardest," *Boulder Daily Camera*, October 25, 2009, D1; Richard Stengel, "The American Woman," *Time*, October 26, 2009.
[16] Alan Kirkpatrick, "Creating Equity," *Bylines* (CU SJMC alumni publication), Spring 2009, 15.
[17] Bob Witeck, personal communication, August 10, 2012.
[18] Data computed from "Current Population Survey: A Joint Effort between the Bureau of Labor Statistics and the Census Bureau—Annual Social and Economic Supplement," 2011, www.census.gov.
[19] Binyamin Appelbaum, "Where Wealth Declined Most," *New York Times*, June 11, 2012, www.nytimes.com.
[20] Nathaniel Popper and Tara Bernard, "In Era of Cheap Money, Consumers Are Shut Out," *New York Times,* June 8, 2012, www.nytimes.com.
[21] Laurie Burkitt and Bob Davis, "Chasing China's Shoppers," *Wall Street Journal*, June 15, 2012, B1.
[22] "Fast Facts on U.S. Hispanics," *Advertising Age 2012 Hispanic Fact Pack,* supplement to *Advertising Age*, July 24, 2012, 38.
[23] R. Thomas Umstead, "BET: African-Americans Grow in Numbers, Buying Power," *Multichannel News*, January 26, 2010, www.multichannel.com.
[24] Sabrina Tavernise, "Whites Account for Under Half of Births in U.S.," *New York Times*, May 17, 2012, www.nytimes.com.
[25] Taverniese, "Whites Account for Under Half of Births in U.S."
[26] "Country of Birth," *Advertising Age 2009 Hispanic Fact Pack*, supplement to *Advertising Age,* July 27, 2009, 39.
[27] Jack Neff and Emily York, "ANA Urges Marketers: We Must Be the Ones to Lead the Country Out of Recession," *Advertising Age*, November 9, 2009, www.adage.com.
[28] "Mohammad Now Top Male Name in England, World," *NPR Morning Edition*, September 17, 2009, www.npr.org.
[29] Richard Stengel, "The Responsibility Revolution," *Time*, September 21, 2009, 38–40.
[30] Associated Press, "Designers Target Toddlers Who Have $10,000 to Spare," August 13, 2012, www.cnbc.com.
[31] Clair Cain Miller, "Google and F.T.C. Set to Settle Safari Privacy Charge," *New York Times*, July 10, 2012, www.nytimes.com.
[32] Dana Mattioli, "On Orbitz, Mac Users Steered to Pricier Hotels," *Wall Street Journal*, January 26, 2012, A13.
[33] Kate Stein, "Shop Faster," *New York Times*, April 16, 2009, www.nytimes.com.
[34] Everett Rogers, *Diffusion of Innovations*, 3rd ed. (New York: Free Press, 1983).
[35] Sandra Moriarty, Nancy Mitchell, and William Wells, *Advertising & IMC Principles & Practices*, 9th ed. (Prentice Hall: Upper Saddle River NJ, 2012), 97–98.
[36] Don Schultz, personal communication, August 12, 2012.

CHAPTER 6

[1] Shaynidi Raice, "Facebook's New R&D Machine," *Wall Street Journal*, May 16, 2012, B1.
[2] "Cheesy Fun. It's Not Just for Kids," in *Advertising and IMC Principles & Practices*, 9th ed. (Upper Saddle River NJ: Prentice Hall, 2012), 161–162.
[3] J. A. Bargh, M. Chen, and L. Burrows, "Automaticity of Social Behavior: Direct Effects of Trait Construct and Stereotype Activation on Action," *Journal of Personality & Social Psychology* 71, no. 2 (1996): 230–244; C. Pechmann and S. J. Knight, "An Experimental Investigation of the Joint Effects of Advertising and Peers on Adolescents' Beliefs and Intentions about Cigarette Consumption," *Journal of Consumer Research* 29, no. 1 (2002): 5–19; C. Pechmann and S. Ratneshwar, "The Effects of Antismoking and Cigarette Advertising on Young Adolescents' Perceptions of Peers Who Smoke," *Journal of Consumer Research* 21, no. 2 (1994): 236–251.
[4] Steve Lohr, "Computers That See You, Read You and Even Tell You to Wash," *New York Times*, January 2, 2011, 1.
[5] Emily Glass, "The Eyes Have It: Marketers Now Track Shoppers' Retinas," *Wall Street Journal*, July 12, 2012, B1.
[6] "Research for R.O.I.," Communications Workshop, Chicago: DDB, April 10, 1987.
[7] "Social Is the New Normal for Travel Marketers," *eMarketer*, June 5, 2012, www.emarketer.com.
[8] Julia Chang, "More Than Words," *Sales & Marketing Management*, September 2006, 14.
[9] Emily Steel, "Marketers Find Web Chat Can Be Inspiring," *Wall Street Journal*, November 23, 2009, B8.
[10] "Twilight of the Twinkie?," *Wall Street Journal*, January 14–15, 2012, C4.
[11] Stephanie Clifford, "Social Media Are Giving a Voice to Taste Buds," *New York Times*, July 30, 2012, www.nytimes.com.
[12] Kalia Strong, "4 Ways to Use Pinterest for Market Research," *Search Engine Watch*, May 10, 2012, www.searchenginewatch.com; Amber Wallor, "How Local Businesses Can Do Research and Gain an Edge with Pinterest," *SmartBlog on Social Media*, May 7, 2012, www.smartblogs.com
[13] Ilan Brat, "The Emotional Quotient of Soup Shopping," *Wall Street Journal*, February 17, 2010, B6.
[14] Gina Chon, "To Woo Wealthy, Lexus Attempts Image Makeover," *Wall Street Journal*, March 24–25, 2007, A1.
[15] Sue Shellenbarger, "A Few Bucks for Your Thoughts?," *Wall Street Journal*, May 18, 2011, D3.
[16] Shellenbarger, "A Few Bucks for Your Thoughts?"
[17] Leigh Ann Steere, "Culture Club," *Print*, March/April 1999, 4–5.

[18] Shay Sayre, *Qualitative Methods for Marketplace Research* (Thousand Oaks, CA: Sage, 2001), 31.
[19] Dana Mattioli, "Lululemon's Secret Sauce," *Wall Street Journal*, March 22, 2012, B1.
[20] Russell W. Belk, ed., *Highways and Buyways: Naturalistic Research from the Consumer Behavior Odyssey* (Provo, UT: Association for Consumer Research, 1991).
[21] Sayre, *Qualitative Methods for Marketplace Research*, 20.
[22] Ellen Byron, "Seeing Store Shelves through Senior Eyes," *Wall Street Journal*, September 14, 2009, B1.
[23] Antonio Regalado, "McCann Offers Peek at Lives of Low-Income Latins," *Wall Street Journal*, December 8, 2008, B6.
[24] Regina Lewis, personal communication, November 21, 2006.
[25] Larry Soley, "Projective Techniques for Advertising and Consumer Research, *AAA Newsletter* 6, no. 2 (June 2010): 1, 3–5.
[26] Emily Eakin, "Penetrating the Mind by Metaphor," *New York Times*, February 23, 2002, www.nytimes.com.
[27] Sandra Yin, "New or Me Too," *American Demographics*, September 2002, 28.
[28] Mendelsohn, personal communication.
[29] Jim Edwards, "Victory Dance for the Vain: A Reporter Goes 'Under,'" *Brandweek*, October 3, 2005, 23.
[30] Robin Couler, Gerald Zaltman, and Keith Coulter, "Interpreting Consumer Perceptions of Advertising: An Application of the Zaltman Metaphor Elicitation Technique," *Journal of Advertising* 30, no. 4 (Winter 2001): 1–14; Eakin, "Penetrating the Mind by Metaphor"; Daniel Pink, "Metaphor Marketing," *Fast Company* 14 (March 31, 1998): 214, www.fastcompany.com; HBS Division of Research, The Mind of the Market Laboratory, "ZMET," www.hbs.edu.
[31] Karl Weiss, personal communication, August 10, 2012.

CHAPTER 7

[1] Pat Fallon and Fred Senn, *Juicing the Orange: How to Turn Creativity into a Powerful Business Advantage* (Boston: Harvard Business School Press, 2006).
[2] Tom Duncan and Sandra Moriarty, *Driving Brand Value: Using Integrated Marketing to Manage Profitable Stakeholder Relationships* (New York: McGraw-Hill, 1997).
[3] Joyce Wolburg, "College Students' Responses to Antismoking Messages: Denial, Defiance, and Other Boomerang Effects," *Journal of Consumer Affairs* 40, no. 2 (2006): 294–323; Joyce Wolburg, "Misguided Optimism among College Student Smokers: Leveraging Their Quit Smoking Strategies for Smoking Cessation Campaigns," *Journal of Consumer Affairs* 43, no. 2 (2009): 305–331.
[4] J. Scott Armstrong, *Persuasive Advertising: Evidence-Based Principles* (New York: Palgrave Macmillan, 2010), 16.
[5] Armstrong, *Persuasive Advertising*, 16, 25.
[6] Suzanne Vranica, "Ad Firms Heed Diversity," *Wall Street Journal*, November 29, 2010, B7.
[7] Peggy Kreshel, "What Is Diversity and Why Is It Important?," in Sandra Moriarty, Nancy Mitchell, and William Wells, *Advertising & IMC Principles and Practice*, 9th ed. (Upper Saddle River, NJ: Prentice Hall, 2012), 201.
[8] Larry Kelley and Donald Jugenheimer, *Advertising Account Planning*, 2nd ed. (Armonk, NY: M. E. Sharpe) 2011), 68.
[9] Jack Trout, "Branding Can't Exist without Positioning," *Advertising Age*, March 14, 2005, 28.
[10] Giep Franzen and Sandra Moriarty, *The Science and Art of Branding* (Armonk, NY: M. E, Sharpe, 2009), 5.
[11] John Williams, "Emotional Branding: What's Love Got to Do with It? Plenty!," April 16, 2008, www.entrepreneur.com.
[12] Al Ries and Jack Trout, *Positioning: The Battle for Your Mind* (New York: McGraw-Hill, 1981).
[13] Natalie Zmuda, "Pepsi Tackles Identity Crisis," *Advertising Age*, May 6, 2012, www.adage.com.
[14] Carl Bialik, "New Vehicles Leave MPG Standard Behind," *Wall Street Journal*, August 26, 2009, A12.
[15] Nick Bunkley, "With Low Prices, Hyundai Builds Market Share," *New York Times*, September 22, 2009, www.nytimes.com.
[16] Suzanne Vranica, "Veteran Marketer Promotes a New Kind of Selling," *Wall Street Journal*, October 31, 2008, B4.
[17] Suzanne Vranica, "Paula Deen Pitch Hard to Swallow," *Wall Street Journal*, January 18, 2012, B8.
[18] Kelley and Jugenheimer, *Advertising Account Planning*, 66.
[19] Regina Lewis, panel member on "A Creative Brief That Breathes," American Academy of Advertising Annual Conference, March 15–18, 2012, Myrtle Beach, SC.
[20] Joe Ruff, "Research Goes beyond Focus Groups," *Denver Post*, December 6, 2004, 2E.
[21] Regina Lewis, personal communication, November 21, 2006.
[22] "What Is Account Planning? (and What Do Account Planners Do Exactly?)," Account Planning Group, November 9, 2010, www.apg.org.uk.
[23] Susan Mendelsohn, personal communication, January 8, 2004.
[24] Kelley and Jugenheimer, *Advertising Account Planning*, 73.
[25] Laurie Freeman, "Planner Puts Clients in Touch with Soul of Brands," *Advertising Age*, February 8, 1999, www.adage.com.
[26] Kelley and Jugenheimer, *Advertising Account Planning*, 66–67.
[27] Charlie Robertson, "Creative Briefs and Briefings," in *How to Plan Advertising*, 2nd ed., ed. Alan Cooper (London: Thomson Learning and the Account Planning Group, 2004), 62.

CHAPTER 8

[1] Tina Sussman, "Where Ink Is Still King," *Boulder Daily Camera*, January 8, 2012, 4d.
[2] Mark Stuhlfaut and Margo Berman, "Pedagogic Challenges: The Teaching of Creative Strategy in Advertising Courses," *Journal of Advertising Education*, Fall 2009, 37.
[3] Try Montague, Keynote Speech, Effie Awards Gala, June 7, 2006, www.effie.org/gala/montague.html.
[4] Kevin Keller, *Strategic Brand Management*, 3rd ed. (Upper Saddle River, NJ: Prentice Hall, 2008), 76–81.
[5] Melissa Korn and Rachel Silverman, "Forget B-School, D-School Is Hot," *Wall Street Journal*, June 7, 2012, B1.
[6] Bob Garfield, "Anti-Texting PSA Converts at Least One Viewer, "*Advertising Age*, September 2, 2009, www.adage.com; "Hard-Hitting Video Shows Dangers of Texting while Driving," MSNBCcom, August 25, 2009, www.msnbc.com.
[7] Charles Frazer, "Creative Strategy: A Management Perspective," *Journal of Advertising* 12, no. 4 (1983): 36–41.
[8] Ron Taylor, "A Six Segment Message Strategy Wheel," *Journal of Advertising Research*, November–December 1997, 7–17.
[9] William Wells, "How Advertising Works," speech to the St. Louis AMA, September 17, 1986.
[10] Kathleen Hall Jamieson, *Packaging the Presidency: A History and Criticism of Presidential Campaign Advertising*, 3rd ed. (New York: Oxford University Press, 1996); Kathleen Hall Jamieson, *Dirty Politics; Deception, Distraction, and Democracy* (New York: Oxford University Press, 1992).
[11] John G. Geer, *In Defense of Negativity: Attack Ads in Presidential Campaigns* (Chicago: University of Chicago Press, 2006).
[12] Marilyn Roberts, "Does Negative Political Advertising Help or Hinder Citizens?," in Sandra Moriarty, Nancy Mitchell, and William Wells, *Advertising & IMC Practices and Principles*, 9th ed. (Upper Saddle River NJ: Prentice Hall, 2012), 117.
[13] Stuart Schwartzapfel, "Real 'Mad Men' Pitched Safety to Sell Volvos," *New York Times*, March 5, 2012, 13.
[14] Jack Neff, "Funny TV Ads Don't Sell Better Than Unfunny Ones," *Advertising Age*, July 13, 2012, www.adage.com.
[15] Norihiko Shirouzu, "Jeremy Lin Hired to Endorse Volvo," *Wall Street Journal*, March 20, 2012, B4.
[16] Christina Binkley, "Behind the Choice of a Luxury-Bag Pitchman," *Wall Street Journal*, June 7, 2012, D3.
[17] Darren Rovell, Friday June 18, 2010, CNBC.com.
[18] Stephanie Rosenbloom, "Got Twitter? You've Been Scored," *New York Times*, June 26, 2011, www.nyt.com.
[19] Mark Stuhlfaut, "How Creative Are We? The Teaching of Creativity Theory and Training," *Journal of Advertising Education* 11, no. 2 (Fall 2007): 49–59.

[20] Stuart Elliott, "In New Ad, GoDaddy Upgrades Its Image," *New York Times*, July 15, 2012, www.nytimes.com.
[21] Andrew Newman, "No Actors, Just Patients in Unvarnished Spots for Hospitals," *New York Times*, May 4, 2009, www.nytimes.com.
[22] "Top 100 Advertising Campaigns," *Advertising Age*, March 29, 1999, www.adage.com.
[23] Rupal Parekh, "Domination Wanted: VW Dumps Crispin in Bid to Triple U.S. Sales," *Advertising Age*, August 24, 2009, www.adage.com.
[24] James Webb Young, *A Technique for Producing Ideas*, 3rd ed. (Chicago: Crain Books, 1975).
[25] Jerri Moore and William D. Wells, *R.O.I. Guidebook: Planning for Relevance, Originality and Impact in Advertising and Other Marketing Communications* (New York: DDB Needham, 1991).
[26] Thomas Russell and Glenn Verrill, *Kleppner's Advertising Procedure*, 14th ed. (Upper Saddle River, NJ: Prentice Hall, 2002), 457.
[27] Tevor Guthrie, "Sometimes It's Better to Study Dolphin Brains Than Advertising," *Advertising Age*, July 17, 2012, www.adage.com.
[28] Sheri J. Broyles, "The Creative Personality: Exploring Relations of Creativity and Openness to Experience," unpublished doctoral dissertation, Southern Methodist University, 1995.
[29] Broyles, "The Creative Personality."
[30] Graham Wallas, *The Art of Thought* (New York: Harcourt, Brace, 1926); Alex F. Osborn, *Applied Imagination*, 3rd ed. (New York: Scribner's, 1963).
[31] Linda Conway Correll, "Exercise Your Creative Muscles," in Moriarty et al., *Advertising & IMC Principles and Practices*, 249.
[32] David Droga, "Sweating Ad Copy Like 'Mad Men,'" *Wall Street Journal*, June 11–12, 2011, C12.
[33] Idea Champions, "The 10 Personas of a Good Brainstorm Facilitator," March 30, 2012, www.ideachampions.com.
[34] Goeffrey Fowler, Brian Steinberg, and Aaron Patrick, "Mac and PC's Overseas Adventures," *Wall Street Journal*, March 1, 2007, B1.
[35] Doris Willens, *Nobody's Perfect: Bill Bernbach and the Golden Age of Advertising* (self-published using Amazon's CreateSpace, 2009).
[36] Al Ries, "Advertising Could Do with More of Bernbach's Genius," *Advertising Age*, July 6, 2009, www.adage.com.
[37] Janet Forgrieve, "Ad Agency's Colo., Fla. Offices on Same Team," *Rocky Mountain News Rocky Business*, March 8, 2007, 6.

CHAPTER 9

[1] Tom Murphy, "Drug Brand Search Extends from A to Z," *Boulder Daily Camera*, January 18, 2008, 9A.
[2] "The Advertising Century: Top 10 Slogans," *Advertising Age*, March 29, 1999, www.adage.com.
[3] Gail Collins, "Come Visit. Live Life. Eat Cheese," *New York Times*, April 25, 2009, www.nytimes.com.
[4] Ennis Higgins, "Conversations with David Ogilvy," in *The Art of Writing Advertising* (Chicago: Advertising Publications, 1965).
[5] Susan Gunelius, *Kick-Ass Copywriting in 10 Easy Steps* (Irvine, CA: Entrepreneur Press, 2008).
[6] Brent Kendall, "Skechers to Pay $50 Million to Settle Ad Suit," *Wall Street Journal*, May 17, 2012, B3.
[7] Federal Trade Commission, "Kellogg Settles FTC Charges That Ads for Frosted Mini-Wheats Were False," April 20, 2009, http://ftc.gov/opa/2009/04/kellogg.shtm.
[8] Bruce Horovitz, "Critics Blast Kellogg's Claim That Cereals Can Boost Immunity," *USA Today*, November 2, 2009, www.usatoday.com.
[9] Tiffany Hsu, "FDA Warns General Mills over Cheerios Cholesterol Claims," May 12, 2009, www.latimesblogs.latimes.com.
[10] Sanette Tanaka, "A Motivated Seller by Any Other Name . . .," *Wall Street Journal*, October 5, 2012, M4.
[11] Karen Mallia, "Practice: Where Is Creative Headed?," *Advertising & IMC Principles and Practices*, 9th ed. (Upper Saddle River, NJ: Prentice Hall, 2012), 262.
[12] Yumiko Ono, "Sometimes Ad Agencies Mangle English Deliberately," *Wall Street Journal*, November 4, 1997, B1.
[13] David Droga, "Sweating Ad Copy Like 'Mad Men,'" *Wall Street Journal*, June 11–12, 2011, C12.
[14] David Ogilvy, *Ogilvy on Advertising* (New York: Vintage, 1985).
[15] Sandra Dallas, "Road to Pave? Remember Burma-Shave!," *BusinessWeek*, December 30, 1996, 8; Frank Rowsome Jr., *The Verse by the Side of the Road* (New York: Dutton, 1965).
[16] Paul D. Bolls and Robert F. Potter, "I Saw It on the Radio: The Effects of Imagery Evoking Radio Commercials on Listeners' Allocation of Attention and Attitude toward the Ad," in *Proceedings of the Conference of the American Academy of Advertising*, ed. Darrel D. Muehling (Lexington, KY: American Academy of Advertising, 1998), 123–130.
[17] Peter Hochstein, "Ten Rules for Making Better Radio Commercials," Ogilvy & Mather's *Viewpoint*, 1981.
[18] Jenna Wortham, "Coining Terminology for Life on the Web," *New York Times*, May 6, 2012, 3.
[19] Blessie Miranda and Kuen-HeeJu-Pak, "A Content Analysis of Banner Advertisements: Potential Motivating Features," Annual Conference Baltimore, Association for Education in Journalism and Mass Communication, August 1998.
[20] Edward Hall, *Beyond Culture* (Garden City, NY: Anchor Press/Doubleday, 1976).

CHAPTER 10

[1] Laura Ries, "Repositioning 'Positioning:' Connect with Consumers with a Visual Hammer, Not Verbal Nails," *Advertising Age*, March 12, 2012, www.adage.com.
[2] Sandra Dolbow, "Brand Builders," *Brandweek*, July 24, 2000, 19.
[3] Charles Young, "*The Essence of an Ad*," Ameritest Special Report, 2011, 1–2.
[4] Todd Cunningham, Amy Shea, and Charles Young, "The Advertising Magnifier Effect: An MTV Study," Ameritest Research Report, 2006, 15–16.
[5] "Shepard Fairey, Obama Poster Artist in Legal Battle with AP, Makes Major Admissions in Case," *Editor & Publisher*, October 16, 2009, www.editorandpublisher.com; "Protecting AP's Intellectual Property: The Shepard Fairey Case," Associated Press, October 20, 2009, www.ap.org/prights/fairey.html; "The Shepard Fairey-AP Case: A Clearer Picture," *Los Angeles Times*, November 1, 2009, www.latimes.com.
[6] Chad Bray, "Artist Gets Probation in Dispute over 'Hope,'" *Wall Street Journal*, September 7, 2012, www.wsj.com.
[7] Kunur Patel, "Lessons from the Microsoft Photoshop Fiasco," *Advertising Age*, August 31, 2009, www.adage.com.
[8] Loretta Chao and Betsy McKay, "Pepsi Steps into Coke Realm: Red, China," *Wall Street Journal*, September 12, 2007, www.wsj.com.
[9] Bill Marsh, "Warmer, Fuzzier: The Refreshed Logo," *New York Times*, April 31, 2009, 2.
[10] Noreen O'Leary, "Legibility Lost," *Adweek*, October 5, 1987, D7.
[11] A. O. Scott, "Finding Drama in Newfangled Filmmaking," *New York Times*, August 30, 2012, www.nytimes.com.
[12] Charles Goldsmith, "Adding Special to Effects," *Wall Street Journal*, February 26, 2003, B1.
[13] Stuart Elliott, "JanSport Sings 'Do-Re-Mi' to Teens," *New York Times Direct*, April 29, 2003, www.nytimes.com.
[14] Stuart Elliott, "Is That Honda Commercial Real?," *New York Times Direct*, June 10, 2003, NYTDirect@nytimes.com; "Honda's Cog Does It Again, Taking the Grand Clio," *AdForum Alert*, May 19, 2004, www.adforum.com.
[15] Barbara Haislip, "Picture (Not) Perfect," *Wall Street Journal*, May 21, 2012, R7.
[16] Laura Ruel and Nora Paul, "Eyetracking Points the Way to Effective News Article Design," *Online Journalism Review*, March 13, 2007, www.ojr.org.
[17] Heather McWilliams, "Zooming in to Web Video," *Business Plus*, March 5, 2007, 3.

CHAPTER 11

[1] Erwin Ephron, "Engagement Is Many Different Things," *Admap*, April 2006, 41–42; Joe Mandese, "Medialink," *Admap*, April 2006, 10.
[2] "Sports Ad Spending Roars Back," *Sports Business Journal*, May 2–8, 2011, 1; "McDonald's Unveils Sponsorship Plans for London 2012 Olympic Games," press release, July 20, 2011; McDonald's Announces Eight-Year Extension of Top Olympic Sponsorship through 2020," press release, January 13, 2012; Stephanie Clifford, "An Online Game So mysterious Its Famous Sponsor Is Hidden" *New York Times,* April 1, 2008, www.nytimes.com; Olympic Marketing Fact File 2012, International Olympic Committee, www.freedownloadb.com.

[3] Laura Bright, "Media Planning Education in 2012 and Beyond," American Academy of Advertising, Myrtle Beach, SC, March 15–18, 2012.

[4] Larry Kelley and Donald Jugenheimer, *Advertising Account Planning: Planning and Managing an IMC Campaign*, 2nd ed. (Armonk, NY: M. E Sharpe, 2011), 160.

[5] Yeusung Kim and Sheetal Patel, "Teaching Advertising Media Planning in a Changing Media Landscape," *Journal of Advertising Education*, Fall 2012, 21.

[6] "2009 Set to Show First Revenue Decline for Nation's Top 100 Media Cos.," *Advertising Age*, December 28, 2009, www.adage.com.

[7] Kantar Media Reports U.S. Advertising Expenditures Increased 0.8 Percent in 2011," Kantar Media News Release, March 12, 2012, http://kantarmedia.com/en/press-room.

[8] "About AARP, The Magazine," AARP Press Center, November 15, 2009, www .aarpmagazine.org.

[9] Bright, "Media Planning Education in 2012 and Beyond."

[10] Wayne Arnold, "Beyond 'Gangnam Style:' Why Korea Is a Pop Culture and Products Powerhouse," *Advertising Age*, November 28, 2012, www.adage.com.

[11] Donald Jugenheimer, *Advertising and IMC Principles and Practice* 9th ed. (Upper Saddle River, NJ: Prentice Hall, 2012), 330.

[12] Larry Kelley, personal communication, July 12 and 20, 2012.

[13] Larry Kelley, Donald Jugenheimer, and Kim Sheehan, *Advertising Media Planning*, 3rd ed. (Armonk, NY: M. E. Sharpe, 2012), 7.

[14] "P&G to Slash $10 Billion in Costs over Five Years," *Advertising Age*, February 23, 2012, www.adage.com.

[15] Newspaper Association of America, "The Source: Newspapers by the Numbers 2006," January 2007, 3–4, www.naa.org.

[16] Matt Webb Mitovich, "Ratings: Super Bowl XLVI Is Most-Watched TV Program Ever," *TV Line*, February 6, 2012, www.tvline.com.

[17] Bright, "Media Planning Education in 2012 and Beyond."

[18] "The Multi-Screen Marketer," published by the IAB, May 2012, www.iab.net/media/file/The_Multiscreen_Marketer.pdf; "The Rise of the Connected Viewer," Pew Research Center report, July, 2012, www.pewinternet.org/~/media//Files/Reports/2012/PIP_Connected_Viewers.pdf.

[19] Stuart Elliott, "A Bet (and Tattoo) on an Olympian," *New York Times*, July 4, 2012, www.nytimes.com; Matt Flegenheimer, "M.T.A. Opens Front of MetroCard to Advertising," *New York Times*, July 18, 2012, www.nytimes.com.

[20] Wayne Friedman, "TV Product Placement Delivers for '24,'" *Media Post*, January 19, 2010, www.mediapost.com.

[21] N. E. Marsden, "What TV Is Really Selling," *Washington Post*, October 30, 2009, www .washingtonpost.com.

[22] Beth Bulik, "Layering in Local," "Smart Strategies for Local Marketing," and "Location, Location, Location: Search, Social," *AdAge Insights*, October 1, 2012, 3, 5.

[23] Michael Bush, "What's the Next Marketing Platform? How to Measure Success? Ad Age's Media Mavens Answer the Big Questions," *Advertising Age*, December 9, 2009, www .adage.com.

CHAPTER 12

[1] Erik Sass, "Newspaper Ad Spending Now Half What It Was in 2005," *Media Daily News*, March 27, 2012, www.mediapost.com.

[2] Jason Del Rey, "In USA Today Redesign, Hope for a New Canvas for Web Advertisers," *Ad Age*, September 13, 2012, www.adage.com.

[3] Paul Gillin, "Surprise! Researchers See Industry Growth," *Newspaper Death Watch*, October 12, 2012, www .newspaperdeathwatch.com.

[4] Christine Haughney, "Taking Pointers from Web Sites, *USA Today* Modernizes Its Look," *New York Times*, September 13, 2012, www .nytimes.com.

[5] Alan Mutter, "Twin Threats Peril Preprint Newspaper Ads," *Reflections of a Newsosaur* (blog), August 29, 2012, www.newsosaur. blogspot.com.

[6] Tim Nudd, "The Spot: High on the Hogs," *Adweek*, May 8, 2012, www.adweek.com.

[7] "eMarketer: Magazines to See Positive Ad Spending Growth in 2012," *eMarketer*, September 25, 2012, www.emarketer.com.

[8] Jerry Schwartz, "*Newsweek* Axes Print Magazine," *Boulder Daily Camera*, October 19, 2012, 2A; Christine Haughney and David Carr, "At *Newsweek*, Ending Print and a Blend of Two Styles," *New York Times*, October 18, 2012, www.mediadecoder,blogs.nytimes.com.

[9] *2009–2010 Magazine Handbook* (New York: Magazine Publishers Association, 2009), 17.

[10] Emily Steel, "Meredith Builds Up a Sideline in Marketing," *Wall Street Journal*, February 25, 2010, B6.

[11] "*Ladies' Home Journal* Lets Readers Write the Magazine," *Advertising Age*, January 8, 2012, www.adage.com.

[12] "*Ladies' Home Journal* Lets Readers Write the Magazine"; Stuart Elliott, "Ad Campaign Will Encourage People to Love People,'" *New York Times*, September 11, 2012, www.mediadecoder.blogs.nytimes. com; Stuart Elliott, "*Woman's Day* Turns 75 While Looking Forward," *New York Times*, September 16, 2012, www.nytimes.com; Stuart Elliott, "*Glamour* Campaign Tries to Claim a Generation, *New York Times*, September 9, 2012, www.nytimes.com.

[13] David Carr, "How Esquire Survived Publishing's Dark Days," *New York Times*, January 22, 2012, www.nytimes.com.

[14] John Jannarone, "'Yellow Pages' Last Lifeline: Clinging to Each Other," *Wall Street Journal*, August 22, 2012, B1; Cathie Gandel, "White Pages Phone Books Fading Away," *AARP Magazine*, October 2009, 8.

[15] "Pittman Envisions New Life for Radio," *Wall Street Journal*, October 15, 2012, B1.

[16] "Pittman Envisions New Life for Radio," B1.

[17] Paul Farhi, "Limbaugh's Audience Size? It's Largely Up in the Air," *Washington Post*, March 7, 2009, www.washingtonpost.com.

[18] Ron Winslow, "Watching TV Linked to Higher Risk of Death," *Wall Street Journal*, January 12, 2010, D1.

[19] John Jurgensen, "Reinventing the Music Video," *Wall Street Journal*, May 6, 2011, D1.

[20] Matthew Futterman, Sam Schechner, and Suzanne Vranica, "NFL: The League That Runs TV," *Wall Street Journal*, December 15, 2011, B1.

[21] David Carr and Tim Arango, "A Fox Chief at the Pinnacle of Media and Politics," *New York Times*, January 20, 2010, www.nytimes.com.

[22] Anthony Crupi, "Good News/Bad News: Cable Notches Record Upfront Haul, but Market Is Slumping," *Adweek*, September 17, 2012, www.adweek.com.

[23] Bob Lodice, "10 Events That Transformed Marketing," *Advertising Age*, January 18, 2010, www.adage.com.

[24] Brian Steinberg, "Cartier's Three-Minute Gem Extends Demand for Longer Sports," *Advertising Age*, March 7, 2012, www .adage.com.

[25] Andrew Martin, "The Fitness Revolution Will Be Televised (after Leno)," *New York Times*, March 29, 2011, 1.

[26] Paul Bond, "The Growing Use of DVRs," *The Hollywood Reporter*, April 28, 2009, http://hollywoodreporter.com.

[27] Brian Stelter, "Battle over Dish's Ad-Skipping Begins as Networks Go to Court," *New York Times*, May 24, 2012, www .nytimes.com.

[28] Marisa Guthrie, "Ralph Lauren to Sponsor PBS' 'Masterpiece,' Create Special 'Downton Abbey' Ads," *The Hollywood Reporter*, September 10, 2012, www .hollywoodreporter.com.

[29] John Kubicek, "Super Bowl XLVI Is the Most-Watched TV Program of All Time," *The Voice*, February 6, 2012, www.buddytv.com.

[30] "Boomer TV," *AARP Magazine*, June 2012, 7.

[31] Arian Campo-Flores and Sam Schechner, "Disney's ABC, Univision Mull News-Channel Launch," *Wall Street Journal*, February 7, 2012, B1; Christopher Stewart and Arian Campo-Flores, "Univision, ABC to Start News Channel—in English," *Wall Street Journal*, May 8, 2012, B1.

[32] Daisuke Wakabayashi, "Sony Pins Future on a 3-Revival," *Wall Street Journal*, January 7, 2010, A1; Suzanne Vranica, "Marketers Face Zooming Costs as ESPN Launches 3-D Channel," *Wall Street Journal*, June 10, 2010, B1.

[33] Tanzina Vega, "An Upgrade for the Show before the Show," *New York Times*, April 5, 2012, www.nytimes.com.

[34] *The Signage Sourcebook* (South Bend, IN: The Signage Foundation, 2003).

[35] Rhodina Villanueva, "Country's 1st Plant Billboard Launched," *Philippine Star*, June 24, 2011, www.philstar.com.

[36] SayaaWeissman, "Cool Stuff: TNT Electromagnet Dots Billboard," *Digiday*, July 20, 2012, www.digiday.com.

[37] Stephanie Clifford, "As Storefronts Become Vacant, Ads Arrive," *New York Times*, May 12, 2009, www.nytimes.com.

[38] David Dunlap, "New Territory for Ads, with a Moving Target," *New York Times*, September 16, 2012, www.cityroom.blogs.nytimes.com.

[39] Kit Eaton, "Online Ads Turn a Corner: More Spent on Internet Ads Than TV in U.K.," *Fast Company*, September 30, 2009, www.fastcompany.com.

[40] Mike Orcutt, "Online Advertising Poised to Finally Surpass Print," *Technology Review*, October 7, 2012, www.technologyreview.com.

[41] Shayndie Raice, "Facebook Combats Criticism over Ads," *Wall Street Journal*, June 13, 2012, 13B; Geoffrey Fowler, "Facebook: One Billion and Counting," *Wall Street Journal*, October 5, 2012, B1; Tanzina Vega and Stuart Elliott, "At Ad Week, the Vital Role of Digital Marketing," *New York Times*, October 2, 2012, www.nytimes.com; "Big Spenders Push Ad Line, but Facebook Holds Ground," *Advertising Age*, May 27, 2012, www.adage.com.

[42] Beth Bulik, "Location, Location, Location: Search, Social," *Ad Age Insights*, October 1, 2012, 7.

[43] Amir Efrati, "Google Near Ad Triple Crown," *Wall Street Journal*, September 20, 2012, B7.

[44] Fowler, "Facebook."

[45] Michael Wolff, "The Facebook Fallacy," *Technology Review*, May 22, 2012, www.technologyreview.com.

[46] Rosalind Gray, "Catching New Customers," *The Costco Connection*, February 2012, 23.

[47] Suzanne Vranica, "Element of Choice Draws in Online Viewers," *Wall Street Journal*, February 4, 2010, B11.

[48] Brad Stone, "Craigslist Expands Legal Battle against Spammers," *New York Times*, October 8, 2009, http://bits.blogs.nytimes.com.

[49] Esther Thorson, personal communication, April 20, 2009; Abbey Klaasen, "The State of Search Marketing: 2009," *Advertising Age*, November 2, 2009, www.adage.com.

[50] Brad Stone, "Google Adds Live Updates to Results," *New York Times*, December 8, 2009, www.nytimes.com.

[51] Emily Steel, "Pricing Tensions Shake Up Web Display-Ad Market," *Wall Street Journal*, September 21, 2009, B6.

[52] Emily Steel, "Target-Marketing Becomes More Communal," *Wall Street Journal*, November 5, 2009, B10.

[53] Emily Steel, "Web Sites Debate Best Values for Advertising Dollars," *Wall Street Journal*, August 13, 2009, B7.

[54] Amir Efrati, "New Display Ad Push Adds to Bag of Tricks," *Wall Street Journal*, January 20, 2012, B6.

[55] Will Oremus, "The Chart That Shows How Google Ate the Newspaper Industry," Slate.com, November 11, 2012, www.slate.com.

[56] Martha Woodroof, "In a 24/7 World, What Is a Magazine?," NPR, August 30, 2009, www.npr.org; Suzanne Vranica, "WPP Chief Tempers Hope for Ad Upturn," *Wall Street Journal*, September 21, 2009, B1.

[57] Theresa Howard, "CBS, Pepsi Max Put Video in Some Magazine Ads," *USA Today*, August 19, 2009, http://usatoday.com.

CHAPTER 13

[1] Lynn Elber, "McDonald's Adds TV to Menu," *Boulder Daily Camera*, September 27, 2012, 6B.

[2] Karl Greenberg, "Nissan Expands GT Academy for 2012," *Marketing Daily*, May 7, 2012, www.mediapost.com.

[3] Elie Mystal, "True Story: Harvard Law Sells Naming Rights to Its New Bathrooms," *Above the Law*, February 1, 2012, www.abovethelaw.com.

[4] Chris Herring, "Coke Bottle Is Part Plant," *Wall Street Journal*, January 25, 2010, B7.

[5] Eric Pfanner, "Old Medium Dusted Off," *International Herald Tribune*, July 9, 2007, 11.

[6] Evan Ramstad, "Big Brother, Now at the Mall," *Wall Street Journal*, October 9, 2012, B6.

[7] Lisa Lacy, "Beneful Lets People Play with Digital Dogs," *ClickZ*, May 7, 2012, www.clickz.com; Spencer Ante, "Billboards Join Wired Age," *Wall Street Journal*, February 4, 2011, B10.

[8] Jerry Bennett and Mike Ramsey, "Drivers Seek Help with Techie Cars," *Wall Street Journal*, October 5, 2012, B8.

[9] Rachel Pannett, "Aussie Delicacy Vegemite Loses Some of Its Savory Appeal," *Wall Street Journal*, May 10, 2012, A1.

[10] Evan Hessel and Taylor Buley, "How to Know Your Web Ad Is Working," *Forbes*, April 29, 2009, www.forbes.com.

[11] Eleftheria Parpis, "VW Plays 'Truth & Dare' Online," *Adweek*, May 5, 2009, http://adweek.com.

[12] "Top 10 Social Media Stars," *Fortune*, May 7, 2012, www.money.cnn.com.

[13] Douglas MacMilan, "Blogaola: The FTC Takes on Paid Posts," *Business Week*, May 19, 2009, www.businessweek.com; N. E. Marsden, "What TV Is Really Selling," *Washington Post*, October 30, 2009, www.washingtonpost.com.

[14] Beth Bulik, "Location, Location, Location: Search, Social," *AdAge Insights*, October 1, 2012, 7.

[15] "Mom & Pops Beat Walmart on Facebook," *Advertising Age*, September 20, 2012, www.adage.com.

[16] James Stewart, "When the Network Effect Goes into Reverse," *New York Times*, August 17, 2012, www.nytimes.com.

[17] Andy Sernovitz, "How National Geographic Uses Social Media to Get Fans Talking," *SmartBlog on Social Media*, May 4, 2012, www.smartblogs.com.

[18] Elizabeth Olson, "Grey Poupon Ups the Ante on Assuming an Elite Image," *New York Times*, September 22, 2012, www.nytimes.com.

[19] Stacy Nunnally, "Dos and Don'ts: Scheduling Social Media Activity," *Nashville Business Journal*, May 9, 2012, www.bizjournals.com.

[20] Dan Zarrella, "5 Questions and Answers about Facebook Marketing," Dan Zarrella blog, January 14, 2011, www.danzarrella.com; Nunnally, "Dos and Don'ts."op cit.

[21] "Facebook to Brands: You're Posting Stuff Wrong," *Advertising Age*, May 6, 2012, www.adage.com.

[22] Al Ries, "We're So Quick to Crown Social-Media Successes That We Forget What They're Actually Based On," *Advertising Age*, May 6, 2012, www.adage.com; Ronald Grover, "'Hunger Games'" Success Spells Trouble for TV Ads," *Reuters*, May 4, 2012, www.reuters.com.

[23] Brandon Bornancin, "Off the Wall Overview and Capabilities," *Resource Interactive*, 2009, slide 29, www.slideshare.net/BrandonBornancin/off-the-wall-by-resource-interactive.

[24] Michael Learmounth, "Mobile Marketing Fact Pack 2012," *Advertising Age Mobile Fact Pack*, August 20, 2012, 1.

[25] Rimma Kats, "Starbucks Taps Mobile Advertising to Boast Product Awareness," *Mobile Marketer*, September 11, 2012, www.mobilemarketer.com.

[26] "Mobile Ad Spending," *Advertising Age Mobile Fact Pack*, 2012, August 20, 2012, 6.

[27] Kunur Patel, "Google Wins Inaugural Cannes Mobile Grand Prix," *Advertising Age Mobile Fact Pack*, August 20, 2012, 22–23.

[28] Julie Jargon, "Domino's IT Staff Delivers Slick Site, Ordering System," *Wall Street Journal*, November 24, 2009, B5.

[29] Joe Mandese, "Simultaneous Research Study Reveals Consumers Buzz Most over Word-of-Mouth, Not Ads," *MediaPost Publications*, January 19, 2007, http://publications.mediapost.com.

[30] Steve Knox, "Why Effective Word-of-Mouth Disrupts Schemas," *Advertising Age*, January 25, 2010, www.adage.com.

[31] "Matching the Medium with the Message in Word-of-Mouth Marketing," *Knowledge @ Wharton*, April 11, 2012, www.knowledge.whaton.upenn.edu.

[32] "The Buzz Starts Here: Finding the First Mouth for Word-of-Mouth Marketing, *Knowledge @ Wharton*, March 4, 2009, www.knowledge.wharton.upenn.edu.

[33] Hairong Li, quoted in *Advertising & IMC Principles and Practice*, 9th ed., ed. Sandra Moriarty, Nancy Mitchell, and William Wells (Upper Saddle River, NJ: Prentice Hall, 2012), 397–398.

[34] "HP, Ford, and Sony Top Social Mentions List of Brands, *Search Engine Watch*, August 3, 2012, www.clickz.com.

[35] Brandon Griggs and John Sutter, "Oprah, Ashton Kutcher Mark Twitter 'Turning Point,'" *CNN*, April 18, 2009, www.cnn.com.

[36] Elizabeth Mitchell, "Republicans' #areyoubetteroff Hashtag Backfires When Twitter Responds 'Yes,'" *PR News*, September 7, 2012, www.mediabistro.com.

[37] Suzanne Kapner, "Citi Won't Sleep on Customer Tweets," *Wall Street Journal*, October 5, 2012, C1.

[38] David Streitfeld, "The Best Reviews Money Can Buy," *New York Times*, August 26, 2012, 1, 6.

[39] "Top 10 Social Media Stars," *Fortune*, May 7, 2012, www.money.cnn.com.

[40] Jack Neff, "P&G Embraces Facebook as Big Part of Its Marketing Plan," *Advertising Age*, January 25, 2010, www.adage.com.
[41] "Five Questions with Babytree CEO Allen Wang," *Advertising Age*, August 23, 2012, www.adage.com.
[42] Sean Ludwig, "Pinterest Now the Third Most Popular Social Network after Facebook & Twitter," *VB(Venture Beat)*, April 5, 2012, www.venturebeat.com.
[43] "U.K. Pinterest Contest Highlights Dangers of Driving in Heels," *Advertising Age*, April 11, 2012, www.adage.com.
[44] Natasha Singer, "Learning to Chase Online Word of Mouth," *New York Times*, May 26, 2012, www.nytimes.com.
[45] "Beware of Dissatisfied Consumers: They Like to Blab," *Knowledge @ Wharton*, March 8, 2006, www.knowledge.wharton.edu.
[46] Personal conversation, January 5, 2013.
[47] Somini Sengupta, "Facebook's False Faces Undermine Its Credibility," *New York Times*, November 12, 2012, www.nytimes.com.
[48] "Overheard," *Wall Street Journal*, November 27, 2012, C10.
[49] Jack Neff, "Unilever's CMO Throws Down the Social-Media Gauntlet," *Advertising Age*, April 13, 2009, www.adage.com.
[50] Natalie Zmuda, "Alex Bogusky Takes on Coca-Cola, Soda Companies," *Advertising Age*, October 9, 2012, www.adage.com.
[51] Beth Bulik, "Army of Tweeting Tax Pros Leads H&R Block Social Push," *Advertising Age*, January 4, 2010, www.adage.com.
[52] Claire Miller, "Google Wants to Join the Party, Not Crash It," *New York Times*, October 14, 2012, www.nytimes.com.

CHAPTER 14

[1] Katerina-Eva Matsa, Jane Sasseen and Amy Mitchell, "Magazines by the Numbers," The State of the New Media 2012: A Pew Report, http://stateofthemedia.org/2012.
[2] "Northwestern University Reader Experience Study Tool Kit," Magazine Publishers of America, December 12, 2012, www.magazine.org; Northwestern University Media Management Center, *Magazine Reader Experience Study*, www.mediamanagementcenter.org.
[3] Andrew Brandt, "Super Bowl 2012 Facts and Figures," *Huff Post Sports*, October 22, 2012, www.huffingtonpost.com.
[4] Sandra Gonzalez, "'Chuck' Series Finale React: Were You Satisfied with the Ending?," *Entertainment Weekly*, January 27, 2012, www.popwatch.ew.com; Emily Bryson York, "Subway Caught Up in Fan Effort to Save NBC Series 'Chuck,'" *Advertising Age*, April 27, 2009, www.adage.com.
[5] Jack Neff and Rupal Parekh, "Dove Takes Its New Men's Line to the Super Bowl," *Advertising Age*, January 5, 2010, www.adagecom.
[6] Courtney Rubin, "Shoppers Combine Search, Social Media to Fuel Decisions," *Inc.*, February 25, 2011, www.inc.com.
[7] "9 Things to Know about Influencing Purchasing Decisions," *ConversionXL*, March 19, 2012, www.conversionxl.com.
[8] "Audi: The Art of the Heist, Effie Awards Brief of Effectiveness, 2006, www.edwardbouches.comwp-content/uploads/2012/01/art-of-heist.pdf.
[9] Alex Porter, "FMOT vs. ZMOT: A Conversation with Morgan McAlenney," Location3, May 4, 2011, www.location3.com.
[10] Tom Van Riper, "Super Bowl Ads: A Whole New Ballgame," *Forbes*, January 13, 2010, www.forbes.com.
[11] Chrissy Wissinger, "Prosper MediaPlanIQ: Telecom Companies Need to Reallocate Ad Expenditures," BIGresearch press release, February 5, 2009, www.bigresearch.com.
[12] Laura Bright, "Media Planning Education in 2012 and Beyond," American Academy of Advertising 2012 Conference, Myrtle Beach, SC, March 15–18, 2012.
[13] "Sweet Talk," *Evolution Bureau*, downloaded September 17, 2012, www.evb.com.
[14] Bright, "Media Planning Education in 2012 and Beyond."
[15] Beth Bulik, "Layering in Local," *Smart Strategies for Local Marketing*, an Ad Age Insights Report, October 1, 2011, 3.
[16] Beth Bulik, "Location, Location, Location: Search, Social," *Smart Strategies for Local Marketing*, an Ad Age Insights report, October 1, 2011, 7.
[17] "Validated Campaign Essentials, comScore, October 21, 2012, www.comscore.com.
[18] Carla Lloyd, "Modern Media Planning," in *Strategic Media Decisions*, 2nd ed., ed. Marian Azzaro (Chicago: The Copy Workshop, 2008), 183–184.
[19] Jim Rutenberg, "Secret of the Obama Victory? Rerun Watchers, for One Thing," *New York Times*, November 12, 2012, www.nytimes.com.
[20] Stelter, "'Idol' Grapples with Its Own Competition," *New York Times*, May 22, 2012, www.nytimes.com.
[21] Mike Shields, "Ad Network Business Dominated by Big Players," *Media Week*, January 14, 2010, www.mediaweek.com.
[22] Tanzina Vega, "The New Algorithm of Web Marketing," *New York Times*, November 18, 2012, www.nytimes.com.
[23] Suzanne Vranica, "CBS, ABC Win Higher Rates," *Wall Street Journal*, June 13, 2012, B8.
[24] Emily Steel, "Web Sites Target Oscars Fans; Ads Will Reflect Show Events," *Wall Street Journal*, March 4, 2010: B7.
[25] Terry Stephan, "You've Come a Long Way, Baby," *Northwestern*, Winter 2012, 18.
[26] Bob Garfield, *The Chaos Scenario* (Nashville, TN: Stielstra Publishing, 2009).
[27] Ken Mallon and Duncan Southgate, "Where Digital Marketing Is Heading in 2010 (Part I)," *Advertising Age*, December 29, 2009, www.adage.com.

CHAPTER 15

[1] Glen M. Broom and Bey-Ling Sha, *Cutlip and Center's Effective Public Relations*, 11th ed. (Upper Saddle River, NJ: Pearson Prentice Hall, 2013), 2.
[2] Kimberly Castro, "Best Jobs of 2012: Public Relations Specialist," February 27, 2012, *U.S. News & World Report*, http://money.usnews.com.
[3] Natalie Zmuda, "Can ING, Timex, Others Stomach Increasing Outrage about NYC Marathon?," November 2, 2012, www.adage.com.
[4] Claire Atkinson, "Rubenstein: PR Maestro," *Advertising Age*, October 11, 2004, 46.
[5] Pranay Gupte, "Integrity, Not Image Fixing, Is 'Real' Public Relations," February 8, 2005, *New York Sun, www.rubenstein.com/files/NY_Sun.pdf.*
[6] Public Relations Society of America, www.prsa.org.
[7] Tom Duncan and Sandra Moriarty, *Driving Brand Value: Using Integrated Marketing to Manage Profitable Stakeholder Relationships* (New York: McGraw-Hill, 1997).
[8] Lance Madden, "Nike's Jordan Brand Goes Mobile to Promote New Shoes," July 7, 2012, www.forbes.com.
[9] Thomas L. Harris, *Value-Added Public Relations: The Secret Weapon of Integrated Marketing* (Lincolnwood, IL: NTC Business Books, 1998).
[10] Sandra Moriarty, "IMC Needs PR's Stakeholder Focus," *AMA Marketing News*, May 26, 1997, 7.
[11] Fraser P. Seitel, *The Practice of Public Relations*, 11th ed. (Upper Saddle River, NJ: Pearson Prentice Hall, 2011), 72–73.
[12] John Paluszek, personal communication, August 3, 2009.
[13] Rupal Parekh, "The Implosion of Lance Armstrong's Endorsement Empire: $30 M and Counting," October 19, 2012, www.adage.com.
[14] Jonathan Salem Baskin, "CMOs Go beyond a PR Plan to Prepare for an Inevitable Product Crisis," March 8, 2010, www.adage.com.
[15] Stephanie Simon, "Hard-Hit Schools Try Public-Relations Push," *Wall Street Journal*, August 17, 2009, A3.
[16] Broom and Sha, *Cutlip and Center's Effective Public Relations*.
[17] Nate Silver, "Google or Gallup? Changes in Voters' Habits Reshape Polling World," *New York Times*, November 11, 2012, www.nytimes.com.
[18] Tamara Gillis, "In Times of Change, Employee Communication Is Vital to Successful Organizations," *Communication World*, March–April 2004, 8.
[19] Claire Atkinson, "PR Firms Praise Janet Jackson Breast Stunt," February 9, 2004, www.adage.com.
[20] Michelle Chapman, "Denny's Promotion Hits Grand Slam," *Tampa Tribune*, February 4, 2009, www2.tbo.com.
[21] Jack Neff, "Duracell Brings Charging Stations to Battery Park after Hurricane Sandy," October 31, 2012, www.adage.com.
[22] Shareen Pathak, "Pizza Hut Backs Out of Presidential Debate Stunt, Shifts Campaign Online," October 12, 2012, www.adage.com.
[23] Paul Holmes, "Senior Marketers Are Sharply Divided about the Role of PR in the Overall Mix," *Advertising Age*, January 24, 2005, C1, C2.

[24] "High Marks: Target Puts Education at the Center of Corporate Responsibility," October 22, 2012, www.abullseyeview.com.
[25] Andrew Adam Newman, "Tough on Crude Oil, Soft on Ducklings," *New York Times*, September 25, 2009, www.nytimes.com.
[26] Jack Neff, "Dawn's Wildlife Rescue Efforts Shine in Gulf Coast Oil Spill," May 4, 2010, www.adage.com; Leslie Kaufman, "Ad for a Dish Detergent Becomes Part of a Story," *New York Times*, June 15, 2010, www.nytimes.com.
[27] Thomas Harris, "iPod, Therefore iAm," *ViewsLetter*, September 2004, 3.
[28] Fraser P. Seitel, "E-Mail News Releases," *O'Dwyer's PR Services Report*, March 2004, 37.
[29] "Parade History," www.social.macy.com.
[30] Seitel, *The Practice of Public Relations*: 360.
[31] Jill Whalen, "Online Public Relations," *High Rankings Advisor* 109 (August 18, 2004), www.highrankings.com.
[32] Michael Markowitz, "Fighting Cyber Sabotage," *Bergen Record*, October 4, 1998, www.bergen.com.
[33] Lisa Belkin, "Moms and Motrin," *New York Times*, November 17, 2008, www.nytimes.com.
[34] Mark Suster, "If It Didn't Happen on Twitter It Didn't Really Happen. Here's Why." November 13, 2012, www.bothsidesofthetable.com.

CHAPTER 16

[1] Amir Efrati, "Google Shifts Tack on Android," *Wall Street Journal*, May 16, 2012, B4.
[2] Louise Marsland, "SAMRA Convention 2006 News," Bizcommunity.com, March 15, 2006, www.bizcommunity.com.
[3] Stephanie Gleason, "Fuller Brush Goes into Chapter 11," *Wall Street Journal*, February 23, 2012, B8.
[4] "Direct Sales Giant Avon Ranked 9th 'Most Successful Brand of 2010,'" *MLM The Whole Truth*, December 21, 2009, www.mlm-thewholetruth.com.
[5] Camille Sweeney, "Avon's Little Sister Is Calling," *New York Times*, January 13, 2010, www.nytimes.com.
[6] Dennis Berman, "Inside the Amway Sales Machine," *Wall Street Journal*, February 15, 2012, B1.
[7] John Mazzone and John Pickett, "The Household Diary Study: Mail Use & Attitudes in FY 2008," U.S. Postal Service, March 2009, 40.
[8] Belinda Luscombe, "Using Business Savvy to Help Good Causes," *Time*, March 28, 2011, 65.
[9] James Arndorfer, "A Loyalty Even Man's Best Friend Can't Beat," *Advertising Age*, January 21, 2010, www.adage.com.
[10] Teresa Day, "How Direct Sellers Are Leveraging New Technology," *The Ultimate Social Business Model*, Special Supplement to the *Wall Street Journal* by *Direct Selling News*, June 24, 2011, 18.
[11] Ken Mallon and Duncan Southgate, "Where Digital Marketing Is Heading in 2010," *Advertising Age*, December 29, 2010, www.adage.com.
[12] Day, "How Direct Sellers Are Leveraging New Technology."
[13] Teresa Day, "The Equity in Social Selling," *Wall Street Journal* Special Supplement on Social Selling, June 18, 2012, 1, 4–6.
[14] Dana Mattioli, "Stores Smarten Up Amid Spam Flood," *Wall Street Journal*, March 10–11, 2012, B1.
[15] Wendy Davis, "Twitter Sues 'Spammers' for Violating Service Terms," *Online Media Daily*, April 6, 2012, www.mediapost.com.
[16] Brad Stone, "Facebook Joins with McAfee to Clean Spam from Site," *New York Times*, January 13, 2010, www.nytimes.com
[17] Don Peppers and Martha Rogers, "The Principles of Data-Driven Relationships," in *Advertising Principles & Practices*, 8th ed. (Upper Saddle River, NJ: Prentice Hall, 2009), 458.
[18] Fatemeh Khatibloo, "Personal Identity Management," A Forrester Research Report (Cambridge, MA: Forrester Research, September 30, 2011).
[19] "Cultivating Comprehensive Data Privacy throughout Your Organization," TRUSTe Whitepaper, September 12, 2012, 1, www.truste.com.
[20] Spencer Ante, "As Economy Cools, IBM Furthers Focus on Marketers," *Wall Street Journal*, July 18, 2012, B3.
[21] Jenna Wortham, "Privacy, Please: This Is Only for the Two of Us," *New York Times*, June 3, 2012, 3.
[22] Kara Swisher, "Silicon Valley, the Long View," *Wall Street Journal*, June 4, 2012, R6.
[23] Sam Schechner, "EU Officials Try to Clarify Privacy Rules for the Web," *Wall Street Journal*, June 11, 2012, B3.
[24] Natasha Singer, "More Companies Are Tracking Online Data, Study Finds," *New York Times*, November 12, 2012, www.nytimes.com.
[25] David Rittenhouse, personal correspondence, September 14, 2012.
[26] Julia Angwin, "Online Tracking Ramps Up," *Wall Street Journal*, June 18, 2012, B1.
[27] Anton Troianovski, "New Rules on Kids' Web Ads," *Wall Street Journal*, August 1, 2012, B1.
[28] Anton Troianovski and Danny Yadron, "Child Web Privacy Law Gets Updated," *Wall Street Journal*, December 19, 2012, B1.
[29] Geoffrey Fowler, "Facebook Sells More Access to Members," *Wall Street Journal*, October 2, 2012, B1.
[30] Wortham, "Privacy, Please."
[31] Natasha Singer, "When the Privacy Button Is Already Pressed," *New York Times*, September 16, 2012, 4.
[32] Claire Cain Miller, "Google and F.T.C. Set to Settle Safari Privacy Charge," *New York Times*, July 10, 2012, www.nytimes.com.
[33] "Cultivating Comprehensive Data Privacy throughout Your Organization," 3.
[34] Giles D'Souza and Joseph Phelps, "The Privacy Paradox: The Case of Secondary Disclosure," *Review of Marketing Science*, 7, no. 4 (2009), www.bepress.com/romsjournal/vol7/iss1/art4.
[35] Julia Angwin, "Digital-Privacy Rules Taking Stronger Shape," *Wall Street Journal*, March 27, 2012, B1.
[36] Stephanie Clifford, "A Little 'I' to Teach about Online Privacy," *New York Times*, January 27, 2010, www.nytimes.com.

CHAPTER 17

[1] Arlene Gerwin "Sale Promotion Planning," in *The Power of Point-of-Purchase Advertising: Marketing at Retail*, 3rd ed., ed. Robert Liljenwall (Washington, DC: Point-of-Purchase Advertising International, 2008), 63.
[2] Natalie Zmuda, "Macy's Brings Brazil to Customers," *Advertising Age*, May 8, 2012, www.adage.com.
[3] American Marketing Association, www.marketingpower.com/mg-dictionary.php.
[4] Gerwin, "Sale Promotion Planning," 63.
[5] Bob Garfield and Neal Conan "Bob Garfield's 'Chaos Scenario,'" August 6, 2009, www.npr.org.
[6] "Cutest Social Media Campaign of the Year? Get a Heinz Bean with Your Name on It," *Advertising Age*, August 23, 2012, www.adage.com.
[7] Leo Jakobson, "Incentives without Borders," *Incentive*, March 2006, 12–17.
[8] Gerwin, "Sale Promotion Planning," 63.
[9] James O'Toole, "J.C. Penney Offers Kids Free Haircuts," *CNN Money*, September 10, 2012, www.money.cnn.com.
[10] Tim Nudd, "Oreo Crowdsources Its Final 'Daily Twist' Ad Live in Times Square," *Adweek*, October 2, 2012, www.adweeek.com; Stuart Elliott, "For Oreo Campaign Finale, a Twist on Collaboration," *New York Times*, September 24, 2012, www.nytimnes.com.
[11] Doug Brooks, "How to Balance Brand Building and Price Promotion," *Advertising Age*, December 29, 2009, www.adage.com.
[12] Motoko Rich, "With Kindle, the Best Sellers Don't Need to Sell," *New York Times*, January 23, 2010, www.nytimes.com.
[13] Bruce Horovitz, "Match the Food to the Logo," *USA Today*, May 27, 2009, B1.
[14] Miguel Bustillo and Jeffrey Trachtenberg, "Wal-Mart Strafes Amazon in Book War," *Wall Street Journal*, October 16, 2009, A1.
[15] Warren Brown, "Chrysler's PT Cruiser: Time for Fad to Fade," *Daytona Beach News Journal*, May 15, 2009, 6A.
[16] "Stores Are Media: BIGresearch's Simultaneous Media Survey Ranks the Influence of In-Store Media on Purchase Decisions," September 20, 2006, www.bigresearch.com.
[17] Jill Stravolernos, "78 Percent of Americans Get Coupons from Newspapers," *Boulder Daily Camera Business Plus*, January 11, 2010, 8; John Waggoner, "Consumers Open Wallets, but Not for New Stuff," *USA Today*, May 19, 2009, B1, www.usatoday.com.
[18] "Old Navy Creates Human Coupon to Celebrate 5 Million Facebook Fans," *Advertising Age*, October 10, 2012, www.adage.com.
[19] Stephanie Clifford and Claire Miller, "Merchants and Shoppers Sour on Daily Deal Sites," *New York Times*, August 17, 2012, www.nytimes.com.

[20] Julie Jargon, "Coupons Boost Starbucks," *Wall Street Journal*, November 2, 2012, B6.

[21] Lucette Lagnado, "In the Land of Giveaways, Mr. Cohn Is the Sultan of Swag," *Wall Street Journal*, January 26, 2012, A13.

[22] "Dads Stake Out Their Role in the Household and Online," *eMarketer*, September 18, 2012, www.emarketer.com.

[23] Karlene Lukovitz, "Green Giant to Throw Giant N.Y. Veggie Pledge Event," *Marketing Daily*, September 24, 2012, www.mediapost.com.

[24] Dick Blatt, "Foreword," in Liljenwall, *The Power of Marketing at-Retail*, 9.

[25] William M. Welch, "Skydiver's Space Jump Pays Off for Red Bull," *USA Today*, October 15, 2012, www.usatoday.com.

[26] Suzanne Vranica, "NBC Universal Tees Up Cause-Related Shows," *Wall Street Journal*, October 19, 2009, B4.

[27] Jennifer Valentino-DeVries, "New Approach to Ads in Games," *Wall Street Journal*, June 24, 2011, B5.

[28] Adam Thompson and Shai Oster, "NBA in China Gets Milk to Sell Hoops," *Wall Street Journal*, January 22, 2007, B1.

[29] Michael Grynbaum, "New York Traffic Experiment Gets Permanent Run," *New York Times*, February 11, 2010, www.nytimes.com; Libby Nelson, "Broadway's Car-Free Zones: This Space for Rent," *New York Times*, July 9, 2009, www.nytimes.com.

[30] Shareen Pathak, "Meet the Man behind Nike's Neon-Shoe Ambush," *Creativity*, August 20, 2012, www.creativity-online.com.

[31] Jack Neff, "P&G and Kroger Call It Quits on Coupon Partnership," *Advertising Age*, December 22, 2009, www.adage.com.

[32] Eleftheria Parpis, "Disney-Pixar, Aflac Duck 'Up' to New Tricks," May 7, 2009, www .adweek.com.

[33] Dashiell Bennet, "'Fan Cans' Let You Chug for Alma Mater," August 31, 2009, http://deadspin.com/5342510/fan-cans-let-you-chug-for-alma-mater; John Hechinger, "FTC Criticizes College-Themed Cans in Anheuser-® Busch Marketing Efforts," *Wall Street Journal*, August 25, 2009, B1; Emily Fredrix, "Anheuser-Busch Pulls Promotions at Some Colleges," AP and Boston.com, August 25, 2009, www.boston.com; "A-B Ends Some Bud Light 'Fan Cans' Promotions Amid Complaints," *Street & Smith's Sports Business Journal*, August 26, 2009, www .sportsbusinessjournal.com.

[34] Gerwin, "Sale Promotion Planning," 63.

CHAPTER 18

[1] Wayne DeLozier, *The Marketing Communications Process* (New York: McGraw-Hill, 1976), flyleaf.

[2] Kris Hudson, "China Gets Tony Hotel Line," *Wall Street Journal*, March 20, 12, B4.

[3] Tom Duncan and Sandra Moriarty, "How Integrated Marketing Communication's 'Touch Points' Can Operationalize the Service-Dominant Logic," in *The Service-Dominant Logic of Marketing*, ed. Robert Lusch and Stephen Vargo (Armonk, NY: M. E. Sharpe, 2006), 240.

[4] Giep Fanzen and Sandra Moriarty, *The Science and Art of Branding* (Armonk, NY: M. E. Sharpe, 2009).

[5] Stan Richards, "It's Been a Rocket Ride," *Dallas Business Journal*, April 7, 2006, www .dallas.bizjournals.com.

[6] Tom Duncan and Sandra Moriarty, *Driving Brand Value: Using Integrated Marketing to Manage Profitable Stakeholder Relationships* (New York: McGraw-Hill, 1997).

[7] Suzanne Vranica, "Ads to Go Leaner, Meaner in '09," *Wall Street Journal*, January 5, 2009, B8.

[8] Julie Ruth, "Implementing Strategy for Success," *AAA Newsletter*, June 2010, 5–6.

[9] Jon Steel, *Truth, Lies and Advertising: The Art of Account Planning* (New York: Wiley, 1998); "Tests Ahead for Account Planning," *Advertising Age*, September 20, 1999, 36.

[10] Franzen and Moriarty, *The Science and Art of Branding*, 88.

[11] Bill Lindelof, "Tiger's Fall Cost Sponsors $12 Billion," *Boulder Daily Camera*, December 29, 2009, 3C.

[12] "AmEx Plans Jerry Seinfeld-Meets-Superman Internet Show," *Advertising Age*, February 4, 2004, www.adage.com.

[13] Steve Kelly, personal communication, January 11–13, 2010.

[14] Elaine Wong, "Unilever Signs On as Sponsor of *Today Show*'s 'Cooking School,'" *Brandweek*, January 12, 2010, www .brandweek.com.

[15] Ingvi Logason, "Match CR-V to Your Lifestyle," in *Advertising and IMC Principles & Practice*, 9th ed., ed. Sandra Moriarty, Nancy Mitchell, and Bill Wells (Upper Saddle River, NJ: Prentice Hall, 2012), 544–546.

[16] "Dentsu Launches Next-Generation Communication Planning System IMC ver.2.0™," Dentsu press release, April 13, 2006; "Integrated Communication by Use of ContactPoint Management® ," PowerPoint presentation, Tokyo, November 2006, presentations at IMC consulting visits by Tom Duncan and Sandra Moriarty with Dentsu, Tokyo, Japan, April and November 2006.)

[17] Troy Young, "It's Not the Impression That Counts. It's What You Do with It," *Advertising Age*, January 19, 2010, www.adage.com.

[18] Todd Bishop, "First Windows 8 Ad Touts 'Reimagined Operating System," October 14, 2012, www.geekwire.com.

[19] "P&G to Slash $10 Billion in Costs over Five Years," *Advertising Age*, February 23, 2012, www.adage.com.

[20] Brian Steinberg, "Putting a Value on Marketing Dollars," *Wall Street Journal*, July 27, 2005, 25.

[21] Emily Steel, "After Ditching Tiger, Accenture Tries New Game," *Wall Street Journal*, January 14, 2010, B1.

[22] Katherine Frith and Barbara Mueller, *Advertising and Societies: Global Issues* (New York: Peter Lang, 2002).

[23] Tom Duncan, "The Evolution of IMC," *International Journal of Integrated Marketing Communication* 1, no. 1 (Spring 2009): 17.

[24] Nick Bartle, "Finding the Real Bottom Line," *Advertising Age*, January 27, 2010, www.adage.com.

[25] Scott Hamula, quoted in Moriarty et al., *Advertising Principles & Practice*, 561.

[26] Duncan and Moriarty, *Driving Brand Value*.

[27] Duncan, "The Evolution of IMC."

[28] Bob Liodice, "Essentials for Integrated Marketing: As More Power Shifts to Consumers, Need Grows for Common Metric and 'Renaissance Marketers,'" *Advertising Age*, June 9, 2008, www.adage.com.

[29] Aaron Patrick, "Publicis Chief Seeks Unity Within," *Wall Street Journal*, July 12, 2006, B3.

[30] Bill Vlasic, "Ford's Bet: It's a Small World After All," *New York Times*, January 10, 2010, www.nytimes.com.

[31] Tom Duncan and Sandra Moriarty, "How One Agency Re-Organized to Walk the New IMC Talk," *Admap*, September 2007, 35–38; Thomas Duncan, "IMC and Branding: Research Propositions," *International Journal of Integrated Marketing Communications* 1, no. 1 (Spring 2009): 17–23.

[32] IMC consulting visit by Tom Duncan and Sandra Moriarty with Dentsu, Tokyo, Japan, January 2006.

[33] Liodice, "Essentials for Integrated Marketing."

CHAPTER 19

[1] "What Is Engagement and How Do We Measure It?," Jason Falls, Social Media Explorer, January 4, 2010, www.socialmediaexplorer.com/ social-media-marketing/what-is-engagement-and-how-to-we-measure-it.

[2] Louise Marsland, "How Much Advertising Actually Works?" *SAMRA Convention 2006 News*, March 15, 2006, www.bizcommunity .com/Archive/196/119/9593.html.

[3] John Philip Jones, *When Ads Work: New Proof That Advertising Triggers Sales*, 2nd ed. (Armonk, NY: M. E. Sharpe, 2007), xvii.

[4] Simon Broadbent, *When to Advertise*, Henley-on-Thames, UK: Admap Publications, 1999.

[5] Natalie Zmuda, "Marketing Quant 101: Universities Gear Up for Data Talent Crunch," *Advertising Age*, March 18, 2013, www.adage.com.

[6] www.cnbc.com/id/41624240/page/3.

[7] Jones, *When Ads Work*.

[8] Institute for Public Relations, "Using Web Analytics to Measure Impact," e-mail release, February 15, 2010.

[9] Eric Webber, "You Can't Quantify Everything," September 9, 2008, www.adage.com.

[10] www.socialmediaexplorer.com/social-media-marketing/what-is-engagement-and-how-do-wemeasure-it.

[11] Melissa Read, personal communication, March 13, 2013.

[12] Melissa Read, personal communication, March 13, 2013.

[13] Brian Morrissey, "New Campaign Metric: Social Chatter," *Adweek*, January 27, 2010, www.adweek.com.
[14] Chris Reidy, "Locals Plan Twitter Experiment on Super Bowl Ads," *Boston Globe*, January 30, 2009, www.boston.com.
[15] Gerard Tellis, *Effective Advertising* (Thousand Oaks, CA: Sage, 2004), 6.
[16] Bob Liodice, "Essentials for Integrated Marketing: As More Power Shifts to Consumers, Need Grows for Common Metric and 'Renaissance Marketers,'" *Advertising Age*, June 9, 2008, www.adage.com.
[17] "Unaided Advertising Recall Significantly Higher with Mix of Radio and Internet," *Research Brief*, February 23, 2007, www.centerformediaresearch.com.
[18] Dong Lee and Chan Park, "Conceptualization and Measurement of Multidimensionality of Integrated Marketing Communication," *Journal of Advertising Research* 47, no. 3 (September 2007): 222–236.
[19] Melissa Read, personal communication, March 13, 2013.
[20] 2004 Effie Brief provided by UPS and the Martin Agency.
[21] www.burson-marsteller.com/About_Us/Pages/EvidenceBasedCommunications.aspx.
[22] Marlene Bender and Art Zambianchi, "The Reality of ROI: Dell's Approach to Measurement," *Journal of Integrated Marketing Communications* 2006: 16–21.
[23] Jack Myers, "Jack Myers' Weekend Think Tank: Can the Rules of Research Change?," *MediaPost Publications*, January 5, 2007, http://publications.mediapost.com.

Index

A

AARP Magazine, 339, 369
AbbaSez, 270
Accenture, 272, 579
Accountability
  brand communication, 82
  current trends in, 57–58
  era of, 46–47
  sales promotion, 533–534
Account executive, 54–55
Account management, 54–55
Account planning
  consumer insight and, 225–231
  research and, 55
Account Planning Group, 228–229
Accounts, advertising agencies, 51
Account services, 45
Account supervisor, 54–55
Acquired needs, 161
Act/do facet, advertising and, 143–146
Action
  direct-response brand communication, 503–504
  messages and, 255
  in video production, 324–326
  web page design, 327
Active publics, 482
Acute need strategy, 249
Adaptation
  creativity and, 264
  in media, 343
AdChoices program, 524
Added value, 70–71
  sales promotion, 535
Addressable advertising, 379
  online catalogs, 515–517
Addressable media, 340
Addressable television, 382
adese, in copywriting, 277–279
Adidas, 387
Adoption process, 174–175
Ad-skipping, 144–145, 380–381
Advertainment, 355, 402, 428
The Advertised Mind (Du Plessis), 135
Advertising
  accountability and integration era, 47–48
  audience protection from, 92–93
  basic functions, 36–37
  changes in, 56–58
  creative era of, 46–47
  current practices and concepts, 43–48
  defined, 36–43
  demand creation and, 91
  effectiveness evaluation, 600–603
  eras and ages in, 43–48
  freelancing in, 52
  future trends in, 58
  honesty and transparency in, 95–96
  key components of, 38–39
  key players in, 48–52
  lack of respect for, 103
  in magazines, 338–339, 369, 371–372
  media for, 38, 50–51
  media review of, 112
  message of, 38
  in movies, 382–383
  in newspapers, 368–370
  online sales, 393–394
  organization of, 48–50
  professional suppliers and consultants, 51
  public relations vs., 476–477, 486–494
  regulatory environment, 108–109
  roles of, 40–43
  sales impact of, 591–594
  scientific era in, 44–46
  self-regulation in, 112–116
  social values and, 92
  strategy behind, 38
  television, 379–382
  types of, 39
  writing style for, 273
Advertising Age, 338, 363, 380, 416, 534, 582
  audience demographics, 339–340
  public relations research, 484–485
Advertising agencies, 503
  A-list of, 52–53
  full-service agencies, 53
  function of, 50
  history of, 43–44
  in-house agencies, 53
  networks and holding companies, 54
  organization, 54–56
  payment system, 56
  specialized agencies, 54
  types of, 52–56
Advertising allowances, 546
Advertising Review Council, 113
Advertising Specialty Institute, 541
Advertorials, 372
Advocacy advertising, 146, 489
Adweek magazine, 218, 339
Adwerks agency, 340
Affect, Facets Model of Effects and, 134–136
Affective responses, 134, 226
Affiliates, radio, 375–376
AFLAC (American Family Life Assurance Co.), 362–363, 393, 395, 480
Age demographics, 166–167
Agency-client partnership, 51
Agency networks, 54
AIDA (attention, interest, desire, and action), 127
  consumer decision making and, 155
Aided recall, 599
Akron Children's Hospital, 257
Ali, Muhammad, 253
All Art layout, 313
Alliance for Audited Media, 437, 604, 605
"All In" campaign, 428
Allon, Aaron, 122
Ally, Carl, 221, 563
"All-you-can-afford" budgeting, 578
Alma, 53
Alternative media, 353–358, 605
Altoids, 300–302, 328
Alvarado, Glenda, 463
Amazon.com, 514, 516, 538–539
Ambush marketing, 551
American Advertising Federation (AAF), 218
American Association of Advertising Agencies (AAAA), 44–46
American Eagle Outfitters, 401
American Idol (television program), 354, 361, 439, 461
American Legacy Foundation, 88, 114
American Newspaper Publishers Association, 367
Ameritest research company, 138, 192–193, 596
Amway, 507
Analytics
  direct mail campaigns, 511
  media planning and, 455–460
  monitoring of, 462–463
Android, 208
Animation, 294, 323
  web page design, 326–327

Annual reports, 491
Anomaly agency, 348
Answer print, 326
Anti-smoking campaigns, 89–90, 212
Aperture
  cost negotiation, 461–462
  media scheduling, 453–454
Appeal, of messages, 250–251
Appearance, corporate media, 402
Apple Computer, 42, 49–50, 522. *See also* iPad; iPhone
Applied Imagination (Osborn), 262
Apps, mobile marketing and, 417–418
Arabian Gulf League, 399
Arbitron ratings, 375–376, 604
"Arctic Home" campaign, 304, 321
Argument, 143
Ariga, Masaru, 365
Armstrong, J. Scott, 213–214
Armstrong, Lance, 253, 480, 573
Arnell, Nikki, 314–315
Arnold Worldwide, 53, 89–90
Art, science and, 240–246
Art direction, 308–309
  video production and, 321–326
Artifact creation, 201
Art nouveau style, 314
Assertions, in headlines, 282
Assistant account executive, 54–55
Association facet, brand communication and, 139–141
Association networks, 140
Associations
  in advertising, 139
  in headlines, 283
Atlantic Monthly, 576
AT&T, 374
Attention
  brand communication and, 122
  as message objective, 253
  perception and, 131–132
  trade promotions, 546–547
Attitude
  defined, 141
  psychographics, 170–171
Attributes
  in messages, 253
  tangible and intangible, 255
Audience
  media planning for, 349
  for radio, 374
  radio audience data, 438
  share, 439
  size and profile, 339–340
  stakeholder audience, 569–570
  television audience data, 438–439
Avatar (film), 323
Average frequency, media planning, 445–446
Aversion, 135–136
Avis ad campaigns, 221, 592
Avon, 506
Awareness
  consumer promotions, 542
  perception and, 132
Aware publics, 482
Axe products, 91, 95, 135, 355, 356

B

Babytree online community, 422
Bacardi Rum, 271
Backgrounding, 565–567
Back translation, 296
Bale, Christian, 383
Banana Republic, 512
Banco Bradesco, 405
Band-Aid, 77
Banded packs, 539
Bandwagon appeals, 143
Banner ads, online advertising, 294–295, 390–392
Barre, Bill, 226
"Barriers to Purchase" research, 190–191
"Barrio" studies, 199–200
Barry, Ann Marie, 138, 162, 191
Bartle Bogle Hegarty (BBH New York), 206, 207, 369
Baumgartner, Felix, 548
Bavaria beer, 551
BBDO (Batten, Barton, Durstine and Osborn), 45, 53, 302
Beard, Fred, 101–102, 278
"Beautiful Messy" style, 314–315
Beck, Heather, 441
Beeper diaries, 200
Beer industry, 100
Bees, colony collapse for, 473–474, 482, 488, 495
Behavioral segmentation, 164
Behavioral targeting, 174–175, 517–518
  privacy issues, 521–524
Behavior facet, 143–146
Believability, 143
  of messages, 254
Benchmarking, 481–482, 569
Bendinger, Bruce, 343
Benefits
  in messages, 251
  segmentation based on, 164
Benetton campaign, 101–103, 5733
Ben & Jerry's, 473
Bennewith, Daryl, 214
Bernbach, William, 46–47, 264
Bertucci's, 453
Better Business Bureau, 113
"Be Young, Have Fun, Drink Pepsi" campaign, 221
Big Idea
  copywriting for, 275
  evolution of, 256–263
  management of, 263–265
  in public relations, 484
  in sales promotion, 538
  visual impact of, 304
BIGresearch firm, 419, 447
Billboard advertising, 533–534
  place-based media, 384–388
Billboarding, 403
Billings, Montana direct mail campaign, 195, 508–509, 539
Billing systems, monitoring of, 462–463
Binding, print production, 320–321
Bisquick HeartSmart, 139–140
Black Enterprise clusters, 519–520
Blackberry, 208
Bleed, 371
Bleed-throughs, 463
Blind headline, 282
Bliss, Jeanne, 512
Blogola, 98
Blogs, 414
  microblogs, 421
  online influence of, 493
Bloomberg, Michael, 475–476
Blue Bloods (television program), 382
"Blue Books," 44
Blue Diamond®, 251
BMW
  branded media, 402
  direct marketing, 516
Boating story, 442
Bodine, Kerry, 125
Body copy, in print advertising, 283–284
Body image, 94
Bogusky, Alex, 264, 425–426
Bonuses, 546
Bonus packs, 539
Books
  promotional materials in, 405
  public relations and, 491
The Book of Doing, 256
The Book of Gossage (Gossage), 280
Boomer-plus group, 173–174
Bottom-up creativity, international IMC campaigns, 580–581
Boyle, Susan, 290
BP Deepwater Horizon disaster, 480, 489
Brag-and-boast copy, 278
Brain, cognition and, 138–139
Brainfag, 261
Brainstorming, 262
Erand
  building strategies, 470, 536, 592–594
  human foundation for, 118–119
  as perception, 74–75
  public relations and perception of, 476–477
  website development of, 412–414
Brand advertising, 39
Brand advocacy, 420
"Brand ambassadors," 250

Brand association, creation of, 256
Brand communication
ad copywriter in, 275–279
basic principles of, 119
change and, 81–84
copywriting challenges, 295–297
debates and issues concerning, 93–99
defined, 64–65
direct-response brand communication, 500–506
direct-response writing in, 279
evaluation of, 590–594
First Amendment and, 107
function of, 72, 74
hierarchy, 70
interaction and, 124–125
internet writing and, 294–295
language of, 270–273
legal environment, 105–106
legal imperatives in, 274
marketing and, 65–71
mechanics of, 122–129
media planning for, 346–347
media presentation in, 277–285
mobile marketing, 416–418
multiplatform media, 424–427
power of, 146–148
principles of, 32–33
public relations writing and, 277
radio messages, 287–289
regulation of, 105–114
regulatory environment, 108–109
research, 183
ROI measurements, 606
seeking seekers and, 175–176
social impact of, 90–101
on social media, 414–416
strategic planning, 215–216, 274
television messages, 289–295
types of writing in, 274–279
writer's role in, 270–274
writing styles in, 273–274
Brand communities, 160
Brand Connections, 161
Brand development index (BDI), 452
Branded apps, 418
Branded entertainment, 95, 355–356, 402–403
Branded media, 355, 402–403
strategies for, 449
Branded Memory (Young), 139
Branded reputation, 418
Brand equity, 79–81, 470
Brand essence, 570–571
Brand experience, 174, 189–190
Brand extension, 81
Brand framework, 74
Brand icon, 252
visual communication through, 305
Brand identity, 75–78
language of copywriting and, 271–273
strategies, 218–219
Brand image, 78–79, 220, 536
visual communication of, 305
Brand integrity, 564
Brand intelligence, research and, 228
Brand licensing, 81
Brand liking, 573
Brand linkage, 139–140, 599
Brand loyalty, 80–81, 143, 146, 220, 525–526
Brand management, 72
Brand meaning, 74–75
Brand names, 45–46
Brand optimizer model, 594
Brand personality, 78, 219
Brand position, 78, 219
integrated marketing communication, 570
location of, 224
message strategies, 246
strategy for, 221–223
visual communication of, 305
Brand preference, 220
Brand promise, 78, 220
Brand relationship, 80–82, 470
integrated marketing communication, 560–561
Brand reminders, 406, 543
Brand rewards, 406
Brand stewards, 81
Brand strategy, integrated marketing communication, 570–571
Brand touch points, 562
Brand transformation, 75–79
Brand usage, 174
Brand value, 79–80, 561
Break-even analysis, 602
"Breakfast of Champions" slogan, 306, 548
Breakthrough advertising, 259–260
Breakthrough Advertising, 161
Brewer, John, 195, 509, 539
Bright, Laura, 338
Brinker, Nancy G., 531–532
Brioschi, Edoardo, 303
Britain's Got Talent, 290
British Airlines, 276
Broadcast media, 339
digital issues in, 394
direct-market advertising, 507–508
evaluation of, 605–606
evolution of, 342–345
radio, 374–376
strategies for, 448
television, 376–382
Broadcast network, 378
Broadsheets, 510
Brokers, media, 345
Brookes, Doug, 536
Brooks, David, 163
Broyles, Sheri, 133, 147–148, 244
Budgeting
integrated marketing communication, 576–578
international IMC, 579–581
Budget Travel, 457
Bud Light fan cans, 554
Bu Jin, 82
BumpTruck campaign, 357–358
Bureau of Alcohol, Tobacco, and Firearms, 108
Burger King, 84, 213
sales promotions, 538
viral marketing, 425
word of mouth advertising for, 357
Burma Shave campaign, 286
Burnett, Leo, 46
Burson-Marsteller, 275–276, 421, 610–611
Bursts, media advertising, 454
Business ethics, 48
Business magazines, 370
Business philosophy, 210–211
Business planning, 209–211
Business-to-business (B2B) advertising, 39, 41
brand reminders and rewards, 406
consumer decision making and, 155–156
corporate culture, 157–158
decision making influences, 162
direct marketing, 502
event marketing, 549–551
lists in, 519–520
markets, 66, 69–70
newspapers, 368
personal sales, 409
Sunkist "Ka-ching" campaign, 213
word-of-mouth interactions and, 420
BusinessWire, 490
Buyers, decisions by, 156
Buyer's remorse, 162
Buying, advertising call to action, 145
Buying allowances, 546
Buying centrals, 464–465
Buzz marketing, 125
monitoring of, 191
word-of-mouth interactions and, 419–420

C

Cable radio, 374–375
Cable television, 378–379
direct-response advertising on, 508
global saturation, 464–465
Café de Coral, 585
Call centers, 513–514
Call-outs, in copywriting, 280–281
Call to action, 145, 281
"Campaign for Real Beauty," 153–154, 157–158, 177
Campaign planning
integrated marketing communication, 564–578
obesity awareness campaigns, 589–590
Campbell's Soup, 191, 413, 464
Canada, citizenship campaign, 141

Cancer awareness campaigns, 433–434, 466, 531–532, 555
Caples, John, 45
Captions, in copywriting, 281, 283–284
CareerBuilder, 57, 444
Carey, Tom, 463
Carlson Marketing, 532
Carnival Cruise Lines, 517
Carrot mobs, 142
Carryover effect, 454, 606
Cartier, 380
Casting, in media advertising, 291
Catalina's ValuePage website, 541–542
Catalogs, 512
  online, 514–517
"Catch that Pepsi Spirit," 221
Category development index (CDI), 452
Category dominance, 225
Category sell problem, 229–230
"Cat Herders" commercial, 321–326
Catmandu Branded Entertainment, 95, 254, 355
Cause marketing, 79–80, 479, 548–549, 581–582
Caveman ad campaign, 527
Caywood, Clarke, 458, 477
CBS RIOT, 345
CDNow, 514
Cease-and-desist orders, 112
Celebrities, 272, 573
  in messages, 252–253
Celestial Seasonings®, 78
Cell phones. *See also* Smart phones
  advertising on, 389–390
  mobile marketing and, 356, 416–418
  polling surveys and, 482
Center for Studies in Creativity, 261
Central Hudson Gas and Electric v. Public Service Commission of New York, 107
Centrally conceived IMC campaigns, 580–581
Cents-off deals, 539
Chambers, Jason, 218
Chambliss, Ed, 583
Champ, Janet, 285
Change agents, 483
Channel Four, 231
Channel markets, 67
  trade promotions, 544
Channels of communication, 123–124
  integrated directed marketing, 524–525, 562
  media and, 336–337
  message conduits for consumers, 333
"Chantilly Peach" creative process, 316
The Chaos Scenario: Amid the Ruins of Mass Media the Choice for Business Is Stark: Listen or Perish (Garfield), 147–148
Charity ad campaigns, 334–336, 358
Charles Atlas exercise system, 507
Charmin ad campaigns, 578
Cheerios, 274
Chen, Holly, 507
Cheyenne Mountain Zoo, 385
Chicago school of advertising, 46
Chick-fil-A ad campaigns, 273
Children, advertising to, 110
Children's Food and Beverage Advertising Initiative, 93
Children's Online Privacy Protection Act, 522
Children's Television Advertising Practice Act, 110
Chinese folk art, 404
Chrysler, "Imported from Detroit" campaign, 120–122, 130, 134, 140, 148
Chuck (television program), 439
Cinema Advertising council, 382–383
Circulars, 369
Circulation
  magazines, 438, 605
  in media, 349
  of newspapers, 369, 605
Citizen Brands (Gobe), 47–48
City Hunters (television program), 355, 356
Claims, 251
  substantiation, 110–112
Clairol campaign, 166
Claritas PRIZM system, 437
Clark County Desert Conservation Program, 484
Classified advertising, 368
  online, 392
Claymation, 324
Clichés, 256–257
  in copywriting, 278
Click art, 309
Click-through rates, 295, 391–392
  monitoring of, 462–463, 602
Clients
  advertising agencies, 51
  agency-client partnership, 51
  information on, 435
Clift, Simon, 425
Clip art, 309
Closing paragraph, 284
Closings, in print media, 463
Cloud marketing, 344
Clow, Lee, 42
Clutter, 131
  television audience data, 438–439
Co-branding, 81, 553
Coca Cola, 76–77
  "Arctic Home" campaign, 304
  color branding by, 310–311
  as global brand, 83
  "Hilltop" advertising campaign, 135, 289, 417–418
  New Coke campaign, 202
  product placement strategies, 354–355
  qualitative research techniques, 201
  undifferentiated strategy at, 163
Code of Professional Ethics (Public Relations Society of America), 476
Coffee Rush ad campaign, 286–287
"Cog" commercial, 325
Cognition facet, 136–139
Cognitive dissonance, 162
Cognitive learning, 137
Coke Zero, 221, 225, 541, 568, 570
Cold call, 513–514
Collaboration, creativity and, 242
Collateral materials, 256, 491
Colony collapse disorder, 473–474
Color, visual design and, 310–311
Colorado Pass Club, 609
Color separation, 318–320
Columbia House Online, 514
Co-marketing, 552–553
Commands, in headlines, 282
Comments
  as research tool, 198
  on social media, 421–422
Commercial speech, 107
Communication
  advertising and, 40–41
  campaign plan, 485
  media objectives and, 444–447
  objectives, 217–218
  public communication campaigns, 480
Communication audit, 481–482
Communication brief, 230–231
Communispace, 198
Communities, online, 422
Community regulatory advertising groups, 113–114
Comparative advertising, 96
Comparisons, in messages, 252
Competitive advantage, 68, 223–224
Competitive advertising expenditures, 435–436
Competitive analysis, 190
Competitive budgets, 578
Competitive sell problem, 229–230
Compiled list, 519–520
Complaints
  in earned media, 423–424
  on Twitter, 421
Composition, 316–317
Comprehension, 137
Comprehensives (layout), 316
Computer graphics, 322–326
Computer-vision software, 188
Concepting, 256–257
Concept testing, 192, 594
Conceptual thinking, 261
Conditioned learning, association and, 140
Cone, Carole, 581–582
Conferences, promotional interactions, 410–411
Confessions of an Advertising Man (Ogilvy), 141
"Connectivity Chain" commercial, 348

Consent decree, 111
Considered purchase, 142
Consolidated services, 465
Constant Contact, 412, 515, 540
Consultants, advertising and, 51
Consumer activist groups, 114
Consumer behavior, sales promotions and, 534–535
Consumer Behavior Odyssey, 198
Consumer-generated content, 352
Consumer insight, 190–191, 225–231
Consumer markets, 66
Consumer promotion, 538–543, 601–602
Consumers
advertising and role of, 57
behavioral research on, 156, 182–188, 437
characteristics, 74
control by, 352
decisions by, 155–156
influences on decisions by, 156–162
loyalty development, 525–526
media consumption by, 340–341, 351–353
message conduits for, 333, 340
panel of, 198
privacy of, 523
redress for, 112
research on, 183
sales promotions targeting, 536–543
Contacting
advertising and, 145–146
qualitative methods for, 195
Contact points
integrated marketing communication, 562, 573–576
management, 574–575
in media, 338
Content analysis, 190
Content management, 55
in public relations, 476–477
Contests, 540–541
trade promotions, 544
Contingency planning, 480
Continuity in advertising, 454
Continuity programs, 143, 552
Continuous strategy, 454
Continuous tone, 318
Contrast advertising, 135
Contreras, Diego, 348–349, 412
Control
international IMC, 579–580
in public relations, 476–477
Controlled circulation, 369
Controlled media, public relations and, 485–488
Controversial products, 99
Convergence, in media, 332, 343–344
Converse ad campaign, 348
Conversion rates, 503, 602
Conviction
in messages, 254–255
persuasion and, 143
Cooking School website, 548, 574
Cool hunters, 174
Cool watchers, 198
Co-op advertising, 367–368, 546
Copycat advertising, 259, 263
Copyright protection, 107
Copytesting, 194, 264–265
Copywriters
defined, 275
grammar and adese, 277–278
guidelines for effective writing, 276–277
Copywriting
challenges in, 295–296
for global brands, 295–296
humor in, 278
for internet, 294–295
language of, 270–273
for print media, 280–287
for radio, 287–289
strategies and legal imperatives, 274
styles for, 273–274
for television, 289–295
types of, 274–279
for various media, 279–295
Core values, 157
Cormier, Jason, 195, 493
Corporate advertising, 39
blogs, 414
identity advertising, 489
public relations and, 487–489
Corporate Angle Network ad, 280
Corporate culture, 157–158
Corporate history books, 405
Corporate interactive media, 408, 450
Corporate media consumption, 340–341
strategies for, 449
Corporate presence media, 401–402
Corporate publications, 370
Corporate relations, 479
Corporate reputation management, 479
Corporate social responsibility, 479
Corrective advertising, 112–113
Correll, Linda, 261
Cosmopolitan, 371
Cost efficiency, media planning and, 457–458
Cost negotiation, media buying and, 461–462
Cost-per-lead metric, 602–603
Cost per thousand (CPM) strategy
direct mail, 509
direct-response brand communication, 506
media planning, 458–460
Council of Public Relations Firms, 484–485
Counterarguing, 146
Coupons, 540, 541–542
Couzens, Shawn, 55–56, 242, 269–270, 572
Coverage, 438, 605
Craig, Daniels, 355
"Crash the Super Bowl" competition, 263
Crawl, 322
Creative Aerobics, 261–262
Creative brief, 230–231, 240, 243–245
Creative concept, 256
Creative copy, 45
Creative development and production, 55–56
Creative director, 242
Creative leap, 260
Creative personality, 244
Creative process, 261–262
Creative risk, 260
Creative strategy, 242–246
management of, 263–265
Creative thinking, 256–263
Creativity
adaptation and, 264
dialing up of, 260–261
marketing communication and, 240–246
return on investment of, 257–260
role of, 242
Creativity magazine, 256
Credibility, 143
in public relations, 477
Crisis management, 480
Crispin Porter + Bogusky, 51, 53, 84, 180, 183, 213, 225, 245, 257, 264, 357, 405, 425, 541
Critical touch point, 562
Crocs, 210
Cross-cultural factors, 157
Cross-functional management, 564
Cross-media, 345
buying and selling, 464
integration of, 576
Cross-promotions, 553–554
Crowdsourcing, 198, 423
idea creation and, 263
Cues, in brand communication, 126–127
Cue System, 409
Cultural archetypes, 46
Cultural cohort, 164
Cultural imperialism, 93–94
Cultural relevance, 95
Culture
global advertising and, 93–94
global media buying and, 464–465
influences on consumer decisions, 156–158
Cunningham, Jennifer, 242–243
Curiosity, perception and, 131–132
Customer Bonding (Smith and Cross), 146
Customer characteristics, 74
Customer referral, 420
Customers
direct marketing and, 503
follow-up with, 506
Customer satisfaction, 143
Customer service, 70, 409–410
Twitter complaints and, 421

Customer-to-customer (C2C) advertising, 420
Custom publishing, 370
Cutouts, 383
Cut (video production), 325

D

Dailies, 325
"Dance" (T-Mobile commercial), 407
Dangerous products, 99–100
Dark Knight (film series), 322
DART for Advertisers service, 464
Databases
  circular processes, 518–519
  direct-response brand communication (DBC), 517–524
Data brokers, 523
Data collection, methodology, 195
Data mining, 520–523
Dattolico, Michael, 173, 283, 305, 344–345, 510, 513, 582
Davie Brown Index, 253
DaVinci, Leonardo, 244
Davis, Joel, 373
Dawn liquid detergent, 489
Dayparts, 374
DDB (Doyle, Dane and Bernbach) agency, 46–47, 171, 185, 190–191, 264, 405
DDB Group Hong Kong (HK), 558–560
Dealer loader, 546
Debossing, 321
Decay level, media advertising, 454
Deception, regulation of, 110
Deceptive advertising, 110
  remedies for, 111–112
Decision making, consumer brand decisions, 155–156
Decoded message, 124–125
Deen, Paula, 225, 253
DeGrasse-Cabrera, Tammie, 55
Delayed effects, 147
Deloitte University, 492
Demand creation, 91
  push and pull strategies, 546
Demographics
  age, 166–167
  defined, 166
  education, occupation, and income, 168–169
  gender and sexual orientation, 167–168
  geography, 170
  race, ethnicity, and immigration status, 169
  religion, 170
  research and, 183–184
  targeting and profiling, 166–170
Demographic segmentation, 164
  magazine publishing, 371
Demonstration, 251
De Mooij, Marieke, 157
Dentsu marketing company, 420, 574–575
Deprivation strategy, 213
Designated market area (DMA), 170, 437, 452
  weighting strategies and, 455
Desires, 161
  in advertising, 135
Deutsch New York, 254
DeVito/Verdi, 257
Dex, 374
Di María, Angel, 399
Diagnostic research, 192
Dialog, in radio and television advertising, 291
Diaries
  as research tool, 200
  television audience data, 439
Die cutting, 321
"Diet Coke/Mentos Experiment," 425
Differentiation, 137, 223–224
Diffusion of innovation, 174–175
Digital Advertising Alliance, 524
Digital displays, 383, 355
Digital ecosystem, 602
Digital era, 48
  blurred boundaries and media convergence in, 57
  creativity in, 236–237
  media evolution in, 343
  newspapers in, 206–208, 221–223, 231–232, 367–370
Digital installations, 408
Digital media
  catalogs, 512
  effectiveness evaluation, 602–603, 605, 607–609
  integrated marketing communication, 602–603
  integration with physical media, 426–427
  marketing strategies for, 450
  misleading advertising and, 98
  online advertising and, 389
  owned digital media, 411–416
  public relations and, 491
Digital overlap, media convergence and, 343–344
Digitization, 319–320
  video production and, 322
  web page design, 326–327
Dignity of the person, respect for, 303
Dillon, Mary, 84
Dinkies, 173
Direct action, 144
  headlines, 282
Direct advertising, 408
Directed group interview, 197
Directional advertising, 373–374
Direct mail, 508–511
  lists, 519–520
  testing of, 511
Direct marketing, 70
  brand communication and, 501–506
  evaluation of, 602
  owned media and, 408, 450
Direct-marketing agencies, 503
Direct Marketing Association, 501
Direct Marketing News, 108
Direct observation, 199
Directories
  ad copy in, 286
  advertising in, 372–374
Direct-response advertising, 39
  direct marketing and, 507–508
  owned media and, 408
Direct-response brand communication (DBC)
  catalogs, 512
  databases, 517–524
  data mining, 520–521
  defined, 500–506
  global issues, 526
  internet and, 514–517
  personal sales, 506–507
  privacy issues, 521–524
  process, 503–506
  telemarketing, 513
  tools and media for, 506–517
  trends and challenges, 524–526
Direct-response marketing, 501
  key players in, 502–503
Direct response writing, 274, 279
Discretionary income, 169
Display advertising, 368, 389
  trade shows, 410–411
Display allowance, 546
Displays
  copywriting for, 280–281
  public relations and, 491–492
Dissonance, 162
Distilled Spirits Council, 100
Distribution, 69–70
Divergent thinking, 260
Diversity
  advertising and, 93
  defined, 218–219
  strategic planning, 218–220
Divvy app, 478
"Does She or Doesn't She" campaign, 166
Doha, Qatar, city branding campaign, 566
Do-it-yourself online communities, 443
Domino's Pizza Company, 180–182, 203, 250
Donnelly Marketing Information Systems, 520
Do Not Call Registry, 514
"Do not track" option, 522–524
"Don't Mess with Texas" campaign, 272
Doritos, 553
DoubleClick, 464, 522–524
Double-page spread, 371–372
Douglas, Britton, 239–240

Douglas, Graham, 238–240, 265
Dove advertising campaigns, 152–154, 157–158, 177, 540, 582
Downton Abbey (television program), 381–382
Dramas, message strategies using, 250
"Drivers Wanted" ad campaign, 247
Droga, David, 262, 278
Droga5 agency, 53, 262, 278–279
Drug advertising, product placement ethics, 355
Dubbing, 326
Duluth Trading Company, 512
Duncan, Tom, 424, 470, 561
Dunham boot campaign, 311–313
Dunkin' Brands, 96, 98
Dunkin' Donuts, 96, 98, 200, 227
Du Plessis, Erik, 135
Duration of advertising, 454
DVR technology, 380–381

E

Eagle Shirtmakers, 280, 537
Earned media, 342
  interactive media, 418–424, 451
Earned publicity, 418–419
Eastwood, Clint, 122
"Eat MorChikin" slogan, 206–208, 231–232, 273
eBags, 514
Ecological preservation campaigns, visual communication and, 307
E-commerce, 412–416
  direct marketing and, 514–517
  spam issues, 516–517
Economics, advertising and, 41, 43
Eddie Bauer, 515
Edelman, Richard, 37
Edelman Agency, 36, 53
Editing, video production, 322–326
Editorial content, magazines, 371
Education demographics, 168–169
Edwards, Steve, 103
Effective frequency, 446
Effectiveness of advertising, 38, 47–48
  celebrity effectiveness ratings, 253
  current trends in, 57–58
  effects behind, 127
  IMC evaluation and, 594–599
Effective response, 134
Effects, of effectiveness, 127–128
Ego strategy, 249
Eight O'Clock coffee, 226–227
Einstein, Albert, 209, 244
Electronic Data Systems (EDS), 321–326
Electronic walls, 408, 492
Ellison, Larry, 521
E-mail, 411–412
  promotions on, 541–542
Embedded advertising, 377–382
Embossing, 321
Emotional appeals, 135
  advertising and, 43
Emotional branding, 221
Emotional facet, Facets Model of Effects and, 134–136
Emotional pivot, in television advertising, 289
Emotions
  driving factors in, 135
  message strategies and, 247–248, 254
  research and role of, 188, 202
  visual communication and, 307–308
Empathy, 218–219
Employee relations programs, 402, 478–479
Encoding, 123
Endorsement, 98
Endorser, 262
Engagement
  advertising and, 142–143
  evaluation of, 601
  media research on, 435–440
  media tools for, 337
  sponsorships and, 549–550
  of stakeholders, 569–570
Ennis, Gary, 242, 269–270
Environmental design, 317
  corporate media, 401–402
Environmental issues, direct mail campaigns, 511
E score ratings system, 253
Esmail, Khamis, 399–400
ESPN, media mix on, 447
Estée Lauder Companies, 531–532
Ethical consumerism, 170–171
Ethics
  in advertising, 101–105
  defined, 101
  international standards and codes, 105
  personal and professional ethics, 102–103
  of product placement, 355
  Professional Codes of, 104–105
  public relations and, 475–476
Ethnicity demographics, 169
Ethnographic research, 199
European consumers, 169
Evaluation
  alternative decisions, 155
  brand communication, 590–594
  creative process and, 261, 264
  importance of, 593–594
  integrated marketing communication, 578
  performance monitoring, 462–463
  in research, 192, 194
Event advertising, 388
  interactive promotional media, 410–411
Event marketing, 548, 549–551
"Every Touch Counts" campaign, 399
"Everyday Wildlife Champions" campaign, 489
Excitement
  in advertising, 135
  trade promotions, 546
Execution, 244
Exhibits, 545
  public relations and, 491–492
  trade shows, 410–411
Experian Simmons, 185, 604
Experience, creativity and, 261
Experiential marketing, 562, 602–603
Experimental research, 187–188
Expert panel, 198
"Expired" parking meter campaign, 253
Exposure, 439
  evaluation of, 604
  frequency of, 445–446
  in media, 349
  media planning and, 442
  perception and, 131–132
Extensions, 385
Exterior transit advertising, 388
External communication, public relations and, 493–494
External noise, brand communication and, 124
Extranets, 492
Exxon Valdez disaster, 489
Eye-tracking technology, 188
eZineArticles.com, 491

F

Fab.com, 423
Facebook, 414–416
  affective responses on, 254
  consumer promotions on, 540
  mentions on, 420–421
  newspaper editions for, 208
  online advertising and, 389–394
  privacy issues, 522
  social games on, 423
  "Unleash Deadly" campaign, 399
  user revolt, 462
Facebook Exchange (FBX), 389
Facets Model of Effects, 129–146, 217–220, 245–246
  association facet, 139–141
  behavior facet, 143–146
  broadcast media and, 374–376
  cognition facet, 136–139
  emotional facet, 134–136
  media and, 337
  message strategies and, 247, 253–255
  perception facet, 130–133
  persuasion facet, 141–143
  print media and, 363
  visual impact and, 304
Fads, 173–174
Fairey, Shepard, 309–311
Fairwood, 585
Fakes, in earned media, 423–424
Fallon, Pat, 209
Fallon Worldwide, 209, 321–326
Falls, Jason, 591

False advertising, 95
Family, advertising and role of, 160
"Fan Can" promotion, 554
Fan pages, 422
Fan support, 439
Farmers Ending Hunger (FEH) campaign, 410–411
Farm magazines, 370
"Farmville," 423
Fast Company magazine, 478
Feature analysis, 223–224
Features, 223
  in messages, 251
Feature stories, 279, 490
Federal Communications Commission (FCC), 108–109, 379
Federal Trade Commission Act (1914), 105
Federal Trade Commission (FTC), 108–110, 252, 274, 392–393, 514, 522–524
Feedback
  brand communication, 123–124
  research and collection of, 190
  suggestions and comments, 198
Feelings
  emotional appeals, 134–135
  thought vs., 138–139
FEI company, 545
Fill in the blanks technique, 200
Film. *See* Movies
Filming techniques, 322–326
Film-to-tape transfer, 323
Financial relations, 479
Fine screen, 319
Finishing, print production, 320–321
Firefox, 522
First Amendment
  Brand communication and, 107
  media review of advertising and, 112
First moment of truth (FMOT), 442
Flagg, James Montgomery, 144–145
Flash mobs, 144, 407
  public relations and, 484
Flickr, 336, 422
Flighting strategy, media advertising, 454
FM radio, 375
Focus groups, 197
Fogarty Klein Monroe (FKM), 332
Foil stamping, 321
Font, 312
Food and Drug Administration (FDA), 108–109, 274
"Football Challenge" outdoor board, 387
Foot Locker, 69–70
Footprint, satellite, global media buying, 464–465
"The Force" campaign, 321–322
Ford Motor Company, 49
  product placement strategies, 354–355
Foreman, George, 272, 508
Forrester Research, 166, 412
Foss, Eric, 577
Four-color printing, 318–320
Four Ps of marketing, 65–66, 68–70
Fox Movies, 428
Fractional page space, 372
Fraud, telemarketing, 513–514
Frazer, Charles, 248
Frazer's six creative strategies, 248
Freberg, Stan, 287–288
Free association, 262–263
Freelancing, in advertising, 52
Freestanding inserts (FSI), 369
Frequency distribution, 445–446
Frequency objective
  direct-response brand communication, 506
  gross and targeted rating points and, 455–457
  in media planning, 350–351, 445–446
Frequency program, 552
Frequency quintile distribution analysis, 445–446
Frequent-flyer clubs, 552
Friendship focus group, 197
Fringe (television program), 439
Frontier airlines, 246, 268–270, 292, 296, 313, 541–542, 572
FTC Improvement Act (1980), 106
Fulfillment systems, 503, 506
"Full Color Sound" campaign, 310
Fuller Brush Man, 506
Full-service agencies, 53
Fund-raising, 479
Futures Company, 171–172

G

Gaffer, 325
Gallup, George, 45, 482
Gallup-Robinson, 599
Games
  as branded media (*See* Movies)
  consumer promotions, 541
"Gangnam Style" media phenomenon, 343, 423
Gannett Newspapers, 367
Gap analysis, 481
Garcia, Mannie, 309–310
Garfield, Bob, 147–148, 247
Gargan Communications, 502
Gatefold, 371–372
Gatekeepers, in public relations, 476–477
Gatorade online advertising, 389
GCHQ surveillance network, 223
"Gecko" ad campaign, 246, 323, 415–416, 498–500, 527
Geer, John, 250
Geico, 246, 323, 415–416, 498–500, 502, 508, 525, 527
Gender demographics, 167–168
General Electric, 49, 91
  branded media, 402
  public relations, 480
General Mills, 82, 274
General Motors, 391, 409
Generative creativity, 263–264
Gen Xers, 167, 347
Gen Yers, 167, 349
Geographic segmentation, 164, 170
  magazine publishing, 370–371
  media planning and, 451–453
Geotargeting, 418
Gerwin, Arlene, 534, 535, 547, 554
"Get Met. It Pays" MetLife campaign, 254
GfKMediamark Research & Intelligence (MRI), 185–186, 596
Gift bags, 541
Gillin, Paul, 367
Giveaways, 538–539
Glamour, 371
Global advertising
  copywriting for, 295–296
  cultural differences and, 93–94
  direct-response brand communication, 526
  international IMC, 579–581
Global brands, 80, 82
Global marketing, 82–83
Global media buying, 464–465
Global research, issues in, 202–203
Goals, business planning and, 211
Gobe, Marc, 47–48
GoDaddy company, 256
"GoDaddy Girls" campaign, 256
Golin/Harris Communications, 492
Go/no-go decisions, 264
Goodby, Silverstein & Partners, 472, 473, 495
Goodwill, 81, 475–476
Google
  local targeting on, 453
  mobile marketing by, 417–418
  online advertising and, 389
  privacy issues, 522–524
Google Adworks, 465
Google Maps, 336
Google Offers, 540
Gorbachev, Mikhail, 253
Gossage, Howard, 280, 537
"Got Milk?" campaign, 141, 259
Gottfried, Gilbert, 363
Government agencies
  advertising regulation, 108–109
  research, 183
Grammar, in copywriting, 277–279
Gran Turismo 33, 383
Graphics, print production, 317–321
Gray market, 173–174
Green Giant "One Giant Pledge" campaign, 542
Grey, 53, 242
Grey Poupon, 415–416
Grip, 325
Gross impression, 439
  in media, 349–350, 606
Gross rating points (GRPs), 455–457
Groth, Tom, 257–259, 553
Groupon.com, 540

Group text messaging software, 416
Group texts, 125
Grow, Jean, 285
Grunge design, 313
GSDM agency, 262, 272
GT Academy, 402
Guaranteed circulation, 438, 605
Guardian newspaper, 206–208, 221–223, 231–232, 369
Guerilla marketing, 357–358, 406
Guitar Hero Smash Hits, 412
Gunelius, Susan, 274
Guppies, 173
Gürün, Doğan, 483
Gutter, 371–372

H

Häagen-Dazs, 90–91, 472–474, 482, 488, 495
Habitat for Humanity, 406
Halftones, 318–319
Hallmark Hall of Fame, 381
Hamula, Scott, 79, 582
Hanley, Michael, 417
Hanson Dodge Creative agency, 353
Hard-sell, 247
Harley-Davidson, 160, 257–259
Harley Owners Group (HOG), 160, 422
Harris, Thomas, 477, 489, 492
Harris Interactive research organization, 522–524
Hashtags, 142, 294, 421
HBO, 554–555
Head and heart message strategy, 247
Headlines, in copywriting, 251
Health care reform, 101
"Healthy People" campaign, 282–283
Heavy-up scheduling, 452
Heinz, 534
Heuristic evaluation, 603
Hewlett-Packard (HP), 143
High-context cultures, 295–296
High-definition television (HDTV), 382
"Hilltop" advertising campaign (Coca Cola), 135, 288, 417–418
"The Hire" (BMW mini-films), 402
Hirschhorn, Abigail, 229
Hispanic market segmentation, 169
  audience size and profile, 339–340
Historical budgeting, 576–577
Hits, 419
H:N Marketing Communication, 189, 260–261, 337, 350–351
Hochstein, Peter, 289
Hofstede, Geert, 157–158
Holding companies, advertising agencies, 54
Holiday Inn, 119
Home Depot, 414, 506
Home Shopping Network, 508
Honda "Cog" commercial, 325
Honda CR-V campaign, 574, 580
Hong Kong, 558–560, 585
Hoover, 537–538
Hopkins, Claude, 45
Horizontal publication, 370
Horizontal reach, 350–351, 444–445
Horn, Marty, 185
House ads, 369, 486
Household Diary Study, 508–509
Households, advertising and role of, 160
Households using television (HUT), 439, 606
House list, 519–520
How-to headlines, 282
Huge, 53
Hugo (film), 322
Humor
  in copywriting, 278
  in messages, 252
Hunger Games (film), 416
Hurricane Sandy, 475–476
Hyundai, 444

I

IBM, 304
  repositioning strategies, 225
Idea Champions, 262
Ideas
  with legs, 263–265
  techniques for creating, 262–263
Ideation, creative process and, 261
Identification
  advertising as form of, 37
  in headlines, 282
"I'd Like to Teach the World," 135, 288, 417–418
IKEA, 83
Illumination, 261
Illustrations, visual communication and, 309–310
Illustrators, 44
I Love You More Than My Dog (Bliss), 512
Image advertising, 253
Image transfer, 289
Imagine: How Creativity Works (Lehrer), 256
IMC Brand Optimizer model, 594
"I'm Amazing" campaign, 558–560, 568, 585
"I'm Lovin' It™" campaign, 62, 64, 84, 580–581
Immersion, creative process and, 261
Immigration status, demographics on, 169
Impact
  of communication, 127–129
  creativity and, 257–260
  evaluation of, 590–591
  public relations writing, 279
Implied third-party endorsement, 419, 477
"Imported from Detroit" campaign, 121–122, 130, 134, 140, 148
Impressions, 439
  direct marketing and, 502
  in media, 349
Imus, Don, 284
Inbound telemarketing, 513
Incentives
  survey research, 194–195
  trade incentives, 544
Income demographics, 168–169
Incubation, 261
Independent stations, 376
In-depth interviews, 196–197
Indirect action, 144
  headlines, 252
Indirect advertising, 107–108
Industrial magazines, 370
Industry self-regulation, 113
Influence, persuasion and, 142
Infomercials, 380, 508
Information
  advertising as form of, 37
  database collection of, 518–519
  market information, 189
  media search and mobile marketing, 355–356
  in messages, 225
  search for, 155
  trade promotions, 548
Information processing, 136–139
  association and, 141
Ingredient branding, 81
"Inherent Drama" philosophy, 250
In-house agencies, 53
Injurious deception, 110
Ink-jet imaging, 370
Inner directed consumers, 160
Innovation, 174–175
Inquiry tests, 599
Inside information, media buying and, 460–461
Insight mining, 228–229
Insight research, 228
Instagram, 399, 422
Instantaneous effects, 606
Institute for Advertising Ethics, 104–105
Institutional advertising, 39, 41
Institutional markets, 66
In-store promotions, 541
Integrated direct marketing, 524–525
Integrated marketing communication (IMC), 48, 58
  brand building and, 470–471, 592–594
  brand integrity, 564
  brand perception, 563
  budgeting and scheduling, 576–577
  campaign planning, 564–578
  campaign strategy, 567–571
  contact points, 562
  defined, 71–72
  digital components evaluation, 602–603
  evaluation of, 594–599
  internal integration, 563–564
  international campaigns, 578–581
  key communication problems, 567
  key concepts, 560–564

management and campaign controls, 576–578
marketing analysis and, 214–215
media and, 336–338, 573–576
media planning and, 440–460
message strategy, 572–573
message synergy, 562–563
obesity awareness campaign, 589–590
organizational case study, 584
primary effects, 571–572
public relations media planning and, 458
research in, 183, 203
ROI measurements, 606
strategic planning, 214–216
synergy requirement, 132
360° programs, 581–584
tool performance evaluation, 599–603
Integrated perception, 132, 220–221, 563
Integration
era of, 46–47
sales promotion, 554–555
Integration triangle, 582
Integrator, 228
Integrity, 475–476
brand integrity, 564
Intention, persuasion and, 143
Interaction
brand communication and, 124–125
web page design, 327
Interactive communication, 124–125
consumer promotions, 540
direct marketing and, 501
earned interactive media, 418–424
internet copywriting, 294–295
media and, 336–337
media buying, 463
media evolution, 353
owned interactive media, 407–418
promotional media, 410–411
social media, 340
strategies for, 450–451
targeted conduits, 340
television, 382
Interest
message generation of, 253
perception and, 131–132
Interior transit advertising, 388
Interlock, 326
Intermediaries, 70
Internal communication, 494
Internal integration, 563–564, 582–584
Internal marketing, 478–479, 569–570
Internal noise, brand communication and, 124
Internal operations, 56
International advertising, 94
consumer demographics and, 169
evaluation of, 609
integrated marketing communication, 578–581
International brand, 82
International laws and regulations, brand communication and, 107–108
International marketing, segmentation questions, 164
Internet
advertising on, 338–339
direct-response brand communication, 514–517
interactive consumer promotions, 540
online advertising, 388–394
privacy issues, 521–524
sales promotion on, 541–542
secondary research and, 184
Internet Explorer, 522
Interviews, in-depth interviews, 196–197
Intranets, 492
Intrusive attention, 131
Intrusiveness of media, 351
telemarketing, 513–514
Investment spending, 455
Involvement, 142
public relations strategies, 483–484
iPad, 208, 418
iPhone
direct-marketing on, 516
privacy issues, 522
"Iron Eyes Cody," 379–380
Irving, Kyrie, 425
"I saw it on the radio" slogan, 288
Issue management, 479
Ivory Soap, 44
"I Want You" poster, 144–145

J

J. Crew catalogs, 512
J. P. Morgan, 166
J. Walter Thompson, 43–46
Jackson, Janet, 484
Jackson, Michael, 252
Jamieson, Kathleen Hall, 250
JanSport, 324
JetBlue, 270–271
Jingle houses, 288
Jingles, 254
radio advertising, 375
in radio advertising, 288
Jobs, Steve, 42, 48, 492
John E. Powers, 44
Johnson & Johnson, 49, 282–283
John West Beer, 597
Jolie, Angelina, 253
Jones, John Philip, 147, 598
Jordan, Michael, 277
Journal of Advertising Research, 607
Jugenheimer, Donald, 220, 225–226, 229, 338, 344
Juicing the Orange: How to Turn Creativity into a Powerful Business Advantage (Fallon and Senn), 209
"Just Do It" campaign, 254
"Just Say No" campaign, 146

K

"Ka-ching" campaign, 213
Kaká, 399
Kantar/TNS, 339
Kaplan Thaler Group, 199, 363, 393
Karmic Marketing, 410–411
Keillor, Garrison, 374
Keller, Kevin, 246
Kelley, Larry, 219, 225–226, 229, 332–333, 338, 340, 343–344, 351, 426
Kellogg's, 251–252
Kelly, Steve, 574
Kerry, John, 522
Ketchum public relations firm, 479
Key frame, 293
Key influencers, 493
Key performance indicators, 608–609
Key publics, identification of, 477–478
Key visual, 293
Key words, 264, 392
KFC, 538–539, 585
Kick-Ass Copywriting in 10 Easy Steps (Gunelius), 274
Kiip, 548
Killer ads checklist, 258–259
Kindle, 208
Kiosks, 387–388, 408
KISS (Keep It Simple Stupid), 312–313
Klein, Naomi, 47–48
Kleppner, Otto, 260
Klout influence measurement site, 142
Knowledge structure, association networks, 140–141
Kodak, 225
Kraft Food, 301
multiplatform publishing, 370
Kreshel, Peggy, 218–219
Kroc, Ray, 84
Krugman, Dean, 376–377
Kuni Automotive kits, 544

L

Ladies' Home Journal, 91, 371
Lady Gaga, 253
"Lake Michigan" commercial, 286–288
Lands' End, 512
Lang, Tia, 84
Language
in ad copywriting, 270–273, 275–276
global advertising and, 295–296
Lanham Act (1947), 105
Lasker, Albert, 44
Latent publics, 481–482
Latshaw, Mike, 253–255
Lauder, Evelyn, 531–532
Layout categories, 312–316
LCD touch screens, 408
Lead agency, 580
Leadership, brand positioning and, 220
Lead generation, 70
Lead-in shows, television audience data, 439

Lead paragraph, 284
Lead time, 367, 453
Learning relationship, 518
"Leather Seats" commercial, 291–292
Lectures, message strategies using, 250
LED billboards, 385
Lee, Ang, 402
Left-brain thinking, 260
Legibility, 312
Lehrer, Jonah, 256
Leo Burnett agency, 250, 264, 302, 405
Lerner, Melissa, 353–354, 384–386, 573–574
"Let Me Play" campaign, 284, 285
Levy, Maurice, 582–583
Lewis, Regina, 32–33, 118, 154, 182, 200, 209, 226
Li, Hairong, 420, 423
Libânio, Edinalso Batista, 399–400
Licensing, 552–553
Life-stage segmentation, 164
Lifestyles, 171
  media-driven lifestyle, 352
Lifestyles of Health and Sustainability (LOHAS), 171
Life Style Survey, 171
Lifetime customer value, 526
Liking, 573
  in advertising, 135–136
  brand personality and, 220
Limbaugh, Rush, 374
Limbic system, 138–139
The Limelight (preshow), 383
Lin, Jeremy, 252
Line art, 318–319
Liodice, Bob, 606–607
Liquor advertising, 100
Lists, direct mail, 519–520
LiveWell Colorado, 588–590, 611
Live Wire Euphonic Pack commercial, 324
LivingSocial.com, 540
Lobbying, 479
Local adaptation, international IMC, 579–580
Local brands, 82
Localization, 578
Loeck, Elisabeth, 390
Logason, Ingvi, 189, 260–261, 337, 350–351, 574
Logic, marketing communication and, 240–247
Logos
  cues in, 126–127
  visual communication through, 305
Long-form ads, 380
Look-alikes, avoidance of, 263
L'Oreal, 96
"Lottery of Life" ad campaign, 334–336, 358
Louis Vuitton, 252–253
Low-context cultures, 295–296
Low involvement, 142
Low-power FM, 375
Lowe Brindfors agency, 334, 335, 336
Loyalty programs, 143, 552

M

Ma, Qing, 404
"Mac vs. PC" campaign, 262
Macy's, 532
Madison Avenue and the Color Line (Chambers), 218
Mad Men (television program), 49
Magazine Publishers Association, 369–372
Magazines
  ad copy in, 286
  advertising in, 338–339, 369, 371–372
  circulation, 367
  industry structure of, 369–371
  readership data on, 438, 605
  types of, 370–371
Magnuson-Moss Warranty/FTC Improvement Act (1975), 105
MailNow, 515
Make goods, 463
Mallia, Karen, 240, 242, 276, 326, 507
Management supervisor, 54–55
Manganiello, Rachel, 285
Mann, Lara, 293
Manning, Harley, 125–126, 166, 412–413, 603
Man of Steel (film), 353
Manufacturer-sponsored coupons, 540
Mark company, 506
Marketers, 502
The Marketer's Guide to Public Relations (Harris), 480
Marketing
  advertising and, 40–41
  brand communication, 65–71
  Guerilla marketing, 357–358
  key players in, 65–66
  mobile marketing, 355–356
  privacy issues, 521–524
  public relations, 480
  social media marketing, 426
Marketing at retail, 532–538
Marketing communication
  audit, 190
  defined, 64–65
  functions, 216–217
  future trends in, 84
  plan and strategy overview, 241
Marketing imperialism, 93–94
Marketing mix, 68–70
  strategies for, 214–215
Marketing partners, 66
Marketing plan, 211–215
Marketing portfolio management, 577
Marketplace changes, sales promotion and, 534–535
Market research, 183, 189
  media sources, 435
  online surveys, 195–196
Markets, types of, 66–67
Market segmentation, 163–164
Market selectivity, 367
Market share
  consumer promotions and, 543
  sales promotions and, 534–535
Marlboro Man, 257
Marmot Mountain Works, 327
Marsteller, Bill, 275–276
Martell, Charlie, 226
Martin, Brian, 161
Martin agency, 499–500
Mary Kay, 506
Maskulka, James, 386
Maslow's hierarchy of needs, 161
Mass communication, model, 123–124
Mass media, 339
Materialism, advertising and, 92
Matrix (film series), 322
Maven marketing, 493
Maxim's, 585
MBC2 channel, 428
McCain, John, 522
McCann agency, 44, 199
McConaughey, Matthew, 272
McDonald, Ronald, 99–101
McDonald's, 62–64
  brand building, 536
  branded media, 402
  brand transformation, 84
  Coffee Wars, 248, 250
  coupon offers, 540
  environmental design, 401–402
  global market, 82–83
  Hispanic market segmentation, 169
  international campaigns, 580–581
  marketing plan, 211
  Olympic Games sponsorship, 337
  Scooter Bug recall, 538
  on social media, 142–143
McDonald's Restaurants Hong Kong (HK), 558–560, 568, 585
McGarryBowen, 52
McGraw-Hill campaign, 162–163
McGuinness, Mike, 357
McKinley & Silver media team, 442
McNiven, Michael, 376–377
Measurable objectives, 569
Measured media, 339–340
Mechanicals, 316
Media
  adaptation in, 343
  advertising and, 50–51
  allocations, 458
  alternative forms, 353–358, 605
  audience size and profile, 339–340
  blurred boundaries and convergence in, 57
  branded entertainment in, 355
  brokers, 345
  buying decision process, 349–351, 460–466
  categories and terminology for, 339–342

changing use patterns, 351–353
conduits for, 333, 340
consumer use of, 340–341
contemporary landscape, 344
convergence in, 332, 343–344
corporate use of, 340–341
cost efficiency strategies, 457–458
defined, 336–337
digitization and, 332, 394
earned media, 341–342
engagement research, 435–440
evolution of forms and functions, 342–345
exposure in, 349
guerrilla marketing and, 357–358
industry, 338–339
integrated marketing communication and, 338, 573–576
intrusiveness of, 351
metrics and analytics, 455–460
morphing and convergence in, 332
negotiation strategies and, 460–465
objectives, 444–447
optimization strategies, 460, 604
owned media, 341
paid media, 341
performance monitoring of, 462–463, 603–606
personal contact media, 408–410
place-based media, 383–388, 406–407
plan, 346
plan creation, 434–440
planning steps, 440–460
planning trends, 465–466
platform integration, 426–427
print media requirements, 284–287
professionals in, 345–346
promotional media, 541–542
public relations and, 476–477, 485–491
reach and frequency in, 350–351
relationships in, 478
research, planning, and buying, 56, 345–346
review of advertising by, 112
salespeople in, 345
sales promotion and, 534
scheduling strategies, 453–454
sharing on, 422–423, 451
size, position, and weighting strategies for, 455
sources, 435
strategic fundamentals for, 346–351, 447–455
unbundled planning and buying, 465
vehicle-by-vehicle evaluation, 604–605
vehicle selection strategies, 461
waste, 446
word-of-mouth marketing and, 356–357
writing for, 279–295
Media buying, negotiation and, 460–465
Media-buying companies, 346
Media coverage area, 437
Media-driven lifestyle, 352
Media flowchart, 454
Media kits, 409, 437, 490–491
Mediamark Research Inc. (MRI), 435–438
Media mix, 346, 447
gross rating points, 455–457
Media plan, defined, 440
Media reps, 345
Media research, 191–192
current trends in, 465–466
Media tours, 410–411, 491
Media vehicle, 339
Mega Box McDonald's, 559, 585
Melissa DATA, 520
Membership programs, 552
Memorable messages, 254
Memory model of advertising, 138–139
Memory tests, 598–599
Mendelsohn, Susan, 203, 229, 445
Mental ray technique, 323
Mental rehearsal, 145
Mentions
earned publicity, 419
on social media, 420–421
Merchandising materials, 403–404
Mercury Marine, 442
Meredith publishing company, 370
Merging, database lists, 520
Message, 123
branding and positioning strategies, 246
design, 247
development and diagnostics, 192
direct mail message design, 509–511
evaluation research, 592–599
formats, 251–252
length of, in television writing, 293
media conduits for, 333
objectives, 245–246, 253–256
psychological appeals, 250–251
selling premises in, 251
strategies, 246–256, 572–573, 590
synergy, 562–563
telemarketing messages, 513
Metaphors, 201
Metrics
in measured media, 339–340
media analytics and, 455–460
MetrixLab, 596
MetroCards, advertising on, 353
Michelin tires, 260–261
Microblogs, 421
Microflex, Inc., 510, 513
Micro-sites, 390
Microsoft, 387, 522
Microtargeting, 165
Middle East, 399–400, 428, 483, 566
Military ad campaigns, 222
Millennials, 167, 347, 349
Millward Brown, 84, 596, 600, 605
Milne, George R., 523
Mini-me segment, 173
Mini-sites, 390–391
Misleading claims, 96
Missed closing, 463
Mission marketing, 210
360° communication programs, 581–582
Mission statement, 210–211
Mixer, 325
Mobile marketing, 355–356, 416–418
direct-response and, 516
strategies, 451
Mobile tracking, 522–524
Mojave Max, 484
Molson Beer, 277
Moments, in media planning, 442
Moments of truth, 442
Monetary criteria, direct-response brand communication, 504
Monitoring buzz, consumer behavior, 191
MONITOR™ lifestyle survey, 171–172
Monsanto, 405
Monster.com, 387
Montague, Ty, 240, 242
Moonfruit, 534
Moore, Charlotte, 285
Morals, defined, 101
Morning drive time segment, 376
Morphing
media convergence, 332
video production, 322
Motivation, trade promotions, 547–548
Motive and motivation
persuasion and, 141–142
psychological influences in advertising and, 162
Motorola Talk About™ campaign, 283
Motrin, 494
Mountain Dew, 48, 93, 103
Movies
advertising in, 382–383
as branded media, 402–403
Mozilla, 522
MRI CrossTabs, 435–436
MTV, 376–377
Mudo City, 483
Mullen ad agency, 605
Multichannel media, 345
buying and selling of, 463–464
integrated marketing communication, 338, 574
Multimedia, 333
Multiplatform media, 333, 346
brand communication, 424–427
integrated marketing communication, 338, 426–427, 574
magazines, 370
promotions, 548–554
Multiscreen marketing, 352–353
Multitargeted media, integrated marketing communication, 338
Multitasking, media-driven, 352
Multiuse media consumption, 333
Murray, Keith, 607–608

Museum of Islamic Art, 566
Music
in radio advertising, 288–289
in television advertising, 291
in video production, 324–326
Musion Creative LLC, 173, 582
Mustache March campaign, 432–434, 466
MyLink system, 409
MySpace, mentions on, 420–421
"My Spar" campaign, 214–215
Mystery shoppers, 409

N

N. W. Ayer agency, 43–44
Naming rights, 388, 402–403
Nani, 399
NAPA Auto Parts, 247
NASCAR, 548–549
Nasri, Samir, 399
National Advertising Division (NAD) (Better Business Bureau), 110, 113
National Advertising Review Board (NARB), 113
National Advertising Review Council, 113
National Breast Cancer Awareness Month, 531–532
National Decision Systems, 520
National Geographic, 415
National Humane Society, 326
National Public Radio, 375
Navigation
web page design, 327
on websites, 413
NCIS (television program), 382
Needs, 160–161
acute need strategy, 249
brand communication and, 137
recognition of, 155
Negative advertising, 135, 250
Negatives, in earned media, 423–424
Neiman Marcus Christmas Book, 512, 516
Nelson, Willie, 272
Netflix, 71
Network effect, 414
Network marketing, 516
Network of associations, 140, 200
Network radio advertising, 375–376
Networks, advertising agencies, 54
Network television, 376–382
Neuromarketing, 162, 191
News conferences, 410
News headlines, 282
The Newshour, 382
Newspaper Advertising Bureau, 367
Newspaper Association of America, 347
Newspaper National Network, 367, 464
Newspapers
advertising declines in, 338–339, 367–369
circulation declines, 366–367
digital editions, 206–208, 221–223, 231–232
industry structure, 367
readership data, 437, 605
traditional advertising in, 365–369
News release, 279, 489–490
News value, 489–490
Newsworthiness, 279
New York City Marathon, 475–476
New York Times, 174, 198
on breast cancer awareness, 531–532
circulation declines, 366
media convergence in, 343–344
Niche marketing, 163, 442
Niche media, 339
Nichols, Mary, 410–411
Nielsen, A. C., 45
ClusterPlus system, 437
media research by, 339, 604
single-source research, 598
television audience data, 438–439
television ratings, 376
Nightlife Navigators campaign, 219, 224
Nike, 428
Nike ad campaigns, 284–285, 551
Niman Ranch, 165
"1984" Apple commercial, 42
"97-Pound Weakling" ad, 507
Nintendo, 520, 550
Nintendo Power, 520
Nissan Motors, 402
Niswonger, Amy, 308, 401
Nobody's Perfect (Willens), 264
Noise, 124
No-l-ita, 302–303
No Logo (Klein), 47–48
Nonprice, emotional appeals, advertising and, 43
Nonprofit advertising, 39
direct-response brand communication, 503–504
Nontraditional media, 353–354
Norms, 157, 596
NYNEX Yellow Pages campaign, 275

O

Obama, Barack, 98, 309–311, 460
Obesity awareness campaigns, 589–590, 611–612
Objectives
brand communication, 590–591
in brand communication, 127
business planning and, 211
direct-response brand communication, 503–504
integrated marketing communication, 569, 609–610
in media, 446–447
in public relations, 482–484
sales promotions, 535
strategic planning, 209
Objective-task budgeting, 577
Observation research, 198, 226–227
Occupation demographics, 168–169
"Ocean Speaks" internet ads, 295
Odden, Lee, 601
Odorono campaign, 91–92, 95
Off camera, 291
Offensive advertising, 94
Offers, direct-response brand communication, 505–506
Office Depot, 126
Offset printing, 319–320
Ogilvy, David, 46, 123, 141, 273, 280–281
Ogilvy and Mather, 46, 225, 273, 405
O'Keefe, Georgia, 244
Old Navy, 540
Old Spice ad campaign, 34–36, 50, 59
Olympic Games, 551
Omega watches, 355
On-demand programming, 379
One-order, one-bill ad buys, 367
One-step offer, direct-response brand communication, 505–506
Online catalogs, 514–517
Online communities, 422
do-it-yourself online communities, 443
Online directories, 373–374
Online media
audience data, 440
classified ads, 392
increases in, 338–339
media buying strategies, 461, 435
public relations and, 491–494
sales statistics, 393–394
strategies for, 449
structure of, 388–394
video ads, 390
video games, 383
Online Publishers Association, 393–394
Online survey research, 195–198, 482
Online video, 379
On location, 291
On-premise signs, 401
OnStar Global Positioning System, 192
Open-ended questions, 196
Opinion leaders, 142, 475
Optimization services
direct-response brand communication, 505
media planning and, 460
"Optimizer" program, 460
Opt-in strategy, 418, 517
Opt-out strategy, 517
Oreo "Daily Twist" campaign, 535–536
Organization identity, 74
Originality, creativity and, 257–260
Osborn, Alex, 261–263
Outbound telemarketing, 513
Outcome evaluation, 601
Outdoor advertising
ad copy in, 286
design tips for, 318
evaluation of, 604–605
geographic segmentation and, 452
moving billboards, 344–345

place-based media, 384–388
viewership data, 440
Outer directed consumers, 160
Out-of-home advertising
evaluation of, 604–605
nontraditional media and, 353–354
place-based media, 383–388
signage, 401
Out-of-register color, 463
Output evaluation, public relations effectiveness, 601
Outside In: The Power of Putting Customers at the Center of Your Business (Manning and Bodine), 125
Overlines, in copywriting, 280
Owen, Clive, 402
Owned media, 341, 400–418
branded media, 402–403
corporate presence media, 401–402
digital media, 411–416
interactive media, 407–418, 450–451
public relations and promotions, 405–407
retail media, 403–404
strategies for, 449

P

Pace, 293
Pacific Life, 599
Package design, visual communication through, 305–306
Packaging, 403–404
Pac-Man, 383–384
Page views, 602
Paid media, 341
broadcast media, 374–382
movie advertising, 382–383
place-based media, 383–394
print advertising, 364–375
strategies for, 448–449
video game advertising, 383
Paid postings (blogs), 414
Painted outdoor bulletins, 385
Palmer, Volney, 43
Palm Pilot, 320–321
Paluszek, John, 479
Panel/grid layout, 313
Papa John's, 181
Pareto rule, 174
Parity products, 223, 535
Participant observation, 198
Participation commercials, 381
Partnership programs, 552–553
Pass-along readership, 459
Passion branding, 581–582
Patrick, Danica, 256
Patrick, Mike, 357
Paul Harvey show, 376
Payment systems, monitoring of, 462–463
Payout analysis, 534, 602
Pay-per-click, 392
Pechmann, Cornelia, 188
Pele, 253
Peltier, Jimmy, 523
Pemsel, David, 231
People meters, 439
Pepsi Cola, 221
branded media, 402
cause marketing, 475
color branding by, 310–311
viral marketing, 425
Perceived risk, 175
Percentage-of-sales budgeting method, 577–578
Perception
Facets Model of Effects, 130–133
public relations and brand perception, 476–477
selective perception, 130–132
Perceptual mapping, 224–225
Performance
monitoring of, 462–463
products, 69
sales promotions, 537–538
Permission marketing, 517, 561
Permission to believe, 256
Personal contact media, 408–410, 450
Personal sales, 70, 409, 506–507
interactive communication in, 343
Persuasion
advertising as form of, 37–38
defined, 143
in messages, 254–255
visual communication and, 307
Persuasion facet, 141–143
Persuasive Advertising (Armstrong), 128, 213–214, 216
Peters, Kevin, 126
Pfizer, 49
Phelps, Joseph E., 523
Phone surveys, 194–195
Photoboard, 294
Photo elicitation, 201
Photography
public relations and, 491
visual communication and, 309–310
Photo sorts, 201
Physical characteristics, magazines, 371
Picture window layout, 313
Pillsbury Doughboy, 323
Pinkham, Lydia, 70
Pinterest, 191, 422–423
Pitch letters, 490
Pizza Hut, 181, 585
"Pizza Turnaround" campaign, 182
Place-based media, 406
strategies for, 448–449
Placement
marketing and, 69–70
media targeting and, 340
Podcasting, 375
public relations and, 491
Point of differentiation, 68
Point-of-purchase promotions, 403, 544–548, 601–602
Point-of-sale media, 344
Point-of-view advertising, 489
Pokrywczynski, James, 549
Political advertising, 250, 309–311
Poor taste, in advertising, 94
Pop-behinds, 390
Pop-ups, 390
Port of Vancouver campaign, 128
Positioning, of brands, 78, 220, 221
international integrated marketing communication, 579
location of, 224
media planning and, 455
message strategies, 246
strategy for, 221–223
Positioning: The Battle for Your Mind (Trout and Ries), 221
Postaer, Steffan, 302
Postcampaign evaluations, 462
Posters, 387–388
ad copy in, 286
Posterscope, 384
Postmodern style, 313
Postproduction, television commercials, 325–326
Post-purchase evaluation, 155
Post-testing, 194, 600–603
The Practice of Public Relations (Seitel), 479
Prairie Home Companion, 374
Predictive dialing, 513–514
Preference, persuasion and, 143
Preferred-position rate, 368
negotiations for, 462
Premiums, 406, 540
Preprints, 369, 371
Preproduction, television commercials, 324
Prescription drugs, advertising for, 100–101
Press conferences, 410, 490–491
Press kits, 405
Prestige pricing, 69
Preston, Ivan, 96–97, 139
Pretesting, 192, 594
Prevention, advertising for, 146
Price deals, 538–539
trade promotions, 544
Price/value proposition, 69
Price wars, 539
Pricing
sales promotions and, 534–535
strategies, 69
Primary research, 184–185
Prime time, radio and television advertising, 376, 380
Printed poster billboards, 385
Printer's Ink magazine, 44
Print media
ad copywriting for, 280–287
art reproduction, 318–319
binding and finishing, 320–321
declines in, 338–339

Print media (*continued*)
digital issues in, 394
direct marketing advertising, 507
evolution of, 342–345
history of, 43–44
magazines, 369–372
newspapers, 365–369
production requirements, 317–321
publicity and, 490
published print media, 364–365
requirements, 284, 286
strategies for, 448
typography, 311–312
visual impact in, 304–305
Prism surveillance program, 223
Privacy, direct-response marketing and, 521–524
Privacy Managers, 514
Prize-pack deals, 539
Prizes, 406
PR Newswire, 490
Problem avoidance message, 252
Problem solution message, 252
Problem solving, creativity in, 261
Process colors, 318
Process for Progress, 581–582
Procter & Gamble, 34–36, 76–77
advocacy advertising, 489
brand building, 536
consumer promotions, 541
media sharing, 422
TREMOR metric, 605
Prodigy, 520
Product
deceptive claims concerning, 111
differentiation, 223
features and attributes, 223
in marketing mix, 68
Product-as-hero, 252
Production, print media, 317–321
Production notes, 324
Product launch, 68
Product placement, 353–354
video games, 383
Professional Codes of Ethics, 104–105
Professional magazines, 370
Profiles
customer targeting, 505
marketing, 166–177
psychographics and, 170–173
Profit, 211
Programmatic buying, 461
Program preemptions, 463
Projective techniques, 200
Promise, 251
Promotional campaigns, 542
Promotional designs, 404
Promotional media, 541–542
Promotional pricing, 69
Promotional tools, 39–40
Promotional video networks, 402–403
Promotions
consumer promotions, 538–543
interactive media, 410–411, 450
loyalty programs, 143, 552
multiplatform promotions, 548–554
owned media, 405–407
sales promotions, 532–538
strategies for, 449
support for, 552
trade promotions, 543–548
ProPoint Graphics, 326
Prospects
data mining, 521
for direct marketing, 503
Psychographics, targeting and profiling, 170–173
Psychographic segmentation, 164
Psychological influences in advertising, 160–161, 250–251
Psychological pricing, 69
Public advertising regulatory groups, 113–114
Public affairs, 479
Public Broadcasting System (PBS), 379
Public communication campaigns, 480
Publicity
earned publicity, 418–419
media and, 405, 451
public relations and, 476–477, 484, 489–491
Public opinion, 475
research on, 482
Public radio, 375–376
Public relations, 40
Big Idea in, 484
brand perception and, 476–477
defined, 474–477
effectiveness evaluation, 601
functions of, 479–480
integrated advertising and, 458
interactive media, 450
objectives and strategies, 482–483
owned media, 405–407
planning decisions, 481–484
research and SWOT analysis, 481–482
skill requirements, 481
strategies for, 449
tools for, 484–494
types of programs, 477–480
writing style, 273–274, 279
Public Relations Society of America, 476
Publics, identification of, 474
Public service advertising, 39, 274
Public service announcements (PSAs), 379, 381, 486–487
Public television, 377, 379
Published print media
advertising in, 364–365
directories, 372–374
magazines, 369–372
newspapers, 365–369
public relations, 405, 491
Puffery, 44, 96
Pull strategy, 455, 546
Pulsing strategy, media advertising, 454
Puma, 69–70, 262
Punxsutawney Phil, 484
Purchase decisions, 155
Purchase intent, 185, 187
Pure Food and Drug Act (1906), 105
Purging, 520
Purpose-driven brands, 79
Purpose-driven games, 201
Push money, 546
Push strategy, 455, 546
Puzzles, in headlines, 283

Q

Qatar, Doha city branding campaign, 566
QR (quick-response) codes, 343, 353, 393
direct-response advertising, 408
Q score ratings system, 253
Q-tips, 77
Qualitative research, 187, 195–201
diaries, 200
ethnographic research, 199–200
focus groups, 197–198
in-depth interviews, 196–197
observation research, 198
suggestions and comments, 198
Quantitative research, 185, 187, 194–195, 201–202
sampling and data collection, 195
survey research, 194–195
QVC, 508

R

Race demographics, 169
"Race for the Cure," 531–532
Radio
ad copywriting for, 287–289
audience data for, 438
evolution of advertising on, 45
industry structure, 374–376
Radio Ad Effectiveness Lab, 607
Radio Advertising Bureau, 287–288
Radio networks, 375
Radio Ranch, 374
Radio script, 289
Ralph Lauren, 134, 381–382
Random sampling, 195
"The Rant" ad campaign, 277
Rate card, 367
Ratings, 439
gross and targeted rating points, 455–457
in media, 350, 605
Rational economic decisions, advertising and, 43
Ration strategies, 249
Razorfish, 53
Reach objective
gross and targeted rating points and, 455–457
in media, 350–351, 444–445
Read, Melissa, 602–603, 605
Reader's Digest, 461
Readership data, 605
"Real Beauty Sketches," 154

Real-time search, 393–394
Reasonable consumer perspective, 110
Reason to believe, 143
Reason why premise, in messages, 253
Rebates, 539
Recall test, 137, 598
  perception and, 132
Receiver, 123
Recency criteria, direct-response brand communication, 504
Recognition
  perception and, 132
  test, 598
Recruitment, 479
Redbook magazine, 541
Red Bull, 548, 570
Redemption rates, sales promotions, 537–538
Reeves, Keanu, 322
Reference group, 159–160
Referrals, advertising and, 146
Refunds, 539
Regional brand, 82
Register of Known Spam Operations (ROSKO), 516
Registration, 317
Regulation
  data privacy, 522–524
  impact on advertising of, 109–110
Regulatory bodies, advertising regulation, 108
Regulatory environment, advertising and, 108–109
Reinman, Sally, 187, 228
Reisman, David, 160
Relational databases, 520
Relationship marketing, 82
  in public relations, 477–480
  stakeholders, 560–561
Relationships
  data-driven, 518
  direct marketing communication, 506
Release prints, 326
Relevance
  creativity and, 257–260
  perception and, 131–132
Reliability, in research, 201
Religion demographics, 170
Reminder advertising, 256
Repetition, in messages, 254
Repositioning of products, 225
Research
  applications, 188–194
  brand intelligence, 228
  consumer behavior, 182–188
  consumer insight, 190–191
  design, 185–188
  effectiveness research, 594–599
  future trends in, 203
  global issues, 202–203
  integrated marketing communication, 203
  media research, 345–346
  methodology, 194–202
  primary research, 184–185
  in public relations, 481–482
  scanner research, 598
  secondary research, 183–184
  selection of methodology, 201–202
  single-source, 598
  strategic planning and, 210–211
  trends and challenges in, 202–203
  types of, 183–185
Resonance
  creation of, 136
  in messages, 253
Resor, Stanley and Helen, 45
Response Alliance database, 519–520
Response list, 519–520
Response rate, sales promotions, 537–538
Response strategies
  direct-response brand communication, 505
  market communication, 176
  media search and mobile marketing, 355–356
Retail advertising, 39
  owned media, 403–404
  spam issues, 516–517
  strategies for, 449
Retailer kits, 544
Retailer-sponsored coupons, 540
Retail industry, 535
Return on investment (ROI)
  accountability and, 82
  business planning and, 211
  of creativity, 257–260
  integrated marketing communication, 606
  public relations effectiveness, 601
  sales promotion, 534
Reviews, 421–422
Richards, Jef I., 97
Richards, Keith, 253
Richards, Stan, 564–565
Richards Group, 159
Rich media, 387, 389
Ries, Al, 221, 225, 264
Ries, Laura, 225, 306
Right-brain thinking, 260
Rimes, LeAnn, 272
Risk taking, 175
Ritchie, Guy, 402
Rittenhouse, David, 333, 352–353, 426–427, 521
Ritual view, 248
Roadblock advertising, 380
Road Crew social marketing campaign. 245–246, 257
Road Scholar, 163
Roberts, Kevin, 134
Roberts, Marilyn, 135, 250
Roesch, Orville, 226
Rogers, Everett, 174–175
Romney, Mitt, 421
Ronald McDonald House, 63
Room 214 agency, 493
Ross, Bill, 226
Rotfeld, Herb, 487
Rotfeld, Robert Jack, 97
Rough cut, 326
Rough layouts, 316
Routine strategy, 249
Rubenstein, Howard, 475–476
Rubicam, Raymond, 45
Runners World, 457
Run-of-paper rate, 368
Ruppies, 173
Rusbridger, Alan, 207
Rushes, 325
Ruth, Julie, 568

S

Safari, 522
Safeway Stores, 525
Sainsbury's, 83
Sales force, sales promotions targeting, 536–537
Sales kits, 409
Sales promotions, 40, 532–538
  big ideas in, 538
  brand building, 536
  break-even analysis, 601–602
  defined, 532–533
  growth of, 533–538
  integration, 554–555
  marketplace changes, 534–535
  performance estimation, 537–538
  planning, 535–538
  primary targets, 536–537
Salience, 246
Salton-Maxim Juiceman infomercial, 508
Same-sex marriage, 168
Sampling
  challenges in, 202
  consumer promotions, 539–540
  methodology, 195
  owned media, 410
Sapient, 596
Sasser, Sheila, 242, 260
Satellite radio, 375
Satellite television, 379
Satellite transmission, 370
  global media buying, 464–465
Satisfaction, 161–162
Saudi Arabia, 428
"Save a Life" campaign, 238–240, 263, 265
"Save the Children Sweden" ad campaign, 334–336, 358
Sayre, Shay, 198
Scanner research, 598
Scanning, reading vs., 282
Scappaticci, Sonia Montes, 95, 254, 356
Scarborough Research, 605
Scatter market, 462
Scenes, 293
Scheduling strategies, media planning, 453–454
Schroeder, Karl, 128, 286–287, 305, 323–324, 545
Schultz, Don, 175–176

Science, art and, 240–246
Scientific Advertising (Hopkins), 45
Scientific era in advertising, 44–46
Scorsese, Martin, 322
Scott, Ridley, 42
Scott, Tony, 402
Scott lawn care, 159
Screen values, 318–319
Screenvision, 383
Search advertising, 392–394, 466
Search and reapply, international IMC, 579–581
Search-engine advertising, 355–356, 392–394
Search marketing, 355–356, 392–394
Search optimization, 393
Sears catalogs, 512
Secondary research, 183–184
Seeker consumer model, 175–176
  media consumption and, 341
  mobile marketing, 355–356
  search advertising and, 392–393
Segmentation
  behavioral patterns and, 174–175
  demographics, 166–170
  psychographics, 170–173
  seeking seekers and, 175–176
  sociodemographic, 173–174
  strategies for, 163–164
  types of, 164
Seinfeld, Jerry, 220, 573
Seitel, Fraser, 479, 492
Selective attention, 131
Selective binding, 370
Selective perception, 130–132
Self-discipline in advertising, 112–113
Self-identity, 169
Self magazine, 457
Self-promotion, 369
Self-regulation
  in advertising, 112–116
  data privacy, 522–524
Self-Regulatory Program for Online Behavioral Advertising, 524
Selling premise, 251
Semicomps, 316
Semicontrolled media, public relations and, 486
Semiotics, 126, 192, 594
Senn, Fred, 209
Sensory strategy, 249
Sentence completion test, 200
Service firms, 503
Sets, 294
72andSunny, 53
7-Up ad campaigns, 226
Sex appeal, 94
Sexual orientation demographics, 167–168
Shape-versus-mirror debate, advertising and, 92
Share
  of market, 213
  market share, sales promotions and, 534–535
  media audience, 350
  of mind, 578
  of voice, 457–458
  of wallet, 578
Sheehan, Brian, 134, 344
Shelf-talkers, 403–404
Shell, 100
Shoot sequence, television commercials, 324–325
Showing, 387
  outdoor advertising, 440
Shrek (film series), 323
Side by Side (documentary), 322
Signage, 401
Signaling, in brand communication, 126
Sign spinners, 406–407
Silo mentality
  internal integration, 582–584
  media research and, 466
Silver, Nate, 482
Simmons Market Research Bureau (SMRB), 185
Simmons-Scarborough Syndicated Research Associates, 437
"Singin' the Rain" campaign, 154
Single-source research, 598
Situation analysis, 211, 589
  integrated marketing communication, 565–567
Six Flags amusement park, 592
60 Minutes (television program), 382
Size strategies, media planning, 455
Skechers, 274
Skippies, 173
Skyfall (film), 355
Skyscraper ads, 390
Slice-of-life message, 252
Slim Jim crowdsourcing campaign, 423
Slogans, 254, 271–273
Smart phones, 412
"Smart Start" ad campaign, 251–252
Smart USA Insider website, 422
SMCR model of mass communication, 123–124
Smile Train, 511
Smoking, advertising and, 188
Smoky Bear campaign, 271
Snowden, Edward, 223
Social class, 158–159
Social games, 423
Social influences in advertising, 158–160
Socialization, owned media and, 414–416
Social learning, 140
Social media
  brand communication on, 414–416
  costs of, 424
  direct-response marketing, 516
  evolution of, 342–343
  influence measurement, 142
  as interactive media, 340
  marketing on, 48, 426
  mentions on, 420–421, 451
  online advertising and, 389–394
  online communities, 422–423
  privacy issues, 521–524
  public relations and, 492
  sales promotions on, 534
  search advertising and, 393–394
  usage patterns, 353
Social Media Check-Up, 421
Social responsibility, 47–48
  advertising and, 90–91
  brand communication, 90–101
  product-specific issues, 99–101
Social selling, 516
Social strategy, 249
Societal marketing philosophy, 210
Societal role of advertising, 41, 43
Sociodemographics, 173–174
Soderbergh, Steven, 322
Soft sell, 247
Software, web page design, 327
Soley, Larry, 200
SoLoMo (social/local/mobile marketing), 453
SORPA ad campaign, 47–48, 260
Sound effects, radio advertising, 288–289
Source, 123
Source credibility, 143
South China Research, 585
Spamhaus.org, 516
Spam issues, e-commerce and, 516–517
SPAR advertising campaign, 214–216
Speakers' bureau, 491
Special events, 492
Specialized agencies, 54
Specialties, 541
  advertising, 40
Specialty advertising, 541
Speeches, promotional interactions, 410–411
Spherical branding, 564
Spider-Man movies, 552
Spiffs, 546
Spokes-character, 252
Spokesperson, 252–253
Sponsored stories, 389
Sponsorships, 381, 388, 548–549
  public relations and, 492
Spoofing, 516
Sports advertising, 337
  naming rights, 402–403
  sponsorships and event marketing, 548–551
Spot advertising
  radio, 375–376
  television, 381
Spot color, 311
Stakeholders
  characteristics, 74
  integrated marketing communication, 560–561

in public relations, 474–475
targeting of, 569–570
Standard advertising unit, 367
Standardization, 578
Starbucks, 198
Coffee Wars, 248, 250
social media marketing, 426
Starch, Daniel, 45
Starcom MediaVest Group (SMG), 398, 399, 428, 465
Star Wars (film), 321–322
Stasiowski, Peter, 67, 502
States' Attorneys General, 109
"Steak for Your Ears" campaign, 257–259
Stealth advertising, 414
Steel, Jon, 569–570
Stein, Kate, 174, 198–199
Stengel, Jim, 57, 82, 224
Stengel, Richard, 170–171
Stereotypes, in advertising, 93
Stern, Aaron, 52, 372
Stickiness, 131
of websites, 413
Stock footage, 321
Stock music, 288–289
Stop and Grab, in headlines, 281–282
Stop motion technique, 323
Store-based merchandising, 403–404
Story, Mark, 601
Storyboard, 294, 317
Storytelling
in radio advertising, 288–289
in television advertising, 291
visual storytelling, 306
Straightforward message, 251
Strategic business unit, 210
Strategic consistency, 563
Strategic philanthropy, 479
Strategic planning
brand communication/IMC, 215–216
brand identity strategy, 218–221
brand positioning strategy, 221–225
business plan, 209–211
consumer insight and account planning, 225–231
decision making, 217–218
defined, 208–209
international integrated marketing communication, 578–581
key decisions in, 217–225
marketing communication functions, 216–217
marketing plan, 211–217
Strategic research, 180–203
defined, 183
Strategies
for copywriting, 274
direct-response brand communication, 503–504
formats, 248–253
media strategies, 346–351, 447–455
message strategies, 246–256
in public relations, 482–484
systems of, 248
Streaming video, 382
Street-based media, 406
Strong, Kaila, 191
Strong effects, brand communication, 146–148
Structural analysis, 264
Stuffers, 404
Stuhlfaut, Mark, 256, 263–264, 593
Subheads, 280
Subliminal advertising, 132
Subscription television, 378
Substantiation
in messages, 251
regulation of, 110–111
Suggestions, as research tool, 198
Suliminalism, perception and, 132–133
Sunkist, 213
Super Bowl advertising, 381–382, 439, 550–551
evaluation of, 599, 605
SuperCuts, 253
Superstitials, 391
Supplements (newspaper), 368
Suppliers, advertising and, 51
Support, 251
Surrogate effects, 141, 147, 594
Survey research, 194–196
Survivor (television program), 354
Susan G. Komen Foundation for the Cure, 530–532, 555
Sweeney, John, 337
Sweeps, 439
Sweepstakes, 540–541
Switchers, 174
SWOT (strengths, weaknesses, opportunities, threats) analysis, 211, 213
integrated marketing communication, 567
in public relations, 481–482
Symbolism, association and, 140
Syndicated radio advertising, 376
Syndication, television, 379
Synergy
integrated marketing communication, 71, 606–607
message synergy, 562–563
perception and, 132
Synthesizer, 228

T

Tagging, 421
Tagliabue, Sebastian, 399–400
Taglines, 254, 271–273, 281, 284
Take (film production), 324
Talent, 291
Tang, Yvonne, 560
Tap.Me, 548
Target audience, 165–177
behavioral patterns and, 174–175
demographics, 166–170
directory advertising, 373–374
gross and targeted rating points and, 455–457
interactive media conduits, 340
media planning for, 349–350, 440–443
psychographics and, 170–173
sales promotions, 536–537
seeking seekers and, 175–176
strategic planning and, 218–219
targeting relationships, 176
television advertising, 381–382
Target Corporation, 354, 478, 550, 581–582
Targeted cost per point (TCPP), media planning, 458–460
Targeted cost per thousand (TCPM), media planning, 458–460
Targeted rating points (TRPs), 455–457
Targeted reach, 444–445
Targeting
behavioral, 174–175
defined, 165
direct-response brand communication, 505
magazine advertising, 371–372
media search and mobile marketing, 355–356
message strategy, 246
microtargeting, 165
movie advertising, 382–383
in public relations, 482
of radio advertising, 374–376
of stakeholders, 569–570
strategic planning and, 218–219
television advertising, 381–382
Targets, in headlines, 281
Tasteless advertising, 263
Taviloğlu, Mustafa, 483
Taylor, Bob, 226
Taylor, Ron, 248–249
Taylor's strategy wheel, 248–249
TBWA/Chiat/Day, 42, 264, 478
Tchotchkes, 411
Teaching, in messages, 254
Teasers, 252
Technical problems, monitoring of, 463
A Technique for Producing Ideas (Young), 259
Tech support, 409
Teen smoking, campaigns against, 89–90
Telemarketing, 513–514
Telemarketing and Consumer Fraud Act and Abuse Protection Act (1994), 106
Telemarketing Sales Rule, 514
Television
ad copywriting for, 289–294
audience data, 438–439
dominance in advertising of, 339, 363
emergence of advertising on, 46
industry structure, 376–382

Television (*continued*)
media mix and, 447
production process, 324–326
product placement on, 354
scripts, 294
technology evolution in, 382
Television Standard Dayparts, 380
Tellis, Gerard, 606
Tested Advertising Methods (Caples), 45
Testimonial, 98
Test marketing, 606
Texting, 416–418
Texture/Media, 327
Theater of the mind, radio advertising and, 287
Theater techniques, 201
Think/Feel/Do, 127
consumer decision making and, 155
Thinking, feeling and, 138–139
Thinking outside the box, 260
"Think Small" campaign, 246
This Old House, 457
"Three Artists One Song" campaign, 348–349
3D film production, 324
3D printing, 321
3D television, 382
"Three Little Pigs" ad campaigns, 206–208, 221–223, 231–232
Three Little Pigs commercial, 369
360° communication planning, 561–562, 564–565, 581–584
Thumbnail sketches, 316
Tie-ins, 553–554
Tiffany's, 512
Time blocks, television advertising, 380
Timeliness, 279
Time-shifting, 380
Timing strategies, media planning, 453–454
Tint blocks, 318–319
Tip-ins, 321
TiVo systems, 380
T-Mobile, 407
TNS Global, 596
Tobacco advertising, 99–100
Today Show, 549, 574
Tom's of Maine, 210–211
Toms Shoes, 91
Tone of voice, 245, 277
Top Chef cooking show, 550
Top-of-mind awareness, 246
Torture tests, 254–255
Toscani, Oliviero, 102, 302–303
Total audience data, 438, 605
Total communication, integrated marketing, 561–562
Touch points, 562
Touch screens, 408
Tougas, Joe, 277
Tours
promotional interactions, 410–411
public relations, 492
Town hall forums, 492
Toyota, 443, 480
Tracking research, 597
consumer behavior, 191
Trade advertising, 544
Trade associations, 183–184
sales promotions targeting, 536–537
Trade magazines, 370
Trademark protection, 106–107
Trade promotions, 543–548, 601–602
Trade shows, 410–411, 545
Trade support, 546
Traditional media consumption, 347
Traffic Audit Bureau for Media Measurement, Inc., 604–605
Trailers, 383
"Trailhead" campaign (Billings, Montana), 195, 508–509, 539, 553
Training programs
corporate employees, 402
personal contact media, 409
Transformation, association and, 140
Transit advertising, 353, 388
Transmission view, 248
TREMOR metric, 605
Trend spotters, 174
Trial, 145
Trials, 145
consumer promotions, 542–543
"Triple bottom line," 171
Trout, Jack, 219, 221
Trust, 475–476
TRUSTe organization, 522–524
Truth® ad campaign, 88–90, 114, 480
"Truth & Dare" website, 414
Tsai, Wanhsiu Sunny, 157
Tsui Wah, 585
Tsunami disaster, 365
Tumblr, 422–423
Tupperware, 506
Tweets, 231, 243, 421
24 (television series), 353
Twitter, 414–416, 421
codes and syntax in, 294
consumer promotions on, 540
evaluation of, 605
Guardian ad campaign, 231
spam on, 516
"Unleash Deadly" campaign, 399
2BLIKE.com, 548
Two-step media platform, 451
Two-step offer, 505
Tylenol, 480
Typography, 311–312

U

UEFA Champions League, 399
Unaided recall, 599
Unbundled media planning and buying, 465
Uncola ad campaign, 226
Uncontrolled circulation, 369
Uncontrolled media, public relations and, 486
Underlines, in copywriting, 280
Underwriting, 375, 379
Undifferentiated strategy, 163
Unfair advertising, remedies for, 111–112
Unhealthy products, 99–100
UNICEF, 503–505
Unified brand vision, 563
Uniform resource locators (URLs), protection of, 107
Unilever, 152–154, 548
Unique selling proposition (USP), 251
United Airlines, 214
United Arab Emirates (UAE), 399–400, 428
"United Breaks Guitars" video, 608
"United Colors of Benetton" campaign, 102
Univision, 464–465
"Unleash Deadly" ad campaign, 398–400, 428
Up (film), 323
Up-front market, 462
Up in the Air (film), 353
Urban Decay Cosmetics, 65, 73
U.S. Newswire, 490
U.S. News & World Report, 370
U.S. Postal Service, 108, 526
Usage rates, 174
USA Today
Ad Meter, 550
circulation declines, 366
User-generated ads, 423
USRobotics, 320–321

V

Vail Resorts, 609
VALCON (Value Contact Point Tracer), 574–575
Validity, 201
VALS™ Lifestyle Framework lifestyle, 171–173
Value-added media services, negotiations for, 462
Value-added premiums, 406
Value-Added Public Relations (Harris), 477
Values
advertising and, 92
culture and, 157
segmentation based on, 164
Vampire creativity, 264
Van Persie, Robin, 399
Variable data campaigns, 508
Vasoline Intensive Care Lotion, 306
Vaughan, Stevie Ray, 272
Vertical publication, 370
Vertical reach, 350–351, 444–445

Video
editing, 326
filming and editing processes, 322–326
news releases, 279, 490
online video, 327, 392–394
production guidelines, 321–326
public relations, 405
streaming video, 382
Video games
advertising, 383–388
branded games, 402
Videography, 316–317
Viral communication, 356
word-of-mouth interactions and, 419–420
Viral marketing, 425–427, 466
Viral videos, 425
Virtual communities, 422
Virtual dressing rooms, 515
Vision statement, 210
Visual branding, 401–402
Visual communication
art direction, 308–309
brand image and position in, 305–306
composition, 316–317
designer's tool kit, 309–312
design principles, layout and styles, 312–316
emotion and persuasion, 307–308
environmental design, 317
impact of, 302–304
importance of, 302–308
production requirements, 317–321
storytelling in, 306
video production, 321–325
web design, 325–328
Visual impact, 302–304
Visualization
creativity and, 261
design and, 309
Visual storytelling, 306
Voice-over, 291
Volkswagen, 46–47, 144, 246–247, 257, 306, 321, 414

W

Wagner, Carson B., 131–132
Wallas, Graham, 261
Wall Street Journal, 65, 174, 191, 198, 221, 326–327
advertising campaigns for, 221, 563
circulation declines, 366
on direct response marketing, 514–517
media convergence in, 344
privacy issues in, 521
on television industry, 377
Walmart, 539
Walters, Trent, 159
Wansink, Brian, 174, 199
Wants, 160–161
in advertising, 135
needs vs., 137
Ward, Ted, 499–500
Warhol, Andy, 309–310, 314
Warner-Lambert v. FTC, 112
"Warrior" video collaboration, 348–349
Waste
media waste, 446
reach, 444
The Watcher (film), 554
"We, On Death Row" campaign, 102
Weak effects, brand communication, 146–148
We Are Social for Heinz, 534
Wearout, 454
Weatherproof apparel company, 98
Webisodes, 402
Web radio, 375
Websites
advertising on, 390–394
copywriting for, 294
design considerations, 326–327
evaluation of, 603
owned digital media on, 412–416
privacy issues, 521–524
public relations and, 494
Wegmans grocery chain, 57
Weighting strategies, media planning and, 455
Weiner, Matthew, 49
Weintraub, Bill, 32–33
Weiss, Karl, 195, 196
Wells Fargo, 272
"We Try Harder" campaign, 221, 306, 592
Wheaties, 306
Wheeler-Lea Amendment (1938), 105
White space, 318–319
"Whopper Freakout" campaign, 213, 257
Widgets, 391
Wieden + Kennedy, 34–36, 50, 57, 120–122
Wii, 550
WikiLeaks, 208
Wikipedia, 336
Willens, Doris, 264
Williams, John, 221
Williams-Sonoma, 512
"Wire dancers" billboard, 387
Witeck, Bob, 167–168
Witeck Communications, 167–168
Wolburg, Joyce M., 212
Wolff, Michael, 389
Wolfit, Sir Donald, 278
Woman's Day, 371
Women's Wear Daily, 370
"Wonderful World of Words" campaign, 275–276
Woo, John, 402
Woods, Tiger, 253, 573, 579
Word association, 200
Word-of-mouth marketing, 83–84, 125
interactive earned media and, 419
media role in, 356–357
online influences, 493
strategies, 451
Word of Mouth Marketing Association, 98
"Words with Friends," 423
The World Is Not Enough (film), 354
Writing, media objectives, 446–447

X

Xavi, 399

Y

Yahoo!, online advertising and, 389–391
Yaneura, Lisa, 219, 340
Yankelovich lifestyle profile, 171–172
Yellow Pages, 372–374
Young, Charles, 138–139, 144–145, 192–193, 290, 308, 591–592
Young, James Webb, 259
Young, John Orr, 45
Young and Rubicam, 45, 259
Your-name-here copy, 278
YouTube, 343, 422
brand communication on, 415–416
"Lottery of Life" campaign, 335–336, 358
promotions on, 405
Yuppie puppies, 171
Yuppies, 171

Z

Zaltman, Gerald, 200
Zapping, 380–381
Zappos.com, 410
Zenithoptimedia, 465
Zero moment of truth, 442
Zines, 491
Zipping, 380–381
ZMET (Zalman Metaphor Elicitation Technique), 201
Zommir, Wende, 73–74
ZO Multicultural, 465
Zynga, 423